THE WORLD TODAY SERIES®

Western Europe 1999
18TH EDITION

Wayne C. Thompson, Ph.D.

with Mark H. Mullin—*The United Kingdom, Ireland*

STRYKER-POST
PUBLICATIONS
HARPERS FERRY
WEST VIRGINIA

NEXT EDITION–AUGUST 2000

Graphic Materials Acknowledgments

For their generosity in providing certain visual material for use in this book, and in order of their appearance, special thanks to the following:

European Community Information Services
North Atlantic Treaty Organization
German Information Services, New York
Press and Information Office, Bonn
The Embassy of Austria
The Swiss National Tourist Office
The Government of Liechtenstein
French Cultural Services, New York
The Royal Netherlands Embassy
The Embassy of Belgium
The Embassy of Luxembourg
The British Embassy
The Embassy of Ireland

The Swedish Embassy
The Royal Norwegian Embassy
The Royal Danish Embassy
The Embassy of Finland
The Embassy of Iceland
The Embassy of Italy
The Embassy of Malta
The Sovereign Military Order of Malta
The Government of Monaco
The Embassy of Greece
The Embassy of Spain
The Embassy of Portugal
The Government of Andorra

First appearing as *Western Europe 1982,* this annually revised book is published by

Stryker–Post Publications
P.O. Drawer 1200
Harpers Ferry, WV. 25425
Telephones: 1–800–995–1400 (U.S.A. or Canada)
 Other: 1–304–535–2593
 Fax: 1–304–535–6513
 VISA–MASTERCARD

Copyright © 1999 by Stryker–Post Publications

All rights reserved. This publication, or parts thereof, may not be reproduced in any form whatsoever without permission in writing from the publisher.

International Standard Book Number: 1–887985–23–9

International Standard Serial Number: 0084–2338

Library of Congress Catalog Card Number: 83–643780

Cover design by Susan Bodde

Typography by Maryland Composition Company, Inc.
Glen Burnie, MD 21060

Printed in the United States of America by United Book Press, Inc. Baltimore, MD 21207

Photographs used to illustrate *The World Today Series* come from many sources, a great number from friends who travel worldwide. If you have taken any which you believe would enhance the visual impact and attractiveness of our books, do let us hear from you.

www.Strykerpost.com

DEDICATION

To the memory of my mother and father

ACKNOWLEDGMENTS

I am especially grateful to the Alexander von Humboldt Foundation, a far-sighted German organization which, since 1869, has persistently nurtured the spirit of intellectual discovery and has sought to tighten the links between Europe and the rest of the world, for having granted me a two-year research fellowship at the University of Freiburg in Germany. Without its aid, I would have been unable to complete the first edition of this book.

No author could possibly write a book with the breadth of this one without the assistance of numerous persons and organizations. Mark H. Mullin, a Harvard graduate who earned an M.A. as a Marshall Scholar, Oxford University, and who is presently Headmaster of the Casady School in Oklahoma City, wrote all but the political and economic sections of the chapters on the United Kingdom and the Republic of Ireland. His personal familiarity with Britain and Ireland far surpasses my own. Detlev Hoffmann, a political scientist in Freiburg, who specializes in Italy and Greece, wrote the first draft of the section on Italy. My wife, Susan L. Thompson, translated his work from German, and I have updated it and added some background material and elaboration to aid the American reader. He also helped me to write the history section on Greece. Without his collaboration, treatment of both Italy and Greece would have lacked much of its depth and insight.

I wish also to thank my colleagues and acquaintances throughout Western Europe and the U.S. who took the time to read or to comment upon various chapters dealing with their own countries or specialties. They include: James Cathy, Thomas Davis, Per-Gören Ersson, William Goodman, Michael Jones, Jean-Claude Joseph, David M. Keithly, Klaus and Mary Jo Kusatz, Yrjö Länsipuro, Daniel R. Leamy, John A. Miller, Mario Musella, Jacky Paris, Jacques Piens, Prince Waldemar and Princess Anne Lise of Schaumberg-Lippe, Hans Sennhauser, Arni Stefansson, Countess Irene von Strachwitz, Philippe Vidal, David Vogelsanger, Jürg H. Walser, and Maureen and Peter Ward. Catherine Lowe thoroughly read the entire manuscript in order to comb out style, spelling and typographical errors. I am very indebted also to Jon Markham Morrow for allowing us to use his galaxy of beautiful photographs appearing throughout this book, touching only on a few of the 145 countries which he has visited. Susan L. Thompson took some of the photographs and carefully proofread much of the manuscript. W. Claude Thompson, Jr., and Victor Thompson also assisted in the photographic work.

I am grateful to those cadets at the Virginia Military Institute who collaborated on the updating of this edition. They are: Thomas Coley Campbell, Brian J. Curtis, Augustine O. Ekpoudom, Justin D. Fertick, Jeremy S. Labore, James E. Shircliffe, Jr., D. Scott Thompkins, and Douglas K. Whalen II. I thank also the VMI Foundation and the VMI Research Committee for generous grants which permit me to do research and to remain informed about Western Europe. I am grateful to Pro Helvetia, which arranged and financed a week-long study tour of Switzerland, as well as to numerous embassy and foreign ministry officials who provided information and arranged visits to Western European capitals to speak with representatives of parties, parliaments, universities, research institutes and news media about this book. A Fulbright Teaching Fellowship to Estonia in 1995–96 enabled me to visit Finland several times. Philip Stryker is without doubt one of the most competent, encouraging and congenial publishers with whom an author could work.

W.C.T.

Lexington, Virginia, June 1999

Wayne C. Thompson ...

Professor of Political Science, Virginia Military Institute, Lexington, Virginia. Ohio State University (B.A. in Government); Claremont Graduate School (M.A. and Ph.D., *with distinction*). He did further graduate study at the universities of Göttingen, Paris/Sorbonne and Freiburg im Breisgau, where he has since been a guest professor. He has studied and researched many years in Germany as a Woodrow Wilson, Fulbright, *Deutscher Akademischer Austauschdienst*, Earhart and Alexander von Humboldt Fellow. He has served as scholar–in–residence at the *Bundestag* in Bonn and as a Fulbright professor in Estonia. During the 1999–2000 academic year, he is a visiting professor at the Air War College in Montgomery, Alabama. He is the author of *In the Eye of the Storm: Kurt Riezler and the Crises of Modern Germany* (Iowa City, University of Iowa Press, 1980), *The Political Odyssey of Herbert Wehner* (Boulder, CO: Westview Press, 1993), *Historical Dictionary of Germany* (Metuchen, NJ: Scarecrow, 1994), and *Canada* in The World Today Series. He also co–edited *Perspectives on Strategic Defense* and *Space: National Programs and International Cooperation*, and *Margaret Thatcher: Prime Minister Indomitable* (Boulder, CO: Westview, 1987, 1989, 1994). He has written many articles on European politics, philosophy and history which have appeared in such periodicals as *The American Political Science Review, Western Political Quarterly, East European Quarterly, Journal of Politics, Central European History, The American Review of Canadian Studies, German Studies Review, Current History, The Yearbook on International Communist Affairs, The History Teacher, Armed Forces and Society, Freedom at Issue, Communist and Post–Communist Studies,* and *Contemporary French Civilization*.

Mark H. Mullin ...

Headmaster, Casady School, Oklahoma City, OK. Harvard University (B.A. *Cum Laude* in Government), where he was First Marshal of his class and Ivy League and Intercollegiate Mile Run Champion. He was a Marshall Scholar at Oxford University (B.A., M.A. in Philosophy, Politics and Economics) and studied at The General Theological Seminary, New York (M. Div.). Before coming to the Casady School, the Reverend Canon Mullin was Dean of the Choate School, Wallingford, Connecticut, where he also taught European History, Assistant Headmaster at the Blue Ridge School, Virginia, and Headmaster of St. Albans School, Washington, D.C. He is author of *Educating for the 21st Century: The Challenge for Parents and Teachers* (Lanham, MD: Madison Books, University Press of America, 1991). He and Mrs. Mullin have led many student tours to Great Britain and Ireland.

The Mullins chat with Prince Charles

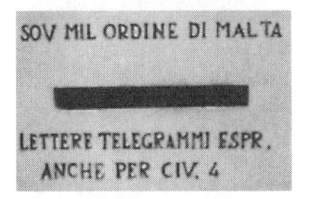

CONTENTS

Western Europe Today 1

The German–speaking Democracies
    Germany... 8
    Austria 102
    Switzerland 120
    Liechtenstein 140

The French Republic
    France 146

The BENELUX Countries
    Introduction 192
    The Netherlands 196
    Belgium 218
    Luxembourg... 234

The United Kingdom and the Republic of Ireland
    Great Britain and Northern Ireland (UK) 242
    Ireland 286

The Nordic Countries
    Introduction 302
    Sweden... 314
    Norway... 334
    Denmark... 352
    Finland 364
    Iceland 378

Mediterranean Europe
    Italy.. 388
    San Marino.. 424
    Vatican City 426
    Malta.. 429
    The Sovereign Military Order of Malta 434
    Monaco... 438
    Greece.. 440

The Iberian Peninsula
    Introduction 472
    Spain.. 476
    Portugal 504
    Andorra 520

Bibliography 524

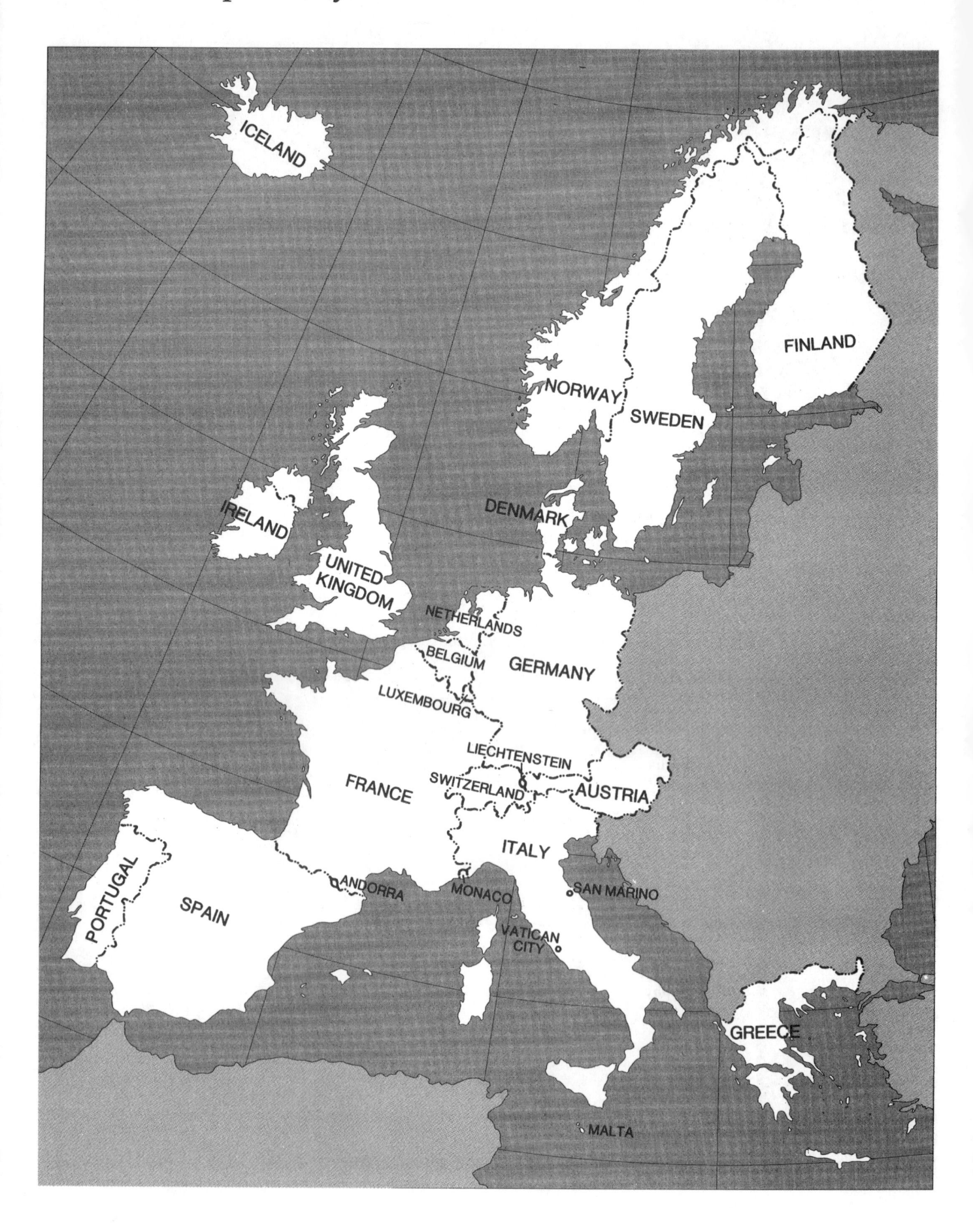

Western Europe Today

Western Europe Today

In 1945 much of Europe lay in ruins, its peoples destitute and demoralized following a war on its own soil more destructive than any conflict in history. Two world wars in the 20th century (World War I from 1914 until 1918 and World War II from 1939 until 1945) had brought Europe's dominance over world affairs to an end and had led to a rise of the United States of America and the Soviet Union as the world's most powerful nations. These wars also ended Europe's colonial hold on much of the world, a hold which, despite some negative effects, had spread European civilization to the Western Hemisphere, Africa, the Middle East and the Far East.

Western Europe is a region rich in diversity, with a population of 382 million persons (compared to about 260 million in the U.S.), speaking at least 13 different major languages and scores of dialects. It is also the world's largest trading area, accounting in 1991 for about a fourth of world trade, compared with 16.5% for the U.S., 10.5% for Japan, and 4.5% for Canada.

Geographically, Western Europe is much smaller than the U.S. The entire region is scarcely more than twice the size of Alaska and would easily fit into the continental U.S. west of the Mississippi with much room to spare. Like the U.S., Western Europe offers a very rich diversity of climates and landscapes, from the permafrost and midnight sun of northern Norway to the hot, dry, sunny Mediterranean, from the fog and rain of northern Germany to the warm blue skies of the Azores and to the snows and arctic winds of Iceland, from the Alpine peaks of Austria and Switzerland to the flat and sub–sea level terrain of the Netherlands.

With the collapse of Communism in Europe, the unification of Germany, and the dissolution of the Soviet Union, Europeans are faced with the most significant alteration of their continent's political map since World War II. Because two hostile Europes no longer face each other, Europe has doubled its size from 382 to 700 million people. From Moscow to Lisbon and Dublin to Budapest democracies exist in which free elections provide the only legitimate claim to power and which are basically committed to freedom, individual rights, and some variant of capitalism.

Looking eastward, Western Europeans see more than a dozen independent nations emerging, all in difficult economic circumstances, with borders in dispute, ethnic scores to settle, and millions of discontented and frightened citizens who may decide to seek a better future in the West. Most are clamoring for admission to the plentiful Western European table and a place under the Atlantic Alliance's security umbrella. The August 1991 putsch in the former Soviet Union destroyed central authority and dispersed power among its various republics. Western European countries led the way in recognizing the newly independent Baltic states of Estonia, Latvia, and Lithuania, which are reaching out to the West. Moldova, carved out of Romania at the beginning of World War II, may one day find its way back into union with that struggling state.

In December 1991 Ukrainian voters chose independence, thus paving the way for the creation of an historically–conscious sovereign state of 52 million people, the fourth largest in Europe with more territory than France and a sizable armed force. Following the collapse of the Soviet Union later that month, it joined Russia and Belarus to form the Commonwealth of Independent States (CIS), to which all former Soviet republics except the Baltics belong. The CIS is a loose organization to coordinate policies mainly in the economic field, but it also performs limited political and military functions. In the South, Yugoslavia came unglued and became the scene of the first full–scale war in Europe since 1945.

Western Europe still has many cultures and many lands and regions with characters and appearances of their own. However, there are many things which make much of modern Western Europe and the U.S. look more and more similar: large shopping centers, fast food stores, freeways, modern cities with some skyscrapers and much concrete, many automobiles and everywhere signs of prosperity.

Americans and Western Europeans also face many of the same problems and have many of the same concerns, though in differing degrees: the "generation gap," the role of women in modern society, a declining birth rate, equal rights for women, illegal immigration, the integration of racial and religious minorities, a flood of political refugees, urban violence and terrorism, the protection of the environment and the quality of life, the defense of their homeland and values in the nuclear age, the provision of adequate supplies of energy and raw materials and the maintenance of prosperity and generous social security programs despite the dangers of inflation, unemployment and declining economic growth rates.

"McDonald's? Me? Always!!!"

Young Americans and Western Europeans have similar cultural tastes for music, films (70% of the film market in Western Europe is from Hollywood), language expressions (especially English ones!) and dress. Jeans, jogging shoes, T–shirts and hair styles no longer provide accurate clues to nationality; they have become international. Western European students and scientists are strongly attracted to American universities and research institutes, and European businessmen have, on the whole, been very successful in adapting production and management techniques to European conditions. Americans also continue to be drawn culturally, emotionally, politically and economically to Western Europe. In short, the American or Western European no longer enters a "different world" when he arrives at the other side of the Atlantic.

The reader will confront numerous abbreviations and acronyms, and one must understand not only what the letters signify, but also what function the indicated institutions serve. Therefore, in the following pages, these acronyms will be presented in the context of a more general discussion of some of the more important Western European bodies and organizations.

Today, Western Europe is a region which is, on the whole, highly prosperous, though it is relatively poor in natural resources. It has a large industrial base, much capital and know–how and a highly skilled work force. It is also relatively secure militarily. Such prosperity and security are partly due to the countries' high degree of voluntary cooperation, formalized in numerous international organizations. All major Western European countries except Switzerland are full members

1

Western Europe Today

of the United Nations (UN), and all participate in the many organizations linked to the UN, such as the UN Educational, Scientific and Cultural Organization (UNESCO), the UN Conference on Trade and Development (UNCTAD), the World Court, which sits in the stately Peace Palace built with funds contributed by Andrew Carnegie in the Hague, Netherlands, the International Labor Organization (ILO), the UN Industrial Development Organization (UNIDO), the World Health Organization (WHO), the Food and Agriculture Organization (FAO) and a number of others.

Most Western European countries would be unable to defend themselves alone. Therefore, the majority has chosen to join the North Atlantic Treaty Organization (NATO), also known as the Atlantic Alliance. Created in 1949, NATO links the power of the United States and Canada, and the geographic position of Iceland (which has no army) with the military resources of Belgium–Netherlands–Luxembourg (BENELUX), Great Britain, Norway, Denmark, the Federal Republic of Germany (FRG or Germany), Italy, Portugal, Turkey, Greece, France, Spain, and (since 1999) Poland, Hungary and the Czech Republic. The only major Western European countries which remain neutral are Ireland, Switzerland, Austria, Sweden, and Finland.

When the question arose concerning the organization of a European military combination, France, Italy and West Germany initiated in 1952 a treaty creating a European Defense Community (EDC). It was intended to bring into being an integrated European army under a unified command structure, which would ultimately include troops from West Germany and the BENELUX countries. However, in 1954 the French National Assembly rejected this plan, fearing the possible loss of its sovereignty if it relinquished command over its army.

NATO members

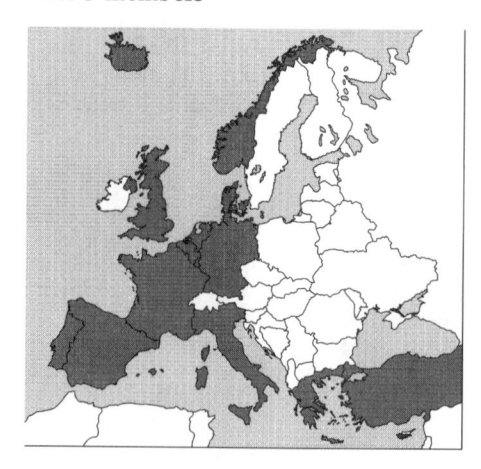

NATO Headquarters

As a compromise, Great Britain proposed a Western European Union (WEU), now composed of the BENELUX countries, France, Italy, Germany and Great Britain, Greece, Spain and Portugal, with headquarters in Brussels. Turkey, Norway and Iceland are associate members. It conducts contingency planning, organizes and controls small all–European military operations (with the possibility of using NATO units and equipment), and attempts to coordinate the defense policies and armaments programs of its members.

At the 1991 European Union (EU, known until 1993 as the European Community—EC) summit meeting in Maastricht it was agreed that the WEU will be Europe's own defense system, albeit "linked to" NATO. It now serves as a vehicle for military operations in which the U.S. does not wish to participate. It has no sovereign or supranational aspects and has functioned as a forum which some European states within NATO use to discuss their special defense needs. A similar function is performed by an informal organization within NATO known as the "Eurogroup," composed of all European members of NATO except France, Portugal and Iceland.

NATO itself has both political and military components. The highest political organ and decision–making body is the North Atlantic Council (NAC). It selects the Secretary General of NATO, who chairs all meetings and seeks consensus among members. By tradition he is always a European. Since 1995 the post is filled by a Spanish *Socialist* and ex–foreign minister, Javier Solana Madariaga. A physics professor and former Fulbright fellow in America, Solana overcame earlier misgivings about NATO and Spain's joining in 1986. Each member country sends a permanent ambassador to NATO Headquarters in Brussels, and these ambassadors meet once a week. Less frequently, the member countries' heads of government, foreign, defense or finance ministers meet to iron out higher level political problems. All decisions are reached by consensus, not by majority vote. In other words, *each* member has an actual veto power although such vetoes are seldom cast.

The ambassadors or ministers of all but those nations which do not participate in the integrated defense system (presently France, Spain and Iceland) also take part in the Defense Planning Committee (DPC), which is assisted by a variety of committees and working groups. A staff of about 1,000, divided into divisions of Political Affairs, Defense Planning and Policy, Defense Support and Scientific Affairs are in Brussels to assist in the NATO effort.

The highest NATO military authority is the Military Committee, made up of the chiefs–of–defense from all states participating in the NATO military command plus France (since 1995). By tradition it is chaired by a European officer. Although the chiefs–of–defense meet infrequently, their permanent representatives meet regularly in their absence. The Military Committee's primary role is to advise the DPC.

NATO has an integrated system of commands. The Strategic Command Europe (SCE) is headed by the Supreme Allied Commander Europe (SACEUR), who by tradition is always an American. He also commands all U.S. forces in Europe. His deputy is alternatingly a British or Ger-

Western Europe Today

man officer. The SCE is based outside Mons, Belgium, at what was formerly called the Supreme Headquarters Allied Powers Europe (SHAPE). In case of war, the SCE is responsible for military operations in the entire European area. One of its two top regional subcommands, the Regional Command North, in Brunssum, Netherlands, is commanded alternatingly by a British or a German general. The Regional Command South in Naples, Italy, is always entrusted to an American admiral. The French, supported by the Germans, advocate turning this command over to a European officer. However, the United States, whose Sixth Fleet provides the most potent naval forces in the Mediterranean area, rejects this suggestion. The other major NATO command is the Strategic Command Atlantic (SCA), commanded by an American admiral or Marine general and headquartered in Norfolk, Virginia.

Only the U.S. engages in Strategic Arms Reductions Talks (START) or negotiations aimed at limiting nuclear forces in Europe. But Western European members are consulted about any American negotiating positions which might affect European interests. Europeans have developed bodies, such as the NATO Nuclear Planning Group (NPG) and the less formal Special Consultative Group, which serve as channels to inform the U.S. of its allies' views and to keep the latter informed of U.S. objectives. In 1973 most NATO members joined the U.S. in the unsuccessful Mutual Balanced Force Reduction (MBFR) talks, conducted in Vienna with members of the Warsaw Pact, a military alliance that combined forces of the Soviet Union, Poland, East Germany, Czechoslovakia, Hungary, Romania and Bulgaria before the pact was dissolved in 1991.

In 1989 the moribund MBFR talks were replaced by the Conventional Forces in Europe (CFE) negotiations in Vienna. This culminated in an agreement between NATO and the Warsaw Pact in 1990 to thin out their military equipment in the center of Europe. It did not apply to troops. Several years after the Warsaw Pact collapsed, the terms of the CFE Treaty began to be reexamined, at Russia's insistence, to take account of the fact that Moscow no longer has allies and has potentially serious internal instability.

In 1991 President George Bush announced unilateral nuclear cuts which went far beyond the START agreement reached in July. European allies and Soviet President Mikhail Gorbachev gave Bush's plan unanimous backing. The greatest impact was on Europe, where the only targets for NATO's tactical nuclear weapons were in areas which are no longer enemies, such as Poland and eastern Germany. Officially endorsed by NATO, the cuts did not make Europe nuclear–free: NATO retains some atomic bombs on dual–capacity aircraft to provide a measure of nuclear deterrence against unknown threats. Also, Britain and France retain some of their nuclear systems. But European defense has become almost entirely non–nuclear.

The sweeping American disarmament proposals, following the disappearance of a clearly identifiable foe, prompted Europeans to try to develop a distinct European Security and Defence Identity (ESDI). A consensus exists that such an identity is necessary, while preserving NATO in one form or the other. No European country wants the total withdrawal of American troops, which had already been drawn down from 320,000 to fewer than 150,000 by century's end. Americans have called on Europeans to bear a greater responsibility for their own defense, but not in competition with NATO, which remains the major pillar for American leadership in Europe. One American diplomat said: "Sure, we want the Europeans to do more, but we're always going to be wary of anything that looks like it could push the U.S. out of Europe."

In order to facilitate greater European security independence, NATO in 1998 reduced the number of its command headquarters from 65 to 20, emphasized a multinational approach to the manning of these headquarters, and arranged them in a way that they can support both regular NATO tasks as well as Combined Joint Task Forces (CJTF), authorized in 1994. If certain members, such as the U.S., do not wish to participate in a certain military operation, a coalition of those that do can use NATO units and assets under the leadership of the WEU as long as NATO is asked first to deal with the crisis. Non–NATO countries can also be included in such Combined Joint Task Forces.

International military groupings that are dedicated to the ESDI concept have proliferated in Europe since the end of the Cold War. Within NATO, a Dutch–German corps under alternate command has been formed. British, German and Belgian troops constitute a multinational division with an air mobile brigade. The Dutch navy has merged its naval headquarters with those of Belgium. A corps has been created with headquarters in Szczecin, Poland, that comprises Polish, German and Danish troops. This unit was modelled on the French–German Eurocorps in Strasbourg, France, created in 1992. A U.S. combat division serves in a German–led corps, while a German division is part of a U.S.–led corps. Outside NATO, Italy, Austria and Slovenia have created a joint land–based force, and the Spanish, French, Portuguese and Italians have formed a rapid operational force called EUROFOR based in Florence. Many NATO troops serve alongside other European and non–European soldiers in the Stabilization Force (SFOR) to guard the peace in Bosnia Herzogovina.

In 1991 NATO was transformed into a more political organization seeking to reach out to its former enemies. It created a North Atlantic Cooperation Council (NACC, renamed in 1997 the Euro–Atlantic Partnership Council—EAPC) comprising 44 countries at century's end to provide for regular consultations between NATO and the former Soviet republics and eastern European nations on subjects ranging from security issues, arms control, and the conversion of defense industries. In 1994 NATO initiated the Partnership for Peace (PFP), which links 27 countries, including Russia, in bilateral treaties with NATO. The purpose is to expand and intensify political and military cooperation and to strengthen stability and peace, primarily through training forces for peacekeeping operations. A special NATO–Ukraine Commission was es-

North Atlantic Council Meeting, NATO Headquarters ("A Free Spirit in Consultation")

Western Europe Today

European Commission (EU) Headquarters, Brussels

tablished to deepen cooperation with that important country.

These nations are also linked in the 55–member Organization for Security and Cooperation in Europe (OSCE, known until 1994 as the CSCE), to which all European states, former Soviet republics, and the United States and Canada belong. It meets irregularly to consider how to defuse threats to peace through mediation, crisis management, and the dispatch of observers.

Many countries regard PFP as a crucial stepping–stone to full NATO membership. In principle, the alliance is prepared gradually to accept new members, on the condition that they have solid democratic credentials, including a firm civilian grip on the armed forces, and can make a genuine military contribution to the common defense. At their Madrid Conference in May 1997 NATO members opened their door and admitted Poland, Hungary and the Czech Republic in March 1999. That door remains open to a select group of European democracies.

There are still important factors that slow down NATO's enlargement in the East: Western publics are hesitant to give pledges that they would go to war to defend some former Communist states. NATO planners fear the effects an increase in membership would have on already complicated decision–making mechanisms, which require unanimity and consensus. Finally, Russia strongly opposes such enlargement, especially insofar as former Soviet republics, such as the Baltics, are concerned. To assuage Moscow's fears, the Atlantic allies signed with Moscow in 1997 a NATO–Russia Founding Act. This is not a legally binding treaty, but it states that NATO has no need, intentions, or plans to create additional capabilities or permanently station troops or nuclear weapons in the new member states. NATO also created a Permanent Joint Committee at its headquarters in which Russian officials can discuss, though not veto, NATO policies and decisions.

NATO's outdated doctrine of containing Soviet power through "forward defense" and "flexible response" was replaced by one which gives NATO a reason to exist in the changed European environment. Smaller, highly mobile, conventional, and multilateral forces are being created which can be deployed on short notice anywhere within NATO territory, and which can help manage unpredictable crises and instability in eastern Europe, the Balkans, the Mediterranean area and beyond.

No region in the world has been so successful in creating voluntary economic unions of sovereign states as Western Europe. In 1922 the Belgium and Luxembourg Economic Union (BLEU) was created, which made the two countries a single unit for importing and exporting purposes and established a unified currency. In 1944 the Netherlands joined to form BENELUX, which was later extended to include even non–customs matters.

In order to help the devastated countries of Europe recover economically, the United States offered Marshall Plan aid in 1947, but insisted that all countries receiving such aid sit down together and decide as a group how the money should be spent. Thus, the U.S. provided an important initial impetus for a unified Europe.

In response, the Europeans created in 1948 the Organization for European Economic Cooperation (OEEC) for making the decisions and the European Payments Union (EPU) for administering U.S. funds. In 1960, the U.S. and Canada joined the OEEC which was renamed the Organization for Economic Cooperation and Development (OECD), with headquarters in Paris. Later other Western industrialized nations, and Japan, Australia and New Zealand, joined OECD, which does economic analysis and forecasting for industrialized countries, including estimates of future growth, inflation, unemployment, and Gross Domestic Product (GDP, a measurement of an economy's total production of goods and services. A related and less used term, Gross National Product—GNP—adds to this value citizens' foreign earnings and subtracts foreigners' income within the country.) The OECD also attempts to coordinate members' economic and development aid, and it provided a forum for member states to hammer out an anti–bribery convention in international commerce. All Western European countries belong. Wanting closer contact with the world's industrial leaders, the Czech Republic, Hungary, Poland and Slovakia joined, and Russia decided to enter. With only 16% of the world's population, its 29 members produce two–thirds of the world's economic output.

The Council of Europe was created in Strasbourg in 1949. Its 40 members include all Western European countries and most newly independent countries in eastern Europe. Its assemblies of parliamentarians from the member states serve as a forum for discussing political, economic, social and cultural issues of interest to all European countries. Perhaps its main contribution has been its various conventions, especially its Convention for the Protection of Human Rights and Fundamental Freedoms (known as the European Convention on Human Rights—

EU Members

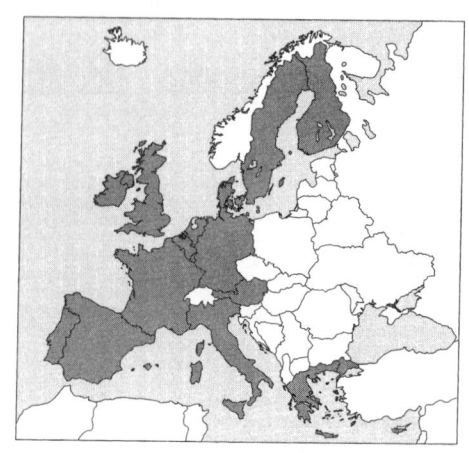

Western Europe Today

ECHR), adopted in 1950. Since 1991 it has been particularly active in trying to strengthen democracy and human rights in eastern Europe. It was because of possible human rights violations in Chechnya that there was criticism of Russia's entry in 1996. The United States requested and was granted observer status in 1996 in order to be able to promote democracy more effectively in eastern Europe.

The BENELUX countries, together with France, West Germany and Italy, made in 1951 the first significant move toward transferring a portion of their national sovereignty to a supranational organization by creating the European Coal and Steel Community (ECSC). Many persons could scarcely believe at the time that six countries which had been locked only six years earlier in a bloody struggle would be willing to transfer sovereignty over questions relating to these commodities, which are so crucial for heavy industry. Not only was it bold and far-sighted to share these important goods rather than to fight wars over them, but the ECSC gave these nations the practice in economic cooperation needed to convince the six that a move to create a unified Europe could succeed.

The same six nations signed the Treaties of Rome in 1957 which created both the European Economic Community (EEC, frequently called the "Common Market") and EURATOM, which seeks to coordinate the six countries' atomic research and policy. Both came into existence the following year and merged with the ECSC under the same overall organization. This union provided for the elimination of tariffs and customs among themselves, common tariff and customs barriers toward non-members, the free movement of labor and capital within the union and equal agricultural price levels through the establishment of the Common Agricultural Program (CAP). To avoid giving the impression that the three communities were only *economic* in nature and to express the fact that they are managed by common institutions, they were referred to in the singular as the European Community (EC).

The 15 member states (with about 375 million citizens in 2000, one-third more than the U.S.) which now include the BENELUX countries, France, Germany, Italy, Great Britain, the Republic of Ireland, Denmark, Greece, Spain, Portugal, and since 1995 Austria, Finland, and Sweden, have agreed to transfer a portion of their national sovereignty to the union. The irresistible logic of European unity has affected countries all over the continent.

Most European countries formally applied for EU membership. Norway was offered membership in 1972 and 1994, but its voters rejected it both times. In December 1997, EU leaders decided how expansion would proceed. They invited the six countries that had made the most economic progress to begin negotiations: Poland, the Czech Republic, Hungary, Estonia, Slovenia, and Cyprus (despite its continued division). Five other applicants were offered "pre-accession partnership" with considerable financial aid and an annual review to determine when they would be ready for negotiations: Latvia, Lithuania, Slovakia, Romania and Bulgaria. The most stinging rebuke went to Turkey, which already belongs to a customs union with the EU. Its 33-year bid to join the EU was rejected because of its poor human rights record, determined Greek opposition, and fears by countries like Germany that a flood of Turkish immigrants would arrive at their doorstep.

The issue of immigrants and refugees is a very sensitive one. Some Western Europeans fear that they bring in crime and terrorism and overburden their generous welfare states at a difficult time when their economies are suffering under the challenges of the global economy. Controlling the movement of outsiders who have entered Western Europe has been made more difficult by the Schengen agreements of 1985 and 1990 that aim to eliminate Europe's internal border controls. The idea is that one need only go through border formalities when entering one of the fifteen participating countries; then one can pass freely into the other 14, submitting only to occasional spot checks. All EU members except the UK and Ireland have joined, and since the Nordic countries long since abolished internal border controls, Norway and Iceland are automatically included. There are many problems to work out, and not all of the 15 participate entirely in the agreements. By 1998 only the BENELUX countries, France, Germany, Austria, Spain and Portugal were full members.

On November 1, 1993, the Maastricht treaty came into force, bringing with it terminological confusion. It created a European Union (EU), which added common foreign and security policy and cooperation in justice and police matters to the EC. But unlike the EC, the EU has neither a single decision-making process or a legal persona; it cannot conclude international agreements. Although the EC and EU are technically not exactly the same entities, most scholars and journalists now employ the term EU instead of EC. The term EU will be used throughout this book.

It is this political element which had prevented some other European states such as Switzerland from joining the EU, but the EU has successfully dealt with this problem by granting associate membership (which generally excludes agricultural aspects only) to most non-full-member states in Western Europe. Regular contacts are also maintained with 70 African, Caribbean and Pacific (ACP) countries linked to the EU through the Lomé Convention of 1975.

Most of the success which the EU can claim has been in the economic field. The record is most impressive. With only 6% of the world's population, the EU accounts for a fourth of the world's economic output, a third of the world's monetary reserves and 36% of the development aid. The EU is the United States' second largest regional export market after Asia, but the U.S. enjoys balanced trade with Europe, which is not the case with Asia. No single country in the world rivals Canada as America's major trading partner. The EU countries' investment in the U.S. exceeds that of the U.S. in the 15 EU nations.

Having cornered a fourth of global trade, it is the world's largest trading power. Politically, Western Europe is and will probably remain a region of largely

European Parliament building, Strasbourg, France

5

Western Europe Today

sovereign states, which make their own decisions about the vital matters which affect them.

The EU has a well–developed institutional apparatus. It has a dual executive: the Council of Ministers is the major decision–making body and is composed of the heads of government or ministers with responsibilities for finance, agriculture, etc., depending upon the specific matter which is pending. The Council meets three or four times per month, and representatives at the meetings carry instructions from their home governments. Decisions are made upon the basis of a weighted voting system, with the more populous member states receiving more votes than the less populous. But *each* member has a veto over issues which it considers to be of vital concern to its own interests. Thus, no important decision can be taken which appears to be wholly opposed to the interests of any member state. There is strong support for a reform which would eliminate the veto.

The Council is assisted by the Committee of Permanent Representatives (COREPER), composed of 15 EU ambassadors representing each member state. Since 1970 links among the member states' foreign ministries have been tightened through the European Political Cooperation (EPC) which prepares materials for them. The Single European Act (SEA) of 1987 put the EPC on a treaty basis. The EPC's key features are a commitment to consult, cooperate and agree by consensus on coordinated positions and joint actions regarding foreign policy issues of general interest. Meeting at the levels of heads of state or government, foreign ministers or senior foreign ministry officials, the EPC discusses such matters as human rights, terrorism, nuclear non–proliferation, and problems involving other regions. The opening of a secretariat in Brussels for European Political Cooperation (EPC) is an important symbol for European unification because member states tend to regard foreign policy as one of the last prerogatives of a sovereign state.

The second part of the executive which directs the day–to–day business of the EU is the European Commission which meets in Brussels and which is composed of 20 members, two each from France, Germany, Italy, Spain and Great Britain and one from each of the smaller member states. Each member is chosen by the government of his country for five–year renewable terms. After selection, each commissioner is expected to make decisions based not upon the interests of his home country, but instead on the interests of the EU as a whole. The commissioners decide issues by a simple majority vote; none has the power of veto. The chairmanship of the Commission rotates on a yearly basis among the member states. The decision of the Council of Ministers and the European Commission are carried out by a 17,000–member staff, working mainly in Luxembourg, Strasbourg, and the large EU headquarters in Brussels. The highest EU official is the European Commission President, selected by member countries for a ten–year term. The current president is Romano Prodi, former Italian prime minister, who replaced Jacques Santer of Luxembourg 1999.

A 626–seat European Parliament has 81 members from each of the most populous countries (except unified Germany, whose number was raised to 98), 60 from Spain, 25 from the Netherlands, 24 each from Belgium, Greece and Portugal, 16 from Denmark, 15 from Ireland, and six from Luxembourg. The rest go to the organization's three new members—Austria, Finland, and Sweden. It meets seven to eight times a year for one–week sessions. Formerly, the Parliament met in both Strasbourg and Luxembourg. However, in 1981 the Parliament voted to hold all its sessions in Strasbourg. Since 1979 its members have been elected directly in their home countries according to each country's own preferred method of election. Its members do not sit in national delegations, but in party groupings, such as the Communists and Allies, Socialist European People's Party (Christian Democratic), European Progressive Democratic and Liberal and Democratic Groups. There are a few unaffiliated members.

The European Parliament is officially entitled to oversee the work of the European Commission and to approve or reject the EU's budget. Since the SEA was introduced in 1987, the Parliament's power and influence have grown. Some legislation, most importantly that covering measures to bring into effect a unified European market, can be altered or amended by the Parliament. It can now veto the accession of new member states to the EU, as well as new trade agreements with non–EU countries. Finally, it oversees the Commission, a power that was dramatically demonstrated in 1999.

For years it had been asking questions about waste and mismanagement, but the Commission responded with arrogance and indifference. In January 1999 the Parliament threatened a vote of censure; a two–thirds majority could have removed all the Commissioners. This threat was averted when a panel of five independent experts were appointed to investigate financial impropriety. In March the panel published a devastating report accusing the well–paid Commissioners ($200,000 salary and expenses in 1999) of tolerating widespread fraud, corruption, nepotism, favoritism and mismanagement. All twenty felt compelled to resign. The consequence of this scandal is not only more democratic accountability, but a dramatic alteration of the political balance of power in favor of the elected European Parliament.

Finally, there is a European Court of Justice with its seat in Luxembourg and composed of fifteen justices, each chosen by member states for six–year terms. The Court judges violations of three major documents, the ECSC, EU and Euratom Treaties.

The SEA amends the European treaties by spelling out certain EU objectives: completion of the European internal market, creation of a great area without frontiers, technological development, progress toward economic and monetary union, improvement of the environment and working conditions, creation of more effective and democratic institutions, and institutionalization of cooperation among member states in the field of foreign policy. The target year 1992 was chosen for its symbolic importance: 500 years after the discovery of the New World.

From 1979 the European Monetary System (EMS) attempted, not always successfully, to coordinate the monetary affairs of certain Western European countries by attempting to link their currencies. At their 1991 Maastricht summit, EU leaders agreed to create a single European currency (called the "Euro") and a European Central Bank (located in Frankfurt, with Dutch banker Wim Duisenberg as its first

Italian election poster for the European Parliament: "Your vote for your Europe"

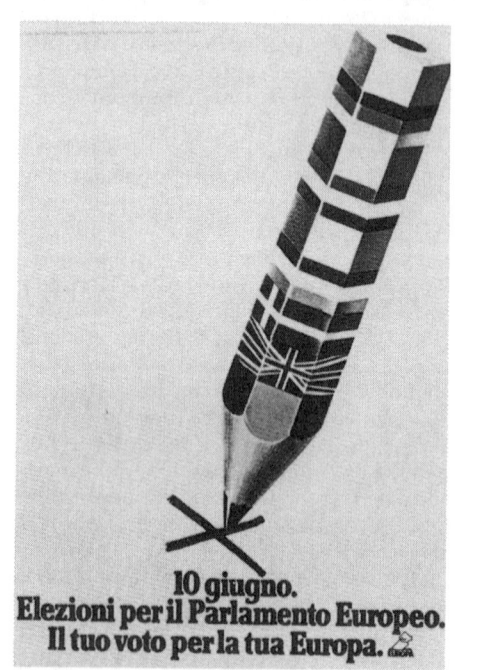

10 giugno.
Elezioni per il Parlamento Europeo.
Il tuo voto per la tua Europa.

Western Europe Today

president). The criteria for joining this Economic and Monetary Union (EMU)—a budget deficit of not more than 3% of GDP and a total national debt not in excess of 60% of GDP—placed enormous political strains on member governments. The inevitable austerity policies were resented by many of their voters. Many Europeans thought that the price to be paid for the Euro was not worth it.

But in 1998 the governments of 11 members (known unofficially as "Euroland") decided to adopt the Euro as of January 1, 1999, with Britain, Sweden, Denmark, and Greece waiting until later to join. Internal exchange rates are locked in, and the Euro floats in relation to outside currencies, such as the Dollar and Yen. Government borrowing and the prices of more and more consumer goods are quoted in Euros. Customers can pay in Euros with credit cards and checks. The quoting of stock and bond prices in Euros intensified efforts to combine the London and Frankfurt exchanges, with those in Paris, Amsterdam, Madrid and Milan showing interest in an eventual merger also.

Over the following three years, the participating countries will phase out their own currencies and phase in the Euro until it becomes the exclusive currency of members in July 2002. In order not to hurt national feelings, the new Euro bills will bear generic European designs: Gothic arches, bridges, windows, and a map of Europe. No scene from a particular country will be recognizable. The only national concession was made to Greece, which does not use Roman letters. The word for the currency will appear both as "EURO" and "EYPO."

A few countries which are not full members of the EU belong to the European Free Trade Association (EFTA), which was created in 1959 and whose headquarters are located in Geneva. Whereas the EU has a huge bureaucracy and budget, EFTA is a shoe-string operation, with 62 full-time staff, spending only $7 million in 1987. English is the working language, even though no member nation uses it as its mother tongue. EFTA has no political objectives, and its members have not relinquished a shred of sovereignty.

EFTA eliminated tariffs and customs on all industrial products bought or sold from all member nations, but it does not include agricultural or fishing products. All EFTA members have separate free-trade agreements with the EU. EFTA's economic importance declined after Great Britain, Ireland and Denmark left to join the EU in 1972 and Finland, Sweden and Austria in 1995. To restore EFTA's significance, its members—Switzerland, Liechtenstein, Norway, and Iceland—signed a trade agreement with Estonia, Latvia and Lithuania, effective 1996, calling for the free exchange of industrial goods and processed food and fish products. They also concluded cooperation agreements with Egypt, Morocco and Tunisia.

In 1991 the EU and EFTA countries agreed to form a European Economic Area (EEA), which creates a market of 380 million customers extending from the Mediterranean to the Arctic and accounting for over 40% of world trade. Within the EEA, EFTA members enjoy the EU's "four freedoms": of goods, services, capital, and people, but EEA does not include agriculture, fish, energy, coal and steel. EFTA members live under many EU rules although they have no voice in their writing; this lack of representation gives them added incentive to join the EU as full members. In 1991 the European Court of Justice rejected certain juridical aspects of the accord, and Swiss voters decided in 1992 not to join this single market.

All Scandinavian countries are in the Nordic Council, which meets regularly to discuss non-military problems which they have in common. Eleven nations belong to the European Space Agency (ESA) which, with American assistance, launched the first European Spacelab into orbit at the end of 1983. On board this Spacelab was the first European astronaut to travel into space with Americans—Dr. Ulf Merbold, a German physicist. In 1988 ESA also joined with the U.S. and Japan to begin construction of the Space Station Freedom.

Western European countries are also active in such international economic treaties or organizations as the General Agreement on Trade and Tariffs (GATT), the World Trade Organization (WTO), which since 1995 attempts to resolve disputes relating to the GATT Treaty, the International Monetary Fund (IMF), which provides funds for countries with balance-of-payments problems, the International Bank for Reconstruction and Development (World Bank), and the European Bank for Reconstruction and Development (EBRD). Headquartered in London, the EBRD was created after the collapse of Communism to help Central and Eastern European countries make successful transitions to free-market economies.

The International Energy Agency (IEA) exists to insure that all industrialized nations have minimally sufficient energy supplies in times of crisis. No European country belongs to the Organization of Petroleum Exporting Countries (OPEC), whose headquarters is in Vienna. Nevertheless, those Western European countries which export large quantities of oil, such as Great Britain and Norway (from the North Sea), note what is charged by the OPEC countries before setting their own prices.

Possible designs for the Euro

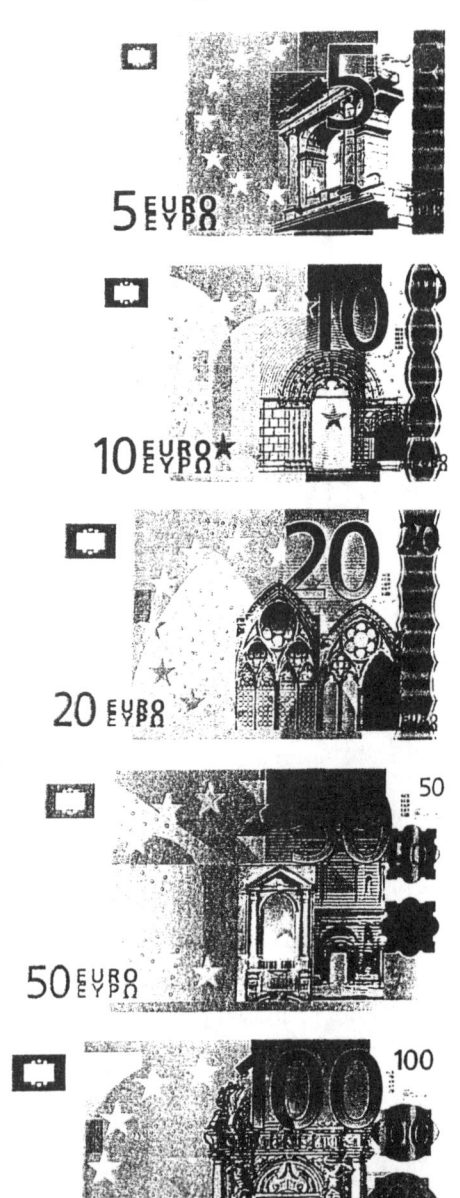

This high degree of cooperation and organization explains in great measure the tremendous growth of the economy of Western Europe. In a sense it may be likened to the United States, which, after discarding the Articles of Confederation and creating the present Constitution two centuries ago, abolished tariffs on goods shipped between the states and laid the groundwork for ever-closer cooperation among formerly sovereign entities. Through the many organizations they have formed and joined, Western European nations are better equipped and prepared to face the complicated problems of today.

The Federal Republic of Germany

Germany (FRG)

Midnight, October 2–3, 1990: UNIFICATION as throngs converge on Berlin's Brandenburg Gate which for over 40 years symbolically divided East from West of the now restored capital city of Germany.

Area: 137,691 sq. mi (357,050 sq. km., slightly larger than the combined size of Ohio, Pennsylvania and New York).
Population: 82 million, estimated.
Capital City: Berlin (became official capital by parliamentary vote in June 1991, following German unification on October 3, 1990), Pop. 4.1 million. Bonn remained the temporary seat of government until April 1999.
Climate: Northern temperate.
Neighboring Countries: France, Luxembourg, Belgium, the Netherlands (West); Denmark (North); Poland, the Czech Republic (East); Austria, Switzerland (South).
Official Language: German. The German language, structure and pronunciation varies widely according to region.
Ethnic Background: Indo–Germanic: Saxon and Teuton, plus an admixture of Slav and other tribes such as Goths.
Principal Religions: Protestant (Evangelical Lutheran), and Roman Catholic-Christianity, plus other and non–religious.
Chief Commercial Exports: Machinery, automobiles (Volkswagen, Mercedes–Benz, Audi), chemicals, iron and steel.
Major Customers: EU 54% (France 13.1%, Netherlands 8.4%, Belgium–Luxembourg 7.3%, Italy 9.2%, U.K. 7.6%), other European, 17.8%, OPEC, 8.3%, U.S. 6.3%, Eastern Europe ca. 10%.
Currency: *Deutsche* Mark.
National Day: October 3 (Day of German Unity).
Chief of State: Johannes Rau, President (since May 1999).
Head of Government: Gerhard Schröder, Chancellor (since October 27, 1998).
National Flag: Three horizontal stripes of black, red and gold.

Few people of the world have such a rich and varied past as do the Germans. Yet theirs is a history full of mountains and valleys. Without German science, theology, philosophy, music, literature and the other arts, Western civilization would have been left with gaping holes. But Germans have known times of shame and destitution so deep and dark that many could not be sure that the sun would ever shine again.

German history is one of religious, class and territorial division. Austria's Foreign Minister Prince Klemens von Metternich said in the early 1800s that Italy was mere-

Germany (FRG)

ly a *geographical conception*, but he could have said exactly the same about Germany. For many centuries there existed the fiction of a unified, almost universal German empire stretching from the North Sea to Sicily. Yet, until 1871 Germany was, in fact, a highly fractured scene of independent and rival kingdoms, principalities, ecclesiastical states and independent cities. Even though most of their subjects spoke one of hundreds of German dialects, few considered themselves *Germans*; rather they felt themselves to be Saxons, Bavarians, Prussians, Rhinelanders, or Frankfurters.

When political unity finally came in 1871, many Germans were left outside the new German Empire, such as the German–speaking Swiss and Austrians. This unity lasted only three–quarters of a century and ended in disgrace and destruction. Not until the Berlin Wall came tumbling down on November 9, 1989, did reunification become possible; on October 3, 1990, Germany became one country again, and that date is now celebrated as the national holiday.

Germany is populated by a dynamic, talented and imaginative people who for centuries have defied definition. Two thousand years ago, the Roman historian Tacitus called the Germanic tribes (which later migrated to most other parts of Western and Eastern Europe) warlike, but until the 20th century the Germans brought war to other nations far less frequently than did others. Germans were deeply involved in tragic wars in the 20th century, and even in 1950, the U.S. High Commissioner for Germany, John J. McCloy, joked "Just give me a brass band and a loudspeaker truck. Then let me march from Lake Constance in the South to Kiel up North, and I will have an army of a million men behind me—all eager–eyed."

He was badly mistaken. Germany is, in fact, now a country in which pacifist sentiment is perhaps stronger than in any other European or North American country. One young German noted with pleasure and with some exaggeration that "Europeans have always wanted a pacifist Germany; well, now they have one!" Indeed, a major source of American irritation toward Germany was the unwillingness of many Germans to defend themselves.

The French–Swiss writer, Madame de Staël, described the Germans almost 200 years ago as a pacific, poetic and romantic people, but Germans also acquired a reputation for diligence and order. German politics has often been described as romantic and irrational. But it was a German statesman (Bismarck) with whom one most directly associates the term *Realpolitik*, which describes a carefully measured, rational policy based on a realistic assessment of a nation's interests and means. The Germans' road to democracy was very bumpy and they have made several wrong turns. But today Germany is one of the world's most stable and tolerant democracies, about which former Chancellor Willy Brandt could say in the early 1970s: "Germans can again be proud of their country."

Germans are still, to a degree, haunted by their history. No people today tries so hard to come to grips with with its own past, and almost no one is more critical of Germany and its past than is the German himself. But the Germans' critical eye to their own past has brought some undeniable benefits to the present. It has helped to harden both the democratic consensus in Germany and the determination to bend over backwards to respect and protect human rights and dignity.

Clichés are never more than half–truths, but those relating to Germans are much more in need of revision than those about most other peoples. Germany is a country in the process of rapid change, in part because of industrialization familiar to Americans and other Western Europeans, and in part because of a lingering reaction to their own experience under Hitler, a dictator almost universally regarded outside and inside Germany as the most evil and brutal individual in recorded history. One can witness change in Germans' attitudes on politics, social problems, religion and work and in almost all German societal institutions, including the family and the schools. The process of integrating the former German Democratic Republic (GDR), which had been ruled by a Communist dictatorship for 40 years, is altering Germany even further. In short, Germany is a country which one must approach with a fresh and open mind.

The People and Place

Germans are the largest nationality in Europe west of Russia, where more than 1.5 ethnic Germans still live. The FRG has 83 million inhabitants after absorbing 17 million East Germans. Germany is a very densely populated country, with 250 inhabitants per square mile. The only European countries where the people live more closely together are the Netherlands and Belgium. The FRG's population is unevenly dispersed, though. The most thickly settled part is the Ruhr–Rhine area around Düsseldorf, Cologne (Köln), Dortmund and Essen (a conglomeration of cities and heavy industry often called "Ruhr City").

Other large urban concentrations are the Rhine–Main area around Frankfurt, the Rhine–Neckar area around Mannheim and Ludwigshaven, the Swabian industrial concentration around Stuttgart, as well as the cities of Berlin, Leipzig, Dresden, Bremen, Hamburg, Hanover, Nuremberg and Munich. There are, however, very thinly settled areas in the Northern German

Germany's highways

Germany (FRG)

Crop fields in a medieval pattern radiate from a Bavarian village   Jon Markham Morrow

Plain, the Eifel Mountain region, the Upper Palatinate, the Bavarian Forest and the peripheral areas adjacent to the earlier border with the GDR. Those latter areas on both sides of the former dividing line are experiencing rapid growth in unified Germany as they become the new heartland.

The FRG, as other countries, has experienced a rapid flight from farms into cities and towns; the rural population dropped from 23% in 1950 to less than 5% today. But about half of all Germans live in towns or villages of less than 20,000 inhabitants. Unlike countries such as France, Britain, Italy or Denmark, no single German city dominates the political, cultural and economic life of the entire country, although Berlin may gradually assume this position in the twenty-first century.

Germany has for centuries been called the "land of the middle" because it occupies the heart of Europe. This is a major reason why other European powers have often sought to keep Germany divided and weak. It has no natural frontiers, and the North German Plain, which is interspersed with hills, has always been and remains an ideal invasion route. Only the Alpine foothills in the Southeast offer uninviting terrain for invading commanders. Because the altitude rises from the North Sea to the Alps, most of Germany's rivers, which provide the country with an excellent inland waterway system, flow north and empty into the North Sea via the Rhine, Ems, Weser and Elbe rivers. The only exception is the Danube, which flows southeast toward the Black Sea.

The visitor to Germany now looks in vain for physical traces of the pauperized and demolished land which in 1945 began to dig itself out from under a pile of rubble. In the western part one sees a highly prosperous country with a well-fed, well-clothed, well-cared-for and predominantly middle-class people. Germans in the eastern part will enjoy roughly the same prosperity early in the next century. The FRG is ribboned by highly modern highways traveled by millions of private automobiles. (There is no speed limit on most superhighways.) Its modern cities in the West show few signs of urban blight, but cities in the East show their four decades of mindless and tasteless urban renewal or neglect. It is an economic giant in the world and now operates in European politics with far more confidence, effectiveness and respect than almost any other nation dreamed would be possible after Germany's total collapse in 1945.

The FRG has even become a less tense and far more pleasant place to live. With high incomes in the West, a short (35 hour or less) work week and a commitment to "quality of life," Germans have become world champion travellers abroad. When they stay home, they enjoy swimming pools, tennis courts, saunas and "free time centers," which have proliferated everywhere.

Their cities contain museums, concert halls and pedestrian zones fill with sidewalk cafes, street-shows and pleasant street life. When the University of Reading (in the UK) made a study of European cities in 1986, it considered such factors as social and environmental conditions, the state of the urban economy, per capita income, unemployment, net migration and supply of hotel bedrooms (as a measure of how many people visit them). The study concluded that the top two cities were Frankfurt and Munich. Eleven of the top 20 cities in Europe were West German, and not a single city in the western part of Germany figured among the bottom 20! Germans are increasingly enjoying their comfortable lives with a spontaneity which invites a much closer look at this modern country.

HISTORY

Roman Penetration

Around four centuries before Christ, Germanic tribes, which were of Indo-European extraction, began entering from

Germany (FRG)

the North and East of what is now Germany and displacing or mingling with the Celtic peoples whom they found there. These tribes were, however, not the only people to be attracted by the soil, rivers and strategic importance of this area in the heart of Europe. In 58 B.C. Julius Caesar led a Roman army which defeated the Germanic tribes in Alsace and in other Germanic areas west of the Rhine River. A good cultural observer as well a a good commander, Caesar wrote the earliest description of the tribes which he had just defeated and thereby sparked the interest and imagination of other Romans who later came to colonize or develop the area.

The Romans extended their frontier eastward toward the Elbe River in 9 B.C., but this expansion survived only two decades. A German chieftain, Arminius, (later known to Germans as Hermann) in 9 A.D. led an army which practically decimated the Roman occupation forces during a furious battle in storm and rain in the Teutoburg Forest, which is said to be located southeast of the present–day city of Bielefeld. The remnants of the Roman forces withdrew westward and southward again beyond the Danube and Rhine rivers. Thenceforth, the Romans remained behind their heavily garrisoned frontier stretching from Cologne (Colonia) to Bonn (Bonna) to Augsberg (Augusta Vindelicorum) and all the way to Vienna (Vindobona). Here the Romans built beautiful cities such as Regensburg (Castra Regina) and Trier (Augusta Treverum) with their stone structures, warm air heating underneath their floors, aqueducts, baths, coliseums and even running water in some villas and public buildings.

They introduced advanced Roman agricultural methods, a money economy and Roman law, administration and culture. Trier even served temporarily as a seat of the Roman emperor, especially for Constantine the Great from 306–312 A.D. What we now know about the Germanic tribes at that time came to us from Romans such as Tacitus, who in his book *Germania* described the tribes' legends, customs, appearance, morals and political and economic systems. His characterization of these tribesmen as particularly warlike helped launch a cliché about Germans which is by no means an inherent trait nor is valid today.

In the latter half of the 2nd century A.D., Germanic tribes began hammering away at the Roman front and, attracted by stories of great wealth in the Italian peninsula itself, actually invaded the heartland of what had become a decadent Roman Empire in the 5th century, causing it to collapse in the West. For centuries the Roman cities were left largely to decay, and much of the legal, administrative and cul-

Roman-built *Porta Negra* in Trier

tural advancements of the past were forgotten. Yet the Romans left their traces in the grammatical structure and some words of the German language, in the German concept of law and the cities which after the first Crusade in 1095 began to gain significance in Germany again.

Some historians have dated the beginning of German history at 9 A.D. when Arminius defeated the Romans at Teutoburg, but the various German tribes which he led against the Romans certainly felt no common identity among themselves as *Germans*. There can hardly be a *German* history without a *German* people and some kind of *German* state. It is a mistake to identify Germany with the various tribes which began to enter what is presently Germany before the arrival of the Romans and with those such as the East and West Goths, Vandals, Burgundians and Langobards which swept into the area during the great migrations before and after Roman supremacy. Those migrations almost completely changed the racial make–up of Europe from the 2nd through the 5th centuries A.D. The German nation was formed only very gradually over many centuries through the conquest and integration of a great number of Germanic tribes. Of course, some such as the Angles, some Saxons, the Danes, Swedes and Norwegians never became a part of the German nation. Others were initially conquered, particularly by the larger tribes—the Friesians, Franks and Swabians, Bavarians, Saxons and Thuringers—and ultimately grew into a community larger than any single tribe.

It is highly doubtful that a German nation would ever have emerged if a Carolinian empire had not taken shape after the Roman rule had effectively ended. This far–flung empire, composed 80% of Germanic peoples and encompassing those speaking Latin–based languages in the West, reached its peak under Charlemagne ("Charles the Great") who ascended the throne in 768 A.D.

During his rule the empire extended from northwestern Europe south to Rome and from Hungary to northern Spain. Charlemagne was a leader of extraordinary personal qualities who spent half his time in the saddle holding his vast territory together. His empire survived only a few years after his death in 814. It was divided in 817 into Kingdoms of East and West Franconia and Lorraine. After bitter and complicated inheritance quarrels, two realms faced each other along roughly the same line as the present border between Germany and France. By 843 this border had become more or less fixed, and in the year 925 it became firmly established. Only in the East could subsequent German expansion take place.

Although Charlemagne's huge empire had been considerably reduced after his death, he had created the indispensable foundation for the formation of a German nation and a German consciousness. There were no other geographic, racial, cultural or strictly linguistic factors which could have pulled Germany together without Charlemagne's political and military acumen. During his reign some persons began to refer to the tongues spoken in the Eastern part of the empire as "Deutsch" (*Doich*)—German, a word derived from "Diutisk," meaning "common" or "popular." In the following three centuries more and more inhabitants of what is now Germany developed a consciousness of being *German*.

Germany (FRG)

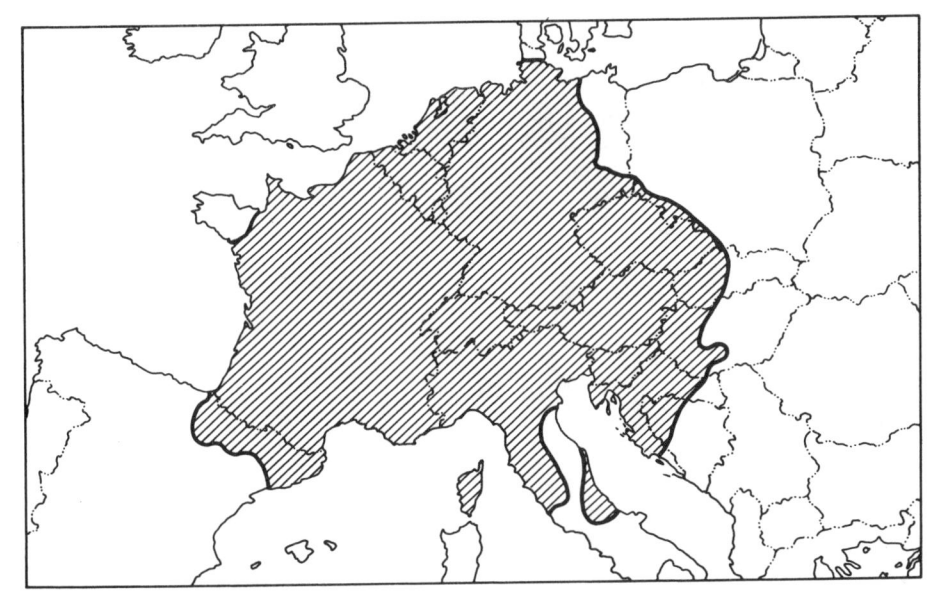

Charlemagne's Empire in 814

The eastern Franconian realm in 919 became the German Empire. "Empire," however, is a somewhat misleading word, since it connotes a centralized, unified power. In Germany there was a strong degree of unity, but until almost the end of the 19th century, rule was by a multitude of heads of local states and independent cities. However, by the 11th century these states and cities had become the most powerful in Europe and were able to claim the title "Roman Empire." In the 13th century this was dignified to the title "Holy Roman Empire," and in the 15th century "Holy Roman Empire of the German Nation." The reach and power of this empire expanded and contracted, but it always retained certain organizational features: the highest nobility (usually called "electors") actually *elected* an emperor.

Although this position was not hereditary as was the case with other European monarchies, there was a dynastic element in that, with very few exceptions, the new emperor had to be a blood relative of his predecessor. There was no capital city; he moved around continually, ruling from wherever he happened to be. He usually resided in various bishoprics or in a collection of buildings known as a *Pfalz*. As one can now see in the charming medieval city of Goslar in the Harz Mountains, the *Pfalz* contained a royal residence, buildings and stables for the emperor's retinue, at least one church or chapel and surrounding farms, mines and businesses from which the emperor could derive his income.

Since no taxes were levied, he was compelled to finance his activities from the various imperial estates throughout the empire. Finally, the major and minor nobility met infrequently in an imperial diet called the *Reichstag*, a body whose work cannot be compared to a modern democratic parliament, but one which displayed how much the emperor depended upon the lesser noblemen if he wanted to conduct a war, increase his revenues or the like.

Germany always has been a mixture of central and regional power, of unity and disunity. There were endless struggles over who should *lead* in the empire, and the emperor's actual power was never assured, even after he had been elected. He had to maintain a powerful army and forge delicate alliances among the rival dukes in the realm and powerful archbishops who ruled such important cities as Mainz, Cologne and Trier. This is why German provinces and cities became much more important in Germany than in other countries.

During the 8th and 9th centuries the Hungarians posed a constant threat to the German Empire. The fortresses which Romans built had long since fallen into ruin. To cope with this threat, the German kings and emperors erected fortresses around the imperial estates, royal and ducal palaces, abbeys and cities with the treasured right to maintain a market place. Erfurt, Meissen, Merseburg, Frankfurt, Ulm, Gosler and Aachen originated from fortified royal estates and palaces, and Augsburg, Passau, Strasbourg, Trier, Worms, Cologne, Mainz and Speyer, originated from fortified abbeys and monasteries. Martin Luther's characterization of God as "a mighty fortress" specifically refers to the safety found in these walled cities. The Hungarians were decisively defeated in 955 and were rooted out of what is now Austria, thereby permitting Bavarian settlers to pour into this "East March" (whence the German name for Austria: Österreich).

The Zenith of the Empire

The German emperors focused their attention far beyond what is now the German-speaking world, particularly on Italy. In 962 the Saxon King Otto I was crowned emperor by the Pope in St. Peter's Cathedral in Rome, a tradition which was to last over 500 years. This unique privilege, which was bestowed on no other ruler, entitled the German monarch to be called "emperor." It also gave the German Empire a universalistic claim to rule over the entire Western world as the protector of Christianity. This claim never became reality.

The special relationship which was established between the emperors and popes proved to be of questionable value for both. German emperors became embroiled in Italian and papal affairs for more than three centuries, a costly diversion from the more important task of creating a unified Germany. Emperors became active in papal selections and on occasion succeeded in driving popes right out of Rome. At the same time, popes often connived with Germany's enemies and bitterly fought again emperors' attempts to gain control of the Catholic Church within Germany.

A showdown between the two occurred in 1077 when Emperor Heinrich IV replaced Pope Gregor VII when the latter refused to permit Heinrich to appoint bishops and other high Church officials in Germany. Gregor struck back by taking away Heinrich's imperial crown, releasing all of Heinrich's subjects from their loyalty to the Emperor and excommunicating Heinrich. The latter soon realized how much he had overreached his power and authority and felt compelled to go to the fortress of Canossa, where the Pope had sought protection. Dressed in the simple garb of a penitent, Heinrich pleaded three days for forgiveness. Then with outstretched arms, he threw himself at the Pope's feet, who had no alternative but to forgive him. Heinrich's act of prostration at the feet of the Pope was a turning point in German history. Soon thereafter, a revengeful Heinrich drove Pope Gregor into exile and lonely death in southern Italy, and for centuries the German emperors could always count the popes among their enemies, even though they continued to influence their election until about 1250.

The perennial activity of the emperors in Italy tended seriously to weaken their ability to contend with the domestic challenges to their authority. One of the few exceptions to this was Emperor Friedrich I of the Swabian dynasty of Staufen, which from 1138 ruled Germany for about

Germany (FRG)

a century. Known as Barbarossa because of his red beard, Friedrich was a strong monarch from the moment he ascended the throne in 1152 at the age of 30. He was a handsome and imposing man, intelligent and well–educated. A highly charismatic figure who attracted loyalty and devotion like a magnet, he was a model knight whose martial skills he continued to display by participating in tournaments until age 60. Despite a determined challenge within Germany by the Saxon duke, his aims were clear: supremacy in northern and central Italy without suppressing the Italian cities' freedoms, and continued influence over the papacy without directly *controlling* Rome. He wanted to crown his reign with a triumphant crusade, but after forging a mighty army and guiding it toward the Holy Land, he drowned in a river in Saleph in Asia Minor.

After his death a legend was circulated by bards throughout Germany that the red–bearded Emperor was not really dead, but instead had sunk into a magic slumber within the mountain of Kyffhäuser, sitting on an ivory throne, his head resting on a marble table. He would leave Kyffhäuser only when his land signalled that it needed his help; if, however, all was in order, ravens would fly around the mountain, and Barbarossa would return to his sleep for another hundred years. Those ravens are still circling the mountain.

The Decline of "The Empire"

The German emperors' attention had become so fixed on Italy that the last Staufen emperor, Friedrich II, an erudite and far–sighted ruler, tried to rule the enormous empire from Sicily. Yet, by the time he died in 1250 and his successor, Conradino, had been executed in 1268, the German emperors could hardly pretend anymore to control large areas outside Germany. They had lost much of their power and influence within Germany as well. Due largely to the emperors' obsession with crusades and Italian campaigns, rather than for consolidating and increasing their power within Germany itself, a process of erosion of their power set in which left some free cities, several hundred German noblemen and the Church largely free of imperial control.

By 1268 no one could speak any longer of a powerful and supreme *emperor* over all of Germany. He could not call on the princes to support him in wartime without their approval; there was no common foreign policy, nor was there an imperial army. The only imperial laws which had any chance of being obeyed were those which had been approved by all three segments of the *Reichstag*—the "electors," the other princes and the cities—which the emperor convened infrequently in Worms, Frankfurt, Regensburg, Augs-

The Bamberg Knight, one of the 13th century's finest examples of statuary

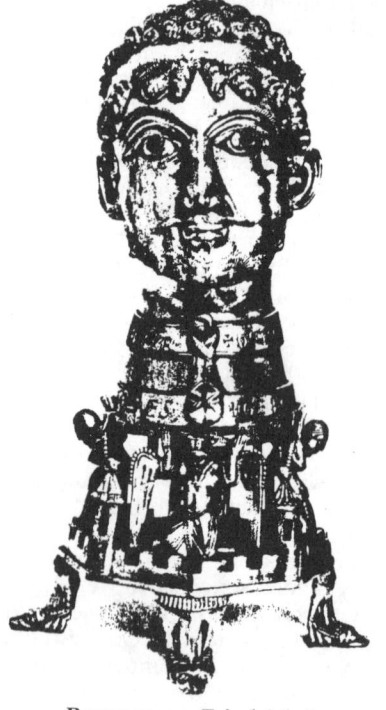

Romanesque **Friedrich I**

14

Germany (FRG)

burg or some other important city in southern Germany.

From the 13th century on, the parts of the Empire predominated over the whole, the regions over the Empire, the princes, kings and high clergy over the emperor. The absence of any strong, centralizing power in Germany prevented for six centuries the development of a unified German nation, as the French and English had been able to do. For six centuries, German politics was largely characterized by conflict between ruling houses. After 1438 the imperial crown practically became the sole possession of the House of Hapsburg, and Austria gradually became the predominant German–speaking territory and one of the most powerful countries in Europe.

The Rise and Fall of "City Power"

By the end of the 14th century the population of Germany had risen from less than a million in the year 500 A.D. to 13–15 million, despite the great plague which had reduced the European population by about a third. Most Germans lived on the land or in villages, and many were tied to the ground they worked and were compelled to deliver a considerable part of their produce to large landowners. Cities had begun to sprout up everywhere by the 10th century, primarily to provide protection. They also provided peasants with a place of refuge from the bondage which was widespread in the countryside.

The Crusades also had provided a mighty stimulation for cities, whose prosperity was often reflected in the mighty cathedrals which were built. Ulm built one, for instance, which could hold two and a half times as many people as lived in the city. Tradesmen and craftsmen in the cities began to develop *guilds* to protect their economic existence and to maintain a good reputation by assuring that quality work was done. These guilds also sometimes forcefully challenged the elite, patrician rule of the cities.

The power and influence of German cities was greatest when they joined together in *leagues.* The most important league was that of the Hansa cities. In 1241 Lübeck and Hamburg forged an alliance in order to protect the land and sea lanes between them from robbers, and gradually more and more cities along the North and Baltic Sea coasts, and even deep within the interior of Germany, Poland, the Baltic area and Scandinavia, joined. By the time the Hansa League had reached its height in the first half of the 15th century, it embraced such cities as Cologne, Brunswick, Bremen, Wismar, Rostock, Danzig, Königsberg, Breslau and Cracow, and the League had large trading colonies in London, Brugge, Gotland and Novgorod. Seldom did the Hansa cities conduct traditional military warfare; they preferred the far more effective trade war. Not until the end of the 15th century was the Hansa League's dominance over the North and Baltic Sea area broken.

By the 15th century, Germany had become a comparatively rich part of Europe, but, like today, its economic strength far outstripped its political influence. Although they remained far smaller than the leading cities in southern and western Europe, German cities had very much to do with such prosperity. The wars which were to ravage Germany in the 17th century, and especially the shift of the trade routes westward following the discovery of America, brought about the decay of the great German cities. This stagnation tended to clip the wings of the middle classes, which cities produce and strengthen, and therefore tended to stifle the development of democracy in Germany. It also left Germany primarily an agricultural country until the middle of the 19th century.

Intellectual Awakening

The 15th and the early 16th centuries were ones of intellectual awakening. This discovery of man and the world was the focus of humanism, which has remained controversial to this day and age, and the *Renaissance.* The latter was an Italian creation of the 14th and 15th century and for Europe signaled an important turning point. It meant an inclination on the part of a few to question all previous religious, scholarly, scientific and political authority which had placed limitations on man. It was a time when Leonardo da Vinci showed that natural science must be based on exact observation and experimentation, when Christopher Columbus dared to cross the ocean to disprove previous theories about the shape of the earth, when a Florentine political figure named Niccolò Machiavelli ripped the idealized cloth from politics to show it in its raw, non–ethical reality.

Germans were very much a part of this burst of discovery. Nikolaus Kopernicus, a clergyman from Frauenburg in Prussia, showed that the earth was not the center of the universe and was merely one of the many bodies in a much larger planetary system. Martin Behaim constructed the first globe of the earth. Peter Henlein produced the first pocket watch. Berthold Schwarz discovered shooting powder quite by accident and thereby revolutionized warfare. An ingenious goldsmith from Mainz, Johannes Gutenberg, developed the first printing press using mov-

The Holy Roman Empire, mid-14th century

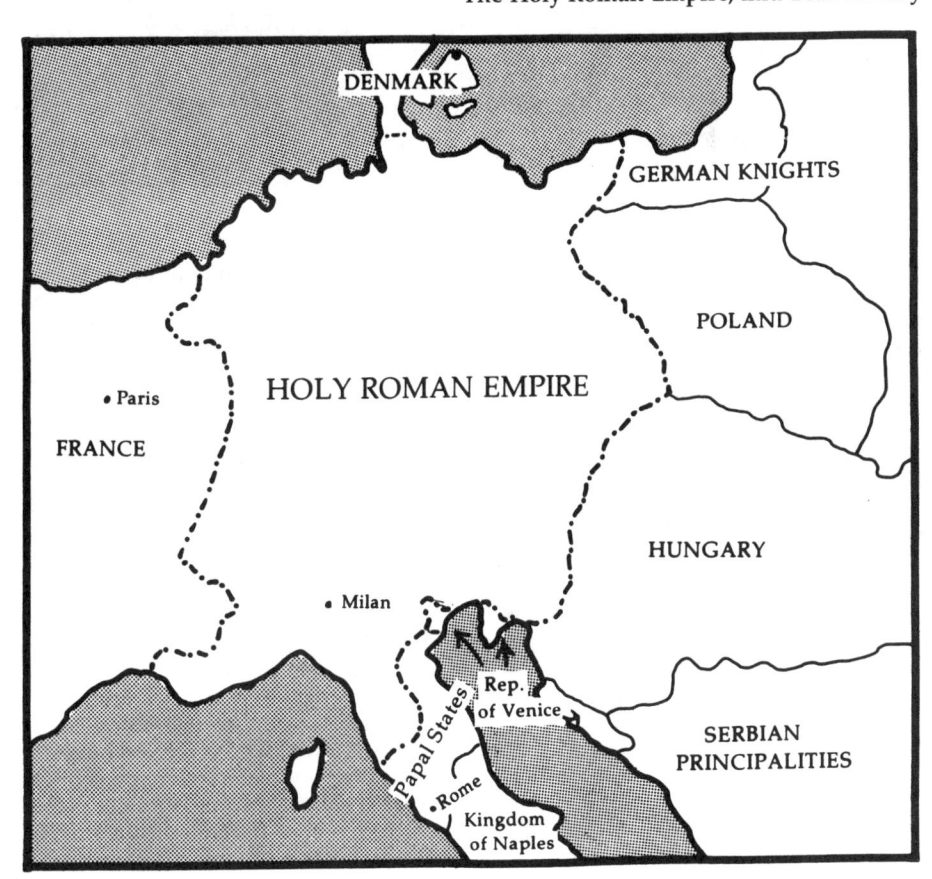

Germany (FRG)

Martin Luther

able type which was a prerequisite for taking the written word out of the libraries of the rich, the noble and the clergy and into the reach of the masses. In art, Albrecht Dürer, Hans Holbein and Mathias Grünewald achieved deserved recognition throughout the civilized world. Universities sprouted up all over Germany in this time of inquiry and became important centers of research and learning to the present day.

In this time of serious questioning it is not surprising that the practices and teachings of the Roman Catholic Church were also examined by critical minds. The master of all humanists was Erasmus of Rotterdam (1465–1536), who lived a part of his life in Germany and has amused the educated world with his *Praise of Folly*, in which he pointed to the grotesque difference between what men profess in *this* world and what they actually do. He also challenged the theologians to reexamine the New Testament in light of "the original sources." He criticized the abuses, pomp and ceremony of the Church and demanded a rational basis for the Catholic faith and a return to the "simple, pure Christ." He never broke with the Catholic Church, nor joined forces with those who later did, but he helped establish the theological foundation from which a Catholic monk in the provincial town of Wittenberg launched a powerful attack which shook the Church to its very roots.

Martin Luther

Martin Luther was the son of a minister from Thuringia who was able to save enough money to send his gifted but brooding son to the University of Erfurt to study law. Luther was reportedly shocked by a sudden flash of light and decided instead to become a monk, pastor and professor in Wittenberg. In 1511 he left for a long-awaited voyage to Rome as a firm believer, but he returned to Germany with his faith in the Church badly shaken. His anger and frustration built up as the Roman pontificate devised a method for raising its own revenues by selling to Catholics forgiveness from their sins.

In countries with strong central rulers, such papal financial maneuvers could be resisted, but until 1517 the Church's agents needed not fear resistance in the weak and fragmented Germany. When a papal representative knocked on Martin Luther's door to present the scheme one day, the glowing kettle boiled over. On October 31, 1517, he published his "95 Theses" branding the Catholic Church as an insult to God and challenging it to an open debate over fundamental theological issues. It is not certain that he tacked this highly explosive writing on the cathedral door at Wittenberg. What is certain, however, is that the Vatican was never the same after this angry monk rolled his weighty stone in its direction.

The Church decided to enter into a three-year debate with Luther, but this merely stimulated the interest which curious and critical Europeans paid to the stream of speeches and writings which poured from Luther's mouth and hand. When the Pope finally decided to silence this troublesome monk, it was too late. Martin Luther merely burned the Papal Bull (writing) in public and defiantly proceeded to the *Reichstag* in Worms. There he presented his views on April 18, 1521 to Emperor Charles V and to the leading German nobles, clergy and bourgeois in Germany. Luther held firmly to his views and asserted that "as long as I am not contradicted by the Holy Scripture or by clear reasoning, I will recant nothing since it is difficult and dangerous to act against one's conscience."

In order to protect this renegade with an enormous following in Germany, sympathizers captured him during his journey back to Wittenberg and took him to the Wartburg fortress outside of Eisenach. There he lived for a year under the assumed name of "Junker Jörg" far away from the furious controversies of the day. In 1522 he completed a German translation of the New Testament. This was not the first translation of the Bible into German; over 170 handwritten ones in the same language had appeared in the Middle Ages, and since the invention of the movable type printing press there had been 14 previous High German (northern Germany) translations. But Luther, the scholar, was able to penetrate deeply into the Greek and "Vulgata" texts and produce a translation, which, as he himself said, forced the prophets and apostles to speak a comprehensible German. Only

Germany (FRG)

such a text could enable the Christian to read and understand the Bible on his own, without the guidance or interpretation of the Church. In 1534 he published his final translation of both the New and Old Testaments, which found its way into enthusiastic hands all over Germany. In this way, Luther's German became the standardized *High German* which was spoken by the educated in every corner of Germany. Although a multitude of dialects continue to be spoken in Germany, Luther gave a land which was fractured into many tiny splinters a common language, which is essential for any collection of people which hope to be called a nation.

His call for a liberation from the theological confines of Rome unleashed demands for change and other forms of liberation which seriously shook the social structure of Germany. In all of these conflicts, the ultimate victors were the German princes.

There was a rebellion of knights in 1522 led by Franz von Sickingen, about whose origins we shall read later. Compared with the growing bourgeoisie (middle–upper class), which was becoming more and more prosperous in the cities, the economic importance of that portion of the lower nobility which had also been knighted (barons, etc.) was steadily declining. Also, armored knights on horseback had become militarily obsolete since Swiss infantry armed with halberds (a wide–shaped axe on a long pole) had learned to decimate their opponents with relative ease. Because of this, Swiss foot soldiers, not knights, became the treasured military mercenaries in half of Europe. The knights had lost most of their income and all justification for existing. Their rebellion was a desperate attempt to turn the clock back in Germany, but it was crushed by the princes. The status of knighthood was thereby eliminated once and for all as a power factor in Europe.

Although the princes became powerful, the people also became more assertive. In 1524–5 an idealistic priest, Thomas Müntzer, led a futile revolt of poor artisans and day workers against the princes in order to establish a "Christendom of the poor." A far more serious convulsion occurred when thousands of German peasants, primarily in the southern part of Germany, revolted. This was the largest and most forceful revolution in the history of a people who have manifested very little attraction to revolutionary causes. Almost four centuries later, the professional Russian revolutionary, Vladimir Ilyich Lenin, remarked scornfully that if would–be German revolutionaries wished to storm a train station, they would first buy a ticket before setting foot on the platform.

Revolt

The peasants revolted against the remnants of serfdom which still bound many of them to the higher nobility. The nobles tended to despise all simple people who worked the land as persons without rights. The peasants resented the steady increase in payments and work days owed to the lords, and they demanded protection for fishing and hunting rights, as well as a return to community use of much of the grazing and watering facilities which the lords had simply appropriated for themselves. They demanded a reestablishment of earlier institutions, which had granted them some self–rule, and they insisted on a return to "the earlier justice," to German law, rather than Roman law. The latter was preferred by the lords because it denied peasants any freedom whatsoever.

Those who joined this revolt found in Luther's words about the "freedom of a Christian man" a divine justification for their goals and actions. Initially, Luther sympathized with the peasants' demands and encouraged the lords to take their pleas seriously. But when the bands of rebels began to attack fortresses and churches and to dispatch with bloody swiftness those who wielded earthly authority, Luther became furious and lashed out against those whom he accused of turning Germany into a battlefield.

When it came to "things belonging to Caesar," Luther did not hesitate to decide in favor of order and princely authority. His reaction to this social revolution and its ultimate cruel suppression had serious consequences for Germany. Peasants remained poor, despised, unfree and without political influence for almost 300 years, until reforms in the wake of the French Revolution finally eliminated the formal chains which had been placed on them. Perhaps more important, Luther's stand left a legacy of freedom in Germany which was interpreted only as inner, purely mental freedom, but *not* political freedom. Thus, this man who had led the charge against the limits placed on man through Catholic theology actually justified external obedience to the princes and thereby strengthened the hierarchical political order within Germany. This helped to retard the victory of democracy within Germany until the middle of the 20th century. It even allowed some Germans who strongly disapproved of National Socialism *(Nazism)* after 1933 to remain within a brutal dictatorship, but nevertheless to persuade themselves that they could embark upon an "internal emigration."

The new Protestant faith spread quickly throughout northern Germany and Scandinavia. By 1555, about four–fifths of all Germans had embraced the new belief. In that year the Peace of Augsburg was reached which recognized that the Protestant faith had an equal status with the Catholic and that each territorial prince and free city would decide which faith should be practiced by *all* residents under their control. *Cuius regio, eius religio* ("whoever rules chooses the religion") was the formula for a kind of religious

Document signed in 1529 by Charles ("Carolus") V, the Holy Roman Emperor

Germany (FRG)

freedom which was restricted to the rulers. Those subjects who could not accept their rulers' preference had to move to another territory or city, and thousands of Germans did just that. Thus, the religious division of Germany was sealed for centuries.

The Time of Troubles

The Peace of Augsburg did not permanently settle the religious question in Germany. A Catholic counter–reformation, set in motion in Rome and supported by the Hapsburg emperors, heated tensions between German Protestants and Catholics, who formed a Protestant Union and Catholic League in 1608 and 1609 respectively. All that was needed was a spark in Bohemia to ignite an almost indescribably destructive "Thirty Years War" on German soil which ravaged this weak and divided land from 1618 until 1648.

In the early years of the war the Catholic states, particularly Austria and Bavaria, won brilliant victories, penetrating northern Germany to the Baltic Sea and reconverting by the edge of the sword many Germans to Catholicism. Catholic successes stemmed largely from strong internal friction within the Protestant camp between Lutherans and Calvinists and from extraordinarily capable generals, Tilly and the dashing and overly ambitious Wallenstein.

These initial successes under Hapsburg leadership prompted other European powers to enter the war. It was soon obvious that this war was not even primarily a religious struggle for the souls of Germans. Fearing Hapsburg control over a strategically important part of the Baltic Sea, and noting suspiciously a Hapsburg alliance with Catholic Poland, the Danish King, Christian IV, and then the Swedish King, Gustavus Adolphus, took over leadership of the Protestant cause. They received financial support from England and Holland. More importantly, the Swedish King was able to receive aid from Catholic France, which was always determined to prevent the Hapsburgs from growing too strong, especially when in control of Spain as well as Austria.

Thus, Germany was criss–crossed by marauding foreign armies which lived off the land in a manner summarized by Wallenstein: "The war must feed the war." No door, wall or fortress could protect the civilian population from the armies which cut wide swaths through the countryside and cities, followed by hordes of often disease–ridden camp followers, and leaving a trail of wreckage, ashes and corpses behind them. Ironically, some of the powerful, comforting and assertive Lutheran hymns were written during this devastation. An example of how arbitrary such destruction could be was Rothenburg ob der Tauber, today one of Germany's most beautifully intact medieval cities. Field Marshal Tilly offered in 1631 to spare the town and its leaders only if one of the city councilmen could drink about a gallon of wine *in one draw*. The elderly mayor stepped forward and accomplished this incredible feat, thereby saving his city and colleagues!

Contemporary drawings of the Thirty Years War

The Treaty of Westphalia

Who won this 30–year nightmare? A quick glance at the Treaty of Westphalia in 1648 gives the answer. Sweden took control of the city of Wismar, the Dukedom of Bremen–Verden (except the city of Bremen), the islands of Rügen, Usedom and Wollin, and part of Pomerania, thereby depriving Germany of the outlets to the sea via the Elbe, Weser and Oder rivers. France got most of Alsace, the cities of Metz, Toul, Verdun, Breisach and the Rhine, and achieved protector status over ten German imperial cities. Germany's western border, which had existed since the 9th century, was thus fundamentally altered. Switzerland and the Netherlands were granted full independence from Germany.

The German princes' official right to determine the religious beliefs of all their

Germany (FRG)

subjects was withdrawn, at least in theory. But the German princes were granted full sovereignty within their own territories, including the right to make treaties with foreign powers. The proviso that these treaties could not be directed against the emperor or the Empire remained valid only on paper. Germany was left with almost 2,000 sovereign states ranging from the large territories of Brandenburg, Austria, Saxony and Bavaria, 83 free and imperial cities (including Hamburg and Frankfurt am Main), countless ecclesiastical and other small units, some of which included as few as about 2,000 inhabitants. The map of Germany now looked more than ever before like the face of a child with measles. At a time when centralizing, centripetal forces were at work in England and France, centrifugal forces were prevailing in Germany, throwing it farther and farther away from national unity. There could no longer be any serious talk of "imperial politics"!

Germany was left breathless, devastated and demoralized from the plunder and destruction. In some areas such as Württemberg, the Palatinate, Thuringia and Mecklenburg, two–thirds of the inhabitants had been eradicated, and overall losses in Germany ranged from a third to a half of the total population. The total population dropped from about 20 million to 10–14 million. Thus, Germany, which at the beginning of the 17th century had the largest number of inhabitants in all of Europe, fell behind that of France for the next century and a half and behind that of Russia to the present day. It was more than a century before it reached its pre–1618 level. In addition to human deaths, 1,600 cities and 18,000 villages had been totally demolished, and livestock, farmland and the rest of the economic infrastructure had been left in shambles. In comparative terms, the destruction to Germany was far greater in 1648 than in 1945. One could say that only an atomic war could produce comparable damage today.

**Alien Forces Move In;
Germans Leave for America**

It is not surprising that the Turkish Ottomans and the French took advantage of Germany's plight to try to enrich themselves further. While Prince Eugene of Savoy was able to stop the Turkish invasion at the gates of Vienna in 1683, the French were far more successful under King Louis XIV to acquire what Cardinal Richelieu called *une entrée en Allemagne* ("a gateway into Germany"). In several campaigns France snatched about 600 cities, villages and fortresses in Alsace. It took Strasbourg and a large tract of territory between Alsace and Lake Geneva, and its decision to "burn the Palatinate" left such lasting traces as the ruins of Heidelberg Castle.

One of the many consequences of the seemingly perpetual war and religious strife in this era was that many beleaguered sects, such as the Mennonites, Quakers and Dunkers, decided to seek their peace and happiness in the New World. There they could escape the political and religious hierarchy, as well as the earthly corruption into which the European nobility had apparently fallen. The first German immigrants to America tended to settle in New York, Maryland and Virginia, but in 1681 William Penn established the first religiously free state in Pennsylvania. The German exodus to Pennsylvania began with 13 Mennonite families from Krefeld in Westphalia, who landed in Philadelphia on October 6, 1683, a day still celebrated in some parts of the United States as "German Day." They created Germantown on the outskirts of Philadelphia. They were followed by the Moravians, so–called because they came from the Hapsburg province of Moravia, and the Amish (erroneously called Pennsylvania "Dutch") from the area of Bern, Switzerland, who have retained to this day, in large part, most aspects of a life style characteristic of pious Germans in the 17th century, including the Bern dialect of German.

Not all Germans found in America the "quiet, honest and God–fearing life" of which they had dreamed, but their reports back to Germany helped open the flood gates for further waves of refugees from religious persecution in the 18th century. One Protestant group from the area of Brunswick set sail in 1707 for New York, but unfavorable winds forced them to land in Philadelphia. They decided to settle in New Jersey, which in 1733 became the home of an immigrant named Johann Peter Rockefeller, who founded what later became one of the richest families in the world. By 1776 there were more than 250,000 Germans living in the thirteen colonies. Germany's religious quarrels were America's gain.

Movement to the Northeast

By the middle of the 17th century, the Germans had been reduced largely to mere spectators and objects of European politics. However, the next 50 years saw this situation change; a highly dynamic

The extremely fragmented Holy Roman Empire after the Treaty of Westphalia: 1648

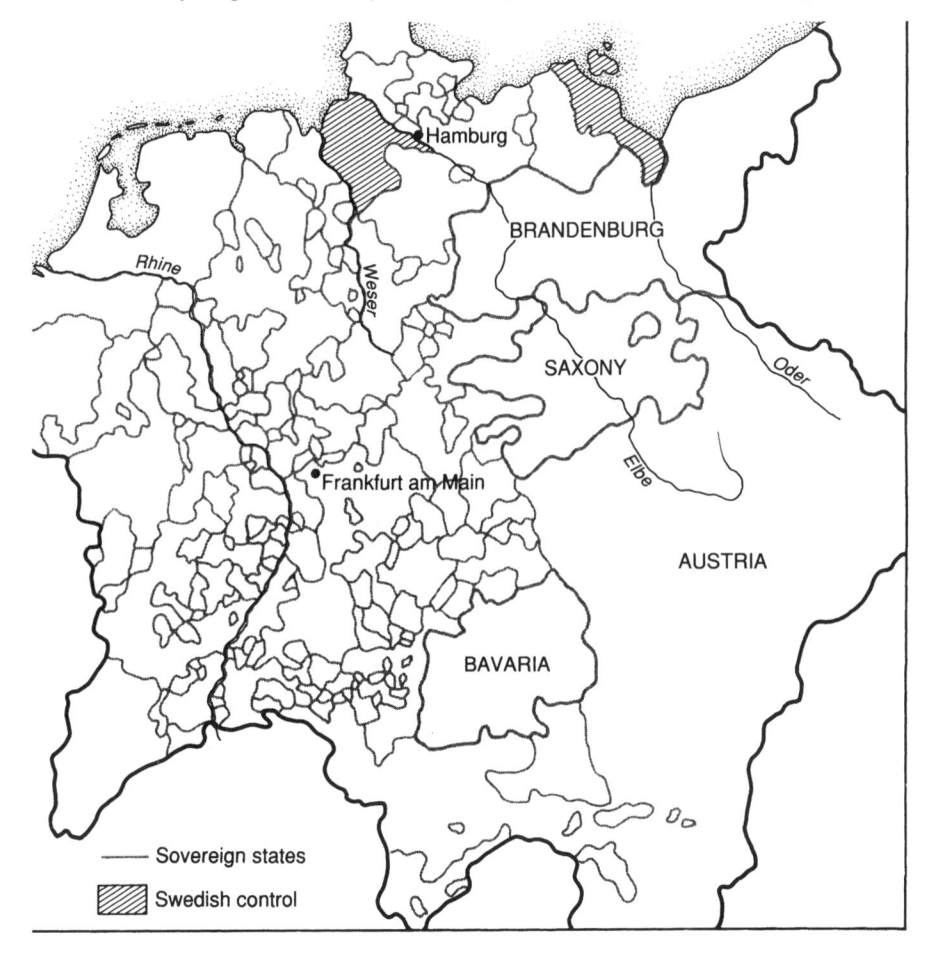

19

Germany (FRG)

state arose on the sandy soil in the eastern part of the Empire which forced its way into the ranks of world powers by sheer force of will, hard work and discipline: Prussia.

Before the 12th century Germany had consisted of two basic parts: a Romanized Germany west of the Rhine and south of the Danube and a Germanic territory east and north. After the 12th century a third part began to take shape: in the Slavic and Baltic East which came to include Mecklenburg, Brandenburg, Pomerania, Upper Silesia and East Prussia. This development involved the often violent conquest of Slavs and Balts and the partial absorption of these peoples. With the conquest and colonization of the East, the Empire's center of gravity slowly began to move eastward.

The motives of those Germans moving East were by no means nationalistic, but rather materialistic and idealistic. German farmers sought land and more independence from their earlier masters; noblemen wanted to open new ground and to gain income from it; skilled craftsmen and businessmen sought new opportunities and markets. However, none of these desires could have been fulfilled if another powerful motive had not been at work as well: the Christianizing of "heathen" peoples.

Medieval Knights

The Crusades which began at the end of the 11th century sparked the imagination of a class of persons which had begun to emerge before the 10th century: the knights. Warfare had been revolutionized in such a way that foot soldiers were replaced by well–armed knights who often fought on horseback. Therefore, the high nobility required knights to live in their vicinity or in fortresses or estates which the lords placed at their disposal. Most of the knights in the earlier days were not of noble birth, so they attempted to make up for their humble status by developing certain virtues such as bravery, courage, loyalty and consistency. The highest virtue was moderation in every situation but battle.

One of Friedrich Barbarossa's sons founded a "German Order of Knights" in 1198, whose mission at first was to care for pilgrims and crusaders in the Holy Lands. It soon joined the active military struggles against the Islamic disbelievers who had laid an allegedly unjust claim to the Holy City of Jerusalem. The Order took in both knights, priests and other brothers who could perform useful services, and its uniform was a white cloak with a black cross on it. Their rules were as strict as those in a monastic order. Since they saw themselves as fully dedicated to the service of Christ, they did not marry. They were also forbidden to own property and swore to maintain absolute loyalty and personal poverty.

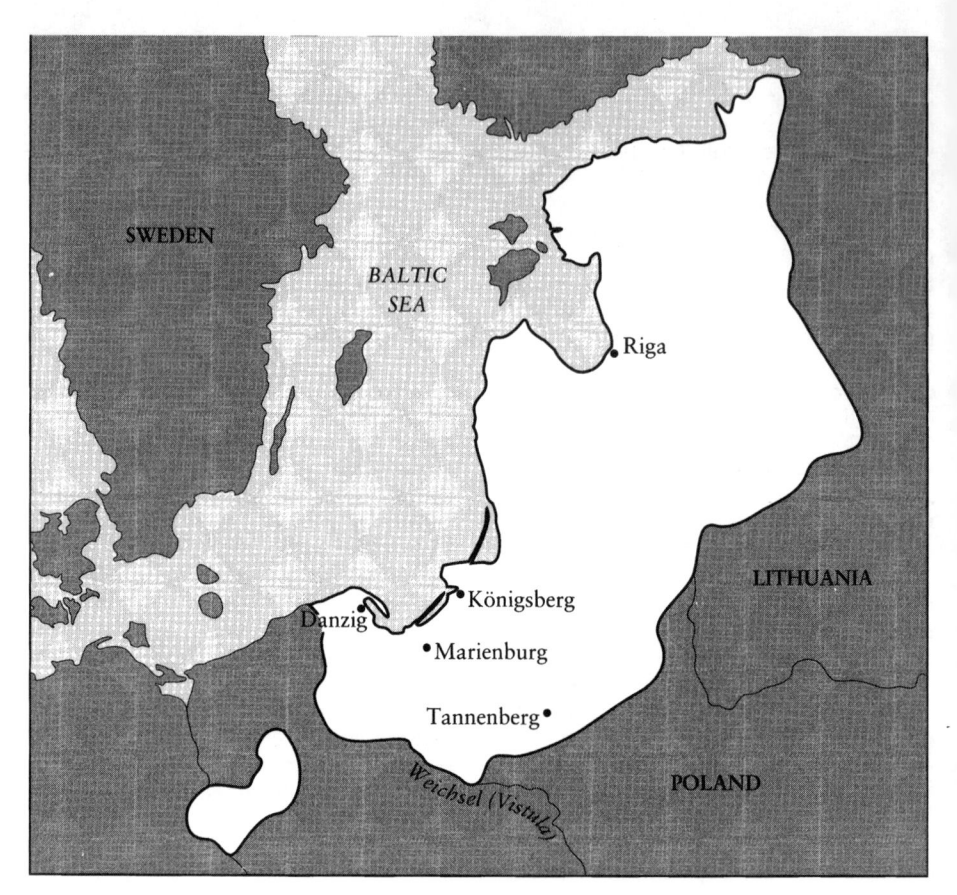

The German Order of Knights at its pinnacle

The Rise of Prussia

Less than a quarter of a century after the Order was founded, its sights were cast in an entirely different geographic direction. A Polish Duke, Conrad of Masovia, asked for the Order's help in 1226 to assist in crushing a hardy tribe of "heathens" called "Prussians." This was a Baltic people related to the Lithuanians and Latvians and regarded by Germans and Poles alike as barbarians. They had no written language, but they had strange customs such as polygamy and placing unwanted babies out to die. The conquest and Christianizing of such a tribe received the blessing of the Pope and the approval of the Holy Roman Emperor. With such encouragement and advancement under the call of "Death to Disbelievers," this conquest was bound to be a cruel one.

The German Order crossed the Vistula River in 1231 in order to engage the Prussians. Not until 1283 was the bloody job completed and the entire territory from the Vistula to the farthest border of East Prussia (that portion of Prussia east of the Vistula estuary) brought under the Order's control. The struggle had devastated much of the land and almost completely eradicated the Prussian tribe. The remnants were converted to Christianity upon the threat of death and were ultimately absorbed by the German conquerors. Their language disappeared completely, and all that remained of them was the name "Prussia," by which the territory came to be known and which became the official name of the state in 1701.

The German Order created a holy republic over the land, and in 1309 the Order's Supreme Master, who was elected by the other knights, moved his seat from Venice to the fortress of Marienburg in Prussia (now in Poland). From there commands were issued to fortresses and cities throughout the entire area. It became a German–led, rigidly organized land administered by the knights, who since they were forbidden to own property, possess wealth or marry, were more like ascetic civil servants than feudal lords. They directed the systematic colonization of the land and were responsible for the establishment of more than 1,000 villages and 100 cities, including the major ones, Danzig (now Gdansk in Poland), Elbing and Königsberg (now Kaliningrad in Russia). Until well into the 15th century, the history of Prussia is the history of colonization, and in some areas this was more violent than in others.

Germany (FRG)

Nowhere were the Slavic or Baltic populations forced to move, and Germans, Slavs and Balts lived side–by–side, although in most places the key political and economic positions were occupied by Germans. The nobility and bourgeoisie were predominantly German, but the agricultural population was mixed. This condition continued more or less to exist until Hitler and Stalin launched massive exterminations and expulsions in the 20th century to homogenize the ethnic composition in these areas.

The German Order of Knights reached its pinnacle in the 14th century, but its hold over the area was broken in the 15th century. Poles and Lithuanians attacked Prussia in 1410 and delivered the knights a crushing defeat on a wet and stormy day in the woods of Tannenberg. This was the first major military defeat which the Order had ever suffered, and sensing the way the wind was blowing, many German noblemen sided with the Poles. Only Marienburg remained unconquered, but new battles eventually drove the Order out of all the area except East Prussia, which in 1466 became a tributary of Poland. The Order was compelled to swear loyalty to Poland.

One area in the German East which had resisted domination by the Poles was the Elector Principality of Brandenburg, a relatively insignificant, poor and backward territory on the periphery of the German Empire, and ruled by a dynasty from southern Germany, the Hohenzollerns. Brandenburg and East Prussia had become linked in 1525. Taking advantage of the severe turmoil caused by the Reformation, the last Supreme Master of the German Order, Albrecht von Brandenburg–Ansbach from the family of Hohenzollern, simply assumed in 1525 the earthly title of "Duke of Prussia," and in 1660 the last ties which bound East Prussia to Poland were severed.

The Hohenzollern dynasty, which had made its residence in Berlin and whose heartland remained Brandenburg, was able to gain control of West Prussia, Pomerania and Silesia, and ultimately it acquired huge chunks of territory in the Rhineland and Westphalia as well. From a poor land known derisively as "the sandbox of the Empire" with no raw materials and a population of little over a million persons grew a huge and powerful kingdom ultimately embracing about two–thirds of all Germans and serving as the foundation for the first truly unified German Empire in 1871.

Perhaps more than any other European state, Prussia did not evolve, but was made by the human hand. A series of extraordinarily able rulers in the 17th and 18th centuries enabled Prussia to rise like a meteor to the ranks of the major European powers. From 1640 to 1688, Friedrich Wilhelm, "the Great Elector," laid the cornerstone for a powerful Prussia. He had spent three years in the Netherlands during his youth, and there he had been deeply influenced by the Calvinist dynamism and sense of obligation. He married a woman from the ruling House of Orange. From the Thirty Years War he had drawn the lesson that his state needed to enhance its military prowess. He said "Alliances are good, but one's own power is even better; one can more safely depend on that." He therefore enlarged the Prussian army from 3,000 to 30,000 soldiers.

He also established an oft–forgotten Prussian tradition which lasted for a century and a half and which was both humanitarian and strengthened Prussia. When the French King invalidated the Edict of Nantes in 1685, which had granted considerable religious and civil liberty to the Huguenots (French Protestants), Friedrich Wilhelm responded with the Edict of Potsdam opening the Prussian gates to the religiously persecuted. More than 20,000 French Huguenots, most of them skilled craftsmen and businessmen, poured into Prussia, and by the year 1700 one out of three residents of Berlin was French. Far from attempting to Germanize these newcomers, foreigners were permitted to retain their own language and customs.

The Huguenots built their own schools and churches and powerfully contributed to the arts and to the vibrant economic life of Prussia. Many of the area's greatest names until the present day are of French origin. More than 20,000 Protestants from Salzburg fled the counter–reformation and in the course of the 18th century there was a steady stream of emigrants and religious refugees to Prussia: Mennonites, Scottish Presbyterians, Jews and sometimes Catholics. In some ways, Prussia in the 18th century was to the persecuted of Europe what America was in the 19th century: a religiously tolerant land which offered enormous opportunities to the talented and hard–working.

Prussia Becomes a Center of Culture

Friedrich I ascended to the throne in 1688. He was a well–educated and cultured man who maintained a glittering, but excessively extravagant court. He established another Prussian tradition which is also frequently overlooked today: he established Prussia, especially Berlin, as a leading home for science and the arts. He founded the Academies of Art and Science, and he ordered the building of many edifices, such as the Charlottenburg Palace, which changed the face of Berlin from that of a peripheral and provincial town to that of one of the most dignified cities in Europe. He also achieved through patient and skillful diplomacy an important political goal: in 1701 he won the Emperor's approval for the Prussian Elector to bear the title of "king." This was a considerable boost for the prestige of a still poor country on the outskirts of the German Empire.

The Soldier King

When Friedrich Wilhelm I (so numbered because the earlier Friedrich Wilhelm had not been a king), was crowned in 1713, Prussia gained a ruler who was capable, but greatly different from his predecessor. What one now most often associates with Prussia was largely due to the new King's influence: the spirit of Spartan simplicity and the conscientious fulfillment of one's obligations to the state, which was to be ruled by the king alone, but for the good of the subjects. As he told his son, "The dear Lord placed you on the throne, not in order to be lazy, but in order to work and to rule his lands well." He discarded the luxurious court life his father had conducted to compete with the glittering courts of France and Austria, and introduced an austere court. He also created a first–rate civil service staffed by duty–conscious, highly respected, but poorly paid officials.

His popular name, "the Soldier King," indicates where his primary attention was paid. Although during his entire reign he led his country into only one short war, he poured four–fifths of all state income into the army, whose size he doubled to 70,000 men. The stunningly rapid growth of the Prussian army in size and importance prompted the Frenchman Mirabeau to remark shortly after the death of Friedrich Wilhelm I: "Other states possess an army; Prussia is an army which possesses a state!"

Located in the middle of Europe with a conglomeration of often unconnected territories and no natural frontiers and a relatively small population, Prussia had to have a strong army to maintain itself in the kind of international setting which prevailed at that time. One could argue the Prussian army was disproportionately large in relation to the country's population and financial strength. But it must be remembered that the new army was still considerably smaller than those of Austria, France and Russia and that "militarism" was by no means restricted to Prussia during this "Age of Absolutism." Further, the Prussian army never "possessed" the state, as Mirabeau charged. It was the most disciplined army in the world and never made the slightest attempt to rule the state.

The army was, without a doubt, first

Germany (FRG)

Voltaire's room at Sans Souci

rate. Carlyle once wrote that Prussia had a shorter sword than Austria, France and Russia, but that it could draw it out of the sheath much more quickly. It was open to the newest military technology. Also, the Prussian army became more and more a national army and less and less a mercenary army. Prussia was one of the first countries in the world to learn that its own citizens serve better than the troops of a foreign country. Its discipline and well–planned supply system was also a blessing for the civilian population in those areas where the army operated. In an age of undisciplined armies which "lived off the land," the civilian population was constantly subjected to plunder, murder and rape. Civilians seldom needed to fear such horrors from the new Prussian army.

Friedrich Wilhelm I was interested solely in establishing the best–organized, most modern and efficient state and military in the world. Unlike his father and his son, he was utterly disinterested in art and education. This brought him into violent conflict with his son. The father was a stern ruler who was wholly absorbed in enhancing his state's power. In 1758 his son, who in 1740 had become King Friedrich II, wrote this about his father: "Books, flutes, writings—if he could ever get his hands on them, they were thrown into the fireplace, and the burning of my books was always accompanied by several blows or by very emphatic rebukes."

Friedrich "The Great"

The son was a sensitive, highly intelligent humanist, who composed flute concertos which are still played in concerts, and who preferred all his life to use the French language. He even wrote thoroughly respectable poetry and essays in French. Most of his writings, which now fill 25 volumes, are in French rather than German, which he never learned to write without numerous mistakes. He was a close friend of the French philosopher and satirist Voltaire, whom he invited for prolonged visits to Berlin and Potsdam. In general, the young Friedrich was open to all the cultural, philosophical and liberal political ideas of his day. He was an enlightened man with a strong sense of taste, as his favorite residence in Potsdam, Sans Souci (French for *Carefree!*) manifested his nature. He despised the absolutist government of his father, even if it was aimed for the good of the people. Once, at age 18, he even tried to flee his father's kingdom with a close friend, but they were caught and delivered back to an irate parent and placed in prison.

What should his father have done? Have the heir to the throne and his friend both hanged for treason? Disregard the law of the land and forgive both for a treasonous act? The father's solution: he had the friend executed for treason right in front of Friedrich's eyes! This paradoxical mixture of strict justice, mercy and reason of state has troubled many people ever since.

Finally, at the age of 28, Friedrich II ascended to the throne in 1740. The young King's reaction to this event was characteristic: "How I abhor this job to which the blind coincidence of birth has condemned me!" Many persons saw in the new King the first philosopher to ascend a throne since the Roman Emperor Marcus Aurelius. Friedrich announced that "any man who seeks the truth and loves it, must be treasured in any human society." Within the first week of his rule, he abolished torture in all cases but high treason. Throughout his 48–year reign, he demanded of every subject a strict performance of his duty. But he was always inclined to permit anything else which did not directly hurt the interests of the state. This tolerance was applied not only to religious practices, intellectual and artistic pursuits, but to personal behavior as well. For instance, when a case was reported to him of a cavalry officer who was caught committing a heinous act of sodomy upon his horse, Friedrich merely ordered that

Germany (FRG)

the poor man be transferred to the infantry!

After Friedrich became King, he for all practical purposes put his flute away forever. Before he had been crowned, he had referred to a military uniform as "a gown of death," but afterwards he was scarcely ever seen wearing anything else. His transformation from a sensitive humanist to "the first servant of the state," as he later called himself, is one of the intriguing mysteries of history. Few would have ever guessed in 1740 that he would become known as "Friedrich the Great" as a result of his leadership. As King, he had become a lonesome figure with a tortured soul, inwardly unhappy, but restlessly active, working 18 hours per day. He was always unkempt and ungroomed, and he loved nobody and was loved by nobody. He had especially troubled relations with women and preferred the company of men in his beloved San Souci palace in Potsdam. Against his will, he was pressured by his family to marry Elisabeth Christine von Braunschweig. He relented, but no sooner was the ceremony over than he packed her off to a separate palace and saw her only a few times the rest of his life. It need not be said that their marriage was childless.

The first half of his reign was a time of almost constant war, which at times seemed to threaten his country's very existence, but which in the end elevated Prussia to the rank of a great European power. The newly–crowned King had just published an elegant attack on Machiavelli's immorality and duplicity in politics; within weeks Friedrich unleashed an unprovoked and unjustified attack on Austrian–owned Silesia. Certainly he was no more unscrupulous than most other rulers of the time, but in this and in almost all other wars during his reign, justice happened to be on the side of his enemies.

Friedrich later said that he had started what was known as "The War of the Austrian Succession" because of "the satisfaction of seeing my name in the newspapers and later in history had seduced me." However, one should not take very seriously such remarks made by a cynic such as Friedrich. What really motivated him was a unique opportunity: in the same year he had become King—1740—a young and politically inexperienced woman, Maria–Theresia, had ascended the Austrian throne. He calculated that she would not have known how to respond to such a brazen act on Prussia's part. There were few Austrian troops in Silesia, so the venture promised to be a military cake–walk. Perhaps surprisingly, the young Austrian Empress rejected Friedrich's ultimatum to withdraw from the province, so the latter unleashed his troops in late 1740. The two armies clashed in furious battle at Mollwitz, and things looked so hopeless for the Prussians that the young ruler actually fled from the battlefield, an offense normally punishable by death. But he was saved by a Prussian victory later that day. Ultimately, two campaigns were necessary to secure Prussian domination of Silesia, and by also taking a substantial portion of land from the Poles, Friedrich was able to unite East and West Prussia into a single territory.

Friedrich tried to justify his action in 1743: "I hope those who will later judge me . . . will be able to differentiate in me the philosopher from the prince, the honorable man from the politician. I must confess that whoever is dragged into the mess *(Getriebe)* of high–level European politics finds it very difficult to preserve his own character frankly and honestly." He wrote that the art of politics appears in many ways "as the opposite of private morality. However, it is the morality of the princes, who . . . do only that which promises to be to their advantage." The Prince had no alternative to "following the practice which authorizes deceit and the abuse of power."

His qualms were not such that he could resist the temptation in 1756 to swoop into Saxony and thereby to become embroiled in a "Seven–Years War" with Austria, which lasted until 1763. Friedrich's troops met with initial success. He published

Friedrich the Great

23

Germany (FRG)

Maria–Theresia's secret plans which were found in the Saxon state archives, which the Prussian troops had captured. These plans showed that the Austrian empress was by no means above duplicity when her state's interests were at stake.

This war provided clear examples of the extent to which the fate of whole nations depended at that time upon the personal preferences and whims of their absolutist rulers. When the Russian Tsarina Elizabeth, the daughter of Tsar Peter the Great, was informed that Friedrich had cracked a joke about her at the dinner table in Sans Souci, she exploded with rage, and joined Austria, France, Bavaria and Saxony in a war against Prussia. Her decision almost dashed Friedrich's kingdom to its destruction. Soon the Russians were at the gates of Königsberg, the French were approaching the Elbe, and the Austrians reentered Silesia. Friedrich tirelessly led his almost hopelessly outnumbered troops from one edge of his kingdom to the other, meeting first one enemy and then another. He was imaginative and bold, and his administration in Potsdam, which his predecessors had built up, worked like a perfectly constructed and oiled machine.

Though he received money from England, which as usual was very interested in weakening France, the Prussians stood alone against all the great European continental powers. Friedrich's army had lost almost all its artillery by late 1760. Berlin had fallen to the enemy and England had stopped sending money to a ruler so near to defeat. But in early 1762 a wonder occurred. Tsarina Elizabeth died, and her successor, Peter III, was a glowing admirer of Friedrich the Great. He not only left the enemy coalition, but he entered into an alliance with Prussia, thereby saving that country from certain defeat. Peter III was assassinated a year later, and his wife, who was later called Catherine the Great, quickly withdrew Russia from the war entirely. But by that time Austria was physically and financially exhausted and had to sue for peace in 1763.

Peace for 23 Years

In the Peace of Hubertusburg, the situation seemed to revert to that which it had been prior to the start of the conflict, with Prussia retaining Silesia and East Prussia, and with Saxon independence being reestablished. But in reality this was a great triumph for Prussia. By maintaining itself successfully against three great powers in Europe, it won recognition as a great power in its own right. Prussia also learned that good relations with Russia were absolutely essential, and until 1890 such relations remained a primary goal of every Prussian leader.

After the war's end, Prussia under Friedrich the Great enjoyed 23 years of peace. Prussia was able, however, to continue to enlarge itself by participating in the partition of Poland with Russia and Austria. Seeing that Russia was perfectly willing to intervene militarily in Poland in order to prevent any strengthening of the Polish state, Friedrich suggested the first partition in 1772. Maria–Theresia had serious qualms about such a dastardly act of political immorality, and Friedrich gleefully reported later that "she wept, but she took." In 1793 and 1795 these three powers partitioned Poland again, creating a potentially dangerous domestic political situation within Prussia by rendering the Poles a majority of all inhabitants within the borders of Prussia.

Friedrich II was one of the most brilliant military leaders of all time. It has been said that one of Adolf Hitler's favorite films was one about Friedrich the Great. It can only be considered unfortunate that one obvious lesson Hitler learned from the Hohenzollern ruler's almost miraculous victory in 1763, despite overwhelming material and manpower superiority of the enemy coalition and crushing military defeats, was that an iron will and bitter determination not to surrender can ultimately carry the day. His tragic attempt to repeat Friedrich's feat almost two centuries later brought scarcely describable death and misery to Germany, its people and its neighbors.

Friedrich II was called "the Great" during his own lifetime. This was not only because of his wars and his successful, but

Middle Europe in 1740 when Maria Theresia (22) became Empress of Austria and Friedrich the Great (28), King of Prussia

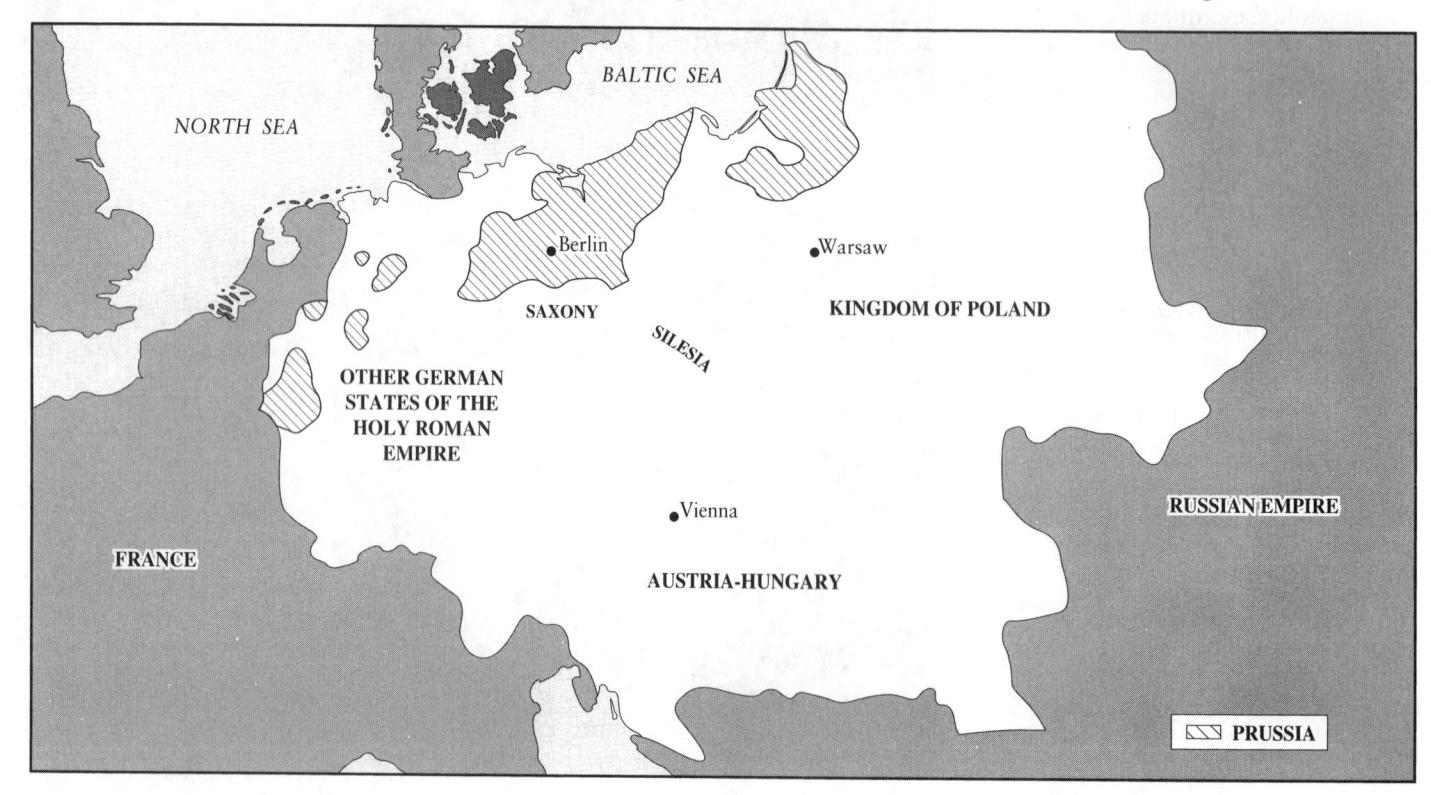

Germany (FRG)

sometimes morally questionable foreign policy, but also because of his reforms, his intellectual and cultural achievements as a young man, and the kind of state which he helped to create. The Prussian state was feared by its neighbors because it was militarily strong and prepared and because of its qualities as a state. It had an uncorrupted administration, an independent judiciary, and a state of law (*Rechtsstaat*) in which there was more legal equality for all citizens than could be found in most other European states at the time. Journalists could write relatively freely, although Friedrich did have a newspaperman beaten who once wrote uncomplimentary things about the King.

Prussia's tolerance toward all religions was considered in Europe to be a very bad example during most of the 17th and 18th centuries. It was also very tolerant toward the different nationalities within its own borders and toward enlightened learning of all kinds. By the standards of the 18th century, which are those which should be used to judge the state ruled by Friedrich the Great, Prussia was a modern and enlightened state. It was certainly no democracy, but enlightenment in politics at first meant basing the affairs of state on reason. Such manifested itself in Europe initially in the form of absolutism, and France under Cardinal Richelieu was an early model. Not until the French Revolution, when a brand of enlightenment which stresses human rights and popular sovereignty and when the call of "liberty, equality and fraternity" caught fire in Europe (outside Holland and England), was Prussia challenged by a state and by ideas which were clearly more modern than its own. Indeed, after Friedrich's death in 1786, the newly risen Prussia had only two more decades before it crumbled in the face of Napoleon's France.

The years 1789 to 1815 were for the German states years of unrest, of war, but also of almost unparalleled genius, talent and productivity in literature and pilosophy. It was a time of openess to new ideas, including political ones.

Admiration of America

The American Revolution had sparked the imagination of many literate Germans. The Americans were celebrated as the "Hellenes of our time," who, by challenging the exclusive rule of the "breed of the nobility," had shown feudal Europe the way to "sweet equality." The greatest German poet of all time was Johann Wolfgang von Goethe, who along with Friedrich Schiller was the greatest exponent of both the impetuous Storm and Stress (a literary age when writers rebelled against the restraints of classicism and the enlightenment) and of the restrained Classical peri-

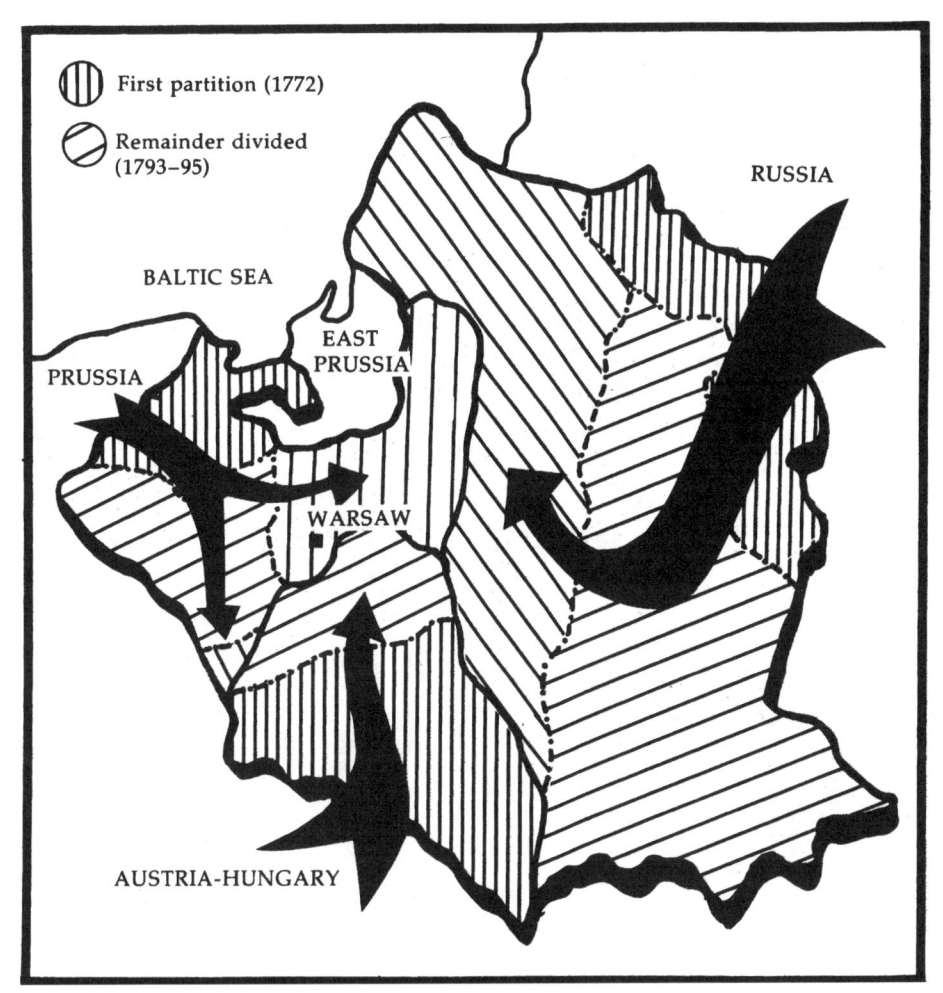

Poland: A Land Devoured

od in German literature during the second half of the 18th and early part of the 19th centuries. Goethe wrote in *Poetry in Truth* that the youthful United States was "a magnificent country," "a magnet for the eyes of the whole world." He wrote "America, your lot is fairer than ours."

In 1781 Friedrich Klopstock wrote a hymn to the new nation entitled "The Present War." It said, *inter alia* "You are the rose dawn of a great new day . . . that will last for centuries." Two years later an anonymous poet gave expression to the popular feeling: "The nations of all Europe will respond with echoes of this holy victory."

While many Germans were inspired by the American ideas and events, it was the French Revolution in 1789 which brought the spark of democratic revolution to Europe. Prussia had been a state well–ordered from above; France was now a nation whose most powerful inspiration came from below—from the people. Revolutionary France was able to fuse ideals, whose force had already been put into practice in America, with national power to an extent that no country on the conti-

nent of Europe could resist. The French Revolution was a declaration of war against the old Europe. To underscore this, French revolutionary leaders promised in the early years of the revolution to help any people which rose up against despotic rulers, and Napoleon's Grand Army later carried the message through the heart of Europe and all the way to Moscow.

Napoleon—Admired and Despised

Some leading Germans greeted Napoleon and the French Revolution. The philosopher Friedrich Hegel called this mighty convulsion "the end of history," while his compatriot Immanuel Kant admired the idealism of the French masses as did Friedrich Schiller, whose admiration, like that of many others, diminished when the guillotine began doing its grisly work. Goethe went to meet Napoleon in Erfurt, where the Frenchman was greeted by the masses and princes with such flattery and servility that Talleyrand wrote disgustedly: "They kiss the hand which could destroy them today or tomorrow." In Germany, Napoleonic power was recognized and, for one reason or another, re-

Germany (FRG)

Napoleon on campaign

spected. Wherever it was not, Napoleon sent his armies, and by 1807 all German states had been compelled one by one to make peace with France.

French domination over most of Germany brought an enormous territorial reshuffling at the expense of the smaller territories, which he eliminated. He abolished all religious rule over sovereign territories, gave the medium–sized states more territory and elevated Bavaria and Wurttemberg to kingdoms. In 1806 he grouped 16 middle–sized states, including Bavaria, Wurttemberg and Baden into a Rhenish League with one of Napoleon's brothers as the monarch, all under French protection. They were obligated to supply 64,000 troops to Napoleon, who assumed control over their armies. All were compelled to declare their exit from the German Empire, which thereby lost a third of its territory. This, combined with Napoleon's defeat of the Austrians and Russians at the battle of Austerlitz, 60 miles (100 kilometers) north of Vienna in 1806, spelled the end of the German Empire, which had existed for almost a thousand years, although it had been weak and very divided. Shortly thereafter, Emperor Franz II cast off the German imperial crown, and the Holy Roman Empire of the Germans came to an end.

Napoleon's objective was clear: he wished to create in Germany states which were strong enough to support France but too weak to constitute a threat to it. The French occupiers were loved nowhere in Germany, and French rule was absolute, in the sense that all orders came from above. Yet it was in some respects very progressive and liberal. Everyone was equal before the law, class privileges were reduced or abolished, schools were taken over by the state, the legal systems were simplified and the churches' active hand in politics was reduced or eliminated. This liberal influence was most lasting in the Rhineland, where it henceforth always outweighed the absolutist tradition.

Prussia had made peace with Napoleon in 1795. This gave it a decade without war, but also permitted Napoleon a free hand in Germany. When Prussia finally had to act against France, it stood alone. At first Napoleon had been friendly toward Prussia in order to keep it out of any coalition directed against France. There was no need for such friendliness once Austria had been defeated, so Napoleon simply marched his troops through Prussia. When the Prussian King, Friedrich Wilhelm III protested this, Napoleon unleashed his armies against Prussia, delivering humiliating defeats in the battles of Saalfeld, Jena, Auerstädt and Friedland.

At the end of October 1806 Napoleon led his troops into Berlin, where he declared his continental blockade against England. He also helped himself, as he did in every land which he dominated, to art treasures, including the four horses on top of the Brandenburg Gate, and shipped them off to Paris. In the summer of 1807 Prussia was compelled to join France and Russia in the Peace of Tilset. This peace treaty permitted Prussia to continue existing as a state, but it lost half its territory, including all Prussian lands west of the Elbe, and was compelled to provide France with money and troops. In short order, Prussia had been reduced to an insignificant country completely in the hands of Napoleon.

Partial Reform

After this devastating defeat, the Prussian King declared that the Prussian state

Germany (FRG)

must replace through intellectual and cultural strength what it had lost in material strength. He knew that Prussia had to reform and modernize itself, so he appointed such men as Karl von Stein, Karl August Hardenberg, Neidhart Gneisenau, Gerhard von Scharnhorst and Wilhelm von Humboldt to make all Prussian citizens, in Gneisenau's words, "free, noble and independent so that they believe that they are part of the whole."

Prussia now experienced a burst of reform activity, brought to a head by the misery of defeat. The overall strength of that country seemed to indicate the strength of the new ideas coming out of France. The social, political, military and educational reforms were not sufficiently democratic in the modern sense, and some of them were undone after 1815. But they were without a doubt steps in the right direction, and they aroused much enthusiasm throughout Germany at the time.

Serfdom was abolished, although the serfs were obliged to pay for their emancipation by incurring debts or by ceding much of land they had tilled to the former landowners. Thus, many Junker (aristocratic landholder) estates actually grew larger, and many former serfs became landless agricultural workers whose lot in life had improved very little, especially since the landowners still maintained control over police and the lower–level judiciary within their districts. Still, it was an important turning point which allowed peasants to win back much of what they had lost in 1525. Noblemen were allowed to practice bourgeois professions, such as law and commerce, and the bourgeoisie was permitted to acquire former knightly estates. Also, Jews were granted social and economic equality, though they still did not gain equal political rights.

The cities were given a greater measure of self–rule in that public officials were to be elected by all property owners. Right into the 20th century, local government in Prussia was admired throughout Europe, even though it stood in sharp contrast to the semi–absolutism in the countryside.

General Scharnhorst wrote in 1798 that "we will not be able to win battles until we learn like the Jacobins to awaken the community spirit." The model was the new French army, and the goal was to create an army motivated by patriotic spirit. All degrading punishments were abolished. Universal military service was introduced in order "to unify the army and the nation," and foreigners were no longer permitted to serve. Ability was to become the sole criterion for advancement, so the officer ranks were opened up more to non–noblemen. The change was slow, but the percentage of commoners in the officer corps rose from 7% in 1806 to 21% by 1848.

The far–sighted Minister of Culture, Wilhelm von Humboldt, introduced educational reforms aimed at opening up the system to the talented from all classes. Elementary schools were created for all, and humanistic high schools (each called a *Gymnasium*) were created for those destined to rise to higher positions. In 1810 the University of Berlin was created. This was the first university in Germany to combine free research and teaching, and it was permitted to administer itself in order to guarantee it continuing freedom.

From 1807 until 1812, the Germans had experienced a peace which was really more like a slow preparation for war. In 1812 the great part of Napoleon's Grand Army, which at the time included some 30,000 Bavarians, 30,000 Austrians and 20,000 Prussians, froze in the snows of Russia. German statesmen stuck their wet political fingers in the air and began to make secret preparations for a change of alliances. Napoleon feared that the worst was ahead of him. In mid–1813 he called the Austrian Chancellor Metternich to his headquarters in Dresden and announced that he "would not withdraw from a single inch of territory . . . I was brought up on the battlefield, and a man like me worries little about the lives of a million persons." Metternich asked icily why he said such a thing behind closed doors instead of announcing it from one end of France to the other. Napoleon replied: "It may cost me my throne, but I will bury the world underneath its rubble." Just 132 years later another defeated dictator who had brought war and destruction to all of Europe would say the very same thing from an underground bunker in Berlin.

Within four months after his meeting with Metternich, Napoleon's hold on Germany, Italy and Spain had been broken. Napoleon suffered a crushing defeat in late 1813 at the "Battle of the Nations" near Leipzig, a battle which brought a scarcely believable carnage: 70,000 Frenchmen and 52,000 allies lost their lives. On March 31, 1814, the Russian Tsar and the Prussian King marched into Paris at the head of their troops. The following year an English army under Wellington and a Prussian army under Generals Blücher and Gneisenau played the key roles in defeating Napoleon once and for all at Waterloo.

Napoleon's occupation of Germany was not a total disaster—he left the German nation far less fragmented than it had been before—about three hundred German states, cities and territories had been joined into fifty, and the Vienna Congress would reduce that number even further. This paved the way for a united and aggressive Germany in the future. The French also brought a valuable reform impulse.

As in 1918 and 1919, it was most unfortunate that democratic ideas had been

The Rhenish League, or *Confederation of the Rhine*

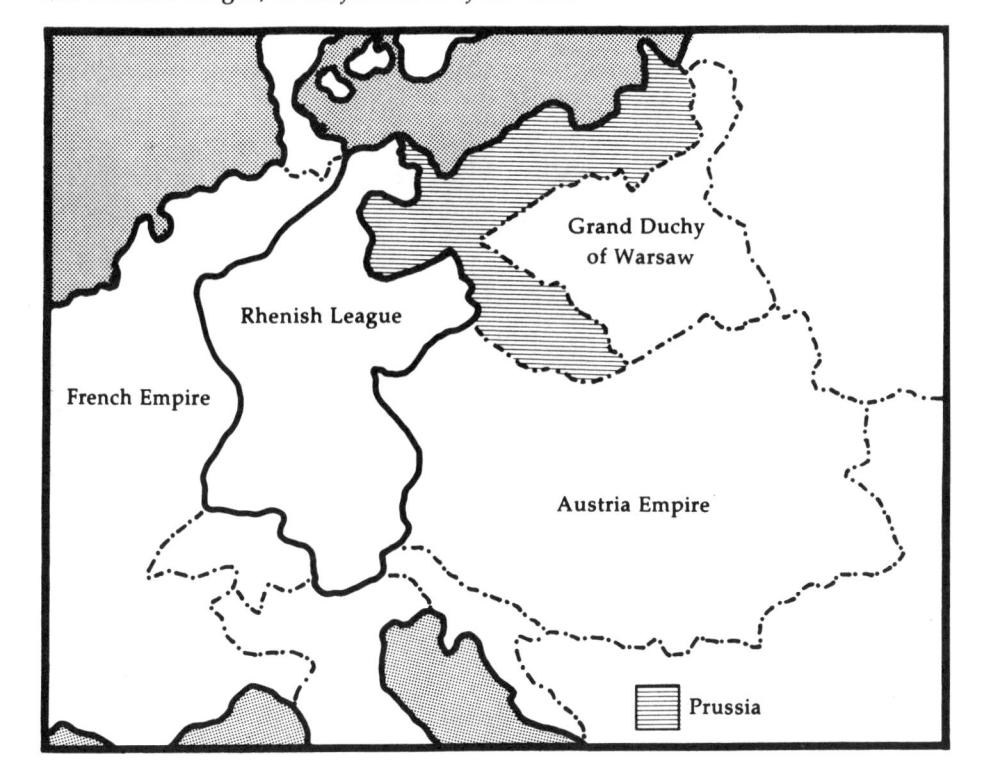

Germany (FRG)

brought into Germany by the troops of an alien occupation power. The French Revolution therefore ultimately created in the minds of many influential Germans considerable enmity toward France and toward democratic ideas. Initially, some leading Germans greeted this momentous event, and in Mainz a revolutionary republic inspired by France was established briefly. However, the excesses of the Revolution became increasingly visible and it progressed from civil war within France to an international struggle for power, largely on German soil. These excesses led some important Germans, such as Goethe and Schiller, to reject revolution as a valid means of change, and it therefore strengthened the traditional German allergy toward revolution. The bloody excesses in France also led many to doubt that the French Revolution was in fact a step in the direction of eliminating political tyranny and social injustice.

The French occupation of Germany also spawned German nationalism by enabling persons in all parts of Germany to put aside some of their local patriotism and to struggle side–by–side to rid Germany of a foreign power. From then on, German nationalism became an increasingly important factor. Since no unified German state yet existed, German nationalism took on an idealistic and romantic character. Also, since it was born in reaction to a conqueror who seemed to understand how to achieve French national interests under the cover of high–sounding calls for "liberty, equality and fraternity," German nationalism and the struggle against alien rule became linked in the minds of far too many Germans with resistance against the ideals of the French Revolution, known in Germany as the "ideas of 1789."

This unfortunate link helped conservative rulers throughout Germany to water down or undo reforms which Napoleon had introduced or promised before 1815. It also established in many German minds a strong resistance which lasted until at least 1945 to the ideas of democracy, equality, civil rights, popular sovereignty, mass participation in politics and representative government legitimized by the consent of the governed.

The Congress of Vienna

The statesmen at the Congress of Vienna were tired of revolution and were interested in restoring much of which had existed a quarter of a century earlier. None wanted a unified Germany and none wanted the dissolution of his own state. Their chief objective was to protect Europe from a renewal of the kinds of shocks and challenges which had come out of France. None talked of popular sovereignty, but all spoke of legitimate monarchy. In the end, Prussia gave up some land to a newly–created Kingdom of Poland, but received the northern part of Saxony, Swedish Pomerania and the island of Rügen, as well as territory in the Rhineland and Westphalia. These new territories were separated from the rest of Prussia by Hanover, Brunswick and Hesse–Cassel, but they placed it along a common border with France. Its job was one which was earlier performed by Austria—to prevent France, whose 1789 borders remained practically unchanged, from threatening central Europe. As a result of the settlement, Prussia grew *into* Germany, while Austria grew *out* of Germany toward Northern Italy and the Balkans. The mineral resources in upper Silesia and the Rhineland provided Prussia with the potential to become the greatest industrial power in Germany and ultimately in Europe.

The Congress of Vienna had, as we saw, no interest in a unified Germany, but it did create a German Confederation to replace the old empire which had died a quiet death almost a decade earlier. The Confederation was a loose association of 35 sovereign German principalities (including the five kingdoms of Prussia, Hanover, Bavaria, Wurttemberg and Saxony) and four free cities. Its sole institution was a Federal Parliament (*Bundestag*) in Frankfurt, whose chairman was always an Austrian and whose delegates were not elected, but were appointed by the member states. In other words, it was a diplomatic organization, not a real parliament. It was dominated by Austria and Prussia, whose main goal by now was to prevent all change. They were not alone.

The violent events which had shaken Europe in the past quarter century had left many Germans and non–Germans alike longing for peace, order and authority. All members of the Confederation pledged, however, to introduce constitutions, which, if they were observed, would always place limits on rulers. Such constitutions never saw the light of day in most German states until more than three decades later. This included Prussia and Austria, where absolutism was quickly restored and which joined with Russia in a "Holy Alliance" in 1815 to suppress signs of revolution anywhere in Europe. Only in southern Germany were constitutions introduced which established monarchies and brought more citizens into political life. The most shining example was Baden where the first signs of parliamentary democracy in Germany became visible.

Conservatism and Obedience

After 1815 there was an ultra–conservative reaction led by the governments of Prussia and Austria, a development which sorely disappointed many Germans, especially the youth. Many had hoped during the wars of liberation from French domination that Germany would become democratic and united. Indeed, they believed that the despotic power of the indi-

Prussia and Austria after the Congress of Vienna: 1815

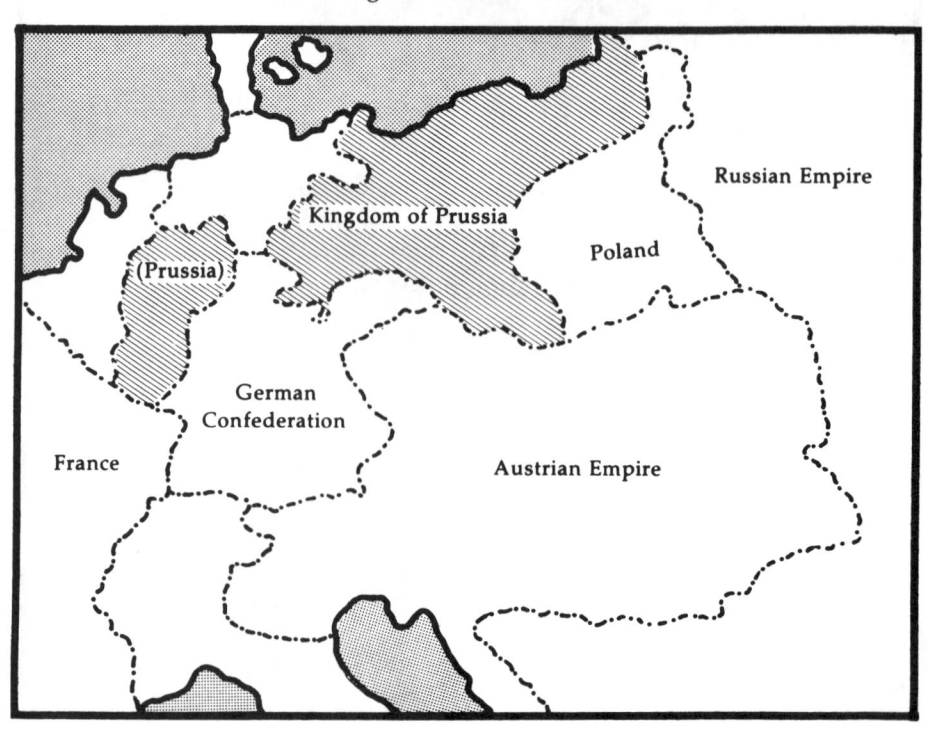

Germany (FRG)

vidual German sovereigns could be broken by creating a unified Germany. Until the 1860s the aims of unity and freedom went hand in hand. Nowhere were these hopes stronger than at the universities, where idealistic students formed highly politicized fraternities under the banner of "honor, freedom, fatherland." The fraternity members dressed in clothing fashionable in Germany in much earlier days, and their colors were black, red and gold, which had been the colors of volunteers during the wars of liberation, and which thereafter became the symbolic colors of republicanism in Germany. They are Germany's colors today.

The fraternity at the University of Jena sponsored in 1817 a mass assembly at Wartburg Castle for persons from all over Germany on the fourth anniversary of the Battle of Leipzig and the 300th anniversary of Luther's Reformation. Thousands came, and passionate speeches were given calling for individual liberty, constitutional government and German unity. Reactionary policies of the leading German states were criticized. At the end of this nationalistic rally, the father of the popular gymnastic associations, Friedrich Ludwig Jahn, organized a particularly unfortunate ceremony which was repeated 116 years later in Berlin: not only the symbols of authority, such as a pigtail and a Prussian corporal's cane, but "un–German" books were thrown into a huge bonfire.

Among the books thrown to the flames were those of a playwright, August von Kotzebue. Two years later a deranged and fanatical theology student assassinated him, calling him a "traitor of youth." This senseless act was just what the leaders of most German states needed to declare the "Carlsbad Acts" in 1819. They called for rigid censorship, prohibition of any political activity directed against the authoritarian order in most states, the outlawing of fraternities (which continued to operate underground), and close scrutiny and supervision of the universities. The Prussian King dismissed all his reformist ministers, and Prussia and Austria remained the centers of conservative reaction.

Romanticism

For the next three decades, Germans were intellectually as divided as ever. This era has been called the "Biedermeier" period: a time of relative peace and security in which the bulk of Germans passively did not look very far beyond their family and village lives. This view of life is well–portrayed by the paintings of Carl Spitzweg and the operas of Albert Lortzing. Another artistic and philosophical movement, romanticism, emerged at roughly the same time. Romanticism stressed feelings and was a reaction against the rationality of the enlightenment. The romantic sought to break all barriers, including those of reason and sought refuge in the past, in nature, in art or in fantasy. He was drawn to legends and fairy tales, especially following publication by Jacob and Wilhelm Grimm of German fairy tales in the years 1812–1814 and of legends a few years later.

Caspar David Friedrich's *Two men gazing at the moon* (1819)

Romanticism in art was best portrayed by the painter Caspar David Friedrich, whose superb landscape paintings showed the links between man and nature; in literature the Schlegel brothers, E.T.A. Hoffmann, Clemens Brentano, Ludwig Tieck, Joseph von Eichendorff and Eduard Mörike; in music by Franz Schubert and Carl Maria von Weber. At first romanticism was not political. But by the end of the 19th century it had seeped into the political thinking of many Germans and lent their views an often unrealistic and immoderate air.

A third and expressly political trend was liberalism, that longing for the previously promised, but largely undelivered, constitutional government and individual freedom. The uprising in Paris in 1830 spread to cities all over Germany and forced the introduction of constitutions in Brunswick, Hanover, Hesse–Cassel and Saxony. There were further uprisings in 1832.

Queen Victoria ascended the British throne in 1837 which nominally included the Hanover crown. The linkage had been established in 1713 when the Hanover monarch George became King of England. Tradition, however, forbade women from ruling Hanover. The new Hanoverian king abolished the constitution, an act publicly opposed by seven prominent professors at the University of Göttingen, including the Grimm brothers. When the seven were promptly dismissed and given three days to leave the kingdom, loud voices of protest were heard throughout Germany.

It was in reaction to the reestablishment of authoritarian rule in a politically fragmented Germany which gave rise in the early 1830s to the "Young Germany" movement, to which a number of German writers belonged, most notably Heinrich Heine and Ludwig Börne. These young writers were convinced that literary figures should become politically active and socially critical. Their influence was so feared by the authorities that their writings were forbidden by the German Confederation in 1835 and their leading exponents were driven into exile, particularly to Paris.

Like most German intellectuals of their time, these writers saw German nationalism and liberalism as goals which went hand–in–hand. It was in this spirit that Hoffman von Fallersleben wrote a song, "Deutschland, Deutschland über alles," ("Germany, Germany above all others") in

Germany (FRG)

Deutschland Über Alles

Hoffmann von Fallersleben. (1841.)
Joseph Haydn. (1797.)

Courtesy: Irmgard M. Baylor

the 1840s. The melody had earlier been written by Austrian Joseph Haydn and was a well-known hymn tune in protestant churches. This song, which became the national anthem for a united Germany and whose third verse is Germany's anthem today, is often misunderstood as having been a call for German domination over the whole world. In fact it was directed against the disunity of Germany. It was a call for placing the goal of a united and democratic Germany above all provincial loyalties and above all inclinations to find happiness in one's own private corner. The final verse sums up the song's message: "Unity and Law and Freedom for the German Fatherland." It was assumed that all these goals were inseparably linked.

A final powerful intellectual force at the time was the Berlin philosopher, Friedrich Hegel, whose almost encyclopedic work gave rise to at least two contradictory traditions: one supporting authoritarian rule and one supporting revolution. In some of his writings Hegel described the state as an organism which is not a mere instrument in the hands of the citizens, but which grows and has needs of its own. Such growth, he argued, was completely rational; in fact, he maintained that reason reaches its highest perfection in the state. Which state had reached the highest existing perfection? The Prussian state, he answered. A state's power reflects the rationality of the state. "What is rational is actual and what is actual is rational," he wrote. The life of the individual human being has meaning only within the state, he argued. Authoritarian rulers could not have been more pleased with a philosophical doctrine than with this one.

However, Hegel also developed a doctrine called the dialectic, which involved the clash of opposites and the development of something entirely new. Hegel meant the clash of ideas, but one of his bright German Ph.D. students, Karl Marx, converted this concept of clashing ideas to one of clashing economic forces. The explosive implications of this theory became clear very soon. Marx, who was born in Trier, the son of a Prussian customs official, and who married a woman of minor nobility, was forced to flee Germany in 1843 because of the biting social and political criticism which he wrote in his Cologne newspaper, *Rheinische Zeitung*. In his London exile he wrote in 1848 the *Communist Manifesto*, which predicted a violent revolution as a result of which the working (proletarian) class would replace the capitalist overlords who owned the land and factories. This powerful tract ended with the words: "Proletarians of the world, rise up; you have nothing to lose but your chains!" Such a rising never came in England or in Germany, but Marxism became and remains a far more significant intellectual and political doctrine in Germany than in the United States.

Closer to Unity

The German Customs Union was established in 1834 by all German states except Austria, Hanover, Mecklenburg, Oldenburg, Holstein and the Hansa Cities. This far-sighted move which created a unified inland market not only became the cornerstone for a united Germany 37 years later, but it became an important model years later for the EC. The German Customs Union greatly stimulated the industrialization of Germany, whose population at the time was three-fourths agricultural. At the same time it diminished the position within Germany of Austria and enhanced the economic predominance of Prussia.

The authoritarian German princes seemed to be firmly in their saddles when they were severely shaken in 1848 by a spark of revolution which had started in Sicily and southern Italy and which, as usual, arrived in Germany via France. But the rebels' objectives in Germany and France were different. What many Germans wanted was unity and freedom, things which had already been realized in whole or in part in France a half century earlier. As a student in Bonn, Carl Schurz, wrote in his memoirs, "The word democracy was on all tongues and many thought it a matter of course that, if the princes should try to withhold from the people the rights and liberties demanded, force would take the place of mere petition." Few Germans wanted a revolution as in France in 1789, but many wanted the traditional authorities to approve of more freedom for the people and of a constitutional monarchy which would include the principle of popular sovereignty. What specific demands were made became clear very quickly. In frightened response to the spontaneous demonstrations and assemblies in the first week of March 1848, many princes granted freedom of press and assembly, the creation of citizen's militias, jury trials, reform of the electoral system and collaboration in constructing a federal German state.

In Prussia, King Friedrich Wilhelm IV waited a little too long to make concessions. Not until he had been informed that Metternich had been driven out of Austria did he decide to grant Prussia a constitution and to support the move toward a united Germany. An unfortunate incident in the square before the royal palace, where nervous troops fired a volley of shots into a crowd which had presumably assembled to applaud the King's concessions, touched off a rampage of violence in Berlin which was not to be duplicated until the end of World War I. The Prussian troops, which had not engaged in combat since the Battle of Waterloo, were baffled and quickly demoralized by fighting street battles against snipers who fought

Germany (FRG)

from rooftops and from behind barricades and who disappeared into side streets and alleys when regular troops closed in on them.

After one day of such fighting, the army was compelled to withdraw from the city, but the King valiantly chose to stay with his "dear Berliners." He was thus a sort of captive of the revolutionaries and was forced to call together bourgeois and intellectual groups to discuss reforms. He later looked back with regret on that humiliating time: "We were on our bellies then." It seemed that the death–knell for the loosely–organized group of mainly authoritarian states called Germany had been rung, but time would reveal that the princes had just temporarily lost their nerve. By the end of March 1848 all German states, including Austria and Prussia, had concluded that there was no alternative to allowing representatives to be elected by universal manhood suffrage to a national parliament to draft a liberal constitution for a German federation. This first German national parliament convened on May 18 in the Paul's Church in Frankfurt on the Main.

The Parliament of the Professors

This has often been called the "parliament of the professors" because of the fact that an overwhelming number of delegates were professors, lawyers or university–educated civil servants who had little practical experience in politics, and in typical German scholarly fashion spent weeks on end discussing abstract notions of law, freedom and the state. The delegates had good intentions and produced an admirable document called the Fundamental Rights of the German People. However, they were unable to unite on the question of parliamentary control of royal power. Gradually, their slow, deliberate and discursive work was overtaken by events outside the Paul's Church. The demands for reform were not quite strong enough to realize themselves, and the resulting frustration led to outbursts of violence in Vienna, Frankfurt, Berlin and elsewhere which in more and more Germans' eyes discredited the entire reformist movement.

The reestablishment of firm monarchical control in Vienna stimulated a longing for order. Suspicions among the states and the classes began to reassert themselves. Nowhere was this more evident than in Prussia, where the King soon began resisting any diminution of his power. The King's disposition was strengthened by a renewal of mob violence in Berlin in June 1848, in which weapons in the state armory were seized and distributed among the rebels. This violence frightened the middle class citizens and played into the hands of the King.

He ordered the troops back into their Berlin barracks in November, an order which ignited more resistance and which could be carried out only by force. But this order ended the revolutionary activity in Prussia. Friedrich Wilhelm caught many of his critics off guard by decreeing a constitution. Revised in 1850, this document provided formal safeguards for Prussian subjects' liberties and established a bicameral legislature which was clearly designed to prevent truly innovative action by more radical elements. The upper house was composed mainly of the nobility and the lower house was elected in a complicated way based on the amount of taxes the citizens paid; two–thirds of the seats were thereby elected by 15% of the population which paid two–thirds of the total taxes. This strange electoral system remained a thorn in the side of the Prussian working class and liberal reformers until it was finally abolished in 1918. Despite its many shortcomings, though, this constitution was a step away from absolute government and toward constitutional, parliamentary government in Prussia.

19th Century Hamburg

Germany (FRG)

After entirely too much debate, the Frankfurt Parliament made two fundamental decisions: first, the majority recommended a "small German" solution to German unity, with close links to Austria, rather than a "large German" solution under the Hapsburgs of Austria. It was decided that it would be nonsense to establish a German nation–state which would include Milan, Venice, Budapest, Prague and Cracow. Second, it offered the German imperial crown to the Prussian King in 1849.

Friedrich Wilhelm IV bruskly rejected this gift with the words "If the thousand–year–old crown of the German nation, unused now for 42 years, is again to be given away, it is I and my likes who will give it!" No doubt, it was not his idea of monarchy to see it based on the sovereignty of the people and offered by lawyers and professors who had been elected by the people. It is possible that he would have accepted it from other princes. But the King was aware that accepting such a crown might very well have meant war with Austria, which, as later events showed, was not prepared to accept German unity under Prussian domination without a fight. He could also not forget his heritage nor muster enthusiasm for a new state in which the Prussian identity might ultimately disappear.

His rejection of the crown sealed the fate of the revolution. Nevertheless, for the rest of the year he continued to send diplomatic feelers to some other German princes to explore the chances of establishing a form of German unity more to his liking, but these came to nothing. More successful was his troops' suppression of the last acts of rebellion in Saxony in 1849, where they restored the Saxon King to the throne, and during the summer in Baden and the Rhineland–Palatinate, where they crushed a rag-tag "people's army" of intellectuals, poets and professional and amateur revolutionaries. That last victory enabled the King of Wurttemberg to disband the Frankfurt Parliament, which had dwindled to about a hundred die–hards, who had fled to Stuttgart. His comment: "Against democrats only soldiers will do. Adieu!"

Migration to America

As was the case after Hitler jolted Germany with his brutal intolerance after 1933, America greatly profited from the events which had shaken Germany in 1848–9. Revolutionaries and sympathizers fled by the thousands to the United States, which had been one of the few countries in the world to send a message of encouragement to the Frankfurt Parliament. These German exiles brought their ideals and their zeal with them, and many of them spoke out elegantly against slavery, streamed into the new Republican Party and fought mainly on the side of the North during the Civil War. Frederick Hecker organized an all–German regiment for Lincoln; the young Graf (Count) Ferdinand von Zeppelin made his first ascent in a balloon in America and acted as an aerial observer for the North in the Civil War.

The former leaders of the Baden Revolutionary Army, Franz Siegel and Carl Schurz, fought for the North. Siegel led an army in the Battle of New Market on May 15, 1864, against Confederate units which included the Virginia Military Institute corps of cadets. Partly because of the young cadets' legendary bravery, Siegel's forces were badly beaten. Schurz was a particularly towering figure among the "1848ers." He campaigned for Lincoln in

Carl Schurz

the 1860 election, was named by the winner as ambassador to Madrid, but he resigned this post later in order to return to America to command a division in the Union Army. Under President Rutherford B. Hayes he was Secretary of the Interior and introduced civil service reform and advocated the integration of the Indians into American society.

The end of the American Civil War stimulated even greater numbers of Germans to seek a better life in America. In the years between 1866 and 1896 Germans were the largest immigrant group to go to America, reaching a peak of a half million in 1882, or more than two–thirds of all immigrants in that year. In fact, Germans led in overall immigration between 1820 and 1920, and in 1907 alone 1.3 million Germans arrived in the United States. Most settled in the quadrangle of New York–Minneapolis–St. Louis–Baltimore, where they established German communities with their own schools, newspapers, churches, hospitals and clubs. They also opened breweries and beer gardens. Their habit of engaging in more pleasant Sunday activities, such as sponsoring band contests, festivals, or simply walking with the family or chatting in a beer garden contributed to lightening the Sunday severity found all too often in 19th century America.

Prussian Power Emerges

The 1848 revolution was over. It has often been said that the Germans' main problem was that they had never had a successful revolution. Of course, as the case of England demonstrates, revolutions are not absolutely essential in the establishment of democratic government, as long as reform is possible. However, Germany was to experience too little reform in years to come. Many liberals who had participated in the "March Revolution" became very self–critical after its failure and became convinced that they had to adjust their political objectives much more to the prevailing political conditions. They thus became more open to ideas associated with Otto von Bismarck, who had become the Prussian chancellor a few years later: of *Realpolitik* (politics which recognize the hard facts of the world) and the inclination to tone down the demand for freedom if the possibility of national unity is at stake.

During the two decades following the events of 1848–9, Prussia not only steadily increased its industrial base and power, but it moved aggressively to establish the preconditions for German unity under Prussian domination. One step was the submission by the new King, Wilhelm I, of a bill to reorganize and double the size of the army, a measure hotly opposed by a majority in Prussia's lower house. The majority did grant a large sum to strengthen the existing army units, but when Wilhelm simply used this money to finance his desired reorganization, the Parliament refused to grant any more funds until the King canceled his unauthorized army reform. The result was such a serious deadlock and tension that the King reportedly considered resigning. Only a person of extraordinary skill could lead Prussia out of this crisis. That man was soon found: Bismarck.

Bismarck's background and reputation seemed to be just what a conservative king like Wilhelm I would have wanted. An East Elbian aristocrat, his disdain for scholarly things and his youthful love for beer–swilling and disorderly conduct had caused him to be banished from the city limits of Göttingen where he had been sent for an unsuccessful year of university study. Yet, since 1850 he had gained much diplomatic experience, first as the Prussian representative to the Parliament of the German Confederation in Frank-

Germany (FRG)

furt, then as a envoy in St. Petersburg and Paris. These assignments helped him to broaden his scope beyond Prussia and to conclude that Prussia should become the heart of a unified Germany *without Austria*. Already in 1856 he had written: "Germany is clearly too small for us both . . . In the not too distant future we shall have to fight for our existence against Austria . . . since the course of events in Germany has no other solution."

Appointed Prussian chancellor in 1862, Bismarck was unsuccessful in persuading Parliament to accept the King's plans for reforming the army. For awhile he simply ignored Parliament, but he knew that he could not continue to do so forever. Thus, he decided to initiate a bold foreign policy which would capture the imagination of nationalists and liberals alike and which would ultimately achieve German unity. The success of this policy won the admiration of many of his countrymen for generations to come.

Bismarck's first years as Chancellor of Prussia were ones of armament and war. In 1864, 1866 and 1870, he conducted short but significant wars against Denmark, Austria and France. The war conducted by *both* Prussia and Austria against Denmark in 1864 over Danish control of the predominantly German–populated territories of Schleswig and Holstein gave Prussian commanders useful battlefield experience. The Prussian victory at Düppel in Jutland also stimulated patriotic feeling in Prussia and in other German states. It weakened liberal opposition to the army reform bill, and inclined more and more Germans to look to Prussia for leadership.

It is hardly surprising that the joint administration of Schleswig–Holstein agreed upon by the Prussian and Austrian victors did not go well. Friction was inevitable, and Bismarck was very astute in exploiting it to force a show–down with Austria, which would never have peacefully acquiesced to his designs for German unity. In mid–1866 Bismarck ordered Prussian troops to occupy Holstein, and after declaring the German Confederation dissolved, he declared war on Austria. It lasted only seven weeks. With new breech–loading rifles which had just been used so successfully in the American Civil War, and with the capacity to move their troops to the battlefield on new railroads, the far better prepared Prussians were able to deliver a stinging defeat to the Austrian and Saxon armies at the Battle of Königgrätz. This victory eliminated Austria from the soon–to–be unified Germany.

North German Confederation

In mid–1867 a North German Confederation composed of 22 German states north of the Main River came into existence, with the King of Prussia as its president. Bismarck's very moderate treatment of the defeated Austrian Empire enabled Prussia to gain in Austria a trustworthy ally for a half century. When in 1870 Prussia launched its final war to establish German unity, Austria did not support that last active opponent to a united Germany: France.

With increasing nervousness the French looked east across the Rhine where Bismarck had created momentum toward German unity. Feverish French diplomatic activity in the south German states and Austria failed to create determined opposition to Prussia. The crisis erupted in midyear when the Prussian government announced that Prince Leopold of the House of Hohenzollern had accepted the Spanish throne, which had been vacant since 1868. As Bismarck well knew, the French would never tolerate a Hohenzollern on the Spanish throne, since they would then face a hostile dynasty on their eastern and southwestern borders. The French ambassador to Prussia, Benedetti, persuaded Wilhelm I at the spa, Bad Ems, that it would be a good idea to withdraw Leopold's candidacy.

Wilhelm politely refused to assure the French diplomat that the Hohenzollern candidacy would not be renewed in the future. The King wired his description of the talks to Bismarck, who then published the telegram after intentionally shortening it in such a way that Wilhelm's reply to Benedetti seemed far more abrupt and impolite than it actually had been. The French were infuriated by this "Ems Telegram," and in an atmosphere of inflamed emotion, the French government declared war on Prussia on July 19th.

The Birth of the German Empire

To French surprise, the south German states immediately joined the Prussians in the war. Never known for indecision, the Prussians struck quickly and fatally. Smashing through Lorraine, the Prussian Army cut Paris off from the two main French armies and delivered a devastating blow to the French at Sedan on the Belgian border. By January 1871, all resistance ended. A humiliated France looked on as the German Empire was proclaimed in the Hall of Mirrors in the Palace of Versailles on January 18, 1871. For the first time in history, there was a united Germany. The Prussian king became Kaiser Wilhelm I.

Bismarck was probably mistaken in acquiescing to pressures from the Kaiser (Caesar—i.e. "emperor"), Prussian military leaders and others by imposing a harsh peace on a prostrate France. Germany annexed Alsace and most of Lor-

Kaiser Wilhelm I

raine, with their advanced industry and rich iron deposits. Also, France was required to pay a very large indemnity and to allow German occupation troops to remain in France until the sum was paid. For the next half century, French policy would revolve around undoing these terrible losses, and the pigeons which German leaders had turned loose in 1871 would in 1919 come back to roost with a vengeance.

These limited wars were models of the primacy of political over military objectives. Military actions ceased the moment Bismarck's political objectives were achieved. Faced with demands to crush entire armies or to humiliate defeated enemies by way of triumphant marches through their capitals, Bismarck always insisted that the business at hand was the

Otto von Bismarck

Germany (FRG)

Germania, overlooking the Rhine Valley, commemorates the unification of 1871.
Courtesy: Jon Markham Morrow

conduct of Prussian or German politics, not an attempt to administer "justice" or to humiliate or destroy great powers. Bismarck strove after 1871 to protect what Germany had gained. Above all, he guarded Germany's most vital interest, the European center. He did not allow Germany's attention to be dangerously diverted by numerous colonial adventures. He once said, pointing to a map of Europe: "Here is Russia and here is France, and here we are in the middle. That is *my* map of Africa."

To insure Germany's protection, Bismarck built up one of the most complicated and delicate alliance systems ever known in peacetime. He saw Germany threatened from two sides and sought to eliminate this threat by preventing the French and Russians from forming a coalition against Germany. He accomplished this by maintaining friendly relations with Britain, by isolating France diplomatically, by establishing a "Dual Alliance" with Austria in 1879 and the "Reinsurance Treaty" among Austria, Russia and Germany in 1887. The latter obligated Germany to stand by whichever partner was attacked by the other, thereby discouraging potential aggression from either Austria or Russia. Bismarck did not regard this treaty as incompatible with the Dual Alliance with Austria because in neither agreement was Germany obligated to aid any aggressor. Of course, one factor gave Bismarck great flexibility: he alone could determine guilt for any outbreak of hostilities, and this decision would always have been in accordance with German national interests.

Of course, the legacy which Bismarck left Germany was not all positive. His alliance system was exceedingly complicated, and he failed to train successors to continue the policy. His followers, who wished to simplify the alliance system, did not renew the Reinsurance Treaty in 1894. Also, his style of *Realpolitik* demanded great skill, the sober and unimpassioned recognition of the limits of power, the exercise of moderation and the respect of other nations' vital interests. His successors often imperfectly understood his policies, and they tended to remember the gestures of his statecraft and not its substance. Bismarckian *Realpolitik*, if understood only in fragments, could be a dangerous inheritance for any nation.

The legacy which Bismarck left German domestic politics was also by no means entirely positive. The German Empire had the outward appearance of being democratic. However, while some other European countries, such as England and France, were in the process of becoming more democratic in practice, Germany was not. It remained a country in which the most important decisions were made by people who were not elected and not directly subject to popular or parliamentary control. Bismarck's skill as a politician prevented a process of democratic reform from gaining any momentum.

The chancellor, like many of his countrymen, felt uncomfortable about political and cultural pluralism in Germany. This was especially revealed in laws which Bismarck introduced to limit the influence of the Catholic Church and the *Social Democratic Party* of Germany *(SPD)*. His campaign against the Catholic Church, called the "Cultural Struggle," was similar to campaigns conducted in many European countries in the 19th century to limit the Church's influence over education and other social affairs. Bismarck also resented the growth of the *Catholic Center Party* and suspected that the Vatican was trying to stir up opposition to the Imperial government among the Polish minority within Germany and among the other Catholic countries in Europe. A series of laws whittling away at the Church's privileges was passed starting in 1873, but these laws unleashed such an outcry among Catholics and Protestants alike that Bismarck was forced to repeal most of them by 1881.

Germany (FRG)

The leader was also unable to view German socialists as loyal citizens because of their Marxist revolutionary program and their talk of internationalism. He blamed the socialists for two unsuccessful assassination attempts against the Kaiser in 1877, and in October of the following year he succeeded in persuading Parliament to pass an Anti–Socialist Law forbidding all associations which aimed to subvert the existing order or which showed "socialist tendencies." This law forced the *SPD* to operate underground, crippled the growing labor unions, deprived socialists of the customary protection of the law and drove many of them into exile abroad. Like the laws against the Catholic Church, these anti–socialist laws also backfired and actually stimulated an increase in the membership and overall strength of the *SPD*.

At the same time, Bismarck linked these repressive measures with progressive social welfare laws to help the needy and working classes. The first social insurance laws were introduced in 1881, and in 1883 there came a Sickness Insurance Law, one–third of the premiums for which were to be paid by the employers, and an accident insurance financed entirely by the employer; finally in 1889 old–age disability insurance financed by employees, employers and the government was introduced. These laws were far in advance of those of any other nation and were the model for the National Insurance Act of 1911 in Britain; not until the 1930s were such programs introduced in the United States by the Federal Government. Even today, Germans are very proud of their social welfare legislation.

Industrialization and Urbanization

Some Germans hoped for an era of liberal reform when Wilhelm I died in 1888. But his son, Friedrich III, who was known to favor such reforms, died of throat cancer only 99 days after his coronation, and a young, inexperienced and impetuous Wilhelm II became Kaiser. The new ruler hoped to become popular by canceling the Anti–Socialist Law, introducing some domestic reforms and conducting an energetic German foreign and colonial policy. Noting that Bismarck had wholly different ideas, he fired the "Iron Chancellor" in 1890. He was then free to take the lead over a people who were enthusiastic about the prospects for Germany's future. The Kaiser, who was rather intelligent and superficially interested in many different things, but who was unable to focus his attention on anything very long, was boastful about Germany's power. He also had a way, as one of his biographers noted, of approaching every matter with an open mouth. Although in actual crises, the young Kaiser tended to be cautious, he seemed to many non–Germans to represent a restless country with more power than it could use well.

German unification and rapid economic

The unification of Germany, 1871, showing only the major states and areas

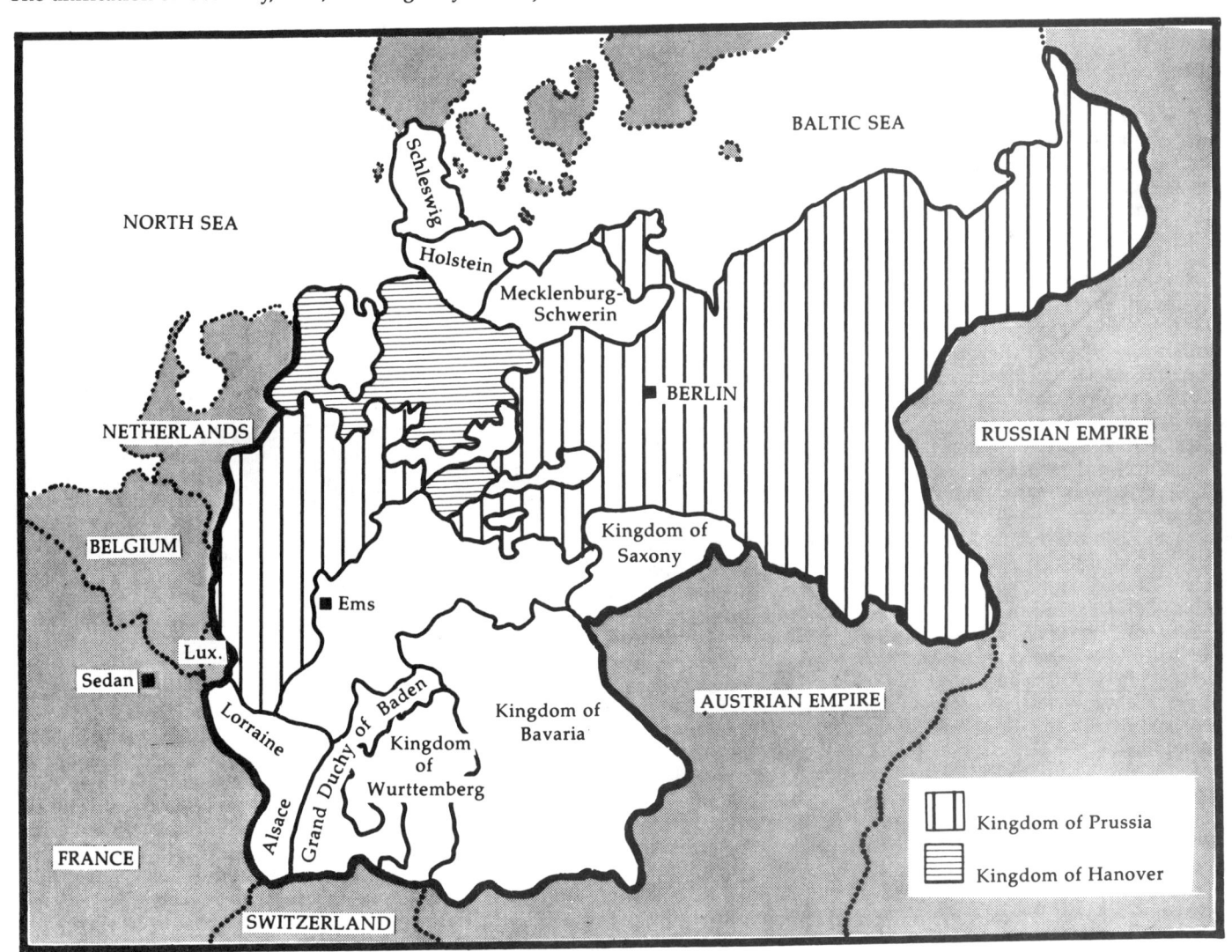

Germany (FRG)

and population growth had given Germany a strong hand to assert its claims in the world. By the end of the 19th century the extremely rapid industrialization and urbanization had transformed Germany into one of the world's foremost industrial, trading, banking and urbanized countries. All Western countries experienced difficulties in adjusting to the social consequences of industrialization. However, the suddenness of German economic and population growth had no equal in Europe.

Between 1816 and 1913 Germany's population almost tripled from 25 to 67 million, and more and more Germans moved into the cities. In 1830, four–fifths of the population lived outside of towns and engaged in agriculture, but in 1895 barely one–fifth did so. Berlin's population alone grew from three–quarters of a million in 1870 to over two million in 1910. The increasingly urbanized people were hard at work making Germany the most economically powerful country in Europe. With Alsace–Lorraine, Germany became the leading producer of iron and steel. It almost quadrupled its domestic rail net between 1871 and 1914, and it built one of the world's largest merchant marine fleets. Its industries were very diversified, ranging from armaments producers such as Krupp and electrical plants such as those of Siemens, Halske and the General Electric Company (AEG), to chemical industries such as Bayer, Agfa and I.G. Farben. Overall German industrial production had already surpassed that of the French in the 1870s, caught up with that of Britain in 1900 and had overtaken it by 1910, when only the United States outproduced Germany.

Imperial Germany also exploded with artistic and scholarly creativity. Its universities and research laboratories became places where the most imaginative thinking in the world was being done. For instance, Wilhelm Konrad Roentgen discovered X–rays, Max Planck the *quantum* theory and Albert Einstein the theory of relativity. Robert Koch did ground–breaking research on tuberculosis, cholera and sleeping sickness, Paul Ehrlich on syphilis and Rudolph Virchow on pathology. The work of such great professors as Theodor Mommsen and Heinrich von Treitschke in history, Wilhelm Dilthey in philosophy, Ferdinand Tönnies, Georg Simmel and Max Weber in sociology, and Adolf Wagner, Lujo Brentano and Werner Sombart in economics, are still admired today.

Berlin also gained a reputation as an exciting cultural center. There Johannes Brahms and Richard Strauss composed their music. The sympathetic Prussian social critic, Theodor Fontane, wrote his novels, focusing on the Prussia which he loved, but which he saw in decline. Also, after the opening of *Die Freie Bühne* (The Free Stage), such talented playwrights as Gerhard Hauptmann and Frank Wedekind were able to introduce a new element of criticism and expressionism into the German theater. Unlike France then and today, Germany's culture and scholarship was not concentrated in the nation's capital, but was also distributed among such cities as Hamburg, Cologne, Leipzig, Munich and Frankfurt on the Main. Despite the cultural creativity of the time, many educated Germans were gripped with a kind of cultural pessimism. They looked around themselves and saw what they considered to be excessive materialism and consumerism, values which they viewed as British and American. German spirit was in decline, they lamented, and many agreed with the philosopher Friedrich Nietzsche, who in 1888 claimed "German spirit: for the past 18 years a contradiction in terms."

Social Division, Foreign Adventurism and Nationalism

Industrial and population growth changed the face and character of German society. The German Empire, which had become united territorially in 1871, became increasingly divided socially. Expressed in an over–simplified way, German society became more and more polarized. A class conscious, somewhat doctrinaire and fairly well–organized proletariat confronted a ruling class which was, in the main, stubbornly conservative. Nationalism grew to be very strong in Germany, but it could never overcome the extreme antagonisms which arose out of this split in German society.

The robust and assertive foreign policy on which Wilhelm II embarked in the 1890s, when Germany enjoyed relatively good relations with the other major countries in the world, led Germany by 1914 into a diplomatic situation in which it felt encircled and distrusted. By building a powerful navy, pursuing colonial ambitions in Africa, and frequently brandishing the sword, Germany's rulers created more problems than they were able to solve.

Bismarck had kept the German Empire within the limits which were imposed upon it by its geographic position in the middle of Europe. He had avoided colonial adventures, which would only have antagonized the other European powers, especially Britain. However, supported by German public opinion, his successors changed this, and by the turn of the century the German flag flew in Africa (Cameroons, South–West Africa and Tanganyika), there was a tiny foothold in China and a smattering of Pacific islands (named, ironically, the Bismarck Archipelago).

In order to try to protect this usually unprofitable empire, Germany decided to build a battle fleet which would enable it to conduct a major naval war against the great powers. Kaiser Wilhelm II announced in 1898 "Our future lies on the water." This decision was a major factor in the deterioration of good relations between Britain and Germany. A German navy which challenged Britain, which, as an island, was completely dependent upon open sea lanes, was bound to be destabilizing and to drive the English into the arms of Germany's potential enemies.

Undoubtedly the chief influence on German naval thinking was Captain A.T. Mahan of the United States Navy. In *The Influence of Sea Power on History* he argued that mastery of the oceans is identical with world domination and that any strong land power fighting against an amphibious master which also has land forces is destined to lose. Mahan visited Germany in 1893 and was received like a hero. He was invited to dine aboard the Kaiser's yacht. The ruler wrote in 1894 to a friend "I am just now not reading but *devouring* Captain Mahan's book and am trying to learn it by heart... It is on board all my ships and constantly quoted by my captains and officers."

Capt. Alfred Thayer Mahan

What worried the British and the French was that Germany was willing to *use* its new navy. In mid–1911, Wilhelm sent a gunboat to Morocco's Atlantic port of Agadir in response to France's dispatching a military mission to Fez. France's action was a clear violation of the 1906 agreements of Algeciras, but the German overreaction to this move caused other Europeans to overlook this point. Ger-

Germany (FRG)

man bellicosity concerned Europe more than a questionable French interpretation of a treaty. Thereafter, German political calculation had always to include the possibility of a war with Britain, which was now firmly on the side of the *Entente* (France and Russia).

The German Chancellor's chief foreign policy advisor, Kurt Riezler, who later emigrated to the U.S., viewed with concern the kind of nationalism which was gripping his countrymen. He wrote in 1913 that too many Germans exaggerated the "power of force." Due to their craving for international recognition, they lacked political sense, judgment and goal orientation. Their nationalism showed "the manners of a young dog" and was laden with "envy and resentments," both of which were poor advisors for an "upstart" who did not know how to "let things ripen." The most vocal spokesman for this kind of impatient nationalism was the Pan–German Union, about which Chancellor Bethmann–Hollweg declared in 1912 almost in despair: "Politics cannot be made with these idiots!"

Long before June 28, 1914, the day on which the Austrian Archduke Franz Ferdinand was assassinated in Serbia, there had been much dissatisfaction in the capitals of Europe. The preceding decade had produced numerous crises which could have served to ignite a war. However, in order for a crisis actually to lead to war, several powers must conclude that they are in a favorable position to gain from such a conflict. That feeling of confidence prevailed in many European capitals in July and August 1914.

Within six weeks after the assassination of the Austrian Archduke, all of Europe's major nations were locked into a war which was to last four years and which far exceeded all previous wars in terms of casualties and destruction. Of course, no European leaders had contemplated, let alone wanted, the kind of war which actually came in August 1914. In the minds of most statesmen at the time, war was a relatively violent action lasting a month or six weeks and conducted as a part of intricate diplomatic games. The memory of the Napoleonic wars having faded, they had not yet had the opportunity to observe the consequences of wars which unlocked powerful emotions stemming from nationalism and democracy. They also vastly underestimated the capacity of countries in possession of modern industry and technology to conduct theretofore inconceivably destructive wars for long periods against one another.

World War I

There was general shock and indignation in all of Europe when Archduke Franz

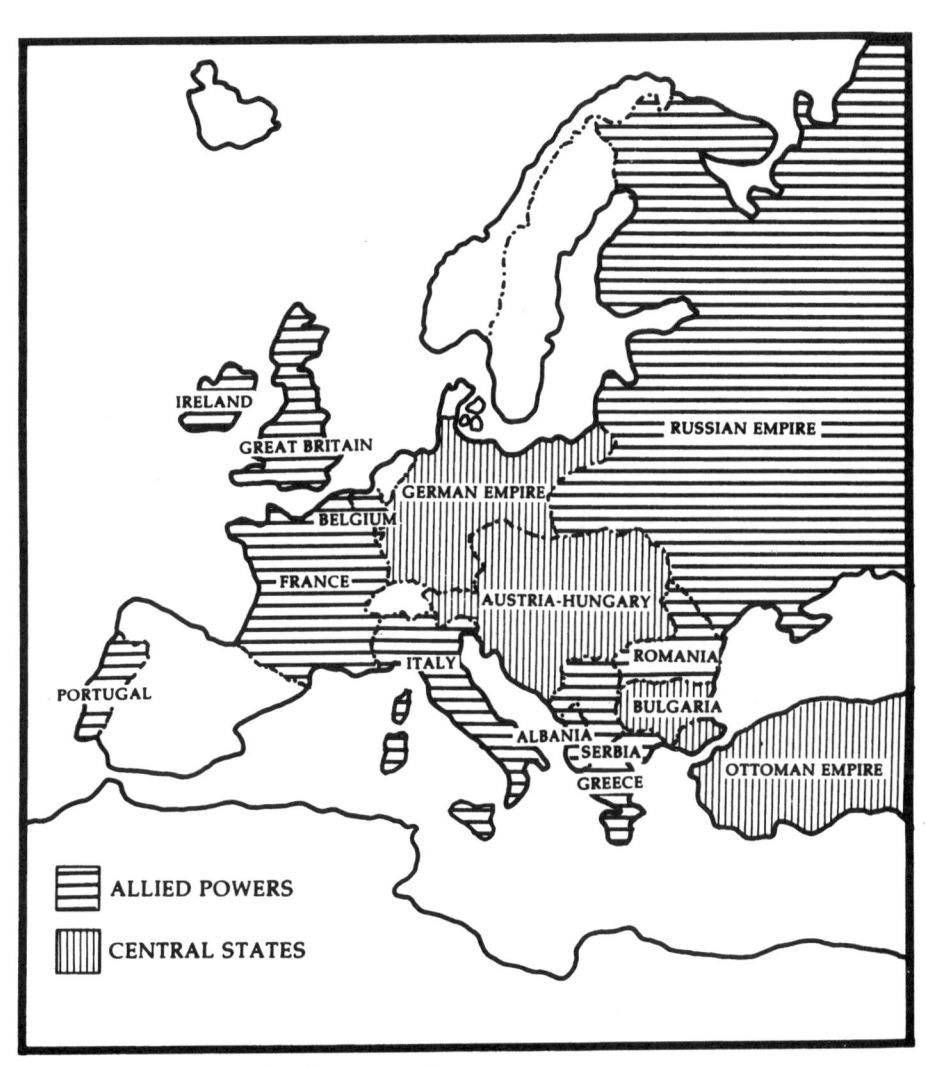

The combatants in World War I, 1915–18

Ferdinand's assassination was announced. On July 5 and 6 Germany granted its ally, Austria–Hungary, a free hand to deal with the matter, and Russia (and indirectly France) gave the Serbians a similarly free hand. Only in the final days of the crisis did the German Chancellor desperately try to regain control of the situation. Subsequent events revealed that German interests would have been better served by a tighter German rein on Austrian policy. However, in the eyes of German leaders, there appeared to be no alternative to their policy of allowing Austria to deal harshly with Serbia at this time.

On July 28 Austria–Hungary declared war on Serbia, and two days later Russia made the critical decision to order general mobilization, thus indicating its unwillingness to allow the Austrian–Serbian war to remain localized. German leaders had for a long time made it clear that they perceived a Russian general mobilization to be a direct potential threat to Germany itself. When Russia refused to withdraw its call to arms, Germany sent a last warning to both Russia and France, but when the German note remained unanswered by August 1st, Germany declared war on Russia. It did not immediately declare war on France, but France mobilized its army anyway on August 1st. With Russia, Germany and France carrying out general military buildups, a European war had become unavoidable. When Germany violated Belgian territory in order to gain easier access to France, Britain also entered the war, thereby transforming the European war, which Germany probably would have won, into a world war.

All the European powers shared the responsibility for the outbreak of World War I. Some, such as Austria–Hungary and Serbia, bore the greatest responsibility. Germany, Russia and France must be blamed for not having sufficiently restrained their respective allies and thereby having allowed a local Balkan squabble (where there had already been two wars in 1912 and 1913) to ignite a world war. Without doubt, Britain bears the least responsibility for the war which came.

Germany (FRG)

General von Hindenburg, Kaiser Wilhelm II, General Ludendorff

Nevertheless, crowds of people in *all* belligerent countries greeted the outbreak of war with a gaiety which is usually reserved for carnival time. Two million German, more than a million French, a million British, a million Austrian, a half million Italian and countless Russian soldiers were to perish in the four–year blood–letting which followed. The war also destroyed the old Europe, and what could be pieced back together collapsed a mere two decades later.

Almost immediately after the start of hostilities, German troops knifed through Belgium and into France according to a carefully laid "Schlieffen Plan," but by mid–September at the Battle of the Marne, they had been stopped in their tracks before reaching Paris. For four years two opposing armies faced each other in trenches stretching from the English Channel to the Swiss border and protected by mazes of barbed wire, machine–gun nests, mortar and heavy artillery batteries. Chemical warfare (gas) was also introduced during the grisly conflict. Occasionally massive attacks were launched against the opposing trenches which sometimes brought infinitesimal gains and always huge human losses. For instance, in the inconclusive Battle of the Somme in 1916, the Germans lost 650,000 men and the Allies 614,000.

It was a different story in the East, where warfare was highly mobile and brought huge gains and losses of territory. After an initial Russian advance into East Prussia, German forces scored stunning victories against the Russians at Tannenberg and the Masurian Lakes. Out of these victories was born the legend of military genius and invincibility which surrounded the victorious Generals Paul von Hindenburg and Erich Ludendorff for the remainder of the war. By 1916 their authority over military and political questions alike exceeded even that of the Kaiser and the Chancellor.

The German successes in the East enabled their armies to march right into the heart of Russia. Still, the badly shaken Tsarist Empire managed to put up stiff resistance. It became clear to the Germans that the two–front war was a vice which could eventually crush Germany. This became especially apparent when the United States entered the war on the Allied side in the spring of 1917. President Woodrow Wilson had been determined to keep the Americans out of the war, but the Germans made several blunders which drew the United States into the conflict. A high official in the Foreign Office, Arthur Zimmermann, sent a telegram to the Mexican government promising territorial rewards north of the Mexican border if it would support Germany in the war. This telegram was intercepted by the Americans and understandably antagonized American leaders and public opinion.

The most serious German mistakes involved its naval warfare against neutral shipping. By the spring of 1915 German surface ships had been swept from all the major seas except the North and Baltic Seas. Because of the ever–tightening British blockade of the North Sea and English Channel outlets, the bulk of the German Navy, which had been built up with so much fanfare and political sacrifice, remained bottled up in Germany's northern ports. This blockade also brought increasing hunger and deprivation to the German population and gradually led German leaders to use submarines to strike at Allied shipping. Submarines were regarded as a particularly hideous weapon at the time since they torpedoed ships without warning and without any capacity to help survivors. A particular outcry had gone up in the United States when a large passenger liner, the Lusitania, was torpedoed off the coast of Ireland in mid–1915, with a loss of 1,198 lives, including 139 Americans. The indignation in America was such that the Germans promised not to repeat such attacks.

For awhile German submarine activity died down, but by early 1917 Generals Hindenburg and Ludendorff, backed by their immense popularity, forced the adoption of unrestricted submarine warfare on the unwilling Chancellor. The head of the German Admiralty misjudged the ultimate effect of America's entry into the war to be "exactly zero;" in any case, it was widely believed that Britain would be forced to its knees before Americans would arrive. Although the first American divisions did not arrive in France until almost a year later, the immediate boost to Allied morale and the military contribution made by American soldiers in the final months of the war were decisive in the defeat of Germany.

Germany (FRG)

Ending the War on the Eastern Front

American entry into the war made it essential that the Germans eliminate the Eastern front. Because the weapon of war had not worked entirely, they selected another weapon: that of revolution. On March 15, 1917, the Russian Tsar abdicated, but to the Germans' surprise, the new government decided to continue the war. Therefore, German leaders decided to transport a group of Russian revolutionaries from their exile in Switzerland through Germany to Scandinavia from where they could return to Russia. This group was composed of Marxists who were known to favor Russian withdrawal from the war and included most predominantly Vladimir Ilyich Lenin. The Germans incorrectly figured that Lenin would be an ideal marionette for Germany, since he and his faction–ridden *Bolshevik* party would presumably be unable to hold power more than a few weeks without German support.

Neither the Germans nor Lenin had any concern for each others' interests. As Leon Trotsky wrote in his memoirs: "In the case of Lenin's trip two opposite plans crossed at a definite point, and this point was a sealed [rail] car." The train, which departed from Zurich with 32 Russian revolutionaries, had such high traffic priority that the German Crown Prince's own train was kept on a side track in Halle for two hours until Lenin's train had passed. The group arrived at Petrograd's (now St. Petersburg) Finland Train Station on April 16th and was greeted by thousands of supporters. It cannot be doubted that the transport and subsequent German financial assistance was vital to the Bolsheviks before their seizure of power in Petrograd on November 7, 1917.

Lenin did indeed announce Russia's withdrawal from the war, but the Germans imposed an extremely harsh peace treaty upon the new Bolshevik leadership at the Russian border town of Brest–Litovsk in early 1918. The Soviets, as the Bolsheviks had come to be called, were forced to relinquish huge chunks of territory from the Russian Empire. This treaty, along with the reparations demanded of Russia in August, set a most unfortunate precedent. It merely stimulated the *Entente's* will to resist and reinforced the enemy's moral self–confidence to impose on the Germans nine months later a peace no less dreadful than this one. That moral self–confidence was also strengthened by weakness which Germany demonstrated during both world wars: its lack of moderation. Without such moderation, no negotiated settlement was possible, only a dictated one. German occupation authorities after 1871 tended to mistreat or try to "Germanize" conquered nations, which could have been potential allies. The highest German diplomat in Russia in the summer of 1918 made a bitter comment about his own people: "Never was a *Volk* more capable of conquering the world and more incapable of ruling it!"

Collapse of the War Effort

Early in 1918 Hamburg, Leipzig, Cologne, Munich and the heavily industrialized Ruhr area had experienced serious strikes, and in Berlin 200,000 munitions workers struck. Hunger was causing the "home front" to collapse—the average rations for German civilians had been cut to only 1,000 calories per day. The tensions were greatly increased by a worsening of the military situation. Large numbers of fresh American troops began arriving in France in the spring of 1918. Germany's last great offensive was launched on March 21, 1918, but the exhausted German troops were unable to cope with the Allied counter–offensive, which began on July 10. On August 8, known to Germans then as "Black Friday," British infantry broke through the German lines at Amiens and threw the German troops in France into a mass retreat. On August 14 Ludendorff was forced to admit that the war could not be won militarily, and on September 29 he communicated to Supreme Headquarters that "the present condition of our army demands an immediate cease–fire in order to avoid catastrophe." On October 3, Hindenburg told the

Labor unrest in Germany's Ruhr area

Germany (FRG)

Chancellor that "under these circumstances it is necessary to break off the fight in order to spare the German people and its allies needless victims."

Despite such calls of desperation at the time, these men and many others had the audacity to claim later that it had been the civilian leadership, especially those who had founded the new Republic, who had "stabbed Germany in the back" by losing nerve and suing for peace at a time when Germany's armies had allegedly not been defeated in the field. This legend placed an unbearably heavy burden on Germany's postwar democratic leadership.

Its armies retreating, its allies crumbling, its people starving, Germany sent a delegation to seek peace with the *Entente*. It met French Marshal Foch in a rail car at Compiègne (in which Hitler later conducted the French surrender ceremonies almost 22 years later!). There the French Marshal delivered undiscussable conditions which Germany could take or leave: the 34 articles included the withdrawal of the German Army from France, Alsace-Lorraine and Belgium to the Rhine, *Entente* occupation of the left bank of the Rhine and delivery to the *Entente* of all German submarines and heavy military and transport materials. The disheartened Germans had no alternative but to accept. The war officially ended on November 11, 1918.

Collapse of the Empire and Birth of the Republic

Even before the cease-fire could be signed, the German Empire ceased to exist. Kaiser Wilhelm simply could not bring himself to abdicate, as the victors had demanded, so Chancellor Max von Baden simply announced the Kaiser's abdication on November 9. A short time later, the *Social Democrat* Philip Scheidemann, was informed that German communists were about to declare a Republic, so he rushed to the window of the *Reichstag* building and announced "The Emperor has abdicated . . . Long live the German Republic!"

The new Social Democratic Chancellor, Friedrich Ebert, made no secret of the fact that his emphasis would be on creating order and a parliamentary-democratic political structure in the badly shaken country. But no sooner had the Republic been declared than demands began to be made for a second, more radical revolution. The Polish revolutionary theorist and activist Rosa Luxemburg remarked sarcastically: "Oh how German this German Revolution is! How proper, how pedantic, how lacking in verve and in grandeur." It was not long before some groups chose to use force against Ebert's government, and Germans witnessed significant events which threatened the Republic in its infancy. In late 1918 the *Communist Party of Germany (KPD)* was formed, and on the same day the Steel Helmet League, a right-wing para-military organization of disenchanted war veterans, was created. The fatal split in German society which would paralyze and ultimately destroy the Republic continued to widen. The regime clearly found itself in a crisis from which it would never be able to extricate itself.

The communists made two unsuccessful violent attempts to seize power in Berlin. More than a thousand lives were lost in defeating the first attempt from January 6–12, 1919. The second erupted during the first two weeks of March 1919 and caused 2,000 deaths and considerable destruction to the city of Berlin. The government crushed a leftist uprising in Munich in May 1919 with such brutality that many observers accused the new republican government of being "blind in the right eye." That later right-wing strikes against the Republic were not suppressed with equal brutality stemmed from the fact that the postwar German Army of only 100,000 soldiers (*Reichswehr*) and the Free Corps troops, which were hastily assembled to cope with the crises were, on the whole, anti-republican and far more sympathetic to the right; they were never successfully transformed into reliable instruments of the Weimar Republic.

The government found itself in the predicament of having no alternative to the use of troops to restore and maintain order who were, in the main, unruly, disillusioned freebooters who had become far too accustomed to violence during a war which had severely shaken their sense of values and proportion. Such troops were extremely difficult to control, and the blemish of partiality toward the right was placed on the new Republic itself.

The Weimar Republic and a Disastrous "Peace" Treaty

In the spring of 1919 delegates to a National Assembly met in Weimar, a city chosen because it lay outside the storm of revolution which raged in Berlin and because of its association with the humanists Goethe and Schiller, who had lived and worked there. This assembly, whose venue gave the new Republic its name, had three tasks: to form a government of Germany, to sign a peace treaty and to draft a new constitution. It legitimized the "Weimar Coalition," composed of the *SPD*, *Center* and *German Democratic* parties, which had ruled Germany since the November Revolution of 1918. However, the necessity of fulfilling the second, highly unpopular task of signing a peace treaty caused this coalition of the Republic's supporters to lose its parliamentary majority in 1920, which it never regained.

The first major problem with the Versailles Treaty was the manner in which it was written. In contrast to all previous peace settlements in Europe, the vanquished (in this case, the Germans) were not included in the negotiations. If the Germans had been included, perhaps they would have felt some responsibility for the Treaty, but as it was, it represented a dictated peace towards which the Germans never felt any moral obligation to subscribe to its terms. The settlement had a strong whiff of "victor's justice."

Prior to American entry into the conflict, President Woodrow Wilson had proposed a "peace without victory" and later issued a written document containing "Fourteen

The colossal *Reichstag*, Berlin

Germany (FRG)

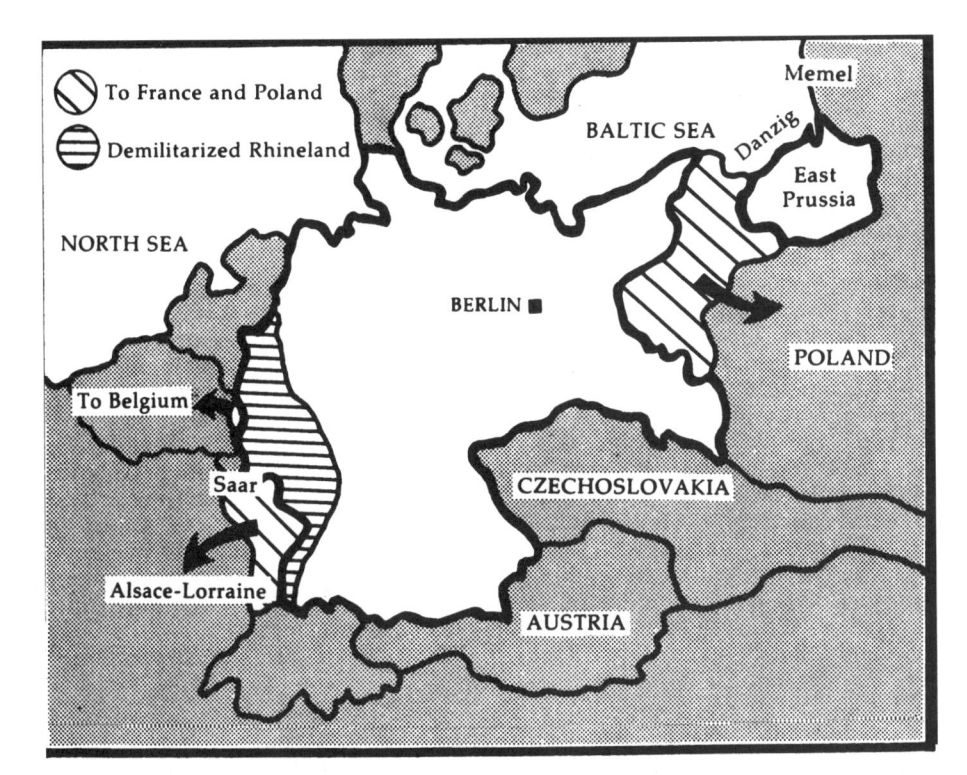

German territorial agreements with the Allies following World War I

Points" as a basis for European peace which contained very lofty language. The Germans later accepted the text, but it faded into the background at Versailles as French Prime Minister Georges Clemenceau ("the old tiger") virtually dictated the terms of what turned out to be an attempt at revenge. Little did he know that he was helping to sow the seeds of disaster, particularly in the mind of a wounded Austrian corporal, Adolf Hitler.

When the terms were forwarded to Berlin in mid–May 1919, with the warning that non–acceptance would result in an immediate resumption of hostilities, the Germans could hardly believe their eyes. They had expected to lose all territory conquered during the war, as well as Alsace–Lorraine, but they also lost a tenth of their prewar population and an eighth of their territory. The city of Danzig and the province of Posen were ceded to Poland, and a narrow corridor was cut right through West Prussia to connect these areas with Poland. Worse, the coal–rich Saar region was placed under League of Nations and French control for 15 years.

This, combined with the loss of practically all its merchant marine fleet, made it far more difficult for Germany to pay the shockingly high reparations demanded of it. The Rhineland was occupied by Allied soldiers and was to be demilitarized permanently. Germany's high seas fleet was to be turned over to the Allies, a requirement which prompted the Germans to scuttle all their naval ships, which had been interned at Scapa Flow in the Orkney Islands north of Scotland in mid–1919. The future German Army was to be restricted to 100,000 career officers and men with no military aircraft, tanks or other offensive weapons.

Perhaps worst of all, Article 231 of the "Treaty" placed sole responsibility for the outbreak and therefore for all destruction of the war on the shoulders of Germany and its allies. This article had been written by a young American diplomat, John Foster Dulles, as a compromise to the French, who had wanted to annex the Rhineland and to have even higher reparation payments from Germany. But Dulles had to admit later that "it was the revulsion of the German people from this article of the Treaty which, above all else, laid the foundation for the Germany of Hitler."

At the time of the Treaty, Adolf Hitler was only beginning to emerge from the political shadows. Born in Austria, he drew around himself a growing circle of enthusiastic admirers. Soon he helped found an energetic and anti–democratic party, the *National Socialist Workers' Party of Germany (NSDAP)* with the acronym *Nazi Party*). Although he had little formal education, Hitler was a fiery speaker, capable of stirring his listeners with haranguing, emotional tirades. For the next quarter of a century he never ceased to rail against the weak Weimar government and the wickedness of the Versailles Treaty.

The document actually made a mockery of many of Woodrow Wilson's Fourteen Points, such as "open covenants openly arrived at," freedom of the seas, the "impartial adjustment of all colonial claims," and of course the self–determination of nations. The victors permitted this latter right only where people wanted to detach themselves from Germany, such as in northern Schleswig and part of Upper Silesia. Wherever an area's population clearly wanted to join Germany, such as Austria or northern Bohemia, no referendum was permitted. Such hypocrisy stimulated within Germany cynicism toward both the Treaty and toward any German government which would sign it. Of course, Germany's harsh policy toward a collapsing Russia at Brest–Litovsk had provided a disastrous precedent. Nevertheless, Germany's short–sightedness in 1918 could not reasonably be invoked to justify an equally short–sighted Allied policy a year later.

As Chancellor Scheidemann said to the National Assembly in 1919, "Which hand would not wither up which put itself and us into these bonds?" The Treaty was a millstone around the neck of the new Republic. It not only helped create a deep division in German society, but it seriously hampered the normalization of Germany's relations with the outside world. It could only be maintained by force, but the United States quickly withdrew from Europe's military affairs, and Britain and France gradually lost the will to enforce it energetically. One day a spell–binding demagogue would be able to untie the "fetters of Versailles" right before the eyes of a weary and lethargic Europe and reap much applause within Germany for this.

Goethe and Schiller Monument in Weimar

Germany (FRG)

An Attempt at Democracy, Runaway Inflation and Anarchy

It was unfortunate that national humiliation coincided with the birth of the first democracy in Germany. When at last it had adopted the political organization extolled by the victorious allies, it had become an international outcast. The new German constitution reflected the democratic spirit of the "Weimar Constitution." The delegates sought to accomplish what the delegates of the Frankfurt Assembly had tried to do in 1848: to combine liberty with national unity and strength. It guaranteed basic individual rights and created a strong lower house of Parliament (*Reichstag*) which had the right to initiate legislation. It also maintained certain traditional German political institutions, such as a federal form and a strong presidency elected every seven years (as a Republican substitute for a strong Kaiser).

The Weimar Constitution did include several weaknesses. In order to give parliamentary representation to as many different groups as possible, it established the proportional representation electoral system. The unfortunate result was not only that anti–republican splinter groups, such as the *Nazi Party*, could publicize their causes in Parliament, but the large number of parties which could win parliamentary seats made the formation of a majority almost impossible. The result was predictable: parliamentary instability and ultimately paralysis.

A second weakness was the provision for initiatives and referendums. While such instruments of direct democracy often appear progressive, they can frequently be manipulated by enemies of the democratic order as Hitler did after 1933. The third mistake was the inclusion of emergency powers in Article 48, which could be invoked in the event that "public order and safety be seriously disturbed or threatened." As we shall see, this article was later used to circumvent Parliament and thereby to undermine the democratic intentions of the framers. This constitution on the whole was an admirable document, but the German nation was too divided on fundamental political values to be able to live by it. To be respected and observed, a constitution must fit a nation and a society well. If it does not, then it will ultimately be cast off like an ill–fitting garment.

The Weimar Republic experienced continuous crisis. The population had been impoverished by the long war and postwar chaos. The Republic saw no other way of keeping up its reparations payments than to borrow money abroad and to produce new money as fast as it could be turned out by the printing presses. The devastating result was inflation. At the beginning of 1922 the German mark was worth only one–fiftieth of its prewar value; one year later it was worth one ten–thousandth. In 1914 the U.S. dollar had been worth 4.2 marks; in 1923 it was worth 25 billion marks! The hero in Erich Remarque's novel, *Three Comrades*, gave an idea of what this meant in personal terms: "In 1923 I was advertising chief of a rubber factory . . . I had a monthly salary of 200 billion marks. We were paid twice a day, and then everybody had half an hour's leave so that he could rush to the stores and buy something before the next quotation of the dollar came out, at which time the money would lose half its value." There finally was a currency reform in 1923 in which one new mark (*Rentenmark*) was equal to a *trillion* old marks. But this dizzying inflation had already had the effect of a second revolution in Germany. It had financially wiped out millions of Germans and had spread fear and cynicism throughout the land, which merely weakened the Republic further.

The Republic was continuously battered from the left and the right. During the night of March 12–13, 1920, Free Corps troops marched on Berlin, singing military songs and flying the black–red–white flag of Imperial Germany. On their helmets was a popular Free Corps symbol: the swastika, the distorted cross which was also the Nazis' chief symbol. The troops faced no armed resistance since the majority of generals in Berlin refused to allow their soldiers to fire on former comrades from the front. The leader of the *coup d'etat* was Wolfgang Kapp, who had been brought up in the United States. He installed himself as chancellor and forced the government to flee the city. But a general strike called by the government before departing was observed by virtually all groups in Berlin: socialist labor unions, radical leftist militants, shopkeepers and the government ministries. Factories, schools, banks and stores were closed, streetcars and buses ceased running and water, electricity and gas were shut off.

Rampant inflation in the Weimar Republic's darkest days: a thousand marks is hastily overprinted to make it worth a million . . . then a billion mark note!

Germany (FRG)

Caricaturist George Grosz catches the cynical attitude of the times as he satirizes the wealthy in the badly divided, economically hard-pressed Weimar Republic: (left) "The Landlord" and (right) "View of Tauentzienstrasse" which depicts a blindman, prostitute, and a corrupt capitalist.

This resistance finally forced Kapp and his supporters to flee Berlin only five days later. Almost immediately after the Kapp effort, the communists staged disorders in Berlin, Münster and the Ruhr area, especially Düsseldorf.

Former Finance Minister Matthias Erzberger, who had signed the Versailles Treaty, was gunned down in the Black Forest in 1921 by a right–wing squad, and the following year Foreign Minister Walter Rathenau was felled by assassins' bullets. The next day, Chancellor Joseph Wirth declared in the *Reichstag*, where Rathenau's body lay in state: "The enemy is on the right!" He was correct. Although the radical left tried to destroy the Republic, the right *did* present a greater danger, primarily because it was so well–placed in the civil service, the judicial system and the army.

Stagnation and Loss of the Ruhr

The year 1923 saw the suppression of a Nazi attempted *coup* in Munich and of communist disorders in Hamburg, Saxony and Thuringia. It also saw the French military occupation of the Ruhr area, Germany's industrial heartland. The German government temporarily suspended all reparations payments and called upon Rhinelanders to practice passive resistance by refusing all cooperation with the French, but this form of retaliation merely meant more hunger and inflation for Germans. The French action was partially a reaction to Germany's signing the Rapallo Pact with the Soviet Union in 1922, calling for a normalization of political and trade relations between the two countries. The two armies began to maintain secret contacts with each other, and German officers began training in Russia with weapons which the Versailles Treaty forbade: tanks, airplanes and submarines. The Soviet Union was also an international outcast at the time and was seeking some support against the Western Allies.

That the storm over the Ruhr finally blew over was the work of the man who became chancellor for a few months in August 1923 and who served as foreign minister until his untimely death in October 1929: Gustav Stresemann. Before and during World War I, Stresemann had been a fervent nationalist who had strongly advocated German expansion. But he was one of those persons who had learned from Germany's past and who had concluded that its future was best served by cooperating with the West, not by fighting it. Like Konrad Adenauer after World War II, he helped to restore Germany's position in the world without having much military power at his disposal. However, unlike Adenauer's policy, Stresemann's foreign policy failed to win much domestic support and legitimacy for the Weimar Republic.

The Golden Twenties: Satisfaction and Dissatisfaction

Stresemann ended passive resistance in the Ruhr, and he set out to reach an international agreement which would enable Germany to pay its reparations. In 1924 the American banker Charles Dawes led a committee of experts which drew up a plan to regulate German reparations payments and to channel foreign credit into Germany to stimulate its recovery. This plan set the stage for a remarkable increase in German living standards and wages in the second half of the 1920s. The results were so promising that five years later the Young Plan, also of American origin, sought even further economic stimulation by scaling down the payments scheduled in the Dawes Plan.

The overall result was that more than 25 billion marks worth of foreign capital was poured into Germany, mainly from the United States. This inflow of capital actually exceeded the outflow of reparations

43

Germany (FRG)

payments from Germany. Thus, in the long run, the payments did not have as adverse an economic effect on Germany as agitators constantly charged.

Stresemann also reached out to France. In the Locarno Treaty of 1925 Germany agreed to recognize the permanence of its borders with France and Belgium, to foreswear (with France and Belgium) the use of force against each other except in self–defense, to submit any disputes to arbitration or conciliation, and finally to enter the League of Nations, which Germany did in 1926. Although Germany did not recognize the permanency of its eastern borders, it agreed to seek their modification only by peaceful means. It underscored this commitment by signing in 1926 a pact of friendship, the Berlin Treaty, with the Soviet Union. The foreign minister's main focus remained on the West, though. His cooperation with the British and French leaders created considerable enthusiasm in Europe and greatly cooled tensions for the rest of the decade, which because of its increasing prosperity, optimism and cooperation was known as "the golden twenties."

The second half of the 1920s was also a time of relative political stability, thanks not only to Stresemann's influence, but also to another event: the election in April 1925 of Field Marshal Hindenburg, the "Wooden Titan" and "Hero of Tannenberg," as President of the Republic. At the time, many democrats threw up their hands in despair that such a man who was mentally embedded in the imperial past could become the highest political leader in Germany. But he actually took seriously his pledge to defend the Weimar constitution, and with this war hero in the presidential palace as a kind of substitute monarch, many German conservatives began for the first time to accept the legitimacy of the Republic and to tone down their attacks against it.

This was also a period of extraordinary cultural achievement, although the roots of "Weimar culture" no doubt were planted during Imperial Germany. It was a time in which the Mann brothers, Thomas and Heinrich, Gerhard Hauptmann, Bertold Brecht, Kurt Tucholsky, Erich Kästner, Oskar Kokoschka and Gottfried Benn were reaching huge audiences and were producing works which in some ways supported the new political order.

Still, many writers continued to capture the attention of those whose ideals had been crushed by the fall of the Empire and the loss of the war and who could not view civilian life in the new democratic Republic as a satisfactory replacement. Erich Remarque's novel *The Road Back* portrayed a disillusioned returning soldier, who asked: ". . . what are we doing here? Look about you: look how flat and comfortless it all is. We are a burden to ourselves and others. Our ideals are bankrupt, our dreams are *kaputt,* and we wander around in this world of rotten opportunists and speculators like Don Quixotes in a foreign land." Such feelings were intensified by the immensely popular battle–front novels by authors such as Ernst Jünger, Werner Beumelburg and Edwin Erich Dwinger, which called for a return to heroic virtues.

Some of Germany's most respected academic minds, such as Martin Heidegger and Carl Schmitt, focused on the shortcomings of liberalism and democracy. Also, many anti–liberals were able to sooth their consciences by reading such best sellers as Oswald Spengler's *The Decline of the West,* which decried the Republic and the alleged death of culture in the materialist West, and Arthur Moeller van der Bruck's *The Third Reich,* which called for a new and better political and social order.

For the first time in its history, Germany had a city which was not only the political, but also the cultural and intellectual center of the country. In fact, Berlin in the 1920s equalled or even surpassed Paris as the cultural center of Europe. Painters, writers, dramatists and film makers from all over Europe found Berlin to be the most stimulating place to work and live, and entertainers like Marlene Dietrich and American–born Josephine Baker found wildly enthusiastic audiences there. However, some Germans were repelled by the experimentalism in art, sexuality and living styles which was taking place in Berlin and rejected the city as a center of decadence. In fact, one of the first things to be swept out of Germany when the Nazis came to power was the Weimar culture.

Two things brought the "golden years of the twenties" to an end. First, Stresemann died of a stroke in late 1929. He had been the only leader who had made parliamentary government work acceptably well, had brought about compromise between labor and capital, and had enabled Germany to take an equal place among the nations of the world. His death was an untimely tragedy for a nation entering a grave crisis, for he was perhaps the only leader who could have successfully competed with Hitler for control of Germany's destiny. Only ten days after his death came the second blow to the Republic: the American stock market collapsed and overnight the chief source of credit for Germany dried up. Germany was thrown into a fatal economic crisis.

By 1930 the Weimar Republic was practically dead, although it limped on for another three years. Dr. Heinrich Brüning became chancellor and attempted to master the economic crisis by reducing government spending, rather than by trying to stimulate the economy through decisive government economic programs. This policy earned him the name "hunger chancellor." He had no parliamentary majority. The *SPD* sometimes supported him begrudgingly in the absence of any acceptable alternative, but Brüning was compelled to resort to the emergency powers granted in Article 48 of the Weimar Constitution, which had been designed originally to enable the president to "restore public safety and order" in times of crisis.

Article 48 was never intended to enable a president or chancellor to rule for long periods of time semi–independently of the Parliament, as all chancellors did during the imperial time and which all did again after March 1930. When the *Reichstag* voted its no confidence for the government for this violation of the constitution, Brüning dissolved Parliament and called for new elections for September 1930. He disregarded all warnings that elections in the middle of such an economic depression and widespread unemployment could only benefit the extremist parties of the left and right. After all, unemployment had risen from 1.37 million in 1929 to 3.15 million in 1930. Such warnings were absolutely correct.

President von Hindenburg's signature (actual size)

Germany (FRG)

The *Communist Party* increased its number of seats in Parliament from 54 to 77, and the *Nazi Party* grew from 12 members to 107, thereby becoming the second largest party after the *SPD*. The Nazis were thereafter in a position to hammer away at the Republic through parliamentary obstruction. Unemployment continued to rise to over 6 million in 1932, while production by 1932 had fallen to barely half the 1929 level. Such economic desperation and governmental paralysis gave a man with a small, socially unpolished minority of followers, but with great demagogical skill, the power to sway the frightened masses—the chance he had awaited for a decade.

Throughout the 1920s the *Nazi Party* had great difficulty gaining political momentum and a significant following. It had first taken shape in the confusion and frustration following the end of World War I and had aimed its appeal toward the disillusioned and impoverished, first in Austria and shortly afterwards in Germany. Its official name indicated the wide spectrum of groups which it tried to encompass: *National Socialist German Workers' Party*. Throughout its entire existence, it was not a party which aimed to serve one particular class, as the *Communist, Social Democratic* or *Conservative* parties tried to do. Instead, the Nazi party was one which attracted the social scrap of all classes. This is why it was and is difficult to put a political label on the party or movement. It was not exactly conservative because it attacked the capitalist economic system and the *status quo*, and, as a rule, German business leaders did not support the party financially or otherwise until after it had actually come into power in 1933.

In a famous speech before the Industrial Club in Düsseldorf in 1932, Adolf Hitler made it unmistakably clear that he considered German business leaders to bear a heavy share of the blame for the 1918 disaster and that business interests would never achieve primacy over political interests in the soon–to–be Third Reich. He always kept this promise. Hitler sought many social changes. In many ways he advocated and introduced a revolution (called by many a "conservative revolution") against bourgeois and industrialized society. National Socialist policy and aims were not leftist either. They were blatantly nationalist, a fact which attracted many conservative supporters who abhorred his means of gaining power. Also, he openly attacked the *Communist Party* and *Social Democrats* as unnational and, in the case of the communists, as handmaidens of the Soviet Union. He detested liberalism, democracy and the Weimar Republic, aversions which he of course shared with the communists.

Adolf Hitler leaves a Nazi party meeting

An Early Attempt in Bavaria

Hitler made an almost comical attempt to seize power in Bavaria in 1923 by having his followers "arrest" government leaders in the Munich Bürgerbräu beer hall (now razed). He had hoped this brazen act would set in motion events which would result in the crash of the Weimar Republic. Instead, he was arrested and there was a highly publicized trial which gave this well–practiced demagogue the opportunity to capture the attention of all Germany and to articulate his attack against the Weimar Republic. He was sent to Landsberg prison for a five–year sentence, although in the end he served less than one year. While in prison he produced his rambling, often raving, book *Mein Kampf* ("My Struggle"), put into writing by his loyal follower, Rudolf Hess.

Hitler's unsuccessful "beer hall putsch" and his imprisonment convinced him that he must try to gain power by means of the ballot box. While in prison, he told a friend: ". . . it will be necessary to pursue a new policy. Instead of working to achieve power by an armed *coup*, we shall have to hold our noses and enter the *Reichstag* against the Catholic and Marxist deputies. If outvoting them takes longer than outshooting them, at least the result will be guaranteed by their own constitution. Any lawful process is slow . . . Sooner or later we shall have a majority—and after that, Germany."

Ten years later he accomplished his goal, but it is mistaken to argue that Hitler came to power entirely legally. When the critical elections came in the years 1930–1933, he unleashed his two private armies, the *Sturmabteilung* (Storm Division—SA) and *Schutzstaffel* (Protective Troop—SS), to break up other parties' rallies and meetings, to beat up opponents in the streets, to terrorize those who manifested an inclination to vote for another party, and to make other kinds of unnerving demonstrations, such as throwing up blockades around Berlin at election time. No person with democratic convictions and a rudimentary knowledge of the Weimar Constitution could call such tactics "legal."

Party Organization

In the 1920s Hitler set about the reorganization of his party from top to bottom. He divided all of Germany into districts, each called a *Gau* and led by a hard–core Nazi called a *Gauleiter*. These districts were subdivided into circles (each called a *Kreis*) and groups. Such units were also created for Austria, Danzig, the Saarland

Germany (FRG)

and the Sudetenland, which at the time were not even a part of Germany, but which gave a clue as to what Hitler had in mind for the future. At the top of this party organization was the leader (*Führer*), Hitler himself. Such rule from the top was called the "leadership principle." Until he committed suicide in 1945, Hitler's leadership within the party was only once seriously challenged by a group of military officers who sensed that Germany was committing suicide under the *Führer* during the waning days of World War II. Indeed, it is inconceivable that the party would have been so successful without Hitler's powerful will and his ability to coordinate a diverse collection of ambitious Nazis.

Throughout most of the 1920s the Nazi Party found members and votes primarily among fanatical, nationalistic patriots, anti–Semites and social misfits fascinated by militarism. They had a psychological need for rabble–rousing rhetoric which was well supplied by party rallies and a daily reading of the party's newspaper, the *Völkischer Beobachter* ("People's Observer"). But the party was getting nowhere fast, with 32 parliamentary seats in 1924 and only 12 in 1928. However, after the economic disasters of 1929 and 1930, more and more Germans began to look to the former corporal from Austria, who had gained German citizenship through the back door of Bavarian citizenship only shortly before becoming Chancellor of all Germany in 1933. As the novelist Erich Kästner wrote: "people ran after the pied pipers down into the abyss."

When Brüning was dismissed as chancellor in May 1932 because of his inability to muster a parliamentary majority, German politics was dominated by the senile octogenarian von Hindenburg and three intriguers, Hitler, General Kurt von Schleicher and Baron Franz von Papen. The latter had been the German military attaché in Washington during the first part of World War I who later was expelled from the U.S. for spying. In the twilight of the Weimar Republic, many Germans had the impression that there were only two alternatives: the conservatives, with their established position in the army, coupled with the civil and diplomatic service on the one hand, and Hitler, who stood at the head of a dynamic mass movement on the other. It turned out that Hitler, who had a much clearer idea of what he wanted than did his political opponents, had the clear advantage.

He was no democrat, but he was a populist, whose power was based on the masses, not upon the country's elites. It is true that Hitler was in some political trouble: in the parliamentary elections of November 1932 his party had lost two million votes. In this last free election in pre–war Germany, two out of three Germans voted *against* Hitler, and most of those who voted for him in that election had not voted for all that he was to do in the following 13 years. Hitler refused to participate in any coalition in which he was not Chancellor, and Hindenburg wearily tried every conceivable conservative combination to prevent the chancellorship from going to Hitler, whom he personally despised. But all efforts were to no avail. Von Papen finally persuaded the aged President that he, von Papen, could control the upstart Hitler. So on January 30, 1933, Hindenburg, literally backed to the wall, appointed Hitler Chancellor in a cabinet containing only three Nazis.

Political responsibility usually moves radicals and ideologues to more practical viewpoints, a historical fact which must have quieted Hindenburg's worries at the time. In any case, Hitler came to power by miscalculation, rather than by overwhelming popular demand. His ascension to power in Germany was neither inevitable nor a culmination of a thousand years of German history as he asserted; such an evaluation honored Hitler far too greatly. In some unsteady situations such as in 1933, power is like a ripe piece of fruit waiting to be picked by that person who is most ready to act decisively. On January 30, 1933, in Germany that person was Adolf Hitler.

Hitler Seizes Total Power

For a few weeks, Hitler had to be cautious because he had no parliamentary majority, by coalition or otherwise, and because Hindenburg, who was still very cool toward him, had not given him permission to exercise emergency powers. But an incident during the night of February 27, 1933, gave Hitler the chance to throw off most of the restraints on his power and to fire the *coup de grace* into the drooping head of the Weimar Republic. In that night the *Reichstag* was gutted by fire. Controversy still surrounds this incident, but it is probable that the fire was set by the Nazis themselves. Hitler acted "quickly as lightning" (which along with "ice cold" was one of his favorite expressions!). He declared that this had been an act of communist violence and won Hindenburg's formal approval the next day to suspend constitutional guarantees for individual and civil liberties.

During the first four weeks of Hitler's chancellorship the courts had dared to reject many of the high–handed methods employed by Hermann Göring's Prussian police force to victimize the Nazis' political opponents. That was no longer possible because Hitler now wielded emergency powers and thereby had the ability to terrorize Germans through instruments of the state. His storm troopers were now able to race through the streets arresting socialists, communists and liberal party leaders, taking sledge hammers to newspaper presses, breaking up all opposition political meetings and terrorizing the entire nation. Neither Hindenburg nor the German army resisted these moves.

In this atmosphere of violence and intimidation, the last election of the Weimar Republic was held on March 5, 1933, in which the Nazis were still unable to receive more than 44% of the popular vote. Yet, by scaring and arresting enough members of Parliament, Hitler was able to manipulate a majority in the *Reichstag* in favor of the so–called "Enabling Act," which in effect suspended Parliament's power and made Hitler the sole leader of Germany. Only the *SPD* dared to vote against this. Only a few more steps were necessary to give him full dictatorial power.

Anti–Semitism and Repression

Hitler and his party proceeded to enforce a so–called *Gleichschaltung,* an untranslatable German word meaning the destruction or restructuring of all independent groups or institutions so that none could exist without supporting Nazi rule. In March and April 1933 he abolished the federal organization of Germany, and for the first time in its history, Germany became entirely centralized, with governors (*Reichsstatthalter*) carrying out Hitler's policy in the various regions. By June all independent labor unions had been outlawed and a Labor Front was created under the leadership of the invariably intoxicated Robert Ley, with the task of keeping labor under firm control. By July all political parties except the *Nazi Party* had been abolished and concentration camps were established, where alleged enemies of the state could be "concentrated" and controlled.

By October, all communications media, including film, were brought under Nazi control and all newspapers editors were required to be Aryans (non–Jewish members of an ancient race which, according to Nazi doctrine, Germans belonged). They could not even be married to Jews. This was only one of the first of a steadily growing number of measures directed against Jews within Germany, who, according to Nazi ideology, were social parasites who weakened the German nation. Many Jews, including brilliant intellectuals and scientists, began to flee Germany during the ensuing years. One of them was Albert Einstein, who came to the United States. These anti–Jewish measures reached a pre–war crescendo in the night of November 9–10, 1938, when hundreds of Jewish homes, stores and syna-

Germany (FRG)

gogues were systematically damaged and plundered. The amount of broken glass which this senseless and criminal rampage left gave the event the name of *Kristallnacht* ("Crystal Night"). Although many Germans were sickened by this incident, none dared to resist.

This event increased the tempo of the stampede of Jews from Germany which started in 1933 when all non–Aryans and people who were "no longer prepared to intercede at all times for the National Socialist state" were excluded from civil service and ultimately from posts in the universities. Many young Germans had streamed into the Nazi student organization and assumed the right to control the lectures and writings of their professors for "un–German" or other politically revealing utterances. Youthful idealism can sometimes have a beneficial effect in politics, but it can also be disastrous. In 1933–1934 an estimated 1,684 scholars, including 1,145 professors, were dismissed from the universities. At the universities of Berlin and Frankfurt am Main, about a third of the faculty was fired, and in all of Germany the size of the student body fell by about one–third, due largely to the inclusion of Nazi Party membership into the admission procedure.

This policy of *Gleichschaltung* issued an almost fatal blow to the cultural and intellectual preeminence of Germany. But there was one country which benefited enormously from this self–defeating and short–sighted policy: the United States. Before the outbreak of war, approximately 200,000 Germans, half of whom were Jewish, had fled to the U.S. American immigration quota restrictions, which had been tightened during the economic depression of the 1930s, were such that a large portion of the German refugees to the United States were intellectual or cultural leaders who could find sponsors more easily. They were attracted by such universities as the New School for Social Research in New York, Princeton University, the University of Chicago or to such magnetic cultural centers as Hollywood or New York City.

Even an abbreviated list of these refugees gives an idea of the enormous loss to Germany: in addition to scientists Albert Einstein and Edward Teller, in literature practically the entire Mann family (Thomas, Heinrich, Klaus, Erika and Golo), Bertold Brecht, Stefan Zweig, Carl Zuckmayer, Alfred Döblin, Leon Feuchtwanger and Erich Maria Remarque. In film there were Fritz Lang, Marlene Dietrich and Otto Preminger, in theater Max Reinhardt, in music Arnold Schönberg and Kurt Weil, in art, Georg Grosz and Max Ernst, in architecture, Walter Gropius and Ludwig Mies van der Rohe; in publishing, Frederick Praeger and Kurt Wolff, and in

Burning of the *Reichstag*

Germany (FRG)

scholarship, Paul Tillich, Erich Fromm, Hans Morgenthau, Theodor Adorno, Ernst Bloch, Leo Strauss, Erich Vögelin, Hannah Arendt, Ernst Cassirer and Kurt Riezler. By 1938 the New York columnist Dorothy Thompson could claim with justification that "practically everyone whom the world considers to be representative of German culture before 1933 is now a refugee." Of course, some stayed in the United States only until Hitler was defeated, but most stayed for good.

"Night of the Long Knives"

In the dark hours of June 30, 1934, known as the "night of the long knives," Hitler had hundreds of potential challengers to his authority *within his own party* murdered, especially the SA leadership, including Ernst Röhm. While his assassination squads were at work, he also eliminated many prominent non–Nazis, such as von Schleicher and some of von Papen's closest aides, as well as leading authors, lawyers, civil servants, Catholic politicians, and harmless citizens who at some time had caused irritation to one or the other Nazi bosses. Von Papen and Brüning escaped by the skin of their teeth, the latter eventually landing in a professorial chair at Harvard. These cold–blooded acts were enough to intimidate most resistance to Hitler within or without the Nazi party until his death in 1945.

The senile Hindenburg died August 2, 1934, and Hitler simply combined the offices of President and Chancellor and declared himself the absolute *Führer* of party and state. He then required that the nation give retroactive approval of this unconstitutional act in a plebiscite, a favorite maneuver of dictators whereby one may vote "yes" or "no" under the watchful eyes of party henchmen. Despite intimidation measures, five million Germans voted "no" to this act. Hitler then proceeded to require all officers and soldiers to take an oath of allegiance not to Germany, but to *him alone*. Many German officers had grave misgivings about taking such an oath. But Hitler's shrewd treatment of the army gradually eliminated it as an immediate threat to his power, although high–ranking officers would later prove to be his most daring, though ill–fated, foes.

The Third Reich

By fall 1934, Hitler stood as the undisputed leader of a dictatorial state which he called the "Third Reich." This name was used to remind Germans that he had created anew a Germany worthy of the two earlier German empires: the one created by Heinrich I in 919 and the one formed by Bismarck in 1871. His path to power had been washed by blood and strewn with corpses. Many of his subjects had been driven through fear to passivity. Yet in 1939 he could claim with justification that he ruled a people which generally supported him. How was this possible? In the first half of his 12–year rule he was able to achieve certain things which many Germans and non–Germans alike regarded as little less than miraculous. His accomplishments confused and disarmed his opponents, who in 1933 were still the majority within Germany. But their numbers had dwindled considerably by 1938, even if most of them did not actually become Nazis.

Before 1933 Hitler had shown himself to be an unparalleled organizer and hypnotic speaker, but few Germans expected him actually to succeed in conducting the complex affairs of state. Before he came to power, he remained largely in the realm of fuzzy generalities. For example, he made no concrete suggestions on how to combat the problem of unemployment. He also seemed to reveal his cards very quickly after coming to power, inflicting a heavy dose of terror on the German people. Indeed, that his rule always rested in part on terror indicated that the whole German people never entirely embraced National Socialism. But terror gradually declined and remained at a level just sufficient to keep the population in a state of fear without driving them into desperate resistance. His orchestration of terror within Germany and his skillful use of his own undeniable charisma were psychological masterpieces from which all would–be dictators could learn.

In retrospect, Hitler has been diagnosed by some professionals as clinically paranoid. Continuously tense and expectant, he was sensitive and suspicious. He had no close relationship with anyone, not even with his mistress, Eva Braun, whom he finally married moments before committing suicide. Untrusting, he always felt that his failures resulted from the enmity or failure of others, even those close to him. He was able, however, to maintain his conduct within nominally acceptable bounds, and some persons considered him to be no more than a "crank."

Initial Successes

What were his specific accomplishments? By far his most important and popular was his dealing with the economic crisis. In early 1933 there were more than six million Germans out of work; by 1936 Germany achieved full employment without creating inflation. Germans had been put to work building an admirable network of superhighways known as *Autobahnen*, as well as other public works. Industries were given tax relief, and the government's financial leaders, especially Dr. Schacht, channeled investments to desperately needy economic sectors and successfully manipulated government funds and the money supply so that the economy would not be choked for lack of money. Also, Hitler revitalized the arms industry in Germany. This provided an important stimulus for the economy, but it should be noted that most of Germany's unemployed found jobs in civilian industries, not in arms industries. In the three years after Hitler had assumed power in Germany, the country's GNP and national income had doubled, and Germans had begun to enjoy a modest prosperity.

Within Germany the mood had changed from one of hopelessness to one of confidence in the future. Of course, the facts should not be overlooked that by 1939 many Germans had become soldiers and approximately 300,000 were in concentration camps. Hitler's economic performance was so successful that many persons in and out of Germany gained the impression that this man could indeed perform wonders. Others in countries all over Europe began to see totalitarianism, cooperation with and imitation of Germany as attractive.

A second accomplishment was that he accelerated a process which had begun several decades earlier in Germany, namely the breaking down of class differences. The Nazis were officially in favor of this. They did not speak of a "classless society," as do communists, but of "community" (*Volksgemeinschaft*). This latter term had become very attractive to many Germans who were sick and tired of conflict and who wanted to see central authority established in Germany. "Community" as interpreted by the Nazis required a high degree of social mobilization of youth, women, farmer and other groups. In fact, Germans were expected to become so active in politically dominated groups that they could not possibly go their own way and be individually free. Still, in the Third Reich there was much upward and downward mobility, mixing of classes and open opportunity for the talented (so long as they were not Jewish or openly critical of the new political order!).

It is certainly incorrect to say that Hitler's rule was "class rule," because no one social group dominated the party and state. For that reason, it is technically incorrect to call National Socialism fascism, which in southern Europe meant upper class domination over the other social classes and groups, all bundled together and cemented by artificially produced mass enthusiasm. No social groups fared badly in Hitler's Reich. Yet it would be indeed wrong to argue that Hitler eliminated class conflict entirely. Despite the rapid economic recovery, the problems between capital and labor, big and small business,

Germany (FRG)

in on that which had been already dying. He had seen when the Weimar Republic had reached the end of its road, and Hitler merely gave it the *coup de grace.* He also could see that the international system which had emerged from Versailles was collapsing. At that conference, one of the four pre–1914 great European powers, Austria–Hungary, had been destroyed, and another, Russia, had been excluded from the victorious coalition. The United States refused to help enforce the Treaty, so only Britain and France remained to hold the dictated settlement together. In the course of the 1920s Britain grew tired of its role and began to seek a policy of moderation and accommodation toward Germany. French leaders did not favor such a policy of appeasement, but France had become so weakened by pacifism and political division from within that it could no longer oppose Germany energetically.

Hitler violated the Locarno Treaty in 1936 and remilitarized the Rhineland. In March 1938 Germany swallowed up Austria in the face of virtually no opposition from it or any other country. Six months later, Germany obtained French and British approval at a conference in Munich for Germany's absorption of the Sudetenland, the predominantly German–speaking western part of Czechoslovakia. Hitler's appetite was whetted, so in 1939 he declared Bohemia (capital: Prague) and Moravia to be German protectorates and occupied the Memel area. He had marched his troops a long way while the rest of Europe slept, but when his troops entered Prague, Britain woke up and resigned itself to the bitter fact that it would have to prepare for war against Germany. France reluctantly agreed.

The Start of World War II

By the spring of 1939, Britain and France had already allowed Germany to become the dominant power in Europe. Hitler's greatest mistake was that he cast this enormous accomplishment away by leading Germany into war. After 1938 he had no further diplomatic victories. But from 1939 to 1941 he led Germany to dazzling successes, but all were of a military nature. With relative ease his newly created army *(Wehrmacht)* rolled over part of Poland, Denmark, Norway, Holland, Belgium, Luxembourg, Yugoslavia and Greece.

The most miraculous victory, in the eyes of the world, was the victory over France. Most German generals shuddered at the thought of attacking France, remembering the failure of the 1914 advance and the four–year war of attrition which had sapped Germany's strength and will. But Hitler had great faith in the tank warfare tactics developed by General Heinz Guderian and in the brilliant strategic plan

Autographed portrait of the *Führer*   Courtesy: David W. Staton

or industry and agriculture were not solved. But the important fact is that there was less social inequality in Germany during the Third Reich than there had been before, and both East and West Germany greatly profited from and continued this process after 1945.

A third accomplishment which won the admiration of many of his countrymen was Hitler's rapid rearmament of Germany. In January 1933, Germany had a 100,000 man army without an air force and modern weapons. By 1938 it had a conscript army and was the strongest military power in Europe. Hitler also made the significant decision, against the advice of many military experts, to integrate armored units with other combat forces. This later proved quite successful in overrunning most of Western Europe. The military buildup may have been a curse for the rest of Europe, but it was approved by many Germans, who saw it as a means for revising the despised Versailles Treaty.

A fourth accomplishment was a string of almost stunning diplomatic and military victories. Until 1942 Hitler had always been a master of recognizing when houses of cards were about ready to collapse and then of acting decisively while others wavered. He had the instinct of a buzzard which told him when to swoop

Germany (FRG)

devised by General Friedrich Erich von Manstein. He also recognized the most important factor: France was simply unwilling to fight a war even before German tanks crossed its border.

In six weeks, Germany had rolled into France via a flank attack around its famed Maginot line of supposedly impregnable fortresses. The amount of French military activity is vividly evident even to this day. If one inspects the war memorials in the towns and cities of France, the names of those who perished in World War I outnumbers by ten, twenty and even thirty to one the names of those victims of World War II.

By the summer of 1940 Germany controlled Europe from the Arctic Circle to the Pyrenees and from the Atlantic Ocean to the Soviet Union. If Hitler had made a generous peace offer to France, he might have destroyed Britain's and other countries' will to resist, but Hitler never thought of such a possibility. He could not grant a magnanimous peace because, as he himself later wrote, the victory of the stronger always involved "the destruction of the weaker or his unconditional subservience." He had a knack for seeing the weakness in his enemies, but he was unable to build anything lasting. Also, because he considered himself to be infallible and irreplaceable, he insisted on doing everything quickly; he could not plant anything which required time to grow.

Based upon his writings and actions, one can say with reasonable certainty that Hitler sought to establish German hegemony in Europe and direct domination over the Soviet Union, which along with the older European powers' overseas colonies, would occupy the bottom of Hitler's power pyramid. Above them would be the rest of the European countries, divided into Germanic lands bordering on Germany, servant peoples, such as the Poles, and satellites and quasi–independent states. On top would be an all–powerful Germany. This German–dominated order would place Hitler in a good position later to struggle against America and Japan for world domination. That he did not accomplish this stunning goal was due in large measure to serious mistakes which he himself made after such stunning successes.

The Beginning of the End

In 1940 he launched an aerial attack against Britain which left rubble piles throughout the kingdom, but which also inspired heroic British action in what Prime Minister Winston Churchill called Britain's "finest hour." While still involved in this furious struggle, violating the treaty whereby Germany and Russia had split up Poland between them, Hitler unleashed his armies against the Soviet Union in mid–1941, against the advice of his generals, thereby creating a two–front war which had been such a nightmare for Germany during World War I. The attack was launched too late, so in a repeat of Napoleon's humiliation, "Mother Winter" saved the weaker Russians. Cold weather and snow closed in on the German troops, many of whom had not been issued proper winter equipment. After initial victories against an enemy which Hitler had grossly underestimated, the German advance slowed to a freeze. Hitler saw his dreams of grandeur buried under Russian snow and ice.

In the midst of this truly desperate situation, Hitler compounded his difficulties even further. On December 7, 1941, Japan attacked the U.S. fleet at Pearl Harbor in Hawaii, and the U.S. responded by declaring war on Japan, but *not* on Germany. Germany had no treaty obligation with Japan, but inexplicably and without conferring with anyone, Hitler declared war against the U.S. Germany had no military means for conducting military operations against the Americans, but this step decisively tipped the scales in favor of his opponents and ultimately sealed Germany's defeat. Thereafter, he had no idea how to extricate Germany from ruin. For example, he could not follow up on General Erwin Rommel's victories in North Africa in the summer of 1942, and, of course, he excluded the very idea of a political settlement. His only order was "Hold at all costs!" In 1942 Germany began losing territory in the East, especially after a disastrous defeat at Stalingrad in early 1943.

After 1941 Hitler withdrew more and more from public view and spent most of his time in military headquarters. Since his first goal—to dominate Europe—was slipping out of reach, he turned toward a second goal—the eradication of the Jews. He began astonishing the world not with diplomatic and military victories, but with crimes the extent of which the world had hitherto not known and the extent of which would only be discovered at the end of the war. Earlier and contemporary dictators or would–be world conquerors such as Alexander the Great, Napoleon

German Expansion, 1935–39.

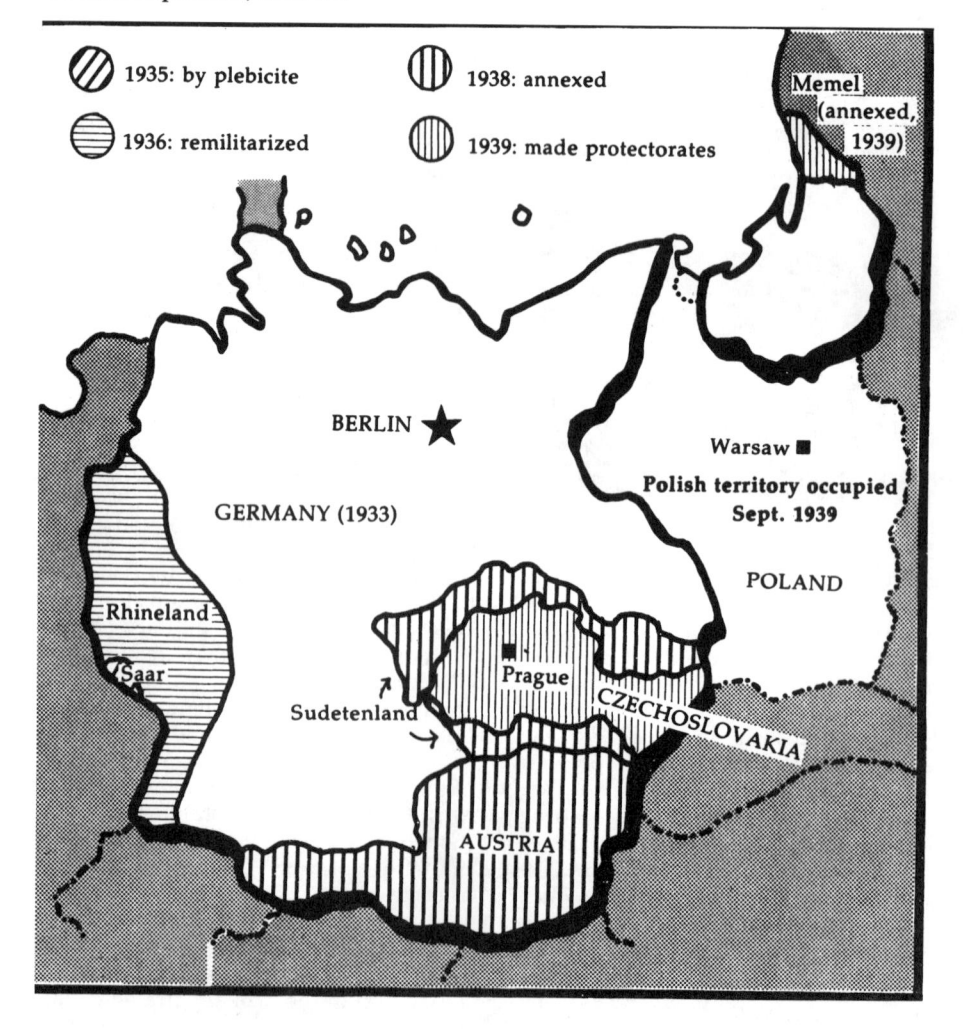

Germany (FRG)

German officers examine a captured Polish banner

and Stalin, had caused thousands or millions of deaths. But whether one agreed with them or not, they usually had political or military motives for their brutality. Hitler had none. Strictly speaking, his crimes were not *war crimes*, because his murder campaign of the Jews worked against his political and military objectives. This campaign was not only morally repugnant, but it sapped further the strength of a weakening Germany.

The "Final Solution"

From the time he first began making public speeches, Hitler left no doubt that he was intensely anti–Semitic. He put this in writing in *Mein Kampf* and underscored it with anti–Jewish legislation after coming to power in 1933. On January 30, 1939, the sixth anniversary of his acquisition of power, he spoke publicly of "eradicating the Jewish race in Europe." This actually was another manifestation of his paranoia. His delusion was that the Jews were responsible for Germany's failure in World War I and were a threat to his current ambitions for Germany. Sometimes, a paranoid's delusions are directed against one person, but Hitler's were directed toward millions.

In mid–1941 Hitler began having Polish and Russian Jews rounded up and shot beside mass graves. At the Wannsee Conference at the outskirts of Berlin on January 20, 1942, the decision was made to extend this policy to Jews in Germany and other occupied countries as well. Special extermination camps were constructed in Treblinka, Sobibor, Maidanek (Lublin), Belzec, Chelmno (Kulmhof) and Auschwitz for this grisly purpose.

By the spring of 1942 the "final solution," which of course "solved" nothing but caused the needless death of four to six million innocent people by 1945, was in full swing. This policy was pursued with such single–minded determination that the German war effort itself was greatly hampered. Manpower which was badly needed at the front or in domestic industries was either sent to extermination camps as victims of this policy or to SS units or other special military units (called *Einsatzgruppen*) as executors of this policy. Railroad rolling stock was diverted, and rail lines were clogged. Also, this policy of murder prompted the western Allies to declare as a major war aim the "punishment of those persons responsible for these crimes"; the Soviet Union proclaimed the same in November 1943. This new war aim made any kind of compromise peace with Germany unthinkable and prompted Hitler's enemies to demand Germany's "unconditional surrender."

How much did the German people know about this ghastly policy at the time? Certainly all Germans of a sound mind knew that their country had adopted an official policy of discrimination against Jews, and all had been informed that their government was "resettling" Jews in the East. However, for a variety of reasons, the regime did not reveal to the German population details about the policy. The most important reason, no doubt, was that Hitler did not trust his own people and suspected that they would not approve. He had noted that most Germans had supported neither the nationwide boycott of Jewish businesses in 1933 nor the "Crystal Night" of 1938. which actually produced more pity for Jews, shame and irritation (but no more than that) among non–Nazis than anything else.

Further, in mid–1941 Hitler had to suspend a policy he had introduced publicly in 1939 to eliminate 70,000 to 80,000 patients in convalescent and nursing homes, 10,000 to 20,000 sick and invalids in concentration camps within Germany, all Jewish patients in mental hospitals and about 3,000 children between the ages of three and 13 in orphanages and special schools for the handicapped. One of the major reasons for the suspension was the increasing unrest within the German population and the active opposition of the churches.

Hitler spared the Jews no misery, but he was careful not to allow most Germans to know *for sure* what was happening to the Jews. The exterminations were conducted in Eastern Europe, outside Germany, and careful precautions were taken not to enable unauthorized persons to witness what was happening within the camps. He even took the special measure, whenever possible, of sending German Jews first to large ghettos such as Theresienstadt in Bohemia, where they were able to

Germany (FRG)

Hitler addresses a Nazi rally

write postcards back to Germany for awhile before being transported to death camps. Of course, rumors about what was really happening filtered into Germany, but the absence of confirmation enabled anyone to reject the rumors or to remain in doubt if he chose to do so. Most Germans did just that, as did most non–Germans in the other occupied areas, for that matter. In Germany and in other occupied areas there were persons who took risks by hiding or helping Jews. But *nowhere* was there the kind of mass uprising which would have been necessary to put an end to that shameful policy. In fact, only the military power of Hitler's enemies brought the Third Reich to its knees.

Other Genocide

Hitler's policy of liquidating people whom he considered to be racially inferior was, of course, not restricted to the Jews. The Jews were not the only group which fell within his definition of *Untermensch* ("subhuman"). Only about a fifth of the 25,000 Gypsies living in Germany in 1939 survived by 1945, and estimates of the total number of European Gypsies murdered at Hitler's order range up to a half million. In October 1939 German leaders began a five–year campaign to destroy the entire Polish elite and culture. Polish priests, professors, journalists, businessmen and earlier political leaders were systematically liquidated. When one considers that the Soviet Union conducted a similar policy against the Poles in those areas under its domination, most dramatically in the Katyn Forest in 1939, when Soviet forces murdered 10,000 Polish officers and elites and dumped them into mass graves, it is almost miraculous that Poland was able to survive the war as a nation. In the end, Poland had lost about six million countrymen, about half of whom were Jews and not more than 300,000 of whom had fallen in battle.

The German treatment of the Russians and of subject peoples under Russian control was even worse than that of the Poles. German policy in the Soviet Union revealed the extent to which Hitler's racial theories thwarted Germany's national interests. Many peripheral peoples in the Soviet Union who had never joined with it voluntarily greeted invading German soldiers more like liberators than conquerors. A far–sighted German policy to transform these people into allies might have been successful and extremely beneficial to Germany.

Instead, Russians and non–Russians alike were treated with the same brutality. Unlike in Poland, the German Army was involved in the actions directed against the civilian population in the Soviet Union. Soviet prisoners of war were especially mistreated by the Germans. According to German military records, by May 1, 1944, more than five million Russian soldiers had been captured by the Germans, mostly in 1941. However, at that time, fewer than two million remained alive. Almost a half million had been executed, 67,000 had fled and almost three million had died in the camps, mostly of hunger. German mistreatment of the Soviet population helped Stalin to unify the population in the war effort against the Germans. The many acts of brutality committed later by Soviet soldiers in occupied Germany, as well as the strong distrust which the Soviet Union showed toward Germany after 1945, must be seen against this background, although nothing can excuse the bestial acts committed by these two peoples against each other.

Minimal Internal Resistance

There were, of course, some symbolic acts of resistance to Nazi rule within Germany. In early 1943 two young Christians in the Catholic youth organization, Hans and Sophie Scholl, brother and sister, passed out flyers on the streets of Munich for a few minutes calling Hitler a tyrant and demanding acts of sabotage in the arms factories before they were whisked away and promptly executed.

The most serious opposition to Hitler came from within the German Army, supported by a unique coalition of aristocrats,

Germany (FRG)

civil servants, clergymen from both churches and trade unionists. The German military traditionally had considered itself superior to Nazis, whom it tended to regard as uneducated, rowdy troublemakers. On July 20, 1944, this coalition made a bold attempt to assassinate Hitler, but the bomb placed under the table during a meeting in Hitler's eastern headquarters miraculously failed to harm the *Führer* seriously when it exploded; it had been placed there by Colonel Claus Schenk von Stauffenberg, a decorated war hero who had lost an arm and an eye in battle. Assuming that the Nazi leader was dead, the plotters moved to take control of the major governmental and military command centers in Berlin. However, Hitler quickly went on the air to announce that he was alive, and he ordered that the plotters be arrested. Within hours the leaders were executed. Hitler suffered nerve damage to an arm and appeared shaken by the incident.

The assassins were without question prompted to act by information they had of Hitler's grisly extermination policies. When asked about his motive before the "People's Court" following the attempt, Count Yorck von Wartenburg said, "I thought about the many crimes," before he was shouted down by the hated chief justice, Roland Freisler. But there were other motives as well. Germany was entangled in a war which it could not win, and there was no attempt on the part of Germany's leaders to reach a political settlement. It was characteristic that after the July 20 plot Hitler ordered mass arrests of more than 5,000 former cabinet ministers, mayors, parliamentarians and civil servants (including such important post–war figures as Konrad Adenauer and Kurt Schumacher), whom the enemy coalition could have viewed as a possible alternative to the Third Reich. For Hitler, the only conceivable alternatives were Germany's holding on under his own leadership or facing total destruction.

The Allies Close In

By the fall of 1944 enemy armies were advancing on Germany from the East and West, and more and more Germans saw the hopelessness of the situation and began to regard conquest by the Western allies as liberation. But Hitler did not share this secret war aim of many Germans. He had personally assumed command of the German forces. He had unleashed a torrent of powerful rockets on London and its suburbs using technology only recently developed. These attacks by what he called his "wonder weapons" merely served to harden even more the determination of the British and their American ally. Disregarding warnings from military advisers that the Red Army was poised for a massive strike from the East, Hitler ordered his last military offensive against the Western Allies in the Belgian Ardennes Forest in late 1944. The element of surprise and extremely bad weather which kept Allied aircraft grounded for a few days helped the Germans to gain initial success and to stop in its tracks the Western powers' advance on Germany. However, once American and British air power could be brought into the action, the German offensive was stopped, and by the first week of January the German forces were being decimated or rolled back. As some of Hitler's generals had warned, the Red Army crashed through the German line in the East and in one violent movement pushed from the Vistula to the Oder Rivers. Because Hitler had squandered his last reserves in the Ardennes offensive, he had nothing left to stop the Russian advance.

Hitler's decisions which had slowed down the Western Allied advance and favored a rapid Russian advance into the heart of Germany had unfortunate consequences for post–war Germany. In the first half of February 1945, President Roosevelt, Prime Minister Churchill and General Secretary Stalin met in Yalta in the Crimea area to discuss the postwar control of Germany and to divide Germany into zones of occupation. The lines which they drew were heavily influenced by the calculations of where exactly the Allied armies would be in Germany at the end of the war. At the time, it appeared that Russian troops would be somewhat farther within Germany than was actually the case when hostilities ceased. However, based on the decisions made at Yalta, U.S. troops had later to be pulled back from Saxony and Thuringia, which were within the designated Soviet zone. Also, the collapse of cooperation among the four Allies after the war left the temporary line drawn between the Soviet zone of occupation and the zones of the Western Allies as the dividing line between East and West Germany until 1990.

Seeing enemy armies advancing within his own country's territory and with no hope for stopping them, any rational and responsible leader with a concern for his own people would have done anything to salvage whatever would be necessary for his people's survival. Hitler was not such a leader. In late 1941 he had made a chilling statement to the Danish and Croatian foreign ministers: "If ever the German people is no longer sufficiently strong and willing to sacrifice its own blood for its existence, then it should fade away and be destroyed by another, stronger power.... In that situation, I will lose no tears for the German people."

The Collapse

On March 18 and 19, 1945, he gave two orders which demonstrated that he had not changed his mind and that he now thought it was time to carry through with the end of Germany. He ordered all Germans in areas threatened by the invasion forces in the West to leave their homes and set out on what could only have been a death march eastward. The following day he gave the so–called "Nero order": "to destroy all military, transport, communications, industrial and supply facilities as well as anything of value within the Reich which could be used by the enemy for continuing his struggle either immediately or in the foreseeable time." When Albert Speer, his trusted confidant and munitions minister, objected to this policy, which would have completely eliminated the Germans' ability to survive after defeat, Hitler answered "ice–coldly": "If the war is lost, then the people will be lost also ... In that case the people will have shown itself as the weaker, and the future would belong solely to the strengthened Eastern people. Whoever survives this struggle would be the inferior ones anyway since the superior ones have already fallen."

Hitler himself chose not to be among the survivors. On April 30, 1945, a few hours before his underground bunker in Berlin was captured by Soviet troops, he stuck a pistol in his mouth and pulled the trigger. Speer and others did their best to prevent these orders from being carried out. But the important effect of these orders was that most Germans, at least in the Western part of Germany, did view the enemy occupation of Germany as a liberation. While the occupation forces expected to find a nation of fanatic Nazis on their hands, they found instead a shell–shocked, seriously disillusioned people who had been far more than thoroughly "denazified" by Hitler's treatment of Germany in the closing months of the war than the carefully planned denazification and reeducation program would otherwise ever have been able to accomplish. The occupation powers interpreted Germans' passivity and willingness to cooperate as typical German servility, but it was rather a reflection of the extent to which Germans felt themselves to have been deceived and betrayed by Hitler.

The Early Postwar Period

Hitler had unwittingly strengthened the chances for democracy to succeed after he had left the stage. Thirty–three years after Napoleon had been defeated in 1815, a new Napoleon was elected President of France. By contrast, in post–1945 Germany, no one who invokes the name and legacy of Adolf Hitler would have the slightest chance of gaining power. Thus, one can be

Germany (FRG)

In Germany . . . desolation

thankful that Hitler and his party had so thoroughly discredited themselves in German eyes. But what kind of Germany did Hitler leave behind? Seven million Germans had perished; only the Russians suffered greater human casualties as a result of the war. Germany lost a fourth of its territory, and what remained was divided into two German states.

Not since the Thirty Years War from 1618 to 1648 had the Germans suffered so much destruction or loss of life. Not a single great German city survived the war undamaged by saturation bombing by the Western Allies and, later, artillery shells. One–fifth of the nation's housing was destroyed, and in the larger cities the situation was genuinely desperate. Only 47% of the buildings in Hamburg were left standing and most others were severely damaged. In the commercial city of Frankfurt, only about a fourth of the houses survived, and in Nürnberg, where Hitler had held some of his most impressive party congresses and rallies, only about one–tenth of the dwellings remained unscathed. Shocked and hungry Germans without shelter were cramped in houses and apartments belonging to others, in hotels, in make–shift structures, or even in former bomb shelters. Everywhere were mountains of rubble with narrow paths cut through them to enable pedestrians, carts and vehicles to pass. Bridges, viaducts, water mains and power lines were cut. All bridges over the Rhine, Weser and Main rivers had been destroyed, and these three key waterways were closed to shipping. Power facilities, even if left intact or repaired, were often unable to function for lack of coal. Home heating was almost non–existent for all but the occupation forces, and often the only warmth the Germans could get was at warming stations in certain places in the city, where they could go for a few minutes a day.

The German population had suffered frightful losses in the war, which for the first time since 1814 had been fought in the heart of Germany. Over two million German soldiers had been killed in action, two and a half million had been taken prisoner, over a million and a half were missing and at least an equal number had been crippled by the war. Civilian deaths and injury were in the hundreds of thousands, and far more than a million German children had been orphaned.

There was very little food, especially in the Soviet and French sectors, where occupation troops and authorities were compelled to "live off the land." Pre–war Germany had never been self–sufficient in food, and during the Weimar Republic it had to import about 20% of its needs. Because of the economic disruption and the loss of extensive agricultural areas in the East, this figure rose to 50% in the three western zones after the war. In those zones, the official target in the immediate post–war years was a mere 1,550 calories per day, but in the heavily populated British zone in 1946 the actual rations sank to 600 to 1,000 calories per day. Malnutrition was especially harmful to the young. Hamburg reported 10,000 cases of hunger edema (abdominal swelling), and in towns and cities in Hesse 90% of the children developed rickets. The mortality rate for infants and young children rose to 154 per thousand in the Ruhr area and 160 in Berlin.

For most Germans, finding the next meal was immensely more important than the political future of their country. The defeated country had suffered economic collapse. For a couple of years the Allied occupation powers restricted production, delayed recovery and decentralized or dismantled industrial plants in order to reduce the power of industrial leaders or to provide reparations to some of the victorious Allies, particularly the Soviet Union, which transported whole factories to mother Russia. As a result of this economic turmoil, the great majority of the population had become pauperized, and many were reduced to selling or swapping their most treasured heirlooms for a pittance in order to obtain food or other necessities, often on the thriving black market and at exorbitant prices. In some cases, honorable women actually had to resort to prostitution among the occupying forces in order to provide food for their families and relatives. Former President Herbert Hoover reported in February 1947 that the situation in western Germany was worse than in any other part of Europe. He told President Truman bluntly: "You can have vengeance, or peace, but you can't have both."

Migration from the East

The available food, housing and jobs had to serve not only the pre–war residents of the three western zones, but also the flood of refugees who poured in from the East. Million of Germans were expelled from Southern European countries or from former German lands east of the Oder and Neisse rivers, which now form the border between Germany and Poland. These lands in 1938 had amounted to about 44,000 square miles (70,400 sq. km., or 24% of Germany's entire land area), and they had supplied a large part of Germany's food and coal. Most of these areas became a part of Poland to compensate Poles for their lands which had been seized by the Soviet Union. Germany officially relinquished these lands to Poland within weeks after it regained its unity and full sovereignty in 1990. The rest (a part of East Prussia, including the city of Königsberg) was absorbed by the Soviet Union. These expulsions of ethnic Germans from Eastern Europe reached a height in the winter of 1945–46. Those affected were often given 24 hours notice and were able to take with them only 50 to 60 pounds of baggage apiece. Other Germans fled the Soviet occupation zone in order to escape the kind of authoritarian political order which was being established there. These refugees placed severe strains on the Western occupation authorities and on the previous residents, who were required to share their meager incomes with the often

Germany (FRG)

highly unwelcome newcomers in order to distribute the nation's material burdens more fairly. By the time the Berlin Wall was erected beginning August 13, 1961, approximately 12 million refugees had poured into West Germany.

Adding to the refugee problem was that of the displaced persons (DP's), whom the Nazis had brought to Germany to perform forced labor. They numbered about six and a half million persons by the end of the war, and about two million of them refused to return to their homelands in the Soviet Union or in the Baltic states which had been annexed by the USSR. They were fed and clothed largely by the U.S. through the UN Relief and Rehabilitation Administration, but they often occupied jobs and housing which were therefore denied to Germans.

The German people were largely disgraced and demoralized. Hitler had greatly changed German society, having reduced or eliminated permanently the power and influence which, for example, noblemen, military officers or large Prussian landowners had wielded earlier. Unlike 1918, the collapse of the Third Reich eliminated the nation's entire political elite. Germany's highest surviving Nazi leaders were placed on trial in Nuremberg from November 1945 until October 1946, and most were given either death sentences or long prison terms in Spandau Prison in West Berlin. Only one prisoner, Rudolf Hess, remained there. Blind and crippled, he died in August 1987 at age 93, and the prison was razed.

The highly controversial denazification programs of the occupation powers required that those Germans who had held positions of obvious authority or influence under the Nazis be jailed, fined or demoted. Others, such as civil servants, teachers, journalists or industrial leaders, most of whom had no choice about joining the Nazi Party, were at least temporarily removed from their jobs. In the end, all the elites under the previous regime had been deprived of their status, except church leaders. It is questionable that most of the denazification measures were necessary at all. Defeat and utter destruction under the leadership of Hitler had been the best antidote to Nazism. Although it took several more years to convince many Germans that even the general idea of National Socialism had been wrong, their approval of the concrete form which Nazism had taken had disappeared almost completely by the end of the war.

The German Army was completely disbanded, and when a Federal Army was created in 1956, the military's influence and prestige in political and social life had been almost entirely eliminated. The various classes had not been eradicated, but they had been brought more closely together during the Third Reich and the aftermath of the war. Germans now mingled more easily with one another. Although an end to hostilities brought no political revolution or social upheaval, as had been the case in 1918, the quiet social and political revolution which culminated in 1945 was much more far–reaching than that of 1918. Germans were now clearly divided territorially, but they were no longer so clearly divided domestically. The old conservatives had been discredited and the romanticism of war, assertiveness in the world and ideas about German national unique superiority had been extinguished. Ideologies had little appeal anymore, and most Germans had become convinced that a flight from the much debunked "bourgeois values," including especially parliamentary democracy within a rule of law, solves no problems, and can bring immense suffering to human beings. Many Germans emerged from the war politically apathetic, but important changes in their political attitudes had occurred which would augur well for a new German democracy.

Collapse of Allied Cooperation

The Soviet Union and Poland annexed large chunks of German territory in the East, and Germany was reduced to about three–fourths its prewar size. What remained of Germany was divided into four occupation zones: the Soviet zone was former East Germany; the British zone was in the North; the French zone was in the Southwest and the American zone was in Bavaria, Hesse and the port of Bremerhaven in the North. Berlin was also divided into four sectors. Full power was in the hands of the four Allied commanders, who bore enormous burdens in bringing order to the chaos, feeding the population, reestablishing a tolerable economic situation and creating political conditions which would make impossible the return of National Socialism.

The Allies tried to work together, and the United States even pulled its troops out of Saxony and Thuringia in July 1945 in order to honor its agreement on occupation zones established at Yalta in February 1945. Also in July, the leaders of the three major Allies—the Soviet Union, the United States and Great Britain—met at Potsdam, outside of Berlin, to discuss Germany's future. France had not taken part in the Yalta Conference and, to the ire of General de Gaulle, was not invited to the Potsdam meeting.

There were many disagreements on details, but the three basically agreed that Germany should be denazified, that the Oder–Neisse frontier would at least temporarily be the border between Germany and Poland, that Germans in Hungary, Czechoslovakia and Poland would be transferred to Germany, that Germany would be required to pay reparations so long as these payments would "leave enough resources to enable the German people to subsist without external assistance," that "during the period of occupation Germany shall be treated as a single economic unit," that the German political structure would be decentralized and, finally, that German political life should be reconstructed on a democratic basis.

It soon became obvious that Allied cooperation was impossible, given the differing definitions of such terms as "democratic" and the four victors' greatly different security and political objectives in Europe. The Allies' disharmony was West Germany's opportunity which permitted it to rise so quickly from the ashes of defeat. Talks involving the political and economic future of Germany stalled, and American soldiers became impatient to go home. Toward the end of 1945 there were spontaneous GI demonstrations in Paris and Frankfurt which left no doubt in the minds of American leaders that the large part of the three million U.S. soldiers in Europe had to be demobilized very quickly. GI's were sent back to the U.S. at a stunningly fast rate; clearly a long occupation of Germany was not among American plans. Nor was a permanent feeding and economic subsidy of a part of the German people among those aims. Despite the agreements at Potsdam, Germany was not operating as an economic unit. It had become increasingly clear to U.S. leaders that the resulting prolongation of German poverty and economic stagnation would not only greatly harm Germany's neighbors, who were traditionally dependent upon trade with Germany, but would perhaps make Germany vulnerable to communist appeals.

The Beginning of Political Activity

The excessive political indoctrination and activity during Hitler's rule had extinguished political interest in the minds of most Germans by the spring of 1945. Most Germans' thoughts were directed toward food, warmth and privacy, and this fact helped divert their attention both from a horrible past and the very uncertain politics of the present. Still, political activity began to bubble from below, on the municipal and land (state) level and always under the surveillance and supervision of the occupation authorities. The future direction of German politics was far from clear. German communists had high hopes, and a number of right–wing parties began to take shape. Anti–democratic attitudes among some Germans also persisted for awhile. But there was also a

Germany (FRG)

democratic movement which gathered steam and which was especially encouraged by the three Western occupation powers. The memories of National Socialist crimes prompted many thoughtful Germans to reintroduce morality and religious principles into politics and to construct a new political order around basic human rights and democracy.

American leaders soon became convinced that U.S. policy should shed all its punitive aspects and shift toward wholehearted support of the democratic potential in Germany. The former aspects had been advocated by President Roosevelt's Treasury Secretary, Henry Morgenthau, who had wished forcefully to change Germany from an industrialized nation back to an agrarian society. His proposals had never become official U.S. policy, but elements of it had been incorporated in the official American occupation guideline, JCS 1067. However, U.S. Secretary of State James Byrnes announced in Stuttgart on September 6, 1946, a significant change in U.S. policy. In the opera house of that bombed–out city, he aimed to quiet German fears by assuring them that "as long as an occupation force is required in Germany the army of the United States will be part of that occupation force." He went on to propose a greater measure of German self–government and, as a first step, the merging of the American and British zones. A British observer commented on the dramatic effect of this speech: "At the time they were spoken these were bold words and they came to the millions of Germans who had heard or read them as the first glimmer of dawn after a long, dark night. Their moral impact was incalculable."

One month later the Berliners revealed in their first municipal elections how receptive they were to a democratic direction. Despite the Soviet presence in East Berlin and the Soviets' open support of their German Communist creation, the *Socialist Unity Party of Germany (SED)*, which ruled the GDR, communists received less than one–fifth of the votes. The Soviets and East German communists quickly saw that they dared not agree to any settlement of the German question which involved free elections.

Secretary of State and ex–armed forces Chief of Staff George C. Marshall foresaw that Europe would economically stagnate for an unnecessarily long period of time unless massive American aid were poured into the war–ravaged countries. The generous American offer, known as the "Marshall Plan," even included the Soviet Union and what were slowly developing into its satellite states which it had occupied militarily.

The year 1947 saw the end of any possibility that the four victorious Allies could work together in harmony and good faith. The failure of the Foreign Ministers Conference in Moscow in April, the refusal of the Soviet Union to allow itself or those countries under its domination to accept Marshall Plan assistance, the break–down in June of a meeting of all German land government chiefs in Munich, and the founding in October of the *Cominform* in Moscow, calculated to coordinate a communist propaganda offensive against the "imperialism of the United States and its Western Allies," all reflected a degeneration of East–West relations.

The year 1948 brought no improvement. In February the British and Americans created a sort of economic government, which was joined in the summer by the French zone (except the Saar, which was not reunited with Germany until 1957 following a plebiscite). This union, at first called "Bizonia," tightened the links which had already emerged between the two zones. This new body brought together leading German political figures, who began discussing future German government and thereby established an early foundation for the FRG.

Leaders of Bizonia elaborated the future guiding West German economic principle of the "social market economy," which combined a free market approach (which helped West Germany rapidly to become prosperous in contrast to its counterpart in East Germany) with a commitment to the social welfare of its citizens, which was crucially important for social peace within Germany and, more important, for democracy. Bizonia also used the Marshall Plan assistance to improve its citizens' well–being. In July 1947 representatives of 16 European countries receiving Marshall Plan aid had declared in Paris that "the German economy should be integrated into the economy of Europe in such a way as to contribute to a raising of the general standard of life." It is, of course, possible that the other nations sought through economic means with this measure to insure that Germany could not again become an aggressive political enemy.

In the next few years West Germans received almost $4 billion in money and supplies from the Marshall Plan. This not only enabled West Germans to rebuild their industrial plants with the most modern tooling, but it established the foundation for West European cooperation, which the Plan required and which culminated in the European Community (EC), now called EU. It also introduced a long–range liberalization of European trade and payments, which has been a key to the economic prosperity of many European nations.

Further Economic Progress

West German economic recovery also got an important shot in the arm from a bracing currency reform in mid–1948 through which the increasingly worthless Reichsmark was replaced by a new

Germany after World War II

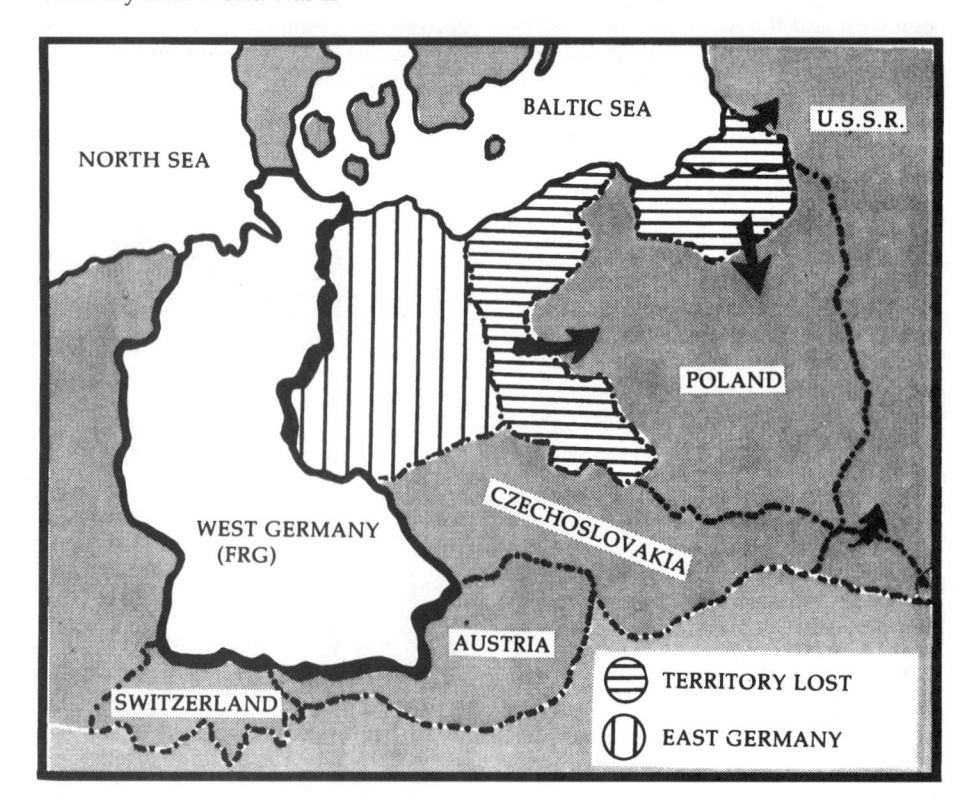

Germany (FRG)

The Berlin Airlift — A/P Wide World Photo

Deutschmark. Every German started at the same point, with only 40 marks in his pocket. This reform was followed by a scrapping of all rationing and price controls—a bold move widely criticized at the time, but one which the chairman of the Bizonal Economic Council, Professor Ludwig Erhard, and the U.S. occupation governor, General Lucius Clay, considered essential. They proved to be right. Suddenly goods reappeared in the stores and markets. One witnessed a disappearance of the black market, whose more treasured items had come from the U.S. military post exchanges (PXs). For awhile Germans had a *de facto* "cigarette economy," in which American cigarettes, not old German Reichsmarks, were the country's actual currency. After several years, many Germans could actually begin smoking cigarettes again rather than hoarding them as a money substitute! The economic improvement was so dramatic that in 1949 Erhard's party could enter the first West German elections with the convincing slogan *Es geht wieder!* ("It's working again!")

The Cold War Begins—
The Berlin Blockade

The "Cold War" which resulted from the severe differences between the Soviet Union and the Western Allies ultimately helped to seal Germany's division, but it also offered the three Western zones the chance to regain a large part of German sovereignty. The sense that the Western Allies and the West Germans had important common objectives was stimulated by the communist seizure of power in February 1948 in Czechoslovakia although the country had functioned since 1945 as a parliamentary democracy.

Especially revealing was the blockade of all road and rail routes to West Berlin from June 1948 until May 1949. This was in response to increasing political and economic unity among the three Western zones, most visible in the currency reform. No doubt the Soviets expected that the Western Allies could be forced to relinquish their rights in Berlin and to abandon the city. The American response was to organize an aerial supply line between the Western zones and the besieged city. This seemingly impossible task (which even included transporting coal!) sparked American and West German imagination and admiration. Several hundred American and British aircraft carried up to 12,000 tons of supplies to Berlin each day. The success of this heroic operation, combined with the effect of adverse world opinion, forced the Soviets to lift the blockade and further cemented West German–American solidarity.

The Federal Republic of Germany—
Konrad Adenauer

From the winter of 1948–49 on, the great majority of West Germans would accept no foreign policy which did not merit the confidence of the U.S., whose protection over Berlin and West Germany were considered indispenable. Despite all the Atlantic disturbances since that time, this West German foreign policy pillar still exists today.

The disagreements among the four occupation powers reached such a low state that the three Western Allies decided in the summer of 1948 to permit German leaders in their three zones to write a constitution and to found a West German state. The Constituent Assembly met in Bonn under the chairmanship of the elderly former mayor of Cologne, Konrad Adenauer, and under the watchful eyes of the three occupational authorities. Things were finally settled in May 1949, almost four years to the day since the capitulation of the Third Reich.

What was created was seen to be strictly "for a transitional period," and the document was called a Basic Law, not a constitution, a word which might connote something more permanent. The founders wrote into the preamble that they had acted also in behalf of those Germans living under Soviet occupation and that "the entire German people is called upon to accomplish, by free self–determination, the unity and freedom of Germany." Thus, West German leaders imposed upon themselves the obligation to bring the two parts of Germany back together, even though that goal seemed to be slipping farther and farther into the distant future.

On August 14, 1949, most of the eligible voters in West Germany went to the polls to elect their first parliamentary representatives. Adenauer's *Christian Democratic Union (CDU)*, along with the *Bavarian Christian Social Union (CSU)*, captured 31% of the votes, and the *SPD* 29.2%. Several other parties also won seats, and Adenauer was able to patch together a coalition government with only a one–vote majority, *his own* vote! Adenauer was to serve as West German chancellor until 1963, longer than the entire Weimar Republic had existed. This shrewd politician was seen by the voters as a comforting father–figure (*Der Alte*—"The Old One"), who took a firmer control of West German politics than any other chancellor since. As a confident (some say authoritarian) ruler, he was able to place his imprint on the young democracy as no one since. The Soviet Union responded to the creation of the Federal Republic of Germany by converting its occupation zone into the German Democratic Republic (GDR), ruled by the communist–led *SED*.

The FRG's new capital was not established in a major West German city such as Frankfurt on the Main, chiefly because such a seat might appear as a permanent capital city for a state which was expressly intended to be provisional. Instead, the

57

Germany (FRG)

sleepy Rhenish university town of Bonn was selected as the "temporary" seat of government, and an architecturally unattractive former teacher's college became the new Parliament and governmental center. Until late 1987, West Germany's capitol remained the least impressive governmental seat in all of Europe. Some liked to call it "the federal village." The new government ordered that the gutted *Reichstag* building, located a few meters within the Western sector of Berlin, be reconstructed so that it could again serve as the capitol of a "soon to be" reunified Germany. Work on the renovation was finally completed in the 1970s.

NATO is Created

The Cold War froze the division of Germany, but it also provided West Germany the opportunities which its crafty first chancellor knew how to exploit for the benefit of his country and his party. There were intense fears in Western Europe and North America that the Soviet Union sought direct or indirect domination over all of Europe. This fear led to the establishment of NATO (the North Atlantic Treaty Organization) on April 4, 1949, several months before the creation of the FRG. When NATO planners began working on plans for defending Western Europe, it was quickly apparent that the necessary forces could not be provided by the Western Allies and smaller West Europe countries alone. This was especially true since the United States had no intention at that time of permanently maintaining large numbers of American troops in Europe. Western European defense was conceivable only with the help of Germany. In the fall of 1949 the U.S. General Staff drafted a plan for the inclusion of German troops in NATO.

Adenauer listened very carefully to the message which was coming from Western capitals: "No NATO without Germany; no Germany without NATO." He reflected on his country's three principal goals and the best way it could achieve them: 1) West Germans, painfully viewing the plight of their countrymen in East Germany, wanted protection from Soviet domination; 2) they wanted political and economic recovery from the ashes of disgrace, to regain much of their national sovereignty, to create jobs, to rebuild their cities, to share in international trade and thereby to acquire material prosperity and to be respected as equals in the Western world, whose values they shared; 3) finally, they wanted their country to be reunified within the German borders of 1937.

The Chancellor decided to strike a bargain with the NATO countries. On November 11, 1949, the 31st anniversary of the cease-fire ending World War I, Adenauer announced in an interview with the French newspaper, *L'Est Republicain*, that "if a common Supreme Command could be created, the Federal Republic would be willing at an appropriate time to integrate itself into a European defense system." He presented this decision to his own people as the "politics of necessity," and he stated the issue very simply: "We are faced with a choice between slavery and freedom. We choose freedom." In the years to come, Adenauer was successful in getting an important political advantage for each increase in German activity or responsibility in NATO. He helped to establish the United States as the permanent guarantor of West German security and to counteract the goal which many American leaders had well into the 1950s of withdrawing U.S. troops from Western Europe. He set a course which was never fundamentally changed by his successors in the Chancellor's office.

There was, however, a problem with Adenauer's bargain with the West which the opposition *Social Democrats* simply could not get out of their minds: how would this integration with the West, especially the military part of it, affect the goal of German reunification, a goal which most Germans at that time wanted very much and which was an obligation placed on all West German governments by the framers of the Basic Law? *Social Democrats* strongly sensed at the time that by seeking to achieve the goals of security and recovery through political, economic and military integration with the West, the FRG was greatly reducing the chances that the Soviet Union would permit the reunification of Germany.

Social Democratic Opposition to NATO

The *SPD's* order of priorities was almost the complete reverse of Adenauer's. Throughout the 1950s, reunification was the *SPD's* top priority. The party was not in principle opposed to reconciliation and integration with the West, nor was it ever opposed to a military defense for Germany, but it believed that the military and economic commitments the FRG had assumed in order to achieve Adenauer's goals would reduce or eliminate the chances that the pieces of Germany would find their way back together again. With the FRG integrated economically in Western Europe, with NATO and Soviet troops facing each other along the Elbe River and with each part of a divided Germany serving as an essential element in the European balance of power, the Soviet Union would be far less inclined to withdraw its troops from East Germany. This would especially be the case if a reunified Germany were free to join NATO, as Adenauer always insisted it should be. The *SPD* feared that the military balance in Europe would require a perpetually divided Germany and therefore showed much greater willingness than the Adenauer government to examine closely Soviet proposals for reunification and to assume that the Soviets were acting at least partly in good faith.

Adenauer continued to argue that his policy was not hostile to the aim of German reunification. He, like the *Social Democrats*, aimed toward German reunification "in peace and freedom." He argued that in return for the FRG's entering the Western Alliance, the three Western powers had formally committed themselves to seek German reunification. He also cast an eye on the West's greater industrial capability to arm itself quickly, on the high degree of Western political and economic integration in the future, and on the prospects of unrest in Eastern Europe which would be directed against the Soviet Union's tight and self-serving grip on its satellites.

He therefore predicted that in time the balance of power would shift in favor of the West, and this shift would make possible negotiations "on the basis of strength" with the Soviet Union. He argued that the Soviets held the key to reunification and would ultimately see themselves compelled to settle the German question on Western terms. This latter element of Adenauer's reunification policy was, as the *SPD* correctly foresaw, an illusion. With the Soviet Union's acquisition of nuclear weapons, there could be no serious talk of rolling back what Churchill had so aptly named "The Iron Curtain" through demonstrations of military strength.

Adenauer was right in his assessment of what West Germans wanted most and of the enormous advantages for his disgraced and impoverished country which Western European unity, crowned by the creation of the Common Market (EC) in 1957, offered: the FRG would be an equal member of such a community and would derive all the economic benefits which the trade and pooling of raw materials would bring. The position of the *SPD*, although it appeared to be grounded on the desire of many Germans for reunification, actually caused an erosion of the *SPD's* domestic political position within the FRG. Social Democrats had to watch with dismay and bitterness how Adenauer's party grew progressively stronger while the *SPD* stagnated.

Political Tensions of the 1950s

The domestic battle over the crucial foreign and security policy decisions made in the 1950s was so intense and emotional that it is almost a wonder that the young democracy survived them. The

Germany (FRG)

issues were serious ones related to the future of Germany and the German nation, and these bitter controversies of the 1950s never completely disappeared, and in part resurface periodically, even in the 1980s.

German rearmament was a truly explosive issue which dominated West German politics until the FRG's formal entry into NATO in 1955. From the point of view of the Western Allies and the Adenauer government, the major problem was how to place international controls on West German troops. The FRG's future allies who had fought against Germany only five years earlier, wanted security *from* West Germany, as well as security *for* it. Well aware of these fears, which he found entirely justified, and desiring German integration and equal status with the West, Adenauer also stubbornly refused to consider establishing an independent German national army. In an effort to solve this problem, the French had presented the "Pleven Plan" in 1950, calling for the establishment of a European Defense Community (EDC). West German military units would be completely fused with a larger European army, and no German generals would command German corps. The FRG would technically not have NATO status, but it would be included *de facto* since the EDC itself would belong to NATO.

The link between the FRG's entry into the EDC and the regaining of West German sovereignty was clear from the very beginning. In 1951 the FRG was permitted to establish a Ministry for Foreign Affairs and to establish diplomatic relations with other states. Also, the *Deutschland Vertrag* (Germany Treaty, also known as the Bonn Conventions) was drafted and was to be signed together with the EDC Treaty. The Bonn Conventions provided for the abolition of the Occupation Statute and of the Allied High Commission, which formally ruled Germany, and prepared the way for West German sovereignty, with certain restrictions.

The issue of a German military role became acute again when in 1954 the French National Assembly rejected the EDC, which an earlier French Foreign Minister had proposed. Surprisingly quickly, however, the foreign ministers of Great Britain, Canada and the U.S. met with the prospective members of the EDC to discuss alternatives. In October these powers signed the Paris Treaties calling for the direct entry of the FRG into NATO, an end to Germany's occupation status and the restoration of full German sovereignty. The three Western powers retained their authority on matters relating to German reunification, Berlin and a final German peace treaty. In late 1955 Adenauer traveled to the Soviet Union to establish full diplomatic relations with that victor and to negotiate a trade treaty and the release of the last German prisoners of war remaining in Soviet hands.

The West German debate over foreign policy remained very polarized. In January 1956, less that a year after the FRG had become a full member of NATO, the first thousand volunteer soldiers entered the Federal Army *(Bundeswehr)*, whose creation the *SPD* had opposed. There was a powerful pacifist strain within the *SPD* which opposed all forms of German rearmament, and this element was a part of an emotional mass movement known by the slogan *"ohne mich"*—"without me." Because of the recent memories and the direct experience which Germans had with the war, the *ohne mich* movement enjoyed widespread support among the general population. For instance, one opinion survey in 1955 revealed that while 40% of the respondents were in favor of a West German army, 45% were opposed. Among those respondents identifying themselves with the *SPD*, only 21% were in favor of the Federal Army and 71% were opposed. Opinion polls also indicated that West Germans were not happy about the stationing of American nuclear weapons on German soil or about the Federal Army's acquisition of dual capacity weapons which could fire or deliver nuclear warheads.

Minimal SPD Gains at the Polls; Continued German Division

The *SPD* went into the federal parliamentary elections of September 15, 1957 confident that it could make significant gains, but the results stunned the *Social Democrats* and probably Adenauer as well. The *SPD* vote did rise from 29% to 32%, but this rise was partially due to the fact that the *Communist Party of Germany (KPD)* had been ruled unconstitutional a year earlier and was therefore not permitted to participate in the election. However, the *CDU/CSU* vote rose from 44% to over 50%, and it gained an absolute majority in the *Bundestag,* the only time this has ever happened since the founding of the FRG. The election was widely interpreted as approval of Adenauer's foreign and economic policies.

This election disaster, plus another Berlin crisis in 1958, convinced the *SPD* to change its foreign policy tack and to support Adenauer's policy of rearmament and integration with the West. Although there were quarrels between the parties occasionally, by the time of Adenauer's re-

NATO maneuvers

Germany (FRG)

tirement in 1963, a foreign policy consensus had taken shape in the FRG which continued to exist throughout the 1960s.

With the FRG firmly planted in the Western alliance, West German leaders began to look eastward to see how they could improve West Germany's relations with the Soviet Union and its satellites. The construction of the Berlin Wall in August 1961 had made it clear that the two Germanys would not be reunified for a long time. Before August 1961 East and West Berliners could pass freely from one part of the city to the other. But the ugly wall which cut right through Germany's largest city destroyed the last hope of national unity.

From the very beginning West Germany's foreign policy was heavily influenced by the fact that Germany was a divided nation in the middle of Europe. After 1955 the FRG did not pursue a determined policy of German reunification, preferring instead to focus on Western economic and military integration, while preventing the legitimization of the *status quo* in central Europe.

Once the signals for a relaxation of tensions between East and West began to be given by France and the U.S., culminating in such agreements with the Soviet Union as the nuclear test ban treaty in 1963, German Foreign Minister Gerhard Schröder began in the early 1960s a "policy of movement." This involved a loosening of the "Hallstein Doctrine," which had forbidden West German diplomatic contact with any country except the Soviet Union which officially recognized East Germany. The FRG established trade missions in Warsaw, Budapest, Sofia and Bucharest. This policy was an important beginning, but it did not go far enough. The FRG neither discarded the Hallstein Doctrine altogether, nor recognized the Oder–Neisse border between the GDR and Poland. Worst of all, it still aimed to isolate the GDR diplomatically.

The FRG had always worked closely with East German officials on practical, day–to–day questions, especially involving economic matters. For instance, the FRG insisted as a condition for its entry into the EU that trade between the two Germanys be conducted as if there were only one Germany. Such free trade was enormously beneficial for the GDR, providing it with an open entry to the EU and serving as a basis for the relatively high economic prosperity in the GDR as compared with other Eastern European countries. Yet, top level *political* contacts were studiously avoided.

In 1966 the FRG's two largest parties formed a "Grand Coalition," with Kurt Georg Kiesinger of the *CDU* as chancellor. Although the parliamentary system was operating very smoothly and although the war damage and mass poverty had given way to visible prosperity, the major parties' leaders saw economic troubles ahead. The *SPD* also wanted to participate in such a coalition government in order to demonstrate that it also was capable of ruling the FRG.

The Grand Coalition stimulated considerable domestic opposition, especially in 1968 when its majority in the *Bundestag* passed a series of constitutional amendments and laws granting the government certain emergency powers in times of crisis. Although it argued that any truly sovereign state had to be able to take special measures in times of emergency to defend the democratic order, many West Germans pointed out that similar emergency laws had been misused during the Weimar Republic to undermine democracy. This controversial issue, combined with doubts about American policy in Vietnam, sent thousands of mainly young Germans into the streets. They employed confrontation tactics which they had learned from the civil rights and anti–war movements in the U.S., even using the American terms for these tactics, such as "sit–in" and "go–in." They called themselves the "extra–parliamentary opposition" (APO), which they claimed was necessary since the opposition within Parliament had sunk to a negligible 5%.

Far less controversial in the eyes of young Germans was the Grand Coalition's policy of seeking improved relations with the East. This received a particular push from Foreign Minister Willy Brandt and the crafty Minister for All–German Affairs, Herbert Wehner, both of the *SPD*. The Kiesinger government took steps toward overcoming the impasse in German reunification. It announced that it was prepared to accept the East German regime as a *de facto* government, and it even exchanged letters for the first time with East German leaders on a semi–official basis. It established a trade mission in Prague in 1967, and its diplomatic recognition of Romania in 1967 and Yugoslavia in 1968 indicated that the Hallstein Doctrine was in fact dead, even if not wiped off the books.

The Brandt Government

In 1969 the *SPD* and *Free Democratic Party (FDP)* won a razor–thin victory in parliamentary elections, and Willy Brandt became chancellor. The new government had no intention to change the FRG's policy toward the West, but it was determined to conduct a dynamic and innovative policy toward the East. Fundamentally, the

Germany's armed forces

Germany (FRG)

Brandt government decided to overturn two decades of West German foreign policy and to recognize the territorial *status quo* in Europe, including the division of Germany. The word "reunification" was dropped from the government's terminology. The first dramatic step in August 1970 was a German–Soviet treaty in which both states renounced the use of force in Europe. West Germany also declared that it had no territorial claims against any country and that the borders of all European states are inviolable, including the Oder–Neisse line and the border between East and West Germany. This treaty was the first West German recognition of East Germany's international legitimacy. Brandt was no doubt correct in commenting that in actual fact, "nothing is lost with this treaty that was not gambled away long ago."

The second step was a German–Polish treaty in late 1970, containing basically the same points as in the German–Soviet treaty, but underscoring the acceptance of the Oder–Neisse frontier. The treaty also provided for normal diplomatic relations and, in a separate accord, Poland agreed to exit permits for some ethnic Germans living in Poland. To demonstrate his sincerity in introducing a new era of Polish–German relations, Brandt dropped to his knees in reverence before a monument in Warsaw honoring the Polish Jewish victims who were killed or mistreated by Germany during World War II. The Poles have never forgotten this electrifying gesture.

A third step, not involving the FRG directly, but strongly encouraged by it, was the Four–Power Agreement on Berlin in 1971. The FRG had linked its ratification of the German–Soviet Treaty with a successful resolution of the Berlin problem. Brandt reasoned that if the FRG was willing to recognize the *status quo* in Europe, the Soviet Union should be willing to recognize the *status quo* in Berlin. The Four–Power Agreement contained a Western Powers' acknowledgment that West Berlin was *not a constituent part of the FRG* and the Soviet Union's recognition that there were *ties* between the FRG and West Berlin. Further, the FRG would perform consular services for West Berliners and represent then in international organizations and conferences. The Soviet Union also promised that transit traffic to and from West Berlin from the FRG would proceed unimpeded. That was deemed necessary, since the East German government had frequently hampered access to the city which it surrounded in order to place pressure on the Bonn government. The Soviet Union admitted that West Berlin was neither located *on* the territory of the GDR nor was it an entity *entirely separate* from the FRG.

From the Main River Bridge, the Franconia statue ignores the castle of Würzburg
Photo by Jon Markham Morrow

The last significant step was the Basic Treaty between the two Germanys themselves. Bonn knew that it could not by–pass East Berlin despite the fact that the East German regime was defensive, rigid and determined to exact a very high price for any concession. After many months of frustrating negotiations an agreement was signed in late 1972 and ratified in mid–1973 which normalized the access between the FRG and West Berlin and made it possible for West Berliners to visit both East Berlin and the GDR. By signing the Basic Treaty the FRG publicly accepted the GDR as a legitimate state and agreed to deal with it as an equal. Yet, Bonn continued to insist that there was only one German nation (even if there were two German states) and that the GDR would not be treated like any other foreign country. To underscore this, the FRG maintained a permanent liaison mission in East Berlin, *not* an embassy, and Bonn's dealings with the GDR were conducted by the Chancellor's office, the Ministry of All–German Affairs or a special office in the Interior Ministry, but *not by* the Foreign Office. The official relations between the two Germanys improved as a result of the Basic Treaty. But the two countries' relationships remained ambiguous and tense, charged with conflict and suspicion.

A major scandal occurred in 1974 when it was revealed that one of Brandt's chief aides, Günter Guillaume, was an East German spy who had access not only to top secret information, but also was privy to knowledge of Brandt's intimate private life, which was reported to be spicy. This embarrassing revelation and intra–party

Germany (FRG)

criticism against Brandt's leadership led to his resignation from the office of chancellor in May. Helmut Schmidt took his place. This was during a time of global economic difficulties associated with tremendously increased oil prices. The energy crisis and the resultant economic problems began increasingly to replace the Eastern policy focus of the government. Although Schmidt signed the Helsinki Accords at the Conference on Security and Cooperation in Europe (CSCE) in 1975, his attention became more directed toward the West and away from the East. His goal was to maintain what had already been achieved, and to preserve or reestablish the economic health and military security of Western Europe.

Plagued by continual dissension within the *SPD* and recurrent coalition crises with the *FDP*, the Schmidt government collapsed in 1982, when the *Free Democrats* switched partners and enabled the *CDU*, led by Helmut Kohl, to take power. The following year, voters confirmed this *Wende* (change) by giving the new *CDU/CSU–FDP* coalition government a solid endorsement in the *Bundestag* elections. The Kohl government set about tackling the problems of unemployment and the emotionally charged deployment of American Pershing and cruise missiles on German soil. The Schmidt government had agreed to do the latter in the 1979 NATO "Twin-track" decision, which was designed to counter a renewed Soviet nuclear missile threat. At the same time, the Kohl government pursued the policy of detente with the GDR and the USSR with as much vigor as had the *SPD* while in power. Like most West German leaders, Kohl no longer believed that German reunification could be achieved in the present era. In 1987 he stated in Moscow that he personally would never live to see the day when the two Germanys would become one country. Like virtually everybody else, he was caught completely by surprise as the GDR collapsed before his unbelieving eyes, and the elusive German unity fell into his lap.

HISTORY OF THE GERMAN DEMOCRATIC REPUBLIC (GDR)—EAST GERMANY

At first the Soviet Zone of Germany was governed by the Soviet Military Administration, but the Soviet authorities had long-range plans for Germany which involved re-educating the people and eventually winning them over to communism. German communists who had spent the Nazi years in the Soviet Union were brought back, put in charge of local governments, and given control over the press, radio, and book publishing. Their instructions were to educate the people in anti-fascism and to gain their cooperation for Soviet occupiers. On April 30, 1945, Walter Ulbricht returned from the USSR in a Soviet aircraft and in June announced the reestablishment of the *Communist Party of Germany (KPD)*. It combined with the *CDU*, *SPD*, and *Liberal Democrats* to form an "Anti-fascist Democratic Bloc," which was soon dominated by the *KPD*. The Soviets had expected that the communists' long record of anti-fascism would make the *KPD* popular among workers, but the latter clearly preferred the *SPD*. In April 1946 this prompted the forcible uniting of the two parties into a *Socialist Unity Party (SED)*, with Ulbricht as General Secretary.

The GDR before German reunification

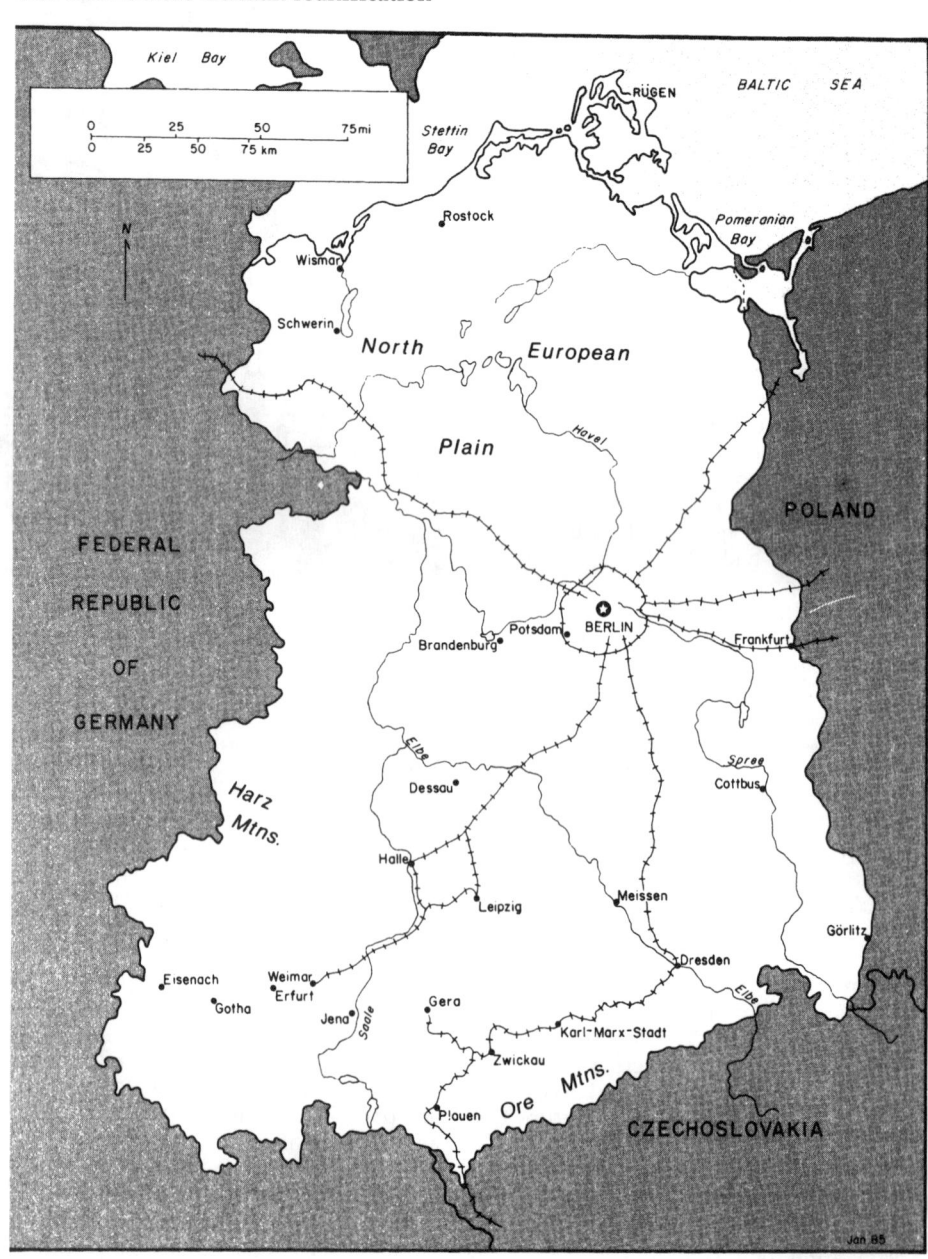

Germany (FRG)

The other parties declined in significance until they were little more than a facade.

In 1948 work on a new constitution began, and on October 7, 1949, the GDR came into being. Industry was nationalized and agriculture was collectivized, creating a state–controlled economy. *SED* domination was tightened through a pervasive state police (*Stasi*) which spied on the citizenry and stifled dissent in every form. On May 26, 1952, the border between the two Germanys was sealed by barbed wire, mine–fields, watchtowers, and free–fire zones.

Revolt and Suppression

Stalin's death in March 1953 and the gradual rise of a new Soviet leadership undermined the positions of all orthodox leaders in Eastern Europe. Although Stalinist from the beginning, Ulbricht managed to hold onto power until 1971. He faced occasional challenges to his leadership. Almost immediately after Stalin's death, the Politburo disregarded Ulbricht's will and adopted a "New Course" which moved toward greater political and economic pluralism. Enraged by onerous reparations to the USSR, higher production quotas, and the lack of personal freedom, workers revolted on June 17, 1953, but Soviet forces brutally put down the insurrection. Until German unification in 1990, this date was commemorated in the FRG as the "Day of German Unity." The revolt may have saved Ulbricht's career; the Soviets now backed him against the moderates, who found themselves removed from their positions of authority.

On January 29, 1956, the GDR joined hands militarily with the Soviet Union by creating a National People's Army (NVA) and joining the Warsaw Pact. In 1956 Soviet leader Nikita Khrushchev delivered a dramatic speech attacking the Stalinist heritage. This message emboldened communist intellectuals in the GDR who wanted to make the *SED* more responsive to the people and to create a more popular, humane form of socialism. Their chief spokesman, Wolfgang Harich, was arrested and sentenced to ten years. Other reformers were branded as "revisionists" and forced to retreat.

Ulbricht met his most serious political challenge on August 13, 1961, when, backed by the Soviets, he authorized the sudden construction of a wall between West and East Berlin, where hundreds of thousands of East Germans had continued to flee. This sealed the last escape route and forced East Germans to come to terms with their plight and their government; there was no longer any alternative. This was the only historical instance in the world that a wall was erected to keep an entire people *confined*, rather than to keep enemies out. The constant drain on manpower, particularly skilled persons, had been an important economic reason for the wall. Despite the devastating blow it delivered to the international prestige of this socialist state which presented itself as the model for Germany's future, it led to greater prosperity in the GDR after 1961 and helped provide East Germans with the highest standard of living within the Soviet empire.

Ten years later the Soviet Union concluded that its interests required closer relations between the two Germanys. When Ulbricht opposed this, he was replaced in 1971 by Erich Honecker, a roofer who had grown up in the Saarland. In 1935 he was jailed by the Nazis and spent ten years in a Berlin prison. After the war he became chairman of the communist *Free German Youth*. Following political training in Moscow, he oversaw the military and security services. He had opposed any form of "revisionism" and was totally loyal to the Soviet Union. He strongly supported the erection of the Berlin Wall and was deemed responsible in 1990 with the orders to shoot to kill along the dividing line between the East and West Germany. About 350 persons were killed trying to cross the border. For this he was charged with manslaughter in the newly united Germany. To rescue him from German justice and the embarrassment he might cause the USSR by his testimony, Soviet leaders first protected him in a military hospital outside of Berlin and then whisked him off to the USSR in March 1991, violating German sovereignty in the process. When the Soviet Union itself ceased to exist at the end of 1991, he was told he would have to leave. He took refuge in the Chilean Embassy. On July 29, 1992, he was forced to return to Germany to face charges of manslaughter, corruption, and breach of trust. East German bosses are the only leaders in the ex–Soviet empire to face justice in Western courts. His trial began in November, but in January 1993 he was proclaimed terminally ill and was released. He immediately joined his family in Chile, where he died a year later.

When Mikhail Gorbachëv launched his reformist policy of *perestroika* in 1985, Honecker and other members of the *SED* leadership resisted introducing it in the GDR on the grounds that the East German economy had already been reformed in the 1970s and was allegedly working well. Their rejection of a market economy was ideologically motivated. They argued that if the GDR adopted a market economy, then little or nothing would distinguish it from the FRG; consequently there would be no further justification for the GDR to exist as a separate state. They also resisted introducing more freedom in the political realm and even prevented the distribution of some free–thinking Soviet newspapers, such as the *Moscow News*. It was extremely embarrassing for a party which had been so servile to the Soviet Union to be in a position of having to resist its leadership. The *SED* found itself in a fatal dilemma from which it could never extricate itself.

Collapse of GDR

In 1989 one of the most dramatic post–war developments began taking place before the very eyes of a stunned world public: German reunification. In late summer a human hemorrhaging westward commenced, as East German vacationers began crossing the newly opened border between Hungary and

A "freedom train" to the West: October 5, 1989

Germany (FRG)

Austria. Budapest informed the irate East German leaders that the human rights agreements accepted at the Helsinki Conference in 1975 superseded earlier bilateral treaties preventing the free movement of peoples. The next avenue of escape was through Czechoslovakia. After thousands had taken refuge at the West German embassy in Prague, "freedom trains" took East Germans through the GDR into the West. The stampede grew when Czechoslovakia opened its western borders.

Under enormous stress, the GDR celebrated its 40th and final anniversary on October 7, 1989. The *SED's* slogan for the event was "Ever Forward—Never Backward!" The prediction was accurate, but the communist chiefs were badly mistaken about which direction was forward. The honored guest was Gorbachëv himself, who at that time was the most popular political figure in Germany. However, rather than to lend his prestige to the struggling East German leaders, he made it known that they would have to pay a high price if they did not learn the lessons of history and adopt timely reforms. He informed them that they could not expect the support of Soviet troops in the GDR to prop up their rule against the people. Without Soviet military backing communist rule could survive nowhere in Germany.

This was a very important message in a country in which public demonstrations had been going on for some time. An umbrella opposition group, *New Forum*, had come into existence a few weeks earlier, and huge demonstrations had spread to all major East German cities. Things came to a head on October 9 in Leipzig. Honecker reportedly issued an order to security forces to put down the demonstration by any means. Communist leaders in Leipzig, fearing a massacre such as had occurred in China the previous June, decided to prevent such a bloodbath in their city. With Kurt Masur, director of Leipzig's Gewandhaus Orchestra, as spokesman, and joined by Protestant Church leaders, they issued an appeal for calm. They coupled this with a call for non–violence and "a free exchange of opinions about the continuation of socialism in our country." Such a dialogue would occur "not only in the Leipzig area, but with our national government." On October 18 Honecker was ousted from power and replaced by Egon Krenz.

The End

The Berlin Wall came tumbling down on November 9. It is ironic that a wall which had been constructed in 1961 to keep East Germans in was opened in 1989 for the same reason! Within minutes millions of East Germans began pouring over the border. Germans, who for decades had suppressed displays of national feeling, experienced a deeply emotional outpouring. While millions sat in front of their televisions and wept, Berliners danced together on top of the Wall, embraced each other on the streets, and chiseled away at the ugly barrier. When word arrived at the *Bundestag*, many members, including some *Greens,* stood up and spontaneously sang the third verse of the national anthem, which stresses "unity and justice and freedom." The rest of Europe looked on with mixed feelings, uneasily remembering a frightening German past, but stirred by the sight of people casting off their shackles and demanding freedom and self–determination.

Krenz proved to be only an interim figure. Unable to put an end to either the demonstrations or the continued emigration to the West, he promised "free, democratic and secret elections," a move toward a market economy, separation of party and state, freedom of assembly, and a new law on broadcasting and press freedom. He also appointed as prime minister Hans Modrow from Dresden, one of the very few East German communists who was personally popular. Honecker was arrested, but he was released for health reasons and was soon taken under the wing of the Soviet Army in the GDR. Krenz could not save his party or himself, and he and the other members of the East German Politburo resigned on December 3. Five days later, a special *SED* party congress met and installed Gregor Gysi, a lawyer who had made a name for himself by defending dissidents and the opposition *New Forum*. Upon accepting the leadership, Gysi admitted that a complete break with Stalinism and a new form of socialism was needed and that the *SED* was responsible for plunging the GDR into crisis. Feeling betrayed, 700,000 of the 2.3 million party members quit within two months; it renamed itself the *PDS* in an attempt to escape the impending doom.

There was an outpouring of disgust and rage among East Germans as massive corruption on the part of their former leaders was revealed. They had enriched themselves while in office. Television broadcast images of the "proletarian" leaders' luxury compound in Wandlitz, estates with as many as 22 staff members, hunting lodges, deer parks, well–stocked wine cellars, and satellite dishes for better reception of Western broadcasts. Their living standards had been totally removed from the meager everyday existence of normal GDR citizens long fed on exhortations for austerity. Even worse were revelations of shady financial dealings totalling millions of marks, involving illegal arms sales to Third World countries and foreign currency maneuvers, the profits of which ended up in personal Swiss bank accounts. Said one rank–and–file *SED* member: "We did not expect this of communists and their creed of equality."

At the last moment, Honecker was whisked out of Germany on a Soviet military plane, an act that the Kremlin admitted was a 'technical violation of German sovereignty. The FRG tolerated the incident with little more than bland diplomat-

Young Germans on the Wall: November 9, 1989. Sign attached to the wall: "Cement Demolition Technique"

Germany (FRG)

ic protests because it did not want to antagonize the declining superpower. An American diplomat put it this way: 'The Soviets have done things that are not nice, but the Germans have their eye on the ball, and the ball is a timely troop withdrawal. The German interest is to smooth over any bumps.' The arrest of the GDR's former premier, Willi Stoph, defense minister Heinz Kessler (who was planning to flee to the USSR) and two other *SED* leaders was ordered.

Reunification

Suddenly German reunification was back on Europe's and the superpowers' agenda, and developments toward it raced faster than any government's ability to react. The rapid collapse of communist rule left a political vacuum in the GDR. Demonstrators in East German streets unfurled banners bearing "Germany–One Fatherland!" Aware of his constitutional mandate to seek German unity, and wishing to calm the waters and head off right- and left-wing extremists, Kohl announced on November 28 a 10-step plan for reunification, which included humanitarian assistance to refugees, freer travel between the two Germanys, massive economic aid contingent on free elections in the GDR, and ultimately reunification if that was the will of the German people, especially of East Germans. He applied no timetable. To reassure his NATO and EU allies, he stressed that any reunified Germany would be embedded in the Western community of nations and NATO. To those who fear for stability in Europe, which until now has been guaranteed by a divided Germany, he asserted that "freedom does not cause instability." West Germans no longer needed to sacrifice unity for freedom, as they had done since 1949.

In March 1990 the last communist government, led by Modrow, collapsed. East Germans had conducted the only successful revolution in German history, and it was a bloodless one. The pace of the reunification movement quickened with the first free elections in East German history on March 18, 1990. The surprise victor was the conservative coalition, "Alliance for Germany," led by the *CDU–East*, which won 48% of the vote by promising prosperity and union with the FRG. The *SPD–East* was a distant second. The communists, running under a new name—*Party of Democratic Socialism* (PDS)—won only 16% and temporarily sank into irrelevance. As in 1949, Germans turned to the *CDU* as the party of prosperity and assured democracy. A "grand coalition" of conservatives and *SPD* formed a government and entered negotiations with the Kohl government to overcome the political, economic and military obstacles to "One United Germany."

The train was speeding toward unity, and the best the Bonn government could do was to make it an orderly, legal process. There was no time for a transition, no pause to "study the problems." A breathless Kohl saw a unique opportunity and had announced in February: "We are jumping with a single leap!" He waved aside *Social Democrats'* call for a more deliberate process and the demand of many intellectuals for a "better" East Germany treading a "third path" between capitalism and socialism.

The next steps toward unity on October 3, 1990, were taken with dizzying rapidity. On July 1 the West German mark was introduced in the GDR in a currency reform without precedence on such a large scale. In a stunning diplomatic breakthrough, Kohl went to the Soviet Union July 14–16 to get Gorbachëv's assurances that he would not stand in the way of German unity and that a united Germany could decide "freely and by itself if, and in which alliance, it desires membership"; in other words, Germany would not have to leave NATO in order to be united. Returning to Moscow on September 12, Bonn's leaders joined GDR Chancellor Lothar de Maisiére and the foreign ministers of the four Allied Powers to sign the "two plus four" treaty granting full sovereignty to Germany and suspending the four powers' rights. The *Conference on Security and Cooperation in Europe* endorsed the agreement in New York on October 1. It went into effect at midnight on October 2, when unity was rung in by a "Liberty Bell" which the U.S. had given to Berlin four decades earlier.

Unity left much unsettled business for a part of Germany in which the economy had to be privatized and in which the secret police, *Stasi*, supported by 85,000 officers and over a half million informants, had penetrated every niche of GDR society and maintained files on six million persons. Germans were left to wrestle with the problem of what to do with such files, which had been assembled with complete disregard for the individual's privacy. They hold many of the keys to rooting out and punishing those persons who suppressed citizens' freedom, but their misuse could again endanger that freedom. They shed light on the GDR's extensive contacts with and training of terrorist organizations, the sheltering of fugitive West German Red Army Faction killers, and the staging of antisemitic attacks in the FRG to discredit Bonn. They also help Bonn uncover spies who had infiltrated the FRG more thoroughly than had ever been imagined.

One set of files the German government did not receive is that containing identities, code names and other vital data of thousands of Stasi foreign agents, most of whom worked in western Germany. The CIA spirited them away after the fall of the Berlin Wall. It refuses to turn them over to the Germans, saying that the archives would expose many friendly agents still operating in the West to retaliation by their victims. This became an emotional test case for the German government, which considers the files to be its property, as it seeks to reassert the full sovereignty of a reunited Germany and establish a more equitable partnership with Washington.

Discussions on German reunification, Bonn, May 5, 1990

Germany (FRG)

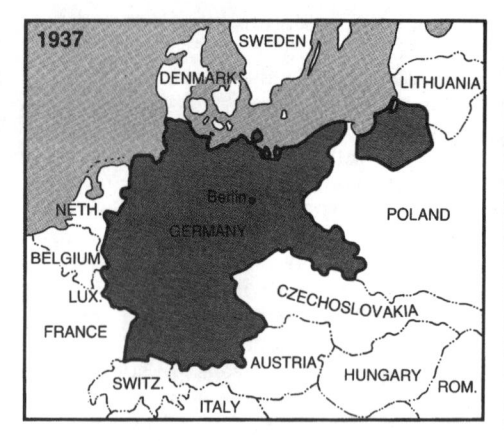

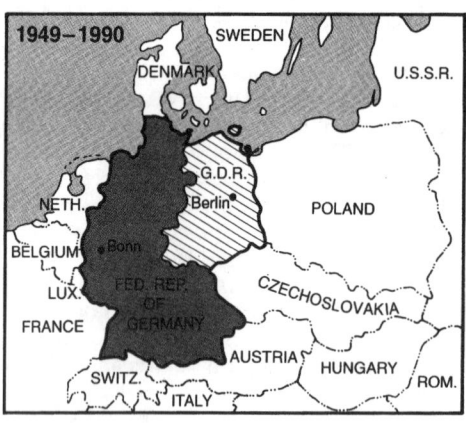

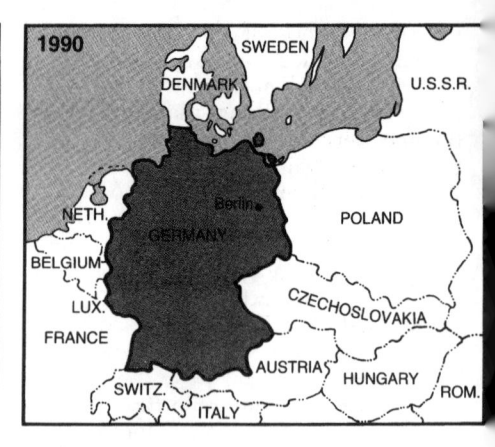

Not wishing to announce open season for witch hunts, but wanting to protect the rights of citizens, the government decided in 1991 to allow individuals access to their own files, while threatening journalists with three-year jail terms if they published information from them without permission. Joachim Gauck, director of the agency that investigated the *Stasi* files, admitted: "Charges, accusations. The memories, the pain and sadness, the failures—that will last very long. We must face it. We must show ourselves that injustice, and especially injustice in high places, does not pay."

This prompted charges of press muzzling by civil liberty advocates, who called the decision the most serious effort at limiting freedom of the press since the Hitler era and a repetition of earlier times in the FRG, when many prominent Nazis were permitted to resume their careers after 1945 without a review of their histories in well-kept Nazi records. Other former GDR citizens must confront their own troubled past. The legendary former head of East Germany's foreign intelligence service, Markus Wolf, returned to Germany from exile in the Soviet Union and was released on $30,000 bail, a paltry sum for a man who is paid at least that much for interviews with the sensation-hungry Western press. When his treason trial began in 1993, he asked: "What country am I supposed to have betrayed?"

Because such cases had the hint of retroactive justice since the defendants were fairly operating under the laws of their country at the time, the Constitutional Court ruled in 1995 that former East German spy masters like Wolf cannot be prosecuted for conducting Cold War espionage against the West. His conviction was overturned, but he was tried and convicted again in 1997 on charges of kidnapping three Germans on both sides of the Berlin Wall 30 years earlier. His sentence was suspended. However, in 1998 he was jailed once more for refusing to identify a Western informer during a spy trial. Again he was freed quickly.

But amnesty applies neither to East German agents caught in the West (although the court urged mercy in such cases), to West Germans who committed treason by spying for the GDR, nor to former East German spies accused of such offenses as kidnapping or bribery, crimes condemned by the GDR's own laws. Thus, prosecution continues.

In 1996 appeals by the GDR's former defense minister, Heinz Kessler, his aide, and top party boss Hans Albrecht, convicted for killing people attempting to escape across the Wall, were denied. By 1997, more than 30 former GDR officials and border guards had been convicted of shootings. In August 1997, for the first time, former members of the GDR political elite were held accountable for deaths along the border. Its last leader, Egon Krenz, and his co-defendants, Guenter Schabowski and Guenter Kleiber, were convicted of manslaughter. Krenz was sentenced to six and one-half years in prison, and the other two received three-year jail terms. Krenz defiantly shouted: "The political persecution is revenge for the fact that East Germany existed!"

The prelude for the first free all-German elections in almost six decades, scheduled December 2, 1990, were state elections in the five newly recreated *lands* in the East; on October 14 the *CDU* won in four of them. Therefore, few observers were surprised to see the *CDU/FDP* coalition win a resounding victory in December and Kohl reap the electoral reward for presiding over the mending of Germany's division.

Columbia University historian Fritz Stern noted that "Germany had been given something uncommon: another chance. The century is ending as it began, with a major German lead in Europe based on economic clout, technological advance, and human efficiency and performance ... [but] under much more favorable circumstances than in the pre-1914 age of rough-hewn nationalism." Prussia has not been recreated, despite the reburial of Frederick the Great at his beloved Sans Souci Palace in Potsdam outside Berlin and the return of the Prussian eagle and iron cross to the newly-restored statue of the victory goddess atop the Brandenburg Gate in 1991.

Kohl and Foreign Minister Hans-Dietrich Genscher knew that while no European country wanted to thwart German unity, there was uneasiness about the possibility that an economically powerful Germany, 43% larger than before and more populous than any country west of Russia, would dominate Europe. Most European leaders were too polite to express these fears publicly. To minimize these fears, Germany signed landmark treaties with the USSR and Poland. On November 9 it signed a friendship treaty with the Soviet Union which amounted to the closest links the Soviets had with any major Western nation. It contains a section affirming that both nations "will refrain from any threat or use of force which is directed against the territorial integrity or political independence of the other side." Neither country would aid an aggressor against the other. Bonn insists that this agreement, ratified in the USSR in March 1991, was aimed at forging a new relationship with the USSR in a way consistent with Germany's obligation to NATO, which is a defensive alliance.

The ink was hardly dry when Germany signed a treaty with Poland on November 14, 1990, fixing their mutual border along the Oder-Neisse Line. The former German land to the East of this demarcation constituted a third of Poland's territory. Genscher stated bluntly that "we Germans are aware that the treaty does not surrender anything that was not lost long ago as the result of a criminal war and a criminal system." But he also admitted that settling this last major dispute of the war hurt: "For those who have lost their homelands, who suffered expulsion [after 1945], it is an especially painful one."

Germany (FRG)

POLITICAL SYSTEM

In 1949 West Germany's founders called their new constitution a Basic Law in order to emphasize that it would apply only temporarily until reunification. But in 1990 the newly-formed eastern German states chose to be absorbed by the FRG through Article 23, which was then scrapped to assure neighboring countries that no other former German territories could enter the FRG that way. Thus, the Basic Law became, in effect, a permanent constitution. It reflects several objectives which the founders hoped to achieve: individual freedom, political democracy, stability (to prevent a repetition of the Weimar experience), built-in safeguards against the emergence of another dictatorship and links with some aspects of the German political tradition.

In contrast to the U.S. Constitution, which has a Bill of Rights attached at the end, the Germans placed in the first 20 articles of the Basic Law guarantees for unalienable rights and liberties and the protection of life. Also in contrast with the U.S. document, the Basic Law explicitly grants Germans, who had never experienced a successful democratic revolution, the right of revolution. Article 20 reads in part: '. . . all Germans shall have the right to resist any person or persons seeking to abolish the constitutional order, should no other remedy be possible.'

A Powerful Court

To underscore its commitment to the principles in this document, the founders, with the full support of the American occupation authorities, created the Constitutional Court which would have the power of judicial review and therefore would be the final arbiter in constitutional questions. With two chambers located in Karlsruhe, where founders thought it could remain freer from political influences, the court reviews legislation, adjudicates disputes between the national and *Land* (state) political institutions, rules on questions concerning individual rights, and can even ban groups or parties if it believes that their activities are not in harmony with the principles of the Basic Law. For instance, in the mid-1950s it banned the neo-Nazi *Socialist Reich Party* and the *Communist Party* for this reason.

The court has a clearly political character, as the selection of the justices reveals: half of the 16 justices are chosen by the lower house of Parliament, and half are selected by the upper house (in order that *state* interests are not overlooked). They serve 12-year terms. The court is administratively independent and cannot be impeached by the Parliament. It has not been afraid to lock horns with the government. For example, it struck down Chancellor Adenauer's attempt in the mid-1950s to create a second television channel under national control because this would have clearly violated the states' constitutional jurisdiction over mass communications media.

In 1983 it decided to postpone the national census on the grounds that the questions which the state intended to ask would have violated the citizens' right of privacy. In 1995 it struck down Bavaria's requirements for schools to hang crucifixes in every classroom, and it prevented the punishment of pacifists caught shouting the slogan, "soldiers are murderers." The first female chief justice, Jutta Limbach, faced further parliamentary criticism for agreeing to rule on parliament's power to restrict political asylum, as it did in 1993.

The court also sometimes upholds the government's policies, as it did in 1993 when it ruled that the Maastricht treaty for European unity and the FRG's participation in UN-sponsored peace-keeping operations outside of Europe are not unconstitutional. All parties in disputes before this powerful court, including the national government, have always complied with its decisions.

State Government

More than any other state in Europe with the exception of Switzerland, Germany has decentralized and fragmented political power. Such decentralization is traditional in Germany, which consists of what had been a myriad of states and free cities. The only experience with highly centralized government—the Third Reich—left a bad taste in Germans' mouths. The FRG is now broken down into 16 states (each called a *Land*). Most of these states were newly created after 1945 and the five in the former GDR, plus a unified city of Berlin, were recreated in 1990. In May 1996 Eastern German voters rejected unequivocally an effort by all major parties, except the *PDS*, and the governments of Brandenburg and Berlin to merge these two states.

The massive influx of refugees into the western occupation zones did much to break down the formerly strong regionalism of the various areas of Germany, but Bavaria has by far retained its own unique character, visually, culturally and politically, more than any other state. It proudly calls itself the "Free State of Bavaria" and, curiously, has never formally ratified the Basic Law, although it has abided by it since 1949.

Each state has its own government, the specific form of which is left entirely up to each. The state constitutions differ considerably in some respects, but they all call for forms of parliamentary government. A government, led by a Minister President, is chosen by a unicameral Parliament, called a *Landtag*, elected by proportional representation. State issues play the dominant role in such state elections, but since the early 1960s these elections, which are seldom held at the same time as national elections, have increasingly become indicators or bellwethers for citizens' approval of national policies or leaders. Therefore, national leaders lend their active support in local campaigns, an important reason why the voter turnout is very high by American standards, averaging about 70% since the early 1950s.

In accord with German tradition and to prevent a single leader or group of leaders in the central government from gathering all strings of power, the founders granted specific exclusive power to the states: education (although the national government does contribute to the financing of universities), law enforcement and internal security (although the central government does maintain an Office for the Protection of the Constitution, roughly equivalent to the FBI in the U.S., and a Federal Criminal Office, which maintains data that is useful to the state police authorities), the administration of justice and mass communications and media. Only in the areas of defense and foreign policy is the national government largely free of the state governments. As in the U.S., all powers not expressly granted to the national government belong to the states. Although this has substantial meaning in Germany, the principle has, of course, largely been circumvented in the U.S. by the "power of the purse."

States used their powers over regional broadcasting to resist a unified national satellite television policy. State leaders travel around the globe and conduct their own foreign policy to a degree. Some have

The 16 states (Länder) of the FRG

Germany (FRG)

even opened offices in Brussels to influence EU policy and seek financial favors. The upper house (*Bundesrat*), which the states control, has been used to force the federal government to consult with them on any foreign policy deals which affect them. New, small state–based political parties are complicating the work of the major national parties to win majorities in the states. All these trends underscore the fact that regional politics is more significant in the FRG than in any other European country. Almost all important political figures in federal politics rose from a strong base in the states.

There are two factors which prevent the states from being as individualistic as American ones: legal uniformity and shared taxation. German law, which was decisively influenced by Roman law and by the Napoleonic Code, was codified in the last three decades of the 19th century. Since the 1950s the criminal code has been in the process of revision. The point is that German law is the same in every state. In general, the national government wields the most legislative power while the state governments has most of the administrative power. The staffs of most federal ministries are relatively small. Indeed, if one excludes the employees of the Federal Railways and the Federal Postal Service, only about 10% of public employees work for the national government, whereas roughly a third work for local governments and over half work for the states.

The states largely finance and set operating rules for local governments in the communities (*Gemeinden*). Local government differs from state to state, but all communities have an elected council (*Stadtrat* or *Gemeinderat*). Also, each county (*Kreis*) has an elected council *Kreistag* led by an executive officer (*Landrat*).

Parliament—The Upper House

The states' interests are also guaranteed by their legislative role at the federal level. The upper house of Parliament, the *Bundesrat,* is composed of delegates from the state governments and, like all upper houses in federal states, exists primarily to protect states' rights. Seats in the *Bundesrat* are apportioned on the basis of each *land's* population; each of the most populous states (including North Rhine–Westphalia, Bavaria, Baden–Wurttemberg and Lower Saxony receives five seats; each of the medium sized states (such as Hesse, the Rhineland–Palatinate, Schleswig–Holstein, and the five new lands in the East) receive four, and each of the three smaller states (Hamburg, Bremen and the Saar) receive three. The *lands* send specific delegates depending upon the subjects being discussed; sometimes they are administrators and sometimes they are leading politicians, including perhaps the Minister Presidents. Delegates are always bound by instructions from the state governments, and each delegation must cast *all* of its votes for or against a matter.

The *Bundesrat* can initiate legislation, and it must approve all legislation relating to the states' constitutional or administrative responsibilities. Also it must approve any legislation affecting state boundaries, national emergencies and constitutional amendments. Presently, about 60% of all legislation falls within the *Bundesrat's* veto power. In many cases, party lines do not decisively affect votes in this body. For instance, smaller or poorer states often have more in common than do larger or wealthier ones, regardless of which parties rule in the state capitals.

Parliament—The Lower House

The lower house of Parliament (*Bundestag*) is the most important chamber. It is normally composed of 656 members elected at least every four years by Germans 18 years of age or older. The electoral system is a complicated mixture of proportional representation and single–member districts. Half the members are elected by plurality vote (more votes than any other single candidate) in 328 constituencies with an average size of approximately 250,000 residents.

The other half is elected by proportional representation from *land* party lists. Each voter casts *two* ballots, one for the constituency candidate and one for his preferred party. The party vote is the more important because it determines the percentage of total seats in the *Bundestag* each party will receive. A further complication is the concept of "overhang votes." If a party wins more seats in the "first vote" than it would be entitled to under strict proportional representation, it keeps the extra seats, and the size of the *Bundestag* expands accordingly. Thus, in 1994 the *Bundestag* swelled to 672 seats, giving the *CDU/CSU–FDP* governing coalition a 10–seat majority instead of a one–seat advantage. The same happened in 1998, when the *Bundestag* grew to 669 seats, benefiting the new *SPD–Green* government, whose majority was enlarged to 21 seats.

With German unity, Berlin became the official capital, but that did not automatically mean that the seat of government would be transferred to Berlin. Faced with the daunting costs of integrating and modernizing the bankrupt economy of the GDR, many shirked from the price tag of moving all their operations to Berlin. A massive move severely affected the economic livelihood of Bonn and its suburbs. There were also political considerations. North Rhine–Westphalia and some western German politicians did not want to transfer the capital from Bonn, which is located close to Brussels and other EU centers, to a faraway city with a reputation for past militarism and present rebelliousness and a thriving counter–culture. Also, until 1994 Berlin was surrounded by a large number of Soviet troops, who could possibly have intimidated the German government if relations between the two countries were to become strained.

On June 20, 1991, in one of the longest

Former Chancellor Kohl addresses the opening session of the *Bundestag* of a united Germany: December 22, 1990

Germany (FRG)

Sie haben 2 Stimmen

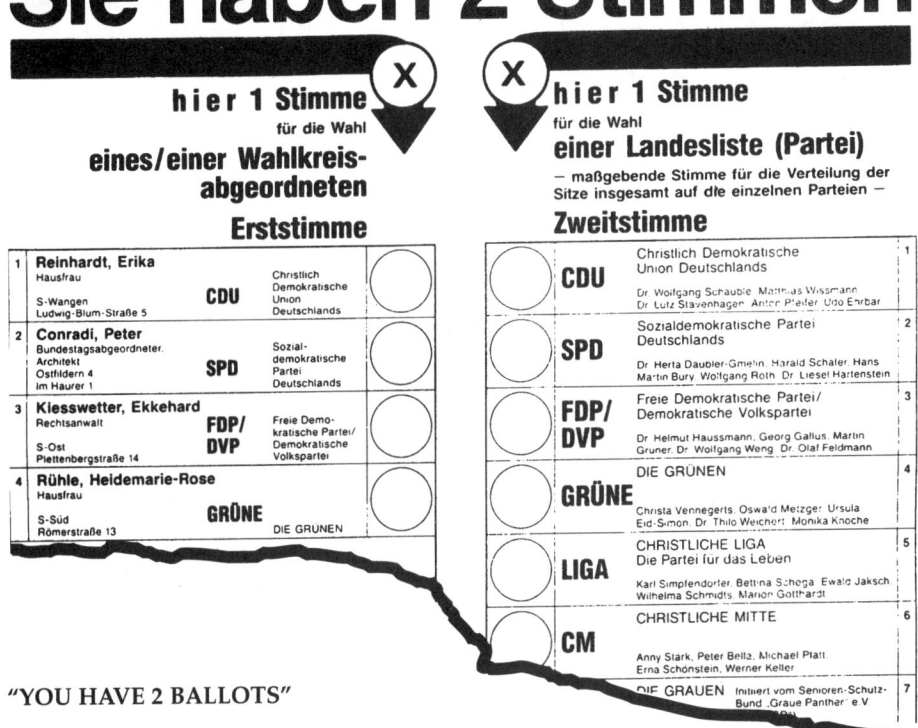

hier 1 Stimme für die Wahl eines/einer Wahlkreisabgeordneten
Erststimme

1	Reinhardt, Erika — Hausfrau, S-Wangen, Ludwig-Blum-Straße 5	CDU	Christlich Demokratische Union Deutschlands
2	Conradi, Peter — Bundestagsabgeordneter, Architekt, Ostfildern 4, Im Haurer 1	SPD	Sozialdemokratische Partei Deutschlands
3	Kiesswetter, Ekkehard — Rechtsanwalt, S-Ost, Plettenbergstraße 14	FDP/DVP	Freie Demokratische Partei/ Demokratische Volkspartei
4	Rühle, Heidemarie-Rose — Hausfrau, S-Süd, Römerstraße 13	GRÜNE	DIE GRÜNEN

hier 1 Stimme für die Wahl einer Landesliste (Partei)
— maßgebende Stimme für die Verteilung der Sitze insgesamt auf die einzelnen Parteien —
Zweitstimme

CDU	Christlich Demokratische Union Deutschlands — Dr. Wolfgang Schäuble, Matthias Wissmann, Dr. Lutz Stavenhagen, Anton Pfeifer, Udo Ehrbar	1
SPD	Sozialdemokratische Partei Deutschlands — Dr. Herta Däubler-Gmelin, Harald Schäfer, Hans Martin Bury, Wolfgang Roth, Dr. Liesel Hartenstein	2
FDP/DVP	Freie Demokratische Partei/Demokratische Volkspartei — Dr. Helmut Haussmann, Georg Gallus, Martin Grüner, Dr. Wolfgang Weng, Dr. Olaf Feldmann	3
GRÜNE	DIE GRÜNEN — Christa Vennegerts, Oswald Metzger, Ursula Eid-Simon, Dr. Thilo Weichert, Monika Knoche	4
LIGA	CHRISTLICHE LIGA — Die Partei für das Leben — Karl Simplendorfer, Bettina Schega, Ewald Jaksch, Wilhelma Schmidts, Marion Gotthardt	5
CM	CHRISTLICHE MITTE — Anny Stark, Peter Bella, Michael Platt, Erna Schönstein, Werner Keller	6
	DIE GRAUEN — Initiiert von Senioren-Schutz-Bund „Graue Panther" e.V.	7

"YOU HAVE 2 BALLOTS"

(12 hours) and most emotional debates ever held in the *Bundestag*, a narrow majority (338–320) voted to make Berlin the seat of government. Younger legislators tended to favor Bonn, whereas those old enough to remember the earlier Berlin and its grandeur, such as Kohl and Brandt, favored Berlin. The outcome was a powerful message of reconciliation to eastern Germans. But the latter played a decisive role in the vote: whereas narrow majorities in both the two largest parties, the *CDU/CSU* and *SPD*, voted for Bonn, it was the 25 members from the small eastern German parties, the *PDS* and *Alliance 90*, who tipped the scales for Berlin. Seven ministries, including defense and agriculture, remain in Bonn and maintain offices in Berlin. But the rest, along with at least 20,000 government workers, were transferred to Berlin in 1999. Some 140 embassies had to move, along with countless organizations, such as lobby groups and industry representatives, who must be close to the center of power.

On April 19, 1999, Chancellor Gerhard Schröder spoke at the inaugural session of the newly renovated *Reichstag* building, with its massive glass dome that symbolizes, in his words, "the openness and the transparency of our democratic politics." He emphasized that "equating *Reichstag* with *Reich* makes no sense," given the strong and stable democracy in today's FRG. But exactly what to call the new capitol, if not *Reichstag*, consumed months of debate. Finally the all–party Council of Elders declared a solution that satisfied no one: *Deutscher Bundestag—Plenarbereich Reichstagsgebäude* (German Federal Assembly—Plenary Area, Imperial Assembly Building).

The President

The federal chief of state is the president. Remembering how the powerful Weimar presidency had overshadowed

FRG President Johannes Rau

and, to a certain extent, undermined Parliament, the founders decided to grant the president largely ceremonial powers, such as formally naming the chancellor and his cabinet, signing all laws and appointing and dismissing national civil servants and federal judges. In each case, however, he merely carries out the will of the government or Parliament. He could possibly be an important mediator and conciliator in the event of a parliamentary crisis, but that has not yet occurred in the FRG.

Former president, Richard von Weizsäcker, was a patriarchal *Christian Democrat* whose style and substance have earned him almost universal respect by transforming the presidency into a post of real authority. He used the office to describe broadly the direction in which he believed the FRG should go. He spoke out at carefully chosen moments on the meaning of Germany's past, the potential dangers of nuclear power, the importance of trade unions in the society, the significance of German unity, and the need to move the seat of government to Berlin. His successor in May 1994 was also a *Christian Democrat*, Roman Herzog, former president of the Constitutional Court. Herzog was followed in May 1999 by *Social Democrat* Johannes Rau, popular ex–minister president of the FRG's largest *Land*, North Rhine–Westphalia.

In order to prevent the president from claiming a superior role based upon a popular mandate upon direct election by all the people, the founders decided to have the president *selected* every five years by a Federal Assembly (*Bundesversammlung*) composed of all members of the lower house of Parliament and an equal number of delegates from the various *land* parliaments. In fact, the founders decided that *no* national figure should be elected directly by all voters and that there would be *no* element of direct democracy (such as initiatives, referendums or plebiscites) at the national level. They did not wish to create a useful tool for a popular demagogue like Hitler which could undermine the authority and responsibility of Parliament, the very heart of democracy. The president has a villa in Bonn, but he resides in Bellevue, the presidential palace in Berlin.

Political Parties

A crucially important point is that a person can be elected to the *Bundestag* only as a member of a political party. In the past, Germans had regarded parties with considerable distrust. Parties allegedly divided the body politic, and their log–rolling and pursuit of particularist interests had an undignified and illicit air in the eyes of the average German. This condescension before 1945 greatly weakened the prestige

Germany (FRG)

of Parliament and therefore of democracy. Also, so many parties had seats in the Weimar Parliament that it was almost impossible to construct a stable and lasting majority.

Therefore, the Basic Law (in contrast to the U.S. Constitution) granted political parties official recognition and status, as well as the responsibility to organize the country's political life. Also, the Basic Law requires any party to receive a minimum of 5% of the votes cast nationwide in order to win any seats in the *Bundestag*. In the first election in 1949 many parties cleared this hurdle, but since 1953 only five parties have been able to accomplish this. The *Bundestag* is made up of parliamentary parties (each called a *Fraktion*) which practice a high degree of party discipline; almost nine out of ten votes are straight party votes. Since 1959 the major political parties have received increasing amounts of financial subsidies from the national treasury. Many observers have called the FRG a "party state" and they are largely correct.

For the first time in German history, the Parliament was granted exclusive control over the country's government and bureaucracy, and it has supervisory power over the military. Although most legislation originates with the government, the *Bundestag* must debate and approve all. Debates in the *Bundestag* plenum are conducted in a very free and relaxed atmosphere. They are punctuated with humorous or pointed quips, boisterous interruptions, laughter, applause and desk pounding. Members from the environmentalist–"anti-nuke" ("Greens") movement added unconventional color by riding bicycles to the sessions, wearing jeans and other casual dress (Conservatives' attempts to impose a dress code failed!), carrying plants to their desks and unravelling signs with critical remarks against U.S. policies while the chancellor addressed the *Bundestag*.

Major debates are televised in order to bring the activity of the Parliament closer to the attention of the citizens. The *Bundestag* combines the role of a debating parliament, such as the British House of Commons, with that of a working parliament, such as the U.S. Congress. Most of the work is actually done in the 19 standing committees, which though not as powerful as U.S. congressional and senatorial committees, thoroughly examine and amend legislation.

They also increasingly use their investigatory and information–gathering powers quite effectively to perform their function of being a responsible critic of the government. An interesting feature is that seats *and chairmanships* in the committees are distributed according to party strength in the *Bundestag* itself. Thus, the opposition party will occupy many committee chairmanships, and by tradition will always occupy that of the finance committee.

The *Bundestag's* function as a "working parliament" is enhanced by the fact that almost half its members are civil servants, who, in contrast with U.S. civil servants, are freed from their normal jobs while serving in political positions and can return to the civil service at any time. Even their promotions and pay raises are continued while they are in political office. Civil servants are represented in the *Bundestag* at a rate ten times higher than their proportion in the larger population, and workers, farmers, housewives and those in business and professional occupations are greatly under–represented. The FRG is a parliamentary system and the most important of the functions of the *Bundestag* is to choose a government. A majority chooses the chancellor, the most powerful political figure in the FRG, from among its own members, and he then chooses his cabinet, most of whom have seats in the *Bundestag* and who are then directly responsible to the chancellor, *not* to the *Bundestag*. The chancellor is always responsible to the lower house. However, in order to prevent the continuous cabinet instability which plagued the Weimar Republic, he can be voted out of office only if a majority is immediately able to choose a replacement. This requirement for a "constructive vote of no–confidence," which has been attempted very infrequently, insures that Germany will always have a government.

The chancellor's office (*Bundeskanzlerant*)—the equivalent of the U.S. Executive Office of the President, has a staff of about 500 in six departments, and the chancellor directs the work of all governmental ministries, which answer to him. Since Konrad Adenauer, chancellors have been very powerful figures, whose popularity always runs ahead of that of their own party or challengers. Some observers have even called the FRG a "chancellor's democracy."

The Christian Democrats and Christian Socials

The major opposition party in the *Bundestag* is the *CDU*, which is linked in Parliament and in federal elections with its Bavarian sister party, the *CSU*. The *CDU/CSU* is the first successful political party in German history which did not rest on a single confessional or class base. It is a union of diverse groups who after the Nazi catastrophe wanted to put Christian principles back into political life and to take ideological rigidity out of it. They wished to give Germany a new moral, democratic and socially just beginning. Adenauer's Economics Minister, Ludwig Erhard, introduced a brand of capitalism with a social conscience (called the "social market economy") which brought not only prosperity, but a broad net of social assistance for the uprooted, the hungry, the unemployed, the old and the sick.

Germans are very proud of their generous social legislation, and the creation of the FRG's modern social net is primarily the work of the *CDU/CSU*; the *SPD–FDP* coalition only tightened this net in a few places during the 1970s. It is thus a democratic, reform–oriented party, which attracts votes primarily from Catholics, independent business people, white collar employees and civil servants. It would not be considered a conservative party in the U.S. political sense, even though it does win the votes of most conservatives in Germany. However, this does not weaken or embarrass the *CDU/CSU* since almost all conservatives in the FRG, in contrast to the Weimar Republic, support the democratic system. For years the party grappled with the problem of how to put aside the internal struggles within its talented and experienced leadership in order to present a picture of unity.

Catholic Bavaria is the FRG's most conservative state and the *CSU* is therefore also conservative. The *CSU*, which especially appeals to Catholics, rural and small city dwellers, craftsmen, small business groups and, increasingly, those in the service industries, easily wins *land* elections in Bavaria (though not in Munich, the state capital), as it did in 1998 two weeks before the *Bundestag* elections. Its leader is Minister–President Edmund Stoiber.

"Yes to Germany, Yes to the Future, together we'll do it . . . freedom, prosperity, security"

Germany (FRG)

The political and economic success of Kohl, the first German chancellor to have been too young to have played any role in Nazi Germany, helped restore in many citizens an interest and pride in being German. Kohl and his party believed that Germans have atoned enough for the nation's past sins. Former President Weizsäcker occasionally deflates such self–satisfaction by reminding Germans of the seamier side of their past, while encouraging them to be proud of what they have accomplished since 1945. Kohl frequently spoke of the "Fatherland" and the *Heimat* ("Homeland"). He also encouraged displays of patriotism and the frequent playing of the national anthem. In Baden–Wurttemberg, school children may be taught all three verses of the *Deutschlandlied* (*Germany Song*, often mistakenly called *Deutschland, Deutschland über Alles*).

Before Germany's dramatic move toward unity, it appeared that Kohl's party, which was ridden with dissatisfaction about what appeared to be a bumbling chancellor, was heading for defeat in the December 2, 1990, federal elections. However, Kohl instinctively knew that, faced with the challenges of melding two Germanys into one, German voters would choose that leader who was decisive and exuded confidence that future problems could be solved. Therefore, the Union parties adopted the slogans, "Yes to Germany, yes to the Future!" At each of its election rallies, a campaign song was sung in English: "Feel the power, touch the future, reach the heart!"

The first all–German election in 58 years was a plebiscite on unity, after the fact. Those parties which had seized the opportunity to bring it about were handsomely rewarded, and those which seemed petty and afraid and who cast doubt on unity were punished. With voter participation falling to a new low of 77.8% (74% in the East), the governing *CDU–CSU–FDP* coalition won 55% of the votes and actually performed better in the East than in the West. The *CDU–CSU* captured 44% of the votes and 319 seats. It won big in the former GDR, where few Catholics live. Half of East German workers voted *CDU*, and it was the preferred party for young voters in both parts of Germany.

The *CDU's* standing in the East was troubled after the election by the cabinet resignation of the GDR's last prime minister, Lothar de Maizière. As a lawyer and high lay official in the East German Protestant Church, he was shown to have maintained contacts with *Stasi* from 1981 to 1988. He maintained that these were necessary for his efforts to defend his clients and church. He was cleared of allegations that he had actually spied for *Stasi*, but he was forced to relinquish his party vice–chairmanship to another eastern German, Angela Merkel, who became the party's general secretary in 1998. Other leaders of the old eastern *CDU*, one of the bloc parties which had cooperated with the Communists, were gradually forced out of their posts.

Before the October 1994 federal elections, it seemed that the Kohl era would be brought to an abrupt end as widespread dissatisfaction over the economic and psychological effects of unification was vented against the chancellor. But then he presided over an impressive recovery from Germany's worst recession since the war, ushered out the last Russian troops from German soil, and persuaded his countrymen that he was the only person who could form a government with a majority in the *Bundestag*. The *CDU/CSU* won a narrow victory, capturing 41.5% of the votes (42.2% in the West and 38.5% in the East) but slipping to 294 seats. Together with his *FDP* partners, his government's majority declined to only 10 seats.

He and his party were not so lucky in September 1998. Voters had grown tired of Kohl, who had not been able to solve Germany's main problem: unemployment. For the first time in the FRG's history, they voted to throw out an incumbent chancellor and to remove *all* the parties in the ruling coalition from power. The *CDU/CSU* fell to 35.2% of the votes (the first time it had ever ended up below 40%) and only 245 seats. It lost its footholds in the East, North, and much of the West. Only in the South did it remain strong, especially in Bavaria; this elevates Stoiber's influence in the union.

Kohl was gracious in defeat, took full responsibility for the fiasco, and announced that he was stepping down. He was replaced as party leader by Wolfgang Schäuble, the *CDU's* popular parliamentary leader, who was almost killed by an assassin's bullets in 1990 and who is confined to a wheelchair. The road to recovery seemed long and steep. But the *Christian Democrats* bounced back surprisingly well, profiting from the divisions in the new *SPD–Green* and from the ruling coalition's unpopular policy to offer dual citizenship to many of the foreigners living in Germany. With that as its main issue, the *CDU* won state elections in Hesse in February 1999 and were thereby able to wrest from the government its majority in the *Bundesrat*. By the time of its party congress in the eastern German city of Erfurt in April 1999, opinion polls showed the *CDU* either level with or a bit ahead of the *SPD*.

The Kohl Government

In many ways, Kohl's chancellorship had been a success: both the "peace movement" and the bitter debates over the installation of new American missiles in Germany died down and were muted by arms control treaties and unification. He maintained close relations with the U.S., Britain, and France while getting along as well with Moscow as his *SPD* predecessors had. He signalled a strong interest in protecting the environment by creating a ministry of the environment.

He had to take the blame for some embarrassing reversals. In 1985 he persuaded the American president to pay homage to the German war dead buried in a cemetery in Bitburg, without learning in time that SS soldiers were also buried there. The president's visit unleashed a storm of protest among Jewish and veteran groups in the U.S., and both houses of the U.S. Congress passed resolutions imploring the president to reconsider the visit. What had been intended as a gesture of reconciliation and friendship actually revived memories of the Holocaust and the war, and it seriously strained relations between these two friendly nations.

Dissatisfaction in the East was dramatized by massive street demonstrations there and Kohl's own pelting with eggs when he strolled the streets of Halle. His credibility suffered, as western Germans remembered his earlier "read–my–lips" pledge. He had clearly miscalculated the expenses and problems involved with integrating eastern Germany into the FRG.

In November 1996 he surpassed his political hero, Konrad Adenauer, as the longest–serving chancellor in the twentieth century: 14 years. Both sought to bring Germany greatness, not through military strength and *Realpolitik*, but by making it liberal, democratic, trusted and prosperous. In some ways Adenauer's job was more difficult. He had led a defeated, despised, divided, and impoverished country that was occupied and partly ruled by foreign troops. His compromises prompted critics to call him "chancellor of the allies." By contrast, Kohl led a Germany that was unified, rich, and powerful, with a mature democracy and the third–largest economy in the world. He almost completed Adenauer's dream of "a free and united Germany in a free and united Europe."

No one can deny Germany's strength: with only 11% of the EU's land mass (compared to France with 17%), it has 82 million people, 22% of the EU's total (France and the UK have 16% each). It produces 28% of the EU's GDP (compared to 18% for France and 13% for Italy and the UK) and more than 10% of the world's exports, twice as much as its nearest EU rival. But by working closely with Germany's European allies, especially France,

Germany (FRG)

Former Chancellor Dr. Helmut Kohl

as well as with the U.S. and by pressing for a unified Europe more vigorously than anybody else, Kohl helped solve the perennial problem that has vexed European statesmen for years: how to make Germany strong without terrifying the rest of Europe.

The "Liberals"

For a long time, the *FDP* (often called the "Liberals") was the only small party to survive in the *Bundestag*. It has never received more than 13% of the vote, and at times it danced dangerously close to the 5% line. Yet the *FDP* plays a role in German politics far out of proportion to its size or voter strength. Only once (in 1957) has a party ever won an absolute majority of seats in the *Bundestag*. Thus, German governments must almost always be coalitions of two parties, and the *FDP* has been and remains the linchpin for almost every governmental coalition. Since 1949 it has been excluded from only three cabinets.

The *FDP* sees itself as the heir to the traditional German liberal movement, which was always composed of two strains: a strong nationalist commitment and the protection of individual rights through minimizing state intervention in the economy and society. In the early 1970s the nationalist strain largely left the party, so throughout the 1970s the *FDP* could be more comfortable in the center–moderate left coalition in Bonn. The *FDP* attracts most of its votes from the middle class mainly in urban areas. Like the *SPD*, it has attracted some critical and confrontational elements which have become difficult or impossible for the party to digest. From 1969 to 1982, the *FDP* was in the governing coalition with the *SPD*. However, it is economically more conservative than its former partner, and it increasingly disagreed with the *Social Democratic* medicine for coping with unemployment and the rising public debt.

It sensed a conservative wind blowing in West Germany, and a string of electoral disasters in state elections reminded it that it was in danger of being dragged down by the *SPD*. Therefore, in 1982 it decided to change partners, thereby enabling the *Christian Democrats* to rule in Bonn. The *FDP* was widely criticized for the way in which it brought the Schmidt government tumbling down. Thousands of its members and some of its parliamen-

"Courage for Freedom."

tarians left the party in protest, and it appeared it would fail to clear the 5% hurdle in the next *Bundestag* elections. But its indispensable role as a moderating coalition partner was again recognized in 1983 and 1987. In 1990 it gained dramatically, winning 11% nationwide and 79 seats. Its two top politicians, Genscher and Wolfgang Mischnick, had grown up in the GDR and could therefore present themselves to voters as both easterners and westerners. That helps explain the *FDP's* 12.9% result in the East and impressive harvest of party members there.

Facing what some observers saw as certain death in the 1994 federal elections, the *FDP* won 6.9% of the votes (only 4% in the East) and 47 seats. This was thanks to *CDU* voters who gave it their second vote rather than see it fall below 5% and cause the Kohl government to collapse. The *FDP* is scared, with few roots below the federal level. The buzzards seemed to be circling in the lead–up to the 1998 elections, but its dynamic party secretary general, Guido Westerwelle, succeeded in scaring some of them away. This experienced survival party arose from the dead and captured 6.2% of the votes and 44 seats. But for the first time in almost three decades the *FDP* found itself neither in the government nor in possession of the foreign minister's post. It needs to reexamine and reorganize itself. It must especially do that in *Land* elections, where it has not done well in the past few years and where political rejuvenation usually begins.

The Social Democrats

The *SPD* is a traditional working–class party which is the only one in the FRG having had a continuous existence since before the German Empire. In the Weimar Republic it was one of the regime's staunchest supporters, and during the Third Reich its leaders either found themselves in concentration camps or went into exile. After the war it fully expected to become Germany's governing party because of its former opposition to the Nazis, but its leaders badly misread the voters' minds. The West Germans, gripped by poverty, were less interested in the *SPD's* socialist solution than they were in the prosperity which its opponents promised and actually produced. Also, *Social Democrats'* focus on strong national policy directed against all four occupation powers and especially aimed toward German re-unification proved to be far less appealing than Adenauer's policy of winning West German sovereignty, international respect and military security through military and economic integration with the West.

In order to break out of the "one–third ghetto" (winning only a third of the votes) within the electorate and in order to attract more Catholic and middle–class voters, the *SPD* changed its program at the party congress in Bad Godesberg in 1959. It cast off the Marxist ballast in its party program and made the basic decision not fundamentally to challenge the capitalist order, but instead to seek to correct its flaws through social reform. The following year the party's chief strategist, Herbert Wehner, announced in the *Bundestag* that the *SPD* would accept Adenauer's foreign policy of integration with the West.

Having become in theory as well as in fact a mass social reform party anchored in the democratic West, and with a new young chancellor candidate, Willy Brandt,

Change in Germany ... W 94
("W" stands for "Election")

Germany (FRG)

who remained the party's chairman until 1987, the party began attracting increasing numbers of middle class voters. These included gains among civil servants, white collar employees in industry and the service sector, and especially youth; these groups soon gained a far greater share of the party's leadership positions than workers. This opening of the party to the middle class was crucial to the *SPD's* gaining power in 1969, but it also converted the *SPD* into a broad–spectrum party whose main problem became that of unifying such diverse groups behind a common leadership.

In 1990 the *SPD* picked as its chancellor candidate its biggest vote–getting provincial politician, Oskar Lafontaine, Minister–President of the Saarland and earlier one of the party's most outspoken leftists. He belonged to a new generation of politicians who did not directly experience Nazism or the onset of the Cold War. His political outlook was significantly shaped by the student rebellion of the 1960s, and his politics are post–industrial, post–materialist "new politics" emphasizing environmental issues. He was brought up in a divided Germany and showed no emotions toward the idea of a united country, to which he derisively referred as a "provisional entity" until the nation–state became superfluous. He hated words like "fatherland," and on the occasion of Germany's unity at midnight October 2 to 3, 1990, he alone among political leaders refused to sing the national anthem. He was unable to notice, let alone tap, the emotions released by the opening of the Berlin Wall. This antagonized many of his party comrades, including former chancellors Brandt and Schmidt.

In his campaign, during which he was almost killed when a deranged women slit his throat with a butcher knife, he harped on the problems and costs associated with unification and was perceived as a prophet of doom. His message was depressing, and his leftist themes did not interest German voters in 1990, especially those in eastern Germany, who wanted prosperity within the FRG. *Die Zeit* called him "the wrong man at the wrong time," and the electoral disaster proved this. The *SPD* dropped to 33.5% of the vote and 239 seats. Its 24.3% in the East, which had been the party's electoral fortress before Hitler's take–over, was shocking. It got the votes of only a fourth of East German workers.

Having led the *SPD* back into the "one–third ghetto" from which it had worked so long to escape, Lafontaine fled back to the Saar and left his party to rebuild itself. Rhineland–Palatinate Minister–President Rudolf Scharping assumed leadership. He was the first national par-

Chancellor Gerhard Schröder

ty leader in Germany to be selected by means of a poll of 870,000 party members throughout the country. He is a moderate, hard–working, but uncharismatic leader, who became defense minister in 1998. Voters ignored his calls for change in the 1994 federal elections although the *SPD* was able to increase its votes to 36.4% (37.6% in the West and 31.9% in the East) and seats to 252. In the aftermath *Social Democrats* began bickering among themselves, and many blamed the party's deep malaise and plunging popularity on Scharping's vacillating policies and weak leadership. In 1995 he was replaced as party leader by Oskar Lafontaine.

Lafontaine was a traditional left–wing politician who enjoyed enthusiastic support by many of the party's rank–and–file. But another *Social Democrat* was showing himself to be a more promising vote–getter in general elections, and this became very important for a party that had lost four straight *Bundestag* elections in 16 years. When Lower Saxony's Minister–President, Gerhard Schröder, won an impressive reelection victory in March 1998, the *SPD* turned to him as chancellor candidate, while Lafontaine continued as party chairman with responsibility for keeping a party united that had historically been prone to self–destructive divisiveness. Both leaders performed their assignments very well.

Schröder came from humble origins, the son of a widowed cleaning lady. Born in 1944, he is the first chancellor with no memory of the war. As a student he was a Marxist who took part in the student rebellion and became chairman of the Young Socialists, the *SPD's* youth organization. However, being ambitious and a skilled political tactician, he saw that his dreams could be fulfilled only in a "new center." Despite an insecure private life (he is on wife number four) and criticism that he lacks deeply rooted convictions and vision, he has made full use of his extraordinary speaking abilities, his telegenic good looks, and his pragmatic bent. He has forged close ties with Germany's business community, serving on Volkswagen's governing board. Because of his ties with VW, he is the first chancellor not to be chauffeured by Mercedes–Benz automobiles; Audis whisk him around. In the September 1998 *Bundestag* elections, he led the *SPD* to a decisive victory. It captured 40.9% of the votes and 298 seats, seriously reducing the conservative presence in the East, North, and much of the West. For the first time in FRG history, the combined parties of the left won both a majority of votes and of seats in the lower house.

Many observers (reportedly including Schröder himself) had expected a grand coalition of *SPD* and *CDU/CSU* to rule Germany after the elections. But the *SPD's* dramatic gains and the conservatives' shocking loss of 8% of its votes enabled the *Social Democrats* to form a coalition with the *Greens* that enjoyed a 21–seat majority. That coalition turned out to be very divided during its first half–year. Traditionalists (led by Lafontaine, who took the post as finance minister), who advocated anti–business neo–Keynsian policies, clashed with modernists (led by Schröder) who wanted to work with business to overcome unemployment. Schröder seemed not to be in full control. This perception was strengthened by serious conflicts with his *Green* partners, who pushed hard for a quick timetable for phasing out Germany's nuclear power. The *Frankfurter Allgemeine Zeitung* spoke of a "madhouse," and *Die Woche* wrote of "no guts, no power, no new departure." In March 1999 the boil was lanced, and Lafontaine resigned all his political posts and seat in the *Bundestag*. Schröder assumed the chairmanship of the party and set about to establish order in his party and government.

Communists

The German Communist Party (DKP) in the western part of Germany, and its equivalent in Berlin, the Socialist Initiative (*SI*, formerly the Socialist Unity Party of West Berlin SEW), remain as irrelevant as ever. They were badly battered by the collapse of Communism in the GDR, to which they were always uncritically servile. They suffered great losses in membership and capacity for action; the cut–off of funds from the GDR shattered their party organizations, and their leaders no longer have the confidence of the rank–and–file. They have lost their theoretical bearings. Only the highly diverse collection of Marxist–Leninist, Trotskyite,

Germany (FRG)

anarchist and autonomist sects, which maintained independence from the ruling Communist parties in East Berlin and Moscow, remains stable. As always, they are impotent at election time and have only a minuscule following, but they can make their presence known in demonstrations, squattings, and terrorist actions.

Only the *Party of Democratic Socialism* (*PDS*) is a credible electoral and parliamentary political force in former East Germany. However, it is burdened by its own history, being the heir to the *SED*, which misruled the GDR for 40 years. Antipathy against the party is kept alive by continuing revelations about financial scandals and outrageous *Stasi* activities, such as its harboring and training former West German terrorists in the GDR. Prosecutors issued arrest warrants for former top East German leaders for ordering that persons attempting to escape from the GDR be killed. From 1961 to 1989, about 350 lost their lives this way. As Joachim Gauck, director of the agency investigating *Stasi* files, admitted: "Charges, accusations. The memories, the pain and sadness, the failures—that will last very long. We must face it. We must show ourselves that injustice, and especially injustice in high places, does not pay."

Its appeal is restricted to the eastern parts of reunified Germany and Berlin. It casts itself as a party which has purged itself of Stalinism, but not of socialism. In the 1990 and 1994 federal electoral campaigns its leader was the only media star in a very mixed bag of socialists. Gregor Gysi is a witty, brilliant East Berlin lawyer who, being Jewish, is a rarity in modern German politics. He had made a name for himself by defending dissidents in the GDR. He declared: "I was already defending political victims when your Kohls and Strausses gave Honecker billions in credits!" He tried to give the party a modern, fresh image, and his followers wore buttons in 1990 reading in English: "Take it easy Gysi!" He filled halls whenever he appeared in the West, and the victors were predominantly young people who liked his unconventional and open style and refusal to speak in communist "functionary's Chinese."

For the 1990 federal elections it formed a "*Left List/PDS*," of which it was the senior partner. This alliance garnered only .3% of the votes in the West and 11.1% in the East, for a total of 2.4% nation-wide. For this election only, the 5% hurdle was waived for new parties, so the *PDS* was given 17 seats in the *Bundestag*. Gysi won a directly elected seat in East Berlin's Hellersdorf–Marzahn, a very unusual feat for a candidate from a small party.

The 1990 elections made it seem that the party's downward trend, beginning with

PDS's Gregor Gysi

the March 1990 GDR elections, was continuing. It was viewed as the heir to the discredited *SED* and as representative of the interests of former *SED* members, who make up a majority of the *PDS's* membership. It capitalizes on the problems felt in the East: disappointment, insecurity, unemployment, comparatively lower wages, and the view that eastern Germany has

"The first time—PDS. Close your eyes when kissing. Open them when voting"

been taken over by arrogant West Germans and their uncaring capitalist economic system. It receives many protest votes against the established national parties, which seem to focus their attention mainly on the West.

The party's momentum continued in 1994. In Saxony–Anhalt its votes became crucial in keeping a minority *SPD* government alive. In the federal elections it captured 19.8% of easterners' votes (but only .9% of westerners'). More important, by capturing four of the five directly–elected seats in its stronghold of eastern Berlin, it benefited from an almost forgotten route around the 5% clause into the *Bundestag*: to give regional parties the possibility of gaining a significant parliamentary presence, the founders decided that any party that can win at least three direct mandates should receive a number of seats proportional to its overall percentage of votes. Thus, the *PDS,* which won 4.4% nation–wide, was awarded 30 *Bundestag* seats in 1994. This was a very colorful mixture of representatives, which included nine westerners, about half women, a lesbian activist, the great grandson of Otto von Bismarck, an author of steamy short stories, and several non–party members. One was Stefan Heym, a former Jewish emigre to the U.S. He fought as an American soldier against Germany and then settled in the GDR in 1952 to become one of its most acclaimed novelists. He defeated the top *Social Democrat* in the East, Wolfgang Thierse (who became *Bundestag* president in 1998). As the oldest member of the *Bundestag*, Heym opened the first session. *Christian Democrats* demonstrably ignored his words. In 1995 he resigned his seat.

In the 1998 *Bundestag* elections the *PDS* continued its climb by winning 5.1% of the votes, almost all in the East. Although it again won four direct seats in eastern Berlin, this is the first time that it cleared the 5% hurdle and would have entered the *Bundestag* anyway. It gained five seats for a total of 35. Its electoral gains in 1998 were even more significant in *Land* politics in the East. In Saxony–Anhalt it already tolerates and thereby keeps in power an *SPD* minority government. By winning 24.4% of the votes in the Mecklenburg– West Pomeranian elections, held on the same day as the *Bundestag* vote, it was able for the first time to enter a *Land* government; it is the junior partner in history's first *SPD–PDS* governing coalition. It was widely expected that similar coalitions would follow elsewhere. But as the only major German party to oppose NATO's bombing campaign against Yugoslavia in 1999, the *PDS* at least temporarily became too awkward a partner for the *SPD*.

Germany (FRG)

Greens

The *Greens* were the first new party in over 25 years to find its way into the federal parliament. Their presence affected not only the ability to form stable governments, but also the tone and style of parliamentary government. In the late 1980s it helped reduce the radicalism which had buffeted the FRG from the mid–1960s to the early 1980s. The key to their earlier success was their focus on environmental problems, which most Germans view as having reached crisis proportions. This is why all parties turned their attention to this issue and robbed the *Greens* of their monopoly on it. Ecological problems are particularly acute in eastern Germany, where the former Communist rulers showed appalling disregard for the environment.

Atomic power? No thanks!
The Greens

In 1990 their eternal in–fighting, rejection of German unity, absence of a positive program, and ambivalence toward taking responsibility in government caught up with them. Grossly misreading the popular mood supporting unity, western *Greens* adopted the slogan, "Everybody talks about Germany; we talk about the weather!" Failing to unite their parties for the *Bundestag* elections, Western German *Greens* received only 4.8% of the votes in the West and were therefore ejected from parliament, to their shock and dismay. An election coalition of eastern German *Greens* and *Alliance 90*, a collection of eastern German grassroots groups which organized the 1989 revolution, won 6% of the votes in the East (1.2% nationwide) and eight seats under the special election law which applied only to the 1990 elections.

The party was split between realists (*Realos*), who favored accepting government posts to achieve the party's goals, and the fundamentalists (*Fundis*), who argued that the party had tarnished its image by ceasing to be an exclusively opposition force and by entering an "arrangement with capitalism." In 1991 the inevitable occurred: The *Fundis* broke away from the *Greens* and formed their own *Ecological Left/Alternative List*, which vowed to concentrate on strengthening non–parliamentary opposition, but it became politically irrelevant. This split made the *Realos* more respectable in the eyes of some voters. In 1993 the eastern and western parties merged, calling themselves *Alliance '90/Greens*, or *Greens* for short. They staged a political comeback in 1994, winning 7.3% of the votes (7.8% in the West and 5.3% in the East) and 49 seats. In 1998 the party dipped slightly to 6.7% of the votes and 47 seats. But this was sufficient to enable the *Greens* to enter the federal government for the first time. Its leader, Joschka Fischer, a school dropout and activist, who once gave his profession as "street–revolutionary," became foreign minister. He is a brilliant and humorous speaker with great political skill in forging unity in a party that was created to oppose party discipline and establishment politics. Fischer proved himself to be a reliable partner to Gerhard Schröder, even though his party was forceful in pressing on the *SPD* its ideas concerning ecological taxes and a rapid shut–down of Germany's 19 nuclear power plants.

Perhaps Fischer's greatest challenge is to reconcile the *Greens'* anti–establishment roots with a yearning to prove that they are capable of serving as responsible ruling partners. He labored to keep his party unified behind the NATO bombing of Yugoslavia to stop ethnic cleansing in Kosovo. He argued that Germany had emerged from the Second World War with two firm convictions: "never again war" and "never again Auschwitz." Recognizing the contradiction, he reasoned that in order to prevent crimes against humanity, Germany must sometimes be prepared to put aside its pacifism, which runs deep in German society and especially in the *Green* party.

Not all of his party comrades agree. In a raucous special party conference called in May 1999 to discuss a bombing halt, Fischer was pelted so hard by red paint that he suffered a perforated ear drum. A human chain tried to block delegates' entry into the hall, and posters depicted Fischer and Schröder with Hitler–style mustaches. Stink bombs were set off in the arena, fights for control of the microphone broke out, and one man strolled naked in front of the dais to mock the leaders' efforts to maintain some decorum. Fischer was decried as a "warmonger." In the end, a proposal calling for a permanent halt to NATO airstrikes was turned back, but delegates voted in favor of a temporary suspension of the bombing. Polls show Fischer as Germany's most popular politician with a 72% approval rating, and he is the party's most potent political asset.

Perhaps more important than the *Greens'* parliamentary presence was their ability to mobilize hundreds of thousands of persons for mass demonstrations against the federal government's defense policy, or against a state government's plans to build a nuclear power, or reprocessing plant or to expand the Frankfurt airport. Some feared that it could threaten the democratic regime.

In the past, mass movements weakened and ultimately destroyed the Weimar Republic. For this reason, the founders of the FRG created a purely parliamentary democracy, rather than one in which a plebiscite is possible. The ad–hoc groups in the western part are often held together by idealistic, romantic and frequently impractical political conceptions with anti–statist overtones. Most of their supporters are non–violent, but a minority is quite prepared to disregard the law, property and public order.

These groups did not encompass the small group of urban terrorists who belonged to such underground groups as the *Red Army Faction (RAF)* who displayed precious little regard for the sanctity of life and limb and who failed to provoke the kind of extreme reaction they have sought. In 1998 the *RAF* was disbanded, and in May 1999 one of the last members still at large, Barbara Meyer, turned herself in to German authorities.

Leftist parties in Germany can no longer assume that they can easily attract the country's youth, whose attitudes have changed considerably since the late 1960s. Recession and unemployment have concentrated young minds and caused radicalism to give way to conservatism among many young Germans. Succeeding in the existing system is more important than changing it.

Right–Wing Parties

The 1990s witnessed a strengthening of parties on the far right, a development which causes anxiety in both the FRG and abroad. They range from illegal neo–Nazi groups to legal parties which feed on myriad dissatisfactions, including hostility toward immigrants, tight housing, high unemployment, and rising crime. Some Germans bemoan what they see as a

Germany (FRG)

breakdown in law and order caused by the leftist alternative subculture.

The *Republicans* claim to be a nationalist, not a neo–Nazi party, but in 1992 the government ordered intelligence surveillance of it to determine if it is antidemocratic. It found a warm reception in western Berlin, where more than 10% of the population is foreign; the 150,000 Turks living there constitute the largest Turkish community outside of Turkey and the third largest in the world. The *Republicans* call for repatriation of foreign workers in stages and for tough measures to stem the flow of asylum–seekers into the FRG, noting that "a multiracial society is a red flag to our party." It decries the Maastricht treaty as "Versailles without war" and a sell–out of German interests. The party's image has been tarnished by unpopular skinhead violence against foreigners, including the American national sledding team in the eastern German city of Oberhof.

The *Republican's* 1.8% showing in the 1998 *Bundestag* demonstrated its electoral irrelevance. The same can be said of the *National Democratic Party of Germany (NPD)*, once a refuge for unreconstructed Nazis. It is more conservative than the *Republicans* and won only .3% of the votes in 1998. Also fishing for votes on the rightist fringe is the *German People's Union (DVU)*, which in 1998 captured only 1.2% of the votes. The three parties' puny total of 3.3% in the 1998 *Bundestag* elections was a great relief to the FRG. However, their ability to score as high as 12.9% in certain *Land* elections, as they did in Saxony–Anhalt earlier in 1998, where they won many young persons' votes, shows that they can be useful collectors of protest votes.

In 1992 the government outlawed six neo–Nazi groups, including *German Alternative*, which was involved in anti–foreigner violence. In 1995 it banned the small, militant *Free German Workers' Party*. The scores of right–wing nationalist and neo–Nazi groups do not follow one leader. But they are better organized, more dangerous, and in closer contact with each other than most Germans had thought they were. Their effect on Germany's international image can be devastating despite their electoral impotence.

Republicans' Franz Schönhuber

The FRG: A Stable Democracy

The significance of the current problems facing the established political parties in the wake of unification should not be exaggerated. The FRG has weathered other serious problems in the past: moral, political and economic regeneration after 1945, a student rebellion in the late 1960s, urban terrorism, fundamental political changes such as the Eastern Treaties and the economic shocks of the 1970s. The democratic order of the FRG has over the years earned and received a reservoir of good will from its citizens to help it survive serious crises. This reservoir springs not from the actual constitutional structure, but from Germans' political attitudes. That is, it depends on the political culture—those political ways of thinking which provide the basis for a workable political system. The FRG has become more than a fair–weather democracy which would collapse quickly if confronted with a crisis.

There are, of course, problems. Prof. Kurt Sontheimer argued that the intense student protests of the 1960s and 1970s radicalized a portion of Germany's intellectuals and created a less tolerant, liberal, more aggressive, uncompromising political and intellectual climate. He feared that the resulting negatively critical and marxist–oriented approach which became popular could weaken the theoretical underpinnings of liberal democracy and induce many citizens to misuse the free political order in order to destroy it, as had happened during the Weimar Republic.

It was fear of such misuse which prompted the *Social–Liberal* coalition to adopt the Extremists Decision in 1972 (known by its opponents as the *Berufsverbot*—"bar to profession"). This was an attempt to serve the constitutional requirement that West German democracy be on guard against those who might attempt to misuse personal freedoms to undermine the democratic order. The Weimar Republic is often remembered as a "democracy without democrats," in which far too few civil servants were prepared or inclined to defend the government. Therefore, the Basic Law stipulates that all applicants for civil service must guarantee that they are prepared actively to support at all times the free and democratic order.

There was considerable wisdom in the framer's decision to create a "democracy on guard," but there are many problems in attempting to achieve this goal. As memories of Nazi terror fade, Germans find it more difficult to define convincingly democracy and democratic behavior. Few would argue with ex–Chancellor Schmidt's observation that a person who smears obscenities on Jewish grave stones does not belong in state service two weeks later. But, as one astute observer stated, "democracy is the right of the majority to be wrong, and if that majority is 2/3, it can be wrong about anything it wishes."

However, should a person who *in his youth* joined a radical movement which

Germany's largest banking center: Frankfurt/Main

Germany (FRG)

preached the destruction of pluralist, parliamentary democracy be considered an anti–democrat the *rest of his life?* This question of whether the Extremists Decision should be applied to former communists is relevant in eastern Germany today, where many judges, professors, teachers, researchers, and civil servants have been removed from their jobs because they had been active members of the *SED*.

One sometimes hears of radical criticism of "bourgeois society" and of the allegedly "pseudo–democratic" and "illegitimate" political order. Such criticism is very audible and is also scribbled on the walls. Yet, there is, in fact, no "legitimacy crisis" in the FRG. During its entire existence as a state, the FRG has not faced a single truly serious challenge to its legitimacy; this stands in stark contrast to the Weimar Republic, which was born into such a crisis and never extricated itself from it. The FRG made remarkable strides to win the approval and support of its citizens. The challenge now is to win eastern Germans' support as well and to make them feel like "first–class citizens." A 1991 poll revealed that 90% of eastern Germans considered themselves to be "second-class citizens" in their new country, and a third of their western countrymen agreed.

Sensible observation of the FRG, combined with an examination of relevant public opinion surveys, indicates that the West German political culture had changed considerably over the past four decades, and that the FRG is a stable and democratic country with a politically interested, informed, involved and tolerant citizenry. Immediately after the war, after excessive political mobilization and propaganda under Hitler, Germans tended to withdraw from public affairs and to seek refuge in private and family circles. Now Germans in both parts are no less active in public or political affairs than their counterparts in older democracies such as the U.S. and Holland. In terms of party membership, attendance at political gatherings and especially in voting, they are even more active than those counterparts.

A few facts help demonstrate Germans' overall satisfaction with their regime, at least in the western part. In 1951, 90% of all adult West Germans believed that Germany had been better off during an earlier German regime, and a third even favored *restoration of the Hohenzollern monarchy.* By 1976, however, ninety percent thought they were better off under the present scheme, and almost no one wanted the restoration of the monarchy. This is due to many western citizens' positive experience under democracy. Their country has had a high level of accomplishment. Prosperity and the expanded social welfare system smoothed class conflicts and allowed all groups in the society more benefits from the system and a greater opportunity to advance.

The FRG is a functioning democracy in which only a small percentage of Germans are asking whether the FRG should remain a democracy. The criticism that Germans have become very materialist is certainly valid. But while materialism might be rejected in principle (but seldom in practice) by some leftists and intellectuals, it has no doubt made the FRG far more governable and respected as a political democracy.

KAL, Baltimore Sun

© 1991 Cartoonists Writers Syndicate

U.S. as Ally

The U.S. relationship has always been and remains very important for the FRG; indeed, no ally supported German unification more resolutely than did the U.S. Like most Europeans, Germans are generally mystified by the American political system. The U.S. is a large, highly decentralized country whose national powers are separated and distributed to competing and sometimes almost hostile institutions in the nation's capital. Such separation of powers is particularly significant in foreign policy because it often makes it impossible for a president to *produce* that which he had *promised* foreign leaders. The American political system enables unknown persons of various professional backgrounds to rise to the highest national political offices through a painfully long and complicated electoral system largely unfathomable in Europe. Because of the parliamentary system in the FRG, aspirants for the highest offices must enter politics at an early age and deal with a wide variety of political problems while they slowly work their way to the top.

In stark contrast, the unique American selection system permits a person to arrive in the White House who had pursued a non–political career and who might have little political experience. This is why many Germans are so shocked to see that a former peanut farmer or actor could almost suddenly appear in the White House. Since Europeans focus almost exclusively on American national politics, they are often unaware of presidents' prior political activity at the state or local level.

Germans are particularly troubled by the fact that a newly–elected president may have notably little experience in foreign affairs and that it is he who has the power to select a maze of foreign policy advisers, secretaries and under–secretaries and agency chiefs, many of whom might also have had little or no foreign policy experience. Such a presidential

Germany (FRG)

"team" is often permitted to operate in what seems like an uncoordinated way and frequently sends off widely differing signals, something which inevitably creates doubts about American leadership capabilities and about the continuity of American foreign policy. Americans must remember that the image of the U.S. and its leaders is in itself an important factor in European politics.

Foreign and Defense Policy

The FRG became more independent and critical of the U.S., and it is more willing to side with its European allies on some issues, such as supporting the French demand in 1996 that the U.S. relinquish its leadership of NATO's Southern Command in Naples, Italy. It is less restrained by the embarrassing German past and has been confronted with a diminution of Russian, French, and British power in Europe. Also, Washington was absorbed during the 1960s and early 1970s with Vietnam and a new relationship with the Soviet Union and the People's Republic of China. The FRG increasingly shouldered political responsibilities and exercised diplomatic flexibility throughout the world. Because of its past, the FRG prefers a low–key, quieter diplomacy which would be least likely to arouse fear or envy in other countries. For the first time in its history, Germany has clearly defined borders not disputed by any nation. It has neither destabilizing minorities abroad nor any claims to former German territories. Nevertheless, the cliché that the FRG was an "economic giant and a political dwarf" is outdated.

In his first policy statement in the all–German *Bundestag*, ex–Chancellor Kohl pledged that "there is no comfortable niche in international politics for us Germans, and we must not shirk our responsibility." The united nation will, he promised, not be a "restless *Reich*." A new Germany in a new kind of Europe has emerged, and it is realistic that the continent's largest and richest democracy bears more responsibility in a world with a considerably weaker Russia. This is not a role which Germany seeks, but one which is thrust upon it.

The new Germany displayed its willingness to use its new political clout in 1991 when it muscled its EU partners to recognize the independence of the Yugoslav republics of Slovenia and Croatia, despite serious misgivings in London, Paris, Washington, and the UN. It was especially noteworthy that Bonn did not even reply to a formal U.S. request to withhold such recognition. Uncomfortable with bad feelings that unilateral action caused, Germany was careful to get allied backing before recognizing Macedonia in 1993, a move which Greece bitterly opposed.

In 1992 it asked the EU to grant the German language equal status with English and French in meetings and documents, even though surveys show that Germans are more likely to speak foreign languages than any other EU citizens except the Dutch. Since unification German is the most widely spoken language in the EU and is experiencing a revival in eastern Europe. Said one German diplomat: "We have the size and the importance now to work in our own language."

Germany and the Second Gulf War

Germany dealt clumsily with its first test as a strengthened power. When fighting broke out in the Gulf on January 17, 1991, it took a week for the government to show solidarity with its allies. The fear that Germany would be dragged into the war by joining a defense of Turkey, one of Germany's NATO allies, prompted the government to insist that it would not become involved. No other ally had disputed Turkey's right to be defended by the full force of NATO.

While it was paralyzed, opponents of the war efforts took over in the streets and denounced the U.S. and Iraq both as aggressors. "Say no!" and "No blood for oil," read the posters. The mayor of tiny Pfedelbach in the Black Forest was forced to withdraw his invitation to General Norman Schwarzkopf to visit the town from where his ancestors came when angry anti–war residents branded the war hero as a "mass murderer." An exasperated finance minister, Theo Waigel, exclaimed: "Again and again we see a misconceived pacifism which does not restore peace but puts up with the aggressor!" The *Frankfurter Allgemeine Zeitung* agreed: "What distinguishes the Germans from other peoples is not that they fear war, but that they fear war more than they love freedom." It added: "Many Germans have obviously not understood what is being fought for in the Middle East." Polls a few days after hostilities commenced revealed that four out of five Germans indeed agreed with the allies' war effort and were critical of the anti–American rallies, but three out of four opposed German participation in the war.

Germany's allies and Israel were furious, and matters were made worse when it was revealed that firms from Germany had sent Iraq the technology for chemical and nuclear weapons. It is the world's fifth largest arms exporter and world's leader in exports of missiles and launchers; arms account for 5% of its exports. Even worse, it also had built military bunkers, including the Iraqi dictator's luxury bunker in Baghdad. It was also alleged, though later disproved, that German firms had helped Iraq extend the range of its Scud missiles so that they could reach targets in Israel. The devastating impression created of the Jewish state being bombarded, with German help, by rockets thought capable of delivering gas (some of which was related to the Zyklon B used in the Nazi gas chambers) and chemicals, was too much. After regaining its composure, the Kohl government acted decisively by criticizing the 'one–eyed' protestors, cracking down on firms breaking its arms export laws, and sending emissaries to Israel. It agreed to deliver weapons, including Patriot missiles, to the Jewish state, violating Germany's long–standing policy of not sending weapons into 'areas of tension.'

The German government went even farther, crossing some important thresholds: It dispatched a thousand soldiers to Turkey equipped with 18 fighter aircraft and Roland and Hawk missiles to protect NATO airbases; this was the first time since the Second World War that German military forces had been sent abroad in response to a threat of war. It also sent 2,200 naval forces with minesweepers and frigates to the eastern Mediterranean and offered more than $11 billion to aid the allies. It served as the hub of the resupply effort, provided doctors for allied military hospitals in Germany freeing allied doctors to serve in the Gulf, gave precision–guided weapons and vehicles to its allies for use there. It gave the U.S. Army alone 1,000 vehicles, including Czech–made tank transporters, which former East German soldiers had to instruct the Americans how to use.

Arguing after the conclusion of hostilities for the need to render humanitarian

Germany (FRG)

On winter maneuvers

aid to the war's victims and to open up the Persian Gulf to free trade, Germany sent 2,000 troops and airlift assets to Iran to help Kurdish refugees, as well as minesweepers to the Gulf to help clear out Iraqi mines. Although these measures met with almost no protest in the FRG, it emerged from the crisis damaged by the charges that it had shown ingratitude for the diplomatic help it had received to achieve unification and had let its allies down in time of emergency.

Kohl's intention to amend the constitution to allow Germany to join in international coalitions was successfully blocked by the *SPD; it* refused to allow *Bundeswehr* troops to participate in anything more than UN peacekeeping forces. Germany seeks a permanent seat on the UN Security Council, not for itself but for the EU. In 1992 it sent three spotter aircraft and a naval destroyer to help enforce the UN sanctions against Serbia and Montenegro, and it sent a *Bundeswehr* unit with a UN mission to Cambodia, where Germans suffered their first fatality since joining peacekeeping operations. In 1993 it assisted in the American airlift of humanitarian aid to Bosnia. That same year the Constitutional Court ruled in a landmark decision that it was not unconstitutional for German airmen to serve in AWACS reconnaissance planes supporting NATO enforcement of a no–fly zone over Bosnia. They became the first *Bundeswehr* soldiers to take part in a potential combat mission since 1945.

In 1993 the FRG dispatched 1,700 troops to join the U.N. effort in Somalia; these were the first German soldiers to serve in Africa since General Rommel's *Afrikakorps* in the Second World War. In 1994 the Constitutional Court ruled that German troops may join military ventures abroad as long as they are acting under the aegis of the United Nations or another international group (such as NATO) to which Germany belongs and provided that a majority in the lower house of parliament approves. In 1995 the FRG dispatched 14 Tornado fighter jets for duty over Bosnia. This was the first German combat unit deployed since 1945. It also sent peacekeeping forces to help implement the Bosnian peace agreement later in the year. Each of these "out–of–area" operations was subjected to intense and emotional debate within Germany. But when the government agreed to commit 3,000 troops, including armored infantry, to the 30,000–soldier "Stabilization Force" in Bosnia in 1997, almost no one in Germany raised any objection. The *Social Democrats* and *Greens*, then in the opposition, backed the plan.

Germany is cautiously but steadily overcoming its postwar aversion to the use of military force. With the Balkans as a testing ground, the *Bundeswehr's* emergence as an international intervention force is helping to diminish Germany's subordinate role within NATO. When the alliance launched an air war against Yugoslavia in the spring of 1999 to stop brutal ethnic cleansing in Kosovo, Germany was a full participant. It sent eight combat aircraft and a warship, and it dispatched several thousand troops to neighboring Macedonia. This was the first time since World War II that Germany engaged in warfare against a sovereign state. In Chancellor Schröder's words, "we are trying to contain the on–going human catastrophe—to stop the killings and deportations. . . . NATO has to win this military conflict."

According to opinion polls, most Germans agreed. One survey even suggested that a stunning 90% of young Germans aged 18 to 24 now support NATO. But there is a clear split between western Germans and those in the East: 64% in the West back the bombing, compared with only 40% in the East. The *PDS* is the only major political party that opposed the war. The war over Kosovo helped Germans, who emerged from the Third Reich with a powerful aversion to any use of force, to cross a large and significant psychological boundary. Leading them across this line were three persons—Chancellor Schröder, Foreign Minister Fischer, and Defense Minister Rudolf Scharping—who are products of the "1968 generation" and who as young men were critical of America and skeptical of NATO.

Armed Forces

Unification and the collapse of the Soviet empire in central Europe profoundly affected the size and the mission of the Federal Armed Forces (*Bundeswehr*). Since 1991 the military's budget has been cut by 15%; by 1999 the FRG was spending only 1.7% of its GDP (compared with 3.6% in the U.S.) on defense. However, it remains the largest NATO land army in Europe and also contains a formidable air force and a small navy which operates in the North and Baltic Seas. Almost all German soldiers are assigned to NATO, the supreme commander of which is always an American general.

Soon after unification the *Bundeswehr* began a unique effort of merging two formerly hostile armies into one. About 25,000 professional East German soldiers who were judged to be reliable defenders of Germany's democratic order became a part of a combined force which, in compliance with an agreement made with the Soviet Union in July 1990, numbers 340,000 troops, only half of whom are draftees.

The same agreement specified that no western German units were to be deployed on former GDR territory until Rus-

Germany (FRG)

FRG army officers confer during maneuvers

sia had withdrawn its 375,000 troops by August 31, 1994, and that no foreign troops and nuclear weapons will ever be stationed there. On September 8, 1994, the last Allied soldiers departed from Berlin, leaving the city free of foreign troops for the first time since 1945.

Germany retains its conscript army on the principle that it is a vital link between the military and society. The founders of the *Bundeswehr* feared the creation of a "state within a state," as was the case during the Weimar Republic. Males in both parts of Germany are required to perform 10 months of military service, unless they are judged to be conscientious objectors, in which case they must perform 13 months of alternative civilian duty. As more and more of its NATO allies abolish conscription and create professional armies, and as the shrinking *Bundeswehr* inducts progressively fewer young males so that the system might seem to become patently unfair, more voices are being raised to advocate a professional army, such as those the U.S., UK, and France have. In a 1996 poll 56% of Germans favored a volunteer army, while only 29% opposed the idea. Another aspect of military service is also being rethought and debated: the role of females. Currently they are only permitted to serve in the medical and musical corps. But there is little enthusiastic support among women's groups, and an expanded use of female soldiers is not likely soon if ever. Almost all German units are assigned to NATO, the supreme commander of which is always an American general.

NATO strategy has been reexamined in a fundamental way to adapt to the post–Cold War era in which the Warsaw Pact has ceased to exist. It was discovered in 1993 just how threatening and prepared that pact had been. Documents found in the former GDR revealed that East German and Soviet planners had drawn up detailed and regularly updated plans for a military invasion of West Germany. They had already made street signs for western cities (renaming such streets as Düsseldorf's Königsallee "Karl Marx Allee"), printed money for their occupation government, built equipment to run broad–gauged Russian trains on western tracks, stocked more ammunition for the 160,000–man National People's Army than was possessed by the half–million–man *Bundeswehr*, and made up medals for officers who performed well in the conquest.

Germany's strategic situation dramatically changed in the 1990s. Its eastern flank used to confront directly the Warsaw Pact countries with no buffer against a heavily–armed, suspicious and unpredictable Soviet Union. Now a larger Germany faces an unthreatening group of eastern European democracies who desperately want to become NATO and EU partners. Beyond them is an unstable Russia with a demoralized and poorly–equipped military and an elected government that is trying to strengthen democratic and capitalist reforms. No longer is the focus on blunting an all–out Russian attack on NATO forces concentrated in Germany, necessitating a "forward defense" by "layer–caked" NATO forces along an inter–German border. The future danger might come from undetermined threats to any NATO member state, from Norway to Turkey; they might emanate from non–European countries, such as Iraq against Turkey, or from unknown dangers springing from violent national unrest in Central Europe or the former Soviet Union.

To respond to a wide range of threats in the 21st century, Germany has integrated some of its units into multi–national divisions and corps within NATO: a Dutch–German corps under alternate command has been formed. British, German and Belgian troops constitute a lightly–equipped multinational rapid–reaction force with an air mobile brigade. A corps has been created with headquarters along Germany's eastern border in Szczecin, Poland, that comprises Polish, German and Danish troops. This unit was modelled on the French–German "Eurocorps" in Strasbourg, France, created in 1992. A U.S. combat division serves in a German–led corps, while a German division is part of a U.S.–led corps. Like all these joint units, it can be used to defend member states, serve in peacekeeping missions, or operate under WEU aegis.

American forces permanently stationed in Europe have shrunk to about 100,000, with about 75,000 in Germany. No European country, including Germany, wants the total withdrawal of American troops. While insisting that "the Alliance and the presence of U.S. troops in Europe remains indispensable for our security," the German government believes that a common European foreign policy must, in the long run, include a common security and defense policy in some form. Europeans are discussing a distinct European Security and Defence Identity (ESDI). Karsten Voigt, in charge of U.S. policy in the foreign ministry, stated that "you cannot ask about a European identity if Germans don't take part." A consensus exists in the EU that such an identity is necessary, while preserving NATO in one form or the other. Americans have often called on Europeans to bear a greater responsibility for their own defense, but not in competition with NATO.

NATO still retains a diminished role for nuclear weapons. Traditionally, FRG governments have always supported a NATO defense strategy which calls for the use of nuclear weapons in the event that an enemy attack cannot be stopped by means of conventional arms. Considering the collapse of the Soviet Union, Foreign Minister Fischer called on NATO in November 1998 to rethink its nuclear "first–use" policy. However, this request was dropped when the U.S., UK and France rejected the notion as premature. Since the FRG refuses to possess nuclear, chemical or biological weapons (although it does possess multi–purpose weapons capable of delivering nuclear warheads), it must rely on its allies, particularly the U.S., to provide the kind of nuclear deterrence which would be necessary to dissuade a potential aggressor from either attacking the FRG in the first place, or from continuing such an attack.

Germany (FRG)

To underscore its determination to defend the FRG, the U.S. maintains a drastically declining number of nuclear weapons in the western part of the FRG. The nuclear strategy presents the FRG with a certain dilemma, however: Germany's defense (and ultimately its very existence as a free country) is dependent upon weapons which are under the exclusive control of foreign, albeit friendly, powers. But it does not want to have a finger even close to a nuclear trigger, as it showed again in 1995, when it politely rejected France's invitation to develop a joint nuclear policy and to share the French nuclear umbrella.

Severe domestic criticism of the FRG's defense policy was unleashed by NATO's "Two–Track Decision" in 1979 to deploy American intermediate–range nuclear forces (INF) in Europe. Schmidt was the most persistent and influential proponent of the plan, and his government fully supported it. The FRG's key role in having this decision adopted, and the domestic reaction to it reveal a unique German problem as far as U.S. nuclear weapons are concerned. On the one hand, the FRG has always harbored fears that the United States might disengage its nuclear forces from the defense of the FRG; that is, it fears that the "American guarantee" could be withdrawn.

On the other hand, many Germans fear nothing more than that the Americans might just decide to use their nuclear weapons to defend Western Europe after all. Failure to prevent the Pershing missile deployment in 1983 left the "peace movement" divided and disillusioned. Nevertheless, the government is compelled to pay heed to domestic opinions on defense questions. It must explain to the public far more persuasively the necessity and rationale for the country's defense and for its military collaboration with the NATO and the United States.

This was enormously alleviated by dramatic announcements in 1991 of unilateral American nuclear cuts which were matched by the shaken Soviet Union. The greatest impact was on Europe, where the only targets for tactical nuclear weapons were in areas which are no longer enemies, such as Poland and eastern Germany. Germans, who lived in the midst of the world's heaviest concentration of atomic weapons, were especially delighted, as Kohl indicated: "President Bush's decision implies that all American short–range nuclear weapons and the nuclear artillery will be removed from German soil. In the name of all Germans I want to thank the President for that." By 1992 all U.S. tactical nuclear weapons had been withdrawn from Europe.

The "Peace Movement"

By the 1980s it had become visible to the entire world that the FRG's defense policy was being challenged not only within the established parties, but in public opinion as well. The "peace movement" was an extremely varied group of activists. Its ranks included party members from the *SPD* and *FDP*, ecologists, church circles, a multitude of smaller humanitarian groups, a blue ribbon assemblage of intellectuals, well–organized, highly visible but numerically small communist splinter groups and several security experts.

The majority consistently opposed the total withdrawal of U.S. troops from Germany (the largest concentration of American armed forces overseas). Nevertheless, Germans increasingly felt the physical burden of almost a half million allied soldiers on their soil. They called for drastic reductions in bothersome low–level train-

Copyright 1987 by Herblock in *The Washington Post*

Germany (FRG)

ing flights and ground maneuvers, even after the 1991 war in the Persian Gulf. Such calls came in the wake of almost universal revulsion caused by a disaster in August 1988 at an air show at Ramstein Air Base, which left 70 persons dead. There have been frequent accidents in the FRG involving NATO aircraft which caused Germans to ask themselves about the blessings of so many foreign troops in their country.

Pacifism can scarcely be detected within the established political parties and institutions. But largely unpolitical pacifist motives inspire the left, church circles, the ecology movement and generally the young persons who swell the ranks of the "peace movement." Pacifists do not oppose nuclear weapons in Europe merely because they are horrified of a possible nuclear war on German soil. More than that, *they oppose the very idea of a military defense of their country.*

No other NATO country has such a large percentage of its population which seeks to avoid compulsory 10–month military service by claiming status as conscientious objectors. This right is anchored in the Basic Law, but it was originally intended for a small group of truly *conscientious* objectors. There are scores of C.O. organizations, and many churches and other groups are active in giving advice about how to apply and successfully to argue for such exemption. In 1996 a record total of 160,000 young Germans refused military service. Uneasiness over the Gulf War in 1991 caused a three–fold increase in the monthly applications, as 22,000 refused military service in January. What was more dismaying was that more than 60 of the *Bundeswehr* soldiers deployed to Turkey during the crisis declared their intention to seek C.O. status. It is no wonder that an exasperated Turkish President Ozal uttered: "I think Germany has become so rich that it has completely lost its fighting spirit."

Just how little the *Bundeswehr* is tolerated was revealed in Bremen in 1987, when a monument to the "Unknown Deserter" was publicly displayed. The defense minister waived off explanations that the statue applies only to deserters during the Second World War and argued that it might encourage Germans to avoid military service today. There can be no doubt that soldiers in uniform are not accorded automatic respect. In 1986 a female pastor unleashed a national debate when she refused to commence a marriage ceremony until the groom doffed his military jacket and put on a civilian jacket borrowed from a guest. Such would have been unheard of in pre–1945 Germany. But Germany is a different country. In a 1996 poll to determine the most prestigious occupations in the FRG, military officers placed last, just behind journalists and politicians. In the total population there is some sympathy for a vaguely articulated pacifism. Yet, few Germans are willing to take a concrete step, such as scrapping the *Bundeswehr* or withdrawing from NATO to underscore such sentiments.

After intense domestic debates, Germans, by and large, have come to accept military deterrence as a means to maintain peace. But until the war over Kosovo in 1999 few could accept the notion that the actual use of force is ever justified. There was little room in their minds for a concept of the "just war." For example, the *SPD's* former leader, Björn Engholm, stated baldly while the street demonstrations were occurring in January 1991: "There is no just war."

Many Germans had persuaded themselves that nobody knows the horrors of war better than they do and that they are therefore particularly sensitive to the victims. This is partly a result of western Germany's efforts for decades to drive home the lessons of two world wars that militarism is wrong and war never pays. This black–and–white message is taught in the schools, propagated in the public media, and expressed on public monuments. Everywhere are "peace museums." The idea that war is always wrong had become a kind of ideology in Germany and prevented many Germans from seeing parallels between Hitler's aggression and that of modern dictators. Such perceptions had changed considerably by the end of the century. But Germany's NATO allies should never assume that Germans' caution and hesitancy toward using military force have disappeared.

ECONOMY

The FRG deserves its reputation as an economic giant. It has the strongest economy in Western Europe and is economically the most important member of the EU. Its economic activity is guided by the principle of the social market economy. This means that while it does not permit unrestrained economic competition whatever the social costs, it does openly advocate and support a liberal (free) world trade.

Integrating Eastern Germany's Economy

Germany's unification in 1990 presents the FRG with awesome difficulties and challenges which threaten the peace and stability of German society and which tax the imagination of German leaders. In a way, the problems are even greater than when the FRG had to rebuild a devastated land after 1945. During the 12–year Nazi regime, Germany had maintained the institutional infrastructure of a market economy, private property, a private sector legal code, and an administrative sector which understood the market system. Eastern Germans could not fall back on such continuity in 1990.

During 40 years of communist rule, the economy was continuously plundered, first by the Soviet occupiers in the form of

Auto assembly plant

Germany (FRG)

war reparations, and then by the *SED*, who let the country's capital stock, housing, transportation network, communications systems, and environment degenerate. Enterprises had no resources of their own for investment; profits were sent to the central government, which was stingy in returning money for modernization. The economy was planned from the top, and the country was isolated economically from the capitalist world. Trade of generally shoddy goods was on a state–to–state basis and directed primarily toward the GDR's communist partners in Eastern Europe and the Soviet Union. This "command economy" created hopeless bottlenecks and shortfalls and robbed individuals and firms of the opportunity to apply their own initiative and creativity to improve their economic situation. Only 5% of the workforce worked independently in repair shops, small stores, and restaurants. Citizens were nurtured to be passive, obeying the leaders at the top in return for a guaranteed job and income, which was the highest in the communist world.

Thus, when western Germans woke up from the initial euphoria of unification, they found an economy in the East in which roughly half the workforce in the average company was unproductive, a majority of the companies were uncompetitive in the world market, a third of the country's production had traditionally been exported to countries in the East which could no longer pay for poorly–made and overpriced eastern German goods, most of the property used for industry and farming had been taken out of private hands, environmental neglect had reached crisis proportions and citizens had huge pent–up consumer expectations they hoped would be gratified immediately. Perhaps worst of all, citizens had forgotten over the past four decades how a market system, a private company, and a western legal system operate.

It was in this setting that ex–Chancellor Kohl, who like most German politicians genuinely underestimated the economic difficulties involved with the unparalleled merger of two so different economic systems and who wanted to win the first all–German federal elections, announced that "no one will be worse off" after unity. Such unjustified optimism rapidly instilled disappointment, pessimism, cynicism, fear, deep unrest and rage among eastern Germans when they soon experienced the worst economic collapse in Germany since the Great Depression in 1929–33. Within a month after unification, eastern German industrial output and employment (including short–time work) had fallen by more than a third and was getting steadily worse.

Why did this collapse occur? On July 1, 1990, the western *Deutschmark,* one of the world's hardest currencies, was introduced in the GDR at an exchange rate of one–to–one, even though experts estimated the east mark to have only a quarter of a west mark's value. The Kohl government regarded this as a political necessity to keep the momentum of unity going, but it made no economic sense. Eastern Germany's former communist trading partners could no longer buy its goods, so a third of its customers disappeared. These markets could not be replaced in the West because of the low quality of eastern products. The problem was further aggravated by the fact that East Germans themselves wanted to buy higher quality western goods, rather than goods produced in their own part of Germany. Thus, demand for their products declined even further, while western Germany's economy boomed because of the huge demand in the East.

New Marina for yachts in Hamburg, Germany's second largest city
Courtesy: Germany Information Center

Production costs rose because pay was in a more valuable currency while output was going down. At the same time, wages also rose as East Germans desired to have the same pay level as their countrymen in the West. Within a year of monetary union wages had risen 50% to 80% in many eastern firms, and East Germans' pay had risen to about half that in the West and was steadily going up. These rises occurred despite drastic cuts in productivity; therefore, eastern companies' competitive advantage from cheap labor was destroyed. Run–down East German companies which have had to pay employees at western German wage levels cannot produce goods at prices that people are willing to pay. By mid–1991 fewer than one in ten companies in the East was economically viable. Unless productivity increases, the higher wages climb and more employees have to be laid off to meet the payroll. But

Germany (FRG)

Worker in the electrical industry: Siemens in Berlin

to increase productivity enough to pay high wages, companies need to be dramatically modernized. That is, they desperately need investment, but this was perhaps the greatest disappointment.

It was expected that western companies would invest heavily in the East and thereby cushion the shock of transition to a capitalist economy, but several factors held them back: first is precisely the fact that eastern enterprises are not economically viable. Investors do not want to buy companies which lose money, have antiquated equipment, bloated workforces, unrealistically high wage levels compared with productivity, and environmental liabilities which could bankrupt an investor. East German firms were so careless in polluting the air, soil and water that the clean-up costs could be prohibitive. Legal changes were necessary to relieve new owners of the responsibility for a firm's past pollution. East German factories used high-polluting energy sources, such as brown coal, with a high sulfur content, which will have to be replaced with cleaner fuels at high costs. In many cases it would be cheaper to create new companies rather than to take over problem-ridden old ones.

A second problem was a complicated jumble of property claims resulting from earlier expropriations by the Nazis, the Soviets, and the *SED*. Property taken and redistributed by the Soviets between 1945 and 1949 is not to be returned to former owners, in contrast to that confiscated before and after, with some qualifications. More than a million claims to such property were filed, but the litigation is complicated and time-consuming. This is especially true since local and land government administrations are understaffed and practically bankrupt, and since many East German judges were removed because of their earlier collaboration with the communist state.

Investors are naturally fearful of time— and cost-consuming—litigation involving property claims, and they are therefore inclined to wait until such problems are sorted out before sending in their money. Realizing the difficulty, the federal government, working together with the eastern *Land* governments, finally agreed that property could be sold to investors rather than returned to prior owners (who would be compensated) if this were necessary to create jobs. Not only does the government want to protect jobs in order to quiet fears and unrest in the East, but in order to prevent a massive migration of East Germans into the West. Most want to remain in eastern Germany, but in 1991 an estimated 10,000 persons a month, often those with dynamism and badly-needed skills, were moving westward; several hundred thousand more commute up to eight hours per day to work in the West.

A further problem in stimulating economic activity is that eastern Germans are understandably mystified by the intricate complexity of western German laws and regulations which have been introduced into the East. Anxious East Germans who are suddenly having to live under totally different and unfamiliar rules are buying hastily published paperbacks with titles like *Your Rights as a Tenant, Your Rights as an Employee,* and *How to Deal with the Tax System.* Few know how a capitalist business works and how to start one up; they lack management and financial know-how and are unprepared to dive into a free-market system. Leipzig's mayor spoke of "a whole society far more complicated than any of us realized—everything here is new." Investors, as well as ordinary East Germans, are dismayed to see that management in struggling East German firms, at least below the top level, is still largely the same as during the communist era. Not only are there doubts about how much such managers know about a capitalist system, but also how much they believe in it. Although they may be well educated and experienced, their presence is a psychological blow to those East Germans who had dreamed of starting anew.

Finally, the infrastructure needed for modern business was antiquated: a 1920s vintage telephone and communications system, an absence of modern and pleasant office space, a road network which has barely been maintained since Hitler's time, and a largely non-computer-literate workforce.

To help guide the transition from an unproductive socialist economy to a modern capitalist one, a Trust Agency *(Treuhand)* holding company was established. With a staff of 3,000 by mid-1991, its job after unity was to try to privatize at reasonable prices and as quickly as possible the huge empire of former East German state assets, consisting of more than 8,000 companies, 60% of the forests, and 35% of the farmland. It also had to divide up state assets among the various levels of government, distribute liquidity cash, supervise the restructuring of companies not yet fit for sale, and prevent the creation of monopolies.

No agency could accomplish such a massive task easily. It assumed from the start that a third of the companies could be privatized quickly, another third only after considerable restructuring, and a final third would have to go under. Some flagship East German companies were allowed to fail when the right kind of buyers could not be found, such as the Interflug airline and the Wartburg automobile manufacturer.

The Trust Agency's work went painfully slowly. By 1993 nearly 9,500 companies had been sold (95% to West German companies), and 435 had been closed. When

Germany (FRG)

large street demonstrations took place in the spring of 1991, the Trust Agency was instructed to shift its emphasis to making companies viable which were not ready for sale, while still officially aiming to transfer ownership of the eastern German economy to private hands. This amounted to massive infusions from the federal treasury, including from a German Unity Fund, to keep the companies afloat and to save jobs.

This assistance could not prevent the Trust Agency, which in 1995 was broken down into smaller agencies, from becoming a scapegoat for the downturn in the eastern economy and for capitalism's slow start. Amid mounting protests against unemployment and soaring costs for rent, energy, and transportation, its chairman, Detlev Rohwedder, was assassinated in his Düsseldorf home. His violent death eliminated the last hopes that the merger of two unequal parts into one harmonious whole could be done without upheaval.

In the meantime, the federal government sought ways to speed up the recovery. This was an unaccustomed challenge because West Germany had created its economic prosperity and strength by slow, steady, balanced growth, not by quick action, as is being demanded for the East, which produces only 10% of the FRG's GDP. From 1991 to 1997 the West transferred $700 billion to the East, a sum equivalent to about 40% of the East's GDP and 5% of the West's GDP. This cash infusion provides buying power to eastern Germans and replaces the decrepit communist infrastructure. But it has failed to generate more jobs in the East and has left the eastern German economy unable to function without subsidies.

The Kohl government subjected itself to intense criticism in the West for raising taxes in 1991 to help rebuild the East's economy after promising before the federal elections not to do that. Included were a 7.5% surcharge on income and corporate taxes, higher social security levies, and hefty tax increases on gasoline and cigarettes. In 1993 this national belt–tightening to pay for unity was renewed through a "Solidarity Pact," which includes a surcharge of 7.5% on earned income, wage restraints, and revenue–sharing.

Its commitments, combined with the $11 billion in aid to fight the war in the Gulf and $9 billion to pay for the withdrawal of Soviet troops from Germany, caused the federal government deficit temporarily to balloon to 7% of GDP before settling down to 2.9% in 1998. However, because the German savings ratio is three–times the U.S. level, the federal government can draw on those larger domestic savings to help finance the budget without borrowing abroad. By 1996 the German national debt was 58% of GDP, lower than that of many Western European countries.

There was a temporary silver lining in this: the foreign trade problems were in part created by the rise of demand in the East. To meet this, western German firms worked to capacity to produce more for the eastern German market and less for the foreign market. GDP in the West grew by 4.5% in 1990, but such growth stalled by 1992, and the FRG entered what its leaders admitted was a "recession." By 1999 unemployment had soared to almost 10% in the West and 16% in the East for a national average of 10.7%. With 410,000 out of work, Germany is experiencing the highest joblessness since the 1930s. The *Bundesbank's* tight money policy held inflation to .4% in 1999.

There are some encouraging signs: 300,000 new (mainly small) businesses created since 1990 have survived. The fact that most eastern companies broke out of the practice of nationwide wage accords has meant that the work force there can protect some jobs by adjusting wages and working hours to what their companies can pay. Much red tape has been slashed. Thus, despite productivity that in 1998 still lagged a quarter behind the west, easterners are showing the kind of adaptability that all nations must have in order to thrive in the globalized economy. This and subsidies have helped induce 1,700 foreign firms to invest in the East during the 1990s. Nevertheless, few large companies have moved their head offices to Berlin; Sony and Coca Cola are exceptions. The East's infrastructure has improved immeasurably.

The telecommunications network is better than that in the West. Roads are much improved, universities are being modernized, and crumbling city centers are being restored. The vast majority of Easterners are far better off materially that they were in the GDR although many may be worse off psychologically. Nevertheless, employment in the East has fallen to only 6 million, compared with 9.3 million in 1991. Only subsidies and temporary "measures to create work" (known as ABM) put checks into the pockets of many frustrated eastern Germans.

Taxation and Federalism

The federal government and the *lands* try to coordinate their policies through such advisory bodies as the *Konjunkturrat* (economic council) and *Finanzplanungsrat* (finance planning council). But the central government cannot order the *lands* to follow its policy, largely because it has no monopoly on taxing power. According to the Basic Law the living standards in all states must be uniform; this became a very problematic requirement after unification

A steelworker at his automated controls

Germany (FRG)

in 1990, which linked a prosperous West with a pauperized East. Thus, the complicated taxing system in the U.S., which permits the per capita tax receipts in some states to be three or four times as high as in other states, is not found in the FRG, at least not before unification in 1990. But Germany's overall taxation rate of 43% is high, compared to 33.8% in the UK, 30.7% in the U.S., and 29.6% in Japan.

Whereas in the U.S. prior to World War II the states were virtually financially independent, in the FRG the question has revolved around of how to divide common tax revenues. The financial relations between the national government and the states is extremely complicated, but it involves roughly the following: federal payments to poorer states, the sharing of common tax revenues, payments by richer states (such as Hesse and Baden–Wurttemberg) to poorer ones (such as Schleswig–Holstein and the new *Lands* in the East), intergovernmental grants and subsidies, and federal payments to states for administrative services rendered.

Individual and corporate income taxes, the biggest source of revenue, is divided in a way that the national government gets 40%, the states get 40% and the cities 20%. Thus, there is no need for a German citizen to file two different income tax returns. The states receive 44% of the second biggest source, the Value Added Tax. This tax means what its title literally says; thus, if, for example, parts from several companies are used to make an automobile, a tax is imposed on the value added to the parts after they have been assembled to manufacture the car. The federal government gets all taxes on gasoline and alcohol, the lands all on car taxes, and the cities all property taxes.

In all, the central government receives about 55% of all taxes, but makes less than 45% of all expenditures, including national defense. The states, on the other hand, spend more than they receive, and the federal government must make up the difference. No one is entirely satisfied with the present tax system, but as yet no one has found an acceptable alternative to the continuous haggling over the distribution of revenues. In 1986 the Constitutional Court demanded a fairer equalization of payments between richer and poorer states. In 1990 the controversy flared again, as cash–strapped new *Lands* in the East clamored for a full share of the pie. Some politicians in both parts advocated tax breaks for eastern Germans during the difficult transition. In any case, the system of redistributing tax resources has not succeeded in evening out the economic gaps between rich and poor lands.

In the federal government a "dynamic tension" often exists between the separate ministries of economics and of finance. They receive expert advice from the FRG's five leading economic research institutes and from the government's own council of economic advisers, known as the "five wise men." To help maintain stability are two government banks. The *Kreditanstalt für Wiederaufbau* (Loan Corporation for Reconstruction) was founded in 1948 to channel Marshall Plan funds and now helps finance German trade, foreign aid and domestic investment. Owned 80% by the central government and 20% by the lands, it receives funds from both the budget and the capital market to help provide long–term investment capital on favorable terms for small and medium–size companies, environmental protection, hard–hit sectors such as shipbuilding, and regional development.

The powerful and prestigious *Bundesbank* (Federal Bank), located in Frankfurt as are most German banks, was one of the world's most independent central banks. Since the introduction of the Euro on January 1, 1999, it has lost some of its power to the European Central Bank, located across town and operating with a much smaller staff (600 vs. 2,600). The *Bundesbank* was charged with issuing bank notes and defending the currency's value against inflation. Remembering how political manipulation helped cause the hyperinflation in the 1920s, the FRG's founders ensured that the new central bank would be impervious to government pressure. All presidents of the *Land* central banks are on its council, as well as up to 10 directors appointed for eight–year terms upon recommendation by the federal government. Also located in Frankfurt is the *Deutsche Börse*, which runs Germany's stock markets. In January 1999 it launched a pan–European trading alliance with the London Stock Exchange that is open to other European stock exchanges.

The Governments' Role in the Economy

Before unification in 1990 FRG governments were more hesitant than many other Western European countries to intervene directly in the economy and to protect or prop up lame–duck industries. The state participated in the ownership and management of some public services such as the telephone, rail and airline systems. Federal and state governments have given financial assistance to service, aerospace, computer, automotive and energy related industries. The bulk of subsidies was paid to service industries, especially transport. The average farmer also receives handsome subsidies.

The central government moved to fulfil its promise to sell off a large part of its shares in private industry. The FRG had sold its stakes in such groups as Veba (energy), Volkswagen, Viag (metals and chemicals), and Salzgitter (steel and engineering). In 1996 it privatized a part of Telekom, the Post Office's telecommunications corporation, which had been split from the postal service in 1989. This was Europe's largest public offering to date, and more than two million retail investors participated. By 1999 more than 1,500 companies were offering telephone–related services in Germany. Such competition has reduced phone charges and forced Telekom to improve its service. The state sold its 53% stake in Lufthansa and its 66% stake in the Rhine–Main–Danube waterway authority, which in 1992 completed the last canal, opening a maritime link between the Atlantic Ocean and the Black Sea. The Federal Railway (*Bundesbahn*) is to be sold into private hands. Direct state aid to failing sectors in the West was significant in the coal, shipbuilding and electrical industries.

The states are also involved in such pragmatic (not ideologically inspired) intervention. For example, Bavaria offered BMW DM190 million not to create a new plant in Austria. Baden–Wurttemberg also offered Daimler–Benz, the country's biggest company, DM140 million to keep a new plant within the state. In fact, Baden–Wurttemberg devotes one–tenth of its budget to science and research facilities to enable its companies to stay ahead in technology. These subsidies can create conflict with EU authorities, as was seen in 1996 when the government of Saxony insisted on providing assistance to Volkswagen plants despite objections that they violated EU guidelines. But without subsidies eastern states are unable to attract large investments.

Natural Resources and Energy

The economy suffers from several important handicaps. Except for modest deposits of iron ore, of natural gas and especially of hard coal in the Ruhr and Saar regions, and of brown coal in the foothills of the Harz mountains, near Cologne, and in the East, the FRG is poor in natural resources. In general, it must import raw materials and export finished goods. Since raw materials are usually priced on the international market in U.S. dollars, the FRG's strong currency lowers its bill for imported materials.

In no sector is the FRG's dependence upon imports so critical as in energy, especially oil, which accounts for 35.6% of the FRG's needs. It has succeeded in reducing its dependence on oil imported from the Persian Gulf; its main supplier now is the U.K. Most of its natural gas, which provides 15% of the FRG's energy, must be imported. The only significant domestic energy source is coal, from

Germany (FRG)

which 37% of the FRG's energy is derived. It accounts for about 28% of the West's needs and a far higher percentage of the East's. However, German coal must be subsidized since its extraction costs are higher than the costs of importing foreign coal. By 1999 it cost about $60,000 in yearly subsidies to protect each of 85,000 jobs in the coal mining industry. Alternative forms of energy, including hydroelectric power, account for only 2% of energy consumption.

Although conservation measures have had some success, total energy consumption continues to rise. The government had planned to cope with this through nuclear power, which in 1999 accounted for a third of the country's electricity. The FRG had 19 nuclear power plants by the end of the century. Their number were to have been increased, but planners were stopped in their tracks by the intense domestic protest to the construction of nuclear power plants and of facilities for the reprocessing and storage of nuclear wastes. By 1991 the FRG government had shut down all the Soviet–designed reactors in the East because they failed to meet safety standards. At Greifswald a meltdown almost occurred in the mid–1970s.

The *SPD–Green* government pledged to shut down Germany's 19 plants, but the two parties differ on timing and tactics, with the *SPD* wanting a longer phase–out period done with the collaboration of industry. Germany has contracts to use French reprocessing facilities and temporarily store wastes at the power stations, and it also has nuclear commitments with Britain. Thus a quick shutdown of nuclear generation would create difficulties not only with allies, but with the industry within German itself. Also it is not clear how the third of electricity produced by atomic plants would be recouped by other means. The inability to expand nuclear power generation at a more rapid rate and to develop alternative sources, despite the fact that many government research subsidies are devoted to energy–related projects, prevents the FRG from improving the structural weaknesses of its energy position. It remains the highest per capita importer of energy and food of any major industrialized country.

Foreign Trade and Investments

Foreign trade remains the essential pillar of the FRG's prosperity. It is one of the world's leading exporters, and exports account for over half of its manufacturing jobs; 38% of its GDP is derived from exports, a fact which makes the FRG very sensitive to world economic climates. It has the advantage of not being overly reliant on the U.S. market, to which only 6% of its exports flow, versus 40% of Japan's and 80% of Canada's.

Export success has provided the FRG with enormous amounts of investment capital, much of which is invested in the U.S. Of the $300 billion German foreign investments in 1999, nearly 60% are in the U.S., compared with 19% in Great Britain, 9% in Italy, 5% in France. In the 1990s there was a surge of foreign investment by German companies; in 1996 a third of them announced intentions to relocate production facilities outside of Germany; a fourth had already done so since 1993. Two–thirds cited labor costs as the main reason, while a fifth mentioned high taxes. This relocation abroad, which helps explain Germany's unemployment problem, is not counterbalanced by foreign investment. In 1996 foreign direct investment in Germany shrank for the first time since records began in 1961. By 1999 Germany had twice as much capital invested abroad as foreign companies had invested in Germany.

To avoid high production costs, German automakers, who make a third of the EU's cars, are cutting jobs and shifting production abroad. BMW built a factory in South Carolina. Daimler–Benz, which laid off thousands of workers, had a training program in "southern American English" before opening its plant in Alabama. In 1998 it entered a super–merger with Chrysler to create the world's third biggest automaker after General Motors and Ford (both of which have major operations in Germany). Volkswagen, which purchased the Rolls Royce factory (while BMW acquired the famous RR brand name), is producing in Spain, the Czech Republic, and Mexico, and it makes half the cars produced in China.

An estimated one million Americans work for more than 3,000 German–owned subsidiaries. Many may not even know it: A & P is owned by Tengelmann; Budd Car Co. by Thyssen (now merged with Krupp); *Scientific American*, Henry Holt, St. Martin's Press, and Farrar, Strauss & Giroux by Holtzbrinck publishing company in Stuttgart; Chicago's Spiegel mail–order house by Otto Versand of Hamburg; Clorox and Loctite by Düsseldorf's Henkel; Allis–Chalmers' agricultural equipment division by Klöckner of Duisburg; Celanese by Hoechst in Frankfurt (which also acquired Marion Merell Dow, Cargill Hybrid Seeds of Minneapolis, and French Rousel–Uclaf pharmaceutical). Bertelsmann, which already owned Bantam, Doubleday, Dell, RCA and Arista records, seven American magazines (including *McCalls, Family Circle, Parents,* and *Fitness*), and half of Barnes & Noble Internet book–selling service, bought Random House in 1998 to become the world's

The Air Bridge Monument in Berlin which commemorates the land blockade of the city in 1948/49

largest publisher of English–language books. Siemens, the Munich–based electronics conglomerate, the majority of whose employees work abroad, owns Westinghouse's non–nuclear power plant operations.

The stampede abroad is not restricted to manufacturing. When Europe's largest insurance company, Allianz, purchased Assurances Générales de France, it became the world's biggest insurer. Although in 1999 it still required approval by U.S. regulatory authorities, Germany's largest bank, Deutsche Bank, announced its intention to take over Bankers Trust of New York. This would create the world's largest banking and financial services conglomerate with a balance–sheet total of

Germany (FRG)

more than $865 billion. To qualify for this, Deutsche Bank had to spin off its subsidiaries in vast industrial holdings in Germany. Unlike American commercial banks, which are forbidden from owning shares in industries, German banks dominate the German industrial sector. Other banks are watching this development because if the American market becomes irresistible, the required restructuring will change the nature of German banking.

Global integration has brought an unexpected negative by-product to German companies. As Swiss banks discovered, expansion into the U.S. market makes foreign companies vulnerable to suits filed in American courts. In 1999 more than two dozen class-action lawsuits were filed against German companies that had used slave labor (90% of whom were not Jewish) and had reaped profits from the Holocaust during the Second World War. Deutsche Bank admitted that it had financed the building of Auschwitz, and marquee names like Daimler-Benz, Volkswagen and Siemens were called to the dock. The Schröder government seeks to fashion a universal settlement that would create a compensation fund of billions of dollars on the condition that further outstanding claims against them be dropped. Not only German, but also American, British and other European companies are being pursued. Their subsidiaries in Germany also allegedly used slave labor. They include GM, Ford, Chase Manhattan Bank, and J.P. Morgan.

Economic Advantages

While the FRG has a number of economic handicaps, it also has undeniable assets. It is located in the middle of Europe and has an excellent net of road, rail, water and air connections which tie it to all the world's major markets. Largely because a great part of its industry was destroyed or dismantled during and after World War II, the western part has ultra-modern plants and equipment, as will the eastern part by the end of the century. It also continues to enjoy a tradition of efficiency and quality production and service. When after World War I the victors wanted to place the loser's goods at a disadvantage, they required the words "Made in Germany" to be stamped in English on all German products. However, this measure boomeranged: German goods and service were of such high quality that purchasers did not *avoid*, but instead *sought* goods with those words stamped on them.

This reputation for excellence also is the key to success of the FRG's small weapons industry, which exports tanks, armored vehicles, artillery, submarines, frigates, combat aircraft and helicopters mainly to NATO and clearly friendly countries, such as Japan and Australia. The FRG ranks fifth in the world in terms of arms sales, after the U.S., Russia, France and Britain. Its armaments industry employs little more than 1% of the labor force and accounts for only 5% of the GDP.

Labor, Unions, Employers' Organizations

The supply and cost of labor is a problem for Germany. For years, the FRG had a shortage of labor and even brought in "guest workers" from southern Europe and Turkey, now numbering about four and a half million. While a majority of these guest workers remain indispensable for many sectors of the economy in which few Germans care to work, they do present the FRG with immense and potentially explosive problems of social integration which will tax German ingenuity and tolerance for years to come.

Also, labor costs in the West exceed those in the U.S. and are among the highest in Europe. In 1995 average German wages were $31.40 an hour, versus $17.36 in the U.S. Employees receive a thirteenth month's pay at Christmas time. At 35 hours, Germany has the world's shortest workweek. The average American worker works longer hours and receives twelve days of paid vacation versus six weeks and 13 to 16 holidays for the German. Social benefits applied to each American job are half as high as in the FRG, where they add 80% to basic wage costs. In the past, productivity was raised to match rising labor costs, but the country's ability to do this in the future is clouded. Although Germany remains one of the world's largest exporters, it ranked only 24th in business competitiveness, according to a 1999 OECD report. The FRG has some of the highest tax rates in the OECD. It has a higher percentage of its work force in industrial production than in most EU countries although its service sector is growing while its manufacturing is shrinking in the face of fierce international competition.

The FRG has a highly skilled labor force, and equally important, a high degree of labor peace, despite restlessness among frightened eastern German workers faced with unemployment and retraining, and despite periodic tensions between employers' and employees' groups, which are called "social partners." Both vigorously represent their members' interests, but since the early post-war period when these groups cooperated closely to help the FRG recover from the war, they have both assumed that they share responsibility for the economy as a whole. The success of this partnership is seen in the facts that strikes are relatively few and that wage contracts increased wages above the inflation rate, but not so high that inflation would be seriously stimulated. The latter fact has helped produce and protect Germans' prosperity.

After unification, East German unions merged with those in the West. The structure of labor unions (to which about a third of all workers and employees belong) helps to assure a great measure of labor peace. The 17 major individual trade unions each follow the principle of "one union, one industry." For example, instead of metal workers in the entire country being organized by many different and competing unions, any one of which can paralyze an industry through a strike, *all* metal workers who wish to join a union, join only one labor negotiating partner, not with many. All 17 unions then belong to the German Trade Union Federation (DGB) which, like all individual trade unions, is independent of political parties and religious denominations. The DGB helps to coordinate trade union goals and activities, and is listened to very carefully by all German governments on labor matters. In addition to the DGB there are a few other trade union organizations, such as the Union of Salaried Employees (DAG) and the German Civil Servants' Federation (DBB). By law the latter is forbidden to enter collective bargaining and to call strikes.

Unions are on the defensive. They are composed largely of blue-collar workers in a white-collar world, and are harder to organize. They are not attracting enough young Germans, and they are weakened by the recession and downsizing of companies' workforces. Union membership has fallen from about 30% of the labor force in 1991 to 22% in 1997. In the East, it has halved since 1990. Firms may choose to opt out of collective bargaining if their works councils agree, and three-quarters of eastern workers are outside of it compared with a third in the West. On the other side of the fence are several hundred employer organizations, many of which are part of a larger umbrella organization called the Confederation of German Employers' Associations (BDA), which coordinates fundamental employer interests.

Another institution which helps to insure labor peace is co-determination (*Mitbestimmung*). In all but the smallest firms, all workers, including foreigners, 18 years or older can elect representatives to a works council, which has many rights, especially in social welfare and personnel matters. Workers in large companies also send representatives to the supervisory councils which are the control organs for the companies' management. The exact composition of these supervisory councils has been since the 1950s and remains a hot-

Germany (FRG)

ly debated issue because of its implications for policy–making within the various industrial units. Workers elect half the members in the large mining and steel companies and slightly less than half in other large companies. In any case, despite the many disagreements, co–determination does provide a far larger scope for worker participation in decisions made in German firms than in most other countries, including the U.S. It thereby gives labor more responsibility in the firms' policies and serves as an important stabilizing element in the economy and society.

Agriculture

A final economic advantage is a fairly efficient agriculture in the West, which was able to produce about three–fourths of western Germany's food needs. This is remarkable when one considers that before the war the western part of Germany was predominantly industrial, whereas the eastern part was the country's agricultural bread basket. The main crops are flour and feed grains, potatoes, sugar beets, vegetables, fruits and wine, and most farmers also raise livestock, mostly cattle. Government–sponsored land consolidation schemes have raised the number of large and medium–sized farms considerably, although small farms still predominate in the West. Cooperatives, which link together about three–fourths of the western farms, strengthen small farmers' competitiveness. Western German farmers exercise impressive political clout; they have been able to prevent the government from accepting in GATT negotiations freer trade in agriculture, which the Americans especially demand.

Agriculture was collectivized in East Germany in 1958, creating large collective farms and fields. Many former owners retained title to their land, but it was non–negotiable and therefore worthless to them. In the GDR, 12% of the work–force was engaged in agriculture, compared with only 5% in western Germany. Farmers in the East enjoyed certain privileges, compared with their countrymen in industry: they escaped the worst pollution, many had their own homes and private plots, they were heavily subsidized, and they enjoyed the time–off and sick–leave that private farmers in the West do not have. Despite the large scale of their farms, East German farmers produced only 40% as much per capita as their western German counterparts, although they had made the GDR self–sufficient in food. Like everybody else in the East, farmers are undergoing a tortured transition to other jobs or to a forgotten form of private agriculture.

Present Economic Challenge

The danger that a disappearance of economic success could threaten democratic values applies more or less to all countries. But in the case of Germany it applies to a far greater extent. Germany's first real experiment with democracy during the inter–war years was rocked from the beginning by staggering economic problems, and the Weimar Republic finally fell in January 1933 in part because of an economic depression had left more than six million Germans out of work. The FRG was able to win and maintain legitimacy in the eyes of its own citizens largely through its almost stunning economic accomplishments.

Main control room of a pipe-making plant

Now it faces the daunting challenge of absorbing a once bankrupt, unproductive socialist economy in its eastern lands, whose people had been deprived of prosperity for four decades. It has proven to be more difficult than expected to stimulate western investment in the East in order to create jobs and raise the standard of living.

In 1993 the government published a much–debated report questioning whether Germany can remain a competitive producer in the world economy. Its labor costs are the world's highest, its working year the shortest, its productivity below its peers in America and Japan, its average retirement age 59, and its social spending enormous. The call for some economic "rethinking" is being echoed by some and vehemently rejected by others, who regard the status quo as a birthright, regardless of global economic realities.

Despite the problems, Germans are unlikely to alter their economic system. Asked what the fundamental purpose of an economy is, most would answer "for social stability," while most Americans believe it exists to raise the living standards of persons willing to work hard and imaginatively. Few Germans want the social consequences of America's emphasis on efficiency and individual economic freedom. They are willing to pay the necessary taxes to enable the government to alleviate the pain that capitalism can create. Chancellor Gerhard Schröder won in 1998 by promising that his government could create new jobs while preserving the generous social welfare network. Germany must confront the grim reality that both promises cannot be kept.

CULTURE

One German Culture?

Germany is politically and legally unified, but the two sides have not yet formed a harmonious blend, and the resentments which separate west from east are deep. For decades Germans on each side of the Wall had assumed that they were basically the same, speaking the same language, reading the same literature, sharing the same historical and cultural traditions. They thought they knew and understood each other, but they were wrong. Germans are not psychologically unified, and so far a sense of national solidarity is lacking to complete the unification process. *Ostpolitik* expert Egon Bahr remarked at the time of unity that "we Germans got married in a hurry and enjoyed it. Now we must get to know each other. Normally it is the other way around, but, then, what is normal in Germany?" Foreign Minister Genscher likes to tell the joke about the *Ossi* (eastern German) saying that "We are one people!",

Germany (FRG)

A festival in Munich . . .

to which the *Wessi* (western German) replies: "So are we!"

Many western Germans believe they have inherited an unknown, problem–ridden country populated by German–speaking strangers. Eastern Germans, in turn, are baffled by the new Germany of which they are now a part and had expected more sympathy from westerners than they have gotten. They are stunned to see how little remains of the society in which they grew up; western German laws and traditions are so much the norm that many easterners agree with psychologist Margit Venner: "This is not unification, it's an annexation!" President von Weizsäcker always says it best: "We cannot deny how much divides us still. . . . The form of unity has been determined: now we must give it substance."

Visually the two parts are beginning to look more like each other. Although the East is still drab and polluted by comparison, it is undergoing a face–lift. Facades of shops are being freshly painted and city streets refurbished. Stores are bountifully stocked with consumer goods, and western firms, banks, and gasoline stations are opening branches everywhere. But anyone visiting both parts of Germany hears an earful about the other and quickly realizes that misunderstandings abound: *Ossis* are allegedly petty bourgeois, narrow–minded, provincial, ungrateful despite their outstretched palms, and want all the benefits of capitalism now despite the fact that they are lazy (a questionable impression given the fact that eastern Germans created 300,000 new businesses in the first seven months of unity!). By contrast, *Wessis* are seen to be rich snobs, arrogant, inconsiderate, insensitive, egotistical, distrustful, and less kind toward children. Many eastern Germans suffer from an inferiority complex toward western Germans, whom they find to be more decisive, independent, more open to the world, more confident, and more able to achieve and to master problems.

The economic disparity is enormous, although it will narrow dramatically within a decade. In 1992 East Germans earned half as much as West Germans in an economy with about 40% of the real output per worker. Per household the easterners had half as many cars (to say nothing about the low quality of East German automobiles!), deep freezers, and color televisions, 7% as many telephones, and a seventh as many automatic washing machines. In 1991 the average East German household had financial assets valued at DM20,000 vrs. DM100,000 in the West. The *Bundesbank* noted that "the financial situation of the population in the new federal states is similar to the situation in western Germany in the early 1970s." They had only 27 square meters of living space per inhabitant (compared with 35.5 in the cramped West) in decrepit housing, 40% of which was built before the First World War. Although about 42% of East German housing was privately owned before 1989, the bad effects of rent control and centralized allocation were visible. The poor condition of housing was the price East Germans had to pay for having to spend only 3% of their disposable income on it. Finally, toxic pollution and poor medical delivery kept East Germans' life expectancy lower than in the West: 69 years for men and 75 years for women, compared with 70 and 77 years in the West respectively.

However, one should not dwell exclusively on the differences. East and West Germans voted in much the same way in 1990, and many polls revealed similar opinions after unification: Both prize the same thing: high income. A total of 71% of Germans see the environment as the top priority, with 82% of eastern Germans and 87% of westerners favoring increased spending in that area. Both sides reject any suggestion of increased spending on the military, although rising crime, drug use, violence against foreigners, and soccer hooliganism prompt 40% of eastern Germans, but only 22% of westerners to desire more respect for state authority, and 65% and 25% respectively to want greater police presence. Two–thirds of Germans in both parts were "proud to be German," although western Germans had a greater sense of being European than did their eastern countrymen, who had been kept largely isolated. They generally agree who their favorite nationalities are: French, American, and Austrian, although the easterners put the Austrians ahead of the Americans. They also dislike the same peoples—Poles, Turks, and Gypsies—although eastern Germans' antipathy is somewhat stronger. Asked what country should be the new Germany's model, 40% said Switzerland, because of its "wealth and independence," and 29% said Sweden; only 6%, 8%, and 2% respectively cited the U.S., France, and Britain as their models!

Family Structure and Life

German society was already in a process of change when two different German societies were grafted together in 1990. For the third time since 1933, Germans in the East must adjust to a very different kind of society. From an earlier German society characterized by authoritarian behavior and institutions and by great social and economic differences among citizens has emerged in the West a predominantly middle–class society with widespread prosperity and with more opportunities and education and upward social mobility. Some of these changes are clearly reflected in important social institutions.

Particularly since World War II, the authoritarian family structure has given way to a more relaxed family organization. This breakdown actually started during the Third Reich, when children were mobilized in activities outside the family and were even encouraged to report on their parents' opinions and behavior, if they veered from Nazi ideology. One now sees more and more permissiveness in the contemporary German family, and it is also increasingly fashionable in middle and upper–middle class families for children to call their parents by their first names.

That this trend toward a less rigid family structure will probably continue is indicated by comparative polls. In 1953 a third of all young respondents between the ages of 13 and 24 indicated they would like to raise their children "exactly the same as I was raised." In 1975 the figure was only 14%. Also, 28% of young respondents indicated in 1951 that independence and free will were the values which should be stressed in the family, whereas 25% believed that obedience and deference were the most important values; in 1976 the corresponding percentages were 51% and 10%.

The combined effects of weaker religious beliefs, Marx's attacks on the family as "legalized prostitution," the former practice of favoring single mothers in the distribution of apartments, and the fact that 91% of women in the East worked, compared with only 51% in the West, contributed in eastern Germany to considerable family differences compared with the West. In the pre–unification GDR, 32% of children were born out of wedlock, compared with 9% in the West. The divorce rate was a third higher in the East. Among the thousands of legal and social issues which had to be resolved before unification, very few were so controversial that no agreement was possible.

The most celebrated example was abortion, and the GDR's law permitting legal abortion on demand within three months was left in place there, while the West's more restricted Paragraph 218 applied in the old FRG. Polls after unification revealed that 57% of East Germans favored legal abortion on demand, compared with only 28% in the West. In 1995 a single law came into effect: abortions are illegal, but a woman who has one anyway will not be prosecuted provided that the abortion takes place during the first twelve weeks of pregnancy and she attends compulsory counseling geared to "the protection of unborn life." Abortions on medical grounds and in the event of rape are legal and are paid by the national health system.

The Education System: Experimentation

A similar breakdown of authoritarianism is taking place in the schools. One sees very few traces of the former stern discipline. The school environment is relaxed, and pupils' relations with their teachers are often close and warm. Discussion and the free expression of opinion are generally encouraged, and discipline and orderliness are far less evident than in most American schools. Americans' most probable reaction when visiting a German school is that it is considerably more permissive than the schools to which they are accustomed.

Reforms since the late 1960s have attempted to open up the school system in the West to permit more working and lower class children better educational opportunities, as had already been done in the East. The unspoken model for some of these reforms has been the American school system, which has always been more oriented upon providing education opportunity equally for all rather than exclusively producing an academic elite. Since education is a *state* responsibility, there is considerable diversity in the school systems within the FRG. Roughly half of the children between the ages of three and six attend kindergartens, which are not a part of the state school system and for which fees are normally charged.

All children at age seven enter unified primary schools (*Grundschule*), which they attend for four years (six in Hamburg, Bremen and Berlin). After this, children enter one of three different kinds of higher schools. In 1990 a third of the girls and 40% of the boys (compared with two–thirds of both in 1969) complete a five–year short–course secondary school (*Hauptschule*) until age 15, followed by three years of part–time vocational school combined with on–the–job training. In an intermediate school (*Realschule*), 39% of girls and 33% of boys (compared with 24% and 20% in 1969) complete a course lasting six years leading to a graduation certificate (*mittlere Reife*) which permits persons to enter certain advanced technical schools and the medium levels of business and administration. Some continue on for a "limited" *Abitur* (called a *Fachabitur*), which then allows university–level study in a limited number of subjects.

The third kind of school, the *Gymnasium*, offers a more academically demanding nine–year course, aiming toward a diploma called the *Abitur,* which entitles one to enter the universities; 28% of all girls and 26% of boys attend (compared with 10% and 15% in 1969) For many years critics argued that such a tracked system merely hardened class distinctions within the society by favoring the children of civil servants, salaried employees and the independently employed. In contrast to workers, these groups traditionally en-

. . . and less "traditional" blue jeans crowd

Photo by Jon Markham Morrow

Germany (FRG)

The relaxed atmosphere . . .

courage their children to enter the more academically demanding schools, and to make financial sacrifices by entering their future jobs much later in life. On the other hand, one can argue that because German schools have only a 10% drop-out rate, compared with about 25% in the U.S. and 45% in the U.K., and therefore prepares young Germans better for the workforce, the school system actually narrows social and economic differences more effectively than do the U.S. and U.K. Nevertheless, certain reforms have been introduced which are praised by some and severely criticized by others.

First, some pupils in advanced classes are given state financial support in order to reduce the monetary burdens for poorer families which longer schooling entails. Second, a "second educational path" was introduced for those pupils who later conclude that they made the wrong decision at age 11 concerning what higher school they should attend. This path involves demanding evening courses for three to six years, but these pupils with determination can receive *Realschule* or *Gymnasium* certificates and gain access to higher educational institutions. A third reform was the creation in some cities of "comprehensive schools" (*Gesamtschulen*). Like the American high school, the comprehensive school combines all pupils under one roof, but nevertheless permits certain interior tracking for pupils with different interests and objectives. These schools were never widely accepted and are attended by only 5% of all pupils. Fourth, a far greater percentage of students has been allowed to attend the formerly elite *Gymnasium*, which is the essential way-station towards the universities and well-paid, prestigious professions. Now, a fourth of student-age Germans study at the universities, as contrasted to only 6% in 1950.

Elementary schools teach the new simplified spelling and grammar rules finally agreed upon in 1996, after 15 years of discussion, by the culture and education chiefs from all German-speaking countries. The 212 spelling and punctuation spellings were dropped, and the peculiar "s-z" character was replaced by a double "s." The official dictionary of the German language, the *Duden*, has been revised accordingly. Not surprisingly, this reform unleashed furious criticism in the land of Goethe and Schiller. Hundreds of writers, journalists and publishers signed petitions against it, and the German Academy for Language and Poetry called on teachers, editors, publishers and writers to ignore the new rules altogether.

While the education system has been considerably opened up, criticism against it still abounds. Some argue that the reforms have left too many traditional elements in place. Others counter that the reforms have greatly lowered education standards. Noting western Germany's economic success, some observers from abroad focus on four strengths of the German school system. First, secondary school pupils are educated according to their aptitudes. Second, they avoid over-specialization. They most show competence in at least 10 subjects before graduation and must achieve a minimum standard, judged by authorities from outside each school, in the core subjects of mathematics, science, German, and for all but the least able, a foreign language. Third, teachers are treated as members of the professional middle class, with high social status, the best pay in the world ($51,000 a year for a 35-year-old with two children in 1991), tenure as civil servants, and a short school day from 8 AM to 1 PM. Fourth, future workers are given top training. Three-fourths of all graduates (almost all who are not going to the university) spend at least three years in a rigorous apprenticeship working for a fourth the normal pay under the guidance of a qualified "master." At the same time, they go a day or two a week to vocational schools learning the theory of their chosen trade. They cannot get a good job until they have served their time as apprentices and have passed a difficult practical and theoretical examination.

East German schools always tried to narrow social differences by merging tracks within the old German educational system and giving pupils a "polytechnic" education: one which brings all pupils into the working world for practical experience. Unfortunately, those schools also included heavy doses of propaganda in their curricula. Therefore, after unification in 1990 a shake-down began. Many schools were renamed so that their original names replaced their communist-inspired ones. Former textbooks were discarded and replaced by ones from the West. Courses on communist ideology

. . . in German schools

Germany (FRG)

were dropped, and the approach in civics and history courses was altered. Former teachers who belonged to the *SED* had to fill out questionnaires and survive a screening process to continue teaching.

When Russian was made an elective, rather than a required course, 90% of the pupils dropped it and picked up English instead. East Germans had never liked Russian, and very few ever mastered it despite the years they were compelled to study it. Studies in 1990 showed that their competence in English equalled that of Russian, even though their exposure to English in school had been scant. Of course, thousands of teachers of Russian had to be hurriedly retrained to teach English. A study of schools in both parts of Germany a few weeks after unification revealed astonishing similarities in kids' attitudes and cast doubt on the effect of intense communist propaganda over 40 years. In both parts of Germany, children wanted an "interesting job," safe from economic ups and downs, and with maximum free time; both preferred free enterprise and believed that pay should be linked to performance; they were not interested in political activism; and English was their foreign language of choice.

Thirty percent of young Germans attempt university studies. The extremely rapid increase in pupils who finish the *Gymnasium* has led to serious overcrowding at the universities. For instance, the University of Munich has an official capacity of 25,000, but 63,000 are enrolled. At the Free University of Berlin 60,000 students occupy 29,000 places. No wonder 40% of all students give up before graduation, and those who finish have an average age of 28. Although more than 20 new universities have been built in the West since the mid–1960s, students have great problems receiving admission to the programs and universities of their choice. Budget cuts prevented the universities from expanding their staffs to cope with the high numbers of students. Many students are highly dissatisfied with the lack of sufficient facilities and staff. This problem is exacerbated by the fact that the average student now spends 13 semesters at the university before taking final examinations, thereby strengthening the *ewiger Student* (eternal student) image.

The university system, designed by Wilhelm von Humboldt in the early 19th century is not suited to an era of mass education. In 1997 a half million university students, joined by hundreds of thousands of high school students, launched the largest wave of strikes and demonstrations since the heady student rebellion in the late 1960s. Most politicians and university officials admitted that there is much justification for the students' complaints of declining higher education due to sharp spending cuts (from 1.32% of GDP in 1977 to only .92% in 1997), a doubling of university enrollment (to more than 1.8 million in 1998) in the same period, overcrowded classes in poorly maintained university buildings, understocked libraries and computer centers, and unconcerned professors, who in some institutions are outnumbered by as many as 600 students to one. With the looming prospect of unemployment even if they complete their studies, students reject talk of paying tuition or shortening their study time. The lands, which are responsible for education, complain that they lack the money to solve the problems. They call on the federal government to help, but it claims to have empty pockets because of the weak economy and the costs of unification.

In order to offer an alternative to the crowded universities, the first private German universities were founded in Witten–Herdecke, Koblenz and Ingolstadt. Modeled largely after American private colleges, the future of these sole private universities remains uncertain. The uneasiness of the students is exacerbated by the increasingly restricted job market which awaits them after they finish their studies. Until well into the 1970s, an economically booming FRG, with expanding industries and financially strong and generous state treasuries, could absorb almost all university graduates. In 1974–75, for example, 85% of university graduates were given public service jobs. Those prosperous years have waned, and the paucity of jobs in the East darkens employment prospects even further.

The University of Freiburg im Breisgau

Religion

About 90% of western Germans belong to Lutheran Protestant or Catholic churches. Protestants and Catholics are divided roughly equally in the western part of the FRG although they are not evenly dispersed throughout the country. In general, the North is predominantly Protestant, whereas the South and the Rhineland are predominantly Catholic. The East was traditionally solidly Protestant; only 6% of East Germans are Catholic, compared with 43% in the West. Thus, a united Germany became more Protestant. The churches' hold over the school system has long since been severed, and there are few denominational schools left. Religious instruction is, however, offered in the schools on a voluntary basis and in separate classes for Protestants and Catholics.

There is no clean separation of church and state in the FRG as in the U.S., and both major churches are supported by a church tax which the state collects with the income tax. A person may be excused from paying the tax if he officially leaves the church of which he is a member. Such a step used to bring a person great social or professional handicaps. A doctor or a kindergarten teacher could be denied employment at a church related hospital or kindergarten because he had formally left his church. But this is the exception today, and more people are formally leaving the churches. Attitudes sometimes change, however, when it is time for a baptism, wedding, funeral, or when children are being raised.

The churches, which were the only institutions to survive the Third Reich practically unscathed, have contributed significantly to establishing a moderate and

Germany (FRG)

compromising political culture. However, questions remain concerning the extent to which they should actively enter the political arena. The Protestant Church is very visible in the "peace movement" in both parts of Germany. It was particularly important in the East, where atheism had been officially encouraged by the communists, but where churches were tolerated if they did not meddle in politics. Protestants could not agree with the latter stipulation, and their church became a sanctuary for growing oppositional groups in the 1980s; because of this, young people took a new interest in it. In the GDR it opposed the militarization of society through military education in the schools. It advocated a right of conscientious objection which did not exist in the GDR. Under the banner of "Swords to Plowshares" it opposed all countries' arms build–ups.

It brought into the limelight the GDR's first massive, organized opposition to the regime by protecting it, providing it with meeting rooms and a podium for all persons interested in a critical dialogue. It supported civil courage to question the regime and urged dissidents to remain in the GDR to build a better country. It made bold and articulate demands for freedom. Perhaps most important, it succeeded in keeping the revolution against the *SED* regime non–violent. The Leipzig demonstrations every Monday, which broke the back of the regime in the fall of 1989, always began in the Nikolai Church with a "peaceful God's service." It was there on the critical date, October 9, that the call for non–violence, penned by symphony conductor Kurt Masur and five others including clergymen, was proclaimed. In the non–communist government which ruled the last half–year of the GDR's existence, Protestant clergymen were the largest single professional group in it.

Catholic bishops and priests, especially in Bavaria, have not been above trying occasionally to influence the voting of their parishioners through messages from the pulpit. Yet the strength of religion as an influencing factor in politics and society has declined greatly. It has little bearing on voting. Only about a third of the Catholics and a tenth of the Protestants in the West attend church regularly, and most of those who do have become largely secularized. There are differences in religious beliefs between Germans in the two halves of the country: two–thirds of eastern Germans were either never baptized or left the church, compared with only 7% in the West. Also, only 7% of eastern Germans say they believe in life after death, compared with half of western Germans.

Fascination with Things American

Perhaps nothing is more noticeable for visitors to the FRG than the attachment of Germans, especially youth, to virtually anything which is American. On the radio, one hears far less German music than American and British. As a form of protest against the massive influence of American culture, there was a tendency among youths in the "alternative scene" to avoid English expressions and to insist upon German–language music. By 1986 this "new wave" had run its course in rock music, and the trend was back to English lyrics. Only two out of the top 30 singles were sung in German, even though a third of the songs had been produced in German–speaking countries. For young singers, sales outside of Germany were more important than nationalist urges. Even the *CDU's* 1990 electoral campaign

Germany (FRG)

was sung in English: "Feel the power, touch the future, reach the heart!"

There is seldom an evening in which an American television show cannot be seen. Jeans, T–shirts and jogging shoes are worn by young Germans, who crowd into fast–food chains such as McDonald's and Burger King, which one finds in every city of any size. Their parents often shop in large supermarkets or shopping centers or fill their cars' tanks at gasoline stations which seem to offer everything from groceries and magazines to car washes. An estimated 85,000 Germans, inspired by Karl May's novels, belong to American Indian clubs. In 1994, six thousand Germans showed up at a "pow–wow" in Essen with native garb and paint on their faces, calling themselves names like "Old Powderface." American slang has mightily invaded the German language, and young people, businessmen and scholars seldom express themselves for long without using some English words. But, unlike many French, most Germans do not seem to be distressed by this lingual invasion.

The *Financial Times* quoted the deputy editor of the daily *Die Welt*, who discovered that one could write German articles while using hardly any German words: "Unser Way of Life im Media Business ist hart, da muss man ein tougher Kerl sein. Morgens Warm–up und Stretching, dann ein Teller Corn Flakes und ein Soft Drink oder Darjeeling Tea, dann in das Office— und schon Brunch mit den Top–Leuten, meeting zum Thema: Sollen wir die Zeitung pushen mit Snob Appeal oder auf Low Profile achten? Ich habe den Managern ganz cool und businesslike mein Papier presentiert: Wir müssen News powern und erst dann den Akzent auf Layout und Design legen, auf der Front Page die Headline mehr aufjazzen und die Deadline beachten. Für jede Story brauchen wir ein starkes Lead. Der Cartoon muss gut plaziert sein. Das Editorial muss Glamour und Style haben, unsere Top Priority bleibt: Action und Service!"

Many German protest movements, such as those against war, for women's and minorities' rights and in favor of environmental protection, are largely based on American examples. Never have more Germans visited the United States than in the 1980s and 1990s. Scholars and students especially find it important to work or study for a time in the U.S. In a 1994 *Spiegel* poll, 31% of Germans aged 14 to 29 indicated that they would prefer to live in another country other than Germany. Of those, far more (24%) named the U.S. than the next competitors, Canada (10%) and France (9%).

Ambivalence toward America

Yet, despite the undeniable and seemingly irresistible attraction which many Germans have toward aspects of American culture, many observers, including some Germans, have noted anti–Americanism in the FRG. But, in fact, only among the militant leftist circles does this come blatantly to the surface. Anti–American sentiments are largely silent among a part of the politicized youth and left–leaning intellectuals. Anti–Americanism, to the extent that it exists, should not be confused with criticism against certain American policies, such as high military budgets or tacit support for authoritarian regimes in Latin America, policies which are also criticized within the U.S. Nor should anti–Americanism be seen in terms of a general aversion against the U.S. or its people.

Criticism of America is more a general way of expressing anti–capitalist, anti–growth attitudes. It involves cultural rejection of a scientific and technical civilization which the U.S. seems to represent. It is also an outgrowth of a conflict between generations. On the one hand is an older generation in the West which admired American democracy and prosperity and which has never forgotten the Marshall Plan and the U.S. defense of West Berlin in the late 1940s and 1950s. One TV journalist said at the time of unification: "We had help from the Americans, who had thought carefully about what should become of Germany, and this enabled us to make something of ourselves." Helmut Kohl frequently told campaign audiences in the East that if they had been occupied by the Americans, their lives would have been as democratic and prosperous as in the West. On the other hand, a younger generation grew up amidst material prosperity and talk of détente. Their political

Just window–shopping

consciousness was shaped at a time when the shock waves of severe racial tension in American cities, the Vietnam War and Watergate were being felt outside the U.S. In eastern Germany much propaganda had been directed against America, but polls reveal very little anti–Americanism there.

More than anything else, anti–Americanism means protest against the prevailing culture of the westernized FRG. It is linked with longings, observable in other Western European countries and the U.S. as well, to drop out of a highly competitive, urbanized society oriented toward comfort, economic prosperity and individual success, and to adopt so–called alternative forms of living which are poorly defined. Thus, anti–Americanism is less a political call to arms against the U.S. than it is a code word for a change of values among a part of contemporary German younger people which embodies a conflict among several cultures within the FRG itself.

Anti–Americanism is statistically almost invisible. How little overall impact anti–American tendencies have on the West German population is revealed by virtually every opinion poll which seeks to measure it. Opinion polls have consistently indicated that more Germans would want to emigrate to America if they had to leave their own country than to any other country in the world, and that more would want to be Americans than any

Germany (FRG)

A Turkish grocer in Hamburg Courtesy: German Information Center

other nationality, if, in some hypothetical situation, they could no longer be Germans.

One frequently hears clichés in Germany about Americans: that they always chew gum, wear their pants too short, generally dress tastelessly (in loud colors, plaid pants, and Bermuda shorts), are fanatic joggers and sport addicts. Some Germans find that many Americans are overweight, uncultured, slightly naive and politically uninformed about the rest of the world, even though Americans have an almost missionary desire to spread the American way of life. Yet, opinion polls reveal different, more positive descriptions of Americans: that they have a good business sense, are individualistic, energetic, patriotic, progressive and technically talented. Less than a fifth of all Germans consider Americans to be ill–mannered or ruthless, and only 4% consider them to be insecure.

Except in certain areas where there are large concentrations of American soldiers, Americans and Germans mingle rather well with each other although there are differences between them. Like some other European nationalities, Germans tend to be more private than Americans. They often do not know their neighbors and are more apt to put fences around their houses to insure their privacy. They also observe certain social conventions that somewhat slow down the development of intimate social contact. For instance, the German language has two different words for 'you.' The German says *Sie* if he wants to keep formal and at a distance and *Du* if he wants to be more familiar. The English equivalent of a formal 'you,' *Thee*, fell into disuse years ago, even among small religious sects which had retained it. In Germany, colleagues who have worked with each other for years might still address each other as *Herr* (Mr.) or *Frau* (Mrs.). *Fräulein* (Miss) has fallen into disuse because there is no male counterpart, and there is no German equivalent to Ms.!

Europeans, including Germans, are uncomfortable about answering such personal questions when one first meets as where one works, for whom one voted or how one acquired a certain painting or piece of furniture in his abode, questions which the American generally feels free to ask in order to open a conversation. This is not to say that Germans do not form firm friendships. They certainly do, even if it takes longer to do so. But while Germans seem to like the more relaxed American manner, they do generally recognize and mildly criticize the superficial aspect of Americans' personal interaction. Unlike most Americans, Germans tend not to call other people by their first names and to use casual expressions like "drop by sometime," unless they really mean it and wish to give an unmistakable signal of friendliness to a person.

Foreigners

The FRG was highly successful after 1945 in absorbing and integrating more than 14 million German refugees and expellees from East Germany and the former eastern territories. Now Germany is faced with the very difficult problem of integrating racially and culturally diverse groups of non–Germans.

Because of Germany's economic prosperity, political tolerance, liberal asylum laws, and constitutional guarantee of asylum "for persons persecuted on political grounds," it has become a magnet for refugees, although it does not accept as high a percentage of immigrants per capita as does the U.S. Also, in the 1950s and 1960s, West Germany recruited southern Europeans, particularly Turks, in order to overcome severe labor shortages in low–paying jobs. Together with about 120,000 foreigners in eastern Germany, foreigners now number about 7.4 million, or approximately 9% of the population. All but 3% live in the West. In 1999 the largest group was Turks (2.1 million), followed by a million from the former Yugoslavia, Italians (558,000), Greeks (346,000), and Poles (286,000). Their numbers are rising because of their far higher birth rate and because members of their families are arriving from their countries of origin to join them.

Most foreigners intend to stay in the FRG forever. Relatively few foreign workers accepted governmental bonuses to return to their countries. Although an estimated 20% of foreigners were born in Germany, few were granted citizenship. For example, of the 2.1 million Turks in Germany in 1999, no more than 160,000 are German citizens. Turks are especially hesitant to give up their Turkish citizenship because they would become ineligible for inheritances in Turkey. Chancellor Schröder's *SPD–Green* vowed to change Germany's citizenship law. After a furious debate that focused especially on initial plans to permit dual citizenship, parliament accepted an amended law in 1999 that nevertheless represents a landmark overhaul of the 1913 citizenship law. It cuts the link between German blood ties and nationality. Beginning in 2000, children born in Germany to foreign parents are granted German citizenship if at least one parent has lived legally in Germany for eight years or longer. These children can hold dual citizenship until age 23, when they must renounce their foreign citizenship if they choose to retain their German one. No naturalized citizens may hold dual citizenship.

Foreigners are especially concentrated in certain large industrial cities, where they often form foreign ghettos in poorer sections of the cities and serve as convenient scapegoats for certain alarming urban ills, most notably, rising crime. For example, foreigners constitute a quarter of Frankfurt's residents. Although most Germans are disgusted by anti–foreigner violence, most seem to believe that the number of foreign residents has become too high.

Glasnost in the Soviet Union seriously

Germany (FRG)

affected emigration. In 1989 alone, 377,000 ethnic Germans from Eastern Europe (especially Poland) and the USSR joined 344,000 Germans from the GDR and the steady stream of non–German refugees into the FRG. This was the largest wave of ethnic Germans entering the FRG since 1949, and the influx continued in 1995, when 218,000 entered. The sudden outpouring temporarily swamped the procedures in funds. All compete for limited accommodation and employment and, as polls and city elections show, are testing Germans' patience. About two million Germans remain in the former Soviet Union. Many of these also wish to emigrate, even though it is not easy for them to adjust to working and living in a less protective state like the FRG. Ethnic Germans from Eastern European countries, enjoy an open–door immigration policy, and 700,000 ethnic Germans from outside of Germany poured into the country in the year following the collapse of the Berlin Wall; many could speak no German. By 1997 the numbers of both asylum–seekers and German resettlers had declined dramatically.

Turks display a greater resistance to social integration than do other nationalities. This unwillingness to become an integrated part of German society creates particular problems in the schools, where the percentage of foreigners in classes sometimes rises to over 50%. Thus, Germans must tackle the problem of bilingualism in the schools, of resultant lowered standards in the classrooms, and of an increasing inclination on the part of German parents to avoid sending their children to schools in which there is a high percentage of foreign children enrolled. This is an extremely delicate problem for a country which tries very hard to be tolerant, compassionate and just. Germans' deep concern about the plight of Turkish guest workers was revealed in 1986-7 by the astonishing high sales (over a million copies) of Günter Wallraff's book, *Ganz Unten (Rock Bottom)*, which depicts the difficult lives of Turks in Germany. By the mid–1990s many Turks had ascended to the middle class, and 37,000 run their own businesses. 15,000 study at universities, and Turks have become lawyers, software experts, and in one case (Cem Ozdemir, of the *Greens*) a member of the *Bundestag*.

Fears that the FRG might become swamped by foreigners persist, and the federal and *land* governments have found it necessary to warn against xenophobia, which is strongest in the East, although only about 2% of the population there is foreign. The GDR was a far more isolated society, so its people had far less contact with outsiders. Also, the Communist regime in the GDR had never accepted responsibility for the crimes of the Second World War, so its citizens had not grown up with the same feeling of guilt toward wrongs done to other peoples, such as the Jews, as people in western Germany had been. About 100,000 guest workers had been sent there from communist countries like Angola, Cuba, Vietnam, and Mozambique, and many refused to return to their homelands when the GDR collapsed. It is noteworthy that xenophobia in the East is stronger among young people than among older, whereas the opposite is true in the West.

In 1992 and 1993 violence against foreigners reached such an intensity that Kohl found Germany's democratic system "being put to the test," and President von Weizsäcker asserted: "Let us entertain no illusions. Something evil is afoot." Sporting swastikas, shouting Nazi slogans, and cheered by some bystanders, right–wing youth gangs attacked an asylum hostel in Rostock and battled police for several days. Such attacks continued throughout the autumn. Most embarrassing was an outbreak of anti–Semitism and attacks against Jewish shrines. After 4,600 anti–foreigner crimes and 17 deaths, the Kohl government declared that it would "use all possible legal measures to fight violence and political extremism." It ordered a far stronger focus on law enforcement and a broader effort to crack down on forms of racist and neo–Nazi expression.

It established a special task force to confront rightist extremism, and it raided neo–Nazi hideouts all over Germany, confiscating arms and Nazi paraphernalia. It outlawed the neo–Nazis' main party, *German Alternative*, and asked the Constitutional Court to apply a never–used clause and strip two leading neo–Nazis of their rights of expression and assembly. In 1995 one of the largest and most radical neo–Nazi groups, the *Free German Workers' Party*, was banned. By 1997 violence against foreigners had declined markedly. The reason is partly because there is so little support among the general population for such behavior.

Many Germans blamed the untenable situation partly on Article 16 of the Basic Law, which granted political asylum to all who claim it. It had been inspired by the fact that many German anti–Nazis had been saved during the Hitler era because they found asylum in democratic countries and by the fact that thousands of Jews perished because other countries had turned them away. In 1993 the government and opposition *SPD* agreed to revoke Germany's liberal asylum law. Asylum seekers arriving from countries Germany has declared to be free of political repression are automatically denied refuge. Border patrols have been tightened. Economic migrants are no longer treated as refugees, and illegal migrants are immediately expelled.

Germany still receives about half of all asylum–seekers in Europe, but by 1995 the number of applicants had declined from about 37,000 per month to 10,000, and only 7% are granted sanctuary. One political result was that this issue played no role in the 1994 elections, and the right–wing parties were demolished at the polls. Like many other EU countries, Germany has, in effect, adopted a zero–immigration policy. It continues to have no legal system for immigration, and the number of newcomers continues to decline. In 1996 the government began forcing Bosnian refugees to return to their homeland; over 350,000 had fled to Germany, more than in all other countries combined. But when the Yugoslavian government commenced ethnic cleansing in Kosovo in 1999, Germany offered to accept many of the refugees.

The Media

Germans are relatively well–informed about politics. Roughly 50% of all adults read the political coverage in a wide range of daily newspapers. Although the daily sale of newspapers has risen, the total number of independent dailies has declined; most are regional papers. More and more newspapers and magazines have become concentrated in publication groups, and the majority of dailies are no longer editorially independent. The largest such group is that controlled by Axel Springer, who produces about 25% of the total national output of daily newspapers. This includes the most widely read daily, the *Bild–Zeitung* (literally "Picture Newspaper"), a sensationalist mixture of conservative politics, crime, sex and gossip, and read by more than a fourth of all adults. With a circulation of almost five million, it is the world's largest–selling newspaper outside of Japan. Even this boulevard newspaper shares Germans' post–war restraint. When the German and English soccer teams faced each other in the semi–finals of the European championships in 1996, British tabloids displayed headlines like "Watch Out Krauts!", "Achtung! Surrender", and "Filthy Hun!". German papers refused to respond in kind, and the Germans went on to win the cup.

The Springer enterprise also publishes one of the four informed, serious, nationally distributed elite newspapers, *Die Welt*. The others are the moderately conservative *Frankfurter Allgemeine Zeitung*, the slightly left of center *Süddeutsche Zeitung* (published in Munich) and the outspoken left-liberal *Frankfurter Rund-*

Germany (FRG)

schau. The authoritative *Handelsblatt* is the German counterpart to the *Wall Street Journal,* and the lively *taz* aims at an alternative audience.

The political party press no longer plays a significant role as it did in the Empire and Weimar Republic days. The *CSU* puts out its weekly, *Bayernkurier.* Also, the *PDS* continues to publish the daily *Neues Deutschland,* which has changed greatly from its dogmatic *SED* days; it reports news more objectively and is free to criticize some *PDS* policies. All other newspapers in the GDR had been censored and controlled at least indirectly by the Communists. In 1991 they were put on the auction block, and all but two of the 15 eastern German dailies were sold; the Trust Agency intervened to ensure that they did not all fall into the hands of the four major media magnates.

West German publishers bought the East German regional papers and gave them a new look. But none of western Germany's newspapers caught on in the East; only one-eighth of the total circulation is western. *Berliner Zeitung, Freie Presse* (Chemnitz), *Sächsische Zeitung* (Dresden), *Mitteldeutsche Zeitung* (Halle), and *Volksstimme* (Magdeburg) are widely read.

There are widely read weeklies. The highly influential *Der Spiegel,* with a circulation of one million, originally modeled itself after America's *Time.* Now it is far more opinionated, investigative, critical and crusading in its reporting. In the words of *The Economist*, it "has probably done more to raise German blood pressure over the years than any other single publication." *Stern*, with sales of 1.4 million, is also investigative (some would say "muck-raking"); since 1983 it has sported a black eye for publishing faked Hitler diaries, for which it had paid a fortune. *Die Zeit* is intelligent and politically moderate, the *Deutsche Zeitung* conservative and Protestant, and the *Rheinischer Merkur* conservative and Catholic.

In 1993 three new weeklies entered the market to challenge the supremacy of the established news magazines. *Focus* has an American-style format and includes short news items and heavy use of graphics and glossy color photos. *Die Woche* also has a color format, shorter articles, and provocative interviews to "organize controversy." *Die Wochenpost,* a serious journal founded in the GDR in 1953 and bought by *Stern* after unification, has been revamped. It emphasizes on-the-spot reporting and includes long articles. It is a favorite among intellectuals in eastern Germany, where 80% of its copies are sold.

Approximately 85% of all Germans watch one of the two half hour nationally televised daily news programs, and political programs constitute about one-third of all television public programming. Public radio and television are administered by non-profit public corporations which are financed chiefly by monthly fees paid by those who own televisions or radios and by limited advertising. There are nine regional radio-TV corporations, which combine to form the "Association of Public Broadcasting Corporations" (ARD) in the Federal Republic. The ARD sponsors the first TV channel, televised nationally, and the third channel, televised regionally. It also encompasses the two radio corporations, the *Deutschlandfunk* (Germany Radio), which broadcasts within all of Europe in German and 14 other languages, and the *Deutsche Welle* (German Wave), which transmits on short and medium wave all over the world in more than 30 languages.

A second German television channel, based in Mainz, transmits nation-wide on the second TV channel. All channels reach audiences in former East Germany, in which some TV broadcasting survived the momentous changes of 1989. In order to insure that the radio and TV corporations remain politically independent, their legal basis is in *state* laws, and they are overseen by broadcasting councils composed of representatives of all important political, ideological, social and religious groups. Although they are duty-bound not to favor any particular political party,

Germany (FRG)

"One doesn't become the darling of the audience through violence"

their programming and the appointments to their councils and management do sometimes become subject to controversies among the parties. Since the 1980s ARD's and ZDF's ratings have dropped significantly as private TV channels capture a larger and larger share of the audience. For example, 56% of young people age 14 to 29 watched private channels in 1995. A growing number of adults watch a private all–news channel (N–TV) similar to CNN, and Phoenix, which is equivalent to C–Span. Private TV provides a lucrative market for U.S. companies; of the foreign programs purchased by German networks in 1997, almost 90% were American.

Artistic Traditions and Theatre

Germany has a glittering cultural tradition, but Nazi rule drove its cultural elite abroad, especially to the U.S., and Germany has never regained its earlier pre-eminence. It can still claim a reputation for music, however. It has 72 orchestras and music theaters in the West, generously subsidized by the states or cities. Some are highly regarded internationally, such as the Berliner Philharmonik, the Sinfonieorchester of Munich, the Stuttgarter Kammerorchester, the Bach–Orchester of Munich and the Berlin Amati–Ensemble. An American, John Cranko, who died in 1973, helped Stuttgart to develop into a ballet center equal or superior to Munich. Further, many foreign musicians such as Ingrid Bjoner, Evelyn Lear, Jess Thomas, Tomas Stewart and, it should not be forgotten, the Beatles, received their first significant stage experience in the FRG. Since the 1980s Anglo–Saxon musicals, especially those composed by Sir Andrew Lloyd Weber, have become popular. For example, by 1995 three of his shows had run for eight years in specially rebuilt theaters: *Starlight Express* in Bochum and *Cats* and *Phantom of the Opera* in Hamburg. Major cities in the GDR also enjoy an excellent quality of performing arts.

In painting and sculpture no post war German artists have been able to establish a distinguishing German style which is internationally recognized as such. The FRG does have many artists who produce recognized works in styles coming from abroad. This is particularly visible in pop–art and hyperrealism, movements which emanated from the U.S.

In literature, German writers after 1945 strove to make a clean break from the past. In their writings they tried to come to grips with their nation's experiences under dictatorship, in war and in postwar misery. In the 1950s and 1960s, though, new themes emerged, which focused on the materialism and egotism of a prosperous society. Many German writers became unmistakably political in their writings and, in a few cases, in their public involvement. The best known of such writers in the West are Heinrich Böll and Günter Grass. Böll, who in 1972 became the sixth German to win the Nobel Prize for Literature and who died in 1985, wrote with grace and simplicity. He was an avowed moralist, who was in the forefront of the contemporary "peace movement." Grass' German is full, rich and imaginative, and through his fantasy characters he bitterly criticizes the shortcomings of his society. He is a staunch if often critical supporter of the *SPD*. He campaigns actively for the party and even wrote about his electoral activities in a book, *From the Diary of a Snail*.

Much of contemporary western German literature is characterized by anxiety, malaise, self–doubt and social criticism. Many writers show impatience with traditional literary themes and styles, reject fixed criteria, focus sharply and without humor on the individual's problems in society, and above all, criticize their society which they often view as unjust and hostile to individual freedom and identity. Many see themselves as initiators of resistance to the social order. The predominant picture of western Germany presented in its contemporary literature is that of a sick society. The German public is also very receptive to another kind of critical literature, namely that coming from East Germany, where much of Germany's best writing now originates. GDR authors like Stefan Heym (who had been an American Army major during the war), Christa Wolf, Ulrich Plenzdorf, and Jurek Becker, were widely published in the West. They were popular enough to disregard the simplicity of "socialist realism," and to criticize certain characteristics of the *SED* state. Wolf was criticized for withholding some of her criticism of the regime until after the GDR's fall, when she published *Was Bleibt (What Remains)*, written ten years earlier, describing how she was watched by the secret police.

In addition to their inclination to criticize their own society, western German writers have sought to improve their monetary position within that society. In 1969 they formed the Association of German Writers (VS), which has won for writers certain material benefits, such as a law requiring libraries to pay a small fee for every book it lends, which goes into a fund to finance such things as writers' supplementary pensions. The VS also has won the possibility for free lance writers to sell their writings to the mass media at higher prices.

German theatre thrives today, but partly because of massive state subsidies. Ticket sales yield only 15% of theaters' income. Only about a fifth of western FRG's 300 theaters are privately owned. While many persons argue that state support enables more artistic guidance, rather than commercial ambitions, government cuts are hitting the arts hard. In 1993 two of Berlin's most famous theaters, the Schiller and the Schlosspark, were closed. Several dramatists have won international recognition, such as Heinar Kipphardt, Franz Xaver Kroetz, Martin Walser and Peter Weiss. Rolf Hochhuth's play, 'The Representative,' dealing with Pope Pius XII's at-

Germany (FRG)

A Munich pedestrian area

titude toward Hitler's extermination of the Jews stirred up much impassioned discussion after the war; this gives an idea of how Germans searched their souls to understand their recent past.

The works of several East German authors, such as Peter Hacks and Ulrich Plenzdorf, were played with much success on western stages. East Germany had succeeded in maintaining a high standard of theater. Bertolt Brecht had returned there after wartime exile in the U.S. and provided an important impetus to it. After 1989 eastern German theater has been able to become more experimental.

Until the mid–1960s it appeared that the German reputation in film, established before the war by such directors as Fritz Lang, Ernst Lubitsch, F.W. Murnau and G.W. Pabst, would be lost forever. The first two decades of postwar productions were mainly provincial, unproblematic entertainment films, which could be summed up in one German word: *Schmalz* (corniness). The need to compete with television for viewers helped keep the level of films low. Between 1956 and 1976, the annual production of German films and the number of cinemas dropped by 50%. Even today, a fourth of all films shown in the FRG comes from the U.S. and a fifth from Italy and France. Only a fifth come from Germany itself, and fewer than 6% of all western German film viewers went to see them.

In 1994 *Der Spiegel* asked young Germans what their favorite films were. The top ten were *all* American, led by *Schindler's List,* followed by *Dances with Wolves, Dirty Dancing,* and *Pretty Woman.* Partly because of the 1968 Film Promotion Measures Act and a Film Promotion Agency, which channels state subsidies to producers of feature, documentary, short and youth films, a wave of creative filmmaking, known as "the young German film," emerged in the 1960s.

German directors in this wave have succeeded in winning international recognition. They include Alexander Kluge, Volker Schlöndorf, Johannes Schaaf, the late Rainer Werner Fassbinder, Hans Jürgen Syberburg, Bernhard Sinkel, Margarethe von Trotte and two directors who particularly like to place their films in American settings, Werner Herzog and Wim Winders. However, since they often fail to attract sufficiently large audiences, the federal government decided to curtail funding for heavily experimental and purely artistic films after 1983. Like their literary counterparts, German film directors tend to focus on the blemishes of Germany's social and political order.

A refreshing exception is Doris Dörrie, a self–assured young director. She went to the U.S. to become an actress, but instead she studied film and theater in California and New York. In her box office success, *Männer (Men)*, the characters laugh about themselves and each other, and their laughter is contagious for the audience. She reflects the waning ideological inclinations of contemporary Germans: "I grew up with pop concerts, not with political discussions. . . . The fact that I do not deal with big political themes is directly linked to that."

Eastern Germany's film future was uncertain. The Trust Agency announced in 1991 that it would try to save the DEFA film production studies in Potsdam–Babelsberg. Founded in 1946, it was the site of the entire GDR film industry and included a college for film and TV and an agency for film exports and imports. Before 1989 it had annually produced about 20 feature films, 25 TV films, 170 documentaries, and many animated films. In 1992 Volker Schlöndorf stepped in to rescue the Babelsberg studio, acting as its business manager and attracting investors. By 1996 it had again become one of the world's most advanced film facilities, producing more than one feature film a month, as well as soap operas and TV dramas.

THE FUTURE

1999 was a jubilee year in Germany: 50 years of the FRG; 50 years since the Berlin Air Lift; 10 years of German unity. But the FRG faces daunting challenges and has not yet found a consensus for bearing the political and economic costs of unity. A poll in 1996 showed that 47% of Germans believed the differences between the two parts of Germany are growing, while only 43% believe they are diminishing. Social and economic conditions in the new Germany are more polarized than in the old West Germany, and the political environment is less settled and predictable. Many people feel disenchanted and bitter. All

Germany (FRG)

are worried about growing unemployment and the prospect that their living standards will not be sustainable. Easterners are especially unsettled by economic uncertainty. Although most have a higher standard of living than before 1990, others are waiting for the upturn they were promised. Westerners are losing patience at having to shoulder the expense of unification, with no end in sight.

Germany's problems are relatively minor compared with those it faced in the 1940s and 1950s. By world standards, it has a workable economy in the West, a good track–record for achievement, and a well–trained work force in the East to fall back on. None of its current difficulties threaten to derail democracy.

As a fully sovereign, unified nation, it shows more independence in its foreign policy, as its participation in the air war over Yugoslavia demonstrates. In general, Berlin's partners should welcome the shift from restrained passivity to restrained activity. It will remain a conscientious partner in the restructuring of NATO, at the same time that it promotes a unified Europe and some form of European defense identity.

As in all Western European and North American democracies, Germany is experiencing a disturbing malaise directed toward the political establishment and the mainstream parties. Voters sent a stern report card to Helmut Kohl in the September 1998 *Bundestag* elections. They handed the reins of power to *Social Democrat* Gerhard Schröder with a 21–seat majority. What demoralizes Germans most is that by 1999 unemployment had soared to 10.7% with little likelihood that the new chancellor's "Alliance for Work" can do anything about it; the problem is especially severe in the East. With 410,000 out of work, Germany is experiencing its highest joblessness since the 1930s, and political leaders do not know how to combat it. Berlin economist Michael Burda argues that "the global revolution in markets has taken away the power of political leaders to deliver on their most important promises to the voters."

At the same time the government led the country into a common European currency without having convinced many Germans that the "Euro" will be good for them. Many believe that it will be weaker than the *Deutschmark*, long an emotional symbol of German economic stability, and the first months of its existence have confirmed that fear. In the lead–up to the 1998 elections, the 16–year–old center–right governing coalition was paralyzed and weakened in the face of rising unemployment and reports of fading German economic competitiveness. Some international economists even called Germany a "newly declining country."

Germany's much–praised system based on consensus, to which many have long attributed Germany's political and social stability since the war, now seems to have become a catchword for paralysis. The German Language Society chose *Reformstau* ("reform blockage") as the "word of the year" in 1997. The Kohl government tried and failed to achieve the "tax reform of the century," as well as to revamp pensions and health insurance.

The elections produced a workable majority, despite divisions within the *SPD* and between it and the *Green* partners. They also brought an entirely new generation of leaders to power, one that has no memory of the Nazi era. The young rulers in their 50s govern from Germany's former imperial capital, a dynamic city that is steeped in history. All are graduates of the 1968 protest movement, all certified war–haters, all anti–nationalists. Within weeks of becoming chancellor, Schröder stated that Germany's self–confidence is that "of a nation that has come of age, that feels neither superior nor inferior to anyone." On another occasion he said: "Having to say *mea culpa* about the past should not interfere with the way we deal with the present and future." He sat silently when leftist novelist Michael Walser said when receiving a book prize: "We are confronted all the time with our guilt. Auschwitz has become a moral stick to beat our people. Over time this has become an empty ritual." Finally Germany could put its past behind it and look into the future. Or so the new chancellor thought.

The American novelist William Faulkner once wrote that "the past is never dead. It is not even past." This is certainly true for Germany today. Schröder was faced with a chorus of critics, including Jewish groups, who claimed that he was pushing too fast to disclaim Germany's legacy of guilt and to free himself and his government from past complexes. He was quickly reminded of just how alive Germany's past is: his government had to decide on a Holocaust memorial in the heart of Berlin close to the Brandenburg Gate and right behind the future American embassy. What is the proper way of honoring victims? Should a memorial be a place of reflection or (as in Washington D.C.) of learning? After much emotional debate, it was agreed that there would be a toned–down memorial with a wall–shaped library containing a million books, and a research center for scholars. Then he had to confront the multi–billion dollar demands to compensate foreign laborers who had been forced to work for German companies during the war. As of mid–1999 the talks remained deadlocked.

A few days before he inaugurated the Berlin republic on April 19, 1999, a chastened chancellor reflected whether his generation has a different attitude about the Holocaust: "No. This event will always influence the way German politicians think and act. Even if one says there is no such thing as collective guilt, it is still our task to see to it that people remember what happened because by remembering we can assure it will not happen again." Such remembering remains part of Germany's future.

View of Berlin's Unter den Linden boulevard with the Brandenburg Gate at upper left.
Courtesy: German Information Center

The Republic of Austria

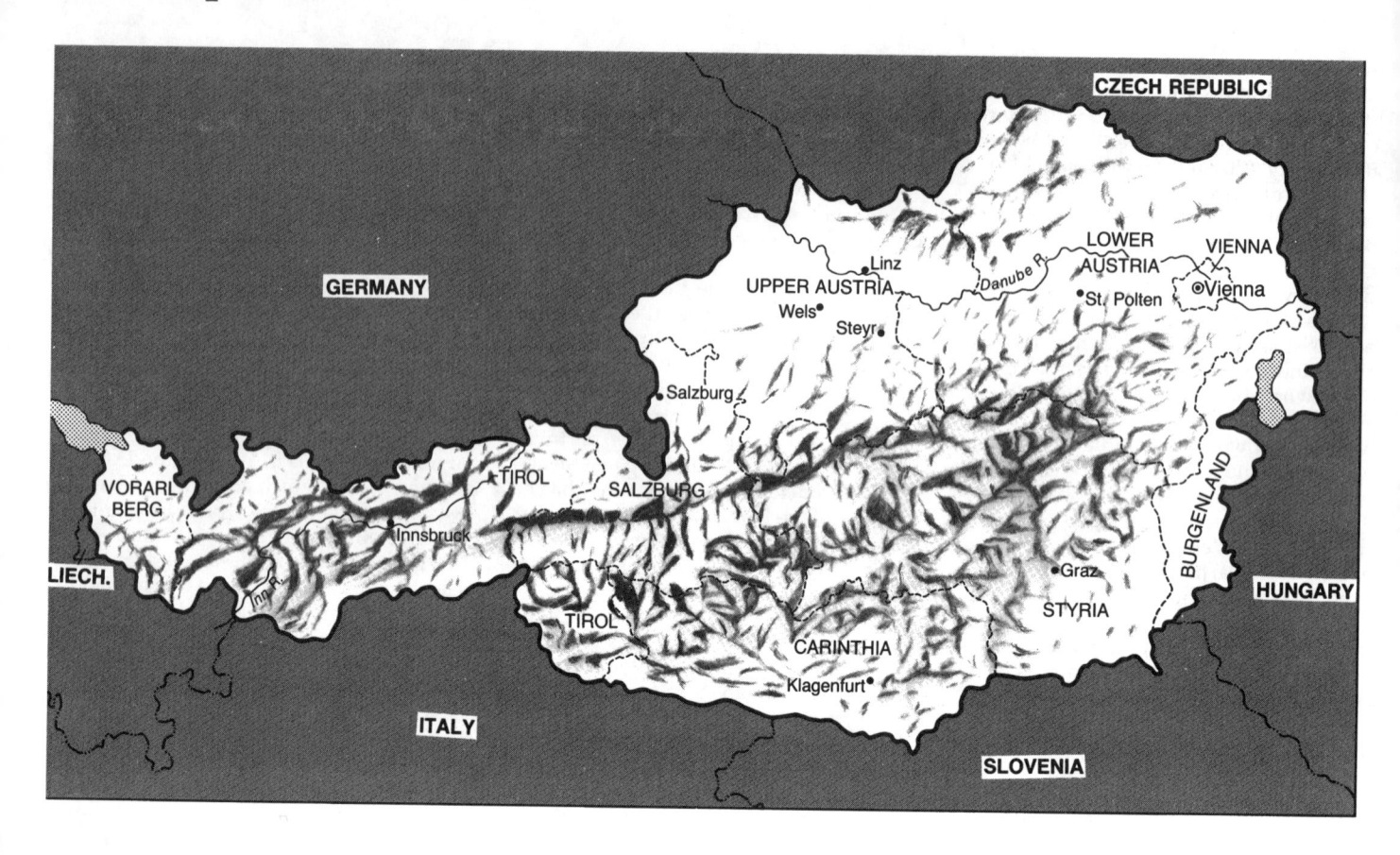

Area: 32,369 sq. mi. (83,835 sq. km.).
Population: 7.9 million.
Capital City: Vienna (Pop. 1.6 million).
Climate: Alpine. Temperate, with rainy days from late October to mid–December. Snowfall begins in the mountains in mid–November, with the air clear and the days cold but sunny.
Neighboring Countries: Czech Republic and Germany (North); Switzerland and Liechtenstein (West); Italy and Slovenia (South); Hungary and Slovak Republic (East).
Official Language: German.
Ethnic Division: German (98.1%); Croatian (.7%); Slovene (.3%) other (.9%).
Principal Religions: Roman Catholic (85%); Protestant (7%); other or none (8%).
Main Exports: Iron and steel products, machinery and equipment, lumber, paper products, textiles, chemicals, hydroelectricity.
Main Imports: Machinery, vehicles, chemicals, metal goods, raw materials, fuels, foodstuffs.
Principal Trading Partners: EU 66%, Germany 42%, Italy 9%, Switzerland 5%, Eastern Europe 11%.
Currency: Schilling.
National Day: October 26 (1955), when U.S., Allied and Soviet occupation was ended.
Chief of State: Thomas Klestil, President (since May 1992).
Head of Government: Viktor Klima (since January 1997).
National Flag: Three horizontal bands—red, white and red. Flags may also have the national emblem, a double–headed, black eagle centered in the white band.

Austria is a landlocked Alpine country. Three–fourths of its territory, particularly in the West and South, is covered by some of the most majestic mountains in the world. About the size of Maine and twice the size of neighboring Switzerland, it is but a small piece of the huge, multinational Austro–Hungarian Empire which collapsed in 1918. It was always a hub for North–South European traffic, and the Danube River, which flows from southern Germany through northern Austria and Vienna, through Eastern Europe and empties into the Black Sea, has always been an important transportation link between Eastern and Western Europe.

This nation borders more countries than does any other Western European land. About three–fourths of Austria is embedded geographically within what has been known since World War II as Eastern Europe; this fact made the former Soviet Union particularly interested in Austrian neutrality. It also has made Austria a natural meeting place for leaders of Eastern and Western Europe, as well as a land of refuge for several hundred thousand Eastern Europeans since 1945.

Austria is a country of truly extraordinary natural beauty. Its snow–capped peaks overlook lush green valleys, countless streams and lakes and picturesque mountain villages. Austria is filled with architectural reminders of its imperial past. Everywhere one sees elaborately decorated baroque churches, imposing castles and palaces, and large, serene monasteries and cloisters. Every major city, especially Vienna, has rich museums and elegant theaters which keep alive the artistic tradition of the country. Also, more than a dozen musical festivals take place in Austria every year, the most famous being in Salzburg. These testify to a creative musical past almost unparalleled in the entire world.

The visitor is greeted by a people who are relaxed, friendly, hospitable and strongly traditional, especially outside the capital city of Vienna, where about one–sixth of the country's population lives. Almost nine out of ten of its people are Roman Catholic, and 99% speak dialects of German which have a distinctive and pleasant musical ring to them. There are three small language minorities in Carinthia, where 20,000 Slovenes live

Austria

along the border of Slovenia, and in the Burgenland along the southeastern border, where 25,000 Croatians and some Hungarians live. Small Czech and Slovak minorities have also survived in Vienna. There are about 180,000 foreign workers in the country; about 120,000 are from former Yugoslavia and a large percentage of the remaining 60,000 are from Turkey.

In some ways Austria is strikingly similar to neighboring Switzerland. Both are naturally beautiful and economically prosperous countries. Despite a high degree of cultural diversity, both are politically stable democracies. Both are federal states, although Austrian politics are more centralized than is the case in Switzerland. Both pursued neutralist foreign policies. Yet there are also undeniable differences. Whereas the Swiss established a secure national identity centuries ago, Austrians until recently lacked a clear consensus on what it actually meant to be an Austrian. Also, in Switzerland a stable democracy was able to evolve slowly and was therefore able gradually to gain the backing of the overwhelming majority of its citizens. By contrast, Austria remained a highly stratified and traditional country until well into the 20th century and has confronted an almost traumatic change of its political, social and economic practices and values.

HISTORY

The Early Period

Historical evidence indicates that what is now Austria has been settled since the late Ice Age almost a thousand years before Christ. Indications of earlier human presence are uncertain. Between 35 and 15 B.C. the Romans conquered the Celtic inhabitants and divided the area among three Roman provinces. The new masters gave the region many of the same benefits which they bestowed on other lands: Roman law and administration, a well–developed network of good roads, aqueducts and new forms of agriculture, including wine–making. They founded most of Austria's cities, such as Vienna, Salzburg and Linz, and between 150 and 350 A.D. they introduced Christianity.

When the Roman Empire began to crumble, the area which is now Austria became vulnerable to invasions by Germanic, Hun and other tribes, which brought much destruction to the area from the 5th through the 8th centuries. Not until Charlemagne established a bulwark in the extreme eastern part of his huge empire in 799 did the area become relatively stable and secure. He called this area his East March (frontier), whose present name in German, Österreich, reflects the area's earlier role. From 799 on, Austria's destiny was very closely tied to that of the rest of the Germanic world.

Part of the Holy Roman Empire and Hapsburg Rule

Austria became a part of the Holy Roman Empire in 962 and a few years later the House of Babenberg began its 270–year reign over the country. The Babenbergs gradually moved their capital eastward, and in the 12th century finally established it in the Hofburg (literally the court fortress) in Vienna. The last Babenberg ruler fell in 1246 in one of the countless struggles against the Hungarians.

Count Rudolf of a family from the "Habichtsburg" in the Aargau area of Switzerland was selected Holy Roman Emperor in 1273. This Hapsburg family ruled Austria for the next 600 years, and under its leadership Austria rose to be one of the grandest powers of all of Europe. This extremely rapid growth inevitably changed European politics drastically. The Hapsburg genius was to be able to expand its empire more by wise marriages than by war. By the 16th century they had acquired an empire over which the sun never set. Flanders and Burgundy had been gained through a marriage with Mary of Burgundy. In 1516 Spain came under Hapsburg rule, and in 1521 two Hapsburg brothers saw a need to divide administratively the last empire between themselves. This was not the end of growth; in 1526 Bohemia and Hungary were unified with Austria. Most of Latin America except Brazil came under Hapsburg rule, as did the Netherlands, the rest of Belgium, Naples, Sardinia, Sicily and a few provinces in eastern France. This huge empire was geographically divided with major centers as diverse as Vienna, Brussels, Zaragoza and Naples; it had no unifying elements except the ruling House of Hapsburg.

Defense Against the Turks

Austria was often forced to perform its duty of defending Europe from the East. In 1529 and 1683 the Turks actually reached the gates of Vienna and besieged the city. Both times the Austrians pushed them back. The second time the Austrians were led by a foreign prince, Eugene of Savoy, a grand nephew of the French Cardinal Mazarin. Eugene drove the Turks out of Hungary, thereby stemming once and for all the Turkish tide westward. An influential national hero, Eugene ordered the construction of one of Vienna's most beautiful palaces, Belvedere, which served as his summer residence. His winter palace is now the office of the Austrian minister of finance. His time was an era of the Baroque, a style which reached its zenith in Vienna and Salzburg, and which can still be admired everywhere in Austria.

Street closed to motor traffic in downtown Vienna

Austria

Empress Maria Theresia

A salon in the Schönbrunn Palace

Maria Theresia

The Austrian Empire had become the envy of other rising European states, which looked for a chance to snatch attractive chunks of its holdings. When the Austrian emperor Karl VI died in 1740, one rising power moved particularly swiftly: Prussia. In both Prussia and Austria, two young monarchs ascended to the thrones in 1740. They dominated much of the European scene for the next four decades and converted Germany into a loose bundle of many states with *two* dominant powers. In Prussia, a philosophically inclined 28–year–old Friedrich II, later known as Friedrich the Great, who had composed chamber music and had written books condemning war and immorality in politics, was crowned king. In Austria a 22–year–old woman who had shown great interest in the arts, but virtually none in politics, became Empress—Maria Theresia. Preferring to reside in the more gracious Schönbrunn Palace rather than the Hofburg, she became a devoted wife and the mother of 16 children to whom she gave as much love and concern as any mother could.

She presented herself to her people as a happy, sincere, pious, philanthropic and folksy ruler, and she was loved and respected by almost all her subjects. Yet she was a courageous and hard–working ruler who had a knack for choosing able advisers and was stubbornly determined to defend her empire and the Catholic faith. Calling herself the "first and supreme mother of her lands," the Austrians under her leadership tenaciously fought Friedrich in three wars and was forced in the Treaty of Hubertusburg in 1763 to concede only the province of Silesia to Prussia, which had risen to the status of a major European power as a result of the wars. She had moral qualms about taking advantage of some of the diplomatic opportunities which offered themselves, such as participating in the partition of Poland, but for reasons of state she did it anyway. It is no wonder that Friedrich the Great referred to her as "the only man among my opponents."

During her reign Vienna bloomed. Today both the works of Haydn and Mozart as well as the streets in the city which boasts palaces, fountains and statues, attest to the greatness of her era. Vienna became the cultural center of the German–speaking world. It also became the sole center for administering the far–flung Austrian Empire, and Austrian politics still reflects the high degree of centralization which Maria Theresia intensified. She was absolutely opposed to religious toleration and attempts to reform her Empire "from below." She herself introduced lasting reforms, though. She separated the judiciary from the administration, abolished torture, established elementary schools, and removed the universities from Church control.

Her son, Josef II, a liberal ruler, accelerated the reform process after her death in 1780 by eliminating all traces of serfdom and by granting his subjects the right to choose their preferred religion. Hapsburg rule at this time was conscientious and in some respects far–sighted, but it nevertheless was "enlightened absolutism." The principles of democracy and equality were greatly distrusted and persistently opposed, which is one reason why Austria was unable to resist the tide set in motion by the French Revolution in 1789.

Napoleon

When Napoleon created in 1806 a "Confederation of the Rhine," dependent upon France, Kaiser ("Caesar," or "Emperor") Franz renounced the crown of the "Holy Roman Empire of the German Nation," and that long moribund entity ceased to exist entirely. Napoleon's Grand Army crushed the Austrian forces in 1809 at Wagram, and the French Emperor was able to dictate a humiliating "Peace of Schönbrunn" from the once beloved residence of Maria Theresia. Austria had its revenge after the bulk of Napoleon's experienced troops had frozen to death in the bitterly cold snows of Russia. An Austrian general, Prince Karl Schwarzenberg, commanded the victorious Allied forces at the "Battle of the Nations" against Napoleon near Leipzig in 1813.

The Congress of Vienna and the "Holy Alliance"

An Austrian Foreign Minister, Prince Klemens von Metternich, was a Rhinelander who led Austria from collaboration with Napoleon to an alliance with his enemies and therefore insured victory. He was able in 1814 to assemble six emperors and kings, 11 princes and 90 accredited envoys at the Congress of Vienna for eight months in order to reconstruct Europe after the fall of Napoleon. The flood of political figures and their entourages provided many Viennese the splendid opportunity to rent out their houses at exorbitant prices and to escape to the countryside to count their windfall profits.

Those foreign notables who could not afford the high prices either slept in the city's beautiful parks or in or under their carriages. Most envoys spent their time in cafes, at balls, at receptions or at tournaments trying to amuse themselves while the major powers, Britain, Austria, Prussia, Russia and, surprisingly, the loser—France—were deciding Europe's fate behind closed doors. In the final settlement, Austria's hold over peoples in Eastern and Southern Europe was recognized. The Austrian monarch thus continued to rule over a multi–national empire led by Germans and composed of Czechs, Slovaks, Poles, Hungarians, Italians, Croatians, Slovenes, Serbs and others.

Austria's attention now more than ever had to be directed away from the German world. Still, it was determined to compete with Prussia for dominance within Germany. Prussia had been granted German lands in the Rhine and Palatinate areas in order to help keep a potentially revengeful France from springing beyond its borders. This arrangement, which led Prussia into the heart of Germany and Austria out of it, ultimately helped Prussia to defeat Austria in the struggle for control of Germany.

Emerging from the Vienna Congress was a "Holy Alliance," which was dedicated to preventing further reform within Europe. Britain left this pact almost as soon as it had been created, but Russia, Austria and Prussia remained. All three ultimately paid very dearly for their determination to dig in their heels and to ignore the signs of the times.

The spirit of the "Holy Alliance" matched Austria's mood very well. It had a conservative elite, who ruled over a very hierarchically organized society. The nobility owned most of the land and provided the bulk of the army officers, diplomats and upper civil servants. Most of the peasants were poor and powerless while the bourgeois scrambled for whatever authority or titles they could obtain. To this day, Austrians probably remain the most title–conscious people in Western Europe. Fortunate is he who can attach a "Herr Doktor" or a "Herr Professor Doktor" to his name—and female spouses are permitted to borrow their partner's titles! Others use such titles as "Herr Engineer (or Businessman) with Diploma," "Herr Government Counselor," or "Herr Chief Postal Official."

Prince Metternich took the task of opposing change as seriously as did Kaiser Franz, who proclaimed in 1831, "I won't have any innovations!" The press was heavily censored, and mail was opened and read by government agents. Spies were sent into university lectures, and school authorities were obligated to report any sentiments which might be considered subversive. Students were forbidden from studying in foreign universities, and until 1848 all reading materials used in schools or universities required government approval.

Revolutionary Stirrings

Given the repression of individual freedoms and of the right of national minorities to manage a part of their own affairs, it is not surprising that the wave of revolution in 1848 also shook the Austrian state. A Hungarian nationalist, Louis Kossuth and others, demanded constitutional government for Hungary, but Kossuth admitted that this would be impossible so long as "a corrupting puff of wind that benumbs our senses and paralyzes the flight of our spirit comes to us from the charnel house of the cabinet of Vienna." Fighting soon broke out in Vienna, where a flabbergasted Kaiser asked, when told that rebels were taking to the streets: "But are they allowed to do that?" The rebels had momentary success until the revolutionaries themselves became hopelessly disunited over the objectives which should be sought.

The Hapsburgs were forced to dismiss Metternich, and the incompetent Kaiser abdicated in favor of his 18–year–old nephew, Franz Josef, a serious and hard–working monarch who ascended the throne with the words "farewell youth!" and who ruled for the next 68 years! A constitution, albeit authoritarian in character, was accepted, and Austria sent representatives to the Frankfurt Assembly, which sought unsuccessfully to draft a liberal constitution for all German–speaking people. Ultimately the revolution failed in Austria, as it did almost everywhere else in Europe. Nevertheless, it had badly shaken the Empire and revealed deep dissatisfaction with a form of government which was not democratic and which did not recognize the rights of subject nationalities. Yet, once the revolutionary storm had blown over, the new ruler showed how little he had learned by enforcing a policy characterized by absolutism and tight centralization.

Competition and Partnership with Prussia

In 1866 Austria suffered a crushing defeat at the hands of the Prussian army at the battle of Königgrätz. With new breech–loading rifles, which had been used so successfully in the American Civil War, and the capacity to move their troops to the battlefield on new railroads, the Prussians were far better prepared than the Austrians, whose wealth had been spent to construct the stately Ringstrasse in the center of Vienna rather than to modernize their army. This defeat finally wiped away any Austrian dreams of dominating or sharing power over all of Germany and cleared the way for a "small German" unification clustered around Prussia and excluding Austria.

For more than a century the dualism within Germany pitting Austria and Prussia against one another had powerfully influenced the European constellation of nations. That dualism was destroyed, and the relationship between the two states became one of partnership. The Prussian Chancellor, Otto von Bismarck, refused his generals' request for permission to make a victory march straight through the heart of Vienna in order to humiliate Prussia's long–time rival. Bismarck remarked that it was not his aim to humiliate or judge, but rather to serve Prussia's interests. Prussia needed a trustworthy ally, and for the next half century Austria played that role. For instance, in 1870 Aus-

Seat of the Congress of Vienna

Austria

Archduke Franz Ferdinand and Emperor Franz Joseph

tria did not try to prevent Prussia's unification of Germany by supporting the French in the Franco–Prussian War of 1870.

Continuing Nationalities Problems

The new German Empire, which was proclaimed in the Hall of Mirrors at the Palace of Versailles in January 1871, had acquired an ally which would become increasingly weakened by its nationalities problem. The 19th century saw the birth of nationalist movements all over Europe. A multi–national state like Austria had to swim against the current of the age and could survive only by introducing timely reforms to satisfy the aspirations of national minorities. Austria was never able to do this.

The German–speaking minority of the Austro–Hungarian Empire was able to reach a compromise with the Hungarians in 1867 as a direct consequence of the defeat at Königgrätz. The Hapsburg Empire was converted into a dual monarchy, composed of two independent and equal states, with the Austrian emperor serving also as the Hungarian king. Military, diplomatic and imperial financial affairs were handled in Vienna, but Hungary had its own parliament, cabinet, civil service and administrative system. While this settlement did increase the efficiency of governmental operations within the Empire, it stimulated yearnings for independence or autonomy on the part of the Empire's other nationalities, especially the Czechs. From time to time there was talk in the Empire of federal reforms which might extend the same privileges to all subject peoples, but these always foundered on the rocks of Hungarian and Austrian intransigence.

Despite a short–lived liberal era in the late 1860s and 1870s, the last decades before World War I displayed growing tension within and along the borders of the Austro–Hungarian Empire. As elsewhere, these were decades of rapid industrialization which not only increased the country's wealth, but also gave birth to a powerful working class movement and to a *Socialist Party* which demanded better pay and working conditions. Although the socialists were moderate in their aims and methods, they were bitterly opposed by conservatives who saw in them a mortal threat to the state.

The steady collapse of the Turkish Empire and growing Russian interest in Balkan affairs (clothed in idealistic terms of Pan–Slavism) seriously threatened the very existence of Austria–Hungary, which sought to preserve the *status quo* at all costs. In 1912 the Balkan states had fought against Turkey in order to enlarge themselves at Turkey's expense, and in 1913 the same Balkan states fought each other over the booty. To Austria's chagrin, the chief winner in both was the rising and highly ambitious Serbia, which began to serve as an attractive model for the Southern Slavs within the Austro–Hungarian Empire. Also, in 1913 a high military official, Col. Alfred Redl, was revealed to have been a spy for the Russians for over ten years. This shocking revelation shook Austrians' confidence in their own governmental structure and weakened its international reputation.

World War I

Thus, the Austrians tended to overreact when one of the most important events in world history occurred on June 28, 1914, a Serbian holiday commemorating the assassination of the Turkish sultan in 1389 by a Serbian patriot. Austrian Archduke Franz Ferdinand and his wife were murdered in Sarajevo, now Bosnia's capital, by a Bosnian student, Gabriel Princip. The Archduke had become successor to the throne after the Kaiser's only son, Rudolf, had become entangled in an extramarital love affair and finally killed himself and his mistress in 1889. The shots of Sarajevo sounded the end of an almost 50–year absence of major wars among European great powers. Austria held Serbia responsible for this act and, ultimately, backed by Germany, made unacceptable demands upon Serbia. All over Europe, alliances were invoked, threats were made, "blank checks" and ultimatums were issued. In the end, all major powers had painted themselves into a corner with their many commitments, and could not get out. By the first week of August Europe was locked into a war which lasted four long years and which far exceeded all previous wars in terms of casualties and destruction. Shortly before his death in 1897, Bis-

Austria–Hungary until 1918, showing the nations carved from its borders

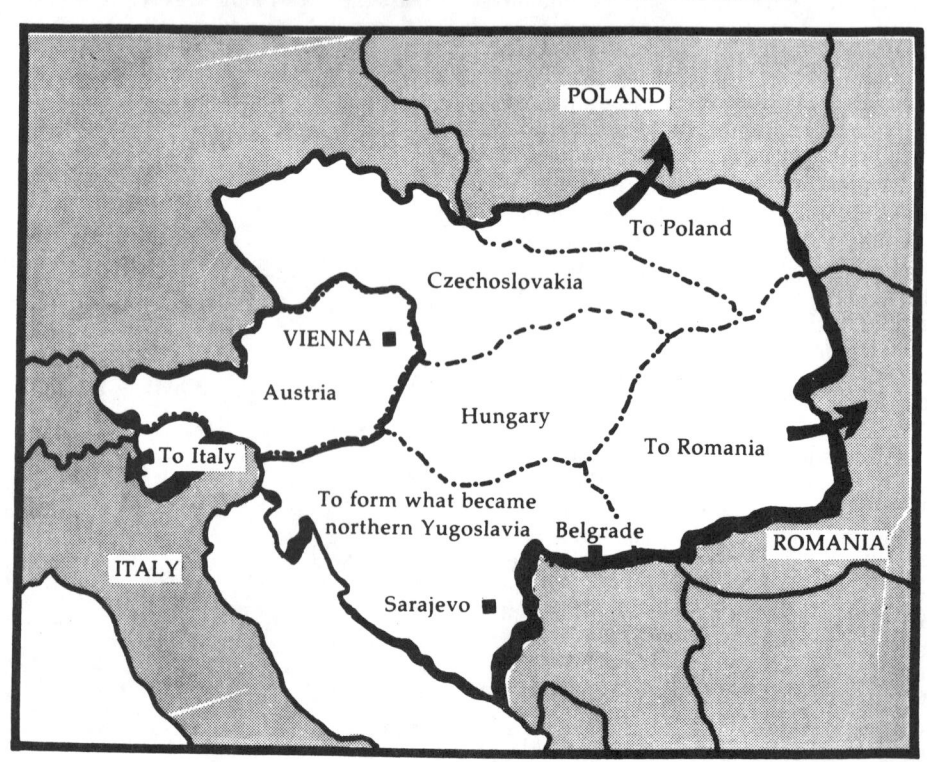

106

Austria

marck had correctly predicted that "one day the great European War will come out of some damned foolish thing in the Balkans."

During World War I Austria–Hungary primarily sought to retain some control over the Balkans. As Germany's military power ebbed, Austria became increasingly bewildered and confused. Proportionately, Austria–Hungary's losses of men were greater than those of Germany: 1.2 million killed and 3.6 million wounded.

By the fall of 1918 the various non–German nationalities within this empire had begun to mount opposition movements. An exhausted Austria simply ceased to fight in the face of such resistance and the quite imminent and predictable collapse of Germany in the fall of 1918. Another casualty of the war was the mind of wounded Austrian Corporal Adolf Schickelgruber, a reject of the prestigious Austrian Academy of Art in Vienna. This mind was further inflamed by the Germanic defeat as he fumed in prison. It would come into full bloom in just 15 years when he would become master of Germany, using the name Adolf Hitler.

On November 11, 1918, Kaiser Karl, who had ascended to the throne upon the death of Franz Josef in 1916, abdicated. The next day the Austrian republic was proclaimed. Soon a democratic constitution was put into effect. The new republic was not more than the small German part of the former Empire. The Treaties of Trianon (with Hungary) and St. Germain distributed the rest of the territory to Romania, Poland and Italy, or was used to construct the new states of Hungary, Czechoslovakia and Yugoslavia. In the process, Austria lost 4 million of its German–speaking population to Hungary, Poland, Czechoslovakia, Yugoslavia and Italy. It also lost access to the sea. Proportionately, it lost much more territory than Germany. Such fragmentation destroyed the Austrian economy. This was the worst possible atmosphere for an untried democracy, and for the next two decades Austria was unable to regain its balance. In desperation, many Austrians demanded in 1920 a referendum to join the newly formed German republic to the north, but the victorious powers vetoed such a combination, fearing that it would strengthen Germany.

Hopeless Internal Division

From the start, Austria was hopelessly divided into two hostile camps, represented politically by socialists, whose strength was in Vienna, and the *Christian Social Party*, which was strongest in rural areas. These camps not only created social institutions such as sports clubs, reading circles and youth groups, which isolated their members from those in the other camp, but they also created large and well–armed paramilitary units. The socialists had their *Schutzbund* ("Protective League"), and the opposing *Heimwehr* ("Home Guard") had become so heavily armed by 1933 that it reportedly had tanks and howitzers and enough material to equip 500,000 men for a military campaign of moderate length.

Inflation, unemployment and working class and rural poverty eroded the sympathy and patience for a formally democratic state, which could be kept alive during the 1920s only by loans from the League of Nations. The world–wide economic depression which shook Europe so violently in the early 1930s eliminated whatever shreds of stability were left in Austria and opened the door widely to political extremism.

An authoritarian Chancellor Engelbert Dollfuss, a diminutive man who reportedly liked his nickname of "Mini–Metternich," sought to convert Austria into a corporatist state (one in which all citizens belong to highly organized groups which are bound together by the political leaders in order to achieve the state's goals) on the model of by then fascist Italy. In 1933 he dissolved Parliament, and in early 1934 he ordered the arrest of political opponents, especially socialists, liberals and trade union leaders. He even ordered that artillery fire be directed against workers' tenements in Vienna, and that ruthless methods be used to suppress any resistance within the working class districts. He promulgated a constitution which allowed him to rule Austria as a dictator, but his time was very short. In July the Austrian *Nazis* attempted an unsuccessful *coup d'etat* in Vienna. They were able to seize the chancellery for only a few hours, during which time they murdered Dollfuss.

"Union" with Germany

He was replaced by Kurt von Schuschnigg, who tried to retain Austrian independence, but who soon discovered that he had very little support. The socialists and trade unions had been crushed, and the middle classes liked more and more the idea of a union with the increasingly dynamic Germany. When Adolf Hitler, Nazi leader of Germany, decided that the time had come for Austria to become a part of Germany, there was little which Schuschnigg could do. Under orders from Berlin, the pro–Nazi Austrian interior minister, Arthur von Seyss–Inquart, assumed Schuschnigg's functions and called upon the German *Reich* to save Austria from alleged communist chaos. On the night of March 11, 1938, three days before a scheduled national referendum to determine whether Austria should become an integral part of Germany (which the unifiers were expected to lose), German

Austrian Chancellor Dollfuss ("Mini–Metternich")

Austria

Germany's Hitler enters Vienna, 1938

troops entered Austria. Two days later it became a province of the German Third Reich. By the time that Hitler greeted the cheering crowds at the Heldenplatz in Vienna, 70,000 Austrians had already been put into jails or concentration camps.

This *Anschluss* ("joining") of the two countries lasted seven years, a time of almost continuous war, destruction and suffering for the Austrian people. Loss of Austrian lives during the war, although not as severe as in World War I, nevertheless was substantial. Altogether 6% of the population, almost 400,000 Austrians, including 65,000 Jews, perished during the Nazi period. Of course, Austrians were both victims of and participants in the Nazi terror. In 1945 more than a half million Austrians were members of the Nazi party, a higher proportion of the population than in Germany. Also, about a fourth of the convicted Nazi war criminals were Austrian. On the other hand, Austria had, in fact, been occupied against its peoples' will in 1938 and had been forced to fight alongside the Germans. Beginning in 1944 the victorious allies emphasized that Austria would be treated as a victim of Nazism; they did this to encourage Austrians to surrender. After the war, many Austrians gladly accepted this interpretation of occupation along with the collective absolution it offered.

Memories of this war experience helped to convince almost all Austrians that they had a destiny which could not be linked directly to Germany. In prisons, concentration camps and resistance groups, many Austrians who had earlier professed widely different political views learned to know and admire each other. This helped create a sense of tolerance and determination to work out political differences peacefully. Also, the need to rebuild the country after the war helped Austrians to put aside their ideological differences and to work together for the good of all Austria.

Thus, out of the ashes of destruction, a strong commitment to democracy was born. Also, the looting and raping for which some Soviet soldiers were responsible in the post–World War II period horrified and alienated most Austrians. This antipathy helped prevent the communists from winning the active support of the Austrian people and thereby from accomplishing the Soviet goal of quickly consolidating power in Austria and then of legitimizing this power through controlled national elections.

The Postwar Occupation Years

The four principal victors divided Austria into four occupation zones: the Russians occupied the eastern part of the country surrounding Vienna; the Americans occupied the north–central part which included Salzburg; the British occupied the southern and the French the western portions of the country. In mid–1946 restrictions on interzonal traffic and trade were lifted. The inner city of Vienna itself was declared an international zone and placed under four–power occupation, a fortuitous factor which made it more difficult for any one power to coerce the Austrian government. The Allies declared that Austria had been illegally occupied by Germany in 1938 and had been 'liberated' in 1945. Therefore, on May 1, 1945, Austria's constitutuion of 1920 as amended in 1929 and all laws passed prior to March 5, 1933 (the date Dolfuss took power) went into effect. Unlike Germany, Austria was permitted to have its own civilian government from the very beginning, so allied control was always indirect, rather than direct, as was the case in Germany.

At first, political conditions in Austria seemed to be just to the Soviets' liking: there was no strong and popular non–communist partisan group to liquidate (as was the case in Poland) nor (or so it seemed at the time) was there a strong non–communist political party which had to be intimidated into submission. Despite the fact that the communist cadres, who had spent the war years in Moscow, were generally unknown and distrusted by most Austrians, they were aggressive and confident that they could control the political future of Austria. They thought their opposition to Hitler had increased their popularity and that the presence of Soviet troops could enhance their political status and influence.

The Soviet occupiers looked for a leader of a multi–party Austrian government which, they hoped, would be dominated by their compliant Austrian comrades. They thought that they had found just the right man—Karl Renner, a popular and highly respected socialist who had been the first chancellor of the earlier Austrian Republic. Because he had hesitatingly supported the *Anschluss* in 1938, the Soviets assumed that he could be blackmailed, if necessary. Best of all, they falsely assumed his old age would rob him of the stamina to deal with detailed problems of governing, and this would make him more amenable to compromise with the communists.

Renner skillfully and tactfully proceeded to dash the Soviet hopes. He formed a three–party government composed of the *Communist Party*, the *Socialist Party of Austria (SPÖ)*, and the old *Christian Socialist Party,* now purified of its former authoritarian ideas and renamed the *Austrian People's Party (ÖVP)*, which shared executive and administrative positions. The ministries of Interior, which controlled all police and security forces, and of Education, Public Information and Worship were given to communists, but Renner devised an ingenious way of minimizing the potential dangers of having such important ministries guided by communists.

He proposed that two undersecretaries be appointed to each ministry so that all three governing parties would be represented at the top of each ministry. The communists were delighted because they though that this arrangement would enable them to exercise influence in every ministry. The real result, though, was general inefficiency and deadlock in most departments. If any undersecretary vetoed a matter, it was sent to the cabinet for consideration. To get the cumbersome 35–member body to act quickly on matters of importance, he established the pol-

Austria

icy of serving wine and food to the cabinet members after each session. Because normal rations in Vienna in 1945 were a near–starvation 400 to 800 calories, the meals which followed the meetings were often of greater importance to the participants than the business at hand.

Renner held the most controversial matters until the end, so that the cabinet could reach an agreement very quickly and with a minimum of controversy. Further, after June 28, 1946, the decisions of the Austrian government could not be reversed unilaterally by the Soviet authorities. Austrian legislation was submitted to the Allied Control Council (ACC) for approval, but if a *majority* of the Allied commanders did not disapprove it within 31 days, the legislation automatically became law. The significance of this was that the Austrian government could continue to function even when the Allied powers were in disagreement. As was clear by 1947, an unfortunate single vote arrangement doomed the ACC in Germany to impotence.

In the fall of 1945 the Allied powers agreed to permit elections for the newly established Austrian Parliament to be held in November. Austrian communists confidently assured the Soviets that they could gain 25 to 30% of the votes, but Russian and Austrian communists were stunned by the results: the ÖVP received 49.8% of the votes, the *SPÖ* 44.6% and the communists a mere 5.42%, which gave them only four seats in Parliament. The Soviets had clearly misread the political temper in Austria, and the election was one of the most important events in postwar Austrian history. It brought to a halt the communist hopes to gain control of the country.

Until 1966 the *ÖVP* and the *SPÖ* ruled Austria together in a *Proporzsystem* (proportional system) whereby cabinet and administrative posts, and many other jobs down to janitorial positions, were distributed to leaders and members of the two parties according to their electoral strength. This system allowed the two largest to work together as a team rather than have to join with extremist parties. It also enabled the government to defend the country's interests against the Allied occupation forces and to combat attempts to destroy or pervert democracy in Austria.

After the election disaster, the Soviet Union had no consistent and clearly defined aims for Austria except economic exploitation. The Soviet Union originally had demanded that Austria pay it reparations because Austrian soldiers had served in the German army and had participated in the destruction of the Soviet Union. The other three Allies refused this, pointing out that this would be inconsistent with their agreement that Austria was to be treated as a liberated country. Therefore, the Soviets demanded and were granted the right to administer the many economic assets which the German government had acquired in the Soviet zone in Austria.

In 1946 it assumed ownership of the Danube Steamship Company which had come into German ownership *after Anschluss*. Through the Soviet Petroleum Administration (SMV), the Russians controlled most of Austria's petroleum reserves. The Administration of Soviet Property in Austria (USIA) operated 420 confiscated industries and agricultural holding by 1955 and employed about 10% of industrially employed Austrians.

Fearing further Soviet expropriations, which in the end would leave very few industries and resources in eastern Austria for the Austrians themselves, the Renner government dropped all ideological reservations and began in 1946 to nationalize the nation's three largest banks and all heavy industry, including all principal mines, the largest steel, iron and aluminum plants, most petroleum facilities, the main electrical plants, the automotive, locomotive and shipbuilding industries and the Danube Steamship Company. In 1947 they nationalized the power industries. The Russians, who controlled about 60% of these nationalized industries, were greatly angered and simply refused to recognize the Austrian legislation. In return, the Austrians refused to recognize most of the Soviet holdings. In the years that followed, the Austrian government nationalized the railroads, civil aviation, public utilities, radio and television, and the salt, tobacco, liquor and match monopolies.

By the early 1950s Austria had established a stable domestic political order, and Marshall Plan aid from the U.S. helped to create the conditions for the rapid reconstruction of the country and for the gradual return of prosperity. In fact, in the time period from July 1948 to June 1949 Marshall Plan aid alone accounted for 14% of the Austrian national income, a far higher percentage than in any other European country. However, the country was still occupied and divided, and it was therefore not yet sovereign. Austria was caught in the great power tensions which had replaced the unified Allied effort to crush Hitler. Leopold Figl said before Parliament in 1952: "The Austrian people know that it is not because of technical or objective matters that the treaty is being held up: it is purely power political considerations to which justice must give way."

Within the first decade after occupation of Austria, more than 300 meetings of the Allied deputy foreign ministers had been held to discuss a settlement in Austria, but the results were always the same. Suddenly in February 1955 an important break in the stalemate came when Soviet Foreign Minister Molotov announced that the Soviet Union would consider signing a state treaty with Austria. The following month it called on Austria to send representatives to Moscow to discuss the matter. When a rather skeptical Austrian delegation, which included the state secretary for foreign affairs and Bruno Kreisky (who later served as Chancellor of Austria), got off the plane in Moscow and was greeted by all the major Soviet leaders, it was clear that something good was about to happen. Kreisky whispered into Vice–Chancellor Schärf's ear, "If they receive us with such pomp and circumstance, they cannot send us home without pomp and circumstance."

The talks went extremely well, and the concluding "Moscow Memorandum" outlined the major provisions for the subsequent treaty. First, Austria was to adhere to a policy of neutrality on the Swiss model. Second, occupation forces would be withdrawn from Austria by the end of 1955. Third, all Soviet economic holdings in the country would be returned, for which Austria would pay over $152 million and ship a million tons of oil to the Soviet Union each year for ten years. The Western Allies accepted this settlement very quickly, since its terms were far more favorable than they had ever sought. On May 15, 1955, the Austrian State Treaty was signed in the Belvedere Palace by the Allied Foreign Ministers Molotov, McMillan, Dulles and Pinay, and by Austrian Foreign Minister Figl.

Full Sovereignty Again

Austrian surprise and joy at this formal ending of Austria's occupation status was

Dr. Karl Renner

Austria

indescribable. In the West, reactions were a mixture of perplexity, pleasure and uneasiness. Why, after ten years of delay, did the Soviets leave Austria? There are many reasons, but the main one is probably that the Soviet Union wanted to make a final attempt to prevent West Germany from entering NATO, whose founding in 1949 Soviet leaders had been unable to prevent. Many Germans desperately wanted to see their country reunified, and by dangling before their eyes an attractive example of what a low price must be paid for national unity and a withdrawal of foreign troops, the Soviet Union hoped to persuade them to remain neutral and to work out a form of German national unity acceptable to the Soviet Union.

As the *New York Times* noted: "The Kremlin is producing a little miracle play for the benefit of the Germans, not the Austrians." However, neither the Western Allies nor a majority in the West German Parliament could overlook the fact that the stakes in Austria were not nearly so high as in Germany. Austria is a small country with little influence on that balance of power which had prevented the Soviet Union from seriously considering attacking Western Europe. By contrast, Germany *is* a key to maintaining that balance of power. This fact made many West Germans highly skeptical that the Soviet Union would be as willing to tolerate for long an independent and neutral Germany as it would an independent and neutral Austria.

POLITICS

Military Limitations

As a fully sovereign state, Austria spelled out the precise status of its neutrality in a constitutional amendment enacted on October 26, 1955, now the country's national holiday. The amendment explicitly forbade Austria from entering any military alliances or permitting any foreign troops to be stationed on Austrian soil. It also pledged to use all the means at its disposal to maintain and defend its neutrality.

Austria formed no military links with the Soviet Union, but it has its own army, which the treaty severely limited in size. The army has only 50,000 ground troops, most of whom are draftees who must serve six months after completion of their 17th birthday, and who must participate in periodic military exercises after discharge, as in Switzerland. (But in 1978 a reform was adopted to establish a militia 180,000 strong by 1986 and 300,000 by 1998.) This army is forbidden by the treaty to possess guns which fire farther than 30 kilometers or to possess nuclear or special weapons, including missiles.

Although Austria is not forbidden to have an air force capable of protecting its own airspace, NATO and Warsaw Pact aircraft violated that airspace for more than three decades. As its army commander noted, the country's defense "stops ten meters above the ground." Even with an improved air defense capability, it is still doubtful that Austrian troops could defend their country against a well-equipped and determined attacker, in contrast to the Swiss military which would probably be able to do.

Foreign Policy

Austria's chief foreign policy goals are to preserve its independence and to promote peace and stability in the community of states. This called for a form of neutrality which Austria calls *active*. Austrians interpreted theirs as military, *not* political neutrality. From the beginning Austria rejected Swiss practices by seeking to join certain international political organizations. In December 1955 it joined the United Nations, and the following year it entered the European Council (which does not deal with military questions).

Austria has supplied troops for UN peacekeeping missions in the Congo, Cyprus and the Middle East, especially on the Golan Heights between Israel and Syria. Since joining the EU in 1995, Austria has participated in practically all international missions in the Balkans. In 1996 alone, 1,200 Austrian soldiers served in UN missions, including Bosnia, and in 1997 it sent soldiers to Albania to help stabilize that country that had temporarily fallen into chaos. Austria's commitment to the UN was particularly conspicuous while Kurt Waldheim served as UN Secretary General from 1972 to 1982. Certainly the policy of neutrality placed no muzzle on either politicians or private citizens. As Foreign Minister Leopold Gratz stated in 1984, "Our neutrality binds the State, but not the individual and not the press, and not our thinking. So we never left any doubt as to which political system we adhere to." Also, that neutrality did not necessarily prevent Austria from considering sanctions against other countries.

Austria also had no problems entering purely economic organizations. In 1960 it entered EFTA, a free trade organization whose economic importance is steadily declining. Its association with the EU, with whose members two-thirds of its trade is conducted, was much more problematic because of the EU's stated goal of political unity. The Soviet Union objected to the possibility of Austria's full membership, but it was prepared to accept Austrian associate membership with no *political* role. After five years of difficult negotiations, Austria reached an agreement in 1972 which provided for the almost complete dismantling of customs and trade restrictions on industrial and agricultural goods between it and the other EU countries by 1977.

In the early 1990s Austria formally applied for full EU membership. The EU required Austria to give assurances that its neutrality would not stand in the way of a common foreign and security policy. In 1994 former Chancellor Vranitzky indicated that his government was contemplating entering the WEU, though not NATO. Even though two-thirds of Austrians voted in a June 1994 referendum for EU entry, he made it clear that "we aren't throwing neutrality overboard overnight." But the entry of Poland, the Czech Republic and Hungary into NATO in 1999, perhaps followed one day by Slovenia, affects Austria's security deliberations. It prompted

The Austrian Parliament

Austria

President Klestil to say in 1996 that his country will have to redefine its role in Europe. His remarks sparked a lively debate.

Although public opinion remains opposed, the junior member of the governing coalition, the *People's Party*, supports entry, arguing that neutrality no longer makes sense after joining the EU. But Chancellor Viktor Klima ruled out applying for early NATO membership. Austria joined the Partnership for Peace (PfP) in order to strengthen its ties with NATO. In 1998 it also hosted the Alliance's supreme commander, General Wesley Clark, who stressed that its proximity to the Balkans and other flash points makes membership an attractive proposition to Austrians and to NATO. The country would provide a convenient land bridge to NATO peacekeeping forces in the Balkans and to Hungary, which shares no border with a NATO partner. He said; "Austria would be most welcome."

There were many opponents to EU entry. They include over–protected farmers, persons who fear for the anonymity of their bank accounts, and ecologists who are afraid that Austria's tough environmental rules would be undercut by weaker EU ones. By 1997 opposition had grown further, as it became clear that rich Austria would have to contribute to EU coffers and as the government justified unpopular budget cuts by pointing to the need to slash benefits and raise taxes in order to meet the EU criteria for a single currency.

Finally, there were unarticulated fears that its entry would somehow increase the weight of a "German bloc" within the EU. Already, Austria's economic relations with the FRG are crucial. By 1991, 40% of its industry and 70% of its daily newspapers were owned or controlled by German investors, and 40% (and rising) of its exports were directed toward an enlarged Germany. Nevertheless, Austria became a full member of the EU on January 1, 1995.

Austria stands outside all military alliances and provides for its own security by making a contribution to peace in the world. At least since the Congress of Vienna in 1814–15, Austria has been the location for important international meetings. It sees itself as especially qualified for the role of a "bridge–builder" between East and West. President Kennedy and Soviet party chief Nikita Khrushchev met in Vienna in the early 1960s. From 1970–72 most of the meeting between American and Soviet negotiators to work out the SALT I Treaty were held in Vienna, and President Carter and Soviet President Leonid Brezhnev signed the Salt II Treaty there in 1979. After 1989 NATO and Warsaw Pact nations conducted Conventional Forces in Europe (CFE) negotiations in Vienna, aimed at achieving reductions of conventional weapons in Europe. The CSCE decided in 1990 to create a conflict prevention center in Vienna.

The Hofburg, once offices of the emperors, now of the presidents

Austrians see themselves in a totally new situation. Before 1989 they were in a kind of *cul–de–sac,* surrounded on three sides by the communist bloc; now that dead–end has been transformed into an intersection with a bustling thoroughfare opening into the East. One Austrian diplomat put it this way: "We used to be on the eastern fringe of western Europe; now we are in the center of Europe again." Austria and Hungary liberalized their border relations so much that in 1989 Hungary dismantled the electronically monitored fences and watchtowers along the Austro–Hungarian border. Austrian officials fear a flood of refugees from other Eastern European countries and therefore deployed troops along the border to prevent illegal crossings and speeded up the procedure for asylum applications. Austria played a central role in the westward exodus of East Germans in 1989. This opportunity to render a dramatic humanitarian gesture strengthened its application to the EU by demonstrating that it is a useful and trusted Western country with excellent connections in Eastern Europe. Concerned that too many Bosnian refugees had arrived, it began in 1997 offering them monetary incentives to return home.

It helped form the *Pentagonale,* joined by Italy, Hungary, Czechoslovakia, and Yugoslavia, to foster a project–centered approach to issues of international affairs, such as the environment, where more progress can be made through regional negotiations. Austria is looking nervously at the former Yugoslavia. The republic of Slovenia is pressing for new economic and political ties with Austria. Because of the tension between the Czechs and Slovaks, the latter, whose capital Bratislava is close to Austria, is increasingly turning more to Vienna. Involved in more than 8,000 joint ventures with its eastern neighbors (4,000 in Hungary alone), Austria is becoming more deeply integrated with Eastern Europe. But it finds itself besieged by cheap imports and immigrants from the East. Therefore, it introduced protective measures against sensitive imports and, for the first time in decades, halted the flow of immigrants.

Vienna is the location for many permanent international organizations. For instance, the headquarters for OPEC is located there. The city is rapidly becoming one of the three major centers for activities of the UN. Austria built, at its own expense, a huge and ultra–modern Vienna International Center, which it rents to the UN for a symbolic one Schilling per year. This "UN on the Danube" houses the International Atomic Energy Agency, the UN Industrial Development Organization (UNIDO), the UN Relief and Works Agency for Palestine Refugees, most UN offices dealing with drug traffic and abuse, the UN Commission on International Trade Law, and many others. Austria also sets aside public funds amounting to about .3% of its GDP for aid to developing countries.

In sharp contrast to Switzerland, Austria never believed that its neutrality should prevent its political leaders from speaking out publicly on important international questions. For instance, Austria always sharply condemned the Soviet Union's disrespect for human rights and its use of military force in Eastern Europe and in Afghanistan. In 1983 it issued a blistering condemnation of the Soviet's shooting down of a South Korean civilian airliner.

Toward the end of his long chancellorship which ended in 1983, Kreisky, who died in 1990, approved sales of Austrian–made arms to military dictators in Argentina, Bolivia and Chile, as well as to certain key Middle Eastern countries, such as Tunisia, Egypt and Saudi Arabia. In 1991 his successor as chancellor, Fred Sinowatz, along with Sinowatz's foreign and interior

Austria

The Vienna Opera House

ministers went on trial for covering up and failing to halt illegal arms shipments to Iran and Iraq. Kreisky openly supported the idea of the Palestinian right to a homeland and met personally with Yassir Arafat, the controversial leader of the Palestine Liberation Organization (PLO), which maintained a permanent representative in Vienna. Kreisky did strongly condemn its representative in 1981, however, because of the latter's contacts with Arab terrorists. His concern grew even greater when a terrorist planted a bomb in a Jewish synagogue in Vienna a few weeks later. His sympathy for the Palestinian cause and willingness to sell arms to moderate Arabs, despite the fact that he himself is a Jew, reaped the public scorn and personal hatred of Israel's former prime minister, Menachem Begin.

Territorial Losses and Claims

In addition, Austria's neutral stance did not prevent it from defending its own territorial claims which it found entirely legitimate. After the end of hostilities in 1945, Yugoslavia again raised its claim to part of the Austrian province of Carinthia and underscored this by occupying the province. However, the British, in whose zone the province was located, ordered the Yugoslav forces out of the area. After the split between Yugoslavia and the Soviet Union in 1948, there was no major power which continued to support the Yugoslav claim. Therefore, in 1955 it recognized Austria's possession of the region in exchange for some promises to make cultural concessions to the Croatian minority located there.

Austria was less successful in gaining control of the largely German-speaking and traditional Austrian area of South Tirol, which the Treaty of Saint Germain had awarded to Italy in 1919. For more than two decades, Austria unsuccessfully demanded that the South Tirolians be permitted to determine in a referendum whether they wished to belong to Austria or Italy. After World War II none of the victorious allies supported Austria's claims. Therefore, it was forced to enter long negotiations with the Italian government to achieve the highest possible cultural autonomy for German-speaking residents of the area of Bozen, which the Italians combined with the overwhelmingly Italian-speaking region of Trentino.

These talks were periodically marred by bombings in South Tirol by German-speaking Tirolians who favored annexation by Austria. Finally, in 1969 an agreement was reached whereby the language rights of the South Tirolians would be respected, and certain governmental responsibilities would be transferred to Bozen, which would become autonomous. Also, low income housing, public service jobs, funds for kindergartens and schools and many other subsidies are distributed on a proportional basis depending on the size of the respective population groups. The formula has been German: 60%, Italian: 30% and Ladiner (a small minority isolated in two valleys, speaking a Latin-based language and related to the Romansch minority in southeast Switzerland): 10%. Though falling short of their original demands, South Tirolians approved this solution in a referendum and Austria pledged to relinquish all its claims over the area as soon as the language rights were fully realized. Some South Tirolians still assert that Italy has not yet fulfilled its promises.

The Emergence of Democratic Trends

Also like Switzerland, Austria is an economically prosperous and stable democracy with a federal form to help accommodate diversity and a consensus approach to political and economic problems which helps guarantee political and labor peace. This contrasts almost completely with Austria before 1918; with numerous ethnic minorities demanding independence, a militant working class demanding a world socialist revolution, rampant anti-Semitism (which helped produce both Hitler's anti-Jewish ravings and Theodor Herzl's Zionist dream of a Jewish homeland), anti-capitalism, anti-communism and anti-clericalism, all dangerously blended to generate constant tension, hatred and violence.

In contrast to Switzerland, whose democratic system has evolved slowly over centuries, Austria has undergone radical changes in political and social values and practices. German-speaking Austrians often had no clear national identity. Did they belong to the German nation or to a separate Austrian nationality? In a poll taken in 1956, 46% indicated that they belonged to the German nation, but in 1991, three-fourths said that an Austrian nationality already exists, with only 5% rejecting Austrian nationhood. This explains why there was unease in Vienna in 1990, when the German government adopted plans to include Austria in the new German History Museum in Berlin. The polls reflect an important change, but one former U.S. ambassador still asserted that "there is no Austrian . . . The Austrians are the creoles of Europe. Look at the Vienna telephone book. It's like a final exam in Germanic and Slavic pronunciations."

During the first republic after 1918, far too few Austrians held firm democratic values. Most had formed their political views under the authoritarian Empire, and many were outright antagonistic and scornful toward democracy. In addition, there was a weak liberal tradition. The chief enemy of the socialist and Catholic subcultures (called *Lager*) was liberalism, which stressed individual rights and free economic activity largely uncontrolled by the state. Finally, common experiences during and immediately after World War

Austria

II had a great effect on the minds of many Austrians, in that extremist politics of the left and right were discredited. Of course, the basic subcultures did not immediately disappear after 1945, but most Austrians strongly supported their government, which sought to rid the country of foreign occupation and to establish a democratic Austria. They shared a widespread determination not to allow the country to devour itself as it once had.

Government Structure–The President

Austria has a parliamentary form of government. The head of state is a president, who is elected directly for a six–year term, with one reelection possible and with all citizens of voting age *required* to vote. The presidency is largely a ceremonial post, but the office would potentially have much power in times of political instability.

A shadow hung over the 1986 presidential election. Kurt Waldheim was haunted by revelations that he had served on the staff of a German general who had been executed in 1947 for war crimes in the Balkans area.

The charges did not help him in his campaign against the *Social Democratic* candidate, Kurt Steyrer. Waldheim received 53.9% of the vote to Steyrer's 46.1%. His election was not a vote for Nazism or anti–semitism. Austrians had grown tired of 16 years of *Socialist* rule, which had been marked by political scandals, wasteful bureaucracy, money–losing nationalized industries and ineffective economic policies. Therefore, voters elected the first conservative president since 1945.

Indeed, Waldheim's past increasingly made him unable to perform his largely ceremonial duties. In his first year in office, he became known to some as the "prisoner of the Vienna Hofburg." He could not receive foreign heads of state. Nor was it possible for him to travel abroad until 1987. Switzerland, Belgium, Japan and Canada politely communicated that he would not be welcome.

The most stinging rebuke came from the United States. In April 1987 Waldheim was put on the "watch list" after the Justice Department concluded that there was evidence that he had "assisted or otherwise participated in the persecution of persons because of race, religion, national origin or political opinion." This was the first time the U.S. had declared a friendly country's head of state an undesirable alien barred from entry. In spite of reassurances, many Austrians viewed the action as an insult to their nation; popular reaction within Austria was intense and negative at the time. The exact nature of the charges were made public in early 1994, and indeed, Waldheim was correctly found to have aided and participated in the Nazi efforts directed against Jews and foreign nationals.

More and more Austrians agree that their country must 'come to grips' with its past. An ominous reminder was given in 1991 when a Gallop poll conducted for the American Jewish Committee revealed that 39% of Austrian respondents held the view that 'Jews have caused much harm in the course of history'; 31% preferred not to have Jews for neighbors, but even higher percentages were averse to living near Poles, Slovenes, Croats, Serbs and Turks. Unlike the Germans, the Austrians have never engaged in a cathartic debate about their Nazi past, hiding behind the comfortable official interpretation that they had been Hitler's first victims. For the first time, Chancellor Franz Vranitzky acknowledged in 1991 that many Austrians had supported Hitler and had taken a hand in his crimes; he apologized for the atrocities Austrians had committed. Textbooks were subsequently changed to emphasize the complicity of many Austrians in Nazi crimes and the fact that Austria was not merely a victim of Hitler. Vienna's mayor decreed that the film, *Schindler's List*, is required viewing for all school–children. In 1993 Vranitzky had become the first chancellor to visit Israel, where he acknowledged that Austrians had been not only victims but also "willing servants of Nazism."

In 1995 parliament voted for the first time to pay compensation to 30,000 victims of Nazi persecution. In 1996 the government finally agreed to abide by the terms of the 1955 Austrian State Treaty that obligated it to return to the Jewish owners or heirs those art pieces that had been confiscated by the Nazis. In a gesture of atonement, it handed over 8,000 items to the Federation of Jewish Communities in Austria, which auctioned

President Thomas Klestil

them for more than $14.5 million, donating the proceeds to Holocaust victims. After two paintings by Egon Schiele, which Austria had lent for a show in New York, were seized because of suspicions that they had belonged to Holocaust victims, Culture Minister Elisabeth Gehrer ordered that once prior ownership is certified, all art confiscated by the Nazis would be returned to their rightful owners. In 1998 parliament unanimously approved this decision, which may strip more than 100 masterpieces from Vienna's leading museums.

Chancellor Viktor Klima, the first Austrian chancellor born after the Second World War, emphasized in 1997 that his government is committed to confronting and studying the Nazi past; "it must teach us." He reiterated this in 1998 on the sixtieth anniversary of the *Anschluss*. Also in 1998 the government gave the go–ahead to construct a holocaust memorial in Vienna. Critics had decried the structure, which they likened to a "concrete bunker" located close to the spot where hundreds of Jews had committed suicide in the midst of an anti–Semitic pogrom in 1421.

In the 1992 presidential elections Thomas Klestil of the conservative *Austrian People's Party* won with 57% of the votes; in 1998 he was reelected, receiving 63.4% on the first ballot, with a voter turn–out of 74.7%. A former ambassador to Washington and Number 2 in the foreign ministry, Klestil quickly succeeded in reestablishing ties with countries that had boycotted Austria and in enabling his country to assume a higher profile in international affairs.

In 1992 the Hofburg Palace, where the president has his office, was partly destroyed by fire. The 18th–century Redoutensaal ballroom and conference hall was gutted. The priceless National Library and Spanish Riding School were spared, and passers–by escorted 69 Lippizaner horses to safety in the middle of the night.

The Chancellor and the Parliament

In normal times, the most powerful political figure is the federal chancellor, who must control a majority in the National Council, by far the most powerful chamber in the bicameral legislature. By means of a complicated proportional representation electoral system in 25 districts, 183 members are elected by voters aged 20 or over for four–year terms. Despite this proportional representation system, which in other countries usually enables a large number of parties to win seats in the parliament, only five Austrian parties have been able to win any seats at all. The share of votes won by Austria's two main par-

Austria

ties, the *SPÖ* and the *ÖVP*, was 66% in the December 1995 federal elections.

The *SPÖ*, which renamed itself in 1991 the *Social Democratic Party of Austria*, is the country's largest party, and it ruled alone from 1970 until 1983. Its socialist appeals have been increasingly moderated, and it has become a pragmatic, reform-oriented party. Some of its members are still attracted to "Marxist" doctrine, but its program stresses that it welcomes all supporters who embrace the party's ideals as a result of religious, philosophic, humanistic or "Marxist" analysis. The party is openly anti-communist and was often critical of the former Soviet Union. It refuses any form of political cooperation with the *Communist Party of Austria (KPÖ)* which has sunk to political insignificance. The *SPÖ's* strength is found mainly in urban and industrial areas, especially in Vienna. The *SPÖ* dominates the trade union movement and attracts the votes of most workers, which give it a base of 38% of the electorate.

The *SPÖ* was led by a pragmatic, successful banker, who is on good terms with conservatives and the business community—Franz Vranitzky. His no-nonsense approach to solving the nation's economic problems helped the party in the 1995 elections. It won 38% of the vote and 72 seats, again becoming the senior member of the ruling coalition.

Exasperated with constant political feuding within his fractious coalition with the *People's Party*, and with the continued electoral success of Jörg Haider—whom he called a "racist hatemonger," Vranitzky stepped down as chancellor in January 1997. Having been in office for almost 11 years, he admitted to having underestimated Haider. He was replaced by his former finance minister, Victor Klima. Well-versed in economics, Klima has the right background to lead his skeptical countrymen along the tough road of austerity to the common European currency.

Two environmentalist parties—the conservative *United Greens of Austria (VGÖ)* and the more leftist *Alternative List of Austria (ALÖ)* all but disappeared in the 1994 elections. None of the other parties in parliament would consider joining a government with these unorthodox parties. But the more politically adroit *Greens* captured 8 seats.

The *Austrian People's Party (ÖVP)* was founded in 1945 by the anti-fascist elements of the former *Christian Social Party*. The Catholic Church now abstains from direct political activity, but the *ÖVP*, which does not view itself as a specifically Catholic party, can usually count on the support of most practicing Catholic lay organizations. The party is also successful in gaining the votes of farmers, independent merchants and industrialists, lawyers and doctors, and generally the middle class. The *ÖVP's* program favors a social market economy and private property, but it also supports social welfare and workers' participation in the management of companies. The 1992 election of the *ÖVP's* Thomas Klestil to the presidency had given the party a temporary shot in the arm and a new sense of purpose.

Chancellor Viktor Klima

The *ÖVP* entered a "grand coalition" as a junior partner with the *SPÖ*. Under its new leader, Wolfgang Schüssel, it continued its downward slide in 1995, capturing only 28% of the votes and 53 seats. This was a disappointment for a party which had hoped to make impressive electoral gains after breaking up the grand coalition when the *SPÖ* refused to accept more cuts in the budget. The *ÖVP* rules in coalition with the *SPÖ*, but it leaves open the possibility of an eventual coalition with the *Freedom Party* if cooperation with the *SPÖ* proves impossible.

The two parties had ruled together until 1966. During this time, they devised a "proportional system," which called for the fair distribution of governmental and administrative posts to members of the two major parties. For instance, cabinet members are often aided by state secretaries who belong to the opposite party. The Transport Ministry, with its patronage in the railways and highways, is a fiefdom of the *SPÖ*, while the Ministries of Agriculture and Defense are in the *ÖVP's* domain. Even jobs with the EU in Brussels are allocated according to this outdated practice. This system rested on a fundamental consensus about the nature of the democratic regime.

Nevertheless, there is a widespread feeling that the "proportional system" has outgrown its usefulness and that it has encouraged corruption and inefficiency since jobs are distributed on the basis of political affiliation, rather than competence. Among its absurdities is the fact that the state-controlled Austrian Airlines and the Vienna Airport each have two presidents. It is already being phased out in the state industries that have been privatized, but it remains strong in banking. A growing number of voters think it should be abolished in the civil service. Jörg Haider hammers relentlessly and successfully against this outdated system of patronage. After his *Freedom Party's* stunning success in the 1994 elections, he boasted that "we have finally succeeded in putting post-war Austria behind us."

The *Freedom Party of Austria (FPÖ)*, has risen dramatically, winning an astonishing 22.5% and 42 seats in 1994, mainly at the expense of the *ÖVP*. In 1995 it slipped to 22% and 41 seats. In 1996 it shocked the political establishment by soaring to 28% of the votes in Austria's first elections to the European Parliament and also in the Vienna city elections, where it deprived the *Social Democrats* of the absolute majority for the first time since 1945. These were the greatest electoral successes in recent years by a far-right party in Western Europe. Particularly potent were Haider's anti-EU appeals. He captured half of Austria's blue-collar workers and growing numbers of disaffected young people and women. Haider continues to fulminate against EU eastward enlargement and the massive influx of Central Europeans that might unleash. All Austrian politicians concede more politely and privately that fears of being swamped make enlargement a hard sell domestically. The three neighbors of the Czech Republic, Hungary and Slovenia have a combined population nearly three times larger than Austria's. The government estimates that five million foreign workers live within commuting distance of the main Austrian cities.

Wolfgang Schüssel
Vice Chancellor and Foreign Minister

Austria

The FPÖ's Jörg Haider

The *FPÖ's* main objective is to limit the state's influence in the economy and society. It generally appeals to the same voters as the ÖVP. But in order to raise its vote nationally, it has tried in recent years to stress the liberal components of its program and to move closer to the political center. It tries to prevent the formation of a dominant, completely two–party system; its present leader has branded the present grand coalition as a "marriage of elephants." In 1983, for the first time, it succeeded in entering a governing coalition itself. However, it was the ouster in 1986 of its moderate leader, Norbert Steger, by a more strident conservative, Jörg Haider, which cracked the coalition with the *SPÖ* and brought about the 1986 elections.

Haider is a fiery orator and a charismatic crowd–pleaser, who calls for a more nationalistic policy and denounces corruption, privilege, and the influx of immigrants. He called for stricter controls. The government felt obliged to respond by doing just that in 1993. It introduced some of Europe's toughest immigration laws. The vigor with which it intends to enforce these laws was revealed in 1999, when the interior minister admitted that a Nigerian asylum–seeker had been bound and gagged so tightly while being deported that he suffocated. One of the *FPÖ's* election posters read: "Don't let Vienna Turn into Chicago!" It is said that many ex–Nazis are attracted to the *FPÖ*.

Haider also appeals to young Austrians who are fed up with politics being dominated by the two big parties and who want change. Since Haider became chief, the *FPÖ* has gained seats in every provincial election. In 1989 he was chosen as provincial governor of Carinthia, a post he held until 1991, when provincial legislators voted him out for daring to compliment the Nazis by saying that "they had a sound employment policy in the Third Reich." In 1995 he again harmed his party by making sympathetic remarks to Waffen SS veterans. But he and his party roared back into prominence. In the 1994 and 1995 elections, the *FPÖ* got more seats in a national parliament than any other European far–right movement. In the March 1999 provincial elections in Carinthia it defeated all rivals by capturing 42% of the votes. Haider again became governor

The influx of immigrants, including 60,000 from Bosnia alone in 1992, brought the number of foreigners living in Austria to 550,000 by 1993. They experienced none of the violence that afflicted Germany, but the issue was propelled to the top of Austria's political agenda. One 1992 poll indicated that 79% of Austrian respondents do not want more newcomers. Haider tried to exploit this resentment by calling on a million Austrians to sign a petition demanding a temporary halt to all immigration, a 30% limit on foreign children in any school class, and a constitutional amendment stating that Austria is "not an immigrant country." The petition failed by getting only 417,000 signatures.

In the resulting clamor, the *Freedom Party* split in two, with five of its parliamentarians forming the *Liberal Forum Party* under the leadership of Heide Schmidt, temporarily ending any prospect of a coalition between the *FPÖ* and the *ÖVP*. *Liberal Forum* captured 9 seats in 1995. In 1993 the broad–based coalition of artists, writers and church leaders, called "SOS Neighbor," became the target of an ugly letter-bomb campaign by right–wing extremists. Vienna Mayor Helmut Zilk lost two fingers. In 1995 four Gypsies were killed in terrorist bombings. This wave of terrorism came as a shock to a country which had been spared the kind of neo–Nazi violence wracking Germany.

A Federal State

Austria is a federal state composed of nine provinces: Vienna, Salzburg, Vorarlberg, Carinthia, Upper Austria, Lower Austria, Burgenland, Styria and Tirol. Each province (called a *Land*) has a popularly elected legislature, which elects a governor and members who serve four to six–year terms in the 58–member Federal Council, the upper house of the Austrian Parliament. The number of seats allotted to each province depends upon its population. The smallest receives at least three seats, whereas the largest may receive no more than 12. Unlike the U.S. Senate, the Federal Council has far fewer powers than the lower house. It may only review and delay legislation, and it has the right to veto only the annual budget.

The provinces are not as powerful as states in the U.S., since most government authority, including police power, rests with the central government. The provincial governments do have certain authority over welfare matters and local government, and strong provincial loyalties persist. However, in general, Austria, despite its federal structure, is highly centralized politically. This condition prompted citizens in one province, Vorarlberg (which after World War I attempted to join the Swiss Confederation), to vote in a provincial referendum in 1980 for negotiation with the federal government to achieve more say over political decisions affecting its citizens, such as taxes and the allocation of funds.

Other Government Elements and Considerations

The Austrian constitution provides for a Constitutional Court whose members are appointed by a number of federal institutions and leaders. This court has the task to review all cases involving constitutional questions and to decide on jurisdictional conflicts between the various levels of governments.

The constitution also calls for the election of chambers financed by taxes and representing various segments of the economy, especially the Chambers of Agriculture, of Labor and of Commerce. These have the right to present advisory opinions on government bills and actions affecting their particular interests. Such chambers are no doubt holdovers from the former corporate state. However, they do play an important role in bringing diverse interest groups into the governing process and they contribute to establishing a political consensus which helps to maintain stability. Thus, they reflect the nature of democracy in Austria today, which aims to reduce conflict and to promote compromise in a land which historically was tragically torn. The process of compromise places much responsibility on the shoulders of political and economic elites, who must tie together various groups in the Austrian society.

This is one rationale for the rule of proportionality, by which offices are distributed among members of both major parties. The Austrian system would be fundamentally changed if one party or group would take all the spoils on the grounds that it won more votes in the last election. Of course, electoral campaigns are hotly fought and are filled with exaggerated rhetoric about how disastrous it would be if the other party were to win.

However, between elections the parties and economic groups cooperate with each other. To make this cooperation work effectively, political leaders must enjoy much freedom from their constituents or supporting subcultures. Some critics argue that this fact somewhat weakens popular control over the elites and weakens political participation of lower levels.

Austria

The Spanish Riding Academy with its world-famous Lipizzaner stallions being put through their paces

Also, young protesters in the 1980s maintain that their actions are in part directed against a political system which leaves far too little room for young people to determine their own future. But the democratic experiment in Austria has been so successful since 1945 that very few voices demand a fundamental change of the political system.

ECONOMY

Austria has basically a free enterprise economy in which the market determines what is produced and at what price. Economic competition exists and is encouraged, although it was traditionally not as highly valued as in the U.S. Still, today almost any market activity requires authorizations, licenses and certificates, and there are numerous 'free trade' restrictions. Further, since 1945, a higher percentage of the economy was under government ownership in Austria than in any other country in Western Europe. Almost two–thirds of all corporate capital belonged to the public sector, and a quarter of the entire labor force worked in nationalized industries or in industries controlled by nationalized banks. These were permitted to operate in large part independently of government control and account for about one–fifth of the country's GDP and one–third of its total exports.

On the whole, the Austrian economy is efficient, and the country is visibly prosperous. From the 1950s the economy grew steadily by about 5% annually until the mid–1970s, when Austria was also affected by the dizzying rise in oil prices and by the worldwide recession, which slowed down growth, sent the budget and balance of payments into severe deficit and produced flurries of inflation (1.5% in 1999) which caused Austrians some concern.

The largest trade union, the Austrian Trade Union Federation (ÖGB) represents about two–thirds of all wage and salary earners, one of the highest percentages of unionization in all of Western Europe. The ÖGB is a moderate labor organization which aims not toward revolution, but toward securing good pay and working conditions for its members. Its willingness to cooperate in order to help Austria maintain its economic health by stabilizing key

Austria

prices and by keeping wage increases from becoming inflationary is demonstrated by its participation in the Joint Price and Wage Commission along with representatives of the government and the Chambers of Labor, Agriculture and Commerce. Chaired by the Federal Chancellor, this commission meets once a month to discuss not only wages and prices, but also long–term economic changes, such as the length of the work week.

Its decisions are almost always honored because all groups concerned realize that this social partnership or industrial consensus is crucially important for the entire country. Though this partnership is formalized, it is based upon a frame of mind, namely, the readiness to solve problems and to achieve harmony together rather than to resort to militant confrontation. No doubt, memories of bitter social tensions in the past and the small size of the country help enable such social partnership to work.

There are other important results of close cooperation among labor, management and government. Strikes are almost unknown in Austria. Statistically, the average Austrian worker strikes a few seconds per year, compared with 192 minutes in the U.S., 215 in Britain and 553.5 in Italy. Second, Austria had relatively low unemployment: 4.3% in 1999. Employers are traditionally hesitant to lay off workers, a fact which helps maintain labor peace, but which sometimes hurts the financial situation of particular firms.

Some restructuring in traditional branches is necessary, and the coalition government is in agreement on how this should be accomplished. It vowed to stem the growing national debt and to reduce the budget deficit, which in 1987 amounted to 5.4% of GDP. In 1998 its deficit was only 2.2%, well below the 3% required for the common European currency (Euro), which it adopted in 1999. It did this chiefly by pay freezes to the public sector, pension and welfare cuts, and reductions in subsidies to state–owned firms, railways and farmers. Overall, a third of the workforce in state–run industries was cut.

Vranitzky announced plans to privatize many state companies: "In Austria, the shelter that the state has given to almost everyone—employee as well as entrepreneur—has led to a situation in which a lot of people think not what they can do to solve a problem but what the state can do. . . . This needs to change. Once people have sniffed the fresh air of self–initiative, it will change." His conservative coalition partners could not agree more. Shares were sold from the country's largest oil and gas company, the largest utility, and Austrian Airlines. The principle is to reduce the state's shareholdings and to remove day–to–day political interference in management.

A third reason for labor peace is that the real earnings of workers and employees steadily increased during the second half of the 1970s, although economic conditions in the 1980s made it necessary to hold wage increases to the level of inflation in order to protect jobs and hold down inflation. The reverse side of the coin, insofar as Austria's trading position is concerned, is that labor costs are very high. Although wages are on a par with those in Germany, the cost of fringe benefits, including payments for the very generous social security system, add about 80% to wage costs, as opposed to about 60% in Germany. The states' claim on the national tax income, in the form of taxes and other payments, now exceeds 40%.

Austria is fortunate to have some important natural resources: gas, brown coal (peat), iron ore, zinc, aluminum, magnetite, lignite, copper, timber and others. These can be traded or used in their own diversified industries, which produce iron and steel, chemicals, capital equipment and consumer goods.

Exports account for about one–third of Austria's GDP. Two–thirds of its trade is with the EU, which it formally joined on January 1, 1995. Germany is by far Austria's most important trading partner, and unification greatly stimulated its sales to the FRG. Austria likes to see itself as a bridge between East and West, and its trade with Russia and Central Europe is growing. By 1998 its trade with Eastern Europe had more than doubled since 1989. But it remains far less than with the EU. The U.S. accounts for only about 5% of the nation's foreign trade. General Motors is the single largest investor of any foreign company in Austria.

As in most other European countries, maintaining sufficient energy supplies is a major problem. Because of its mountain water, it is able to supply about two–thirds of its electrical power through hydroelectricity. Over the entire year, Austria is actually a net exporter of this kind of power, but in the winter when there is little water, it must import electricity. Its oil reserves are becoming rapidly depleted, so Austria must now import almost 90% of its petroleum, thus sometimes throwing its balance of payments into deficit. Its natural gas reserves are also declining, thus requiring Austria to import about 60% of its needs, largely from Russia and Eastern Europe. It must also import about 80% of the coal it needs. Overall net imports account for about two–thirds of its energy, up from 63% in 1974. About a fourth is supplied by Russia.

It was intended that nuclear energy would be able to supplant the country's needs, and a nuclear power station was built at Zwentendorf near Vienna, which could have supplied 11 to 15% of the country's electrical needs. However, in a 1978 referendum, a narrow majority voted against putting the power station into actual operation. Leaders of both industry and labor want to activate the plant, but the nation's political leaders and public opinion remain divided on the question. The nuclear disaster and subsequent discharge of radiation at Chernobyl in the former Soviet Union has increased the anti–nuclear power sentiment within the country. Austria intensely opposes Czech nuclear power stations and Czech plans to expand its atomic generation and sell electricity to Germany.

The pictures of scenic mountain landscapes, Alpine villages or stately baroque cities, and of singing, yodeling and waltzing Austrians, dressed either in ballroom finery or in leather pants and Alpine hats, thoroughly enjoying life, have always attracted virtually millions of tourists each year. Austrians have the highest per capita income from tourism in all of Europe, and without this source the Austrian economy would collapse almost immediately. Tourist receipts can no longer balance the trade deficit, however, as they once could, but it keeps such a deficit within bearable limits. As in Switzerland, it also helps retard the flight from rural to urban areas and stimulates businesses outside the major industrial areas which support the tourist industry. The economic drawbacks of tourism are that it is seasonal and very heavily dependent upon German, Dutch and British economic prosperity. Germans account for about three–fourths of the overnight stays and the Dutch for about 10%.

Only about 4.4% of Austria's work force is engaged in farming and forestry, compared with 48% in industry and mining and about 46% in services. Farms are predominantly small– or medium–sized, family owned, often fragmented and located in the northern and eastern part of the country. Mountains cover three– fourths of the country, and half its farms are located in mountain regions. Generous subsidies from Vienna and the EU help make them viable. Austrian farmers can still supply about 90% of the country's food needs. Some items, such as cheese and beef can be exported. About 46% of Austria is covered by forests, which provide the country with a valuable natural resource: timber. However, as in neighboring countries, the knotty problem of acid rain is seriously endangering Austria's forests.

CULTURE

Despite its small size, Austria is a land with an enormously rich scholarly and

Austria

The woodcarver (19th century print)

cultural heritage. Europe's oldest remaining German–speaking university was founded in Vienna in 1365. During the Empire it became famous the world over for learning and research, especially in medicine as exemplified by pioneering work in antiseptic and brain surgery of Theodor Billroth and Theodor Meynert. Now there are 12 universities and six art academies in Austria, which charge no tuition for citizens of Austria or of countries in the "Third World." As in most European countries, the school system is tracked horizontally into general education, trade or commercial and basic education courses. The first two can provide access to the universities.

One can scarcely think about classical music without thinking of Austria. The first opera performance north of the Alps took place in Salzburg, and in Vienna opera and orchestra music thrived. Joseph Haydn, Wolfgang Amadeus Mozart, a child prodigy from Salzburg, and Ludwig van Beethoven, who chose Vienna as his second home, helped give Vienna the reputation as the music capital of the world, especially toward the end of the 18th century. Some critics argue that the American movie *Amadeus* completely distorted musical history. They maintain that Antonio Salieri was a good friend of both Haydn and Beethoven and was regarded as a top–flight conductor during his lifetime, although his compositions are seldom heard today. Although he disliked him, Salieri allegedly had nothing to do with the imagined poisoning of Mozart, who died of typhoid fever. Mozart's *Requiem* was completed after his death by his student and good friend, Franz Süssmayer, not by Salieri.

In the 19th century, Viennese–born Franz Schubert became one of the forerunners of the musical romantic movement, and Anton Bruckner, Johannes Brahms and Hugo Wolf produced their musical treasures. Richard Strauss' opera, *Der Rosenkavalier,* whose words were written by Hugo von Hofmannsthal, premiered in Vienna in 1911. Light comedy became a particular Austrian specialty, with such masters as Johann Strauss, Karl Millocker ("The Beggar Student") and Franz Lehar ("The Merry Widow").

Today, one has many reminders of Austria's musical past. There are many traditional musical festivals in the nine provinces and Vienna. Especially well–known is the festival in Salzburg, where many of the best conductors and musicians in the world assemble. The Vienna Boys' Choir was founded in 1498 by Kaiser Maximilian I to sing in daily masses and occasionally at the royal table. Some of its notable members were Haydn and Schubert. Since 1950 the boys, organized in four choirs of 24, have made many foreign tours and have become musical ambassadors for Austria. But in the midst of the Choir's 500th anniversary, its artistic director, Agnes Grossmann, the first woman to hold that distinguished post, resigned in protest against the punishing concert and academic schedule. She argues that up to 100 annual concerts on top of demanding musical and academic studies overburdens the boys physically and emotionally. "When I arrived two years ago, the boys were emotionally dead. They wore masks and showed no sense of childhood joy."

Austria also has a rich literary heritage. In the 12th and 13th centuries the chivalrous and court poetry of Walther von der Vogelweide was admired throughout the German–speaking world, and he remains one of the greatest writers of middle (high medieval) German. The greatest German medieval epic poem, the *Niebelungenlied* (about 1200 A.D.) was partly set in the Danube area. In the 18th and early 19th centuries, Franz Grillparzer was an especially important Austrian literary figure, and Adalbert Stifter's novel, "Indian Summer," written in the 19th century, is one of the greatest novels in German literature.

Around the turn of the century Vienna experienced a burst of artistic creativity. This time, known as the *fin de siècle,* was one in which Austria was experiencing social and political disintegration, a condition which created a fertile breeding ground for all that was new and for artists who wished to break with their past. So new and different were the young artistic products that one spoke of "Young Vienna."

"Viennese schools" developed in psychology, art and music and reached their full maturity by the outbreak of World War I. One poet described the city at that time as "the little world in which the big one holds its tryouts." Salons and cafes became lively places where intellectuals, professionals and businessmen met and discussed the issues of the day.

Sigmund Freud gave psychology a new direction which he elaborated in his mon-

Austria

umental work "The Interpretation of Dreams." Having moved man's sexual urges to the center of man's subconsciousness and behavior, he influenced the way humans view themselves and their motives as did few thinkers in history. At the same time, Konrad Lorenz analyzed animal behavior to look for important clues to that of human beings. In art, the work of Gustav Klimt, Franz von Stuck and Kolo Moser was so unique that it was referred to as the "Vienna Secession." In music, Vienna became a rich terrain for the experiments of Gustav Mahler (who was allowed only one première in Vienna!), Franz Schmidt, Alban Berg and Arnold Schönberg. The last dispensed with traditional tonality and was perhaps the greatest musical revolutionary of the 20th century. His concerts often unleashed cries of "garbage!" and conspicuous rushes to the exits! The work of these experimentalists no doubt was partly a protest against the values of their society and was not very well received in their time.

In literature, Hugo von Hofmannsthal and Arthur Schnitzler appear as the very mirror of Vienna in their day. The first wrote mystical novels and a comedy in 1921, "The Difficult One," which vividly portrays the Austria which collapsed in 1918. Schnitzler's works, with their mixture of irony and sentimentality, were entertaining, but they also reflected the influence of Freud and contained effective attacks on the social ills of the day. Psychological insights into the human soul were also particularly revealing in the fascinating biographies of Stefan Zweig.

At the same time, Prague became an important German literary center within the Austrian Empire. Franz Kafka was a lonely figure who described man entrapped in a bureaucratic world. Rainer Maria Rilke, a master of German lyrical poetry, and Franz Werfel were also products of that intellectual crossroads between the Germanic and Slavic worlds.

World War I represented a true collapse with which the writers Joseph Roth and especially Robert Musil, in his fascinating portrait of Austria in "The Man Without Qualities," tried to come to grips. In art, Austria showed its independence. It remained practically untouched by impressionism, but was deeply touched by expressionism and surrealism, as was shown by the works of Oskar Kokoschka and Alfred Kubin. The interwar years also produced one of the world's greatest movie directors: Billy Wilder.

The end of World War II signaled a new beginning for Austrian artists and writers. Many young and highly experimental authors, such as Gernot Wolfgruber, Franz Innerhofer, Peter Henisch and, especially, Peter Handke, have attracted serious attention. Handke's works are within the spirit of the anti–theater, which aims to break from the restraints of the traditional stage and to shock and teach the viewer. Some of Austria's talented authors and novelists chose to live and work in Germany. Austria does produce some internationally acclaimed films. An example, *38*, directed by Wolfgang Glueck, depicts a Jewish writer who searches desperately for a hiding place in Austria after the German invasion in 1938. 38 was nominated for 'Best Foreign–Language Film' at the 1987 Academy Awards. American viewers also saw one of the world's best German–language actors, Klaus Maria Brandauer, who played the philandering Swedish baron in *Out of Africa*. Now as earlier, Austria provides a fertile home for traditional as well as *avant–garde* artistic movements.

With EU membership, Austria is unable to maintain the state broadcasting monopoly through the Austrian Broadcasting Corporation (ÖRF). Beside's ÖRF's two television programs, about half of Austrian households can watch German channels through cable television. Private radio stations were permitted in 1994. German newspaper concerns have purchased large stakes in some of Austria's largest publishing groups, and many newspapers depend on German money. Its quality newspaper market is led by the lively *Der Standard*, which was launched by the Axel Springer group in 1988. The second–largest daily is *Kurier*, which owns several important magazines and is itself partly owned by the German *Westdeutsche Allgemeine Zeitung*. They are followed by the stodgier *Die Presse* and the *Salzburger Nachrichten*. Most papers backed by political parties have folded.

THE FUTURE

In 1996 Austria celebrated its millennium. It will continue to have much to be proud of. Since 1945 Austria has developed a stable and harmonious political and social order which can be expected to survive all but the most devastating economic and political crises. Economic prosperity, which has resulted from social peace, active cooperation of all economic groups, low defense budgets (under 1% of GDP) and relatively productive industries will be maintained. Austria's policy of neutrality is being changed to become compatible with its membership in the EU, but NATO membership is unlikely any time soon. The country is preparing for parliamentary elections in the fall of 1999.

Newsstand in downtown Vienna

The Swiss Confederation (Confoederatio Helvetica)

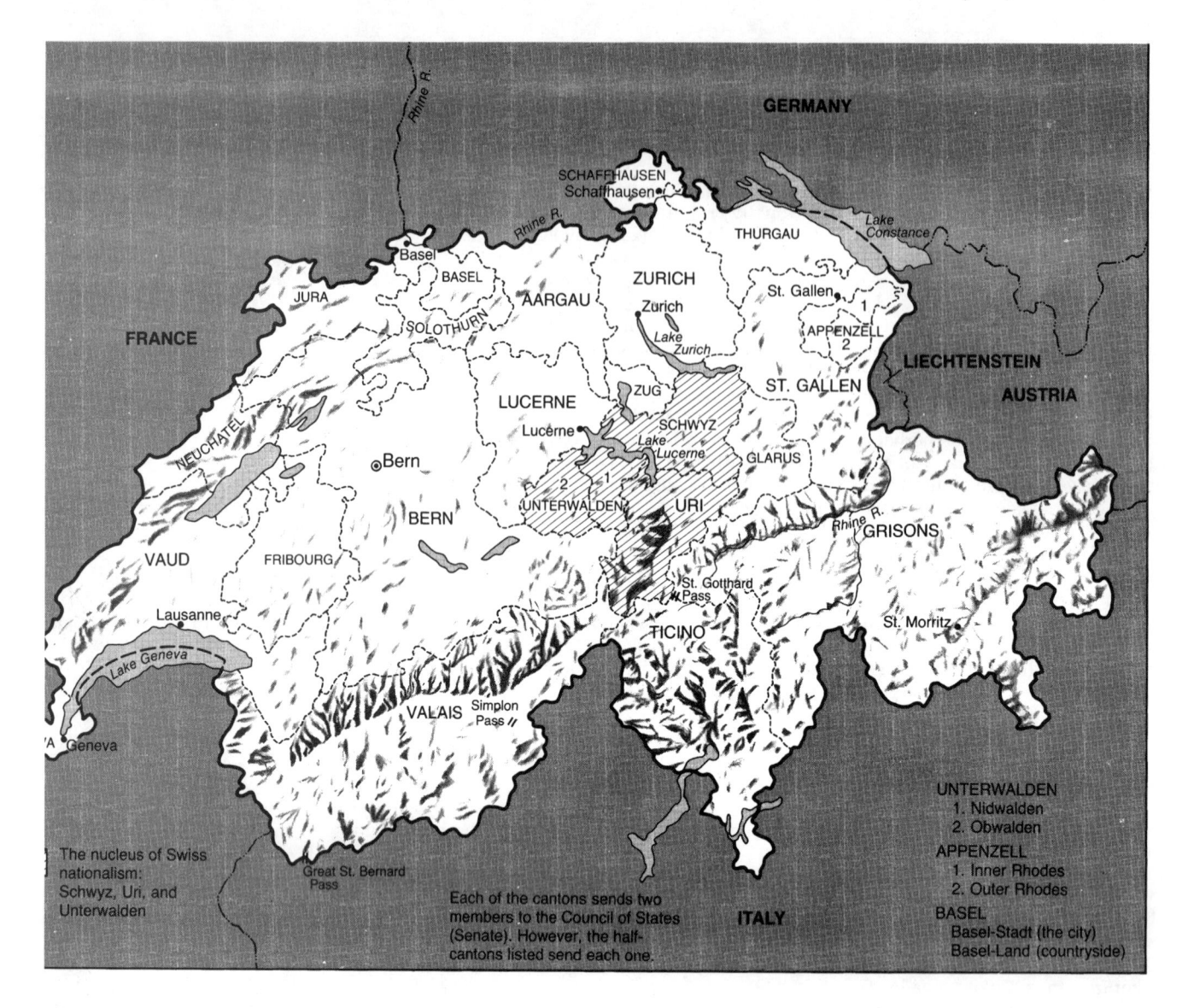

Area: 15,943 sq. mi. (41,292 sq. km.). Roughly the size of Vermont and New Hampshire together.

Population: 6.91 million. Average annual growth rate is .1%. 14.3% of residents are foreigners, primarily Italians, Germans and Spaniards.

Capital City: Bern (Pop. 152,000).

Climate: Owing to great variations in altitude, rapid changes in weather are typical.

Neighboring Countries: France (West); Germany (North); Austria and Liechtenstein (East); Italy (South).

Languages: Swiss nationals—German (64%); French (18%); Italian (8%) Romansch (.5%), Other (9.5%). Total population: German (64%); French (19%); Italian (8%); Romansch (.5%); other (8.5%).

Ethnic Background: Swiss nationals—German (74%); French (20%); Italian (4%); Romansch (1%); other (1%). Total population: German (69%); French (19%); Italian (10%); Romansch (1%); other (1%).

Principal Religion: Swiss Nationals—Protestant (55%); Roman Catholic (43%); Jewish (.2%); other (1.8%). Total population: Protestant (47.8%); Roman Catholic (49.4%); Jewish (.3%); other (2.5%).

Main Exports: Machinery, chemicals, precision instruments, metal products, watches, yarn and textiles, dyestuffs, processed foods.

Main Imports: Machinery and transportation equipment, metal and metal products, chemicals, foodstuffs, textile fibers and yarns.

Major Trading Partners: EU (58% and rising)—Germany (22%); France (11%); Italy (9%); UK (7%), EFTA (7%), Austria (9%); U.S. (7%).

Currency: Swiss franc.

Independence: August 1291.

National Day: August 1.

Chief of State: A seven–man collegiate Federal Council; ceremonial functions are performed by the Federal President, a member of the Federal Council chosen by Parliament for a one–year term.

Head of Government: The Federal President's position is merely "first among equals" in the Federal Council.

National Flag: Square with a white cross on a red field. The flag of the International Red Cross is exactly the same, except that the colors are reversed.

No visitor ever left Switzerland without feeling that he has been in one of the most extraordinary countries in the world. With its stark Jura Mountains, jagged snow-capped Alps with tidy, rustic villages dotting their valleys, clean, mountain–fed lakes with cosmopolitan, manicured cities such as Geneva, Lausanne, Lucerne, Zurich and Basel on their shores. Switzer-

Switzerland

land seems to be the epitome of natural beauty, cleanliness, prosperity and stability. Its people speak a polyglot of languages, but such diversity does not threaten the country as it often does elsewhere.

In general, the Swiss are disciplined, thrifty, realistic, cautious, prudent about change and ingenious about using the resources which they have at their disposal. They are not an exceptionally outgoing people, but they are renowned for their tolerance. Therefore, Switzerland is a dreamed refuge for political and economic disadvantaged and advantaged from all over the entire world.

A small, land–locked, mountainous country, Switzerland is located in the heart of Western Europe. New Hampshire and Vermont could easily fit into the entire country, and 41 of 50 American states are larger than Switzerland. The Jura mountain chain covers approximately 10% of the country in the west and northwest and separates the city of Basel from the rest of the nation. Of the country's entire land area, 60% is located in the Alpine mountain chain, which runs roughly west to east through the southern part of the country. Often called "the mother of rivers, Switzerland, or more precisely, the Gotthard Massif, is the watershed for some of Western Europe's most important rivers: the Rhône flows through the canton of Valais, Lake Geneva and France to the Mediterranean Sea. The Rhine forms the border with Liechtenstein, Austria and Germany; it flows through Basel, where because of its large harbor, one has the impression of being closer to the sea than to the Alps. It forms part of the border between Germany and France, and after flowing through Holland, it empties into the distant North Sea. The Ticino River flows into Italy and into the River Po, which ultimately empties into the Adriatic Sea. Finally, the Inn River, rising in the Swiss Engadine Valley flows through Austrian Tirol, the city of Innsbruck and empties into the Danube, which is destined for the Black Sea.

The remaining 30% of Switzerland's land area is composed of the rolling lowlands of the Central Plateau, extending from the northern shore of Lake Geneva (Lac Leman), northeast past Lake Lucerne and Lake Zurich to Lake Constance (Bodensee). This part of Switzerland is one of the most densely populated and heavily industrialized areas in Europe. Here are located three–quarters of the country's population, the bulk of its industry and agricultural crops, and most of its large cities, which by comparison with many other European cities, are relatively small. The largest is Zurich, with only about 720,000 inhabitants, including suburban residents.

Switzerland's central location has made the country a transportation hub for at least 2,000 years. Through it runs important arteries connecting Paris with the Balkans, Munich with southeastern France, and northern Europe with Italy. This central location has, throughout the centuries, brought both prosperity and war to the fiercely independent Swiss people. It has presented them with their greatest opportunities and their greatest problems.

HISTORY

The Early Period

Since about 4000 B.C. the fertile plain between the Jura and Alpine mountain ranges had been settled by Celtic tribes. One such tribe, which had moved from the banks of the Rhine, called themselves Helvetians. Scribes at that time described the Helvetians as "wealthy with gold" and as "outdoing all others in martial valor." They also knew how to write, applying the Greek script to their own spoken tongue. These ambitious warriors had been seriously bitten by the restless spirit of the migrations and set their eyes on the lands of the richest empire in the known world: Rome. When they tried to move into what is now southeastern France in 58 B.C., they clashed head on with the legions of Julius Caesar, which decimated the Helvetian army. For the next four and one–half centuries, Switzerland was a Roman outpost, an important buffer between the Germanic tribes in the North and the Roman Empire.

An Alpine village, Château d'Oex, in the canton of Vaud

Switzerland

The Helvetians prospered under Roman domination. The new masters built cities in which trade, arts and crafts flourished. They secured the mountain passes and opened the Great Saint Bernard Pass for wagon trains in 47 A.D. Thus, military and trade routes between the two halves of Europe separated by the formidable Alpine mountains were created, which proved to be of lasting importance for the future development of Europe. The Roman legions also brought Christianity to Switzerland in the 4th century A.D.

As a Roman rampart and thoroughfare leading to the heart of the Roman Empire, the Helvetians were among the first to face the attacks by northern "barbarian" tribes who were bent on moving south against Rome. By the beginning of the 5th century, the Romans were compelled to withdraw, and the entire area lay open to invading Germanic tribes.

Two Germanic tribes moved to fill the rich vacuum left by the Romans. Christianized Burgundians settled in the western part of the country and gradually adopted Latin as their language. Ultimately their Latin idiom was the source of the French language. Shortly afterwards, the hardy and uncivilized Alemans from north of the Rhine River moved into the central plains and the Alpine area. They refused to give up their Germanic tongue and eventually displaced the Latin language and the Roman culture wherever they settled. Only the Rhaetians, who were firmly settled in the southeastern part of Switzerland (now the canton of Grisons), and the inhabitants of the valleys on the southern slopes of the Alps (now the canton of Ticino) escaped Burgundian or Aleman mastery. They were able to continue speaking Latin, which gradually became vulgarized into Romansch and Italian, respectively. By the 6th century the division of Switzerland into four separate language zones was established—three of Latin origin and the last, spoken by the majority, German.

From the 6th century on, another Germanic tribe, the Franks, established their control over large parts of Europe north of the Alps. During the reign of Charlemagne, who crowned himself Emperor in 800 A.D., the future Switzerland was absorbed into an Empire which scarcely survived his death. Switzerland was partitioned in the 9th and 10th centuries between the Kingdom of Upper Burgundy and the Dukedom of Swabia, both parts of the Holy Roman Empire. Switzerland's history from then on was closely linked to Germany, particularly to the House of Habsburg in Austria.

Although the new masters tried very hard to impose feudal ties on the Swiss, these attempts were never completely successful. The Helvetians and Alemans both had firm traditions of local autonomy and of personal freedom, traditions clearly visible in Switzerland today. By the 13th century, when Europe's feudal orders had been severely weakened by the crusades, important developments began to take place which ultimately resulted in an independent Switzerland.

In the year 1230 the St. Gotthard Pass was opened. Earlier, only two major, direct roads for crossing the Alps had been open, one in the West and one in the East of Switzerland. The opening of the Gotthard Pass now brought traffic to and from Italy through the heretofore relatively isolated central portion of the land. The great powers of Europe now eyed with much greater interest this valuable piece of territory astride a crucially important trade route.

At the foot of the northern slope of the Gotthard Massif, at opposite ends of Lake Lucerne, are located two small areas: Schwyz (from which Switzerland later got its name) and Uri. Far in advance of their time, these rugged mountain people met in assemblies to elect their leaders and to decide on the administration of common lands. In the 13th century they rebelled against the local dynasties and achieved a semi–independent status linked with the Holy Roman Empire. Schwyz had adopted its own banner, a white cross on a red field, the present Swiss flag.

The Beginning of Independence and Allegiance

The Habsburg ruler Rudolf I died in 1291, and two weeks later, representatives of Schwyz and Uri, joined by those of a third Swiss area, Unterwalden, which is located on another arm of Lake Lucerne, met on the meadow of Rütli. There they signed a peace alliance in the beginning of August 1291, declaring their right to

The Oath of the Three Swiss (18th century)

choose their own judges from among men of their own valleys and pledging reciprocal aid if one of them were wronged by an outside power. Indeed this alliance proved effective in 1315 when a thousand Swiss mountain men trapped and slaughtered two to three thousand knights sent to reestablish full Habsburg control. Although this alliance does not seem very revolutionary today, it was a momentous step at the time and established the cornerstone for modern Switzerland.

What it created was a loose confederation with neither central authority, army, police, court nor executive. Ultimate power remained with the individual states (called cantons after 1803). Decisions were made in regular meetings among the cantons' leaders, and were made not by majority vote, but by consensus. In other words, solutions had to be found to which *all* parties could agree. These principles of reaching agreement for all decisions, known in Switzerland today as "amicable agreement," and of working out problems in a confederal, not centralized way, have

Huge mural in Parliament—Lake Uri where Switzerland was founded

Switzerland

become deeply rooted in Swiss democracy.

The legendary William Tell of Uri, immortalized in Friedrich Schiller's drama, remains a symbol for the liberty which these three "forest cantons" on the shores of Lake Lucerne pledged to defend. Forced by the tyrannical bailiff Gessler to shoot an apple from the head of his own child, Tell took revenge by shooting a fatal arrow at Gessler himself.

Present–day Switzerland gradually took shape in the following centuries as other cantons or cities joined this original alliance. The major motive for the cantons' joining or remaining in the alliance was usually to defend themselves against the Habsburgs' repeated attempts to regain or tighten control over them. The cities and territories of Lucerne, Zurich, Bern, Glarus and Zug joined in the 14th century. At about the same time Uri conquered the Italian–speaking Levintina, a valley along the Ticino River on the southern slope of the Alps. This was the first time that a non–Germanic speaking area became a part of the Confederation. In 1477 Bern snatched stretches of land in the Vaud from the Duke of Savoy. Again, people who did not speak German were incorporated into the Confederation. Later in joining were Fribourg and Solothurn in 1481, Basel and Schaffhausen in 1501 and Appenzell in 1513. The land between these cantons was gradually purchased or conquered, so that by the early 16th century, Switzerland was a more or less contiguous territory.

Initial Alliance Organization

The terms for each entry were often different, and most maintained their own alliances with outside powers. Thus, Switzerland was at this time a "system of alliances," a patchwork of independent countries with different political systems. What they agreed to do was to assist each other militarily, to consult one another and to hold conventions (Diets) at fixed times and places. Only unanimous decisions were binding. There were certainly powerful disagreements among the members, which sometimes led to wars among themselves. This system of alliances was the first in Europe to combine cities with rural states, and there were persistent disputes stemming from the different interests of town dwellers and peasants. Also, some cantons wanted the Confederation to expand in a westerly direction toward France, while others wanted it to expand in a southerly direction toward Italy.

The Swiss temptation to become a great power through territorial expansion was rapidly extinguished in 1515, when the French decisively defeated the Swiss forces at Marignano. The bravery of highland infantrymen was no match for modern cavalry and artillery in the plain. This disastrous battle, in which only about one–half the cantons chose to participate, made the Swiss realize two things: first, the headless Confederation, with its web of alliances and no overall executive, did not permit ambitious Swiss projects beyond their territory. It decided thenceforth to make key decisions by majority vote, but it was no longer a match for the surrounding monarchies. Second, having eliminated the last vestiges of Habsburg influence from Switzerland in 1499, the Swiss decided to pursue a policy of maximum independence from the alliances and political intrigues of all other European countries. A treaty signed in 1521 with France became the only alliance signed by all the cantons of the Confederation with a foreign power.

Arms, Mercenaries and an Independent Tradition

In return for French protection and the right to trade freely with France, the Swiss obligated themselves to provide soldiers for the French king's infantry. At the same time, the Swiss were permitted to provide military units to other European states. This practice meant that on occasion, Swiss troops faced each other on the battlefield. It was, nevertheless, often economically important for Swiss communities which accepted contracts for the troops. The hiring of mercenaries did not end until 1859, with the one exception of the colorful Swiss guards who still staff the Vatican today.

Due to the outstanding reputation of Swiss troops throughout Europe, these soldiers were very much sought after. Louis XI of France paid Swiss troops premium wages for their services, and when the word got around the Swiss were being paid so well, men from all over the French–speaking world attempted to enlist under the guise of being Swiss. Thereupon, Louis decided that a Swiss was only a person coming from a German–speaking canton, and anyone else who claimed to be Swiss was hanged promptly for "fake advertising."

The excellent Swiss military reputation stemmed from several things. First, Swiss troops served their own cantons' interests, fought under their own cantons' banners, obeyed their own officers and were governed by their own codes. This made them far braver than other mercenaries, who were well known for the speed with which they left the battlefield at crucial times. Swiss troops, with their capacity to stick together and to offer themselves wholly to a collective, were prepared to fight to the last man.

The Swiss soldiers also had certain capabilities which were highly valued. They could march with great rapidity and they could operate very effectively in mountainous areas. Because they could scale cliffs so easily, they could capture fortresses better than any others. Therefore, before heavy artillery was perfected, the best weapon against a fortress was a unit of Swiss troops.

The Swiss infantry units also were the first to use a weapon which was terrifying to knights in armor—the halberd. This hand–wielded weapon, now frequently carried by the Swiss guards at the Vatican, basically stood in the same relationship to a knight's armor as a can–opener now stands to a can. Johannes von Winterthur recorded in his chronicle of a ghastly picture of row after row of dead knights lying on the battlefield, their helmets split wide open.

The Swiss were, and still are, a people in arms. This fact has been a key to Switzerland's survival as an independent country in the heart of Europe. It has also been a key to its establishment very early of an exceptionally high degree of personal freedom for more and more of its own people. Among the first things which European feudal lords did, in order to insure their mastery over serfs, was to disarm them. Thus, in the rest of Europe, fewer persons were armed than in Switzerland. This meant not only that peasants and other citizens of Swiss cantons were treated with greater respect by their rulers, but it underscored the principle which gradually became accepted in Switzerland that the people were sovereign and that no ruler could rule legitimately without their consent.

Although many Swiss did not achieve equality until the 19th century, the ruling nobility in other European countries were well aware after 1291 that a different kind of society existed in some parts of Switzerland, especially in Schwyz, Uri and Unterwalden. They harbored fears that the Swiss example might destabilize the nobility and lead to the liberation of peasants all over Europe. For example the Burgundian King, Charles the Bold, once ordered that all captured Swiss soldiers be exchanged immediately so that they could not infect peasants from elsewhere in Europe with their independent ideas.

While noblemen throughout Europe regarded Swiss progress toward democracy and respect for personal freedom as an ominous development, the Swiss themselves were never crusaders for their own ideas. They satisfied their yearning for freedom neither by trying to spread an abstract idea of justice throughout Europe, as the French did after their revolution, nor by trying to establish a *Pax Helvetia* in the entire known world as the Romans

Switzerland

had done. Swiss democracy was always linked with moderation and the willingness to compromise. The Swiss almost always showed common sense by recognizing their own limitations.

The Reformation

Switzerland in the 16th and 17th centuries was shaken and divided by a development which changed the soul of Europe: the Reformation. From Swiss soil the great humanist Erasmus had long criticized the all–too–worldly popes and the many petty clerical abuses, and had advocated a return to the simplicity of the earlier Church. Only two years after Martin Luther had tacked his revolutionary 95 Theses on a cathedral door in Wittenberg, Germany in 1519, Ulrich Zwingli, a priest, army chaplain and humanist known as the "Reformer of Zurich," denounced on his own the abuses of the Catholic Church and began to preach sermons no less inflammatory than Luther's. Several Swiss cities followed his call, but the more rural cantons around Lake Lucerne resisted Zwingli by force. Ultimately he was killed in the violent atmosphere he helped to create. In the Peace of Kappel (1531) the cantons accepted a confessional division of the country into Protestant and Catholic cantons. Thereafter, all citizens in the same canton had to subscribe to the same form of Christianity. Where this was difficult, cantons split into half–cantons, as Appenzell did in 1597.

In another city linked by alliance to the Swiss Confederation, Geneva, a Frenchman named Jean Calvin successfully established in 1541 a strict, Protestant religious government. His pious religious ideas spread quickly to central Europe and across the Netherlands to England and Scotland. Geneva itself became a strict city, where frolicking and frills of all kinds were frowned upon. For example, it was forbidden to wear chains, bracelets, necklaces and gold objects. It became known as the "Protestant Rome." Interestingly, Calvinism as a faith had almost no impact on the rest of Switzerland; its theological radiation was felt chiefly outside the country. It did attract thousands upon thousands of skilled, ingenious, but brutally persecuted French Huguenots into Switzerland during the 17th century. These French Protestants were the first of many waves of immigrants seeking political or religious asylum in Switzerland. The Huguenots also brought skills in banking, trading and manufacturing (especially watchmaking) which were of enormous economic benefit to Switzerland.

To its great fortune, Switzerland was able to remain almost completely uninvolved in the confused, bloody conflict known as the Thirty Years War, which ravished parts of Europe from 1618 to 1648. The religious split a century earlier did slow the development of central institutions in the Confederation. Yet, Switzerland was always fortunate to have its internal divisions overlap one another. The many differences among language and religious groups, as well as between urban and rural areas, had and now have the effect of pulling the Swiss back together. For example, two residents of the city of Zurich may belong to different religions, but the fact that they are German–speaking city dwellers means that they have important things in common. A French–speaking and a German–speaking Swiss may both live in a rural environment and belong to the same religion. These overlapping divisions and the traditions of tolerance, moderation and readiness to compromise are important reasons why a multi–lingual, multi–national, multi–religious Swiss state is still able to manage the searing problems of division so well.

Statue of Zwingli, Zurich

Industrialization

Swiss ingenuity and the economic shot in the arm which the Huguenots provided were especially crucial in the 17th and 18th centuries because the discovery of America gradually led to a shift in the center of world trade toward the Atlantic coast. One could almost say that Christopher Columbus had placed severe strains on the economic progress of Switzerland and of many other central European lands. In order to overcome the resultant economic stagnation, the Swiss had to raise capital to develop the country's manufacturing facilities, to expand Swiss banking operations and to build a world trading network. These efforts later put Switzerland in a position to be one of the first countries on the continent of Europe to undergo an industrial revolution, a fact which has enabled the country to achieve a level of prosperity which is still envied throughout the world.

Democratic Ideals

Switzerland in the 18th century became a cauldron bubbling with explosive democratic political ideas which were to have a dramatic impact all over Europe. One reason for this was that a trend had gathered momentum in Switzerland since the 17th century which saw a narrowing ruling class, rich and often highly cultured, gaining hold over almost all the coveted public offices, monopolies or privileges. Zurich became known as "the little Athens of the North," and after the 1760s Geneva became a magnet for brilliant minds such as Gibbon, Voltaire and Rousseau. Jean–Jacques Rousseau, a citizen of Geneva whose politics made him unwelcome in France, challenged the very legitimacy of all contemporary regimes and societies. His opening to the famous *Social Contract* became a starting point for many revolutionaries, including Karl Marx—"Man was born free, but everywhere he is in chains." In Geneva, which had become known as the "political laboratory of Europe," such ideas helped ignite an unsuccessful revolution in 1782. This was the first in Europe since the American Revolution and seven years before the outbreak of the French Revolution.

As Germany's greatest poet, Goethe, said at that time, "With Rousseau a new world begins."The momentous events in France after 1789 unleashed aftershocks which ultimately tottered the fragile confederal structure of Switzerland. In 1792 Geneva exploded, and the revolutionary fever spread throughout the Confederation. Republican France intervened openly in Swiss affairs, and in 1798 French troops invaded Switzerland, partly in order to secure the Alpine passes. This was the first time since the Thirty–Years War (1618–48) that the Confederation had been occupied by foreign troops. Further, in 1799 Austrian and Russian troops also entered Swiss territory, but they were driven out by the French. The ease with which the well–commanded armies conquered Switzerland was another reminder of its inherent weakness. Such an excessively decentralized Switzerland was completely unable to withstand a determined attack. By the end of 1799 large parts of Switzerland had been ravaged by war and

Switzerland

the French held the cantons firmly under their control.

The conquerors created a "Helvetic Republic," which was a highly centralized state modeled after France. This new republic was almost the complete opposite of the traditional Swiss Confederation and therefore sparked severe disorders within the country. It was replaced in 1803 by a new constitution drafted by Napoleon and called the *Act of Mediation*. This document permitted more decentralization, and it drew considerable inspiration from the newly–developed U.S. Constitution in that it combined federalism, separation of powers, popular sovereignty, individual rights and the central government's authority over foreign and military policy. It reestablished the cantons, and to the older ones it added six new ones: French–speaking *Vaud*, Italian–speaking *Ticino*, partly Romansch–speaking *Grisons* and the three German–speaking, *St. Gallen, Aargau* and *Thurgau*. Thus, under French influence, Switzerland, which had hitherto been a predominantly German–speaking country, was converted into a truly multi–lingual state.

For the next ten years Switzerland remained a scarcely disguised French protectorate. Much to the disgust of many Swiss, it was compelled to supply a contingent of 16,000 men to the French army. In 1812 Napoleon's dominance of Europe received its fatal blow in the snows of Russia, and in 1813 Napoleon's enemies marched through Switzerland on their way to conquer France. When Napoleon escaped from Elba the following year and attempted to pick up his tattered imperial flag, Switzerland joined France's enemies in burying the Napoleonic Empire once and for all.

It received its reward at the Congress of Vienna, which put Europe back together in 1815. The European powers added three cantons: two French–speaking ones (*Neuchâtel* and *Geneva*), and the bilingual *Valais*, thereby completing the boundaries of present–day Switzerland. The Congress also proclaimed the neutrality and inviolability of Switzerland, and from that date on, Swiss neutrality has been an established principle of international law.

Although the French Revolution had been crushed, its ideals retained their force and popularity in many countries, including Switzerland. Pressure mounted in the cantons to achieve more democracy. Such efforts received a powerful boost at the time of the Paris uprisings in 1830, which prompted some cantons to regenerate themselves by establishing fully elective governments. They were also furthered by the industrial revolution, which created a confident middle class and a growing urban working group. Both demanded greater influence in the political affairs of their cantons. The democratic movement rapidly gained steam, and between 1830 and 1848 conservatives throughout Europe viewed Switzerland as a carrier of dangerous democratic germs which could infect the rest of Europe.

By 1847 proponents of an even more democratic national constitution had won the majority in more than a dozen cantons. As in the U.S., a civil war had to be fought between those insisting upon states' rights and those advocating a stronger federal government. The conflict lasted little more than a month and claimed only about a hundred lives. But the federal victory was necessary for the pact among cantons to be converted into a truly federal constitution with institutions under which Switzerland still lives. A Swiss federal state with a democratic constitution inspired by the American Constitution and the 1803 Act of Mediation was created. This actually occurred before many revolutions had erupted throughout Europe in 1848, all of which ultimately failed. The only consequence of these outbreaks as far as Switzerland was concerned was that the European powers were far too busy with their own domestic problems to interfere in Swiss affairs at this crucial time. From 1848 on, Switzerland has been a democracy in the modern sense of the word. The industrial revolution, with a Swiss emphasis on watchmaking and fine machine tools and equipment, continued steadily during the balance of the century and the 20th century. Brilliant engineering enabled construction of a comprehensive rail system through the rugged terrain.

Rumblings and Difficulties During World War I

During World War I, tension between the German and French–speaking populations erupted over a scandal involving a high–ranking Swiss military officer who had passed intelligence information to the Germans. Also, thousands of refugees poured into the country; many continued political activity involving other countries from Swiss soil, a practice which threatened the country's neutrality. Perhaps the best known of these was Vladimir Ilyich Lenin. He was living in Zurich in 1917 when the Russian Revolution erupted, and he reportedly screamed in exasperation that he would gladly sell his soul to the devil for the chance to return to his country to take control of the upheaval. German leaders, desperately wishing to eliminate Russia as a battlefield foe, decided to support the Russian revolutionaries, who promised peace to their war–weary countrymen. Of course, the Swiss authorities were delighted to be rid of him and many other Russian radicals. The Germans provided him passage in a train

The church in Meiringen (Bern canton) has frescoes from the 11th and 12th centuries

Switzerland

Scenic valleys in the canton of Bern

closed to German officials of all kinds. As Winston Churchill later wrote, Lenin was sent "like a plague bacillus from Switzerland to Russia."

European wars always threaten the markets and raw materials which trade–dependent Switzerland needs in order to survive. Price controls and rationing had to be introduced during World War I, and the Swiss economy suffered greatly. In November 1918 the social discontent created by such setbacks exploded into a general strike with Marxist revolutionary overtones. Timely concessions, such as the introduction of a proportional representation electoral system, enabled the government to end the strike quickly, and thereby to avert the danger of further domestic tensions.

Switzerland made three significant foreign policy decisions in 1920–21. It turned down a request by the Austrians living in the Alpine area of Vorarlberg to become a part of Switzerland. It agreed to form a customs union with its small eastern neighbor, Liechtenstein. Third, it decided to become a member of the League of Nations, whose headquarters had been established in Geneva. Thus, it decided that membership in international organizations did not violate Swiss neutrality so long as (1) the organization publicly recognized Swiss neutrality, (2) Switzerland be permitted to abstain from sanctions against other countries and (3) Switzerland be permitted to maintain its universal economic relations with all countries of the world, a principle which it considers essential for its prosperity.

The Depression and World War II

The great depression of the 1930s inevitably affected Switzerland because of its dependence upon foreign trade. The social unrest which the economic shocks helped to create spawned some radical political movements such as the youthful *Front* groups which demanded a fascist order. Nevertheless, Switzerland managed to preserve its democratic order at a time when most of the democracies in Europe collapsed.

It also managed to remain neutral during World War II, which followed on the heels of the depression. Such neutrality was not entirely a gift of the neighboring fascist dictators. Switzerland mobilized 430,000 soldiers and threatened to destroy all major tunnels and bridges. It declared its determination to fight to the last man if it were invaded, although it was revealed after the war that only the heartland, including the St. Gotthard Pass and the Simplon tunnels, were to be defended to the end. This threat, backed by the Swiss military reputation and determination, helped to dissuade Hitler and Mussolini from attacking the country, which the former scornfully called "the anus of Europe."

But Switzerland did not remain free as a result of military deterrence alone. Faced with the prospect that it could share the fate of other occupied countries, it made compromises with Nazi Germany in the name of "neutrality" that now make it seem to many Swiss and non–Swiss that the country may have bought its freedom at a very high moral price. It continued to trade with Germany and Italy, and some of the products which it sold were obviously used for armaments. Further, thousands of Jews and political refugees were denied entry into Switzerland and therefore ended up in prisons or extermination camps. An agreement with Germany in 1938 required Jews to obtain visas and have a special stamp in their passports. Elie Wiesel argues that the idea of stamping German passports with a "J" for "Jewish" came from the Swiss. Police officials who allowed Jews to enter the country illegally were punished.

Recently declassified Allied intelligence documents reveal the extent to which the Swiss also reaped handsome profits by serving as bankers both for the Nazis and their Jewish victims. Prominent Nazis were steady customers of Swiss banks: Hitler reportedly deposited royalties from *Mein Kampf,* and Hermann Goering made regular trips to Zurich to deposit art masterpieces stolen from museums in occupied countries. The banks purchased from the Nazis hundreds of millions of dollars of looted gold, and other looted funds were invested in Swiss enterprises. Bank secrecy was introduced in 1934 to accommodate Jews who wanted to deposit their assets quietly outside of Germany, and then those same secrecy laws were used to prevent the heirs from claiming those assets after the war. Jewish groups estimated in 1996 that the banks hold about $7 billion, including interest, that belonged to Jews who perished in the Holocaust, in addition to gold and other valuables looted from Jews. After years of denial, the government admitted that the Swiss secretly used some of these funds to compensate their own citizens for property confiscated by the Communists in Poland, Hungary and Czechoslovakia.

The Swiss refusal to discuss or deal with these problems cracked in 1996 under intense pressure from Jewish organizations, the American Senate Banking Committee, and other foreign governments. Attempting to contain this gigantic public relations disaster, it formed one commission, chaired by former U.S. Federal Reserve Chairman Paul A. Volcker, to oversee the search for dormant accounts left by Jews. A second international historical panel was appointed to investigate

Switzerland

the extent and fate of Jewish wealth and Nazi loot sent to neutral Switzerland during the war. In 1997 it agreed for the first time to use the funds in Holocaust victims' unclaimed bank accounts to help survivors. It also set up a separate fund of about $200 million contributed by private banks to distribute to individuals who survived the Holocaust. In August 1998 the two largest Swiss banks reached a $1.25 billion settlement of a lawsuit by Holocaust survivors and their descendants. Two major European insurers also reached an accord on life insurance claims for victims. In return, U.S. cities and states canceled an economic boycott against all Swiss banks, institutions and companies, and a $20 billion class–action suit brought against the banks was dropped. Ursula Koch, president of the *Socialist* party, said that "we have to come to grips with our history."

While few Swiss are proud today of such past policies, Swiss national survival seemed to require them at the time. On the positive side, Switzerland was a base during the war for allied spies, such as Allen Dulles, as well as for international Jewish agencies operating in Europe. It also offered protection to thousands of refugees who would otherwise have joined the many victims of fascism. Switzerland did not entirely escape the destruction meted out in other parts of Europe. In April 1944 U.S. squadrons mistakenly bombed the Swiss city of Schaffhausen, the only major Swiss city located entirely north of the Rhine River. Other localities, such as Basel and Geneva, were also attacked by Allied bombers.

In April 1999 the Swiss government disbanded a special crisis task force looking into the country's role in the war. But it will take much longer for the bruised feelings to heal. The myth of wartime Swiss neutrality was exposed. Yet nothing in recent years unified this highly decentralized country as thoroughly as the world's condemnation of its actions during the war. The crisis opened Swiss eyes to their contemporary isolation. Many Swiss believe that their European neighbors and the U.S. had abandoned them by bearing down on them so forcefully over Nazi gold.

POLITICAL SYSTEM

In many countries of the world today, ethnic, lingual and regional diversity often create almost insolvable problems of political and social instability. This has not been the case in Switzerland. Thanks to its tradition of tolerance and compromise, its economic prosperity and its decentralized democratic order tailored to its particular needs, Switzerland enjoys a level of political stability envied in much of the world.

The constitution, adopted in 1848, was considerably revised in 1874 to establish national responsibility for defense, trade and many legal matters. On the whole, it has served Switzerland well. Some Swiss now consider the much–amended constitution to be unwieldy and outdated, and since the 1960s the government studied the possibility of rewriting the document. In April 1999 voters, backed by all the major parties, approved a new constitution that abolished the gold standard for the franc and enshrined new rights in law, including the right to strike and the principle of equal opportunities for the handicapped.

The central elements of Swiss democracy remain unchanged: a federal form of government composed of powerful and confident cantons, jealously protective of their own powers; the participation of all major parties in the national, cantonal and communal governments; a collegial executive elected by, but not responsible to the Parliament, rather than a one–man executive elected directly or responsible to the Parliament; a method of decision–making known as "amicable agreement" involving consensus and respect for minority opinions, rather than the majoritarian approach and, finally, a system of semi–direct democracy at the national, cantonal and communal levels.

Canton Customs and Government

A Swiss person tends to consider himself a citizen of his commune or canton, and secondly of Switzerland. Only communes can grant citizenship, but communal approval is normally a mere formality when the person meets all federal requirements. About 12,000 foreigners become naturalized citizens each year. Federalism, reinforced by strong regional pride, is very much alive in Switzerland, and as a result the 26 Swiss cantons have been considerably more successful in resisting the trend toward government centralization than most other countries, including the U.S. As is nominally true in the U.S., Swiss cantons in reality exercise all powers not explicitly granted to the federal government. In general, they have their own taxing authority, and the Swiss pay most of their income taxes to their cantons. The cantons have the right to manage their own affairs and the responsibility to enforce the law within their own boundaries.

A proposal in 1978 to create a federal police force was rejected in a national referendum. In 1982, 74% of the voters agreed to increased penalties for violent crimes, such as terrorism and hostage–taking, but they also overwhelmingly rejected the creation of a federal anti–terrorist unit. They also have the authority to decide who has the right to vote in cantonal elections.

Because 60% of all voters in a 1981 referendum agreed to amend the constitution in order to give women and men equal rights, it was inevitable that women would ultimately get to vote at every level. In 1990 the Federal Tribunal ruled that Article 4 granting equal rights overrides Article 74 giving cantons the power to decide their own voting rules. Thus, in 1991 the last hold–out, Appenzell–Inner Rhodes, counted women's votes in its open–air assembly. The trend toward full equality for women was continued in a 1985 referendum which granted them equal marriage rights. The husband will no longer be the legal head of the household who could decide where to live, to what schools the children should go or whether the wife could open a bank account or take a job. Since 1971 all women

The government procession at Nidwalden

Switzerland

have been allowed to vote in national elections. Cantons also have the right to decide what kind of governments they will have, so long as they are democratic and conform to the federal constitution. All have chosen to have a collegial executive with a unicameral legislature.

On the last Sunday in April and the first Sunday of May the citizens of the five mostly rural Swiss cantons of Obwalden, Nidwalden, Glarus and the two Appenzell half cantons of Inner Rhodes and Outer Rhodes gather in annual open air assemblies to elect their leaders and judges, vote on important laws, approve the budget and change their constitutions. In the early days attendance at such assemblies, which date back to 1231, was required for all male citizens old enough to fight, which was usually 14 years. Participants came to the assemblies armed. Male citizens in Appenzell must still appear with sidearms in order to vote; women were granted an exception to this rule. A large, ornate sword, which is the symbol of cantonal authority is carried into the assembly area (called the "ring") with great pomp. In Glarus, the presiding official (called the *Landammann*) even wraps his arm around the sword during the entire session. In the past, the people dismissed the *Landammann* by the simple act of taking the sword away from him.

The assemblies begin, proceed and end with ceremony and colorful folklore, which give vivid glimpses into Switzerland's past. Honored participants and guests are led into the ring by full–bearded attendants in long robes, baggy striped pants, fur or pointed hats, or plumed helmets. They carry the cantonal insignias, seals, banners, keys and other relics with them. The leaders stand on a wooden stage surrounded by attendants, while the citizens stand or sit on long wooden benches. In Nidwalden, the assembly is opened by the blowing of a large curled horn, a word from a priest, the introduction of honored guests and an oath of the leaders to respect the constitution.

The visitor is usually so fascinated by the ceremonial aspects of the assembly that he forgets that the citizens have gathered in order to make policy, not to view a parade. There is a serious air, and participants in modern business suits and dresses far outnumber those wearing ornate traditional jackets and bonnets. All voters receive detailed information in advance on the issues which are to be discussed. Except in Appenzell, where there is no discussion at the assembly, each citizen has a right to speak. Speeches are well–prepared and short, and normal voting is done by raising hands, with officials in red robes judging the results from an elevated platform.

A 1982 vote showed how uncertain the outcomes can be. In Obwalden the president of the federal senate, Jost Dillier, one of Switzerland's leading national politicians, was voted out of office, even though he had no opposing candidate. Newspapers the next day wrote of "an absolute sensation," a "bomb which exploded." The Swiss emphasize continuity and stability so strongly that elected officials have no formal limits on the time they may serve. However, most retire when their terms expire. Dillier had violated two fundamental rules of Swiss politics. He had assumed too many offices in politics and business and thus had too much power in his own hands. Also, he paid more attention to politics in Bern than in his canton. Many said that he personified the "arrogance of power," and in Switzerland there is almost nothing which is more distrusted than obvious political ambition or heavy–handedness.

The vote is taken in Glarus

At the end of the four to six hour assemblies, ceremony again glosses over the differences which arose in the debates. The attendants lead the procession out of the ring and to the church or city hall, where the newly elected leaders are greeted before attending a banquet. The other citizens spend the rest of the day in a holiday manner.

In order to accomplish anything in such annual meetings, the canton must be rather small in size. It must also have a small and homogeneous population. Granting women the right to take part has created a particular problem by doubling the number of participants. Serious divisions between Catholics and Protestants or city and country dwellers have wrecked such annual assemblies. There are many tales of brawls at meetings, even though such disturbances of the peace traditionally carried a higher sentence than at other times. To reduce the likelihood of these outbreaks, the consumption of alcoholic beverages at such meetings has long been strictly forbidden. Success requires concentrating on a few important issues, as well as discipline on the part of the individual citizens. Long–winded speeches would seriously try the patience of the participants, and filibusters would be a catastrophe.

One can call this form of direct democracy antiquated or mere ballast tradition. Yet every form of democracy has its advantages and disadvantages. This kind of colorful, but serious, gathering brings together several thousand citizens for public debate on political issues immediately affecting their lives. There have been practical reasons why some such assemblies have had to be abolished. But none has ever been cancelled because of lack of public spirit or citizen interest.

Trends Toward Centralization

There is an undeniable trend toward greater governmental centralization because of the many knotty problems of modern life. Such issues as environmental protection, nuclear energy and especially economic matters including unemployment, inflation, foreign trade, currency controls and planning are increasingly seen to be problems with which single cantons cannot easily cope effectively. A rule of thumb is that whenever the Swiss economy is in a slump, there is the strongest demand for shifting more powers to the central government. When the economic picture is rosier, then the resistance to such transfer stiffens.

Over the years the principle has developed that "federal law is superior to cantonal law." The cantons are, nevertheless, far from helpless in the face of this powerful pull toward the federal capital city

Switzerland

of Bern. Any constitutional change requires a "double majority" in a national referendum—a majority of all Swiss voters and a majority in more than half the cantons. For instance, in 1973 a majority of Swiss voters supported a proposal to give the national government authority to unify the country's schools, traditionally a cantonal power. However, a majority of the cantons rejected the proposal, so each still maintains its own preferred school system.

The Bicameral Legislature

All national legislation must be approved by both houses of the national Parliament, including the Council of States. This upper house, modeled after the U.S. Senate, is composed of two representatives from each canton regardless of size—and the cantons vary in population from 50,000 to more than a million. The cantons are free to decide how these representatives are chosen; in fact, the 46 members are elected directly by the people in all but four. This Council of States tends to be far more conservative than the lower house of the national Parliament, especially insofar as cantonal prerogatives are concerned. As is true of other Swiss political offices, that of parliamentarian carries neither great influence or prestige. Parliament meets for approximately 16 weeks a year divided into four sessions. Deputies are given only a part-time wage for their service and are even freed two days per week during the sessions to perform their regular jobs.

As the United States' leaders saw in the 1780s and as Belgium's leaders realized in the 1970s, federalism is a very important means of enabling a heterogeneous population to live together in harmony; it certainly has been a key ingredient in Switzerland's success as a multi-national, multi-lingual state. Switzerland has had the flexibility to adjust its federal order when a serious problem developed, such as that which emerged in the bilingual canton of Bern. The French-speaking inhabitants in the Jura mountains which border France sensed discrimination by the canton's German-speaking majority and desired to live in an autonomous canton of Jura. Mass demonstrations were organized, and a few extremists even planted bombs in prominent public places to underscore this separatist demand. In a national referendum held in 1978, 82% of all voting Swiss and a majority in virtually all cantons approved the creation of a new Jura canton, the first new canton to be created in 130 years. Thus, instead of suffering a festering problem with a separatist minority, Switzerland now has an additional canton exercising all the powers enjoyed by all the other cantons. Again, federalism was able to act as a tranquilizer.

Below the cantons are more than 3,000 communes of greatly differing size. They choose their own system of local government (with approval of the cantons), elect their own officials and assume general responsibility for granting citizenship, administering public lands, such as the forests, and supplying citizens with water, gas, electricity, bridges, city administrative offices, schools, swimming pools, sanitation facilities, fire services and police protection. Swiss communes have to submit to some supervision by cantonal governments, but their right to self-rule is guaranteed by the federal constitution, and they can appeal to the Federal Supreme Court if their autonomy is excessively infringed upon.

The Swiss Parliament, Bern

Political Parties

At all levels of government in Switzerland, political parties play a key role. In contrast to most other Western European parties, Swiss parties did not grow out of parliamentary groupings or honorary societies, but were mass parties from the very beginning. This was because Switzerland had introduced universal manhood suffrage as early as 1830. As in the U.S., Swiss parties were, and still are, organized primarily at the communal and cantonal level, and the national parties are little more than umbrella organizations for local parties, some of which even have different names than the larger national parties. As decentralized bodies, the national parties are all able to perform an important integrative function by cutting across most subgroups in Switzerland. The major Swiss parties encompass all

Switzerland

language, regional, religious and occupational groups. Decentralization also permits maximum flexibility for local and regional solutions to problems.

Swiss parties have a few other important characteristics. First, organized interest groups are represented formally in the parties to an extent unknown in most other countries. Second, the parties demand almost no "party discipline." Members are left more or less free to vote as they please, and it is therefore often difficult to pin a particular policy to a particular party. Third, conflicts within the parties are settled by the principle of "amicable agreement." The majority tries to find solutions acceptable to the minority rather than merely voting it down. This is widely accepted as the best means of finding a common denominator for all the diverging language, religious and economic interests. At the same time, it makes parties and governments very cautious and deliberate and therefore helps give Swiss government and all major parties their rather conservative hue.

The principal parties' voting strength has remained stable since the end of World War I. In 1919 the four major parties received 88% of the vote; 60 years later they still received approximately 80%. All four strongly support the existing political order in Switzerland, and none sees itself as an opposition party. For this reason, no major party and no government in Switzerland has a firm party or governmental program against which one could easily evaluate its performance. Because of the proportional representation electoral system, votes for the 200–seat National Council (lower house) seldom produce dramatic shifts in political power. Elections normally renew the governing coalition. The four ruling parties slipped from 159 to 146 seats in the 1991 elections, but nevertheless retained a comfortable three–fourths majority.

The most traditional and oldest Swiss party is the *Radical Democratic Party (FDP)* which now has 44 seats. Founded in the 19th century as a radical (which in the traditional European sense means anticlerical) and liberal (meaning traditionally that it favored an expansion of individual rights and a reduction of governmental power) party, it now defends the economic and social status quo. It has very close connections with private economic groups and influential molders of opinion in the mass media, schools and universities. It is perhaps the most influential party in Switzerland.

The *Christian People's Party (CVP)* received 36 seats and has obtained approximately 20% of the vote since 1919. The bulk of its voters are practicing Catholics. It does recruit members and voters from all language and occupational groups; but although it has attempted to leap beyond the confessional barrier by attracting Protestants, it has not been very successful in doing so. The party sees itself as a "dynamic center" party, with a social policy slightly to the left of the *FDP*.

Since 1935 the *Social Democratic Party (SPS)* has received more votes than any other party and now has 41 seats. Founded in 1904, it was originally a working–class party dedicated to the class struggle. But the fascist threat and the economic crises in the 1930s convinced Social Democrats that support of reform policies in the existing Swiss state was its best course. It officially changed its program in 1959 and is now a moderate party which wants to reform the capitalist economic system by expanding the social security net, reforming the tax structure and evening out incomes. Its voters were once found only in the working class, but many intellectuals now support it. It helps to form every government in Switzerland, but it is the only major party which tries to project an image of the "opposition within the government."

For instance, the party pushes hard to relax the bank secrecy laws, which the party believes attracts money to Switzerland from criminals and right–wing dictators. Within the party there are intense conflicts which have been fueled by the violent youth protests of recent years. There is a growing demand within the *SPS* to present the party as a leftist, anti–capitalist force, even if this means that it cease cooperating with the other parties. The intra–party quarrels have become so serious that the *SPS* faces the possibility of a split into a reformist social democratic and less compromising socialist party.

Finally, the *Swiss People's Party (SVP)* retained its 25 seats. The *SVP* tries to represent the interests of farmers, small businessmen and craftsmen. Because of its narrower social base and the fact that it is organized in only 14, mostly German–speaking, cantons, its voter strength had, until the 1979 election, steadily declined. It is traditionally more conservative than the *FDP* in the sense that it has been openly skeptical of any sign of a welfare state and European union.

A few other parties receive a smattering of seats. The ecologically–oriented Greens continue to gain, winning 12 seats in 1991. The Swiss, who in 1991 had experienced several fire–bombings of dwellings harboring immigrants, woke up to find that 13 right–wing representatives, 11 of whom from the *Motorists' Party*, demanding curbs on newcomers, had won seats in the lower house; this is the strongest xenophobic contingent in two decades. There is also the *Workers Party (PdA)*, a communist party founded in 1944 to replace the outlawed *Swiss Communist Party*. Its base is almost exclusively in French and Italian Switzerland. It was traditionally an orthodox Marxist–Leninist, Moscow–oriented party, but it has now advocates a "Swiss way toward socialism" and respect for individual freedoms. It fashions itself as Switzerland's only real opposition party, even though it has become politically irrelevant.

Foreign Workers

The *Swiss Democrats*, formerly called the *National Action for People and Homeland (NA)*, aims its arrows toward what it sees as a threatening perversion of the Swiss character caused by foreign workers, rapid urbanization and growing concentration of power in Switzerland. This openly patriotic and nationalist party reached its zenith in 1970 when a majority of Swiss voters was almost persuaded in a referendum to limit the numbers of foreign workers. In the 1990s the less democratic, neo–Nazi *Patriotic Front*, entered the anti–immigrant scene.

In their opposition to foreign workers the *REP* and *NA* unquestionably touch a very sensitive nerve in Switzerland. The country has traditionally been very hospitable to political exiles; for example, it took in 16,000 Hungarians after 1956 and 14,000 Czechoslovaks after 1968. Swiss industry learned very early that high levels of production could be achieved only by attracting foreign workers. No one doubts that the hotel and restaurant industries would never be able to survive without foreign workers. About half of these workers are Italians, followed by Germans and Spaniards. By 1987 foreign workers accounted for 25% of the labor force.

These groups certainly integrate themselves into Swiss society more easily than do Turks in Germany or Arabs in France. While all Swiss are aware of the foreigners' economic indispensability, they are nevertheless uneasy about their very visible presence. This visibility has been especially enhanced by a wave of arrivals: Sri Lankan Tamils, Kurds, Pakistanis and Congolese. In a 1987 referendum, voters accepted by a margin of two–to–one a new law tightening rules even more regarding immigration and political asylum. It extended to peacetime the government's emergency powers to close the border to all refugees. The Swiss government also maintains a fund to send asylum seekers arriving by air back to their homelands on the next flight. As classrooms in Swiss schools sometimes swell with foreign children and as run–down areas with predominantly foreign residents begin to appear in some cities, cultural clashes are inevitable. In fact, this same problem is seriously testing the tol-

Switzerland

erance of many Western European countries. In a 1994 referendum, a majority of voters accepted a government ban on all forms of racism, including a belittling of the Holocaust, and 53.6% rejected in 1996 a proposal to tighten regulations over asylum–seekers from Africa and Asia.

In numerous referenda, Swiss voters, not wishing to tarnish Switzerland's image as a land of refuge or to harm its economy rejected proposed laws to limit the percentage of foreigners to 12^1/$_2$% (by a 2 to 1 margin in 1988). Nevertheless, the Swiss government has been very attuned to the discontent and has quietly reduced the percentage of foreigners in Switzerland to 17% of the total population. It can do this because, although foreign workers enjoy many rights and social benefits while in the country, many must renew their work permits every year. A third of the work force is foreign; those with permanent work permits, with the same employment rights as Swiss nationals, slightly outnumber those with limited rights. By carefully restricting the number of renewals, the government can slowly reduce the foreign population. Further, foreign workers must live in the country four years before they are permitted to bring their families. A 1987 referendum ratified new laws tightening rules on immigration and political asylum. This policy is not always appreciated by the countries from which the guest workers come; they often accuse Switzerland of "egotism" and of "exporting unemployment." But this policy enables Switzerland both to control its own employment and to pacify Swiss fears of an excessive foreign presence.

The Federal Government

The federal government, with its seat in Bern, is composed of a bicameral parliament similar, in some ways, to the U.S. Congress and of a powerful seven–man executive elected by Parliament. The National Council, elected every four years by male, and by 1971, female voters over 18 years of age, represents the interests of all Swiss. Because elections almost never produce significant changes in the parties' strength in Parliament, Swiss elections are never the heated, highly publicized affairs they are in the U.S. and many other Western European countries.

As in the U.S., both houses have equal powers. Although all bills are now drafted by the government and presented to Parliament, they must be examined by both houses. Once both have passed a piece of legislation, the executive may not veto it, and the Supreme Court may not declare it unconstitutional. In drafting legislation, the government, by tradition, consults all interested groups inside and outside Parliament. This is a clumsy, time–consuming process, but it helps to insure better results in that potential objections to the legislation are ironed out in advance; it also reduces the possible danger of a law's being overturned in a referendum.

Both houses meet to elect the seven Federal Councilors (*Bundesräte*), who have steadily become more powerful in the Swiss political system. They are carefully selected by the parties on the basis of party membership and political experience at the federal or cantonal level. Highly charismatic figures are very seldom chosen because of the traditional Swiss aversion to a personality cult of any kind. The recommended candidates are almost always elected. Their terms are four years, during which time they cannot be removed by Parliament for any reason. They are traditionally reelected until they voluntarily choose to retire. Thus, strictly speaking, Switzerland does not have a parliamentary system as in most Western democracies.

Since 1959 they have been selected according to a so–called "magic formula": two councilors are chosen from each of the three largest parties in the National Council and one from the fourth largest. By 1999 it was no longer clear which party was fourth. The anti–EU *Swiss People's Party* had caught up with the *Christian People's Party* in popularity and demanded that this be recognized in the National Council. At least two councilors must be from the French or Italian–speaking sections, and it is usual that one comes from each of the country's three largest cantons—Zurich, Bern and Vaud. Finally, no two councilors may come from the same canton. One can imagine the compromises necessary to satisfy such a "magic formula"!

Each directs one of seven ministries, called departments. Together the seven form the government, and they play the predominant role in drafting legislation, executing laws and dealing with the outside world. They make decisions collectively according to the principle of "amicable agreement." They are nominated by the major parties, but they are expected to cease being "party men" once they are in office. Therefore, they have no coherent government program, and there is no formal opposition either within the government or the Parliament. This does not mean that a particular party cannot oppose a particular issue; what it means is that none of the major parties consistently opposes the government with a view to replacing it. In other countries such an "all parties government," also known as "grand coalitions" are formed only in times of national emergency. Switzerland always has them.

The year 1984 saw a break in the tradition of parliament's more or less automatic acceptance of the parties' nominations to the Federal Council. Polls indicated that 64% of citizens thought it was time to have a woman federal councilor, so the Social Democrats nominated Lilian Uchtenhagen, a respected economist. Reportedly grumbling that she was "too emotional," "too elegant," "not enough of a mother figure" and "unable to stand the strain of high office," a majority in the Federal Assembly in a joint meeting of the two chambers rejected her.

The widespread bad feelings caused by Uchtenhagen's rejection no doubt helped Elisabeth Kopp, a lawyer and leading member of the *Radical Democratic Party*, to win a seat on the Federal Council in 1984. Unfortunately Kopp became implicated in Switzerland's biggest scandal in years. In 1989 she resigned because of accusations that, as justice minister, she had used her

Former President (1982) Fritz Honegger with the author's two daughters, Katie and Juliet Thompson, April 1982.

Switzerland

influence to protect her lawyer husband against charges of complicity in a major drug money–laundering operation by leaking confidential information to him about the inquiry. She was later acquitted of violating the official secrecy laws.

In 1993 it was time for another woman to be named to the Federal Council. She had to be a *Social Democrat* from a French–speaking canton, and parliamentarian Christiane Brunner fit that bill. However, an overwhelmingly male parliament rejected her, some say for sexist reasons: she was a thrice–married blond who liked flashy clothes, opposed the military, and was said to have had an illegal abortion and posed in the nude. She denied the latter charge. Switzerland had never experienced what followed: thousands of women gathered in front of parliament, spattering paint and eggs, and chanting: "We have lost the first battle, but only the first!" They were right. Ex–trade unionist Ruth Dreifuss of the SPS was promptly elected as interior minister. A close friend of Brunner, she concluded that "I reassure people because I look a little plain." In 1999 she became the country's first female and Jewish president.

Every year the Parliament elects from among the seven a President and a Vice–President for one–year terms. They are not permitted to succeed themselves immediately, and by tradition, the Vice–President is elected President the next year. The President of the Confederation is only a "first among equals," representing the government in ceremonial functions. In times of emergencies he may assume greater powers than the other Councilors. Under no circumstances can he be recalled or impeached.

Swiss presidents are so inconspicuous in comparison to French or American counterparts that most Swiss, when asked, are unable to name their own president in any given year. In a country in which the most glamorous figure is the head of the central bank, the president needs neither bodyguards nor staff cars, and he lives in his own house during his term of office. He goes unguarded to movies or restaurants and probably carries out his own garbage. When Kurt Furgler (1981) traveled to work or around the country, he either drove his own car or went by rail. Only when his schedule was particularly tight was he transported by helicopter. Once, when he was being flown to an appointment, his helicopter developed engine trouble and was forced to make an emergency landing. Undaunted, he merely walked to the nearest road and hitch–hiked the rest of the way.

The Courts

Since the Federal Supreme Court has no

Young woman gathers signatures opposing centralization of power

power to judge on the constitutionality of federal laws, it does not have the same prestige or importance as does the U.S. Supreme Court. It is chiefly the highest court of appeals for civil and criminal cases. Its judges are selected by both houses of Parliament meeting together for six year terms and must be chosen from all language and regional groups in order that the entire population be represented. Its seat is not in Bern, but in Lausanne. The administration of justice remains primarily a cantonal affair, but the supreme civil and criminal laws of the land are the federal code of civil law, in force since 1912, and the federal code of penal law, enacted in 1942.

Direct Democracy

Many Western European democracies permit citizens to vote directly on some particularly important political issues, rather than to leave virtually all such decisions to the Parliament. This is called "direct democracy" because the will of the people is not filtered exclusively through Parliament. In most countries this instrument is used very sparingly, particularly because it has often been a favorite tool for dictators to legitimize their power over a frightened people. The Swiss have never needed to fear such abuse in modern times, and direct democracy is a very important part of the political process at all levels of government. If at least 100,000 voters sign a petition demanding a constitutional change, then such an "initiative" must be submitted to a direct vote of all Swiss. If at least 50,000 demand in a petition that an act of Parliament or an international treaty be approved by all the voters, then a "facultative referendum" is held. Parliament can declare an act to be too urgent to allow time for a referendum, but one is mandatory if Parliament adopts any constitutional changes or approves of an international treaty of supranational or security character which affects the country's sovereignty.

Initiatives and referendums are held on an extremely wide range of subjects: abortion, conscientious objection to military service, mandatory wearing of safety belts, increasing federal powers to tax and to control unemployment and inflation, mandatory retirement ages, gun control, bans on automobile driving and on leaded gasoline, daylight savings time, rent controls, euthanasia, worker participation in management, and many more topics.

By threatening to organize an initiative or referendum, interest groups in Switzerland can almost always secure a serious hearing for their concerns within the government or Parliament. This insures that they will not be overlooked in the decision–making process and that the government will try to establish a consensus for all its acts. Still, the problems associated with direct democracy have increasingly become the subject of discussion. The first problem is that the number of referendums and initiatives at all levels has sharply increased. Between 1914 and 1934 there was an average of 8.5 referendums per year. At present, the average has climbed to more than 30, and this includes neither the many referendums at the communal and cantonal level, nor the up to four national initiatives per year. Consti-

Switzerland

tutional changes since 1871 have been made an average of once every 13 months, and the frequency has risen in recent years. Further, the issues on which the people are asked to decide have become more and more complex, and fewer and fewer citizens are able to form a firm opinion about them. From 1971 to 1997 only five of 68 national initiatives passed.

The cost of gathering signatures by convincing enough people of an issue's importance has become very expensive, and the Swiss government must now spend more than four million Swiss francs (about $3 million) to conduct a referendum. The increasing dissatisfaction with this form of democracy is demonstrated by the rapidly decreasing voter participation. Few referenda, initiatives or national parliamentary elections attract more than 50% of the voters, and no one is surprised if only one–third of the eligible voters choose to vote on an issue; the average was 42% by 1998. In fact, Switzerland is the only democracy in the world where voter participation in major elections is now lower than in the U.S.

Drugs

Youth protests died down significantly in the late 1980s. A greater scourge in the 1990s and beyond is drugs. Nowhere in Europe were they as available as in a park (nicknamed "Needle Park") located a few hundred meters from Zurich's main shopping center; on a normal day, 2,000 people, half of whom under age 22, came to buy or sell drugs, and the number doubled on the weekend. Because of the influx of professional dealers and the rising crime and chaos in and around the park, it was closed in 1992. The drug population merely dispersed to other Zurich neighborhoods.

Drug use is illegal in Switzerland, but the police almost never arrest anyone for mere possession. In 1997 voters overwhelmingly endorsed their government's liberal drug policies, including state distribution of heroin under doctors' care to longtime addicts. However, in 1998 nearly 74% rejected the legalization of heroin, cocaine and marijuana. The Swiss try hard to find acceptable compromises with the youth because they fear that failure could damage or destroy a very delicate but essential ingredient of Swiss democracy: the inclination and ability to solve serious problems by means of consensus. Without its traditional "rules of the game," which include tolerance and compromise, Swiss democracy would lose much of its uniqueness.

Foreign Policy

Swiss foreign policy is based on five main pillars: (1) armed neutrality, (2) universality of diplomatic and economic relations with *all* countries of the world regardless of regime or foreign policy, (3) the readiness to provide its "good offices" to other countries (for instance, Switzerland represents the U.S. in Cuba and Iran, where no U.S. diplomats are allowed; it also represents Cuba in the U.S., Iran in Egypt, and Israel in Ghana), (4) providing its own territory for international organizations and conferences and (5) solidarity with other peoples of the world, especially when it comes to humanitarian actions.

There are many international organizations with headquarters in Geneva, including many UN specialized agencies such as WHO, ILO, ITU, and WTO. Numerous non–governmental organizations have their headquarters in Geneva, such as the World Council of Churches, the International Committee of the Red Cross (for war emergencies) and the International Federation of Red Cross Societies (for natural disasters and peacetime emergencies). The latter organization was founded in 1864 by the Swiss businessman Henri Dunant, who had been shocked by the carnage he had witnessed on Italian battlefields during the campaigns of Napoleon III. Switzerland's close links to the Red Cross are still symbolized by the latter's use of the Swiss flag with reversed colors. The Red Cross is an important vehicle for international humanitarian actions involving prisoners and refugees.

Switzerland is often criticized for its mediocre record for foreign aid. In the mid–1990s, it devoted .34% of its GDP to helping developing countries, compared with .9% for Sweden and .3% for the U.S. Yet, the quality of its assistance is very high, and there is scarcely a people in the world which is more generous in time of crisis.

In general, Switzerland avoids any alliances or actions which might involve it in any kind of political, economic or military action against other states. But it may participate in UN peacekeeping operations. Its troops perform support functions in the former Yugoslavia. It also joined NATO's Partnership for Peace (PfP) in order to strengthen its cooperation with that alliance. The Swiss are armed to the teeth in order to demonstrate their determination to defend their neutrality and in order to dissuade any belligerent in a European war from viewing Swiss territory as a military vacuum and thereby inviting invasion. There is no general staff in peacetime, and Parliament creates the rank of general only in wartime. There is only a skeleton standing army. Nevertheless, defense spending claims about 20% of the Confederation's budget and about 2% of the nation's GDP.

The Swiss buy some of the most sophisticated military hardware available, including U.S. fighter aircraft. They also produce a wide range of military equipment that they sell—subject to certain restrictions—to countries as diverse as Australia, Turkey, Egypt, Saudi Arabia, Burma, Guatemala and Angola. Too, in an emergency, Switzerland could mobilize 625,000 men (one–tenth of the population!) within 48 hours. It also has built a network of bomb shelters that would protect 90% of the population in the event of nuclear attack.

Military Service

Every Swiss male must serve in the na-

Young people ("drop–outs") at their favorite hangout

Switzerland

Swiss soldiers

tional militia from age 20 to age 42 (age 52 for officers and 62 at the latest for generals). It has been aptly noted that Switzerland "has been in a state of war every weekend since 1945" and that "Switzerland does not have an army, it *is* an army!" Although there is a civilian service for those citizens who are morally or religiously opposed to all forms of military service, this service lasts 1.5 times longer than the minimum requirement for ordinary military duty. Those who for any legitimate reason cannot perform military service must pay a fee to the Swiss state. If they want to do so, women can also serve in the armed forces, except in combat missions.

After 15 weeks of basic training, soldiers are assigned to militia units and are required to perform three weeks of duty every other year. Special units such as militia pilots and tank formations, serve two weeks each year. The Swiss soldier is permitted to take his equipment, including his rifle and live ammunition, home with him, and he is required to practice his sharpshooting regularly in rifle associations. The Swiss ability to shoot straight is widely respected. As the Swiss often remind listeners: "William Tell was a man of courage and integrity—and he was a good shot!" The last German Kaiser, Wilhelm II, was also given a friendly reminder of this. Once, after inspecting a Swiss army unit, he turned to one of the Swiss soldiers and asked what his comrades would do if the German army were to invade Switzerland with twice as many soldiers. The answer: "In that case, each of us would have to fire twice!" In 1989 the government decided to add some American firepower by acquiring several thousand shoulder-fired Stinger anti–aircraft missiles and 34 F/A–18 fighter airplanes.

In 1989 the revered armed forces, which in a country with so many ethnic divisions is one of the few truly national institutions, was seriously buffeted by the winds of détente. In a referendum, in which 68.6% of the eligible voters participated (the largest turnout in 15 years!), 35.6% voted to abolish the military. Although the President at this time, Jean–Pascal Delamuraz, had called the initiative "an idiocy as big as the Matterhorn," (one of the highest and best known mountains in Switzerland), the results severely shook the armed forces. Even though it had survived, the vote pointed to resentment against the army's influence in Swiss society. In an 1989 opinion poll, three–fourths of respondents said officers had a better chance of being promoted in their civilian jobs, 59% believed their boss was a officer, and 34% thought that the boss treated them like soldiers in the office. Today an officer's career is no longer as important because there are considerably more civilian leadership and management courses than before. The vote also revealed resentment against the male network in Swiss society from which women are barred.

The army embarked on reform and rehabilitation. Former General Heinz Häsler admitted that "everything must be done to restore the people's confidence that military defense is needed." In 1994 voters were asked to decide on the questions: "Does Switzerland really need an army?" and "Does Switzerland need 34 new fighter airplanes?" Both votes passed by a small majority. By 1995 the Swiss Armed Forces were reduced from 600,000 to 400,000 soldiers and converted from a "static force" to a "dynamic force." The professional support comprises about 1,500 instructors, pilots and professional soldiers (to protect the underground installations). As a result of the most extensive armed forces reform since 1907, called "Army 95," the minimum total service time (after basic training) is 295 days for soldiers, 900 days for officers up to the rank of captain, and 1,200 days for colonels.

Switzerland is not a member of NATO, and its and Austria's neutrality separates NATO's northern and southern halves. But Swiss neutrality is defined much more narrowly than merely refusing to join a military alliance such as NATO. The Swiss government is considering joining the "Partnership for Peace" within NATO, and there will be a vote on it in the future. Earlier, its political leaders never publicly commented on foreign political events, such as elections or *coups d'état* or on foreign military actions such as the Soviet Union's invasions of Czechoslovakia in 1968 and of Afghanistan in 1979. This changed in August 1990, when for the first time Switzerland applied the UN sanctions against Iraq, which had invaded Kuwait.

Although the Swiss conception of neutrality has also prevented the country from joining the UN, Switzerland has joined many of the specialized UN organizations, and it pays more than half a billion Swiss francs (more than 72 Swiss francs per inhabitant). Geneva is the seat of the UN's European headquarters. It has held that the UN's provision for sanctions against member states is incompatible with Swiss neutrality. The Swiss Federal Council and Parliament gradually reached the conclusion that Switzerland could no longer remain outside the UN, which they believed would officially take note of Swiss neutrality. They were supported by most university educated Swiss and by the country's most prestigious newspapers. Nevertheless, three out of four Swiss citizens still oppose entry. In a 1986 referendum, Swiss voters overruled their government and all main parties by three to one on this issue. An overwhelming majority in every canton, including Geneva (which has an income of $600 million from the UN headquarters there), voted against membership. The magnitude of the no vote makes it unlikely that the government would dare submit it to another vote in the coming years.

Switzerland does help finance UN

Switzerland

peacekeeping operations. In 1989 it took the bold step of actually sending unarmed but uniformed medical personnel, administrators and observers to Namibia, and later to Western Sahara. Since the Swiss constitution forbids sending troops abroad, this was not an ordinary military unit: all were volunteers; a third were women, only a few of whom are members of the country's tiny women's military services (known best for their former work with carrier pigeons that has been abandoned with "Army 95"). Nevertheless, this marked the first deployment of Swiss troops abroad since the Battle of Marignano in 1515. Switzerland also sends officers and aircraft to assist the UN in the Middle East. In 1996 it broke with its tradition by allowing NATO troops to pass through its territory on their way to implement the peace in Bosnia. By giving sanctuary to 400,000 refugees from former Yugoslavia, it also turned its back on its refugee policy before and during the Second World War. The growing internationalism is strongest in the French- and Italian-speaking parts of the country.

ECONOMY

The economy is one of the most efficient and prosperous in the world. Its per capita GDP and income is the highest in the industrialized world—slightly ahead of the United States (but less than that of tiny, neighboring Liechtenstein with its postage stamps and tremendous number of banks). The Swiss work longer than any nationality in the OECD (44.5 hours average per week). The economy is firmly based on the principle of free enterprise.

Swiss chocolate factory

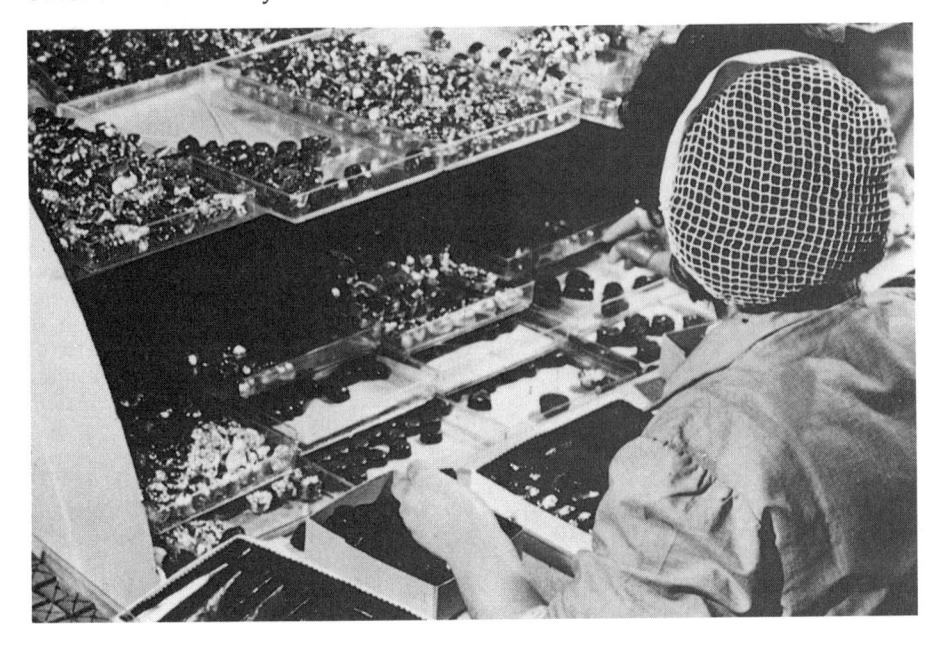

The public sector accounts for a lower percentage of GDP than in most other Western European countries, and some public companies, such as telecommunications, are being privatized. There has traditionally been little protection for their industries, so Swiss companies have always been stimulated by international competition to adapt in order to survive. However, as in all modern states, the Swiss state intervenes more and more in the economy. It offers export risk guarantees to exporters who doubt the viability of their customers. But it scorns central planning and other attempts to limit the flexibility of private firms.

The Swiss economy is influenced heavily by several basic factors. First, Switzerland is a very small country with almost no exploitable raw materials. This includes, most importantly, oil. Switzerland meets more than three-fourths of its energy needs with oil, and almost every drop must be imported from as many diverse sources as possible. It must also import natural gas—which constitutes about 4% of its energy consumption—and nuclear fuel for its four nuclear plants, which produce a about 20% of its electricity. One of its few natural resources is mountainous terrain for water power, which provides the country with about 60% of its electricity. The only other natural resource is wood, available because one-fourth of the country is covered by forests.

Second, Switzerland has insufficient farmable land to feed its population. Since it has pasture lands, much of which is in or at the foot of mountains, it has a productive dairy industry. Milk has always been plentiful, and long ago the Swiss discovered that by converting it to cheese, it could export its milk to the world. This discovery made it famous for cheese. Its sunny hillsides also enable every single canton to produce excellent, mostly light dry white wine, which supplies well over one-half the Swiss market. Unfortunately, there is very little left over for export. Only 6.3% of Switzerland is suitable for grain crops, and this is the chief reason for its excessive dependency upon food imports. In terms of calorie intake, Swiss agriculture produces only 55% of the national requirements, or 45% if one takes into consideration the imported feed component of milk and meat production.

Third, the lack of raw materials and sufficient home-grown food has forced the Swiss to make the most of their human resources. This means that they have had to industrialize and, above all, to become a trading nation. Almost no European country with such a high standard of living has reached such a high degree of dependence on the world economy. Almost two-thirds of its GDP is derived from foreign trade in goods and services. This high volume of foreign trade is also made necessary both by Switzerland's small domestic market stemming from a small population and by its high level of prosperity.

Germany is its most important trading partner. The lion's share of Switzerland's trade is with European countries, particularly with the members of the EU: 60% of its exports and 80% of its imports. Of course, it benefits from being strategically located at the junction of Europe's main trade routes and from having an excellent road and rail network which plugs into the transportation nets of its neighbors. Nevertheless, about 30% of its exports are sent outside of Europe, and about 7% of its exports are to the U.S. This points to an almost unique problem for a European trading nation: Switzerland is landlocked. It does have one important port on the Rhine–Basel. It maintains 29 merchant ships on the high seas and is in 50th place among 111 nations which maintain a merchant fleet. However, its lines to its overseas trading partners are very vulnerable. This is one reason why it maintains its important air link through Swissair, a semi-public corporation in which the Confederation, cantons and communes have a 30% equity. The airports at Zurich and Geneva are among the busiest in the world.

Swiss industry, which was fortunate to survive World War II almost unscathed, produces a wide variety of quality, precision goods. It has some heavy-weight multinational corporations, 12 of which are on the Fortune 500 List, led by Nestlé (which ranked number 12). However, most of its factories are by world standards relatively small and widely dispersed

Switzerland

throughout the country. About half of all employed persons work in industry, one of the highest percentages in the world. But only a third of the GDP is derived from industry, compared with almost two-thirds from the growing service sector.

About one-sixth of all employees work in the machine and equipment sector, which provides one-third of Switzerland's exports. It specializes particularly in equipment which does not lend itself to mass production, such as generators and turbines. It produces over 15% of the world's textile machines and roughly 13% of the precision instruments. The country provides about 1% of the world's arms exports. In 1997 three-fourths of voters approved continuing arms sales despite reports that Switzerland had delivered about a fifth of the equipment for Iraq's atomic program. It is also a leading chemical exporter. Three Basel firms alone produce roughly 10% of the world's need for medicines, and Swiss chemical plants provide 13% of the world's production of paint materials.

The chemical industries in the Basel area created great concern and international consternation in November 1986. Accidents at the chemical plants of Sandoz and Ciba-Geigy spilled masses of toxic waste into the Rhine, undoing much of the hard work in the preceding 15 years to revive a river which had been declared ecologically dead. Countries all along the Rhine protested the Swiss handling of these disasters and the fact that information about them was withheld for many hours by Swiss authorities. These incidents were also a rude awakening for the Swiss, who had comfortably contended that nothing like this could happen in their country because their technology was too good and they were so careful.

Two of Switzerland's traditionally most important industries, watchmaking and textiles, have faced serious challenges. The textile industry is a victim of high labor costs and the rising value of the Swiss franc, which has priced many textile products out of the market; they cannot compete with Asian products which are cheaper.

In 1970, Swiss watchmakers had a third of the world's sales. By 1984 that share had fallen to 10%. Benefiting from the technological spin-offs of space exploration, the U.S. watch industry moved rapidly into the field of digital, electronic and quartz watches regulated by computer chips, and Japan was close behind. Swiss watchmakers responded by restructuring and investing effectively, diversifying into such products as heart pacemakers and by shifting some of the production facilities to foreign countries with low labor costs. To the horror of traditionalists, many "Swiss" watches bear the stamp "Made in Hong Kong under Swiss supervision." Two Swiss firms, (SSIH and Asuag) have also merged to form the world's second largest watch producer—*Industrie Horlogère Suisse*—and have met the challenge of the electronics revolution by introducing robots to produce such big, mid-price sellers as the "Swatch," which make a lifestyle statement. As a result, the watchmaking industry has recovered steadily since 1982. It is also making advances in microchips for watches. Switzerland now has a 60% share of the world market. Watches account for 8% of exports, and brands such as Rolex and Omega are among the most coveted in the world.

Strikes in key sectors of the economy have been almost unknown since 1937, despite the fact that nominal wage increases are traditionally the lowest of all industrialized countries. This fact is crucial for Switzerland's ability to maintain its international competitiveness. Consensus and conservative continuity are the foundation of the country's stability and steady economic progress. Wage negotiations are conducted at the local level, and the government stays out of them.

A chronic problem had been a shortage of labor. This helped insure that Switzerland did not have the kinds of unemployment which other Western European nations face: 3.1% in 1999. The former labor shortage compelled Switzerland to attract foreign workers, who comprise a third of the labor force and are essential to Swiss prosperity. In earlier years the country could cope with the threat of unemployment by simply sending some guest workers home. However, criticism of this policy shamed the government into granting more permanent visas. The resulting higher jobless rate has so driven up welfare costs that the public sector deficit had reached 3% of GDP by 1994.

Since the 16th century Switzerland has been among the world's major banking nations. Geneva became an extremely successful banking city, which aroused admiration and exasperation throughout Europe. Voltaire once advised that if one sees a Genevese banker jump out the window, one should jump after him because there is bound to be gold on the pavement! The French novelist, Stendhal, called them "the foremost money men of the continent. In this *metier*, they have the foremost of virtues, that of eating less each day than they earn!" The U.S. also profited from this talent when the scion of a wealthy Geneva family, Albert Gallatin, was appointed Secretary of the Treasury in 1801. Later, as the U.S. Ambassador to France and Britain, Gallatin adroitly negotiated commercial relations between the U.S. and Europe.

Switzerland has more banks than it has dentists—one per 1,400 residents. They have a reputation for secrecy, security and efficiency. However, they have begun to lose ground to the three big world banking centers of New York, Tokyo and London. A third of its smaller banks have merged or closed. Even two of its largest banks, Union Bank and Swiss Bank, announced a merger, and the three largest banks reported financial losses in 1997. The banks' dealings with the Nazis have also tarnished their reputation. In 1997 California, New York City and other U.S. cities even started boycotting their services.

Swiss banks have profited from Switzerland's political stability and hard currency, which is the most highly treasured in the world. By attracting funds to Switzerland the "Gnomes of Zurich," as the Swiss bankers have been called, in turn help to drive up the value of the franc. Combined with the Swiss National Bank's successful policy of restricting the domestic money supply, the high value of the franc has kept Switzerland's inflation rate (.6% in 1999) under control. This is because with its valuable franc, it can buy raw materials abroad more cheaply than it could if its currency were worth less. Of course, the rise in the franc's value can increase the price of Switzerland's exports, thereby hurting Swiss industry. However, the extremely low inflation rate helps keep down the price of Swiss exports and thereby keeps the export industries competitive.

A very important ace which Swiss bankers hold in their hands is the country's bank secrecy laws, which sometimes make their banking system look like the Ali Baba caves. These laws were introduced initially in 1934 to protect Jewish victims of Nazi persecution. They differed from bank secrecy laws in other countries in that bank information was also withheld from revenue authorities, and any breach of banking secrecy was a criminal offense. Yet since 1991 absolute secrecy is no longer possible. Swiss courts can order banks to divulge information or to freeze accounts, as they did when the U.S. Congress began investigating insider trading.

A 1973 treaty with the U.S. permits the divulging of bank information in cases where U.S. authorities can prove that a criminal offense is under investigation. This does not include U.S. tax evasion, which does not violate Swiss laws. After 1983 Swiss authorities were willing to extend legal assistance to other foreign governments seeking evidence to convict persons accused of tax fraud or other penal cases. The code was tightened in 1989 when the laundering of money obtained through illegal activities was made a criminal offense. This law was in part a result of American pressure, as was a 1985 measure dealing with insider stock trading. The trail leading to the conviction of Ivan Boesky began with a Swiss account. In 1990 the Swiss handed over bank documents on his and his associates' deposits. They froze assets of deposed dictators Nicolae Ceausescu (Romania) and Manuel Noriega (Panama) and of the Medellin drug cartel, and they divulged information on accounts needed in the trial of Elizabeth Kopp. They agreed to cooperate with investigations on unclaimed Jewish assets from the Second World War. In 1997 they for the first time took action against a ruler still in office, Zairian President Mobutu, who by the time of his death was said to hold $4 billion in Swiss bank accounts. In 1998 Switzerland's highest court ordered $500 million in assets belonging the late Philippine ruler Ferdinand Marcos to be returned to the Philippine central bank.

The Trade Union Federation and the *Swiss Socialist Party* have long demanded that banking operations be opened even more to public scrutiny, and American law gave strength to these demands. Many other Swiss grew uncomfortable with the notion that their prosperity might partly be based on the huge deposits of dictators and drug kings, especially as drug consumption is a growing problem in Switzerland itself. Finally in 1991 Switzerland abolished its "Form B" accounts, which allowed clients to conduct bank transactions through intermediaries without revealing their own identities. Banks must now know who is behind each account.

A further essential aspect of the Swiss economy is tourism, which accounts for about 8% of the overall national income, although Swiss tourists re–spend about one–half of that income outside Switzerland. This industry is threatened by the high value of the franc. Anyone who has seen pictures of Switzerland's majestic mountains, its sparkling spring–fed lakes and streams, or its beautiful meadows and valleys has no difficulty understanding why the tourist industry is so successful. It has also been the salvation for rural areas which would have become almost completely depopulated due to the economic and cultural attractions of the cities. Since the tourist trade is concentrated largely in otherwise economically disadvantaged areas, rural Switzerland has been kept alive and prosperous. Of course, some veteran travelers miss much of the color and folklore of the earlier rustic Switzerland, but they sometimes forget that such folklore often masked great poverty.

Switzerland is a member of several economic international organizations. In addition to the OECD, IEA and the WTO, it

Switzerland

Cheese–making

has belonged since 1960 to EFTA, which is now largely irrelevant. Although Switzerland signed an agreement with the EU which removed all tariffs on industrial products in 1972, it could not become a full member for three reasons: first, it would have had to relinquish a portion of its sovereignty to the EU; second, its neutrality could be affected; third are economic reasons. For example, the free movement of labor guaranteed within the EU would undermine the Swiss policy of reducing the number of foreign workers. Also, Switzerland gives much higher subsidies to its farmers than the EU allows.

The EU's push toward greater unity stimulated fears in Switzerland that it could be isolated, and in 1992 the Federal Council formally applied for membership. In that year Swiss voters voted to join the IMF and the World Bank. But in December they rejected their country's entry into the European Economic Area (EEA), a link between the EU and EFTA. German–speakers in the large cities said yes, but they were outvoted by rural and small town German–speakers, whose traditional fear of being absorbed by a larger Germany was revived by the EU. By contrast, French–speaking Swiss, who have no fear of France, said yes. The rejection of the EEA put the application to the EU, for which there is no parliamentary or popular majority, temporarily on ice. Its laws have already been made "Euro–compatible" in most sectors. If it were ever to enter, it would be the second–biggest financial contributor after Germany.

In a step to align their fiscal policies to the EU and to lower the budget deficit, voters approved in a 1993 referendum the introduction of a Value Added Tax (VAT). Refusal to join the EU hurts some industries, such as chocolate. To retain their market shares in other European countries, chocolate makers are having progressively to shift their production outside of Switzerland, thereby dulling the magic ring of "Swiss chocolate." At least they retain a huge market at home: the average Swiss consumes more than 22 pounds of chocolate per year, more than do Americans (10 pounds) or any nationality.

It is willing to pay a high price to keep farms operating in remote areas of the country in order to reduce the wartime vulnerability of its food supplies. Swiss farmers comprise only 5.5% of the labor force, compared to 22% prior to World War II, the lowest proportion of any continen-

Switzerland

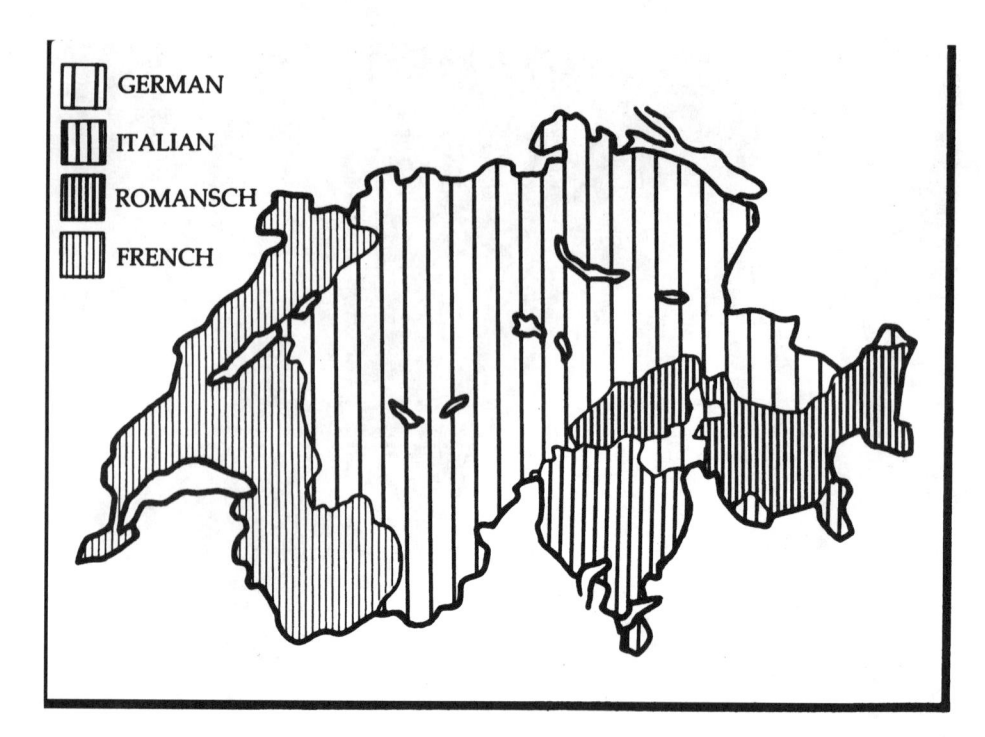

LANGUAGE AREAS

tal European country except Belgium. They produce only 3.5% of the GDP, but they earn an average of 50% more than other European farmers. This is not due entirely to subsidies, but also to heavy mechanization and to the government–sponsored effort to combine more than half the arable land into larger farms which are more suited to efficient farming.

CULTURE

Switzerland is a multi–lingual country. The most widely used official language is German, spoken by 64% of the citizens. Actually, most German–speaking Swiss speak one of many different dialects of Aleman German, which differs from valley to valley and which is spoken very differently from that which is heard in Berlin. The other official languages are French, spoken in pure form by 18% of the Swiss, and Italian is spoken by about 8%.

A fourth "national language" is Romansch, a collection of five not always mutually intelligible Latin–based dialects spoken mostly in the more isolated valleys of Grisons. Some linguists argue that it is the closest living language to the late Roman Empire vernacular. It is spoken by about 40,000 (.5%) of the Swiss. That number has been declining as tourism has helped encourage slightly more than half the residents in Grisons to speak Swiss German. To fight against this trend, linguists are busy standardizing the idioms and spelling and translating many texts, including income tax forms, into Romansch. T.V. and radio air–time is also being increased and broadened to include comedians and such local pop groups as Ils Hades ("Hell's Boys"). In 1996 the Swiss voted in a referendum to elevate Romansch to the status of a "semi–official" language, meaning that speakers may use it in dealings with the federal government.

Although only a minority of Swiss is fully multilingual, as are Luxembourgers, the fact that the language groups are separated and largely concentrated in single–language, autonomous cantons prevents the language diversity from being a major problem as in Belgium. It is true, though, that French and Italian–speaking Swiss somewhat resent the dominance of German in the federal institutions in Bern. In 1998 a new language problem emerged: the most populous canton, Zurich, decided that English, not French, should begin at an early age, perhaps in the first grade. Its officials argued that in the contemporary world pupils need more than the one or two years of English they used to get before age 16, when they can leave school. This produced an uproar, especially in the French–speaking cantons. But with no national ministry of education, it is difficult to establish and maintain one common policy in the cultural field. Some other cantons are sure to follow Zurich's lead.

Switzerland is also multi–religious. While Protestants outnumbered Catholics by nearly three to two in 1900, Catholics, who now comprise 49.4% of the population, presently outnumber the Protestants, who comprise 47.8% Each canton is free to decide whether or not to have complete separation between church and state, as in Geneva. The federal government does exercise some control over the churches by reserving the right to approve bishoprics and by banning members of the clergy from the National Council. Not until the 1970s did the government permit the Jesuits to resume activities in the country. However, one cannot say that serious tensions exist among religions or between the churches and the state. Religion also plays an insignificant role in Swiss politics today except when such issues as abortion are the subjects of referendums.

The cantons organize their own school systems, and this enables the schools to reflect their religious, lingual and cultural uniqueness. All children enter primary school at age six or seven. After four or five years of primary school, the children enter one of three different kinds of "upper school": an extended primary school makes the lowest academic demands; a second type, called a *Realschule*, prepares pupils for a commercial or technical career and a *Gymnasium* prepares pupils for the universities. After the mandatory eight or nine years of schooling, pupils can enter an apprenticeship, and roughly 80% do this; or they can continue their general education, aiming toward specialized training or the university. There are seven cantonal universities, one business and social science university in St. Gallen and two federally operated technical universities in Zurich and Lausanne.

Radio and TV operate under government license and are administered by a mixed state and privately owned body, the Swiss Broadcasting and Television Corporation (SRG). The SRG broadcasts in four languages from six radio studios and in German, French and Italian from three television stations. Of course, broadcasts from neighboring countries are also received in most parts of Switzerland. In 1983, the cabinet approved the establishment of Switzerland's first local radio and TV stations, which would supplement the existing national broadcasting network. These new stations will be non–profit, and advertising will be limited. With about 231 newspapers, the country also has the greatest number per capita in Europe, although it has declined by 40% since 1939. Zurich has one of the most highly respected newspapers in Europe, the *Neue Zürcher Zeitung*.

Switzerland has a wealth of folk art and music and a rich cultural tradition of its own. The Swiss foundation, Pro Helvetia, seeks both to preserve and stimulate Swiss cultural activities. Yet the cultural and intellectual life of Switzerland has always been enriched by foreigners who were drawn to it or who sought refuge there.

Switzerland

Such towering figures as Hans Holbein the Younger, Germaine de Stäel, Franz Liszt, Richard Wagner, Friedrich Nietzsche, Thomas Mann, Jules Verne, Albert Einstein, Karl Barth, Karl Jaspers and Hermann Hesse chose to live and work part of their lives in Switzerland. The proximity of great cultures which surround the country both stimulates Swiss writers and thinkers and draws their minds away. Any Swiss writer who does not feel himself a German, French or Italian, or who does not share in the intellectual life of the neighboring country where his native language is spoken, risks becoming narrow and provincial. But if he takes a much wider view, his work risks losing its Swiss character. Indeed, many Swiss writers have been frustrated and bored with the narrow confines of the small bourgeois and neutral Switzerland. The Swiss psychoanalyst, C.G. Jung, once described Switzerland as a country "beneath the battle," and two of the 20th century's greatest playwrights, Max Frisch and Friedrich Dürrenmatt, both Swiss, have expressed in their works gruesomeness and disillusionment and have generally debunked the lives of those around them.

Still, many Swiss artists have found great international recognition. Paul Klee, who was brought up in Bern and who later fled Nazi Germany, brought Swiss painting to the world stage. His modern art is represented in the great galleries around the world. The art theoretician and one of the greatest architects in history, Charles–Edouard Jeanneret (better known as Le Corbusier) designed buildings throughout the world, although he built very little in his native Switzerland. The modernist sculptor, Jean Tinguely, with his "free and joyous machines," ranks as one of the world's most inventive contrivers. An ingenious example of his work can be found in the town commons of Columbus, Indiana. Using pieces he had found in the Columbus junk yard, he created his indescribable "Chaos" with such intriguing moving parts that the viewer can neither wholly understand nor forget it.

Without a doubt, one of the most important influences on the Swiss culture has been and always will be nature. Perhaps the greatest pages in its literature and its greatest art focus on the incomparable Swiss landscape. They evoke those magic moments when a person surrenders himself completely to the beauty of the world around him, when a person feels himself included for a moment in a great harmony. Foreign writers could scarcely escape this magic effect of the Alps. Friedrich Nietzsche conceived his *Zarathustra*, which expressed his bold, heroic, over–proportional philosophy in the Alpine Engadine, and Thomas Mann set his *Magic Mountain*, one of the 20th century's greatest novels, in the crisp, sanitary Alpine air above Davos. Perhaps Hermann Hesse, who had been drawn permanently to Switzerland, expressed this magic best: "Everything merges into one, distance vanishes and time is done away with."

FUTURE

In 1991 Switzerland celebrated the 700th anniversary of its birth. Instead of patting themselves on the back for the peace and prosperity they have enjoyed, the Swiss are ruminating about their role in the modern world. Such problems as political scandals, laundering of dirty money, and rising drug use have prompted the country, in the words of a Swiss official, "to redefine Switzerland by examining our internal problems and by looking at our future role in Europe and in the 21st century."

That reexamination has dramatically been extended to the country's wartime dealings with Nazi Germany and the possible misuse of bank secrecy laws to prevent the return of Jewish assets to Holocaust victims. The debate will continue whether Switzerland had paid too high a moral price to remain neutral.

It will continue to enjoy a relatively high degree of domestic stability. Its industry is well–equipped and prepared for increasingly intense international trade competition. Therefore, Switzerland will remain a prosperous country. Its foreign policy will have a more international orientation, and its policy of neutrality will undergo change. Voters prepare for legislative elections in October 1999.

Jean Tinguely's *Chaos I* on the commons in Columbus, Indiana Photo by Claude and Victor Thompson

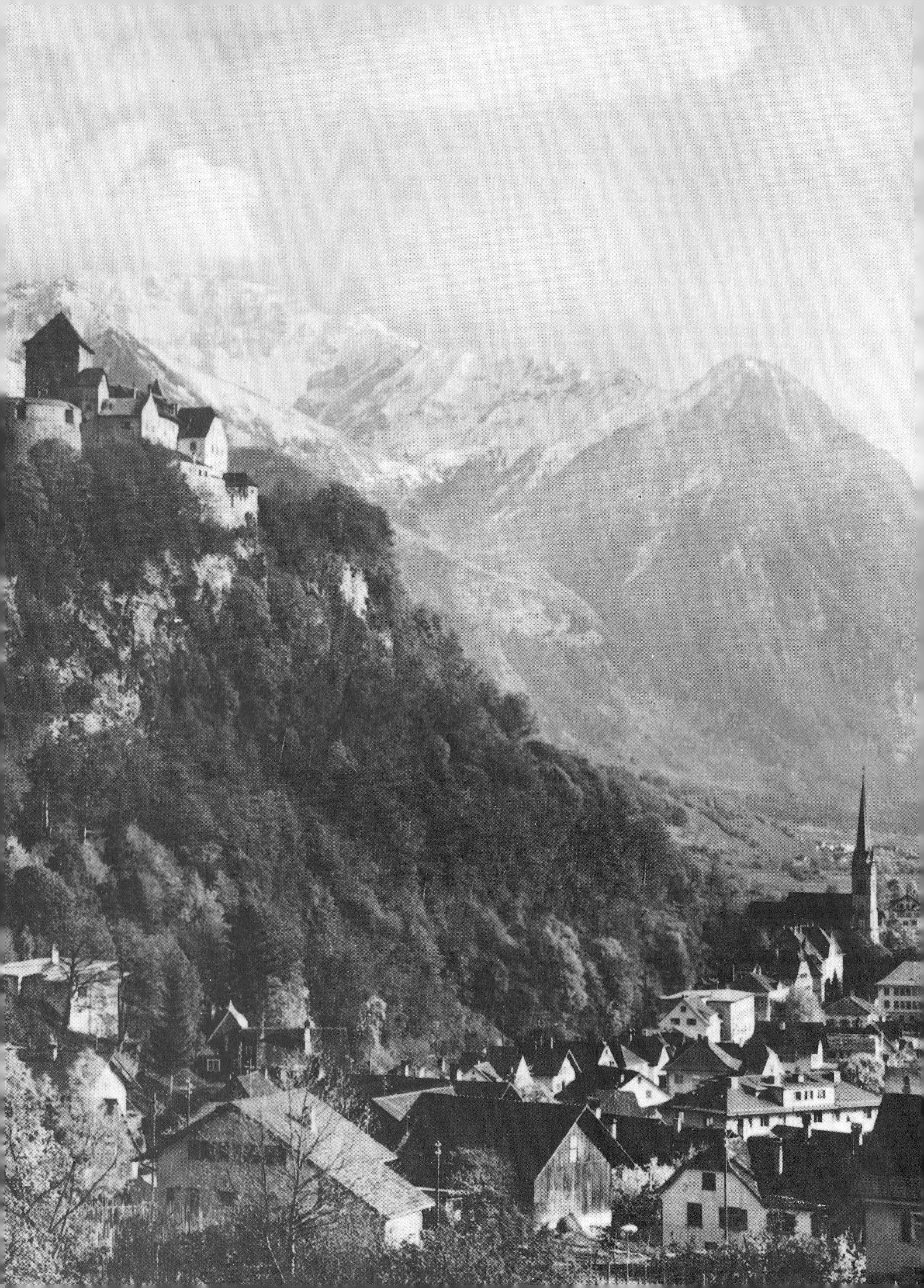

The Principality of Liechtenstein

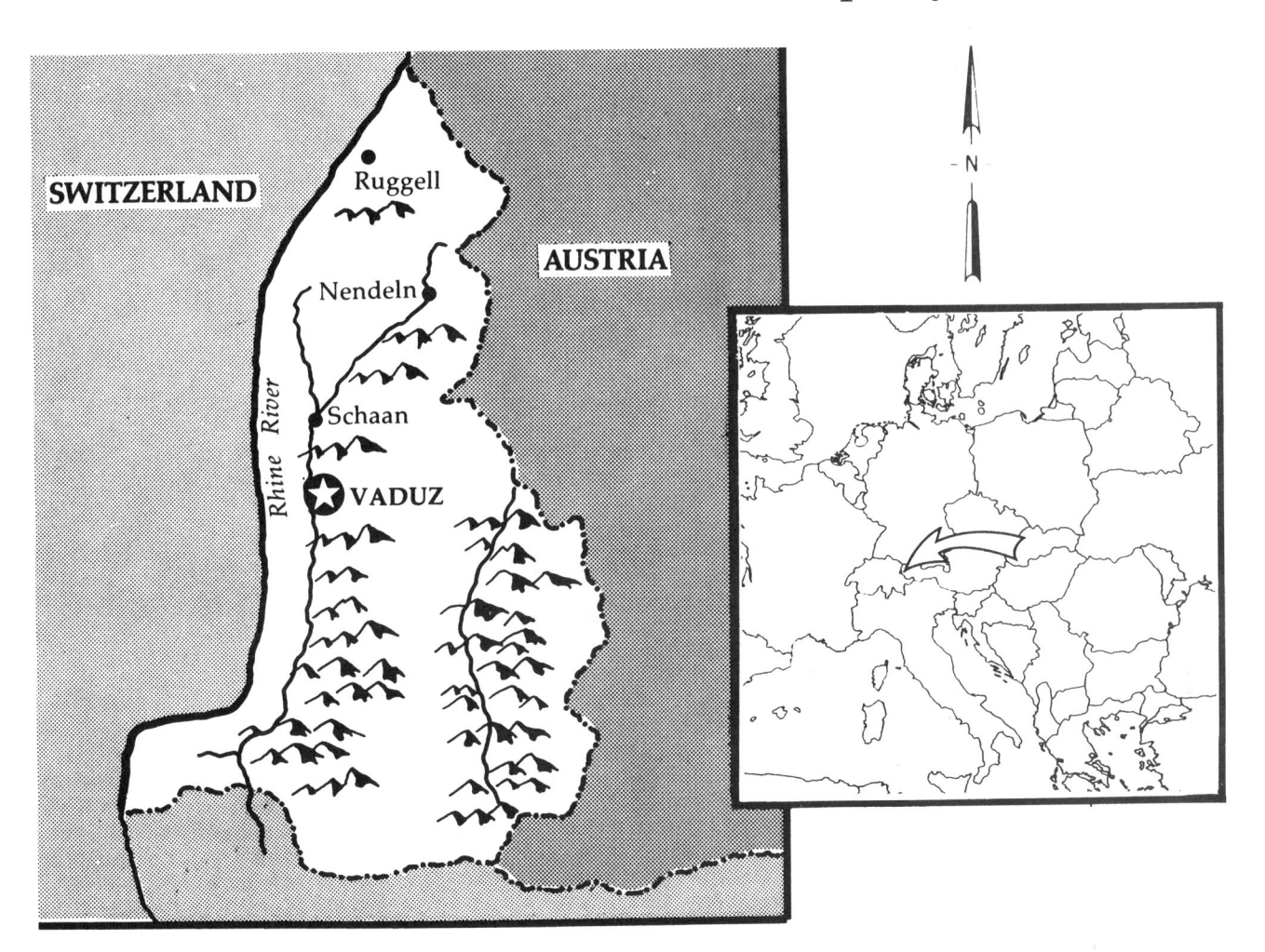

Area: 62 sq. mi. (160 sq. km.)
Population: 31,000, estimated.
Capital City: Vaduz (Pop. 5,000, estimated).
Climate: Alpine, with cool summers and cold winters.
Neighboring Countries: Switzerland (Northwest); Austria (Northeast); Italy (South).
Official Language: German (Aleman dialect).
Ethnic Background: Alemannic German. More than one–third of the residents are foreigners, chiefly Swiss, German, Austrian and Italian.
Official Religion: Roman Catholic (92%).
Main Industries: High technology, metal industry, especially production of small machines, textiles, ceramics, chemicals and pharmaceuticals, timber, hydro-electric power, building equipment, processed foods, tourism, postage stamps.
Main Customers: EU (45%), EFTA (19%), Switzerland (27.3%).
Currency: Swiss Franc.
Date of Independence: January 23, 1719.

Government: Hereditary constitutional monarchy.
Head of State: His Serene Highness Prince Hans Adam II (b. 1945).
Heads of Government: A five–man collegial board including the head of government, Mario Frick (since 1993).
National Flag: Two horizontal bands, blue over red, with a gold crown in the blue field. (The colors of the House of Liechtenstein are gold and red.)

Liechtenstein is an almost unknown Alpine country with a territorial size slightly smaller than the District of Columbia and one–twentieth of that of Rhode Island with a population of only about 31,000. In fact, about the only thing big about this pint–sized state was the name of its late ruler, who died in 1989: Prince Franz Josef II Maria Aloys Alfred Karl Johannes Heinrich Michael Georg Ignatius Benediktus Gerhardus Majella von und zu Liechtenstein, Duke of Troppau and Jägerndorf, Count of Rietberg. It is the last existing intact remnant of the Holy Roman Empire and is the world's only remaining German–speaking monarchy. Its people, who have a strong feeling of independence and tradition, maintain their country's sovereignty without soldiers.

Separated from Switzerland by the Rhine River, a torrent rushing straight down from the mountains which at times threatens the country's fertile valley, Liechtenstein is squeezed between the Swiss cantons of Grisons and St. Gallen to the west and the Austrian province of Vorarlberg to the east. One third of the country, which is approximately fifteen miles (twenty five kilometers) long and an average of four miles (six kilometers) wide, is a rolling, green and fertile area located in the Rhine valley. Most of the country's population, industry and agriculture is located in this area. The remaining two–thirds is composed of the rugged foothills of the Raetian Massif, with peaks ranging from 5,900 feet (1,735 meters) to 8,600 feet (2,599 meters), that form part of the central Alpine chain which runs east and west through the southern half of Switzerland. This forward–looking relic of the past is a land of almost unsurpassed natural beauty, colorful tradition and economic prosperity.

Liechtenstein

HISTORY

The Early Period

Situated on one of the oldest north–south transit routes in Europe, Liechtenstein was a logical area for continuous settlement since the Stone Ages.

In 15 B.C. the Romans under Caesar Augustus conquered the Celtic inhabitants and established an important highway through the area. This road helped open the land which is now Germany to Roman conquest, trade and administration. Later, it provided good access for German tribes or troops seeking wealth and power in Italy. Liechtenstein also lies astride the Basel–Vienna route, a thoroughfare which also brought soldiers and traders to the area. The remains of Roman villas and the castle in Schaan testify to the former Roman presence. Parts of the Alemannic (Germanic) tribe moved into the region in 264 A.D. Like many other tribes of northern and eastern Europe at the time, the Alemans had pulled up stakes and sought richer territories in western and southern Europe. They drove the Romans out of the area very quickly and have remained ever since. Today's citizens are descendants of these ancient Alemans and still speak their melodic dialect of German, which is also spoken in sections of eastern Switzerland and southern Germany.

The land was subsequently ruled by a variety of noble houses until Prince Hans Adam von Liechtenstein, an Austrian nobleman with a family residence near Vienna, purchased the Lordships of Shellenberg in 1699 and Vaduz in 1712. The calculation of the Prince, who had tried for years to buy territory anywhere between Italy and the Elbe River, was that by purchasing these two independent lordships which were fiefs of the Holy Roman Empire, he could persuade the Austrian Kaiser, Karl VI, to upgrade the united lordships to the status of the Imperial Principality of Liechtenstein. Karl did just this on January 23, 1719, and the House of Liechtenstein, which gave its name to the new Principality, thereby gained a coveted seat in the Imperial Diet of the Holy Roman Empire. Karl's declaration made Liechtenstein the 343rd state in the Empire and gave the Principality its present form. The new ruling family remained in Vienna, caring very little for the small land which had brought it privilege and honor. For 187 years, Liechtenstein was ruled from a distance by an absolute monarch.

Napoleon

In 1806 Napoleon drove out the Austrian troops which had occupied the principality since 1794 and made the country a member of the Confederation of the Rhine. Its ties with the Holy Roman Empire ended with the demise of that long paralyzed conglomerate of states, which, as was often said, was neither holy, Roman, nor an empire. Liechtenstein officially became a free and sovereign state. Napoleon respected Liechtenstein's independence, which was confirmed later by the Congress of Vienna in 1815. It is, in fact, the only part of the Napoleonic territorial system which survived unchanged to this day.

It is almost inconceivable that a country as small as Liechtenstein could exist without some form of economic union with a greater power. It joined the German Confederation after the fall of Napoleon and in 1852 it joined a customs union with the Austro–Hungarian Empire. From 1876 until 1918, the Principality was a part of an even tighter customs and tax arrangement with the Austrian province of Vorarlberg. Its close ties with Austria made it unavoidable that it lent its support in Austria's feud with Prussia over the future shape of a unified Germany. Nevertheless, Liechtenstein maintained a rather free hand. It resisted all efforts to draw it into the First World War as an ally of Germany–Austria.

After World War I

The links between Liechtenstein and its eastern neighbor were severed in 1918 with the collapse of Austria–Hungary. World War I brought about the collapse of centuries–old dynasties all over Europe in the face of revolution, famine, misery and the widespread evaporation of former ideals. Liechtenstein's partner, Austria–Hungary, had been whittled down to its German core, a mere splinter of the earlier multi–national empire. Such a ruined and chaotic country could no longer offer a promising future to Liechtenstein. In fact, Austria's collapse and dizzying post–war inflation wiped out Liechtenstein's entire savings. Therefore it saw the need for far–reaching changes. It both proclaimed the present democratic constitution on October 5, 1921, and reoriented itself toward its other, more fortunate neighbor: Switzerland. A customs treaty was signed with that nation in 1923, and this relationship, updated and deepened by subsequent agreements, is now firmly established.

Depression and World War II

In the 1930s Liechtenstein was severely shaken by the economic depression and narrowly escaped being swallowed up by Hitler's Third Reich. Austria was absorbed by Germany in 1938 and the shadow of the swastika was cast over Liechtenstein's border. The 85–year–old monarch, Franz I, was without heirs, and he feared that his death would be the signal for a Nazi takeover of the Principality. He therefore appointed as regent one of his grandnephews, the present monarch's father, Franz Josef II. On July 26, 1938, Franz Josef II ascended the throne. A small minority of Liechtensteiners had actually been attracted to Nazism, and in March 1939 local Nazis attempted unsuccessfully to overthrow the government. This determined minority remained undaunted and continued to publish a semi–weekly Nazi news-

Prince Hans–Adam and Princess Marie

Liechtenstein

paper; a few of them even joined the armed sections of the Nazi SS.

Liechtenstein, which was not included in the Swiss defense system during World War II, miraculously managed to maintain its neutrality throughout the conflict. German troops could have captured the country within a half an hour, especially since the fifty–man auxiliary police corps was under orders to offer no actual or symbolic resistance whatsoever. This corps occupied itself chiefly with trying to control the great number of foreign deserters, conscientious objectors and refugees who streamed into the country.

After Germany's collapse, the border posts were strengthened and a barbed–wire barricade was strung along the entire border with Austria. However, in the night of May 2, 1945, the barricade was trampled and crossed by armed soldiers of the First Russian Army of Liberation, who were fleeing from Red Army units which had been ordered to send them back to the Soviet Union. They were disarmed and interned with thousands of other refugees in camps near Ruggell and Schaan. Despite attempts by a Soviet investigating team which came to Vaduz to demand possession of all Russians, these refugees remained until 1948, when they were permitted to emigrate to Argentina.

POLITICAL SYSTEM

Liechtenstein is a constitutional monarchy in which sovereignty is theoretically shared by the hereditary monarch from the House of Liechtenstein and the people. The country has a 25–member unicameral parliament elected by proportional representation for four–year terms. The voter turnout at elections is quite high, ranging from 76% to 95%, and citizens twenty years of age or older are permitted to vote. Not until 1984 were women granted the right to vote and to hold public office. Earlier, an antiquated law stripping all locally born women of their citizenship if they married foreigners was repealed. Liechtenstein has ceased being politically a "man's world."

As in Switzerland, the highest executive authority is a collegial board. All five members serve four–year terms; the leading member (called the Head of Government) is selected by the majority in parliament. The Deputy Chief is also chosen in this manner, and by tradition is from an opposition party. Parliament also chooses the remaining three members (called Government Councillors). All are formally appointed by the Prince. The leaders of the government are chosen by the parliament and must be approved by the Prince; they are responsible to both parliament and to the Prince.

The Prince must formally approve all legislation, although he has not vetoed a law since the 1960s when he disapproved of the legislature's proposed change in hunting rights. He has the right to introduce legislative proposals in the parliament. In time of emergency, he can, with the permission of the Head of Government, decree laws without seeking approval from parliament. In normal times he 'reigns but does not rule.'

But in 1993 he flexed his constitutional muscles by dissolving parliament and calling new elections after the ruling party revolted against its leader, Markus Büchel, whom it accused of incompetence. Such a rejection of a parliamentary no–confidence vote is inconceivable in any other European monarchy. The Prince noted: "There is no majority for a figurehead."

In the past the Prince has normally made no attempt to dominate the political process. However, in 1997 he demanded the right to appoint judges. Final approval rests with the voters, but he says he will pack up his family and move to Vienna if this power is denied him. Even one of his critics in parliament, Peter Wolff, admits that losing the Prince would be a terrible setback: "The monarchy gives us our national identity." The Prince has found almost universal support among the political parties and the people. According to custom, he receives no pay from his subjects, although he accepts a token expense allowance of 250,000 Swiss francs. His popularity helps give stability to the country's politics.

Liechtensteiners know how to reconcile their love for the royal dynasty with their right to self–rule. Thus, their traditionally firm attachment to the monarchy is rather surprising to the outsider, considering the facts that the first time their ruler even vis-

The Prince and Princess of Liechtenstein with their children—(on the stairs) H.S.H. Princess Tatjana and H.S.H. Prince Maximilian, and (left and right) H.S.H. Prince Constantin, H.S.H. Hereditary Prince Alois.

Liechtenstein

The Castle at Vaduz, residence of the Reigning Prince of Liechtenstein

ited the tiny country was in 1842 and that the rulers declined to live permanently in the land until 1938. Until then, Princes always preferred the splendid family palace, Burg Mödling, near Vienna. But when he ascended the throne in 1938, the quiet and unassuming Prince Franz Josef II, who had been born in 1906 and educated in agriculture and forestry in Vienna, chose to reside in the 100–room medieval castle perched on a high cliff crowning Vaduz. The Prince of Liechtenstein's family possesses an art collection whose estimated value is from $150 million to $500 million.

In 1989 Franz Josef II died, less than one month after the death of his wife, Princess Gina; he collapsed at his wife's bedside and never recovered. The new Prince, Hans–Adam, is an economist who has long administered the family's wealth, estimated at more than $2 billion. This includes a bank with subsidiaries in London and New York, electronics and "software" investments in the U.S., and land holdings in Austria twice the size of Liechtenstein. He is also demanding that the Czech Republic return lands confiscated after World War I ten–times the size of the principality. It also owns jointly with the International Paper Company a 75,000–acre farming operation in Texas.

The Prince is married to Prague–born Countess Marie Aglae Kinsky, and they have four children. When Prince Alois was married to Duchess Sophie of Bavaria in 1993, the entire Liechtenstein population was invited to join the festivities.

Political Parties

Except for the *Free List (FL)*, the two main political parties have programs that are difficult to distinguish from each other. They appeal to electors who, not surprisingly in such a small country, are often inclined to vote for the man rather than the party. In the 1997 elections to the 25–seat parliament, the conservative *Progressive Citizens' Party (FBP)* won 10 seats. The centrist *Fatherland Union (VU)* won 13 seats and formed a government headed by Mario Frick. The *Christian Social Party* failed to capture a single seat. A left–wing environmentalist group, the *Free List*, entered parliament, and won two seats.

Liechtenstein has an independent judiciary and a legal system based on Swiss law. For administrative purposes, the country is divided into eleven communes, which are governed by mayors and city councils elected locally every three years. A civil service staff of approximately 400 officials administers the government's political decisions.

This is a sovereign state which, because of its extremely small size, has chosen to align itself politically and economically very closely to Switzerland. This places severe limits on its powers, but as a sovereign state, Liechtenstein is free to take back its full powers at any time. It does differ with Switzerland on some diplomatic issues. In 1980 Liechtenstein broke with the Swiss policy and supported the U.S.–led boycott of the Moscow Olympics to protest Soviet intervention in Afghanistan. Also, it endorsed a high level of European military integration and the creation of a European nuclear deterrent force. As the prince noted, 'We have to think about European stability, even though we are neutral.'

He also announced Liechtenstein's entry into the UN, rather than to wait for the Swiss to make up their minds. In 1992 it announced that it would not enter the EU, even if Switzerland decided to do so. The referendum on the European Economic Area (EEA) treaty was accepted by voters in 1992 under the condition that the customs union with Switzerland be maintained. Unlike Switzerland, it joined the EEA in 1995. EEA membership gives it most of the advantages of EU membership and few of the burdens. Prince Hans–Adam called it "the best of all possible worlds for Liechtenstein. We have our cake and eat it too." The greatest beneficiary is its manufacturing sector, which accounts for almost half of the country's 20,000 jobs and which is almost totally dependent upon exporting. Liechtenstein belongs to several special organizations associated with the UN, such as the International Court of Justice, the International Atomic Energy Agency and the UN Conference on Trade and Development. It belongs to EFTA (to which a substantial amount of its exports go), the Council of Europe in Strasbourg, and the OSCE.

Liechtenstein maintains embassies only in Bern, Switzerland, (which in turn represents its tiny partner throughout the world) and in Austria. It has agreed not to conclude trade or customs treaties with other states, but is bound by most treaties into which Switzerland enters. In general, it avoids any international dealings that would displease Switzerland. It has renounced its right to coin its own money, with the exception of gold coins that have no legal value as currency; Swiss currency has been used since 1921. Swiss officials have full responsibility for all customs questions arising out of the 1924 customs union.

Beautiful postage stamps are printed in Liechtenstein, which it sells profitably throughout the world. In fact, such sales provide 10% of the government's revenues. Switzerland shares responsibility for the postal, telephone and telegraph systems, although Liechtenstein owns the equipment. Swiss border guards also control Liechtenstein's boundaries. Officially, all able–bodied males to age sixty are required to be ready for military service, but there has in fact been no army since 1868. Liechtenstein maintains merely a 55–man police force.

ECONOMY

The visitor to Liechtenstein most often remembers the romantic side of this Alpine retreat, which seems to have slumbered almost unnoticed into the modern age. What he often overlooks is the fact that this principality is the second richest,

Liechtenstein

second most industrially productive country in the world when measured in per capita income terms. Only Brunei, with its tremendous oil deposits, earns more per person each year. This economic prosperity tends to change the traditional, overall picture of this nation. Though traditional in so many ways, it has shown itself to be extremely open to progress in research, technology and production. Before World War II more than a third of the population worked on the land, and there were only four factories.

Now only 1.7% of the population is engaged in agriculture, and there are forty-five factories. This leap into the modern industrial age is a result not only of extraordinarily stable political conditions, but also of minimum investment requirements, a very liberal tax policy and strict bank secrecy. The tax laws have encouraged from 20,000 to 30,000 foreign businesses, often called "letter box companies," to maintain nominal headquarters in Liechtenstein. About a third of Liechtenstein's total fiscal revenues are derived from such companies. It is untrue that no individual or company pays taxes there. Income taxes range from 8% to 10% for individuals and 6% to 18% for companies. Property is also taxed.

Liechtenstein's industry is very diverse. High technology and the metal industry, which specializes in small machines, are the leading ones, followed by the ceramic, chemical and pharmaceutical industries. The country produces a wide range of goods, including artificial teeth, ultra-high vacuum technology, miniature calculators, boilers, textiles, furniture, varnishes, fountains, canned foods, prefabricated houses and protective coatings for spaceship windows. One of its companies even produced a component for a solar wind experiment that went to the moon with the Apollo astronauts.

Because it has practically no natural resources, Liechtenstein has no heavy industry. The relatively small size of factories and the fact that the firms have been consciously dispersed throughout the country away from urban areas has had the favorable effect of both preventing large industrial plants from dominating the landscape and of preserving the country's environment from the kind of damage which has often accompanied rapid industrialization in other countries. This fortunate situation greatly benefits not only the inhabitants, but also the country's tourist industry, which is the nation's fourth most important source of income.

The thriving economy has enabled the residents to enjoy a high standard of living and a generous social welfare system. It has also brought certain economic and social problems to the country. First, since there is almost no domestic market for its high technology products, Liechtenstein is overwhelmingly dependent upon exporting. It is extremely vulnerable to international developments which might adversely affect world trade. Second, with only 2% of its population working in agriculture, it must import 70% of the food needed to nourish its well-fed population. Third, the small size of the domestic work force has necessitated the importation of foreign workers. Approximately 12,000 such workers, who come chiefly from Switzerland, Austria, Germany and Italy, and who are often accompanied by their families, now constitute a third of the country's population. Adding 6,500 commuters who come daily to work, about 60% of the workforce is foreign.

This large percentage of foreigners has placed strains on the highly tolerant and hospitable Liechtensteiners. They can seldom be absorbed into the political life of the country; an ancient practice permits foreigners to become citizens only if they are individually approved by the popular assemblies in one of the eleven communes. Few of the foreigners ever gain the right to vote.

Many native Liechtensteiners became concerned about the possibly negative social effects that the presence of so many foreigners might have on the country. Therefore, since 1962 the government has placed severe limits on the influx of foreign workers. This policy has produced undeniable economic difficulties. Without an available pool of labor, Liechtenstein's domestic industry cannot grow. Because of this limitation, almost all of the country's major industries, which need to expand because of the high volume of orders, have begun to transfer substantial portions of their production activities to foreign countries. Unemployment stood at 1% in 1996.

Liechtenstein has a good network of roads, but has no airport and no rail service to the capital city. The railway facilities in the north of the country linking Switzerland and Austria are owned and operated by the Austrian Federal Railways.

CULTURE

As a small country with very few citizens, Liechtenstein is heavily dependent culturally on its German-speaking neighbors. Two German language newspapers appear in the capital city of Vaduz: the *Liechtensteiner Vaterland* published three times weekly by the Catholic-oriented *Fatherland Union*, and the *Liechtensteiner Volksblatt*, published four times weekly by the *Progressive Citizens Party*. All radio and television programming comes from Switzerland, and the Liechtenstein Postal Ministry pays fees for this service.

Cultural efforts receive generous subsidies from the government. Permanent art collections are maintained in two museums in the so-called *Engländerbau* on the main street of Vaduz. In the second half of the 1980s a new art museum was supposed to be built in Vaduz to display the bulk of the Prince's collection of paintings, sculptures, old weapons and furniture. However, bickering and red tape have held up the construction. Most of these treasures are stored in the royal castle in a five-story depot as large as a medium sized department store. A few can be seen in the *Engländerbau*. An impatient Prince Hans-Adam reportedly thought about establishing his own art museum by blasting a huge cavern into the cliff under his castle in Vaduz. The high cost of constructing the new museum was such a political hot potato that it prompted new parliamentary elections in 1989 to try to sort it out. *Theater am Kirchplatz* in the town of Schaan attracts leading performers from throughout the world.

The school system offers kindergarten, elementary and secondary educations, and is modeled largely after the Swiss school system. There is one elite *Gymnasium* (high school) in Vaduz for those pupils who wish to pursue university studies. Students must enter universities outside the country, since none exists locally. The literacy rate among the country's citizens is 100%.

FUTURE

Liechtenstein's close association with Switzerland and its highly advanced and diversified economy will continue to be crucial for its existence as a sovereign micro-state in the modern world. It can be expected to remain politically stable, despite the fact that over one-third of its residents are foreigners. Liechtenstein will remain somewhat vulnerable economically because of its excessive dependence upon exports and its static domestic labor pool. Also, rapid industrialization and sudden wealth can be expected to intensify certain urban problems, such as rapidly increasing land values. In June 1999 Europeans took notice of this minuscule principality when it hosted the small Olympics, held every other year for little European countries.

The French Republic

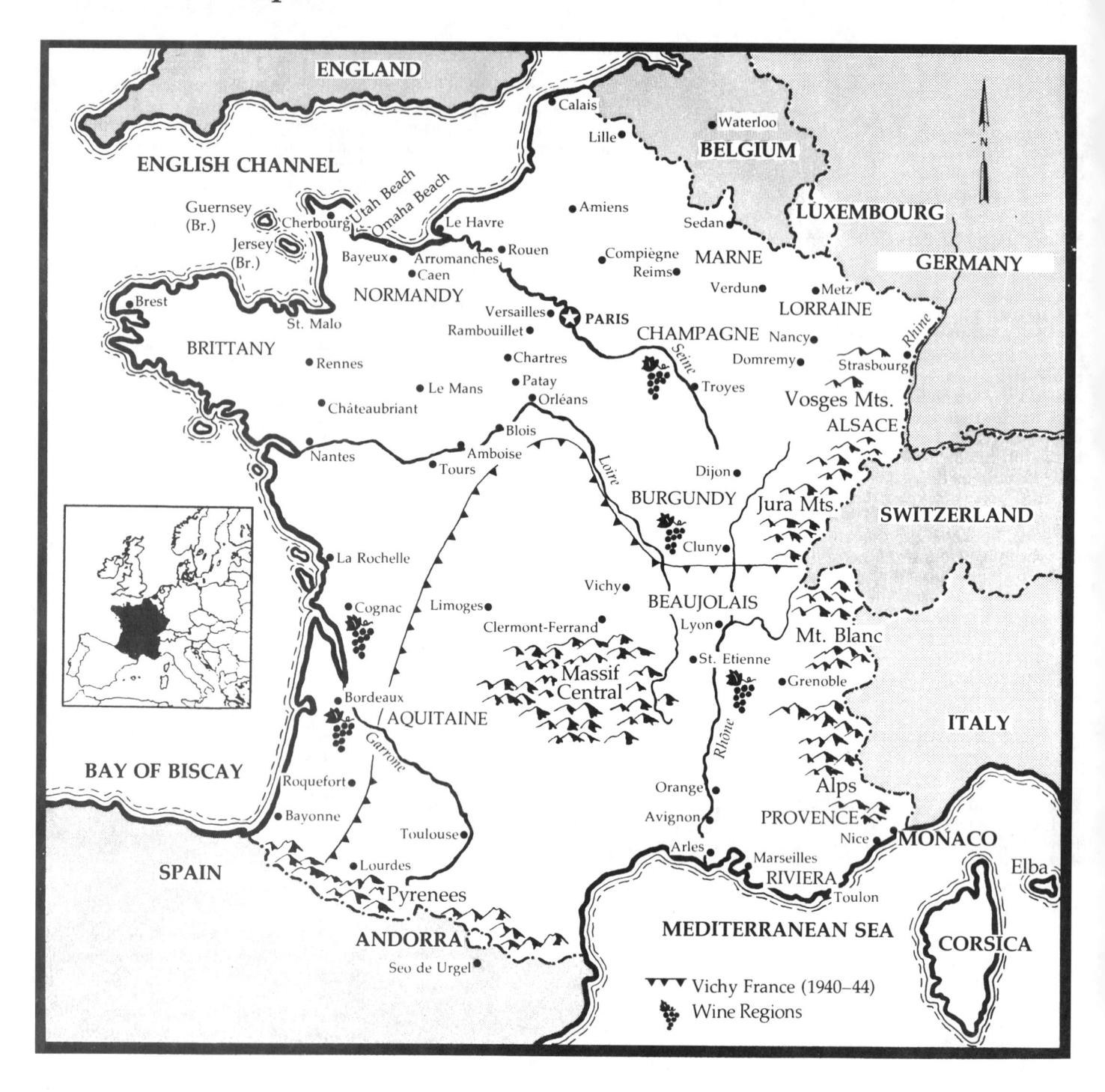

Area: 211,208 sq. mi. (547,026 km.) This is the largest country in Western Europe, four fifths the size of Texas and four times the size of New York State).
Population: 58.2 million. Average annual growth rate 0.4%.
Capital City: Paris, population 2.4 million within city limits, 9.1 million within Metropolitan Paris.
Climate: Pleasant, rather temperate, except in the south, where the weather resembles that of Florida.
Neighboring Countries: Belgium, Luxembourg, Germany (North and Northeast); Switzerland (East); Italy and Monaco (Southeast) Spain and Andorra (Southwest).
Official Language: French.
Ethnic Background: Indo–European, of diverse origin.
Principal Religion: Roman Catholic (83%), Protestant (2%), Jewish (1%), Unaffiliated (13%).
Chief Commercial Exports: Textiles and clothing, machinery, automobiles (Peugeot, Renault, Citroen), iron, steel, agricultural products, expensive fine wines and cheaper, ordinary wines.
Main Imports: Crude petroleum, machinery and equipment, chemicals, iron and steel products, foodstuffs, agricultural products.
Major Trade Partners: EU (about 50%), petroleum exporting countries, U.S., Japan.
Currency: Franc.
National Holiday: July 14, anniversary of the storming of the Bastille Prison in Paris in 1789, the spark which brought the French revolution to an explosion.
Chief of State: Jacques Chirac, President (since 1995).

France

Chief of State: Lionel Jospin, Premier (since June 1997). Unlike many nations where the presidency is merely ceremonial, France has a Chief Executive with broad powers; the Premier concerns himself primarily with the daily workings of the government, and he also can wield great power if he is from a different party than that of the president, as is the case following the 1997 elections.

National Flag: The tricolor—three broad vertical stripes, blue, white, red.

France is a land of visible contrasts. In many ways it appears divided. Within the past two centuries, during which time the United States has had one continuous political system, France has experienced three monarchies, two empires, a half dozen republics and more than a dozen constitutions; its history is strewn with revolutions, counter–revolutions and *coups d'etat*, and its political party system is extremely fragmented. General de Gaulle, the founder of the present French Republic, once asked in exasperation how one could *ever* rule a land which has more than 300 different cheeses! Yet there is an underlying stability in contemporary France and a strong consensus concerning the importance of respecting individual rights and of maintaining a republican, democratic form of government. Indeed, France is one of the few stable democracies in the world and is therefore a haven for political refugees.

France also is highly centralized politically, economically and culturally. The predominance of Paris is undeniable. No successful revolution ever began outside of Paris, and King Henry IV's famous statement in 1593, justifying his conversion to Catholicism, that "Paris is worth a mass" was an early reminder that control over France must emanate from Paris and not from the provinces. The French capital often seems to be the place where French history is made and then merely presented to the provinces as the finished product. With a population as great as the entire continent of Australia (roughly one out of five Frenchmen lives in Paris or its suburbs), it is the residence of a fourth of France's civil servants and doctors, a third of its students and half of its university professors, two thirds of its artists and authors, a fifth of its factory workers and factories employing more than 25 persons and two–thirds of its company and bank headquarters. Efforts since 1955 to decentralize the French economy have met with little success.

At the same time, France is a land of great diversity in terms of religion, landscape, language, customs and styles of living. Such ethnic minorities as the Basques, the Alsacians, the Bretons, the West Indians and the Corsicans preserve their own languages and cultures, but only in Corsica is there a movement for autonomy which enjoys any appreciable popular backing. In general, ethnic diversity does not threaten the present French state to the degree that it does other European countries such as Ireland, Belgium and Spain.

France, it has often been said, is "weighed down by history." Frenchmen have a long memory for their own past, although they do not always agree about its high and low points. Yet, far from being a country exclusively living in the past, contemporary France is a highly dynamic and forward–looking nation. It is among the wealthiest, most technologically advanced

From atop Notre Dame Cathedral, a stone gargoyle stares vacantly over the Seine River and the rooftops of Paris to the distant Eiffel Tower
Courtesy: Jon Markham Morrow

France

and influential countries in the world. Clearly, France has a future, but Frenchmen would say that they have a *destiny*. From the time of the Crusades, the first of which was practically an entirely French affair, to the present day, Frenchmen have felt a sense of mission to civilize the world.

Perhaps no one expressed this mission better than the great realist de Gaulle, who opened his war memoirs with the following words: "All my life I have had a certain idea of France. This is inspired by sentiment as much as by reason. The emotional side of me tends to imagine France, like the princess in the fairy stories or the Madonna in the frescoes, as dedicated to an exalted and exceptional destiny. Instinctively I have the feeling that Providence has created her either for complete successes or for exemplary misfortunes... But the positive side of my mind also assures me that France is not really herself unless in the front rank; that only vast enterprises are capable of counterbalancing the ferments of dispersal which are inherent in her people; that our country, as it is, surrounded by the others, as they are, must aim high and hold itself straight, on pain of mortal danger. In short, to my mind, France cannot be France without greatness." The General, who once admitted that he preferred *France* to *Frenchmen*, disdained the petty squabblings of everyday politics. He denied that the essential France was to be found in the yawning provincial bureaucrat, the scandalous French president (Felix Faure) who died in the presidential palace while making love to his mistress, or the impetuous Parisian pamphleteer who plots to bring down the regime. He believed that one must inhale the heady air of the mountain peaks in order to see the true France: "Viewed from the heights, France is beautiful."

France is at the same time an Atlantic, Continental and Mediterranean country, and it is territorially the largest country in Europe west of Russia. The country is somewhat hexagonal in shape with rather regular contours. It stretches roughly 600 miles (960 km.) from north to south and west to east. Through it flow five great rivers, the Seine, Loire, Garonne, Rhone and Rhine, which originate in the central land mass (Massif Central) or in the mountains of the Alps and the Pyrenees. It faces three seas (the North Sea, the Atlantic Ocean and the Mediterranean), and has a coastline of more than 1,200 miles (1,930 km.).

In the North, there are no natural barriers to separate France from northern Europe. Elsewhere, the Rhine River separates France from Germany, the Alps from Switzerland and Italy, and the Pyrenees from Spain. The geographical relief of France begins from the coastline to the valleys, and then rises to plateaus, highlands and finally to mountains, the highest being Mont Blanc in the Alps (15,777 feet, 4,809 meters) and Mont Vignemale in the Pyrenees (10,804 feet; 3,293 meters).

Although France is large, it has the lowest population density in the European Union (EU). Its total population and economic riches are very unevenly distributed geographically. If one were to draw a line on the map of France from the northern port of Le Havre to Grenoble and then on to Marseilles, one could see two halves of a country as different from one another as northern Italy is from southern Italy. The western half of France contains 56% of the territory, but only 37% of its people, and is steadily losing population. It tends to be less industrialized, and its agriculture is based on small farms and is therefore less efficient. East of the line one finds 80% of France's industrial production and three–fourths of the industrial employees. Economic development is particularly rapid in the northeast of France, and recently in Rhône–Alps and Marseilles regions. Farming tends to be more intensive and efficient, and a far smaller percentage of inhabitants live agriculturally.

Geographic and demographic statistics can hardly convey the beauty which for centuries has been called *la belle France*. The visitor invariably finds himself charmed by the smell of rich vines heavy with grapes, by the rolling green countryside studded with more castles than one finds in any other country, by the towering cathedrals whose bells resound throughout the countryside, by the warm beaches along the Riviera and by the majestic, snow–capped peaks. As one begins to realize how this beauty blends with the Frenchman's proverbial *joie de vivre* ("joy of living"), one sees why the Germans have always described the good life as "living like God in France."

HISTORY

The Early Period

Although France has played a prominent role in European history for at least 1500 years, it did not become a national entity or even approximately achieve its present shape until the 16th century A.D. The legend of French unity goes back to Vercingetorix, the chief of a Gallic tribe called the Arverni, who led a coalition in an uprising against the Roman occupiers in 52 B.C. Although he placed his foot soldiers in a hopeless strategic position and squandered his cavalry before the critical phase of the battle had begun, resulting in his troops' and his own capture, he is seen as the first patriot and resistance hero of French history.

The French profess a close kinship to the Gauls. But the latter were a people who left no literature, no language, no laws, who worshipped many gods and practiced human sacrifice, and who, according to the Roman arch at Orange, fought naked, their hair buttered and in a long looped knot, with drooping mustaches and long narrow shields. It is doubtful that such a race had a profound impact on the French people and their civilization. Frenchmen today are very amused by the caricature of the early Gaulois in the popular *Asterix* comic books. They no doubt owe far more to the Romans, who occupied for centuries much of what is now France. The Romans built towns, roads, aqueducts and theaters. They provided examples of centralization, efficient bureaucracy, written law and a periodic census. They brought education and culture to France and gave the French an appreciation of abstractions. They also left a tradition of grandeur, spotting France with statues and monuments. Finally, their language—vulgarized by common usage, later developed into French.

Even before the fall of the Roman Empire in the 5th century, France had become an invasion ground for tribes from all over the known world: Visigoths, Burgundians, Alemans, and Franks (Germans who eventually gave the country its name). In the 8th and 9th centuries, Charlemagne, the warrior king who established himself as "Emperor of the West," absorbed what is now France into a huge political unit encompassing much of present Europe, from Saxony to the island of Elba, including Bavaria and most of Lombardy in Italy. This great empire, however, did not survive his death in 814 A.D., and France again became fragmented.

The Capets Claim Paris

Not until a century and a half later did conditions begin to develop which were favorable to unity. In 987 the Capet family, which owned large tracts of land around the region now called the *Île de France*, raised a claim of dynastic leadership over France. The Capetians chose as their capital a small town nearby, which had been established in 100 B.C. on a five–acre island in the middle of the river Seine by a curly headed Celtic tribe of fishermen and navigators called *Parisii*. The Romans had named this city Lutetia and had built it up to a town of from 6,000 to 10,000 inhabitants. The city had also served as capital for the Frankish King Clovis, who had defeated the last remnants of the retreating Romans in 486.

The Capetians adopted *Francien*, a Latin–based dialect spoken around Paris, as their official language. Hugues Capet, born in 938, was the first Frankish king who could speak no German, and as a re-

France

Crusaders and Saracens in Battle
(From a 12th century stained-glass window)

sult of the Capetian example, German and Latin soon disappeared from the early French court. French became the language of the elite, both at the court and abroad (for example, Marco Polo wrote about his travels to China in French!), and the political and military successes of the French dynasty gradually led to the language's adoption by all the people. This language became a powerful agent in the formation and expansion of the French nation and civilization. For that reason, few peoples in the world try so hard to preserve and spread their language as do the French.

Crusades

The first Crusade in the 11th century, sponsored by the French Pope Urban II, and organized by the French cleric Peter the Hermit, was conducted almost exclusively by the French knights. While building castles in Lebanon and establishing a Kingdom of Jerusalem (which endured at least in name until the 15th century), they showed a zealous sense of mission in extending French civilization, which they tended to see as embodying Christian values. This became a major rationale for most French military and colonial enterprises in the centuries to follow.

A crucially important by-product of the Crusades was the weakening of the feudal bonds which tied serfs to their lords. French noblemen were often left penniless by the military expenses which they bore, and many times they obtained needed money by freeing serfs and selling charters to cities. By the 13th century, serfdom had almost disappeared in France, and cities had sprung up everywhere, partly because of the trade which the Crusades had created. Spices and textiles from the Orient were highly desired by the Europeans, and cities became the crossroads for such trade. France prospered.

Another indirect example of French expansionism occurred when William (the Conqueror) invaded England in 1066, conquering the Anglo-Saxons by 1070. Although initially French largely displaced Anglo-Saxon, at least at the court, the latter soon revived, and the two languages were combined, enriching each other. Court decisions and proceedings by the twelfth century were written in a curious combination of English, French and Latin. But William retained his holdings in Normandy, Maine, Touraine and Anjou within what is now France; this later became a source of friction between the French and the English. William's great-grandson, the incompetent King John of England, lost many of the French territories in the early 13th century.

By the end of the 12th century, France, especially Paris (which by that time was the most populous city in Europe) was considered to be the world center of science and culture, having replaced Athens and Rome. By the 14th century one-half of the people in the Christian world lived in what is now France.

Disorganization and Weak Monarchs

Despite the establishment of a unique language and a French dynasty, French history, until the 16th century, continued to be characterized most of the time by weak kings struggling against foreign rulers and by powerful, rebellious French noblemen, who often did not hesitate to ally with foreign powers against their king. Such division exposed France to the danger of absorption into a large kingdom dominated by England because of its control over much of France. But in the 13th and 14th centuries, three powerful French kings, Philippe Augustus, Louis IX (canonized in 1297 as Saint Louis) and Philippe IV (the Fair), succeeded in wresting control of some of the English domains in France. They began the slow process of patching France together, sometimes by legitimate feudal claims, often by intermarriage, and very often by war. However, England maintained its huge foothold in Aquitaine, acquired in 1154 and encompassing most of southwestern France below the Loire River; England was also allied with the Burgundians north of the Loire. In the 14th and 15th centuries, the French kings waged a "Hundred Years War" to finally drive the English out of France.

Joan of Arc

In the midst of this struggle, a female savior emerged from the small village of Domremy in Lorraine. At the age of 16, Joan of Arc, the daughter of a French shepherd, claimed to have heard the voice of God commanding her to free the besieged city of Orléans and to have the French King crowned in Reims. Having persuaded a French captain to give her a horse and an armed guard, and flying a white flag, she set off to find the King. She told a distrustful Charles VII that she would drive the English out of France and be "the lieutenant of the king of heaven who is king of France."

France

Joan of Arc triumphantly enters Reims

Dressed in a man's armor, and displaying remarkable skill in improving offensive military operations, she liberated Orléans, defeated the enemy forces at Patay and Troyes, and amidst enthusiastic crowds, proceeded to Reims to have the 26-year-old Charles VII crowned on July 17, 1429, in the way traditionally prescribed for French kings. Whenever she addressed the crowds as "Frenchmen," the response indicated that a new nationalism mingled with a divine mission was emerging.

Short-lived was the fortune of this girl. Dressed in men's clothing and violating the feudal law barring women from combat, she was distrusted by the clergy, the nobility and even the newly-crowned king. Mounted on a beautiful horse, she led her forces in a vain attempt to storm Paris and Compiègne, and though wounded by an arrow, she tried unsuccessfully to rally her troops. She was captured in May 1430 and delivered to the Duke of Burgundy, who was allied with the English and who sold her to them for a high fee. She was tried in Rouen by a French ecclesiastical court and, despite her own eloquent defense, was pronounced guilty of heresy. On May 30 she was burned at the stake in Rouen's marketplace, without the ungrateful king having made the slightest effort to save her.

Even for centuries afterwards there was no consensus in France concerning the legacy she had left. A monarchical France before 1789 had little use for saviors from the masses, and her mystical, religious aura made her out of place in an enlightened, revolutionary France. Nevertheless, Napoleon had a beautiful statue of her erected in Orléans in 1803, and the process to have her made a saint was initiated in 1869. Not until the humiliating defeat of France at the hands of the Prussians in 1870 was she embraced as a symbol of vengeance toward an outside power which had taken her native Lorraine. She was finally canonized in 1920.

Joan of Arc is to many Frenchmen the ideal symbol of patriotism: a pure lady warrior with a sense of mission who placed God solidly on the side of the French. She is undoubtedly the Madonna in de Gaulle's memoirs who incorporated France, since the great French leader also adopted the cross of Lorraine as his own symbol. His stubborn, righteous defense of France's destiny moved an exasperated Englishman, Sir Winston Churchill, to remark that "of all the crosses I have had to bear, the heaviest was the Cross of Lorraine."

Further Union Followed by Religious Wars

By 1453 the English had been driven from France, except for a tiny foothold in the northern port city of Calais. The "Hundred Years War" had nevertheless been a cruel disaster for the French people. Within a century, the war and the plagues which had struck at roughly the same time had reduced the population by almost one-half. In the closing years of that century Brittany, which had been independent, was integrated into France. The union had been sealed by Anne of Brittany, who married the French King, Charles VIII in 1491, taking her native Brittany as a dowry, and who upon his death married the next French King, Louis XII, in 1499 in order to preserve this union. Though France had made impressive strides toward territorial unity in the 15th century, the century to follow was not to be one of peace and unity.

In 1519 a minor German priest named Martin Luther courageously raised a challenge of faith to the powerful Catholic Church and began the Reformation which spread throughout the Christian world. A Frenchman, John Calvin, also developed a religious doctrine hostile to the Church and was forced to flee to the Swiss city of Geneva, which he soon shaped into a Protestant "capital." He left behind a France seriously divided into two sects: the Huguenots (protestant) and the Catholics. From 1559 until 1598, the Wars of Religion raged in France; this was a chaotic period dotted by eight distinct wars, assassinations and massacres. These unfortunate events were related to the issue of the king's and other nobility's respective powers, as much as to theological matters.

The situation became particularly grave in 1572 when 4,000 Protestants gathered in Paris for the wedding of the 19-year-old King Henry of Navarre to Charles IX's sister. Henry, whose life was under threat, had announced his conversion to Catholicism, ostensibly to heal fanatical religious divisions in France. The Protestants were massacred on orders of the French king, and they promptly re-

France

sponded to this "St. Bartholomew's Day Massacre" by announcing that such a treacherous king was no longer to be obeyed. Henry quickly reassumed the Protestant faith and the wars raged on. When all involved finally realized in 1598 that the strife was without any redeeming value, Henry, upon becoming king, issued the Edict of Nantes, which promised Frenchmen religious freedom. Nevertheless, the religious issue continued to gnaw away at the unity of France for more than three centuries.

The French Century

The 17th century became "the French century" in all of continental Europe. This was a period when forceful French kings and brilliant royal advisers succeeded in reducing much of the French nobility's powers and in establishing the present borders of France. The glitter of the royal court soon dazzled Europe.

When in 1624 Louis XIII chose an ambitious cardinal to be his chief adviser, he gained at his side a tireless servant of the French crown and the French state. Cardinal Richelieu was not a man given to courtly debauchery, theological hairsplitting or listening for voices from God. "Reason must be the standard for everything," he said, and "the public interest ought to be the sole objective of the prince and his counselors." *Raison d'état* ("reason of state"), the interests of the community, became for him the overriding concerns.

Since Richelieu was convinced that only absolute monarchical authority could elevate his country to the highest rank in the world, he proceeded to neutralize any powers which could challenge the central authority of the King. He had torn down all castles not belonging to the King which could be used to resist royal authority. In a swash-buckling era presented so vividly in Alexander Dumas' *The Three Musketeers*, Richelieu dared to ban duelling, a favorite pastime of the nobility, on the grounds that weapons should be drawn only against enemies of the state. While not attacking religious principles, he whittled away at the privileges granted in 1598 to Protestants, believing that a free, powerful Protestant party in France could easily undermine the centralized power of France.

At the same time he sent money and troops to support the Protestants in the Thirty Years War which ravaged Germany from 1618 to 1648. His reasons were simple: although Austria and Spain were fighting in the name of Catholicism, their victory in the struggle would have strengthened these great powers and thus presented a greater threat to France. Further, by sending French troops southward, eastward and northward, France acquired territory along the way. France's borders thus moved outward. Clearly, the Cardinal did not think religiously; he thought *French*. When he died in 1642 (followed in death a few months later by Louis XIII), he left behind an almost unchallenged central authority, a powerful French army, a small but effective fleet and a highly organized professional diplomatic service. He also established French as the new diplomatic language for the world, a position it enjoyed for more than 250 years. Above all, he left a tradition of total dedication to the power and glory of France.

Louis XIV, Cardinal Mazarin and Anarchy

This renowned monarch became king in 1643 at the age of five. He was able to build on the great works of Cardinal Richelieu and on the works of another Cardinal who, though extremely unpopular, held France together against an angry and dangerous storm until the young king was ready to assume the reins of government. Cardinal Mazarin was a wealthy Italian, whose love of money did not prevent him from energetically serving the young king's mother and regent, Queen Anne, with whom Mazarin reportedly had more than just cordial relations.

Picking up where Richelieu had left off, Mazarin led France to victories over Austria. The Treaty of Westphalia in 1648 and subsequent victories over Spain left France the foremost power in Europe. Austria was seriously weakened, and Germany was fragmented, depopulated and exhausted. *French strength and German "weakness" through division remained a cornerstone of French politics until 1990.* Indeed, Frenchmen have always liked to say ironically that "we like Germany so much that we want there to be many of them."

Having achieved a position of power in Europe, France became seriously weakened internally. From 1648 to 1653 it was rocked by a complicated series of civil disturbances which threatened the young king's hold on the throne, and which in some ways anticipated the French Revolution which came a century and a half later. The parliament, the bourgeoisie (a class of persons who had risen socially above the level of peasants and manual laborers, but who had no titles of nobility), and the Parisian mobs, all for their own reasons, created such an anarchial situation in Paris that the king and his mother were forced to flee to the palace of St. Germain, where they lived at Mazarin's personal expense.

Some French nobles invited the Spanish troops to reenter France, and Parisian mobs erected barricades and took law into their own hands. In the prolonged confusion, battles raged in the countryside and the streets of Paris, and finally Mazarin was forced to flee to Germany. However, after all order had disappeared, the key figures of this uprising, known as the *fronde* (named after the French word for slingshot, used by rioters to smash windows in Paris) surprisingly lost their nerve, and this revolt against the centralized monarchy and the unpopular Mazarin gradually collapsed.

The 14–year-old Louis led his loyal troops in 1652 into a tired and shamed Paris. Louis never forgave the rebellious city and wasted little time in removing himself from the clutches of this beautiful, but temptuous and unfaithful mistress. The rupture between the king and Paris

Paris in the 17th century

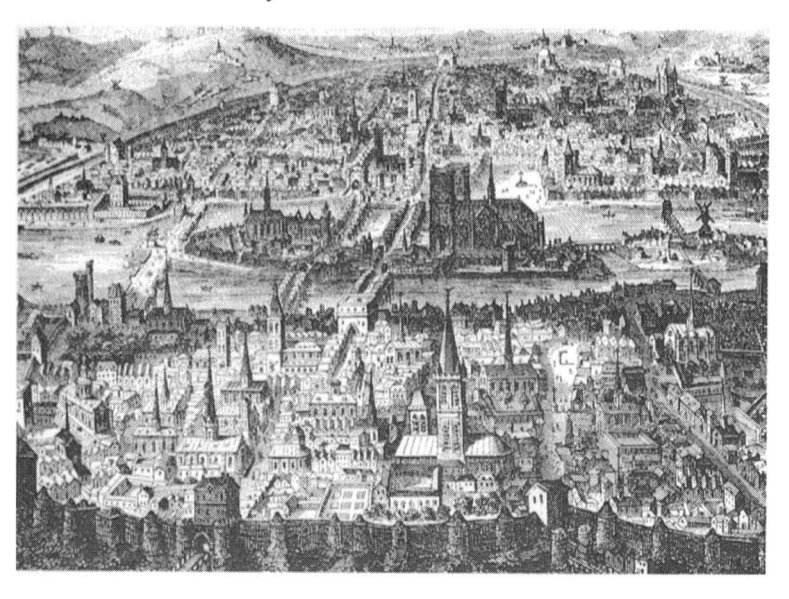

France

Louis XIV, the "Sun King." Probably painted at about age 55+, it indicates he had lost his teeth, was overweight, had bunions from wearing high heels, and a double chin.

would later have disastrous consequences for the monarchy.

Louis Comes of Age

Immediately after Mazarin's death, the young king called a meeting of all the court's advisers and announced: "Now it is time that I rule!" No one questioned this. By then, the 23–year–old monarch's imposing physical dignity and his polished manners, combined with an unhesitating decisiveness, rapidly brought him respect within France, which sometimes bordered on worship. France was weary of chaos and was ready to kiss the hand which ruled with firm authority. His prodigious lovemaking at the court, which has certainly lost nothing in the telling, greatly irritated his mother, but it did not prevent him from being a hard–working and effective king. Almost no state affairs escaped his attention; in 1661 he commanded his ministers not to sign or seal any order without his permission.

The entire kingdom increasingly felt the impact of the royal government. When the affairs of state became too great for one man to handle, he developed a bureaucracy and efficient procedures to enable his government to absorb the workload. All aspects of French foreign affairs, defense, finance, commerce, religion and the royal household were channeled through the king's court. He appointed officials to secure royal control over all activities in the various regions in France. He supervised all major appointments in his bureaucracy and the army. Though there is no evidence that he ever really said "I am the state," there was no question that he would have readily agreed with such an assertion. He actually worked very hard to live up to his rather arrogant motto: *Nec pluribus impar* ("None his equal").

As a symbol of his magnificence, the "Sun King" ordered that a royal palace be built in Versailles, which would not only be at a safe distance from Paris, but would be unsurpassed in all of Europe for its beauty and dignity. For 20 years he had this gigantic structure, with its surrounding gardens, fountains and smaller palaces, built and rebuilt. His finance minister, Colbert, was exasperated by the project, which almost emptied the royal treasury and which could only be financed by selling many of the state's treasures. However, once finished, this palace became the assembly point for much of France's ambitious nobility. There Louis could keep an eye on them and busy them with ritual duties, such as buttoning his coat or escorting the servants who brought his food to the royal table. Louis' preeminence was such that nobles competed for the honor of performing even the most menial functions at his court. For instance, the Princess of Ursins, who later became the Queen of Spain, was considered one of the luckiest persons at the Court of Versailles because she performed the task of handing the king his dagger and night pot each evening as he retired to his private bedroom.

Under the conscientious guidance of Louis XIV, France achieved an incomparable political, military and cultural ascendancy. The arts bloomed, and France was the richest and most populous country in Europe. It also acquired the most powerful army on the continent, and Louis was more than willing to use it. He conducted almost continuously destructive wars. He thereby was able to establish France's present borders, but he ultimately converted almost every country in Europe into an enemy of France. He ordered that the Palatinate in the western part of Germany be burned, resulting in the destruction of Heidelberg, Mannheim, Speyer, Worms and hundreds of smaller towns. His soldiers ripped the bones of earlier Holy Roman emperors out of their graves in Speyer, a sacrilege which was not soon forgotten in Germany. An uneasy peace was finally established in 1713, two years before the king's death, by the Treaty of Utrecht.

Even if France gradually exhausted itself financially and physically through almost continuous warfare, it was certainly well administered. Louis' powers were broad, and he used them with great energy. However, he could by no means be called a dictator in the modern sense. He had to deal with a limited national treasury, an absence of a national police force, ineffective and slow means of communication and regions which still jealously guarded their remaining powers. All in all, he gave Frenchmen an era which they still proudly call "the grand century."

Stirrings of Discontent

The "Sun King" long outlived all of his children, and upon his death his five–

France

year-old great-grandchild was crowned Louis XV. The new King ruled until 1774, when Louis XVI, a good man who never wanted to be king, succeeded to the throne. Both were rather weak and increasingly unpopular kings who were unable to guide their country's adjustment to the changes which occurred in French society during the 18th century. This was a formula for revolution. Greatly contributing to and benefiting from France's prosperity, the bourgeoisie resented its exclusion from political responsibility, which was almost entirely in the hands of the aristocracy. The rural peasantry, which comprised 80% of the population and owned 40% of the land, resented the aristocracy's rights to hunt on their land, their local police power and their near monopoly over rural mills, bakeshops and wine presses. The manorial lords appeared to live well without performing an obviously useful function.

The dissatisfaction with the aristocracy was fed by the enlightened ideas of the time. In the course of the 18th century, thinkers such as Montesquieu, Voltaire and Diderot had brilliantly chipped away at the foundations of aristocratic society. An irreverent Frenchman named Jean-Jacques Rousseau had written in his bombshell book, *The Social Contract*, that "man was born free, but everywhere he is in chains," and he had proposed provocative ways of breaking these chains and creating a society of free and equal human beings. Rousseau was driven from France because of these ideas, and died in 1778.

Events in America that same year prompted an inpouring of revolutionary ideas which brought the soup to a boil. A young revolutionary named Thomas Jefferson from Virginia had written that "all men are created equal and are endowed with unalienable rights." In rapid succession, the 13 colonies began to produce democratic constitutions, which were translated almost immediately into French and avidly read by intelligent persons grown weary of social hierarchy and inherited privilege. Benjamin Franklin, who was sent to France to persuade the government to help the American colonies in the struggle against the English, was lionized by France's high society. His rustic, egalitarian wisdom was the talk of Paris. Most importantly, he persuaded France's leaders, who had lost their colonies in North America to the English in the Seven Years' War (1756–1763), to enter the struggle against the British. French assistance to the rebellious colonies was a very important contributing factor in the American victory; without the French army and navy, perhaps the ill-equipped and militarily untrained colonists would never have prevailed against their masters.

While the French government slapped its traditional enemy in the face, it had unknowingly allowed the bacillus of freedom to enter France through the back door. Some officers and many non-commissioned officers returned to France deeply moved by the events in America of which they had been a part, and they were very sympathetic and supportive of revolutionary movements in their own country. The world now had a concrete model of a large country ruling itself in a republican way.

**Financial Woes Lead
Toward Revolution**

Another unforeseen consequence of France's aid to the Americans was that it brought France to the brink of bankruptcy; it doubled the national debt and consumed more than one-half of the crown's income. France's desperate financial situation was not caused by an extravagant court; only 5% of the public expenditures were devoted to the entire royal establishment. The French Revolution did not spring from a naive, spendthrift Queen Marie Antoinette (called by the people "Madame Deficit") who was reported (incorrectly!) to have asked why the peasants did not eat cake if they had no bread.

One-fourth of France's budget was devoted to war costs, and a whopping one-half was needed to service France's debts. Other countries, such as England, had similar expenditures, but France's financial crisis could not be solved because of its archaic and unequal tax system. The aristocracy and the wealthy bourgeoisie either evaded or won exemptions from taxation. The Church also refused to pay taxes, so the tax collectors could turn only to the poorest French citizens. Thus, although the country was generally prosperous, the public treasury was empty.

Louis XVI, who like his predecessor had often opposed the aristocracy and sought strength from the bourgeoisie, well understood the problem, but he was so weak and unpopular that he could do nothing about it. In desperation, he convened an Estates General in May 1789, the first such meeting in a century and a half. However, the class antagonism in France was such that the three classes assembled (clergy, aristocracy and bourgeoisie) simply could not work out reform in cooperation.

The Palace at Versailles

France

On June 17, 1789, the bourgeois element (the "Third Estate") decided to declare itself the "National Assembly." When the king panicked and closed the hall in which the Third Estate met, the latter moved to a nearby indoor tennis court and proclaimed in the "Oath of the Tennis Court" that it was the true representative of the people and that it would not disband until it had produced a constitution for France. This was a revolutionary step, unleashing explosive events which an irresolute king could not control. It was the first act in the French Revolution, which went through many stages and lasted ten years. Whether or not these events represented "the end of history," as the Prussian philosopher Friedrich Hegel maintained, neither France nor the world would thereafter be the same.

Revolution

The events at the Versailles meetings stirred up crowds in Paris, which began to look for weapons in arsenals and public buildings. On July 14, 1789, a crowd went to the Bastille, which, like the Tower of London, was a stronghold built during the Middle Ages to overawe the city and to provide a place of detention for influential prisoners. When the official in charge of the stronghold refused to distribute any weapons, the crowd successfully stormed the fortress. The mob, infuriated that almost a hundred persons had been killed, slaughtered the guards who had surrendered. They then beheaded the commanding official with knives and paraded around Paris with the heads of their victims on spikes. This bloody skirmish and macabre display was a harbinger of ferocious acts to come. Nevertheless, July 14 is celebrated by Frenchmen today as their major holiday.

The unrest and violence spread to the countryside as manorial lords saw their properties sacked and burned by bitter peasants. The more fortunate escaped with their lives, but royal power vanished quickly. The Marquis de Lafayette, a revolutionary–minded aristocrat who had served on George Washington's staff during the American War of Independence, was given command over the guard in Paris. He designed a flag for the new France to replace the blue and white *fleur de lis* ("lily flag"). He combined the colors of the city of Paris, red and blue, with the white of the House of Bourbon. Thus, the tricolor, which is France's flag today, represented a fusion of the new and old regimes.

The sudden acts of violence had frightened the ruling group into granting important concessions. On August 4, 1789, the nobles relinquished their feudal rights, and on August 27 the National Assembly promptly proclaimed the Declaration of the Rights of Man. The U.S. ambassador to France and author of the American Declaration of Independence, Thomas Jefferson, had been asked to read and improve this French equivalent before its publication, a request which he declined for diplomatic reasons. This French document was one of history's most eloquent assertions of equality before the law, of the opening of public service to all classes and of freedom as an unalienable individual right, limited only by the freedom of others. An enlightened constitutional monarchy was established. The king was forced to return to the Tuileries palace in Paris. There he would be under the watchful eye of France's new, moderate regime, guided by the aristocrat Count de Mirabeau, who, like many aristocrats, had concluded that the future lay with the Third Estate.

Revolution Out of Control

It is always a great misfortune when moderate and democratic revolutionaries cannot control the beast of revolution once it has been uncaged. As in Russia a century and a quarter later, a more radical "second revolution" often overtakes the first one, wiping away many of the democratic gains in the process. This misfortune befell the French Revolution.

The first signal for such a change came on the night of June 21, 1791, when the king and his family attempted to escape to Germany. Caught at Varennes, close to the border, two days later, they were ungloriously brought back to the Tuileries and locked up in their palace. After this clumsy move, the king's commitment to the new order was no longer credible, and the people's loyalty to the king, which had already been eroded, disappeared entirely.

This new situation greatly angered the other monarchies of Europe, especially those of Prussia and Austria. The moderate "Girondists," members of a revolutionary club whose name derived from the department (state) of Gironde and who had gained a majority in the National Assembly in 1792, responded to what they saw as a clear external threat to the Revolution. They declared war on Austria. It went badly for France, but it quickly added a new element to the Revolution. Seeing the "fatherland in danger," the citizens took up arms, and patriotism rose to fever pitch. Nationalism and revolution joined hands as the French national anthem, the *Marseillaise,* indicates.

The newly unleashed popular tide became extremely difficult to control. The Tuileries palace was stormed by a mob and forced a humiliated king to wear a red hat of the Revolution and to drink

France

with them from a common bottle. The constitutional monarchy was overthrown, and in September 1792 suspected royalists were hunted down and massacred in prisons, monasteries and elsewhere. In December the king was tried and convicted of conspiring with the enemy (a charge which was no doubt true), and he was beheaded one month later. Scarcely had the king's head fallen into the basket of the guillotine before France found itself at war with all the major monarchies of Europe.

Faced with a frenzied, imperiled nation, the moderates were pushed aside by the radical Jacobins, a revolutionary club which had met regularly since 1789 in the Jacobin Convent in the Rue Honoré and which was led by the fanatical Robespierre. A Committee of Public Safety was formed to cope with enemies abroad and at home. On October 10, 1793, the new revolutionary leadership declared that the government of France must remain "revolutionary until the peace." In clear text, this meant a "reign of terror," and political "trials" were begun at once.

On October 16 Queen Marie Antoinette was guillotined, followed by all the Girondists who could be arrested. For the next nine months the guillotine would never cease from doing its grisly work. Until Robespierre and his followers' own execution in July 1794, France was subjected to a dictatorship in the hands of fanatically self–righteous people who asserted that "terror is nothing else than swift, severe, indomitable justice; it then flows from virtue."

Enlightened democrats make no claims to know absolute truth and therefore tolerate other men's views and weaknesses. By contrast, the ideologues who controlled France in those bloody days had such an abstract conception of liberty that they lost sight of man. Out of love for humanity and the truth, they would have eradicated the human race.

The noted French author, George Sand, wrote that "during the terror, the men who spilled the most blood were those who had the strongest desire to lead their fellow men to the dreamed–of golden age, and who had the greatest sympathy for human misery . . . the greater their thirst for universal happiness, the more relentless they became." Charles Dickens was no doubt correct when, in the opening sentence of his *A Tale of Two Cities*, he referred to the French Revolution: "It was the best of times, it was the worst of times, it was the age of reason, it was the age of foolishness . . ." Perhaps at no other time could one see so clearly the worst and best in man.

Although Frenchmen today tend to remember mostly the noblest aspects of the Revolution, the terror made it difficult then and now for persons outside of France to have a unified opinion of this first great European revolution. No doubt, many of the 17,000 victims of the terror were in fact enemies of the new republic. Only 15% of the executions took place in Paris, and more than half took place in western France, where the resistance to the new order was the greatest. Only 15% of the victims were aristocrats or clergymen. To some extent, then, the terror was a defensive measure. However, the number of innocent persons who were caught in the grinder was so great that the new republic disgusted highly respected friends abroad. Also, although France's foreign enemies were ultimately defeated, the French Revolution was knocked off its democratic path, and it was almost a century before France was able to return to relatively stable, republican government.

Napoleon

Robespierre was overthrown and beheaded on July 27, 1794. That date fell within the month of Thermador in the revolutionary calendar, which had been introduced on August 18, 1792, the date the constitutional monarchy began. The notables who assumed power moved rapidly to restrict suffrage and eliminate the masses from political influence in a tired, internally paralyzed France. In 1795 they created a *Directory*, led by five Directors, but this new form of government could not create order in France.

In the midst of such instability, a brilliant young general saw his great opportunity. Born into an Italian family from Corsica in 1769, Napoleon Bonaparte had been educated in French military schools and had gained notoriety by suppressing an uprising against the Directory shortly after its founding. An ingenious innovator of lightning military tactics combined with effective use of field artillery, he understood how to win the unswerving devotion of his soldiers. He achieved great victories in Italy, and in 1799, while his troops were conducting a major campaign in Egypt, he returned to Paris and seized power at bayonet point.

For the next 15 years, France followed this man, who though slight of stature (barely five feet tall), was a great leader in many ways. He clearly preferred order to liberty, and he quickly moved to establish order in France. Despite his authoritarian style of rule, he was an immensely popular leader who quickly showed that he was, at least to some extent, a child of the Revolution. He introduced financial reforms and tightened the centralized administration of France. He promulgated a new constitution and a civil code which reflected the major accomplishments of the Revolution: popular sovereignty, underscored by Napoleon's practice of submitting every constitutional change to a plebiscite; trial by jury and equality before the law; a citizens' army; office holding based on competence; abolition of feudal privileges; freedom of religion; and freedom of speech and press (at least in theory). Though they had often been ignored in practice during the ten years since 1789, liberty and equality had within a decade become so embraced in principle that they have remained permanent elements of French public life.

Napoleon may appear today as a greater friend of monarchy than of the Revolution. He signed a Concordat with the Catholic Church in 1801, reintroduced slavery in French colonies in 1802 and allowed emigrés to return to France and reclaim their unsold properties. In 1804 he crowned himself "Emperor of the French," and during his reign he divorced his wife Josephine in order to marry an Austrian princess. He also placed his brothers, son and marshals upon thrones throughout Europe as he proceeded from conquest to conquest. Nevertheless, in his own day, he was seen by the other peoples of Europe as a very embodiment of the Revolution who carried its ideals to every part of Europe. These principles were always among his most effective weapons.

Napoleon remained a great military leader who sought both to secure France's "natural borders" and to pacify Europe under French leadership. This was essentially accomplished by 1802. However, his ambition was to be more than a peacemaker, and his lack of moderation not only sapped his own country's vigor, it ultimately doomed him to defeat. In May 1803 he began an endless series of wars aiming far beyond the mere protection of France's frontiers. Due to stunning

France

At the Court of Napoleon I

victories, French domination by 1806 extended from Holland and the German North Sea coast to the Illyrian Provinces along the east coast of the Adriatic Sea. Italy was completely under French control, and some territories (including Rome itself) were annexed to France. But his very successes helped to bring about his downfall.

His invasions stimulated nationalism outside France, and the other governments of Europe felt compelled to imitate France by making popular reforms and raising citizens' armies. Soon Napoleon discovered that he faced opposition, not just from hostile governments and ruling groups, but from entire nations in Europe. He fought an unsuccessful guerrilla war in Spain, and in 1812 his Grand Army suffered a disastrous wintertime defeat in frigid Russia. The following year he was defeated at the "Battle of the Nations" in Leipzig which pitted France and its allies, chiefly the Rhineland Germans, against Prussia, Austria, Russia, Sweden and England. His enemies pursued his disintegrating army into the heart of France, capturing Paris itself on March 31, 1814.

Napoleon was forced to flee to the island of Elba, where the victors erected a small kingdom for him, but in less than a year he returned to France in order to regain his empire. Though exhausted from long sustained warfare, the French succumbed once more to Napoleon's magic. In a hundred days he prepared a new army, but his dreams were crushed by a united Europe on the Belgian battlefield of Waterloo on June 18, 1815. This time he was held as prisoner on the small British island of Saint–Helena in the South Atlantic while the victorious European powers gathered at the Congress of Vienna to reconstitute Europe.

Napoleon died in lonely exile in 1821, but this "little corporal," as he was often called, still casts a giant shadow in the memories of Frenchmen. He brought France pride, and he rests in magnificent glory in the Invalides, a military hospital in Paris, where the mutilated from his Grand Army were cared for. To this day, the elite professional officers of the French army descend at midnight to their knees at the foot of Napoleon's giant illuminated statue to receive their commissions at St. Cyr, the military academy which he had created.

The Monarchy Returns

In 1815, with 150,000 occupation troops on French soil, the Bourbons were again placed on the throne. Although one spoke of a restoration and although 70,000 returned from exile abroad, few believed that the clock was to be turned back before 1789. The royal family was compelled to live in Paris under the eyes of a population which had never made the kings'

France

lives comfortable. The new King, Louis XVIII, the brother of the ill-fated Louis XVI, wanted no part of the revolutionary flag, the tricolor. He did accept a constitutional order which left things more or less as they were before 1815; feudal customs and special privileges of the nobility were not reintroduced, and France's law code, formalized under Napoleon, the tax system, personal freedoms, centralized administration and the principle of equality before the law remained.

Louis' other brother, who was crowned Charles X in 1824, showed that he had learned little about France since 1789. He believed in the divine right of kings to rule, and he tried to restore the earlier authority of the Catholic Church. His men sought revenge against former Jacobins and Bonapartists, and the ultra-royalists demanded restitution of their properties. In 1830 he made his final mistake by suspending liberty of the press, dissolving the French legislature and so restricting the electorate that practically only noblemen could vote. While the oblivious king was hunting in Rambouillet, dissidents publicly waved the tricolor and erected barricades in the streets of Paris, some of which reached a height of up to 80 feet. One nobleman, sensing danger, noted to his friend: "Things look bad. They are singing La Marseillaise!"

Three days of bitter street fighting (known as the *troix glorieuses*) convinced Charles that he could not master the situation, so he set sail immediately for Scotland. No Bourbon ever ruled France again; their last King had failed to notice that although the French population had grown tired of revolution and war, it nevertheless continued to take equality and liberty seriously. However, unlike the Americans, the French did not experience one successful 18th-century revolution which established a new democratic political order once and for all. The French Revolution had to be refought at intervals, and each revolution left France divided. It remained a country with a seed of civil war.

Another monarchy was established in 1830. The new King was the 57-year-old Duke of Orléans, Louis-Philippe, the son of the renowned Philippe *Egalité* ("equality"), who had voted for the beheading of Louis XVI and who soon thereafter was also beheaded in the name of the Revolution. Louis-Philippe had fought for the Revolution at Valmy and Jemmapes and then had gone into exile, visiting the United States at one time. Despite his romantic past, the new king was an uninspiring man. He was intelligent enough to disavow the divine right of kings and to proclaim himself the "citizen's king." He restored the revolutionary tricolor as the nation's flag, lifted censorship and doubled the suffrage (although only about 200,000 in a nation of 32 million had the right to vote).

He was a moderate, business-oriented king who brought France more prosperity at home and peace abroad. But the fact that he was the target of more than 80 assassination attempts indicated that his rule was not universally acceptable to Frenchmen. He did not pursue glory, a fact which the poet Lamartine lamented: "France is a bored nation." Although an admirer of the king, even Victor Hugo wrote in that great work of fiction about post-Napoleonic France, *Les Misérables*, that "his great fault was that he was modest in the name of France.... His monarchy displayed excessive timidity which is offensive to a nation that has July 14 in its civil traditions and Austerlitz in its military annals."

An economic crisis in 1846 made the voteless urban workers in Paris nervous, and the middle classes wanted an end to the narrow elite composed of a few thousand noblemen and upper bourgeoisie. The influence of the extremely unpopular premier, François Guizot, who was reputed (incorrectly) to have advised those in power to "enrich yourselves," helped fan the republican and democratic revival which was gaining momentum. On January 27, 1848, Alexis de Tocqueville, who had gained a great reputation for his perceptive study *Democracy in America*, told the French Parliament, "I believe that at this moment we are sleeping on a volcano." The volcano erupted in Paris only a few days later. Wanting no bloodbath on his conscience, Louis-Philippe abdicated and departed for England.

The Second Republic, More Anarchy and another Napoleon

The Second Republic was declared immediately, and a highly idealistic government under Lamartine's leadership proceeded to introduce universal male suffrage, to abolish slavery in the colonies again and to guarantee every citizen a job by establishing national workshops at the state's expense. To the new leaders' surprise, their government suffered a crushing defeat in the first parliamentary elections in the spring of 1848. A new legislative majority eliminated the costly socialist experiments, most notably the national workshops. This action provoked desperate workers and idealists again to erect barricades in the streets of Paris and to resist the reaction which always follows each radically democratic experiment in France. In four bloody "June Days" of street fighting in Paris, General Cavaignac crushed the rebels, killing 1,500 and arresting 12,000 in the process; 3,000 persons were hunted down and executed later.

The frightful events in Paris set off rebellions in capitals all over Europe. French workers were left bitter and smoldering, and class hatred in France was hardened, feelings which remained a part of French life for the rest of the century and which, to a limited extent, continue to exist in France today.

After the June convulsion there was a widespread desire for a return to order. A new constitution was written, calling for presidential elections by universal male suffrage. In elections held late in 1848 the winner by a landslide was a man who in the past had not displayed any political talent. He was not a dashing figure. He was short and rather paunchy, and his appearance was once described as that of a "depressed parrot." However, he enjoyed two immense advantages: his name was Louis Napoleon Bonaparte and he was the nephew of the former emperor.

He had been raised in Germany and always spoke French with a slight German accent. He had served as a captain in the Swiss army and had participated in revolutionary events in Italy. In 1836 and 1840 he had made two almost comic attempts to overthrow the dull regime of Louis-Philippe. In his trial in 1840 he had cried: "I represent before you a principle, a cause, a defeat. The principle is the sovereignty of the people; the cause is that of the Empire; the defeat is Waterloo!" Though he did not persuade the court, he managed to associate his name in the minds of many Frenchmen with the Napoleonic legend, which had been experiencing a rise in popularity at the time. Streets in Paris had been named after Napoleonic victories, the Arch of Triumph which Napoleon I had ordered had been finally completed, and the "little corporal's" remains had been brought back to France and solemnly transported through the city before the wet eyes of thousands of nostalgic Frenchmen.

For his revolutionary activities in France, Louis Napoleon was imprisoned for life in the fortress of Ham, where he spent his time in luxurious confinement, writing tracts on such topics as "The Extinction of Poverty." One morning early in 1846, Louis Napoleon slipped into workman's clothes, and with a pipe in his mouth and a board over his shoulder, he walked out the front gate of the fortress. He was in England the next day, where he awaited his opportunity. In May 1848 his chance came, and he returned to France; by the end of the year he had been elected France's president.

Louis Napoleon invoked the revolutionary principle of popular sovereignty, but he left little doubt that his would be an authoritarian regime. He once remarked: "I do not mind being baptized in the water of universal suffrage, but I do

France

not intend to live with my feet in it." With his four–year term of office approaching its end, and with a hostile parliament which refused to change the constitution so he could succeed himself, he sent his troops to occupy Paris the night of December 1–2, 1851, and to arrest most of his opponents. When Parisians awoke the next morning, they learned that a *coup d'état* had just effectively put an end to the Second Republic.

In characteristic post–1789 style, Louis Napoleon asserted the sovereignty of the people as the first law of the land and promised a referendum on all constitutional changes. Also, in characteristic fashion, the Parisian population refused to accept this change without a fight. The barricades went up again; at one across the Boulevard de Montmartre near the Saint–Denis Gate, a military column panicked under the insults of the mob and opened indiscriminate fire on the fleeing citizens. Two hundred persons lay dead as a result of this unfortunate carnage. Although a terrified Parisian populace did not rise up again for 20 years in 1871, Louis Napoleon's hope for a bloodless takeover was dashed; the December massacre was never forgotten or forgiven. Years later his wife Eugénie confided to a friend: "A *coup d'état* is like a convict's ball and chain. You drag it along and eventually it paralyzes your leg."

Observing the usual practice, Louis Napoleon proceeded rapidly to rewrite the constitution. He created a weak legislature and a strong president who could appeal directly to the people by means of plebiscites. After a year, he could no longer resist one last temptation: on the first anniversary of his *coup d'état*, he submitted a referendum to the people asking whether they favored "restoration of imperial dignity." Almost eight million votes indicated yes against only a quarter of a million who said no. On December 2, 1852 he was proclaimed Napoleon III, Emperor of the French.

For all his talk of restoring France's glory, Napoleon III desired above all to establish order and to make it a prosperous, industrially advanced country. He expanded credit and stimulated new investment. Everywhere new industry and railroads sprang up. He liberalized trade, which boosted French commerce. Overall, French industrial production doubled under his rule; signs of dynamism were everywhere.

Perhaps the most lasting of his public works can be seen in the large cities such as Marsailles and Paris. Napoleon III appointed Baron Haussmann to administer the department of the Seine in which Paris is located. Haussmann completely transformed the city. He built the Paris Opera. He destroyed the narrow, medieval streets and laid wide boulevards and broad squares (such as the Place Étoile) with radiating avenues. It was noticed immediately that such wide boulevards would make barricade building, a periodic Parisian pastime, almost impossible and would facilitate military mobility inside the city. Nevertheless, these changes were badly needed to accommodate the capital's rapid growth and to make it a more modern, livable and beautiful city. During the Second Empire Paris was a prosperous, carefree and culturally active city which attracted admirers from all over the world.

In the first decade of his rule, Napoleon III restricted political parties and freedom of the press. He was a very popular ruler in France, however, and seeing that he had nothing to fear he introduced greater political freedoms in the 1860s. He even took what at the time seemed to be a very radical step: he legalized trade unions and granted workers the right to strike. His regime certainly did not come to an end due to domestic resistance. Instead, he shared the fate of his uncle, falling victim to foreign policy entanglements. He conducted a very active colonial policy in Af-

Foyer of the Paris Opera

France

rica, the Near East, China and Indochina, bringing the latter under French control in the 1860s.

In 1861 he decided to take advantage of the United States' preoccupation with its own Civil War by trying to establish a monarchy in Mexico dominated by France and ruled by Archduke Maximilian of Austria. In 1863 French troops entered Mexico City and placed the Archduke on the newly–created throne. But he never developed popular backing and as soon as the American strife ended in 1865, the U.S. invoked the Monroe Doctrine and demanded that France get out of Mexico. Napoleon III complied, and when by 1867 no French troops were left in Mexico, the naive Maximilian, who had decided to remain with "his people," was executed by a firing squad. The Mexican adventure was a blunder which greatly diminished Napoleon III's prestige at home.

The fatal blow to the Second Empire was delivered in 1870 when the emperor tried to enforce France's long–standing policy of keeping Germany permanently divided. Provoked by the Prussian Chancellor Otto von Bismarck, who sought to create a unified Germany under Prussian domination, the French government declared war against Prussia. Napoleon calculated that the southern German–speaking states would not support Bismarck and might even side with France, but he had made a grave miscalculation; southern Germans were swept up in the new tide of German nationalism.

War and Defeat

France entered the war extremely unprepared. Prussia had a far superior general staff, supply system and strategy. Also, because of their faster mobilization, the German soldiers outnumbered the French two to one. Smashing through Lorraine, the Prussian Army cut Paris off from the two main French armies and delivered a devastating blow to the French at Sedan on the Belgian border. Napoleon III and more than 100,000 French soldiers were captured there, and the Empire came crashing down. In Paris, a republic was declared and the Parisians prepared for a long siege. The new government's 32–year–old leader, Léon Gambetta, escaped from the surrounded city of Paris by balloon and tried to raise a new army in the Loire area. However, the capture of the last trained French army in Metz in October 1870 demoralized the remaining untrained troops in France. In early 1871, after every last scrap of food in the capital had been consumed, including the rats in the sewers and the animals in the zoo, and after the trees in the Bois de Boulogne and the Champs Élysées had been chopped down for fuel, Paris and the troops in the provinces surrendered.

A humiliated France looked on as the German Empire was proclaimed in the Hall of Mirrors at the Versailles Palace. Germany then proceeded to set a very bad precedent by imposing a harsh peace on a prostrate France: Alsace and most of Lorraine, with their rich iron deposits and industry, were annexed by Germany. Further, France was required to pay the victor a very large reparations sum and to allow German occupation troops to remain in France until the sum was paid. For the next half century, French policy would revolve around undoing these terrible losses. Referring to the lost provinces, Gambetta told his countrymen: "Never talk about them, always think about them."

France Drifts

While a new government under Adolphe Thiers saw no alternative to accepting this bitter peace, hundreds of thousands of Parisians saw the matter differently. They had suffered the most during the war and had been humiliated both by the Prussians' triumphant entry into Paris and by the transfer of the French capital to Versailles. Further, this traditional hotbed of republicanism resented the monarchist sentiment which dominated both the provinces and the newly elected National Assembly. Finally, Parisians greatly resented the new government's termination of the wartime moratorium on rents and debts and of all payments to the National Guardsmen, who had defended Paris, and who, because of France's financial collapse, were now out of work and without subsistence. Again, Paris became a powderkeg.

On March 18, 1871, the government sent two cavalry troops commanded by two French generals to remove the guns from the promontory of Montmartre which overlooks the city. An angry mob attacked the cavalry and lynched the generals. Violence spread throughout the city, prompting the government's troops to withdraw hastily. Recalling the radical days of 1793, a new Commune of Paris, composed of radical republicans, socialists and National Guardsmen was formed. However, this strange mixture of idealists and rowdies spent more time debating socialist and political experiments than in preparing for their own defense. The government immediately besieged the city and, reinforced by French prisoners of war whom the Germans had released for just that purpose, prepared to storm the city.

The troops struck on May 21, and for one bloody week the street battle raged. In the closing days of the struggle, the Communards, as the dissidents were called, shot their hostages, including the Archbishop of Paris, and set fire to many public buildings, including the Tuileries palace and the Palais Royal. Finally the remaining Communards were trapped in Père–Lachaise Cemetery, where they were executed against the Mur des Fédéré (now highly revered shrines for socialists and communists all over the world).

The government's vengeance was severe: any person caught wearing a National Guard uniform or army boots was shot immediately without trial. In all, about 20,000 Communards were killed in battle or executed without trial. Thousands more were imprisoned or driven into exile. Both sides, fired by hatred, had fought literally like animals. Reflecting on the events, the French novelist Flaubert wrote: "What an immoral beast the mob is, and how discouraging it is to be a human being." Karl Marx, in his widely read pamphlet *The Civil War in France*, made a legend of the Commune, and these violent events widened the gap created in 1848 between the workers and the political left, on the one hand, and the rest of France on the other. A constant reminder of this gulf is the beautiful white Sacre Coeur (Sacred Heart) church which overlooks Paris from the top of Montmartre. Built to commemorate the suppression of the Commune, it remains for the French left a prominent and hated symbol of a reactionary France.

For awhile a monarchist majority in the National Assembly pressed for the restoration of the monarchy, and Bourbon, Orléanist and Bonapartist pretenders waited for the call. There were very good prospects for the aging Bourbon pretender, the Count de Chambord, who would rule as Henry V. But the Count quickly showed how little he had learned about his own country. He insisted that the king have absolute authority, unrestrained by any constitution. He also insisted that the old *fleur–de–lis* flag of the old monarchy replace the revolutionary tricolor. Even the most die–hard royalists could see the folly of such demands.

Meanwhile the French people, who in the past 100 years had experienced about every conceivable regime and who were growing tired of provisional governments, pressed for a decision. In 1875 important constitutional laws were adopted calling for the establishment of a two–house parliament and a weak president. The wheel which always alternates in France between a strong parliament and a strong executive had again come full circle. This Third Republic lasted until 1940, longer than any French scheme of government since the Revolution.

The capital was moved back to Paris from Versailles in 1880; July 14 was established as the national holiday and *La Marseillaise* was made the national anthem.

France

Renoir's *The Luncheon of the Boating Party* (1881)

Paris began to bustle with artistic creativity. By the time the Eiffel Tower was unveiled at the World Exposition in 1889, it had assumed the place, in many foreigners' minds, as the intellectual and artistic capital of the world, of which one often said: every person in the world has two capitals—his own and Paris. One can scarcely imagine contemporary culture without the creative contributions of artists, writers and scholars in Third Republic France: impressionism in music and art (*e.g.* Renoir, Monet, Degas, Debussy) and the reaction to it (*e.g.* Bracque, Picasso, cubism or fauvism); the positivism of Auguste Comte, the "*élan vital*" of Henri Bergson, and the discoveries of Louis Pasteur in medicine or Pierre and Marie Curie in physics.

Stung by its territorial losses in 1870, France, with Bismarck's encouragement, sought to reestablish a world empire such as the one it had lost a century earlier. It created French Equatorial Africa and protectorates in Tunisia and Indochina (presently Vietnam, Cambodia and Laos). Thus, by 1914 the tricolor flew in most of North, West and Equatorial Africa, in Madagascar, in several West Indian and South Pacific islands and in small holdings elsewhere. Such a policy was not universally popular in France, but a colonial empire offered France the opportunity to resume expansion of its culture overseas. It also offered some economic benefits to France, which was experiencing a slower rate of population growth and economic progress than Germany and Britain.

Many French industries remained small, family-owned and cautious, a situation which persisted in France until after World War II. At the same time, there was considerable worker unrest and violent strikes during the Third Republic. Legalized trade unions tended to remain dedicated to direct, sometimes violent action, rather than to pursue gains through the parliamentary political process. Such "syndicalist" tendencies (to which French trade unions are still attracted) reveal that the deep wounds of the Paris Commune never healed entirely.

At the beginning of the Third Republic, more than half of the population lived in rural areas, and this number had declined to only about one-third by 1940. While the visitor to France has always been struck by the amount of acreage which is cultivated, many farms remained small and relatively inefficient. In the 1870s plant lice threatened the wine industry with extinction. Only by importing American plant grafts was this precious jewel saved. Thus, in a certain sense, French wine is actually American wine!

Third Republic Politics

The Third Republic was seriously rocked by religious disputes, parliamentary instability, scandals, a world war and serious economic depression. The new republic moved in traditional French revolutionary fashion to reduce the influence of the Catholic Church. Its anti-clerical policies included the permission to divorce and the loosening of the Church's grip on the school system. The result was a total separation of church and state in most of France by 1905.

The absence of party discipline and the distrust of any president who tried to play a guiding role in French politics (Third Republic presidents were said to be merely "old men who wore evening clothes in the afternoon!") produced a constant rotation of weak parliamentary coalitions. The resulting "parliamentary game" inclined French citizens to view politics with increasing cynicism and decreasing trust. Representatives rarely hesitated to vote themselves frequent and large salary increases. At the occasion of one such increase in 1905, a socialist member of parliament was heard to say "my indignation is matched only by my satisfaction."

Scandals further shook the confidence in France's political institutions. In the 1880s a dashing general named Boulanger was reputed to have wanted to put an end to the republic after gaining power legally. When he was summoned to the Senate in 1889 to answer to charges of conspiracy against the state, he lost his nerve and fled to Belgium, where he committed suicide two years later. Scarcely a year after his death, another scandal came to light, Since the 1870s a private French company had been attempting to build a canal across the Isthmus of Panama. Unwise engineering and yellow fever bankrupted the company in 1889, but its directors bribed politicians and press in order to secure public subsidies for the project. The revelation of such bribery in 1892 helped convince many Frenchmen that all politicians were corrupt, an attitude which has by no means disappeared from France today. The French still tend to be far less shocked by political scandals than is the case in the United States.

A further scandal convinced many Frenchmen that it was not only politicians who could not be trusted, but military leaders as well. In 1894 Captain Alfred Dreyfus, the first Jewish officer to be assigned to the French general staff, was convicted of selling military secrets to the Germans and was sent to the infamous Devil's Island off the northern coast of South America. Later, probing journalists, aided by a skeptical army officer, discovered that the documents presented by the military had been forged and that Dreyfus had been framed. The army, seeing its honor at stake, refused to reopen the case, and many French conservatives and clergymen openly supported the army. Dreyfus was later pardoned, promoted to lieutenant-colonel, and awarded the Legion of Honor. But for more than a generation this sordid affair, with its implications of anti-Semitism, the army, the Church and democracy in France, weakened the re-

France

public. Not until 101 years later, in 1995, did the French military formally and publicly acknowledge that the army had been wrong. On January 13, 1998, the 100th anniversary of Emile Zola's sensational headline article, "J'accuse" (I Accuse) in *L'Aurore* newspaper, Prime Minister Lionel Jospin laid a wreath on Zola's tomb in the Pantheon and called the Dreyfus affair "one of the founding events in the history of our country."

Until the 1890s Germany's Chancellor, Bismarck, managed to keep France diplomatically isolated in Europe. However, after the Chancellor's fall from power in 1890, France was able to improve its relations with Italy and in 1894 to forge a military alliance with Russia. France's intense colonial activity led it into frequent conflicts with the greatest colonial power of the time, Britain. Nevertheless, after the turn of the century France gradually settled its differences with England, and military and political cooperation between the two countries became much closer. Thus emerged the outlines of the Triple Entente alliance against Germany and Austria–Hungary before and during the First World War. Eventually, crises in Morocco and then in the Balkans brought about the devastating explosion which Bismarck had predicted shortly before his death in 1897: "One day the great European war will come out of some damned foolish thing in the Balkans." It did (see Austria, history).

World War I

The outbreak of World War I in August 1914 unleashed an outburst of patriotic sentiment in all major countries of Europe. Even workers rallied to the French cause, and trainloads of enthusiastic troops left their hometowns in railroad cars with words "à Berlin" written on the sides. Although not openly avowed, many French undoubtedly viewed the affair as an opportunity for revenge of the dismal defeat of 1870 and recovery of the "lost provinces." Never since that time did France experience such unity of purpose.

The British and French armies were able to stop the German advance within heavy artillery range of Paris. Thereafter, the armies faced each other during four weary and bloody years of trench warfare. This unimaginative method of fighting made it exceptionally difficult for either side to win. The enthusiasm faded quickly as 300,000 French soldiers lost their lives in the first five months. Colonel de Grandmaison's axiom that "there is no such thing as an excessive offensive" produced untold carnage on battlefields such as Verdun, where a half million soldiers were slaughtered in the spring of 1916. A young second lieutenant named Charles de Gaulle, who was wounded and sent to a German prisoner–of–war camp for two years, noted: "It appeared in the wink of an eye that all the virtue in the world could not prevail against superior firepower."

The defeatism and demoralization which such mindless frontal assaults produced led to large–scale mutinies on the French front from April to October 1917. Miraculously, the Germans never heard about them at the time. They also produced a frame of mind which the novelist Jules Romains described in his book, *Verdun*, which first appeared at an unfortunate time—1938: "Men in the mass are seen to be like a school of fish or cloud of locusts swarming to destruction. The individual man is less than nothing—certainly not worth worrying about . . . My most haunting horror is not that I see men now willing to suffer and act as they do, but that having so seen them, I shall never again be able to believe in their good intentions."

Ultimately a million fresh American troops in France tipped the balance, and on November 11, 1918, the exhausted and starving Germans saw no alternative to capitulation. France had technically been victorious, but it was left breathless and demoralized; 1.3 million Frenchmen had been killed and more than a million crippled. Northeastern France, the country's most prosperous industrial and agricultural sector, was largely devastated. France's enormous human and material losses inclined French leaders to demand a heavy price from Germany in the Treaty of Versailles.

Germany and its allies were branded as solely responsible for the war, and Germany was therefore required to pay exorbitant reparations. France regained Alsace and Lorraine, established temporary control over the German Saar, stationed its troops in Germany west of the Rhine and obtained mandates in the former German colonies of Togo and Cameroons, and in Syria and Lebanon as well. While France's demands were somewhat understandable, they played into the hands of a future German rabble–rouser named Adolf Hitler, who promised to undo the hated treaty. The settlement is a glaring example of the fact that policies which may be righteous are not always wise.

The Post–World War I Era

The French expected to rebuild their land with the reparations from Germany, but when it became apparent that an impoverished Germany could never pay the sums demanded, the French set about to do the work themselves. Displaying remarkable resilience, the French had, by the mid–1920s, cleared away the rubble, rebuilt homes, factories and railroads, and achieved a measure of prosperity which exceeded even that of Britain. Unfortunately, many of the economic gains were wiped away by the great depression which spread to France by 1932. The last European country to be affected by "Black Friday" on Wall Street, France was so jolted that when democracies all over Europe toppled, France tottered also.

The Nazi seizure of power in Germany in 1933 further destabilized France by pumping new life into right–wing and, in some cases, openly fascist groups in France. The best–known was the *Action Française*, which had emerged from the Dreyfus controversy, and whose leader, Charles Maurras, powerfully and eloquently railed against Jews, Protestants, foreigners and the French Republic generally. Offshoots and competitors of *Action Française* such as the *Camelots du Roi* or the *Francistes*, bullied people in the streets, dressed like Hitler's storm troopers, and ceaselessly pointed to the difference between the vigor and effectiveness of the dictatorships in Italy and Germany and the tired, ineffective parliamentary system in France. Royalist and fascist groups, supported by thousands of students and some communists gathered on February 4, 1934, at the Place de la Concorde and stormed the National Assembly, located just across the Pont de la Concorde. The police stopped the assault, but 21 persons lay dead and more than 1,600 were injured in this violent action against the feeble republic.

Storm Clouds and Paralysis

As storm clouds gathered over Europe, France had only short–lived, stop–gap governments which could not begin to cope with the mounting crises. In desperate economic straits, no French government could propose military increases to counter the dictators. Also, the memories of the First World War were so horrifying in the minds of many Frenchmen that they could not tolerate the thought of participating in another war, for whatever cause. *Surtout pas la guerre* ("Above all, no war!") was the slogan of *Action Française*. It was uttered with all the energy of "Hell no, I won't go!" in the America of the 1960s and 1970s.

Pacifism was widespread and was manifest in the writings of many of France's literary figures. In a letter to a friend, novelist Roger Martin du Gard wrote: "I am hard as steel for neutrality. My principle: anything, rather than war! Anything, anything! Even fascism in Spain . . . even fascism in France! . . . Anything: Hitler rather than war!" The highly respected writer, Jean Giono, dared to write: "I prefer to be a live German than a dead Frenchman!"

France

Even the Minister of Public Works, Anatole de Monzie said publicly that "I prefer to receive a kick in the behind than a bullet in the head." French patriotism after World War I had become tinged with the fear that the costs of war were simply too great.

A state of mind jelled which prepared France for defeat in the next war. As noble as it may seem sometimes, pacifism usually plays into the hands of the world's bullies, as France was soon to see.

With the fascist leagues active in the streets of France, the parties of the left began to speak of unified action for the first time. In 1935 the Socialists and Radicals formed a *Popular Front* which won a great victory in 1936 parliamentary elections. Under Léon Blum, the first Jew and first Socialist to serve as Prime Minister of France, the *Popular Front*, with the parliamentary support of the communists, proposed a forty–hour work week, paid vacations, collective bargaining and the partial nationalization of the Bank of France. Blum was unable, however, to find a solution to the problem of lagging production, and in 1938 the government fell.

France was the helpless observer of an aggressive German government which in the mid and late 1930s reoccupied the Rhineland, sent troops and squadrons to Spain to fight for Franco in its Civil War, absorbed Austria and occupied part of Czechoslovakia. After World War I, France had not only constructed the Maginot line, it sought to protect itself by surrounding Germany with enemy powers. It forged military alliances with Belgium, Poland, Czechoslovakia, Romania and Yugoslavia. Hitler merely pointed to this encirclement to justify his own aggressive policies.

In 1930, before Hitler came to power, just 12 years after the end of World War I, the French Parliament voted funds to build an allegedly impregnable defensive line against invasion from Germany. The *Maginot Line* consisted of an elaborate system of underground bunkers, fortifications and anti–tank devices and extended all the way along France's border with Germany. It was based on a conclusion drawn from the previous war that all advantages lie with the defense. Colonel Charles de Gaulle disagreed. He warned at the time in his controversial book, *The Army of the Future*, that modern warfare requires great mobility with tanks and aircraft. Regrettably the book was read only by the German commanders, who reportedly carried it with them when they invaded France in 1940. Unfortunately the designers of the line forgot one of the basic principles of fortress–building: protect all sides.

This shield–mentality naturally meshed with the pacifist feelings in the French population and political circles. Léon Blum, who apparently believed in the power of a strong world conscience which hated war, opposed the extension of military service from one to two years and continued to speak of the need for France to take unilateral steps toward disarmament, as if such a French policy could incline Hitler to be more peaceful. As his government fell, France was literally frozen with fear. Political parties and alliances were such that the country was ungovernable. Complicating the scene was journalism at its lowest. Most political parties and groups printed their own newspapers which daily printed untruths about opposing parties, groups and people. There were 39 regularly published in Paris alone.

World War II

Thus, when Germany invaded Poland on September 1, 1939, and when France reluctantly and finally felt compelled to declare war three days later, France entered a disastrous conflict militarily and emotionally unprepared and half–consciously aspiring more to an armistice than to a victory. Germany and the Soviet Union quickly partitioned Poland, but Hitler delayed military action against France for three–quarters of a year. In France, one spoke of a "phoney war" or a *Sitzkrieg*, and precious little was done to prepare for a future onslaught. The German tank commander, Guderian, later wrote that "the relatively passive attitude of the French during the winter of 1939–40 incited us to conclude that the adversary had little inclination for war."

On May 10, 1940, Hitler unleashed his armies against France. Invading the Netherlands and Belgium (thereby avoiding the face of the Maginot Line which was unprotected from the rear) German forces used lightning warfare (*Blitzkrieg*) tactics against a French army which was poorly and lethargically led and in some respects technologically outdated. French leaders refused to withdraw troops from the Maginot Line to confront actual German advances to the north, and their administrative confusion prevented badly needed French aircraft and artillery from being transferred to the actual front. This produced such disastrous reversals that the French government was forced to abandon Paris within one month. British Prime Minister Winston S. Churchill testified that French soldiers fought valiantly, but that their political and military leaders were so quickly seized by defeatism that the French cabinet could not muster the tenacity or eagerness to persist after the shock of initial defeats.

Britain pleaded urgently that France both honor its earlier agreement not to seek a separate peace and even consider a political union of the two countries. The latter proposal was understandably unwelcome to a country which had spent centuries ridding itself of English domination and influence. A demoralized French cabinet, under the influence of the First World War hero, aging Marshal Pétain, chose instead to surrender on June 22, 1940, barely 40 days after the German attack. The degree of French resistance to the onslaught can be seen today in French cities and towns which have memorials to soldiers who died in the two World Wars. The names of World War I victims outnumber those of the subsequent conflict by uncounted numbers.

The surrender terms were very harsh. The northern half of France, including Paris, as well as the whole of the Atlantic coast to the Spanish border, were to be occupied by German troops at French expense. The rest of France was to be ruled by a French government friendly to Germany. This government was to supply its conquerors with food and raw materials needed for the German war effort. The French army was to be disbanded and its navy placed in ports under the control of the Germans and the Italians.

The fate of the French navy especially distressed the British. They were unaware that the French naval commander–in–chief, Admiral Darlan, had secretly ordered his fleet commanders to scuttle his ships if the Germans or Italians tried to seize them by force. When the British tried to take control of the French Atlantic squadron in Mers–el–Kebir in Algeria, the French commander resisted. The British destroyed the squadron, an action that caused a wave of anti–British feeling in France. This sentiment played into the hands of the cunning Premier Pierre Laval and the 80–year–old Pétain, who had long opposed the Third Republic as a decadent, inefficient regime.

They quickly abolished the Third Republic and established a repressive *Vichy Republic* (named after the spa in France where the new government established its seat of power). Without prompting by the Germans, they denied Jews and Freemasons the protection of the law. In all, 75,000 Jews were, with the help of the French police, deported from France during Vichy, and only 2,600 returned. Foreigners who had come to France to escape Hitler's persecution were penned up in French concentration camps and, unless they were able to escape, were later returned to Germany where an uncertain, usually fatal, future awaited them.

Many Frenchmen were relieved to have achieved a peace at any price; nevertheless, a numbing feeling of humiliation and an awareness that this was a tragic deba-

France

German troops enter Paris, 1940

cle which had befallen the French nation was felt. What followed was as much a French civil war as a war against the Germans. For the next four years there were two Frances, one fighting against the Germans and one trying to ignore the conflict and to minimize damage to the French population. The individual Frenchman could find sound patriotic reasons for supporting each, and it was up to the individual to decide which France was his. France still has not fully recovered psychologically from the terrible tension of the *Vichy* years. A poll in 1992 showed that 82% of Frenchmen considered the Vichy government to be guilty of "crimes against humanity," and 90% thought that their country should admit it.

In 1994 the trial of Paul Touvier captivated France. Convicted of murdering Jewish hostages in 1944, he became the first Frenchman charged and convicted of a crime against humanity. This was also the first time a French court blamed Vichy for its role in the Nazis' Final Solution. In 1995 Jacques Chirac became the first president to accept the responsibility of the French state for the arrest and deportation of Jews during Vichy. In 1997 the Bishop of St. Denis admitted for the first time the French Catholic Church's guilt in "acquiescing by its silence" in the persecution of the Jews: "We beg God's pardon and we ask the Jewish people to hear our words of repentance."

Maurice Papon was a police supervisor in Bordeaux from 1942–4, who, according to documents first revealed by the satirical *Le Canard Enchaîné*, was instrumental in the arrest and deportation of 1,690 Jews; very few returned. Still defiantly maintaining that he had been a loyal member of the resistance, he became de Gaulle's post–war police chief in Paris, member of the National Assembly, Gaullist party treasurer, and budget minister under President Giscard d'Estaing. He was found guilty in 1998 and sentenced to ten years in prison although the lengthy appeal process practically ensures that the 87–year–old will never serve time.

While working together with the Germans, the Vichy government introduced what it called a "National Revolution." Although this was, in some cases, fascist in inspiration, it sought among other things to strengthen the role of France's regions, to introduce economic planning at the highest political level, to concentrate small agricultural holdings into larger, more efficient farms and to stimulate population growth through family allowances for children. Postwar France actually built on some of these Vichy innovations.

The Vichy government's powers were drastically reduced at the end of 1942 when the Germans, in response to Anglo–American military landings in North Africa, occupied all of France. Vichy's prestige declined rapidly and when Frenchmen were sent to Germany involuntarily in order to work in German war industries, the ranks of the resistance began to grow.

By 1943 command over the entire French resistance movement had been gathered into the hands of General de Gaulle, who had fled to Britain in 1940 and who had organized there the Free French Movement. He reminded his countrymen by radio that "France has lost a battle, but not the war." His claims to be the legal French government in exile and the sole spokesman for France greatly irritated Churchill and Roosevelt, who, for a time, found it politically wise to maintain diplomatic recognition of the Vichy government. Further, when Admiral Darlan was assassinated three weeks after he scuttled the French navy, Britain and the United States recognized another French General as "chief of state" in French North Africa. Roosevelt greeted him warmly in Washington, which infuriated de Gaulle. His wartime experiences with the British and Americans did not leave him with a strong admiration for the two countries, and his resentment was to disturb these two nations' relations with France even after 1958 when he became France's leader.

The French resistance fighters helped protect unfortunate Allied pilots and often provided useful military intelligence and other support to the Allies. There is no doubt that resistance against the Germans was very dangerous business. De Gaulle later estimated that 20,000 French resistance fighters had been executed and more than 50,000 deported from France before the Allied landings in Normandy. But German documents reveal that this movement had not constituted an effective military threat to the Germans, as had the resistance movements in the Soviet Union and Yugoslavia. Still, when the Allies landed on the Normandy beaches (which are sobering and moving sites for visiting and reflecting today), the French resistance played an important part in destroying bridges, assembling paratroops for action and providing Allied units with useful information. Also, French military units which had been organized in London under de Gaulle's overall command fought side by side with the Americans, British and Canadians.

Local resistance forces and delegates from de Gaulle's headquarters in London assumed political control in liberated France, arresting or executing Vichy officials. On August 19, 1944, resistance fighters rose up in Paris against the German occupiers. Six days later, Free French

Gen. Charles de Gaulle, London

France

Allied invasion of Normandy, June 6, 1944

units commanded by General Philippe Leclerc took control of the city, which a disobedient German commander had saved from senseless destruction by refusing to burn and destroy as ordered by Hitler. De Gaulle arrived with the French troops, and the following day he led a triumphant march down the broad Champs–Élysees.

The Vichy government fled to Germany, and for the next year and a half, de Gaulle's provisional government exercised unchallenged authority in liberated France. The resistance movement had brought together persons from all backgrounds and political convictions, and de Gaulle hoped that this predominantly young, patriotic, idealistic, but at the same time practical core of Frenchmen would provide the spark for national revival and change. He announced during the war that "while the French people are uniting for victory they are assembling for a revolution."

His movement also encompassed French communists although he was always suspicious that his desired revolution was not the same as theirs. French communists displayed undeniable courage and commitment after Germany had attacked the Soviet Union in 1941, "but never, as an army of revolution, losing sight of the objective, which was to establish their dictatorship by making use of the tragic situation of France . . . I was quite as decided not to let them ever gain the upper hand or by–pass me, or take the lead." He successfully blocked their efforts to gain a ministry controlling foreign affairs, defense or the police. French Socialists and other groups also learned then and later what a mixed blessing cooperation with communists can be.

The End of Conflict and the Beginning of Bickering

De Gaulle engaged in feverish diplomacy in order to reestablish France's position in world affairs: he traveled to Moscow in November 1944, helped create the United Nations, fought successfully for a permanent French seat on the Security Council and secured a French occupation zone in Germany as a victorious power. He also initiated a program of nationalizing the nation's coal mines, electrical production, natural gas, some banks and other basic industries, such as the Renault auto company. Since many French business leaders had collaborated with the enemy during the Vichy years and since a national effort to rebuild the French economy was so obviously necessary, few people opposed such a policy.

Frenchmen shared an almost universal desire for the creation of a Fourth Republic, but they split on the perennial French dispute concerning the *kind* of republic which was appropriate for France. De Gaulle stood aloof from these controversies, although it was widely known that he preferred a strong executive and a weak parliament. "Deliberation is the work of many men. Action, of one alone!" Sensing that the old bickering party and parliamentary activity was about to re–emerge, that his coalition was collapsing and that his views on the future republic were not gaining support, he announced in January 1946 his resignation as temporary president. He apparently expected a wave of popular support to swell in his favor, allowing him to strengthen his hand in shaping the new republic, but such a movement failed to materialize. For seven years he tried to return to power, but in 1953 he withdrew completely from direct involvement and lived for the next five years in the political desert, awaiting a crisis which would direct his countrymen's eyes again on de Gaulle, the savior.

In 1946 that kind of political regime was created which de Gaulle had most feared: a parliamentary system with a weak president—practically a restoration of the Third Republic which, in his eyes, had so thor-

France

oughly discredited itself and France in 1940. In the plebiscite of late 1946, a bare majority voted in favor of the new constitution, an ominous sign for the new Fourth Republic. There was no clear majority, either in the parliament or the nation, so subsequent political instability was hardly surprising. There were ten governments in the first five years, and by 1958 Frenchmen had witnessed no fewer than 25 governments. A coherent policy was very difficult to achieve, and the "parliamentary game" appeared more and more to be divorced from the pressing needs of the public.

The governments of the Fourth Republic were faced with many crises in economic, foreign and colonial policy, some of which they mastered and most of which weakened or destroyed them. Nevertheless, it is a great mistake to view France from 1946 until de Gaulle's return to power in 1958 as a hopelessly paralyzed country. France had a resilient population, a rather competent and dedicated bureaucracy and a few leaders with sound judgment.

Economic Growth and European Cooperation

France set about very quickly to repair the destruction from the long war and to reestablish economic strength. The results, with massive assistance of the United States' Marshall Plan, were impressive. Between 1949 and 1957 its GNP increased by 40%, and from 1952 forward, its growth rate was more than 10% a year, consistently among the highest in Europe. Frenchmen poured into the urban areas from the countryside, thereby dramatically changing the face of French society. Fortunately, French industry was able to absorb them. At the same time, agricultural production increased by 24% from 1949–1957. Government financial subsidies for families with children, coupled with the people's increasingly optimistic view of the future, helped bring about one of Europe's highest birth rates, a welcome development for a country which for more than a century had experienced relatively low population growth.

France's rapid economic growth was greatly aided by economic planning, which, in contrast to planning in communist countries, is entirely non–compulsory. These periodic plans set targets and suggest investments to French industry, with a view to making the economy as efficient and modern as possible. Perhaps most important, such planning has helped Frenchmen believe strongly in the possibility of progress. The Marshall Plan assistance which the United States gave to France and other Western European countries encouraged such planning and even had a further long–term benefit for Europe: a condition for aid was that European countries discuss and agree among themselves how such help should be used. These discussions opened possibilities of European cooperation which laid the foundations for the creation of NATO and the EU.

The fruits of this were not long in coming. In 1950, France's brilliant Foreign Minister, Robert Schumann, proposed an imaginative European Coal and Steel Community, which within two years provided a common market for these two critical commodities among West Germany, France, the BENELUX countries and Italy, a step unthinkable five years earlier. Seven years later, Schumann and his countryman, Jean Monnet, de Gaulle's wartime representative for economic negotiations with Washington and London, and from 1946 to 1952 chief of France's General Planning Commission, were key figures in the creation of the EU by the same six powers. The French were not inclined to transfer any French sovereignty to the EU; indeed, de Gaulle later reiterated that this was to be a "Europe of Fatherlands," i.e., of entirely sovereign nation–states. Yet they have clearly recognized that French interests are best served in a cooperative,

De Gaulle leaves Notre Dame Cathedral after the liberation of Paris

France

democratic Europe and they have strongly supported such a Europe.

At one time France sought to extend European cooperation into the military sphere as well. When the Korean War began in 1950, there was fear in Europe that the Soviet Union might be considering an aggressive assault against Western Europe. When the United States suggested that West Germany be permitted to rearm, the French became uneasy. Therefore, the government proposed a European Defense Community (EDC) which would integrate German soldiers into an overall European command. There would be no German general staff. However, Britain refused to join and French public opinion also gradually turned against it. In 1954 the parliament, not wanting French troops to be under supra–national control, rejected the proposal. After the vote the Gaullist and communist deputies stood up and sang the *Marseillaise*. France, however, remained a member of NATO, which had been formed in 1949 and which West Germany also joined in 1955.

The Empire Crumbles

While France's economic recovery and contribution to a unified Europe, which included former enemy powers, were glittering successes of the French Fourth Republic, the government was brought to its knees by the painfully traumatic disintegration of the colonial empire. The two world wars had stimulated a desire in colonies all over the world for independence, but many Frenchmen believed it was impossible to restore French power, prestige and prosperity without aid from the colonies.

The first disaster occurred in Indochina, which the Japanese has occupied during the war. When the French attempted to reestablish control after liberation, they were opposed by a powerful native communist resistance movement called the Viet Minh, led by Ho Chi Minh. Fighting broke out in December 1946 and all French political parties, including the communists, initially supported the war effort. However, eight unglorious years of fighting without victory created powerful domestic opposition to continuation of the conflict. The United States refused to assist the French in a colonial war; when in 1954 France sought a quick solution to the war by asking that the U.S. use atomic bombs against the Viet Minh, the request was understandably turned down. After the Viet Minh captured the French stronghold of Dien Bien Phu in 1954, the French agreed to a temporary division of Vietnam and to a permanent withdrawal after free elections. For complicated reasons, such elections were never held.

Having had no time to recover from the shock of loss of Indochina, the French had to immediately turn their attention to a rebellion in Algeria which erupted in November 1954. Algeria was a much more complicated problem. Legally it was not a colony, but an integral part of France, as Hawaii is part of the U.S. Located directly south of France, it (unlike Indochina) had an immediate strategic importance for the country. Further, there were more than a million French settlers living there, some of whose families had been in Algeria for more than three generations. Many were farmers, producing semi–tropical foodstuffs for France.

The Algerian rebellion shook France to the core. It unleashed conspiracies against the government, assassinations and ill–fated military *coups d'état*. It also brought an aging man out of retirement from the eastern village of Colombey–les–deux–églises: Charles de Gaulle. When the French military seized power in Algeria's capital city, Algiers, in May 1958, and soon thereafter on the island of Corsica, Napoleon's birthplace, many, especially French generals, believed that only de Gaulle could save Algeria or protect the country from civil war.

De Gaulle haughtily said that he would respond to the call of his fellow citizens only on his own terms: that he be granted unrestricted authority to cope with the crisis. In mid–1958, he was appointed Prime Minister, and he quickly went to Algeria and gave an enthusiastic French throng the highly ambiguous assurance "I have understood you!" He undoubtedly knew the situation was hopeless. In late 1958 he was elected President of the Republic by an electoral college of notables. This spelled the death knell of the Fourth Republic and the birth of the present Fifth Republic.

The de Gaulle Years in Power

Always a realist under his mantle of magnificence, de Gaulle was convinced that Algeria could no longer be held by force, but he proceeded very cautiously in seeking a settlement of the crisis. He did not want to provoke a military *coup d'état* in France itself. He shrewdly allowed all groups to think that he shared all of their own objectives. Sensing that the right time had come, he announced a referendum for early 1961 to decide whether Algeria should be granted self–determination. Fifteen million said yes; only 5 million said no. He thus had received a free hand to pursue negotiations with the *Algerian National Liberation Front (FLN)*, and he directed France's Prime Minister, Georges Pompidou, to lead the negotiations.

This was an extremely unstable time in both France and Algeria, and de Gaulle felt compelled to assume sweeping emergency powers to master the situation. The cloud of a military takeover loomed over the country. Indeed, some French officers regarded the President's policy as "treachery" and formed the *Secret Army Organization (OAS)* with the aim of keeping Algeria French by any means possible, including terror, bombings and assassinations. De Gaulle himself barely escaped three attempts in 1962.

A breakthrough occurred in March 1962: France granted Algeria full sovereignty in return for the Algerian promise to respect the French settlers' lives and property, as well as French oil interests in the Sahara and military interests in a port city. Ninety percent of the people approved this settlement in a referendum, and three–quarters of a million French settlers from Algeria (known in France as *pieds noirs*—"black feet" since many had been farmers) left for mainland France. The promise regarding oil interests was not fully kept by the Algerians.

De Gaulle had already offered all the other French colonies the option of becoming independent while retaining cultural ties with France. By 1960 all had accepted this option, with the exception of Guinea, dominated by a mentally disturbed communist, which rejected all ties with the *French Community* which was to be established. Thus, by 1962 the French empire had practically ceased to exist. It now possesses five overseas departments (Guadeloupe and Martinique in the Caribbean, French Guiana in South America, Réunion in the Indian Ocean, and Saint–Pierre and Miquelon in the Atlantic near Newfoundland) and five overseas territories (New Caledonia, French Polynesia, Wallis and Futuna in the South Pacific, Mayotte in the Indian Ocean and a smattering of islands in the Antarctic in the southern part of the earth). The inhabitants are French citizens with a right to vote and economic subsidies that enable them to enjoy a standard of living comparable to that of metropolitan France. Far from weakening France, the shedding of the colonial burden freed its hand for a more assertive foreign policy in Europe, the Middle East, and elsewhere and it eliminated the searing domestic division which stemmed from unpopular colonial wars. In the years which followed, de Gaulle was able to show his countrymen that it was possible to have a measure of grandeur without a colonial empire.

Prosperity and Social Benefits

While de Gaulle provided France with a constitution which could maintain a greater measure of political stability, he also sought to eliminate the bases of social conflict by introducing needed social reforms. The often enigmatic, but always pragmatic General was a point of intersection between two seemingly contradictory forces. He was an agent of French modernization and also the guardian of the idea of French mission and grandeur. His task was to change France without discarding her glorious tradition. Among his followers were traditionalists, technocrats, social reformers, French nationalists, dreamers and realists.

He continued work begun before 1958 to expand education opportunities, thus facilitating greater mobility, especially for workers and other formerly underprivileged groups. He stabilized France's currency and helped bring about a rise in real wages. He expanded the social security net which protects Frenchmen against ill health, unemployment and old age. He also proposed that large firms distribute a portion of their shares to employees and include workers in the firms' decision–making practices, which some companies such as Renault actually adopted.

In general, he furthered efforts to provide his countrymen with prosperity and higher common consumption standards shared by all. He could write with pride that "once upon a time there was an old country hemmed in by habits and circumspection . . . Now this country, France, is back on her feet again."

Foreign Affairs—Estrangement from U.S. Hegemony

With social peace and economic prosperity at home, de Gaulle could turn full attention to that which was undoubtedly his major interest: foreign affairs. He had been greatly displeased with France's position in the world when he came to power. Colonial wars had sapped almost all of France's attention and military strength. What was worse, the fate of Europe had been determined by the Soviet Union, the U.S. and Britain, and after the advent of the Cold War in 1946-7, French security had fallen almost exclusively into the hands of NATO, with an American general in command. That is, France's security was basically in the hands of the U.S., a friendly, but *foreign* country, which in his words, "brings to great affairs elementary feelings and a complicated policy."

De Gaulle and all his successors knew that the Soviet Union posed a threat to Western Europe, which ultimately needed American protection. He also knew that the United States' tolerance level toward its European allies was high. He therefore decided that France needed and could achieve foreign policy independence. He unquestionably also had bitter memories of what he considered a personal snub by Churchill and Roosevelt during the struggles of World War II.

His first step was to develop French atomic weapons. When he was informed in 1960 of the successful French explosion in the Sahara, he exclaimed: "Hurray for France!" This nuclear capability, known in France as the *force de frappe* has come to be supported by most of the French political parties, including the *Communist Party*. It now includes 33 *Mirage IV* A–bombers carrying 60–kiloton nuclear bombs, 18 land–based nuclear missiles on the Albion Plateau in Provence and 5 nuclear missile–bearing submarines, with an additional 2 in the planning stage.

Seeking to strengthen the center of Western Europe, he signed a treaty with West Germany in 1963. It basically called for regular consultation and semi–annual state visits between the leaders of these two European powerhouses. A disappointed de Gaulle later referred to this treaty as a "faded rose" because it had failed to persuade the West Germans to loosen their own ties with the U.S., as he had hoped. Nevertheless, it was an extremely important and imaginative policy observed by all his successors. For example, the first

France

meeting which President Mitterrand had with a foreign political leader after his election was with the West German Chancellor. Further, Helmut Kohl's first foreign visit after becoming German Chancellor in 1982 was to Paris. De Gaulle had provided an enormous boost for a development which few Europeans would have considered possible in 1945: *for the first time in European history, the idea of a war between France and Germany had become unthinkable.*

In 1967 he announced an "opening to the East" which amounted to direct French contact with the Soviet Union and actual participation in the era of détente. In 1967 when war broke out between Israel and its Arab neighbors, de Gaulle, unfettered by a colonial policy in North Africa, chose to adopt an openly pro–Arab position. Although many Frenchmen were displeased by his anti–Israel (and occasionally unconcealed anti–Jewish) remarks, this policy was not reversed by his next two successors, who were only too well aware of France's dependence upon Arab oil. President Mitterrand promised a more even–handed policy toward Israel and the Arabs.

The U.S. reluctantly honored de Gaulle's demand that American troops (whom he called "good–natured but bad mannered") be withdrawn from French soil, a move which greatly increased NATO's logistical problems. This was a logical step to follow his announcement a year earlier that France would withdraw from NATO's integrated command (although not from NATO itself). He did not oppose the presence of American troops elsewhere in Europe because he did not want to remove France from the NATO shield. It was always assumed that France would support NATO in the event of a Warsaw Pact attack against Western Europe. This assumption was underscored by the fact that France continued to maintain 70,000 troops in West Germany and participates in many joint military exercises. De Gaulle was convinced that in case of a ground war in Europe, Frenchmen would be more willing to make sacrifices to defend Europe because they would see this as primarily a *French* defense effort, not an American one. Thus, in his opinion, the Western alliance would be strengthened, not weakened.

American leaders in 1967, bogged down in a hopeless Vietnam war, had little understanding for such logic. Many Americans remembered that there are possibly more American soldiers buried in France as a result of World War II than there are French who fell during that conflict. However, after 1968, the White House had far more admiration for de Gaulle's character and policy. Kissinger noted in his memoirs that de Gaulle's policies "so contrary to American postwar preconceptions, were those of an ancient country grown skeptical through many enthusiasms shattered and conscious that to be meaningful to others, France had first of all to mean something to herself."

The changes were by no means universally supported in France at the time, but by the early 1970s they had been embraced by all political parties, including the communists. The basic Gaullist goal to create an independent Europe under French leadership, and thereby to diminish Soviet and U.S. influence in Eastern and Western Europe, respectively, has not been accomplished. Nevertheless, his design to create an independent French foreign policy has been followed by his presidential successors, despite some changes in emphasis and style. He gave France a role of which it could be proud, and he ultimately won the world's respect for his country. Kissinger recalled that the General "exuded authority " and told of de Gaulle's attendance at a reception given by former President Nixon on the occasion of General Eisenhower's funeral in Washington: "His presence . . . was so overwhelming that he was the center of attention wherever he stood. Other heads of government and many senators who usually proclaimed their antipathy to authoritarian generals crowded around him and treated him like some strange species. One had the sense that if he moved to a window, the center of gravity might shift and the whole room might tilt everyone into the garden."

The "Events of May" and de Gaulle's Exit

Under de Gaulle, France had not become a land of complete satisfaction and harmony. Many Frenchmen grew weary of his paternalism. His preoccupation with foreign affairs gradually slowed down the reformist impulse. Some notice that while most Frenchmen shared in the increasing prosperity, income differences had actually widened during the Fifth Republic. Further, despite the educational reforms, only 1% of the children from the working class families entered the universities. Class stratification was not breaking down as much as some would have liked. At the same time, some Frenchmen, especially the young and the educated, were becoming afraid that the new consumption–oriented society was not good for France; it became apparent that France's traditional schizophrenia about change and modernism had not been entirely erased.

"... the whole room might tilt everyone into the garden."

France

Before departing for a state visit to Romania in May 1968, de Gaulle announced that France was an "island of calm" in a very troubled world. Scarcely had he arrived in Budapest when a furious storm erupted in France which brought the Fifth Republic to the brink of extinction. Student unrest at the new University of Nanterre, a slogan–besmeared concrete complex located at the edge of Paris, spilled over to the Sorbonne and to other universities in the country. Many small groups of anarchists, Trotskyite and Maoist students believed that the university was the ideal place to launch a revolution against the capitalist society. Trying to reestablish order, the police violated an old taboo by entering the university grounds. This tradition stemmed from the time when the universities actually exercised the privilege of ruling themselves, a privilege long since revoked by a highly centralized French regime.

With vivid pictures of the Paris Commune in their heads, students erected barricades in Paris, and night after night they battled police with bricks from the cobblestone streets for control of the Latin Quarter. (For this reason, Parisian authorities later paved over all of the city's cobblestone streets, thereby eliminating this arsenal of projectiles!) Miraculously, the chaos claimed only two dead.

De Gaulle's number two man, Prime Minister Georges Pompidou, was very conciliatory toward the students, but before he could restore order, French workers were on strike and the French economy practically came to a standstill. The Paris Stock Exchange was burned and the threat of civil war was in the air.

De Gaulle developed a bold plan of action. He quietly flew by helicopter to Baden Baden, the headquarters of the French Forces in Germany, in order to assure himself that the French military no longer bore grudges against him and would help him in the crisis. Returning to Paris, he announced new parliamentary elections in a radio speech which reversed the entire situation.

The campaign which followed was one of the shortest (19 days) and crudest in France since 1945. De Gaulle presented the basic issue as a choice between himself or anarchy. He successfully raised the spector of a communist danger to France. He also freed the remaining OAS prisoners in order to placate the army and right–wing elements. Opposition collapsed when the communists decided that it was not yet time for a revolution in France and advocated a return to order. The elections held in June 1968 were a virtual landslide for the Gaullists. The left lost half its seats and found itself in utter shambles.

The "events of May" had so shaken de Gaulle's grip on power he decided that he needed to restore his authority. He announced a referendum for April 1969, and, as usual, warned that if his recommendations were not accepted, he would resign. He combined a rather unpopular reform (a change in the election of senators), with a more popular measure designed to strengthen the French regions. It was clear, however, that the chief issue was de Gaulle's popularity and his continued presidency, and on election day 53% voted against him. The General was thus handed the first referendum defeat in French history—a stinging rebuke.

Never tempted by dictatorship over his country, he resigned immediately and returned for the last time to his estate in Colombey–les–deux–églises in eastern France. Many Frenchmen asked whether this would be the end of the Fifth Republic, but they soon saw that he had not left a political void. He had left a sturdy constitution, in many ways well tailored to French needs, and had begrudgingly left a successor who easily won the presidential elections and whose greatest contribution to France was that he showed how the Fifth Republic could survive its creator.

Street scene in Tours

Georges Pompidou and Valery Giscard d'Estaing

The new president, Georges Pompidou, had been educated at one of France's elite *Grandes Ecoles* and had quietly taught French literature in a Paris *lycée* during World War II. He was characteristic of many successful French political leaders, including Mitterrand: highly literate and intelligent, with a humanistic education and a sharp, practical sense for the realities of modern and political economic life.

In foreign policy, Pompidou was only slightly less Gaullist than de Gaulle himself, although he was always more modest and less abrasive than the General had been. He did break with his predecessor's policy by allowing Britain to enter the EU. He stressed continued industrial growth and the protection of French economic interests in the world. He also sought to modernize Paris by constructing urban freeways and skyscrapers in the city. However, Frenchmen, who are always sensitive to any alterations of their capital, widely condemned this "Manhattanization" of Paris, and his successor therefore abandoned this face–lifting operation.

France

Pompidou died in 1974 and was succeeded by Valery Giscard d'Estaing, who won a razor–thin victory over Socialist leader François Mitterrand. A product of the super–elite *Ecole Nationale d'Administration (ENA)* and a former finance minister, Giscard, who possessed distinguished aristocratic looks and a logical and photographic mind, had emerged as leader of a cluster of parties in the center and moderate right of the French political spectrum which came to be known as the *Union for French Democracy (UDF)*.

Giscard entered the presidency determined to establish a more relaxed style in the Elysées Palace. Calling himself a "conservative who loves change," he wore a business suit instead of formal wear to his inauguration and after the ceremony walked instead of motored down the Champs–Elysées. He allowed himself to be photographed in a V–necked sweater and took a ride on the Paris Metro. For awhile, he even ate monthly dinners in the homes of ordinary Frenchmen, and once he invited a group of Parisian garbagemen to breakfast in the presidential palace. But he, like U.S. President Jimmy Carter, discovered that his people did not necessarily respect folksiness in their highest leaders. Soon he withdrew to the dignity of his office and eventually assumed such an aloof and aristocratic air that his political opponents were always able to score points with voters by attacking his "monarchical" style.

Giscard did introduce some social changes. During his term the minimum voting age was lowered from 21 to 18, divorce laws were liberalized, abortion was legalized, a minimum wage was made available to agricultural workers, and most of the emigrants housed in embarrassing shanty towns, known as "Bidonvilles," on the periphery of France's metropolitan areas, were resettled in newly–built public housing.

In foreign affairs he observed the basic Gaullist principles of French independence and active presence on the international scene. He modernized France's *force de frappe*, sent warships to the Persian Gulf to underscore French interests in the area and took an active hand in Zaïre and the former French West Africa. About 6,000 French troops, including Foreign Legionnaires, are stationed in Africa, where about 300,000 mainland French still live. The largest units are in Djibouti, Senegal, Côte d'Ivoire (formerly Ivory Coast) and Gabon.

He sent French troops in 1977–8 to Shaba (formerly Katanga) Province in Zaïre to halt an invasion of Angolan and rebel forces. While France continued to sell arms to Libya, Giscard approved French military operations against Libyan moves in Mauritania (1977 and 1979) and Tunisia (1980). He joined anti–Libyan efforts in Chad. He also approved the use of French soldiers in 1979 to help depose the butcherous leader of the Central African Republic, Jean Bedel–Bokassa, a man who figured in one of Giscard's most embarrassing and damaging scandals: while finance minister under Pompidou, he had accepted gifts of diamonds from Bokassa.

Giscard prided himself for his support of European cooperation. He increased France's role in NATO planning and exercises although he never hinted at any willingness to lead France back into full participation. Sometimes, though, he chose to act alone, reaping condemnation not only from France's western allies, but from many French as well.

Giscard's main objectives were to re-order in a systematic and long–term way French industrial priorities. Industries such as textiles or steel which could no longer compete in international markets were denied government subsidies and were therefore often forced to reduce their operations. Future–oriented sectors, such as telecommunications, micro–electronics, nuclear and aerospace technology and seabed research, which could compete successfully, were granted support. To reduce French energy dependence on oil from over one–half of energy needs to less than a third, Giscard supported an atomic energy policy which made France Western Europe's largest producer of nuclear power.

On the whole, France was more prosperous and economically prepared for the future than when Giscard entered office. Yet, fickle French voters' evaluation of his economic performance was seriously affected by two notable failures. First, inflation stood at almost 14% by 1981. Part of the reason was indexing—many wages, pensions, rents and prices in France were automatically raised at least to keep pace with inflation. Although indexing helps to protect wage earners and pensioners in the short term, it almost always further fuels the flames of inflation. The second reason is that Giscard's effort to strengthen the economy by making firms more competitive put many Frenchmen out of work. By election time in April 1981, over 7% were unemployed. This statistic, combined with growing revulsion of Giscard's aloof and aristocratic manner and the scandals which surrounded him and his family, convinced a majority of the French

Subway entrance, Paris
Photo by Susan L. Thompson

voters in 1981 that it was time for change. The *Socialists* came to power.

GOVERNMENT IN THE FIFTH REPUBLIC

In his famous Bayeux Manifesto of 1946, de Gaulle had repeated the rhetorical question posed by the ancient Greek thinker Solon: "What is the best constitution?" He answered: "Tell me first for *what* people and during *which* period." He suggested to his countrymen "Let us take ourselves as we are." He asserted that French political parties, as indeed most individual Frenchmen, traditionally obscured the highest interests of the country and thereby created confusion in the state. He admitted that a parliament is necessary, but that it could not be entrusted with the destiny of the French nation. Due to its very nature, France requires a powerful, popularly elected president who stands above the parties, focuses on the "national purpose," and wields the supreme power of the state.

The constitution of the Fifth Republic, adopted in 1958 and still in force, reflects these convictions. It contains a workable compromise between the need for national unity and the legitimate expression of many political ideas, social classes and interests; between the need for a strong executive and a representative parliament; between lofty politics and common, day–to–day politics. It also incorporated the Napoleonic practice of involving the citizens directly in the political process. Since 1962, they directly elect the president for a seven–year renewable term, and, through referendums, they are called upon occasionally to give opinions on major national policy issues.

The Presidency

The French president's constitutional powers are immense, and the character of the presidents since 1958 expanded these powers far beyond the letter of the constitution. He appoints the prime minister and cabinet, chairs all cabinet meetings and actively directs the work of the cabinet ministers. Within any one year period, he may dismiss the National Assembly (lower house of the parliament) for whatever reason he chooses and call new elections. He may question the constitutionality of any law and require parliament to reexamine any piece of legislation. He may submit any issue to a referendum, but he is not bound by the results, except insofar as constitutional amendments are concerned.

These infrequently held referendums almost always demonstrated confidence in the president and therefore invariably strengthened him with respect to the parliament. He is commander–in–chief of the nation's military forces, and he negotiates and ratifies all treaties. He may not issue decrees. But if, in his opinion, the Republic is in danger, he can assume emergency powers which enable him to wield full executive, legislative and military authority. He is formally obliged to seek the advice of the Constitutional Council and is not permitted to dismiss Parliament during this time. There is no provision for terminating such emergency powers. In effect, the French president determines domestic and foreign policy and has veto power over every imaginable aspect of policy, including constitutional amendments. Unlike his American counterpart, though, he cannot veto an act of parliament. He can be removed from office only if he is convicted in a special tribunal (not by the parliament!) of high treason.

Hon. Valery Giscard d'Estaing

De Gaulle in 1964 described the presidency which he had created in breathtaking terms: "It must of course be understood that the indivisible authority of the State is confided in its entirety to the President by the people who have elected him, that no other authority exists, neither ministerial nor civil nor military nor judicial, which is not conferred and maintained by him . . ."

Clearly this is hardly presidentialism of the American type! The U.S. president must deal with 50 powerful states and what has become the most powerful and assertive legislature in the world. One foreign minister complained that in matters involving the United States he had to deal with 535 secretaries of state!. The French president traditionally appoints the prefects (governors) in the 96 departments (states) and until 1986 faced neither serious regional resistance nor a powerful legislature. Whereas the American president must deal with such nonconstitutional checks as an influential, independent and often fiercely investigative press and electronic news media, the French president faces a meeker press. Until 1984, radio and television networks were controlled by the government and were hesitant to attack the president openly.

In contrast, the American president must operate in an environment in which the Freedom of Information Act and various "sunshine" laws have made more visible the working of government. The French traditional cult of secrecy and more impenetrable bureaucracy are a haven for the chief executive. The public appears to be more used to viewing the state as something which is walled off.

Some prefer to describe French presidentialism as *monarchy*, in which the incumbent's whims and favors are crucially important. The French satirical magazine *Le Canard Enchaîné* ("The Chained Duck") once put it: "There's the President, and under him there's a vast void. And afterwards there is a nothing. And below that, nothing. But finally one stumbles over the government." Edouard Balladur asked: "In which other democracy is the president in charge of the executive and the legislature and the judiciary; in charge of the order of business in parliament, where by intimidation, force or a reverential majority he gets the votes he wants; in charge of the promotion of magistrates and of the public prosecution that sends them cases; in charge of a government that moves only at his whim?" The powers of the presidency grew so much that President Mitterrand pledged to reduce them and to pass back to parliament some of the powers it had lost. He had always been a vocal critic of the Fifth Republic's constitution, as the title of his 1964 book indicated: *The Permanent Coup d'Etat*. In office, he did nothing to diminish presidential powers.

The Prime Minister and Cabinet

The prime minister and the cabinet ministers (the "government") have usually been drawn from all the parties in the president's majority coalition, although some have belonged to no political party. They are forbidden from having seats in the National Assembly. Ministers, including prime ministers, must give up their seats to substitutes, and if they later leave the government, they can reclaim their seats only by persuading the substitutes to stand down and by winning a by–election. If the prime minister and president are from the same party, the former is responsible for explaining and gaining support for the president's policies and for insuring that the president's overall directives are carried out in practice. The

France

prime minister executes the laws. He supervises the drafting of the budget, which is submitted to the parliament for overall approval, but which parliament rarely alters. Finally, he determines the agenda of parliament; government legislation always take priority. He is the president's lightening rod and is dependent on him; from 1958 to 1991 only one prime minister resigned voluntarily and none survived a full five–year legislative term.

If the president's party does not have a parliamentary majority, then the president must select a prime minister whose party or coalition can get a majority of votes in the National Assembly. In this case, the prime minister is a very powerful political figure who establishes the main lines of French domestic and economic policy and shares with the president responsibility for foreign and defense policy. He appoints and instructs the top officials in the foreign ministry.

Parliament

The parliament has two houses; the Senate and the 577–seat National Assembly. Deputies to the National Assembly are elected for five years by universal suffrage. The president can call new elections before the end of the five year term. The Senate has 260 members elected for nine–year terms by municipal counselors and members of the National Assembly. One–third of its members are elected every three years.

The asparagus vendor

Both houses of Parliament have essentially the same powers with two exceptions: the National Assembly has the privilege of examining the government's budget first. Further, only the National Assembly can force the government to resign by assembling a majority against an important piece of government legislation. However, the Fifth Republic's constitution places severe limits on this latter practice, which in past republics had been abused and which therefore brought a merry–go–round of governments with extremely short life spans. Such a vote may be submitted only once during any legislative session, and all abstentions or blank ballots count automatically for the government. Also, if such a vote succeeds, the National Assembly is dissolved immediately and new elections are called. This latter provision takes the fun out of the former "parliamentary game" of shooting down the government for the most trivial reasons and makes such a vote of censure a much more serious step for the parties and the individual deputies.

An additional limitation of the parliament's powers is that much of what is considered "legislation" in other democratic countries is defined in the French constitution as "rule–making." The president has the right to issue decrees on the latter, thereby circumventing the parliament altogether. Finally, the number of parliamentary committees (which enable a parliament to develop the expertise to challenge the executive), is limited to six, and even these few committees are not permitted to amend a government bill before it comes to the floor. Such an increasingly weak parliament has been called "a device to provide majorities." There is little public interest in its debates, and people turn to their mayors rather than to their local deputies to pursue causes and grievances.

A final striking innovation in the constitution is the Council of State, composed of nine members appointed by president of the Republic and the two houses of Parliament for nine–year terms. This body was designed to guard the constitution, and upon request of the three above mentioned presidents or the prime minister it can review the constitutionality of laws, treaties, elections and referendums. The Council cannot be compared to the far more prestigious United States Supreme Court, which possesses the power of unlimited judicial review. From 1986 to 1988, though, when for the first time since 1958 the prime minister came from a different party than the president, the Council of State was called upon to make important judgments concerning which powers and responsibilities belong to each office. It became the ultimate referee in the political system.

Political Parties

It has always been difficult to rule France from the center, long referred to as the "swamp." Since the founding of the Fifth Republic there has been a steady reduction in the number of parties with any hope for electoral success. There has also been an obvious polarization between parties of the political left and right, although the *Socialists* have moved closer to the center. The major parties on the right are the *RPR*, the *UDF* and the *National Front*. On the left are the *Communists* and the *Socialists*.

Rally for the Republic (RPR)

The *Gaullist Party* after numerous name changes is now called the *Rally for the Republic (RPR)*. Founded in 1976, it seeks to preserve the fundamental Gaullist values: foreign policy independence, distrust of a more united Europe, maintaining the institutions of the Fifth Republic and economic and social expansion and progress. Even a quarter century after his death, de Gaulle basks in widespread approval. His predictions seem to have come true in the 1990s: the collapse of communism and the USSR, upheaval in Eastern Europe, the unification of Germany, which Frenchmen accepted with only a little uneasiness, an emergence of a Europe more independent of the superpowers. "Europe from the Atlantic to the Urals" was his concept before Mikhail Gorbachev picked up on it. In

1990, to celebrate his famous call for resistance on June 18, 1940, the obelisk at the Place de la Concord was draped with a 35–meter high radio model blaring popular songs of the time and coded messages from London to the Free French.

In May 1995 Jacques Chirac was elected president. But he was reduced almost to the status of a figurehead after the 1997 parliamentary elections, when the *RPR* crashed from being France's largest party with 258 seats to a minority with only 134 seats. Philippe Séguin was named party leader to try to lead a stunned and humiliated party out of opposition, but he gave up and resigned in April 1999. The *RPR* struggles to unify itself and to find a new identity more compatible with the rise of a global economy and the EU and the reduced French role in the world.

The Union for French Democracy (UDF)

Former President Giscard d'Estaing had founded his own *Independent Republican Party* in 1966, renamed the *Republican Party* (PR) and then *Liberal Democracy (DL)* in 1997. The *DL* is right–wing, anti–statist, free–market, and quasi–Thatcherite. In order to enlarge his electoral and parliamentary base, he forged in 1978 a larger, loosely–knit group of parties called the *Union for French Democracy (UDF)*, which is more pro–Europe and free–market oriented than the *RPR*. The *UDF* has several thousand direct members who strive to unify all disparate groups within the umbrella organization. In addition to the *DL* and diverse centrist political groups, the *UDF* includes *The Democratic Force (FD)*, formerly the *Center of Social Democrats (CDS)*. Now centrist, devolutionist and strongly pro– European, this is the last remnant of the postwar reformist *Popular Republican Movement (MRP)*, which had played such an important political role in the Fourth Republic. It also includes the *Radical Party*, a pro–Europe social democratic product of 19th century liberal tradition and one of France's oldest parties. During the Third Republic it almost dominated French politics and led a particularly determined campaign against the power of the Catholic Church in politics and society. This always undisciplined party shrank in importance after World War II, and in 1971 its more leftist–oriented members broke away and formed the *Leftist Radical Movement (MRG)*, a tiny party which closely cooperated with Mitterrand's *Socialist Party*. A final party in the *UDF* is the pro–European *Popular Party for French Democracy (PPDF)*.

The *UDF* was never a sufficiently powerful political base for Giscard, although it was constructed around him. Conservatives are plagued by divisions and bickering. In 1996 the former president retired from politics. In the 1997 elections the *UDF* captured 108 seats, down from 206 in 1993, and entered the opposition. François Bayrou assumed the leadership in 1998, but it is a difficult task to make this loose collection of disparate parties into a credible political force. It has been torn by a dispute over whether local party leaders should deal with the *National Front*; three regional leaders were expelled for doing so. Finding itself in disarray, it formed an *Alliance* of various conservative groupings in May 1998 to present a unified image for the June 1999 European

**Hon. Jacques Chirac
President of the French Republic**

elections and beyond. But this experiment has not succeeded. Without an undisputed leader to present a clear, bold program, the respectable right will remain in the wilderness.

The National Front

The phenomenal rise of the extreme right–wing *National Front (FN)*, led by the former paratrooper, Jean Marie Le Pen, was the 1986 election's biggest surprise. Foaming against France's 4.2 million immigrants, whom he accused of being responsible for high unemployment and crime, Le Pen's party won 9.7% of the votes. It did particularly well along the Mediterranean coast, where there is much hostility to North African immigrants.

The timely abolition of proportional representation in 1988 practically eliminated the party from parliament. This time its 9.7% of votes translated into only one seat. But its 14% showing in the 1988 presidential balloting and 15% in 1995 indicate that racist fears and resentments on which the party feeds are strong in French society. Its high vote (*eg*. 28% in Marsailles) in regions, towns and suburbs with large concentrations of immigrants, unemployed, and crime is a warning to the government to eliminate the seeds of discontent which keep the *National Front* alive.

Although Le Pen insists he is not a racist, a court ordered him to pay a fine of FF900,000 (ca. $180,000) to nine French deportee organizations for his reference to Nazi gas chambers as a mere "detail of history." Because of this remark the European Parliament, in which he won a seat in 1994, lifted his immunity, clearing the way for the prosecutor's office in Bavaria to proceed toward an indictment of Le Pen. He also found himself convicted in court for assaulting a *Socialist* politician at a 1997 rally; he was banned from voting or holding office for most of 1999. He complains repeatedly about Jews having excessive power in the French media, a view that, according to a poll, was shared by 88% of the delegates at the party's 1990 congress. The other conservative parties have refused to deal with this overtly racist, xenophobic party, which opposes greater European unity. A populist, he presents himself as a supporter of the "little guy" against a corrupt establishment. Le Pen's supporters are predominantly young, urban, poor and unemployed. In 1997 it won 15% of the votes in the first round, but because of the electoral system it received only one seat in parliament, which it lost in a byelection in 1998.

Le Pen's 15% result in the 1995 presidential elections might have been higher if he had not been challenged on the right by an aristocrat, Philippe de Villiers, and his *Movement for France*, which won two seats in the 1997 parliamentary elections. The latter's softer opposition to further immigration, European Union, free trade, corruption and abortion, appeals to older, rural, bourgeois voters. A dozen other right–wing politicians not aligned with the *FN* and *Movement for France* won seats in 1997.

In January 1999 an intraparty putsch was launched against Le Pen by his number two, Bruno Mégret, a well–educated man with a master's degree from Berkeley. Mégret seeks to turn the party into an acceptable mainstream party although his political views differ little from those of Le Pen, who expelled him and 19 other leading party officials from the party. Mégret then called a congress of 2,000 disaffected party members that included about half the party's elected politicians and officials, had himself elected the new president (and Le Pen named as "honorary

France

president"), and sought to carry off the party under his own banner. However, in May a court ruled that only Le Pen had the right to use the name, *National Front*, and declared null and void the January vote by Mégret's splinter group to take control of the party. The party has been left in tatters.

The Communists

The main reason why the left had difficulty assuming power in France is that it has always been fragmented, with two parties particularly prominent: the *French Communist Party (PCF)* and the *Socialist Party (PS)*. The *PCF* was founded in 1920 when delegates to the *Socialist Party* congress walked out to join the *Comintern*, the external arm of the Soviet's party. It converted the Socialist newspaper, *L'Humanité*, into an organ through which the new party consistently advocated a hard-line, class-conscious revolutionary policy, closely attuned to the aims of the Soviets. In 1936 the *PCF* refused to join the *Popular Front* because Socialists dominated the coalition, and it loyally supported Stalin's non-aggression pact with Hitler, which was the prelude to the devastating German attack on France in 1940. Once the Soviet Union was invaded by Germany, though, the *PCF* joined the resistance to Hitler's Germany and fought valiantly, thereby winning the admiration of such diverse persons as de Gaulle and Mitterrand.

When the Cold War poisoned relations between the West and the Soviet Union, the *PCF* did not hesitate to orient itself toward the latter. The Soviet suppression of uprisings in Eastern Europe in 1953, 1956 and 1968 all ultimately won the *PCF's* approval. In the 1970s a thaw in the party began to occur. It officially disavowed the Marxist–Leninist concept of "dictatorship of the proletariat" and accepted in 1972 Mitterrand's offer of a common program of the left, including both socialists and communists. The course was an entirely new concept for Western European socialists, who had seen clearly what happened in Eastern Europe after socialist and communist parties had agreed to cooperate.

The *PCF*, led until 1994 by former steelworker Georges Marchais, showed itself to be a difficult partner. Mitterand's *PS* could count on only about 5% of the vote in 1972, whereas the *PCF* consistently received over a fifth of the vote in any election (and a third of all workers' votes). Therefore the *PCF* believed that it would soon be able to control its "junior" member. It was badly mistaken. During the decade the *PS* grew very rapidly in voter appeal and eventually overtook the *PCF*. Not wishing to be the smaller member of a parliamentary majority, the *PCF* torpedoed the chances for a leftist victory in the 1978 parliamentary elections.

The *PCF* had second thoughts about its *Eurocommunist* course. It openly supported the Soviet invasion of Afghanistan and was returning to its pro–Soviet position. This was disastrous. To halt its stunning erosion, the *PCF* saw no alternative in 1981 to joining forces with the *Socialist Party*, but this alliance collapsed within three years. The *PCF* has suffered a steady decline in votes and membership, especially among the young and intellectuals. By 1991 it had little more than 100,000 card-carrying members. The *Socialists* overtook the *Communists* in the traditional "red bastions" in the north. The *PCF* declined to where it stood a half century ago. In 1997 it managed to climb from 24 to 38 seats. Led by Robert Hué, a jovial former male nurse and judo champion, the *PCF* has shed such dogmas as the pledges to "abolish capitalism" and "nationalize the means of production." It remains staunchly opposed to Europe's single currency and the Maastricht Treaty, which many French identify with the government's austerity measures. Nevertheless, it entered the *Socialist Party's* governing coalition in 1997 and has three ministerial posts. Other leftist groupings won 14 seats in the 1997 parliamentary elections.

The Greens

The French public now focuses greater attention on environmental protection because of such highly-publicized problems as the Chernobyl nuclear accident in the Ukraine, chemical factory accidents which polluted the Rhine and Loire rivers, depletion of the ozone layer, global warming and deforestation. They are also untainted by scandals, which have shaken other parties. French Greens are on the left of the political spectrum, although they advocate protecting the high material standard of living, rather than radically changing the structure of French society. They call for restraints on foreign capital in France and the preservation of small neighborhood stores, which are increasingly threatened by supermarkets. The *Verts* (Greens), led by Dominique Voynet, who is environmental minister, captured seven seats in 1997. A *Citizens' Movement* also won seven seats in 1997.

Because of France's electoral system and because it lacks a tradition of pacifism, nuclear protest or respect for the environment, the *Greens* do not have the political clout that their German counterparts do, even though both are in their respective national governments. Desiring to overtake the *Communists* as the second-largest party on the left, they chose as their standard-bearer in upcoming elections a German citizen, Daniel Cohn–Bendit. Known earlier as "Dany le rouge" (Dany the Red), he had been expelled from France for playing a leading role in the 1968 student rebellion. Known for his pugnacity, charisma and rhetorical skills, he is an outspoken Europhile who already represented the German *Greens* in the European Parliament. He is the first foreigner to head an electoral campaign in France.

The Socialists

The chief opposition party is the *Socialist Party (PS)*. After it lost its parliamentary majority in 1993 and the presidency in 1995, Lionel Jospin took the reins of the party and has breathed new life into it. He imposed his authority on this fractious party and was successful in having a new

Le Pen campaign poster

program adopted in 1996 which he calls a "new New Deal." Like its American forerunner in the 1930s, this aimed to "break with the blindness and sterility of conservative policies which dominate the western world and are threatening the European social model." It called for the creation of jobs for young people, a reduction of the work week from 39 to 35 hours with no pay reduction, improvement of housing and decaying inner cities, and the cancellation of recent tax cuts and privatizations. Also, women candidates would be presented for at least 30% of the parliamentary seats.

The *PS*, entered a new period of cohabitation after the 1997 parliamentary elections, when it won a resounding victory, electing 253 members (including 12 *Radical Socialists*) to the National Assembly, up from only 63 four years earlier. The new parliament doubled its female membership to 11% thanks to the *PS's* policy of fielding women for nearly a third of the seats. This compares with an EU average of 17% and 11% in the U.S. House of Representatives and 7% in the U.S. Senate. In French local government, 6% of the mayors and 12% of regional councilors are female. Of Prime Minister Lionel Jospin's 27 ministers, 30% are women. They include Martine Aubry, his second–in–command, and Elisabeth Guigou, France's first justice minister.

The *PS* was created in 1971 from the staunchly anti–communist *French Section of the Workers' International* (SFIO,) François Mitterrand's own *Convention of Republican Institutions* and various other socialist elements. Its rapid growth was partly due to the decline in some social groups which traditionally supported parties of the right: farmers, small shopkeepers, wealthy bourgeois families and non–working women. But the *Socialist Party's* success can be attributed mainly to the work of a man who was both far–sighted and persistent, but who, like de Gaulle, was also mysterious, elusive and unknowable: François Mitterrand.

He was born into a piously Catholic bourgeois family in the Cognac region of France in 1916. His father was a railway stationmaster who inherited a thriving vinegar business. Brought up on Balzac's panoramic novels, Lamartine's romantic poetry and Barrè's patriotic fiction, he acquired a love for literature; which remained his primary passion. He authored ten books himself and certainly ranks with Léon Blum and de Gaulle as one of the most literary figures in French politics. His career did not always follow a consistently left–wing course. At age 18 he joined the youth group of the far–right *Croix–de–Feu* (Cross of Fire) and wrote for right–wing journals.

He studied law and political science at the Sorbonne in Paris. A sergeant in the army, he was wounded in the chest at Verdun in 1940 and was sent to a POW camp after his capture. After two unsuccessful attempts to flee, he finally succeeded. Asked many years later why he thought he could win the presidency after two unsuccessful attempts in 1965 and 1974, he noted that in 1941 he had succeeded in returning to France only on his third try! He became a civil servant and admirer of Marshal Pétain. He was awarded the highest honor given by the Vichy state, the *Francisque* in 1943, and from 1986 to 1992 he lay a wreath on Pétain's tomb every Armistice Day. He also maintained personal contact with a number of collaborators, such as René Bousquet, who had overseen the deportation of French Jews. Joining the resistance movement under the cover name of "Morland" in 1943, he gained respect for French communists and a strong distaste for de Gaulle, who had demanded that he subordinate his activity to the General's leadership.

Mitterrand was hardly a new face in Fifth Republic politics, having occupied many ministerial seats during the Fourth Republic under diverse governments. His political views continued to be very changeable, leading to charges that he was a political opportunist. In the Fifth Republic, though, he was a consistent and ferocious opponent of Gaullism and a man determined to unify the left in order to take control of France's destiny.

His first task was to establish a program acceptable to his own heterogenous party. He set a clear leftist course for the 1981 elections. However, he never mentioned the word "Marxist" in the campaign, even though the party's program does contain some Marxist references and principles. In the campaign, Mitterrand hammered away at the rising unemployment rate, the many inequalities in French society and Giscard's unpopular style. He presented himself as the "tranquil force" which France needed. His countrymen listened.

Mitterrand's 1981 Election

In the first round of the presidential elections of 1981, Mitterrand fell only about 2-1/2% behind Giscard, but since no candidate received a majority, Giscard and Mitterrand, as the two top vote–getters in the first round, had to face each other in a runoff two weeks later. It was in this second polling that the success or failure of the two candidates hinged on the support they could muster from the other parties. The *PCF* saw no alternative to jumping on the Socialist train in order to share the ride into the leftist victory station. It strongly encouraged its followers to vote for Mitterrand, and about 90% of

France

Premier Lionel Jospin

them did so, thereby giving the new president his 4% margin of victory. His triumph was the first time that an entire generation of Frenchmen had experienced a transfer of presidential power from *right to left*.

One of Mitterrand's first acts in office was to dissolve the National Assembly and to call new elections. This reveals a fundamental characteristic of the French political system. Despite the extremely powerful office of the presidency, no incumbent had been able to rule long in the face of a determined, reasonably cohesive opposing majority in the National Assembly because of its budgetary and legislative approval powers. For the first time in the history of the Fifth Republic, a president faced a hostile parliamentary majority. The elections in June produced a landslide victory for the *PS*, which won an absolute majority with 288 out of 491 seats in the assembly.

In the government which President Mitterrand formed, the most surprising appointments were of four *PCF* members. The only price was that the *Communists* agree to support the president's domestic and foreign policies. This price eventually proved to be too high, and in 1984 the *PCF* left the governing coalition.

The new government wasted little time in seeking legislation for the most far–reaching of its proposed reforms: the nationalization of certain industries and the decentralization of the French political system. Although Mitterrand's plan to extend state control over more of the French economy appeared at first glance to be a radical move, three things had to borne in mind: first, France has a long tradition of extensive state intervention in the economy, at least since the time of Louis XIV.

France

Mme. Martine Aubry

Laissez–faire economics (believing that the government should intervene as little as possible) never really took hold in France, and for a long time the government has heavily subsidized industries for one reason or another. Second, 12% of the French economy had already been nationalized before Mitterrand was elected. The state–owned sector was already France's largest employer and responsible for 30% of all industrial output.

Third, the French state has supervised economic planning since the end of World War II. "Le Plan" has always been drawn up by managers, union representatives and government officials, and parliament debates and approves it. It usually extends for a five–year period and sets economic targets, investment priorities, statistical analyses of past, present and future economic performance and needs. The aim is to sustain balanced economic growth; under Mitterrand it clearly was designed especially to increase employment. Traditionally, there have been no coercive measures associated with the plan, but the state has always offered industries many incentives to participate: it provides useful statistics and analyses, grants tax relief and tariff concessions, awards government contracts or provides loans for investment funds.

Over half of all French investments were controlled by the state and this percentage gained under Mitterrand. Finally, the state finances roughly two–thirds of all scientific research, although it actually conducts only half the work itself. If completed, Mitterrand's program would have raised the state's share in the economy from 12% to roughly 17%. Over a decade later, by 1993, the state's role in the economy had actually been pruned. But France still runs the most state–dominated economy among the "Group of Seven" industrial powers: 25% of all workers are on a government payroll (up by 20% since 1980 and in contrast to one in six in the U.S.), and an additional 12% work for state–owned enterprises. The state still spends 46% of GDP.

Decentralization

The second fundamental reform was the decentralization of the political system. Since at least the 17th century, French national leaders consistently strengthened the powers of the central government at the expense of the regions and communes. Napoleon I divided France into 96 departments, each headed by a prefect, a powerful and uniformed official appointed by and answerable to the national government. The prefect oversaw the work of locally elected mayors and councils in the 37,500 municipalities. For economic and administrative purposes, 22 regions, whose borders roughly approximate those of France's ancient provinces, each headed by a regional prefect, were created. The essential fact is that all important initiatives had either to originate or be approved in Paris. For example, the designs for school cafeterias, soccer fields, swimming pools and other public facilities had to clear numerous bureaucratic and political hurdles in Paris.

This not only required personal connections and caused serious delays, but many Frenchmen feared that it was creating excessive visual uniformity in a land admired for its rich diversity. Many observers also believed that centralization stifled individual civic action and stimulated suspicion toward the French state. Mitterrand took seriously his pledge to reduce the power which the central government and the prefects had over sub–national political units and to allow popularly elected regional and local assemblies and executives to handle their own affairs. Within two years, his government announced ten devolution laws and 50 decrees designed to decentralize France. Perhaps the most significant change was that the prefects, renamed "Commmissioners of the Republic," were stripped of many of their administrative, financial, judicial and technical powers. During the 1980s local governments were granted more autonomy in spending, taxation, and borrowing. The result has been much more local activity to build new airports, wider streets, pedestrian zones, museums, concert halls, and stadiums. However, the shift of power from civil servants to local politicians has also brought a higher level of local indebtedness and corruption.

A political problem which devolution presented to the Mitterrand government was that his conservative opponents did very well in local and regional elections after 1982. Regional assembly presidents, such as Giscard d'Estaing (Auverne) and Jacques Chaban–Delmas (Aquitaine), emerged as powerful provincial barons. Further, the *National Front,* which was traditionally untouchable in the National Assembly, bolstered its power in the regions, where its votes were vital in electing five conservative presidents. Thus, Mitterrand created a troublesome territorial set of checks and balances that provide departmental and regional restraints on the Paris government.

Mitterrand proposed a special statute for Corsica and a separate department for the Basque area, in order to grant autonomy to these two areas which have their own distinct ethnic and lingual characteristics. Corsica was allowed to elect its own assembly in 1983, ahead of other regions. This enlargement of autonomy was an important testing ground for devolution, but, through acts of terror, the Corsican separatist minority showed that the changes had not gone far enough to suit it.

The New Conservative Outlook

The *Socialists* promised France in 1981 fundamental changes, but few persons expected to see France emerge as a more pragmatic, conservative country with a more robust brand of capitalism. In his first year, Mitterrand nationalized some industries which the conservative government began to undo in 1986. Other reforms, such as a reduced work week and retirement age and increased minimum wages and paid annual vacation of all Frenchmen, are reforms which *no* future government dares undo. But after it was

Hon. François Mitterrand

France

clear by 1983 that his socialist revolution had failed, the Mitterrand government pursued a more austere economic course and stressed modernization, rather than socialization of France. His failure to combat growing unemployment by reflating the economy and the specter of large-scale nationalization of more industries strengthened the ideas of free-market and sound economic management. He even ordered the newly nationalized industries to cut their work forces and make a profit, and most are now in the black.

As an intellectual force, Marxism became far less popular than it once was. Partly because of Mitterrand's maneuverings, the *Communist Party* became practically impotent and is locked in a steady decline. The trade unions, a traditional pillar of the *PCF,* have almost never been weaker in modern France, partly because of the scourge of unemployment. Thus, France experienced very little industrial unrest. He succeeded in doing something which no conservative government could have done without serious unrest: breaking the indexing of wages to rising prices, thus lowering inflation.

As French Socialists began to talk about modernizing France and going "back to the basics" in schools, French society was beginning to manifest more conservative changes as well. Support for government-subsidized Catholic schools was so great that the Mitterrand government had to back down from efforts to restrict their independence. The government grip on the airwaves was also loosened, as private radio and TV stations sprung into life.

Cohabitation—1986 to 1988

The 1986 electoral results created something entirely new since the beginning of the Fifth Republic in 1958: a president whose party is a minority in the National Assembly. The traditional conservative parties won a whisker-thin majority. Therefore, Mitterrand was compelled to appoint a conservative prime minister, Jacques Chirac.

Chirac studied international relations at Harvard, paying his way by working as a waiter at Howard Johnson's. During the Algerian War he served in the French Foreign Legion, after which he entered the prestigious *Ecole Nationale d'Administration.* His subsequent political rise was meteoric, working, as always, so energetically that Pompidou gave him the nickname "the Bulldozer." From 1974–76 he had served as Prime Minister under Giscard. However, believing that he was given too little leeway to pursue his own policies, he became the only prime minister in the Fifth Republic to quit due to disagreements with the president.

Observers coined the word "cohabitation" to describe the relationship between a strong president and an equally strong prime minister who is not willing merely to execute the will of the president. This relationship changed the basic rules of the French political game from 1986 to 1988. It also showed that the institutions of the Fifth Republic are more adaptable and resilient in democratic politics than even de Gaulle had ever imagined.

The president's actual powers diminished somewhat, but they nevertheless remained formidable. "Cohabitation" was not a return to the parliamentary politics and "games" of the Third and Fourth Republics because the powers which the president lost fell to a powerful prime minister, not to parliament. Nevertheless, it was a difficult relationship with which the French had almost no experience. Both the president and the prime minister had an interest in making this power-sharing succeed. French politics has traditionally been characterized by polarization between the left and the right; the new experiment proved that two ideologically opposed sides can find common ground and cooperate with each other in the interest of the French nation. In fact, by election time in 1988 it had helped diminish the ideological gulf separating the major parties. Therefore, it actually strengthened

Reading the latest novel Photo by Susan L. Thompson

French democracy. "Cohabitation" proved to be a workable alternative, and 70% of the French found it to be good.

As soon as Mitterrand appointed Chirac prime minister, the latter declared that he would play an active role in French foreign and defense policy, fields traditionally reserved for the president. Although Chirac and Mitterrand thought almost alike on these issues, their struggle was over constitutional power, not policy substance. Mitterrand turned down several of Chirac's choices for cabinet posts, but the prime minister nevertheless assembled a staff of foreign policy advisers to rival those of the president.

In domestic affairs, Chirac moved extremely quickly, hearing loudly and clearly the count-down to the 1988 elections. His government probably put through the largest number of reforms by any French government since 1958. Some critics said that his impatience damaged French democracy because he often chose to impose key measures by decree, thereby limiting parliamentary debate. He abolished the proportional representation electoral system, which Mitterrand had intentionally introduced in order to reduce the *Communists'* parliamentary seats and to prevent any party from winning a majority. An unfortunate by-product of this system had

177

France

been that it enabled the *National Front* to win 35 seats and thereby reduced Chirac's usable majority to only two deputies, even though the right, as a whole, had won 55% of the vote.

Although Mitterrand initially balked at some of the conservative government's initiatives, he could not stop a single policy which the prime minister wanted to pursue. He was the first Fifth Republic president to have his wings clipped while still in office. He watched most of his power drain away from the Elysée to the Matignon palace. However, by knowing how and when to assert his residual authority, he succeeded in halting the trend. Having preserved his authority, his popularity soared. By standing above the political fray and focusing on the nation's interests, he let Chirac, who was in the trenches doing day–to–day combat, acquire some serious political bruises. Mitterrand thereby enhanced his own chances of reelection in 1988 and diminished Chirac's chances to win the presidency.

1988 Elections

The strength of de Gaulle's constitution had been demonstrated by the two–year "cohabitation" experiment, which coupled a *Socialist* president with a conservative prime minister. The 1988 elections led the country into yet another untested experiment: a minority government.

The presidential election in May was perhaps the least ideological struggle in recent French history. Having been cured by 1983 of any hope of successfully implementing a leftist program, Mitterrand called for an "opening to the center." Shouldering the blame for much that displeased voters and unable to unite the conservatives behind him, Chirac garnered only 46% of the votes to Mitterrand's 54%.

Ignoring statements he had made during the campaign, the reelected Mitterrand called for parliamentary elections in June, expecting to see the momentum of his victory produce a solid *Socialist* majority in the National Assembly. His plan backfired as the *PS* fell 14 votes short of a majority. He appointed a popular and capable rival within his party, Michel Rocard, as prime minister with a cabinet containing some non–*Socialists*.

The minority government had to work with other parties to make the system work. But this is nothing unusual in Western Europe, where most major democracies have coalition or minority governments. The constitution had been designed in 1958 to enable a country with a fractious parliament to enjoy stable rule. No new elections can be called for 12 months, and governments cannot be brought down unless a majority unites against it. In other words, it is the opposition, not the government, which needs a majority. Rocard went far in introducing non–socialist ideas on how an advanced economy should be run. He deserves much of the credit for transforming the *PS* from a party of doctrine to one of government.

Although Rocard's popularity soared after France's participation in the 1991 Gulf War, Mitterrand appointed France's first woman prime minister, Edith Cresson, to head a government containing seven women; she lasted less than a year. She was abrasive, but the main problem was that her politics pointed leftward while the rest of the political spectrum was shifting rightward.

1993 Parliamentary Elections

In many ways Mitterrand had done more to transform French society and politics than de Gaulle. No one would have expected that he would be so able to convert the French to an acceptance of a market economy and the need for stable and rigorous economic management. In foreign policy he swept away some of the most important cornerstones of Gaullist foreign policy by nurturing a more trusting relationship with the United States and by championing greater European integration, including in the field of defense. It was in the context of greater European integration and closer Franco–German relations that he sought to contain an enlarged, unified, and dynamic Germany within a Europe whose map is being redrawn.

He also oversaw the most ambitious building program in Paris since Haussmann remade the capital more than a century earlier. I.M. Pei's glass pyramid in the court of the Louvre had shocked Parisians at first, but it gave new life to one of the world's finest museums. The Grand Arch at the heart of the suburb of La Défense, completed for the bicentennial in 1989, is a majestic, modern, 360–foot steel–and–glass version of Napoleon's Arc de Triomphe. The Bastille Opéra, opened in 1989, has been less successful in winning public admiration, but numerous other *Grands Travaux*, such as a new National Library, leave Mitterrand's stamp on Paris.

Voter disillusionment was rampant, and more than 30% of the electorate refused to vote, one of the lowest voter turnouts in recent French history. Mitterrand's party, which had been in power too long and had run short on vision, ideas, and energy, was swept from power in the most devastating defeat in modern French electoral history. It was a hard verdict, but it was not an ideological one, since the *Socialist Party* had already shed most of its socialist ideology. Before stepping down in May 1995, Mitterrand admitted that with all the formal powers a French president has, he had "underestimated the ponderous nature of society, the slowness of its wheels, the weight of its traditions. You don't change society by an act of legislation."

The conservative victors captured 80% of the seats in the National Assembly, and for two years France again experienced

Autumn in Paris . . . Susan and Wayne Thompson

rule by cohabitation. The conservative government of Edouard Balladur had to cope with unemployment and racial tension. He moved to revitalize the economy by selling state companies, lowering taxes on employers to enable them to hire more workers, cracking down on illegal immigrants through expulsions and tightened border controls, and advancing resolutely toward greater European unity. The latter goal was a challenge after a hair–thin 51% voted *Oui* for the Maastricht treaty in a 1992 referendum. The narrowness of that margin in one of the EU's founding nations was a stinging blow to France's political elite.

1995 Presidential Elections

Balladur had become France's most popular politician and leading presidential prospect, but his star fell precipitously in 1995. He could not overcome his patrician aloofness and present himself as a man of the people. A technocrat who had never held public office until his mid–50s, he was an inept campaigner. His government was put on the defensive by a series of corruption scandals, including illegal wiretapping.

It was also embarrassed by charges of American industrial espionage in France and subsequent expulsion of four U.S. diplomats. This was the first time France had publicly sought the removal of alleged American agents from its soil. It was also a setback for the two countries' intelligence cooperation, which had been instrumental in France's 1994 capture in the Sudan of the world's most wanted terrorist, known as "Carlos the Jackal." The government's handling of the spy affair widened a serious breach in the cabinet between Balladur's supporters and those of party leader Jacques Chirac. The latter had put Balladur into the prime ministerial hot seat to free himself to run for the presidency, which had eluded him twice before. Boosted by temporary popularity, Balladur's ambition grew, and he decided to make a bid for the presidency himself. Chirac felt double–crossed, and the stage was set for a tense race.

The first round of balloting in April 1995 revealed deep public discontent with mainstream politicians; almost 40% of the voters supported candidates representing the far right or left. Jean–Marie Le Pen of the *National Front* made his strongest showing yet, winning 15%; combined with the votes of nationalist candidate Philippe de Villiers, the far–right captured more than a fifth of the total. On the left, 17% cast their ballots for Communist leader Robert Hue, Trotskyite militant Arlette Laguiller, and *Green* candidate Dominique Voynet. *Socialist* Lionel Jospin was the surprising victor in the first

I.M. Pei's glass pyramid at the Louvre Photo: Susan L. Thompson

round, with 23.3%, ahead of Chirac with 20.8% and Balladur with 18.5%. Chirac's first–round percentage was the lowest for any president since 1965, when elections under the present system began.

In the second round in May, neither Chirac nor Jospin agreed to bargain with Le Pen, even though unemployment and immigration were the dominant issues on the minds of voters. As a result, nearly half of Le Pen's voters abstained or cast blank ballots, and only 40% voted for Chirac. Chirac campaigned energetically under the banner, "France for All," to try to show that he stood above party politics. He repeated in his standard stump speech that French society "is more divided and dangerous than ever." Although he criticized Balladur for not taking bolder measures to heal social divisions and improve the economy, Balladur supported him publicly in the final round and delivered 85% of his first–round voters to the new president. With a turnout of 80%, Chirac won 52.6% of the votes, doing best among farmers, business people, shop–keepers, artisans, and the professions, such as doctors and lawyers. For the first time, a conservative candidate won a majority of voters under age–35, as well as more than 40% of blue–collar workers and French describing themselves as under–privileged. Since a record 6% of blank ballots was cast, he actually won only 49.5% of the votes cast, making him the first president to be elected with fewer than half the total votes.

Chirac's victory left the right in control of the presidency, 80% of the seats in the National Assembly and two–thirds in the Senate, 20 of 22 regional councils, four–fifths of the departmental councils, and most of the big cities. Never in the history of the Fifth Republic has there been such a concentration of power. According to exit polls, two out of five voters supported Chirac in order to prevent another seven years of socialism. Considering the *Socialists'* unpopularity after 14 years in power, Jospin's 47.4% in the final round was impressive.

Growing public cynicism toward the political establishment has emboldened journalists to break hallowed taboos against reporting on politicians' private lives. In 1994 the weekly *Paris Match* published a cover photo of Mitterrand in public with his daughter born from an extramarital affair two decades earlier. Mistress and daughter had been housed in government guest houses and had travelled at taxpayers' expense. Although the magazine was sold out within hours, there was an outcry among public figures that it had crossed the line. Unlike in the U.S., neither Mitterrand, who made no attempt to conceal his daughter's paternity, nor his party was harmed by this. At his funeral in January 1996 his wife, Danielle, stood for the first time with his daughter out of wedlock, Mazarine Pingeot, and her mother Anne Pingeot. He died of prostate cancer. He had been informed of this condition several months after his election in 1981, but he ordered that it be kept secret.

On the first day of his presidency Chirac traveled to Colombey–les–Deux–Eglises to emphasize his political roots by laying a wreath at the burial site of his mentor, Charles de Gaulle. On the following day, he lunched with German Chan-

France

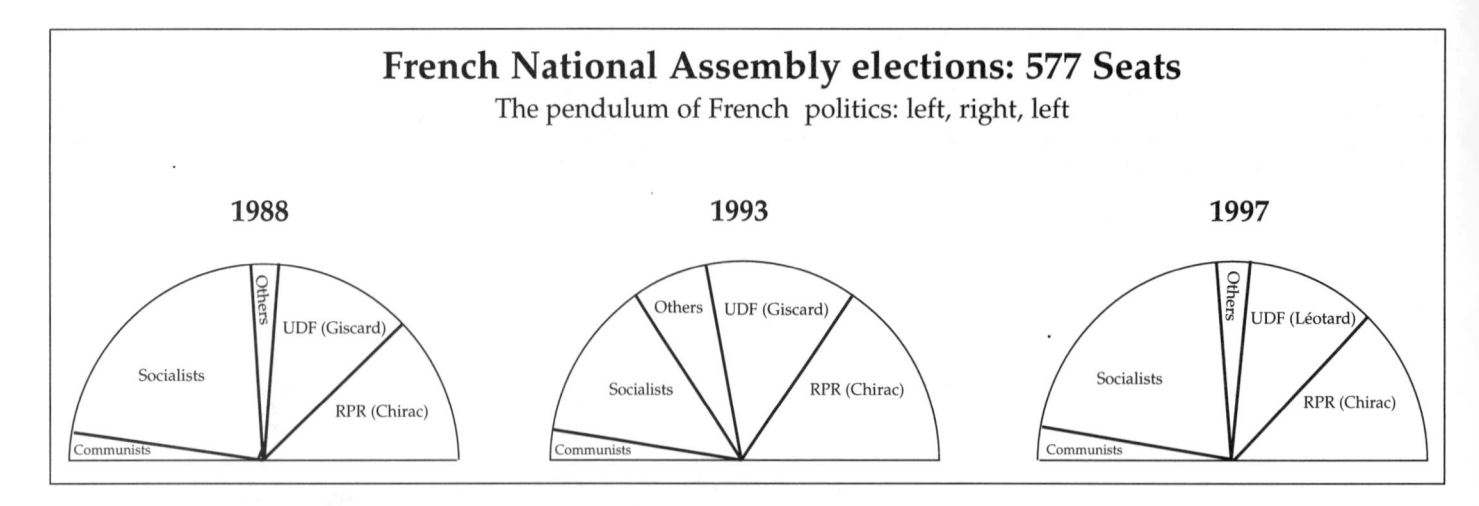

French National Assembly elections: 577 Seats
The pendulum of French politics: left, right, left

1988 — Socialists, Communists, Others, UDF (Giscard), RPR (Chirac)

1993 — Socialists, Communists, Others, UDF (Giscard), RPR (Chirac)

1997 — Socialists, Communists, Others, UDF (Léotard), RPR (Chirac)

cellor Helmut Kohl in Strasbourg to underscore the importance of France's ties with its powerful neighbor. He promised a less monarchical presidency than that of his predecessor. He promptly ordered that the fleet of military jets and helicopters at the disposal of the president and cabinet be disbanded and that ostentatious signs of power, such as motorcades with screaming sirens and motorcycles racing through the streets, be banned.

During his campaign, Chirac promised "profound change" and an attack on unemployment as his "priority of priorities." He did not explain exactly what that meant. His chosen prime minister, Alain Juppé, was left to fill in the gaps. Observers were understandably perplexed about how the conservative government's expensive new programs with no tax increases or budget cuts could result in the reduction of the deficit. Clearly the day of reckoning could not be postponed for long. As it became obvious that Chirac could not fulfill his campaign promises of lower taxes and bountiful jobs, his approval rating plummeted. Without preparing the public, he suddenly announced an abrupt reversal of his economic policy from creating jobs to cutting the deficit in order to ensure that France would be able to join Europe's monetary union in 1999.

The sense of betrayal over the unexpected U-turn from job creation to austerity ignited in 1995–97 the worst strikes since 1968, involving millions of citizens, from civil servants and truck drivers to students, actors and doctors. Unlike in 1968, though, there is no unified political idea behind the unrest. Demonstrators in 1968 had risen up against materialism and an allegedly soulless affluent society. Many French now revolt, not just because they refuse to relinquish treasured welfare benefits and special privileges, but also because they have a feeling that life is getting worse and worse and that affluence and security might be slipping away from them. This is why strikers today enjoy strong public support and why the government caves into them so often. French also dislike having welfare reforms imposed upon them without adequate preparation or explanation. Juppé came to symbolize the cold-blooded, technocratically-trained elites who have little concern for the common people.

1997 Parliamentary Elections

In the June 1997 final round of elections, control of the National Assembly changed hands for the fifth straight parliamentary election in 16 years. Tired of Chirac's broken promises made only two years earlier to protect the social net and reduce France's 12.8% unemployment, while lowering taxes and government spending, voters turned back to the *Socialists,* led by Lionel Jospin, a former diplomat, economics professor, and education minister. They rejected the conservatives' austerity program ineffectively presented to the nation as essential for joining the common European currency in 1999. They believed in Jospin's promises to create 700,000 jobs for the young—half of them in the public sector, to create more jobs by reducing the work week from 39 to 35 hours with no loss of pay, and defending the welfare state without raising taxes. While not entirely disavowing the common currency, Jospin pledged to allow neither it nor global market forces to condemn France to the "cruelties of 19th century capitalism," which many French identify with American-led economic reforms sweeping the industrialized world.

The *Socialists* captured 253 seats (including 12 *Radical Socialists*) in the 577-seat Assembly. Since that is short of an absolute majority, the government formed by Prime Minister Jospin had to rule with the support of the *Communist Party,* which won 38 seats, and the *Greens,* which got seven. In opposition, the conservative *RPR* and *UDF* together won 242 seats, and Le Pen's *National Front* got one seat even though it won a half million more votes than the *Communists*. Other rightist parties got 14 seats. President Jacques Chirac, who disastrously misread the mood of the French public, was obligated to accept cohabitation for the third time in 11 years. The balance of power favors the *Socialist* prime minister this time since cohabitation came about in a way particularly demeaning to Chirac. While presidents normally claim full control over foreign and defense policy, Chirac had to agree to "act in concert" with Jospin.

Foreign and Defense Policies

German unification in 1990 led many French to fear that their country would be overshadowed by Germany and would be driven to the margins of international politics. That has not happened. France plays an important role as a medium-sized power willing to use its force abroad. It preserves its independence and has not rejoined NATO's integrated command structure, although it has intensified its contacts with the alliance. For example, in 1994 it began attending NATO defense minister meetings again. In 1995 it rejoined NATO's military committee, which brings the service chiefs together, and its officers began working more closely with SHAPE.

In part because of defense cuts in all Western European countries, the French now talk of creating a European defense pillar within NATO, rather than in competition with it. President Chirac's meeting with British Prime Minister Tony Blair at St. Malo the end of 1998 agreed on a blueprint for such a new European defense.

The wars in the Persian Gulf and the former Yugoslavia convinced France that it cannot do much in military operations without NATO assets and American help. It put some of its ships and aircraft under American control in the Balkans. Its troops that enforce the Bosnian peace settlement serve in a NATO force. France dispatched the largest foreign contingent—4,000 troops—to Bosnia to play the leading role in the UN Protection Force, led initially by a French general. Its combat pilots helped enforce the "no–fly zone" over that war–torn country. When NATO created a rapid–reaction force in 1995 to protect UN peacekeepers in Bosnia, France contributed 1,500 elite troops and assumed overall command. France was a major participant in the Implementation Force (IFOR) in Bosnia, assuming responsibility for maintaining peace in the most complicated spot imaginable: Sarajevo. Its troops remained after IFOR ended.

Many of the country's leading intellectuals embraced the cause of direct military intervention in the Balkans, fearing that "ethnic cleansing" could spread across Europe. This mood reflects a sharp break with the pacifist traditions of French intellectuals. That support continued in 1999 when France contributed 61 combat aircraft and five ships to conduct an air war against Yugoslavia in a NATO attempt to stop ethnic cleansing in Kosovo. France's pragmatic Atlanticist Foreign Minister Hubert Védrine noted in April 1999 that "in contrast to Bosnia, there's been no major disaccord at any point among Europeans or between Europeans and the United States. It doesn't happen often, but this time we've had a remarkable identity of views on the cause of the problem and what to do about it."

What has replaced antipathy toward America is fear of the sole remaining superpower's domination of world affairs. Polls in April 1999 revealed that a large majority dislikes this, and most French discounted the idea that American policy abroad, including in the Balkans, is motivated by ideals of human rights and democracy. Védrine remarked that "without a counterweight, there is a danger of a unilateralist temptation, a risk of hegemony. So, depending on the situation, we will be friends and allies of the United States; but sometimes we will need to say No without acrimony, in the name of our legitimate interests or those of Europe." It is ironic that this mistrust occurs at a time when military cooperation between France and the U.S. is closer and more harmonious than at any time since de Gaulle took France out of NATO's military command in 1966.

This is not to say that France is always in agreement with the U.S. In 1996 Paris proposed reforms in the NATO command structure as a price for its further reintegration into the alliance. Specifically, it demanded that the Southern Command headquartered in Naples be led by a European officer, preferably by a Frenchman. The U.S., whose Sixth Fleet comprises the main military force in the Mediterranean, refuses. Both the Gaullist president and the *Socialist* prime minister, who agreed to "act in concert" on matters of foreign affairs and defense, believe that France's reintegration into NATO must be contingent upon a European's receiving that southern command. The important thing is that the strong Gaullist antipathy toward both the U.S. and a more united Europe is gone. A survey in 1998 revealed that 77% consider the EU a "good thing" for France; 51% would like to see an acceleration in the European integration process.

Another important departure is a dramatic increase in France's military cooperation with Germany. The two neighbors created an experimental joint brigade, whose command alternates between French and German officers. In 1991 they agreed to expand that unit to a corps size—35,000 troops. The French eased some of America's and NATO's fears by conceding that this "Eurocorps" could operate under NATO for international peacekeeping and in time of war. The creation of a Combined Joint Task Forces (CJTF) allows some of NATO's European assets to be used in military operations where the U.S. has no interest in participating. The concept is meant to work within NATO and not against it.

France seeks to tighten its already close links with the FRG. Bilateral ties, EU integration and NATO tether Germany securely to the West. German unity made Germany, not France, the leader of a strengthened Europe, and France seeks to act with Germany's support in the name of "European interests." When Gerhard Schröder became chancellor in 1998,

Typical World War I monument seen in every French village

France

French leaders worried about his talk of tighter links with Britain and feared that this might destroy the special relationship between Paris and Berlin. The French had a host of disagreements with the new German government ranging from financial contributions to the EU, possible German cancellation of nuclear reprocessing contracts, Germany's questioning of the NATO nuclear "first–use" doctrine, and London–Berlin plans to merge British Aerospace and German's DASA (the air wing of the Daimler–Chrysler conglomerate) to form a European rival to giant American arms industries. France wants its state–owned Aerospatiale to be included, but the Germans and British resist this until the latter is privatized. By 1999 French fears of a new Berlin–London axis were quieted.

The end of superpower confrontation meant that France had to reexamine the three pillars of its defense policy—its nuclear forces, its draft army, and its operational independence from permanent alliances. Without a Soviet threat it had problems defining a clear purpose for its atomic *force de frappe*. It became difficult to maintain its expensive triad of forces, which in 1991 consumed a fifth of total defense spending.

Its underground nuclear test series in 1995–96 unleashed a violent world outcry, especially in Asia and the Pacific, where they took place. Taken aback by the world–wide protest, Chirac swore that these tests were needed to perfect computer simulation programs that would make further testing unnecessary. They enabled France to sign an international treaty banning nuclear testing in 1996. In 1991 the French had finally signed the nuclear Non–Proliferation Treaty to emphasize the need to stop the spread of atomic weapons.

France continues to maintain the largest and most diversified military capability in Western Europe, as well as a credible nuclear force. Despite the changed security environment in Europe following the end of the Cold War, a consensus remained to maintain as the ultimate security guarantee a minimal nuclear force posture for the purpose of *"dissuasion,"* the French version of deterrence. A significant change is that these nuclear weapons are intended to be linked to European security, not just the defense of French territory and interests. The French are aware that there is little current interest in Europe for such a link and that the establishment of a European defense identity would be a precondition.

The consequence of France's decision to maintain only a minimal *dissuasion* policy is that major reductions in its nuclear force posture and infrastructure became possible. In the course of the 1990s, France reduced its nuclear spending by more than 50%. It started eliminating its 18 land–based nuclear missiles on Plateau d'Albion (to be completed by 2005), reduced to four its planned new ballistic missile submarines, and began closing its plants at Pierrelatte and Marcoule that produce fissile material for atomic weapons, to be completed by 2002. Of the five nuclear submarines in use the end of the century, four are always operational and two at sea. One sub has 16 M4 missiles, each carrying six warheads. Four new strategic subs carrying upgraded missiles have or will enter the force: "Le Triomphant" in 1996, "Le Téméraire" in 1999, "Le Vigilant" in 2002, and the final one in 2007. This submarine force represents four–fifths of the French nuclear arsenal. An airbourne component remains: three squadrons of Mirage 2000 N planes are equipped with ASMP missiles; and two fleets of Super Etendards, equipped with ASMPs, are stationed on aircraft carriers.

The aircraft carrier *Clemenceau* was decommissioned in 1997, and the following year it was announced that the aged *Foch* would also be withdrawn from service. Coming on line in 2000 after a four–year delay was the *Charles de Gaulle*. This is the first French carrier constructed to be interoperable with U.S. Nimitz–class carriers. It has compatible catapults, can receive U.S. aircraft, and carries U.S.–built Hawkeye planes flown by U.S.–trained pilots that control the airspace around the carrier and guide planes to their targets.

The 1991 Gulf War revealed that France's conventional forces were not equipped or structured to cope with faraway crises. Its draftees could not be sent out of France, and its equipment was found wanting. The war reinforced the case for a more professional army. Consequently, France began in 1996 to phase out its 10–month conscription and to create an all–volunteer army. Over a five–year period, it is disbanding 38 of its 180 regiments, including 12 in Germany, where only 3,000 out of 20,000 soldiers will remain. Army manpower is being reduced from around 400,000 to 140,000, along with cuts in the land–based nuclear deterrence force, military bases, schools and hospitals, and civilian defense contractors; 16 warships are being decommissioned. The professional officer corps remains at 38,000. Despite these defense cuts, France still spends the most on defense of any European country: 3.1% of GDP in 1999

Finally, its independent stance was challenged by the reality of emerging European defense identity which the French government advocates. More than any Western country, France was rocked by the break–up of the old world order. It can no longer pose as an independent force between two superpowers— such a state of affairs has ceased to exist.

Activism in Foreign Policy

France always tried to remain largely independent of other western industrialized nations in its dealing with the "third world." In 1984 it created a 47,000–man "Rapid Action Force" (FAR). This highly mobile force was designed not only to plug holes in NATO defenses in Western Europe, but also to be sent to trouble spots anywhere in the world to back up French interests, such as in Africa.

No other country of comparable size maintains as big a military presence abroad; it has more than 60,000 soldiers stationed in some 35 countries and territories. The French maintain military bases in six African ex–colonies and have troops in more in order to protect French interests and citizens, who number about 130,000 in Sub–Saharan Africa. They station 4,000 troops in Djibouti on the East coast and smaller forces in West and Central Africa. France also sends two–thirds of its foreign aid to Africa, making it the continent's major patron. Since 1990 it encourages the trend toward democracy in Africa by linking its aid to democratic reforms.

Until 1994 it provided 13 African countries belonging to the *Communité Financière Africaine (CFA)*, also called the "franc zone," with the benefits of a hard currency pegged to the French franc. Then it decreed that such pegging would cease; this caused widespread African hardships. The establishment of a common European currency will further weaken what is left of French support of African currencies.

Although it convenes a Franco–African summit each year, it decided to trim its costs on that continent. Its military interventions have become rarer, although in 1992 it joined other allies to participate in the UN humanitarian relief operation in Somalia. It was the only European country to send troops to Rwanda in 1994. Its 2,500 soldiers managed to interrupt the first round of genocide and save thousands of lives. In 1997 its troops in the Central African Republic were used against mutinous local soldiers who opposed the local president and who had killed two French soldiers.

In 1997 the *Socialist* government called for a complete rethinking of France's policy in Africa. It ordered a reduction in French troops permanently stationed in Africa from 8,400 to 6,000 in 1999 and declining further to 5,000. Two bases in the Central African Republic were closed, and military cooperation agreements with 23 countries were reviewed. President Chirac reiterated at a Franco–African summit in 1998: "The period of outside interference is over."

France

France has long-standing interests in the Middle East. It sent a powerful 12,600-man air, naval and ground contingent in 1991 to help drive Iraq out of Kuwait. This was a bold move, considering the large Arab population in France and the fact that Iraq had been France's best Middle Eastern customer, and owes France $3 billion. In doing this it violated one of de Gaulle's most basic teachings: French troops should never be under U.S. command. Former President Mitterrand answered critics, saying "we are linked, we are allies, and we intend to do what we are committed to do."

Other countries look to France to take the lead in deciding how the West should respond if Algeria, to which France annually provides $1 billion in aid, becomes a fundamentalist Islamic republic. France is torn between the desire to prevent Muslims from coming to power and fear of making irreconcilable enemies out of potential rulers of Algeria. It supports the military junta in power, reinforced by its election, even though it has outlawed the popular Islamic Salvation Front (FIS). This policy creates problems within France itself. To punish France, the Armed Islamic Group renewed it terroristic activities within France, using bombs, which killed four innocent bystanders in ugly carnage at the Montparnasse underground rail station in late 1996.

France's nervousness is understandable. By 1995, a third of the 78 foreigners killed in a year and a half of Algeria were French, and the threat of violence on French soil had become real. About three million persons of Algerian origin, in addition to a million other Muslims, live in France, and authorities believe that fundamentalists wield influence over a small but growing minority of them. This was demonstrated in 1994, when terrorists hijacked an airliner in Algiers, intending to blow it up in the skies over Paris. It was intercepted in Marseilles when police stormed it.

France's pro-Arab foreign policy, driven in part by domestic considerations, has put the country in conflict with the U.S.'s basically pro-Israel leaning. Its viewpoint has been reflected in 1996–7 by "shuttle diplomacy" calculated to resolve differences between Israel and the militant *Islamic Hezbollah*. It refused to support U.S. air strikes and an expansion of the "no-fly zone" in Iraq in August 1996.

France also must deal with domestic terrorism from Corsica. Since the 1970s Corsicans have suffered an average of 400 explosions a year by various and divided nationalist groups, who finance their operations by extorting "protection money" from local businesses. Supported by no more than one Corsican in ten, these groups do not agree among themselves

Parakeets for sale, Paris

Photo by Susan L. Thompson

about whether they are seeking independence or more autonomy. But in 1996 they took their struggle to the French mainland, bombing a courthouse in Aix-en-Provence and the Bordeaux office of the prime minister. The Corsican National Liberation Front (FNLC) claimed responsibility for the multiple explosions.

In 1998 the troubles escalated on "the impossible island." France's prefect, Claude Erignac, was murdered, and the assassins were never found. He was replaced by Bernard Bonnet, who was given *carte blanche* to crack down on separatist terror, corruption, organized crime and clan vendettas. He succeeded in reducing bomb attacks to 96 in 1998, armed robbery fell by two-thirds, and scores of separatist extremists were arrested. Dozens of local politicians and dignitaries were placed under investigation in some 80 corruption scandals. Then in April 1999 five paramilitary gendarmes from an anti-terrorist squad were sent to burn down a beachfront restaurant. They bungled the job and were caught after fleeing. They claimed they had been sent by the island's top gendarme, who in turn explained that he had acted under orders from the prefect himself. *All* were put in prison awaiting charges and trial; this was the first time in the history of the Fifth Republic that a prefect had been fired or jailed. Prime Minister Jospin had to admit that it was a "very serious and unacceptable affair."

ECONOMY

After World War II France experienced an economic miracle no less impressive than that of West Germany. The U.S. Marshall Plan, economic planning, membership in the EU and decolonization were important factors in this success. It possesses enough raw materials to supply about half of its overall needs, and it has a diversified and modern industrial base and a highly skilled labor force, about 40% of which is employed in industry and more than 60% in commerce and services. Women constitute 43% of the work force,

France

compared with 36% in 1968. With its cultural riches and geographic beauty, France employs many people in its tourist industry; it is the world's most visited country, just ahead of the U.S., Spain and Italy. It had 60 million visitors in 1996, but the French do not reciprocate. With more second homes than any other nation, 90% of them stay in France for their holidays.

By 1995 it had become the fourth richest country in the world, despite the fact that it has only 1% of the world's population. Household assets doubled from 1970 to 1995. Overall production rose threefold between 1946 and 1966, after having only doubled between 1889 and 1940. In the two decades following 1967, its economy grew an average of 3.3% per year. Its trade surplus continues to grow, and its high–tech industries in aerospace, transportation, electronics, telecommunication, and software are among the most competitive in the world.

At .4% in 1999 its inflation was the lowest in four decades. By contrast, unemployment, while slowly declining, stood at 11.5% in 1999 (more than twice that among the young and 22% and rising for unskilled workers). One major reason for the problem is the high cost of French labor ($17.10 per hour on average in the manufacturing sector). Employers must pay a minimum wage of FF6,000 ($1,200) per month, plus an added 40% in benefits. It is politically impossible to create new jobs by cutting the pay and benefits of those working.

The work week was lowered to 35 hours for private companies with more than 20 employees beginning in 2000 (smaller companies by 2002). After fighting hard against the new law, employers discovered that by averaging the hours over 52 weeks they now have more flexibility to increase hours in busy periods and reduce them during slower times. They can respond better to seasonal demands. Thus workers find themselves doing shiftwork at awkward hours and six–day weeks. Also coffee breaks do not count in the 35 hours. Although wages are seldom cut, they are often being held down. It became clear that the new law would not create new jobs. These unintended results disappointed many employees, who did what frustrated French workers always do: many went on strike against the 35–hour week!

France has usually had relatively peaceful labor relations. In part, this is because France's social security programs have taken much of the heat out of the issue of unequal income distribution. Under 9% of the French work force belongs to labor unions, and membership continues to decline, except in white collar unions. This gives France the least unionized work force of any industrialized country. Some non–unionized French, especially in the public sector, belong to so–called "coordinations," *ad hoc* bodies which serve as liaisons between competing unions or spring up in protest at the unions' feebleness. The communists dominate the largest, the *General Confederation of Labor (CGT)*. The *French Democratic Confederation of Labor (CFDT)* displays moderation, as does the leftist but anti–communist *Workers Force (FO)*. The powerful *National Education Federation (FEN)* and the *Confederation of Supervisory Grades (CGC)* organize teachers and engineers and skilled technical personnel.

Despite many small family farms, only 4% of Frenchmen are now employed in agriculture (compared with more than a third in 1945). It is self–sufficient in all foodstuffs except tropical produce and it is the major agricultural country in the EU, producing 21% of the Community's total output. Only the U.S. exports more food and drink products. France is one of the world's leading producers of wine. As in other Western European countries, the farm lobby wields influence out of all proportion to its numbers. French farmers get a fourth of the EU's agricultural subsidies (CAP). The combined EU and French government subsidies account for half the farmers' income, but they are distributed very unevenly. A fifth of the largest and richest farmers, especially the grain growers, receive 80% of the funds. Some, such as wine producers, can compete well on the world market and therefore have no need for the assistance.

The importance of agriculture, not only for the French economy but for the country's emotional rural roots in *la France profonde*, was demonstrated in the farmers' violent reaction to a compromise reached in 1992 between the EU and the U.S. regarding GATT limits on agricultural subsidies. They took their tractors and manure to the streets of France, targeting not only the National Assembly and the European Parliament, but also McDonald's restaurants and Coca–Cola plants. All of them use only French farm products. However, the facts that Coke had cornered half of the soft drink market by the mid–1990s and McDonald's continued to grow steadily gave them symbolic value. The emotion and fury of their clashes with the police underscored their intense concern about the effects a slash in subsidies would have on rural France. Already barely surviving economically, many farmers would be forced off the land and into crowded cities, leaving depopulated regions behind them. From 1970 to the end of the century the number of farms declined from 1.6 million to 700,000, of which only half were run by full–time farmers; 40,000 farms go out of business each year

Its economy is still troubled by certain traditional structural weaknesses, such as an overcentralized state bureaucracy. It has a clumsy system of distribution due partly to the relatively large number of small retail shops. In 1973 parliament passed a law giving locally elected officials and representatives of commerce and crafts the right to veto the opening of new supermarkets, so one sees considerably fewer large grocery and discount stores in France than in the U.S. Not until 1989 did supermarkets do more business than small neighborhood stores.

France is concerned about its future energy sources. Its energy consumption doubled during the 1970s. It is heavily dependent upon the importation of fossil fuels. It imports 96%. It obtains roughly half its needs from Persian Gulf countries, one-fourth from Mediterranean countries and one–eighth from Black Africa. It imports 90% of its natural gas. Some is produced in the southwestern region of Aquitaine, but these wells are rapidly being depleted.

Nevertheless, France produced about half the total energy it needs. The reason is that it launched a full–scale program to develop nuclear power, especially fast breeder reactors. Now Western Europe's largest producer of nuclear power, producing half the EU's nuclear energy, it is the world's fourth richest country in uranium, with 10% of all known reserves. Its *Eurodif* enrichment plant at Tricastin represents a third of the Western world's capacity and feeds a third of the world's nuclear reactors. By 1999, 75% of France's electricity (compared with 19% in the U.S., 28% in Japan, and 33% in Europe as a whole) was generated by 56 nuclear reactors. In 1994 it fired up the world's only working fast–breeder reactor, which creates plutonium while it generates electricity. Nuclear power provides the country with the EU's cheapest electricity, except in Denmark. France even has an overcapacity in electrical generation which allows it to export about 13% of its production.

There are critics who argue that France has become overly dependent upon a single energy source and that such heavy use is unsafe. But its reactors are among the safest in the world. Its decision to build a single standard reactor design not only reduces construction costs but enables technical personnel to be used interchangeably in all the sites, rather than being trained to work only in one site. Because of violent local opposition, it has still not succeeded in finding a deep–storage site for nuclear waste. In the meantime, low–level waste is stored above ground, while high–level waste is stored in vitrified form in both steel canisters and concrete pits at La Hague and Marcoule.

France

CULTURE

The French have long fought what some critics see as a futile battle to preserve the purity of the French language, which is spoken as a native tongue by about 90 million persons throughout the world. This struggle is waged particularly against the powerful onslaught of the English language. One author even wrote a book with the provocative title *Parlez-vous Franglais?*, "franglais" being a combination of the words meaning French and English. The number of pupils learning English in school quadrupled in the 1980s. French scientists find it increasingly necessary to publish their works in English, and they often choose to deliver their lectures in English at international conferences held *in France*.

Ordinary Frenchmen have adopted English words so quickly that in 1975 the parliament passed the Bas-Lauriol law requiring that trade names, advertising material, product instructions and receipts use only the French language. The text of the law even specified French replacements for such common expressions: "savoir-faire" (for "le know-how") "boutique franche" (for "le duty-free shop"), "mini-marge" (for "le discount"), "aéroglisseur" (for "le hovercraft"), "credit-bail" (for "le leasing"), "matériel" (for "le hardware"), "grosporteur" (for "le jumbo jet"), "astronef" (for "le spacecraft"), "boteur" (for "le bulldozer"), "retrospectif" (for "le flashback"), "spectacle solo" (for "le one-man show"), "palmarès" (for "le hit parade"), "baladeur" (for "le Walkman"), "mercatique" (for "le marketing"), and "zonage" (for "le zoning"). Some words escaped the sharp eyes of the language legislators: "le football," "le shopping," "le parking," "le living," and "le footing" (a word which is gradually being replaced in common usage by "le jogging"!).

Economic-Cultural Influences

Whether "le come-back" of pure French will succeed depends in part on "le marketing" of American investors in France. In 1983, the state's High Committee of the French Language stepped in to ban English words in the audio-visual field. Thus, "cameraman" and "close-up" became "cadreur" and "gros plan," and "drive-in theater" gave way to "ciné park." It also banned Anglo-Saxon terms in all government publications and speeches, legal contracts and schoolbooks. The counterattack has been generally successful in the computer field despite the persistence of a few terms such as *un batch* of data or *un floppy disk*. In 1996 the High Committee sued the American sponsors of an English-only site on the World Wide Web because the material is not also available in French. It was thrown out of court in 1997 on a technicality. President Chirac argued that "the stakes are clear. If, in the new media, our language, our programs, our creations are not strongly present, the young generation of our country will be economically and culturally marginalized."

Feeding the pigeons　　　　　　　　　　Photo: Susan L. Thompson

The French government wages a difficult battle. By 1995, 83% of high school pupils in EU countries learn English (84% in France itself), compared with 32% learning French and 16% German. In an editorial, the *Washington Post* spoofed the apparent obsession with enforcing language purity by imagining a bureau in Washington sending a disk jockey a letter like this: "It has come to our attention that you have repeatedly used the word 'taco' to describe the comestible for which the officially sanctioned word is 'corn meal crispette.' Please be advised that . . . " A *Dictionary of Official Terms* contains 3,500 new French words for advertising, broadcasting, public notices, official documents and those dealing with goods, services and conditions of work. All international conferences held in France must allow participants to speak in French if they want and must provide French translations of foreign-language speeches and documents.

French is the mother tongue of about 100 million people in the world and the occasional language of another 30–40 million. As such, it ranks only ninth in the world, behind English, Spanish and Portuguese. The French insist that it remain one of the two official languages in most international bodies, but only a tenth of the documents produced by the UN Secretariat are in French. In an attempt to promote use of the language world-wide, France also foots the bulk of the bill for *Francophonie*, an assortment of 53 countries from Congo to Cambodia who enjoy "a shared use of the French language." Since French need not be the country's dominant or official language and since the membership includes such lands as Egypt and Moldova, it is doubtful that this organization is effective in achieving France's lingual goals.

The government's policy of rejuvenating France's cultural life did not work well, despite a doubling of the Culture Ministry's budget since 1981. The number of French feature films exported declined even though subsidies to the film industry were increased by 800%. Sixty percent of the films French cinema fans go to see are American, double the proportion a decade ago, and below the EU average of 70%. In 1991 the top ten films in terms of attendance were all American. In 1995 audiences in France for French films were half as large as a decade earlier, while audiences for American films had not changed. This worries many French: in a 1996 poll, 70% of the respondents feared that American culture has an "excessive" influence in TV, and 59% in movies.

Nevertheless, the French still make more films than do their European neighbors. In 1990 French film makers put the swashbuckling and poetic classic, *Cyrano de Bergerac*, on screen, staring Gérard De-

France

pardieu, who won the best actor award at the Cannes Film Festival and was nominated for an Academy Award.

Television has been influenced even more strongly by America. The most popular soap opera in 1992 was called "Santa Barbara," and a French clone of the game show, "Wheel of Fortune," topped the popularity charts. Ratings for American programs are as high as for French ones. About 70% of foreign TV shows purchased are from the U.S. Nevertheless, by law, 60% of TV programming must be European (of which two–thirds French); 40% of songs on FM radio must be French, instead of less than 20% before the law was passed. Many of the teeth were extracted from this law in 1995, though, when the Constitutional Council ruled that it conflicted with freedom of expression.

Anti–Americanism still exists. De Gaulle's humiliation during World War II is no longer relevant, and thanks in part to the writings of Alexander Solzhenitsyn the Soviet model has fallen from grace in French eyes. *Le Nouvel Observateur* even criticized anti–Americanism as "socialism for imbeciles." Many Frenchmen are hurt by the dethroning of French as the world's cultural leader. However, as ex–communist and singer Yves Montand remarked, "if America has succeeded in invading us culturally, it is because we like it."

Perhaps "invasion" is the wrong word: a 1991 poll revealed that whereas two–thirds of U.S. respondents believed French culture was important to America, only 44% of the French repaid the compliment. In 1999 two–thirds of French respondents said they "do not feel close to the American people," and 60% believed the U.S. is too influential culturally. These feelings were strongest among young and educated. One sign of America's acceptability was the hard–won contract negotiated by a *Socialist* government to build a $4 billion Disneyland 20 miles east of downtown Paris. It opened in 1992 promising to create 12,000 new jobs. The only saving grace for hard–line Americanophobes is that Disney, himself, is of French lineage; the family's name was not Disney at all, but *D'Istngy*!

Academie Française

Since 1635 the "Academie Française" has striven, in the words of its first patron, Cardinal Richelieu, to "preserve the purity of the French language." Forty distinguished literary figures known as "immortals" are selected individually by the body itself and meet every Thursday in order to compile a French grammar book (finally completed in 1932) and a dictionary which is to serve as a criterion for good usage rather than as a list of all the words in the French language. Each word

Poster for the French census

proposed for inclusion is first brought up before a special committee and then is voted on by the Academy as a whole. In 1986 the Academy added 912 new words; three–fourths of them were based on English or technical terms.

Such great French writers as Voltaire, Racine and Victor Hugo were members, but no female writer, such as Madame de Staël or George Sand (pseudonym for Aurore Dupin, later Baroness Dudevant), ever managed to break the Academy's all–male tradition. Finally, in 1980 it chose Marguerite Yourcenar, who at age 16 had begun to publish her string of poems, novels and historical works, culminating in her monumental *Memoirs of Hadrian*. When World War II broke out, she decided to join the faculty of Sarah Lawrence College in New York, and she became an American citizen in 1947. After teaching ten years, she moved to a wood frame house on Mount Desert Island in Maine, where she could escape the literary circles and gossip of Paris and New York, which she detested.

In 1989 the French Academy found itself in the midst of a storm over a proposal to simplify French spelling by, for example, eliminating the circumflex accent in such words as *être*, replacing the "x" on the end of plurals such as *bureaux* with a simple "s," writing "f" instead of "ph" (thus *filosofes*!), and doing away with unexpected double consonants in words like *traditionnel* when the noun is *tradition*. A government survey had revealed that about 20% of the adult population is functionally illiterate, twice the percentage in Britain. One poll of teachers revealed that 90% favor making French easier to write in order to combat both such illiteracy and to enable French to hold its own as a world language.

Proponents of simplification point out that French has in the past been changed by decree and that another change is long overdue since the last one came in 1832 when King Louis–Philippe ordered all public servants to conform strictly to the French Academy's dictionary. As expected, the opposition to change is strong and furious. One teacher warned his colleagues acidly to "keep your filthy hands off our language." Therefore, the Academy ruled in 1991 that changes should not be enforced, but should instead be subject to the "test of time." They have been blithely ignored.

The language watchdogs were stirred again in 1998 when the Academie Française, whose members wear green medieval costumes and carry swords when they meet, stoutly resisted female government ministers having themselves referred to as "Madame *la* Ministre" (the word being masculine). The "immortals" cringed when the education ministry declared that all women's job titles should be linguistically feminized: a female member of parliament should be a député*e*, a lawyer an advocat*e*, an inspector an inspect*rice*. Just how much the French admire their wordsmiths was revealed again on November 23, 1996, when André Malraux, a wartime hero, adventurer, and writer was reinterred in the Panthéon. The ceremony was televised live on national TV, and his creative career was discussed exhaustively in the other media.

Although all citizens of France can speak French, there are many tongues spoken by ethnic minorities, primarily on the periphery of the country. These languages include Provençal, Breton, Corsican, Italian, Catalan, Basque, Flemish and Alsacian. In 1993 the government faced protests because of its refusal to sign the European Charter on Minority Languages, adopted in 1988 by the European Parliament.

France's World Cup championship soccer team in 1998 demonstrated how multicultural France has become. Of 22 players, eight were non–white (most of whom born and bred in France), another four of recent Armenian, Argentine, Kalmyk or Spanish descent, not including the Bretons and Basques on the team. France has always been a magnet for foreigners, and today a third of all Frenchmen have at least one foreign grandparent. In 1991, 11% of residents were foreign–born. Six percent of the population had foreign passports in 1994. This is the same percentage as 25 years ago, but then three–fourths were Europeans compared with only 40% now; 39% of foreigners come

France

from North Africa and 6% from Sub–Saharan Africa.

Partly as a result of frightening unemployment, non–European immigrants face growing rejection and violence in communities where they live in large numbers. Except for music and sports, non–whites are noticeably underrepresented in business, politics, media and the professions. In parliament some non–whites represent overseas French colonies, but only one has a seat from metropolitan France; only one out of 36,560 mayors is not white. Yet they are visible in the streets; mosques spring up next to empty churches, and exotic North African commercial establishments are everywhere. Some Muslim girls wear scarves to school, igniting emotional debates about whether such headgear should be permitted in secular schools. Violence has escalated in crowded schools and bleak housing blocks heavily occupied by North African immigrants; in 1998 alone 8,000 cars were burned by rampaging youths. Eight in ten Frenchmen said in 1999 that urban violence has reached "unprecedented proportions," and many blame foreigners and call on the government to act.

Called *Beurs*, French–born Arabs also face resistance from their own families when they try to integrate into French society. The animosity toward them has helped far–right parties, such as the *National Front*, to make significant electoral gains in those areas. In their defense, an anti–discrimination lobby, *SOS–Racisme* has emerged. It is needed, as a 1993 poll indicated: 94% of the French regard racism to be widespread, and 42% confess to be "a bit" or "quite" racist themselves. There was an element of racism in the public reaction in 1996 to the proposed sale to Korean investors of Thomson SA, a state–owned defense and consumer–electronics firm. The French government has been selling off state–owned companies for a decade, but when 20,000 workers protested the sale in front of the National Assembly, saying that they did not want to be owned by Koreans, it backed down and cancelled the offering. France in the 1990s is also experiencing another outbreak of anti–Semitism, which especially manifested itself in the appalling desecration of Jewish graves at Carpentras.

There is widespread uneasiness over the presence of an estimated 4.5 million immigrants, half of whom are Arabs and blacks. A 1998 poll revealed that almost 60% of respondents thought there were too many Arabs in France (down from 71% five years earlier); over a quarter believed there were too many blacks (down from almost a half), and 15% said there were too many Jews. Four out of ten admitted to being "racist" or "fairly racist," almost twice as many as in Germany, Britain or Italy. Other polls revealed that half no longer feel "at home" in France and want a "large number" of immigrants to leave. Half expressed a belief in the "inequality of the races."

Earlier immigrant groups are often among the opponents of the new arrivals. Portuguese– and Spanish–born workers in the Marseilles area are among Le Pen's most fervent supporters. But the polls

LE PARIS FANTASTIQUE DE McDonald's®

France

show that racist feeling goes far beyond the 15% who vote for the *National Front*. About 28% of those who say they are "racist" or "fairly racist" vote for leftist parties. Le Pen's rantings against "invading Muslim hordes" who allegedly threaten Frenchmen with the same fate as America's "Red Indians—annihilated by immigration," prove so seductive that the leaders of more respectable parties borrowed from his xenophobic vocabulary. Chirac once criticized their "odor" and "noise." Giscard d'Estaing warned of an "invasion" and called for nationality laws based on blood to replace the statutes which grant French citizenship automatically to anyone born on French soil. By 1996, almost a half of respondents said they share some of Le Pen's ideas although two–thirds claimed to have been "shocked" by his comments that races are unequal and that the French national soccer team was not "representative" of the country since so many of the players are non–white.

There is positive news, though. A study in 1998 showed that six in ten white Frenchmen say they have friends among "minority groups." The same number says they would not try to stop their child or sibling from marrying a Muslim. In fact, half of boys and a quarter of girls of Algerian origin in France have their first steady relationship with a white. Fremainville, a tiny farming hamlet just outside Paris, even adopted a black Marianne, the potent bare–breasted symbol of French republican liberty springing from the French Revolution.

The government responded by declaring that France "can no longer be a land of immigration." It introduced policies to stop the influx of foreign workers, refugees, and their families, as well as to tighten citizenship rules, while buckling down to speed the integration of foreigners already there. In 1993 a policy of "zero [illegal] immigration" was proclaimed. In 1995 France opted out of the EU Schengen agreement to abolish all border controls among signatories. In 1996 it sent riot police storming into a French church to remove 300 African immigrants barricaded inside to resist expulsion; ten of them had conducted a hunger strike for 50 days and had to be carried out on stretchers. These policies succeeded in reducing the number of asylum–seekers from 61,000 in 1991 to 20,000 in 1996 (only 3,000 were accepted), and the number of other foreign immigrants was cut by a third. From 400,000 to a million illegal aliens remain underground, despite a dramatic increase in forced deportations. By 1999 the Jospin government had awarded legal status to 80,000 of them.

Religion

Almost nine out of ten Frenchmen are baptized Roman Catholic, and two–thirds describe themselves as Catholic. Since 1905 churches in France have been separated from the state, except in Alsace, Lorraine and the Moselle Department, which then belonged to Germany. In these areas, church–state relations are governed by the Concordat which Napoleon I signed with the Vatican in 1801. Protestants constitute barely 2% of the population, but their influence far outweighs their numbers in business, the civil service and intelligencia. Three of 14 prime ministers, including Lionel Jospin, Michel Rocard and Couve de Murville, are Protestants. In the French public mind, Protestantism is almost synonymous with austerity and moral rigor.

Fewer than one in ten French still goes to Mass regularly. A 1997 poll by the Catholic newspaper, *La Croix*, indicated that two–thirds of the youth believe that the church has little influence on their lives. Because of the principle of "secularity," whereby the state must be strictly separated from religion, the government's involvement in the Pope's visit to France in 1996 sparked months of controversy and hostility. Also, many French resent any attempt by the Catholic Church to interfere in their private lives. Contraception is widely practiced, and abortion is common. By 1994 the number of weddings had fallen to 254,000, which is 40% fewer than in 1972, and only half those weddings took place in church, compared with almost all of them only a quarter century earlier. France now has the lowest marriage rate in Europe after Scandinavia. In 1998, one in seven couples lived together without marriage, a number seven times higher than a couple of decades ago and double the proportion a decade ago; only 7% of French respondents found such an arrangement "living in sin."

With the average French woman bearing only 1.8 children in the mid–1990s, the country faces the prospect of a declining native population. More than 40% of all babies are now born out of wedlock, the highest rates in Europe outside the Nordic countries. Clearly illegitimacy no longer carries a stigma. When President Chirac proudly announced in 1996 the birth of his first grandchild, no one seemed to care that his daughter Claude was not married to the child's father, an ex–judo champion turned television presenter.

EDUCATION

Control over the school system is concentrated in Paris. Education is free and compulsory between the ages of six and 16, and approximately five out of six children attend public schools. Mitterrand stirred up much controversy by promising to do away with private schools, which receive state subsidies, and to create a unified, secular school system. A half million persons protested in the streets against this policy, the largest public demonstration in French history. Such widespread protests prompted him to withdraw the contentious private school bill in 1984.

From ages five to 11 children attend elementary school, and then they spend four years in an "intermediate school," called a "college." After this, they proceed to a high school, called a "lycée," which provides either vocational training or a baccalaureate degree leading to university study. In 1998, 75% were still in school pursuing the "bac," double the proportion only a decade earlier. Over half pass it.

The examination for the baccalaureate is a traditional intellectual one, and France is one of the few countries which still includes philosophy as one of its obligatory high school subjects.

About 700,000 students are enrolled in the 57 universities or special advanced schools, and about a third of these students are in the 13 universities in the Paris region. In 1968 a fourth of 18–year–olds and 4% of 20–year–olds were in a school or university; in 1990 the comparable figures stood at 55% and 22%. The rapid growth of enrollment has brought severe overcrowding. Graduates find that their degrees are now worth less and that there are too few jobs for them after graduation.

The unemployment line never threatens graduates of the elitist *Grandes Ecoles*, who are selected by highly competitive nation–wide examinations (*concours*) following two further years of intensive preparation in the Lycée after the "bac." Many students at the universities still suffer from a sort of second–class status, as they watch the best jobs being filled by graduates from the *Grandes Ecoles*. Some of the best university students are admitted to these highly selective institutions, which are very prestigious and produce an elite in teaching, industry, government and the armed forces. In 1794 the military *Ecole Polytechnique* was established to train top public officials. Following the military debacle of 1870, the *Ecole des Sciences Politiques* (called "Sciences–Po"), which offers advanced training in political science and economics, was created to improve the quality of senior civil servants.

After the defeat in 1940 and the shame of Vichy, the *Ecole Nationale d'Administration* (*ENA*, whose graduates are called *Enarches*), which accepts fewer than 100 students (a fourth to a third female) by examination from the other *Grandes Ecoles* each year for the 27–month program, was set up to train elite administrators who would put the interests of the state above their own. All were in Paris until 1992 when ENA was moved to Strasbourg. Study at ENA is particularly important to those persons aspiring to top civil service positions.

Presently about two–thirds of such offices are held by Enarches, who form a highly useful informal network of contacts for each other. Among its graduates were *all* the major contenders for the presidency in 1995—Jacques Chirac, Lionel Jospin, and Edouard Balladur—as well as former President Valery Giscard d'Estaing. Prime Minister Lionel Jospin and five out of seven of his predecessors are Enarches. The mayor of Montpellier spoke bitterly of the influential Enarches: "France is still run by civil servants. There is no difference between a socialist Enarche and a neo–Gaullist Enarche. They are intelligent, incorrupt and absolutely convinced they are right. The country is run by thousands of little Robespierres." One conservative politician, Alain Madelin, even said in 1997: "Ireland has the IRA, Spain has ETA, Italy the mafia, but France has ENA."

In addition, there are the *Ecoles Normales Supérieures*, such as Rue de Bac and St. Cloud for men, Sèvres and Fontenay for women, and ENSET for men and women. They train the top Lycée and university professors, who must pass a rigorous final examination called the *Agrégation*. Finally, there are the *Hautes Etudes Commerciales*, (*HEC*) and other business–oriented schools, the *Ecole des Mines,* and similarly specialized schools, such as the military academy at Saint–Cyr.

In protest against underfunding, overcrowding, decrepit buildings, insufficient security at inner–city schools, and bleak employment prospects, especially in non–technical fields, thousands of lycée and university students again took to the streets in 1998 and engaged in pitched bloody battles with the police. One 15–year–old demonstrator was killed. The education minister admitted that the system is "archaic," but he pleaded for patience until reforms could be enacted. Teachers sympathize because half their classes have over 30 pupils, and some have over 40. One result is that one in four teachers requests a transfer or job change every year.

The American film, *Dead Poets Society*, which portrayed a rebellion against a hidebound educational system, had a profound effect on debates in France concerning reform of the school system. The government proposed reforms to humanize the gruelling "bac." A major stumbling block for change has been the resistance of powerful teaching unions. In the meantime, many French ask why their once excellent educational system is soaking up more and more resources and producing students with less knowledge.

The Press

Financial difficulties have steadily reduced the number of daily newspapers to less than a hundred. The most widely read are the conservative *France Soir* and *Le Figaro*, and the moderately leftist, intellectual *Le Monde*, all from Paris, and *Ouest–France* published in Rennes. In order to halt the growing concentration of the French press and, as critics charge, to limit the influence of conservative publishing magnate Robert Hersant, who died in 1996, the *Socialist* government approved in 1984 a law prohibiting publishers from owning both Parisian and regional newspapers, and from controlling more than 15% of either Parisian or regional circulation. Many educated French read certain political and economic weeklies, such as *L'Express, Le Nouvel Observateur, Le Point, L'Evenement du Jeudi* and *Le Canard Enchaîné*, which offer more in–depth analysis, criticism and, in the case of *Le Canard Enchaîné*, satire. Many French have turned increasingly to television and radio for news.

As a result, newspaper readership has dropped over three million since 1970. Even *Le Monde* was rapidly losing money and circulation; it is owned and operated by its employees and improved in sales and financial condition by 1985, making its format more attractive and by selling and leasing back its headquarters building near the Opera. More and more of its critical readers had turned to the intellectual leftist newspaper *Liberation,* whose daily circulation has doubled since 1981 to 130,000. Ninety percent of all households own television sets, and the average French family spends 18 hours per week watching television, a fourth of which is spent viewing newscasts.

Until 1984 the state had a monopoly on television and radio. Radio programs are produced by the Radio–France company, and French government holding companies partially own three independent radio stations (Radio Luxembourg, Europe No. 1 and Radio Monte Carlo), which broadcast from outside of France. Radio–France and the state–owned television companies are financed by annual license fees paid by those persons owning sets.

Critics charge that these companies, although nominally independent and responsible for their own programming, have been manipulated from the Elysées Palace. Mitterrand proposed reducing government influence over them by placing control into the hands of an independent board of directors which would include government officials, media specialists and private citizens. In fact, little has changed in the management of the state–owned media.

The big changes in 1984 came with the legalization of private radio and television stations. So many private radio stations

A farmyard near Tours

France

had cropped up that they could no longer be controlled. By legalizing them, the state broadcasting monopoly had been so irreparably punctured that it was only a matter of time until private television was permitted. More than 800 private radio stations exist already, providing a voice for all kinds of minority interests. Eventually, about 80 local TV stations will be set up around the country. In 1987 the government took another momentous step by selling the largest of the old state networks (TF1) to the private sector. This was the first sell–off by any government of a state–owned TV network. The state kept two of the six channels.

The Arts

France continues to be a land rich and creative, and performing arts, although no longer occupying undisputably primary position in the world, are topnotch. Its artists have also declined from their pinnacle, but their past greatness is preserved for the world to admire in such great French museums as the Louvre, the Musée d'Orsay, the Beaubourg, and the Picasso Museum. Traditions date back hundreds of years in literature, art, music and the theatre. The writings of Voltaire and Rousseau are landmarks in rich French enlightenment. The music of father and son François Couperin were classic; that of Frederic Chopin, Jules Massenet, Camille Saint–Saens and Claude Debussy richly romantic. During the Third Republic before World War I, Paris was enriched by impressionism in art, e.g. Renoir, Monet, Degas, and the reaction to it (Bracque, Picasso, cubism or fauvism). During the same period there was the positivism of Auguste Comte, the *élan vital* of Henry Bergson, in medicine the discoveries of Louis Pasteur and in physics the discoveries of Pierre and Marie Curie. In 1988 Maurice Allais became the first Frenchman to win the Nobel prize for economics, for his study of markets and efficient utilization of resources.

The job of French minister of culture is one of great influence and patronage. Today, the arts in France, as almost everything else, receive state subsidies and are highly concentrated in Paris. To try to spread French cultural activity into the provinces, de Gaulle's minister of culture, André Malraux (himself a leading French writer and art critic, who incurred the wrath of Parisian traditionalists by ordering that all public buildings in Paris be sandblasted to eliminate centuries of soot which had accumulated on them) created cultural centers in ten provincial cities, financed and operated jointly by the central government and the municipalities. These centers are designed to promote artistic creativity and to bring the performing arts into the provinces. They also serve as places for discussions on contemporary problems. Despite such attempts, many persons still speak with some justification of "Paris and the desert."

FRENCH REVOLUTION IN RETROSPECT

The year 1989 marked the 200th anniversary of the French Revolution, and 5,000 events around the country commemorated this great convulsion. It created the opportunity for Frenchmen to look both back into their past and forward into their future. Not all Frenchmen cherish the spirit of 1789, as was shown by Catholic counter–demonstrations to remember martyrs in the Place de la Concorde on August 15, 1989, the production of a movie called *Vent de Galerne* which depicts the savage repression of peasant rebels in the Vendée, the tracing of descendants of the 3,000 persons executed in Lyons by the Jacobins, and the widespread apathy in many parts of the country.

There has been a fundamental rethinking of the causes and meaning of the revolution, and many simplistic explanations have been replaced by a much more complex picture. Some myths were corrected: only seven prisoners were freed at the Bastille; execution by guillotine often took several "chops," and only 10% of those beheaded were nobles; most of the revolution's victims were shot, burned or drowned, rather than beheaded; the statement attributed to Marie Antoinette, "Let them eat cake!", appeared in Rousseau's *Confessions* at least two years before Marie arrived in France in 1770.

Frenchmen have even become more ambiguous about their heros and villains. Polls indicated that the era's most revered character is the Marquis de Lafayette, who broke with the Jacobins and fled France. Also, a televised re–enactment of Louis XVI's trial with the ending left open so that viewers could decide his guilt or innocence produced astounding conclusions: only 27% of viewers favored beheading him, versus 55% who voted to acquit him. It is therefore not surprising that the government decided to focus as little as possible on the bloody elements of the past and almost exclusively on the idealistic achievements of the revolution which have undeniable relevance for France's future, such as the Declaration of the Rights of Man and the Citizen. This focus on human rights and the question of what it means to be a citizen in a free and modern republic relate directly to France's future as a multi–racial, multi–cultural society. Some citizens are also beginning to ask whether France needs to have such a brutal national anthem, which calls on them to "drench our fields" with the enemy's "tainted blood." According to a July 14, 1992, poll, 40% of the French find the lyrics too bloodthirsty, but 75% are staunchly opposed to altering the hallowed verses.

FUTURE

All past attempts to put France on a leftist course failed, as did Mitterrand's. A popular Prime Minister Lionel Jospin, who still had high approval rating above 60%, was elected on a left–wing platform, but he pursues a social–democratic course that he calls "left–wing realism." The *Socialist* government finds itself politically limited by global competition and by France's commitments to the EU, which require a tight hold on the budget deficit, down to 2.9% in 1999. Former Prime Minister and now National Assembly President Laurent Fabius, who was acquitted in a blood–tainting scandal, commented: "The left should not expect to be able to tear up every rule in the economic book. It needs to keep certain realities in mind. International competition is a fact. Our capacity to adapt will be decisive." It is doing rather well.

The central problem for the new government will be the same as for the old: how to reconcile France's European obligations with its chronic unemployment. Since 1981 France has changed governments five times. Each time the new government promises to make jobs its "priority of priorities," and every time it is thrown out of power because it fails in this. The Jospin government faces a formidable dilemma in attempting to reduce persistent and growing unemployment, now 11.5% (more than twice that for young people), while keeping the deficit low.

The outbreak of strikes and other violence shows how little leeway the government has. In 1998–9 truck drivers blocked highways again. Railway workers shut down the train system. Air France pilots disrupted the opening of the World Cup soccer championship, and their mechanics struck to show displeasure over the terms of the new 35–hour workweek. Bus drivers in the South stopped driving to protest their work conditions and the robberies and physical abuse to which they are subjected. Pig farmers demonstrated against low pork prices. Jobless protested to get a $600 bonus in their unemployment checks while retirees marched to lament their pensions and social security. Teachers and librarians stopped working while students demonstrated in the streets. Journalists struck to rescue their tax breaks. Doctors, dentists, ski instructors, cabbage growers and cognac makers also put down their tools and took to the streets. Even Eiffel Tower elevator operators struck, as did the 40 actors who impersonate Disney characters at Disneyland outside Paris. They carried signs reading "Mickey, you are not the boss. Scrooge is running the show!" Strikes and demonstrations became so frequent that Paris's morning newspapers publish maps of zones to avoid because people are marching in the streets, or because trains or subways are not running.

In 1998 Jospin gave his countrymen a dose of economic realism, saying that the budget deficit must be controlled and welfare payments capped. "I want a society of work, not a society of assistance." This seemed like a reversal for a politician who had been elected by opposing austerity. Most French view American capitalism as the law of the jungle; even conservative President Chirac declared: "I do not want that model." In 1998 Jospin travelled to the U.S. with Finance Minister Dominique Strauss–Kahn and Education and Research Minister Claude Alègre, both of whom have taught in the U.S. The *Socialist* prime minister returned saying that "my view of the United States has changed" and that France could learn much about America's economic dynamism, research and innovation, competitive spirit and capacity for renewal.

Jospin still aims to "create more jobs," and by 1999 he had created 150,000 of the promised 350,000 public–sector jobs for young people (dropping his campaign pledge of 700,000 jobs). He maintains his popularity by sticking with this and other campaign promises, such as raising the minimum wage by 4%. His government lowered the work week to 35 hours with no loss of pay by the year 2000, but the unexpected consequences of this were not popular. Although he had pledged to stop, or at least slow down, the privatization of industries, he organized the biggest French privatization ever, selling off a quarter of France Télécom and 49% of Air France. In fact, his government sold more state assets in its first 18 months than the previous conservative government had in its two years. The government's efforts are aided by some positive economic news: booming exports, a positive trade balance, a thriving technology sector, and low inflation.

Jospin entered office promising open and honest government, and the judiciary has been energetic in investigating the kind of corruption that Frenchmen used to consider acceptable on the part of politicians. After all, Mitterrand's son, Jean–Christophe, had run the president's Africa office; ex–Culture Minister Jack Lang had employed his own wife as his official adviser, and President Chirac's daughter is paid as his chief publicist. A former prime minister and two ex–ministers were tried in March 1999 in connection with a scandal over HIV–contaminated blood, and one of the ministers was convicted of criminal neglect. At the same time, France's first female prime minister and one of the country's two members of the European Commission, Edith Cresson, engaged in such blatant misconduct (such as hiring her dentist as her "science adviser") that the European Parliament ultimately prompted a mass resignation of all Commissioners in Brussels. Another former prime minister, Alain Juppé, is under investigation for charges that he let public money be used illegally to pay salaries of dozens of Gaullist party officials. Roland Dumas, head of the Constitutional Court, the supreme guardian of France's laws and institutions, was placed under investigation and had to step down in the face of charges that he had received more than $10 million in gratuities from the former state oil giant, Elf, while he was foreign minister. The funds were allegedly channeled to him through his mistress, Christine Deviers–Joncour, herself under formal investigation, who described the sordid affair in her best–selling book, *The Whore of the Republic*.

It is very difficult to change France. President Chirac, whose approval ratings reached 79% for his handling of the Kosovo crisis and for his willingness to work constructively with *Socialist* Prime Minister Jospin, has seen his responsibilities shrink to little more than foreign and defense policy. He spoke in 1997 of the "extreme difficulty of changing anything at all in a profoundly conservative and fossilized country." This is not the first time that France has experienced "cohabitation," whereby the president is from one political camp and the prime minister and cabinet are from another. However, this is the first time that such a divided executive might last a full five years. In fact, polls in 1998 indicated that a majority likes the existence of such a system of checks and balances that honestly reflects the divisions within the French public.

Finally, Notre Dame's gargoyles . . . possibly pondering the mysteries of French politics
Courtesy: Jon Markham Morrow

The BENELUX Nations

Belgium, the Netherlands and Luxembourg are located at the crossroads of Western Europe. Although they are collectively called "BENELUX," a word derived from the first letters of each country's name, these small countries have developed differing traditions, national characters and problems. Still, they have many things in common, and it is no accident that they cooperate with each other more closely than any other nations of the world. In fact, their example of international cooperation and their steady encouragement of tighter European integration have made them the core and motor for greater unity. The vast majority of the EU's institutions are located in Belgium and Luxembourg.

All three countries are very small and have no natural frontiers which could serve as barriers to unwanted intruders. They have therefore suffered recurrent invasion by all the great European powers. For a century and a half they tried to keep themselves out of the grips of the major powers by declaring a policy of neutrality. But two disastrous world wars in the 20th century, which spared only the Netherlands from 1914 to 1918, left such a policy and the three countries in shambles. No one can easily forget the lines which the poet John McCrae wrote after visiting the Flemish battlefields: "In Flanders fields the poppies blow between the crosses, row by row. . . ."

Having paid a heavy price for their neutrality, all three countries became founding members of NATO in 1949. Its political headquarters are now located on the outskirts of Brussels, and its military headquarters, the Supreme Headquarters of the Allied Powers in Europe (SHAPE), is located outside of Mons, Belgium.

The Netherlands and Belgium have the highest population density of all Europe. All three have great numbers of foreign workers who bring both needed labor and social problems with them. These countries are not particularly rich in raw materials, but they have productive economies which have provided standards of living and social welfare systems for their populations which are almost unmatched in the world. Their central location and access to the sea made them prosperous trading nations, and the ports of Rotterdam and Antwerp are the largest and most active in Europe. With relatively small populations and high prosperity, these countries are heavily dependent upon trade, and, therefore, upon economic and political conditions beyond their borders. Roughly half of these countries' GNPs results from foreign trade. This heavy volume is an economic blessing as well as a possible liability for the future.

To help secure their trade, they were pioneers in economic unions. In 1922 Belgium and Luxembourg formed the Belgium Luxembourg Economic Union (BLEU), which made the two countries a unit for importing and exporting purposes. It also established a unified railway, customs area and currency for the two countries. Luxembourg does coin and print money below one hundred francs for local circulation, but Belgian currency remains dominant in both countries. The three countries' governments– in–exile in London in 1944 formed a customs union called BENELUX, which was later extended to include even non–customs matters. Because of the striking difference in postwar recovery, BENELUX did not come into effect until January 1948.

In 1952 they were founding members with France, West Germany and Italy of the European Coal and Steel Community (ECSC), with headquarters located in Luxembourg. Not only was it a farsighted idea to share these commodities, so crucial for heavy industry, rather than to risk fighting over them, but the ECSC gave these nations the practice in economic cooperation needed to convince the six that a bold move to create a united Europe could succeed. The six signed the Treaty of Rome in 1957 and in 1958 the European Economic Community (Common Market) came into existence. Later the Community grew, and its name was changed first to European Community (EC) and then in 1993 to European Union (EU) in order to emphasize that the union was someday to become a political one, as well as an economic one. None tried harder than the BENELUX countries to keep the idea of a united Europe alive in the 1960s, when the six were seriously split over the question of British entry.

All three countries are constitutional, parliamentary monarchies, whose monarchs are relatively popular, though not powerful. As modern constitutional monarchs, they "reign but do not rule." In contrast to the monarchy in Great Britain, which can be traced back more than a

The BENELUX Nations

thousand years, the BENELUX monarchies are young. The oldest, in the Netherlands, dates back to 1813. Throughout the centuries these small countries have been tossed back and forth among the great powers of Europe and have sometimes been forced together and sometimes split apart. A quick glance at their history shows why they have so much in common and are nevertheless different from each other.

Early History

The early history of these three countries is so intertwined that it is best considered by grouping them together.

About a half century before Christ, after a long and destructive campaign, the Roman legions conquered the tenacious Celtic tribes, including the Belgeai and Treveri. In his commentary *The Gallic Wars*, Julius Caeser used the name "Belgium" to refer to all the territory we now call the BENELUX countries. This area, especially what is today Belgium and Luxembourg, was dominated for more than 300 years by the Romans, who built roads and villas and introduced agriculture, especially vineyards and fruit orchards. They also brought Christianity to the area, but this did not begin to flourish until the 6th and 7th centuries.

When Attila the Hun invaded what is now Germany, Germanic tribes were thrown into the Low Countries (the Netherlands) in about 300. Two centuries later another Germanic tribe, the Franks, invaded the area and established a linguistic frontier which exists today in the middle of what is now Belgium. North of the line the Germanic tongues evolved into the Dutch language and into Flemish, a Dutch dialect spoken in northern Belgium. South of the line, vulgarized Latin, which developed into French, was spoken. Thus in Belgium the Latin and Germanic worlds met face to face and presented Belgium with a problem which many centuries later threatened to tear the country apart.

In the 8th and 9th centuries the entire territory which had been fragmented into many duchies, principalities and other political units, became a part of Charlemagne's empire. This was the time when the political center of gravity in Europe shifted from the Mediterranean to the northwestern regions. His great empire fell apart soon after his death, and for several centuries the BENELUX people saw their land converted into a constant battlefield between French and German contenders for control. During this time the crusades opened up trade with the Orient, and especially Belgium experienced a flowering of trade and urban development. The beautiful canal city of Brugge became a wealthy city of trade and the arts. In the 15th century, the Dukes of Burgundy, who were among the most powerful in Europe, began to acquire control over what is now Belgium and Luxembourg by means of conquest, marriage or land purchase.

Only the Netherlands was able to resist the Burgundian encroachment. As a country whose development had been retarded by its preoccupation with fighting back the sea, the Netherlands was not a very tempting target for Burgundian expansion anyway. At the end of the 15th century the last descendent, Mary of Burgundy, married Maximilian of Austria, and the Burgundian holdings in the area passed into the Hapsburg family. Their son, Philip the Handsome, married the Spanish princess, Juana of Castile; Spain and Spanish America also came under Hapsburg control.

A son born of this union in 1500 in the Flemish city of Ghent was destined to become one of Europe's greatest rulers. He became King of Spain in 1516 and the Holy Roman Emperor in 1519. He was Charles V, and by 1543 he had unified all of what is now the BENELUX area, except the county of Liège, which led a separate existence until the 18th century. Charles

The Holy Roman Emperor, Charles V

The BENELUX Nations

ruled his far-flung empire from Brussels, a city which had been established in 979 on the islands of the Senne River, which was then called "Bruocsella." His reign was a time of great economic prosperity, artistic and intellectual bloom for the "Seventeen Provinces," as the Luxembourg area was then called. This was the time of the great humanist, Erasmus of Rotterdam, of Mercator, the most widely known cartographer in the world, of the painters van Eyck and Pieter Breugal.

The unity of the Seventeen Provinces might have survived if the Reformation which Martin Luther unleashed in 1519 had not divided Europe and with it the Low Countries. Charles V abdicated in 1555 in favor of his son, Philip II who had been raised in Spain; he decided to rule the empire from Madrid, leaving the administration of the Seventeen Provinces to governors. He was, however, determined to defend the Catholic faith, and he was cruel and inflexible in attempting to suppress the Protestant movements, which in its Calvinist form, was particularly strong in the Netherlands. Protestant resistance in the northern provinces was led by William of Orange-Nassau. Because Spain was so severely weakened by its continuous struggles against England and France during the second half of the 16th century, the Netherlands was able to secure its independence in 1581.

Until Napoleon's conquests in the 1790s the Dutch took control of their own destiny, while the Belgians and Luxembourgers continued to be dominated by other powers. In order to give the latter a sense of autonomy, Philip gave the southern provinces to his daughter, the Archduchess Isabella, and her husband, the Archduke Albert of Austria. This was a relatively happy time when the painter Peter Paul Rubens reached the height of his creativity. When Albert and Isabella died childless, the provinces reverted to Spain in 1621, and until 1713 the Hapsburgs fought over control of the area.

In one campaign in 1695, the French Marshal Villeroy, under orders of Louis XIV, bombarded the beautiful Grand Place in Brussels with its majestic town hall, built around 1400; it survived only with its tower and its thickest walls. This disaster merely stiffened the courage and determination of the Brussels population, which began the very next day restoring the structure. The best artistic and architectural talent in the city joined in recreating one of man's greatest architectural treasures. Jan Van Ruysbroeck, the city's master mason, rebuilt the town hall. Wishing to retain the foundation and porch of the old bell tower while extending the new walls as far as possible, he placed the main portal of the town hall off center with the central axis of the tower. Legend wrongly has it that he threw himself to his death when he discovered the error, but the "error" was in fact intentional. The Grand Place remains the vibrant heart of the city and has always been a favorite subject for painters and poets. It is a place for open-air markets, public meetings, political assemblies, royal receptions and coronations. Earlier it was the favorite place for launching revolutions and for public executions. Each year on a summer evening the Grand Place is transformed into its medieval setting for a historical procession called the "Ommegang."

Both Luxembourg and Belgium passed into the hands of the Austrians, who renamed Belgium the "Austrian Netherlands" and who ruled over these provinces until 1794–95, when French troops snatched them away. The Austrians had exercised a benevolent dictatorship, but some Luxembourgers, Flemings and Walloons were infected by the fever of revolution emanating from France and welcomed the changes which came with the French republican troops. Belgium fell to the French in 1794 and the following year Luxembourg and the Netherlands, which had been greatly weakened by its series of wars against England, were conquered by French revolutionary forces.

The French occupation brought fundamental changes to the Netherlands, which had been ruled by an enlightened oligarchy, with a high official called a stadholder (not a monarch!) at the top. Although it was not a modern democracy in that power was not exercised by leaders who had been elected by universal suffrage, the Dutch republic had nevertheless been one of the most democratic countries in Europe with the possible exception of Switzerland. The old republic had been highly decentralized, with each province stressing its independent powers. The new regime which the French created and called "The Batavian Republic," named after one of the tribes which had populated the country in the Roman period and which had revolted against Roman domination, was highly centralized in conformity with the French constitution.

The Napoleonic Code of laws and the selection of members of parliament on the basis of limited but free elections were also introduced. The Dutch grew restive under French control, especially after the Batavian Republic was abolished and Louis Napoleon, the brother of the French Emperor, was made King of Holland in 1806. Quarrels with his brother forced Louis to abdicate in 1810, but only after he had tried unsuccessfully to have his son, who later became Napoleon III of France, crowned in his place. The Netherlands was annexed directly into the French Empire in 1810. Again, Napoleon's reversals gave the Dutch the chance to reassert their independence. In 1813, after Napoleon's defeat in the Battle of Leipzig, the son of the last Dutch stadholder who had fled to England, landed at Scheveningen, not far from the Hague, and was proclaimed William I of the House of Orange-Nassau, King of the Netherlands. For the first time the Netherlands became a monarchy with a Dutch monarch on the throne. Dutch troops took an active part in the final defeat of Napoleon.

In late 1794 French troops besieged the fortress of Luxembourg, which did not fall until mid-1795. It was annexed to France in the fall; French rule was very unpopular at first, but Napoleon was gradually able to smooth out many problems. When the French left the Duchy in 1814 they had left many positive and lasting gifts behind: the idea of equality, centralized and efficient administration and the Napoleonic Code.

The French were at first widely greeted in Belgium as liberators, and the introduction of the Napoleonic Code and an efficient, centralized administration was generally seen as an improvement over the old regime. Almost no one seemed to have realized at the time that decentralization would have helped Belgium's language groups to live together more harmoniously in a unified Belgian state. But the seemingly endless Napoleonic wars soon sapped the Belgians' enthusiasm. After Napoleon began suffering disastrous reversals, especially in Russia in 1812, the Belgians joined the enemies of France. It was outside Brussels near a small town named Waterloo that the little dictator was defeated for the last time.

When the great powers of Europe met at the Congress of Vienna in 1814–15, they combined the Netherlands, Belgium and Luxembourg to form the "Kingdom of the United Netherlands," with the monarch William I as King. The Belgians were distrusted by the European leaders, who suspected that they had supported the French too enthusiastically. They believed that the Belgians, therefore, needed to be controlled by the Dutch King. Further, the East Belgian cantons of Eupen, Malmedy and Saint Vith were ceded to Prussia, whose borders had been moved as far west as possible in order to prevent any future eastward French expansion.

The union of the three countries did not last long. In 1830 the sparks of revolution flying from Paris landed in Brussels. The overwhelmingly Catholic Flemings and Walloons (Belgians who speak French) sensed religious discrimination by the predominantly Protestant Calvinist Dutch, despite the tradition of religious tolerance in the Netherlands.

The BENELUX Nations

Although it was the only thing which drew Flemings and Walloons together, Catholicism was enough to unify them against the Dutch. Such religious unity was later to prove the weakest of glue to hold the state of Belgium together. The use of Dutch in the Flemish area of the north and in Brussels had been resented by the economically and culturally more influential French–speaking Walloons in the South. This determination to elevate the French language above Dutch also was later to create extremely serious problems for this bilingual country. The eruption occurred in 1830 after the performance of an opera with a liberation theme—after a brief skirmish in Brussels, Dutch troops withdrew and a provisional government proclaimed independence within three months. Seeing the usefulness of a buffer state on the European continent, the British announced that they would thenceforth guarantee Belgium's neutrality.

A liberal constitution, which is still in force, was proclaimed placing sovereignty in the people and providing for a constitutional monarchy. A German prince, Leopold I of Saxe–Coburg who happened also to be a British citizen, became king in 1831. Since sovereignty was placed in the hands of the people, there was no doubt that the Parliament, as the representative of the Belgian people, would be superior to the monarch. French was also declared to be the new country's official language.

The Dutch reacted to these events by attempting to invade Belgium, but the French and British announced their determination not to allow the Dutch to reassert their control. At a London Conference of 1831, a border between the Netherlands and Belgium was drawn, but this settlement pleased neither the Belgians, who claimed about half of Luxembourg, nor the Dutch, whose king wanted no settlement at all which would reduce the size of his kingdom. Finally, the Treaty of Twenty–Four Articles, signed in London in 1839, granted the Dutch a slice of northern Belgium. Belgium, in turn, was compensated through a grant of about half of Luxembourg's territory. Further, the great European powers guaranteed the neutrality of Belgium and Luxembourg. This settlement finally satisfied all but the Luxembourgers, who saw their already tiny state reduced to about one-fourth of its pre-1815 size.

The Congress of Vienna had made Luxembourg an autonomous Duchy with the Dutch King as the Grand Duke, but Luxembourg lost all its territory east of the Moselle, Sure and Our Rivers. The congress also made Luxembourg a member of the German Confederation and granted the Prussians the right to man the fortress in the capital city in order to be able to keep a closer eye on the recently defeated French. This arrangement meant that Luxembourg was wide open to Dutch royal ideas, Prussian military demands and Belgium's liberal cravings.

At first the Dutch King ruled in a rather authoritarian way, and when the Belgians rebelled against Dutch rule in 1830 most Luxembourgers outside the capital city also arose. Although they were unable to establish their independence, Luxembourgers were gradually able to establish separate institutions and administrations. Political autonomy was granted in 1839 and in 1848 the country received a liberal constitution similar to that of Belgium. The Dutch became more benevolent rulers and cooperated in Luxembourg's movement toward democracy and independence. Finally, in 1867 the Treaty of London, drawn up in an attempt to reconcile differences between Bismarck of Germany and Napoleon III of France, proclaimed Luxembourg an independent and neutral country. Only a year later Luxembourg adopted a constitution which in revised form remains in force. Upon the insistence of Napoleon III, the Prussians withdrew from the Duchy and the fortress was razed.

The only disappointment for the Luxembourgers was that the Dutch King remained the Grand Duke. However, when in 1890 there were no male heirs to the Dutch throne, Adolf of Nassau, whose family was related to the Dutch ruling family, became the Grand Duke of Luxembourg and chose to reside in Luxembourg City. Nevertheless, the close historical ties with the Netherlands continue to be symbolized by the fact that the two countries have almost exactly the same flag.

From 1890 on, all three BENELUX countries have been fully independent and sovereign states. Proximity, economic interests and political values continue to bind these three democracies very closely together.

The Monnaie Theater, Brussels, where the torch of liberation was lit

The Kingdom of the Netherlands

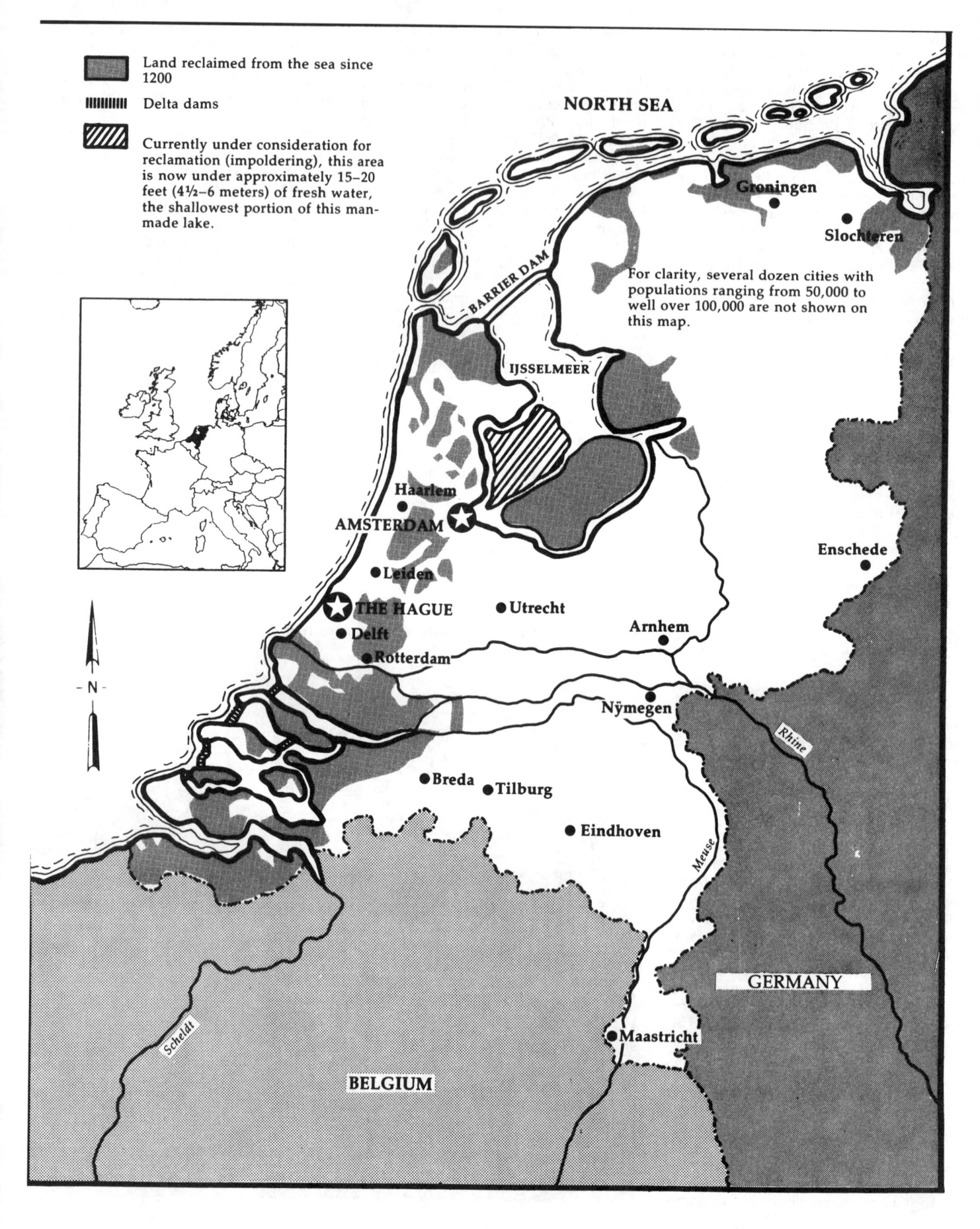

- ▬ Land reclaimed from the sea since 1200
- ▮▮▮ Delta dams
- ▨ Currently under consideration for reclamation (impoldering), this area is now under approximately 15–20 feet (4½–6 meters) of fresh water, the shallowest portion of this man-made lake.

NORTH SEA

BARRIER DAM

IJSSELMEER

For clarity, several dozen cities with populations ranging from 50,000 to well over 100,000 are not shown on this map.

- Groningen
- Slochteren
- Haarlem
- ★ AMSTERDAM
- Leiden
- ★ THE HAGUE
- Delft
- Rotterdam
- Utrecht
- Arnhem
- Enschede
- Nÿmegen
- Breda
- Tilburg
- Eindhoven
- Maastricht

Rhine

Meuse

Scheldt

BELGIUM

GERMANY

N

196

The Netherlands

Area: 16,163 sq. mi. (41,863 sq. km., twice the size of New Jersey and one-half the size of Virginia).
Population: 15.6 million.
Capital City: Amsterdam (Pop. 1,000,000, estimated). but the seat of government is The Hague (Pop. 530,000, estimated).
Climate: Temperate, with mild winters, cool summers.
Neighboring Countries: Germany (East); Belgium (South); England (West, 90 miles across the North Sea).
Official Languages: Dutch, Frisian.
Other Principal Tongues: English, German.
Ethnic Background: Frisian in the North, Saxon in the East and central part of the nation, Frankish south of the rivers.
Principal Religions: Roman Catholic (about 40%), Dutch Reformed—Lutheran (about 36%). About 24% profess belief in no religion.
Main Exports: Petroleum products and natural gas, chemicals and plastics, machinery and electronics, agricultural products, largely dairy, processed foods, fish and fish products.
Main Imports: Cotton, base metals and ores, pulp, pulpwood, lumber, feedgrains, edible oils.
Major Trading Partners: EU (76%), Europe as a whole (85%), Germany(26%), Belgium, Luxembourg, France, UK, U.S. (6%).
Currency: Guilder.
National Day: April 30th, Anniversary of the Investiture of Queen Beatrix. Liberation day, May 5th, is celebrated every year.
Chief of State: Her Majesty Queen Beatrix (b. 1938), married Claus George Willem Geert von Amsberg on March 10, 1966, a German diplomat who was proclaimed H.R.H. Prince of the Netherlands a few weeks before the wedding.
Heir Apparent: His Royal Highness Crown Prince Willem–Alexander (b. 1967).
Head of Government: Wim Kok, Prime Minister (since 1994).
National Flag: Three horizontal stripes of red, white and blue, almost identical to the flag of Luxembourg, which has a *pale* blue stripe.

Benjamin Franklin once said: "In love of liberty and in the defense of it, Holland has been our example." Indeed, when the Dutch declared their independence from Spain in 1581, they justified their act in words which in some ways are very reminiscent of those which Thomas Jefferson wrote in the American Declaration of Independence almost 200 years later: "As it is apparent to all that a prince is constituted by God to be the ruler of the people . . . and whereas God did not create the people slaves to their prince, to obey his commands, whether right or wrong, but rather the prince for the sake of the subjects. . . . And when he does not behave thus, but on the contrary oppresses them . . . they may not only disallow his authority, but legally proceed to the choice of another prince for their defense . . ." Although their independence was not recognized internationally until 1648, the Dutch had already taken command of their own destiny and established a republic based on the ideas that government should be limited and directed exclusively toward the well-being of the people.

A thousand-year struggle against the sea helped to shape a people which are hard-working, persistent, efficient and imaginative. It is a fact of history that nations have expanded their borders at the expense of other nations. The Netherlands, which even the Dutch call "Holland" though North and South Holland were traditionally merely the richest two provinces in the country, is one of the few nations whose expansion has been at the expense of the sea, not of other peoples. According to an old Dutch saying, "the Lord made heaven and earth, but the Dutch made Holland!" For centuries the Dutch built dunes and dykes to hold back the sea. Since the 15th century they constructed windmills everywhere to convert the sea winds into energy to pump water back into the sea. Today, almost one-third of the country is below sea level, and if the Dutch were not constantly vigilant, about one-half of the country would disappear under water or become unusable for any purpose. It is precisely in that half that more than 60% of the Dutch live and work and that most of Holland's industry is located. The visitor flying into Holland can scarcely imagine that Schiphol Airport, near Amsterdam, where he would probably land, is the only airport in the world which was once (in 1573) the scene of a *naval* battle!

Despite the almost miraculous land reclamation which the Dutch have achieved, there is still too little land. The Netherlands is the most densely populated country in Europe, with an average of almost a thousand people per square mile. If the United States were as densely populated, it would have about *three billion* inhabitants. Of course, density is even greater in the horse-shoe shaped megalopolis surrounding a "green heart" of lakes and woods, called the *Randstad* (literally "rim-town"), which encompasses the capital city of Amsterdam, The Hague (the seat of the government and now the royal residence), Rotterdam (the trade center and the largest port in the world), as well as the cities of Delft, Leiden and Utrecht. Its population density is twice that of Japan. Almost half the country's population lives in this area, which covers only about one-fifth of the total land

HOLDING BACK THE SEA: DUNES, DIKES, DAMS

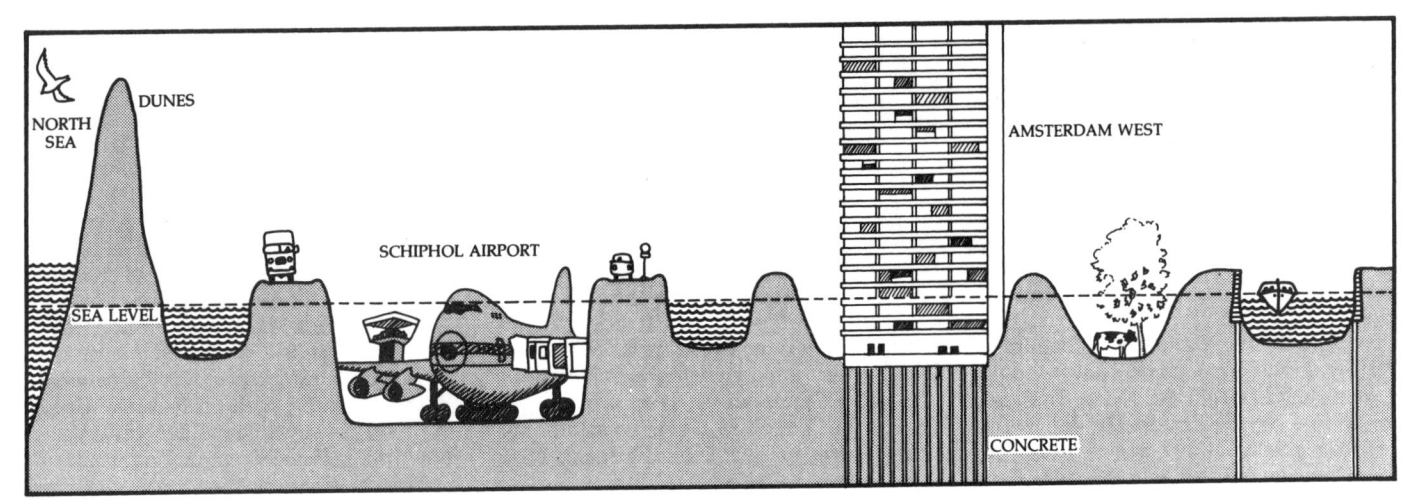

The Netherlands

The Barrier Dam under construction

... and completed in 1932

area. Such concentration has made urban difficulties the most pressing of all Dutch problems although the *Randstad* provides a model for meeting the needs of its seven million inhabitants. In 1997 it created a new metropolitan government to make it easier to manage itself.

The Netherlands is located on the North Sea at the mouth of three large rivers—the Rhine, the Meuse and the Scheldt—and with the large port in Amsterdam as well, it truly deserves the name "Gateway to the heart of Europe." It has a predominantly low–lying, flat landscape, criss–crossed by lakes and waterways, which cover a total of 10% of the country's land area, about half of which consists of polders—land surrounded by dykes and drained artificially. There are many hundreds of such polders because in earlier times the areas were pumped by windmills, which were not powerful enough to drain them. Now, with modern technology, much larger polders can be created. Dutch hydraulic engineers have been among the most ingenious in the world and have successfully tackled projects which one can only call gigantic in scope. In this century the Zuyderzee and Delta projects have attracted particular attention.

The Zuyderzee Project was begun in 1920, with the expectation that it would be completed within 40 years. The idea was to seal off the Zuyderzee Bay in the northern part of the country from the North Sea by means of a 20–mile dam called the Barrier Dam. This created a large, freshwater lake, the Ijsselmeer, parts of which have been pumped dry and converted into farmland and recreation areas. If needed, residential areas for Amsterdam also could be created. The Barrier Dam was completed in 1932, and four out of five of the planned polders have been created. Extremely high costs, environmental worries and disagreements concerning how the reclaimed land should best be used have delayed progress on the fifth. It is now uncertain whether the entire project as originally conceived will ever be completed.

In the 1950s a much larger project dramatically claimed a higher priority in the minds of the Dutch. On February 1, 1953, flood waters from the North Sea surged into the Delta area in the southwestern corner of the country, covering many of the islands there and killing almost 2,000 persons. An audacious plan was promptly adopted to close off most of the waterways of the Rhine, Scheldt and Meuse rivers from the sea by a chain of dams and artificial islands. These would shorten the coastline by 440 miles, and reverse the increasing salinization of the inland waterways. They would also enable the Dutch to claim an additional 25,000 acres of land from the sea, if they ever choose to do so.

Only one dam across the Eastern Scheldt was left to be completed when a violent verbal storm erupted over the effect such a dam could have on the plant and animal life in the estuary. The environmentalists' influence was so great that parliament decided to build a costly storm–surge barrier instead of the planned solid dam. This change, which would better protect the ecological system, added more than a billion dollars to the costs, delayed completion until 1986, required entire new technology and could result in a barrier which might not last more than 50 years.

Queen Beatrix officially opened the Oosterscheldedam, assuring her subjects that "nature is under control but not disturbed." Indeed, this two–mile dam is "the ultimate insurance policy." This barrier, costing $5 billion, is the most expensive maritime project in the nine centuries since the Dutch have been building dykes to hold back the sea. It is a movable barrier, anchored by 65 concrete piers as large as grain elevators, which lowers 62 gigantic steel gates at the touch of a button to block off the rampaging North Sea whenever a serious storm threatens. Unless they are lowered, the tides continue to flow into the Rhine estuary as usual. This "compromise barrier" was a victory for the vocal Dutch environmental lobby. Large, man–made changes in the Netherlands' geography on

The Netherlands

the scale of the past are more difficult, but the Dutch are constructing a storm surge barrier to protect Rotterdam, scheduled for completion in 1997.

Experts calculated that these gates will need to be closed only once every five years or so. When another storm like that in 1953 raged again in February 1995, forcing a quarter of a million Dutch to evacuate their homes, this kind of dam could mean the difference between survival and total disaster for the inhabitants of Zeeland.

In 1995 the Dutch were caught looking the wrong way. Having focused on the North Sea, they were struck this time by man–made perils along the Rhine. Marshes and floodplains once acted as sponges, soaking up surges of water. But in order to create residential and industrial property, people all the way along the river have dried out, asphalted and cemented, and buttressed with embankments the earlier waterlogged land. Changes in farming practices have also reduced the land's capacity to absorb rainwater. Worst of all, stretches of the Rhine have been straightened, reducing the meander to the sea and doubling the water's speed from Basel. This lessens the river system's ability to accommodate flood waters. Holland's dykes held in 1995, but they were weakened by what many called "the flood of the century." Alarm bells were rung alerting the Dutch, more than a third of whom live below sea level, that they must again mobilize for a renewed campaign to salvage their lands.

The Netherlands is still a country where the old can be seen alongside the new. Windmills are plentiful, although they no longer serve their original purpose. For centuries the flower bed of Europe, Holland in April almost seems like a gigantic bouquet of tulips, daffodils, narcissuses and hyacinths. In a few isolated villages one can find men in baggy pants and wooden shoes and women in floppy hats and bustling skirts. Yet the Netherlands is an extremely prosperous and heavily industrialized country, with a people whose dress is now more casual and modern. It is a dynamic country whose modern look prevails over the traditional.

HISTORY

The Emergence of the Netherlands

Protestant leaders in the northernmost provinces of the Spanish empire signed, in 1579, the Declaration of Utrecht swearing to defend liberty and religious freedom. Predictably the Catholic Spanish King was unwilling to accept such freedom in the area he controlled, so in 1581 the northern provinces declared their complete independence of Spain. William of Orange–Nassau, also known as William the Silent, became the first head (Stadholder) of the newly born Dutch Republic. He was assassinated by order of Spanish King Philip II, but the young Republic was able to resist Spanish efforts to reassert control. Aided initially by the English and by a fortuitous storm which decimated a mighty Spanish naval armada in 1588, the Dutch conducted a brilliant land campaign, led by Maurice, son of William the Silent, and forced the Spanish to vacate the Netherlands in 1595. Although more wars with the Spanish followed, Dutch independence was internationally recognized in 1648 by the Peace of Westphalia.

The 17th century was one in which the Dutch were involved in almost constant war, but it was for them also one of commercial success, naval supremacy and cultural bloom. It was the Netherlands' "Golden Age," and Dutch confidence and prosperity were vividly recorded in the paintings of the Dutch masters. It was the century in which Amsterdam quadrupled its population to 200,000 inhabitants and became a major point of departure for the entire world. It was also a city which even at that time was constantly *moving inland* as more and more land was reclaimed from the sea. In 1609 the Bank of Amsterdam was established, 85 years before the Bank of England, and Dutch financiers were among the most influential in the world. It was also a time of philosophical and scientific discovery.

Trade and Colonization

By the middle of the 17th century the Dutch had 16,289 seagoing vessels and 160,000 seamen. Their traders could be found in every corner of the globe, most often representing huge private companies such as the Dutch East and West India Companies, which had been chartered by parliament, called the States General. They traded virtually all over Europe, and their activities extended to Central Asia, where they had obtained the first tulip bulbs in the 16th century, India, Ceylon (now Sri Lanka), China and Indonesia, where they established a colony which they controlled until 1949. In 1652 they es-

Aerial view of the Oosterscheldedam Photo: Aerocamera-Bart Hofmeester

The Netherlands

Manhattan Island about 1627 . . . and today

tablished a colony at a good stopping–off place on the southern tip of Africa.

This Cape Colony was snatched by the British in 1806, but the Dutch descendants packed their belonging in 1836–8 and moved in a "Great Trek" into the interior of what is now the Republic of South Africa and established the Afrikaaner colony of Transvaal in 1852 and the Orange Free State in 1854. Ultimately these Dutch (together with French Huguenot descendants), who speak a dialect of Dutch called Afrikaans, became the predominant White group in the Republic of South Africa which was created from a union of Dutch settled areas and British colonies. Until well into the 20th century the Dutch retained great sympathy for their Afrikaaner relatives, who had created an economically prosperous state in an inhospitable land and who had successfully resisted cultural assimilation by the British who previously had political control of the area as a colony. However, the Dutch gradually turned against the Afrikaaners because of the latters' policy of racial segregation known as *apartheid*, an Afrikaans word meaning "separate." Until majority rule was introduced in 1994, the Dutch were among South Africa's most determined foes.

In 1609 a navigational failure brought the Dutch to North America. In that year Henry Hudson, an English sea captain in the service of the Dutch, sailed westward in search of a passage to the East Indies and China. He failed in his mission, but he bumped into what is now New York and sailed up a hitherto unknown river which now bears his name. It was the fate of America in its earliest days to be visited by seamen who actually wanted to get somewhere else! Hudson's contact with America resulted in the establishment of the Dutch West India Company and in subsequent settlement of the New World.

Six years before the Pilgrim fathers landed, in 1614 the Dutch established Fort Nassau on an island just below the present–day city of Albany, New York, a city which the Dutch incorporated in 1652 as the town of Beverwych. In 1625 an even more important fort and town had been founded on Manhattan Island, and five family farms were established to supply the soldiers and merchants. The name of the town was Nieuw (New) Amsterdam, and it was soon to become the most important city in the Dutch North American Colony, called New Netherland. Only a year later the Dutch Governor made the famous deal with the local Indians, buying the whole of Manhattan Island for 30 guilders' worth of merchandise, which by today's exchange rates is worth only about $12, but which was worth consider-

The Netherlands

ably more in 1625. It was nevertheless an extraordinarily favorable exchange for the Dutch.

In the next two decades New Netherland continued to grow, but at a much slower rate than the British colonies in New England and Virginia, whose populations outnumbered the Dutch settlers by at least four to one. New Amsterdam had a population which did not exceed 700 by 1647. Its boundaries, if one looks at a present–day map of New York City, extended to Pearl Street and to the northern wall, called *de wal*, which gave the name to what is now perhaps the richest street in the world, Wall Street. Under the last Dutch governor, Pieter Stuyvesant, the city grew to 1,500 (1664) and boasted two windmills and one church. It was a very cosmopolitan city in which reportedly 18 languages were spoken. In strict accordance with Dutch West India policy, religious or other discrimination was forbidden. It was therefore much more tolerant than the Massachusetts Bay Colony to the north. It was also much more fun to live in New Netherland. There were many inns for drinking and dancing, and sports were a favorite activity. One such sport imported from Holland was called *kolf*, which developed into modern golf.

The Dutch continued to found cities in their colony. Among them were what is now the Bronx, Staten Island, Breukelen (Brooklyn), Bergen (now Jersey City), Hackensack and Ridgewood. But the growth of New Netherland was halted abruptly by one of the three wars which Holland fought against England in the 17th century. When British ships of war sailed into the harbor of New Amsterdam in 1664, Governor Stuyvesant saw no alternative to surrendering the colony to the English.

Although the Dutch won the colony back for a year in 1673–4, the Dutch foothold on North America was lost. They also lost their settlements in Brazil, although they managed to hold on to Dutch Guiana (since 1975 the independent nation of Suriname) on the northern coast of South America and to a handful of Caribbean islands known as the Netherlands Antilles, which still belong to the Dutch. But Dutch influence did not totally disappear from North America. Governor Stuyvesant returned to his beloved city, renamed New York, to live on his farm on Manhattan Island. His *Bouwerij*, the Dutch word for farm, gave the name for a famous, but now rundown area in New York City known by its Americanized name—the Bowery.

Holland and the United States

In 1775 the Netherlands was the first foreign nation to fire a salute to the newly–designed American flag, and in 1782 it was the second country formally to recognize the independence of the U.S. It was America's major source for loans, although it must be said that Dutch lenders at the same time provided loans to the British. The Netherlands also left influences in the New World which became a part of American history and culture. Many famous Americans, including James Madison, Martin van Buren, Zackery Taylor, Ulysses S. Grant, Jefferson Davis and Theodore and Franklin D. Roosevelt descended from Dutch settlers. Also, some words such as skate (from *schaats*), as well as seafaring expressions as skipper, marline, hoist and yacht entered English through the Dutch language. Perhaps the most famous, however, was the corruption of the popular Dutch name in the 17th century, *Jan–Kees*, which came to be applied to all persons from the United States: "yankees." The first serving American president to visit the Netherlands was George Bush, who in July 1989 paid tribute to the contributions made by the Dutch in America, especially their strong spirit of freedom.

Decline and Political Change

In the numerous wars during the 17th century, particularly against the English, the Dutch did not always fare badly. One time during the reign of Charles II of England, as Samuel Pepys described in his diary, the Dutch Admiral de Ruyter sailed up the Thames, burning British warships at Chatham right outside of London harbor and putting the city into a panic. This event was a high point in Dutch history and is still commemorated in Holland. The Dutch were also able to frustrate the plans of Louis XIV to conquer the Netherlands.

Nevertheless, Holland was exhausted by almost continuous war, and it became clear by the end of the 17th century that the Netherlands had assumed a position in the world which was out of proportion to its resources and size. It was propped up to some extent in the 18th century by a close tie with England. When James II of England decided to remain a Catholic, parliament offered the throne in 1688 to the Protestant Dutch Stadholder, William of Orange, who had fought the English only ten years earlier. William reigned with his wife, Mary, the daughter of the deposed James II. The childless couple ruled until 1702, and it was after them that the College of William and Mary in Williamsburg, Virginia, was named, as well as Nassau Hall at Princeton University for William of Nassau. The 18th century was for Holland one of political and cultural decline. When the French came again in 1795 the Dutch were unable to offer serious resistance.

The Netherlands for the first time in 1813 created a monarchy of their own. In 1848 the revolutionary tide in France, Belgium and elsewhere in Europe reportedly converted King William I into a "liberal overnight." and he accepted a constitutional revision which made the government responsible to parliament rather than to the king. Thereafter, the Dutch monarch *reigned* but no longer *ruled* and became merely the first citizen of the kingdom. This was in effect the same position which the Princes of Orange had earlier occupied as Stadholders of the Dutch Republic and remains essentially true today.

After 1848 the Netherlands was confronted with tensions arising from industrialization. Though it came later than in Belgium or England, it nevertheless spawned a trade union and socialist movement. Holland also was confronted with struggles between the churches and the state, particularly over the creation of religiously affiliated schools which would be financed by the state. Not until 1920 was the present system of full state subsidies for parochial schools established. In all of these disputes, the Dutch displayed their characteristic willingness to abide by established rule of the democratic game and to find harmonious solutions to conflicts and differences.

The World Wars

During World War I, the Netherlands remained neutral and unoccupied. Sniffing the winds of change which this mighty conflagration released, the Dutch did introduce universal suffrage for men in 1917 and for women in 1919. Because it had not joined Germany's enemies, the last German Kaiser fled to Holland after his abdication, living there until his death in 1941. The war radically disrupted the trade on which Holland has always been so dependent, and after the war its prewar prosperity did not return. The economic depression of the 1930s created greater unemployment, which stimulated radical movements on the left and right.

When the German army was hurled westward again in May 1940 the Dutch were unable to remove themselves from the melee. In the first large–scale aerial bombardment of a densely populated city, German dive–bombers destroyed 90% of Rotterdam's city center within 40 minutes. The German attempt to capture Queen Wilhelmina and the Dutch government by dropping crack paratroop units over the Hague failed, and the Queen, Crown Princess Juliana and the cabinet managed to escape to London; they worked during the entire war to bring about a German defeat.

Holland fell within 5 days and the country was ruled for the remainder of

The Netherlands

the war by a Nazi–appointed Dutch Reich Commissioner, an Austrian named Seyss–Inquart. This was an especially hard time for the Dutch, especially for Jews. Although its true authorship has been placed very much into question in recent years, the *Diary of Anne Frank,* whose setting is Amsterdam during the Nazi occupation, remains a moving testimony to the suffering inflicted upon the chief victims of Nazi racial theories and policies. Unfortunately, a few Dutch people were among the persecutors. As late as 1980 an art–collector, Pieter Menten, was imprisoned and fined for his role in the murder of 20 to 30 Jews in Poland in 1941.

At the same time, thousands of Dutch were active in the resistance movement against the occupation forces. Despite the successful Allied landing in Normandy in June 1944, because of strong German resistance north of the Rhine and Allied policy to drive toward Berlin, Holland was not liberated until May 1945. When the horror was over, the Netherlands was left with 280,000 civilian dead, vast expanses of flooded areas, wrecked harbors and industries, and an economy close to total collapse. Dutch memories and emotions remain strong, which is one reason why a West German chancellor's trip to Holland in December 1987 was only the third official visit there in a quarter of a century.

Recovery

The very popular Queen Wilhelmina returned to Holland in 1945 amid enthusiastic cheers of her people, and the Dutch set about to mend their physically broken country, a task which they were able to complete surprisingly quickly. In 1948 Wilhelmina abdicated in favor of her daughter Juliana, and all would have gone well if the Netherlands had not been forced to face the same searing problem which was plaguing several other European powers at the time: decolonization.

The jewel of the colonial empire was Indonesia. In 1619 the Dutch East India Company had created a city it called Batavia (now Jakarta) on the island of Java. From this base the Dutch extended their control over most of the 3,000 or so islands of the Indonesian archipelago; for more than 300 years they retained firm control over the colony, but their policy of drawing a rather distinct line between themselves and the native population was a major factor which fanned the flames of an independence movement in the 20th century. The islands were an attractive target for Japanese expansion after 1940, and the Dutch government which was trying to maintain a policy of neutrality in the Pacific war could not organize a credible defense—they were captured in February 1942.

Decolonization

When the Dutch returned at the end of the war in order to reclaim what they believed was theirs, they found that they were not wanted by a native population whose leaders had declared the islands' independence in August 1945 immediately after the Japanese surrender. After four years of tension and military conflict, a settlement was reached which recognized an independent Indonesia within a kind of union which the Dutch equated with the British Commonwealth of Nations. This agreement by no means settled all the difficulties. The Dutch had insisted on retaining full control of their economic investments which at the time accounted for almost 15% of their national income. Indonesia's flamboyant and unpredictable President Sukarno solved the problem single–handedly by simply nationalizing all Dutch properties in 1957. Relations between the two countries also remained sour because of the Dutch retention of West Irian, part of the island of New Guinea, which the Indonesians claimed. Finally in 1962 an American mediator proposed the face–saving procedure of turning West Irian over to the UN, which seven months later transferred sovereignty to Indonesia.

After a painfully drawn out severance from Indonesia, the Netherlands was more than cooperative in aiding its other colonies to gain their own independence. In 1975 Suriname was freed in the midst of widespread fears among the Surinamese that such independence would lead to violent racial measures against the whites and East Indian Hindustani. More than a quarter of the population fled to Holland in the final days before independence. In order to help Suriname adjust to its new status, the Netherlands promised it aid amounting to $100 million for each of the following ten years, certainly one of the most generous foreign aid programs on a per capita basis in history.

However, because of the Surinamese government's flagrant human rights violations, the Netherlands suspended its assistance programs in 1983. The Netherlands has also notified the six islands in the Netherlands Antilles that they must begin preparing for their independence, although there is no consensus among the islands themselves concerning the precise form this should take. They are now organized into four self–governing communities—Aruba, Bonaire, Curaçao and the Leeward Islands (southern portion of St. Maarten, St. Eustatius and Saba. Only the island of Aruba has announced that it would like to be an independent state by 1996. It is feared that the islands would not be able to find a long–term alternative to their present economic dependence on Holland, although they can be sure of very generous transitional assistance.

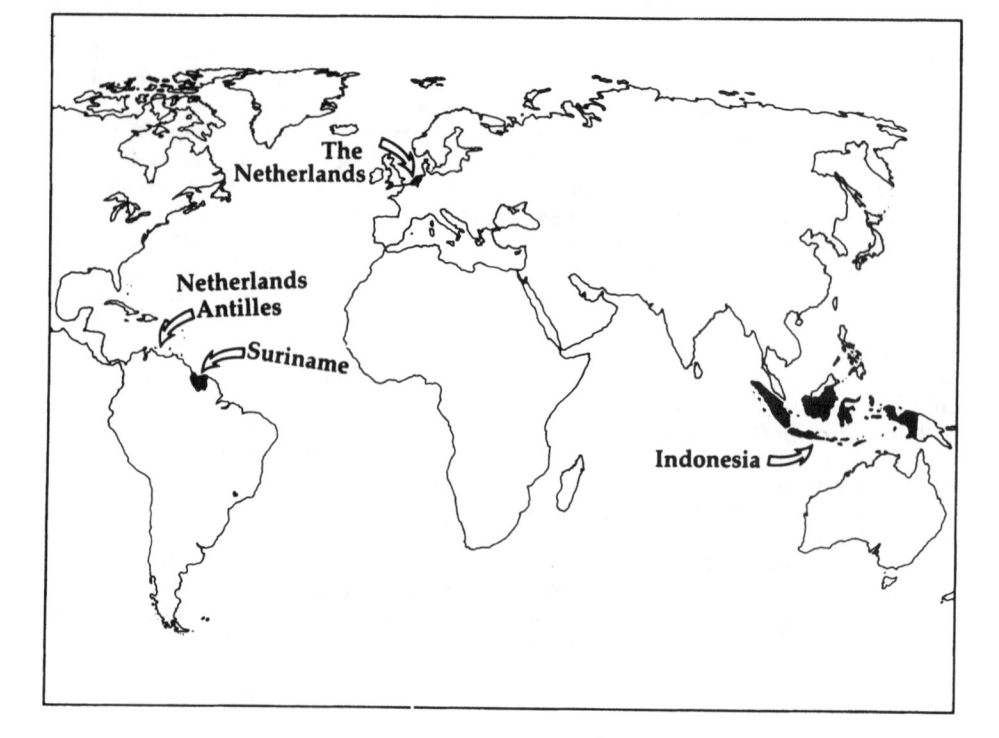

POLITICS AND GOVERNMENT

The Monarch

The Netherlands is a constitutional monarchy whose character is prominently visible during the investiture ceremony when a new king or queen begins to reign. The monarch takes an oath of allegiance

The Netherlands

Prince Constantijn, H.M. Queen Beatrix, H.R.H. Prince Claus, Crown Prince Willem–Alexander, Prince Johan Friso
Photo by Vincent Mentzel

to the constitution. Also, the royal crown is not placed on the head of the new ruler (for which reason the ceremony is called an investiture, not a coronation), but it and the other symbols of royal authority—the orb and the scepter—are arranged on a table *around* the constitution.

The royal family is the House of Orange, whose descendants are inseparably tied to the Netherlands' entire history as an independent state. This is one reason why there is very little opposition to the monarchy in Holland and why most Dutch remain firmly attached to their monarchs. It was therefore a shock to many Dutch to witness the violent disturbances in Amsterdam, Rotterdam and Utrecht on April 30, 1980 when the popular 71–year–old Queen Juliana abdicated in favor of her daughter Beatrix. While orange flags and streamers were displayed everywhere and while the mood around the royal palace in Amsterdam was royally festive, elsewhere several thousand protesters waged such violent battles with the police that more than 50 policemen and 100 demonstrators were injured. The slogan of the protesters was "No apartment, no coronation," which referred to the serious housing shortage in the capital city. No doubt some of the protesters wished also to show disapproval of the monarchy and of a family which is among the richest in the world and which draws over $5 million a year from the state treasury to maintain a royal household with 250 servants and other assistants. The area in which the ceremony was held had to be sealed off by the police.

Queen Beatrix was well prepared for her position, having studied law, politics and history at the University of Leiden. She has a pleasantly dimpled smile, but she tends to be a strong–willed and impatient person whose manner is often stiff and overly aristocratic. For awhile her manner appealed less to her people than did that of her unpretentious mother Juliana, but the nation's respect for her has grown considerably since she became queen. It was her mother's enormous popularity which had enabled the family to overcome an extremely embarrassing scandal in the last decade of her reign; it was prompted by revelations that her husband, Prince Bernhard, had accepted payoffs from the Lockheed Aircraft Corporation for his assistance in helping the company to secure lucrative contracts from the Dutch air force.

Beatrix's marriage in 1966 to a German diplomat, Claus, had created quite an uproar at the time, but the marriage is now accepted, and Claus has proven himself to be an effective promoter of good Dutch relations with developing countries. He acts as an adviser to the Minister of Development. Her sons are preparing for their future roles. Crown Prince Willem–Alexander served as a lieutenant on a guided missile frigate, while Johan Friso went to the University of California at Berkeley to study engineering.

Queen Beatrix is extremely hardworking and spends hours preparing for her speeches and meetings, and reading proposed legislation. She was very frank in her inaugural speech about the unromantic side of being Queen: "It is a task no one would ever seek. The glitter is visible, but not the burden and perpetual self–denial." In most matters she is prevented from making any mistakes by the requirement that the appropriate cabinet member also sign all her acts and decrees.

Forming a Parliamentary Government

She is certainly very capable of performing the one public act which she is charged to accomplish independently: to coordinate the long coalition talks which are necessary to form a government after a parliamentary election. Because the Netherlands uses the proportional representation electoral system, many parties are able to win seats in the lower house, and no single party can even come close to winning a majority on its own. The formation of a government out of almost a dozen parties which win parliamentary seats is therefore a very delicate task, requiring a firm but subtle lead on the part of the monarch. She consults numerous party, parliamentary and other political leaders in order to acquaint herself intimately with the political climate. Then, acting entirely independently, she names an *informateur*, who is usually a leading politician, whose task is to advise her of the most promising formula for constructing a government. She then appoints a *for-*

The Netherlands

mateur, a person who must seek to form a government in which he himself would probably be the prime minister. He is usually the leader of the party which has won the most seats in the election. His task includes the establishment of a program acceptable to several different parties. Such a broad program is necessarily moderate; no remotely radical program would be acceptable to several parties. The entire process usually takes a very long time, usually two to four months. Fortunately the work is done carefully, and normally results in a government which can survive for at least three years.

In the carefully constructed cabinet, ministerial seats are usually distributed according to the proportion of seats the various governing parties have in the lower house, the most important positions being that of prime minister and minister of finance. Cabinet members, including prime ministers, need not be members of parliament, and some ministers are specialists who had never even run for elective office in their lives.

Compared with other parliamentary systems in which a prime minister is the most important political figure, the Dutch system is almost unique in that it calls for a separation between the executive (cabinet) and the parliament. All cabinet members must resign their seats in parliament, and the new government need not seek the formal approval of the lower house. Nor is there such a thing as a vote of confidence in which a majority in parliament can vote against the government, causing it to fall. The government is, however, always free voluntarily to pose a "question of confidence" to the lower house if it chooses. It is acutely interested in maintaining a majority without which it could not gain approval for important legislation, which is almost always written and submitted by the government, not by members of parliament.

The Parliament

The Dutch Parliament, called the States General, remains powerful in comparison to many other parliaments in Western Europe. One reason is that the lower house has permanent committees which correspond to each ministry. Therefore, parliament members can develop the necessary expertise to question and control the work of the ministries. Further, parties in parliament do not require absolute discipline from their members, who according to the constitution represent the entire nation, not a regional or party constituency. Therefore, the government can never be absolutely sure that its measures will pass in both houses. It must design its legislation in such a way that it would be acceptable to more than a slim majority, and it must work very hard to persuade parliaments to support its programs. Parliament is by no means dominated or overshadowed by the cabinet.

The Hague, with the Dutch Parliament in the background

The States General was first established in 1464 by the Burgundian kings as an advisory body. After independence in 1581, it considered itself the keeper of Dutch sovereignty and granted an hereditary official, the Stadholder, the right to exercise executive power. The States General is bicameral, and both the First and Second Chambers meet in the Binnenhof (Inner Court) in the Hague. The First Chamber, or upper house, is composed of 75 members elected by the 11 provincial parliaments for six–year terms, with one half of its membership being elected every three years. Since the provincial chambers are elected directly, the upper house usually has roughly the same party composition as the Second Chamber. This First Chamber cannot introduce or amend bills, but it is far more than a mere advisory or delaying chamber as is the British House of Lords. It has the right to approve or reject all legislation.

The Second Chamber is composed of 150 members elected at least every four years by all citizens 18 years or older. In contrast to most other European countries, elections are not held on Sundays. Nevertheless, voter turnout is extremely high (roughly 87%) in contrast to U.S. presidential elections which are also held on Tuesdays and which now rarely attract more than 60% of the voters. The Second Chamber generally meets three days a week, Tuesday through Thursday, and its members are expected neither to reside in the Hague nor to give up their normal employment while they serve. About a third of its members are women.

Both chambers are regarded as the chief interpreters of the constitution, and together they are empowered to initiate the process to amend the constitution. If a majority in both houses finds a constitutional amendment necessary, then both houses are dissolved, new elections are held, and the amendment can then be accepted by a two–thirds vote in both chambers. No court in Holland has the right to declare a legislative act unconstitutional. The highest court of the land, the Court of Cassation, can only nullify a statute which is in variance with an international agreement. Its chief tasks are to insure the uniform administration of justice and to serve as the court of high appeal for decisions made in lower courts. Presiding over those lower courts are independent judges who apply Dutch law, which is based on Roman law. There are no juries; the Dutch want a professional administration of justice by judges who serve for life and who are as free as possible from popular influences.

Assisting the Queen and government as the highest advisory body is the Council of State, which is composed of a crown prince or princess over the age of 18 and no more than 24 persons appointed for life, although they normally step down at the age of 70. They are expected to have political, commercial, trade union, diplomatic or military experience. The Queen officially presides over the Council, although it is actually guided by a vice–president who is selected from among the members. The

The Netherlands

cabinet can seek expert advice from the Council and is always responsive to any constructive advice it might give.

Political Parties

At all levels of government Dutch political parties play a key role in informing voters about the most important political issues, conducting election campaigns, and then forming coalitions to rule. Dutch political parties have always tended to represent particular subcultures in society, such as Catholicism, various shades of Protestantism, socialism or liberalism. At the same time, they must adjust their aims to those of other parties in order to be able to participate in government, therefore, compromise and mutual adjustment have been their basic rules. In a small country with such a highly homogeneous population, the range of political interests and opinions is somewhat narrower than in a large, multi–racial, multi–lingual and multi–national country. Thus, a consensus regarding the political system and rules of the game has always been relatively easy to maintain in Holland, and this has made it less difficult for such a multi–party state to have such a high degree of parliamentary stability.

It has, however, become increasingly difficult to form coalition governments in Holland, and this results partly from a change which is occurring in party politics. In the past, no Dutch government could ever be formed without the participation of confessional (religious) parties, particularly the Catholic party. Therefore, the secular parties always had to moderate their programs in order to be able to coalesce with them. But as the importance of religion declines in Dutch society, fewer and fewer Dutch vote for a party exclusively for religious reasons. Therefore, the strength of the confessional parties has declined in recent years. Seeing this, the major secular parties have sharpened up their own programs and have moved more clearly to the right or left in order to draw the formerly religiously oriented voters away from the politically heterogeneous religious parties. In other words, the major secular parties often have intentionally tried to polarize Dutch politics in order to attract more votes. They have even publicly stated that they are not interested in entering into any coalition with each other.

In the May 1998 elections a couple dozen parties actually competed for seats. Some of them, such as the *Party for the Liquidation of the Netherlands*, the *God is With Us*, the *Live or Die Together*, and the hard–line *Communist Party of the Netherlands* (CPN), could not seriously hope to win seats. But profiting from proportional representation, which grants a parliamentary seat for roughly 55,000 votes, several parties managed to win seats.

The *Green Left*, which rallies radicals, socialists, pacifists, and communists, won 7.2% of the votes and 11 seats (up from five). Dutch voters are very sensitive to environmental issues. The crowded population, flatness, and the fact that half of it is below sea level make it a first victim to any rise in water levels due to the "greenhouse effect." In fact, in 1989 a Dutch government became the first in Europe to fall in a crisis over the environment. The *Socialist Party* won 3.8% and five seats (up from two). The 1994 elections had seen the startling emergence of two new parties representing the interests of elderly Dutch, alarmed by the *Christian Democratic* proposal to freeze all pensions for four years. The *General Old People's Union* captured six seats, and *Unie 55+* got one. But in 1998 they were wiped out, winning only 1% of the votes and no seats. The blatantly racist *Center Democrats* struck a cord with some voters upset by the influx of foreigners, but in 1998 it lost all three seats, capturing only .6% of the votes.

The more conservative of the two main secular parties is the *People's Party for Freedom and Democracy* (VVD), headed until 1998 by Frits Bolkestein, a feisty man who is the least consensual of Dutch politicians despite the fact that, according to 1996 polls, he was the country's most popular political figure. It is usually referred to as the *Liberal Party* because of its century–long struggle to reduce the influence of the churches in Dutch public life, especially in the schools. Individual freedom is its chief tenet, and it favors lower

The *Liberal Party's* Frits Bolkestein

Prime Minister Wim Kok

taxes, an even lower government deficit, a shrinking of the increasingly costly welfare state, higher criminal sentences, and a strengthening of the police in order to curb crime. It supports a free market economy, but it also favors profit–sharing with workers. It draws voters particularly from the upper and middle classes. It did well in the 1998 elections, rising from 31 to 38 seats, and it is in the governing coalition.

The other main secular party is the *Labor Party (PvdA)*, led by Wim Kok. The son of a carpenter, Kok studied economics and worked in the trade unions for more than 20 years, ten of those as president of the most powerful central workers' union. He entered politics in 1986, and after only two months, he replaced Joop den Uyl as party head. He is a popular leader, whose relaxed and more moderate, democratic style contrasts strikingly with his predecessor's more autocratic and ideological approach. It is a moderate socialist reform party, which traditionally favors what it calls *Nivellering*, or the elimination of differences in citizens' power, knowledge and income. It supports an increased workers' share of profits and decision–making in the factories.

An earlier move to the left caused some of its more conservative members to break off and found a separate party, *Democrats '70*, which has had only negligible electoral success. In 1989 it had joined the *Christian Democrats* to form a center–left ruling coalition, with Kok as finance minister. Because it had helped preside over the most sweeping reform of the welfare state ever undertaken, it alienated many

The Netherlands

of its voters and created discontent within the party. It received the bill in the 1994 elections, dropping from 49 to 37 seats. But because it emerged as the largest party, the queen tapped Kok to form a government. In 1998 it bounced back to 29% of the votes and 45 seats and remained the senior governing partner.

The moderately left–wing party called *Democrats 66,* had been founded in that year in order to present voters with a clear alternative to the established parties, especially the *PvdA,* whose strong, paternalistic leadership was widely resented. It opposes the ideological approach to politics and sees itself as a practical, problem–party. It advocates reforms in the society and the constitution, such as the direct election of the prime minister. Once a trendy, intellectual party which appealed mainly to young voters from the upper and middle classes, it has broadened its base considerably. In 1994 it doubled its seats to a total of 24, thanks in part to its charismatic leader, Hans van Mierlo. But it could not maintain its momentum in 1998, falling to 9% and only 14 seats. The party remains in the government, but party leader Els Borst complained that "we are in the twilight zone."

Fighting for it political life between the secular parties of the left and right is the *Christian Democratic Appeal* (CDA), which emerged from the 1998 elections with 18.4% of the votes and 29 seats. Led by Jaap De Hoop Scheffer, it is in the opposition. Faced with the gloomy prospect of watching their voters run to the increasingly polarized secular parties, the three major religious political parties, which had long since severed their direct ties with the churches, decided in 1973 to join forces for electoral purposes. In a nostalgic ceremony of prayers and hymn–singing in 1980, they went a giant step further by disbanding themselves entirely and becoming full members of the larger *CDA.* Three of Holland's oldest political parties, the *Catholic People's Party* (KVP), the *Anti–Revolutionary Party* (ARP), and the *Christian Historical Union* (CHU) ceased to exist.

All three had always been seriously split into different factions, so the merger in 1980 brought birds of many different colors together, which are very difficult to control. They all agree basically that Christian principles must be applied in politics, and that both a free enterprise economy and the present social welfare system should be defended. The fact that the *CDA* encompasses a broad political spectrum gives it the advantage that the party can easily form a coalition with almost every other party. Therefore, the *CDA* has survived the secularization and polarization of Dutch politics and until

Former Prime Minister Ruud Lubbers

1994 was the key party in any coalition. In 1998 three separate fundamentalist Christian parties captured 1.3% of the votes and eight seats (up from seven).

In 1982 *Christian Democrat* Ruud Lubbers became Prime Minister. He introduced the most austere policy of any Dutch administration since the 1930s. Faced with runaway government spending, zero economic growth, a fall in natural gas prices (which are pegged to oil prices), the highest rate of company bankruptcies since 1900 and the highest unemployment rate in the EU, his government slashed public spending to try to balance the government's books and moved to revive the private sector by reducing business costs through tax reductions and cuts in government red tape. The Dutch felt the sting of these policies. Social welfare benefits were slashed, and the indexing of wages and welfare benefits was suspended because of an adverse inflationary effect.

Lubbers' popularity stemmed from his courage in meeting the Netherlands' problems head on. An example is euthanasia. Passive euthanasia (halting life support systems to allow natural death) has long been permitted, but in the past decade the Netherlands has moved toward permitting voluntary euthanasia ("mercy killing" through fatal injections to hopeless patients), which is practiced about 1,500 times each year, 80% involving cancer patients. One out every 50 deaths is a mercy killing. Polls indicate that three out of four Dutch support this. It is still technically illegal, but Dutch courts have stopped prosecuting and jailing doctors who, according to a 1993 law—the first of its kind in an industrialized nation, follow a detailed 28–point checklist: the patient must be terminally ill and in a clear state of mind, and he or she, not family or friends, must ask repeatedly to die. A second opinion must be obtained. In 1995 for the first time a physician was found guilty of murder for ending the life of a deformed newborn who was unable to ask explicitly that a doctor do so. But as a sign of how torn even judges are over this issue, the court ruled that the doctor's actions were justifiable under the Netherlands' tolerant euthanasia laws and refused to punish him.

The *Christian Democrats* suffered in the 1994 elections from Lubbers' announcement that he was leaving Dutch politics. Dutch voters were troubled by accelerating unemployment, social welfare cuts, alarming crime levels, and an influx of immigrants and asylum–seekers. In a surly mood, many of them turned sharply away from the mainstream parties that had ruled them for decades and supported radical populist parties. The *Christian Democratic* and *Labor* parties could no longer continue their ruling coalition. Therefore, *Labor* constructed a left–liberal coalition with the *Democrats 66* and the *Liberals,* known as the "purple coalition." The Kok government succeeded in achieving its top priority to create new jobs and was reelected in 1998.

Unitary System, Regions, Municipalities

The Netherlands is a unitary, not a federal state. There are elected provincial and municipal governments which deal with matters of regional or local concern, but about 90% of their income is channeled to them by the central government. In each of the 11 provinces voters elect by means of proportional representation a Provincial Council. This assembly appoints from among its own members a Provincial Executive who is responsible for the day-to-day administration; retaining a French practice, the central government appoints a Queen's Commissioner, who presides over the Provincial Council and Executive and seeks to insure that nationwide interests will not be overlooked. The Provincial Councils elect the members of the First Chamber in the Hague, a provision which helps insure that provincial interests in turn will not be passed over by the central government.

Considerably more important in Dutch government are the Municipal Councils, which are also elected by proportional representation in the cities and towns. Each Municipal Council appoints Aldermen from their own membership who serve as an executive. Presiding over both the executive and the Council is the Burgomaster (mayor), who is appointed by the central government for a six-year term. Although he usually does not come from the city in which he serves, he very often becomes the locality's most effective spokesman in the Hague. Increasingly, several municipalities are joining to form regional authorities to tackle such matters as the location of industry, housing, transport and environment. The need for action on a larger scale than the municipality has led to a proposal to increase the number of provinces and to allow the new provincial governments to perform such tasks.

Other very important local bodies in the Netherlands and among the oldest form of democratic administration in Europe are the Water Control Boards. Property owners within a board's jurisdiction elect a general council which in turn elects an executive committee. The central government chooses the executive committee for the most important Water Control Boards. These are responsible for what might be considered the most important task in Holland: defending the land against water.

Housing Shortages

The Dutch government must grapple with some very difficult problems. One of the thorniest is the desperate housing shortage in the Randstad. In the 1980s this drove thousands of young Dutch, often referred to as *Krakers* (literally, "people who break in") to arm themselves with bricks and iron bars, to issue calls on their own private radio station and weekly newspapers to rally their sympathizers and to build barricades in the streets which only army tanks could flatten. They delivered battle to the police before the disbelieving eyes of Dutch television viewers, who never imagined that such violence could ever take place in their own country. Empty houses, apartments and office space were forcibly occupied by the *Krakers*, who are often willing to leave only after a good fight.

No one denies the housing shortage, but people disagree on how such a shortage arose and how it should be eliminated. The shortage is clearly due in part to changed demands for housing. As young people leave home earlier, as the divorce rate climbs and as an increasingly prosperous people demand larger and better quality housing, the demand for existing housing increases. Like other European countries, the Netherlands is experiencing a dramatic increase in homeless persons. In a controversial effort to help them, Rotterdam began in 1993 distributing tent–shaped waterproof cardboard boxes to the estimated 3,500 homeless in that city.

Only 43% of the Dutch housing stock is owner–occupied. Renting is clearly more popular than buying because of rent control laws which had been introduced in the immediate postwar years in order to help the economically hard–pressed Dutch. But as incomes began to rise, it was politically dangerous to eliminate these laws, so the rents, especially on older dwellings, have been kept unrealistically low. Parliament has permitted them to rise only as fast as inflation, and half of the renting population now pays less than 11% of its income for housing. In Amsterdam the average monthly rent for workers in 1989 was 330 guilders ($220). At such a low rate, people with higher incomes are very reluctant to vacate the cheap housing which is so badly needed by those with low incomes. Those who are more prosperous face an acute shortage of luxury apartments for sale in Amsterdam.

Private investors are also discouraged from building more new apartments because the government forbids the returns on housing investments to exceed the returns paid on state bonds. No government has been able to find a way out of this trap. With such low rents, many landlords refuse to pay for the kinds of renewal which much housing needs. According to the Amsterdam municipal council, as much as 60% of the city's housing is in need of renewal. In some districts, three-fourths of the houses have no bathrooms. Thus, rather primitive accommodations are hidden behind many of the stately facades which foreign tourists admire in the capital city.

Social Welfare Problems

The government was confronted with the problem of how to finance the generous social welfare system which the country has built up. Unlike many Western European countries, where welfare states were created after 1945 as a compromise between capitalism and socialism, and as an essential ingredient for social peace and political stability, Holland's welfare system (called the *verzorgingsstaat*) was built more on a Christian imperative, rather than on a political necessity. Most observers believe that it has reached the limits of the welfare state and that it must realistically revise downward its earlier version of a new society. The *Christian Democrats* cut back the welfare system slightly, and Prime Minister Kok is continuing in this direction.

It is understandable why the Dutch want to cling to the present social welfare system. Parents receive special allowances for children, and widows and orphans receive special benefits. State health insurance, including dental care, is provided for all Dutch who earn less than 36,200 guilders (roughly $24,000) per year, and this covers treatment and nursing in institutions for the physically and mentally handicapped, nursing homes, hospitals, sanitoria and similar establishments. Employees and certain self–employed persons receive 70% of their wages if they are unemployed.

Workers who are declared to be fully or partially disabled are entitled to benefits in amounts up to 80% of their wages, depending upon former income and degree of incapacitation. Since 1968 when these disability benefits were expanded, the nation's health has seemingly declined rapidly. In that year 5.5% of the work force was considered to be at least partly disabled. By 1991 over 16% were so catego-

The Royal residence in The Hague: *Palace House in the Woods*

The Netherlands

rized on the basis of complaints ranging from claustrophobia to chronic backache, and this was swallowing up almost 7% of GDP. In 1988 the average worker called in sick 8.4% of all work days.

All in all, only one out of two adults worked by the 1990s (compared with about 80% in the U.S.), which is one reason why economic growth has lagged behind most industrialized countries for years. Government efforts in 1991 to rein in the runaway costs of the disability benefits scheme by limiting the number of years of entitlement ignited a nation-wide strike. The Kok government toughened the conditions for unemployment benefits and broadened the definition of "suitable work" to prevent people from easily rejecting job proposals. As a further incentive to work, the link between wage and benefit rises was temporarily abolished.

Generous retirement benefits await all employees, especially those who contributed to special pension plans. All Dutch who cannot support themselves, including artists, are entitled to state aid. Employers and employees contribute 50–50 to the unemployment and health insurance, but the employers and, in some cases, the state treasury pay for all the other benefits. In 1986, one-fourth of Amsterdam's residents were living from welfare or social security. The Dutch took the steady improvement of welfare provisions so much for granted that it is a small miracle that a majority of voters approved in 1986 of a reduction. Indeed, from 1983 to 1987 welfare support fell by 7.5%. The Dutch grudgingly accepted Lubbers' outlook after his 1986 election: "The role of the government in our society is changing because people are becoming more independent and want to be more responsible for themselves and others."

The luxurious social welfare system grew out of the unpleasant memories of the depression of the 1930s and of the war. At first it was paid for by rising productivity and prosperity, and after large natural gas reserves were discovered in the late 1950s, budget deficits resulting from the social welfare bill were simply paid for by large government revenues derived from the export of natural gas. But the government, wishing to conserve the country's precious supply of natural gas, announced that all export contracts were to be terminated in the 1990s.

The country faced serious choices, with no more gas revenues to look forward to and with a budgetary deficit which has fallen dramatically; in 1998 it was 2.3% of GDP with total debt at 74.5% of GDP. Public sector spending had risen to 54% of GDP. How should the system be financed? By 1991 the combined burden of welfare premiums and taxes was already the second highest in the OECD behind Sweden.

The Dutch government believes that the welfare state can be maintained only if it is operated more strictly and efficiently. Therefore, in 1994 it announced plans to privatize sickness insurance and to shift responsibility for social security from the government to companies. It hopes to improve greatly the ratio of active to inactive persons in a land where almost half the population lives on benefits.

European and Third World Relations

The Netherlands is a founding member of the EU and has long been one of the chief proponents of a more unified Europe. The Hague is the site of several supra–national institutions, including especially the International Court of Justice, which is the supreme UN legal body in theory. This International Court meets in the stately Peace Palace which was built by money donated by the American steel magnate, Andrew Carnegie. Regrettably, its decisions are not always divorced from international tensions and strained relations; the judges are often accused of "taking sides" in disputes based on the country of their origin.

A young Dutch soldier
Royal Netherlands Embassy

Holland has especially distinguished itself in development aid. In 1983 it had given 1.5% of its GDP, the highest in the world, but by 1992 this had declined to .88%. It still donates more on a per-capita basis to Third World development than any other country. One Dutch official commented that "development aid is a breed of sacred cow with us. We carry it out with the zeal formerly reserved for our country's Christian missionaries."

Defense Policy

Its defense policy is based on its membership in NATO. Dutch troops are well-trained and equipped, and are considered to be among the best-prepared forces in NATO. One unique feature of the Dutch military is that it officially recognizes almost a dozen official personnel associations which function very much like labor unions. The main one is the *Union of Conscript Soldiers (VVDM)*, which regards the soldier as an "employee in uniform" and which has done away with the tradition of saluting officers.

Another unique feature is that the Dutch military was the first in the world

The Netherlands

to assign to combat units any woman who volunteers and who can satisfy the physical requirements. They also are permitted to serve on all naval vessels and to fly combat aircraft. The Dutch invested several million dollars on such things as developing backpack straps which do not irritate women's breasts, constructing separate quarters and conducting studies to determine how valid the Israeli experience is that military units are more quickly demoralized when women are wounded than when men are wounded. Other armies, including that of the U.S., watched the Dutch experiment closely, as they did Holland's policy since 1974 to allow gays in the military. Gays have their own Foundation for Homosexuality in the Armed Forces (FHAF), which represents gay interests in the services. For example, when Dutch troops serving in the Balkans in 1993 were sent complimentary copies of *Playboy*, homosexual soldiers were sent issues of a corresponding gay publication. Self–declared homosexuals continue to be welcome in the volunteer army.

The Dutch have abandoned conscription and created a flexible volunteer army designed to be used in rapid deployment actions and UN peace–keeping operations. The force has been cut 37% from 101,000 to 63,800, and stricter discipline and grooming standards have been introduced. Earrings and ponytails have been curtailed, and the use of cannabis has been banned. The nonsaluting policy was not changed.

Some army bases were closed, and almost half the army troops are assigned to a joint German–Dutch corps headquartered across the border in Münster. The command for this joint corps rotates between a German and a Dutch general.

The air force, which since 1977 has used the American F-16 fighter, has the task of protecting Dutch air space and of contributing to the tactical air forces of the alliance. The navy plays a part in defending the Atlantic, the English Channel and the North Sea. Its most important assignment is to keep the Dutch coast clear of mines and to defend the Dutch ports, which are critical for NATO supply lines. Several Dutch naval vessels were sent in 1991 to the Persian Gulf, and missile batteries were deployed to Turkey. The U.S. has had 2,200 troops stationed in the Netherlands, but this force may be scaled down or withdrawn. The American units include the 32nd Tactical Fighter Squadron in Soesterburg, whose personnel are required to wear patches indicating that they are serving Her Majesty the Queen of the Netherlands.

Dutch soldiers serve in the Balkans, both on the ground and in the air. Their humanitarian image was badly tarnished by allegations in 1995 that they had stood aside after Srebrenica fell to Bosnian Serbs while Moslems were butchered, raped and expelled. The Dutch government absolved them of any wrongdoing in that complicated and tragic situation. In 1999 it deployed one ship, 16 combat aircraft, and 738 troops in the NATO air war against Yugoslavia to stop ethnic cleansing in Kosovo.

Nuclear Disarmament Hopes

Even though the Dutch are close to the top in terms of military preparedness, they were at the forefront of a powerful anti–nuclear arms movement in Europe. In the 1990s this movement lost much of its steam as the need for nuclear deterrence declined following the collapse of the Soviet empire and the resultant diminution of the Soviet threat. The campaign cut across class and age groups and was supported by prominent leaders in political parties, labor unions and especially the churches spearheaded by the *Interchurch Peace Council (IKV)*.

Not all Dutch leaders accepted this approach. For instance, *Liberal Party* leader Frits Bolkestein claimed that "these people don't know the world. It is a case of 'stop the world, I want to get off'." He also pointed to something typically Dutch about the campaign: "In a country where religion meant so much, they have been able to infuse the issue with quasi–religious aspects. Everything is seen in terms of 'good' or 'bad'. They are nationalist, parochial, and they want to fix the world and everyone in it."

In 1987 the Lubbers government was vindicated in its view that a decision to deploy cruise missiles on Dutch soil would prod the Soviet Union toward an agreement to scrap all such weapons in Europe. Arms control negotiations culminated in a treaty to remove all medium and short–range missiles from Europe before Holland had to deploy a single one of them. Nevertheless, the debate meant that Holland's NATO partners cannot count on Dutch cooperation in all questions of defense, especially those involving nuclear policy.

Dutch idealism does not always stand in the way of lucrative sales of weapons to countries outside of NATO. About 18,000 Dutch are employed in the arms industry, which produces most kinds of military equipment, including warships, fighter planes, ammunition and electronic and optical equipment for military purposes. Dutch policy is to refuse to sell arms to countries in areas where international tensions are high, but ostensibly for reasons of national security and trade competition, the government tries to keep secret the identity of purchasing countries, as well as the type of equipment sold. Dutch companies sometimes do not cooperate with this policy and with U.N. embargoes, as was the case during the 1991 Gulf War, when the Delft Instruments firm sold and delivered night–sight devices to Iraq.

ECONOMY

The Dutch economy is almost entirely in private hands and the government restrains itself from subsidizing or assuming a direct or indirect ownership of Dutch companies. Nor does it engage in compulsory economic planning. The state nonetheless is very active in the economy. For example, it is a major participant in the Netherlands' Railway, the Dutch States Mines, and the Netherlands Gas Company. It employs 15% of the nation's work force, and including all social security programs, it now spends 51% of the country's GDP.

The government is also closely tied in with the highly structured Dutch system for dealing with conflicts of economic interests. The labor unions (which have unionized about 40% of employees) send representatives to the Joint Industrial Labor Council, established in 1945; employers, primarily the Federation of Netherlands Industry and the Netherlands Federation of Christian Employers, send an equal number of representatives. The Council not only engages in collective bargaining, but serves as an official advisory body to the government.

Another important body is the Social and Economic Council (SER), which is composed of 45 representatives: 15 each from the labor unions and the employers' organizations, 13 academics, and the heads of the central bank and planning agency. The government is required to ask its opinion on all proposed economic and social legislation, and the Council is free

The Netherlands

to give unsolicited advice. The cabinet is not required to follow the advice, but if the Council's recommendations are supported by a large majority of its members it is very difficult for the government to disregard them.

The Netherlands has long since shed its traditional character as an agricultural country. Nevertheless, Dutch agriculture is important. It is very intensive, and farms in Holland, which are predominantly small family operations, are the most productive in all of Western Europe. The percentage of Dutch engaged in agriculture or fishing has dropped by half in the last quarter of the century to only 6% of the total population. Since three-quarters of them are unionized and since their representatives sit in all economic advisory organs and political parties, they still can wield considerable political clout.

Over 70% of the land is used for agricultural purposes, of which 62% is used for grassland, 32.5% for cultivation and 5.5% for horticulture. The visitor notices much cultivation under glass. Of course, no one can overlook the most beautiful crop of all: flowers. The Dutch have grown and exported all over the world a wide variety of plants ever since the first tulip bulbs arrived from Central Asia in the 16th century. Their most splendid showpiece is Keukenhof and its environs, which in the months of April and May must surely be the largest and most colorful garden in the world.

The country is heavily industrialized. Its highly diversified industry employs almost a third of the Dutch work force and accounts for about 70% of the country's total exports. Some of the most prominent industrial names in the world are based in Holland: Phillips, Unilever, Royal Dutch Shell, Fokker–VFW & AKZO. In 1993 the giant music company, PolyGram NV, purchased the legendary symbol of African–American music, Motown Records.

Almost 70% of the industrial turnover is in chemicals and petroleum, metals, biotechnology products, food, drink and tobacco. Chemical and petroleum industries, which include the processing of natural gas and the refining of oil, alone account for over one-third of all exports. The Netherlands does have some lame industries, such as shipbuilding. It is, however, trying to gear up for future trade competition by exporting such sophisticated products as micro–computers and precision optical equipment. The government is strongly supporting the search for new Dutch markets abroad and does offer export subsidies to Dutch companies.

For centuries this has been a trading country, and today it is the world's seventh largest trading nation. Close to 60% of its GDP is derived from the export not only of its goods, but also the services (in which sector half the Dutch work force is employed). It always has invested heavily abroad, ranking second behind the U.K. in total foreign investment in the U.S. It has always been a particularly important transit country because of its ports and inland waterways.

Of all goods loaded or unloaded in the EU destined for or arriving from overseas, 30% pass through Dutch seaports, particularly Rotterdam, the world's largest port. The port moves almost half of all cargo entering or leaving ports between Le Havre in France and Hamburg in Germany. In 1996 the Dutch state and city of Rotterdam launched an investment program valued at $6.1 billion to boost the harbor's capacity. It includes building eight new state–of–the–art terminals capable of serving jumbo container ships. Because a deep channel was dug in the bed of the North Sea, the port can accommodate heavy tankers. Over half the cargo tonnage handled by the port now consists of crude or refined oils, and it is the world's chief oil port and "spot market" on which oil is bought and sold on a supply and demand basis. Pipelines have been constructed which can move petroleum to Germany and Belgium. Rotterdam alone provides more than 10% of the country's GDP.

Because of its inland waterways, which include Western Europe's most important rivers, the Dutch ports of Rotterdam and Amsterdam have the capacity to transport goods by water to markets which serve over 200 million persons. About 70% of the transport between the ports and the European hinterlands moves on water, but Holland also has an excellent road and rail net which is connected with those of neighboring countries. Finally, the national airlines, KLM, links two major Dutch airports, Schiphol near Amsterdam and Zestienhoven near Rotterdam, to cities all over the world.

Holland's chief customer by far is Germany, whose unity was a powerful stimulus for Dutch goods and which accounts for 26% of Dutch foreign trade. Belgium and Luxembourg provide 14% of its imports and buy 15% of its exports. In all, the EU accounts for more than two-thirds of its foreign trade, the U.S. for only about 6%. But the U.S. is still Holland's largest source of private foreign investment; a fifth of American (and a third of British) investment in the EU goes to the Netherlands. The amount of American dollars per capita invested in the Netherlands is larger than in any other European country. The U.S. has 1,100 companies there, including 42 of the top 50 American Fortune 500 companies.

Energy

The Netherlands must, with a few exceptions, import almost all the raw materials its industries need. It has large salt deposits in the eastern part of the country, and it also is able to produce about 5% of the oil it needs. The principal exception is natural gas. Huge gas reserves were discovered in 1959 in Slochteren in Groningen Province. This is now the largest pro-

Offshore gas/oil rigs

The Netherlands

Schiphol Airport

ducing gas field in the world and contains about half of all natural gas reserves in Western Europe. Its gas reserves are the world's fifth largest, after those of Russia, the U.S., Canada and Norway. In energy equivalent, it is equal or superior to Britain's oil reserves in the North Sea. The Slochteren fields produce 84% of the country's gas, the remaining 16% coming from Holland's continental shelf off shore. It exports about one–half of its gas, which is the country's most valuable source of foreign exchange.

The proceeds from these exports have not only kept its balance of payments in surplus since 1982, but the government, which claims a 90% share of all gas export income, derived about 10% of its revenues from this source. In 1980 Holland renegotiated its ten–year gas sales agreements with its Western European customers in order to bring the price more into line with world energy prices.

When the Dutch first discovered their large gas reserves, they decided to exploit them very quickly because they saw that a rapid world–wide conversion to oil was in process. They foresaw the prospect of atomic plants supplying a high percentage of the industrialized world's needs in the future. Therefore, they rapidly converted 90% of Dutch homes and other buildings to gas heat. They also sought to sell their gas quickly while there was still a market for it. Almost all Dutch now regard this decision to have been a very serious mistake.

In the late–1990s natural gas accounts for about half of the nation's energy supplies, while oil accounts for 37%, coal 12.6% and nuclear 1.6%. In order to stretch out their gas supplies at least until the year 2000, the Dutch decided to terminate all gas export contracts in the early 1990s, to limit their own gas use to high–priority needs, such as home heating, and to mandate home insulation and the conversion of industry from gas to coal and oil. They also decided to begin buying gas from abroad, especially from Russia. The government negotiated contracts with Moscow whereby Dutch gas companies would provide assistance in helping it extract gas, which would then be sent to Western Europe.

Oil had to take up the energy slack, a fact which not only damaged Holland's balance of payments, but also made it far more vulnerable to an oil boycott such as the nation faced in 1973–4, when the Arab–dominated OPEC nations singled out Holland for its support of Israel. New discoveries in the North Sea enable the Netherlands to supply 20% of its own oil.

The future reliance on oil can be relieved also by increased use of coal and nuclear power. The Netherlands wanted to raise coal's share of electricity generation from the present 5% to 40% by the end of the century. This is made difficult by the fact that since Holland has already shut down its coal mines, most of the coal will have to be imported. Also, coal has a frightening effect on global warming, a pernicious development which threatens the Dutch almost more than any other nation. Holland has two nuclear power plants, but there is strong opposition to nuclear power generation; a 1990 poll showed 85% opposed building new reactors. The *Labor Party* even advocated the shut–down of the existing plants. With razor–thin majorities, and with the 1986 Chernobyl nuclear accident in the Ukraine still in people's minds, shaky coalitions can seldom afford to touch such hot potatoes, so one cannot expect Holland's energy problems to be alleviated by nuclear power soon.

Current Economic Situation

Dutch industry faces several problems. The work week has fallen to 36 hours. Wage costs are very high, and, if one adds employer contributions to social security, wages are on a par with Belgium. Employers must also pay employees a holiday bonus of 7.5% of their annual pay. Normal wages are not indexed, but pensions and certain benefits are. The trade unions are still moderate, but they are often tempted to seek wage increases which could heat inflation (2.2% in 1999), and they resist reductions in social welfare benefits.

Despite high wage levels and the maintenance of extensive job protections and cooperation with the unions, unemployment has declined to 3.6% in 1999. Part of the success has been the willingness to create incentives to work by lowering unemployment benefits and to make the labor market less rigid by reducing job security and increasing temporary employment. By deregulating work hours and allowing previously unthinkable part–time and temporary work contracts, such jobs now make up a third of all jobs, the highest proportion in all Europe. Such workers also continue to get benefits like vacation and health insurance, and after six months they begin to accumulate pension rights.

Unlike most European countries, the Netherlands actually created jobs in the late 1990s, and this is a particular boon to younger Dutch. Success is due in part to the Dutch tradition of consultation and cooperation. It is also a small enough country that all the key political, labor and employer figures know each other and can work together. There is hidden unemployment, such as early retirement and disability payments. Although the criteria have become stiffer, disability is so loosely interpreted that 700,000 in a workforce of 6.2 million are legally considered to be fully or partially incapacitated.

At the turn of the century the Dutch are showing some of the healthiest economic indicators in the EU. Its economy has grown faster than that of its neighbors since 1993; its growth in 1997 was twice

The Netherlands

that of Germany and France and was 3.5% in 1998. Its budget deficit (down to 1.2% of GDP in 1999), government spending and taxes are sinking, while its national debt, though high at about three–fourths of GDP, is falling. Wages are holding steady while inflation is under control. Its welfare program has become less generous, but unlike most of its EU partners, it faces no "welfare crisis." The Dutch have already tackled most of the economic problems that are now afflicting other EU states.

CULTURE

A largely homogeneous country, the Netherlands has only a small non–white racial minority, and except for a small percentage of persons in the province of Friesland north of Amsterdam who speak a German–Dutch language called Frisian, all whites speak Dutch as their mother tongue. Thus, the country avoids the terrible language problems found in neighboring Belgium. At the same time, the Dutch are very open to the world, and most school children learn English, French and German. Visitors who seek information from or contact with the Dutch are relieved that most Dutch have learned these languages rather well.

Holland is a very pluralistic country in which diversity is institutionalized in a way which the Dutch call *Verzuiling*, or "columnization." This means the coexistence in political and social life of separate religious organizations which operate parallel to one another, but which aspire to the same goals. Such columnization is no longer as rigid as it was two decades ago, but diversity still is found in education, the mass media, sports and social clubs. Dutch school children are free to attend either state or private (mainly religious) schools, all of which are financed entirely by the government.

Primary schooling lasts six years, and 70% of primary school children attend private schools. Secondary school pupils can choose either to go straight into vocational education, which would lead to careers in the trades, services or sales, or into a general secondary education, which paves the way to the university. Approximately 60% of the secondary school pupils attend private schools. There are 12 universities, three of which are private. Only 3% of Dutch students of university age attend them, compared with approximately 50% in the U.S. Over 70% of university students attend state institutions. Many Dutch attend religious schools from the beginning through the university. Aside from some supervision to ensure minimum standards, the government does not attempt to influence the private schools.

Religion

In the Netherlands religion has always been an important force shaping the national character. The Reformation took seed in Holland and it was the attempt of the Spanish king to re–Catholicize Holland that sparked the Dutch rebellion in the 16th century. It remains a tradition for the Dutch royal family to belong to the Protestant Dutch Reformed Church. When the Queen's younger sister Irene left the Netherlands in 1963 to marry Prince Carlos Hugo de Borbon y Parma, a Catholic pretender to the throne of Spain, the very enemy her forefathers fought for almost a hundred years, she threw her family and her country into a rage. But in fact, the Netherlands was never thorough-

Keukenhof

The Netherlands

A residential area in Amsterdam

ly converted to the Protestant sect of Calvinism, and even today over 40% of the population is Catholic, compared with 36% non–Catholic and over 23% which profess no belief in religion at all. Still, those observers are to some extent correct when they say that every Dutchman is somewhat a Calvinist.

The Dutch take a very strong moral approach to most human affairs. One sees this in the tone and content of Dutch politics. Moral arguments are invariably made to support many political issues, including social welfare, human rights, nuclear disarmament, environmental protection and aid to developing countries. Some political parties are organized around religious principles. Although Dutch voters are less likely than they once were to vote primarily out of religious considerations, political parties often cannot resist the temptation to sprinkle their appeal with biblical messages, even if practical political considerations far outweigh religious ones. Most radio and television organizations and some newspapers have religious affiliations.

Further, despite the fact that church and state are officially separated, the school system offers both religious and secular schools, with the state picking up the bill for both.

Despite their religious and moral approach to many human affairs and despite the religious strife that one still finds in the country, the Dutch have never practiced the kind of intolerance which Calvinists practiced in, for example, the Massachusetts Bay Colony. Most of its people continue to display an almost unique measure of tolerance toward other ideas and ways of living without which no democracy can function properly. Some Dutch are increasingly inclined to cast off their tolerance and to attack violently those views which they do not accept. For instance, when the Pope visited the Netherlands in 1985, he was greeted by bottles, cans, bombs and such obscene chants as "Kill, kill, kill the Pope!" A majority of Dutch Catholics *do* oppose the Vatican's teachings on contraception, abortion, celibacy and the ordination of women, and John Paul had gone to Hol-

The Netherlands

land in the first place to *heal* these divisions.

While religion plays a role in many facets of public life, church attendance is actually falling. The importance of religion in everyday affairs is no longer as great as it once was. Polls in 1987 indicated that 27% of Dutch adults attend church regularly (vs. 14% in the U.K. and 12% in France). The fact that both religions draw believers from all occupations prevents them from being linked closely with any particular social class, as is the case in Northern Ireland.

The churches' influence at election time is also declining. In 1963, for instance, 83% of Catholics voted for the *Catholic People's Party*, but in 1972, only 38% did. Still, there are fewer interfaith marriages than in most European countries.

The Dutch remain a very family–oriented people, who tend to treasure family life and prefer private to public amusement. There is very little outright class discrimination. Nevertheless, there is still a large income gap among citizens, and people of different social classes tend not to mix as frequently and as easily as in the U.S.

Tolerance for Minorities

Holland was always a land of refuge. It absorbed religious refugees from England, Belgium and France, and Jews from Spain and Portugal. In fact, because of the tolerant and relatively enlightened and prosperous conditions inside the Netherlands, the Dutch never poured out of their country and colonized foreign lands in great numbers. Presently about 10% of the population is visibly different ethnically from the native Dutch. When Indonesia won its independence from the Netherlands, many people of Indonesian ancestry came to Holland and assimilated rather well. Exceptions were the 15,000 South Moluccans who could not get along with the new rulers and who were permitted to resettle in Holland. Their community has since more than doubled to 40,000. They have borne a deep grudge against the Dutch, for whom these Protestant Christians had fought. They claim to have been led to believe that their homeland would be made independent as a reward for their loyalty and that the Dutch still have an obligation to help them achieve a free South Moluccan republic. They have long refused to integrate into Dutch society, preferring instead to dream of returning to their homeland on their own terms.

In order to publicize their plight in 1975, a group of them besieged both a train in northern Holland and the Indonesian consulate in Amsterdam, actions which resulted in several deaths. Despite such problems, the Dutch have refused to consider washing their hands of these troublesome guests by simply expelling all of them or even their more violent fringe. In May 1986, on the 35th anniversary of their arrival, the Dutch government announced that it would grant annual tax–free payments of $800 and commemorative medals to 3,000 South Moluccan veterans or their widows, and that a museum of Moluccan history would be created.

When Suriname became independent in 1975, approximately 140,000 Surinamese left their newly freed country to go to Holland. The Dutch did almost nothing to stop or discourage them. Referring to these Surinamese, who now number 180,000, one Dutch clergyman spoke for many of his countrymen when he said that "they are here because we were there." The Netherlands continued to provide $1.5 billion of aid to Suriname annually. It strongly criticized the military *coup* which toppled the elected Surinamese government in December 1990.

In the 1960s when the labor–starved Dutch economy was in desperate need of more workers, thousands of guest workers poured in from the Mediterranean area, primarily from Turkey (now 156,000), Morocco (now 112,000), Spain and Italy, and concentrated in the cities of Rotterdam, Amsterdam and the Hague. The influx from non–EU countries has been stopped, but foreign workers and their families already account for about 6% of the Netherlands' population and for 13% of residents in the country's larger cities (a figure which is expected to rise to 20%). This percentage includes neither the Surinamese or the immigrants from the Netherlands Antilles, who are continuing to enter Holland.

The foreign workers are a very convenient target for quasi–fascist extremist groups such as the *Netherland People's Union*, this latter group can be expected to win very few votes in any Dutch election. Although these minorities are not on an economic or social par with the Dutch, and while unemployment is considerably higher among these groups, the Dutch government bends over backwards to serve them if they stay. For instance, mobile caravan schools have been organized for gypsy children, and all minorities are entitled to the same social welfare benefits as are the native Dutch. The Dutch Broadcasting Foundation beams television shows in five languages with subtitles. In 1986 'outlanders' (as the resident foreigners are called) were permitted to vote or run for office in municipal elections, and 49 were elected to city council posts. A 1998 survey on racism in Europe revealed that about a third of Dutch admit to being "racist" or "fairly racist." This regrettable statistic was nevertheless far below that in Belgium (55%) and France (48%).

In 1992 an Israeli cargo jet crashed into an Amsterdam apartment building filled with illegal aliens, killing 43 and leaving many survivors with chronic health problems. An enquiry in 1999 revealed that the plane had had 600 pounds of de-

Motor biking in The Hague

The Netherlands

pleted uranium and components of deadly Sarin nerve gas on board. This led to accusations against the Dutch government that it had misled parliament on the consequences of the crash. This tragic accident sparked calls for expulsion of such illegal residents, who constitute up to 1% of the population. Partly in response, political asylum regulations were tightened to allow faster expulsion of rejected applicants.

Prime Minister Lubbers reaped vehement criticism in 1993 when he commented that the Netherlands had reached the 'critical threshold' as far as the number of resident foreigners was concerned. In 1996 the Netherlands adopted a method of dealing with illegal immigrants so harsh that it caused a wave of protests in detention centers. Some foreigners there complained that cells were overcrowded, that they had been denied access to lawyers, and that they had been forced to pose nude for photographs. Prison authorities acknowledged that the policy is intended to discourage further immigration.

Homosexuals in the Netherlands have wider civil rights than anywhere in Europe. Since 1999 they can register their partnerships in a civil ceremony and have almost the same rights and obligations as heterosexual couples. They can take each other's surname, inherit their property, receive alimony, and enjoy the same tax status. The only restriction is that only one partner in a homosexual marriage may adopt a child. Polls indicate that most Dutch support these reforms.

Drug Policies

In the early 1970s the Dutch had another opportunity to show their toleration when Amsterdam became the favorite destination for long–haired, guitar–toting young people who were called at the time "hippies," as well as other younger people with different lifestyles. While these young people horrified the established citizens almost everywhere they went, the Dutch accepted them with good humor and tried hard to find them temporary shelter and areas where they could meet freely. They also tried to look the other way when the visitors chose to use "soft" drugs or violate the sexual standards of Dutch society.

By the mid–1980s, though, Dutch patience with hard drug trafficking and crime in Amsterdam had visibly begun to wear thin, and neighborhood vigilante groups were organized to protect against lawbreakers. On the whole, the crime rate remains low compared with the U.S. and many other Western European countries. But street crime has increased dramatically. Some politicians suggest that judges hand out sentences which are too lenient.

Moulin de la Galette by Vincent Van Gogh (1853–1890)

In 1986, for instance, a punker who stabbed to death a young man outside a disco was sentenced to four years in prison, two of which were suspended. Dutch jails are known throughout Europe to be the hardest to enter and the easiest to leave. Even hardened criminals in prisons are permitted to vote and to have overnight visits with their families, girlfriends or homosexual partners in special rooms with complete privacy. Two–thirds of all prisoners are hard drug addicts, which points to a further problem.

Polls in 1996 showed that only 5% of the population uses cannabis regularly. It is still technically illegal, but the state taxes the profits from the sale of cannabis, and police put the lowest priority on preventing the sale and use of small amounts of it. Marijuana is so tolerated that 1,200 coffee houses put it on their menus and serve it to customers. There are some legal problems. Dutch law prohibits substances that have been "processed." Does that include mushrooms merely if they have been dried? Authorities are well practiced at turning a blind eye. When ecstasy tablets became popular in the 1980s, they were declared illegal. But the police were told to ignore consumption and to try to curb manufacturing.

Uncomfortable with its reputation as being soft on drug users, Dutch authorities cracked down on the larger–scale commercialization of soft drugs. Neighboring countries put pressure on the Dutch government to enforce stricter laws on drugs. The German government blames it for the vast amount of drugs crossing the German border. France also

215

The Netherlands

feels compelled to maintain its border controls. The Netherlands is responding to those concerns as Europe moves toward tighter economic and monetary unification.

Cafe owners were put on notice not to call attention to their wares, deal in carry-out quantities, sell more than a sixth of an ounce at a time, or sell cocaine and heroin under the counter. Coffee houses caught selling cannabis to children under age 18 are to be shut down. One justice ministry spokeswoman commented: "We want just enough to cater to our own citizens, not to the drug tourists." Police are cracking down on drug dealing at highway rest stops and parking areas. They have especially gone after on the traffic in hard drugs, even though users are not arrested unless they commit other crimes. Authorities believe that their tolerating soft drugs is responsible for the decline in the percentage of young people using hard drugs from 14% in the 1980s to only 1.6% in 1997, compared with 3% in Italy, 2.8% in France, and 1.5% in Germany.

Addicts are steered into treatment and are provided with clean new needles to prevent AIDS. The publicly visible use of drugs has caused some Dutch to wonder if their country has indeed become too permissive. Ed van Thijn, Mayor of Amsterdam, confessed that "in the past 15 years tolerance became synonymous with permissiveness and softness on law-and-order." In 1990 the Washington-based Drugs Policy Foundation awarded the Dutch government a prize for "its effective and humanitarian drug policies." Said one senior Amsterdam policeman: "We do not say that our way is right for them [Americans], but we are sure it is right for us."

The Dutch, as a people, are inclined to cling to tradition and to be conservative. At the same time they are open to new ideas and are relatively tolerant toward all forms of individualism. This is why criticism and protest can be so firmly entrenched in the Dutch tradition, but why the Dutch are at the same time not inclined to be revolutionary. Compromise is a highly developed art in the Netherlands, and protest groups have often been smothered by tolerance. It often saps one's strength to beat one's head against a richly padded, sympathetic wall!

Media and Arts

"Columnization" is also found in the press and electronic media. Newspapers and magazines reflect the opinions of many diverse groups in society, and the average reader expects to find his own opinions expressed in the news he reads. Financial problems have resulted in the concentration of most newspapers in the hands of a few large companies, although 60% of the dailies still manage to take an independent editorial line. To help preserve their independence the government provides financial support to newspapers and magazines which are undergoing reorganization to become profitable again. The major dailies, in order of circulation, are *De Telegraaf* (conservative), *Algemeen Dagblad* (neutral), *De Volkskrant* (progressive), *Het Parool,* (center-left) and *Trouw* (Protestant). Top people tend to prefer the *Nieuwe Rotterdamse Courant* (now called *NRC–Handelsblad)* and the *Financiele Dagblad.* The major magazines are *Elseviers Magazine, Elseviers Weekblad* and *Vrij Nederland.* In 1990 the first Sunday newspaper, called *De Krant op Zondag,* was introduced in 50 years. It is printed in Belgium to avoid Dutch union laws against working on Sunday.

Radio and television programming is in the hands of at least eight larger private broadcasting organizations, which largely operate free of government control. In 1988 a new public educational and cultural channel (Nederland 3) was introduced. Many of these organizations represent the basic pillars of society. For instance, KRO is Catholic, NCRV is Protestant, VPRO is liberal Protestant and VARA is socialist. Unlike many newspapers, however, the broadcasting companies attempt to broaden their appeals to include all social groups. They are, therefore, actually able to overcome some of the cleavages in Dutch society. These four private organizations operate within the framework established by the government-related Netherlands Broadcasting Association. The NOS, a quasi-governmental broadcasting foundation, is charged with producing programs "in the general interest," such as news bulletins. The Ministry of Welfare, Health and Culture is the authority to oversee its operations. The postal service collects fees to finance broadcasting. The NOS also controls the amount of advertising which may be broadcast on radio and television. NOS has a very difficult time, however, controlling a few pirate stations which illegally broadcast and televise in the country from offshore ships. In 1988 the European Court of Justice ruled against Dutch restrictions on advertising by foreign broadcasters, calling them too strict.

When one thinks of Dutch culture, perhaps the first words that come to mind are the names of painters: Hieronymus Bosch, with his powerful and sometimes terrifying scenes, brought to European art in the 16th century a form of symbolism which reflected the mind of a great vision-

The Netherlands

ary. In the 17th century, Rembrandt, Franz Hals and Jan Vermeer established an artistic tradition through their vivid depiction of early Dutch life. In the 19th century J.B. Jongkind became a precursor of impressionism, and Vincent van Gogh, in a short but wild life, helped create the romantic picture that many people have of artists. He sketched the drab and dreary life of persons living in working–class and rural areas in the late 19th century, going later to Paris and southern France where he established his personal style of short brushstrokes in brilliant colors, which pointed the way to a new, expressive style.

In the Dutch artistic tradition of accurately recording the landscape around them, Hendrick Willem Mesdag painted in 1880 the world's largest panoramic painting, portraying Scheveningen, a fishing village on the outskirts of The Hague. Displayed in a museum in The Hague, called the "Panorama Mesdag," the painting completely surrounds the viewer and gives him the most vivid possible impression of Holland in Mesdag's time. Piet Mondrian, the greatest and most consistent renovator of modern Dutch art of the 20th century, began with experimental nature paintings, but gradually he departed from nature and sought harmonious and universal images. His paintings of lines and colors are among the world's most treasured modern art works.

The Dutch consider art to be so important for the society that they maintain, at public expense, some 3,000 artists who are unable to make a living. Although they must demonstrate that they are full– time and professionally trained artists with talent, once they are selected they merely have to deliver a modest number of paintings each year to the state in return for their pay.

Most of the paintings go into storage and are never seen again. Some critics argue that this subsidy lowers the quality of painting and is merely an example of the welfare state run wild. Yet, the taxpayers do not appear to mind bearing the costs for this. The government also helps to finance experimental theater, orchestra, ballet and film companies. Over 4% of the central government's budget is devoted to supporting the arts. Even Dutch businesses are financing a variety of artistic groups from jazz to chamber music artists in order to improve their image with customers.

Historically, Holland is rich with philosophical and intellectual leaders. Hugo Grotius founded the study of international law. René Descartes, a Frenchman who was living in the Netherlands, developed a new starting point for philosophy when he asserted "I think, therefore I am." Baruch Spinoza wrote treatises on the relationships between the human intellect, the state and religious belief. Anton van Leeuwenhoek invented the microscope that thereby revolutionized the study of biology. Christian Huygens invented the pendulum clock, and the Dutch have been a very punctual people ever since.

There are more than 20 million people inside and outside the Netherlands who can read Dutch literature in the original, and the Foundation for Promoting the Translation of Dutch Literature seeks to introduce the nation's writings abroad.

Before the 16th century, literature was primarily composed of plays, religious literature, folk tales and stories of chivalry. In the 17th century Joost van den Vondel's writings were read all over Europe. The most noted author of the 19th century was Multatuli, whose novel *Max Havelaar*, written in 1860, attacked colonialism. The works of novelist Louis Couperus evoke the atmosphere of the turn of the century. After 1945, Holland rapidly lost its rural character. The postwar literature of such younger writers as Jan Wolkers, W.F. Hermans, Harry Mulisch and G.K. van't Reve often deals with the problems arising from life in a highly urban and industrial society.

FUTURE

The Netherlands will remain politically stable because the many diverse groupings in Dutch society are willing to compromise within the political sphere, while continuing to profess different social and religious values. It will remain a reliable ally for its NATO partners, as its participation in the air war over Yugoslavia demonstrated.

The 1998 parliamentary elections retained Kok's ruling coalition in power. However, it resigned in May 1999 over whether to give citizens the right to vote in referenda. Prime Minister Kok hinted that new elections might be necessary: "The voters must have their say." The crisis was solved in June by a compromise allowing more referenda, but they will be consultative, not binding. Kok remained prime minister.

Panorama Mesdag by Hendrick Willem Mesdag

Photo: L. Schepman

The Kingdom of Belgium

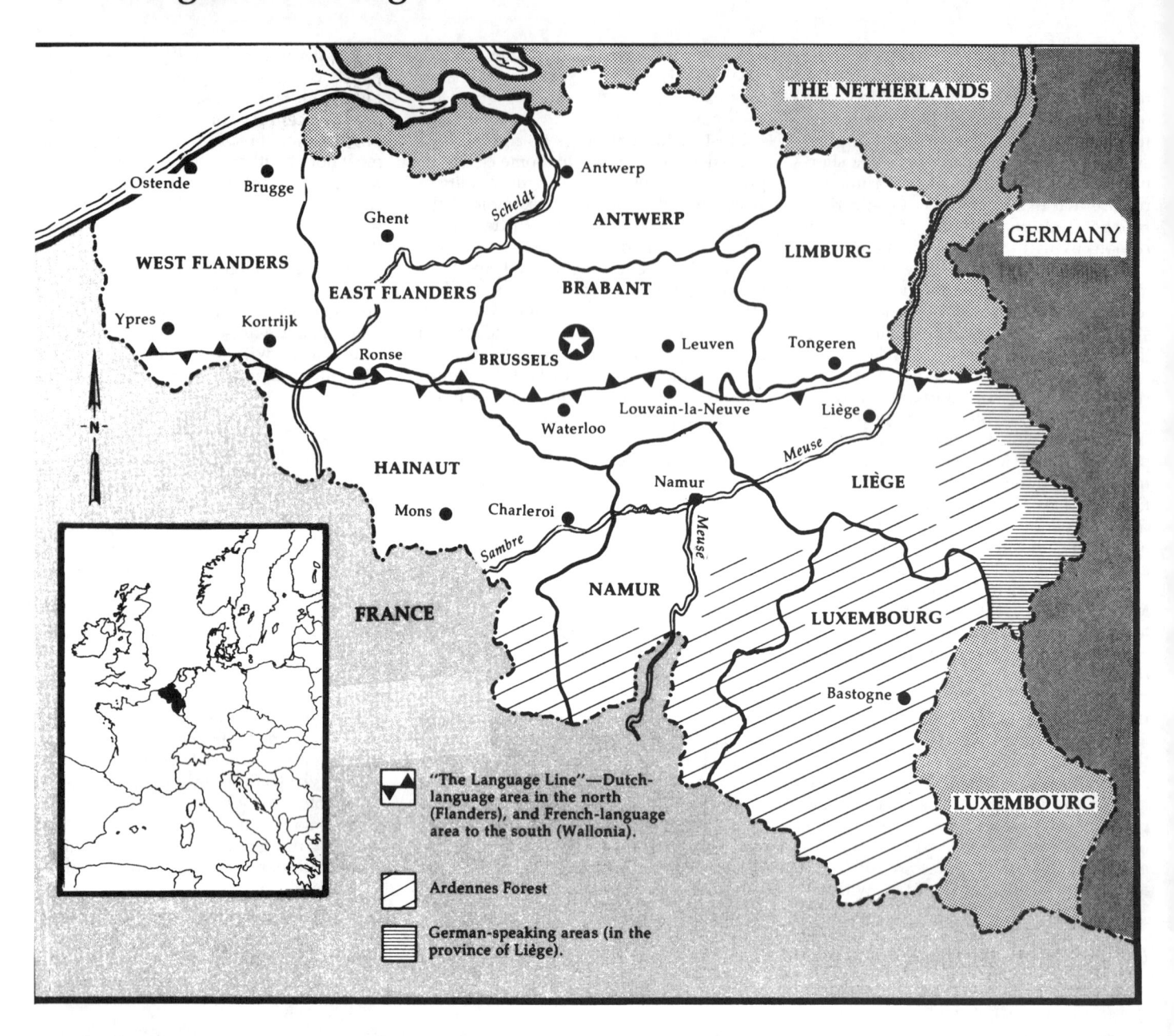

Map Legend:
- "The Language Line"—Dutch-language area in the north (Flanders), and French-language area to the south (Wallonia).
- Ardennes Forest
- German-speaking areas (in the province of Liège).

Area: 18,991 sq. mi. (30,562 sq. km., somewhat larger than Maryland and about 200 miles or 320 km. wide, taken from its northwest to southeast points).

Population: 10.2 million (estimated).

Capital City: Brussels (Pop. 1.1 million, estimated).

Climate: Temperate, with rather mild winters and comfortable summers.

Neighboring Countries: Germany (East); the Netherlands (North); France (South); Luxembourg (Southeast); England is about 54 miles (87 km.) away across the English Channel.

Official Languages: Dutch (57%), French (32%), and both languages are spoken by another 10%, principally those living in and around Brussels, 80% of whose citizens are native French speakers. German is the native tongue for 1%.

Ethnic Background: Indo–European, descendants of the Gauls and Franks.

Principal Religion: Roman Catholic (95%).

Main Exports: Metal manufactures, chemicals, steel products, textiles, food products, 70% of the world's cobalt, 60% of the world's diamond dealing and 40% of cutting.

Main Imports: Motor vehicles, chemicals, foodstuffs.

Major Trading Partners: EU, Germany, France and the Netherlands.

Currency: Belgian Franc.

National Day: July 21st.

Chief of State: His Majesty King Albert II (b. 1934). Ascended the throne on August 9, 1993. Married Paola Ruffo di Calabria (Italy), 1959.

Heir Apparent: His Royal Highness Prince Philippe (b. 1960).

Head of Government: Guy Verhofstadt, Prime Minister (July 12, 1999).

National Flag: Vertical stripes of red, yellow and black, with the black stripe at the pole.

In some ways Belgium is a very unnatural country. It has no natural frontiers, such as a mountain chain or wide river, to set it off from its neighbors. It has therefore always been very vulnerable to foreign invasion. Belgians have no common

Belgium

language and are extremely sensitive about being forced to speak the one not used in their half of the country. Their tradition as a unified country is only a century and a half old and is too weak to give its citizens a strong common identity. Unlike the Swiss, many Belgians never really developed the habit of thinking in terms of a single nation.

It sometimes seems that there are just six million Dutch–speaking Flemings and four million French–speaking Walloons, who must try very hard to live with each other. Unfortunately, the forces which once held them together—Roman Catholicism, economic and political opposition to the Dutch—are no longer strong. During the 1970s, the economic prosperity which in the past smoothed over some of the most important lingual and cultural problems was threatened. In short, Belgium appeared almost like a shotgun wedding—like a hopelessly broken marriage which held together only because the partners could find no other place to live.

Such a view is that of a pessimist, who likes to call half–empty a glass which is half–full. For awhile, Belgium's language disputes showed signs of cooling. Parties which preach language radicalism are still being demolished at the polls. Economic performance and stable government, as well as language issues, are foremost in Belgians' minds. Belgians have many trumps in their hands as they face the future. They are rather cautious, conservative people, a fact which causes some critics to call Belgium a private, family–centered country. It also means that while their conflicts are often verbally bitter and serious and sometimes erupt in street brawls between the rare hotheads, Belgians are very unlikely to resort to outright violence and terror to accomplish their goals. They have always shown a genius for compromise by very small steps. Thus, no one expects the community problems, as the language issue is called, to explode into a bloody and tragic Northern Ireland–style conflict. As was shown at the end of 1987, though, they can still cause a government to collapse.

It still has many valuable economic resources. It has a very skilled work force with a proven willingness to work. Its economy remains highly productive; this has usually kept inflation low and has maintained for Belgians one of the highest standards of living in the world. Its central location in Europe remains a very significant trading advantage for the country. It is an important partner in a unified Europe and in the Atlantic Alliance, and its capital city, Brussels, is in many ways the "capital of Europe," housing the headquarters for both NATO and the EU. One in three residents of Brussels is now non–Belgian. Some countries even have to send three ambassadors to this city: one to the King of the Belgians, one to NATO and one to the EU.

Belgium is a picturesque country with scenery varying from Gothic medieval university cities to countless towns and villages located along winding rivers with steep bluffs. The country is mainly flat, but it rises toward the south, away from the North Sea coast and toward the Ardennes Forest. The country can be divided roughly into three geographic parts. In the North is the Flemish plain, which extends westward from a 41 mile (60 km.) North Sea coastline, with its sandy beaches and luxurious and expensive resorts. Flanders presents a pastoral landscape with small farms and most of Belgium's agricultural production. With 56% of the Belgian population, it is the most densely populated part of the country which itself is the second most densely populated land in all Europe, behind the Netherlands. Here are the Flemish cities of Brugge (with its many bridges which gave the city its name), Ghent and Antwerp, all three towns filled with cathedrals and other medieval structures. Most of Belgium's newer industries are located in Flanders, which is the country's most economically dynamic section, a fact which greatly riles the Walloons today.

At the center of Belgium are rolling fields of grain and many villages with houses grouped around the parish church. In the middle is Brussels, and below it are heavy industrial centers, clustered around the formerly rich Walloon coal fields, which are now largely exhausted and closed. This was the area of the country's industrial revolution in the 19th century, which occurred in Belgium earlier than almost anywhere else in Europe. It is where such industrial cities as Mons, Charleroi and the ancient and dignified city of Liège are located. South of the Sambre and Meuse rivers is the third area, with no large cities or industries. It is a region of fields and pastures with woods thickening as one travels southward into the Ardennes Forest.

Running west to east just south of Kor-

Their Majesties King Albert and Queen Paola

H.R.H. Prince Philippe

Belgium

trijk, Ronse, Brussels, Leuven (Louvain) and Tongeren is an invisible line established 1,500 years ago and now of far greater significance for contemporary Belgium than the geographic areas mentioned above. This is the language line which separates the Flemings from the Walloons. Along the German border is also the German-speaking minority numbering about 64,500 people. Because most Belgians live on "their" side of the language line, they have fewer language problems, now that Flemish (a language which differs from Dutch about as much as American from British English), French or German is used exclusively in all affairs, including education, law, government and business, within each respective region.

The people in the various sections do not look or act very differently, although some observers claim to notice differences in the people's characters—the Flemings being severe and serious and the Walloons being more outgoing, volatile and fun-loving. In fact, the visitor would scarcely notice any difference at all if it were not for the fact that he hears different languages spoken on the streets and sees different languages on street signs and on billboards. The language separation is greatly complicated by the capital city of Brussels, which has 11% (1.1 million) of the country's population, 85% of whom speak French as a mother tongue. This city is situated uncomfortably north of the language line and is surrounded by Flemish speakers. It is over the hurdle of Brussels that all proponents of regional language reform have tripped.

One would not expect language difficulties to trouble this small, cosmopolitan country which is located at the very crossroads of Europe and which has been one of the most persistent and constructive proponents of European integration. But it is exactly this problem which has caused many people to wonder how more birthdays this country will be able to celebrate.

HISTORY

Shaky Independence

Belgium proclaimed its independence from the Netherlands in 1830, and its new king took the name of Leopold I. Because the Dutch king refused to recognize Belgian independence until 1839, his most immediate goal was to win recognition for his new state, a goal which was greatly boosted by his marriage to the daughter of Louis-Philippe, King of France from 1830–1848. Having adopted a modern liberal constitution in 1830, Belgium was scarcely affected by the storm of revolution which blew across Europe in 1848 and could turn its attention to economic development.

Bilingual signs, Brussels: Flemish, then French

Following Britain's example, Belgium adopted a policy of free trade and plunged headlong into industrialization, using its large and easily extracted coal resources. This effort was aided by an agreement with the Dutch in 1863 ending tolls for the use of the Scheldt River, which passes through Dutch territory before emptying into the North Sea. This agreement enabled the Belgians to develop fully the port of Antwerp which now plays such a key role in their trade.

The rapid industrial growth also gave birth to an urbanized working class and ultimately to socialism, which along with liberalism and Catholicism became one of the three main political "families" or social cleavages in Belgian society. These divisions still exist, although they are now less hostile to each other than they once were. The liberal and Catholic "families" squabbled throughout the 19th and early 20th centuries over the relations between church and state, especially insofar as the schools were concerned. Their struggle roughly ended in a draw, and state financial support continues to flow to both secular and denominational schools.

King Leopold II actively engaged in colonial activity. Henry Stanley, the famous Welshman who after emigrating to America fought on both sides of the U.S. Civil War, proceeded on an arduous journey to Africa in search of the Scot missionary, Dr. Livingstone. Leopold summoned him to Belgium and engaged him to explore the Congo area of Africa (not on behalf of Belgium, but on behalf of the king!). Stanley accepted, left for Africa and negotiated many favorable treaties with local chiefs which resulted in the establishment of the Congo Free State. Conditions were harsh, since Leopold reportedly condoned labor and torture as instruments to produce wealth. Some say that about eight million Africans lost their lives during 23 years of Leopold's exploitation. Bowing to strong international pressures after a commission reported that administration of the colony was scandalous, the parliament passed an act in 1908 annexing the Congo state of Belgium. But Leopold had already enriched his treasury with the immense copper deposits in Katanga Province (now Shaba) during his years of possession.

Another problem began to bubble in the 19th century: the conflict between languages. French so dominated the overcentralized bureaucracy, the court system, schools and businesses in the entire country that ambitious Flemings felt obligated to observe the rule "French in the parlor, Flemish in the kitchen." In the long run, such suppression of the Flemings' language, and with it their identity as a people, could not last. In 1898 Belgium officially became a bilingual state, although it was not until 1932 that Flemish could be

King Leopold II of Belgium

Belgium

used in the national administration and not until the 1960s that Flemish became fully equal to French.

Failure of Neutrality and World War I

Since independence, Belgium tried to preserve its neutrality, which had been guaranteed by the great powers in Europe. However, when this was put to a test in 1914, the result was disastrous. Imperial Germany had set its gun sights toward France and demanded the right of free passage through Belgium for its troops. The Belgians refused, and the British announced that they would stand by the treaty of 1839 and support the Belgians to the end. Winston S. Churchill, the First Lord of the Admiralty, wrote later that the British cabinet had been "overwhelmingly pacific" at the beginning of August 1914, but the direct appeal from the King of the Belgians for French and British aid raised an issue which united an overwhelming majority of ministers."

In a meeting with the British ambassador to Berlin, the German Chancellor, who thought he was speaking off the record, expressed amazement that the British would go to war over a mere "scrap of paper." Of course, the treaty rested on more than paper. It was anchored to the British national interest of preventing the North Sea coasts from being dominated by a hostile power and of preventing any European power from dominating the continent, as would have been the case if the Germans conquered France. The Belgians were conquered by the Germans in a few weeks, but their bravery against truly insurmountable odds was one of the most important factors in preventing a German victory in World War I.

The German violation of Belgian neutrality conformed with the German "Schliefen Plan," designed to meet the danger of a two–front war in the East and West through a strike at the heart of France on the well–fortified Franco–German frontier, which extended 150 miles (240 km.) from Switzerland to Verdun. German forces were to be concentrated on the right flank, which would sweep through Luxembourg and Belgium into northern France. Paris would be enveloped and the French troops would be pushed back toward the Moselle where they would be met by the German left flank.

By late August 1914 this plan appeared to have succeeded. German troops, which had bypassed Antwerp and the Belgian coast were dangerously close to Paris, with only a retreating French and British army before them. However, the German commanders grew increasingly nervous about the Belgian army, which was in a position to strike at the Germans' right flank and perhaps even to sever their lengthening lines of communication and supply in Belgium. Therefore, some German troops were detached from the main invasion force in order to contain the Belgian army in Antwerp. Seeing a chance to increase the Germans' nervousness, the British sent a brigade of marines (about 3,000 men) to the Belgian port of Ostende and leaked rumors of much more massive British landings and of totally fictitious British–aided Russian landings involving more than 80,000 troops.

This partly contrived danger to the German right flank, along with the Belgian army's refusal to surrender, influenced the German decision to avoid Paris and to slow down their advance. This interruption of momentum proved to be crucial during the four–day Battle of the Marne in September and turned the tide of the war. The Belgian military effort was an example of how seemingly hopeless defensive operations, when seen in a larger strategic context, can be crucial for overall victory.

The Germans occupied most of Belgium for the remainder of the war although the king and the remains of the Belgian army held out in Ypres on a few square miles of unoccupied Belgian soil on the western tip of the country. This small salient was pulverized by four years of constant bombardment, and by the time the armistice was signed, it resembled a crater–filled lunar landscape.

Initially the Germans found some favor among some Flemings, who saw the possibility of liberation from Walloon control. Such sympathy, which was again manifested in World War II, created great distrust in Wallonia toward the Flemings and has still not been entirely forgotten by Walloons. Further complicating the picture was a feeling on the part of some Walloons that the French had "defaulted" in both World War I and World War II, and that Belgians had to pay a high price in helping pull French irons out of the fire. This strengthened the realization that union with France was unthinkable. Thus, although "estranged," the couple (Walloons and Flemings) had no choice but to remain in the same house.

German plunder of Belgian industry led to high unemployment and the mass deportation of Belgian workers to Germany, creating downright hatred. Even the German military commander in Belgium had to protest the policies he was asked to enforce. He remarked sarcastically that "a squeezed–out lemon has no value and a slaughtered cow gives no milk!"

The Inter–War Period and World War II

After World War I, Belgium entered the League of Nations and was given the German–speaking area of Eupen, Malmedy and Saint Vith, as well as a League of Nations mandate over two former German colonies in Africa, now called Rwanda and Burundi. It also abandoned its earlier policy of neutrality and negotiated a military agreement with France and Great Britain. As the clouds of war became more ominous in the 1930s, however, Belgium again proclaimed a policy of neutrality on October 28, 1936. It was thus without allies when on May 10, 1940, German troops again invaded Belgium. After 18 days of bitter fighting the Belgian army was forced to capitulate. The government escaped to London, but the King of the Belgians became a prisoner of the Germans.

Although Belgium was liberated after the Normandy invasion in the summer of 1944, war returned when Hitler threw his last tanks into the Ardennes Forest in order to recapture Antwerp and break the Allied advance. The decisive action took place at the southern Belgian town of Bastogne, where the surrounded U.S. forces under General Anthony McAuliffe refused to surrender. When called upon to recognize the hopelessness of his situation and to give up, he reportedly answered defiantly, "nuts!" It has long been rumored that the general actually used a different expression, but decorous military historians chose to report it in the now famous way. Fortunately, foggy weather broke and enabled the necessary air support to preserve the general's position. After the war, Bastogne's main square was renamed "Place McAuliffe." The Bastogne Historical Center was opened to commemorate one of the most important battles of the war, and every December a "Nuts Festival" is held.

Postwar Reconstruction and "The Royal Question"

Belgium's postwar reconstruction was accomplished very rapidly. Partly because it had been liberated so quickly, the country had not been as heavily bombed and shelled as the Netherlands, and Antwerp was virtually undamaged. It adopted a financial policy to strengthen the Belgian franc, which soon became one of the most stable currencies in Europe. It also blocked all bank accounts and levied a high tax on fortunes acquired as a result of collaboration with the Germans.

From 1945 until 1950 Belgium was rocked by the so–called "royal question." King Leopold III, unlike his Dutch and Luxembourg counterparts, refused to leave Belgium when the government fled. He argued that as Commander–in–Chief of the armed forces he was compelled to stay where he could help his people more than by leaving. He did deal with the German occupiers, and some of his country-

Belgium

Bastogne: winter of 1944

men claimed he had actually *collaborated* with them. Shortly before liberation, the Germans moved him to Austria, where he remained until 1950. Until his wartime role could be determined, his brother Charles served as regent. A parliamentary commission appointed in 1947 returned a favorable verdict as far as the king's wartime actions were concerned, but the socialists and communists continued to oppose his return. In an attempt to settle the question once and for all, a referendum was held in 1950 in which 57.7% of all voters approved of the King's return. Significantly, 58% of the Walloons were opposed. When he reentered Belgium in 1950, the resulting disorders were so intense that Leopold felt obligated to abdicate in favor of his eldest son, Prince Baudouin, on July 16, 1951.

Ever since the "royal question" divided the country, the Belgian king has never been able to exercise the considerable influence on Belgian affairs which he formerly had. None of his acts is effective unless the responsible ministers countersign his orders. Baudouin was a popular monarch who restored dignity to the Belgian throne while stripping it of much of its earlier pomposity. The monarch is now expected to be a symbol of the nation, but to perform this role he often has to bend over backward to please the Walloons, whose hatred of grandfather Leopold still smolders. Of course, overt efforts to satisfy the Walloons inevitably stimulate criticism among the Flemish.

The king must often play a role in facilitating the formation of cabinets, and since more than 30 have been formed since 1945, this is no small task. It is after parliament has been dissolved and a new cabinet is being sought that the king's influence is greatest. The limited nature of his power was again shown in 1981 when he called together 18 political, labor and business leaders in order to appeal to them to end the country's political instability. Some criticized this, accusing the king of going beyond his established powers. Though there is no republican movement in Belgium, the king is truly a very limited monarch.

One of Belgium's most serious and prolonged postwar crises was the painful decolonization of the Belgian Congo, 80 times the size of Belgium with a vastly larger population. Over 100,000 Belgians had settled in the Congo, and Belgium had certainly developed economic interests there, although it sought to avoid mutual economic dependence between the colony and mother country. Belgium opened up the colony to foreign investment and trade. In the 1950s winds of African independence began to reach gale proportions, especially after the new French President, Charles de Gaulle, offered the French colonies in Africa their independence in 1958. A Congolese leader, Patrice Lumumba, emerged as a highly visible proponent of a free Africa. On January 4, 1959, riots broke out in the Congo; 42 persons died in events which deeply shocked the Belgians.

The Congolese had not been prepared for independence. Belgium quickly granted independence on June 30, 1960. Unfortunately, a series of bloodbaths ensued, sparked by greed for power and wealth as well as by tribalism. It was not until seven years later that the Congo (now Zaïre) became orderly, in part because of vigorous efforts of the Belgians and of UN troops.

The copper, cobalt and uranium mines in the southern Shaba Province are still of great interest to Belgium. When this province was invaded from Angola in mid–1978, Belgium and France sent paratroopers to evacuate White families and to secure the area. In 1979 the Belgian government again sent paratroopers to Zaïre to join its soldiers in training exercises near Kinshasa, the capital city. Thus, Belgium retains a great interest in its former African colonies, and the great bulk of its relatively large development aid (.06% of its GNP) has gone to Zaïre as well as to Rwanda and Burundi, which had been granted their independence in 1962. Zaïre is not always a grateful recipient of such aid, and by the end of the 1980s Belgium's importance as a source of trade and aid had declined. In 1989 Belgium halted all development plans in Zaïre in response to President Mobutu's suspension of payments on Belgian loans. In 1990 it used its diplomatic influence to try to sort out civil unrest in Rwanda, and in 1991 it sent 750 commandos to Zaïre to help evacuate Belgian citizens from the riot–torn country.

GOVERNMENT AND POLITICS

Overcoming the *Barrier*

Any discussion of Belgian politics always has to begin with the ever–present language problem. No major issue could be divorced from it, and it exhausted, paralyzed and fractured coalition governments to such an extent that the country was scarcely able to tackle the extremely important economic problems which it increasingly faced. Belgium was seriously distracted.

Flemings have fought hard and successfully for the complete equality of their language and culture, although some of the victories might strike foreign observers as petty and unnecessary. Now cabinet posts must be distributed exactly equally between the French and Flemish speakers (except the office of the prime minister who remains outside of all language quotas or restrictions), and all discussion in cabinet meetings are conducted through simultaneous interpreters, a concept developed by the father of the editor of The World Today Series. All major political parties are formally split along language lines, as are most military units and labor unions.

Even the prestigious medieval Catholic University of Louvain, which had become a bilingual university, had to be split in 1968 because it was located in the Flemish area a few miles north of the language

Belgium

line. The French–speaking part was moved just below the language line and was renamed *Louvain–la–Neuve* ("The New Louvain"). When it came to deciding how to divide the holdings in the famous university library, one of the oldest in Europe, the only solution which was acceptable was that all books with an even file number would remain in Louvain (now called by its Flemish name of Leuven), and all books with an odd file number would be moved to the new campus!

The tension between Flemings and Walloons has been exacerbated by the economic disparities which have developed between them. In the words of ex–premier Leo Tindemans, whose government foundered on the rocks of language regionalization in 1978, "the basic problem is not linguistic. It is the unequal economic development of two regions which speak different languages, have a different mentality and different dynamics, with the jealousy between them that often results and that can be easily exploited by politicians."

The economic inequality was becoming more apparent. By the turn of the century, Wallonia had become one of the richest regions on the continent while Flanders was a poor, rural area. Then the tables turned with a vengeance. Wallonia's coal industry disappeared, and its antiquated steel plants are in desperate need of streamlining and restructuring. Other traditional industries such as textiles lost out to competition from Third– World countries, where labor costs are very low. Thus, unemployment and labor unrest were higher in Wallonia. The EC declared Wallonia a "development area." Unfortunately, because of the psychological shock caused by crossing the linguistic border, unemployed Walloons are not inclined to move to Flanders to find work. Thus, there is little labor mobility.

While Wallonia faced an uncertain economic future, Flanders is experiencing an economic boom, based on future–oriented industries such as chemicals. Output per capita is higher in Flanders than in Wallonia. Because of Antwerp, foreign investments poured into the area. Earlier, most foreign investment went to Wallonia, but by 1975 it received only 20% of the total. By 1979 the figure had dropped to 10%, while Brussels received the same amount and Flanders a gigantic 80%. Distrust made both decisive governmental action and the establishment of some kind of national consensus, so strong in the Netherlands and Luxembourg, almost impossible in Belgium. But since the mid–1980s Wallonia has experienced an economic turn–around. Investment, including high-technology, has flowed in, industrial output has risen, and the economy has shifted from one in which 53% of the gross regional product is derived from industry and 42% from services to one in which 36% comes from industry and 60% from services. Unfortunately services can still not provide sufficient employment; in 1994 Wallonia's jobless rate was still higher than that of Flanders'.

There was general agreement in Belgium that Wallonia and Flanders had to be given more powers to control their own affairs, but there was much haggling on the details. As early as 1963 the two respective languages were given supremacy in the two main regions, and Brussels was declared to be a bilingual city. In 1971 the constitution was revised to permit the establishment of two cultural councils within parliament with authority over certain cultural and linguistic matters. The revision also established the necessity for special majorities (mostly two–thirds) for legislation touching these matters. Such special majorities were demanded by Walloons, who are outnumbered by the Flemish 60–40 and who have a lower birthrate as well. The amendment called for the establishment of a federal state composed of two lingual communities and three precisely defined regions, each empowered to legislate within carefully drawn limits.

Eight years and a string of cabinet crises later, two–thirds of both houses of Parliament approved an autonomy plan establishing regional assemblies and executives with authority over cultural and family affairs, public health, roads, urban projects, energy, environment, hunting and fishing, water resources, housing and many other matters. They would receive a total of 10% of the national budget to finance these tasks. The central government would, however, retain control over national finances, defense, justice and education. Belgium thereby ceased being a unitary state and became more decentralized. But the new arrangement is messy. In 1990 the federal government could do little to solve a long teachers' strike in Wallonia because it had lost its former powers over education. Also, some ministries at the federal and regional levels share the same responsibilities. In a country with one of Europe's highest tax rates, this seems wasteful.

This act of parliament was an important step, and the establishment in 1981 of regional and community institutions has sparked enthusiasm and energies to improve the life in the language regions. Nevertheless, there are still many problems in the two larger regions which must be solved. There are small language enclaves on the wrong side of "the line." In 1987 the Belgian government collapsed over such an issue. Because of its location, the small, predominantly Walloon town of Fourons (or Voeren, depending on where one stands on this dispute!) had been transferred in 1963 to the Flemish province of Limburg. Although most of the inhabitants of the town actually speak a dialect of German among themselves, two–thirds consider themselves French speakers.

They elected as mayor a militant French–language campaigner, José Happart, who refused to speak Flemish or take a Dutch–language test. The Belgian Supreme Court ruled that Happart's appointment was therefore illegal. This village incident mechanically set off reactions which would be possible only in Belgium: Flemish ministers in Prime Minister Martens' cabinet threatened to resign if Happart were not sacked, and their French–speaking colleagues said they would leave if he were! Evicted from the mayor's office, Happart won a seat in the European Parliament and remains one of Wallonia's most popular politicians. An exasperated Martens had to resign over the issue, which he and many others considered absurd. He was understandably furious that such a parochial dispute could prevent his government from solving the critical economic challenges facing the country. In 1992 power sharing was introduced to such mixed communities. But Belgians remain acutely aware of the underlying message of the dispute: never underestimate the importance of language factors in Belgian politics!

The thorniest of all regionalism problems continues to exist: what to do with Brussels, where Flemings have long been very nervous about certain developments. Brussels has grown rapidly. With the construction of hundreds of office buildings, businesses and international headquarters in the city, those who formerly resided in the heart of the city have increasingly had to settle in the suburbs and surrounding villages, where the schools, administration and cultural activities had traditionally been Flemish. Conflicts inevitably develop because French–speakers demand French language facilities. Proposals to make Brussels a third independent region have always been rejected by the Flemings. They fear that Flemish rights might be trampled and that in the future two French–speaking regions could somehow join forces against Flanders. They insist on a distinct and *unchangeable* line around Brussels to fence in the French–speakers. Virtually no one expects this problem to be solved in the near future.

Belgium's high unemployment rate has created an interesting situation: in the past, the only Belgians who were bilingual were Flemings, since the Walloons traditionally refused to learn Flemish. Brussels' bilingual status has placed a premium in

Belgium

the job market on the ability to speak both official languages, and that means that the Flemings there have a leg up on their Walloon competitors. This economic fact has given rise to a phenomenon which would have been unimaginable even a few years ago: Walloon parents are beginning to send their children to Dutch–language schools in order to improve their employment prospects.

The new regional governments work alongside the traditional provincial and communal governments in Belgium. The country has always been divided for administrative purposes into nine provinces, each with a provincial council of 50 to 90 members and a governor chosen by the cabinet and officially appointed by the king. Four of the provinces are French–speaking—Hainaut, Namur, Liège and Luxembourg (a large chunk of the Grand Duchy of Luxembourg which was transferred to Belgium in the settlement of 1839). Four are Flemish–speaking—East and West Flanders, Limburg and Antwerp. Brabant, which includes Brussels, is bilingual.

In 1989 parliament passed legislation to devolve further power to the regions, and a special court was created to solve problems stemming from devolution. In 1992 an elected regional government for Brussels was approved, and the following year Belgium became even more federalized. The regional governments were granted all powers but those of the treasury, defense, and foreign policy. In 1995 their parliaments, as well as local parliamentary bodies, were directly elected for the first time. There are potential problems in foreign affairs because the three regions have the right to sign treaties with other nations. Flanders signed one on water with the Netherlands and set up a network of 70 economic representatives in five continents; it also has its own diplomats in Vienna, The Hague, Washington, Tokyo and Brussels. Such separate foreign ties could diminish the standing of the federal government.

Local governments in Belgium have a long tradition stemming from the Middle Ages and have had much autonomy. They are governed by an elected council of aldermen, who serve six–year terms. As a holdover of Napoleon's reforms, the mayor (called *burgomaster*) is nominated by the city council, approved by the cabinet and officially appointed by the king. He presides over the city council and is expected to insure that national interests are considered. They very often become skilled defenders of local interests in opposition to the central government.

Since 1971, Brussels is officially a bilingual city, broken down into 19 bilingual and seven Flemish communes and ruled by a metropolitan council elected by proportional representation and a council executive with an equal number of French and Flemish–speaking members. In general, government at the provincial and communal level works rather efficiently and has been able to keep an important part of the governmental machinery running smoothly at times when the central government has been paralyzed. Also, city officials have much influence on the central government; more than 3/4 of the members of the Belgian parliament are at the same time local government officials, and this fact strengthens the ties between the national and local governments.

The National Government

Belgium is a constitutional monarchy in which the king exercises largely ceremonial powers. The established tradition is that he signs all legislation passed by democratic methods. That is why there was dismay in 1990 when former King Baudouin announced that he could not sign a bill liberalizing abortion within the first 12 weeks of pregnancy. The childless, devoutly Catholic monarch asked: 'Would it be normal that I be the only citizen in Belgium to be forced to act against his conscience? Is freedom of conscience a privilege for all except the King?' The pragmatic Belgians found a way out of this dilemma: invoking Article 79 of the constitution on April 3, the government declared the king 'temporarily incapable of ruling,' and it hurriedly promulgated the abortion law in his absence from the throne. Then on April 5 a joint session of parliament, invoking Article 82, offered him his job back. This bizarre episode prompted some Belgians to question again whether their country really needs a monarch after all.

After reigning for 42 years, King Baudouin died suddenly of a heart attack in Spain on July 31, 1993. Though his official powers were limited, he was popular among both Flemings and Walloons, and many credited him for helping preserve Belgian unity. Childless, he was succeeded by his brother Albert. King Albert II is a relative newcomer to the political world, but he is familiar with the leaders of all three regions and is experienced in business. He had stated that he would step aside and allow his son Philippe to assume the throne. However, since the King's influence is considered essential to a smooth transition to greater federalism, he was convinced to become King himself 'in the interests of continuity.'

Real power is exercised by coalitions of parties which can maintain a majority in the Chamber of Representatives, the lower house of parliament. This is never easy because the proportional representation electoral system enables about a dozen parties to win parliamentary seats. Therefore, Belgian governments tend to be very fragile and seldom last the entire four years for which a parliament is elected.

It is striking that few cabinets are overturned by votes in parliament. Members

Brussels—carefully bilingual

Belgium

of Parliament are firmly bound to the party leaders through party discipline, so it is the powerful party leaders who make or unmake governments. Even when cabinets fall, the new governments are usually formed after minor reshuffling of cabinet posts. For example, after 1978 Wilfried Martens was prime minister in six governments, and they came to be known as Martens I through VII. Thus, there is usually more governmental stability in Belgium than meets the eye. This is particularly so because of the nature of Belgian political parties. Although they are very different ideologically and linguistically, they are normally willing to compromise in order to form a government. This stems in part from the tradition of elite cooperation in Belgium which has always helped to bridge some of the differences in the heterogeneous Belgian society. Nevertheless, the delicate compromises necessary to form and preserve a government make it very difficult to attack the country's pressing problems head–on.

The Parliament

The Belgium parliament is bicameral, and both houses constitutionally have the same powers. However, tradition has made the lower house, the Chamber of Representatives, the more important. Its 150 members (reduced from 212 in 1995) are elected at least every four years by all citizens 18 years or older, who are *required* to vote. The great majority of its members continue to perform their normal jobs and commute to Brussels for parliamentary sessions. Most legislation is discussed first with the major Belgian interest groups and is introduced into the Chamber before being passed on to the upper house.

The Senate accepts about 90% of the laws without change. The 181 senators are elected for four year terms in three different ways. Fifty are elected by the provincial councils, 25 by the Senate itself and the rest directly by Belgian voters. The heir–apparent to the throne, presently Prince Philippe, is always a member, and the senate almost always has roughly the same party composition as the lower house.

Both houses are empowered to amend the constitution by simple majority in both houses, although a two–thirds majority is now necessary for certain language and cultural legislation. Acts of Parliament cannot be declared unconstitutional by the highest court in the land, the Court of Cassation, whose chief justice is chosen by the government and formally appointed by the king. In the Belgian legal system, which is modeled on the French, there is no provision for judicial review, but the Court of Cassation can rule administrative acts unconstitutional.

The three arches at the ruins of the monastery at Orval
Courtesy: Jon Markham Morrow

A separate body, the Council of State, is permitted to give advisory opinions on the legal suitability and constitutionality of major legislation.

Political parties in Belgium follow the cleavages of society. There are specific language parties whose main objective is to preserve or extend the language rights of their particular groups. The three "traditional" parties spring from the three great movements in Belgium during the 19th century: Catholicism, liberalism and socialism. Coalitions always require the participation of at least two of these, and one usually leads the opposition. None of the traditional parties is highly ideologically oriented, and all are rather flexible. These parties have been challenged by three language parties whose demands in behalf of Walloons, Flemings and residents of Brussels have been so appealing that these three language parties have increased their electoral strength enormously in the past two decades. This challenge was so great that all three traditional parties have split into separate French–speaking and Flemish–speaking parties which limit their appeal strictly to their own region. However, they are inclined to cooperate with their former party comrades when it comes to constructing a national governing coalition. There are *no major national* parties in Belgium today. One can scarcely imagine governing a nation with only regional parties! Energy is expended on the pettiest of issues.

The *Christian* Parties

The largest twin party, although it has slipped in elections since the 1950s, is the *Christian People's Party (CVP)*, as it is known in Flanders, or the *Christian Social*

Belgium

Party (PSC) in Wallonia. Participation of the *CVP* and *PSC* has been crucial in all coalition governments since 1958, and the recent prime ministers, Leo Tindemans, Mark Eyskens (son of earlier Prime Minister Gaston Eyskens, who played a key role in the development of a satisfactory regionalization plan) and Wilfried Martens have all been from the *CVP*. Martens was a particularly important integration figure for the party. He started his political career as an ultra–nationalist Flemish radical who painted over signs at the 1958 World's Fair which were not written in both Flemish and French. He later became a convinced federalist and a model of hard work, patience and adaptability. He was regarded as one of the few Belgian politicians who is trusted by both language groups.

Formerly a single Catholic party, it severed all its formal ties with the Catholic Church in 1945 in order to become the two mass parties which they are today. Nevertheless, the two parties are still the only parties which many Belgian Catholics find acceptable. Their program endorses a policy guided by Christian principles (liberally interpreted), and they have always been staunch proponents of state support for parochial schools. They favor a free market economy and the protection of private property. At the same time, they advocate equality of opportunity, an active state role in the economy and state assistance for those persons who cannot compete successfully in the capitalist economic order. These positions enable them to work sometimes with the Socialist parties. The *CVP* is relatively stronger in Flanders than the *PSC* is in Wallonia, where the *Christian Socialists* have always taken a back seat to the Socialist parties. Both find the bulk of their voters among the middle class, farmers and Catholic labor movement, particularly within the *Christian Trade Union Federation (CSC)*, Belgium's largest trade union. The *CVP* also attracts upper–class voters, such as prosperous merchants and high–ranking military officers.

Martens' government was the first in many Belgians' memory to survive so long. But in 1991 it crashed on the familiar rocks of Flemish–Walloon linguistic rivalry. This necessitated early elections which left the country even more difficult to govern. Disgusted voters, who were fed up with the language bickering, deserted

Hon. Leo Tindemans

Children during Carnival at Binche, Hainaut Province

Hon. Mark Eyskens

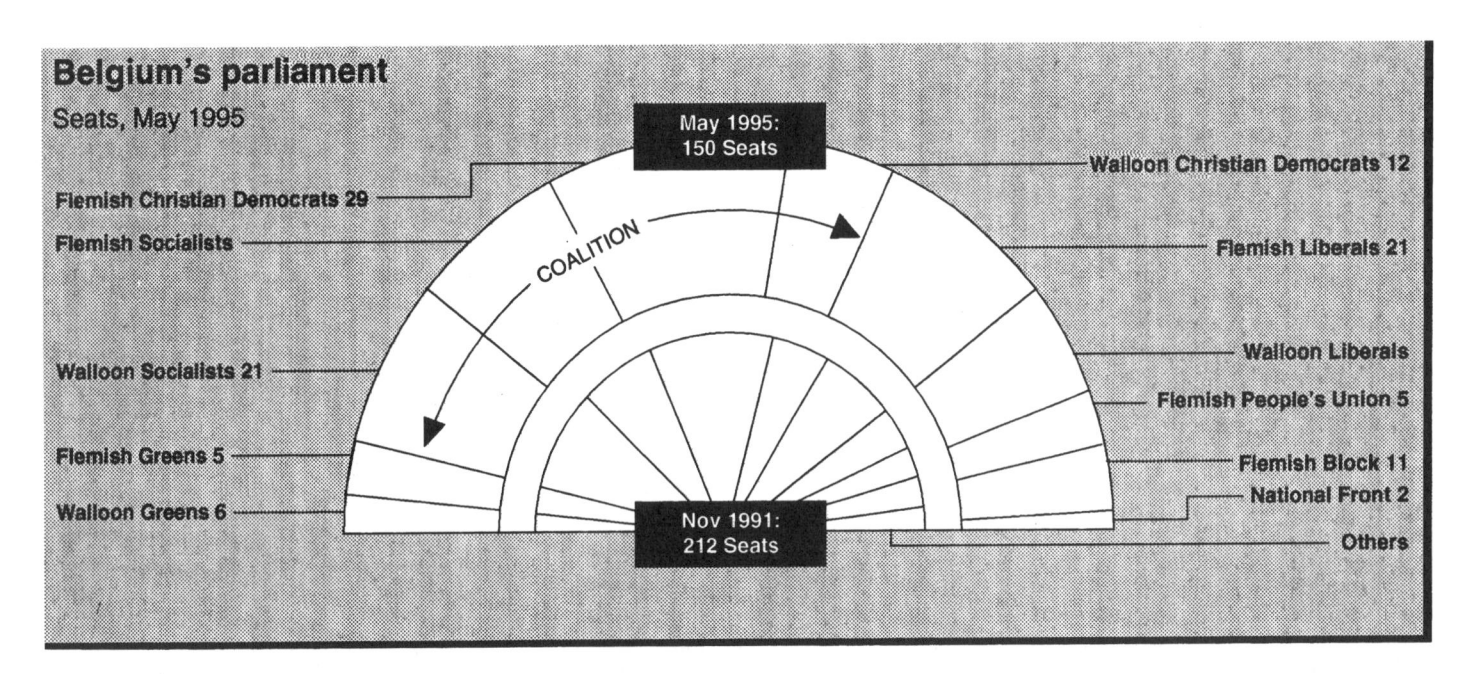

Belgium

Belgium's parliament
Seats, May 1995

- Flemish Christian Democrats 29
- Flemish Socialists
- Walloon Socialists 21
- Flemish Greens 5
- Walloon Greens 6
- Walloon Christian Democrats 12
- Flemish Liberals 21
- Walloon Liberals
- Flemish People's Union 5
- Flemish Block 11
- National Front 2
- Others

May 1995: 150 Seats
Nov 1991: 212 Seats
COALITION

Martens' center–left coalition parties, which lost the two–thirds majority needed to continue their devolution reforms. The old coalition still retained a simple majority, but the linguistic feuding which had made early elections necessary in the first place weakened it after the polling.

The election results added up to one thing: stalemate, a situation which reminded one Brussels journalist of a match during the Karpov–Kasparov world chess tournament: "Everywhere you look for a move there is something to block it. There seems no way out." The problem is that the language issues which destroyed the old government prevent a stable new one from being created. In Belgium it is not enough to gain support from a party; one must also satisfy all potential supporters that one is backing their linguistic claims. In concrete terms, every effort to create a center–right coalition of *Christian Democrats* and *Liberals* or a center–left government of *Christian Democrats* and *Socialists* founders eventually on one or other language wing of a crucial party.

In 1992 Jean–Luc Dehaene, who is from the trade union wing of the Flemish *Christian Democrats,* became prime minister. His coalition is composed of the same four parties whose government fell in 1991. He is known as the "Bulldozer," "Carthorse," and "Plumber" because of his ability to fix problems. What awaited the new government was a host of difficult decisions, such as direct election of regional and communal assemblies. Dehaene pushed hard to get parliament to accept constitutional reforms devolving additional power to the regions. In the May 1995 elections, the *CVP* won 29 and the *PSC* 12 of the 150 seats in the lower house. Together with the *Socialists*, Dehaene maintained his center–left government, which has a total of 82 seats.

The Socialist Parties

The Socialist parties (*SP* in Flanders and *PS* in Wallonia) are an equally strong twin party nationwide. The *Socialist Party* is one of the oldest parties in Europe. It was never an extreme left–wing party and always sought to work within the constitutional system. Winning elections always took priority over doctrine. The best–known Belgian Socialist, Paul–Henri Spaak, former prime minister, foreign minister, first president of the UN General Assembly and NATO general secretary, expressed the character of his party this way: "There are two kinds of Socialists—Socialists and *real* Socialists. Me? I am a Socialist."

Its program presents a parliamentary–reformist path to a socialist society. The party congress of 1974 defined the party's aim as democratic socialism, which gives each individual the possibility for full social, economic and cultural realization. Belgian Socialists seek to change the present capitalist economic system because it

Hon. Jean–Luc Dehaene

Hon. Wilfried Martens

Belgium

allegedly concentrates economic power, dehumanizes the working man's world and increases global tensions between rich and poor. They favor economic planning, nationalization of certain key economic sectors such as energy and banking, and the establishment of a national health service. They find their voters chiefly among lower level employees and workers, especially those without strong ties to the Catholic Church and those who belong to the second–largest trade union, the *Federation of Belgian Labor (FGTB)*.

The Flemish party is generally less friendly to far–reaching reform than the Walloon party, which must stay left in order to compete in the more socialist Wallonia. The Socialists are considered to be especially useful coalition partners because of their ability to help control the powerful Belgian labor movement. Belgian Socialists are among the very few outside the United States who allow their parliamentary candidates to be chosen by means of party primaries, with all party members entitled to vote.

In the 1995 election, the *Socialists* captured 41 seats, 21 in Wallonia and 20 in Flanders. Considering a scandal that had scarred the party in 1995, this result was surprisingly good. The Flemish party reportedly received kickbacks from an Italian arms firm, Augusta, in a sale of 46 helicopters to the Belgium army. In the wake of the scandal, three ministers resigned, one top military official committed suicide, and two internationally prominent figures, Willy Claes, who was economics minister when the deal was made, and EU Commissioner Karel van Miert, were tarnished. In late 1995 Claes had to resign as NATO Secretary General.

The Liberals

The third traditional party group is the *Party for Freedom and Progress (PVV* in Flanders and *PRL* in Wallonia and Brussels), generally referred to as the *Liberals*. They pursue traditional European liberal policies, such as the limitation of the power of the state in society and the greatest possible freedom for private initiative. They generally want to prevent the socialization of the economy, to reduce taxes and to cut state expenditures. Perhaps the only expressly conservative parties in Belgium, they appeal mainly to middle class voters, especially small businessmen and professionals. It is also divided by regions. In 1995 the *PVV* won 21 seats and the *PRL* 20. They form the largest opposition grouping.

Fringe Parties

The Communist Party (KPB) in Flanders and *(PCB)* in Wallonia is a small, politically insignificant party which appeals almost exclusively to workers and which is strongest in Wallonia and Brussels. In 1971 it separated into regional organizations although it did not formally split. Its program is orthodox Marxist and it generally pursued a Moscow–oriented line. For instance, while most Western European communist parties denounced Soviet policy in Poland from 1980 on, the Belgian communists announced that Soviet pressure on Poland to limit or eliminate the free trade unions within the country is "perfectly understandable and exclusively defensive in nature." The party's offer to participate in a ruling coalition has never been accepted. One unique practice observed by the party's representatives in parliament is that each pays his parliamentary salary into the party coffers and accepts in return only a worker's wage from the party. This practice is irrelevant, though, since the communists have been shut out of parliament since 1985.

A relatively new party which scored dramatic gains in 1985 is the *Ecologists*. As in other Western European countries, this party finds voters among those who are concerned about environmental protection and nuclear dangers. It is a convenient party for expressing discontent and protest. They are the only party whose French and Flemish factions cooperate easily in parliament. In 1995 the Walloon *Ecologists* won six seats and the Flemish five.

The oldest of the Belgian autonomy parties is the *Flemish People's Union (VU)*, established in 1954. The *VU* draws almost half its votes from workers and half from the middle and upper classes. It supports a free market economy, and autonomy of Flanders and Wallonia, bound together loosely in a Belgian state. From 1987 to 1991 it was in the ruling coalition, but it skidded to five seats in 1995.

The hard–line anti–immigrant *Flemish Block* won 11 Flemish seats. Marching under the banner, "Our People First!," it is the largest party in Antwerp. It also does well in Brussels, where half the newborns are from Arab parents. Its French equivalent is the *National Front*, which won two seats in 1995. In Brussels the *Democratic Front of French Speaking Brusselers (FDF)*, which advocates a redrawing of the boundaries separating Flemish from French speakers, has become the strongest single party. In a 1998 survey on racism, 55% of Belgians admitted to being "racist" or "fairly racist." This was the highest percentage in Europe.

Foreign and Defense Policy

As a small country, Belgium's foreign policy is anchored in international organizations which seek to maintain peace and prosperity in the world, especially in Europe. The EU continues to give an important boost to this small trading nation, one–half of whose national income is derived from foreign trade.

Belgium is also a founding member of NATO, but in recent years it has been among the alliance's least enthusiastic members, due in great part to its severe financial difficulties and to its preoccupation with its internal problems. Much of its equipment is outdated; its air force has 150 mostly older planes, but it decided to modernize this force by purchasing 44 American F–16 combat aircraft. The navy is mainly a coastal defense force, composed of four frigates and a dozen mine sweepers. In 1987–8 it sent three of those mine sweepers to the Persian Gulf to help in the allied effort to keep that important waterway open to world shipping. In 1991 it again sent four warships, including two minesweepers, to the Gulf, and in 1992 its troops were dispatched to the Congo, where violence threatened the lives of Europeans, and Somalia. In Somalia its soldiers were regarded as tough, unforgiving, disciplined (despite several incidents of racism and violence toward the local population) and skilled, traits acquired in previous interventions in Africa.

It has a conscript army of approximately 62,000 men, separated as much as possible into separate language units and divided generally into two armies. Its Home Defense, staffed chiefly by reservists and ten–month draftees, is stationed in Belgium. In 1993 the government announced plans to reduce by 1997 the army to 27,500 full–time soldiers, the air force to 10,000, and the navy to 2,500 personnel. Critics, including high military officers, fear that such drastic cuts would deprive Belgium of the bare minimum needed to defend the country. In 1993 the government decided to participate in the Franco–German Eurocorps, the embryonic European army. Not surprisingly, this decision provoked criticism in Flanders because Flemish would not one of the languages used. The memory is still alive that Flemish troops sometimes died during the First World War because they could not understand the orders of their overwhelmingly francophone officers.

The U.S. maintains approximately 2,000 military personnel in Belgium, but this force also faces reductions. U.S. cooperation with Belgium expanded to space in 1992, as a Dutch physician joined the Atlantis crew for a 9–day voyage; he became the first Belgian in space. Opposition to the deployment of U.S. medium range missiles had caused the government to postpone a final decision until 1985. The missiles were stationed at Florennes in the southern part of the country, but they were later pulled out thanks to the 1987 INF treaty. Belgium also pushed hard in

Belgium

The port of Antwerp from the Scheldt River

1989 for a postponement of any modernization of short–range nuclear missiles in Europe. Here and elsewhere in NATO countries serious questions are being asked about the need for and method of defending Western Europe after the collapse of the Soviet Union. With most Belgian newspapers and opposition parties demanding his resignation, Willy Claes, who denied all wrongdoing in the Augusta bribery scandal, found it impossible to provide the leadership NATO needs. It seriously eroded his credibility, and he resigned in 1995. In 1998 a court found him guilty, and he was given a suspended sentence.

Extremists

Although the broadly–based peace movement quickly died down after the deployment of the missiles, a murderous group of left–wing terrorists calling itself the "Communist Fighting Cells" (CCC) sprang to life. It has placed bombs in an office of the prime minister, headquarters of conservative and centrist political parties, bank offices, defense contractors' offices, police stations and, above all, NATO facilities. It reportedly has links with similar political terrorist groups in Germany, Italy and elsewhere. Only a few score of Belgians sympathize with or support these killers' objectives, let alone their methods. On the other side of the political fence is a neo–Nazi group called the Westland New Post, who are accused to stealing NATO documents.

Perhaps far more disturbing to average Belgians are so–called "Brabant killers." Showing every indication of being psychopaths, these murderers have raided supermarkets, indiscriminately gunning down shopkeepers and bystanders, including children. In 1989 a former prime minister, Vanden Boeynants, was kidnapped in Brussels and released a month later after a ransom of up to $2.5 million had been paid. In a country so used to quiet and order, these grisly events had a traumatic effect on the public and dramatically elevated the concern for security in the minds of the citizenry.

ECONOMY

Belgium was one of the first countries in the world to become heavily industrialized; this was possible because of large coal, and to a lesser extent, iron ore deposits. The industrialized areas became heavily urbanized, and a well–trained and powerfully organized work force emerged. Today, two–thirds of Belgium's workers are unionized, the highest percentage in Western Europe. They are divided almost evenly between socialist and Christian unions.

As in every other Belgian institution, language separations weaken the unity of the unions. The country experienced its first general strike in 58 years in 1993; it was aimed at the austerity program of a shaky government, which beat a tactical retreat. The government can weather many such labor disturbances because the mainly French–speaking socialist unions and the dominant Christian unions in Flanders cannot pull together sufficiently to bring the government down.

Over the years, a highly elaborate system of formal discussions between labor unions, employers and the government has developed. These discussions facilitate the exchange of conflicting views and aim at establishing the framework for agreements in economic matters which would protect the well–being and future of the entire country.

Sometimes this cooperation breaks down, but as a rule, the unions take a constructive, pragmatic approach to economic matters. They have much to show for their high productivity and cooperative policies: wages which, though declining in real terms, remain among the world's highest, one of the world's shortest work weeks (less than 38 hours), pensions and social security benefits which until the 1980s were fully protected from inflation by means of indexing, which means that they were automatically raised to keep step with rises in retail prices. Such indexing took some of the heat out of labor relations, but it invariably contributed to inflation and to government spending deficits.

As many European countries which were left in a condition of devastation and destitution at war's end in 1945, Belgium, within a few months, passed sweeping social welfare legislation which could give the people some economic hope for the future. Benefits were continually expanded through the 1970s. For instance, generous unemployment benefits take much of the sting out of losing one's job. The state

Belgium

medical insurance reimburses three-fourths of all medical and pharmaceutical expenses and pays persons with long-term illnesses—60% of their salaries for the first two years and 40% for the next two years. Belgium's social welfare net has attracted many admirers, but such a net became extremely expensive. Its nominal costs multiplied twelve-fold from 1960 to 1980, and the government exhausted domestic sources of credit to pay for them.

After 1978 the government has had to borrow heavily abroad, not merely to finance foreign trade, but to meet the budgetary demands created by what many consider to be an overly generous social welfare program. With its high standard of living and small domestic market Belgium is extremely dependent upon foreign trade; about half of its production must be exported. Of course, it has many foreign trade advantages. Its central location in the middle of major European economic centers and its membership in the EU are very significant. Belgium lies within a 200 mile radius of a market containing 100 million consumers. This includes Holland, the Ruhr area, Paris and London. Three-fourths of its exports go to the EU, and 60% flows to its three neighbors—Germany, France and the Netherlands.

Also, it has the second largest port in Europe and one of the most modern, best equipped, efficiently operated and busiest in the world—Antwerp. This port, which is owned by the city, is located within 250 miles of Frankfurt, Düsseldorf, Lille, Paris, Amsterdam and London. Situated 45 miles (72 km.) inland along the Scheldt River, its access to the open sea was always a problem because the Scheldt passes through Dutch territory before emptying into the North Sea. For centuries the Dutch, wishing to minimize competition for their own port of Rotterdam, limited or prevented traffic heading to Antwerp from passing though their territory. Excellent relations with the Netherlands finally enabled the two countries to sign a treaty eliminating such hindrance, and Antwerp now thrives.

The port has the largest underwater warehouse facilities in the world, and is especially noted for its lightning-fast turn-around time. More than 75,000 are employed by the port or by companies which in some way service the port. The port complex, which covers 27,000 acres, contains entire industrial plants, including factories owned by such multinational companies as General Motors and Bayer. About half of the traffic entering and leaving the port is moved by Belgium's 930 mile (1,500 km.) canal system, which links the port to all major Belgian cities and rivers, which are easily navigable because of their slow current. Most important, the inland waterway plugs into the Rhine River, a link which perhaps entitles Antwerp to call itself the gateway to Europe.

Backing up this inland waterway is a very well developed internal transport system. The first railway in Europe formally opened in Brussels in 1835 and now with its 2,536 miles (over 4,000 km.) the Belgian railway net is the densest in the world. Its international motorways are also plentiful and fully lighted at night. Its national airline, SABENA, which is 90% government owned but incorporated as a private company, calls at 67 airports in 47 countries. In the 1990s SABENA found itself deeply in debt.

Many of the factors which once made Belgium an economic powerhouse have now disappeared. Easily extractable coal, traditionally Belgium's only significant raw material, has been almost completely exhausted in the South, where most of the mines are closed. Coal production in the fresher Flemish mines is now eight times higher than in Wallonia. Belgium's steel industry, which grew up around the coal fields, had become inefficient and obsolete; EU policies to reduce European steel production have cost thousands of jobs in Belgium. Steel towns such as Liège, Charleroi and Mons are now economic and political trouble areas. The Belgian government felt compelled to subsidize many lame industries, particularly in the steel and textile sectors. This aid has almost always flowed to Wallonia, which suffered almost 75% of all plant closures in 1979. Such government subsidies only postpone the restructuring of Wallonia's

A panorama of industry in Antwerp

Belgium

industries nec essary to enable them to compete in modern markets. They have also enabled the labor unions to achieve higher wages in the lame industries, especially steel, than those paid in the more productive mills in Flanders. Indeed, the strike record in Wallonia is three times the rate per capita than in Flanders. This only increases resentment toward Wallonia, which many Flemings believe is in essence being subsidized by Flanders.

The world economic turndowns since the oil shocks of 1973–4 struck a hard blow at Belgium's trading position. Four decades ago, Belgium's own coal supplied 90% of the country's energy needs, but that figure has now sunk to about 20%. About 40% of its present energy needs are covered by oil; almost all of it must be imported and most comes from the Middle East. The oil company, Petrofina, provides a small portion of the country's oil through its concession in the U.S., Canada, Zaïre and the North Sea. A quarter of its energy consumption is from nuclear power, and 17% is from natural gas. It hopes to be able to develop on–site gassification of coal, which could have the effect of reviving the lagging coal mining industry.

A very unpleasant development for Belgium was the slowdown in foreign investment caused, in large part, by the country's high wage costs and dramatic drop in profitability of Belgian firms. American investors, who in the 1960s accounted for 65% of all foreign investment in Belgium, had reduced their share to less than a third by the 1980s, and some of the most visible U.S. firms such as RCA, General Electric and Holiday Inn, have withdrawn altogether. This is a very serious problem because multinational companies control an estimated one–third of all manufacturing jobs and almost one–half of all industrial assets in Belgium. Thus, their confidence in the Belgian economy is crucial.

The government is trying to lure foreign investment by providing subsidies, reducing interest rates and giving capital bonuses and tax breaks, but the results are mixed. The French automaker, Renault, found out in 1997 what can happen in Belgium when it decided to close its plant in Volvoorde and lay off 3,100 Belgian workers. Prime Minister Dehaene proclaimed the action as "brutal and unacceptable," and a hundred thousand people staged a protest march in Brussels.

Belgium now has approximately 400,000 foreign workers, who with their families number about 900,000. They are eligible for all social security benefits and cannot be deported for economic reasons. They are concentrated primarily in the Wallonian industrial areas and Brussels. The capital city has a particularly visible foreign presence. The thousands of EU bureaucrats, international businessmen and especially foreign laborers now comprise almost 30% of the city's population.

Foreign workers are a convenient target for extreme right–wing groups such as the *VMO* and *Youth Front,* but they do face discrimination in the larger society. The extent of the problem of integrating the predominantly African and Mediterranean workers was revealed by the passage of a law in 1981 directed against racism and hatred toward foreigners. It is now forbidden by law to put up signs such as "Foreigners unwanted" or "No entry for North Africans," as once one saw in Belgium. Public services may no longer be denied to foreigners.

Like many other rich Western European countries, Belgium has become a magnet for persons from the Third World seeking asylum. A fourth of Brussels' residents are immigrants, mainly Moroccans and Turks. With the situation worsening monthly, the government became a firm advocate of strict border controls. In 1991 the capital saw its worst rioting in years, as bloody fighting and destruction took place in immigrant neighborhoods after an incident of alleged police harassment. The government tightened controls on illegal refugees in 1993 and speeded up the application processing and deportation of such foreigners.

Belgian agriculture is still relatively efficient by European standards and provides 80% of the country's food needs. There are problems, however. Farm incomes have stagnated for years, but farmers have managed to stay afloat because of subsidies from the EU's Common Agriculture Program (CAP). Most Belgian farms are mixed, producing grains and raising livestock and, except for Italy, Belgium has the smallest farms in the EU. Therefore, there is a great need for amalgamation and modernization. But with a high unemployment rate in Belgium, the 3.5% of the population engaging in agriculture must be kept on the land until some can be absorbed by industry.

Despite some improvement, Belgium faces economic problems. Although its government deficit was down to 1.5% of the GDP in 1999, 30% of the budget is devoted to paying interest on the national debt. Its public debt, at 125% of GDP, is the highest in the industrialized world. The country's inflation and unemployment rate were shooting up, and its currency was under constant pressure. It is small wonder that Belgium experienced a rapid turnover of government which survived an average of only 13 months.

The government's stiff austerity program since the early 1980s was partly successful. Increases in the government's borrowing, spending and deficit have all been reduced. Unemployment in 1999 was 11.3%, one of the highest rates in Europe, but inflation was steady at 1.2%. The economy is growing, and disposable income is increasing.

One can no longer call the country "the sick man of Europe," as some observers did. But a certain truth rings in something the director of the Belgian employers' association said about his own country in 1981: "Belgium reminds me of a well–dressed man who inspires confidence until you learn that he has not paid his tailor."

CULTURE

Belgium has more than one culture, and to understand the cultural dimension of this country, one must unravel the strands of Roman, Frankish, Spanish, French, Austrian, German and Dutch influences. With no common culture, there is very little feeling of Belgian national identity, especially among the Flemish. Unlike in Wallonia, there is a vocal separatist movement in Flanders. It is mainly when they are outside of Belgium that many Flemish and Walloons begin to feel like Belgians.

Today, Belgium is secularized, and few Belgians vote primarily along religious sect lines. Also, there is a trend away from doctrinaire religious positions on social and political matters, even among the Roman Catholics. Catholicism is still a significant social force, especially in Flanders. Catholics organize trade unions, youth movements, hospitals, sports clubs, political parties and schools, and these organizations are thriving. Perhaps this helps partly to explain the conservatism of the Belgians, who remain largely a rather private, family–oriented people.

The best example of the vitality of Catholicism is the seperation of the school system into state schools, which accommodate approximately 43% of the pupils, and "free" (chiefly Catholic) schools, which are largely financed by the state and accommodate 57%. The long and emotional dispute over state support for Catholic schools was finally settled in 1958. The compromise which was reached probably put to rest the last religious dispute which would significantly affect Belgian politics.

Children are now permitted to choose English as their first foreign language, rather than learning French or Dutch. There has been an increasing tendency to use English as the common language between Flemings and Walloons. Even José Happart admitted after a fierce TV debate that "after all, everybody will speak English in 20 years." There is, at the same time, an encouraging trend for ambitious francophones to buckle down and learn Flemish. Most educated Flemings contin-

Belgium

The Grand Place, Brussels

ue to speak fluent French. There are many variants of Walloon French, which is closer to the old rather than to the modern Parisian form. There is diversity at the university level. Four universities are Flemish–speaking and four are French–speaking. Some are Catholic, such as Leuven and Louvain–la–Neuve, and some are not, such as the University of Brussels, Ghent and Liège.

The news media uses both languages. The *Radio Television Belge de la Communauté Culturelle Française (RTBF)* and the *Belgische Radio en Televisie (BRT)* are separate public utilities with state financing but without direct state intervention in their management. Both are run by ten–member administrative councils, of which eight are representatives of political parties and are appointed by the parliament. Belgians were pioneers in radio broadcasting and now have one German, three French and three Dutch channels. There is one French and one Dutch–language television channel.

There are newspapers in all three languages. The leading French papers are *La Libre Belgique* (Catholic) and *Le Soir* (independent). Flemish dailies include *Het Laatste Nieuws* (Liberal) and *De Standaard* (Catholic). One daily, *Grenz Echo*, appears in the German language. Most Belgian dailies have a political affiliation and are owned by one of four large chains, although each newspaper has a great measure of autonomy within each group.

Simply by driving through Belgium, one realizes that the country is filled with art treasures. One can see splendid medieval cities such as Brugge, Ghent, Antwerp, Liège, Brussels, Leuven (Lou vain), Tongeren, Namur and Tournai, which are filled with castles, abbeys and venerable public buildings. But it is art museums throughout the world that one can best see the impact of Belgian artists.

Painting was the medium in which artists came to be known best of all, and by the 16th century, Flemish painting with its bold personal expression and vitality marked the high point of the northern Renaissance. Jan Van Eyck was the first Flemish master to arouse the admiration of Italian painters, and his brother Hubert Van Eyck also produced masterpieces of lasting value. Pieter Bruegel the Elder combined religious, moral or satirical subjects with vivid descriptions of the Flemish rural environment. He broadened the art of landscape painting through a masterful, sweeping concept of nature.

Peter Paul Reubens became the most famous exponent of Baroque painting; he also was a noted diplomat and worked for Marie de Medici, Philip IV of Spain and Charles I of England. His collaborator, Anthony Van Dyck, became the court painter of the English royal family. David Teniers was a master at painting highly realistic popular scenes. Flemish artists were pioneers in giving depth to painting, instead of rendering a flat appearance. They paid very close attention to detail and to common people. Thus, they gave us the most vivid picture imaginable of their surroundings and have kept their own time alive in the mind of the modern viewer.

Since ancient times, Belgian literature was bilingual. Until the 19th century its writers were overshadowed by its painters, but after Belgium gained its independence, literature began to bloom. Hendrik Conscience attracted attention to his homeland through his novel *The Lion of Flanders*. Reminiscent of Sir Walter Scott's romantic novels, Conscience rekindled Flemings' pride and interest in their past. He also wrote other delightful novels depicting life in the Flemish countryside and towns which sparked a literary revival. Another great 19th century Flemish figure was the poet, Guido Gezelle, whose poems presented religious sentiment with great eloquence. Karel van Woestijne was also a brilliant poet who wrote about the eternal conflict between body and soul. Perhaps the greatest 20th century authors are Hugo Claus and the late Baron Marnix Gijsen.

Belgium

Walloon literature was revived under the leadership of Max Weller, whose literary review *La Jeune Belgique* encouraged experimentation and cosmopolitanism in the late 19th century. Charles de Coster wrote *Ulenspiegel* in 1867, a ribald tale so filled with the spirit of liberty that it became a symbol of Belgian resistance in both world wars. Perhaps the greatest French-speaking Belgian writers were Maurice Maeterlinck, who won a Nobel Prize in 1911, Emile Verhaeren and Michel de Ghelderode. Paradoxically, all three were Flemish! With such a composer as Cesar Franck and ballet artist as Maurice Béjart, Belgium has also gained world acclaim in music and dance.

In general, Walloon literature is strongly oriented toward France, while Flemish literature is concerned chiefly with maintaining and broadening Flemish cultural identity, without strong reference to the Netherlands. In order to attempt to establish a Belgian cultural identity, the state has established "Houses of Culture" all over the country. These houses enrich the quality of life of the communities in which they are located, but it is doubtful that they contribute much to welding together two so distinct cultures.

FUTURE

Belgium has begun to overcome its serious economic difficulties. It is still wealthy even by the high European standards. It must restructure its traditional industries in order to make them competitive in world markets today. The fact that for years Wilfried Martens had the most solid parliamentary majority in recent history and became Europe's longest-serving prime minister helped put the Belgian economy back on firmer ground. His was one of the rare Belgian governments to serve longer than a year or two.

Belgians show a receptivity to innovation. Proton, a cash-card developed by a consortium of banks, has become the world's largest electronic-purse scheme. A million Belgians can now make even the smallest purchases simply by inserting their cards into a reader at the grocer, the news stand, or many other small and laege businesses. At the end of the working day, the merchant downloads the data into his bank's computer, and the proceeds are credited to his account. Thus he need not guard his cash, count it, or carry it to a bank. Most banks support this card, which reveals that Belgium is a small land where collaboration among competitors still is a favorite way of doing business.

At the turn of the century Belgians are a people who have lost some faith in those who govern them. There is a widespread belief that the country's political and judicial systems have failed the people. The government's credibility was severely undermined by revelations of police and judicial incompetence that tolerated a pedophile ring, led by a man (Marc Dutroux) accused of murdering four young girls and composed of sordid individuals who were police informants. The exposure of this sex-abuse and murder case led to allegations of police bungling and cover-ups by politicians, who may have been protecting persons in the ring. It also aroused suspicion that the assassins of former deputy prime minister André Cools in 1991 may have been linked to the ring. A Belgian court charged a former interior minister, Alain Van der Biest, and four others of murdering Cools. In the hysteria came allegations that the current flamboyant deputy prime minister, Elio Di Rupo, had engaged in sex with boys under age 16. Di Rupo does not deny that he is a homosexual, but he protested the charges and was exonerated.

A series of wildcat strikes and a 300,000-strong march through Brussels in 1996 gave the Dehaene government no alternative but to act, amid fears of a popular revolt. It promised that the political appointment of judicial magistrates would end in order to prevent political patronage and manipulation in the legal system. It pledged to clean up public life. Nevertheless, many Belgians remain skeptical, and the scandals are forcing the entire society to look at itself more honestly and to deal with its faults.

In 1998 the government and opposition agreed to reform the police and justice system by creating a unified federal police force and a single district force and by eliminating the military-style national gendarmerie and municipal police. Justice is one of the few main duties besides social security and defense that remain within the competence of the national government. Politicians lost some of their legal immunity. One benefit of the angry outpouring in 1996 was that it created a rare moment of national unity in Belgium. For the first time in a long time, Walloons, Flemings and immigrants marched together in peace. Perhaps Belgium is not a country "held together mainly by inertia," as one foreign diplomat observed.

Entering parliamentary elections in June 1999, parties now receive public financing, freeing them from reliance on bribes, and agreed among themselves to limit campaign spending. But in the week before the elections Belgians were traumatized by evidence that dioxin had gotten into animal feed and thereby poisoned much of their food. With their grocery shelves empty, angry voters threw out the Dahaene government, which had mishandled the crisis. His *Christian Democrats* fell to 22 seats in Flanders and 10 in Wallonia, while his *Socialist* partners dropped to 14 in Flanders and 19 in Wallonia. The big winners were the *Liberals*, led in Flanders by Guy Verhofstadt, who captured 18 seats in Wallonia and 23 in Flanders. The *Greens* jumped to 9 seats in Flanders and 11 in Wallonia. Also increasing its votes was the Flemish separatist *Vlaams Blok,* which won 15 seats; however, no party will join a coalition with it. The *Volksunie* in Flanders climbed to 8 seats, and the *National Front* in Wallonia dropped to only one. As always, the coalition-building that followed was tricky.

On a canal in Brugge

The Grand Duchy of Luxembourg

Luxembourg's largest castle dominates the village of Vianden   Courtesy: Jon Markham Morrow

Area: 999 sq. mi. (2,586 sq. km., somewhat smaller that Rhode Island).
Population: 410,000, of which 120,000 are foreigners (30% of the total population).
Capital City: Luxembourg (Pop. 81,000, estimated).
Climate: Temperate, with mild winters and summers.
Neighboring Countries: Luxembourg is wedged between Belgium (West); Germany (East) and France (South).
Official Languages: Luxembourgish (a Moselle Franconian–German dialect with numerous additions of French words), French and German.
Ethnic Background: Indo–European, Germanic.
Principal Religion: Roman Catholic (94%).
Main Exports: Iron and steel products, chemicals. International banking activities are extremely important.
Main Imports: Minerals, metals, foodstuffs, machinery.
Currency: Luxembourg franc, equal to the Belgian franc, which circulates in the country.
Major Trading Partners: EU countries (75%), principally Germany.
National Day: June 23rd.
Chief of State: His Royal Highness the Grand Duke Jean, b. 1921. Married in 1953 to Princess Josephine–Charlotte, sister of the late King Baudouin of Belgium. He succeeded his mother upon her abdication in 1964.
Heir Apparent: His Royal Highness Crown Prince Henri, b. 1955.
Head of Government: Jean–Claude Juncker, Prime Minister (since 1995).
National Flag: Three horizontal stripes of equal width, red, white, blue (The flag closely resembles that of the Netherlands).

Since the Roman legions came to what is now Luxembourg in 57 B.C., the Luxembourgers have tenaciously clung to their separate existence. Caesar wrote that the Treveri tribesmen who resisted his troops "never submitted to commands except under the compulsion of an army." In the two millenia which followed, the Franks, Burgundians, Dutch and Germans controlled this tiny land. But, unlike most small nations, the Luxembourgers never allowed themselves to be absorbed entirely by another power. They well deserve their national motto: *Mir wolle bleive wat mir sin!* ("We want to remain what we are!").

Luxembourg is the smallest independent state in the EU, encompassing only 999 square miles, less than the state of Rhode Island. It also has a population of about 368,000, fewer than one–third that of Brussels and one–twentieth that of Paris. Nevertheless, it is one of the most prosperous countries in the world, with an industrial productivity and international significance far out of proportion to its size.

The northern half of the country, called Oesling, is a rugged territory of low mountains and forests. It is a continuation of the Ardennes forest area of Belgium. The southern half is within the Lorraine Plain and is rolling, wooded countryside. Because of its lush pastureland and fertile soil, this area is called the *Gutland* or *Bon Pays* (Good Land). It also contains most of Luxembourg's industrial centers and its capital city.

With its many international organizations and multilingual citizens the capital is a very cosmopolitan city. Having only about 81,000 inhabitants, it is no metropolis, but it is a charming, almost fairytale city built in the late 16th century in Spanish Renaissance style and remodeled at the end of the 19th century. Two rivers, the Alzette and Petrusse, flow through the city, which is located on a plateau, and through the centuries they have cut deep,

Luxembourg

narrow valleys with very steep sides dropping 200 feet. The old section of the city is perched on the highest part of the plateau. Located on one of the many narrow, twisting streets of the old city is the Grand Ducal Palace, built in 1573, with colorful guards always standing or marching in front of it.

HISTORY

The Early Period

Luxembourg's independence was established in 963 A.D. Siegfried, the Count of Ardennes, hewed powerful battlements in the cliffs where Luxembourg's capital city is now located. Until it was demolished by international agreement in 1867, this almost impregnable fortress was called the "Gibraltar of the North." In fact, the word *Luxembourg* meant "little fortress." The visitor can still climb on the ruins of this stronghold and wander in the maze of passages underneath it.

Independent Luxembourg was linked to the Holy Roman Empire, and in the beginning of the 14th century Luxembourg's Duke, Henry VII, was crowned Holy Roman Emperor. Luxembourg ultimately provided four Emperors during this heyday of the Duchy's power. Henry's son, John, a man very fond of travel, women, horses and dice, became the King of Bohemia. After losing one eye in battle and the other to disease, he became known as John the Blind. His bravery became legendary in the Battle of Crecy in 1346 against the English. Unable to see, John galloped to the head of his troops by having his steed tied to those of several loyal aides and then ordering them to advance. Not surprisingly, he did not survive the battle.

John's grandson, Charles IV, was also a Holy Roman Emperor and built the beautiful city of Prague, now the capital of Czechoslovakia. The Luxembourger's golden age of power gradually declined, and in 1443 the Duchy was conquered by the Duke of Burgundy; for more than four centuries, foreign powers gave the orders in Luxembourg.

Neutrality and War

Luxembourg evolved into a neutral country in the 19th century, but this lasted less than a half century. It was violated by German troops in August 1914. The Grand Duchess Marie–Adelheid remained in the country during the entire four–year occupation, and in the opinion of many Luxembourgers she collaborated with the Germans. Whether this was true or not, she felt obliged to abdicate in early 1919, and her popular sister, Charlotte, ascended the throne. A referendum in 1919 confirmed the constitutional monarchy, but proclaimed the people to be sovereign and introduced universal suffrage for men and women. This referendum established a fully democratic parliamentary form of government in the Grand Duchy.

As small countries often do, Luxembourg felt the need to seek a union with a larger power, so in a referendum in 1921, Luxembourgers voted three to one to enter an economic union with France. The latter country, however, advised Luxembourg to enter a close economic relationship with Belgium; both smaller countries agreed to this in 1922.

In 1940 Luxembourg was given another reminder that a policy of neutrality alone cannot guarantee the security of a country. German troops again occupied the tiny state in 1940 and within a few weeks virtually annexed it. In August 1942 Luxembourg was officially incorporated into Hitler's *Reich*. When the population responded with a strike, about 30,000 Luxembourgers, or about 10% of the population and most of country's young men, were deported. Many were forced to serve in the German army and until liberation the population continued to suffer greatly from a brutal occupation.

Having learned from her sister's mistake in 1914, Grand Duchess Charlotte fled in 1940 with her entire government, first to London and then to Montreal. She worked tirelessly to assure that Luxembourg would be recognized as an independent country at the war's end. Her son, Crown Prince Jean, served as an officer in the British army, and landed with

235

Luxembourg

his unit, the Irish Guards, on the beaches of Normandy on June 11, 1944, five days after the first Allied troops had landed. On September 3 his unit entered Brussels and on September 10 it crossed the Luxembourg border between Rodange and Pétange, exactly at the spot where his parents had left the country in 1940. The same afternoon he reached the capital city—his arrival was hailed by thousands of his countrymen. His father, Felix, had reached the city that morning with an American tank division.

Unfortunately, the war was not yet over for Luxembourg. Hitler's forces made a last offensive at the end of 1944 in order to stop the Allied advance toward Germany. During this Ardennes offensive, known as the Battle of the Bulge, the American commander, General Omar Bradley, made Luxembourg City his headquarters, but a large portion of the Duchy was nevertheless recaptured by German troops. In the fiercely fought Battle of the Bulge such destruction was visited upon the land that it took until 1952 to repair all the material damage. American losses were also very great, as one can see at the American military cemetery in Hamm, located about a mile from Luxembourg Airport. There rest 5,000 American soldiers, including General George Patton, who was killed in a jeep accident in December 1945. Most cities in Luxembourg have a street or square named after Patton, who is hailed as the country's liberator. Ettelbruck in the Ardennes unofficially calls itself Patton Town.

GOVERNMENT AND POLITICS

The Grand Duke

Luxembourg is a constitutional monarchy, whose constitution of 1868 was amended in 1919 to invest sovereignty in the people, rather than in the crown. Executive power is formally vested in the Grand Duke Jean, who ascended to the throne in 1964 when his mother abdicated in his favor. The Grand Duke is a very popular monarch, and the Luxembourgers' enthusiastic response to his son's marriage in 1981 demonstrated this sentiment will remain. Crown Prince Henri met a beautiful and intelligent Cuban exile, Maria Teresa Mestre, while both were studying in Geneva. Although she was not of noble birth, he chose to marry her, and their wedding in the Luxembourg Cathedral drew a large assemblage of European nobility.

The Grand Duke, who takes his duties seriously, has considerable influence in the political process. As all constitutional monarchs, he "reigns but does not rule." To be effective, his orders must be countersigned by one or several members of the government, who alone assume political responsibility. Nevertheless, he could be an especially important figure in times of national crisis when either the parties are unable to form a government, or the nation desperately needs a symbol of national unity. In normal times his actual powers are limited.

Executive Power

This is actually exercised by the President of the Government (the Prime Minister) and his Council of Government (cabinet). The latter body is composed of eleven or twelve persons, each usually holding several ministerial posts. During the five years between elections, the cabinets are occasionally reshuffled, but the resulting "new" governments are seldom significantly different from the ones they replace. In order to try to create some separation between the parliament and the executive, as mandated by the constitution, all cabinet members are required to resign their parliamentary seats when they assume a cabinet post.

The cabinet drafts and submits legislation, which is debated in parliament. The most important professional organizations, especially the six official groups representing agriculture, handcrafts, commerce, civil servants, private employees and labor, are consulted on legislation affecting their interests. The smallness of the county enables this process to work smoothly. Passage after two rounds of debate is usually a foregone conclusion, since the governing parties' approval had already been reached in advance. Particularly important legislation can be submitted directly to the voters in a referendum if the cabinet and parliament approve, but such referendums occur very seldom.

Legislative Structure and Powers

Although the Grand Duke must formally sign all legislation and appointments, the President and Council of Government are not responsible to the monarch, but to the lower house of parliament, the Chamber of Deputies. Its 60 members (lowered from 64 in 1989 to reflect the declining population) are elected every five years by a system of proportional representation tailored to a small or medium–size country, in which voters live close to the candidates and may even know them personally. Luxembourg is divided into four electoral districts, and seats are distributed to each depending upon population. The largest receives 23 seats and the smallest seven. Each voter is permitted to cast as many votes as there are candidates to be elected and may even cast two votes for the same candidate if he wishes. The seats are then distributed to the candidates who receive the most votes.

Summaries of parliamentary debates and election information are sent to all citizens of voting age, who are *required* to vote. As in all parliamentary democracies, if the President and Council of Government lost their majority in the Chamber, then the Grand Duke can call new elections, although such early elections are seldom necessary.

Political Parties

Since 1925 no political party has ever been able to win a majority of seats in the Chamber of Deputies, so all governments

Their Royal Highnesses The Grand Duke and Grand Duchess

Luxembourg

are coalitions of two or more parties. Luxembourg's three main parties have led Luxembourg for about 50 years and have helped create a democracy based on party cooperation. Although each major party represents a distinct political subculture, they all seek a solution to problems in a way agreeable to all three, no matter which is in government at the moment. All three are willing to form coalitions with each other. Neither ideologies nor historical resentments prevent them from sharing responsibility for their nation's future.

The largest is presently the *Christian–Social People's Party (CSV)*, which represents the bourgeois values of a predominantly Catholic population. Its votes are drawn primarily from practicing Catholics, although the gradual disappearance of church–state issues has greatly reduced the religious component of its program. It does draw votes from the nation's farmers and workers. The party's program calls for support of a social market economy and special attention to the needs of citizens who earn below the national average. It is a middle–of–the–road party which supports the extension of the country's already generous social welfare system. With a loosening of religious bonds and a decrease of the number of farmers, the *CSV* has begun to lose votes.

After the 1984 elections, it formed a governing coalition with the *Socialists*; this was maintained after the June 1994 elections. The *CSV* has for years been the key coalition party, and no ruling coalition since World War II has been formed without first trying to win its direct participation. In 1994 it fell from 22 to 21 seats.

Jacques Santer, who left office to be EU president from 1995 to 1999, was replaced as prime minister by Jean–Claude Juncker. One of seven children of a steelworker and trade union militant, Juncker studied law at the University of Strasbourg. He came from the left of the *CSV* and joined the cabinet in 1984 at age 29. He quickly gained a reputation as an intelligent, well–connected man in the EU with integrity, a broad mind, and a knack for grasping both practical detail and conceptual problems. He also serves as finance minister.

The second–largest party is the *Luxembourg Socialist Workers Party (LSAP)*, known generally as the *Socialists*. Led by Foreign Minister Jacques Poos, it fell from 18 to 17 seats in 1994, but it stayed in a grand coalition with the *CSV*. This alliance, which in 1994 was reelected for a record third term, is scarcely troubled by squabbling between the partners. The *LSAP* was founded at the turn of the century to protect workers from the seamy consequences of industrialization. Because it views itself as the party of the working class, it is strongest in the highly industrialized South. In the 1960s it showed signs of broadening its base by weakening the socialist components of its program, but this move was strongly resisted by the left wing of the party. The question of collaboration with communists at the local level prompted the party's right wing to split off and form the *Social Democratic Party (SDP)*, which is insignificant today.

The third party is the *Democratic Party (DP)*, usually referred to as the *Liberals*. It lost heavily in 1984 and was forced out of the government. Led by popular mayor of Luxembourg City, Lydie–Wurth Polfer, it climbed from 11 to 12 seats in 1994. But it remained shut out of the government. The *Liberals'* support is found primarily in the middle class, professions and skilled working groups. It strongly supports a free market economy and opposes excessive government control over the economy.

Small parties took a sixth of the votes in the 1994 elections. A one–issue party, calling itself the *Five–Sixths Party* because it advocates raising all pensions to five–sixths of a person's last salary, as government employees receive, won four seats in 1989. In 1994 it ran under the name *Ac-*

Crown Prince Henri and Princess Maria Teresa

Luxembourg

Prime Minister Jean-Claude Juncker

tion Committee for Democracy and Pension Justice (ADR) and received five seats. Two Green parties won five seats. Despite turbulent internal politics which have kept the parties split, they wish to reunite and enter the government some day.

The only party which never participates in governing coalitions is the *Communist Party of Luxembourg (KPL)*. It finds its electoral support primarily in the industrialized South. Its electoral support has continuously declined. A major reason is that it has remained relatively immune from the more moderate form of communism known as *Eurocommunism,* which seeks to respect the democratic process and pursue policies oriented toward the particular needs of their own countries. The *KPL's* ideological rigidity will probably keep it in the political cold, especially following the collapse of communism in Eastern Europe. It lost its only seat in 1994.

Although the parliament is technically a one–chamber assembly, the 21–member Council of State traditionally functions as an upper house. It is appointed by the Grand Duke, acting upon the advice of the cabinet, Chamber of Deputies and the Council of State itself. Mainly an advisory body, the Council of State must be consulted on all legislation and can actually postpone its enactment. Ultimately, however, it can always be overridden by the Chamber of Deputies. Eleven of the Council's members function as the nation's highest administrative court, and, on the whole, the Council plays an important role in the governing process.

Local Government

For administrative purposes, Luxembourg is divided into three districts: Luxembourg, Diekirch and Grevenmacher, which are further broken down into 12 cantons and 118 communes. Each commune has authority over local affairs and elects a Communal Council every six years. To maintain some measure of national control, the central government appoints a Burgomaster (mayor) to every commune, who presides over the Communal Council. All appointments must, however, enjoy the confidence and support of a majority among the locally elected members of the Communal Councils; no mayor is ever imposed on a commune. In order to make the system of local government more efficient, the central government has proposed that all the present communes be fused into a total of 30, with none having a population under 3,000. Local resistance so far has prevented the realization of this plan.

Defense and Foreign Policy

Two world wars in the 20th century convinced Luxembourgers that neutrality offered their country no protection whatsoever. Their government–in–exile supported the Allied cause, and in 1949 the country joined NATO. With such a small population, it cannot contribute many troops to the alliance. It abolished its conscript army, created in 1945, in 1967, but it maintains a voluntary army of battalion size (about 500 troops, plus a 60–man band). More importantly, it provides storage sites for NATO equipment.

Luxembourg was also a founding member of the EU, a fact which has greatly enhanced its prestige. It amended its constitution in 1956 to permit the transfer of certain of its sovereign powers to the EU. At first, the EU's founding fathers suggested that tiny Luxembourg, which is the geographic center of the six nations, become a kind of Washington, D.C., for the new United States of Europe. This never happened, but Luxembourg continues to propose it at EU meetings. Now EU officials travel back and forth from Brussels, Strasbourg and Luxembourg, a necessity which many officials and observers find wasteful and irritating. It is now the home of many EU offices and institutions, a large part of which are located in the Europa Center, one of Luxembourg's few skyscrapers. In all, about 10,000 EU employees and an equal number of foreign business executives live in Luxembourg.

Among the EU offices located in the Grand Duchy are the Secretariat for the European Parliament, the ECSC, Euratom, the European Court of Justice, the European Audit Court, the European Investments Bank and the European Currency Union. In 1988 Luxembourg won an important victory in its bid to become the center of the EU's legal operations. A new court of first instance was created there to assume some of the growing workload of the European Court of Justice.

The European Parliament used to meet there sometimes, and a new European parliament building was constructed for these meetings. But in 1979 the parliament decided to hold all sessions in Strasbourg. This decision infuriated Luxembourg, which turned to the European Court of

Entrance to the Grand Ducal Palace in Luxembourg

Luxembourg

Justice for help. Few people are optimistic, though, especially since a massive office complex is being constructed in Brussels which includes an Assembly Chamber large enough for the European Parliament. Luxembourg tenaciously guards its retention of the parliament's secretariat, a body of about 2,000 European officials who make the parliament work, against Brussels. Most of the parliament's committee work already takes place in Brussels, and all the major political groups within the parliament have established their headquarters there. It has been estimated unofficially that 10% of all retail spending in the city of Luxembourg comes from EU employees and their families. Thus, their disappearance could severely affect retail businesses and property values. Luxembourgers are desperately trying to convert their European Parliament building into a viable international conference center.

Luxembourg's chief foreign policy goals are to be a significant partner in the defense of Western Europe and in the building of a politically and economically integrated Western Europe.

ECONOMY

Luxembourg is a highly industrialized and prosperous country. In 1995 it had the world's second highest per capita GDP, after Switzerland, and the highest in the EU. Since 1945, it has known a high degree of political and social peace. Its economy has always been based so heavily on iron and steel that it is often said that "Luxembourg is as much a gift of iron as Egypt is a gift of the Nile." This has been especially true since 1877, when an English engineer, Gilchrist Thomas, discovered a process for removing the phosphorus from Luxembourg's iron ore. Its largest steel company, *ARBED*, (Europe's third–largest) is partly foreign–owned, but the Luxembourg state is now its major stockholder. Only a fifth of *ARBED's* turnover is in Luxembourg; its operations are worldwide and it has major plants in France, Germany, Belgium, Holland and South Korea.

Luxembourg's reliance on steel is a source of economic vulnerability, as well as of opportunity. The competition among the world's steel producers had become so strong in recent years that production outstripped demand. In response, Luxembourg had to reduce its production. In 1970 the steel industry produced nearly a third of the country's GDP; by 1991 that figure was down to 8%. Steel had fallen by 1991 to a third of manufacturing output, compared with 70% in 1960. This has not only led to huge financial losses, but has forced the Luxembourg steel industry to restructure itself. This was also required by the EU, which now seeks to save the European steel industry by requiring it to modernize in member countries.

The Château de Berg, Grand Ducal country residence

For Luxembourg this has necessitated a gradual reduction of the steel industry's work force from 25,000 in 1974 to 8,000 in 1993 and to 6,000 by 1996. These reductions resulted in a rise in productivity per employee. In order not to disrupt social peace within the country, the reduction has been accomplished by retirement of older workers as early as age 57, rather than by massive layoffs. It is this kind of practice which has enabled Luxembourg to hold its unemployment rate to 3.7% in 1999, among the lowest in the world and best in the EU. But it has a labor shortage, and over 80% of new jobs are filled by cross border workers, called *"Frontaliers."* Together with resident aliens, they constituted 53% of the workforce in 1995.

The country's political and economic leaders saw the problem of excessive dependence upon steel well in advance, and, since 1950, they have made a steady effort to diversify the economy. The Goodyear Tire and Rubber Company began building plants in the Grand Duchy in 1951 and is now its second largest employer. The program got a particular boost from the industrial diversification law of 1962; this has been renewed regularly and provides state financial assistance for industrial development which contributes to the construction, conversion and rationalization of industries, crafts and commercial operations. The program has greatly stimulated the service industries, which now employ 60% of the workforce, and has attracted over 60 new companies to Luxembourg, which have created employment for more than 11,000 persons. The most important newcomers have been American, such as DuPont.

The program has also helped to attract foreign banks to the country; the number of banks increased from 13 in 1955 to 230 in 1998. Luxembourg has become one of the financial centers in Europe. When the Eurodollar market (in which Luxembourg had specialized) declined, and London deregulated the British financial industry, Luxembourg shifted deftly to other retail

Luxembourg

View of the capital

banking services and maintains its place in the world market. This has greatly benefited the country. Banks employ over 9,000 and generate almost 15% of the GDP and 30% of government revenue. One can almost speak of an economic revolution in the Grand Duchy.

In the 1980s, one job in banking was being created for every job which was disappearing in the steel industry. By 1988 the number of Luxembourgers employed in banking exceeded those working in the steel industry. To attract funds to Luxembourg banks, the country has doggedly pursued its right to guarantee total bank secrecy, despite pressure from the EU and U.S. to cooperate more closely in cases involving crime, money laundering and tax fraud. Germany suffers most from the capital flight to Luxembourg. Along with other powerful neighbors, it wants the Duchy to harmonize its low tax regime with its EU partners and abandon its zero withholding tax on foreigners. Because the financial services sector now accounts for more than a fifth of its GDP and employs one in ten persons in the work force, Luxembourg resists these efforts, although it pays lip service to proposals to reform EU banking policies.

The financial services sector has emerged as the economy's largest taxpayer. To keep the economy growing, the government introduced in 1986 the most sweeping tax reform in the nation's history. Taxes were cut and loopholes were closed. Just over half the cuts are enjoyed by the business sector, prompting some critics of the reform to charge that it is a device primarily to improve the financial environment for bankers.

In 1991 further tax cuts went into effect. Luxembourg was the first EU country in 1997 to meet all the Maastricht treaty convergence criteria for economic and monetary union (EMU). The banks have mixed feelings about the new Euro; they quail at the cost of introducing it, estimated to be 4% of their total revenues. They also fear that the Euro could bring with it an EU–wide harmonization of withholding tax, which could be a severe blow to Luxembourg's competitiveness as an offshore financial center. The country's government debt is a mere 6.7% of GDP, its budget is balanced, and its inflation is steady at 1% in 1999.

With a very small population and a high standard of living, Luxembourg is absolutely dependent upon foreign trade. Exports and imports account for 85% of its GDP, compared with 50% for Belgium, 20% for France and 10% for the U.S. Such dependence indicates why Luxembourg's membership in the EU has been a matter of economic life or death. It sends three–fourths of its exports to the EU countries and imports the same percentage from EU members. Its trade with the U.S. remains relatively insignificant. Primary imports are iron ore, coke and all energy sources except hydroelectricity.

Its steel companies own some coal mines in Germany, but its dependence upon imported oil, gas and coal is a major problem. With the highest per capita number of automobiles in Europe, oil is a particularly sensitive import, but by 1991 oil accounted for only 10% of Luxembourg's imports, down from 17% in 1973. To increase its energy supplies, an atomic plant along the Moselle River was planned, which would have supplied most of the power needs until the year 2000. However, the nuclear accident at Harrisburg, Pennsylvania, created political problems which caused the plans for this plant to be dropped. Luxembourg also declined to join with France in developing a nuclear power plant at Cattenom, located only six miles from the Grand Duchy. After the 1986 nuclear accident at Chernobyl in the Soviet Union, the Luxembourg government and, according to polls, 80% of the citizens began to worry more about the safety of the Cattenom plant. However, demonstrations and diplomatic protests have had no influence on the French in this matter.

An important factor in maintaining industrial production in such a small country has been the importation of foreign workers, especially from Portugal, Italy and Spain. Together with their families, they now account for nearly a third of the population. This is the highest percentage of foreign workers in the EU. If trends continue, the proportion will be one–half within the lifetimes of most living inhabitants. Half of Luxembourg City's population is already foreign. Non–nationals, especially immigrants from Portugal and Italy, hold about half of all jobs in the country. Foreigners provide 52% of the workers in all of Luxembourg's industries, although the percentages differ in the various economic sectors. They account for 85% of the construction workers, 66% of the craftsmen and 35% of the laborers in the iron and steel industry. These workers and their families are not permitted to participate in the national political life, although they can vote in European parliamentary elections. But even if there is little integration with the native population, they are generally well–treated. Unlike in many Western European countries, there is no seriously destabilizing anti–foreigner sentiment.

The dependence upon foreign workers seems irreversible, given Luxembourg's alarmingly low birth rate. Unlike the case in most European countries after 1945, there was no baby boom in Luxembourg, and since 1960 the birth rate has steadily

Luxembourg

declined to one of the lowest in the world—since 1968 the native population has declined by about 1,000 each year. This is not only a serious problem for the very survival of a small nation, but it creates an increasingly aging population which must be supported by fewer and fewer persons of working age. A fifth is already over 60 years of age, the largest percentage in the EU.

It is hoped that this unpleasant development can be rendered less serious by automating and modernizing industry. This would establish a productive industrial base which could create a high degree of wealth with fewer workers. The government provides a multitude of inducements to raise the birthrate: increasing family allowances, extending maternity leaves and helping single or divorced women raise children. Few people are optimistic that these measures will reverse the demographic downturn. As one member of parliament worried: "Our country is like an aging couple. We live well, but we don't know what tomorrow brings. We have no grandchildren."

Maintaining economic stability and prosperity will remain a major task for the future. This will require maintaining not only a high level of productivity, but also the labor peace that has prevailed since the end of World War II. There has been scarcely a strike since 1945; this enviable record is due to the well-organized process of consultation among employers, employees and the government, and to the great care taken not to allow the rate of unemployment to increase. In part, this has been successfully accomplished by introducing extensive public works and part–time work schedules with the state paying for the hours not worked.

This daring policy is one that most observers agree will become too costly in the long run. Labor peace was also preserved by indexing incomes and pensions to adjust automatically to inflation, although such indexing fans the flames of inflation and damages trade competitiveness. In addition, this desire to maintain purchasing power clashes with the desire to increase social benefits, which already cover virtually the entire population.

The Belgian government unilaterally devalued its currency in early 1982, making it necessary to devalue Luxembourg's franc, which is linked to Belgian currency. The Grand Duchy's government was unhappy about this move by Belgian leaders, who did not even consult with it beforehand. There was some talk of reappraising the monetary union which has existed since 1922. It had become clear that the economic partnership with Belgium is increasingly a marriage of two divergent economies. After high–level meetings, Belgian leaders agreed to undertake no unilateral devaluations in the future.

Slightly more than half of Luxembourg's land is used for agriculture, of which 54% is used for grazing. A third of the country is planted with forests. Meat and dairy production dominate, accounting for more than 80% of the farm income. Wine production is also important.

Presently only 6% of the population is engaged in agriculture, and this number is steadily declining. Yet even non–farming Luxembourgers are not very far from the natural environment of their rural compatriots. A population density below the EU average, the absence of large cities, and the nearness of wooded areas, together with a relatively unspoiled countryside available for many kinds of relaxation, all contribute to making Luxembourg a pleasant place to live.

CULTURE

Tiny Luxembourg has always been heavily influenced by its neighbors and nothing shows this quite so clearly as the polyglot of languages that every Luxembourger masters. The everyday language of the people is Luxembourgish, an old Moselle–Frankish dialect of German, which has taken on many altered French expressions, such as d'fotell (*le fauteuil*, armchair). The language has become the country's one real symbol of national identity. Even modern Germans have difficulty understanding it.

This native language is spoken at home, in parliament and sometimes in the courts, although documents and formal proceedings are in French. It also has a written form. Despite an official spelling, most Luxembourgers write it phonetically. Some literature exists in the language, and local radio thrives on it. There has been a daily one–hour TV news broadcast in it since 1992. The 1990s are witnessing a renaissance in interest in written Luxembourgish, and more and more foreign residents are learning to speak it.

The German language is primarily used in most primary schools, criminal court proceedings, church, and the press, although it is not uncommon to see articles written in all three national languages on the same page of a newspaper. Finally, French is the language that is used most in administration, civil courts, parliament and secondary education. Two German invasions in the 20th century caused the elite to align itself more toward France and francophone culture. The country lacks a university. Some persons have noted a positive side of this fact: a source of articulate dissent is exported. Young Luxembourgers do demonstrate, but they usually do so over local issues, and they are seldom violent.

All Luxembourgers are completely trilingual, a fact which spares the country of the terrible language conflict which plagues neighboring Belgium. In Luxembourg, culture, including theater, film and literature, is very dependent upon the surrounding French and German worlds, and citizens have realistically accepted this without resentment. Luxembourgers' national identity is so strong and seems so natural that no language issue seems capable of altering it.

Luxembourg introduced Europe's first commercial radio station in 1934. In 1988 it seized the lead in the satellite broadcasting of commercial television when an Ariane rocket placed its Astra satellite into orbit. It has 16 channels which can beam to Britain, France, Germany and the BENELUX and Scandinavian countries. Radio–Télé–Luxembourg (RTL) broadcasts to 500 million viewers across international borders. It purchased a second satellite doubling capacity to 32 channels. It is the first European country to have an entire satellite system for TV. Some EU members, such as the UK and the Netherlands, oppose such open broadcasting, but Luxembourg is determined that the EU's principle of a "Single Market" should apply to TV viewing. This single market can also have other effects: Ufa, the TV and film subsidiary of the German media giant, Bertelsmann, merged in 1996 with the Compagnie Luxembourgeoise Radiodiffusion (CLR/now CLT), one of the pioneers of the European media industry.

THE FUTURE

After a period of rapid economic progress, the economy will grow more slowly. Luxembourg's economic task will be to maintain the productivity, prosperity and social welfare net which it has already achieved. As an exporting nation, it worries about recession in the rest of Europe, especially Germany, and about its increasingly uncompetitive cost structure. It can be expected to maintain the political and social stability which has prevailed since 1945. The Duchy's goal of becoming Europe's capital will remain unfulfilled although its role in Europe is important. In July 1999 it assumed the rotating presidency of the WEU. Parliamentary elections were held in June 1998. Juncker's *Christian Democrats* remained in power. But the *Liberals* overtook the *Socialists* and were thereby in a position to replace them in the governing coalition.

The United Kingdom of Great Britain and Northern Ireland
by Mark H. Mullin

Political power's most coveted address: 10 Downing Street, residence of the Prime Minister

Area: 89,038 sq. mi. (230,609 sq. km., slightly smaller than Oregon).
Population: 59 million (estimated).
Capital City: London (Pop. 7 million, estimated, including the city's sprawling suburbs).
Climate: Mild and temperate, rarely above 86° F (30° C) or below 14° F (−10° C).
Neighboring Countries: Ireland (a short distance across the Irish Sea to the west); France, Belgium and the Netherlands (a short distance across the English Channel or North Sea to the east).
Official Language: English.
Other Principal Tongues: About a fourth of the population of Wales speaks Welsh, and about 60,000 Scottish speak a form of Gaelic. Both are Celtic dialects.
Ethnic Background: Angle, Saxon, Celtic and Nordic.
Principal Religion: In England—Church of England (Anglican) 49%, Roman Catholic 7%. In Scotland—Church of Scotland (Presbyterian) 19%. In Wales—Church in Wales. Methodist, Jewish and other.
Main Exports: Machinery, chemicals, motor vehicles, oil.
Main Imports: Manufactured goods, machinery, foodstuffs, consumer goods.
Currency: Pound sterling.
National Day: Celebration of the birthday of the Queen is in June, although she was actually born on April 21st.
Head of State: Her Majesty Queen Elizabeth II, b. 1926. Married Lieut. Philip Mountbatten (Prince of Greece and Denmark) on November 20, 1947; he had been created Duke of Edinburgh on the preceding day and (in 1957) Prince of Great Britain. Queen Elizabeth II succeeded to the throne on the death of her father, George VI on February 6, 1952; her coronation took place on June 2, 1953.
Heir Apparent: His Royal Highness Prince Charles (b. Nov. 14, 1948), Prince of Wales. His son, Prince William of Wales (b. June 21, 1982) is second in succession to the throne.
Head of Government: Tony Blair, Prime Minister (since May 1997).
National Flag: The Union Jack—a dark blue charged with the white cross of St. Andrew (for Scotland), the red cross of St. Patrick (for Ireland), surmounted by the red cross of St. George (for England) bordered in white.

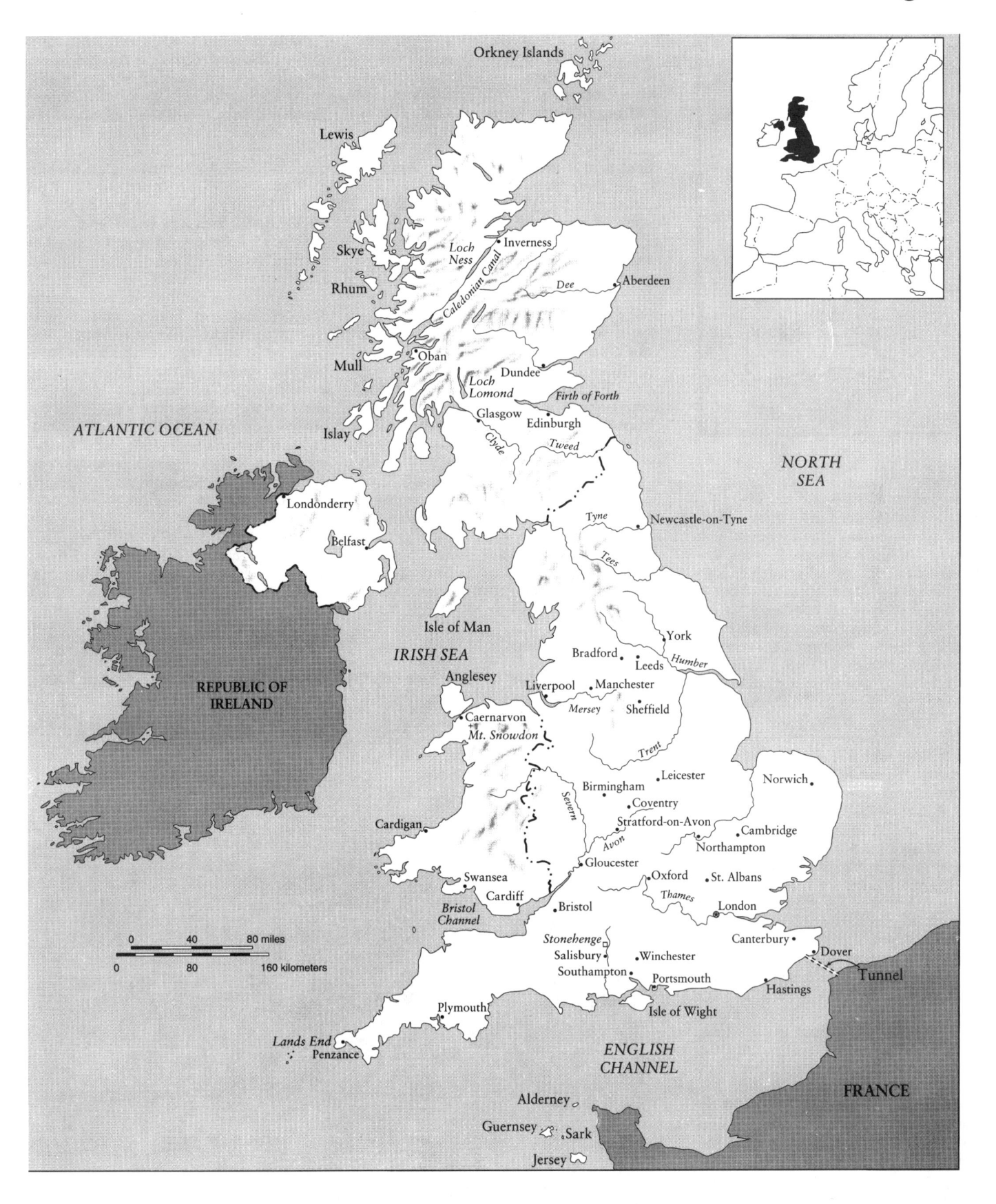

The United Kingdom

The United Kingdom

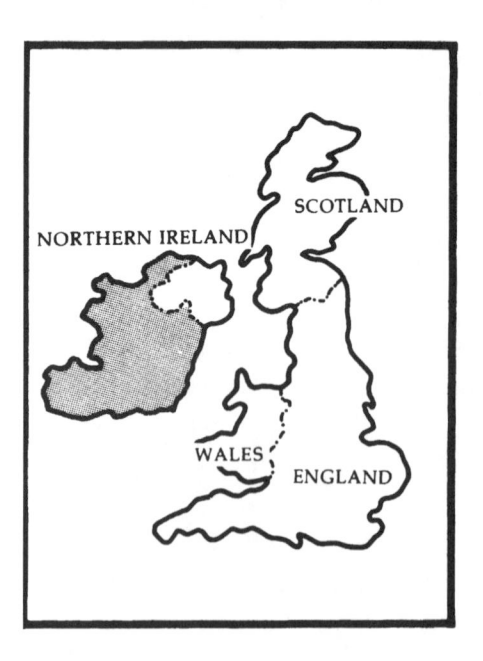

No country in the world has closer ties with the United States in language, history, shared assumptions and emotion than does the United Kingdom. It is not surprising that in the capital of each country there stands a prominent statue of one of the greatest leaders of the other. Abraham Lincoln gazes at the Houses of Parliament in London, and in a prominent section of Washington, Winston Churchill (himself half American) stands giving his famous "V" for victory salute. Although the British influence on the United States is not surprising, what is a remarkable fact is the influence that the United Kingdom has had on the rest of the world. It is striking that a moderately–sized island off the coast of Europe should achieve first a pivotal role in European affairs and then domination of much of the entire globe.

Britain is blessed with a moderate climate, despite its northerly location, due to the warmth of the Gulf Stream, which after originating in the Caribbean Sea crosses the Atlantic. Its waters provide a warmer, albeit moister, climate than would otherwise be the case. Rain is frequent, but not over–abundant. The sun shines in most parts for one out of four to eight daylight hours during the winter. The mountains of the west modify this pattern, condensing the clouds into rainfall, which is more abundant there.

The climate is not suited to plant life needing heat, but it is ideal for water–seeking crops, particularly grasses. With a population density of about 640 persons per square mile, much of Britain is urbanized. In spite of the fertile soil, it is an importer of foodstuffs. The industrial revolution, for which Britain is renowned, resulted in a particularly dense type of city building construction. Wales is a mixture of industry, agriculture and herding. Virtually all sheep and cattle are consumed within the country; the sheep support production of fine woolens, few of which are exported. Scotland, about one quarter the size of England and Wales, consists of a small area of lowlands and the larger highlands, which actually reach a maximum height of only 4,400 feet. The cities of Glasgow on the Clyde River and Edinburgh on the Firth (Bay) of Forth are seats of heavy industry and highly urbanized. The mountains are widely interspersed with valleys where intensive sheep–raising supports the production of world–famous Scotch tweeds and plaids, treasured by tailors throughout the world.

While Roman remains can be found in various parts of England today, the most important architectural work is virtually invisible. London, located at the spot closest to the sea where the Thames could most easily be bridged, was walled and became a Roman center, even though the Celtic name was retained. It became the hub from which spokes of roads headed out to other parts of the island. This pattern still shapes the roads and rails of Britain. The city today extends far beyond the boundaries of the original wall.

Natural resources that were important in the early Industrial Revolution in the late 18th and 19th centuries have been a second blessing. Its island location has protected it from invasion for more than 900 years and encouraged it to use the sea for commercial and political gain. But its greatest blessing has been a relatively stable history which developed quite early in a tradition of freedom and representative government. Americans are sometimes confused by the various names applied to Britain. Its official name is *The United Kingdom of Great Britain and Northern Ireland*. Four areas combine to make up the country: England, Wales, Scotland and Northern Ireland. The word "Britain" encompasses the first three. The last is composed of the six northern Irish counties. Because England is the site of the capital and over the centuries came to control the other areas, the term "England" or "the English" is sometimes (but inaccurately) used to describe the whole country. Residents of Wales, Scotland and Northern Ireland prefer to use the term "Great Britain" or "British."

The growth toward world leadership and representative democracy in Britain has not been smooth or steady, but the history of Britain has been a stage on which royal pageantry has combined with re-

The prehistoric ruins of Stonehenge on the Salisbury Plain which scholars date from 1800 to 1400 B.C.

244

The United Kingdom

markable commercial, industrial and political success of more humble citizens.

HISTORY

The Early Period

It must have been quite a shock for the Roman legionnaires who left the brilliant sunshine of Italy, marched across Gaul, and then made the short but perilous crossing of the English channel. They arrived in a land of soft greens, frequent rains and fearsome warriors who painted themselves blue and drove chariots armed with sharp blades at the axles. These Celts had come to the island during the Iron Age, spoke a dialect known as Brythonic, and thus their land was known as Britain.

Julius Caesar led two expeditions to Britain in 55 and 54 B.C., but it was not until 43 A.D. that the Roman Emperor Claudius began to establish settlements. The campaign to stamp out Celtic Druid beliefs, with all of their mysticism which have faded into the mists of time, produced the first of the great British queens, Boadicea, who managed to kill several thousand Romanizing Britons before finally being captured and committing suicide. While the popular image has always seen the British as chauvinists in their men's clubs, the fact that in the 1980s both the throne and the office of Prime Minister were occupied by women is less surprising when one remembers that the first resistance leader and the monarchs with two of the greatest reigns in English history, Elizabeth I (1558–1603) and Victoria (1837–1901) were women, however different they were. The first was an astute monarch, who is reported to have utilized amorous affairs to advance the affairs of state. The latter was conservative, conventional, prudish and astute, devoted only to her husband Albert. Indeed, rightfully or wrongfully, an entire age is known by the name of each in the English–speaking world.

Celtic tribalism continued in the mountains of Wales and Scotland. Hadrian's Wall ran for miles to seal off the northern borders of the Roman area since the people in the mountains there were beyond conquest. No attempt was made to invade Ireland.

The Early Christian Era

Roman soldiers and merchants brought Christianity with them to the island. Their persecution by Emperor Diocletian produced the first Christian martyr of the island, St. Alban. But after Emperor Constantine legalized Christianity in the empire, the Church began to flourish in Britain.

The Romans occupied England for about 400 years, but, as the empire collapsed inward, barbarian pressure on England increased. Angles, Saxons and Jutes, Teutonic tribes from what is now northern Germany and Denmark, filled the vacuum left by the Romans. Now it was the Celts leading their tribal lives in Wales, Scotland, Ireland and Cornwall, who kept alive the light of Western civilization and Christian culture.

King Arthur may be more legendary than historical, but his story represents the urge to restore Christian order during the dark period which lasted for two centuries. In 597 the monk Augustine (named for the more famous St. Augustine of Hippo) was sent from Rome to convert the English. He established Canterbury as his see and became its first archbishop. As Roman Christianity spread, it came into contact and then into conflict with Celtic Christianity. The synod of Whitby, meeting in 664, decided that Roman Christianity would prevail. This proved to be a most significant decision, for England was thus brought once more under the influence of Rome; its culture, its politics and religion would be shaped by events on the Continent. Nearly 900 years later, when England turned away from Roman Christianity, the effects would be even more important. During the 8th century, English

A castle in Wales

culture flourished. The first English historian, Venerable (later Saint) Bede, wrote his *Ecclesiastical History of the English People*; the great Anglo–Saxon epic *Beowulf* was written; and the Saxon monk Alcuin of York was a leading intellectual of Charlemagne's court.

Viking Invasion and Expulsion

By the 9th century, Vikings (Norsemen, Northmen, Normans) from Norway and Denmark attacked and then conquered much of the British isle. In response, the only English king to be known as "the Great," Alfred of Wessex, whose capital was at Winchester, organized an army, developed a navy, founded schools and stopped the growth of Norse–Danish power. It is ironic that the Norsemen then invaded France, where their region became known as Normandy. Almost two centuries later, one of their leaders would head the last successful conquest of England. Although Alfred died in 899, his son, Edward the Elder, conquered the remaining Danish–controlled areas and thus became the first King of a united England.

For the next 100 years, Anglo–Saxons and Norsemen merged during a golden age of relative peace. As the English historian Trevelyan said, "Had it not been for

245

The United Kingdom

the Scandinavian blood infused into our race by the catastrophes of the ninth century, less would have been heard in days to come of British maritime and commercial enterprise." Again ironically, at about the same time, the Scandinavians were *invited* to Russia to establish order among the belligerent, disorganized Slav warlords.

By the start of the 11th century, a weak king, Ethelred the Unready, allowed his kingdom to fall into confusion. The Danish king, Canute, invaded the island in 1016 and England became part of an empire that included Denmark and Norway. Canute was followed by his two sons, each of whom died shortly after ascending the throne. Ethelred's son, Edward the Confessor, who was half Norman and had lived in Normandy during the reign of Canute and his sons, was placed on the throne. He made two decisions with far-reaching consequences. He founded Westminster Abbey outside of London, starting the separation of the government from the city. Because he was childless, he promised his cousin, William, Duke of Normandy, that the throne would one day be his.

The Final Conquest and the First Plantagenets

The year 1066 is to the English school children what 1492 is to Americans. In that year, Edward the Confessor died. The Witan (national council) elected his brother-in-law, Harold, as his successor. A Norwegian invasion in Yorkshire called Harold to the north. Seizing the opportunity, William landed a Norman force in the south of England. Harold raced south to meet his death—at the Battle of Hastings he was killed by a sword blow and William established himself and his Norman lords as rulers of England.

William chose to rule by a rigorous system of feudalism. He established Normans loyal to himself as lords of all the great manors. But they were tenants on the land; ownership was the King's right. The most important lords made up the Great Council, the forerunner of parliament. William also placed Normans in the most important positions in the church hierarchy and ruled that clergy would be tried in ecclesiastical, rather than secular courts.

All over England, Norman buildings characterized by massive rectangular towers, showed that the conquerers had come to stay. The most notable were the Tower of London and Westminster Hall. Scores of parish churches, castles and monasteries dotted the landscape. William dispatched Norman legal scholars to go among the people and inquire by what laws (including customs which were virtually laws) they lived. These were organized into the *Common Law*—the law of the people, which were to be used in secular courts. This greatly pacified the conquered people, since they corresponded with what had prevailed before the Norman conquest. Writs were established which were an intriguing combination of Latin, Anglo-Saxon and French—*Assumpsit, Trespass Quare Clausum Fregit, Indebitatus,* etc.

William's great-grandson, Henry II (the first of the Plantagenets), came to the throne in 1154. He asserted the power of the king at the expense of the barons by tearing down unlicensed castles, creating a militia instead of depending upon the nobility for armed troops, and created traveling judges. The decisions of these judges were based on the Common Law, which operated by establishing written precedents rather than a codified law. Henry II also invaded Ireland, and, with the permission of the Pope, established himself as King of England's western neighbor. No one could possibly foresee what enormous consequences this would have for England in the years to come— consequences that affect Britain to this day.

Henry might have foreseen the consequences for which he is most remembered. He got into a dispute with his Archbishop, Thomas à Becket, over the issue of whether the clergy should be tried in Church courts or civil courts. Whether Henry ordered that Becket be killed, or merely hinted that it would please him, will never be known. But Becket's murder turned him into a martyr and Canterbury into a shrine. Henry's two sons, Richard and John, were low points in the history of the English monarchy. Richard (who came to be known as the Lion-Hearted) spent most of his reign out of the country as a crusader, trying to wrest Jerusalem and Israel from the Arabs. His absence did England little good, but it did provide that great scene in stories and movies where, when he did return to England, he reveals himself to Robin Hood.

John was not only ineffective but also very unpopular. He lost English possessions on the Continent, including Normandy, and ran up such a debt that the barons were able to force him to sign the *Magna Carta* in 1215. This document was not the forward-looking cornerstone of freedom that it is sometimes portrayed to be, but rather it guaranteed the rights which the nobility and the Church expected. At the same time, it established the principle that there are limits on the powers of the monarch, and thus it was a first step toward the largely unwritten constitutional monarchy of today.

The 13th century was a time of intellectual growth. Groups of scholars gathered at Oxford, and a splinter group later moved to Cambridge. Roger Bacon was a leading teacher stressing scientific experimentation. The King's Council was expanded to include representatives of shires and boroughs; thus the way was prepared for a representative House of Commons. At the end of the century, Edward I epitomized the medieval monarch. Physically imposing, he aided the growing spirit of nationalism by checking the power of the barons and the Church, and by increasing English power in Wales and Ireland. However, unsuccessful attempts to invade Scotland led Edward into financial difficulties, and in 1297 he was forced to sign a confirmation of the Magna Carta. He agreed that the King could not impose taxes without the consent of the new-born parliament.

Edward's grandson, Edward III attempted to reassert English power on the continent. In 1337 the Hundred Years War began. At first, success came to the English and the war strengthened the nation. However, in 1348 the Black Death (Bubonic Plague) swept the country and nearly half the population died. The country sank into economic depression, and by the time the king died in 1377, all the lands he had conquered in France had been lost except for a small area around Calais.

The period produced the first great work of literature in primitive English, Chaucer's *Canterbury Tales*. For centuries, Latin had been spoken by the Church and French by the nobility, but now the nation was uniting with the use of the English language.

The War of the Roses and the House of Tudor

Among Edward's sons were John of Gaunt, Duke of Lancaster, and Edmund, Duke of York. During the first half of the 15th century, the Lancaster branch held the throne, but in 1455 the Wars of the Roses, symbolized by the red rose of Lancaster and the white rose of York, subjected the country to a brutal civil war. Shakespeare puts the words "Uneasy lies the head that wears a crown" in the mouth of Henry IV, the first of the Lancastrian kings. The instability of a monarch's life continued throughout the 15th century. Perhaps the best example was Richard III of the House of York, who gained the crown by allegedly having two of his nephews, young princes, murdered in the Tower of London, and lost his own life in a battle against Henry Tudor of the House of Lancaster. Despite the battles for the throne, the 15th century was one of growing prosperity for England, especially in wool and foreign trade. To this day, the Lord Chancellor's seat in the House of Lords is a wool sack.

The United Kingdom

King Henry VIII

Anne Boleyn

With the arrival of the Tudors, the medieval world drew to a close. During the first Tudor reign (Henry VII), Columbus sailed for the New World. The wealth that Spain acquired there provided constant problems for the Tudors, and it was not until their successors, the Stuarts, that English colonies were firmly established. Soon the winds of the Reformation would bring even greater changes to England. Henry arranged for his eldest son, Arthur, to marry Catherine of Aragon, daughter of the king of Spain. This was a particularly important match for diplomatic reasons, because Spain controlled the Netherlands through which much of English trade entered the continent.

Arthur died in 1502 before his father. Despite both scriptural and canon law injunctions against marrying one's brother's widow, the Pope granted a dispensation allowing Arthur's brother, Henry, to marry the young widow. Henry's sister, Margaret, married the King of Scotland, thus providing England with marital allies on several sides. When Henry VIII assumed the throne after his father's death, he realized the importance of a male heir. But his union with Catherine only produced a daughter, Mary. It is important to note that Henry was initially loyal to Roman Catholicism, and because of a work he authored attacking the doctrines of Martin Luther, the Pope granted him the title "Defender of the Faith." It is ironic that his non–Roman Catholic descendants *still* carry that title.

Because Henry realized that Catherine would not produce a son, and because he was lusting after the attractive, dark–haired Anne Boleyn, he asked the Pope to grant him an annulment of his marriage to Catherine, claiming that it was illegal in the first place. Unfortunately for Henry, Catherine's uncle, Charles V, of the Holy Roman Empire had his troops in Rome at the time. When the Pope refused to grant Henry's request, in an unprecedented move, Henry had himself declared Head of the Church in England. His marriage to Anne Boleyn, however, produced only a daughter, Elizabeth, and Henry then proceeded through four more wives, making six in all, only one of whom produced a son, Edward. Every student learns to keep track of Henry's wives by the saying "Divorced, beheaded, died, divorced, beheaded, survived."

Edward VI followed his father to the throne in 1547 at eleven years of age. His guardians moved the country rapidly in the direction of Protestantism. But the sickness–prone boy died six years later (he was possibly murdered), and the first of Henry's daughters, Mary Tudor, assumed the throne. Had Mary wanted to move England back to the religious position of her father, she probably would have lasted. But she felt a calling to return the nation to full Roman Catholicism and further alienated her subjects by taking Philip of Spain as her husband.

Although the number of resisting protestants who were burned at the stake was actually quite small, there were enough prominent bishops ignited to earn the Queen the historical title of "Bloody Mary." The words of one of these bishops—"Be of good cheer, Master Ridley, we shall today light such a candle as will by God's grace never be extinguished in England" proved to be prophetic. At Mary's death after only five years on the throne, her half–sister, Elizabeth I became queen, and with her, one of the great ages in English history began.

The Elizabethan Period

Since Elizabeth was considered illegitimate by the Catholic Church, she moved the country back toward protestantism. It was a moderate protestant position, with the old forms of worship retained in English and no vigorous attempt to be overly scrupulous in matters of doctrine. As Elizabeth put it, "We shall make no window into any man's soul." At this time, Elizabeth's cousin, Mary Stuart, abdicated the throne of Scotland in favor of her son, James, and fled to England. For years, Roman Catholic attempts to oust Elizabeth flurried around Mary, who was Catholic. Despite "that divinity that doth hedge a king," (or queen), Elizabeth finally yielded to the advice of her court and had Mary beheaded in 1587.

That same year, Sir Francis Drake, having already stolen Spanish gold from the New World, raided the port of Cadiz. In reprisal, the next year Spain sent a Great Armada to invade and conquer England. But a "Protestant wind" and English naval tactics carried the day; less than half of the Armada managed to limp back to Spain.

The United Kingdom

England had established itself as a ruler of the seas, a position it would continue to enjoy for almost 400 years.

The Elizabethan Age was a flowering of English culture and the brightest blooms were uses of the language that still affect our thought and speech. Although William Shakespeare was the most magnificent of the blossoms, others, such as Spenser, Drayton, Donne and Marlowe bloomed in the sunshine.

Thomas Cranmer produced a *Book of Common Prayer* in 1549 whose magnificent collects shaped the way the English-speaking world addressed God and whose words start the most important ceremony in most people's lives: "Dearly beloved, we are gathered here together in the sight of God and in the face of this company to join together this man and this woman in holy matrimony: which is an honorable estate instituted of God, signifying unto us the mystical union that is betwixt Christ and His church." The musical liturgy of the book was done with assistance from Lutherans, who had retained Catholic plain song chant traditions in German; they were adapted to English. Further, harmonized Anglican chant was first produced. All of this is preserved with little change in many churches to this day.

In the last part of Elizabeth's reign, William Shakespeare began to write his plays. Their plots shape our view of history, or romance, and of humor, and his phrases fill our speaking and our reading, even when we do not know the source of the words. Finally, shortly after Elizabeth's death, the language of the *Book of Common Prayer* and the language of Shakespeare came together in the most influential of all English books, the *King James Bible*. Until recently, it was read by more people than any other book in the English language, and for many Americans on the frontier, it was their only book in the English language. It has been only in the past five decades that serious attention was paid to any of the "modern" English translations.

The Tudor monarchs were able to dominate England by their political skill and by the force of their personality. All except Edward and Mary enjoyed considerable popularity, and if those who followed them had enjoyed similar success, the parliament might have melted out of British life. But the Stuarts, of whom it could be said, "They learned nothing and forgot nothing," tried to push the doctrine of the Divine Right of Kings farther than the English wished to have it carried. When Elizabeth died unmarried in 1603, James Stuart, King of Scotland, became James I of England and the whole island was united under one monarch.

The Stuarts Brief Tenure

The second of the Stuarts, Charles I, came to the throne in 1625. He soon began to have trouble with Parliament over taxation, and his inflexibility and demands for royal absolutism only angered the democratic movement within the country. Moreover, Charles was a "high" churchman, with Roman Catholic leanings, and most members of Parliament were Puritan protestant in inclination (i.e. a full, chanted eucharistic service with all ceremonial acts, including incense, holy water, etc. vs. three hymns, a psalm, lessons and sermon). For 11 years Charles managed to rule without Parliament and his persecution of Puritans led to the founding of the colonies in New England. In order to raise revenues, Charles reconvened Parliament in 1640 and soon civil war broke out in England. Catholics, high churchmen, the nobility and the rural people of the north and west supported the King; Puritans, people of trade and commerce and most important, Londoners, supported Parliament.

Religious and Civil Turmoil

Unlike the Wars of the Roses, the Civil War of the 17th century was not simply a fight over who should occupy the throne, but an ideological struggle to determine the very nature of English society. Oliver Cromwell emerged as leader of the parliamentary forces after Charles had been captured. Cromwell purged Parliament of all but his loyal supporters, abolished the House of Lords, and in 1649, had Charles beheaded. He was the only English monarch to die for religious reasons, and the last to be killed for political reasons. Whether Charles was a martyr for the causes of royal stability and the Anglican

Queen Mary I

Queen Elizabeth I

The United Kingdom

Church or whether he justly died for opposing the representatives of the people depends on one's viewpoint—and perhaps both views are true.

The Commonwealth Period and Return of Monarchy

Cromwell had hoped to rule in a liberal and democratic way, but continued factionalism and the threatening anarchy in English society caused him to assume absolute power as Lord Protector. This period was known as the Commonwealth. When Cromwell died in 1658 and the monarchy was restored in 1660, Charles II, the son of the dead king, returned from the continent to which he had escaped and was greeted by a joyful people.

During Charles' reign, English culture extricated itself from the heavy burden of Puritanism and flourished again; Bunyan, Milton and Pepys were the most famous writers. The great fire of 1666 destroyed much of London, but allowed such master architects as Christopher Wren to rebuild a new and even more glorious city. On another continent, the Dutch were driven out of North America and New Amsterdam became New York.

James II followed his brother to the throne, but did not renounce his faith in Roman Catholicism. The English then turned to William of Orange, a grandson of Charles I, who came to England and later defeated James in the July 1690 Battle of the Boyne in Ireland. From then on, the fact that England was Anglican (not Roman Catholic or Puritan) was settled. But both William of Orange and his wife were childless. The most logical successor was Queen Anne, daughter of James II, but she died childless in 1714. What was the answer for a people accustomed to a monarchy?

The House of Hanover (later Windsor) and Parliament Power

Britain turned to George of Hanover (a great–grandson of James I, and a Protestant) to become king. The fact that he could speak no English (only German) was of immense importance. It meant that the king had to leave many of his powers in the hands of the chairmanship of his council, and that person was the leader of the *Whig Party,* with a majority in the House of Commons. Thus, England developed the tradition of having a Prime Minister preside over a Cabinet *which grew out of Parliament.*

During the middle part of the 18th century, the first British Empire took shape. English forces defeated the French for control of much of India and the defeat of the French forces at Quebec in 1759 meant that Canada and the area west of the thirteen colonies were brought under British rule. In 1760, George III succeeded to the throne. Since he believed a *king* should rule the country, he suspended the cabinet government, intending that the king and the "king's friends" would rule.

George III (1738–1820)

As the British Empire expanded with Captain Cook's discovery of Australia, relationships with the thirteen American colonies deteriorated. By 1782 they had been victorious in their revolution and the period of the First British Empire was largely over. With the disaster in North America came the return of the cabinet system to England as William Pitt the Younger became the new Prime Minister. For the next 50 years the Tories would lead the country and maintain a steady and conservative posture while the French Revolution and then the armies of Napoleon forced Britain once again to demonstrate its mastery of the seas.

Nineteenth Century Change

At the turn of the century, the Act of Union dissolved the Irish Parliament and incorporated Catholic Ireland into the United Kingdom. Tragically, religious persecution of the Catholics kept the Irish from full integration into British society and thus, the Union was doomed from the start.

But change was occurring in England. The Industrial Revolution, gradual at first, gathered momentum. Early machines made of wood were replaced by stronger and more efficient ones of iron. James Watt's inventions harnessed the power of steam. Reforms in agriculture improved food production, but caused many farmers to leave the land. Thus, as industry and commerce were growing, along with the wealth and power of those who controlled them, so, too, there was a growing urban class kept in degrading poverty. As populations shifted, Parliament became less representative.

In so–called "rotten" boroughs, a few voters could control who was elected to Parliament. In one district in Cornwall *a single voter* could elect two members! It is coincidental, but symbolic that in 1830, the *Reforming Whigs Party* obtained a ma-

The United Kingdom

John Constable's *Hay Wain* (1821) — National Gallery, London

jority in Parliament and the first railroad line on which the *Rocket* whizzed along at 35 miles an hour was opened.

The Whigs were able to get their *Reform Bill* through Parliament in 1832. This most important piece of legislation abolished many "rotten" boroughs, gave representation to the new towns and significantly lowered the property qualifications necessary to be a voter. Many observers think that this Reform Bill saved the country from revolution, which had become so popular in the rest of Europe. Certainly, it gave new power to the middle classes, and was an important step toward mass democracy.

Victoria

In 1837 the 18–year–old Victoria began the longest reign in British history. As the last half of the 17th century had belonged to Elizabeth, so the 19th century belonged to Victoria. During Victoria's reign, reform acts gradually increased the number of people enfranchised and gave protection to the lower classes. The repeal of the "Corn Laws" and free trade not only stimulated industry, but also reduced the cost of living for the poor. Thus, under the leadership of such greats as Palmerston, Gladstone and Disraeli, Parliament found a course that kept England moving toward democracy without being caught up in the excesses that racked so much of the continent. By 1846 Canada had been made self–governing, and within a few years, Australia and New Zealand were given internal self–government. Thus, the concept of the Empire of free countries bound to the mother country by loyalty to the Queen was born.

Two great events marked the reign of Victoria. The great Exhibition of 1851 demonstrated British industrial might and middle class prosperity, whereas the Golden Jubilee of the Queen in 1887 marked the high point of the Empire. The claim that the sun never set on the British Empire was indeed true. Its members included Canada in North America, British Guiana in South America; the United Kingdom in Europe; South Africa, Kenya, Somaliland in Africa; India and Ceylon in Asia; and Australia and New Zealand in the Pacific. The greatest problem, however, was closest to home, and various attempts to solve the Irish problem through Home Rule were unsuccessful.

Until 1900 the roar of the British lion could be heard throughout the entire world. Britain controlled over one–fifth of the earth's land surface and ruled a quarter of the world's population. Its flag flew on every continent and its magnificent empire was protected by the largest and most powerful navy in the world. At the same time, Britain was invulnerable to foreign invasion. This meant that, unlike many other nations with frontiers instead of shorelines, it could leisurely develop a democratic form of government. Nations under the constant threat of attack often could not afford the luxury of a relatively inefficient and cumbersome governmental order that involved parliamentary meetings, long debates, votes, press coverage and criticism. As a nation equally invulnerable, the Americans shared this advantage with their English forebears.

Also, Britain did not need to maintain a large standing army. As the history of many countries indicates, ambitious soldiers, led by prestigious officers close to the political heart of the country sometimes cannot resist meddling in the political affairs of a nation. The British never had difficulty in maintaining control over their military; a military putsch is unthinkable in the British context. Fortunately, the tradition of civilian supremacy over the military was passed on to many (though not all) of its former colonies, including in the United States.

Political Power Struggles and Social Change

A watershed year in the growth of power of the House of Commons was 1911. The *Liberal Party* government had proposed a land tax, and although tradition had it that only Commons controlled finances, the House of Lords rejected the bill. The Parliament bill of 1911 deprived the Lords of *any* control of finance and limited their power over other bills to a two–year delay. In a move to make the Commons more responsive to the popular will, the maximum life of a Parliament was reduced from seven to five years. When it appeared that the Lords would veto this bill, George V threatened to increase the number of Lords and pack the Upper House with those favorable to the

The United Kingdom

bill. The Lords yielded to the threat and thereafter the House of Commons gained virtual total control of legislation. In the same year, members of the House of Commons began to receive pay, and thus, those without independent incomes could be in Parliament.

World War I not only devastated a generation of Englishmen—it helped to produce changes in society. As recognition for their part in the war effort, women received the vote in 1918. Because they involved so much of the population, both World Wars did much to further popular democracy and reduce the differences between social classes. Shortly after World War I, the southern part of Ireland left the United Kingdom and achieved dominion status as the Irish Free State. Protestants living in the north clung tenaciously to their membership in the United Kingdom and their loyalty to the crown, but their conflict with Catholics living alongside them has not been solved to this day.

Following World War I, trade unions grew in power and were able to call a general strike in 1926. But the great depression of the 1930s significantly reduced the power of the Labour government, and the Conservatives led the country in the years before World War II. The last crisis to affect the monarchy occurred in 1936. Edward VIII ascended the throne, but within months he abdicated so that he could marry the divorced Wallis Simpson, an American.

The Hitler Threat and World War II

As Hitler began to threaten more and more of Europe, Prime Minister Neville Chamberlain practiced a policy of appeasement. This only whetted the German appetite; after an attack on Poland in September 1939, Britain joined France as allies in World War II. In May of the next year, Winston Churchill became Prime Minister. His courage and his words epitomized the best of the British spirit and inspired the nation to withstand withering aerial attacks from bombers and rockets. With tremendous assistance from the U.S., Britain and its allies were victorious, but prostrated and devastated by the end of the conflict in 1945.

The Postwar 1940s and 1950s

Two world wars in the 20th century brought enormous changes. These included revolutions in many European countries, the rise of the United States and the Soviet Union as the most powerful countries in the world and the relative decline of the traditional global powers, including the United Kingdom, in terms of political and military significance. As a victorious ally, Britain gained a veto right in the United Nations Security Council, but it had to liquidate most of its foreign investments to finance its own recovery; these foreign investments had once paid for a third of British imports. The merchant marine was depleted and factories and equipment were either destroyed or obsolete.

The negative economic consequences of the wars reduced Britain's ability to be a global power and stimulated in many British colonies the desire for independence. By proclaiming the Truman Doctrine, the U.S. assumed from Britain the burden of economic and military aid to Greece and Turkey and relieved the U.K. of its responsibility for supporting the struggle against communist forces in the Greek civil war. The British also found themselves in the crossfire between Jews and Arabs in Palestine and Hindus and Moslems in India and were forced in 1947 to abandon both important regions. In 1952 it lost control of Egypt. When Egypt seized the Suez Canal in 1956, Britain, supported by France and Israel, attempted to reconquer that important waterway. However, stiff joint United Nations, U.S. and Soviet opposition to this move, which seemed like the last gasp of colonialism, forced the British, French and Israelis to back down.

In 1959 Britain still ruled over 53 countries with a population of 81 million, and 86,000 British troops were deployed around the world outside of Europe. But the floodgates opened, and by the 1960s a tidal wave of separations swept through Africa, the Middle East and Asia. Having lost most of its Asian empire in the late–1940s, the British recognized the inevitability of African independence. Fortunately, Britain had trained many Africans as capable administrators and had established there a relatively efficient system of local administration. Therefore, when they gradually relinquished their hold, well–trained Africans were usually able to take their places. An exception was Rhodesia, whose tiny white minority took power in 1965 and held it for years before finally handing the reins of power to the new black–ruled state of Zimbabwe.

Britain spearheaded the international U.N. boycott of Rhodesia. But the U.K. was in the throes of such economic distress that it was not only unable to steer events in Africa, but it was also forced in 1971 to terminate most of its military and political responsibilities "East of Suez." This withdrawal was unfortunate for the U.S., which was trapped at the time in the quagmire of Vietnam. The U.S. felt compelled to assume Britain's prior responsibility for maintaining "stability" in the Middle East. It thereby became embroiled in one of the world's least stable regions. This untimely responsibility prompted American administrations in the 1970s to help build up the Shah's power. The hope was that a modernized and well–armed Iran could maintain order in the oil–rich Persian Gulf region and keep the Soviet Union's power and influence out of the area. The Americans paid heavily in the 1980s for this gamble.

Elizabeth II succeeded her father, George VI, on the British thone in 1952. Thirty generations separated her from her ancestor, William the Conqueror, and she began her reign in a nation struggling to find a new role in the modern world. The Empire became a Commonwealth of independent nations, bound together by language, democratic principles and a residue of loyalty to the person (but not the power) of the British monarch. Decolonization had a serious negative economic impact on Britain by depriving it of many protected markets, sources of raw materials at low prices and cheap food. The resulting economic difficulties harrassed the United Kingdom for a quarter of a century following the Second World War.

Domestic Politics before Thatcher

On July 5, 1945, voters delivered a dramatic blow to the *Tories* by electing the first *Labour* Prime Minister with a clear majority of 145 seats in the House of Commons, Clement Attlee. Although the British deeply admired Churchill as a great wartime leader, they associated his *Conservative Party* with the soup lines and unemployment of the prewar depression. *Labour* had ably guided the home ministries in the national government during the war. It had impressed the British as being the best team for creating full employment, housing and better social security and health care for a people which had just sacrificed so much in the war effort.

Although ideologically divided, as always, between more pragmatic and radical wings, the *Labour Party* moved boldly to make many sweeping economic changes, including the nationalization of the Bank of England, hospitals, railways, aviation, public transport and the gas, electrical, coal and steel industries. Unlike France and Italy, though, the newly nationalized industries were placed under the direction of autonomous corporations (subsidied from the state treasury), rather than government agencies and ministries. In 1946 the National Insurance Act and National Health Service Act were the prime examples of popular social welfare legislation which strengthened or created old–age pensions, unemployment compensation, education, social insurance and free health service. No sooner were these innovations in place, though, than the *Labour* government began losing popular-

The United Kingdom

Horse Guardsmen leaving their barracks for duty at Buckingham Palace

ity. It was badly divided, British influence abroad was noticeably eroding, the pound was losing its value, and economic recovery was painfully slow.

At age 77 Winston Churchill was returned to power in 1951, and his *Tories* ruled until 1964, the longest period of continuous party government in modern British history. His government returned the iron and steel industries and road transport to private ownership, although iron and steel were renationalized by *Labour* in 1967. However, accurately sensing the sentiments of the British nation, the *Tories* did not make a radical U–turn. It accepted the national welfare and health services, as well as the commitment to full employment.

Following a stroke, Churchill was finally persuaded to step down in 1955. His successor was his long–time foreign minister Anthony Eden. After only a year Eden had to resign in the aftermath of the Suez crisis of 1956. He was followed by Harold Macmillan, who optimistically predicted a turnaround in Britain's economic fortunes (for which reason he was dubbed "Supermac"!). There was a short-lived economic boom in the late–1950s, and the living standards of some Britishers rose. But inequalities of wealth remained which the government could not alleviate because of a rising imbalance of payments and a serious sterling crisis. Britain was obviously not keeping up with its international trade competitors, and management and trade unions were not inclined to introduce more efficient and modern methods of production. In an attempt to protect the value of the pound, the government had to introduce an unpopular wage freeze and raise the bank rate. Macmillan sought to halt the growing economic malaise and increase British industry's competitiveness by leading Britain into the EU, but French President Charles de Gaulle vetoed its entry in 1963.

Following this humiliation came the *coup de grace* for the Macmillan government: a lurid sex scandal involving Secretary of War John Profumo. He was alleged to be involved with a call girl who had been asked by the Soviet naval attaché to gather information from Profumo on the U.K.'s nuclear weapons. No government could possibly benefit from such a spicy and embarrassing affair. But what forced Macmillan to demand Profumo's resignation was not so much the illicit activity itself as the fact that Profumo had insulted Parliament by lying to it about his involvement. He thereby dragged both himself and the prime minister down.

Macmillan was replaced in the fall of 1963 by the colorless Sir Alec Douglas–Home. Home (pronounced Hume) was a rare example of a prime minister being drawn from the House of Lords, even though he scrambled to win a by–election seat to the Commons. Home could not quiet the growing desire for a change, and with only a razor–thin majority he could not prevent Harold Wilson's *Labour Party* from winning power in October 1964.

A former Oxford University economics don (lecturer), Wilson was from the more conservative, reformist wing of the *Labour Party*. Faced with daunting economic problems, he not only pared down the U.K.'s military commitments abroad, but he applied the traditional conservative policies of increasing taxes and reducing government spending. These unpopular economic policies widened ideological divisions within his own party, sparked industrial unrest and strikes and brought Wilson into a head–on collision with the trade unions. Widening trade imbalances, another devaluation of the pound, and a renewal of strife between Catholics and Protestants in Northern Ireland, all spelled disaster for Wilson in the June 1970 elections, when the *Tories,* led by Edward Heath, returned to power.

Heath's government knew little happiness, aside from Britain's entry into the

The United Kingdom

EU in 1973. His bitter confrontations with the assertive coal miners brought serious economic disruptions and forced the prime minister to declare states of emergency five times. The crippling coal strike in the winter of 1973–4 destroyed what credibility remained for the cabinet. Voters brought Wilson's *Labourites* back to power in February 1974 on the assumption that they would have better relations with the powerful unions.

Wilson had only a miniscule majority. He expended precious energy and patience fending off an ambitious radical left wing within his own party which sniped at him constantly and openly advocated such unpopular policies as a "socialist transformation" of British society, massive nationalizations of large companies, the abolition of elite institutions such as the House of Lords and private schools, withdrawal from NATO and the EU, and unilateral disarmament. These leftist antics ultimately drove some moderates out of the party and led to the formation in 1981 of the now defunct *Social Democratic Party (SDP)*.

It is hardly surprising that Wilson was unable to improve the economic situation. The sky–rocketing price of oil resulting from the 1973 OPEC embargo hit the struggling British economy hard, despite the discovery of oil in Britain's own sectors of the North Sea. Inflation rose to dizzying levels, and for the first time since the war unemployment reared its ugly head. These problems made hopes for harmonious labor relations a pipe–dream, as the spate of disruptive strikes indicated. In 1976 an exasperated and tired Harold Wilson turned the keys to Number 10 Downing Street over to his foreign minister, James Callaghan. The new prime minister was no more successful than Wilson had been in controlling the unions, improving the overall economy, and coping with rising violence in Northern Ireland and growing separatist movements in Scotland and Wales.

It has been said that the world stands aside for a man who knows where he is going. By the spring of 1979, the British voters were prepared to do just that, with one historical twist: they brought to power the first woman prime minister in British politics, Margaret Thatcher. She acted with such determination and decisiveness that by January 3, 1988, she had become the longest continuously serving British prime minister in the 20th century. Ruling over a country with the highest economic growth of any major economy, low inflation, declining unemployment, a rising pound, and tamed unions, she had every reason to believe that she would remain at the helm into the 21st century and perhaps even overtake the record of Sir Robert Walpole, whose 21 consecutive years of service as prime minister began in 1721.

Attitude and Political Change

Terrorism related to the unsolved problem of Northern Ireland, along with rising crime in Britain, helped shift British voters' view of the world in an important way. It helped many of them shape a tough–minded attitude and become more receptive to political appeals based on "law and order," replacing the compromise politics of the 1960s.

The parliamentary elections of 1979 and 1983 took many foreign observers by surprise because they revealed that the political landscape in Britain had dramatically changed. Upon closer scrutiny, it can be seen that these changes are the consequence of important changes in Britain's economy and society in the course of the decade of the 1970s. Those changes broke down much of the class structure of Britain, which traditionally had shaped British politics to such a large extent.

Public opinion polls and election analyses continually confirm that fewer and fewer Britishers spontaneously identify with a particular class, and that class–consciousness has and is declining markedly. Class itself has become only one of many factors shaping individual attitudes and preferences. It has become harder to classify Britons by class, which has increasingly become more a matter of taste and culture, rather than of income and occupation. With less than a quarter of workers in manufacturing jobs, fewer than two workers in five belong to a labor union. Two–thirds of all Britishers own or are buying their homes; even one of three unskilled manual laborers is a home–owner. Also, leisure is no longer the privilege of a few; instead, almost all full–time workers receive four weeks of leave. In short, more workers have become middle–class. Young people from all economic strata mingle more easily and are more likely to intermarry than they used to. Since Britons have become more individualistic, their social attitudes and political behavior have become less predictable. These changes are bound to have a negative effect on political parties whose appeals have traditionally been heavily class–based, especially the *Labour Party*.

Since 1979, Britain's population has barely grown, but the size of the electorate increased from 39.3 in 1970 to 42.2 million in 1983. The voting age was dropped to 18 in 1970, but the number of pensioners has grown, so the average voter today is actually older than in 1970. He is also more highly educated, more likely to be divorced and live alone or in small households, own his own home, and, despite high unemployment, have a higher standard of living than in the 1970s. Disenchantment with unions (see Economy) and changes in social patterns (see Culture) which were occurring in the 1970s set the stage for dramatic political shifts in Britain. After 1979 these effectively altered much of the conventional wisdom about British politics and realigned the structure.

Although the diminishing numbers of unionized workers in the mines and factories retained their traditional loyalty to the *Labour Party* and the managers remained steadfast to the *Conservative Party*, their diminishing numbers hoisted the flag of change on the pole in the 1970s. Soaring inflation and rising unemployment, accompanied by increasingly strident union demands alienated the people. Their revulsion at the excessive "unelected power" which union bosses wielded boiled to the surface in "the winter of discontent," 1978–9, when coal and transportation strikes threatened to paralyze the entire nation.

These changes led to conditions whereby a party leader would advocate a policy based on the notions that the best help was self help, that initiative deserved rewards, than an economic pie must be baked before it is divided, that welfare could not produce prosperity, that private business is better than nationalized industries, that the problem of inflation is more important than the problem of unemployment, and, finally, that the government cannot control the economy. In other words, traditional Keynesian economics (see Economy) was no cure for British problems, but was part of the disease. That leader was Margaret Thatcher, leader of the *Conservative Party* (Tory) since 1975, who was elected prime minister in 1979. Leading a changed party, she captured the mood of an altered society and spoke for the new social realities.

Return to the Conservative Party

When she moved into the prime minister's office, she promised "three years of unparalleled austerity," and for three years the pain of Thatcherism was far more evident than the benefits. Unemployment rose and economic conditions worsened. She was unable to cut government spending significantly because of greater numbers on welfare and pay raises for government workers to bring them into equity with the private sector. Nevertheless, the "iron lady," as she began to be called, held firm to her monetarist policies (restricting the money supply) and vowed that "I will not stagger from expedient to expedient." By 1982 her party was well *behind* the *Labour Party* in the polls and she

The United Kingdom

seemed to be heading for sure defeat in the next elections when the unexpected occurred.

The Falklands War

Argentine troops invaded and captured a small group of off-shore islands which had long been settled and ruled by the British. Mrs. Thatcher galvanized the nation with her firmness and resolution in organizing the recapture of the Falklands Islands. The British basked again briefly in imperial glory, and an overwhelming majority of them applauded their leader for her ability to deal with a crisis, winning back control of the islands, albeit at a tremendous financial cost. The Falklands War boosted her party's popularity, and the economy fortuitously began to revive at the same time, with inflation shrinking to the lowest level in 15 years. The electorate became convinced that her economic medicine had been a harsh necessity and that she was a true leader. Sensing the political winds blowing briskly at her back, she took advantage of the prime minister's privilege to set an election whenever it suits his or her party. It was called for June 1983 and demonstrated beyond doubt that the party landscape had greatly changed and that a new *Conservative Party* had become the dominant force in British politics as of the mid-1980s, and perhaps beyond.

Her astonishing electoral triumph in June 1983, which made her the first *Conservative* prime minister in this century to be reelected to a second term, revealed both her leadership image, established in the Falklands War, and the extent to which most social and economic groups in Britain accepted her diagnosis of the nation's problems. Most voters did not even blame her for the country's most pressing problem: continuing unemployment, which shot up from 5.4% to 13.3% during her four years of rule. They clearly patted her on the back for bringing inflation down.

"The Iron Lady"

She was a fundamentally cautious politician, whose bark was often more powerful than her bite. She did take modest steps to return some of the nationalized industries to private hands, but she did not precipitously withdraw the public from the economy; in 1988 government spending amounted to 42% of GNP, about the same as in 1979. Nor did she dramatically reduce public employment, welfare assistance or taxes; she disliked spending what she did not have. Therefore, most voters did not see in her a fanatic ideologue who wished to turn the clock backward.

She never enjoyed "popularity," as her many nicknames reveal: "Leaderene," Attila the Hen," "Rhoda the Rhino" and "Nanny," to mention only a few of the "kinder" ones. Many saw her as uncaring, cold and obsessed. But she had authority and respect because of what she accomplished and what she represents. She strode firmly forward to remake her country in her own self-image: brisk, hard-working, frugal and self-sufficient. She combined some of the best 19th century values with 20th century energy. She was a strong leader who entered office with a sense of mission: to make Britain great again. Of course, she benefited from an opposition which was in disarray.

Part of Thatcher's appeal was that she represented a new kind of *Conservative Party* which had emerged. The image of the party as the preserve of the landed gentry, bankers or high-level civil servants, which could display charity when needed toward the lower classes, and which assembled in prayer in the Church of England, has changed.

The attitude of most citizens, an overwhelming majority of whom are baptized protestant, is now indifference toward religion—its traditional role in politics has all but vanished. Tory leaders cannot count on the support of the Church of England, containing many clergy bitterly opposed to the government's positions on such issues such as nuclear arms and capital punishment.

Thatcher was an example of the "new" kind of Tory, who worked her way up in the world. The daughter of a dressmaker and grocer from Grantham, Lincolnshire, she lived with her family in an apartment above the shop and worked all her childhood in her father's store. She studied chemistry at Oxford, where she led the Conservative student organization and held off-campus jobs. She later acquired a law degree after marrying a successful businessman, Denis Thatcher, who is now retired and served as the nation's "First Gentleman," staying a discreet half pace behind the prime minister. She was never an insider in "the establishment," and, like Ronald Reagan, she harbored a bias against the party elite. She served only four years in the early 1970s as Education Secretary before gaining the party leadership in 1975.

Having emerged from the middle class herself, she was well able to forge an alliance between skilled workers and the middle class, in a society which is becoming more and more middle class. She capitalized on the dream of owning one's home by giving residents of government-built houses the opportunity to buy them at bargain prices. About a half million gratefully did so. This was the greatest transfer of wealth to the British working class in history. By the time her *Tory* party was voted out of power in 1997, 68% of all housing units were owner-occupied, a higher percentage than in the United States or elsewhere in Europe.

She benefited from a transformation within the party, which extends from the grass-roots all the way up to parliament. Its seats are no longer occupied primarily by traditional local notables, but increasingly by insurance agents, housewives, teachers, salesmen and self-made middle management types. Perhaps as good an example of the new kind of Tory as Thatcher herself was a Speaker of the House, Bruce Bernard Weatherill, a former tailor who always carried in his pocket a thimble to remind himself of his humble background. It is said that when he entered parliament, one aristocratic *Conservative* MP was overheard saying to another: "I don't know what this place is coming to, Tom: they've got my tailor in here now!" The point which needs to be repeated is that the tailor to whom they were referring *was a Tory!*

Mr. Denis Thatcher and former Prime Minister Thatcher

The United Kingdom

GOVERNMENT

Simplicity and Flexibility

Speaking of his country, the great Victorian prime minister, Benjamin Disraeli, stated: "In a progressive country, change is constant, and the great question is, not whether you should resist change which is inevitable, but whether that change should be carried out in deference to the manners, the customs, the laws and the traditions of the people." Americans often imagine the British as a conservative nation. In fact, Britain has skillfully adjusted to change for centuries, and today it confronts fundamental shifts in its society, economy, political system and place in the world. The British genius is to combine astonishing continuity with necessary change; they excel in pouring "new wine into old bottles."

Great Britain remains a monarchy with a noble class which still enjoys certain privileges. However, Britain is the birthplace for the most durable democratic model of government in the world. Unlike the complicated American democratic system, which has almost never been successfully adapted to other societies, the "Westminster model" not only fits the British people and circumstances, but it can quite easily be made to fit other nations as well. Its secret lies in its simplicity and its flexibility. It can be modified and tailored to other peoples' needs and circumstances without losing its essentially democratic character.

British politics operates according to an unwritten constitution which prescribes the "rules of the game" and places limits on the rulers. In Britain voters elect 659 members of the House of Commons, the lower house of Parliament. The leader of the party which wins a majority of the seats (or has more seats than any other party) becomes the prime minister, the most powerful political figure in the land. The monarch is the chief of state, but her role is largely symbolic; she makes no important political decisions. The prime minister selects other ministers, who are also experienced parliamentary leaders in the party, to sit in the cabinet.

Together the prime minister and cabinet are called "the government" which rules "collectively." This means that all members of the government must publicly support its policies or resign from office, in great contrast to the United States. Further, the entire team assumes responsibility for the overall policy. The government rules as long as it maintains a majority in the House of Commons. Thus, it rules until it loses a "vote of confidence" on an important bill. The prime minister must call a new election at least five years after the preceding election, but she or he can call one earlier if that would be to the party's advantage.

Contrasts with U.S.

Unlike the United States, where both houses of Congress are equally powerful, the British upper house, the House of Lords, has far *less* power than the House of Commons, Also, unlike in the United States, there is neither "separation of power" among the executive, legislative or judicial branches, nor a distribution of political powers among the national government and many state governments. Executive and legislative powers are fused, and the prime minister is *both* the chief executive and the chief legislator of the land. Through party discipline the prime minister controls the House of Commons. Further, political power is concentrated in the central government. Britain is a *unitary*, not a *federal* state, so he/she does not have to contend with separate states which wield constitutionally granted powers of their own. Laws cannot be judged unconstitutional by any court in the country. Parliamentary supremacy is the fundamental principle of British government.

This set-up is the basic model for most democracies in the world. Even the founders of the American government, whose political views had been shaped by British political ideas but who had consciously sought to depart from that model, adopted more from the British system than many Americans care to remember. After all, what the founders had deemed to be so unjust and tyrannical was the fact that Americans had been "denied their rights as Englishmen." Even the arguments and wording of the Declaration of Independence bore striking resemblance to the work by the 17th century English philosopher, John Locke, entitled *The Second Treatise of Government*, an important blueprint and philosophical foundation for British government.

The American founding fathers were certainly aware of their debt to Westminster when they included in the American constitution such provisions as the necessity of senatorial confirmation of cabinet ministers, congressional election of the president in the event that no candidate wins a majority in the electoral college, and the possibility for the national legislature to impeach and remove a president. It is indeed fitting that the statue on the top of the Capitol faces toward London, symbolic of the extent to which the American government, the political habits, and the thinking of its people have been shaped by Great Britain.

The Unwritten Constitution

As the British political system is more closely examined, perhaps the first aspect which is striking is the fact that the country's constitution is *unwritten*; that is, there is no single document, as in the United States. One must refer to one or all of five sources to know what is constitutional: first are particularly important documents, such as the Magna Charta (1215), the Habeas Corpus Act (1679), The Bill of Rights (1689) which, unlike the American Bill of Rights, defines rights of Parliament, not rights of individual citizens, the Parliament Act of 1911, and the Statute of Westminster (1931). Then there are interpretations of courts of law and principles of common law (which has itself been in a constant state of change). For example, basic individual liberties, such as the freedom of assembly, speech, religion are all derived from common law. There is the Law and Custom of Parliament, which deals with the special privileges which parliament and each Member of Parliament (known as *MP*) enjoy.

Finally there are wholly unwritten elements, known as conventions. These include such practices as: parliament must meet at least once a year, the government must resign if it loses a vote of confidence, the monarch cannot attend cabinet meetings or enter parliament without permission. However, the monarch always opens parliament with a speech from the throne. She is there in all her finery, displaying the majesty and royal tradition that stretches back continuously over so many centuries. Yet, she is surrounded by members of parliament, freely elected by the people and operating within the context of an effective multi-party system. Her speech does not contain her own ideas, but puts forward the program of the prime minister and the government which holds a majority in the lower house of parliament. It is listened to by members of the opposition party, often called the "Loyal Opposition." Because the monarch delivers the speech, tradition requires that even critics refer to it as "the gracious speech." For example, opposition leader John Major responded to Prime Minister Tony Blair's text read by the Queen in May 1997 as follows: "The road to hell is paved with good intentions, and this gracious speech is very full of good intentions."

Perhaps no other idea has been a more important gift of the British to the growth of free government than the concept of the "Loyal Opposition." That someone may be opposed to the pre sent government in its policies and yet still be loyal to the country and not subject to political punishment, is incomprehensible in totalitarian or one-party states.

No politician could violate these conventions without touching off a serious political crisis. The well-informed and respected *Economist* described Britain's con-

The United Kingdom

Her Majesty Queen Elizabeth II opens Parliament in the House of Lords

The United Kingdom

stitution as a "contraption, stuck together from old laws, bits of precedent, scraps of custom and practice and blind faith in the steering ability of its driver, the prime minister of the day. The machine is notoriously short on brakes: the checks and balances which are a feature of written constitutions."

Why does a nation of 59 million persons have no written constitution? One reason is that Britain is one of the few democracies in the world to enter the democratic age without a revolution. After successful revolutions, winners are far more inclined to put in writing the kind of guarantees and rights which had been denied them by the former rulers. The outlines of the British regime were established before the industrial revolution in the 19th century. Therefore, the economic and social conflicts which that revolution sparked could ultimately be reconciled *within* the system. Also, the British aristocracy had the foresight to make concessions to the middle and working classes, prompting the latter to realize that they could achieve change and satisfaction through reform, rather than rebellion. This is one reason why Marxism was never as potent a political force in Britain as it was on the European continent. Further, Britain is not a federal state, so there is no need for a careful delineation of jurisdictions between various governments, as in the U.S.

Most important, however, is the kind of political culture which one finds in Britain. There is widespread agreement on basic political values, and the leading institutions are broadly supported by the population. This consensus has meant that disagreements over policies have (except under Cromwell) never led to fundamental challenges to the regime and constitution. The British have changed their political system only gradually. Important changes usually only occur after much dialogue and after the major parties have reached general agreement on them. The British also are a law-abiding people, a fact which makes it especially shocking to read about bombings or racial riots in that country. They tend to be moderate and pragmatic and are remarkable for their unwillingness to mount the barricades over abstract or idealistic principles.

They are inclined to boil political disputes down to conflicting interests rather than to conflicting morals or ideas, and this makes compromise much easier. Finally, there is a widespread acceptance of democracy and pluralism. Any foreigner who needs a reminder of the fact that there are many different groups or viewpoints which have a right to exist and be heard in Britain can go to Hyde Park on any Sunday morning to hear the soapbox speeches of dozens of advocates.

Hyde Park Corner, London

The Monarchy

Britain is a monarchy, and in theory the Queen or King has sweeping powers. She theoretically appoints the prime minister, assembles or dissolves parliament, approves of all laws, makes foreign policy, commands the "Armed Forces of the Crown," and appoints officers who hold their rank by "Royal Commission." The trappings of political power would seem to confirm this. The "Queen's government" contains "Ministers of the Crown," who propose laws which always begin with the following words: "Be it enacted by the Queen's Most Excellent Majesty, by and with the consent of the Lords Spiritual and Temporal and Commons in this present Parliament assembled . . ." She is the temporal head of the Church of England, the country's official religion, and she appoints the leading priests. Also, in theory, sovereignty resides not in the people, but in the "Crown," which is not the person of the monarch, but rather the symbol of supreme executive power.

Actually, she no longer exercises any of the above powers. She "reigns but does not rule." The "Glorious Revolution" in 1688 established parliamentary supremacy and spelled the end of any monarchical pretense to rule absolutely. The last exercise of royal veto power was in 1707. By the 20th century, the real reason why "the Queen can do no wrong" is that the government never permits her to make any important decisions. This does not mean that the monarch does not perform any important functions whatsoever. She retains the right "to be informed, to advise and to warn." This right confers no power, but it does confer influence. As constitutional expert Ivor Jennings notes, "she can be as helpful or as obstreperous as she pleases: and she is the only member of the Cabinet who cannot be informed that her resignation would assist the speedy dispatch of business."

In unusual circumstances or in times of crisis, the monarch could actually exercise considerable influence. If a prime minister dies or resigns and a successor has to be appointed from the same party, or if an election yields no majority, the Queen could wield authority, so long as she would not act according to personal preference. For instance, in 1957 when Anthony Eden resigned, it was not clear who would replace him until Queen Elizabeth named Harold Macmillan. The monarch holds other significant "reserve powers," such as dissolving parliament or rejecting requests for dissolution. The ultimate guarantee that the monarch will not overstep her bounds is the British people, who are sovereign in reality, if not in theory. Prince Charles admitted this fact frankly, saying that "something as curious as the monarchy won't survive unless you take account of people's attitudes. I think it can be a kind of elective institution. After all, if people don't want it, they won't have it."

Much more importantly, she symbolizes the unity of the nation and the continuous thread through a millenium of English history. She is thus the focus of national pride. Politics touches not only the mind, but also the heart, and she helps to provide her subjects with an emotional attachment to their country. She is therefore an important cornerstone for the kind of low-keyed, but deeply-rooted, patriotism which most Englishmen share. Finally, because of her dual position as head of state and defender of the faith, she helps to link governmental with religious authority in the minds of many Englishmen.

In his brilliant book published in 1867, *The English Constitution*, Walter Bagehot distinguished between the "dignified" and

The United Kingdom

"efficient" parts of government. The "dignified" parts, especially the glittering monarch and nobility, were useful in securing authority and loyalty for the state from the citizenry, while the "efficient" parts actually used the power and resources of the state to rule. In his book, *The Body Politic*, Sir Ian Gilmour argued that "legitimacy, the acceptance by the governed of the political system, is far better aided by an ancient monarchy set above the political battle than by a transient president, who has gained his position through that battle.... Modern societies still need myth and ritual. A monarch and his family supply it; there is no magic about a mud–stained politician."

Bagehot had written that "we must not let daylight in upon magic." But in an age of non–deferential journalists and citizens in Britain, royal indiscretions have completely exposed that "magic." In the wake of lurid reports in the tabloid press about marital breakdowns and infidelity within the royal family, the succession to the throne and the very future of the monarchy in Britain is being questioned. The concept of a family monarchy, a Victorian–era notion which granted a symbolic and public role to royal offspring and consorts as well as to the king or queen, has been severely shaken.

Three of Queen Elizabeth II's four children have been unable to sustain a stable first marriage. The year 1992 saw the formal separation of Prince Charles from Diana, a superstar princess who overshadowed the estranged crown prince until her tragic death in Paris in 1997. In 1999 he began appearing in public with his long–time love, Camilla Parker Bowles. No one can predict whether the people would ever accept her: a 1998 MORI poll revealed that only 53% of the public thought he should be allowed to become king if he married her, and a mere 19% were prepared to accept her as queen. Prince Andrew is divorced from Sarah Ferguson. In 1992 Princess Anne, who divorced her first husband, Mark Phillips, became the first top–ranking British royal since King Henry VIII to divorce and remarry. She wed a divorced naval commander, Timothy Laurence. The ceremony had to be held in Scotland because the Church of England does not condone second marriages. Edward waited until 1999 to announce his engagement to Sophie Rhys–Jones.

Personal revelations about the royals are dangerously corrosive because an unelected institution in a democracy depends on the popular will for its legitimacy. Despite this bad publicity, an April 1997 MORI poll revealed that 62% of respondents oppose removing the monarch's constitutional powers, and only 19% support it. A MORI poll in December 1996 had already confirmed that the royals still enjoy considerable trust: when voters were offered a choice among 13 candidates for an elected president, the clear favorite was Princess Anne. A 1997 poll taken September 7, the day after Diana's moving funeral and an outpouring of grief that saw 60 million bouquets placed around the royal palaces, revealed that the mood toward the monarchy had changed: 73% of respondents (82% if Diana's eldest son William were to be the next monarch) favored its retention (down from 85–90% a decade earlier); fewer than half thought it would survive the next 50 years; and 39% now think less of the royal family.

An increasingly hostile mood had been shown in the reaction to a fire which caused $90 million worth of damage to Windsor Castle in 1992. The royal family had invented its name Windsor after this favorite castle in 1917 in order to shed its German name (Saxe–Coburg & Gotha) during the war against Germany. Popular outrage greeted the government's decision to pay the costs of the repair, which were completed beautifully in 1998.

The flames reignited the debate over whether the monarch should pay taxes and whether the state should provide annual incomes to the members and staffs of a very wealthy royal family. To quiet the fury, Queen Elizabeth announced that she would pay income taxes amounting to about $4 million annually and about $1.9 million to most members of her family out of her own fortune. She noted in 1997 that the cost of operating the monarchy had fallen by 39% since the beginning of the decade and that the royal yacht, "Britannia," had been decommissioned for financial reasons. It is understandable that on the fortieth anniversary of her coronation she publicly described 1992 as an *annus horribilis*. After Diana's death the royals made a real effort to be more accessible and open. They hired pollsters to help them come closer to the people and to read the public's message. As Elizabeth II admitted: "Read it we must."

Parliamentary Government

The seat of power was once the House of Commons, which elected and controlled the prime minister and the cabinet. It debated the great issues of the day and shaped the laws of the land. It was supreme, and its will could not be blocked by any political institution in the entire kingdom. A century later this was no longer true. The rise of powerful mass parties firmly controlled by party leaders had largely converted the majority in the House of Commons into the tail wagged by the dog in Number 10 Downing Street, the residence of the prime minister. Observers gradually stopped speaking about parliamentary government and began talking first of cabinet government, then prime ministerial government.

The prime minister is not all–powerful. He must face a powerful civil service (collectively called Whitehall), sometimes count his votes carefully in the Commons, and deal with a multitude of quasi–governmental and interest groups. In theory, the British political process is simple; in practice, it is surprisingly haphazard. British governments do at least as much "muddling through" as they command. The need to persuade, coax, beg, threaten or compromise with so many groups and institutions,

The funeral cortege of Diana, Princess of Wales, proceeds through Hyde Park toward Westminster Abbey.

Photo: Edward Jones

The United Kingdom

all with independent standing of some sort, changes the traditional picture of British government, which is centered on the prime minister and cabinet, who can do anything they want. In truth, British government has never been exactly as it appears to be on the surface. While clothed in basically the same institutional garb, the reality of British politics is always changing.

The House of Commons

The House of Commons has 659 Members of Parliament (MPs) elected at either general elections, which must be held at least every five years, or at by–elections, held when a seat falls vacant because of the death or resignation of a member. From the Great Reform Bill of 1832 until the electoral reform of 1970, the suffrage was gradually expanded until all men and women 18 years and older can vote. Also, all citizens of the Republic of Ireland who reside in the United Kingdom are allowed to vote. Compared with American elections, British campaigns are very short.

Usually only about four weeks elapse between the time the prime minister sets the date for new elections and the polling day. Many voters complained that the six–week campaign in 1997, the longest in 70 years, was much too long. The threat of sending MPs out on the hustings with very little notice is a powerful tool of persuasion in the hands of the prime minister. The MP does have certain advantages over the U.S. Congressman at election time: the parties pay the bulk of the campaign expenses. Also, since the MP's constituency has only one–seventh the number of inhabitants as an American congressional district, he or she is able to canvass the voters at their doorstep and get the full blast of public opinion face to face.

MPs are elected by a system which is very simple and controversial: the single–member constituency. The candidate with the most votes in each of the 659 constituencies is elected, even if he or she won fewer than 50% of the votes. This electoral system has the advantage of preventing many parties from gaining seats in parliament. By bolstering the two–party system, proponents say it enhances political stability. Since one or the other of the large parties usually has a majority in the House of Commons, there has never been the need for a formal coalition to rule.

Opponents say that it is undemocratic and unfair because it favors the larger parties by enabling them to win a far higher proportion of parliamentary seats than the percentage of votes they won nationally. For example, in the 1997 election, the *Labour Party* won 43.1% of the total vote, but received 63.4% of the seats. By winning 30.6% of the vote, the *Conservative*

House of Commons. View of the Chamber showing the Speaker's Chair, seating for Clerk of the House and assistants.

Party gained 25% of the seats. The *Liberal–Social Democratic Alliance,* with 16.7% of the total vote won only 7% of the seats. This was nevertheless twice the number of constituencies it had captured in 1992 even though its percentage of the total votes had dropped from 17.9%. It is increasingly common for MPs to be elected with the support of less than half the voters; in the House of Commons elected in 1997, 312 of 659 are in this situation. In 1992 a Liberal Democrat, Sir Russell Johnson, won his Inverness constituency with only 26% of the votes.

It is no surprise that the *Alliance* is strongly in favor of a proportional representation (PR) system, which would award seats in proportion to the total votes won. A 1997 MORI poll revealed that two–thirds of voters agree. The question is: exactly *how* could this be done?

Virtually every other Western European democracy has some form of PR. Prime Minister Tony Blair confessed before his party won a huge majority in 1997 that "I personally remain unpersuaded that proportional representation would be beneficial for the Commons." Aside from the obvious fact that his party benefitted from the old system, he points out that a fair electoral method must not only reflect opinion, but "it must also aggregate opinion without giving disproportionate influence to splinter groups." This is "particularly important for a parliament whose job is to create and sustain a single, mainstream government." The British political system needs an electoral system which offers voters a clear choice between the governing party, whose performance can be judged, and an opposition party, whose promises can be weighed and considered. The clear distinction between the two sides necessarily discourages third parties and splinter groups from developing.

In 1998 Prime Minister Blair appointed a commission under Lord Jenkins to examine the electoral system but with two stipulations: that the need for "stable government" should be kept in mind and that the link between MPs and their constituencies should be preserved. The conclusion was that a "lack of democracy" would have to be accepted at the national level in the interest of retaining stable, one–party government, while proportional representation could be practiced at the regional and local level. That is exactly what was done in regional elections in Scotland, Wales and Northern Ireland.

The very organization and physical structure of the House of Commons depends upon a government and an opposition, *without* a wide spectrum of opinion. The House of Commons is arranged in rows of benches facing each other rather than in seats facing the podium. This arrangement encourages debate and questions because members of the opposition parties sit facing each other across an aisle. By ancient custom, and for good reason, the aisle is wide enough so a man may not reach across it with a sword and skewer his opponent during debate. The government sits on the front row to the right of the Speaker's throne, and the

The United Kingdom

leaders of the opposition (known also as the "shadow cabinet") sit on the first row to the Speaker's left. Because of the massive *Labour* majority after May 1997, some of its members had to sit on the opposition side. MPs on the lower end of the pecking order in their respective parties sit higher up on the back rows and are therefore called "backbenchers."

Debate is directed by the Speaker, who since 1992 is a woman, Betty Boothroyd. Frequently described in tabloids as a "former dancing girl," she spent time in the U.S. working on John F. Kennedy's 1960 presidential campaign and doing office work and speechwriting on Capitol Hill. She observed the tradition of feigning reluctance to assume the post and having to be tugged to the speaker's chair, a throwback to the days when speakers were occasionally beheaded because of their uncomfortable position between the Commons and the monarch. When she strides into the chamber, her aides call for the long–standing ritual of respect: "Hats off, strangers!" But she has broken new ground in other ways. She refuses to wear the traditional long horsehair wig, and she insists on being addressed as "Madame," not "Mr. Speaker." Finally, until May 1997 she was not from the ruling party, being a member of the opposition *Labour Party*.

Unlike in the United States, the opposition party in Britain has an alternative cabinet which is pre–selected and ready to assume office at a moment's notice. Indeed, a major strength of British parliamentary democracy is that talented leaders in a government which loses an election still retain their front–row seats in parliament and are therefore kept in reserve until a later date when the electorate's moods change and their services are again desired. This shadow government leads what is known in Britain as "her Majesty's loyal opposition," a concept grounded in the notion that two persons of good will can disagree agreeably on an important issue. In contrast to America, though, the "loyal opposition" has no means of delaying governmental action through filibuster in parliament.

In theory, parliament checks and controls the executive (the prime minister and the cabinet). In practice, it is normally the other way around. Parliament lacks the facilities to watch over the government competently, and MPs are underpaid, understaffed and under–informed. Despite some recent pay increases, MPs still earn far less than their American counterparts. In 1996 they raised their salary to £43,000 (ca. $67,000), plus $72,000 for secretarial and research assistance. A cabinet minister earned £67,779 and a prime minister £81,956 before the 26% raise in 1996. MPs do receive expenses for travel, phoning, postage and housing allowances (if they must maintain two homes). Two–thirds continue working at their normal jobs, and the hours of the parliamentary sessions are set from mid–afternoon to evenings in order to accommodate that need. One–third even work for private lobbying firms and other businesses with interest in legislation, something forbidden for U.S. congressmen. They have inadequate office space and receive only a modest sum for secretarial and research assistance while the average American congressman has 16 aides and the average senator 36. With such minuscule staffs, ordinary MPs have great difficulty acquiring sufficient information to challenge the government, which has the entire civil service to provide it with facts.

Unlike the U.S. Congress, the House of Commons does not have a well–developed committee system to do the detailed work which cannot be done on the floor of the House. The ad–hoc "standing committees" have too little expertise and are too large to be truly effective. The smaller "select committees" have a relatively permanent membership, are often chaired by an opposition MP, and do play a more important role. In 1980, new committees were set up to oversee the work of specific ministries and to deal specifically with Scottish and Welsh affairs. There is considerable discussion of reforms to improve the committee structure in the House, but in the absence of successful reforms, it is likely to remain more a forum to debate the important issues of the day than a powerful law–making body. In 1988 the Commons voted to allow television to record its often rowdy deliberations.

It remains the government's job to determine what will be the law of the land. All important legislation, including the budget, is drafted by the government and Whitehall. Since the government determines the order of parliamentary business, its proposals always take priority over those of private members or the opposition. Parliament can make amendments and must give its approval, but the government has numerous ways to insure that its policies will be accepted. First, all MPs are party members, and they jeopardize their careers if they defy their party leaders. Renegades are seldom reelected. Second, as many as 110 MPs are actually members of the government, and all are expected to vote with the government.

Finally, since the very survival of the government depends upon maintaining a majority, MPs are under far greater pressure from the cabinet to support the government than is the case in the U.S. Rigid party discipline on most bills has always been essential in order to make the political system work. MPs are permitted to "vote their conscience" on moral issues, such as abortion, capital punishment, and gun control. The demand for the latter became very strong after a deranged man charged into a Scottish primary school in Dunblane with four high–powered rifles in 1996 and massacred 16 children and their teacher. Prime Minister Blair announced in May 1997 that *Labour* MPs would be free to vote on this question as they think right.

Control by the government is much less effective than it once was. From 1945 to 1970 no government lost a vote of the full House of Commons. The 1970s brought a significant change. The *Conservative* government of Edward Heath suffered defeat

Queen Elizabeth II with six former prime ministers celebrate the 250th anniversary of 10 Downing Street as the official residence of the Prime Minister.

The United Kingdom

in parliament six times. Before 1970 it would have been unthinkable for a government so defeated to remain in office, but he returned to the 19th century practice of resigning only upon losing a declared vote of no confidence. The *Labour* government which ruled from 1974 until 1979 suffered 23 such defeats, and Thatcher was defeated twice. The fact that the MPs can now often vote against the government without bringing it down encourages backbenchers to revolt without severely endangering their careers. The days are over when the backbenchers automatically vote as their leaders order.

The House of Lords

Great Britain is a monarchy, and it should therefore not be surprising that its aristocracy continues to enjoy certain political privileges. These are institutionalized in the upper house of parliament, the House of Lords. Of the 1,164 members (known as the "peers") 650 have hereditary titles, which means that all the offspring of these peers who inherit the titles are automatically entitled to a seat in the House of Lords. These titles range, in order of precedence, from Duke, Marquess, Earl, Viscount and Baron, all except Dukes being commonly addressed as "Lord." Some of these peerages have ancient origins, such as the Marquis of Salisbury or the Duke of Norfolk, but half the hereditary peerages have been created in the 20th century "for services to the nation." No new hereditary peerages were created after 1964 until Prime Minister Thatcher ennobled senior minister William Whitelaw and retiring Speaker of the Commons George Thomas.

An irreversible trend was set by a law of 1958 creating "life peers." Such peers are appointed for their learning or their distinguished public service. However, after they die, their heirs cannot claim their seats. Among the life peers named in 1997 was composer (now Baron) Andrew Lloyd Webber. Sir Paul McCartney (now a knight) and "Dynasty" star Joan Collins (now an Officer of the Order of the British Empire) were not awarded peerages. The House of Lords in 1999 consisted of 650 peers by inheritance, about a dozen law lords (who form the highest appellate court in the land), 26 Church of England Bishops and 514 life peers. Among the life peers are 67 peeresses, compared with 120 women in the House of Commons after the 1997 elections.

As the democratic wave caused a steady expansion of the franchise in the 19th and 20th centuries, the powers of the House of Lords came under increasing attack. In the Parliament Acts of 1911 and 1949, its veto right was taken away; now the only kind of bill it can veto is one to prolong the life of parliament beyond five years. Also, its power to delay legislation was reduced; it can now hold up bills for 13 months at the most (only 30 days for a financial bill). Until the Thatcher era, it seldom exercised its power out of fear that if it fully used its powers, it would ultimately lose them.

The *Labour Party* has long sought "to abolish the undemocratic House of Lords as quickly as possible." One of *Labour's* most influential leftists even renounced his title of Viscount Stansgate, giving up his right to sit in the House of Lords. He also shortened his name from Anthony Wedgewood Benn III to the more proletarian Tony Benn. One cannot say, however, that he "put his money where his mouth is" because he did *not* renounce his considerable fortune.

Labour's dislike for this body was understandable in view of the fact that the *Conservative Party* enjoyed a permanent majority in it. However, when one looks only at the 300 or so peers who regularly attend the sessions and do the actual work, the *Conservative* majority is only about five to four. An even closer look at those *Tory* lords reveals that many of them are what Thatcher derisively called "wets": those in her party who disagreed with many of her hard–line economic policies on the grounds that they widened the gulf between rich and poor. A prime minister has no control over them.

In normal times, opposition to the prime minister's policies is exercised in the House of Commons. But Thatcher so dominated that body until 1990 that another institution performed that function: the House of Lords. Said one *Labour* Lord in 1988: "It hurts to admit it, but on many issues we are the government's only real opposition." A *Liberal* baroness added: "As an unelected body, it would obviously be quite improper for us to try to kill a bill outright. But there is nothing to stop us from being an utter nuisance to the government. We call it playing Ping–Pong—holding up a bill for so long that the government is compelled to accept our amendments just to get the thing passed." In fact, by 1988 Thatcher had suffered 107 defeats in the House of Lords, compared with only two in the House of Commons!

Why is such a privileged house, to which *no one* is elected, retained in a democratic country? In fact, debates in the House of Lords are at least as well informed and much less partisan than in the lower house. In order to demonstrate this fact, debates in the upper house began to be televised in 1985. The lords' main job is to examine and to revise bills that have proceeded too hastily through the House of Commons. With such experienced peers, the most active of whom had already distinguished themselves in all walks of life outside parliament, the lords perform an important function in improving legislation. Also, the fact that the most active lords are persons of great prestige and influence in British society means that no government systematically ignores the House of Lords.

Supported two–to–one in a 1997 MORI poll, Tony Blair's *Labour* government moved swiftly to enact its campaign promise to remove "the absurdity of the hereditary element." He appointed a royal commission that produced a white paper in 1999. It recommended that the hereditary peers' right to sit and vote be removed, that the nomination of life peers be accomplished through an independent appointments committee (not the prime minister), that some be indirectly elected by bodies such as the new regional assemblies, and that longer–term reform be considered. To move this reform through the legislative process, Blair agreed to a compromise with the *Tory* leader in the House of Lords: that 91 hereditaries be permitted to stay until a fuller second–stage reform of the house can be undertaken.

Prime Ministerial Government

The nerve center of British politics is "the government," a collective term to describe the prime minister, the 16 to 23 cabinet ministers and the parliamentary secretaries or junior ministers, a team which may total from 70 to 110 members.

In theory, the prime minister is the 'first among equals' within the governing team. The prime minister is the leader of the party that has a majority (or at least a plurality) in the House of Commons. Thus, the holder of this highest office is a MP who has worked his or her way upward through the legislative system. The average prime minister has served a quarter of a century in the House of Commons. It is virtually inconceivable that a stranger to the national capital, such as Jimmy Carter, Ronald Reagan, or Bill Clinton, could become prime minister. In actuality, the powers of the post are so great that the description 'first among equals' is misleading.

The prime minister's powers, which are almost nowhere clearly spelled out in statute, strike the American as sweeping. As the nation's chief executive, chief legislator and chief administrator he is the primary focus of political attention. After the election, he is rather free to appoint and dismiss cabinet members, thereby largely determining the broad political direction the government will take. The convention of 'collective responsibility' prevents his ministers from criticizing him in public, and the tradition of secrecy shields

The United Kingdom

many of his decisions and actions from the public eye. He decides on the agenda for cabinet meetings and appoints the cabinet committees, which prepare government policies or deal with crises and carry out most ministerial business. For example, in 1982 Thatcher formed a 'war cabinet' to manage the Falklands crisis; she also had influential committees for economic, foreign and defense, domestic, and legislative policy. Such grand committees have subcommittees. There are no votes taken in cabinet meetings, and the prime minister interprets the sense of the cabinet.

Regardless of how the debate in the secret cabinet meetings might have gone, he can always announce the meaning in a way which conforms to his own views. As ex–*Labour* cabinet member Richard Crossman revealed, any prime minister who is subordinate to the cabinet is "consciously refusing to make use of the powers which now constitutionally belong to the office." In practice, most issues are decided either in Whitehall or in cabinet committees and are not even discussed in full cabinet meetings, which are normally held twice a week, including each Thursday morning. The modern cabinet is increasingly a reporting and reviewing body and less and less an executive one.

The prime minister selects new peers to the House of Lords. He directs the nation's sizable civil service. He determines the country's foreign and defense policies and can commit Britain to a policy which the cabinet and Commons can do little to alter. He can even enter treaties with foreign nations that need not be approved by parliament; foreign policy was a 'royal prerogative' which was never passed to parliament, although a prime minister does customarily discuss with it treaties and declarations of war. Finally, as leader and chief strategist for the national party, he alone can decide the date of the general election and thus determine when the entire government and Commons must face the voters. He is burdened neither by separation of powers nor by a federal structure. No American president wields such power.

Limitations on the Prime Minister

A closer look at the contemporary British political system reveals that the prime minister's power is far more restricted that initially meets the eye. Although he appoints and dismisses the cabinet members, he can hardly lord over them. Unlike most American cabinet members, the British ones are highly experienced and influential parliament members with whom the prime minister has usually worked for many years. He cannot scout the country for talented individuals whose main responsibility is to carry out the chief executive's policy; he can only choose from his close colleagues in parliament who have powerful political bases of their own in the party and in the nation. He thus does not deal with minions, but with powerful political office–holders, who would be far less afraid to stand up to him in private.

He must retain the confidence of the most important factions within the parliamentary majority party. He must inevitably take into the cabinet some persons who disagree with him on some fundamental issues. This has tended to weaken the convention of cabinet solidarity. In the 1970s it was twice suspended by *Labour* prime ministers so that certain ministers could express themselves freely. Thatcher had to cope with scarcely concealed criticism from those within her own cabinet whom she dubbed "wets." John Major lost the 1997 elections in part because he never succeeded in silencing *Tory* colleagues who opposed his policy toward Europe. Finally, since 1999 he must deal with regionally–elected parliaments in Scotland, Wales and Northern Ireland.

It is often argued that the prime minister enjoys the advantage of not having to direct huge ministries, as cabinet members do. Therefore, he is freer to deal with larger political questions. To some extent, this is true, but the other side of the coin is that he lacks manageable administrative backing. He has no department to provide him with independent analyses and advice. His "private office" at his residence, Number 10 Downing Street, is too small. More valuable to him is the "cabinet office," headed by a top civil servant, which organizes the agenda for cabinet discussions. Thatcher established a "policy unit" at Number 10 composed of some expert advisers. Yet these specialists were no match for the massed expertise available to departmental ministers. Thus, the quality of the prime minister's information is not generally better than that of his cabinet members.

He must deal with a complicated network of ministries and departments with diverse views and a good deal of autonomy in their own areas of responsibility. By American standards, there is virtually no "spoils system" in British politics. The prime minister is able to send to each ministry only one minister and one to three parliamentary secretaries. But when they arrive, often with little or no detailed experience in the particular areas of responsibilities and with no staffs of their own, they are faced with a permanent secretary, the senior civil servant of his department with several decades of experience. He and his subordinate civil servants have the facts at their fingertips and brief the minister.

Although it is his job merely to give technical advice and let the minister set the political direction, it is but a short step from persuasively "giving the facts" to actually determining departmental policy. Usually continuity, not change, wins out. New policies must be negotiated with these bodies, not simply imposed upon them. Nevertheless, if the minister comes to clear, firm decisions, then his officials will almost always carry them out.

Bureaucracy and the Civil Service

As in all advanced countries, much of the work which used to be done by leading politicians has now been delegated to the civil service, which numbers about 640,000 bureaucrats. Most do not actually work in Whitehall, that small area in London where the chief administrative buildings are located. Britain is fortunate to have civil servants who generally work efficiently, who are almost entirely uncorrupted and whose decisions usually arise not from personal or political reasons, but from good administrative ones.

Personnel are frequently criticized because they, the top people, come from too narrow a social background and because they operate under a blanket of secrecy. It remains essentially true that the top 3,500 administrators are drawn overwhelming from the "Oxbridge" (Oxford and Cambridge) universities after having received a generalist's education, despite the fact that the three–class hierarchy was replaced in 1971 by a single, open structure. The recruitment system remains largely unchanged.

Not only the cabinet, but the top 3,500 or so civil servants must take oaths of secrecy. Among cabinet ministers, this convention is breaking down somewhat, as they leak information to the press or write revealing memoirs. The civil servants' oath makes it a crime to disclose any official information, whether it is classified or not; he is bound to remain silent for life.

A vigorous campaign has been launched by a variety of groups to punch some holes in this screen of secrecy by adopting a law similar to the U.S. Freedom of Information Act. One hole appeared in 1991 when for the first time the newly appointed chief of the MI5 counterespionage service, Stella Rimington (the first woman ever to occupy the post), was identified by name; this agency, as well as Secret Intelligence Service (SIS, formerly know as MI6), which deals with foreign intelligence, has long inspired the imagination of thriller writers. When a disgruntled former MI6 agent, Richard Tomlinson, put the names of more than a hundred British secret agents on the World Wide Web in 1999, British security

The United Kingdom

View of London across the Thames, with "Big Ben" (right)

officials conceded that the Internet is so far-flung that no government can control the flow of information on it.

Despite the Official Secrets Act and tradition, the British news media have always been an important check on governmental power. Britain has more newspapers per capita than any other country. Nevertheless, Prime Minister Blair has vowed that his government will introduce a Freedom of Information Act, a reform with the backing of three-fourths of the population, according to a 1997 poll.

Acts of parliament usually merely establish the basic principles of law, and the civil service fills in the details. Bureaucratic regulations now vastly outnumber actual laws, as is the case in the United States. Traditionally, the Treasury, led by the Chancellor of the Exchequer (Treasury minister), has been the main coordinator of the many departments and ministries. Since it was responsible for the budgets of the various departments, it gained the right to comment on any policy proposal from any department. There is some skepticism about the Treasury's ability to oversee and review all policy effectively. But if anybody is master of Whitehall, it is the Treasury and not the cabinet as a whole.

In addition to the huge bureaucracy, the prime minister must deal with a maze of so-called "quasi-autonomous non-governmental organisations," mercifully shortened to "quangos." Depending on how wide the net is thrown, these organizations number up to 5,521 and include such bodies as the Arts Council, the University Grants Committee, the Commission for Racial Equality, the BBC, Trustees of National Museums and the nationalized industries. Many are purely advisory, but some dispense large sums of money. All consider themselves to be more or less autonomous, but most are financed, and most members are named, by the central government, usually by a department of Whitehall. The government can sometimes force these "quangos" to comply with overall policies by giving or withholding grants, but it frequently faces stiff opposition and must often modify its policies in order to win compliance. They have taken over many services formerly performed by local authorities.

Alongside the "quangos" are especially important interest groups which have semi-official status with the government or with various ministries. They include the Church of England, the universities and the umbrella organizations for the unions and industry—the Trade Union Congress (TUC) and the Confederation of British Industry (CBI). The latter is the largest employers' association in the world, with a highly professional bureaucracy. Sometimes the government is driven to very close negotiations with one of these. From 1974 to 1978 the *Labour* government reached a "social contract" with the unions, swapping legal concessions and price restraints for limits on wage increases. More often, the government tries to conduct "tripartite" negotiations with both the TUC and the CBI to maintain economic stability. The fatal flaw in this effort is that the CBI and the TUC (whose constituent unions are autonomous and therefore negotiate their own wage agreements and decide when to strike) are no longer able to bind their members to whatever agreements are reached under the auspices of the government.

The Judiciary

Another limitation on the government's power, which has long been one of the chief cornerstones of British liberty, has been an independent judiciary. Political leaders are forbidden to obstruct the judicial process, even though judges make decisions which significantly influence politics. As with most other aspects of the British public life, the legal structure is fragmented and complicated. There are different court systems: one for England and Wales, one for Northern Ireland and one for Scotland, which has always retained its own separate, Roman-based legal system. There are different layers of courts. At the pinnacle are the 10 to 12 Lords of Appeal (known as the "Law Lords"), who sit in the House of Lords and who, constituted as the Judicial Committee of the Privy Council, can even hear appeals from some parts of the British Commonwealth.

Usually the Law Lords' hearings are dry and poorly attended; they involve less pomp and ritual than does the U.S. Supreme Court. But the eyes of the world were on them in 1998–9, when former Chilean leader, General Augusto Pinochet, went to Britain for medical treatment. While there, Spain and other European countries demanded his extradition because of his alleged international human rights violations. He claimed immunity as a former head of state and current member of the Chilean senate, so the Law Lords were asked for a ruling. Normally these jurists do not have reputations for their political leanings, as do American Supreme Court justices, but their politics became an issue in the long legal battle. In the end, they rendered seven judgments that revealed differing interpretations on points of law. Nevertheless, they ruled that Pinochet could be extradited to Spain to face charges of torture, but only for those acts committed after December 1988 when Britain implemented the 1984 Torture Convention.

Much of criminal law and most civil law in Britain does not come from acts of parliament, but instead from the "common law." Unlike "code law," which most European democracies have, "common law" is based on tradition, a slow development of rules based on previous cases ("precedents") which are reported in writing, indexed and published in an elaborate system for reference. It is law made by judge and jury. In order to make legal language more comprehensible for litigants, civil courts eliminated Latin legal terms from proceedings in 1999, replacing them with plain English.

The United Kingdom

Britain's tradition of parliamentary supremacy excludes the possibility of "judicial review," such as exists in the United States. This would permit the courts to overturn acts of parliament on the ground that they were unconstitutional. But this is theoretically impossible since no body can be superior to parliament. Only a small part of the governing of Britain is carried out by parliamentary acts. Ministers, civil servants, local government authorities and "quangos" must use discretion in applying general laws to concrete situations, and it is precisely this discretion which can be checked by the courts. In the 1970s a group of parents took the minister responsible for education to court on the charge that the way in which he had applied the school reform was illegal, and the court ruled in their favor. In order to deal with concrete cases, judges must decide what the laws mean. It is in such interpretation that judges have most of their power; the whole thrust of a law can be changed or bent by judges. One might ask "who needs judicial review?" when judges have this kind of power.

As in the United States, there is much controversy over the question of whether the courts have too much power and whether they are, in fact, political. There can be no question that judges' ability to assess the propriety of ministerial actions opens up another course of action to persons who oppose the government's policy. Of course, if parliament does not like what the courts are doing, it could make new laws which are clearer and more specific, but parliament has taken that step only once since 1945. It is far too busy to monitor the judges' use of their discretionary power. Whether one likes it or not, the impact of judicial interpretations will remain political and will continue to place limits on governmental power. However, judicial restraint still prevails in Britain to a greater degree than in the United States.

Local Government

Largely because of historical circumstances, the United Kingdom is a unitary, not a federal state. That is, it is not a collection of "united states." Unlike the United States of America, the UK was not consciously created by sovereign states which carefully retained important powers. The English conquered Wales militarily in the 12th century; it was politically integrated with England in 1536. The thrones of England and Scotland were united in 1603, and the process of union was completed in 1707. The question of succession to the throne led to Anglo–Scottish conflict in 1715 and 1745, which culminated in the occupation of Scotland by English armies. Ireland was simply taken by force, and the six northern counties remained in the United Kingdom in 1922, when the southern 26 counties became independent.

Therefore, the British government is, in theory, freed from the problems of getting its policies accepted by powerful states or provinces. This centralization would seem to fit well with the land and its people—it is a small country, no bigger than the state of Oregon, with a population of 59 million. It is highly urbanized, with 40% of the population living in only seven urban centers which account for less than 4% of the total land area.

London, with a population of seven million (over 15% of the United Kingdom's total), is seven times larger than the second largest city, Birmingham. Only four other cities have more than half a million inhabitants: Liverpool, Manchester, Sheffield and Leeds. Unlike Washington, New York, Ottawa or many national capitals, London is simultaneously the center of government, finance, the mass media and the arts. Nearly three–quarters of the people who earned a place in *Who's Who* live within a 65–mile radius of London. Half the MPs never resided in their constituencies before their election, and many of these are from London. Further, most ambitious civil servants climb the career ladder in London.

Nevertheless, unitary government does not mean that orders from Number 10 Downing Street, Westminster, or Whitehall are automatically carried out in all corners of the UK. There are many institutions which give much scope for local resistance to central authority. Let us look first at local government.

It is not a surprise that, like most other British political and legal institutions, the structure of local government is diverse and highly complicated. In 1974 a reorganized structure of local government came into effect in an attempt to produce a fairly uniform pattern throughout the entire kingdom. This reform scarcely made the structure of local government more easily understood by the foreigner. To begin with, local government still differs in England, Wales, Scotland and Northern Ireland. In the first three, there are two tiers of administration, each with elected councils, taxing authority and its own powers. The top tier (composed generally in England of metropolitan or county councils, and in Scotland of nine regional councils) and the lower tier (composed of borough, or district councils) together provide schools, local roads, government–owned housing (known as "council housing"), and an array of services, such as buses, garbage pickup, libraries, swimming pools and (except in London) police protection.

These two tiers often clash with each other, especially in metropolitan areas. To muddle things even more, there is usually even a third tier composed of parish or community councils with powers of their own. In all, there are more than 14,000 local governments in Britain! These local units provide for about half of their own expenses through local property taxes (known as "rates") and fees for services. They employ almost three million people (over 12% of the total work force), far more than the central government.

Former Prime Minister Thatcher locked horns with local authorities. In 1988 she sought to abolish the existing system of local taxes, based on the size and value of personal property, and to replace it with a flat–rate levy, or community charge, which would spread the tax burden to residents of all incomes. Opponents said this was regressive and unfair, while she said that by spreading taxes evenly, the new tax would bring pressure to bear on local councils, many of which are dominated by *Labourites,* to reduce their budgets. Thus, a motive to modernize the tax system was mingled with one to reduce the opposition's power even further. So unpopular was this flat–rate levy that it helped lead to her downfall in 1990.

She also moved to abolish the metropolitan councils, at least in part because some of them had become centers of leftist power. These included the Greater London Council (GLC) and what was sometimes derisively referred to in Tory circles as the "Socialist Republic of Yorkshire." While eliminating the GLC in her 1986 reform, the elected councils in London's 32 administrative areas, such as Kensington and Chelsea, Westminster, and Lambeth and Hackney, continued to exist. Within days of assuming office in May 1997 Prime Minister Blair proposed a referendum for Londoners to create an elected government and mayor. It took place the next year, and 72% voted in favor of a directly–elected mayor. Blair favors the same for other major cities.

Sometimes strong–armed measures toward local governments do work, depending largely on the skill and determination of the prime minister. Nevertheless, it would be more accurate to describe the overall relationship in terms of bargaining between *interdependent* levels of government.

Island Governments

The United Kingdom includes certain island groups, such as the outer Hebrides, Orkney and Shetland, which have more local authority than county, district or metropolitan county councils on the mainland. For instance, Shetland controls oil developments in its own territory and has launched a strong movement toward total internal autonomy. The Isle of Man in the

The United Kingdom

H.R.H. The Prince of Wales

Irish Sea and the partly French-speaking bailiwicks of Guernsey and Jersey off the French coast already have autonomous legal status, Norman-based legal systems, their own parliaments and governments which control domestic, fiscal and economic policy. They are quaint anomalies in that they are not part of the UK, but are Crown dependencies.

The Channel Islands had been occupied by 30,000 Germans during World War II. In 1993 embarrassing evidence was released that islanders had collaborated with, profited from, or slept with the German masters. In one notorious incident in 1942, local authorities helped the Germans identify 2,100 Jews and English-born residents to be deported to camps in Germany. These revelations reopened old wounds and prompted Britons to think about how they might have reacted if Hitler's forces had overrun the entire country.

Wales, Scotland and Northern Ireland

The three large regions on the outer fringe of the United Kingdom comprise less than a fifth of the UK's total population: Wales (2.9 million), Scotland (5.1 million) and Northern Ireland (1.6 million). These populations compare with 48.7 million in England. Until 1999 all were, in varying degrees, Celtic in background and relatively poor economically. All three were ruled by departments of the central government: the Wales Office, the Scottish Office and the Northern Ireland Office, each with a mini-Whitehall at its disposal. The prime minister appointed a secretary of state for each, and these politicians, who never come from the areas they control, sat in the cabinet.

Although these regions' relations with London have rarely been smooth, regionalism was seldom a major factor in British politics. The differences were masked by a common language, the facade of unitary government and economic prosperity. This changed dramatically in the 1970s. Strapped with a disproportionate number of dying industries and unhappy with the remoteness of central government, nationalist parties in Wales and Scotland grew. At the end of the century Westminster transferred important powers to these regions. "Devolution," which resulted in all three having their own elected parliaments in 1999, represents a historic shift in the way Britain is governed.

Wales

Wales is technically a principality whose titular ruler is the Prince of Wales, who is always the heir apparent to the English throne. It lost all traces of political identity through the Act of Union with England in 1535. However, its social integration with England proceeded much more slowly. English was the language of the government after 1535, but until the 19th century the Welsh language, which is a Celtic dialect related to Irish, Scottish and Breton, was spoken by a majority of the people. Now only one-fifth of the Welsh population speaks it, mainly in rural areas and small towns in North Wales, but one-third claims to have "some understanding" of the language. Welsh speakers form a majority in outlying areas in the West inhabited by only 10% of the population.

Unlike Scotland, it was the preservation of the language, more than independence from England, which fired the Welsh nationalist movement in the 1970s. Lacking its own aristocracy, the Welsh always tended to be somewhat more egalitarian in their outlook. The coal mining and basic industry, especially in the more populous South Wales have always made it a *Labour Party* stronghold. In 1978 London offered both Wales and Scotland regional assemblies whose powers would nevertheless fall short of American state legislatures. But in a 1979 referendum, Welshmen rejected such an assembly by a margin of four-to-one, largely because of the revulsion which English-speaking Welshmen felt toward the pretensions of the Welsh-speaking minority.

To help satisfy Welsh nationalist urges, Welsh-language schools were established, and by 1984 they numbered 344 primary and 36 secondary schools. The result is that for the first time since reliable statistics have been taken, the proportion of children who speak Welsh is *rising*: Between 1982 and 1996 the proportion of children aged three to 15 who speak Welsh grew from 18% to 24%. Second, a separate Welsh-language television channel was established (*Sianel Pedwar Cymru*—channel four—S4C), which, due to the small viewing audience, is one of the most expensive television channels in the world. Finally, the Welsh Language Act of 1993, which declared that Welsh and English were to be considered "on a basis of equality," enabled Welsh speakers to be more insistent that Welsh be spoken more. Language disputes are nevertheless mild compared with Belgium or Quebec.

Welsh nationalism is alive though not robust. A nationalist party, *Plaid Cymru* (pronounced "Plide Cumry"), founded in the 1920s amid anti-English feeling, no longer talks much about an independent Wales with a seat in the United Nations since most citizens do not want that. It settled for the referendum leading to an elected Welsh Assembly. In September 1997 a razor-thin majority in Wales, with only half the eligible voters participating, voted in favor of its first elected parliament in nearly 600 years. Its powers are more limited than those of the new Scottish Parliament. It cannot change acts of Westminster, pass its own laws, nor raise taxes. It can decide how to spend the budget formerly administered by the Welsh Office, including for health and education, and scrutinize and alter the administration of Wales.

In May 1999 the first elections were held, and the *Labour Party* captured 35.4% of the votes and 28 of the 60 seats. *Plaid Cymru* garnered 30.5% and 17 seats, while the *Tories* won 16.5% and nine seats and the *Liberal Democrats* 12.6% and six seats. It used a new electoral system modeled on that of Germany: each voter has two votes, the first for his preferred representative (called Member of the Welsh Parliament—MWP) in the 40 constituencies and one for the party of his choice. Thus it is a combination of Britain's "first-past-the-post" system and proportional representation. Secretary of State for Welsh Affairs Alun Michael of the *Labour Party* handed over his powers to himself in his new capacity as first secretary of the Welsh Assembly.

Scotland

Scotland, which is still a kingdom in its own right, joined England by agreement in 1707. Although the Scottish parliament voted itself out of existence at that time, other institutions remained intact, such as the legal system, based on Roman law, a distinctive educational system and a Presbyterian Church of Scotland. By longstanding custom, the Queen worships as a Presbyterian in Scotland and as an Episcopalian in England! One should therefore not wonder at the fact that the Scots have

The United Kingdom

a secure sense of separate national identity which has survived union with England.

Scottish nationalist feeling has simmered for two and a half centuries, but the intensity and strength surged furiously in the 1970s when oil was discovered in the North Sea off Scotland's coasts. The *Scottish Nationalist Party* (*SNP*), founded in 1928, argued that "It's Scotland's Oil!" and that it would make this relatively poor region in the UK wealthy and capable of independence. In the 1974 parliamentary elections, its vote surged to 30%. In the face of such rising nationalism in their traditional party stronghold, the ruling *Labour* government offered to create a popularly-elected Scottish assembly if such a move were approved by a majority in a referendum.

Such an instrument of "direct democracy" means that between parliamentary elections, the people, not parliament, decide. Because of the tradition of parliamentary supremacy, there were no referendums in Britain until the 1970s. Parliament did stipulate that at least 40% of the eligible Scottish voters had to approve the transfer of powers to the region (a process known in the UK as "devolution"). The referendum was held in March 1979, and 51.6% of the voters approved of the assembly; however, only 33% of the eligible voters participated, so parliament repealed the devolution act for Scotland. The *Labour Party*, which had always won most of the Scottish seats, reasserted itself in Scottish affairs and picked up the torch of devolution.

The 1990s witnessed a resurgence of Scottish nationalism and the *SNP*. Polls in 1992 indicated that 80% of Scots wanted either a Scottish parliament or outright independence. One native son, actor Sean Connery, compared Scotland to the independent Baltic states. This was quite a role reversal for "James Bond," who on screen risked everything to serve the British crown. The hit movie *Braveheart* in the mid–1990s also boosted the movement for greater Scottish independence. Even more Scotsmen began saying: "We're not free. We need a William Wallace." This feeling helped fuel a huge upsurge of interest in learning Scotland's Gaelic language, which had declined to only 80,000 speakers. Still there is no language motive to Scottish nationalism, as in Wales. Nor are there religious ones, as in Northern Ireland, or ethnic motives, as in eastern Europe. *SNP* leader, Alex Salmond, remarked that "we are a mongrel nation."

In the 1997 elections the *SNP*, which captured six seats, did not come close to overtaking *Labour*, which won 56 of 72 seats in Scotland in 1997 and for the first time in Scotland's history drove the *Tories*

out completely. With *Labour* dominating Westminster again, a devolution of powers to Scotland and Wales came back on the agenda. A referendum in Scotland in September 1997 paved the way to a democratically elected assembly in 1999. Voters overwhelmingly approved a 129–seat parliament, Scotland's first in 300 years, with wide powers over such local matters as health, education, municipal government, economic development, housing, criminal and civil law, fisheries and forestry. They also voted for the right to raise or lower income taxes by up to 3% and to levy charges, such as road tolls. The polling set the stage for the most important constitutional change in British government in modern times. It also signaled the peaceful rebirth of a nation in an extraordinary way: no guerrilla army, separatist terrorists, civil disobedience, or even mass demonstrations.

On May 6, 1999, voters elected their first Members of the Scottish Parliament (MSP). Using the same mixed single–member constituency/PR electoral system as the Welsh, they favored *Labour*, led by Donald Dewar, which received 33.8% of the votes and 56 seats. The *SNP* was second, with 27% of the votes and 35 seats. The *Conservatives* got 15.4% of the votes and 18 seats, while the Liberal Democrats won 12.5% and 17 seats. This result was a set–back for the *SNP's* independence cause. The low turn–out (58% compared with 71% in the 1997 British elections) also suggested that Scots still value the Westminster Parliament more highly than their new one.

Northern Ireland

The UK's most serious regional problem by far is Northern Ireland. The Irish island can be said to be England's oldest colony, having been invaded by the English in the 12th century and ruled as a colony until 1800, when it received its own parliament. Ireland remained legally a part of the United Kingdom until 1922, when the 26 predominantly Catholic southern countries formed what is now the Republic of Ireland. The Protestant majority in the six northern counties rejected "home rule" (independence from Britain). The British at the time pledged that no change in the link between Northern Ireland and the United Kingdom would occur without the consent of the majority of the people. Every subsequent British government has held firmly to this commitment.

The largely Presbyterian and Church of Ireland Protestants are descendants of Scottish immigrants who began arriving in the 17th century. Their loyalty to the English crown is based upon the monarch's historical status set forth in the 1689 Bill of Rights, as "the glorious instrument

of delivering this kingdome from Popery and arbitrary power." It is not surprising that this historical attitude, along with the Protestants' rejecting unification of the two parts of Ireland, has always antagonized the Catholic minority in Northern Ireland (who comprise 42% of the population of 1.5 million). Although Northern Ireland is officially a secular (i.e. non-religious) state, in actual practice the friction between Catholics and Protestants dominates politics there.

Northern Ireland has been in turmoil since 1968, when a Catholic civil rights movement organized internationally publicized street demonstrations to object to Protestant discrimination in housing, jobs and electoral representation. British governmental pressure on the Northern Irish parliament (which has existed since 1921 and is known as "Stormont" because it met in Stormont Castle) to meet many of the Catholic demands created a Protestant backlash. Peaceful street demonstrations in 1969 gave way to open violence, and British troops were sent to reestablish order.

The Irish Republican Army (IRA) sprang to life again and launched a modern terrorist campaign to remove the British from the territory and reunify the entire island. It has received money and arms from overseas sources ranging from Gadhafi in Libya to the Irish Northern Aid Committee—NORAID—in the United States. Due to bad publicity, IRA fund–raising in the U.S. became more difficult. It found a lucrative substitute: extortion and racketeering in Northern Ireland itself. Because it also seeks the overthrow of the Dublin government, it had been banned in the South since 1936.

In retaliation, some Protestants in the North organized illegal forces. The best known illegal Protestant para–military group, known for its violence, is the Ulster Volunteer Force (UVF). This illegal unit should not be confused with the Ulster Defence Regiment (UDR—the British army in Northern Ireland), the Royal Ulster Constabulary (RUC—the mainly Protestant police force) and the Ulster Defence Association (UDA—a moderate and legal Protestant para–military group). In 1993 Protestant gunmen murdered more people than did the IRA.

The British disbanded Stormont in 1972 and resorted to the unpleasant task of ruling the region directly, through a Secretary of State for Northern Ireland. Successive British governments have sought earnestly for ways to devolve governmental power to the Northern Irish themselves. The problem has always been how to protect the Catholic minority's interests against a perpetual Protestant majority. This difficulty revealed a major weakness

The United Kingdom

of the English model of parliamentary democracy which presents great power to any political group which commands an electoral majority: the model does not work well in societies which are divided religiously, ethnically or racially, because minorities can be voted down so easily.

Realizing this, the British government had to reject in 1975 a proposal by the leaders of the Protestants that a constitution be drawn up for Northern Ireland which would copy British parliamentary practice. Instead, British governments sought some form of "power–sharing" arrangement which would guarantee the minority Catholic parties a place in any Northern Irish executive. This idea infuriated the two Protestant political parties, the *Ulster Unionists* and the *Democratic Unionists*.

The IRA, a dedicated and ruthless band of 400 to 500 paramilitaries operating in small cells called "active service units," is divided into two groups: the "official" IRA was formerly Marxist, but now it seeks power through elections; the "provisional" IRA (Provos) was strictly nationalist, but it shifted to armed struggle to convert Ireland into a Marxist state. This shift was one reason why Irish–Americans became less generous toward the IRA. Both these wings face some competition from the smaller, but more radical *Irish National Liberation Army (INLA*, the paramilitary wing of the *Marxist Irish Republican Worker's Party).*

From 1976 to 1982 the IRA campaigned for special treatment as "political prisoners." After the failure of such tactics as refusing to wear prison garb and smearing the walls of the cells with their own excrement, they resorted to hunger strikes. The deaths of ten IRA hunger strikers in Maze Prison in 1981 sparked renewed militant Catholic nationalism. Shortly before his death, one of the hunger strikers, Bobby Sands, even managed to win a seat in the House of Commons, while he was still in prison.

In response, the British government tried again to restore a measure of devolved government by means of the 1982 Northern Ireland Act. Elections for a 78–seat Northern Ireland Assembly and an executive branch were held in 1982. This new body was to have the power to make proposals to the British government on how to return to self–government. It failed. Neither the mainly Catholic, moderate and law–abiding *Social Democratic and Labour Party*, nor the militant *Sinn Fein* (the political arm of the IRA, pronounced "Shin Fane," receiving only 10% of the total votes), took their seats in it. The *Ulster Unionist Party* also walked out and vowed that it would not return until security had been restored in Northern Ireland.

Mr. Gerry Adams
President, *Sinn Fein*

That is exactly what the British tried to do. In 1975 it ended the detention of both Catholic and Protestant terrorist suspects without trial, and it has refused to declare martial law in the violence–torn area. Because of the risk of intimidation against jurors, non–jury courts (known as "Diplock Courts") were created for those accused of terrorist–related offenses. The British have always contended that the fundamental principles of British justice—a fair trial, the onus on the prosecution to prove guilt, the right to be represented by a lawyer, the right of appeal if convicted—are still maintained for all.

The most effective anti–terrorist measure undertaken by the government in 1983 was the granting of pardon or lenience to onetime terrorists if they would tip off the police (in Northern Irish slang, 'to grass') on the whereabouts of active terrorists. The testimony of such 'supergrasses' led to a dramatic number of arrests in *both* the IRA and Protestant Ulster Volunteer Force. These organizations were so paralyzed that terrorist deaths in Northern Ireland dropped by half in one year, from 97 in 1982 to about 50 in 1983. IRA terrorists did give British Christmas shoppers a grisly indication they were alive in 1983, however, when they exploded a bomb outside of the bustling Harrods Department Store in London, claiming still more innocent lives (including an American teenager, a fact that hurt IRA fund–raising in the U.S.) in their ruthless struggle.

The Brighton bombing of 1984 was another grim reminder of the IRA's intent to wreak as much havoc as possible, this time by assailing the highest levels of British government itself. Having organized into "cells," the IRA became more difficult for police to combat. The violence

Rt. Hon. Marjorie "Mo" Mowlam
Secretary of State for Northern Ireland

prompted the Irish Republic to ratify the European convention on terrorism, which requires the extradition of terrorists.

By 1998 the toll stood at almost 3,400 since 1969. In doing its bloody work the IRA had the tactical advantage over the 30,000 security forces, which were kept on the defensive by the IRA's meticulous planning and constant shifting of tactics. To minimize its own losses, it increasingly struck at "soft targets," such as bands, military hospitals, off–duty RUC officers, and civilian firms which supply goods and services to the security forces. It also acquires state–of–the–art equipment; for example, it has surface–to–air missiles to use against army helicopters.

Democracy still exists at the local level in Northern Ireland, and voters send 27 MPs to the House of Commons in London. Protestants win almost all of these seats. Catholics would take more if the competing *SDLP* and *Sinn Fein* would unify in constituencies with predominantly Catholic populations. In the 1997 elections the two Catholic parties captured an unprecedented 40.2% of the votes. The Protestant Unionist parties also have trouble working together, with Ian Paisley's hardline *Democratic Unionists* taking only two seats and David Trimble's larger *Ulster Unionist Party* winning ten. *Sinn Fein* refuses to take any seat in the British parliament, whose authority it does not recognize. In the 1997 elections it won an all–time high of 16% of the votes in Northern Ireland. Two of its candidates, Gerry Adams and Martin McGuinness (an IRA leader who has served jail sentences), won seats, which remain vacant. *Sinn Fein* does occupy seats in local councils on both sides of the Irish border, though.

There has been some progress in addressing the problem of social and eco-

The United Kingdom

nomic discrimination; unemployment in Northern Ireland declined to 11.6% by 1996. Nevertheless, a Catholic man is still two and one-half times more likely to be unemployed than a Protestant man, and the jobless figure exceeds 70% in some ghettos of Belfast and Londonderry, where the terrorists do most of their recruiting. Northern Ireland has failed to attract large new investment deals, but many tourists are returning to the province, which surprisingly has the lowest rate of violent crime in the UK.

In 1985 former Irish *Taoiseach* (Prime Minister) Garrett FitzGerald and British Prime Minister Thatcher signed an Anglo-Irish agreement on Northern Ireland. This marked the first time the British government formally permitted the Irish Republic involvement in Northern Ireland's affairs, a concession which many Northern Irish Protestants cannot accept. It is regrettable, but perhaps not surprising, that all groups in Northern Ireland condemned this landmark act, despite the fact that its first article states that no change in the province's status would come about without the consent of a majority of its people.

Peace Talks in Northern Ireland

In 1993 optimism was ignited by a joint declaration by the British and Irish prime ministers offering *Sinn Fein* a seat at the bargaining table to discuss Northern Ireland's future if the IRA renounced violence. Former Prime Minister John Major, who admitted that his government had conducted secret contacts with the IRA, promised that Britain would not stand in the way of a united Ireland if a majority of Northern Ireland residents supported such a step. His Irish counterpart pledged that there would be no change in the six counties' status without majority consent.

The following year President Bill Clinton, betting that the IRA wants peace in Northern Ireland, made a risky decision to grant a visa to *Sinn Fein* leader Gerry Adams to come to the U.S. Although the British government criticized him for this, it triggered a series of historic events. On August 31, 1994, the IRA declared a cease-fire, which prompted the Irish government to begin meeting with *Sinn Fein* leaders. Six weeks later Protestant loyalists also declared a truce. While paramilitaries on both sides continued to terrorize their own communities, inter-sectarian violence and IRA attacks on British forces stopped. As a result, the British government relaxed its security measures in Northern Ireland and began drawing down its 18,000 troops. In December London opened direct talks with *Sinn Fein* and, later, with the Protestant paramilitaries. In February 1995 the British and Irish governments issued a "Framework for Agreement," outlining their proposals for Northern Ireland's future.

The U.S. government did its part to keep the momentum going by permitting *Sinn Fein* to open an office near Dupont Circle in Washington in 1995 and to raise money legally in the U.S. Much to London's displeasure, Clinton invited Gerry Adams to a St. Patrick's Day party in the White House honoring Ireland's *Taoiseach* (prime minister). In May the U.S. also organized a Northern Ireland Investment Conference in Washington that brought together more people from more different Northern Irish parties under one roof than ever before. It was also attended by top government officials from the UK and Ireland and was the venue for the first meeting between Gerry Adams and Britain's ex-Secretary of State for Northern Ireland Patrick Mayhew. This was the highest-level meeting between British and IRA leaders in 75 years and a giant step toward Adams' goal of receiving the same recognition and treatment accorded to Northern Ireland's other political leaders.

Clinton gave another powerful boost to the peace process in November 1995 by paying the first visit to Belfast ever made by an American president. It was a triumph. The very approach of his historic visit helped dissolve a stalemate in the talks and revitalized cooperation. Hours before his arrival the Irish and British prime ministers met and agreed to a breakthrough: preliminary all-party talks, led by former U.S. Senator George Mitchell, would be held while an international "decommissioning commission," led by former Canadian chief-of-staff and ambassador to Washington, General John De Chastelain, sought a way around the weapons impasse.

John Major admitted that Clinton's coming helped "concentrate the mind." Greeted everywhere in Belfast by cheering crowds waving American flags, Clinton addressed over 100,000 people, the largest throng in memory to gather in the square of Belfast City Hall. He appealed to everyone to put aside "old habits and hard grudges" and to seek peace. One witness said: "I've never seen anything like this before. Everybody's come together." His American optimism reportedly made a deep impression. He met with all major leaders in the conflict and invited them to a reception at Queen's University; most came, which would have been unthinkable earlier. It was a very different Belfast that he saw: gone are the soldiers on the hunt, the countless roadblocks and the barbed wire. Although the ugly wall topped with razor wire separating Protestants and Catholics, inaptly called the "peace line," still stands, most of the blockaded streets have been reopened in Belfast.

There is very little support in Northern Ireland or elsewhere for immediate reunification of Ireland. But not since 1969 have there been so many grounds for optimism that "the troubles" can end and that the Northern Irish can discuss their future peacefully. As a symbol of returning normalcy with Britain in 1995, Prince Charles became the first member of the royal family to make an official visit to the Irish Republic since 1922. Also in 1995, David Trimble, leader of the Ulster Unionist Party, the main Protestant group, travelled to Dublin and met with the Irish *Taoiseach*. This was the first time since 1922 a Unionist leader was received in Dublin.

In February 1996 the IRA ended an 18-month cease-fire and launched a bombing campaign in Britain and Northern Ireland. Tony Blair's *Labour* government, which for the first time appointed a woman—Marjorie "Mo" Mowlam—as Secretary of State for Northern Ireland, departed from the previous government's policy of not admitting *Sinn Fein* to multi-party talks until the IRA ends its violence campaign. *Sinn Fein* insisted that there could be no preconditions to its participation in negotiations, which resumed in June 1997.

Since the Labour government is not dependent upon Unionist MP's from Northern Ireland to win important votes in parliament, as John Major was, it has more political flexibility on Northern Irish issues. A couple of weeks after becoming prime minister, Blair lifted the ban on official contacts with *Sinn Fein* in order to explain London's position and to assess whether the IRA was really prepared to renounce violence. Gerry Adams accepted the offer. Blair dropped London's insistence that terrorists disarm before joining peace talks. He visited Northern Ireland on May 16, 1997, in order to demonstrate that he is willing to take risks for peace in the six counties.

To continue the negotiation process, he invited Gerry Adams to a meeting in Downing Street in December. This was the first visit by an Irish Republican leader to the prime minister's private residence in 76 years. It was a richly symbolic encounter, with the meeting over tea held in the cabinet room, the target of an IRA mortar attack only six years earlier. A month later, in January 1998, Adams returned to Downing Street to hear from the prime minister that the peace process is an "absolute priority" and that "the status quo is not an option." To balance his gesture to *Sinn Fein*, Blair told Protestants that "none of us . . . , even the youngest, is likely to see Northern Ireland as anything but a part of the United Kingdom."

The United Kingdom

Talks, involving eight Northern Ireland parties and the British and Irish governments continued, despite the outbreak of renewed violence following the assassination of a Protestant terrorist, Billy Wright, in Maze prison just after Christmas. American George Mitchell emphasized the importance of the negotiations: "We're talking about, literally, people's lives, the possibility of the resumption of the terrible conflict that enveloped this society with fear and anxiety. So, frustrating and tedious as it seems—and it is—you have to be patient and recognize how tough it is for them to move."

In the early morning hours of Good Friday, 1998, after a series of marathon sessions, *all* parties at the table reached an historic agreement: a new 108–member Northern Ireland Assembly would be elected using the Irish Republic's system of proportional representation with the transferable vote. To protect Catholics from being permanently outvoted on sensitive "cross-community" issues and to necessitate consensus, a majority of both Catholic and Protestant blocs or an overall "weighted majority" of 60% would be required for decisions. The cabinet would consist of 10 seats distributed proportionally to the four largest parties. The assembly would share power with a new North–South Ministerial Council, composed of ministers from the Republic and Northern Ireland. This gives the Irish Republic its first formal role in Northern Ireland's affairs. In return, Ireland's leaders agreed to give up the Republic's claim to the North. All parties pledged to use their influence to persuade armed groups to turn in their weapons within two years, and imprisoned members of those armed groups would be released within two years as well.

On May 22, 1998, referenda were held on both sides of the border, and 71% of Northern Irish and 94.4% in the Republic approved of the Good Friday settlement. The following month, the first elections to the new assembly were held, and David Trimble's *UUP* came out on top with 28 seats. John Hume's *SDLP* was second, with 24 seats. For their indispensable role in the entire peace process, Trimble and Hume shared the 1998 Nobel Prize for Peace. Hume had declared that "we finally decided that agreement for the whole community is more important than victory for one side." Other seats went to the *DUP* (20), *Sinn Fein* (18), the *Alliance* (6), the *UKUP* (5), *Independent Unionists* (3), and the *Women's Coalition* and *PUP* two each. The great number of parties winning seats demonstrated the effect of the proportional representation electoral system. Trimble became First Minister, and the body met for the first time in the traditional Stormont building on July 4.

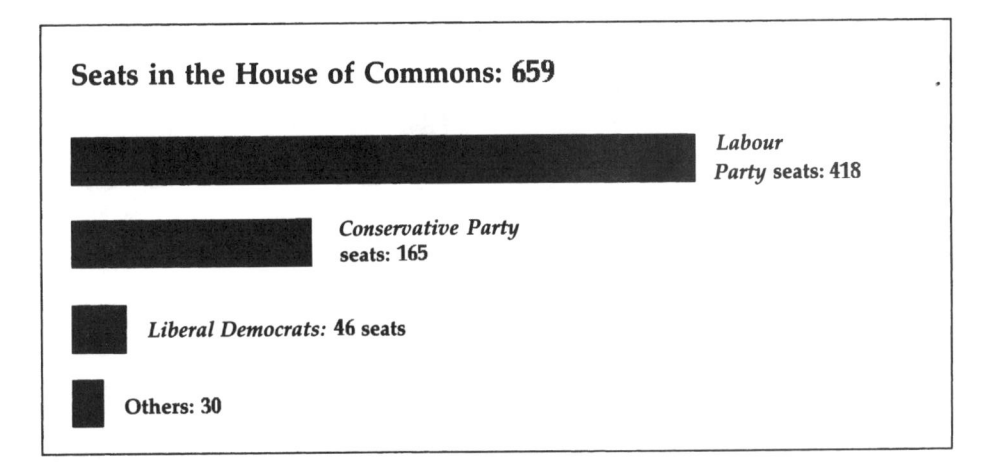

Seats in the House of Commons: 659

Labour Party seats: 418

Conservative Party seats: 165

Liberal Democrats: 46 seats

Others: 30

This being Ireland, an island with so much history and so many memories, things were not destined to go smoothly. In August a fringe Catholic organization calling itself the "Real IRA" exploded a car bomb in the Northern Irish city of Omagh, killing 28 people. The public was so repelled by this grisly act that the "Real IRA" apologized and announced a permanent cease–fire on September 12. To maintain his credibility in the Protestant community, Trimble called for a beginning of "decommissioning" (turning in) of weapons even before the creation of a Northern Ireland cabinet. Noting that this precondition had not been in the agreement, *Sinn Fein* balked at completing the peace process. The world was still waiting as Tony Blair, who in November 1998 had become the first British prime minister to speak in the Irish parliament since Ireland's independence, set a deadline of June 30, 1999, for the creation of a ministry to run the province.

Today's Political Parties

Like any modern democracy, the British system could not function without parties. They recruit and select candidates, define issues which are important, educate voters about them, finance and fight electoral campaigns, put up governments which rule at all political levels, and provide well–organized opposition which continually remind the electorate of the government's shortcomings. For the government, the party is an essential tool for maintaining a parliamentary majority, and for the individual politician, it is the ladder to power. For the political activist it is an important means for putting his ideas into practice. For the voter, it is an indispensable label for a set of politicians, policies, sympathies or interests.

British parties bear some similarities to those of America, but there is a striking difference which stems from a fundamental difference in the two political systems: the real power in American parties is at the bottom of the hierarchy; a national party in America is nothing more than a loose coalition of state and local parties. By contrast, in Britain the real power within the party is at the top.

Basically, all British parties have a similar organization. At the lowest level are party units in the wards, which are grouped together into 659 constituency parties, each of which struggles for a seat in the House of Commons. These ward or constituency parties raise funds (part of which must be passed up to the national party), recruit members, campaign at election time and select candidates.

National parties rarely try to overrule constituent parties' choice of candidates, although the national parties clearly influence the selection. The most obvious evidence is that about a half of all MPs do not reside in their constituencies before their election to parliament. Unlike the U.S., there is no legal requirement for this, and the national party leaders search all over Britain for "safe seats" for important MPs. Constituency party leaders often decide that national party interests override their own local desires. All constituency parties are grouped into regional organizations, which, except Wales and Scotland, have little importance.

At the national level, each party organizes an annual conference to which each constituency sends representatives. This large conference debates and adopts the party's overall policy (which is never binding on the party if it is in power) and, in the case of *Labour*, elects the party's leadership. At the national level, two other party organizations also exist. The central bureaucracy assists the party at all levels. The parliamentary party consists of the MPs and members of the House of Lords belonging to it.

All British parties are coalitions of differing interests and ideologies. It is often assumed that British parties are class parties. While this, to some extent, is true of the *Labour Party*, the *Conservative Party* has always had an appeal which cuts across

The United Kingdom

class lines. In terms of policy, the major parties have normally been far closer together than is often assumed. From 1945 until the early 1970s, there was a large measure of consensus among the major parties. All were agreed on a welfare state, the mixed public–private economy which permitted much state intervention in the economy and employer–union–government collaboration (sometimes referred to as "corporatism").

Some observers even spoke of the "end of ideology" in Britain. That broad consensus collapsed in the 1970s, and both the *Conservative* and *Labour* parties became more ideologically oriented. By the 1983 elections the major parties had become more polarized than they had been in a half century. Margaret Thatcher's embrace of market–oriented economics and rejection of state intervention, of "welfarism," and of "corporatism" was matched by revived class–warfare rhetoric in the *Labour Party*. Its moderate wing found itself placed on the defensive by the left–wing, which demanded radical changes in Britain's social, economic and political power structures. Sir Winston Churchill's observation was no longer correct that "four–fifths of the two major British parties agree about four–fifths of the things that need to be done." But four defeats in a row from 1979 to 1992 prompted *Labour* to move toward the political center. The payoff exceeded its wildest expectations.

The Conservative Party

The *Conservative Party* is conscious of its heritage, which it traces back to the 17th century. Its pragmatic approach has always enabled it to appeal to Britishers from all classes, even though its strongest appeal could be found among those who were well–off economically. At the heart of the *Tory Party*, as it was formerly known, is the unity of the whole nation. It has always preferred voluntary effort to public assistance, and this stems from its insistence on free enterprise in industry, advocacy of the profit motive and of indirect (sales) taxes rather than direct (income) taxes.

It has never argued that the state has no role in the economy, and it even nationalized industries under certain circumstances, such as the Central Electricity Board in 1926 and Rolls–Royce in 1971. Nor has it ever rejected the notion that the state should provide social welfare services sensibly. In her 1987 campaign Margaret Thatcher said that all decent people want to help the ill, the unemployed and the aged, but that a healthy economy is needed to provide the level of services which the British want.

There has, of course, always been divi-

**The Rt. Hon. William Hague, MP
Leader of the Conservative Party**

sion within Tory ranks between proponents of more state intervention and those who favor less regulation and a much freer market economy. Some of the differences in political orientation within the party are reflected in well–established pressure groups: they include the *Bow Group*, which presses for policies which benefit all classes, the *Monday Club* (the old right), the *Tory Reform Group* (progressives) and the *Charter Movement*, who want to democratize the party.

It was publicly known in 1975 when Thatcher defeated Edward Heath for the party leadership that the new leader represented a different Toryism than Heath. After she became prime minister in 1979, those persons in her cabinet who loyally supported her views were dubbed "dries." Those who had doubts about her medicine, especially about how it would affect millions of citizens and their families, were dubbed "wets." In a cabinet reshuffle after the 1983 and 1987 elections, she dismissed the "wets" in her cabinet.

Thatcher's stunning victory in the 1987 elections revealed that although she was an unpopular and unloved leader, British voters respected her no–nonsense competence and will. They grudgingly accepted her bitter economic medicine of sound money, hard work, and standing on one's own two feet. She was the first prime minister to win a third consecutive term in modern British history and surpassed Winston Churchill and H.H. Asquith as Britain's longest serving prime minister in this century. Why did she win?

The first reason is that her opposition was severely divided. Second, the prime minister had won considerable stature and influence in the international arena. She could boast with justification that "we have put the Great back into Britain." The main reason for her victory was the unde-

niable economic success her government had achieved.

Thatcher's Fall

The willingness of France and Germany to relinquish more sovereignty to Europe widened the chasm between the UK and its continental partners. Thatcher's cabinet had been rocked by high–level resignations stemming from disagreements over Europe. In 1986 Michael Heseltine stormed out because he wanted a European consortium, not one from the U.S., to purchase a British helicopter company. In 1989 Nigel Lawson left because he wanted to include the pound in the European Monetary System (EMS). The fatal resignation—and the catalyst for her downfall—was that of Sir Goeffrey Howe, the last surviving member of her original 1979 cabinet and an architect of "Thatcherism." He charged in parliament that her obstruction in Europe carried "serious risks for our nation."

The devastating speech led to a successful challenge to her leadership in November 1990. After an historic eleven–year rule, the longest prime ministership since the Victorian era and the longest consecutive one since the Napoleonic age, Thatcher resigned. The events leading to her fall related to Europe, but the reason why 45% of her parliamentary party colleagues voted against her was that she was guiding her party toward defeat in the next elections. For 18 months her party had trailed in the polls a *Labour Party* that had become more moderate, had overthrown its suicidal commitment to nuclear disarmament, and had embraced the EU. Her country was experiencing high inflation, a growing trade deficit, a slow–down in economic growth, and intense domestic opposition to her poll tax for local governments.

With her passing, the UK entered a period under John Major, Britain's youngest prime minister in this century, until he was evicted from Number 10 Downing by *Labour* leader Tony Blair. Major was a self–made man from a very humble background and with no university education. His father had been a circus performer and minor league baseball player in the U.S. Major was the Iron Lady's protegé and hand–picked successor. Nevertheless, he backed away from strident Thatcherism, abolishing the hated poll tax in 1991. He buried the grudge Thatcher had borne against both the EU and Germany and became a more cooperative European. Like Thatcher, he benefitted from an unexpected war, this time in the Gulf in 1991, which went very well for Britain and its allies.

He entered the 1992 elections with the highest popularity rating of any British prime minister in three decades, but nobody expected his stunning victory in the

The United Kingdom

midst of Britain's worst recession in a half century. He led his party to a 21–seat majority, based on 42% of the votes and 336 seats (down from 376). By the end of 1996 this thin majority had evaporated as a result of defections and by–elections.

The *Tory* party was deeply divided, especially over Britain's role in the EU. Major's government was sometimes held hostage by several dozen vocal "Euroskeptics" in his own party, including Thatcher herself, who were determined to sabotage all moves to closer European union. Not only did the government appear to be at war with itself. It was also dogged by a succession of scandals and sleaze, as well as the fall–out from the "mad–cow disease" debacle, which the government handled ineptly. Voters were tired of *Tory* rule after 18 years. Even the party's most significant achievement—a booming economy and unemployment half as high as when Major took office in 1992—played in the opposition's favor since voters seemed to think they could afford the risk of voting *Labour*.

The election results were devastating for the *Conservative* party. It fell to 30.6% of the votes (down from 41.9%) and to 165 seats (down from 321). The party lost all its constituencies in Scotland and Wales and 30 of its 41 seats in London. Seven cabinet members lost their seats, including several presumed front–runners in the contest for the party's leadership that followed John Major's resignation. He was replaced by William Hague, a young former management consultant with only nine years of parliamentary experience and no major ministerial background. Although he projects a sense of necessary generational change within the party, he is an untested leader. At the 1997 party conference he reminded his fellow *Tories* that "people thought we had lost touch with those we always claimed to represent. Our parliamentary party came to be seen as divided, arrogant, selfish and conceited. Our party as a whole was regarded as out–of–touch and irrelevant." Demoralized after its worst election defeat since 1906, and in opposition for the first time since 1979, the *Conservative* party faces a difficult task of rebuilding.

The Labour Party

Although its roots extend far back into the 19th century, the *Labour Party* was officially founded in 1900. Under the influence of the small but well–connected *Fabian Society*, which sought to reform British society gradually from above rather than through violent revolution or labor union agitation from below, the party adopted in 1918 a new constitution which transformed it officially into a socialist party. It proclaimed that the goal of the party is to "secure for the producers by hand or by brain the full fruits of their industry and the most equitable distribution thereof that may be possible upon the basis of common ownership of the means of production and the best obtainable system of popular administration and control of each industry and service . . ."

That purely Marxist objective helped prevent the *Labour Party* from sharing the fate of many socialist parties in Europe which split apart in the aftermath of the Russian Revolution. However, it became the source of continuous intra–party friction ever since. During most of its history the party was in reality more moderate than its constitution might indicate. It sought to "democratize" the economy by nationalizing key industries and regulating others, to distribute wealth more equally, to expand social welfare services and to eliminate class differences.

During the Thatcher government *Labour* took a leftward lurch and embarked upon an almost suicidal political course. Grossly underestimating Britain's first woman prime minister and the public support for her economic austerity policies, the *Labour Party* committed itself to radical promises: unilateral nuclear disarmament, withdrawal from the EU, massive nationalization of industries and huge increases in public spending.

This led to an electoral disaster, and in the 1983 elections, it suffered its worst defeat in 60 years. Its 27.6% was *Labour's* lowest popular vote since 1918 and was 20 percentage points lower than in 1966. Almost a quarter of those voters who had identified themselves consistently with the *Labour Party* abandoned it.

It failed to win a majority of the votes among the working class or among labor union members. This was a severe setback for a party created by and organizationally linked to the unions; it seriously hollowed out the party's claim to be *the* party of the worker. Only the traditional working class remained more loyal: that segment which worked in nationalized or "smokestack" industries or which lived in council housing, Scotland, Wales or the North of England. This represented the most significant basic shift in the social basis of British politics since World War II.

Within hours after the polls had closed, the move to replace the ineffective *Labour* leader, Michael Foot, began. The choice was Neil Kinnock. He began immediately to mend the gaping, intra–party split between the left and right which had led to electoral disaster and the massive drop in party membership between 1979 and 1983 to a level comparable to that of 1945. He moderated his party's views on the EU, defense and the status of capitalism. With a sharp eye on the social changes which

Rt. Hon. Tony Blair, MP, Prime Minister of the United Kingdom, and Leader, *Labour Party*

have occurred in Britain, Kinnock announced that *Labour* must appeal to the "newly well–off" and should be a party which appeals to the haves, as well as the have–nots.

Going into the 1987 elections, he recognized that if *Labour* were to be electable and to regain the initiative in British politics, which it had lost in 1979, the party would have to shy away from extremism. The platform it prepared purged the earlier pledges to abolish the House of Lords (which has been critical of some of Thatcher's policies), to nationalize much more industry and to control the country's banking system. It accepted the principle of selling public–owned houses, and it no longer opposed the UK's membership in the EU.

The party clung to some of its old cures: more public spending and borrowing, higher taxes for the "very rich," and restoration of trade union immunities by repealing *Tory* legislation. An enormous electoral liability was Kinnock's decision to stand by his party's unilateral nuclear disarmament position. The electoral effect was suicide. The party suffered its second worst defeat in more than a half century, capturing only 32% of the votes and 229 seats.

The 1992 elections showed that the *Labour Party* continued to suffer from an image problem: voters worried about extremism within the party, and they had doubts about its defense and economic policies and, in general, its competence to rule the country. It faced important social changes which worked against it: its traditional support base—trade–union mem-

The United Kingdom

Rt. Hon. Paddy Ashdown, MP, Leader, Social and Liberal Democrats

bers, manual laborers and tenants of state–owned housing—is shrinking.

Party leaders conducted a thorough rethinking of its positions. In order to be able to present a credible challenge to the *Conservatives*, *Labour* had to develop a moderate, non–socialist program. It unveiled its new policy, which scrapped unilateral nuclear disarmament, as well as vote–losing calls for withdrawal from NATO, removal of U.S. military bases in Britain, scuttling the Trident nuclear submarine program, and state ownership of industry. It reconciled itself to the market system.

The year 1992 seemed ideal for a *Labour* victory, but voters handed *Labour* its fourth consecutive defeat, even though it climbed to 35% of the votes and 271 seats. Voters were still unwilling to trust *Labour* with power and continued to associate it with crippling strikes, chaos, and economic decline. Kinnock had begun to introduce the kinds of changes that would ultimately lead his party to victory in 1997, but he had failed at the time to persuade his countrymen that *Labour's* transformation and pragmatism were genuine and lasting.

Kinnock resigned as leader and was replaced by John Smith, whose untimely death of a heart attack in 1994 forced his colleagues to select another leader who could bring the party victory. They turned to Tony Blair. The son of a life–long *Conservative*, Blair was educated at a private boys' school and studied law at Oxford. He took no interest in student politics and spent his spare time singing in a rock band called "Ugly Rumours." He entered parliament in 1983 representing a traditional *Labour* constituency in the North. He bears no scars of *Labour's* dismal rule in the 1970s, and he is its first leader with no roots in the labor movement and with no grounding in traditional socialism.

This made it easier for him to complete the process of modernizing his party. He lessened its dependency upon and identification with unpopular unions. In the 1960s, union money made up 80% of the party's budget; by 1995 that figure was 50% and then 30% by 1998. He remained silent during a 13–week railway strike in 1994, breaking a long tradition of unfailing party support for the unions' actions. He curbed the voting power of union leaders, who had controlled large blocks within the party. Their power was diluted by changes in the complicated rules governing party voting and policy making. He persuaded the powerful NEC to accept his revision of Clause IV of the party constitution, setting aside the party's 1918 commitment to public ownership of key industries. This had been a major obstacle to its return to power. Blair confessed later that scrapping Clause IV had "shown me what I intuitively thought but wasn't sure of: that the party was actually behind change." Since it was a democratic process every step of the way, he was sure that most of the party's rank and file had changed and were behind the reform.

Through his patience, charm, and power of persuasion, he reversed the radicalism within the party and opened it up to fresh ideas. He led *Labour* toward the political center. He ceased regarding *Labour* as a tribal party focusing on the working class. By enhancing its appeal among the middle class in the heavily populated south of Britain, he aimed directly at the bedrock of the *Tories'* support. He is highly confident, disciplined, focused, energetic, and quick to master a brief. He is also sometimes accused of being brutally autocratic when it comes to bringing his party in line with his reforms, a quality Margaret Thatcher is said to admire in him. Unlike Thatcher, though, who relished battering her opponents into submission, Blair prefers logical argument and persuasion.

In the 1997 elections he demonstrated what a skillful campaigner he is. He can orchestrate a tightly organized campaign, present himself convincing in two television debates with his opponent (an innovation in British campaigns), "work a crowd" very effectively, and inspire voters without promising too much. His main challenge was to convince voters that his party had indeed shed the heavy baggage of the past. He stuck to a single message: that his party was now "New *Labour*." "The old ideologies are dead. New *Labour* is offering a new and different form of politics. . . . There has been a revolution inside the *Labour* Party. We have rejected the worst of our past and rediscovered the best. . . . We have made ourselves fit to face the future."

He distanced his party from the "outdated ideology" of high taxes financing expensive government programs, from powerful unions, and from unilateral nuclear disarmament. He established friendly relations with business leaders. He vowed neither to renationalize industries nor raise income taxes. Instead, he pledged to keep inflation low, to spend no more than the *Tories* had already budgeted, but nevertheless to improve the struggling National Health Service and the school system, to introduce a minimum wage, to combat crime, and to reform the constitution.

Seeing too little difference between his program and that of the *Tories*, some observers dubbed him "Tony Blur." He responded by arguing that "I do not think everything that has happened in the last 18 years has been bad. My attitude is: keep what is working and change what is not." Clearly Britain's economy was already working well, with unemployment at a 10–year low of 6.2% on election day. This fact persuaded even more voters that there was little danger in voting for a *Labour Party* which promised not to tamper with one of Europe's most robust economies. Blair assured Britishers within hours after his victory: "We ran as New *Labour* and will govern as New *Labour*."

The electoral payoff for *Labour* was historic: it won 418 of 659 seats on the basis of 43.1% of the votes. Its majority of 179 seats was its best performance ever. It wiped the *Tories* out of Scotland and Wales altogether and made deep inroads into *Tory* strongholds in southern England and London, capturing even Margaret Thatch-

View of Hong Kong

The United Kingdom

er's north London Finchly constituency. In a stunning turnaround women flocked to *Labour*, which won 53% of their votes (compared with 30% who voted *Tory*). The number of women with seats in the House of Commons shot up from 63 to 120, and most of them were from *Labour*. Most of the nine ethnic minorities, including a wealthy Muslim, elected to parliament ran on the *Labour* ticket. Blair's cabinet also contained many firsts: five women, a blind man (David Blunkett, Education and Employment Secretary), and an openly gay man (Chris Smith, National Heritage Secretary).

The Liberal Democrats

In reaction to the *Labour Party's* earlier swing to the left, a group from the party bolted and in 1981 formed the *Social Democratic Party (SDP)*. This new grouping sought to occupy the center ground of the British political spectrum, which had opened up because of the polarization between the two larger parties. Its strategy was to align with the older *Liberal Party* of the center.

The *Liberals* had been one of the two major parties during the 19th century, but it had not been in power since it was eclipsed by the *Labour Party* just after World War I. Their heaviest emphasis has been on individual freedom, and it speaks for decentralization of state power, for a greater focus of local political issues and for workers' (not union) councils sharing control with management. Both the *Liberals* and the *SDP* strongly support European integration and reform of the electoral system in favor of proportional representation.

Just how important such a change would be for the *SDP–Liberal Alliance* was demonstrated in the 1983 elections. It won 25.4% of the vote, the best performance of center parties for 60 years. Its remarkably even support across the entire class spectrum proved that it was not merely a fashionable "wine and cheese" grouping, as critics had charged. But it won only 23 seats in the House of Commons. The *SDP* was reduced to a tiny rump within parliament. Most of the former *Labourites* who had switched their allegiance to the *SDP*, including two of its four founders, were swept from office. The *SDP's* share was only six seats. Under the popular leadership of David Steel, the *Liberals* improved their standing, winning 17 seats.

The *Alliance* did even worse in 1987, falling to 22% of the votes and only 22 seats. It had hoped to gain a surge of new support from voters in the political center, but all it managed to do was to split the opposition vote with *Labour*.

Many analysts had believed that the *Alliance* could supplant the *Labour Party* and that the new *Social Democrats* and the traditionally independent, undisciplined *Liberals* could forge a partnership which could "break the mold of British politics." But the *Alliance* had failed to establish itself as an electable non–socialist alternative. Therefore, in 1988 the *SDP* dismembered itself. It merged with the larger *Liberal Party* to form a new party, the *Social and Liberal Democrats*, led by Paddy Ashdown. The prospect of a hung parliament in 1992, meaning that neither of the large parties would win a parliamentary majority, buoyed the party's spirits. It could then play the "king–maker role" and demand the introduction of proportional representation as the price for entering a governing coalition with one of the large parties. This would have secured its own future and decisively changed British politics. But its hopes were dashed, as the *Tories* won a majority.

Doubling their seats to 46 (from 26 in 1992) on the basis of 16.7% of the total votes (down from 17.9%), the *Liberal Democrats* registered in 1997 the best performance by a third party in three generations. Party leaders and members were elated. But the magnitude of the *Labour* victory meant that their 46 votes in the House of Commons could not be employed to enhance their party's political influence as many *Liberal Democrats* had hoped. Ashdown stepped down as leader in 1999, having accomplished in his 11 years most of what he had wanted. He had rescued his party from the splits and name changes of the 1980s. He had put it close to the center of power, having negotiated a presence on a cabinet constitutional committee that dealt with big constitutional changes, such as devolution, electoral reform, and removing hereditary peers from the House of Lords.

Recent Foreign Policy and Post–Colonial Problems

Today the sun technically does not set on the British empire. Ten dots on the map are still ruled by Britain: Pitcairn in the south Pacific Ocean; Bermuda, British Virgin Islands, Caymans, Leeward Islands, Turks and Caicos in the Caribbean area; the Falkland Islands, St. Helena in the south Atlantic Ocean; Gibraltar in the Mediterranean; and Diego Garcia in the Indian Ocean. Yet it must still deal with many problems which stem from its colonialist legacy. They have included both foreign policy problems and domestic political difficulties, such as how to control and treat millions of immigrants from the former colonies (see Culture).

The Commonwealth of Nations is a loose, voluntary association of the former ruler and the ruled, and the head is the British monarch, even though some of its members are republics. Member states regularly confer at Commonwealth gatherings, and sometimes Britain must assume additional, unwanted responsibilities under the aegis of the Commonwealth, such as in helping to arrange a transition to democracy in the tiny Caribbean island of Grenada after four years of totalitarian rule and an invasion by the United States and six other Caribbean island states.

Britain also faces terribly complicated problems with the smaller enclaves it rules because local inhabitants there fear their larger neighbors and look to Britain for protection. It has declared that the principle of self–determination must not be violated and that the subject peoples can be absorbed by a neighboring land only by their consent. The principle is an admirable one, but it has a high cost. The 2,200 inhabitants of the Falklands, located off the Argentine coast, called upon Britain to defend them from Argentina in 1982. Britain's military victory did not convince Argentina to renounce its claims to the islands. No doubt Buenos Aires also has its eye on the Falklands' potential offshore oil reserves of two to five billion barrels, larger than those of the North Sea. As a deterrent, London stations 2,000 troops on the islands. Although Britain still refuses to discuss its sovereignty over the islands, it has established friendly relations with Argentina. President Carlos Menem received a warm welcome in London in 1998, where he laid a wreath to the Britons who died in the war. Prince Charles visited Argentina the following year.

The 31,000 inhabitants of Gibraltar cling to their rock and are largely self–ruling. But they rely on the protection of 5,000 British troops stationed there because they are afraid of becoming a part of Spain. In 1985 the border between Gibraltar and Spain was reopened, and discussions over its sovereignty and eventual disposition continue.

Painstaking negotiations with the People's Republic of China (PRC) over Hong Kong resulted in an agreement that gave the PRC sovereignty over the colony in July 1997, but that committed China to guarantee Hong Kong's capitalist economy and lifestyle for 50 years.

Britain's foreign policy today involves close cooperation with the United States and a primary focus on Europe. As separate sovereign states with their own interests, the Americans and British sometimes have different views on issues, ranging from the British–French invasion of Suez in 1956 to the American invasion of Grenada in 1983. But many people on both sides of the Atlantic still talk of a "special relationship" between the two

The United Kingdom

The Order of Succession to the Throne

Her Majesty Queen Elizabeth II and His Royal Highness Prince Philip the Duke of Edinburgh

—— *The Heir Apparent, eldest son of The Queen.*
1. His Royal Highness The **Prince CHARLES Philip Arthur George,** Prince of Wales and Earl of Chester, Duke of Cornwall and Rothesay, Earl of Carrick, Baron of Renfrew, Lord of the Isles and Great Steward of Scotland, b. November 14, 1948. Married Lady Diana Frances Spencer (3rd daughter of the 8th Earl Spencer) July 29, 1981.

> The Prince and Princess of Wales separated in 1992 and were divorced in 1996. Diana, Princess of Wales, died from injuries received in a car crash in Paris on August 31, 1997.

—— *The sons of that union,*
2. His Royal Highness **Prince WILLIAM Arthur Philip Louis of Wales,** b. June 21, 1982.
3. His Royal Highness **Prince HENRY Charles Albert David of Wales,** b. September 15, 1984.

—— *The second son of The Queen,*
4. His Royal Highness The **Prince ANDREW Albert Christian Edward,** Duke of York. b. February 19, 1960. Married Miss Sarah Margaret Ferguson July 23, 1986. They separated in 1992 and were divorced in 1996.

—— *The daughters of that union,*
5. Her Royal Highness **Princess BEATRICE Elizabeth Mary of York,** b. August 8, 1988.
6. Her Royal Highness **Princess EUGENIE Victoria Helena of York,** b. March 23, 1990.

—— *The third son of The Queen,*
7. His Royal Highness The **Prince EDWARD Antony Richard Louis,** b. March 10, 1964. Married Miss Sophie Rhys-Jones June 19, 1999.

—— *The daughter of The Queen,*
8. Her Royal Highness The **Princess ANNE Elizabeth Alice Louise,** Princess Royal, b. August 15, 1950. Married (1) Captain Mark Anthony Peter Phillips, November 14, 1973. The marriage was dissolved April 23, 1992. Married (2) Commander Timothy James Hamilton Laurence, RN, December 12, 1992.

—— *The son and daughter of her first union,*
9. **PETER Mark Andrew Phillips,** b. November 15, 1977.
10. **ZARA Anne Elizabeth Phillips,** b. May 15, 1981.

—— *The sister of The Queen,*
11. Her Royal Highness The **Princess MARGARET Rose,** Countess of Snowdon, b. August 21, 1930. Married Mr. Antony Charles Robert Armstrong–Jones, May 6, 1960, later created Earl of Snowdon. The marriage was dissolved July 5, 1978.

—— *The son and daughter of that union,*
12. **DAVID Albert Charles,** Viscount Linley, b. November 3, 1961. Married Hon. Serena Alleyne Stanhope (only daughter of Viscount Petersham, son and heir of the 11th Earl of Harrington) October 8, 1993.
13. Lady **SARAH Frances Elizabeth Chatto,** b. May 1, 1964. Married Daniel Chatto July 14, 1994.

—— *The son of that union,*
14. **SAMUEL David Benedict Chatto,** b. July 28, 1996.

—— *The first cousin of The Queen,*
15. His Royal Highness **Prince RICHARD Alexander Walter George,** Duke of Gloucester, b. August 26, 1944. Married Miss Birgitte Eva Van Deurs (of Denmark) July 8, 1972.

—— *The son and daughters of that union,*
16. **ALEXANDER Patrick Gregers Richard,** Earl of Ulster, b. October 24, 1974.

The United Kingdom

Buckingham Palace

17. **Lady DAVINA** Elizabeth Alice Benedikte Windsor, b. November 19, 1977.
18. **Lady ROSE** Victoria Birgitte Louise Windsor, b. March 1, 1980.
— *The first cousin of The Queen,*
19. His Royal Highness **Prince EDWARD** George Nicholas Paul Patrick, Duke of Kent, b. October 9, 1935. Married Miss Katharine Lucy Mary Worsley, June 8, 1961.
— *The first son of that union,*
   GEORGE Philip Nicholas, Earl of St. Andrews, b. June 26, 1962, is no longer in line of succession having married a Roman Catholic, Miss Sylvana Palma Tomaselli, January 9, 1988.
— *The son and daughters of that union,*
20. **EDWARD** Edmund Maximilian George, Lord Downpatrick, b. December 2, 1988.
21. **Lady MARINA-CHARLOTTE** Alexandra Katharine Helen Windsor, b. September 30, 1992.
22. **Lady AMELIA** Sophia Theodora Mary Margaret Windsor, b. August 24, 1995.
— *The second son of the Duke of Kent,*
23. **Lord NICHOLAS** Charles Edward Jonathan Windsor, b. July 25, 1970.
— *The daughter of the Duke of Kent,*
24. **Lady HELEN** Marina Lucy Taylor, b. April 28, 1964. Married Timothy Verner Taylor, July 18, 1992.
— *The sons of that union,*
25. **COLUMBUS** George Donald Taylor, b. August 6, 1994.
26. **CASSIUS** Edward Taylor, b. December 26, 1996.

— His Royal Highness **Prince MICHAEL** George Charles Franklin of Kent, b. July 4, 1942, brother of the Duke of Kent married a Roman Catholic, Baroness Marie Christine von Reibnitz, June 30, 1978, and under the terms of the Act of Settlement of 1701, he is no longer in line of succession to the Throne. The son and daughter of that union, however, remain in the line of succession:
27. **Lord FREDERICK** Michael George David Louis Windsor, b. April 6, 1979.
28. **Lady GABRIELLA** Marina Alexandra Ophelia Windsor, b. April 21, 1981 (known as *Lady Ella*).
— *The sister of the Duke of Kent,*
29. Her Royal Highness **Princess ALEXANDRA** Helen Elizabeth Olga Christabel of Kent, born December 25, 1936. Married the Honourable Sir Angus James Bruce Ogilvy (second son of the 12th Earl of Airlie), April 24, 1963.
— *The son of that union,*
30. **JAMES** Robert Bruce Ogilvy, b. February 29, 1964. Married Miss Julia Caroline Rawlinson, July 30, 1988.
— *The son and daughter of that union,*
31. **ALEXANDER** Charles Ogilvy, b. November 12, 1996.
32. **FLORA** Alexandra Ogilvy, b. December 15, 1994.
— *The daughter of the union of number 29,*
33. **MARINA** Victoria Alexandra Mowatt, b. July 31, 1966. Married Paul Julian Mowatt, February 2, 1990. They were divorced 1997.
— *The son and daughter of that union,*
34. **CHRISTIAN** Alexander Mowatt, b. June 6, 1993.
35. **ZENOUSKA** May Mowatt, b. May 26, 1990.

The United Kingdom

countries stemming from their common language and heritage, as well as from their alliance during two world wars. They cooperate closely on defense, intelligence gathering and nuclear technology.

This relationship does not exclude disagreement. Ex-Foreign Minister Geoffrey Howe spoke in 1983 of the "special intimacy and a special mutual confidence that we're able to talk with each other with the candor which one would normally expect only between one's own advisers." But some Europeans suspect that Britain is a sort of Trojan Horse for American objectives on the continent. This, among other things, influenced former French President Charles de Gaulle to reject Britain's first attempt to join the European Community.

For centuries Britain was a global power, whose interest in Europe was merely to prevent any one power or combination of powers from upsetting the military balance there and dominating the entire continent. Now its primary focus is on Europe.

Defense

This shift of focus is best seen in defense. It was a founding member of NATO, and until 1990 it organized its defense on the assumption that the chief threat was the Soviet Union. It therefore channeled the bulk of its resources into strengthening NATO rather than defending British outposts elsewhere. In 1971 it abandoned its defense commitments east of Suez.

The "NATO-first" policy necessitated fundamental changes in defense structure. Britain converted the once-mighty Royal Navy into a specialized force whose purpose was primarily to assist the American navy and to defend against submarines. In the 1970s it phased out its attack aircraft carriers. The Falkland Islands war in 1982 revealed how this change in force structure could affect Britain's commitments outside of Europe. It had to lease luxury liners and merchant vessels just to transport its troops and equipment to those faraway islands. The conflict prompted Britain to bolster its capabilities to project military power in the world by canceling the scheduled deactivation of an aircraft carrier and the Royal Navy's last two amphibious assault ships.

The heart of the British defense effort today is the army. It has thousands of soldiers on station in Northern Ireland. It deploys a diminishing number of troops on the European continent, mainly in Germany. The costs for this force are great, especially since Britain has a volunteer army. With the disappearance of the Soviet threat to Europe, NATO faces fundamental restructuring which affects the British military. In 1991 the allies decided to establish a sizable rapid reaction force to confront unforeseen threats anywhere in Europe. This new force is stationed mainly in Germany and is commanded by a British officer.

Within Britain itself, the most controversial aspect of British defense was its nuclear arsenal. Aside from France, the UK is the only European country to possess atomic weapons. The Thatcher government decided to replace the aging Polaris vessels (each carrying 16 missiles) with more modern submarines, capable of firing ultra-modern American-made Trident missiles, each of which could attack eight separate targets. As part of its nuclear modernization program, the UK also equipped Tornado jets with the capability of delivering nuclear bombs. The new *Labour Party*, which took power in May 1997, dropped its long-standing opposition to Britain's nuclear force. But in post-cold war Europe, nuclear weapons have become largely irrelevant. The UK decided in 1998 to halve the number of its nuclear weapons at sea to 200 on four Trident submarines.

Although nuclear targeting is coordinated with the United States, only the British prime minister can order the use of Britain's nuclear weapons. The willingness of the British government since the 1950s to permit the deployment of American nuclear weapons on British soil, which are not under the direct command of the British prime minister, reflects NATO's importance in British defense planning. "Dual-key" safeguards were considered unnecessary because the UK had a firm agreement with the U.S. (which has never been published) that no American nuclear weapons could ever be launched from Britain without the approval of the British government.

In 1991 Britain's participation in the war to drive Iraq out of Kuwait was solidly supported at home. The UK sent a powerful contingent of land, air and naval forces serving under the overall command of American General Norman Schwarzkopf, whom the Queen knighted after the successful campaign. In 1998 it dispatched an aircraft carrier back to the Persian Gulf to show its solidarity with the American and UN efforts to force Saddam Hussein to open his weapons facilities to international inspectors.

No sooner were the warriors home than the government began a steady reduction. From 1990 to 98, it cut the army from 156,000 to 116,000, the navy and marines from 63,000 to 55,000, and the RAF from 89,000 to 75,000. Infantry battalions sank from 55 to 40 and front-line tanks from 699 to 304. The British Army of the Rhine was halved. The navy retains its three small (a fourth the size of America's larger ones) but expensive aircraft carriers and four ballistic-missile submarines (especially the Tridents). But its fleet of 28 attack-submarines was cut to 12, and its 48 frigates and destroyers to 35. The RAF lost nine of its 30 front-line combat squadrons; its total front-line fighters and bombers sank from 630 to 500, some of which are flown by women. The draw-down continues. By 1999 total forces had declined to 210,000.

Defense spending was cut by a fifth from 1990 to 1999, to 3% of GDP, the lowest since the mid-1930s. Critics charge that such a slimmed-down force would never be able to respond to another crisis as big as the invasion of Kuwait in 1990, especially since the UK has increasingly assumed peacekeeping responsibilities. It deployed several thousand troops to Bosnia in a peacekeeping role. It also sent 35 combat aircraft, eight ships and 6,600 troops to participate in the air war over Yugoslavia in 1999.

The ruling *Labour* party produced a long overdue Strategic Defence Review published in 1998. It emphasized mobility, flexibility, sustainability, interoperability, and rapid reaction. It called for a nimble British military capable of going quickly "to the crisis, rather than have the crisis come to us." To back this up, the navy will receive two new full-sized aircraft carriers (the first in 30 years). The army will get an air cavalry brigade, complete with American Apache attack helicopters and paratroop regiments. The air force will acquire giant transport aircraft and sophisticated air-to-ground surveillance systems. The *Labour* government shows an increased interest in a European defense capability that could, when necessary, operate without the U.S. It wants more competitive European defense production. To that end, British Aerospace and DaimlerChrysler Aerospace decided to merge.

ECONOMY

Britain for almost two centuries has been a highly industrialized and developed nation. It led the Industrial Revolution in the 18th and 19th centuries but after World War II it enjoyed less efficiency than some of its newer rivals. Only a fourth of the present gross domestic product now comes from manufacturing, while service industries provide the rest. Although agriculture employs less than 3% of the working population, it produces more than half of the country's food requirements. Two-thirds of Britain's agricultural land is used for grazing; the main field crops are wheat, barley, oats, potatoes and sugar beets.

The United Kingdom

The 600–foot long boring machine which led others in clawing through 7.5 million cubic meters of chalk–marl one mile beneath the sea which divides Britain and France.

Because of the extraction of oil and natural gas from the North Sea, Britain became self–sufficient in these sources of energy in the 1980s. It became the 10th largest oil producer in the world. It is the biggest coal producer in Western Europe. At the present rate of extraction, Britain's coal supplies could last for another 300 years. Nuclear power provides 13% of Britain's electricity.

Economic Changes Since the 1970s

Economically, Britain found itself in a paradoxical position; during the 1970s it achieved economic growth and greater prosperity in absolute terms, that is, when compared to its own past performance. At the same time, it experienced a much lower rate of growth than most other developed industrialized nations. Faced with highly effective foreign competition, especially after entering the EU in 1973, Britain bought more goods abroad than it sold, and it lived beyond its means. Pay rose faster than productivity. This led to chronic balance of payments problems and a plummeting of the value of the British pound. Few British companies were aggressive enough to take advantage of the lower cost of British exports to outselling their competitors abroad.

To fierce competition must be added important world economic developments in the 1970s. The dramatic rise in the world price of oil beginning in 1973 set off a world recession which made it harder for foreigners to pay for imports from Britain. It cheered when it discovered that it had large reserves of oil in the North Sea. However, an unpleasant by–product of Britain's oil wealth was that it pushed up the value of the British pound and made it even harder for British business to sell goods abroad. The cumulative result of this series of economic shocks was that many British businesses, especially in such traditional "smokestack" sectors as steel, shipbuilding and textiles, were either badly shaken or destroyed. Long–term structural unemployment resulted.

The decline in the traditional economic production sectors occurred particularly in the outlying areas of Britain, where such industries had been disproportionately concentrated. Other areas, such as the southeast, which had a more vibrant service industry and newer, high–technology industries, suffered relatively less. This merely exacerbated regional frictions. The decline in the old–style manufacturing industries and mining also meant a decline in the blue–collar working class which worked in them. The changes were dramatic: in 1970 Britain had eight million people employed in manufacturing and 11.5 million in services; by 1983 the corresponding figures were 5.5 million and 13 million. Even these figures conceal a general move within the existing manufacturing and mining sectors of employees from the shopfloor to offices.

At the same time, most manual work-

The United Kingdom

ers shared in the general growth of affluence. This was partly due to the primary political focus since 1945 on income redistribution, rather than on high production and profit. One can see the difference: in 1949 the top 10% in terms of income received a third of the nation's productive wealth, but by 1976 this had fallen to only one fourth. Wealth, on the other hand, remained very concentrated, with the richest fifth possessing three–fourths of all personal wealth, principally inherited.

Decline in Economic Performance

Economic and social shifts in Britain helped to bring important changes in some fundamental assumptions. From 1945 to 1970, it had generally been assumed (and was broadly the case) that despite temporary ups and downs, the economy would always continue to improve, that inflation was unimportant, that full employment was normal and that if the economy got a little out of kilter, it could be put back on course by reducing or raising demand through taxes and public spending (classic economic methods of the late British economist, John Maynard Keynes). It was therefore widely accepted that governments should regulate the economy in order to maintain employment while expanding the welfare state out of ever–increasing national prosperity. By 1975 state spending amounted to more than 60% of national income.

The Keynsian assumptions, which more or less enjoyed an acceptance by both major parties, were torn asunder in the 1970s. At the beginning of the decade inflation began to rise, reaching the stratospheric level of 25% annually in the mid–1970s and 22% in 1980. Unemployment began to rise steadily, and the old cure did not seem to work any more.

As economic growth slowed to a standstill, governments were faced with an unpleasant dilemma: demand for welfare services continued to grow while the national income to pay for them did not. British economic discussions began to be preoccupied with "managing decline." The nationalized industries (most of which had passed to public control in the immediate postwar years) were performing poorly and were becoming an increasing drain on the nation's productivity, thereby discrediting the very idea of public ownership. Everywhere people began talking about the "English disease."

The Thatcher Revolution

Margaret Thatcher brought dramatic economic changes during her prime ministership from 1979 to 1990. Neither the *Tory* government of John Major nor Tony Blair's *Labour* government, which took office in 1997, moved to undo her reforms in any fundamental way. She denationalized more than a third of Britain's nationalized industries, including Rolls–Royce, British Airways and the British Gas Corporation. The sale of these brought more than $40 billion into the state treasury, eliminated the need for taxpayers to subsidize them, and reaped handsome annual tax revenues. In 1987 the government began selling shares of British Petroleum, even though the stock market crash of October had reduced the price it could get for such shares. In 1988 plans were announced to privatize the electric industry in England and Wales. British Telecom was sold, and in 1996 its merger with the American MCI company was made public. Thatcher's large–scale privatization program included two dozen major companies. Nevertheless, state spending still accounts for almost 40% of GDP, roughly the same percentage as when she took office.

Thatcher had argued that the state was overspending, and the shortfalls were being covered by public borrowing and expanding the money supply, rather than by taxes. These expedients stimulated inflation and absorbed the capital which was desperately needed to finance industrial innovation. The cure, she argued, was to restrict the money supply and cut public expenditures, which would both reduce inflation and free investment capital. To create economic incentives, income taxes should be cut. Finally, trade union power had to be curbed.

Her pride and her optimism were borne out by the facts: Since the country began pulling out of recession in 1981, productivity increased at an annual rate of 3.5%. The economy grew at an annual rate of 3%. Inflation was down from a high of 24.2% to 3.3% in 1995. Taxes had been reduced slightly, and the average voter's real pre–tax income had increased by 25% since 1979. From 1971 to 1994 real disposable income grew by almost 50%, and spending on social benefits increased by 168%. Britons live more prosperous lives. Nevertheless, it is the only EU country in which working hours have increased, to 43.4 hours.

Unemployment was higher than the 4.3% when she took office. Nevertheless, a million new jobs had been created under her rule, in part because of incentives to small enterprises. Also, the jobs of those who were employed seemed far less threatened than in the early 1980s. Interest rates were falling, and the pound was much stronger. Its stock market was booming, and the UK had again become a leading creditor nation. Public borrowing had fallen to 1% of national income. Most important, she had restored morale and seemed to have ended decades of relative economic decline.

After her 1987 victory, London's *Sunday Times* pronounced that Thatcher has brought about Britain's "biggest transformation since the Industrial Revolution." Indeed, her economic performance has profoundly changed her country. She has created what she calls a "property–owning democracy," in which "every earner shall be an owner." Two–thirds of Britons now own their homes, compared to 50% in 1979, and car ownership has risen from 54% to 66%. In 1979 four times as many Britons belonged to trade unions as owned shares in the stock market. But by 1989 the number of stock–holders had tripled from 7% to 21%. As a result of a fall in union membership by one–fourth to nine million, the number of union members and stock–holders are now equal.

Thatcher enormously reduced the power of the once–mighty labor unions, which had been able to topple the governments of her two predecessors. She introduced laws which limit unions' legal immunities. They limit picketing rights, ban secondary picketing and political strikes, make national unions financially responsible for the actions of their members, and require unions to have a secret balloting of members before declaring a strike. She rooted out one of the main causes of the "English disease" by taking on the bosses of the most powerful unions and crushing them: the steel workers in 1980, the coal miners in 1985 and the teachers in 1986. By 1987 strikes were at a 50–year low; workdays lost to union disputes declined from 29.5 million in 1979 to 1.9 million in 1986.

The reduction in the number and length of strikes was, in part, due to workers' and employees' fear of losing their jobs and to their realization that real earnings for those with work has risen almost 35% between 1980 and 1987. There has also been a change of attitudes: many workers associate unions with strikes and therefore have increasingly turned their backs on the unions, whose membership has continued to decline. An important result for the overall economy is that the unions are no longer able to block the introduction of state–of–the–art technology in order to protect jobs. Thus, while from 1974–80 output per worker in British manufacturing did not increase at all, from 1981–7 it grew by 40%. So powerful had the unions been that many people wondered: "Who governs?" After she was finished, no one would suspect that it was the union bosses.

More and more workers became homeowners (43% by 1983 and one-third of even unskilled laborers by 1988) thanks in part to Margaret Thatcher's policy of selling many state–owned council houses to

The United Kingdom

their occupants. By the time her party finally left power in 1997, 68% of all households own their own homes. It is not surprising that the percentage of Britons who consider themselves to belong to the middle class increased from 30% of the population in 1979 to roughly 50% in 1987. Their lifestyles became more and more like those of the middle class; this was given added impetus by the education changes in the 1970s which largely did away with the several schooling tracks and brought most British schoolchildren together in one school. The massive occupational shifts and break–down in elite–structure in the educational system fostered increasing social mobility. It is no wonder that persons who lived in several classes in their own lifetime ceased to use class as a major political reference point. It is quite simply no longer accurate to speak of "two Britains," one a deprived working class and the other a traditional upper class.

Thatcher created a more prosperous and productive Britain. But her chief economic legacy was one of the mind. The pursuit of comfort and wealth had become marks of bad form. But she made prosperity an acceptable goal and free–market capitalism morally defensible. Tony Blair's *Labour Party* not only embraces both, but he won the 1997 elections by promising that his government could manage Thatcher's economy even more competently. By the 1990s anybody working in Britain's offices and factories can see that they are much better and more productively run than was the case two decades earlier. Industrial relations have improved dramatically.

Labor Unions

Public sympathy and enthusiasm for labor unions gradually eroded in the 1970s and early 1980s. In order to gain wage restraint from the powerful unions, *Labour* governments made so many concessions to them that many persons began to blame the unions for high prices and many of the economic problems. Their revulsion at the excessive "unelected power" which union bosses wielded boiled to the surface in the 1978–9 "winter of discontent," when coal and transportation strikes threatened to paralyze the entire nation.

Both the economic recession and the *Conservatives'* broadside attacks against the *Labour Party* in general and the unions in particular greatly weakened the latter. Between 1979 and 1992 their membership dropped from 12 to 8 million. In 1979 more than half the workforce was unionized; in the late–1990s less than a third is. By election time in 1983, almost three-fourths of all Britons favored stricter laws to regulate unions; an astonishing three-fifths of all trade unionists also favored legal curbs on union power. Union popularity declined further as the result of a protracted coal miners' strike in 1984–5. Union leader Arthur Scargill fanned the flames of anti–unionism with public pledges to bring down Thatcher's government. He failed, and her ability to break trade union power is her most lasting legacy.

In the 1990s strikes are at their lowest level in more than a half century. In 1979, 29.5 man–days were lost to strikes; in 1995 that figure had fallen to 4.15. One expert noted: "It's much more risky to strike now. If you don't do it right according to the law, you end up in court." The 1.9 million lost workdays were the lowest figure since 1963, a fourth of the average in the 1980s and six times lower than the average in the 1970s. Unions affiliated with the TUC lost a third of their members after the *Tories* came to power in 1979. Even within the *Labour Party* the unions' influence has been drastically reduced, though not eliminated, thanks to the efforts of Prime Minister Tony Blair.

By the late–1990s only 18% of American workers belong to unions, compared with a third in the UK. The gap between the working and middle classes has also been narrowed by the changing composition of the labor unions. The increase in the number of civil service employees, the growth of the service sector within the economy, and the rise of computer–related and other high–technology industries in the south of England and especially around London and Cambridge prompted the growth of so–called "white collar unionism." That is, union members were no longer exclusively manual workers in factories and mines, but they could be teachers, engineers in a nationalized industry, secretaries in Whitehall, etc.

With rising inflation and talk of "paring down the public sector," these white-collar unions even became quite militant in pressing their demands. Thus, Britain began to experience a different breed of striker, from nurses and hospital personnel to civil servants. This militancy among the white collar employees has helped even more to bridge the social gap between workers and employees and to break down class divisions.

Of course, there are still workers concentrated in large manufacturing or mining industries living in rented council housing in working class sections and remaining in a largely isolated social environment. They confront employers and managers whose political attitudes are also traditional and are diametrically opposed to those of their workers. These groups are far more likely to retain a strong loyalty either to the *Labour Party* or the *Conservative Party* and a strong class–consciousness. However, these kinds of workers and managers are becoming a diminishing minority in Britain's more service–oriented economy. Union members in the service sectors work in an environment which bring them into contact with all other classes, a factor which reduces, rather than sharpens class consciousness. As a consequence, their voting behavior is far less class–bound. They can be attracted to parties which portray a new, non–class image and seem capable of overcoming the old social divides.

Britain and Europe

In 1973 the UK entered the EU, a move which has had a dramatic impact on its economy. The EU now buys 43% of British exports, compared to 31% in 1972. The high prices for food, fixed by the EU's common agricultural policy, have been a boon for British farmers. Still, many British remain critical of their country's entry into the EU.

In practice, British governments have tended to put British interests ahead of European interests. They have been cool on a common EU energy policy, a directly elected European Parliament and European Monetary Union (EMU). Britain has shown little interest in expanding European integration, and Thatcher tried hard to reduce the British contribution to the EU budget. In 1989–90 she remained suspicious of "deepening" EU unity on the grounds that it would undermine national sovereignty and that it is no time to create new bureaucracies and weaken national parliaments just when Eastern European nations are digging themselves out from underneath their bureaucracies and breathing new life into their legislatures. Not all British, even all *Tories*, agreed with her foot–dragging, and this contributed to her fall.

At the historic 1991 summit in Maastricht, Britain agreed to greater economic and political union on the condition that the UK could "opt out" of an eventual single European currency, which it chose to do when the Euro was introduced in 11 EU countries in 1999. It also rejected moves to make an EU "social policy" mandatory for all members. Despite much resistance from many *Tories*, Parliament finally accepted the treaty in 1993.

The *Labour* government is more supportive of British membership in a more united Europe although Prime Minister Blair promises to put British interests first. Thanks to the economic accomplishments of his predecessor, the UK does not have to worry about meeting the criteria for EMU. Its budget deficit in 1999 was .4% of GDP, and overall public debt stood at 54% of GDP. One of Blair's first acts as

INDEPENDENT

SATURDAY 3 MAY 1997

WEATHER: Sunny and warm

Everything has changed

THE TIMES

FRIDAY MAY 2 1997

KIDS GO FREE Tickets to Warwick Castle PAGE 32

EMBRACE: HEADING FOR GLORY Caitlin Moran PAGE 38

LYNNE TRUSS: INQUEST ON ENGLAND How good are the World Cup hopefuls? PAGE 50

TOMORROW THE INSIDE STORY OF MILLBANK by Sidney Blumenthal

Landslide forecast for Labour

Tories facing worst defeat this century, say TV exit polls

By PHILIP WEBSTER, POLITICAL EDITOR

Inside today's five-section Guardian with the pocket-sized listings magazine

Labour landslide
15 pages of news, comment, analysis and full results

Kathy Acker meets the Spice Girls
Weekend exclusive

Plus: Jobs&

70p
Saturday May 3 1997
Published in London and Manchester

The Guardian
NEWSPAPER OF THE YEAR   WEEKEND

The history man

he fight over:

Triumphant

prime minister was to transfer the power to set interest rates from the Chancellor of Exchequer (Gordon Brown) to an unelected panel of the Bank of England. Greater independence for central banks is one of the EU's prerequisites for participation in the common currency. EMU remains unpopular in the UK.

The British and French finally agreed to construct a twin–bore, 32–mile channel tunnel (dubbed "Chunnel") through which an auto–rail link between the two countries passes. Road vehicles are loaded on trains at terminals on both sides of the Channel and whisked at a speed of 100 miles per hour from one side to the other. The Channel became what Napoleon had described as "a ditch that will be leaped whenever one has the boldness to try." The two nations' leaders shared not only a bold vision of the future. This multi–billion dollar project created many jobs and made a sizable dent in the unemployment problems which plague both countries. In 1990 the burrowing French and British crews linked up under the Channel, and the Chunnel opened in 1994.

In November 1996 a dangerous fire broke out on a truck–carrying rail car, raising serious questions about the safety of the system. Miraculously no one perished in the inferno, but 800 yards of tunnel were ruined, and one of the system's two transport tubes had to be closed for more than a half year. Traffic in the other tube continued. Despite the accident, the Chunnel is extremely popular, carrying half a million passengers and nearly a quarter of a million tons of freight each month. It has captured 45% of the lucrative cross–channel market. Nevertheless, it is mired in serious financial difficulties, having cost twice as much to build as projected. Repayment of the $13.5 billion debt had to be suspended while its finances were restructured.

The United Kingdom has been heavily involved in overseas trade for many centuries, and the importance of that trade continues to grow. In the last 50 years, the export of goods and services has moved from being one–fifth of the gross domestic product to one–third. Of these exports, 43% go to the EU, 17% to the rest of Europe and 11% to North America.

After the U.S., Britain is the world's largest investor abroad. In 1998 it was actually the largest because of British Petroleum's (BP) purchase of Amoco for $61 billion. Many well–known "American" brands are now British: Brooks Brothers belongs to Marks and Spencer, and Burger King and Pillsbury are owned by Diageo. In 1995 it surpassed Japan to become the largest source of foreign direct investment in the U.S. By 1999 the UK directs 30% of its direct investment to America, while the U.S. sends a fifth of its foreign direct investment to Britain. At the turn of the century only the U.S. and China attract more money from foreigners than does Britain.

The City of London (a small area within greater metropolitan London) is of immense significance in international finance. It has the world's largest insurance market, the lengthiest listing of overseas securities, the highest proportion of the Eurodollar market, and the biggest foreign exchange market. In 1986 a "big bang" occurred in the London financial world: the financial markets were largely deregulated, and foreign companies were permitted to trade in British financial markets for the first time. The overall effect has been to make London the world's most important financial center. Each day, 600,000 people go to work in 580 banks. Big American banks have their continental headquarters there, and London's traders have grown to control 30% of global foreign exchange trading. In 1998 the London Stock Exchange and the Deutsche Börse announced an alliance that is open to other European stock exchanges as well. Britain's financial institutions are fully competent in dealing with the Euro, even though its political leaders are not yet ready for it.

Prime Minister Blair inherited an economy that no one calls "diseased" any more. Its growth rate of 3.2% in 1997 makes it (along with the U.S.) one of the two fast–growing industrial economies in the world. At 6.3% in 1999, unemployment is the lowest of any major western European country and is about two–thirds the EU average. Inflation is a stable 2.1%. Roughly 40% of all foreign direct investment flowing into the 15 EU nations goes to the UK. In part, this is due to the fact that Britain's labor costs (about $14 per hour in 1997) are the lowest of any major industrialized country. But its productivity is a problem, lagging 37% behind that of the U.S. in 1998, and 25% behind that of Germany and France. The Blair government introduced the country's first minimum wage law. But the current economic success is also due to less cumbersome business regulations, cost effectiveness, and a flexible labor market. Privatization is also well advanced although the "new" *Labour* government prefers to search for of a "third way," whereby private money is brought into the service, but outright privatization is avoided.

Britain is the fifth most popular tourist destination in the world, attracting 25 million foreign visitors annually. The 125,000 mostly small tourist businesses employ 1.75 million people, more than agriculture, food production, coal mining, steel, car and aircraft manufacturing, and textiles combined. In the 1990s it was responsible for creating a sixth of the new jobs.

CULTURE

The impact and pervasiveness of British culture on the rest of the world has been out of all proportion to the size and population of the United Kingdom. While those who participated in the Beatlemania of the 1960s might disagree, two British gifts to world culture stand out as most important. First, the achievement of English writers in producing a magnificent body of literature has influenced the way men think around the world. And within English literature, certainly the world of Shakespeare and the King James Bible have been most important.

Second, the development of a constitutional, parliamentary democracy set an example to all the world of how men and

Feeding the pigeons, Trafalgar Square, London

The United Kingdom

women may live in freedom and guide their own destinies, and how compromise and civility rather than coercion are the best ways to pull together the social fabric. In a world in which the majority of human beings do not enjoy political or individual freedoms and other countries that attempt democracy are unable to achieve stability, the United Kingdom stands a worthy example of a free society living under laws.

The widespread knowledge of English as a first or second language throughout the world speaks for itself, be it the Americanized or British version. It has become the language of scientific expression almost worldwide. English is not spoken throughout England, Wales, Scotland and Ireland in an identical fashion. Local expressions and local pronunciations vary widely. The urbanized lower classes of London traditionally speak "Cockney" English which the average American can seldom understand. Language has traditionally been a key to identifying the social class of a British person. The reason lies partly in the educational system.

Education and Religion in Britain

The traditional school system had been tracked in such a way that a child's educational program was more or less fixed at age eleven. After the crucial "eleven–plus exam," some children went into trade or commercial schools. Others went into the more elite, state–supported grammar schools or the independent, privately endowed "public schools" (the most prestigious being Eton, Harrow and Winchester). "Public Schools" were especially geared to preparing pupils for the few seats in universities, especially at Oxford and Cambridge, which held the keys to success in politics, industry and scholarship. In a 1992 study of the top 100 persons in Britain's elite, the *Economist* found that two–thirds had attended public schools, and more than half had studied at Oxford and Cambridge.

Critics had long charged that this system actually hardened and perpetuated class lines in British society and that an American–styled comprehensive school, in which all pupils learn under one roof, would help iron out class differences. However, *Conservatives* charged that the *Labour* government's 1976 reform actually lowered educational standards and were even less fair, since state scholarships to the coveted private schools were eliminated.

Some counties controlled by the *Conservative Party* dragged their feet by continually submitting plans which they knew would be unacceptable, thereby holding out until *Labour* lost power in 1979. Despite the development of comprehensive schools, 7% of all pupils still attend the fee–paying "public schools." Some state schools, educating about 4% of the children, have the right to exclude pupils who do not meet up to their minimal standards.

About a third of university–age Britons (up from one–eighth in 1980) study in one of the 90 universities or polytechnic schools. This dramatic increase in enrollment broke the budget and required that students contribute to the cost of their education. Many of these students were distressed by the *Labour* government's decision to end tuition–free higher education and to levy a £1,000 (ca. $1,600) yearly tuition charge. Those from lower–income families pay less, and the lowest 30% pay nothing. This is on top of the roughly $2,600 room and board costs, much of it borrowed or obtained through grants, including from local governments. Some enterprising British universities attract large numbers of foreign students and charge them American–level tuition.

The educational system remains a target of criticism. Critics argue that spending for it was cut by 10% in real terms under Thatcher. Even her Minister for Information Technology, Geoffrey Pattie, had complained that "schools are turning out dangerously high quotas of illiterate, delinquent unemployables."

In 1993 the government introduced an Education Bill to parliament which took school reform another step forward. But after haphazard and underfunded reforms under Thatcher and Major, British schools still reflect the social stratification of the country. A majority of pupils leave full–time education or training at age 16, as John Major had done in 1959. As a result, less than half the work force is classified as skilled, compared with 85% in Germany and 75% in France. Tony Blair's campaign appeals in 1997 for higher academic standards and lower class sizes fell on sympathetic ears. The feeling is widespread that British schools are not fully prepared for the challenges of the 21st century.

Religion

Polls in 1990 revealed that 71% of Britons believed in God (77% in 1965), 44% in life after death, and 30% in the devil. Although the Anglican Church of England (in Scotland the Presbyterian Church of Scotland) is the official state religion, claiming up to 30 million members on paper, only a fifth of religiously active Britons belong. Church attendance has fallen dramatically in the Church of England. In 1960, 2.1 million attended on Easter Sunday, a figure that had fallen to 1.3 million by 1994. It is estimated that it lost about 1,000 church–goers every week during the 1990s.

Most worshipers are drawn to religions that are better able to satisfy the thirst for spirituality: immigrant religions (mainly Islam, Sikhism and Hinduism), cults, Pentecostal or charismatic Christian churches, or new age, non–mainstream faiths. In an attempt to lure worshipers back to the Church of England, its General Synod voted in 1992 to ordain women, a decision which had to be approved by parliament and the Queen in 1993. In protest, traditionalist Anglicans threaten to split away from the Church, and some may migrate to Catholicism.

The Media

Britain has large London–based newspapers, such as the high–quality *Guardian*, *The Times* and the *Financial Times*, as well as the more popular *News of the World*, *Daily Mirror* and *Sun*. Two–thirds of the papers sold are conservative; in order of circulation, they are the: *Sun*, (which nevertheless endorsed *Labour's* Tony Blair in 1997), *Daily Mail, Daily Express, Daily Telegraph, Daily Star,* and *Times*. Fewer than 10% are non–aligned: *Today, Independent,* and *Financial Times*. Only a fourth are left–leaning, chiefly the *Daily Mirror*, and the *Guardian*. The news wire service, with particularly good international coverage, *Reuters*, is renowned for its meticulous accuracy and avoidance of editorialization. In spite of the fact that ownership of these London dailies is concentrated in a few hands, they keep a sharp eye on Downing Street, Westminster and Whitehall. Bringing the important political news to all corners of the country, they do not stifle the lively regional press. They are also reinforced by widely–read weekly news magazines, such as *The Economist* and *The Observer*.

The written media is supplemented by radio and television, which are controlled by two public bodies, the British Broadcasting Corporation (BBC), whose directors are nominated by the government, and the Independent Broadcasting Authority (IBA), which permits private advertising. Both are expected to remain politically impartial (in stark contrast with commercial American television), and both vigorously resist being used by the government in power. For instance, when the American TV film *The Day After*, portraying the effects of a nuclear war was shown at the end of 1983, the Minister of Defense, Michael Heseltine, demanded the right of reply on BBC. His demand was refused. The BBC also rejected *Tory* charges that it had presented a biased and unprofessional picture of the American bombing raid on Libya in April 1986, an attack made possible by British permission to use FB–111 aircraft stationed in Britain.

The United Kingdom

The new Prime Minister: *Labour Party* leader Tony Blair with his wife, Cherie, and children, from left to right, 9–year–old Kathryn, 11–year–old Nicky, and 13–year–old Ewan, outside his local polling station in Trimdon, northeast England, Thursday, May 1, 1997, after casting their votes in Britain's national election.
AP/Worldwide Photo

Since multi–channel TV came to Britain in 1990, a flood of American shows began to appear on screens. BBC struggles against losing its audience. It launched a 24–hour news service, News 24, to compete against Sky News and CNN. Its best defense is to continue producing its high–quality programs, which Americans like to watch on public television.

Ethnic Changes in Britain
A basic change in British society is ethnic—it had for 900 years experienced almost no immigration, except from Ireland. Now it is no longer a racially homogeneous society. As a consequence of decolonization, Asians and blacks poured into Britain from India, Pakistan, Africa and the Caribbean. The population is 7% non–white (half of them Asians of Indian, Pakistani, and Bangladeshi descent), a percentage that is likely to grow because of the declining birth rate of white Britons. By 1992 half of all West Indian babies in the UK were born out of wedlock (compared with 29% of whites), and two of five marriages in Britain ended in divorce. Since more than two–thirds of single parents are on welfare, and a child raised by only one parent is five times as likely to be poor, many more non–whites seem destined to poverty.

Immigration has been reduced. The 1981 British Nationality Act restricted it, and the inflow was reduced to a trickle. The number of successful applicants for British citizenship in 1993 was the lowest in more than a decade. Britain is now faced with the extremely difficult problem of integrating large groups of non–white minorities, who tend to be concentrated in the decaying inner cities, even though there is less residential segregation by race in Britain than in the U.S. Such concentration gives the impression that the minority presence in the UK is far greater than it actually is. A fifth of London's population belongs to an ethnic minority, and that figure will rise to a third by the year 2010. They often speak little or no English, worship religions which are quite unfa-

The United Kingdom

miliar to most British, dress or groom themselves in very different fashion from the rest of the population.

Ethnic minorities suffer the most from any economic downturn, especially unemployment. In 1998 the jobless rate for blacks was around 22%, compared with under 7% for whites. The comparable figures in the U.S. were 11% and 5%. It is even higher among Pakistani and Bangladeshis: 27%. British blacks have not penetrated the top levels of business, the professions, judiciary, or the cabinet, as the American black elite has. Only 1% of soldiers are minorities (compared with 27% black in the U.S.), 2% of the police (3.3% in London) and 5% of civil servants. This may change as a result of an increase in non–white enrollment at British universities; 12% of students are from ethnic minorities, double their representation in the overall population. In London 29% of nurses, 31% of doctors, and more than 20% of civil servants are already from ethnic minorities.

Britishers began to become uneasy about being swamped by immigrants. When in 1981 dramatic racial riots occurred in such non–white ghettos as Brixton and Southall in London and Toxeth in Liverpool, they began to fear for their own protection. These violent outbreaks were the result of youth unemployment and disillusionment, poor living conditions, racial discrimination and inefficient police practices. The unarmed "Bobbies," who always seemed to symbolize British tact and tolerance, were severely criticized for alleged racism, arrogance and brutality. They still are regarded with distrust and suspicion in many non–white areas. In an effort to improve their public image, the London Metropolitan Police has recruited more black policemen.

The riots helped raise the awareness of the extent to which racial problems fester in a society in which many citizens have not yet accepted the *fact* of a multi–racial Britain. There is no consensus among Britons about race relations. Laws aiming to improve race relations were passed in 1965, 1968 and 1975, mainly modeled on American legislation, except that the provisions for judicial enforcement are much weaker. Also there is no official affirmative action. The government–sponsored Commission on Racial Equality combats discrimination, but its tools are mainly investigative and conciliatory, rather than prosecutive.

Young white gangs of "skinheads" and the "punk–rock" and "heavy metal" set derive morbid amusement from "Paki-bashing." Those whites who want to exploit the rising racial tensions, such as the neo–Nazi *British National Party*, seldom find favor with the voters. But in 1993, promising "rights for whites," it won a municipal council seat in London's East End.

In some ways Britain is a more integrated society than is the U.S. There is more dating and intermarriage between white and black men and women. According to a 1997 survey, half of Afro–Caribbean men born in Britain and a third of women born in the UK have a white partner. This is lower among British–born Indians, but the figures still show progress: 20% for men and 10% for women. In the U.S. only 4% of black men and 2% of black women have a white spouse. Tolerance for inter–racial marriage is strong: 74% respondents said in a 1997 poll that they would not object to one of their close relatives marrying a black, and 70% said the same about an Asian. Bangladeshis, Pakistanis and Indians remain more to themselves, though; fewer than 5% live with whites. Perhaps the most visibly integrated group in Britain was the female rock group Spice, five sassy young ladies exuding "girl–power."

A combination of tough anti–immigration policies, unusually detailed laws against racial discrimination, and the fact that legal immigrants have always been treated not as migrant workers but as permanent settlers, with automatic rights to vote, to run for office, and to claim social security benefits, has prevented the spread of kind of anti–immigrant sentiment and support for racist parties seen on the continent in the 1990s. Nevertheless, the number of racially motivated attacks doubled in Britain between 1989 and 1995.

The immigration issue, so explosive in the 1960s and 1970s, has ceased to have any great significance at election time. Nevertheless, white fears worked politically more in favor of the tough–minded *Conservatives* than of the *Labourites*. On the other hand, *Labour*, which has always presented itself as the party of the underdog, receives the overwhelming majority of non–white votes. In the 1987 election, 27 non–whites ran for office, and for the first time since 1922, non–whites took seats in the House of Commons. In 1992 six non-whites were elected to parliament, including one *Tory*, and in 1997 there were nine. In 1993 there were more than 100 non–white local councilors.

Prior *Tory* attempts to bid for black votes sometimes backfired. For instance, in 1983 the largest of many ethnic minority newspapers, the *Caribbean Times,* refused to print a *Tory* advertisement displaying a neatly dressed black and the slogan, "Labour says he's black, the Conservatives say he's British," on the grounds that it was "insulting, obnoxious and immoral." In fact, 75% of blacks in the UK are British citizens, and most of the rest are Commonwealth citizens who can vote in Britain.

It has been difficult to integrate blacks and Asians into the political process, except in direct defense of their own interests. But there has been progress. Non–whites in the UK have visible positive role models in sports, the arts, business and the professions. There are grounds for optimism that the lauded English tolerance and gradualism will lead more British to accept the immigrants and their children as non–white Britons. It is symbolic that in 1998 a statue of Martin Luther King was placed in the last remaining niche above the Great West Door of Westminster Abbey.

FUTURE

Tony Blair's *Labour* victory in 1997 insures stable government in Britain for at least five years. It was a personal triumph for the prime minister, who had remolded his party into *New Labour*.

During 18 years of *Tory* rule, power was increasingly centralized in the cabinet's hands in London, and the system's already weak institutional checks and balances withered. In reaction, a lively discussion on constitutional change is taking place. Will Hutton, whose book, *The State We're In,* was a bestseller for most of 1995, wrote that "once the courtesies of a 19th–century debating chamber have been observed, the government can make laws almost at will ... Monarchical power has passed in effect to the majority party in the House of Commons." Another bestseller, *Ruling Britannia: The Failure and Future of British Democracy*, offered a similar critique. *Charter 88,* an organization advocating broad structural changes in British government, grew by 1,000 supporters a month.

Polls in 1995 revealed that half the adult population thought the political system is out of date; 79% agreed that a written constitution and a bill of rights to protect individual liberty are needed; 77% favored adopting a referendum system. It is small wonder that Tony Blair wrote a half year before becoming prime minister that "changing the way we govern, and not just changing our government, is no longer an optional extra for Britain. . . . The challenge facing us . . . is to take a working constitution, respect its strengths, and adapt it to modern demands for clean and effective government while at the same time providing a greater democratic role for the people at large." The prospect for significant constitutional change came with the landslide *Labour* victory in May 1997.

The new prime minister wasted no time

The United Kingdom

in announcing an ambitious legislative program, including constitutional reform. With its huge majority in the House of Commons, most of the government's proposals are enacted. Devolution in Scotland and Wales was begun by referenda to establish parliaments there and culminated in elections to them in 1999. His government is working hard on a settlement in Northern Ireland, which will devolve power to that violence-stricken area as soon as the last snags are cleared away. Limited self-government has been introduced for London, and referenda will be used more often to allow British to express their desires between elections.

Something akin to an individual bill of rights will be introduced by incorporating into British law the European Convention for the Protection of Human Rights and Fundamental Freedoms (often referred to as "the European Human Rights Charter"). This convention includes such protections as rights for criminal defendants and freedom of speech, religion and assembly. It has applied to British citizens since the UK entered the EU in 1972, but it has not been enforceable in British courts. A freedom of information act and reform of the House of Lords by eliminating hereditary peers' right to a seat and a vote are to be studied.

The government changed the raucous "prime minister's question time" in the House of Commons by converting it into a more serious, once-a-week half-hour session in which more questions from opposition backbenchers are allowed. The leadership confrontations with the opposition leader, which tend to be the sharpest, most entertaining and sometimes most embarrassing interchanges for the prime minister, have not disappeared.

In addition to such constitutional changes, the Blair government quickly banned handguns and fox hunting and introduced Britain's first minimum wage law. It is preparing laws regulating campaign fund-raising, restructuring the overburdened National Health Service, and improving standards of education. Some of *Labour's* initiatives have created problems for the new government. Seeking answers to the question of how government could do more with less, its overall goal is to take a welfare state built for the Britain of the 1940s and reform it for the Britain of the 21st century. The rising costs of welfare are unsustainable, and the electorate finds them unjustifiable. Blair designed a welfare-to-work plan in an attempt to move young and long-term unemployed workers off the government rolls. This bold move ignited a noisy revolt within his own party.

His legislation to ban tobacco advertising created a storm of criticism when it was learned that an exemption had been made for Formula One auto racing after a Formula One chief had made an earlier contribution of £1 million to the *Labour Party*. Blair issued an extraordinary public apology for his handling of this controversy over campaign money. One of the key reasons for the *Labour Party's* victory in 1997 was Blair's pledge to avoid the repeated scandals that plagued the *Tories*. But his party is not immune from sleaze. Two of his top advisers, Peter Mandelson (Minister of Trade and Industry) and Geoffrey Robinson, had to resign because of a questionable loan. The fact that Blair's popularity (72% in late 1998) was not diminished by Mandelson's and another minister's (Nick Brown, Agriculture) admission to being homosexual says a lot about changing British and European attitudes toward homosexuality. In a 1998 poll 56% of British respondents said it was morally acceptable, and the EU has laws prohibiting discrimination against gays.

Britain remains Europe's healthiest large economy, but there are some economic storm clouds: growth is slowing, unemployment is inching upwards, and the strong pound and economic troubles in Asia have had their effect. Many Britons do not yet feel like they live in the new prosperous Britain, especially outside of London and the relatively prosperous enclaves in southern England. Nevertheless most of the doubt about Britain's future that surfaced in the bitter debates over joining Europe are gone.

Blair's honeymoon with the public has not yet ended, as polls in 1999 confirm: if elections were held, *Labour* would receive 35% of the votes, the *Conservatives* 29% and the *Liberal Democrats* 13%. There has been no collision between the rhetoric of campaigning and the reality of governing. He is not a confrontational politician and prefers to build coalitions across traditional class and political divides. He explained to his country at the end of 1997: "We can't do it all at once. Progress I promised and am delivering. Britain reborn in a day or even a parliamentary session—I never did promise that and could not deliver it." But he is doing quite well, and one could perhaps argue that he is the most successful democratic politician in the world.

Campaign brochure for Charlotte Atkins, April 1997

The Republic of Ireland

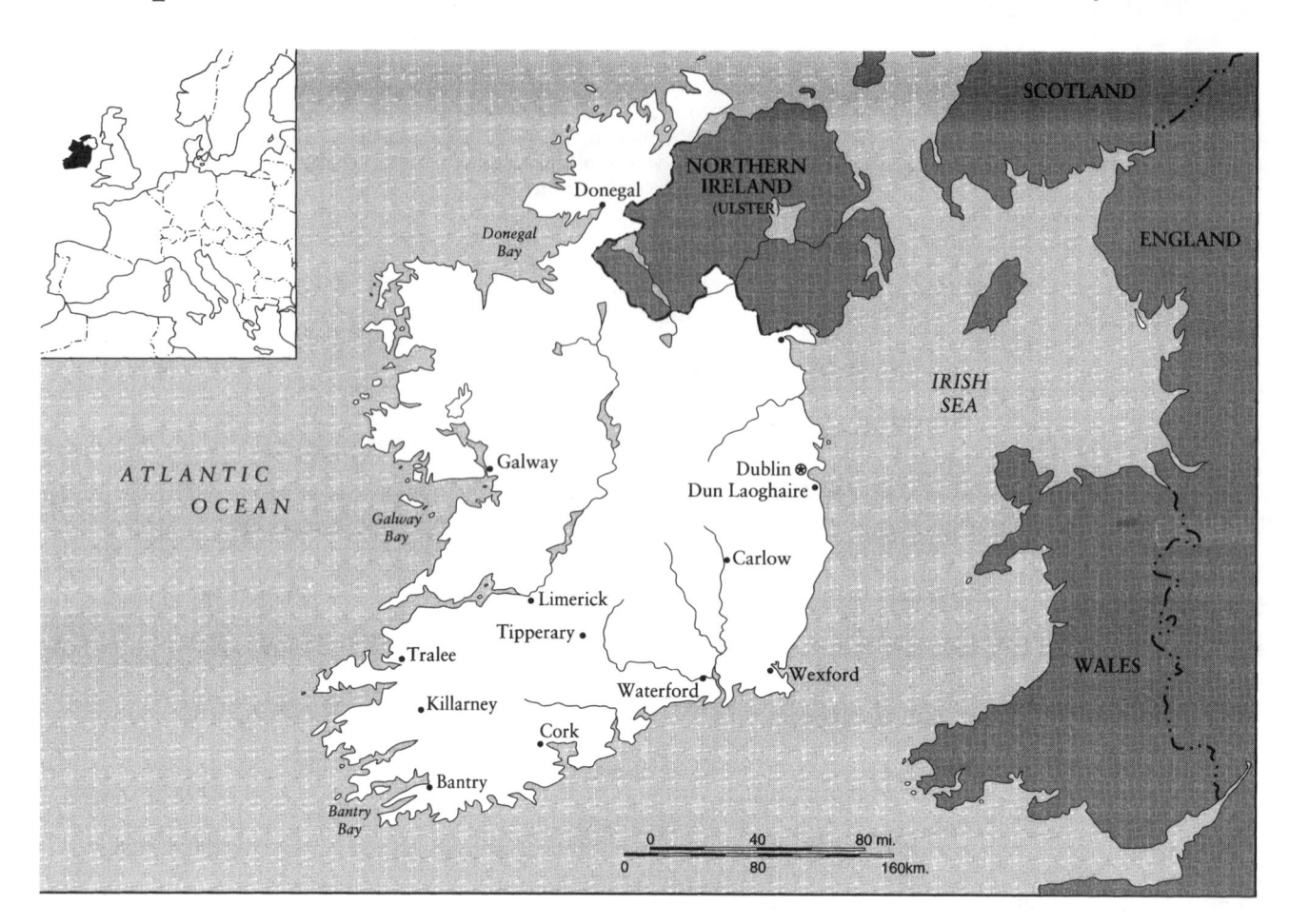

by Mark H. Mullin

Area: 27,136 sq. mi. (70,262 sq. km., slightly larger than West Virginia).
Population: 3.6 million (estimated).
Capital City: Dublin (Pop. 650,000, estimated).
Climate: Cool and damp (rarely above 65|SDF or below 40|SDF).
Neighboring Countries: Great Britain lies a short distance eastward across the Irish Sea.
Official Languages: Irish (Gaelic), English, which is the first language of 98% of the population.
Ethnic Background: Celtic (some Norman and Norsemen).
Principal Religion: Roman Catholic (93.1%). 2.8% are Church of Ireland, .4% Presbyterian, and 3.7 other faiths.
Main Exports: Foodstuffs, high–tech equipment, livestock, machinery, chemicals, clothing.
Main Imports: Machinery, petroleum, chemicals, cereals.
Currency: Irish punt.
Major Customers: EU 70% (including United Kingdom 27%), United States 10%, Germany 10%, France 9%.
Former Colonial Status: "Given" to England in 1155 by the Pope, turbulent English control until 1922; its own parliament, diminishing control until independence.
Independence Dates: December 6, 1921. (Dominion status); April 18, 1949, independent republic.
Chief of State: Mary McAleese, President (since October 1997)..
Head of Government: Bertie Ahern, *Taoiseach*, pronounced "Tea–such," or Prime Minister (since June 1997).
National Flag: Three vertical stripes of green, white and orange.

Green fields, white–washed thatched cottages, leprechauns and men sitting in front of a peat fire spinning tales that are part fact and part fiction are images of Ireland that the first–time tourist seeks. This scene is also found in St. Patrick's Day cards, framed in green. While the tourist may miss much of what is new in Ireland, both the green fields and the confusion of fact and fantasy are still there for him to find. And both are largely the result of Ireland's location—it lies at the spot where the warm air and water of the Gulf Stream confront their cold rivals of the northern latitudes. This produces a climate in which temperature variations are rare; it is an unusual day when the temperature is more than slightly warm or cold.

The confrontation of warm and cold produces air that is frequently moist—thus the lushness of the green, and skies that are always changing—gray and sad one minute, brilliant and joyful the next. If the sky is not constant, why should reality be constant? And, perhaps it is the soft, moist air that blurs fact and fantasy. George Bernard Shaw wrote of Ireland to an English friend, "You've no such colors in the sky, no such lines in the distance, no such sadness in the evenings. Oh the dreaming! The dreaming!"

If one may generalize about the people of a nation, the Irish people reflect their climate. There is a gentleness about the Irish, an essential sadness punctuated by flashes of sparkling wit. And there is a willingness to let the line between reality and dream be as indistinct as that between the distant mountains and the evening sky.

Ireland

If its location has shaped the green beauty of Ireland and the character of its people, its location has been more responsible for shaping its history. Ireland is not merely an island; it is an island off the coast of another island. While its contact with the continent has usually been indirect, its subjugation to England has been of paramount influence. Being one step removed from the mainland has kept continental armies, and the cultural influences that they brought, out of Ireland. Roman legions never tramped across its fields. Although Norsemen settled on the east coast and raided many other areas, Irish culture achieved a flowering of learning and artistic brilliance while the rest of Europe slipped into the Dark Ages.

As nation–states developed on the continent, Ireland was involved in European dynastic wars only when England had a stake in the contest. The last continental troops to be in Ireland made an unsuccessful attempt to export the French Revolution. Ireland even managed to be one of the few European countries to be neutral during World War II. As the English, century after century, negotiated and fought rivals on the continent, they did not want to have to worry about the island on their other side. The English always felt a domination of Ireland was essential to their security. The Irish Sea, after all, varies in width from 120 miles to only 11 miles, thus the fates of England and Ireland have been intertwined for the past 800 years.

Ireland is like a small bowl floating in the Atlantic. Its mountains ring the coastal region; they seldom reach more than 3000 feet (914 km.) into the sky. But the steepness with which they meet the sea gives them the appearance of considerable height. The center of the island is relatively flat, with the Shannon River flowing from north to south like a fine crack in the bottom of the bowl. West of the Shannon, peat bogs provide much of Ireland's fuel. East of the Shannon, the plains are rich grasslands, superb for cattle or horses. In fact, the Curragh, the finest stable and race track in the land, has 5000 acres of grass uninterrupted by either a tree or a fence. But even in the center of Ireland, one is never far removed from the sea, for the whole island is only 150 miles wide and 275 miles long.

Ireland is a beautiful and gentle land. Tragically, its history has not always been so.

HISTORY

The Early Period

The earliest remains of humans in Ireland date from about 7000 B.C. These hunters and food gatherers lived along the coasts and near the rivers. By 3000 B.C. Neolithic settlers had introduced agriculture and pottery. Their most spectacular accomplishments, elaborate Megalithic burial chambers, can still be seen today. At Newgrange one may enter the massive chamber by crawling through a tunnel 62 feet long. It is so constructed that only at the summer solstice does sunlight come down the tunnel and illuminate the interior chamber.

About 300 B.C. the Gaelic Celts used their knowledge of iron weapons to gain control of the island. Celtic Ireland was divided into some 150 local kingdoms under the loose control of the Kings of the Five Provinces. Although Meath later became part of Leinster, the four provinces of Ulster in the north, Leinster in the southeast, Munster in the southwest and Connacht in the west have retained fairly similar boundaries to this day.

Saint Patrick

One of the High Kings who ruled at the Hill of Tara from 380 to 405 A.D. was Niall, an ancestor of the O'Neills, an important family in Ulster until the 17th century. Niall's troops attacked both Britain and Normandy. On one raid, a young Briton named Patrick was brought back as a slave. After several years in Ireland, Patrick escaped to the continent where he entered a monastery. In 432, after being consecrated as a Bishop, Patrick returned to Ireland. He spent Lent in prayer at the top of Croagh Patrick, a mountain overlooking the Atlantic in County Mayo. Bound by age–long tradition, even now, more than 50,000 people a year make the strenuous 2700 foot climb to the top. And it is typical that some do it as an adventurous outing and some do it as a religious penance. In fact, thousands climb over the rough stones with bare, and therefore bleeding, feet. The story is told that two young men were climbing and one of them saw some attractive girls up ahead. He said, "Let's hurry and catch up with those girls." The other one replied, "Oh, I wouldn't dare. It's for too much foolin' with the girls that I'm havin' to make the climb."

Certainly Patrick was one of the most successful missionaries of all time. Within a few years after his death, the whole island was Christian. Celtic Christianity developed in unusual patterns. Instead of the Bishop and his Diocese being the chief authority, the Abbott and the monastery were the center of ecclesiastical life. The emphasis on monastic life had three major effects on cultural developments.

First, monks often practiced extremes of asceticism. To this day, Irish Christianity has maintained an emphasis on self–de-

The ruins of Rocktown Castle, County Limerick

Ireland

nial and penance that affects the Irish character. Second, while the rest of Europe descended into darkness, Irish monasteries kept the light of western culture burning. Piety, painting and learning were combined into one art form: the illuminated manuscript of the scriptures. Flights of imagination turned the letters of holy books into fantastic geometric shapes and celestial beings. The most famous illuminated manuscript, the Book of Kells, may be seen today in the Library of Trinity College, Dublin.

Third, because monastic orders thought beyond the geographic boundaries of the Diocese, Irish missionaries carried Celtic Christianity to Britain and the continent. The Irish St. Colombo established a famous monastery at Iona off the coast of Scotland. But perhaps the most interesting missionary was St. Brendan—medieval manuscripts describe how he and a group of monks sailed in a leather boat from the coast of Kerry. They visited a land of sheep, then an island occupied by giant blacksmiths working at their forges, and later an area of great fog. Finally, they reached a new land of beauty and richness which was divided by a large river. Brendan returned to Ireland just before he died. The story has usually been dismissed as a fanciful legend. In 1977, however, a group of men built a leather boat and sailed from Brendon's creek in Kerry. They were blown to the outer Hebrides (where there are many sheep), wintered in Iceland (where volcanos might be confused with giants' forges), were becalmed in the fog off the Grand Banks, and finally, in 1978, washed ashore in Canada. Perhaps Brendan, not Leif Ericson or Christopher Columbus, was the first European to reach the New World!

Viking Raids and Norse Settlements

Unfortunately, the very success and more particularly the wealth of the monasteries brought trouble. Beginning in the 9th century, Viking raiders began to attack monastic and other settlements, plundering them for gold and valuables. Inevitably, the monks sought refuge in remote places. The most spectacular of these is Skellig Michael, a tiny island off the coast of Kerry. Today, those who brave the four miles of rough seas in an open boat can climb the steps cut into the stone face by monks over a thousand years ago and visit the remains of the bee–hive huts perched 550 feet above the water.

By the 10th century, the Norsemen began to plan settlements. The first cities in Ireland were established by the Vikings near the mouth of important rivers. Dublin, Waterford, Cork and Limerick all began that way.

At times the Celtic Irishmen intermar-

Skellig Michael

ried with the Norse and at times they tried to drive them into the sea. Brian Baru, after defeating the Norsemen in Munster, established himself as High King of all Ireland in 1002. Brian married the beautiful Gormflath whose six feet of height was crowned with flaming red hair. Unfortunately, as so often happened in Irish history, treason destroyed a chance for national unity. Gormflath's half–Danish son by an earlier marriage plotted with his mother, his uncle and other Danish chieftains to attack Brian. At the Battle of Clontarf in 1014 in which 20,000 men took part, Brian's forces were victorious and broke the Viking domination of Ireland. Tragically, at the end of the battle, a Danish soldier broke free and killed Brian in his own tent. Even more tragically, neither Brian's brief unification of Ireland nor his freeing it of foreign domination, proved lasting. No clear successor to him was able to establish control, and strife between local warlords continued as an Irish tradition. Because of these rivalries, new invaders arrived within a hundred and fifty years.

The name Dermot MacMurrough has been a black one in Irish history for eight hundred years. It was he who invited British troops into Ireland. But it is easier to see the tragic consequences of his act in retrospect than it would have been in the 12th century. In fact, it was the Pope himself, Adrian IV, the only Englishman ever to be Pope, who set the stage. Wishing to bring the practices of Celtic Christianity into conformity with the rest of Roman Christianity, Adrian issued the Papal Bull *Laudabilitier* in 1155 which granted Henry II of England permission to control Ireland. For twenty years, Henry did not make a move across the Irish Sea. However, when Dermot MacMurrough lost control of the Kingdom of Leinster, he asked for help from the Normans who had then been ruling England and Wales for a hundred years.

Norman–Anglo Saxon Invasion and Control

In 1170 Strongbow, Earl of Pembroke, led a group of Normans into Ireland. He married MacMurrough's daughter and for a while it appeared that an independent Norman kingdom might be established. A year later, however, Henry II himself brought a large force of British Normans into Ireland. With the murder of Thomas à Becket less than twelve months behind him (see The United Kingdom), Henry may have thought it was a good time for some foreign travel. He not only established Normans loyal to himself as local rulers, but did away with the Celtic form of worship and brought Irish Christianity under the control of the Roman Church.

Two legacies of the Normans are still plentifully evident in Ireland. Many of the great names of Ireland came with the Normans: Joyce, Fitzgerald, Barry and Burke. These names can still be seen on many store and pub fronts. A person driving through Ireland also still sees the remains of castles, the prototypes of which were built by the Normans. These are usually rectangular stone towers three or four stories high. Most are in ruins, but a few such as Bunratty, Blarney, Dungory, Cahair and Knappogue have been restored and are open for visitors or popular medieval banquets. Over 300 castles still stand in Ireland.

As the Anglo–Normans became settled in Ireland, they adopted more and more

Ireland

of the Irish ways. The old saying is that "They became more Irish than the Irish themselves." Eventually, of course, such assimilation began to threaten the rule of the British crown. The attitude of the English was shown in the statutes of Kilkenny in 1366. These provided a punishment of the loss of lands for any Englishman who spoke Irish, married Irish people or adopted Irish customs.

English authority was strongest in the area around Dublin, known as "The Pale." Outside this region, local rulers paid only nominal homage to the British Crown and British ways. Thus the expression "Beyond the Pale" as a term of derision expresses things from the English point of view. While they had only small loyalty to Britain, the Irish rulers could hardly be described as ardent nationalists. Ireland was so fragmented politically that the idea of allegiance to Ireland itself was not an effective alternative. Rather, each local lord simply looked after his own interests.

Religious Intolerance After the Reformation

It is interesting, but futile, to speculate what would have happened to relationships between Britain and Ireland if the Reformation had not come to England. Perhaps Ireland would have gone the way of Scotland and Wales and become part of the United Kingdom. But the Reformation drove an irreconcilable wedge of hatred and mistrust between the English and the Irish.

England vacillated between Roman Catholicism and Protestantism through several monarchs, but with the crowning of Elizabeth I, the English were ready to try to export the Reformation. For the next four hundred years, religion and nationalism would be intertwined in Ireland. In 1579, armed rebellion arose in the southwest of the island. As a reprisal against the rebels and as a reward to her soldiers, Elizabeth confiscated vast areas of land from the Irish and gave them to Englishmen. On one such parcel of land, Walter Raleigh planted the first Irish potato. It was a crop well suited for growing by the Irish and they soon became dependent on it, much to their regret during the potato famine 275 years later, one of the greatest tragedies in Irish history.

By 1588 Elizabeth's rule was strong enough that as the ships of the Spanish Armada wrecked against the rocky shores of Ireland, the Irish obeyed her orders and slaughtered the would–be invaders. Only in Ulster in the north were the Spaniards spared. This was ironic; because Ulster held out against English rule, a sequence of events began that led in the 20th century to the north being the *one* area of Ireland loyal to the British crown.

At the end of the 16th century, Hugh O'Neill led a rebellion in Ulster. He embarrassed Elizabeth's current favorite Essex, but finally in 1601 was defeated at Kinsale by Mountjoy. In 1607 he and other Ulster chiefs fled to the continent in "the flight of the Earls." James I filled the vacuum by sending Scots Presbyterians to settle in northern Ireland. These are the antecedents of today's Protestants in Northern Ireland loyal to the British. It is significant that the only Protestants in Ireland were *imported*.

Upheavals in the British monarchy brought violence to Ireland in the 17th century. Oliver Cromwell beheaded Charles I and in 1649 landed in Ireland. His purpose was to establish *his* brand of Puritanism in Ireland and end the possibility of rebellion. Tens of thousands of Irish were killed or driven into exile. Irish landlords in the fertile east were given the choice of death or migration to the rocky areas of the west. "Hell or Connacht" are still remembered as the only options open to them. By 1660, only one quarter of the country was owned by Irish Catholics.

When James II, a Catholic, came to the throne of England, there was a chance of reconciliation. But there was an immediate rebellion of Protestants against James, who chose William of Orange, a Netherlands Protestant as King of England; the decisive battle was fought in Ireland in 1690. Protestants in Ulster still celebrate the anniversary of the Battle of Boyne, fought on Irish territory, where William defeated the forces of James. This greatly irritates their Catholic neighbors.

As retribution for support of James, the English confiscated more areas of Irish land and imposed the Penal Laws. These forbade Catholics to vote, to hold office, to send their children to anything but a Protestant school or to have wealth above a set limit.

The Georgian Era

Much of Dublin and many beautiful country homes were built by the Protestant aristocracy during the Georgian era of the 18th century. The vast majority of the population, Catholic peasants, subsisted on potatoes grown on tiny plots of land. The success of the American and French revolutions inspired hopes among the down–trodden people. The ideals of equality and fraternity were imported from the continent. Theobald Wolfe Tone founded the *United Irishmen,* a group that sought to include those of different religions in the establishing of a Republic. In 1798 a French force with Tone in attendance landed in Mayo on the west coast. The British commander, Cornwallis, was more successful than he had been at Yorktown, and the French–Irish forces were soon defeated.

The English now tried to have Ireland conform to the pattern which Scotland and Wales had followed years earlier. The Act of Union, passed in 1800, abolished the Irish Parliament and gave the Irish representation in the British parliament at Westminster. Robert Emmet tried an unsuccessful revolution in 1803; his statue stands today in Washington, D.C., but his words were engraved on the heart of

The ancient mansion of Sir Walter Raleigh, Youghal

Ireland

every Irish revolutionary who came after him: "When my country takes her place among the nations of the earth, then and not till then let my epitaph be written."

Further Attempts at Freedom and the Potato Famine

Two names dominate Irish attempts for freedom in the 19th century: Daniel O'Connell and Charles Stewart Parnell. But their periods of influence were separated by the most terrible tragedy Ireland ever knew. In the first half of the century, Daniel O'Connell worked to improve the position of Catholics. He won election to the House of Commons in 1828 even though, as a Catholic, he could not take his seat. A year later, the Penal Laws which accomplished this were replaced. In the 1840s O'Connell developed a large following which demanded the repeal of the Act of Union. However, when he obeyed an order by the British government to cancel a mass meeting in Clontarf, his political support soon failed.

By the 1840s more than half the people of Ireland were dependent on potatoes as their principal source of food. In the wet summer of 1845, blight attacked the crop, and it appeared again in 1846 and 1847. Famine and death spread across the stricken land. The relief efforts of the British government were too little and too late. In a population of 8.5 million, 1 million *starved* and another million *fled* their country. English-speaking countries around the world, particularly the United States, received a transfusion of Celtic, Catholic blood which would, in turn, help shape their destinies. Even as the famine subsided, immigration continued and for the next forty years, 1% of the population left each year. Many found their way to America, where by the onset of the 21st century 44 million persons claim Irish descent, nine times as many as inhabit the whole island of Ireland. One hundred years after the great famine, the population was only one-half what it had been before the blight struck.

As Irish immigrants prospered abroad, many did not forget the cause of Irish independence. Money and occasionally arms or leaders flowed back into Ireland and supported various movements. The *Fenians,* a secret society favoring armed revolution and also known as the *Irish Republican Brotherhood,* was founded in 1856 in Ireland and the United States. In 1879, the *Land League* was founded by Michael Davitt and was supported by American money. It worked through parliament to achieve land reform. Charles Stewart Parnell became the leader of the *Irish Parliamentary Party.* He controlled enough seats in the British parliament to tip the balance of power at various times. His Home Rule Bill passed the House of Commons, but was defeated in the House of Lords. His next try for home rule might have been successful, but in 1890 a scandal broke when Parnell was the cause of a divorce between Kitty O'Shea and her husband. Although Parnell married Kitty, neither Victorian England nor Catholic Ireland would forgive him. How ironic it was that one man's illicit love of a woman delayed the possibility of home rule until it was too late to be effective.

In 1912, after severely limiting the power of the House of Lords, the House of Commons finally passed a Home Rule Bill, but by that time the Protestants in Ulster were afraid of being controlled by a Catholic majority. Sir Edward Casson organized the *Ulster Volunteers,* a military group armed with German guns to oppose the move. The next year the Irish Vol-

The potato famine struck a severe blow to Ireland

Ireland

unteers were formed by the *Irish Republican Brotherhood* and the *Sinn Fein* (pronounced "Shin Fane," meaning "Ourselves Alone") to oppose the Ulster Volunteers.

But the outbreak of World War I caused Britain to postpone home rule for the duration of the war. With British attention focused on the continent, the *Irish Volunteers* and the *Irish Citizens Army* staged an armed rebellion. On Easter Monday, 1916, rebels captured the center of Dublin. At the General Post Office, they proclaimed the Irish Republic: "We declare the right of the people of Ireland to the ownership of Ireland and to the unfettered control of Irish destinies to be sovereign and indefeasible. The long usurpation of that right by a foreign people and government has not extinguished the right nor can it ever be extinguished except by the destruction of the Irish people. In every generation for centuries the Irish people had and have asserted their right to national freedom and sovereignty. Six times in the past three hundred years they have asserted it in arms. Standing on that fundamental right and again asserting it in arms in the face of the world, we hereby proclaim the Irish Republic as a sovereign, independent state, and we pledge our lives and the lives of our comrades in arms to the cause of its freedom, of its welfare, and of its exultation among the nations."

Within a week the rebellion was crushed; because the British were at war, they reacted to the rebellion as treason, and with great severity, executing most of the leaders. Eamon deValera was spared because he had been born in the United States. Those executed instantly became heroes and martyrs to the Irish people, and hatred toward England became even deeper.

When World War I ended, the *Sinn Fein* again proclaimed an Irish Republic. Eamon deValera was President and Michael Collins led frequent terrorist raids on British installations. The British fought back with the *Auxiliary Cadets* (former officers) and the *Black and Tans* (former enlisted men). Atrocities, murders, burnings and lootings were practiced by both sides. The Irish desire for freedom received world–wide publicity when Terrence McSwiney died in a British prison after a 74–day hunger strike. This strategy would later be used in the fight by India for its freedom from Britain and again in Ulster in the 1980s and 1990s.

Strife and Freedom

The three years of fighting are still known by the Irish as "The Troubles," though many years in Irish history could qualify for that title. Parliament passed the Government of Ireland Act in 1920 which allowed for two types of Home Rule, one for the six counties in the north and another for the rest of Ireland. In early 1922 the Republican Government led by Arthur Griffith and Michael Collins accepted a treaty which made twenty–six counties a free state within the British Commonwealth, and left the six northern counties a province of the United Kingdom. DeValera refused to accept the treaty, and for a year and a half led a civil war against his former friends. Collins was killed in a battle and Griffith died, but deValera was forced to give up his fight. William Cosgrave became head of the Irish Free State; the boundary between the Free State and Northern Ireland was accepted in 1925.

Eamon deValera returned to power in 1932 as head of the *Fianna Fail* ("Warriors of Destiny") *Party* which held a majority for sixteen years. In 1937 a new constitution declared Ireland to be "a sovereign, independent, democratic state." Only formal ties with Britain remained. Ireland was officially neutral during World War II, but many Irishmen served in the British armed forces. Further, it was an important refueling stop for transatlantic military aircraft during the strife.

In 1949, a coalition government led by John Costello took Ireland out of the Commonwealth and made it an independent Republic. DeValera served as *Taoiseach*, (pronounced "tea–such"), a Prime Minister, several times, but in 1959 he gave up leadership of the *Fianna Fail* and was elected President of the Republic. During the 1950s, Ireland began a major push toward industrialization. Foreign capital

Ireland

By the sea in County Cork

Ireland

was invited into the country and given tax incentives. By the mid–1960s, industrial output was growing at over 5% a year. Ireland joined the EC in 1973, which gave a great boost to both its agricultural and industrial production. The improved economic situation brought about a rising standard of living. Automobiles and televisions became commonplace.

POLITICAL SYSTEM

A Written Constitution Derived from an Unwritten One

The Republic of Ireland (Eire) is Europe's newest independent state, having been founded in 1921 and having separated itself completely from Britain in 1949. It devotes much attention to strengthening a sense of Irish national identity, and the resentment resulting from recent British occupation is still very strong. Because of its long domination by Great Britain, it is hardly surprising that the Irish political system so closely resembles that of its former conqueror. Before Ireland gained its independence, many Irishmen had served in the British House of Commons. Therefore, they had not only gained their parliamentary experience in Britain, but also contributed to the very development of the British political system.

In some important ways, however, Irish democracy differs from the "Westminster model" of Great Britain. The Republic of Ireland has a *written* constitution which it adopted in 1937. Article 2 of that document mandated the eventual reunification of Ireland: "The national territory consists of the whole island of Ireland, its islands and the territorial seas." This article was removed in 1998 as a contribution to a daring Northern Ireland settlement.

The Catholic Church

The constitution also pledges to support the teachings of the Roman Catholic Church. Except for the Vatican itself, Ireland has traditionally been the least secular state in all of Western Europe. The Catholic Church maintains considerable influence in social affairs. It controls all but 462 of the 3,940 primary and secondary schools. Senator Donal Lydon once noted that "the Church has contacts at every level of society, in every corner. Its influence is everywhere. Any politician who ignores the views of the Church would need to be crazy." Many younger Protestants in Eire left; of the 115,000 Protestants who remain, most are elderly.

In recent years, the church's political influence has declined significantly, as a younger generation is more reluctant to accept Catholic teachings. By the end of the 20th century only six in ten Catholics regularly attend Sunday mass, down from 87% in 1984 and 91% in 1974. Only 38% of Irish Catholics regularly take communion. Contraceptive devices are now legal, but that does not prevent a fifth of all children from being born out of wedlock. Following referenda in 1992 and 1995, Irish women are permitted to have abortions abroad; such abortions may be performed in Ireland if the life of the mother is threatened. As a result of a close vote in 1995 (50.2%, with urban support outweighing rural opposition), couples are allowed to divorce after a four–year separation. The 60% yes vote in Dublin swung the result. It was supported by all the parties and most of the media. The campaign was bitterly fought: opponents' posters read "Hello Divorce, Goodbye Daddy!," while proponents, irreverently referring to the spate of revelations about child–molesting and sexual transgressions by priests, waved signs reading "Let the bishops look after their own families!" These scandals involving clergy have shaken respect for ecclesiastical authority.

The referenda manifest an open revolt against the Church's dominance. President Mary Robinson spoke of the country's "new pluralism," which "means the movement of a predominantly Catholic country, where the Catholic moral code and doctrines had a very significant place, to a society still influenced by the role of the Church but having other voices and having a sense of space between legislators and the Catholic Church." In the spirit of the times, the 30–year censorship ban on *Playboy* magazine was lifted in 1996.

Whereas Protestants in Northern Ireland outnumber Catholics by about 58% to 42%, in the Republic they constitute only about 3% of the population. Since Independence their numbers have declined by two–thirds. Nevertheless, they have played and continue to play a role out of proportion to their size. They were important in creating modern Irish nationalism, from Wolfe Tone and his United Irishmen at the end of the 18th century to Charles Stewart Parnell and the home rule movement in the 19th. The Republic's first president, Douglas Hyde, was one, as were great Irish writers like W.B. Yeats, Samuel Beckett and Oscar Wilde. They were products of the Dublin Protestant middle class. Ireland's premier university, Trinity in Dublin, was opened to Catholics only in recent years. Even such recognizable Irish products as Jameson whiskey and Guinness stout were created by Protestants.

Two Languages

The constitution recognizes two official languages: English and Irish, the latter of which is a Celtic language, closely related to Scottish, Gaelic and more distantly, to Welsh. It was spoken by a majority of Irishmen until the first half of the nineteenth century when it rapidly lost ground to English. Irish is now "used frequently" by only about 5% of the people and is spoken as a native language by only about 2% in seven small pockets by about 70,000 people along the western seaboard, an area known as *The Gaeltacht*. There are three dialects, and the speaker of one will not necessarily understand everything said in the other two.

As the twentieth century closes, Ireland is experiencing a resurgence of the Irish language. In 1996 polls, more than a million claimed "some proficiency" in it, and a half million said they are "fluent" or intend to become so. These numbers justified the creation of an Irish–language television station, called *Teilifís na Gaeilge* (literally "Irish TV"), which broadcasts home–grown soap operas and news and sports programs aimed primarily at educated and urbanized Irishmen. They also prompted the education ministry to create a dozen new all–Irish primary schools.

With state policy to promote the use of Irish, it is a required subject in the schools. Only recently did it become possible to receive a school leaving certificate without passing an examination on the Irish language. Parliamentary documents are translated into it, and parliamentarians sometimes begin their speeches in the lan-

Ireland

guage. After a few sentences, though, they usually switch to English with the words "As I was saying . . .." Also, some persons wonder what good a sign does which reads *Roinn na Plandeolaiochta. Aonad an Leicteron Mhiocrascóip"*, when the following words must be written underneath it to make it comprehensible: "Department of Plant Science. Electron Microscopy Unit."

The Supreme Court

As in most countries, a written constitution also calls for the Supreme Court to uphold that fundamental document. The Republic has a Supreme Court consisting of a Chief Justice and five others, which is empowered to decide upon the constitutionality of laws if the President of the Republic asks for an opinion. This provision, known in the United States as "judicial review," is, of course, not present in Great Britain because there is no written constitution. However, English legal concepts and common law did replace the ancient Irish law (known as the Brehon law) by the 17th century and thus, Irish justice does bear an unmistakable British stamp. The Supreme Court demonstrated its power in 1993 by declaring hundreds of EU directives unconstitutional because they had bypassed the Irish Senate.

The President

The most notable divergence from the "Westminster model" is that the Republic of Ireland does not have a monarch and all links with the British crown were severed in 1949. Instead of a monarch, the Republic has a President, elected by the whole people for a seven-year term. This term can be renewed only once. The office is chiefly ceremonial, but unlike the British king or queen, Irish presidents have been leading political figures who continue to exercise considerable influence within the system, even if their powers are restricted.

The first woman president in Irish history, Mary Robinson, was elected in 1990. For years she had opposed Catholic positions on contraception, divorce, and homosexuality. Although the post is largely ceremonial, her election signaled an important change from traditional social attitudes. She became one of the most popular presidents in Irish history, enjoying a 93% approval rating in 1996. Not inclined to shy away from controversy, she unofficially met *Sinn Fein* leader Gerry Adams in 1993 and shook his hand in public in 1996, a political act which won her countrymen's praise. She became the first Irish chief of state to meet a British monarch. The fact that she is married to a Protestant manifests tolerance on this religiously torn island. In 1997 she became UN High Commissioner for Human Rights.

Her successor is Mary McAleese, a Belfast lawyer and vice–chancellor of Queen's University, who was the candidate of *Fianna Fail*. A resident of Northern Ireland, she is the first British subject to be elected president of Ireland. Under the Irish constitution, residents of the six "partitioned" counties of the North are considered citizens of the republic. She is a conservative Catholic who opposes the legalization of abortion and divorce, but favors the ordination of women. She admits that she is an unabashed nationalist. She was not helped by the fact that Gerry Adams said during the campaign that she would make a fine president and by the fact that she has a cousin serving a life prison term for an IRA murder. She disavows any links with Adams or *Sinn Fein* and pledges to stand above politics, to "seek to heal the hurt of divided Ireland," and to "build bridges."

The Parliament

Despite the differences described, the Irish political system developed by using Britain as a model. Irish *government* is parliamentary. This means that there are no checks and balances among three equal branches of government as in the United States. The Lower House of parliament is supreme because unless the government can find a majority in it to carry forth its policies, that government must resign. Parliamentary government in the Republic of Ireland has usually been quite stable and durable. Conflict in the Republic now takes place almost entirely within the parliamentary traditions and standards of conduct left by the British.

The Irish Parliament (called the *Oireachtas*—pronounced "or–rock–tas") is bicameral. The Upper House is the Senate (*Seanad*) composed of 60 members, 11 of whom are named by the Prime Minister and six by the universities. The remaining 43 are selected from five panels of nominees representing the national language and culture, agriculture and fisheries, organized and unorganized labor, industry and commerce, public administration and social services. The Senate has the power to delay legislation for up to 90 days in order to try to amend bills. However, it can always be outvoted by the lower house.

One might ask why such a weak body should even exist. Upper houses usually have the greatest importance in federal states where regional interests must be represented within the national government; however, the four traditional Irish provinces (Ulster in the north, Connacht in the west, Munster in the south and Leinster in the east) are not political units. Further, the 115 local authorities are supervised by the National Department of Environment. Local budgets are financed partly by grants from the national government, since local property taxes (known as "rates") cannot possibly provide enough revenue. In other words, the Republic of Ireland is a truly unitary state, and political authority rests largely with the central government. This centralized system exists even though local concerns are very important to Irish politicians. Thus, the Senate's purpose was never to represent provincial interests, but instead to give some political power to certain groups which could not win it in free elections before the whole people.

Political power is centered in the Lower House of Parliament known as the *Dáil* (pronounced "Doyle"). This House is composed of 166 members known as *Teachtái Dála,* or TD for short), elected from 41 constituencies. Elections must be held at least every five years, although the prime minister (called the *Taoiseach*—pronounced "Tea–such") may choose to hold earlier elections if he desires to reestablish or widen his party's majority in the *Dáil*. For instance, in late 1982 the third election in 18 months was held because the government could not maintain its majority. The *Taoiseach* is by far the most important political figure in the Republic. With his cabinet, which is composed of from 7 to 15 members, he establishes the country's policies and dominates his party in the *Dáil* in order to get his government's bills through parliament.

Electoral System: Proportional Representation

In any democratic system, parties usually play a key role, presenting candidates and policy issues as alternatives from which to choose. They educate the voters, wage election campaigns and above all, they rule or prepare to rule. Political parties are especially important in the Irish Republic because interest groups are far less tightly organized than in most other Western Europe countries. Thus, Irish parties are particularly important channels for interest groups expressing their concerns and wants at high policy levels.

President Mary McAleese

Ireland

Parties seek seats in the *Dáil* by means of a particularly complex electoral system—a form of proportional representation system involving what is known as a single transferable vote in multi–member constituencies. The voter marks his ballot by placing the number 1 opposite the name of the candidate of his first choice and may then place the figure 2 opposite the name of his second choice, and continues on until he has numbered all the candidates. Thus the voter is able to say in effect, "I wish to vote for A, but if he does not need my vote or if he has no chance of being elected, transfer my vote to B. If B in turn does not need my vote, or he has no chance of election, transfer my vote to C," and so forth.

Thus, the system reflects more completely the voters' preferences for the three to five seats filled by each constituency. This makes it easier for smaller parties and independents to win parliamentary representation. At the same time, it is designed to prevent fringe politicians and a high number of small parties from winning seats in the *Dáil* and thereby adversely affecting the stability of the parliamentary system. It is thus one of the better proportional representation systems in Western Europe. However, this complicated system enormously slows down the tabulation of the votes, and thus it often takes several days to determine the final results of an Irish election.

The Republic's electoral system affects Irish politics in several important ways. By permitting voters to discriminate among candidates of the same party (as does the American primary system), it pits members of the same party against each other. Thus, the individual candidate's appeal must veer from the policy of the national party and be far more closely tailored to local concerns. Politicians compete with each other to perform a variety of services for local constituents, and this strengthens an important characteristic of Irish politics: personality and personal ties become far more significant than national policy issues.

Moreover, the local political clubs, *not* the national parties (which have very small staffs), recruit candidates and wage campaigns. Although it is not required by law, *Dáil* members almost always come from the constituency in which they are elected. Also, most TDs continue to hold local political office at the same time. All of these factors represent a strong decentralized tendency in Irish politics: politicians show strong loyalties to their local constituencies, but at the same time the national party leadership needs to maintain strong party discipline as it seeks a majority in the *Dáil*. Without such discipline, no government could possibly survive.

Political Parties

Irish political parties are noticeably different from British parties whose bases were traditionally rooted in different social classes. The Republic of Ireland is a more homogeneous country, and it has historically been economically underdeveloped. It has no major national, regional, religious or racial differences which could become the basis for different parties. There are, of course, social cleavages, but these do not have the overriding significance that they do in many other Western Europe countries. It is more likely that the dividing line between the two major parties is determined by the position one's father or grandfather took on the signing of the Anglo–Irish treaty in 1921, which divided the island and created the Irish Free State. In 1932, after a bloody civil war followed by intense domestic political rivalry, the party which had accepted the treaty (now the *Fine Gael*, meaning "Family of Irish") suffered an election defeat and relinquished power to the *Fianna Fail Party*, which had originally opposed the treaty. The 1932 elections firmly established democratic government, which stands or falls on the parties' willingness to alternate power peacefully, in response to the wishes of the voters.

The "pro" or "anti" distinction between the two major parties does not really mean very much today, but the importance of family ties in Irish politics inclines Irishmen to vote as their fathers and grandfathers did, and encourages political activists to become leaders in those same parties. It is hardly surprising that parties which are not formed along class or religious lines are not very ideological in their orientation.

North Americans who observe the two major Irish parties have the same difficulties distinguishing between them that Western Europeans express about American parties. Perhaps the 1960s saying of George Wallace about the American mainline parties applies to their Irish counterparts: "There's not a dime's worth of difference between them." Both parties in the Republic are catch–all parties, which attract voters from all social groups. Both parties are rather conservative, anti–secular, nationalistic and predominantly male. Both are what one would call Christian Democratic parties elsewhere in Western Europe.

The Irish party system has developed into two more or less stable blocs. In the past three decades, the government has alternated between the *Fianna Fail* and a coalition combining *Fine Gael* and the *Labour Party*. Traditionally *Fianna Fail* did not enter coalitions, but it must often rely on support from small parties, making its governments more fragile. *Fine Gael–Labour* coalitions were made easier by the fact that there is very little ideological distance between them.

Fianna Fail (pronounced Fee–*anna* Foil) has governed most of the time since 1932. It is moderate to conservative on economic matters; it still has a slightly anti–British attitude, although it has eliminated many of the more militant elements in the aftermath of a party split in 1970 over the question of Irish unification. It attracts considerable support from businessmen and professional people as well as parts of the urban working class. However, its greatest strength remains in the rural western regions. It is solidly supported by the native Irish–speakers because it has stamped itself as a party seeking restoration of the Irish language (at least nominally). It often sees itself as a grass roots party and often demonstrates populist tendencies.

Fianna Fail was able to stay in power after 1989 only by forming a historic coalition with its most bitter political enemies, the *Progressive Democrats*. This was the first time ever that *Fianna Fail* has shared power while ruling. In 1992 Charles Haughey was finally forced out after it had been revealed that he had been aware of police bugging of two journalists' phones. He was replaced as *Taoiseach* by Albert Reynolds, a self–made pet–food tycoon.

Two days after taking office, Reynolds entered an ethical minefield which took him to the root of what kind of society Ireland is and aspires to be. With abortions forbidden in Ireland, his government got a court order to prevent a 14–year old rape victim from going to Britain to end her pregnancy, as several thousand Irish women do annually. This decision triggered a barrage of international criticism and an emotional national debate, which continued even after the court later over-

Hon. Bertie Ahern
Taoiseach of Ireland

Ireland

turned the decision to ban her from travelling to the U.K. In 1992 voters overwhelmingly decided in referenda to permit women to obtain information and to have abortions abroad, though not in Ireland. In 1995 this passed in parliament and was affirmed by the Supreme Court.

After calling his own *Fein Gael* coalition partner "reckless, irresponsible, and dishonest," Reynolds lost a vote of no–confidence in 1992 which prompted a snap election. *Fianna Fail* suffered its worst electoral setback in 50 years. Reynolds emerged from the polling badly wounded and had to enter *Fianna Fail's* first coalition with *Labour* in order to stay in office. With 100 seats, the coalition had the biggest *Dáil* majority in Irish political history until a crisis broke it apart in 1994 and forced *Fianna Fail* out of the government. Bertie Ahern became party leader.

Ahern led the party to victory in the June 1997 elections, winning 39.3% of the votes and 77 seats. Together with its small ally, the *Progressive Democrats*, the government has 81 seats and can maintain an unstable majority only with the votes of a handful of independents. As usual, it took weeks of haggling and deal making before the new prime minister could go to the elegant Phoenix Park residence of the president and ask for permission to form a government. A populist Dubliner from a lower class background who is separated from his wife and lives openly with his girlfriend, Ahern vowed to "cut taxes, cut crime and work for peace in Northern Ireland." Although reputed to be "green" or pro–Catholic on the volatile subject of Northern Ireland, he has pushed hard for progress in the peace talks. This has cost him the support of a few independents' votes.

Ahern has a frail grip on parliament, and his government has been shaken by scandals. Only five months after taking power, his foreign minister, Ray Burke, had to resign for accepting a campaign donation from a man who wanted to develop land in Burke's constituency. The cloud of financial scandal was already looming over the party when a judge found former *Taoiseach* Charles Haughey guilty of accepting a "gift" of 1.3 million Irish punts ($1.9 million) while in office and then stashing it away in offshore bank accounts, presumably in order to hide it from the tax collectors. Ahern had been a close colleague of both men for many years, and their sins greatly embarrassed him and his government.

Fine Gael (pronounced Finna Gwail) is a traditional establishment party which draws a disproportionate share of its votes from the upper and middle classes and from farmers with large holdings. Its leaders also tend to be drawn from somewhat higher social strata. Although it tends to be moderate to conservative on economic matters, the party has moved slightly to the left to accommodate the *Labour Party*. *Fine Gael* is the most centralized and hierarchically organized in the Republic. Led by John Bruton, a wealthy rancher with long governmental experience, *Fine Gael* slipped in 1992 to less than 25% of the votes and 45 seats. Nevertheless, Bruton was able to form a center–left governing coalition with the *Labour* and *Democratic Left* parties in 1994 and become *Taoiseach*.

In June 1997 Irish voters continued a tradition maintained since 1969: never re-elect a government no matter how good its record. Despite the fact that the *Fine Gael* government presided over the strongest economy in the 75–year history of independent Ireland, with the fastest growth rate in the EU that won it the nickname, "Celtic Tiger," and living standards that were near the EU average, it was thrown out of power. It captured 27.9% of the votes (up from 24.5%) and 54 seats (up from 46). But its partner, the *Labour Party*, collapsed in the voting booths. The two parties were rudely reminded of an old saying in Irish politics: No good turn ever goes unpunished.

Unlike in Britain, the *Labour Party* in Ireland has never articulated socialist or Marxist ideologies. In fact, by western standards, it is hardly a party of the left, although it does have a left–wing minority. It had been virtually excluded from urban politics in the eastern part of the country, and most of the working class voted for one of the two major parties, especially the *Fianna Fail*. But its leader, Dick Spring, an astute rugby–playing lawyer with a wife from Virginia, brought *Labour*

**Hon. Mary Robinson
UN High Commissioner for
Human Rights**

more into the public eye. *Labour's* main electoral support is found among rural, agrarian workers. Its importance in Irish politics was greatly enhanced by the fact that until 1997 it had been an essential part of any ruling coalition led by either *Fine Gael* or *Fianna Fail*. Mary Robinson's election as president in 1990 forced Ireland's leaders to take a fresh look at Irish society, which has proved to be more receptive to change than most had realized. She became Ireland's most respected politician and helped pave the way for 20 women to win seats in the 1992 elections.

Labour triumphed in 1992, becoming the king–maker in Irish politics. In 1994 it entered a governing coalition with *Fine Gael*, with Spring as deputy prime minister (*Tánaiste*) and foreign minister. However, it slipped badly in 1997 to 10.4% of the votes (from 19.3%) and only 17 seats (down from 32). It finds itself in the opposition.

Minor Parties

Despite the proportional representation electoral system, which usually permits many parties to enter parliament, small parties had almost entirely disappeared from Irish parliamentary politics. Ten representatives of minor parties and six independents did win seats in the 1997 elections. The *Democratic Left* won 2.5% of the votes and four seats (down from six). It was in the governing coalition from 1994 to 1997. The ecological *Greens* won 2.8% of the votes and two seats in 1997.

The most significant development in the 1987 elections was the rise of a new center–right party, the *Progressive Democrats (PD)*. The *PD* had broken away from *Fianna Fail* in 1985 in protest against its hard–line Northern Ireland policy. It temporarily displaced *Labour* as third largest party, a position that *Labour* had occupied since 1922. The *PD* appeared to break the mold of Irish party politics; it supplanted *Labour* as *Fine Gael's* favorite coalition partner, although *Fine Gael* and *PD* still are likely to compete for the same kinds of voters. In 1993 Mary Harney was elected to replace Desmond O'Malley as party leader. She is the first woman to head an Irish party. In 1997 *PD* received the same percentage of votes as in 1992 (4.7%), but it lost half its seats, capturing only four.

The Marxist–oriented *Communist Party of Ireland* seeks to unify the entire island under an orthodox communist regime. It plays no significant role whatsoever in Irish politics. The Trotskyite *Socialists* captured one seat in 1997. The *Workers' Party* took that name in 1976 following a split six years earlier among the ranks of the small *Sinn Fein* Party, which was the political arm of the Irish Republican Army (IRA). The split resulted in two distinct groups: the first is a "official" IRA, whose

Ireland

political arm—the *Workers Party*—has for years competed in parliamentary elections in the Republic and has accepted the few seats which it has won.

The second group is the "provisional" IRA (Provos), which is has become Marxist and remains fervently nationalist. Until 1987 it refused to recognize the Dublin parliament as a legitimate Irish parliament, and it therefore refused to participate in elections, except for town councils in which it occupies a few seats in both parts of Ireland. Its suspicions that it would win precious few votes were confirmed in the 1997 elections, when *Sinn Fein* won a paltry 2.5% of the votes. Caoimhghin O Caolain became the first member of *Sinn Fein* ever to win a seat in the Irish parliament since independence in 1922. But the *Fianna Fail*-led government did not seek his support. The result underscores two facts: although polls indicate that two–thirds of Eire's population believes ideally that Ireland should one day be a unified nation, the overwhelming majority abhors the violent attempt to unify Ireland by bullets and bombs.

It is precisely to try to overcome its isolation that leader Gerard (Gerry) Adams ended the party's boycott of the Irish (though not of the British) parliament. As he stated: "We've lost touch with the people for the simple reason that we have not been able to represent them in the only political forum they know. To break out into the broad stream of people's consciousness, we have to approach them at their own level." To many traditionalists, this approach smacked of betrayal. As one die–hard remarked, "when you lie down with the dogs, you get up with the fleas."

Foreign and Defense Policies

A central reality in the Republic of Ireland's foreign and defense policy is that the Irish live on a politically divided island and that they are a politically and religiously divided people. Few foreign policy issues can be treated entirely separately from these facts. Most Irish citizens and politicians in the Republic want to see these divisions overcome, and no Irish Republican government has ever recognized the division of the island as permanent. Most people in the Republic do not use the term "Republic of Ireland." which implies permanent division, but instead refer to their state almost exclusively as "Ireland." It is nevertheless true that the unification issue is no longer as important in Irish politics as it once was, even though unification is no closer now than it has been at any time in this century. The old revolutionary elite who fought against Britain for independence has been replaced by younger leaders with no direct memories of the bloody struggle and with far greater interest in Ireland's economic development.

The Republic of Ireland lives in the shadow of Great Britain although it has become a much more confident nation and is no longer obsessed by its ancient hatred of the British. Because of Britain's part in Irish history and the continued presence of the British in Northern Ireland, the Republic is inclined to remain neutral in conflicts where Britain is involved. It remained neutral in World War II—in fact it even refused to observe black–outs in its cities at night. Thus, German bombers were able to orient themselves by regrouping in the skies over Dublin, and then flying in a direct line toward such British cities as Liverpool. In 1982, the Republic also refused to go along with EU sanctions against Argentina when Britain, a fellow member, was engaged in an armed struggle for control of the Falkland Islands.

Ireland's policy of neutrality does not mean that the Republic is ideologically neutral or politically indifferent. It shares the basic democratic, political and economic values of other countries in Western Europe and North America. However, it is the only one of four EU countries which have not joined NATO. This fact does cause disputes sometimes. For instance, when the *Dáil* debated the ratification of the EU's Single European Act (SEA), which calls for majority votes in the EU Council of Ministers and a completely free market, some members questioned how the Republic could engage in the kinds of security and foreign policy cooperation for which the act called and still remain neutral. The Supreme Court found that the ESA's political cooperation section was unconstitutional and therefore ruled that a referendum on amending the constitution was necessary. In the voting in 1987, 70% voted in favor of it and 30% against.

Ireland's long–established policy of military neutrality is increasingly irrelevant since the country cooperates on European security matters and Irish and British troops coordinate the fight against the IRA. In 1999 it decided to establish formal links with NATO through the Partnership for Peace (PfP).

The Republic is so enveloped by the military forces of the Atlantic Alliance that it is able to keep its own defense forces very small. Internal security rests almost entirely with the unarmed police, the 10,000 strong *Garda Siochana*. External defense is the responsibility of the permanent defense forces which number approximately 16,000, about 13,000 of whom are land forces. The Navy does have plans to acquire two further patrol vessels capable of carrying helicopters. The Air Force is composed of less than 40 aircraft, including helicopters. Military service is voluntary, and there is also a reserve defense force of 16,800 which could be mobilized in time of crisis. Ireland has contributed troops to UN peacekeeping units throughout the world, including in southern Lebanon and Bosnia. In 1991 the Irish government supported UN policy toward Iraq. Although Ireland played no direct role in the war, it did permit U.S. military planes to refuel at Shannon Airport, thereby prompting many domestic critics to cry that its neutrality had been breached.

Out of sheer economic necessity, Ireland joined the EU in 1973, at the same time that Britain entered. Ireland stood to benefit from EU regional aid and Common Agricultural Program (CAP), which in 1998 accounted for 4% of its GDP. In its first 18 years of membership, it received 8.7 billion pounds from the EU while paying 1.6 billion to Brussels' coffers. EU aid totals $2.7 billion annually and helps modernize Ireland's infrastructure. For a few years CAP funds were a boon to Irish farmers, but their benefits were not lasting. Adjusting to CAP, western Ireland has been forced to change from its traditional dairy and beef farming economy to tourism and forestry. In 25 years its forestry industry is expected to be as important to the economy as its food industry is now. Its trade volume with Britain (to which a third of its exports still go) remains very high.

EU membership has served to shift Irish foreign trade and political attention away from Britain to a broader view of the rest of Western Europe. Former President Robinson argued that "it lifts the burden of the relationship with our close neighbor. We are now partners with them in Europe. The history is still there, but it is less a tight connection and burden between us." For centuries Ireland had defined itself in relation to Britain, as a victim. That is far less prominent now. Today it is more inclined to define itself in relation to Europe and the EU, in which it is recognized as an equal. It distinguishes itself from Britain and benefits from being the most pro–European anglophone country in the EU. This foreign policy reorientation has not altered the fact that hundreds of thousands of Irish still live and work in Britain, where they enjoy the same political, legal and social welfare rights as British citizens.

Reunification

The vast majority of the citizens of the Irish Republic and virtually *all* of its political leaders share the goal of reunifying all 32 Irish counties. But they eventually wish

Ireland

to see this accomplished peacefully and with the consent of the Northern Irish. In Northern Ireland, about a million Irish Protestants outnumber the half million Catholics, so Irish unity must take a form palatable to the Protestants. As it is, most southern Irish probably secretly abhor the idea of having to deal directly with Northern Irish Protestants as fellow citizens until fundamental changes in attitudes have occurred. Violence spilled over from Northern Ireland to the South. The Irish government outlawed the provisional IRA; government raids and arrests provide frequent reminders that the IRA can expect no tolerance within the Republic. In 1982 a Dublin court convicted an Irishman for possessing explosives, even though the crime was committed in Britain. This was the first application of a 1976 law which was part of an ongoing Irish–British cooperation against terrorism in both countries.

In 1981 a U.S. court convicted the Irish Northern Aid (NORAID) committee for failing to list the IRA as its principal foreign agent. The Irish government ordered its diplomatic representatives in the United States to boycott the 1983 annual St. Patrick's Day parade in New York City because the organizers of the parade had chosen an IRA supporter as Grand Marshal. In explaining its decision, the Irish government noted that the IRA's actions, which include collecting money from unsuspecting Irish–Americans to finance violent operations in Northern Ireland, "have deepened the wounds of our troubled history and continue to postpone the day of Irish unity and reconciliation." Dublin has frequently appealed to Americans not to support violence in Ireland. Funds from NORAID have been declining, and the IRA has sought to fill its coffers by means of extortion and racketeering in Northern Ireland.

The Irish government realizes that unification can be accomplished only in cooperation with Britain and Northern Ireland. This has brought the Irish and British Prime Ministers together for periodic high level meetings to discuss the developments in the area. Former Prime Minister FitzGerald proposed to change the Irish Republic's constitution in a way that would calm Protestant fears by presenting a less stridently Catholic image.

FitzGerald's objectives were not easy on an island where so much blood has been spilled and where so much bitterness has already been created. Nor was it easy for a country whose population is still deeply Catholic and whose religious values are reflected in its laws and constitution. FitzGerald alluded to his preferred path to unity when, with an eye on the Northern Irish Protestants, he said: "If we could create a state down here which they could accept, and they could find the civil and religious liberties in which they believe, they would be willing to think again about this."

A "New Ireland Forum," which he sponsored, issued a report containing proposals to achieve better understanding between Northern Irish Protestants and Catholics, Dublin and London. However, the proposals, which called for a joint Irish British panel, were criticized by Catholics, who found them too conciliatory, by Northern Irish Protestants, who reject any notion of reunification and finally, by the Thatcher government itself. Mrs. Thatcher was no doubt responding in part to the grisly IRA bombing in 1984 of the hotel in Brighton where she was staying. She narrowly escaped death, and several Tory

**Mr. David Trimble
Leader, Ulster Unionist Party**

leaders were killed or wounded. The bombing enflamed anti–Irish sentiments to a height unequaled since the IRA murdered Lord Mountbatten in 1979, and it set back progress towards peace. By 1985 FitzGerald's initiative was dead.

Nevertheless, consultation between representatives of Eire and the UK continues within the rubric of the 1985 Anglo–Irish accord. For the first time, this permitted Dublin some say in Northern Ireland's affairs. The agreement enjoys majority support in the Republic. In 1990 the Pope appointed Bishop Cahal B. Daly, a fierce critic of IRA terrorism, as Ireland's primate. In 1993 optimism was ignited by a joint declaration by the British and Irish prime ministers offering *Sinn Fein* a seat at the bargaining table to discuss Northern Ireland's future if the IRA renounced violence. Prime Minister John Major promised that Britain would not stand in the way of a united Ireland if a majority of Northern Ireland residents supported such a step. *Taoiseach* Albert Reynolds pledged that there would be no change in the six counties' status without majority consent.

The years 1994–5 brought dramatic breakthroughs in Northern Ireland. The Bruton government pledged that there will be continuity in the peace process, and it lifted a half–century–old anti-terrorism state of emergency, which had given police special powers of detention. *Fine Gael* has always been less enthusiastic about Irish nationalists on both sides of the border. Bruton's better rapport with Ulster unionists and supportive attitude toward British policy in Northern Ireland facilitate the ongoing negotiations. facilitate the ongoing negotiations.

As a symbol of returning normalcy with Britain in 1995, Prince Charles became the first member of the royal family to make an official visit to the Irish Republic since 1922. Also in 1995, David Trimble, leader of the Ulster Unionist Party, the main Protestant group, travelled to Dublin and met with *Taoiseach* Bruton. This was the first time since 1922 a Unionist leader was received in Dublin.

A couple of weeks after becoming British prime minister in 1997, Tony Blair lifted the ban on official contacts with *Sinn Fein*. He visited Northern Ireland in May 1997 in order to demonstrate that he is willing to take risks for peace in the six counties. To continue the negotiation process, he invited *Sinn Fein* leader Gerry Adams to a meeting in Downing Street in December. This was the first visit by an Irish Republican leader to the prime minister's private residence in 76 years. In January 1998, Adams returned to Downing Street to hear from the prime minister that the peace process is an "absolute priority" and that "the status quo is not an option." On November 26, 1998, Blair became the first British prime minister since Ireland's independence to speak to the Irish parliament.

Talks, involving eight Northern Ireland parties and the British and Irish governments, continued despite sporadic outbreaks of violence. American George Mitchell emphasized the importance of the negotiations, which he chaired: "We're talking about, literally, people's lives, the possibility of the resumption of the terrible conflict that enveloped this society with fear and anxiety. So, frustrating and tedious as it seems—and it is—you have to be patient and recognize how tough it is for them to move."

In 1998 a majority in Eire backed the deletion from their constitution of the mandate to unify the island. As a result of the 1998 Good Friday Peace Agreement, followed by dramatic "yes" referenda votes for the accord in both the Republic (94.4%) and Northern Ireland (71.1%), Ire-

Ireland

land has reached the doorstep of peace. Only one snag remained to be worked out in 1999: decommissioning of IRA weapons. Trimble and his Catholic counterpart, John Hume, received the 1998 Nobel Peace Prize for their role in reaching an historic peace agreement in Northern Ireland that year. Optimism is greater than it has ever been that "the troubles" will soon end (see United Kingdom).

ECONOMY

In the last half century, Ireland has undergone an economic revolution. The influx of foreign investment as a result of generous incentives and the increase in trade have added significantly to the prosperity of Ireland. More than 800 foreign firms employ close to half of all Irish workers involved in manufacturing. Foreign companies are also responsible for 80% of the country's non-food exports. It has also acquired an impressive high-technology industry. By 1986 it had already achieved the highest ratio of high-tech to total exports of any EU country. At the turn of the century this tiny land is the 19th richest country in the world.

Growth and prosperity in Ireland have been dramatic. Less than 30% of all households are rented, while 80% have television sets and over 50% own a car. The Irish entered the 1990s with a 50% gap between their living standards and those of the EU average. By 1998 income in Ireland had caught up with the European mean and surpassed Britain in per capita GDP for the first time in history. Per capita consumption rose 10.5% from 1990 to 1996, twice the average rate of increase in the rest of Europe. Sustained economic growth, low inflation, a hard currency, and a healthy trade surplus cohabit with high unemployment (9.4% in 1999) and a growing income gap between rich and poor. One sarcastic critic described it as "one of the most successful unemployed economies in the world." One reason for this is that new jobs are increasingly taken by women entering the work force and Irish returning home.

About a fifth of the population is marginalized from the mainstream economy and barely benefits from the upsurge in prosperity. Competing successfully in the global economy has cost Ireland the kind of low-wage, unskilled jobs other countries do more cheaply. *The Economist* spoke of a "tale of two economies." One is a still-backward, unproductive and labor-intensive one owned by the Irish. The other is an extremely productive, capital-intensive and modern one owned by foreigners, including companies like IBM, Intel, Fujitsu, and Motorola, as well as banks and financial institutions, like Citibank, Merrill Lynch, and Daiwa. By 1998, 40% of all American electronics investments in Europe were going to Ireland, and a third of the personal computers sold in Europe were being made there. Many of its unskilled laborers are joining an idle underclass, and drug use and drug-related crime are rising. The problem of organized, drug-related crime in the country was highlighted by the gangland assassination in 1996 of a courageous investigative reporter, Veronica Guerin, who had put the spotlight on ruthless mobsters. Nevertheless, Ireland still has one of Europe's lowest crime rates, with a murder rate one-seventh as high as the United States.

Agriculture has declined in importance in the last thirty years—the percentage of the working force employed in farming dropped from 43% to 16%. Almost a quarter of the country's workers still is directly or indirectly involved in producing food. Agriculture now accounts for only 10% of GDP, compared with industry's share of 44%. The agricultural life of Ireland benefited from EU membership, although income from the CAP helped fuel the rapid growth of welfare spending and thus contributed to the country's present debt problem. Income in the farm sector has doubled in the past three decades, and today one-half of the value of agricultural production is exported. However, family farming remains relatively unsophisticated, and food processing has not developed as far as in most EU countries.

Two other sources of revenue are important to Ireland: tourists and pubs. Each year two million tourists (that is well over half the number of Irishmen there are to receive them) visit the nation despite the fact that Ireland is the only EU nation not directly linked to the continent since the opening of the English Channel "Chunnel" in 1993. Americans account for 14% of the total, although they tend to spend more than other visitors. They find over 11,000 pubs; the ratio of one pub for every 300 people is even more striking when one knows that half the population is under age 25 and thus the ratio of pubs to those old enough to drink is even higher. Despite the unrest, 1.25 million tourists visited Northern Ireland in 1993, and that number is growing as violence ends.

The Irish economy is very dependent on events outside of the country because of the important roles that trade and foreign sources of energy play in the life of the country. It is a land which must import many essential raw materials. It does have a large quantity of zinc ore, as well as copper, sulphur, baryte, gypsum and dolomite. Its only valuable energy source is peat, or turf bogs, which cover parts of the Central Plain and large areas along the south, west and northwest coasts. It lacks sizable coal deposits, and it is only beginning to extract natural gas near Kinsale Head. Although recent discoveries on the ocean shelf may produce oil for Ireland, at this time the country has very little. Yet 70% of its energy needs are supplied by oil. Thus, the Irish economy was drastically affected by changes in oil prices, while remaining dependent upon unstable world trade for its strength. It generates no nuclear power.

Almost 90% of Ireland's GDP is generated by trade. Manufactured goods account for well over half the value of exports. Since almost a third of these go to the United Kingdom (and the percentage is steadily declining) and another third to the continental EU members (a percentage which has steadily risen since 1973), Ireland is very vulnerable to economic ups and downs in those industrialized countries. In an attempt to reduce that vulnerability somewhat, the Irish severed the

U2

Ireland

link between the British and Irish pound in 1979 and tied its currency later to the European Monetary System. In 1999 it joined 10 other EU nations in adopting the Euro, to be fully introduced by 2002. Ireland presents an image of financial stability that foreign investors like.

Ireland finds itself in an economic dilemma, described in 1988 by *The Economist* as follows: "Take a tiny, open ex–peasant economy. Place it next door to a much larger one, from which it broke away with great bitterness barely a lifetime ago. Infuse it with a passionate desire to enjoy the same lifestyle as its former masters, but without the same industrial heritage or natural resources. Inevitable result: extravagance, frustration, debt."

The scourge of high unemployment has had several unfavorable consequences for Ireland. Unemployment compensation helped send welfare spending through the roof. Government spending on social services soared from 29% of GDP in 1980 to 35.6% in 1985. The government simply borrowed money at home and abroad to pay for them. About a fourth of all government expenditures is devoted to interest payments, the majority of which are to foreign lenders. By 1999 the total public debt stood at 55% of GDP (down from 131% in 1987), and its 1997 budget deficit was only 1.2% of GDP, well below the 3% limit required to meet the EU's convergence criterion for the European currency.

Taxes are kept low for foreign firms in order to attract them to invest in Ireland, making it the EU's biggest tax haven. Therefore, wage and salary earners bear a heavy income tax burden (including a 25% VAT, Western Europe's highest). For example, a single man with no allowances sees two–thirds of his pay disappear through taxes and deductions. It is no wonder that tax cheating has become rampant.

The economic growth that Ireland has enjoyed since the mid–fifties continued in 1999, at a rate of almost 9% of GDP, after averaging 6% from 1993–8. The economy is in danger of overheating. Inflation had risen to 2.9% in 1999, and Dublin real estate prices shot up 40% in 1998. Inflation might be even higher were it not for a "social partnership" created by government, labor and business to slow wage–rate increases and secure labor peace. Its 9.4% unemployment is far lower than the 20% posted at the low point of the 1980s and close to the EU average of 10.4% in 1999. It continues to decline steadily. This is partly due to more than three–quarters of a billion dollars in annual investment by off–shore companies, creating directly or indirectly more than 300,000 jobs. Also, as a formerly poor member of the EU, Ireland still gets structural and CAP funds from Brussels 4% of its GDP, although these monies are bound to diminish over time.

Unemployment presents a particularly worrisome problem for a country with the EU's highest sustained growth in population and labor force. It must provide jobs for those Irishmen who continue to move back to Ireland and from the agricultural into the manufacturing and service sectors, but it must also provide work for the growing number of young persons and women who are entering the labor market. The economic boom is also attracting other EU nationalities, including British. At the turn of the century, immigration to this once–poor island exceeds emigration. The government's strategy to create jobs for the EU's youngest labor force has been through rapid industrial development.

In the past high unemployment set in motion a disappointing wave of emigration. Almost a fourth of Ireland's adults have lived abroad at some point in their lives. The impressive economic growth in the mid–1990s reversed the population flight, and skilled workers are returning to Ireland. American firms advertise in American newspapers to fill vacancies in their Irish businesses.

The tradition of spirited trade union activity has remained in Ireland. This is reflected in the 94 member unions of the Irish Congress of Trade Unions (ICTU), which have affiliates in Northern Ireland. About 60% of working Irishmen are members of unions, which were among the strongest and most militant in the world.

CULTURE

Ireland's culture, like its political history, reflects the problem of a native people being dominated by a more powerful neighbor. For centuries the natives spoke Gaelic (usually called Irish); the Norman invaders spoke French; but as they were Anglicized by the English they came to speak that language as it had evolved in the 14th century. As so many of the Irish–speaking people died or immigrated after the Potato Famine in the mid–19th century, English came to be the predominant language. Despite efforts to require school children to learn Gaelic, only 2% of the population (located primarily in the rural areas of the west) speak Irish as a first language. The fact that road signs and official government publications are still in Gaelic is quaint, but hardly necessary. In fact, it is so difficult to find someone who speaks it that fluent speakers can wear a lapel pin called a *fainne* to invite others to address them in Irish.

Because of the poverty in which they lived for many centuries, the Irish developed world–wide recognition in only one art form; it required no capital investment—the use of words. The Irish have always prided themselves in their ability to talk and write. Celtic history is rich in legend and folklore, and more recently, a number of authors, poets and dramatists have achieved international prominence. Whenever one thinks of masters of the English language, the names of Irishmen come to mind. Jonathan Swift, Thomas More, James Joyce, Oliver Goldsmith, John Millington Synge, Sean O'Casey and Brendan Beehan are influential in all of literature. And four Irishmen, William Butler Yeats, George Bernard Shaw, Samuel Becket, and in 1995 Seamus Heaney, have won the Nobel Prize for Literature. Born in Belfast the son of a potato farmer, Heaney's poetry is stamped by the simplicity and nature images of his boyhood farm. With his characteristic modesty, he said that he is a mere "foothill of a mountain range" compared to Yeats and Becket. In the 1990s writers like Colm Toibin, Dermot Bolger, Mary O'Donnell, Evelyn Conlon, and Nuala Ni Dhomhnaill are being widely–read.

The Irish are indeed a musical people, but their music has most often taken the form of widespread participation rather than special expertise of outstanding composers or professional performers. The Celtic harp, along with the shamrock, is one of the most frequently used symbols of Ireland. Harp playing and Celtic dancing (rhythmical patterns formed by four or eight dancers using rapid foot movements, with the arms usually held down at the sides) have spread around the world wherever there are groups of expatriate Irish. Interestingly, many American pioneer songs, bluegrass and country music (but not western) have Irish roots. In rural Ireland, amateur nights where performers display a variety of talent, are still popular. Even today, a visitor to a rural cottage may be told, "Now you mustn't leave until we have a little sing–song." Then all those present will sing together, usually unaccompanied by any musical instrument. The Cork jazz, Wexford opera, and Waterford light opera festivals attract thousands of visitors.

Among the most famous Irish musicians was U2, a successful rock group and winner of two Grammy awards in 1988. Their unmistakable Irishness is revealed by the political content of some of their texts, which deal with fighting and dying on their island. The repertoire of the popular Irish–American rock band, Black 47, is also overtly political, as the title of its debut album, *Fire of Freedom*, indicates. Other musicians, such as Moving Hearts, Fleagh Cowboys, and Mary Coughlan, mix musical styles like rock and tradition-

Ireland

al and demonstrate that Ireland is still fertile ground for creative music. Ireland is also producing world–class films.

Irish step dancing has burst out of the local parish hall and onto a world stage. The dance show–musicals, *Riverdance* by Bill Whelan and *Lord of the Dance* starring Chicagoan Michael Flatley and Jean Butler, are performing before packed audiences everywhere and are receiving global acclaim. After one performance, an observer claimed that "the speed and coordination took my breath away!" Another noted that Irish vernacular is being married to "American razzmatazz." These dance sensations are part of a larger cultural phenomenon in the 1990s. The Irish are becoming more urban, secular, experimental, self–confident, and less attached to nationalist certainties. Their once rural–based arts are being transplanted to Dublin, where they find a new cosmopolitan expression and no longer serve a nationalist agenda.

Irish art in both Celtic and medieval times displayed a wild imagination with brightly colored swirls and fantastic figures best represented in the illustrated manuscripts. Until recently, Irish art has tended to copy work being done in England or on the continent. But in the last quarter century, there has been a revival of crafts which have used the old Gaelic and medieval symbols to create the beginnings of an indigenous modern art.

Until the 20th century, Ireland had only one university, Trinity College in Dublin, which was founded in 1591 by Queen Elizabeth I. Until recently it was not open to Catholics. In 1908 the National University of Ireland was founded. It has branches in Dublin, Cork, Galway and Limerick. Education is free and compulsory for children through the age of fifteen. The system pays its teachers more in relation to average earnings than any other land in the OECD. It produces a well–educated work force, especially at the upper end. This and the use of the English language are very appealing to foreign investors.

Both the postal and telephone services are operated by the government, which claims that 90% of all letters mailed reach their destination within one day. There are seven daily newspapers, five in Dublin and two in Cork. An autonomous public corporation operates radio and television broadcasting; licensing fees are charged and advertisements also produce revenue.

Dublin, whose graceful Georgian buildings are now falling into the shadow of taller concrete and glass structures, continues to dominate the life of Ireland. Eighteen percent of the population lives within the city's boundaries, and a third of Eire's population lives in greater Dublin. This reflects the fact that Ireland has become much more urban than it once was. It also means that some of Eire's poverty, which was largely confined to rural areas, is now more visible in the capital city. Dublin is the center of the nation's cultural, financial and political life.

FUTURE

The major problem which still faces Ireland is its relationship with Ulster. Until recently, every patriot and every successful politician preached the necessity of unifying the whole island. But the violence and economic depression in the North made most citizens of the Republic wary of unification. Election battles have been fought on economic grounds and not the Ulster issue. The prospects for peace are perhaps the brightest in three decades since the "troubles" began.

For 800 years, Ireland was dominated by a foreign power. Those who led the country from the 1920s to the 1950s were men who had helped to expel the British. For the next 25 years, Ireland was able to forget its past and make dramatic strides in modernization and industrialization. Now the people face the challenge of maintaining their new prosperity. But they may be proud that Robert Emmet's vision has come true—his country *has* taken its place among the nations of the earth.

Ireland has acquired the new nickname, "Celtic Tiger." It has undeniable economic strengths. Its growing standard of living during the past 50 years reached that of the EU, and for the first time in history it overtook that of Britain. Small wonder that when Prime Minister Ahern visited China in 1998 the mayor of Shanghai told him: "If there were more Irish here, I think development would be much faster." This wealth and success have significantly increased the expectations of the Irish people and their demands on the government for continued prosperity.

The failure of any party to gain a majority in parliament and the frequent elections point to the difficulty any government will have in satisfying these aspirations. With typical Irish wit, Fitz-Gerald said before the 1982 election, "Whoever wins the election should have first choice on going into opposition."

By electing two presidents in a row, including British subject from Northern Ireland Mary McAleese, voters signaled a receptivity to reforms which enabled the country to enter the 21st century as a modern European nation. In 1994 a bill was passed "without a ripple of controversy" legalizing homosexuality. Abortion and divorce are also legal now in certain circumstances. The traditional bastions of power and paternalism—state, church, and family business patriarchs—are under assault as never before. Ireland's overall political course has not changed under the Ahern government. Ireland is justified in being optimistic about its future.

Ireland's culture is attracting attention far beyond its borders. When leaving for Paris in 1939, Irish dramatist Samuel Becket claimed that he preferred France at war to Ireland at peace. His country has changed dramatically. Frank McCourt, whose bestselling *Angela's Ashes* describes his youth in a poor and hide–bound Ireland before and during the Second World War, said about Ireland in the late–1990s: "When I go back I see it in a way the kids walk. The confidence. It's almost saucy. We have entered the age of Irish sauciness. God help us all."

Aerial view of Dublin

The Nordic Countries

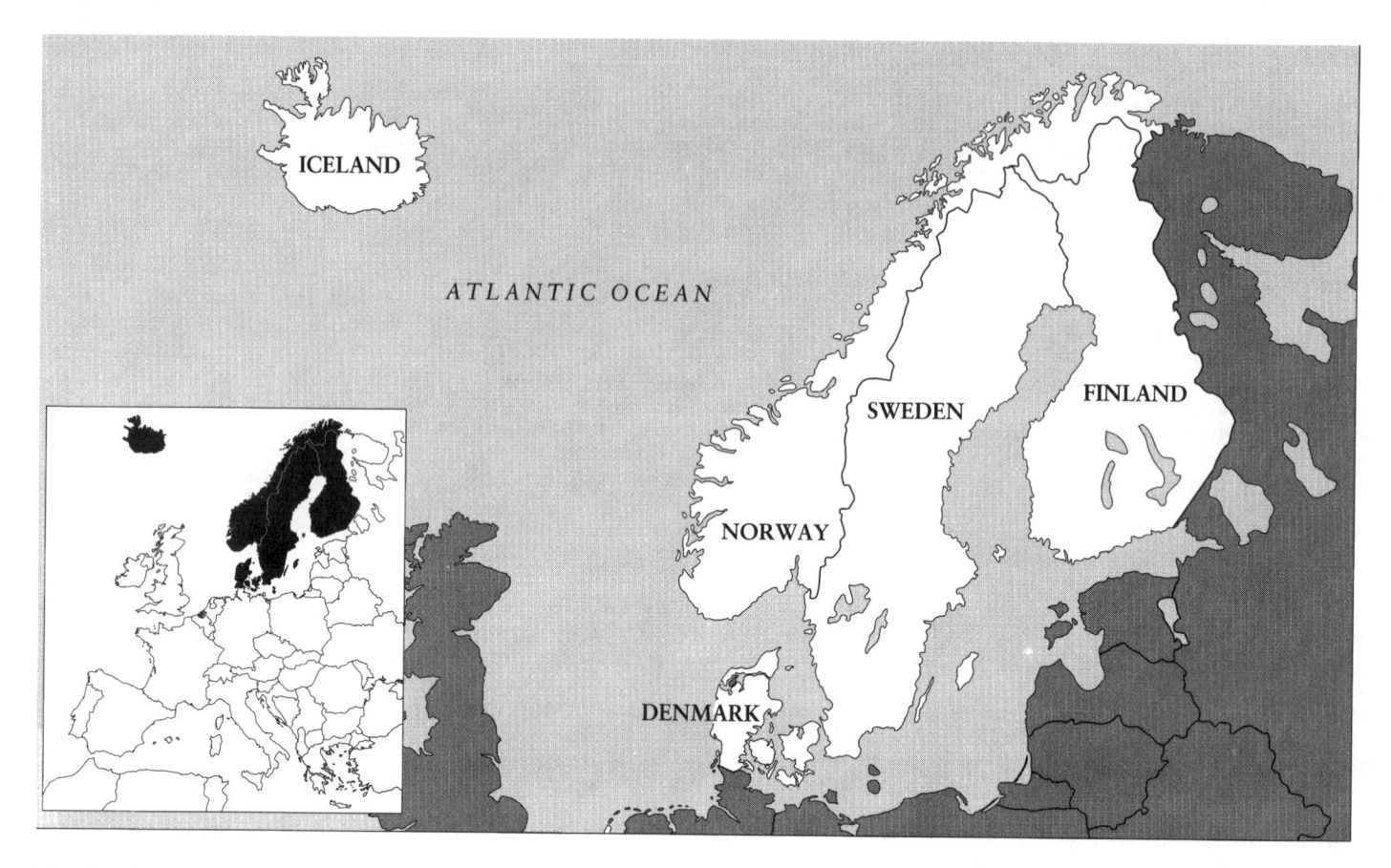

The People

Prosperous, peaceful, harmonious, with a stable, democratic political order and beautiful, unspoiled and sparsely populated territories on the outskirts of Europe are words which typify this area of the world. These are things which are often associated with the Nordic area, which encompasses Sweden, Norway, Denmark, Iceland and Finland, or, more narrowly, to Scandinavia, a term generally applied to the first three. Indeed, at first glance, these countries seem to have escaped many of the most severe problems which have afflicted postwar Europe. Yet, a closer look reveals that they share some important economic and social problems with the rest of Western Europe. Further, they are by no means so isolated from the world as many people often think.

Although the Nordic countries have chosen to take different paths on many matters, they have many things in common. Geographically, they are all located on the same latitude as Alaska and Siberia, but they are warmed by Atlantic currents, which make them more habitable. Also, they are comfortably set apart from Europe, and Iceland, Sweden, Norway (except for a short stretch at the northern tip) and parts of Denmark are separated from Europe by water. Thus, they have been spared many of Europe's violent conflicts. For at least two centuries their populations have been too small to permit any grand–scale political activity outside their sphere. They have therefore had the luxury of being able to concentrate on their own affairs and to develop, to a great extent, at their own speed and in their own preferred way.

Citizens of the Nordic countries have minimal language problems among themselves. Except for Finnish, which is related to Estonian and Hungarian, all other Nordic languages are of northern Germanic origin. To help maintain a lingual tie to the other countries, Finland retains Swedish as an official language together with Finnish. Danes, Swedes, Norwegians and, to some extent, Icelanders can read each others' languages, and with patience and good will they can make themselves understood when speaking, although Danish presents some difficulties to Swedes and Norwegians, and Icelandic presents greater problems to all three. These language ties and close proximity enable Nordic officials to pick up the phone and talk to each other in order to discuss everyday problems.

The Nordic peoples also share many cultural values. One of the most important is Lutheran Christianity, to which most, at least nominally, belong. Lutheranism in Scandinavia is void of religious fanaticism. Although most citizens are baptized and married in the Church and voluntarily pay their church taxes, few attend church regularly. For instance, in Norway today only 3% above the age of 15 attend weekly. Another 6% go once every couple of months. All the Nordic countries are highly secularized in that religious dogma or considerations play a very small role in the everyday lives and politics of the people. By the middle of the 19th century, religious freedom and tolerance were practiced in all Nordic countries and helped to bolster tolerance in the political and social spheres as well.

Most persons in these countries tend to take a practical, unemotional approach to politics which stresses compromise, stability and continuity. Compromise is necessary because all have proportional representation electoral systems, which always grant parliamentary seats to a large number of parties. Therefore, a single party almost never wins a majority of parliamentary seats, and the countries must be ruled by either minority or coalition governments. These lands do have fewer social tensions than some other Western European countries, and over the years, most of their citizens have developed a kind of immunity to totalitarian ideologies or unrealizable political demands.

All the Nordic countries entered the second half of the 19th century as relatively poor agricultural societies and ex-

The Nordic Countries

perienced the industrial revolution rather late. Industrialization brought greater wealth, but it also brought many problems. At the same time that they underwent fundamental social and economic changes, they adopted democratic political practices. As a result of many compromises between the traditional ruling elites and the newly developing or increasingly self–confident middle, working and farming classes, more people were allowed to vote, and the governments became answerable to popularly elected parliaments, rather than to the Swedish, Danish and (after 1905) Norwegian monarchs. In characteristic Nordic style, this process of democratization took place largely without violent revolutions or *coups d'etat*. These peoples generally have had a good sense of timing in changing outdated practices or structures in order to be able to preserve that which is worth preserving. Also, they have had a genius for solving political, social and religious issues in such a way that the losers are never left permanently unreconciled to the system and with bitter determination to revive the dispute later.

The Earliest Period

The common ties among these countries did not emerge overnight, but in the course of centuries of mutual collaboration. In Denmark there is evidence of human settlements as early as 50,000 B.C., and by 10,000 B.C. communities began to be established all over Scandinavia. Although some trade gradually developed with the rest of the continent, Europe did not take much notice of the Nordic area. The Romans did not bother with this region at all, except for a small volume of trade in amber. Tacitus did refer to a tribe of people in Sweden known as the *Svear*, from whom the name *Sverige* (Sweden) was derived. The Romans also engaged in combat with Cimbri, Vandals and other Scandinavian groups.

The Vikings (Norsemen, Northmen, Normans)

This inconspicuous existence ended abruptly in the beginning of the 9th century, when the Vikings burst out of Scandinavia and began venturing in sturdy ships far from their own lands. They sometimes established colonies and traded peacefully, but they often pillaged and plundered, leaving wastelands in their wake. Most Europeans learned to pray for protection from the Viking's ravishings, and the institution of feudalism was, in part, a response to the widespread willingness of a common people to exchange their liberties for protection.

A notable twist probably occurred in Russia. In the 9th century, warlike Slav tribes were weary of rampant strife. The Vikings were using Russian rivers for trade. They, according to *The Primary Chronicle* of the 12th century, actually *invited* the Vikings to become their rulers! The "Varangian Russes," called *Variagi* in Russian, were Norman (Norsemen, Northmen, Vikings), who founded the first Russian dynasty. This part of the *Chronicle* is vigorously disputed in the Soviet Union today—the idea that *outsiders* had to be called in to bring order to the area is distasteful. It is indisputable, however, that the Vikings ventured all the way to the Black Sea, Constantinople and the Mediterranean Sea during this period.

The Vikings sailed to the British Isles, (establishing settlements in England, the Hebrides Islands, Shetlands and Isle of Man), Ireland (whose capital of Dublin was a Viking fortress), Normandy and Iceland. From the latter island, Eric the Red discovered and named Greenland in 981 or 982 A.D., where he established a settlement on the southwest tip. His son, Leif Eriksson, sailed from Greenland to the northeast coast of North America around the year 1000 A.D., beating Christopher Columbus to the New World by about five centuries. In the U.S., Leif Eriksson Day is celebrated on October 9th of each year. By the middle of the 11th century, the Vikings had reached their peak and dominated most of the sea shipping routes around Europe and Orkney. The boldness and restlessness of such modern Norwegian explorers as Roald Amundsen and Thor Heyerdahl show that some Scandinavians still have the adventuresome spirit of their forebears.

Christianity

Viking marauding had brought considerable wealth to the Nordic area, but it also caused a serious drain on the tribes' manpower and threatened to make the Nordic lands vulnerable to outside attacks. They began to settle down, and the regional tribal communities gradually gave way to larger kingdoms. Christianity, which had been introduced to Sweden as early as 830 A.D., along with other European influences, began to filter more and more into the Nordic area through the peninsula of Jutland. By the 12th century, Christianity had spread to all corners of the area, and with the Pope's blessing, the Swedes conducted crusades in Finland, which became a part of the Swedish realm.

Medieval Norway

In the 13th century Norway, which had been united into one nation by the end of the 9th century, reached the peak of its power, taking possession of Greenland and Iceland. Norwegian culture also reached its high point and was described vividly and imaginatively in the sagas of Snorre Snurrlasson. The terrible bubonic plague, known in Europe as the Black Death, from 1349–50 struck the region with full fury. One–half of Norway's population perished. This accelerated the economic and cultural decline of Norway which became a predominantly peasant nation during the following centuries.

The Nordic Countries

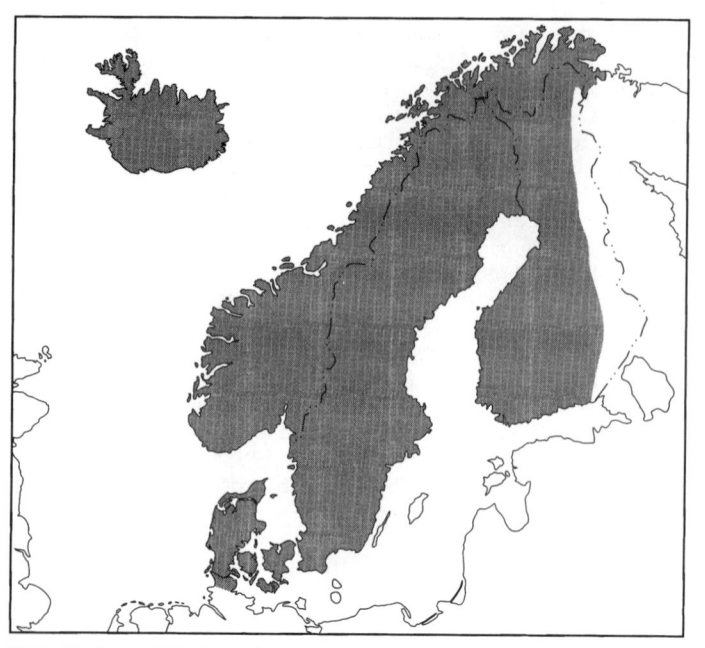

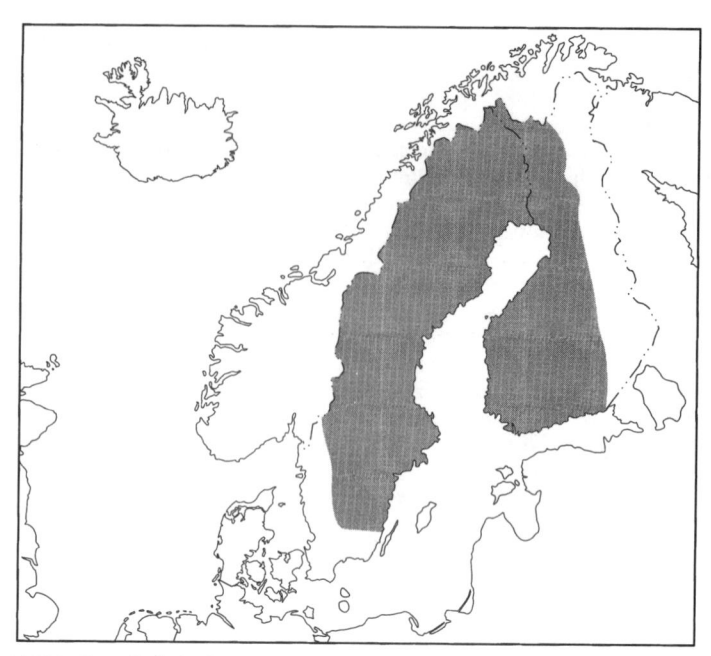

1397: Union of Kalmar (under Denmark)

1523: Swedish independence

Contests for Supremacy

Throughout the ensuing centuries, Denmark and Sweden vied for domination over the Nordic region. Not until the 20th century were Norway, Finland and Iceland able to win full independence. By the end of the 14th century it appeared that Denmark would control all of northern Europe. In the late 12th and early 13th centuries it had already begun to expand to other territories along the northern and southern Baltic coasts. In 1380 it acquired Iceland and the Faroe Islands and by 1387 its domination extended over Norway. Denmark's political domination over the region was formalized in the Union of Kalmar, which was established in 1397; it linked all five Nordic nations together in a single kingdom under Danish leadership. It also helped to curtail German commercial predominance in the region, which had threatened to lead to German political domination as well, especially in Sweden.

The Union of Kalmar began to break down after Queen Margrete died in 1412. Swedish nationalism had begun to grow, and by the middle of the 14th century, Swedes had developed a set of laws which applied to the whole nation. In the 15th century they increasingly resisted Danish domination and in 1434, a peasant uprising, supported by some noblemen, was directed against Danish rule. This event led to the convocation of the first *Riksdag* (Swedish Parliament) in 1435. King Christian II of Denmark sent an army against the Swedes and in 1520 had himself crowned in Stockholm as the hereditary monarch. There was a good chance that he could pacify the Swedes after he had promised a general amnesty for all rebels.

However, he broke his promise and ordered the decapitation of 80 leading Swedes. This disgusting and politically unwise bloodbath prompted the young Swedish nobleman and first genuine national hero, Gustav Eriksson Vasa, to lead a successful rebellion against the Danes. In 1523 Vasa was declared the first truly Swedish king, taking the name of Gustav I and exercising authority over all of Sweden except the southernmost provinces, which continued to belong to Denmark until 1658. The Union of Kalmar ceased to exist, although the Swedes and Danes continued for another century and a half to struggle for supremacy in Scandinavia.

The house of King Gustav I in Delecarlia

The Reign of Gustav I and the Emergence of Sweden

This is generally known as the Vasa period and was extremely important for Sweden's later development. Not only did he establish Swedish independence, but, like Henry VIII of England, he severed Sweden's ties with the Catholic Church in 1527, creating the Lutheran State Church and supported the Reformation. In fact, all over the Nordic area, the Reformation succeeded quickly and with little resistance. Therefore, these countries were left with only tiny religious minorities and were spared the kind of religious divisions and tensions which continued to plague many European countries for centuries. Gustav I also created a centralized national ad-

The Nordic Countries

ministration, which was an essential for Sweden's era as a great European power from 1611 to 1718, generally referred to as the Age of Greatness. During this period, Sweden flourished economically, culturally, politically and militarily.

Today, it is difficult to imagine that a nation of only a million inhabitants could conduct successful military campaigns against the then great powers of Denmark, Poland and Russia. When the Thirty Years' War began to rage in the heart of Europe in 1618, Sweden initially kept out of the struggle and instead continued to concentrate on broadening its foothold in the eastern Baltic. The result of this policy was that the Baltic became a Swedish lake which could be used only under Swedish terms.

By contrast, Denmark rushed headlong into the tragic, ostensibly religious, Thirty Years' War and sought to expand its influence southward. Its military adventures in northern Germany provoked the ravishing of Jutland by marauding Catholic troops. In 1630 a battered Denmark was forced to sue for peace; in the same year Sweden decided to enter the bloody struggle because of the Catholic armies' advances toward the Baltic area and the serious reversals which the protestant princes had suffered in the first half of the war. King Gustavus II Adolphus, grandson of Gustav Vasa, led his Swedish troops brilliantly. He marched them all the way to Bavaria, and by the winter of 1631–2, he could hold court in Mainz and Frankfurt am Main. He was killed in 1632 while leading his troops to victory against Catholic forces at Lützen.

His death sapped the initiative and dynamism from Sweden's policy. Nevertheless, when Denmark attempted to take advantage of the new political void in Sweden by launching a renewed attack, the Swedes were able to respond quickly and successfully. The Danes were forced to accept a peace at Brömsebro in 1645 which underscored and solidified Sweden's predominance in Scandinavia. Not only did Denmark lose much of its territory to Sweden, but it had to renounce its right to levy customs on Swedish goods in Øresund, the narrow strait between the two countries.

Sweden emerged as a great power from the Peace of Westphalia, which formalized the end of the terrible Thirty Years' War in 1648. It received German holdings in Pomerania, the bishoprics of Verden and Bremen and the island of Rügen. When Denmark sought revenge in the Danish–Swedish War from 1657 to 1660, during which Sweden occupied Jutland and other Danish islands several times, it suffered even further losses. In the Peace of Copenhagen in 1660, Denmark lost all its Swedish provinces and thereby all control over the Øresund Strait. The borders between Sweden and Denmark which were established in this settlement remain essentially unchanged today.

This peace signified the end of Danish dreams of being a great power. It bankrupted the country and laid waste to much of its territory. The outcome of the conflict underscored Sweden's position as the leading power in northern Europe, although Denmark occasionally disputed this status in the following decades. Swedish authority extended over Finland, Estonia, Latvia, Ingermanland (in which Leningrad is now located) and several coastal towns, and its empire continued to grow in later years. Sweden fought many wars to expand its empire, but it was fortunate in being able to fight them mostly on foreign soil.

During the 17th century Sweden also was able to acquire a colony in America which it called *Nya Sverige* ("New Sweden"). In 1638 it purchased from Indians a large tract which encompassed southeastern Pennsylvania (including the present city of Philadelphia), a chunk of New Jersey and most of Delaware. The capital of this colony was Christina, which was later renamed Wilmington, in Delaware. Swedish and Finnish Lutheran priests, merchants, soldiers, settlers and convicts were sent to New Sweden. The residents had relatively good contacts with the local Indians and were possibly the first settlers to introduce a particular Swedish invention into the New World: the log house. In 1655 the colony was seized by the Dutch following an intense border dispute, but Swedish continued to be spoken in some communities there until the late 18th century, and the Swedish Lutheran Church established its foothold in America.

The Swedes acquired from France the Caribbean island of Saint Barthélemy in 1784. Very few people settled on this island, whose major population was Black slaves, but the capital was named Gustavia after the Swedish king. In 1878 the island was sold back to France. The Swedish also established temporarily a colony called Cabo Corso in what is now Ghana in Africa. The capital was called Carlsborg, and the present–day city of Accra was the site of a Swedish factory. There were very few Swedes in this colony, beyond a governor, soldiers and merchants.

By the beginning of the 18th century Sweden's empire had so aroused the resentment of Denmark, Russia, Poland and Saxony (in Germany) that the latter powers decided to help themselves to some of the Swedish holdings. Despite some initial successes by the young king, Karl XII, the Swedes revealed that they had neither the manpower nor the resources to resist

1660: Swedish dominance

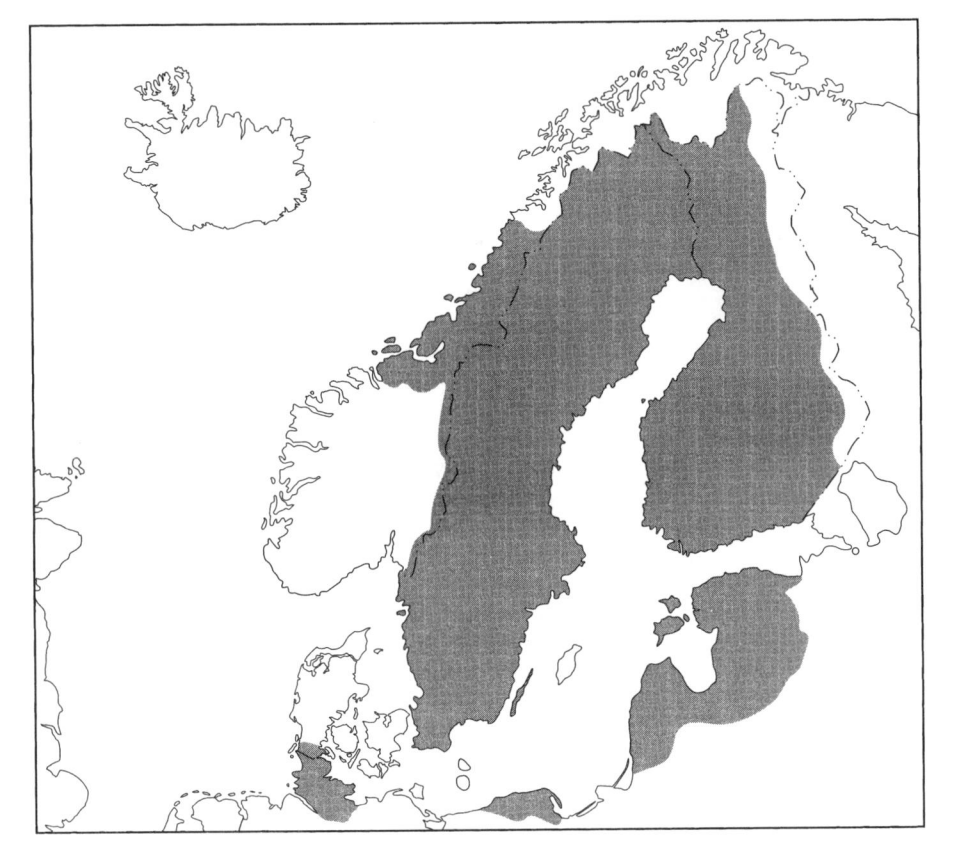

The Nordic Countries

for long. The country had become exhausted by constant war, and at least by 1718 Sweden's decline could no longer be denied. Its northern German territories were ceded to Prussia and Hanover by 1720, and during the Great Northern War (1709–21) the Swedish armies were defeated in Russia, which resulted in Russian occupation of the Baltic countries and of southeastern Finland.

The Napoleonic Wars

These battles from the end of the 18th and beginning of the 19th centuries brought significant territorial changes to the region, and the ideas of the French Revolution influenced political developments in certain Nordic countries, especially Denmark and Norway. In the struggle which gripped all of Europe, Denmark tried in vain to remain neutral. However the English feared that the country might eventually side with Napoleon, so they challenged the Danish fleet a short distance from Copenhagen in 1801 and forced Denmark to enter a formal non–aggression pact with Britain. Six years later the British again grew nervous. They demanded that Denmark hand over to them its high seas fleet and threatened to shell Copenhagen if this ultimatum was not accepted. The Danes understandably balked at this impudence, but after British ships had bombarded the capital city for four days, the disheartened Danes handed over their navy. Out of spite, they then cast their lot with Napoleon against the British, but Denmark ultimately had to pay a high price for this folly. By 1813 it was bankrupt, and in the Treaty of Kiel a year later, it was compelled to hand Norway over to Sweden, which had fought on the side of the victors.

But the Norwegians, who wanted full independence, went to war against Sweden in order to prevent one form of domination from being exchanged for another. A Norwegian national assembly had adopted one of the most liberal constitutions of its time and had selected a Danish prince as its new king. But a combination of Swedish leniency and military power during the armed confrontation of 1814 persuaded the Norwegians to accept a new arrangement. The newly selected Norwegian king abdicated, and the first Norwegian Parliament (Storting) accepted the Swedish monarch as the king of Norway. Sweden assumed overall predominance in foreign policy and the right to appoint a Norwegian viceroy, who performed the normal duties of a prime minister.

Norwegians were left with wide powers over their own affairs and with their own constitution, navy, army, customs and legislature. In effect, Norway had complete liberty and independence within its own boundaries. In the course of the 19th century, Norwegians solidified their sense of national identity and resisted any closer relations with Sweden. Finally in 1905 they requested in the form of a plebiscite complete independence, which Sweden, after some internal debate, granted. At the end of that year, Prince Carl of Denmark was chosen king and took the name Haakon VII.

Sweden's acquisition of Norway in 1814 was mild consolation for its loss of Finland five years earlier. Because Sweden had sided with Britain against the French, Napoleon had granted Russia in the Peace of Tilsit a free hand against Sweden. Thus, in 1809 Russia took Finland, a land which it dominated for a century. This bitter loss of a province which had belonged to Sweden for many centuries cost the Swedish king Gustav IV his crown in a bloodless *coup*. In the same year, the Swedish elite adopted The Instrument of Government (*Regeringsformen*), which, after the U.S. Constitution, is the second oldest written document of government in the world and which is one of the four which makes up Sweden's present constitution.

The Swedes chose in 1810 one of Napoleon's field marshals, Jean–Baptiste Bernadotte, as regent. Turning on his former leader, Bernadotte led Sweden into the struggle against France, a decision which secured allied support for the Swedish acquisition of Norway. After the short campaign against that country in 1814, Sweden withdrew from European conflicts and has not been at war since. Bernadotte was crowned king in 1818 with the title of King Karl XIV Johan; he ruled until 1844 and his descendants still hold the throne. It is an irony of history that the king had once been an ardent opponent of the monarchy in France and had even reportedly had the words indelibly tattooed on his arm: "Death to Kings!" It can be assumed that he never wore short sleeves while he occupied the throne of Sweden!

The 19th Century

The 19th century was for the Nordic countries one of major political, economic and social changes. Except for the war of Prussia and Austria against Denmark, which resulted in Denmark's loss of Schleswig and Holstein which contained about one–third of Denmark's European holdings (see West Germany), this was a century of peace for the Nordic area. The French Revolution had produced a spark of democracy all over Europe, and the Nordic countries, especially Norway and Denmark, were touched by that spark. However, unlike many European countries at that time, the northern peoples al-

1814: Sweden loses Finland to Russia, gains Norway from Denmark

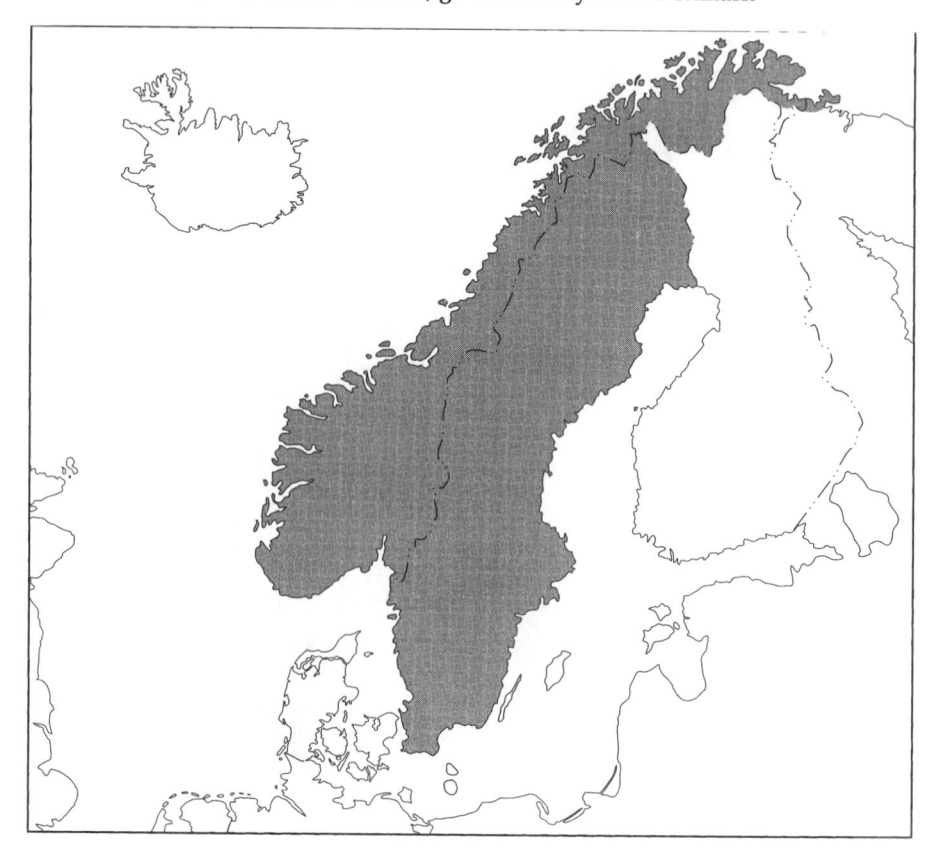

The Nordic Countries

ready had traditions in which some groups had political representation, parliaments had some powers and monarchical authority was limited by constitutions and other barriers.

These foundations for modern democracy were strengthened in the course of the 1800s. Following a short outbreak of civil unrest in 1848, Denmark proclaimed a *Grundlov* (charter) which formally declared the country to be a constitutional monarchy, with guaranteed civil liberties and with a parliament which shared power with the crown. In Norway, municipal self–government was introduced in 1837, and in 1884 the Swedish king recognized the principle of parliamentary government in Norway by agreeing to appoint a prime minister who had the approval of a majority in the *Storting*. In Sweden, political power passed gradually from an aristocracy of birth to a prosperous elite of common birth, and ultimately to the middle and working classes. By the 1870s all Nordic countries had functioning representative assemblies, although full parliamentary government was not introduced into Norway until 1884, in Denmark until 1901 and in Sweden and Finland until 1917.

Democracy and Industrialization

This progress toward political democracy took place at a time of extremely rapid industrialization. It had come late to the region and created wrenching social problems, such as the breakdown of many rural communities, too rapid urbanization, excessive population growth, the weakening of family ties and alcoholism. Nevertheless, the democratic transformation came about without any mass violence. This peaceful change was due in part to the existence in these countries of political institutions and attitudes which could more easily adapt to changing conditions and to increasing demands for greater democratic participation in politics.

More and more citizens were granted the right to vote. Finland achieved universal suffrage in 1906, followed by Norway in 1913, Denmark in 1915 and Sweden in 1921. The absence of mass violence also was due to the steady increase in literacy and to the success of mass movements, such as those for workers' rights or temperance, which could articulate and channel important demands on the political system.

Emigration to America

A further factor which alleviated social tensions in these countries was emigration, which reached massive proportions by the 1860s and which enabled the most desperate to begin new lives elsewhere, especially in the U.S. The possibility of leaving for the New World helped to diminish militant discontent which could have been seriously disruptive at a crucial time when these people were adjusting to the modern age. Sweden produced the greatest waves of emigration—in the 1880s at least 325,000 out of a total population of 4.5 million left for the U.S., and in the following two decades, from 10,000 to 20,000 Swedes left for America each year. By the year 1900 one–fifth to one– fourth of all native–born Swedes were already living abroad. Parts of America, particularly the northern midwestern states around and west of the Great Lakes, where the climate and landscape were very similar to the home country, were decisively shaped by Nordic immigrants. The lives, problems and successes of these people in America was movingly portrayed in the three volumes on this subject written by one of Sweden's outstanding novelists, Vilhelm Moberg. His story was also filmed by the Swedish director, Jan Troell. Edna Ferber's moving "So Big" attested to the hardiness and strength of character of these emigrés. This flood to America is also evoked in the Emigrants House museum at Växjö.

Finland experienced waves of emigration to the U.S. and, later, to Sweden. Many Norwegians also set their sights toward the New World. In fact, no country, except for Ireland, sent such a large percentage of its people as emigrants to the U.S. as did Norway. The first shipload landed in New York City in 1825, and in the years 1866 to 1873, over 100,000 left Norway. From 1900 to 1910 more than 200,000 departed. By 1910, roughly 880,000 Norwegians had left their country for greener pastures in America, especially in the northern Midwest, and their descendants now number close to ten million.

World War I

All Scandinavian countries were able to remain neutral during World War I, but the 1917 revolution in Russia gave the Finns the chance for which many had waited for centuries: the opportunity to declare their country's complete independence. The Danes were able to observe that the wartime threat to shipping was so great that their hold on some faraway islands was simply too tenuous. Thus, Denmark sold its part of the Virgin Islands to the United States in 1917. Denmark also profited from Germany's defeat in the war by winning international approval for a plebiscite in 1920 to determine to which country the population of the province of Schleswig wished to belong. In the North, 75% of the people voted to return to Denmark, but in southern Schleswig, 80% voted to remain with Germany. This latter vote left a small, Danish–speaking minority in Germany which still exists today.

Statue of Norway's King Haakon VII

For decades afterwards, the Danish monarchs would not accept this final loss of southern Schleswig, and they showed their resentment by refusing to set foot in that part of Germany. However, the present Danish queen, Margrete II, discarded this antiquated prejudice of her predecessors and enters the province as a welcomed foreign guest.

Depression and World War II

The citizens of the Nordic countries were not so successful in isolating themselves from the economic shockwaves which were generated by the 1929 stock market crash on Wall Street. Everywhere in the region the 1930s were lean times, filled with bankruptcies, unemployment and anxiety. They were also politically and militarily frightening times, with democratic experiments failing in many European countries, and with the European giants, Germany and the Soviet Union, awakening from their own internal chaos and diplomatic and military paralysis.

During this period all four main Nordic countries, like Nazi Germany, introduced eugenics laws, some of which remained in the statutes until 1976. From 1934 to 1974, 62,000 Swedish women were sterilized, often against their will, because they were judged to be rebellious, promiscuous, of low intelligence, or even of mixed blood. The purposes were to prevent "degeneration of the race" and to save the state the heavy cost of welfare for inferior human beings. The policy was carried out openly

The Nordic Countries

by officials who believed in the science of racial biology and thought they were helping to construct an enlightened, progressive welfare state. Norway and Finland confirmed that each did the same to about 1,000 women.

As the clouds of war gathered in the skies over Europe, the Nordic countries tried to maintain a policy of neutrality. All tried to avoid any steps which especially Hitler, the German dictator since 1933, could interpret as being the slightest provocation. They harbored the hope that the League of Nations, the impotence of which had already been demonstrated on repeated occasions, would somehow be able to maintain the peace. Even after the Soviets attacked Finland at the end of 1939, which temporarily drove the Finns into the arms of the Germans and ultimately created an extremely precarious situation from which the Finns have never been able entirely to extract themselves, the Scandinavian countries did not consider themselves to be mortally threatened. Denmark had entered a ten-year non-aggression pact with Germany in May 1939 and declined thereafter to make any military preparations. Norway ordered that military precautions be taken only in the northernmost part of the country, which touches the Soviet Union. Sweden peered nervously into the horizon.

The Danish During the War

Denmark's strategic location astride the exits from the Baltic Sea to the North Sea, as well as its proximity to Germany, made the small nation perched on top of the continent's most dynamic and aggressive power at the time an irresistible victim. Hitler sent his troops to occupy it in April 1940; with the ominous tones of German heavy bombers in their ears, the Danes offered no significant resistance to the forceful occupation of their country, and in return the Germans promised to respect Denmark's independence and integrity and to allow the Danes to have their own government. Nevertheless, they had to bend to many unpleasant German demands, and the Germans selection of the Hotel D'Angleterre in the heart of Copenhagen as its military headquarters served as a constant reminder to the Danes of who exactly was in charge. They had to orient their economy exclusively toward German needs, to join the anti-Comintern Pact, to crack down on communist political activity within Denmark and to tolerate the official Nazi persecution of Jews.

The Danish population practiced a policy of the cold shoulder toward the occupation forces. Sometimes they chose not to hide their sentiments, such as in 1943 when it became fashionable to wear knitted caps with the colors of the British Royal Air Force. Quite early a Danish resistance movement sprang up, but for awhile the Danish government opposed it out of fear that its policy of cooperation in order to save the country from destruction would be undermined. However, the government's position became increasingly untenable, and in August 1943 the Danish King and Parliament stopped functioning. The center of resistance activity became the "Freedom Council," whose membership included former politicians and officers.

The German occupation forces struck back by arresting resistance fighters, police and Jews, but they could never eradicate the Danish opposition, which enjoyed the sympathy and support of almost all Danes. For this resistance activity the alliance against Hitler recognized Denmark as a victorious power after the British had liberated the country on May 5, 1945. After the war Denmark punished those Danes who had collaborated too closely with the Germans.

Britain occupied Denmark's possession of Iceland and the Faroe Islands at the beginning of the war in order to prevent them from falling into enemy hands. In 1941 the U.S. relieved the British in Iceland and, with the approval of local authorities, has retained a military base on the island ever since. The long severance of Iceland from the mother country after the outbreak of the war enabled the Icelanders, who in 1918 had already been granted an autonomy statute for domestic affairs, to declare their complete independence from Denmark in 1944. Greenland was occupied by American troops and was made a temporary protectorate under U.S. authority. After the war it was returned to Danish jurisdiction, although American troops continued to be stationed there by agreement with Denmark.

Norway and the War

Norway, with its long coast facing not only Britain, but also the North Sea and North Atlantic also presented an irresistibly tempting target for German expansion. Unfortunately, Norway had made military preparations only in the North, and its troops were inexperienced and poorly equipped. Therefore, it was not well prepared when Hitler sent his forces against the country on April 9, 1940, the same day on which his troops occupied Denmark. To the Germans' surprise, the Norwegian government rejected the German ultimatum to surrender peacefully and to cooperate, as the Danes had chosen to do. The king, government and parliament withdrew from Oslo toward the North, from where they conducted war against German troops. Further, by sinking the German cruiser, Blücher, Norway was able to transport its entire gold reserves out of the country.

In the confusion of withdrawal to the north, the chief of the *Norwegian National Socialist Party (Nasjonal Samling)* and former defense minister, Vidkun Quisling, read a proclamation to the Norwegian people in the afternoon of April 9. Quisling criticized the government for turning down Germany's "peaceful" offer of cooperation, and he declared himself prime minister and foreign minister. His call to the Norwegian troops to lay down their arms merely stiffened the army's resolve to fight. The Norwegians so despised him that the Germans had to dismiss him as prime minister on April 15, although he was reappointed in 1942. The name *Quisling* is now inseparably associated with the very concept of treason against one's own country.

Not until May 5 was the southern part of the country conquered. With the help of Polish land and British naval forces, the Norwegians fought bitterly against German troops in the northern part of the country, and the Germans, unused to the bitter cold, suffered considerable losses in taking such strategically important objectives as the port of Narvik from which Swedish iron ore was shipped to Germany. By June 7, the Germans had conquered the northern part and became the undisputed power in Scandinavia.

Once it was clear that the Germans would win, the Norwegian Parliament gave King Haakon VII full powers, and the latter, accompanied by the crown prince and the cabinet left the country for London, where he directed lively resistance against the occupation forces throughout the war. Within Norway, the German commissioner, Josef Terboven, governed with the assistance of some cooperative Norwegian civil servants. Others were not cooperative, as so vividly depicted by John Steinbeck in his novel, "The Moon Is Down"; active and passive resistance was widespread. A few small units of the Norwegian Army were also evacuated to Britain, and they subsequently absorbed other Norwegians who fled by boat through icy seas or were already abroad. These highly motivated units, as well as local resistance movements, conducted sabotage and small attacks against the alien regime.

Their number grew in 1944 when they were permitted to equip Norwegian refugees in Sweden, who could then join in the attacks against the Germans and Norwegian collaborators. They received a steady stream of weapons, ammunition and materials from Britain. Unfortunately, these bold actions often provoked Nazi reprisals against civilians, and about 35,000 Norwegians were sent to prisons or

The Nordic Countries

concentration camps during the occupation. These included 1,000 teachers who, like most of their colleagues, refused to teach Nazi principles in the schools. Also, 95% of the pastors were either dismissed or voluntarily gave up their positions because of their almost universal rejection of the "new order." Not until May 7, 1945, did the unwanted foreign domination come to an end. On that day the joy and relief of the people, who had won their independence only 40 years earlier, was almost boundless. Quisling was tried and executed in September, and general elections were held in October. In 1946 Trygve Lie of Norway became the first Secretary–General of the United Nations; his successor was a Swede, Dag Hammarskjöld.

When Thorbjørn Jagland became prime minister in 1996 his first official act was to commit Norway to pay compensation for property stolen from Jews by the Quisling government during the war. Despite the difficulties of identifying, locating, and allocating the repayments, Norway became the first European country, except Germany, to make this commitment.

Sweden

Only Sweden escaped foreign occupation and active participation in the war. However, it was isolated from the outside world, and, because of its obvious military inferiority to Germany, it made concessions which created some animosity among Danes and Norwegians. These compromises were quietly resented by many Swedes themselves, but most Swedes saw no reasonable alternative at the time.

Sweden conducted trade with Nazi Germany, which relied especially on Swedish iron, steel and ball bearings. In some cases, the Swedish police shared information with the *Gestapo* (German secret police), and in the early war years the government tried to muzzle the press to prevent stories unflattering to Nazi Germany. Swedes suppressed most communist activity in their own country in order to please Berlin's leaders. The Swedish government gave in to pressure to permit a German division to move across Swedish territory in order to reach the Russian front. It tolerated German violation of Swedish airspace for military purposes. Finally, the Swedish central bank and the wealthy Wallenberg financial empire bought looted gold from Germany, which provided Germany with additional funds to engage in profitable trade with Sweden and other neutral countries.

On the other hand, after denying refuge to fleeing Jews in the early war years, Sweden dispatched Raoul Wallenberg to Hungary in July 1944 under diplomatic cover on a mission funded by the United States to distribute Swedish safe–conduct passes to Jews. His efforts saved thousands of Jewish lives before he was arrested by invading Soviet forces in January 1945 and died mysteriously at an undetermined time in a Soviet prison somewhere. The Swedish government agreed in 1996 to launch an investigation into allegations that looted Nazi gold had been deposited in Swedish banks, that Holocaust victims had deposited money in Sweden of which their heirs received only a part, and that Swedes had extended loans and other financial help to Nazi Germany. The Wallenberg family agreed to open its files to examiners.

Despite these unfortunate compromises, it should not be forgotten that Sweden granted refuge to thousands of Hitler's opponents, who would otherwise have ended in Nazi prisons or death camps. Such important post–war political leaders as Willy Brandt of Germany and Bruno Kreisky of Austria were able to live and work in Sweden during the war. As victorious powers, both Denmark and Norway took part in the occupation of Germany, and Brandt even returned to Germany as a Norwegian citizen and wearing a Norwegian officer's uniform. Undoubtedly they brought back to their own countries, which between the wars had been severely polarized politically, lasting impressions of Scandinavian moderation, tolerance and democratic spirit. These were qualities which were badly needed in the new beginning which Western Europe made after 1945.

Because neutrality had failed to protect all of the Scandinavian countries from armed aggression, Denmark, Norway and Sweden discussed the possibility of forming a Nordic Defense Community after the war. However, these talks collapsed over the question of whether this alliance should seek the backing of the Western powers, as Norway wished, or whether it should try to remain free of all Great Power conflicts, as Sweden wanted. Although there was and remains a strong emotional attachment of the Nordic region to neutrality, Norway, Denmark and Iceland decided to break with a long tradition and join NATO. Sweden and Finland chose to move away from their strict neutrality in 1994 and join NATO's "Partnership for Peace," a form of affiliation short of full membership.

Postwar Attitudes and Cold War

All Nordic countries espouse political values oriented toward the rest of Western Europe and North America. All had spoken or unspoken fears about Soviet military power and about a possible Soviet military threat to the Nordic area. All are aware that the region has considerable strategic importance. The exits from the Baltic Sea lead through narrow straits between Sweden and Denmark. Two of the

Norway's Quisling returning the salute of a German officer

The Nordic Countries

countries—Finland and Norway—border on Russia, and Norway and Russia had different opinions as to exactly where the border between their territories in the North should be. Norway is the northern flank of NATO. It is astride the waters which separate the northwestern part of Russia from most other NATO countries and which lead to the Atlantic Ocean, where the NATO countries' most important shipping lanes are located. Finally, all are economically advanced countries with valuable industrial resources and high levels of technology.

Although the Nordic countries share common values and defense needs, they have chosen different roads to military security, while retaining a common objective of preserving stability in the region. There is no strategic bloc or single military alliance in the Nordic world. Iceland has no army at all, but relies on the American Icelandic Defense Force for its own protection. All four other countries have compulsory military service. Norway and Denmark are founding members of NATO, but neither permits the stationing of nuclear weapons or foreign troops on its soil during peacetime. The only exception is Greenland, where an agreement between the U.S. and Denmark enables the U.S. to station conventional (non–nuclear) forces.

Sweden pursues a policy of nonalignment in peacetime and armed neutrality in wartime. Finland is also nonaligned, but it entered a treaty of friendship and mutual assistance with the Soviet Union and agreed to limit the size and quality of its armed forces. None permits the stationing of nuclear or chemical weapons on its territory. Norway and Denmark do permit American and British warships to dock without asking whether there are nuclear weapons on board. In 1988 an election was prompted in Denmark when the left unified to pass a parliamentary resolution demanding that the captain of each visiting warship be reminded of Denmark's ban on nuclear weapons within its territory. This violated standing practice of the British and American navies, who refuse to reveal whether their vessels have such weapons on board. After the election, the victorious conservative government was able to water down the issue by merely sending a reminder to each embassy about respecting Danish laws, without any mention of nuclear weapons. This was acceptable to Washington and London, which had temporarily halted all port calls in Denmark.

All Nordic nations had the goal of mutual restraint toward the Soviet Union, but not of total accommodation with that country, whose political values the Nordics abhorred. A central guideline in all Nordic foreign policies is to maintain the established equilibrium and low level of tension in the area. They would never be able to rely on their own strength for protection. This is a rather large area with an extremely small population. If one disregards Greenland, the world's largest island, the Nordic area is still larger than Great Britain, France, Germany, Portugal and the BENELUX countries combined. But its population, at 22.5 million, is only one–tenth that of those countries. Also, the Nordic countries would have to have enormous navies and mobile land and air forces in order to protect such far–flung possessions as the Faroes, Jan Mayan, Svalbard, Greenland, Bouvet and Peter I (tiny South Atlantic islands, not far from Norway's claim in Antartica).

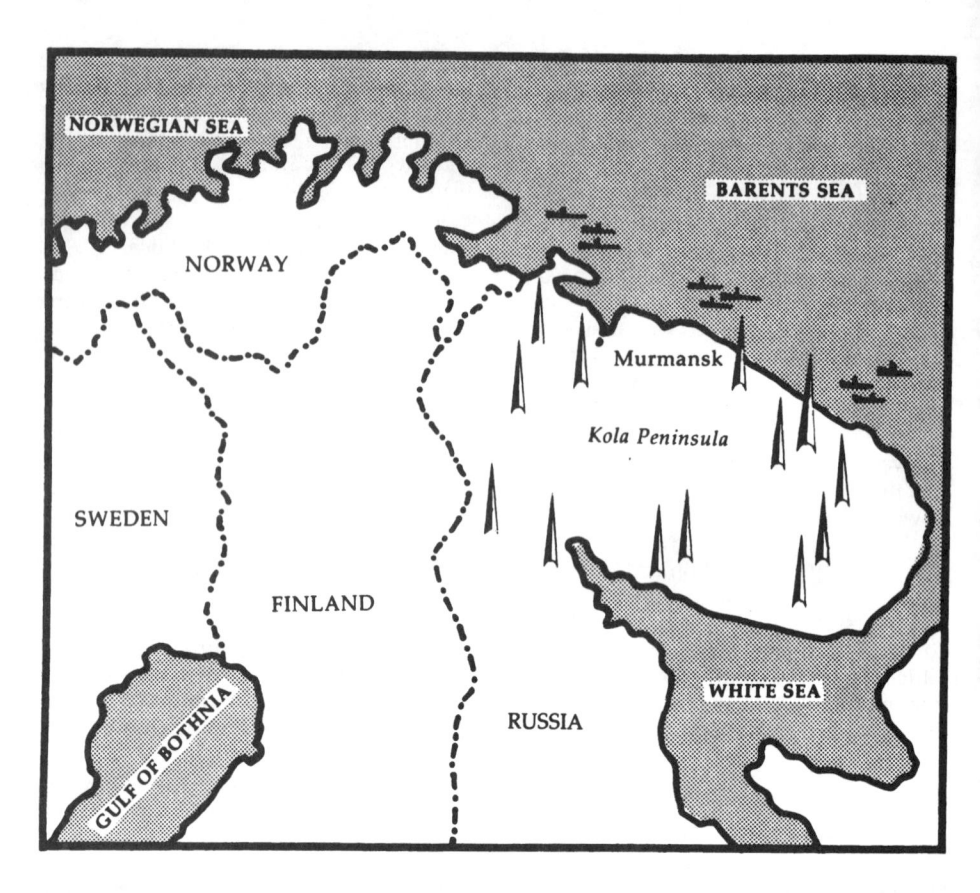

The Kola Peninsula

The collapse of the Soviet Union changed the threat to the Nordic Region, which was under the shadow of the Kola Peninsula, an area at the northwestern tip of Russia saturated with nuclear weapons. At Murmansk (60 miles east of the Norwegian border) and the small, ice–free coast next to the northern tip of Norway, Russia has its only naval and air bases which have open access to the Atlantic. Russia's problem of access to the open sea was described by the late Sir Winston Churchill as "a giant with pinched nostrils." It contains early warning and air defense facilities, as well as major naval bases in every fjord between Pechenga on the Norwegian border and Murmansk. The peninsula is the home port of the Northern Fleet, one of four main Russian fleets and one with a Kiev– class aircraft carrier, about a dozen Kresta missile cruisers and 155 submarines, including more than 65% of the strategic missile bearing subs and 60% of its nuclear powered ones.

The nuclear threat to the Nordic region has shifted from one of weaponry to one of waste: 71 of the submarines were judged in 1995 to be derelict and still have their nuclear fuel on board because there is no place else to put it. Two–thirds of the nuclear waste ever dumped into the world's seas lies off Kola, and much more radioactive waste is stored in ships so rickety they cannot be moved from their moorings near downtown Murmansk. The Kola Nuclear Power Station, which provides 60% of the peninsula's power, is one of the world's least safe and suffered a near–meltdown in 1993. Norwegians sought in 1998–9 to confront another danger to stability in the North: desperation on the part of a million Russians in the impoverished Kola Peninsula, the only place where Russia borders a NATO member. Norway provided tons of food, warm clothing and medicine.

Soviet military power in the Kola Peninsula was not primarily directed against the Nordic region, but rather to maintain

The Nordic Countries

a global balance with the U.S. and to provide the Soviet Union with the military capability to support its interests in all parts of the world. But the concentration of so much nuclear and conventional power in such a close and small area is unnerving to those who live nearby. It also complicated all discussions aimed at establishing a "nuclear–free zone" in the Nordic area.

This proposition was most persistently pressed by Finland, and it is enthusiastically supported by large segments of the population of all five countries, who found themselves caught up in the "peace movement." The Soviet Union rejected any idea of a nuclear–free Kola Peninsula, but, on the other hand, what purpose would a formally declared Nordic nuclear–free zone serve during times of war and peace, so long as the Kola area remains bristling with nuclear missiles?

Further, an embarrassing incident in 1981 involving the accidental grounding of a Soviet Whiskey–class (non–nuclear driven) submarine in Sweden's *internal* waterways understandably increased doubts in Scandinavia that such a nuclear–free zone would be feasible. Swedish inspections of the grounded ship revealed strong evidence that it was carrying nuclear weapons, although Moscow had always claimed that such vessels were armed only with conventional weapons. In other words, how could one be sure that the Nordic area, which includes the waters around it, would really have been nuclear–free, even if Russian leaders put their signatures on such a treaty? Flagrant Soviet submarine incursions into Swedish and Norwegian waters continued into the 1980s. A final problem with any proposed nuclear–free zone is the desire of Norway and Denmark not entirely to tie their hands on the question of nuclear weapons on their soil *in time of war*, even if both plan to defend themselves by means of conventional weapons.

In 1988 Sweden and Russia settled their long–standing dispute over their economic zones in the Baltic Sea, which separates their mainlands by 200 miles. The agreement, which deals with fishing and exploration rights, gives Sweden 75% of the disputed area and the Russians 25%. In 1993 Russia and the Nordic countries demonstrated their willingness to work together, particularly on environmental protection, by signing an agreement on cooperation in the Barents region.

All Nordic countries exercise restraint. Norway, *not* the U.S., or other NATO countries, patrols the Norwegian and Barents seas. No NATO maneuvers take place in the northernmost Norwegian county of Finnmark, thus always leaving a distance of at least 480 miles (800 km.) between any NATO maneuver and the Norwegian–Russian border. Both Norway and Denmark insist that attacks against their own territories can best be prevented if the aggressor can be persuaded in advance that both would call in foreign reinforcements very early in any conflict.

To underscore this, the Norwegians signed an agreement with the U.S. in 1981 providing for the advanced storage of heavy equipment and for Norwegian support of an American marine amphibious brigade, which could be rushed to Norway in an emergency. Reflecting the restraint which Norway always exercises, its leaders decided at the same time that the depots would be located in central—not northern—Norway, where any military confrontation would, at least initially, take place. Russia is still a major worrying presence on the edge of the Nordic world. How it develops economically, politically and militarily greatly influences security in the North. No country there can ignore Russia.

Military Restraint and Preparedness

The fact that the Scandinavian states exercise military restraint does not mean that they are unprepared to contribute to their own defense. All except Iceland have compulsory active military service for males, lasting 9 months in Denmark, 12 to 25 months in Norway and 9 months in Sweden, and followed in all three countries by reserve duty. Thus, for example, Norway's 40,000– man peacetime force could be increased rapidly to 300,000, and Sweden's 70,000 regular force could be increased almost tenfold to 650,000 in wartime 14 days after mobilization. Since 1965 Denmark's armed forces have been roughly halved to 29,000 troops.

The navies of Sweden, Norway and Denmark are equipped with submarines, frigates and torpedo and fast boats. These craft are designed for the defense of their very long and meandering coastlines, which offer so many hiding places for friendly and enemy ships alike. At the end of 1986 Denmark announced that women are permitted to serve on its combat ships and may be permitted to have combat roles in the army and air force. A Danish general or admiral always heads a special Baltic Approaches Command, which must try to control the entrances to and exits from the Baltic Sea in wartime. Denmark also has a limited number of troops stationed in northern Germany. The air forces of both Denmark and Norway are equipped with American F–16 aircraft, parts of which are produced in Denmark and other NATO countries.

Because it is in NATO, Denmark allowed itself the luxury of spending only about 2% of its GDP for defense, which prompted some critics to speak of "Denmarkization," a term which referred to the alleged inclination of a small country to assume that larger and more powerful countries will come to their rescue in time of emergency, regardless of what the smaller country spent on defense during peacetime. The Danes are occasionally reminded of their inability to defend themselves alone. When in 1987 the UK suggested a reappraisal of the role of its UK Mobile Force, which is earmarked for the defense of Denmark and the Baltic approaches, the Danish government became very nervous. The possibility of such a change prompted those parties which support NATO defense policy to agree upon a higher medium–term defense budget. The charge of "Denmarkization" was resented in Denmark, which does not, in fact, neglect its defense, even though most other NATO countries do spend more of their GDP for defense.

Although 12 of NATO's 16 countries have women in their armed forces, and Belgium, the Netherlands and Norway theoretically allow women in all assignments, only Denmark has made real steps toward imposing full equality in all branches. This move was prompted by passage of a comprehensive equal rights law in 1978, and the military was compelled to comply with it. A four–year experiment with assigning females to naval combat duties indicated that male–female crews outperform single–sex units and that women recruits are more highly motivated than men. Therefore, Danish women are now assigned to all naval billets but submarines, and similar experiments are being made in the army and air force. Because of the country's declining birthrate, women may become a crucial factor in maintaining Danish force levels.

Sweden also spends more on military security than Denmark; it expends 2.7% of its GDP (down from 5% in the 1950s), or about 10% of the total state budget. Its policy of nonparticipation in alliances in peacetime and neutrality (which it retained upon entry into EU in 1995) during wartime is supported by an overwhelming majority of Swedes—they are willing to underscore this policy by maintaining a strong total defense capacity, backed up by a well–organized civil defense. The aim of the Swedish defense is to raise the costs to an aggressor to such a level that an attacker, though possibly defeating Sweden in the end, would ultimately lose more than it would gain from such an attack. Such preparedness would, the Swedes hope, dissuade any power from attacking the country in the first place.

There were some real problems with this strategy. If an unprincipled power with vastly superior armaments were to achieve overwhelming victory in Europe,

The Nordic Countries

it would be able to attack Sweden successfully after initially ignoring it. Swedish military strength has declined: its air force has lost half its military aircraft, and its navy has lost a third of its ships. The latter fact partly explains why the Swedes cannot track submarines effectively and why their anti-submarine force can operate only in one area at a time. Of course, the Swedish military still packs quite a wallop. In 1987 it possessed 335 combat aircraft and 60 reconnaissance planes, more than the other Nordic countries put together. After the Soviet Union's demise, Sweden continued to modernize its military. However, in 1995 the defense budget was cut so severely that the country would be left with only 45,000 soldiers and 300,000 territorials. Its top commanders fear that Sweden might have to abandon all pretence that it can repel an attacker without calling for outside help.

In order not to be dependent upon other powers in wartime, Sweden produces about 80% of the weapons (and all the fighter aircraft) which its own armed forces need. In 1987 it unveiled a new Gripen supersonic fighter. Swedish manufacturers may no longer be able to produce the bulk of the country's weapons, and the government is faced with a situation where it is often cheaper to buy abroad than at home. To lower unit costs for its weapons and to earn foreign exchange, Swedish arms industries do sell abroad, despite widespread domestic opposition. Arms constitute 2% of its exports. SAAB exports aircraft, Hagglunds tanks and Kockums submarines. In 1981 the country's major arms manufacturer, Bofors, landed a major contract to provide 40mm anti-aircraft guns for a U.S. Army mobile divisional air defense system. With Swedish defense spending inching downward, Bofors and other Swedish companies hoped to receive lucrative orders from other countries as well, especially from those in NATO.

Sweden creates difficulties for itself by pretending that it sells arms only to countries which would be unlikely to use them and which do not violate human rights. Sales to war zones are against the law. However, many of the 40 or so countries to which it sells arms do not meet those standards. In 1987 a noisy scandal was unleashed concerning clandestine Swedish arms sales (including ground-to-air missiles) to Iran from 1983-5, and to other Persian Gulf states, often through third countries, such as Singapore. Particularly stunning were allegations that Bofors bribed Indian officials to purchase $1.3 billion worth of guns, Sweden's largest-ever export contract and one personally promoted by former Prime Minister Olof Palme, a moralizing public advocate of disarmament. At the turn of the century Nordic arms companies are cooperating with each other more and more, co-producing, for example, ammunition and gunpowder and procuring jointly such big-ticket items as helicopters and submarines. This would have been unthinkable for neutral Sweden and Finland during the Cold War.

Even if the five Nordic countries have different answers to questions related to defense, their foreign policies are similar in the sense that all are very active members in international organizations, especially the UN, and all but Iceland participate in UN peacekeeping operations. Each of the three Scandinavian countries maintains a permanent stand-by force which can be placed at the disposal of the UN at short notice. All were active proponents of East-West détente and vocal opponents of South Africa's *apartheid* policy. In 1988 Sweden, which has a tradition of mediating between Arabs and Jews, played a crucial role in establishing a dialogue between the U.S. and the *PLO*. In 1993 Norway brokered a landmark agreement between Israel and the *PLO* that paved the way to the beginnings of Palestinian autonomy in 1994. Norway again hosted a historic ceasefire deal in 1996 between the Guatemalan government and rebel guerrillas.

All strive to maintain especially close relations with "Third World" countries, and the three Scandinavian nations are among the world's most generous donors to development aid, as measured by percentage of GDP. Sweden's and Norway's contribution exceeded 1% of their GDP at one time, and they and Denmark still meet the UN goal of .7%. The Swedish government shifted its priorities to newly independent democracies in the Baltics and Eastern Europe. It reduced aid to Vietnam and cut it to Cuba altogether.

Nordic Cooperation

A major emphasis of all their foreign policies is revealed by the fact that each has a minister for Nordic cooperation. The nerve center of this broad regional collaboration is the Nordic Council, which began its work in 1953. In all, it has 78 members elected by the national parliaments from among their own ranks, and it is broken down into several standing committees, which submit proposals to the plenary sessions. Members of the various governments also take part in the discussions, but they do not have the right to vote. The Nordic Council has no sovereign authority; its decisions, which must be unanimous, are merely unbinding recommendations to the five governments. Critics charge that the council's advice is ignored by member governments unless they planned to do it anyway. Also, with 23 committees, 74 Nordic institutions, 152 committees of inquiry and working groups, and 2,000 on-going projects, the exasperated Danish minister for Nordic cooperation declared in 1988 that the system had gone mad.

Nevertheless, the Council does discuss many important pieces of legislation before they are passed by national parliaments. This has created a greater uniformity than is found in most other regions in a wide variety of laws dealing with such matters as marriage and child custody, contracts and commercial practices, copyright and patents, transportation and maritime law. The Council has a presidium with a standing secretariat in Stockholm, a secretariat for general affairs in Oslo and one for cultural affairs in Copenhagen.

The five countries decided in 1954 to form a single labor market, in which a citizen of one member country can work in any other country without a work or residence permit and can travel within the region without a passport. In 1955 all agreed that citizens from other Nordic countries should receive the same pension, unemployment, health and welfare benefits as each country's own citizens. The result is that almost a million persons have emigrated from one Nordic land to the other, and in Sweden 60% of all immigrants are from other Nordic countries.

The move toward greater unity received a setback in the late 1950s when a Nordic Customs Union and a wider Nordic Economic Union failed to materialize. Nevertheless, these nations continued to tighten their links with each other. In 1971 a Nordic Ministerial Council was set up to provide a basis for closer practical collaboration among the five governments. In 1973 a treaty dealing with transport affairs went into effect, and for many years a single airline, SAS, has been operated by private and public funds from Sweden, Norway and Denmark. Finally, a Nordic Investment Bank, with its seat in Helsinki, was created in 1975 to finance investment and export projects of common Nordic interest.

The economic interests of the countries are by no means identical. As Iceland's former president, Vigdís Finnbogadóttir, commented, we "are a family, not quintuplets." By 1995 only Norway and Iceland remained in EFTA (European Free Trade Association), which had been founded in Stockholm. The five have different approaches to Europe and its integration although all abide by the EEA agreement with the EU which involves free trade in everything but farm and fish products. Finns are the most enthusiastic about being in EU and are proud of being the only Nordic country to adopt the com-

The Nordic Countries

mon currency, the Euro. Denmark has the most nuanced attitude about the EU, to which it belongs. It has won a record four "opt–outs," including from the Euro. The Swedes joined the EU, but are divided over whether it was a good idea; they have rejected the Euro for now. The Norwegians voted twice to stay out of the EU, and only a small minority in Iceland wants to join.

Sweden had second thoughts about going through with a plan it made with Denmark to build a 16 kilometer (10 mile) road–and–rail bridge over the sound from Malmö to Copenhagen, the final link joining the Scandinavian peninsula to mainland Europe. This will create a city region of 3.2 million people and the most vital region in the Nordic area. For years Denmark had stalled the plans until its own project to build a bridge linking the island of Zealand to the Jutland peninsula was underway. There was opposition in Sweden, where critics claim that such a bridge might cause environmental damage: exhaust fumes might harm trees, and the flow of water might be disturbed, thereby upsetting the ecology in the Baltic. The link will open in June 2000.

Swedish opponents openly expressed another concern: that the moral environment of Malmö could be undermined by Copenhagen's laxer policies on drugs, alcohol and prostitution. A concrete focus of their fears is the "Free City of Christiania," founded in 1972 near Copenhagen. Occupied by anarchists, hippies, drug–pushers and "down–and–outs," this settlement has become so dangerous that most Danes, the police and municipal buses usually avoid it. In 1993 the police arrested 17 persons openly selling hashish on "Pusher Street" and rounded up children wandering the streets during school hours. The government did not succeed in persuading the Danish Parliament to evict Christiania's "citizens." In 1989 the leftist experiment established its own liaison office with the Danish Ministry of Defense, which owns the site, provides water, power and other services free of charge, and accepts Christiania as permanent. Two–thirds of the residents of this seedy settlement live on public welfare.

A problem that has plagued all Scandinavian countries in the 1990s is a long–lasting motorbike–gang war between the Hell's Angels and Bandidos. Violence involving machine guns, bombs and anti-tank missiles had by 1998 left 12 dead and more than 80 injured and had terrorized citizens everywhere. In an attempt to control such warfare, Denmark suspended the right of biker gangs to assemble and put accused offenders on trial. Leaders in all the countries have met to discuss how this threat to the public can be eliminated.

Hiking through a Danish beech forest

Economics and Welfarism

All five Nordic countries have highly productive economies and have experienced rapid economic growth since 1945. In all the five lands economic prosperity depends greatly upon foreign trade. This means that all need industries and agricultures which are competitive. This means also that all are more vulnerable to changes in the world economic climate than are larger countries.

All have, in varying degrees, the general goal of economic egalitarianism (equality). All have developed elaborate social welfare systems which many people outside the region greatly admire and which include largely free medical treatment, high unemployment benefits and generous child allowances. These many benefits are coupled with a widely– spread high standard of living. There is perhaps less economic inequality and poverty in the Nordic states than anywhere else in the world. It must be repeated that this was achieved by peaceful reform, not by violent revolution. The economic prosperity has helped create the high level of political harmony and consensus within the countries and it is therefore an important ingredient in the overall political stability.

At the same time, these countries also presently face a common dilemma: taxes have been raised to stratospheric levels in order to pay for the welfare states. The average tax bite is now around 50%. The high tax levels sparked various forms of tax revolts, and in the 1970s this dissatisfaction culminated in electoral losses in most of the countries by social democratic parties, which had dominated political life for almost a half century, and the election of non–social democratic governments which promised cutbacks in taxes and public spending.

Nevertheless, it became clear that despite the growing conviction that the social welfare systems can no longer be paid for (except in oil–rich Norway), no determined attack against the welfare state can succeed at present because most citizens are unwilling to sacrifice the social services and security which have been created. In other words, the populations want the *advantages* of the welfare state, but they are unhappy about *paying for them*.

313

The Kingdom of Sweden

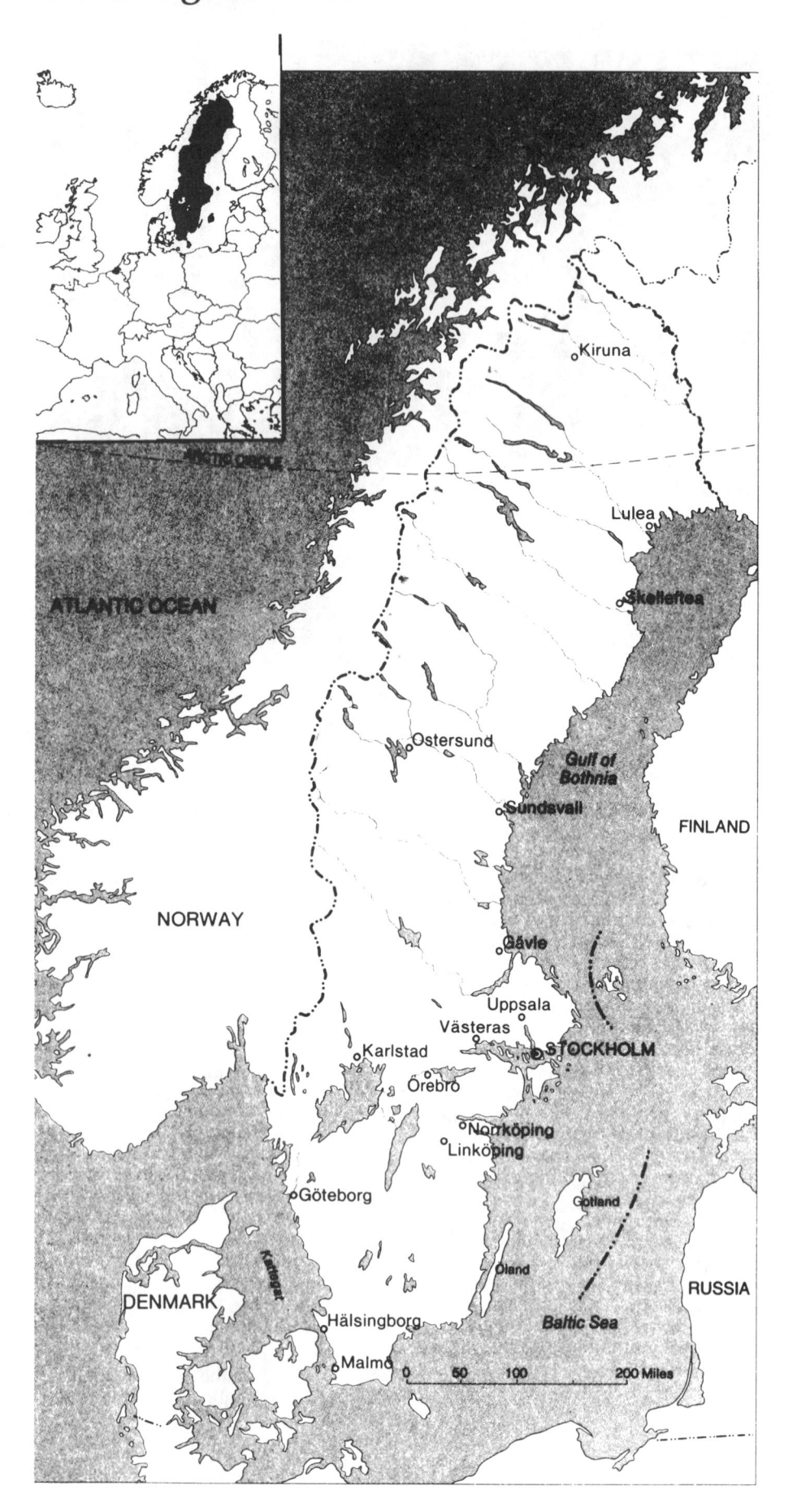

Area: 173,654 sq. mi. (449,793 sq. km., approx. 1,000 mi. from north to south and 300 mi. at its widest point; somewhat larger than California.
Population: 8.8 million (estimated).
Capital City: Stockholm (Pop. 1.56 million, estimated).
Climate: In the south and central portions the climate it rather like New England. The summers are warm and dry and long hours of daylight extend from late spring through early autumn; winters are cold, bitterly so in the northern regions.
Neighboring Countries: Finland (East); Norway (West); Denmark (Southwest); Germany, Poland (South across the Baltic Sea).
Official Language: Swedish.
Other Principal Tongues: Nordic tongues of the region.
Ethnic Background: Scandinavian. (North European).
Principal Religion: Lutheran (Swedish Church), 95%.
Main Exports: Machinery, motor vehicles, wood pulp, paper products, finished iron and steel products, metal ores, processed chemicals.
Main Imports: Machinery, motor vehicles, petroleum and petroleum products, textile raw materials and fabrics, iron and steel, chemicals, foodstuffs.
Major Trading Partners: Germany, Great Britain, U.S., Norway, Denmark, Finland; 55% of its trade is with the EU, a fifth with the Nordic countries.
Currency: Krona.
National Holiday: April 30 (1946), birthday of the King.
Chief of State: His Majesty King Carl XVI Gustaf, b. 1946. Ascended the throne September 19, 1973. Married Silvia Sommerlath (German) June 19, 1976.
Heiress Apparent: Her Royal Highness Princess Victoria, b. 1977.
Head of Government: Goran Persson, Prime Minister (since March 1996).
National Flag: A deep blue field crossed by a yellow stripe horizontally and another vertically, the latter being closer to the pole rather than dead center.

When one thinks of postwar Sweden, one tends to conjure thoughts of many things: enviable prosperity, dynamic industry producing well–designed products, assured future economic progress, an absence of strikes and debt, sky–high taxes which the Swedes willingly pay in order to maintain one of the world's most advanced social welfare systems, permanent rule by a moderate, progmatic *Social Democratic Workers' Party*, open arms to political refugees from all over the globe and, finally, leadership in the sexual revolution.

Sweden

Most of these things have changed by now, and the last point was always grossly exaggerated anyway. Sweden is like a sleek and daring automobile which has recently developed some engine problems and has acquired a few visible dents on its highly polished fenders. It is still a country where a majority of the people relish social experimentation whenever it promises a more just and egalitarian society. It has done away with grades and programs for the mentally gifted in the lower classes, outlawed spankings in every institution of the society, including the family, and introduced the use of first names between students and teachers (including most professors). It has done away with many titles, erased the distinction between the formal and informal words for "you" (a means for maintaining social distance which virtually every other European language retains except English) and extended post–natal maternity benefits to fathers. It remains a healthy, democratic political system which is totally immune from any internal shift toward authoritarian rule. Nevertheless its political consensus is splitting a bit at a few seams. It is visibly prosperous, but it now faces serious challenges to its economic health, as well as to its way of life and its way of perceiving itself. At a time when many citizens of former communist countries' regimes look to the "Swedish model" of the welfare state as the most humane alternative to their former stultifying centralized autocratic systems, that very model has collapsed on its home turf.

Sweden is still the heart of the Nordic region and the keystone for the Nordic balance. It is the largest and most populous nation in the area. It has also been the richest for a long time, and it is accustomed to being regarded with a blend of expectation and envy. But it is now oil–rich Norway which is reaping most of the envy, and for the first time ever, the Swedes must approach their western neighbors as a needy suitor, not as rich and slightly condescending patrons. In terms of GDP per capita, the Danes have surpassed the Swedes in wealth, and the Danes are also beginning to pump oil from the North Sea; Sweden has almost no oil resources. The poorer neighbors to the east, the Finns, have made considerable economic progress, and many of those Finns who had moved to Sweden to find a better economic life are returning home.

Sweden is the third largest country in Europe and is roughly the size of France or slightly larger than California. It is very sparsely populated, with fewer than 20 inhabitants per square kilometer, which is somewhat lower than in the U.S. Such overall figures are misleading because the Swedish population is distributed very unevenly. More than 90% live in the southern half of the country and more than half live in the lower third. For many decades the northern people have migrated southward, and from the countryside into the cities, although there are recent signs that this latter process may be reversing itself slightly. In the year 1880 only 10% of the people lived in towns, and even a hundred years ago Sweden was predominantly rural. During the second half of the 19th century the move into the cities accelerated, so that by now about 83% live in cities or towns. About a third of the people live in the large urban areas of Stockholm (1.56 million), Göteborg (761,000) and Malmö (498,000).

Sweden has been an independent kingdom for at least 1,000 years, and its relative isolation from the political and military storms which have swept the rest of Europe have created a firm national identity and unity, symbolized by the King. For most of its existence Sweden had a homogeneous population, and this was a key factor in the Swedes' ability to create such a sturdy social and political consensus. But this homogeneity has begun to change. This former country of emigrants, which once poured a fourth of its population into the U.S., has itself become a country of immigration. Immigrants and their descendants make up 1.2 million out of a total population of 8.8 million. This means that more than 13% of the population is non–Swedish in origin, and that percentage is steadily rising since immigrants' birth rates are higher than

Four generations in a 1946 photograph: King Gustaf V (d. 1950, age 92), his son, Crown Prince Gustaf Adolf (who succeeded his father in 1950 as King Gustaf VI Adolf, d. 1973), his grandson, Prince Gustaf Adolf (who died in an air accident in January 1947), and his great–grandson, Sweden's present monarch, King Carl XVI Gustaf.

Sweden

Swedes', who have been in a state of negative population growth for several years.

Sweden always had a small Finnish–speaking minority in the north, numbering about 30,000. It also has had a Lapp (called *same,* pronounced sa–may) minority, which now numbers about 17,000 and which has its own language and culture. The degree to which Lapps are integrated into Swedish society varies. The most traditional are the approximately 2,500 nomadic Lapps, whose livelihood is derived from raising reindeer. Sweden requires all Lapp children to attend the minimum nine years of school, although it permits the Lapp language to be used and Lapp culture, which has only a limited written literature, to be preserved. It even provides eight nomadic schools for the children who are constantly on the move, and there is a folk school at Jokkmokk where Lapps of all ages can study their own culture. The state also broadcasts the news and special programs in the Lapp language.

Partly because of the rising concern in the world for the rights of minorities, a somewhat more aggressive consciousness has arisen among some Lapps, who maintain contact with Indian groups in North America. Some even raised a claim for possession of their people's native lands, but in 1981 the Swedish Supreme Court ruled that the Lapps can no longer claim possession of those lands, although they still have preferential hunting and fishing rights. The Court also ruled that the Lapps could not interfere with energy projects or tourism in the mountainous Skattefjällen region of northern Sweden.

Since the 1945 Nordic agreement to allow free emigration within the area, Finns poured into Sweden and now constitute the largest minority, accounting for 40% of the total. Finns in Sweden are not visible to the outsider, and they do not have such problems of adjustment as do many other immigrants. Nevertheless, only 20% of Finns speak Swedish upon arrival and they do not integrate as quickly as some Swedes think they should. The Finns tend to forget that Swedes think they should. Swedes tend to forget that they always resisted complete integration in Finland, where about 6% of the population speaks Swedish as the first language and has Swedish language newspapers, schools and universities.

Stockholm, which was founded in the 13th century as a fortress to seal off the inland waterways from Baltic intruders, is the cultural, financial and government center of Sweden. Unlike Copenhagen, Paris or London, though, the Swedish capital does not overshadow the rest of the country. Göteborg has Sweden's largest port and is in many ways as oriented toward such foreign cities as Oslo, Copenhagen and London as it is toward Stockholm. Malmö is situated on the Øresund sound directly across from Copenhagen and its residents often take a half–hour ferry ride to the Danish capital to do some of their shopping.

Approximately 15,000 years ago Sweden was covered with ice, the movement of which cut deep scars into the land, leaving a long mountain chain along the Norwegian border. These mountains, which cover a fourth of the country, are the source of numerous rivers which flow eastward through the forests into the Gulf of Bothnia.

These rivers are sources of hydroelectric power, which provided the energy for Sweden's industrialization. They also offered rapid and inexpensive transportation for logs from the immense Swedish forests, which cover half the country's territory. Many of the indentations cut during the great ice age are now filled with almost 100,000 lakes, which occupy about 8% of the country's surface. Boats can travel all the way from Stockholm to Göteborg via lakes linked by rivers and the Göta Canal. Along the jagged coast of this country, which stretches 1,000 miles (1,600 km.) are thousands of islands. The average width of the country is 250 miles (400 km.).

As in Norway, all open land which is not cultivated or which is not part of a residence can be used by anyone for camping, hiking, skiing or other outdoor recreational activities, regardless of who owns the land. The vast forests have long provided one of the three most valuable natural resources—wood. The other two are water power and mountains of Europe's highest grade of iron ore, found in the Bergslagen area in central Sweden and in the Kiruna and Skellefteå areas in the north. It also has sizable deposits of ferrous alloys, pyrites, fire clay, zinc, silver, lead, copper and shale uranium. Its greatest poverty is in oil and coal, but with its people's proven ingenuity, it has been able to achieve almost unparalleled prosperity, even without "black gold." A heavy dose of this ingenuity was necessary to make Sweden basically self–sufficient in food, even though its soil is generally not good, its rainfall undependable and its growing season short. Less than 10% of its land area is suitable for agriculture, but Swedish farmers, who now make up only about 5% of the active population, know how to apply a high level of mechanization and scientific farming techniques.

The climate is far milder than would be expected if one merely glanced at the globe. It is on the same latitude as Siberia and Alaska, and Stockholm is as far north as southern Greenland. Yet the Gulf Stream from the Caribbean is able to penetrate, bringing warm water and from it, warm air which produces a climate in the most populous half of Sweden which is similar to that of northern New England.

The country has a varied landscape. The south, or *Götaland,* which includes the islands of Öland and Gotland off the eastern coast, is a region of fertile plains and rolling, verdant hills, dotted with clean, red and yellow barns and farmhouses, freshly painted and surrounded in summer by fields of yellow flowers. Here is the heart of Sweden's industry and agriculture and the home of half the Swedes. Central Sweden is called *Svealand,* from which was derived the name of the entire country, *Sverige,* or *Svea–rike,* which means "Kingdom of the Svear." This region contains the capital city as well as the old university town of Uppsala. It also has many farming communities and countless lakes. The northern half of the country, or *Norrland,* is a rugged, mountainous frontier area of wilderness, timber and mining. In short, Sweden is a beautiful land of many scenic contrasts and of water everywhere.

RECENT POLITICAL HISTORY

Sweden has for a half century been governed by the *Social Democratic Workers Party (SAP)*. The election in 1976 of the first non–*SAP* government since 1936 was a turning point. Swedes had decided that it was a time to have a government which proposed a policy to stimulate the dynamism of the market place, increase productivity in the private sector by stimulating investment and slow the growth of government. It was never a question of dismantling the social welfare net. No Scandinavian government has a mandate from its people to do that. However, the conditions were not favorable for a shaky coalition government with a razor thin majority in parliament. It took over the helm after 44 years of *SAP* rule and at a time when the country was plunging into its worst economic crises in three decades. As the 1982 elections showed, it was a bad time to try to change the direction of economic policy.

The non–*SAP* government did accomplish a few things, but it failed to cope with runaway public spending and to stimulate investment in industry. The *Center Party* was far too obsessed with the nuclear power issue, and the *Liberals* were constantly worried about their decline in the public opinion polls to devote full attention to the pressing problems. The coalitions which ruled after 1976 simply shied away from truly decisive policies which would have been necessary to begin to solve the country's economic problems.

Olof Palme's *SAP* reaped the electoral rewards of this failure. Palme knew that

Sweden

View of Stockholm, with the Royal Palace (center–top)

in the minds of many Swedish voters his party was closely associated with the prosperity and full employment of the past. He also knew that his party's program was in harmony with the electorate's desire to maintain at all costs the social welfare system, which most Swedes have come to regard as permanent.

Palme stood at the zenith of his career when tragedy struck in 1986. Walking home unguarded with his wife late at night, he was killed by an unknown assassin's bullets. He was the first Swedish leader to be murdered since King Gustaf III, who was shot at a masked ball in 1792. Evidence emerged in 1996 that the assassin was dispatched by the *apartheid* regime of South Africa, which was known to be greatly angered by Palme's vociferous opposition to *apartheid*. Sweden also had a policy of funnelling hundreds of millions of dollars into the anti–*apartheid* movement within South Africa.

Swedes mourned not only the loss of this talented, but controversial leader, but the loss of Sweden's totally open society. Scandinavia is one of the last regions in a violent world where close, informal contacts between political leaders and common people was possible. As Ulf Adelsohn, the conservative leader, lamented, "Sweden will never be the same after this."

New Prime Ministers

Palme was replaced as prime minister and leader of the *SAP* by his personal deputy, Ingvar Carlsson. His state visit to the U.S. in 1987, the first such trip in almost three decades, revealed how much the two countries' relations had improved since 1972, when Palme had compared U.S. bombing of Hanoi with Nazi Germany's extermination policy. That dubious statement prompted a mutual withdrawal of ambassadors for more than a year. Carlsson tried to be even–handed in his criticism of the U.S. and Soviet Union. His successor in 1991, Carl Bildt, had always opposed Sweden's foreign policy moralizing and its support for Vietnam during the war. After visiting U.S. military cemeteries in Belgium, he wrote: "Swedes ought to take the time to go and see the row after row of the hundreds of white crosses." In 1994 Carlsson replaced Bildt as prime minister. In March 1996 Goran Persson assumed the prime ministership.

GOVERNMENT AND POLITICS

As in other Scandinavian states, politics in Sweden is characterized by great stability despite the existence of many political parties competing for power. It entered a democratic age without revolution, and violence is an element which has almost never raised its ugly head in Swedish politics until recently. This does not mean that there are no political conflicts or disagreements in the country's political life. It does mean that they are fought out verbally and in the democratic arena and with restraint, and that they are almost invariably resolved by the Swedish talent for cool–headed, pragmatic negotiations and compromise.

The Swedish constitution consists of three separate documents, not just one as in the U.S. The first is the Act of Succession, which deals with the present royal family and which was amended, effective 1980, to permit the *oldest child* of the reigning monarch, not the oldest *son*, to succeed to the throne upon the death of the monarch. This meant that King Carl XVI Gustaf's son, who had been born crown prince, was moved behind his older sister, Victoria, in the order of succession. The second document is the Freedom of the Press Act of 1949. The third and most important writing is the Instrument of Government which went into effect on January 1, 1975, replacing the 1809 Instrument of Government. This change brought no radical reform, but it formally incorporated into the constitution the current governmental practices which had evolved since 1809.

This document explicitly sanctions popular sovereignty, representative democracy and parliamentary government. Thus, while most other constitutionally governed countries have gradually developed actual political practices which are not clearly spelled out in a constitution, Sweden has tried to bring its constitution and actual political practices into harmony. In 1976 and 1979 parliament again passed laws amending the document in a way that strengthened the protection of human

Sweden

rights and fundamental freedoms. Thus, its existing observance of these rights and freedoms now have documentation.

Constitutional Monarchy

Sweden is a constitutional monarchy with a parliamentary form of government. As a result of the recent constitutional changes, the monarch does not have sweeping political powers on paper, as do other European monarchs. He is in theory and fact a symbolic figurehead who exerts no influence on politics and takes no part in it. A Swedish monarch never actually wears a crown, and he performs only purely ceremonial functions, such as opening the annual session of parliament each October and conferring four of the five Nobel Prizes. (The Peace Prize is conferred by the Norwegian government.) The money for these prestigious prizes was donated by the Swedish chemist and inventor, Alfred Nobel, who had made a fortune from his invention of dynamite, blasting gelatine and smokeless explosives, which made the development of firearms and artillery possible.

The monarch does not formally sign government documents, and his former fictitious power to select the prime minister has been taken over by the Speaker of the Parliament. Also, the formal power of government now rests with the cabinet, not with the monarch. The Swedes have stripped their monarch of all his duties and powers, and collect taxes from him as they would any other citizen. As a person worth an estimated $4.5 million, Carl is by no means the wealthiest European monarch, but he can certainly afford to pay his taxes without too much pain. But this stripping of the monarch's formal powers does not mean that the Swedes are indifferent to their royal family. Opinion polls reveal that the King and his German–born Queen, Silvia, a commoner who was serving as a guide at the 1972 Munich Olympics when Carl met her, are by far the most popular public figures in Sweden. In fact, they are far more beloved and respected than are any of Sweden's present political leaders. This is not due exclusively to the fact that many have become cynical and disillusioned about their leadership, however. Having no political responsibilities, the king cannot be accused of doing anything wrong, since in this area he does nothing. The royal family strives to be very near to the people, sending their children to normal public schools and taking a great interest in such charities as those seeking to improve the lot of handicapped children. Without a doubt, their popularity is the best protection against the voices which are sometimes heard on the political left to abolish the monarchy altogether.

Parliament

Since 1971 Sweden has had a unicameral parliament *(Riksdag)*. Almost 90% of Swedes 18 years of age or over go to the polls to elect 349 members by proportional representation. For the election of 310 of the members, the country is divided into 28 constituencies, each of which chooses an average of 11 members. The remaining 39 are selected from national ballots in which all of the country constitutes a single constituency. A substitute deputy is selected simultaneously for each member so that there need not be by–elections if a deputy dies or resigns. In 1994 women captured 41% of the *Riksdag* seats and were awarded half the cabinet posts.

Parliamentary elections are held at least every four years in September, although the prime minister can decide to call earlier ones. Such earlier balloting is very rare, and if it does take place, the newly– chosen deputies merely serve out the remainder of the four–year parliamentary term. Many had found that three year terms, in effect until 1994, were insufficient for a parliament; a government can act more decisively if it does not have to worry about elections so often. Therefore, parliamentary terms were lengthened to four years.

Sweden has a highly organized society. Each occupation group and such categories of citizens as consumers, members of cooperatives, environmentalists, women, tenants and landlords have their own organizations, which deal directly with the government. Before an important piece of legislation is introduced into the *Riksdag*, the government calls together a royal commission composed of members of that body (except communist members), experts from the concerned interest groups and independent specialists to examine the proposals thoroughly and to develop, if possible, a consensus behind the new laws. Representatives of the groups also belong to many administrative agencies. The participating organizations, therefore, are a part of the democratic system itself, and not merely lobbyists.

Once the legislation is presented to the *Riksdag*, one of the 16 standing committees gives it another look, so that when a law is finally adopted, it usually enjoys a broad consensus. This process certainly helps to promote stability, but it has been severely criticized by some Swedes since the late 1960s. They charge that the process takes place behind closed doors and over the heads of most normal citizens and persons within the various occupations. This is mere "democracy at the top," they say. The

(Right to left) King Carl XVI Gustaf, Queen Silvia, Crown Princess Victoria, Prince Carl Philip, Princess Madeleine, and the King's aunt, Princess Lilian

Sweden

parties have taken this criticism seriously and have developed some new proposals on the subjects of decentralization while continuing to practice the traditional method for achieving a consensus.

There is no institutional separation of power between the legislative and the executive branches in Sweden. Nevertheless, since the early part of the 19th century, Sweden has had a tradition controlling the governmental administration. The first form of guarantee against the abuse of power by judges, governmental officials and civil servants is the requirement that all documents be made public, except in rare instances where secrets vital to the nation's welfare are concerned.

The second guarantee is the election by the *Riksdag* of ombudsmen, a specifically Swedish invention, who have the independent authority to act on their own initiative or on the basis of written complaints from individual citizens, newspapers or other organizations. The Justice ombudsman sees whether any public official, except a government minister, has acted illegally or improperly. If he finds evidence of misconduct, he can admonish the erring official or initiate corrective steps, although prosecutions are infrequent. If he finds that the laws are vague or faulty, he can recommend to the parliament a change in the law.

There are also other, more specialized ombudsmen. The Press ombudsman deals with complaints about journalistic ethics. The Anti–Trust ombudsman watches over the economy to see that competition is not stifled. The Consumer ombudsman protects the consumer from unfair marketing methods and the Equality ombudsman primarily is responsible for insuring that there is no discrimination against women on the job or in public life. It is scarcely surprising that the latter office is traditionally occupied by a woman. The ombudsmen can invoke a well–developed body of Swedish law, which is a synthesis of Roman and common law and which is interpreted by courts at three levels: Courts of the First Instance (*Tingsrätter*), Appellate Courts (*Hovrätter*) and a Supreme Court (*Högsta Domstolen*).

In practice, the *Riksdag* is subordinate to the cabinet (*Statsråd*), usually composed of 18 to 21 ministers and led by the prime minister. Together they are called "the government" and must be able to win a majority in the *Riksdag* for their important policies. The government is collectively responsible for policy, but parliament can force individual cabinet members to resign. Of course, they can be dismissed by the prime minister. Cabinet members are normally leading politicians in the governing parties and had won seats in parliament, although their substitutes occupy their seats while they serve as ministers. Occasionally, specialists who are not professional politicians and who were not elected to parliament are included in the cabinet.

The *Riksdag* majority has the last word on whether a matter becomes law or not. That majority may choose to allow the people to express, through a referendum, their opinion on a particularly important subject, but the results of such a nation–wide vote, which occurs very seldom, are not binding on the government. In 1979 the constitution was amended to allow another kind of referendum. If a third of the *Riksdag* deputies desire it, a binding referendum on a proposed constitutional amendment can be held at the same time as a general election.

Provincial Government

Sweden is a unitary, not a federal state. But it does have provincial and local governments which have considerable responsibility. Each of the 24 provinces (*län*) is formally led by a governor (*landshövding*), who is appointed by the cabinet for a six–year term and who presides over a 14–member provincial administration (*länsstyrelse*), which is appointed by an elected provincial council (*landsting*). As in the municipalities, the provinces have plural rather than single person executives; such collective leadership encourages collaboration among all parties, and it therefore fosters nonpartisan, compromising and practical leadership. The provinces lack the independence which the U.S. states have, and since 1971 there is no upper house in the national parliament which would be in a position to guard provincial interests.

Local Government

There are 284 municipalities (*kommun*), each with an elected assembly. The *kommun* does not have the same measure of autonomy as does an American city and is largely occupied with administration on a day–to–day basis of services which have been mandated by the national government. The *kommun's* responsibilities extend to housing subsidies, roads, sewerage and water supply, elementary education, public assistance, health care, child welfare and cultural, social and athletic activities. They have the right to levy income and property taxes. They not only charge fees for some of the services they render, but they receive subsidies from the national government for the services which they are required to perform for it.

Absorption into the National Government

Provincial and local governments have been progressively transformed into administrative extensions of the central government. The provinces apply national policy and have primary responsibility for health care, hospital services, for certain types of education and vocational training. They have the right to impose an income tax to pay for their services. To make things even more complicated, there are also church councils at the local level which are popularly elected and which look after church financial affairs. The state church levies income taxes also, which about 90% of all Swedes choose to pay, rather than leaving the church and lowering their tax burden. This means that the average person pays income taxes to nation, provincial, municipal and church authorities. Fortunately for him, however, he must file only one single tax return which covers all four.

Political Parties

As in other democracies, political parties are very much a part of Swedish government. The proportional representation electoral system produces a multi–party landscape, which is kept within manageable bounds by the requirement that no party can win seats in the *Riksdag* which does not win at least 4% of the vote nationwide, or 12% of the vote in any one electoral district. Those parties who are able to win at least one seat receive state subsidies to cover a portion of their expenses.

There are several different ways of approaching the party scene. One is to see it as a four or five party system, with generally coherent and stable groups which are closely linked to specific occupation groups in the well–organized Swedish society. In a land with no traditional language, ethnic or confessional differences, it is understandable that the parties would form along occupational or class lines. These close ties which most parties have make it more difficult for them to broaden their bases and become mass representation groups which could single–handedly win a parliamentary majority. The one exception is the *Social Democratic Workers' Party (SAP)*, which has dominated Swedish politics for a half century.

Thus, Sweden has a stable, multi–party system which is divided into two roughly equal blocs: one contains a unified, dominant party; the other is fractured into three parties, which have difficulties ruling the country together. Since a hard–lined, anti–socialist front never developed, and since the major parties tend to be unideological and pragmatic, both blocs were always able to cooperate in the political middle. Most electoral shifts are among parties within each bloc, not between the two. Thus, electoral landslides are completely unknown.

Sweden

The Social Democratic Workers' Party (SAP)

In 1989 the *SAP* celebrated its one hundredth anniversary. Since the early 1930s, it ruled Sweden almost continually, with a three–month interruption in 1936. It won a majority five times. Sometimes it has coalitions with the *Center Party* (1936–9 and 1951–7) but it tends to dislike coalitions and is happier to rule as a minority government with the tolerance of another party, whenever it cannot win a majority. In 1976 it went into the opposition, returning to power after the 1982 elections. It reentered the opposition in 1991, but it came back to power in 1994. Ingvar Carlsson, who again became prime minister, vowed to undo many of the conservatives' cost–cutting reforms while preserving the world's most lavish welfare state. But he found spending cuts unavoidable in order to keep his debt–ridden government afloat and to restore confidence in Sweden's economic future.

He stepped down as prime minister and party leader in 1996 and was replaced by his finance minister, Goran Persson, who had won few friends by implementing painful budget cuts in order to reduce the gaping budget deficit. The *SAP's* greatest strength is among the elderly, those living in small towns, and public sector workers. They could not prevent near disaster in the 1998 elections. With the lowest voter turnout in 50 years (81%), the *SAP* fell from 45.3% to 36.6% of the votes and from 161 to 131 seats. Persson formed a minority government that depends on votes from the *Left Party* and the *Greens*.

The secret of the *SAP's* success was its close ties with the Trade Union Federation *(Landsorganisationen—LO)* which links 25 unions and organizes about 90% of all Swedish workers. Sweden is a highly unionized country, and since the founding of the *LO*, most of its members must also be members of the *SAP*. This is not merely formal membership; most Swedish workers actually vote for the *SAP* in general elections. The *LO* supports the *SAP* financially, organizationally and through the trade union press, such as the popular *Aftonbladet*, a leftist newspaper whose circulation has steadily declined. The *SAP* revived it morning tabloid, *Stockholms–Tidningen*, which concentrates on local Stockholm news and on low–keyed presentations of the party's policies. The *LO* and *SAP* have a common committee during election years, and the *LO* chairman has a seat in the party presidium. The *SAP* also has good relations with the Union of Employees *(TCO)*, but its links with the *SAP* are not nearly as close, and its influence not so important as is the case of the *LO*.

The *SAP* party programs since 1897 have always contained some radical elements such as presenting socialism as the long–range goal of the party, but these elements have been disregarded in practice. The party supported socialist economic reforms, but it always took a gradualist approach to change and was willing to cooperate with other parties and with private enterprise. It left private property untouched and allowed Swedish companies to make high profits, as a reward for financing full employment, a tight social welfare system and an ever–increasing living standard for all groups within the society. In 1959 it changed its party program so that it would be in harmony with its moderate, pragmatic politics.

The benefits for Sweden which flowed from this realistic approach were revealed in the country's undeniable prosperity. Some people began to talk of an "end to ideology," but in the late 1960s and early 1970s a "new left" emerged, composed mainly of young, middle class university students, which began directing its sharply pointed arrows at the Swedish political and economic system, admired by so many abroad. New left critics hammered at the inequalities which still existed and at the highly developed process of compromise at the top, which it claimed, took place over the heads of, and therefore beyond the control of the people. The critics also charged that Swedish society was becoming stultifyingly bureaucraticized. They demanded more ideology in politics.

These more radical elements never made up a majority within the *SAP*, to say nothing of the overall electorate, but their attacks jolted the party into taking a noticeable left turn. Olof Palme's outbursts against the U.S. were not enough to pacify these tenacious critics, and the party changed its program in 1975 in order to incorporate more ideological content. The program states that the "struggle for equality is directed against all kinds of class differences—economic, social and cultural." It declared that the existing freedoms and rights should be used to attain economic and social liberation and that economic democracy "should be an immediate goal."

A Swedish journalist, Anders Isaksson, compiled a report in 1986 which shows how far the *SAP* has gone in spawning a new political class, held together by family ties and mutual economic interests. Of the 209 leading *Social Democrats* he interviewed, three out of four came from *SAP* homes, in which most family members were active in the movement. Only a fourth had ever worked in the private sector, and none returned there after having a job in the party. Isaksson concluded that their background and experiences incline them to oppose certain changes, such as permitting private sector competition with public sector services.

Property Distribution

The *SAP* programs had contained such verbiage before, but this time the party was confronted with untiring critics on its left and a trade union partner which was also thinking along lines of a more radical move to achieve a form of economic democracy. At the *LO* Congress of 1975 a trade union economist presented a bombshell report which called for a "distribution of the wealth," and the *LO* chairman even went a step further and spoke of a "special Swedish brand of socialism" which would have the goal of "abolishing capitalism and private property in industry." Indeed, while Sweden has gone a long way in redistributing *income*, it has done very little to redistribute wealth. Property ownership has changed very little since the 1930s. Industry is highly concentrated; the industrial scene is dominated by 15 to 20 corporations, many of which are family–owned. According to a 1982 study, 89% of Swedish households owned no stock in corporations, while a little more than 1% of all households controlled three–quarters of the nations' shares of stock. One half of the shares are owned by 0.3% of the families!

LO proposed a concrete plan of "workers funds" which Swedish employers justifiably called a confiscation policy. A certain percentage of the firms' profits and payrolls are turned over annually to five government–nominated boards, dominated by the trade unions. Each of these boards can purchase up to 80% of a company's stock. Individual wage–earners

Prime Minister Goran Persson

Sweden

would neither own the shares nor draw dividends, but within a couple of decades the trade unions would gain control over every sizable company in Sweden.

The *SAP* in 1978 also embraced the idea of the "funds," despite their unpopularity. In its campaign for the 1982 elections, it pledged to introduce these funds, to protect the large public sector, to restore full employment and to put an end to what it calls a dismantling of the social welfare state, which the *SAP* was chiefly responsible for building. In 1983 Palme submitted the question of the "funds" to a vote in the *Riksdag*, a decision which had prompted 100,000 Swedes to march on parliament, the country's largest demonstration in recent history. The *Riksdag* approved the funds with a narrow majority. This close vote on such an unpopular issue revealed just how far Sweden has departed from the politics of consensus and compromise, and how confrontational Swedish politics has become. In 1984 a watered down fund system went into effect. In 1991 the newly elected conservative government promptly abolished the funds altogether.

The Communists

One party that advocates a leftist ideological course is the *Left Party (VP)*, which split from the *SAP* in 1917. It transformed itself into a "Eurocommunist" party in the 1960s by scrapping its advocacy of a "dictatorship of the proletariat." It also changed its name in 1967 in order to make itself more appealing to left–wing socialists and the *SAP*. It cut its ties with the Soviet Union, a move which led some elements in the party to split off and form other communist groupings. None has mustered more than the feeblest support at election time or has ever won a single seat in the *Riksdag*. The *VP* became a political home for a part of the "new left" in the 1970s, and it defines itself as "socialist–feminist" today.

The *VP* finds its major strength is in the industrial centers. It actively opposes EU membership, as well as austerity and cuts in the welfare budget. It has never been included in a Swedish governing coalition although it is sometimes willing to support the *SAP's* programs as the best alternative to "bourgeois" governments. It is led by Gudrun Schyman, who demands much more spending on welfare and jobs, a slowing down of national debt repayment, higher taxes on wealth, and an end to nuclear power and privatization. It scored its best results ever in 1998, almost doubling its votes to 12% and its seats to 43.

The battered *SAP* was compelled to enter a four–year cooperation agreement with both the *VP* and another party that in 1988 had become the first new party to

Göteborg, Sweden's second largest city and Scandinavia's largest port

win seats since Sweden introduced universal and equal suffrage in 1917—the *Greens*. In 1998 they captured 4.5% of the votes and 16 seats. They advocate strict environmental controls, the extinguishing of nuclear power, the transfer of politics from professional politicians to amateurs and laymen, and a clear distancing from the EU.

The "Bourgeois" Parties

The second block of parties in Sweden is often called the "bourgeois" or "non–socialist" bloc. None of the parties in this group advocates a dismantling of the social welfare system, although all favor some correction of its excesses and abuses. They are not against collective action, which has deep roots in Sweden's heritage, but they do lay more emphasis on individualism and the rights of private property than does the *SAP*. This is why all three advocate a greater degree of decentralization as a barrier against excessively centralized authority and bureaucracy. They also call for lower taxes in order to stimulate and liberate individual initiative again, but they disagree about the precise form of such reductions. In questions of foreign policy they have no fundamental disagreements either with each other or with the *SAP*, especially insofar as Swedish neutrality is concerned. However, the leaders tend to favor more amicable relations with the NATO countries.

The bourgeois coalition ruled from 1976 to 1982, but it was stricken with disunity and problems from the very beginning. Its failure stemmed in large part from its response to the economic problems which had befallen the once–fabled Swedish model of quiet compromise. In the 1988 elections it again lacked unity, and its platform of lower taxes and private competition in the welfare system was not an attractive alternative to the *SAP's* successful economic policies. It therefore suffered its worst defeat since the Second World War. It won the 1991 elections, finding its greatest strength among youth and middle class voters in big cities. It formed a minority government. In 1994 it was replaced by the *SAP*. Voters disliked the bloc's budget–cutting and attempts to reform the welfare state to make it solvent. This brought too much pain and too few immediate benefits. Voters longed to return to the snug security they had enjoyed earlier.

The second largest party after the *SAP* is the *Moderate Unity Party (M)*. In the 1998 elections it held its ground and won 22.7% of the votes and 82 seats. It was one of two members of the earlier conservative government that maintained its electoral strength in 1998. The other is the staid, God–fearing *Christian Democrats*, who soared to 11.8% of the votes and 42 seats in 1998. *M* changed its program and name in 1969 in order to reverse a constant loss

Sweden

of voters, but most Swedes still refer to it as *The Conservative Party*. It has always appealed more to the upper class, but it never was a reactionary party of the extreme right. Like other parties of the bloc, it had to adjust to Sweden's changing social structure and to extend its appeal into the urban areas, where it receives almost half its votes. Its key supporters come from large and small businessmen, big farmers, the upper civil service, and in 1991 from young Swedes. It receives financial assistance from the Confederation of Employers (SAF) and from industry, as well as some sympathy from the union of academics and upper civil service (SACO/SR), but these forms of support are not nearly as significant for it as is *LO* support for the *SAP*.

Many Swedish newspapers support the party, the most important being the respected Stockholm morning daily, *Svenska Dagbladet*, a well–informed, low keyed paper whose circulation is growing. This newspaper does retain its independence and it does not hesitate to criticize the *Conservatives*. The party has always had relatively strained relations with the other two parties in the "bourgeois" bloc, and it left the coalition in 1981 over the issue of tax reduction, which it considers as absolutely essential. Its former leader, Ulf Adelsohn, summed up his party's position tartly by remarking that "things are pretty crazy if a man is taxed so much that he can't pay his rent, but the government is willing to pay him a rent subsidy to make up the difference." That kind of remark sounded like a serious threat to the welfare system and to the role of the state in the nation's economy. In a country in which the *majority* of voters derive their livelihood from public funds or employment, political assaults on the public sector and calls for a "change in the system," however logical they may be, are highly risky.

Hon. Carl Bildt

Its new leader was Carl Bildt, the party's young defense policy expert. In his inaugural address to Parliament in 1991 he called the vote "a question of a revolution in freedom of choice," and declared that "the age of collectivism in Sweden is over." Faced with a stalled economy and declining international competitiveness, voters turned against the power of the large institutions and centralized decision–making process which are the hallmarks of the "Swedish model." Young voters especially opted for the non–socialist parties. Described as the "Interrail generation," they have returned from wide travel with the impression that other Western Europeans enjoy more freedom of choice in their lives.

Bildt, a great admirer of Germany, spent much time in Poland during 1980–1. He returned doubly convinced that "freedom and democracy are conditions for peace and cooperation." As the first Swedish prime minister in this century who is a passionate European, he pressed hard for his country's admission to the EU, which Sweden formally entered in 1995. His victory did not mean that he had a mandate completely to transform the welfare state. He aimed to stop its growth and trim it around the edges. Swedes did not like this and voted his government out in 1994. Bildt was not helped by the fact that he had returned to Sweden with the aura of an international leader after serving two years as UN High Representative to Bosnia.

The *Center Party (C)* also responded to the structural changes in Swedish society by changing its name in 1957 from the *Farmer's Party*. It now draws more votes from workers than from farmers, but its strength is still located largely outside the cities and mainly in southern Sweden. It receives about 70% of the farmers' votes, and its membership, leadership and parliamentary group are dominated by farmers. It also receives financial, organizational and political support from the Farmer's Organization (LRF), with which it has an overlapping leadership. The *Center* has ruled with the *SAP* in the past, and its goal of a "guided market economy" is still very compatible with the traditional economic policy of the *SAP*. In fact, it was its cooperation with the *SAP* over the tax cut scheme in 1981 which prompted the *Conservatives* to leave the governing coalition.

There has always been tension between the *Center* and the *Conservatives*, and this tension was made worse within the government by the *Center's* anti–nuclear energy policy and by its strong ecological appeals which from 1976 on were able to attract many protest votes. It now has a fragile and mixed electorate which merely intensifies its traditional difficulty in

Hon. Lars Leijonborg
Leader, Liberal People's Party

deciding, first, whether and with whom to form a coalition and, second, to what extent it should compete for votes at the expense of the conservatives or the liberals. It continued its downhill slide in 1998 to 5.1% of the votes and only 18 seats.

The third party in the non–socialist bloc is the *Liberal People's Party (FP)*, which has its main strength in the larger cities, especially Stockholm and Göteborg. Its voters are a very heterogeneous group, and unlike all other major parties, it is not backed by any large economic organization, although it does receive some financial support from the employer's organization, SAF. Traditionally it also has been supported by the nonconformist religions and by the anti–alcohol organizations. It does have a strong foothold in the press, especially the largest national morning newspaper, *Dagens Nyheter*, whose circulation started falling rapidly as a result of the more leftist approach it began taking in the mid–1970s, and the afternoon daily, *Expressen*, which has Scandinavia's largest circulation. The *Göteborgs'–Posten* is also liberal. None of these papers is directly connected with the party, though, and all criticize it freely. For a while the *FP* successfully attracted non–socialist voters by stressing *both* the virtues of a market economy *and* of social responsibility through welfare policies. But it has been losing ground in elections, winning only 4.7% of the votes and 17 seats in 1998 under its leader, Lars Leijonborg.

ECONOMY

General Considerations

Sweden has a market economy. One–third of the labor force is employed by the state. It is also very dependent

Sweden

upon exports, which account for about a third of the country's GDP (compared to about 10% in the U.S. and 25% in Canada); 80% of its exports consists of industrial products. It must also import heavily, especially oil. This reliance on foreign trade makes Sweden vulnerable to international economic conditions and prices.

The economy is not socialist, since most of the enterprises and means of production remain in private hands, at least for the present. This percentage had traditionally been about 95%, but it was lowered to 92% as a result of state takeovers under the non–*SAP* government between 1976 and 1982. About 10% of the work force is employed by state–owned enterprises, which include the railroads, iron ore mining in Lapland, post and telephone services, and a large part of the domestic energy production, primarily hydroelectric.

It may seem ironic that the non–*SAP* coalition nationalized more Swedish industry in four years after 1976 than the *SAP* had done in the previous 40. In the worst postwar economic crisis (1975–77) the new government decided that some key ailing industries, especially steel production and shipbuilding sectors, could not be saved through increased state subsidies and mergers. Therefore, it boosted public spending and added more formerly private firms to the State Company (*Statsföretag*), which comprises the major part of the state–owned companies. The result was rapid wage inflation, a loss of international competitiveness and gaping current accounts deficits.

After 1982 the *SAP* returned some state–owned firms to private hands. The Bildt government carried this on in 1992 by launching the privatization of 35 such companies. The *SAP* had returned to the non–interventionist rules of the "Swedish model." Subsidies to lame–duck industries were abolished, and ailing firms are allowed to die. Market forces decide which Swedish firms thrive or fail. Whatever financial assistance it gives is concentrated on research and development and on incentives for high–tech investment. Its overall investment in R & D is 3% of GDP, the world's highest. Almost 60% of this is financed by private industry. Also, it has more industrial robots per capita than any other country.

The *SAP* had always tended to leave the private character of the economy untouched, focusing instead on state influence over private industry and heavily taxing the profits. For the *SAP* it was always more important for the state to be able to gather the eggs rather than to own the hen. What are some of the ways in which the state has influenced the economy and maintained the fabled "Swedish model"?

During its four and a half decades of rule, the priority of full employment was established so firmly that the other parties did not dare to challenge it. Unemployment had never risen above 3% since the 1930s, but it was 5.3% in 1999. It is somewhat higher among young people and women. The total figure would be somewhat higher if the state did not "hide" unemployment by providing emergency work and broad retraining possibilities. Thus, actual unemployment would be about 11%.

Among the reasons for low unemployment formerly was an active policy of tackling unemployment, involving imaginative job retraining and other measures to make Swedish workers more mobile. It offers inducements to firms to locate in the north where employment possibilities have always been limited. To add a stick to the carrot, generous unemployment benefits (about 80% of normal pay) are cut off if an unemployed worker refuses to accept either the training or the job he is offered. It was therefore better at reducing long–term unemployment. For instance, of those unemployed in 1991, only 8% had been out of work longer than a year. Fighting inflation, which stood at .1% in 1999, usually had a low priority. Yet, the fairly tight fiscal and monetary policy which the government pursues helps keep inflation low.

Sweden has a large public sector, high taxes, a generous welfare state, low wage differentials and powerful labor unions, and its economic performance was disappointing in the 1990s. By the end of the century it had slipped to only 15th place among OECD nations in terms of GDP per head. Nevertheless, it has one of the world's highest living standards, and a 1998 UN report cited it as having the lowest incidence of poverty in the world. Its vigorous private companies, such as Volvo, Ericsson, Electrolux, SAAB, ASEA, SKF and Alfa–Laval, are world leaders in their main products. Sweden is not an economic sick man of Europe.

Sweden has a predominantly industrial and service economy, not an agricultural one. Its agricultural population has shrunk rapidly to about 5%, but its modern farming methods have led to such increases in productivity that it can supply about 90% of the country's needs. The state has both helped farmers to maintain their incomes and supported consumer prices for food to keep prices down in supermarkets. When the government suspended some of the food price subsidies in 1981 as a part of its effort to cut down on the overall level of government subsidies, food prices shot up 20% overnight. They are now at such a high level that a foreigner who visits a supermarket is almost stunned at the stickers.

Timber cutting

Sweden

Sweden is no longer the land of lumberjacks—the number making a living from forestry has dramatically decreased in the past decades, which is one reason for the shortage of employment opportunities in the North. The immense Swedish forests still can supply the raw material for the wood processing industry, which is competitive on world markets despite the rather small size of the companies and the stiff competition from abroad, especially from North America. A fourth of all wood pulp and paper materials sold in the world is from Sweden. The export of other forms of raw materials has lost much of its former importance for the Swedish economy, although it still accounts for a seventh of total exports.

Sweden is a country with many large and multi–national firms. The top 20 accounted for half the country's total sales. Many of these giants, such as Volvo (by far the largest single enterprise in the Nordic region), Electrolux or SAAB–Scandia export far more than they sell in Sweden. The large companies have also invested heavily abroad, especially in the U.S., Britain, France and Germany, in order to get closer to their markets. For example, Volvo sells more automobiles in the U.S. than in Sweden itself. In 1999 Ford Motor Company acquired Volvo's passenger vehicle operation, which still operate as an independent subsidiary. Volvo kept its profitable truck, construction equipment, and airplane and marine engine operations. Sweden's foreign subsidiaries employ more workers than do the home companies in Sweden. In 1990 for the first time, Swedish firms invested more capital abroad than at home; 70% went to the EU. In 1996 the 25 largest Swedish companies had 75% of their employment, production, and sales abroad. It is perhaps ironic that in a 1997 study by a Canadian consulting firm, Sweden ranked only behind Canada as the industrialized country with the lowest overall costs of doing business. Nevertheless, at the end of the century many large companies, are considering moving their headquarters out of the country. For example, Ericsson, Europe's leading telecom manufacturer and world's largest maker of mobile phones, is moving key parts of its head office to London.

The best known industry has traditionally been iron and steel. However, its iron ore is of high grade and its steel production is also high. It has actually become a net importer of iron and steel products at present—too much steel is produced in the world and the steel industry everywhere is in dire need of restructuring. The state is trying to guide this partly by encouraging mergers, such as the formation of Svenskt Stål AB (Swedish Steel—SSAB), of which the state owns 50%.

Machinery, automobiles, ships, armaments, metal processing, electronics (the fastest growing Swedish industry) and other engineering products have a lion's share of Swedish production and exports. The weakest at the present time is shipbuilding, a traditional Scandinavian specialty. After the mid–1960s, Sweden had been building more ships than any country but Japan and was selling three-fourths of this production to foreigners. This reached a peak in 1976, but then it declined rapidly. There is no hope that the industry will ever fully recover from this crisis. Beginning in 1977 Svenska Varv (Swedish Wharf) absorbed all the big shipyards and began introducing a rigid program of automation. By 1985 these shipyards had a work force about one–third of their size in 1976. They were also put on notice that they would have to get along without subsidies. Finally, each shipyard is to specialize on a particular market, such as that for offshore rigs and platforms, tankers, cargo carriers or ferries.

About 80% of Sweden's exports goes to the industrialized world, with Germany, Great Britain, the U.S., Norway, Denmark and Finland receiving about half; 8% is shipped to the U.S. Swedish companies want to be in the U.S. market because of its size and so that they can absorb new trends in research and marketing. It buys most of its imports from Germany, followed by Great Britain, the U.S. and Denmark. Taken together, the other Nordic countries account for roughly a fifth of its foreign trade.

The EU accounted for 55% of its trade in 1995. This offers the best explanation why Swedes voted 52.3% to 46.8% in November 1994 to enter the EU in 1995. A united front of most of the country's business and political establishment supported entry. They argued that Sweden needed the EU to bolster its exports, keep companies from moving more jobs and investments abroad, improve its lagging international credit rating, and shore up its troubled economy. Farmers, environmentalists and leftists, especially in rural areas in northern and central Sweden, led the opposition, arguing that Sweden's voice would be drowned out in the European cacophony. Even after entry, opposition remains strong, especially to monetary union. Some changes are not welcome, such as the EU demand that Sweden liberalize its restriction on alcohol, which has been one of the cornerstones of Swedish social policy throughout the twentieth century. It has had to drop state monopolies on the import and wholesale distribution of spirits.

Energy Dependence

Energy is one of Sweden's economic Achilles' heels. Like the other Nordic countries, which are sparsely populated and situated in a cold climate, its energy consumption per capita is among the highest in the world (but behind that of Canada and the United States). It is very dependent upon OPEC countries, espe-

Volvo assembly plant, Göteborg

Sweden

cially Saudi Arabia, for a particularly vital import: oil. Slightly over half of its energy needs must be covered by imports (down from 78% in 1973), especially by oil. Accounting for 15% of its overall needs, water power is its most important domestic source, providing half of its electricity generation; nuclear power produces the other half. Wood accounts for 2%, nuclear power for about 15%, and coal, coke, wastes and other domestic sources for 12%. Efforts were made to reduce reliance on oil. Sweden is trying to do this by continuing its rather effective conservation measures. Between 1976 and 1986, it halved its oil consumption in response to the "oil shock," despite a growing number of automobiles; in 1989 there were 412 cars per 1,000 inhabitants. It has begun to serve clusters of homes with heat produced centrally in nearby heat plants and also is increasing its use of imported coal, peat, its own wood, water power and nuclear power.

Sweden dived deeply into nuclear energy. The *SAP* had developed plans during its last years in power before the 1976 election to build a total of 24 nuclear plants which could provide over half of all the country's energy. The *Center Party* placed the issue squarely in the political limelight during the 1976 election, and in power it refused to permit the fueling and starting up of the seventh and eighth plants. After two years of wrangling within the center coalition and countless demonstrations by the powerful environmentalist groups, the government collapsed on the issue.

When the nuclear accident occurred at Three Mile Island near Harrisburg, Pennsylvania, the government decided to put the issue of nuclear power to a referendum in 1980. The results represented a kind of compromise: Sweden would complete the construction of 12 reactors, but it would shut down all nuclear plants by the year 2010. This defused the issue for awhile. The Chernobyl accident in the Ukraine in 1986 caused limited but highly publicized radioactive contamination in northern Sweden. The heat of the public debate over nuclear power in Sweden again reached melt–down levels. But Sweden is on the horns of an energy dilemma. To buy more time, the government announced in 1991 that plans to abolish nuclear power would be postponed while energy–saving and pollution–free alternatives were sought. The Persson government announced that it would try to close down one plant by 1998, but a 1996 poll found that only 14% believed that the 2010 deadline for closing all reactors should be adhered to.

Sweden's energy problems will increase in the future, rather than decrease. The country's estimated uranium reserves of over 300,000 tons will make it tempting to stick with this important source of domestic energy rather than to scramble to supply an even greater percentage of its total needs with expensive imports. Already it generates half of its electricity from nuclear power, a percentage which is steadily rising—in 1986 it used twice as much nuclear energy as it did in 1980. No adequate substitute sources have been found. Possibly the solution will be found in the development of safer nuclear reactors. The Swedes, with their "Process Inherent Ultimately Safe Reactor" (PIUS), are pioneering in the newest nuclear technology and could turn a bitter necessity into a commercially profitable virtue. Sweden has an excellent record of nuclear safety. Nevertheless, it plans to shut down two efficient and safe plants by 2001. An unfortunate consequence could be that Sweden would have to increase its use of electricity generated by Russian and Baltic nuclear plants, none of which meet Swedish safety standards.

Economic Difficulties

Sweden's economic rose began to fade. Like the U.S., it had entered the postwar era with its factories, cities and economic structure intact. This was a great advantage, especially since it had an ample supply of raw materials and was located close to Western Europe, which had been ravished and partly destroyed by the war. It made full use of its advantage and soon had a highly productive and growing economy which created unimagined wealth. But then certain problems set in. As Western Europe recovered from the war, competition became stiffer, even in sectors which were traditionally Swedish specialties. "Third World" countries also began to snatch markets from the Swedes for such goods as textiles.

World energy costs began to shoot through the roof after 1973 and the resultant worldwide recession led to a reduced demand for Swedish exports. When the competition really became fierce for shrinking markets, the Swedes discovered that their industrial muscles had grown flabby. They found that too much of their wealth had been spent on public and private consumption and that far too little had been reinvested in such a way that a high level of productivity could be maintained.

The high private consumption was reflected partly in the industries' wage costs, which have soared. The worst binge of salary increases came in the mid–1970s, when salaries rose by 40% in two years. By 1981 Belgians and Swedes had the highest pay in Europe. Since 1938, when an agreement between the employer organizations and trade unions was reached at Saltsjöbaden, relations between management and labor have, on the whole, been characterized by cooperation rather than by confrontation. All Swedes benefited from this. Every year or two the highest representatives of the *LO* and the *SAF* met to establish general wage guidelines which were then normally observed down the line. The *LO* was able to insist upon the principle of "solidarity wages," which means equal pay for the same kind of work regardless of the profitability of any specific firm. Thus, struggling firms could be strained even further by having to pay the same wages as the more successful companies.

The concept of "solidarity wages is under attack by skilled workers' unions and employers. Also, the unions, to which 86% of the labor force belongs, carefully guard the pay differentials between certain categories of jobs. When these pay differentials are not observed, rare but serious nationwide strikes can break out. Centralized wage negotiations, abandoned in 1984, often brought stability and labor peace. The non–socialist government proposed in 1991 to dismantle centralized wage bargaining, deregulating the labor market and lowering corporate wage bills. But Swedish unions resist the steep decline suffered by trade unions elsewhere by accepting necessary technological change. They traditionally are innovative, not reactive.

In the mid–1990s Sweden came out of its worst recession in a half century, during which it experienced a soaring budget deficit approaching 11% of GDP, record unemployment of 8% with industrial employment falling by 27%, a depressed real estate market, and a krona which had to be devalued periodically. Central Bank chairman, Burenstam Linder, concluded: "We see that we are not uniquely blessed by God, that we have created a lot of problems for ourselves and that now we have to go about changing various things."

National Debt

To pay for its imports, its budgetary deficits and the foreign travel which its prosperous citizens have come to love, Sweden went deeper and deeper into debt. High wage costs and tax rates deprive industries of investment funds which they need to maintain their productivity. Any drop in productivity strikes at the very heart of Sweden's "middle way." That model, by which social welfare and income redistribution would be paid for by a robust private sector, now seems to work only in times of economic growth.

Sweden's high public consumption is vividly reflected in its comprehensive social welfare system, which some admirers contend make it the most just society in

Sweden

the world. Some observers have called it the perfect "post–industrial" society which has effectively solved its problems of production and can now concentrate on distributing economic and social benefits widely and justly. In other words, the consumption and distribution of wealth had allegedly replaced the *production of it* as the society's major problem. The economic difficulties in the last decade show how the "post–industrial" situation is by no means static, if it ever existed at all, and that there are great dangers in focusing too much on consumption and losing sight of production. It should be stressed, though, that *private* consumption and the growth of disposable income actually dropped during the 1980s, in comparison with such countries as the U.S., and Canada, and Switzerland. According to 1989 OECD statistics, the disposable income of a Swedish production worker was lower than that of a worker in France, Italy or Spain. Also, welfare spending has been significantly trimmed in the 1990s, bringing by 1999 the total national debt down to 77.3% of GDP and the annual budget deficit to an impressive 1.9% of GDP.

Welfarism and Taxation

Swedes understandably do not wish to give up a welfare system which pays almost all doctors' bills and at least half of dental bills, which provides invalids with about 90% of their normal pay until age 65 and which pays the unemployed 80% of their former income. It provides five weeks of paid vacation time and allows the employee to save up his vacation time and take it all in one extended period. By 1995 the average work week for a full–time employee was 36 hours, one of the lowest in all Europe; his average time off work, for all reasons including vacation, is about 25%. Sick pay of 90% of normal earnings encouraged the average Swede to be officially absent from work for reasons of illness 30.7 days (more than a working month!) per year, compared with only 7.8 days in the U.S. and 17.2 days in Germany. In 1988 Volvo suffered 14% sickness absenteeism. Needless to say, this can play havoc with production schedules which depend upon the presence of key employees. After benefits were reduced in 1991 and again in 1993, the sickness absentee rate predictably began to fall. Sick leave became less readily available, and by 1999 the average number of days taken for illness had dropped to 11.

This welfare system is generous, but many Swedes agree that it is impossible to pay for. Costs of maintaining the system have expanded annually more rapidly than has economic growth. But as conservatives experienced in the 1994 elections, it was risky to reduce social programs that Swedes have grown to regard as their birthright. For more than 50 years they had been taught that state and society were the same things and that the function of government was to attempt to solve all problems. The Bildt government's message was that "the state ought not to strive after doing what a free society can manage better or as well." It no longer saw a need for welfare services to be entirely under public management and control; private initiative enjoyed more encouragement. Even the *SAP*, which built the welfare state, supported crisis measures to save Sweden's economy and currency. These included reducing housing subsidies, sickness benefits, and foreign aid, making employers and employees share health benefits and sickness insurance with the state, raising gasoline and cigarette taxes, and changing old age pensions to begin at age 67. Sweden radically restructured its basic taxpayer–funded retirement system and even permits a portion of the funds to be invested in the stock and bond market.

Unlike Norway, Sweden has no oil revenues which can pay the difference. Almost 40% of the Swedish work force is employed by the national, regional or local governments (compared to the OECD average of one–fifth). By 1995 public

Sweden's Stefan Edberg raises his trophy after defeating Boris Becker in the Men's Singles Final at Wimbledon on July 4, 1988
AP Wide World Photo

Sweden

spending represented a whopping 70% of Sweden's GDP, compared with 45% in 1973. The bulk of government spending can only be paid for by direct and indirect taxes that are over half (54%) of the average Swede's wages.

Income taxes are steeply progressive. The top marginal rate in 1989 was 72%, which Swedes pay when their incomes reach about $50,000. The tax code appeared unjust because rich Swedes learned how to use the complex system of deductions to lighten their burden. In 1989 Finance Minister Kjell–Olof Feldt called it "rotten." The major parties agreed to simplify the income tax structure by introducing a three–tier rate structure: 31% for the average payer and 60% for the richer; corporate tax was reduced from 50% to 30%. Many loop–holes were eliminated. Taxes on capital gains were made more equitable with other forms of income. Swedes also pay a VAT of 25%. The rest of government spending is covered by budget deficits which once comprised about a third of the total government budget and which had risen from less than 4% of the GDP in 1976 to 11% by 1995, before dropping dramatically to 2.1% in 1998.

The extremely high tax level has had many negative consequences. It has not only driven such wealthy Swedes as tennis star Björn Borg and skier Ingemar Stenmark into tax exile in Monaco, but it has encouraged tax evasion and "barter work," one of the most primitive forms of work whereby Swedes swap services with each other behind the backs of the tax officials. For instance, a carpenter builds a cabinet for a mechanic who repairs his car in return. By 1987 it was estimated that such an "underground economy" equalled 10–20% of GDP.

The tax system also discourages some Swedes from seeking promotions because most of the added pay would be collected by the state anyway. Working overtime is less attractive for the same reason. For example, in 1979 an employer offered his workers a bonus of $2,000 if they worked between Christmas and New Years, but it was turned down because taxes would make the bonus negligible. Also, a fourth of the total labor force now finds it more attractive to work half–time than full–time because of the tax structure.

The Swedish welfare system would not have some of these negative effects if the former Lutheran work ethic had remained intact. As late as the early 1970s one's social status and self–esteem in Sweden was still largely established by one's occupation and position. However, as in many other industrialized countries, many Swedes' drive to have individual success has weakened, and the importance attached to financial rewards and status has decreased. Fewer people obtain job satisfaction, partly because much work has become automated and routinized, and partly because prosperity created leisure–time activities which became increasingly attractive. In other words, Swedes have fewer qualms about being absent from work.

Finally, the social welfare system has not evened out the differences in income, as many of its proponents had hoped, although these differences are certainly narrower than in most countries, including the U.S. Nor has the welfare system led to a diminution of crime, alcoholism, suicides, juvenile delinquency, vandalism or other anti–social activities, as many of its supporters had argued that it would. In fact, crime has risen so much, especially in the cities, that Sweden became one of the first countries in the world to provide financial compensation to victims of violent crimes.

CULTURE

The Equality Goal

Perhaps no people in all of Western Europe has tried so hard to establish equality in so many segments of its society as have the Swedes. They have been willing to experiment, and their reforms are regarded with great interest from abroad. In many ways they have fallen short of this goal; there are still noticeable differences in wealth, income and social status, and not all Swedes agree that every single effort and policy designed to achieve the goal of equality has been a good one. Many of the policies are being criticized today on the grounds that they are unrealistic or that they place limits on the ability of an individual to use his talents to the fullest and to reap the benefits of his own capacity and effort. Critics contend that the result is often mediocrity, omnipresent and suffocating bureaucracy, or worse, a restriction of human freedom. But Swedes are a tolerant people with a strong pluralistic tradition. They debate these matters openly and do not try to hide the problems or the failures. Also, they have always had a pragmatic inclination and are able to undo those reforms which most might agree have created more problems than they have solved.

One distinction among people which has almost entirely disappeared involves the word "you." The person who speaks English uses the same word for all individuals he addresses, remnants of this lingual distinction having disappeared from English in the last century (the formal usage was "thee," "thou" and "thine"). But all other European languages have preserved different words for "you"—a formal one (in Swedish, *ni*) for persons whom one does not know well, whom one wants to keep at arms's length or whom one wants to show particular respect, and an informal one (in Swedish, *du*) for friends, family or often those beneath one's own social station (such as a maid or gardener). More than in any other European country, the formal *ni* has fallen into disuse, and almost everyone is simply addressed as *du*. The only exceptions are elderly persons who cannot accept such a modern equalizing step in their last years and the King and Queen, whom only journalists dare to address in public as *du*.

In addition to dropping off the formal "you," they are also casting off many of the academic and occupational titles which used to adorn so many persons' names. Swedes were traditionally a very title–conscious people, with many persons attaching to their name a "Dr.," "Mr. Director," "Mr. Chief Postal Inspector," or, of course, a title of nobility in this monarchical country. One uses the titles less often now because they no longer fit easily into the egalitarian movement. Pupils do not call their teachers "Mr.," or "Mrs.," and students at the universities seldom address their professors or instructors as "Professor" or "Doctor." In fact, the few persons who acquire Ph.D. degrees in Sweden today can look forward to a life in which only their families and employers will even know that they have achieved this academic distinction.

The Family

More equality has seeped into the Swedish family, where few fathers are stern disciplinarians who are treated with a combination of love, respect and fear by other members. With women entering the working world in large numbers, the patriarchal character of the Swedish family declined or disappeared and the position of both sexes was equalized. Family members have a more relaxed, comradely relationship with each other, especially in urban, middle class families.

As in most advanced industrialized societies, the extended family no longer lives under one roof. The elderly are financially independent since they receive at age 65 pensions which amount to two–thirds of their earlier working incomes and which are regularly adjusted for inflation. At present, 16% of Swedes receive old age pensions. The state provides them with an array of social services if they are needed. These services include the cleaning of their apartments or bodies in order to keep hygienic standards high, delivery of complete meals, chauffeuring and even special subsidies to enable them to remain in their own homes as long as possible. When they need full care, they

Sweden

can move into state–operated homes for the elderly. This usually occurs at about age 80. This involves many Swedes, since the life expectancy is 74 for men and 80 for women. They must be supported by fewer and fewer persons in the work force because the nation's population was barely growing. But it began climbing fast in the 1990s, reaching in 1991 a total fertility rate of 2.1 per woman, the rate needed to match the number of people dying. There are some persons who find drawbacks in the breakdown of the extended family under one roof, but the absence of the elderly from the homes of their children's families has undoubtedly brought greater freedom to most of those families and has eliminated an authority pattern which tended to bring more hierarchy and less equality into the family.

Not only the Swedish extended family has changed, but the very institution of the family is undergoing radical alteration. By the end of the 1980s the Swedish marriage rate had fallen to the lowest in the industrial world. Non–marital cohabitation, which is now regarded legally and culturally as an accepted alternative rather than as a prelude to marriage, is the highest. Two–thirds of all couples have lived together before marriage; among the young, the rate is close to 90%. Half the babies are born out of wedlock. The average ages for first marriages are 30 for men and 27 for women (vs. 25.5 and 23.3 in the U.S.). A growing number of Swedes are not marrying at all. In today's cohabitation environment, even the arrival of children is no longer a strong reason for marriage. Gone for the most part are engagement parties and elaborate weddings. Divorce is also reducing the number of families, although the Swedish rate is slightly lower than the American one and stopped rising by 1991. Thus, an ever larger percentage of Swedish families have only one parent. In 1995 homosexuals were granted the right to marry, but not to adopt children or have them by artificial insemination.

In a country in which 70% of adult women have full or part–time jobs (encouraged by the tax system, which taxes each partner separately), having children can cause certain strains. The state provides certain payments and allowances to families with children so that their living standards will not fall below those of families in which there are *no* children. These payments vary; the less the parents earn, the more such assistance they receive. When a child is born, both the mother and the father have the right to divide in any manner they choose 12 months of almost fully paid vacation in order to care for the infant. For example, the father could stay home seven months and the mother five,

if they wished. Even non–working parents can receive a *per diem* allowance for 12 months to care for the child. Or, they can put aside six months of this child–care vacation and use them at any other time for any reason until the child is eight years old. Both the father and the mother have the right to take up to 60 days paid sick leave *per child* not only if they are ill, but if their child is ill. Thus, while the law encourages both parents to work, (an undeniable factor in national and personal prosperity), it has to provide benefits to enable them to perform the mother's traditional chores.

The child now enjoys a unique protection of the law against being spanked or hit by his parents: "A child may not be subjected to physical punishment or other injurious or humiliating treatment." One Stockholm youth police officer explained that "if grown–ups don't hit each other, then they can't hit children either." The main argument in favor of the law is that it might limit child abuse; most child abusers, proponents maintain, were once abused themselves as children. Opponents charge that the law is impossible to interpret or to enforce and is merely another example of "Big Brother," i.e. the state intervening in personal and family relationships. Swedish children are very aware of the law, and there is considerable discussion among parents and children on how parents can discipline children without hitting them. In any event, the law reflects the extent to which the child's role in the modern Swedish family has changed.

The woman's role in the family has also

One of Sweden's many rivers—every fifth family owns a boat

changed; 60% work outside the home. Her equality at the work place is protected by law. A special Equality ombudsman, who is usually a woman, is empowered to investigate complaints of discrimination. There are numerous visible signs of women's changed role in society. They can now perform sentry duty at the Royal Palace in Stockholm, a place where the head resident can be a woman now that the law of succession was changed. By 1979 Sweden's UN Peacekeeping Forces included 41 women, and females have broken into the priesthood of the Swedish State Church.

Although her role as an equal in family decision–making is rather secure, she must still do more of the housework than do men. The government–sponsored Equality Commission reported that in families where both partners had full–time jobs, 51% of the women worked 20 hours or more in the home and 10% did more than 40 hours of work, compared with only 18% of the men, who did 20 hours or more and 2% who did more than 40 hours. As the Equality Minister, Karin Andersson, said, "we are still a long way from achieving real equality in Sweden. In the home there is not a lot else we can do, except by keeping the debate alive." For awhile, at least, men will continue to be able to take it a little easier at home than will women.

Sexual Revolution

One form of emancipation which the Swedish woman was reputed to have since the 1950s, at least in the eyes of many foreigners, was sexual liberation. The outward evidence seemed to be clear. Films such as "She Danced Only One Summer," starring Ulla Jacobson, Ingmar Bergman's "Virgin Spring," or Vilgot Sjöman's two films, "I Am Curious–Yellow" and "I Am Curious– Blue" revealed nudity and sexual activity with a vividness which was shocking and sensational by the standards of the times. People did sometimes bathe publicly in the nude. Almost all limitations on pornography were dropped, and it could be displayed almost anywhere, including gasoline stations. In 1955, sex education was introduced as a required subject in the schools, teenage girls were able to get birth control pills, and condom machines were put in many public places, including student union buildings.

Those who actually came to Sweden expecting to find a society where all sexual inhibitions had broken down were badly disappointed, though. As in other Western European and North American countries, sexual attitudes had begun to change, but the changes in Swedish sexual mores never meant promiscuity, and

Sweden

the Swedes were not an *avant-garde* in the sexual revolution. In fact, observers who know Sweden well note that the Swedes are rather prudish compared to other northern Europeans. Nude bathing was mainly a family affair, and although it is practiced somewhat more widely in Sweden today, it is by no means more prevalent than in most other Western European countries, especially in Germany, where this is frequently seen in public parks.

The lead in the production and sale of pornography soon passed to such countries as Denmark and the Netherlands (which never acquired a reputation as sin centers), and pornography is now exploding in such countries as Spain. In short, the image of Sweden as the land of sexual license is one which the Swedes neither deserve, nor particularly desire to have. The constitution protects freedom of expression, including adult pornography. While the publication and distribution of child pornography is banned by law, the fact that Swedes are unique in Western Europe in being permitted to own and view it prompted Queen Silvia to break with tradition and attack it in an outspoken television interview in 1996. Although most Swedes agree with her opinion, the audacity of a monarch to intervene in political debate caused outrage.

The public manifestations of changed attitudes toward sexual matters in Sweden was a reflection of the Swedes' fundamental tolerance. There are many Swedes today who think that tighter limits should be drawn. Many voices have been raised against the law which was liberalized in 1975 to permit abortions until the twelfth week with no questions asked and until the 18th week under certain circumstances. For a couple of decades abortions have been legal under certain circumstances, but many people are distressed by the fact that one-third of all pregnancies are now terminated by abortion. There have also been calls to place limits on prostitution, although no government has attempted to outlaw this ancient profession.

Education

Increasing stress has been placed upon achieving social equality and less on competition since the 1960s. The general idea is that all persons are born with the same talent and capabilities, but an unequal social environment creates the differences among human beings. The schools are seen as an important socializing agent to counteract the unequal environment in other parts of the society. Put in an oversimplified way, the schools should focus more on social development than upon learning.

Only about 1% of the children attend private schools, which do receive some financial assistance from the state. Most children attend the same basic school (*grundskolan*) for nine years. New teaching methods have been introduced, including group work, individualized curricula and special activities, such as learning chess in the fourth grade. The issuing of grades is strictly limited in the first six years, and there are no final examinations during the first nine years. After the nine compulsory years, about 80% continue for two or four years in an integrated high school called *gymnasieskolan*. This combines more than 20 different curricula under one roof. Some pupils take a more rigorous academic course, preparing one for university studies, while others take a more practical course preparing one for a trade or commercial career.

All pupils who finish a course of study at this integrated high school are eligible to apply for a place at one of the more than 30 state institutions of higher education, integrated in a single system of higher education (*högskola*). The major universities are in Uppsala, Lund, Stockholm, Göteborg and Umeå. There are only a limited number of places in each field. Rather than distributing these places strictly on the basis of previous academic performance, a fourth of them are reserved for people over age 25 with four years of work experience or two years at the high school and knowledge of Swedish and English. The rest of the openings are given to those applicants with the best academic records. Women dominate the lecture halls in some fields: 59% of the university graduates are women. Most law and theology students are female, as are four-fifths of students enrolled in medical and diagnostic treatment programs. Men still predominate in departments of engineering, national science and math, and business administration.

Many critics argue that the preferential treatment given to those who did not prepare for the university, but who entered later in life creates at best an equality of mediocrity. They say that the academic standards have gone down considerably, that the university has become easier and that the students cannot write well any more. There are almost no critics against the fact that there is no tuition at the universities and that most students receive loans to help finance their studies. These loans are interest free, but the borrowers must pay back a sum to which intervening inflation has been added. Nor is there any criticism against the well-developed system of adult education, which was created in the 19th century. These kinds of equal opportunity are seen to be good. But the kind of equality which subordinates academic talent and performance to class or social considerations, and which thereby lowers the quality of scholarship, has not been accepted. In general, there is something of a backlash forming against what many Swedes see as a lowering of standards and discipline in schools at all levels. Societies have been formed to press for changes in what they see as a trend toward mediocrity. However, it is too early to say what long-term effect this undercurrent of protest and dissatisfaction will have.

Ethnic Diversity

Further compounding educational (and economic) problems is Sweden's growing ethnic diversity. Unlike some other European nations, Sweden had no colonial possessions in the past several centuries that exposed its society to foreign influences. In the 1960s, Sweden's booming industry was starved for labor, so immigrants were attracted to it from outside the Nordic area. But it never adopted a "guest worker" policy that foresaw immigrants returning to their countries once their jobs ended. The percentage of Nordics among the total foreign population in Sweden fell from about two-thirds in 1971 to slightly more than half today. By the 1980s these included about 50,000 Yugoslavs, 21,000 Greeks, 17,000 Turks, 10,000 Italians and a smattering of nationalities from Iberia, North Africa and the Middle East. Added to these immigrants are about 10,000 political refugees from Latin America, especially Chile, the former Yugoslavia in the 1990s, and a smaller number from Ethiopia and Iraq. The crack-down and declaration of martial law in Poland at the end of 1981 brought many more Poles to the country.

A wave of "boat people" from Vietnam also drifted ashore. They were callously driven from their homeland by a regime which the Swedish government and many Swedes had passionately supported during the Vietnam War, and which still receives a large share of Sweden's development aid. Former Prime Minister Olof Palme had marched in demonstrations in the Swedish capital with the North Vietnamese ambassador, and Stockholm was offered as the venue for "war crime trials" against the Americans who had led the Vietnam conflict. An official Swedish government publication dated April 1979 proudly noted that "Sweden came out early in favor of the Vietnamese people *(sic)* in their fight for independence and protested against the whole American involvement in Indochina." Swedish idealism has greatly benefited many Swedes, as well as many thousands of political refugees and economically desperate people in the "Third World." But like that of other nations, Swedish idealism is neither

Sweden

The changing faces of Sweden

unerring, nor free of cynicism, hypocrisy or irony.

The strong moral undertone of Palme's foreign policy explains why the Swedish peace movement has usually been on good terms with the political establishment. In this respect, it differs greatly from similar movements in the U.S. or other Western European countries. However, Carl Bildt, leader of the *Moderate Party*, reminded Swedes that there is more to politics than morality: "Sweden remains a small state in a vulnerable position. In a world where factors other than morality are also of importance, we would be wise to keep in mind both the limitations and the opportunities of our role as a small state." Indeed, a shift in Swedish foreign policy has already taken place, from Palme's broad internationalism to a lower-key focus on Europe and the Nordic region. As a result, foreign policy is a less divisive issue in Swedish politics today.

Nordic immigrants can become citizens after only two years; for others the minimum is five, and there are inhibiting costs and complications. About 60% of the more than one million immigrants have acquired Swedish citizenship, but even non-Swedes with work and residence permits by law are treated on the basis of equality with native Swedes. This means that immigrants receive all welfare benefits for which they have contributed but little, that they are not forced to go home if they lose their jobs and that they can even vote and stand for election in local and regional elections, so long as they have been residents there for at least three years. Government offices distribute information materials in fourteen languages explaining residents' rights and duties, taxes, insurance, employment and educational possibilities. The state also publishes an immigrant newspaper in six languages. Employers are required to provide foreigners with up to 240 hours of Swedish language instruction on company time, and the schools are required to give auxiliary Swedish lessons to immigrant children for as many years as are necessary to make the child completely competent in the language.

The schools must offer special instruction to an immigrant child in his own mother tongue for as long as the parents desire such instruction. For adults who desire it, the schools also arrange for home study of the non-Swedish native language. The basic principle is that the state should be committed to helping any person residing in the country to *maintain* his own language.

The extent to which Swedish officialdom has gone to accommodate immigrants is perhaps unparalleled in the entire world. Public opinion surveys also underscore that the fact that, while there is widespread opposition to further immigration, there is still considerable toleration toward those immigrants who already are in Sweden. There are no race riots as there have been in certain other countries, such as Britain and the U.S. But many Swedes are having difficulties learning to live with the large number of foreigners within their midst, especially in the larger cities. By the turn of the century, a tenth of the residents are non-Nordic. Assimilation of the one-fifth of the population that is either foreign-born or have a least one parent born abroad has not succeeded. Therefore, a new Integration Office reflects a changed government focus on insuring that individuals in diverse groups have equal rights and opportunities and are not subjected to racism and discrimination.

This difficulty is made worse by the fact that the visible increase in non-European (18%) in 1981, versus only 6% of foreign citizens in 1971 and southern European immigrants has coincided with a frightening rise in unemployment and a growing budget deficit and foreign debt. Immigrants, who most often, but not always, work at the dirtiest, noisiest or most monotonous jobs, are increasingly confronting Swedish prejudice and anxiety about the changing ethnic composition of Swedish cities. In some cities, such as Södertälje, south of Stockholm, the immigrant population was approaching 20% by the late 1970s.

In Western Europe today, any immigrant minority which approaches or exceeds 10% of the city's population usually spells trouble in one form or another. In 1989 a parliamentary commission of inquiry against racism and xenophobia judged the danger to have grown sufficiently that it recommended a law banning racist organizations. The extraordinary campaign to block the 2004 Olympic Games from coming to Stockholm demonstrated the problem. An extremist organization calling itself *We who build Sweden* asserted that it would "never allow a large number of niggers, Latinos and Eurotrash to come here, paid for by the Swedish taxpayer." Two bombs went off, and dozens of explosively racist threats were made. Partly because of this obnoxious campaign by a determined minority, Stockholm was not even among the top three contenders for the games.

Swedes are very hospitable towards guests whom they invite in their homes, but as one observer, Richard F. Tomasson wrote, "There is general agreement on the Swedes as stolid and stiff, shy or reserved, formal and conventional, inhibited—even dull, non-expressive, more interested in things than in people." Even Olof Palme stated in the precise English which he learned as a student at Kenyon College in Ohio that "we're probably shy and reserved, . . . and the humor of hell would have the humor of Sweden. We are distant and perhaps rather dull."

This is still a country with much public decorum, and many Swedes are inclined to withdraw into quiet anonymity. The content of much of Sweden's contemporary literature and of many of its films is the problem which individuals have in establishing meaningful contacts and relationships with others. It is therefore not surprising that many immigrants perceive their official treatment as fair and generous, but on the personal level such

Sweden

treatment is not always warm and friendly, and is sometimes even aloof and hostile. A Stockholm University ethnographer, Aake Daun, confirmed these traits of coolness, shyness and introvertedness in a 1989 study. He reported that only 24% of adult Swedes admitted being moved to tears when hearing of Olof Palme's assassination, compared with 44% of first–generation immigrants to Sweden; 53% of adult Americans said they cried when they heard of John Kennedy's assassination. Swedes see shyness as a positive trait and talkativeness as a negative one; they prefer being silent and alone. There is, of course, a positive side to all this: they shun conflict and do not like to say things for the sake of teasing others. Half as many Swedes as Italians and Finns admit to losing their temper easily if they cannot get their way.

The growing Swedish anxiety has been reflected in much tighter Swedish regulations for newcomers. Almost no one coming from outside the Nordic area can now receive a work permit, and, as a rule, only family members of immigrants already in Sweden are allowed to settle there. Further, Swedish authorities are making faster and stricter decisions on applications by political refugees and are immediately deporting those who are denied this status. Sweden, like most other wealthy Western European nations, has begun to close its open door. It turns away people with unfounded claims to asylum.

Sweden is a tolerant and generous country and wants to remain a refuge for the politically oppressed. But it is not willing to be a land of *unlimited* opportunities for outsiders. Swedish idealism has its limits, especially in time of economic distress.

The ratio of native Swedes to non–Swedes was seven–to–one in the 1990s. The Swedes have one of the lowest population growth rates in the world (less than 0%, with only 8 births per thousand). The average woman has only 1.6 children, while 2.1 would be necessary in order merely to maintain, in the long run, the present number of Swedes. More Swedes die every year than are born, and 16% of the population is already over age 65, a demographic fact which places great strain on the country's social welfare system. One baby in four being born is from an immigrant family; 52% are born out of wedlock, the highest in Europe.

The modest annual population increase is entirely due to the immigrants and their high birth rate, particularly of non–Europeans. In fact, if the present trends continue until the end of the century, one out of every five inhabitants will be of non–Swedish descent. At least it does have the lowest infant mortality rate in the world, and, contrary to a popular misconception, Sweden does *not* have the highest suicide rate in all of Western Europe; Finland, Denmark, Austria, Switzerland and Germany all have higher rates.

State Goals in Culture

Sweden has an ambitious cultural policy and devotes more than 1% of state expenditures to it. One journalist, Anders Ehnmark, told why many Swedes think such an effort to support Swedish culture is necessary: "Sweden is a small country, with a low threshold of resistance to banality arriving from outside. For many years it has been a thoroughly Coca Colonialized country. American soap opera culture holds hegemony in the public mind." The Swedish parliament spelled out in 1974 the objectives in the state's cultural policy. In principle, cultural equality is considered to be just as important as economic and social equality. That means that any individual who so wishes should have the opportunity to develop whatever talents he possesses and to enjoy cultural experiences, regardless of geographic, educational or other hindrances. This policy is underscored in practice by plentiful subsidies for cultural activities at all levels of government.

In order to aid authors, book publication is subsidized. Because the Swedish language is spoken by only about 8.5 million persons, the market is simply too small to make most books commercially viable. Also, in order to provide authors with a greater measure of economic security, the libraries pay the Swedish Author's Fund a small fee for every book which is lent out. These funds are used to pay the authors a guaranteed basic income, pension or special scholarships. This is an effort to keep the Swedish literary tradition alive, which includes many fine writers.

In the second half of the 18th century, Carl Michael Bellman wrote poetry which could be sung. These songs describe the peculiarities and interests of the people of Stockholm in his day and give Swedes both entertainment and insight into their own past. He helped to establish a tradition of concentrating on the country's people and their folk culture, a characteristic of much Swedish literature before 1945.

The end of the 19th and the beginning of the 20th centuries were times of economic poverty and mass emigration, especially to the U.S. However, it was also a rich time for Swedish literature. Gustaf Fröding was a poet who wrote in the dialect of the common people and whose works were filled with folklore. Selma Lagerlöf was a romantic novelist who won a Nobel Prize. Perhaps the greatest literary figure in Swedish history, August Strindberg, produced dramatic works which were deadly serious, deeply psychological, invariably anti–female and often downright depressing. His plays are still presented on stages throughout the world.

The 1930s were also times of economic crisis, and Ivar Lo–Johannsson, one of Sweden's best–loved authors, wrote several books, including *Good Night Earth*, about the landless peasants during these discouraging years. The 1940s were years of disillusionment among many Swedish intellectuals and writers, caused, at least in part, by the destructiveness of World War II and by the feelings of guilt and shame on the part of some Swedes at having been spared from this horrible conflict while other Europeans had suffered so much. This malaise was reflected in the works of such writers as Stig Dagerman and Karl Vennberg.

After the war, many writers tried to come to grips with the effects of a materialistic society on the individual, who can easily become alienated in an environment of cement and individual affluence. Other writers looked back at the Swedish past. Vilhelm Moberg produced a monumental series of books on Swedish emigrants to the U.S. which included *Unto a Good Land*, *The Immigrants*, and *The Last Letter Home*, all of which have been translated into English. Moberg committed suicide in the late 1970s, but his literary description of Swedes in America was filmed by the Swedish director Jan Troell.

Another author, Astrid Lindgren, created unforgettable children's books with such figures as Pipi Longstocking, which have for decades helped children inside and outside Sweden to imagine the countryside, the people, the customs and the spirit of Sweden's past.

In keeping with the country's objective to bring culture to as many people as possible, the state helps to finance theaters in many regions and has frequently subsidized independent theater troupes which perform in the streets, in schools or in factories and which help to bring theater to many groups of people, including children.

When one thinks of Swedish film, one tends to think immediately of such performers as Greta Garbo and Ingrid Bergman, and of such directors as Bo Widerberg, whose films focused on the industrial worker in modern society, and the film giant, Ingmar Bergman, whose films such as "The Seventh Seal," "Wild Strawberries," and "The Silence," helped to make the 1960s a golden decade for Swedish filmdom. However, Sweden's high taxes drove Ingmar Bergman abroad (he has since returned), and the 1970s were meager years for the cinema. There was a decline in the number of films produced, and some people began to ask if the Swedish film talent had dried up. To sal-

Sweden

vage this art form in Sweden, the state assumed more of the costs of production and a 10% surcharge on all movie tickets flows to the Swedish Film Institute to help finance new films. Nevertheless, the industry remains in serious financial difficulties, and even the Swedes seem to show less and less interest in their own films. The average citizen goes to the movies only three times a year; 75% of all visits to the cinema are to see American films, whereas only 15% concern Swedish ones.

Performing Arts

Sweden's newest concert hall is named after Franz Berwald (1796–1868), Sweden's most famous composer of romantic music. The voice of another Swede, Jenny Lind, captured the ear of the musical world at the end of the 19th century, and in the 1980s a versatile pop group called Abba carried the Swedish banner throughout the world by entertaining millions of rock fans with their English-language songs. Since the late 1940s the choreographer and ensemble director, Birgit Cullberg, has been the towering figure in Swedish ballet. As in theater and dance, the symphony orchestras in Stockholm and in the various regions receive generous and essential state financial assistance.

Artists

Swedish art gained an international reputation, especially through the works of Carl Larsson, who died in 1919, and Anders Zorn, who died one year later. Larsson painted idealized and unproblematic scenes of middle-class daily life. Zorn was a pioneer in new art techniques and also painted many outstanding portraits, including ones of American president William Howard Taft and the steel magnate and philanthropist, Andrew Carnegie. As elsewhere in the Nordic countries, modern, abstract art has been popular in 20th century painting.

One of the eight cultural guidelines established by the *Riksdag* in 1974 was that commercialism was to be resisted in the country's culture. Nevertheless, Swedish art is a realm in which commercial and artistic objectives have blended to create well-designed objects for use in the home. They include furniture, textiles, glass and porcelain which are often in bright, fresh colors and are practical and beautiful. In Sweden, where skies are often gray and where the sun sometimes fails to shine for weeks, such objects in the home can have a particularly refreshing and therapeutic effect on the individual.

Religion

All Swedes are born into the Swedish State (Lutheran) Church, but a person can voluntarily leave it. Only about 10%

The Nutcracker **performed at the Stockholm Opera**

choose to do so, and they are largely non-Protestants and former immigrants. An overwhelming majority of Swedes pay their church taxes, which amount to less than 1% of the average income. Nevertheless, Sweden is a very secular country, and only about 5% of Swedes attend church regularly. The Church faces a shortage of priests and has had difficulty organizing new parishes to keep up with the migration from rural to urban areas. In 1989 the Church shed its legal obligation of recording all vital statistics, passing that function over to the Social Insurance Service. It retained its state financial support, though.

In 1995 the Lutheran Church agreed to a government-sponsored separation of church and state beginning in 2000; all political parties accepted this. The rights of the Church will still be enshrined in the constitution under a law guaranteeing freedom of religious expression. Religion plays little role in politics, although the Church does offer more than mere liturgy. Its preschools are crowded, and its youth movement is Sweden's largest youth organization. It has many summer camps and alternative programs, and it still attracts close to 70% of all teenagers for confirmation, providing it with a nine-month opportunity to influence a young person's thinking.

Religious veins can be tapped to win support for such policies as development aid to the "Third World" or stricter controls on the use of alcohol. The latter movement gained momentum in the second half of the 19th century, when the Swedish nation almost seemed to be destroying itself through alcoholism and emigration. Legislation in the 20th century has always sought to control the use of spirits. Alcohol was rationed until 1955; the prices are still kept very high in order to discourage its consumption. Religious motives play almost no role in the popular campaign to stop smoking. The movement's slogan is "A Non-Smoking Generation;" English is used for the slogan because this language is quite fashionable in Sweden today, where it is learned by all school children. As the American discovers to his pleasure, most Swedes under age 45 usually speak English well.

The Media

Swedes buy more newspapers per capita than any other nation except Japan and Iceland. It has about 100 dailies and 85 weekly newspapers, with a total circulation of 4.5 million. The number of newspapers has declined in recent years, and in most localities there is a only one. Most have a definite political line; about three-fourths support the bourgeois parties, and only about a fifth back the *SAP*. *Ny Dag* is the major communist paper and is published twice weekly. The print media's influence remains great. In 1997 a series in *Dagens Nyheter* broke the embarrassing story about Sweden's eugenics policy from 1934 to 1976.

In the 1970s the *Riksdag* passed a series of laws designed to strengthen the economic base of the press and to ensure that there is a diversity of views. Except for the market leaders, all newspapers receive direct and indirect (tax breaks) subsidies, with the money distributed roughly

Sweden

equally between the socialist and non–socialist press. Such state assistance appears not to make the recipients more docile since subsidized papers are generally as outspoken about government policies as are those which are not. Those newspapers which appear in areas with few inhabitants receive especially significant financial support, and those newspapers which utilize the unified distribution system developed for magazine subscriptions also receive state assistance. There were 46 magazines in 1989, but there is no nation–wide weekly news magazine such as *Time* or *Newsweek*.

Sveriges Radio AB is responsible for radio and television activities, which it coordinates through four independent subsidiaries: one for television, which operates two channels, one for national radio programs, which operates three stations, one for local radio and one for educational radio and television programs. The pan–European satellite channels ended the state monopoly over the broadcast media and have changed public attitudes about Sweden's role in Europe. They add an international perspective to debates and contribute to greater diversity of opinions. The stock in Sveriges Radio AB is owned by private industry, the press and various popular movements. In effect, though, it is state–controlled, since the government appoints the director and half the board of overseers. Also, its budget must be approved by parliament, which grants some subsidies and which determines the amount of the users' fee, which all persons who own radios or television must pay.

FUTURE

In 1994 Swedes decided to join both NATO's Partnership for Peace and the EU. Lotta Forsman of the Foreign Ministry explained that "the collapse of the communist dictatorships in Eastern Europe has changed the military map and consequently the basis for Sweden's neutrality." Swedes have serious second thoughts about EU membership; polls a year after the referendum revealed that roughly two–thirds disapprove. Opposition to the European single currency was so strong that the government ruled Sweden out of participation in the first wave in 1999.

On September 18, 1994, voters indicated their dissatisfaction with Carl Bildt's conservative coalition and returned to power the *Social Democrats*, who argue that a slower, more managed approach to reforming the welfare state is needed. Nevertheless, under a new prime minister, Goran Persson, Swedes had to continue taking the bitter medicine of austerity in order to restore their country's economic stability. The consequence was the worst electoral result in 78 years for the *SAP* in 1998. It remains in power, ruling through a minority coalition, but its reliance on ex–Communists and *Greens* makes bold policy initiatives impossible.

Social Democrats found their and their country's moral reputation badly tarnished by shocking revelations of a eugenically–inspired sterilization policy lasting during decades of *SAP* rule. Some 60,000 Swedish women were forcibly sterilized for reasons as trivial as "unmistakable gypsy features." Social Affairs Minister Margot Wallstrom called it "barbaric." Arne Ruth, editor–in–chief of *Dagens Nyheter*, which broke the story, wrote: "The perception both at home and internationally is that Sweden is a clean, well–lit place with no dark spots. But this was barbarism on an incredible scale. It was not just a barbaric measure against social outcasts but against women, who made up 90% of those sterilized." The fact that all four Nordic countries had similar selective breeding programs does not diminish the shame.

There is much that is going well for Sweden. Annual growth at 2% is respectable. Inflation has practically disappeared and unemployment at 5.3% and the budget deficit at 1.9% of GDP are falling. It remains a remarkably comfortable, steady, decent, peaceful and egalitarian land.

A fish market, Stockholm

Courtesy: Hon. and Mrs. Schuyler Lowe

The Kingdom of Norway

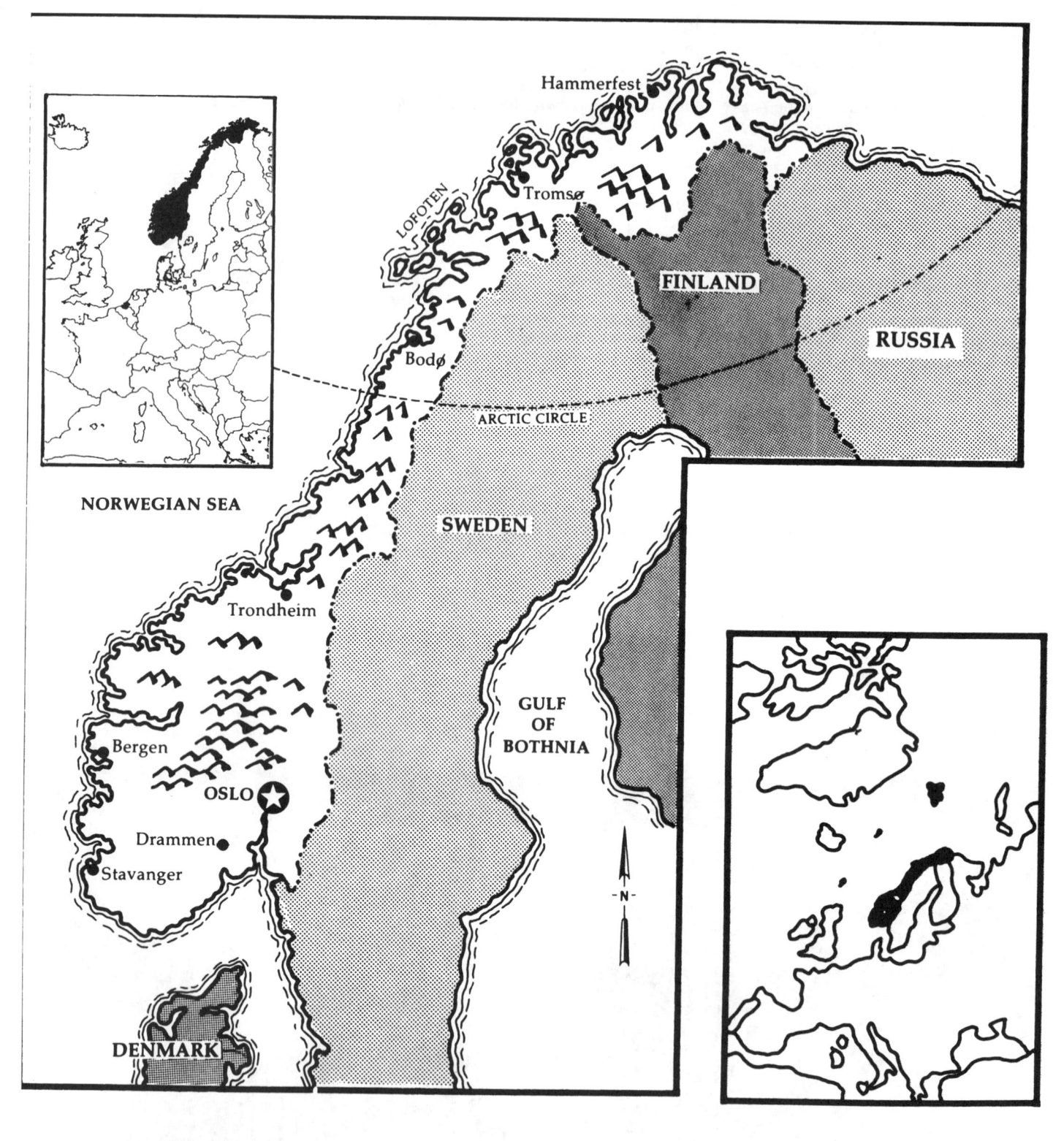

Area: 125,182 sq. mi. (324,219 sq. km., not including Svalbard and Jan Mayen; slightly larger than New Mexico).
Population: 4.3 million (estimated).
Capital City: Oslo (Pop. 500,000, estimated).
Climate: From late spring to August the nights are very short, with hardly any night in June and July, and the sun shines constantly during the summer above the Arctic Circle. The flow of the Gulf Stream keeps the climate temperate along the coast. Bitterly cold winters in the north and higher altitudes.
Neighboring Countries: Sweden (East); Finland and Russia (Northeast); Denmark (South, across the Skagerak), Scotland (Southeast, across the North Sea.

Official Language: Norwegian.
Other Principal Tongues: Other Nordic tongues, English.
Ethnic Background: Germanic, Scandinavian.
Principal Religion: Lutheran (State Church).
Main Exports: Crude oil, natural gas, metals, pulp and paper, ships, machinery,

Norway

fish and fish products, chemicals. Two–thirds of its exports go to EU countries.
Main Imports: Foodstuffs, fuels, motor vehicles, iron and steel, textiles, chemicals, processed and unprocessed.
Currency: Krone.
National Day: May 17, Constitution Day.
Chief of State: His Majesty King Harald V, b. 1937.
Heir Apparent: His Royal Highness Crown Prince Haakon Magnus (b. 1973).
Head of Government: Kjell Mange Bondvik, Prime Minister (since 1997), leader of the *Labor Party.*
National Flag: A red field crossed horizontally and vertically by blue stripes (cross), bordered by thin white stripes.

In many people's minds, Norway is a sparsely populated nation somewhere in the frozen North, with a tortured landscape filled with many majestic, snow–capped mountains, glaciers, isolated valleys, and a long coastline which is dotted by small, quaint fishing villages and countless beautiful fjords. This image is certainly true, as far as it goes. This is a long, narrow country, with a 2,125 mile (3,200 km.) coastline washed by the Arctic and Atlantic Oceans as well as the North Sea. It is the fifth largest country in Europe and occupies 40% of the Scandinavian Peninsula. Half of Norway is located north of the Arctic Circle, and even the capital city of Oslo in the south is on the same latitude as southern Alaska. This means that many Norwegians are able to experience the midnight sun in the summer, but they must go without much daylight in the winter. In the very north, it shares a 118 mile (196 km.) border with Russia and a 430 mile (716 km.) border with Finland. Flanked most of the distance by the Kjølen mountain range is a long, 972 mile (1,619 km.) common border with Sweden, a now friendly country to which Norway belonged until 1905.

Almost two–thirds of Norway is covered by mountains, although they do not give the country an Alpine character. Most of them are barren—without forests—in fact, only a fourth of the entire country lies *below* the timber line. One mountain range, the Dovre, divides the country into a northern and southern part, whereas the Langfjell chain separates the eastern from the western part of the country. The Kj\olen chain marks the country's eastern border. In the highlands are countless cold, clear lakes and ponds, including the Hornindalsvatn, the largest inland body of water in all of Europe. The rivers which originate in these mountains either flow gently in an easterly direction or precipitously into the sea. Its rivers provide Norway with a seeming endless source of hydroelectric power, which was the basis for the country's industrialization.

Edge of fjord valley near Voss Courtesy: Jon Markham Morrow

Over a fifth of Norway is covered by forests, which supply wood, one of its most important raw materials, and 7% of its area is composed of 50,000 islands, only about 2,000 of which are inhabited. Lakes and rivers cover 5% of the territory and only about 3% of the land is arable farmland, the lowest percentage in all of Europe. Despite its extreme northern latitude and the fact that 1.4% of its surface is covered by 1,700 glaciers, Norway is not a gigantic deep freeze. This is due to the North Atlantic Current, which is warmed by the Gulf Stream from the Caribbean and which makes Norwegian winters mild, especially along the coast.

Norway has the lowest population density in all of Europe (except Iceland). It has 13 inhabitants per square kilometer, compared with 372 in the Netherlands, 225 in Britain and 90 in France. Its population is also very unevenly divided, with about half concentrated in the southeastern corner around Oslo and its fjord, with very few inhabitants in the northern part of the

Norway

country. Four out of five live within 10 miles of the sea. Almost three-fourths of the country is uninhabitable. There are many small villages, and a third of the population lives on the land or in towns with fewer than 2,000 inhabitants. Norway has no large cities and only three have a population of over 100,000. Oslo, in which the government and much of the industry and cultural life is concentrated, has about a half million residents; Bergen has about 215,000 and Trondheim about 135,000. A fourth city, Stavanger, with close to 90,000 people, has recently gained additional prominence since the headquarters for the state-owned oil company, Statoil, is located there and because it is the center for the petroleum extraction activities in the Norwegian sector of the North Sea.

The danger that many Norwegians living in the large tracts of sparsely inhabited areas might move into the larger cities has long been recognized by the country's leaders. For this reason, an important element of the government's agricultural and industrial policy is to provide incentives for the people to remain in the less densely populated sections of the country. There is no possibility that these areas could be settled by an increasing Norwegian population, since the growth rate is declining drastically; estimates are that there will be one million fewer Norwegians by the year 2050.

Norway is an almost completely ethnically homogeneous country. There is a small number of foreign workers who came to Norway before the mid-1970s and who have either received Norwegian citizenship or are remaining with permanent residence permits. Except for those coming from other Nordic countries, no additional foreign workers are allowed to work in Norway. In the northern part of the country are two ethnic minorities. The largest are the 45,000 *Sami* (formerly called Lapps) whose language and culture are completely different from those of the Norwegians. About two thirds of all Sami live in Norway and the remaining third live in northern Sweden and Finland. Only about 3,000 of the Norwegian Sami are now reindeer breeders, who lead a nomadic existence and who cling most tenaciously to the traditional Sami culture. The majority of Sami now lead a settled existence. The second minority is composed of about 7,000 descendants of a Baltic people who also entered Norway earlier via Finland. They are called *kvener* and have retained many of their original physical and cultural characteristics.

Norwegians call their country *Norge*, a word derived from the earlier name *Nordvegr*, "the Northern Way." The country is indeed on the northern extremity of Europe and appears on the map to be geographically isolated. But in the 19th and 20th centuries it has been attuned to the developments in the rest of Europe. As a nation facing westward and southward across three seas, it has developed a merchant marine which not only helps it maintain its links with the rest of the world, but also helps other countries maintain links with each other. It does have weather-beaten fishermen, strapping lumberjacks and ruddy-faced farmers, but these groups account for fewer than a tenth of the population. Most Norwegians now work in the manufacturing, service or government sectors of the economy, and by the early 1970s Norwegians had become a very prosperous people. It is now a major producer of oil and gas, which began to be exported in the 1970s. The country is in the enviable position of being a net exporter of energy, while most other Western European countries are energy-starved. Thus, Norway is by no means a backward country lost in the modern world, but is very much a dynamic and prosperous part of the world.

POLITICAL SYSTEM

Norway is a country in which there is a deep consensus supporting the democratic process and institutions. The individual's personal and civil rights are widely respected, and Norwegians are basically inclined to be very tolerant toward other viewpoints and manners of living. They enter into sharp debates with each other over political, economic and social questions, but these debates are always kept within a framework in which recognized rules of the game are respected and observed. The result is a high degree of political stability.

The Monarchy

This is a constitutional monarchy with a parliamentary form of government; there is no aristocracy. Harald V was sworn in as king in 1991, coronations having been abolished in 1908. In 1937 he was the first Norwegian monarch to be born on native soil in 566 years. After the royal family fled occupied Norway, Harald lived with his mother and sister in the U.S., where he attended two years of elementary school. After liberation in 1945 he continued his schooling in Norway, and he pursued a military career; in 1977 he was promoted to general of the Army and Air Force and admiral of the Navy. His wife, Sonja, was the daughter of a Norwegian textile merchant and is the country's first queen since 1938. Harald's older sister could not succeed to the throne because of a law, now repealed, which favored male succession. Since the new law of succession applies only to those born after 1990 (the year of the act), the current crown prince, Prince Haakon (born before 1990) is the heir apparent, not his older sister, Princess Martha Louise.

The monarch performs mainly ceremonial functions, even though the constitution formally grants him considerable executive powers. Even decisions of the State Council (*Statsråd*), or cabinet are denominated decisions of the "King-in-Council," although the king is seldom involved in their deliberations. Thus, the government merely acts in his name.

The king can play a role in facilitating the formation of a government when no party or coalition of parties receives a clear mandate in parliamentary elections. In times of extreme crisis, as was the case during World War II, the parliament can allow the king temporarily to perform the governmental and military functions which are formally granted to him in the constitution, but no Norwegian king would dare attempt to do so under normal circumstances. The crisis during World War II also demonstrated the major function the monarch can perform: he serves as an important symbol of the nation's unity and this can be extremely important, especially to a nation which did not become entirely independent until 1905. The king is the head of the State (Lutheran) Church, and at least half of the cabinet members must also belong to that church.

The king cannot be accused in a court of law for any misdeed. Since he is not permitted to make decisions in normal times, he is protected from making political mistakes. This protection, along with the personal qualities of those who have reigned since independence have made the monarchy a popular institution. There is almost no one in Norway who advocates the abolition of the monarchy.

The Parliament

Real political power lies in the Norwegian people, represented by the 157 members of the parliament, called the *Storting*. A third of its members are now women. Elections are held every four years, and all citizens 18 years of age or older are eligible to vote. The electoral system is a complicated form of proportional representation, which enables many political parties to function. This makes the creation of a workable coalition in the *Storting* difficult, despite a method of distributing seats which favors large and medium-sized parties. A newly elected *Storting* is obligated to serve the full four years, since the constitution forbids early elections. Even by-elections are very rare, since vacated seats are filled by replacements who are elected at the same time as the deputies.

Norway

Thus, substitutes are almost always available at all times. The inability to call early elections forces the various party leaders to negotiate very seriously with each other in order to produce a government whose programs can win majorities in the *Storting*. No party has won an absolute majority since 1961, nor for a decade until 1983 was there even a governing coalition which had a majority. Therefore, the Norwegian talent for moderation and compromise, along with the basic political consensus in the country, have been essential for the maintenance of political stability. Most other countries would have failed the test and fallen into political chaos.

Deputies are elected from 19 counties (*Fylker*) in such a way that 38 representatives are elected from the northern counties, 49 from western and southern Norway and 68 from eastern Norway (of which 15 are from Oslo). In order to try to prevent any domination by the large cities, the rural areas are represented by a slightly greater proportion of deputies than the urban areas.

Voters elect only one parliament, the *Storting*, but after each election, it is divided into two parts. One fourth of the members are assigned to the *Lagting*, or second chamber, and the rest constitute the *Odelsting*, or lower house. These two houses deliberate separately only when the *Storting* must deal with questions touching on the constitution, such as the rights and duties of citizens. However, most matters, including constitutional amendments, are discussed in joint plenary sessions. Once a piece of legislation is approved by a majority in the *Storting*, it automatically becomes law.

The *Storting* also has standing committees which correspond to the various government ministries and which perform most of the detailed work of the parliament. Unlike in the U.S., seniority plays very little role in the assignment of seats and chairmanships in the committees; party membership and special skills are the decisive factors. The *Storting* also has the responsibility of appointing a special committee which selects and awards the prestigious Nobel Peace Prize. When Norwegian economist Trygve Haavelmo was named the 1989 laureate in economics, he had to travel to Stockholm to receive the award and prize.

Storting deputies can be elected only if they represent parties; no independents can be elected, although one may leave his party after the election and retain his seat until the next election. As a rule, deputies vote with their parties, but they do have the right to vote against their parties. On some moral issues, such as abortion, the parties announce that deputies will be permitted to vote according to their consciences, although the party's position on such an issue would be well–known. In order to encourage them to be conscious that they are supposed primarily to represent their constituents, not their parties, deputies are seated according to the alphabetical order of their counties, not according to their party affiliation, as is the custom in most Western European parliaments.

The Norwegian government is headed by a prime minister and a cabinet of at least seven ministers, the foreign minister being the highest in the hierarchy after the prime minister. The government meets in cabinet meetings at least once a week (usually on Fridays), although the various members meet informally several times during the week.

The Judiciary

Norway has an independent judiciary, with courts at four levels. From the lowest to the highest, they are the Conciliation Councils (*Forliksrådene*), the local courts (*Herredsrettene og byrettene*), the courts of civil and criminal appeals (*Lagmannsretten*), and the Supreme Court of Justice (*Høiesterett*), composed of a Chief Justice and 17 justices, of which only five sit for any one case. The framers of the 1814 constitution adopted the American innovation by granting the Supreme Court and the inferior courts the authority to declare as null and void any law which they deem to be incompatible with the constitution. However, the Norwegian courts have exercised this right of judicial review very infrequently, preferring to leave it to the government and the *Storting* to make certain that the constitution is observed.

Constitutional Amendment and Referendums

The *Storting* also has the power to amend the constitution; all proposed amendments must be presented to the parliament, but in order to prevent the basic law from being changed too quickly or by a simple majority which might be available at any moment, any amendment must be approved by a two–thirds majority in a *newly–elected Storting*.

There is no constitutional provision for a referendum. However, in a few instances, the *Storting* has declared that non–binding referendums could be held in order to give the people the opportunity to express an opinion about an important issue.

For instance, in 1972 a national referendum was held on the question of whether Norway should enter the EU. In this vote, 53% said "no," and the government chose to honor this result and not to enter the EU. This rejection was due more than anything else to a general reaction by the periphery (rural) people against a move which, it was feared, could seriously affect the unique and traditional life and culture of the nation (see Culture). The EU was widely seen as a potential danger to Norwegian society. In 1992 the *Storting* voted both to accept EEA and, for the fourth time, to seek entry into the EU. But in a November 1994 referendum, 52% of

Deceased King Olav V in his sailboat. He competed in the Olympics

Norway

The late King Olav V opening the Norwegian Parliament, the *Storting*

the voters, citing many of the same arguments as in 1972, again voted EU membership down.

Citizens' rights are also guarded by the institution of the ombudsman, as in other Scandinavian countries. There is an ombudsman for Consumer Affairs who ensures fair advertising and marketing practices, a Civil ombudsman who sees to it that the administration does not treat any citizen unjustly, and an ombudsman for the Armed Services who deals with grievances of military personnel. All are appointed by the *Storting*.

Regional and Local Government

It is not surprising that a country which is so spread out and cut up by mountains, fjords, lakes, rivers and other natural barriers which make transportation within the country so difficult, would have a lively tradition of local and regional government. There are about 50 municipalities *(bykommuner)* and about 400 rural communities *(landkommuner)*, with their own councils elected every four years midway between the national elections. Non–Norwegians who have resided in the country for at least three years can vote in these local elections. The councils appoint a local government and a mayor, their authority extending to schools, churches, health care, social welfare, zoning and local construction, fire fighting, traffic and a host of other matters.

Between the national and local governments are 19 counties *(fylker)*, each of which is headed by a governor appointed by the central government. The counties deal with tasks for which the national and local governments share responsibilities, such as hospital construction, public instruction, health care and electricity supply. Each county has its own parliament, which is elected at the same time local elections are held. Although much political responsibility is assumed at the local and regional level, it should not be overlooked that the nation's major political priorities are established by the central government in Oslo.

Overseas Territories

The government in Oslo rules over territories flung far around the world. It has a large tract of land called Queen Maud Land on the continent of Antarctica, which could one day have great economic significance. It also has two uninhabited islands near Antarctica: Peter I Island and Bouvet. Situated between Greenland and Iceland is Jan Mayan Island, which covers 380 square kilometers, on which the Beeren Mountain surges 7,400 feet (2277 meters) into the air. First discovered by the Dutch, Jan Mayen became Norwegian in 1930 and now serves as a meteorological station and as a post in the NATO early–warning system.

Closer to home is the Svalbard archipelago, lying halfway between the North Pole and the tip of the Scandinavian peninsula. It is about 575 miles (959 km.) by air from the northern Norwegian city of Tromsø, from which regular civilian air service commenced in 1975. The largest and only inhabited island is Spitsbergen. This rugged area, with mountains rising to 5,585 feet (1,717 meters) and dangerous cliffs overlooking a landscape covered with glaciers and ice, exists in total darkness 112 day per year and in total daylight 127 days. Nearly two–thirds of Svalbard is covered by ice and provides an ideal habitat for polar bears.

These islands were first mentioned in Icelandic journals in the year 1194, and for centuries they were a meeting point for whaling crews from all over the world. At the beginning of the 20th century they became economically significant because of their sizable coal deposits, which continue to be exploited today. Until 1920 the archipelago was a "no man's land," in international law, but in that year a complicated treaty was worked out.

This conferred on Norway sovereignty over the islands in 1925, while at the same time giving all nationals of the contracting parties the right to carry out maritime, industrial, mining and commercial operations on the basis of absolute equality. It also explicitly prohibited the establishment of naval bases or fortifications on the islands, which could never be used "for warlike purposes." Norway was granted responsibility of ensuring adherence to this treaty. At present, the only other country which shows any appreciable interest in Svalbard is Russia, which did not sign the 1920 treaty. The instrument granted the Russians predominance over four of the 40 islands, covering about 6% of the total land area.

Only one Norwegian and one Russian company maintained permanent mining operations on the islands, even though both Norway and Russia lose money on them. In the mid–1990s Russia extracts about 500,000 tons of coal a year, while Norway gets about 400,000. Almost certainly, the real reason for both countries' presence there is strategic. Each is scared of allowing the other to gain exclusive use of the harbors, which are so close to the sea lanes between Russia's northern ports and the Atlantic. No wonder that the British used to call Spitsbergen an "Arctic Gibraltar."

Russia has a larger settlement in Svalbard than does Norway; out of a total population of 3,100, two–thirds are foreigners, mainly Russian. Contact between the two nationalities is increasing somewhat, but it is still the Norwegians who take the initiative. Spitsbergen remains the only place on this globe where a person can walk into a Russian settlement unannounced and without a visa.

The Russians have always had difficulty accepting the idea of Norwegian sovereignty over the islands and have frequently challenged the scope of its authority. They have advanced the view that Norwegian regulations are subject to prior Russian agreement, a view which is wholly unacceptable to the Norwegians, who have established a hearing procedure for Russian citizens on Svalbard to air their grievances, and, on the whole, the two nationalities on the islands get along rather well. But Oslo retains the right to make final decisions. Russia also takes exception to Norway's position that the 1920 treaty deals only with the islands themselves and not to the waters around them. Thus, Norway has established a 200–mile fishing zone which gives it primary rights. It also has raised the claim that the Norwegian continental shelf includes Svalbard and that Norway therefore has the final authority over mining and drilling in those waters.

Norway does not dare begin any drilling operations in these waters until some kind of mutually acceptable agreement can be reached with Russia, which also continues to refuse to accept the Norwegian position on how the Barents Sea should be divided between the two countries. Norway favors the "median line principle" whereby a jagged line would run through the Barents Sea everywhere equidistant from the territory of the two countries. The Russians, on the other hand, insist upon a straight line running due north to the North Pole, with certain adjustments being made around Svalbard.

Such a boundary would run far west of the median line and would add 155,000 square kilometers of oil–rich ocean floor to the Russian sector, an area equivalent to that covered by the Norwegian continental shelf in the North Sea.

The fact that the geological indications for oil in the area are quite positive makes the Russians somewhat impatient for a settlement. At the same time, Norway's ailing fishing industry, as well as its need for future oil extraction, makes Norwegians unwilling to sacrifice such a large area. It is determined to keep the level of tensions with Russia low until some kind of arrangement can be worked out for these maritime boundary disputes, which extend much farther than the relatively short 118–mile land border with its powerful eastern neighbor. However, the economic plans of Russia, which unlike Norway has *not* pledged to forego all oil drilling in the disputed area, may force a settlement far more quickly than the Norwegians would like. Russia has already announced that it will begin prospecting in the Barents Sea, but drilling will probably begin off the island of Novaya Zemlya, well outside the disputed area. Norway has supplied some of the equipment for the Russian oil rigs and has discussed with Russian officials the possibility of joint offshore projects in the Barents Sea outside the disputed waters.

Norway

POLITICS AND POLITICAL PARTIES

There are two ways of looking at Norway's party system. One is to see it as a multi–party system, perpetuated by an electoral system of proportional representation which always favors the proliferation of parties. Such division was further stimulated by the bitter debate over entry into the EU. This emotional conflict hammered Norway at many of its social fault lines. It cracked some of the country's traditional parties wide open and created the conditions for some entirely new ones to spring up. By the 1973 elections, 13 parties were prepared to throw their hats into the electoral ring. In the meantime, most of those which shot up as protest parties in the early 1970s have shriveled or died, and the number which would win seats in parliament had settled back to eight by 1997.

Another way of looking at the country's party system is that it is made up of two clusters of parties, one socialist, or at least social democratic, and the other non–socialist. The votes of each cluster remain more or less equal from one election to the next, although there are noticeable, often dramatic shifts among the various parties within each cluster. However, these shifts are not such that a two–party system would be likely to develop. This existence of two rather firm blocks lends a certain

Their Majesties King Harald V and Queen Sonja

Norway

stability to the political system. Nevertheless, competition for votes within each cluster sometimes makes parties less willing to cooperate with each other than one might expect. Each must always think about the next election.

The Non–Socialist Parties

Norway's third–largest non–socialist party emerging from the 1997 elections is the *Conservative Party (Høyre* or merely *H)*. *Høyre* strongly supported Norway's entry into the EU and experienced dizzying growth during the 1970s, climbing to 50 seats in 1985. Since then it has steadily lost ground, winning only 14.3% of the votes and 23 seats (down from 28) in 1997. It tends to draw the votes of the better–educated and the better–paid, and since these groups grew in prosperous Norway, *Høyre* grew also.

Høyre does not encompass the entire conservative spectrum. Its voters tend to be concentrated in the industrial, urban centers of the southeast, and it does not appeal to the populist, pro–prohibition *Nynorsk*, or religious movements, which are so strong in the periphery (see Culture). It is a modern, urban movement, which defines itself as a "conservative party of progress." It demands protection of individual rights and of private property. It is strongly oriented toward NATO, the U.S, and Europe.

In contrast to the other Norwegian parties, *Høyre* is not ridden with internal divisions, and ideological debates within the party are almost unknown. Like the *Labor Party*, *Høyre* is highly secular, and supports economic growth and a high level of oil and gas extraction. It has basic differences with the other major conservative parties on a range of thorny subjects which include alcohol policy, abortion, environmental protection and oil policy. Its leader since 1994 is Jan Petersen. The pro–European *Conservatives* are wary of their former non–socialist partners after a serious spat over European policy caused their coalition government to collapse in 1990.

The *Christian People's Party (KrF)*, surged to win 13.7% of the votes and 25 seats in 1997 (up from 13 seats). As its name indicates, it seeks to place Christian concerns in the political spotlight. It led a furious battle against Norway's abortion law, which permits abortion on demand. It also appeals to many supporters of strong, anti–alcoholic legislation. Another policy which it thinks is in harmony with the biblical spirit is a rise in Norway's development aid, which is 0.88% of GDP. Even though Norwegians are overwhelmingly Lutheran, the *KrF's* strong whiff of pietism and serious commitment to the values of the Bible has hampered it from attracting a considerably larger following in this largely secular country.

The hard core of *KrF's* votes mainly live in the south and the west and are distrustful of the secular, cosmopolitan *Høyre*. The *KrF* is strong in the periphery and attracts about two thirds of those who support the movement to elevate the social status of *Nynorsk*. The party's leader, Kjell Magne Bondevik, is a Lutheran pastor with much parliamentary and cabinet experience. He became prime minister after the 1997 elections, forging a ruling minority coalition with the *Center* and *Liberal* parties. Since he does not get along well with these parties, his government is fragile and divided. Virtually all members of his cabinet are from the west coast and represent fishermen, farmers, and strict Lutherans, who tend to be suspicious of city dwellers and the EU. His government stresses human rights, family values, higher welfare spending, and Norway's religious and cultural heritage.

Many politicians talk about values, but the Norwegian government put its money where its mouth is. It created a "Values Commission" of social workers, religious leaders and academics to travel throughout the country asking people what they believe in. Noting that divorce ends half of marriages and is four times commoner than three decades ago, that a fourth of women aged 20 to 44 live with men to whom they are not married, and that 48% of children are born out of wedlock, the government pays a mother 80% of her salary for 12 months to stay home with her baby. When the year is up, she may return to her job with at least the same pay as before. It also unveiled an male equal rights program that allows for preferential treatment to men in industries like child care, preschool and primary school teaching, and child welfare in order to provide male role models. Citing the need to strengthen the family, the government pushed through a law stopping larger shops from opening on Sunday.

It adopted in 1999 a $57.7 million package to compensate Jewish families for some of the property that was plundered by the Nazis and to finance projects for the Jewish community. Finally, a year after taking office Bondevik himself publicly admitted to suffering from depression and took three and a half weeks of sick leave. Far from being pommeled for neglecting his duties, he was supported by 85% of Norwegians who thought he had done the right thing by telling the public what was bothering him. His approval ratings soared to historic highs.

The *Center Party (Sp)*, has fallen on bad times, dropping in 1997 to 11 seats (from 32) and only 8% of the votes. Earlier called the *Farmers Party*, it did not change its name and move from an overtly anti–industrial position until 1959. Nevertheless, it is still wary of industrial growth, and, like the *KrF* it is a party of the periphery.

Like some elements within the *KrF*, the *Center* adamantly opposed Norway's entry into the EU out of fear of the damage which membership might do to traditional Norwegian society. In 1994 party leader Anne Enger Lahnstein successfully led the attack against entry, arguing that Norway had to remain out of the control of the Brussels bureaucracy. Like the *KrF*, it calls for a reduction in oil production and it is hard–lined in its support of environmental protection. This issue also creates a kind of wedge between the conservative heart of the party and the younger members. The young wing is even more radical on environmental issues and is especially wary of any form of collaboration with the *Conservative Party*.

Seldom in contention as a member of the government is the *Progress Party* which made spectacular showings in 1981, 1985, and again in 1989 for a party which almost everybody thought was dead. In 1997 it leaped to 25 seats (up from 10) and 15% of the votes. It is the last remaining protest party which arose in the early 1970s, and it opposes the heavy tax burden and the growth of state control over the economy. Its early growth, especially in the Oslo area, reflected many Norwegians' opposition to the extremely high tax level in Norway, which siphons off close to half the income which the average person earns. Led by Carl Hagen, a charming man who projects effectively on television and who defies the Nordic tradition of consensus, the party offers sim-

**Prime Minister
Kjell Magne Bondevik**

Norway

ple remedies for every problem. His party's objections to immigrants make him an especially unacceptable coalition partner. Nevertheless, he continues to rise in prominence.

The final non–socialist party is the *Liberal Venstre Party (V)*, often called "the Liberals." This is one of Norway's oldest parties, but it was never tightly organized, and split in 1973 over the EU issue. In fact, it was the chief victim of the EU battle, and it never recovered. Only that part of the party which opposed entry remained in parliament, and the entire debate drove the party to the left. It now defines itself as a "radical social–liberal party," and it presents itself as committed to environmental protection and more careful exploitation and utilization of Norway's natural resources. In the 1997 elections it garnered six seats in parliament, up from only one, and it entered the governing coalition. A *Coastal Party* captured one seat.

The Socialist Parties

The largest party in Norway is the *Labor Party (A)* which captured 65 seats in 1997. From the 1930s the *Labor Party* dominated Norway and has been the only party since then ever to win a parliamentary majority. Beginning as a democratic reform party, it took a temporary radical turn in the 1920s, but then moderated its course again and now defines itself as a "socialist reform party." The pragmatic character of this group is such that one could hardly call it a true socialist party, even though its party program calls for the creation of a socialist society and the nationalization of large parts of the economy as long–range goals. In fact, its immediate goals are full employment and expansion of the social security net.

After World War II the party broadened its base to include employees, small farmers, fishermen and foresters, in addition to its traditional working class base, which remains the backbone of the party. Geographically, the party is strongest in the North and in the Oslo area. In contrast to most social democratic parties in Western Europe, the *Labor Party* has never been wholly dominated by academically trained persons.

As in the cases of Sweden and Denmark, it sees itself as the political arm of the trade union movement, and it is formally linked to the Trade Union Confederation *(LO)* through interlocking leadership, collective membership and organizational ties. The *LO* traditionally has two seats in the party's presidium, and two party representatives sit in the *LO* directorate. Also by tradition, the *LO* leader is given a *Labor* seat in the *Storting*, and the trade union apparatus is used at election time to support the party.

The *Labor Party* has been plagued by internal division. The youth wing of the party tends always to oppose the more pragmatic economic orientation of the middle–age and older members. But the worst division arises from foreign policy disputes. There is an element in the party which never fully digested Norway's NATO role, and during the Vietnam War the *Labor Party* broke NATO ranks, and, like Sweden, recognized North Vietnam, thereby creating a minor crisis in U.S.–Norwegian relations. The left wing opposed entry into the EU in 1972, although the party officially supported membership. This split spelled disaster for the party in the 1973 elections, and only gradually could it regain its strength after that vigorous struggle. The party's left wing publicly opposed the then–*Labor* government's decision in 1980 to permit the stockpiling of U.S. military equipment in Norway. This issue sparked torchlight parades, mass rallies and petitions. The press published front page pictures of mushroom–shaped clouds and maps showing how close Soviet troops and missiles were to the country.

Judging from this emotional outburst, it almost appeared that the country was on the brink of war. This debate left many scars within the party, and it also led the *Conservative Party* to break out from its long–standing common front with *Labor* on foreign and defense policy and to accuse the former *Labor* government of mismanagement in foreign affairs. As a concession to the left wing of the party and as an attempt to create unity on defense questions, the leadership called for a nuclear–free zone in the Nordic area.

The party withdrew its support for NATO plans to deploy new U.S. INF missiles in Europe in 1983. Tempers against the U.S. bombing of Libya in 1986 also ran high within the ruling *Labor Party*. As a sign of protest, Norway banned American F–111 fighter–bombers from entering Norwegian airspace during NATO exercises. Nevertheless, polls indicate that support of NATO membership remains strong in Norway. During the 1991 Persian Gulf crisis it sent a coast guard vessel and a supply and support ship to the Gulf, and a minesweeper to the Mediterranean, as well as financial assistance to countries affected by the crisis. In 1993 it dispatched 220 peacekeeping troops to Macedonia as part of a UN tripwire to prevent the conflict in Bosnia from spreading. It also sent humanitarian aid to Bosnia. Deputy Foreign Minister Jan Egeland noted: "Norway has two feet—one Atlantic foot and one European foot. This makes us feel very strongly that we need NATO for the Atlantic leg." It was the firm tie with NATO that convinced many Norwegians in 1994 that they did not need the EU for security.

In 1996 Dr. Gro Brundtland, who had been Scandinavia's first female prime minister, resigned and in 1998 was named director general of the World Health Organization (WHO) in Geneva. Her successor as prime minister and party leader was Thorbjørn Jagland. From a working class family, he is self–educated and never received any formal degrees. He has worked in politics all his life. He is credited with having modernized the party and having held it together during the acrimonious EU debate. In the 1997 elections he tied his hands by promising to resign if *Labor* did not receive at least the same percentage of the vote as in 1993. It fell from 36.9% to 35% and from 67 to 65 seats. It is in the opposition.

A unique aspect of the third Brundtland cabinet formed in 1990 was that nine of its 19 members were women. The *Labor Party* requires that 40% of its candidates for public office be women, and 40% of the *Storting's* members since 1993 are women, as are several leaders of major parties. Thus, Norway has a higher percentage of women in top governing positions than any other nation in the world. This does not carry over to the corporate world, though; no women are at the head of any of the country's large companies.

The *Socialist Left Party (SV)* won 9 seats in 1997, down from 13. This party emerged from the political battle against EU entry and was at first an electoral alliance of several socialist groupings, including elements from the *Labor Party*. It preserves an old tradition within the *Labor Party,* especially strong in the 1920s, of radical socialism (albeit within a democratic framework). Its program calls for a radical change of Norwegian society and places much emphasis on problems related to the environment, natural resources and the "Third World." Until 1992 it opposed *Labor's* backing of NATO. Unlike the *Labor Party*, its leaders are almost all from the intelligentsia. In the past it has been willing to support *Labor* minority governments in the *Storting*.

Communists receive very few votes in Norway and are politically insignificant. The Beijing–oriented *Red Electoral Alliance* had garnered only one seat in 1993, but it lost it in 1997. The *Norwegian Communist Party* remains unrepresented in the parliament.

ECONOMY

Norway's geography has always greatly influenced the economic activity of its people. Its long coastline has made the country reliant on fish and now, offshore oil. Facing westward, Norway has directed its trading activity toward other lands

Norway

with access to the North Atlantic. Its mountains have enabled Norwegians to produce more hydroelectric power per capita than any other country and twice as much as the United States or Canada. This cheap, available electricity was the basis for Norway's industrialization, which gradually changed it from a country so poor at the turn of the century that 20,000 of its people chose to emigrate to the U.S. each year into a nation with one of the highest standards of living in the world. The economic growth has been especially dramatic since World War II, a conflict which destroyed 20% of the national wealth, half its merchant tonnage, 40% of its fishing fleet and a third of its industry.

The extremely small size of the Norwegian domestic market of little more than four million inhabitants has forced Norway to export many goods and services abroad in order to maintain its high standard of living and social welfare system. It must also import many raw materials to keep its industries operating, as well as many consumer goods to satisfy the rising demands of its prosperous people. Its major trading partners are Sweden and the U.K., Germany and Denmark. Over three-fourths of its exports now go to the EU countries, compared with 47% in 1974, while more than half of its imports presently come from EU nations. Its exports and imports represent more than 40% of its GDP, a much higher figure than in almost any other industrialized country. This heavy dependence upon trade makes Norway particularly vulnerable to international economic fluctuations, though. Presently, about 40% of the labor force works in manufacturing and related activities, about 30% in the service industry and less than 10% earns a living from the primary sector, which includes agriculture, fishing and lumbering.

Hydroelectricity, Oil and Gas

No other industrialized country has such an abundant supply of domestic energy for its inhabitants as does Norway. Its water power is almost endlessly renewable, and it has developed only about half of its potential for hydroelectricity. It produces coal in Svalbard. Its energy abundance saves it from that painful decision facing most other Western European countries: nuclear power. It neither has nuclear power plants nor plans to construct any. With its long coastline, it will perhaps be possible for it someday to generate power from waves. Its long coastline overlooks other riches of enormous immediate value right now: oil and gas, which in 1995 accounted for a third of Norway's exports.

As a result of an international agreement reached at the 1958 UN Law of the Sea Conference in Geneva, Norway received possession of a sector in the North Sea three times the size of its mainland. The offshore oil and gas resources in the North Sea are expected to be commercial until well into the 21st century. Producing more than 3 million barrels per day in 1997, of which it exports 2.8 million barrels, it became the world's second largest petroleum exporter after Saudi Arabia.

Norway's continental shelf contains more than half of Western Europe's gas resources. A new gas platform named TROLL came on line in 1996, which doubles Norway's gas output and enables it to provide a third of Germany's and France's gas needs. The state owns 75% of the TROLL rig. By the turn of the century Norway's enormous offshore gas reserves accounted for 15% of combined oil-and-gas income. Norway exports all its gas to the EU through underwater pipelines directly from the North Sea fields to a terminal at Emden, Germany. Its oil is delivered by underwater pipeline to Teeside, Scotland. Because of a deep underwater valley just off the Norwegian coast and the resulting precipitous rise of that coast, it is difficult to construct pipelines to the mainland. About 70% of its oil finds its way to Western Europe, and most of the rest goes to the U.S.

Norway must cover about 85% of its own oil requirements through imports, but its oil needs remain relatively small, comprising only about 41% of its total energy consumption; about 2% is provided by coal, while a whopping 57% is provided by hydroelectricity. With its electricity prices half those of oil, it is no wonder that Norway can afford to consume more electricity per capita than any other country in the world. For example, the average Norwegian heats his home with it and uses twice as much electrical power as the average American. It is also able to sell electricity to Sweden and Denmark.

Norway supplies about 10% of the EU's requirements of oil and about 14% of Western European gas requirements. Norwegian governments restrict maximum extraction to 90 million tons of oil and gas annually (extraction is far below that figure). Norway wants to preserve its reserves as long as possible and fears that too rapid exploitation could seriously disrupt Norwegian society and its economy.

Catching a 60 lb. salmon near Bergen

Norway

It informally cooperated with OPEC by lowering production in order to stabilize and ultimately raise prices.

Drilling began in 1966, and in 1971 production started on the Ekofisk field in the southwest corner of the Norwegian sector. By the end of the decade, more fields had begun production, but in line with its policy of restraint, petroleum activities north of the 62nd parallel in the North Sea were delayed. One reason for this was the fact that two offshore disasters stung the nation. The first was in 1977 when a well in the Ekofisk field blew out of control, spilling thousands of tons of oil into the sea. The second, in 1980, occurred when a hotel platform capsized, killing 123. This latter tragedy occurred on the first anniversary of the nuclear plant failure near Harrisburg, Pennsylvania, which ignited a serious debate in all of Western Europe over nuclear power, even though the incident did not cause a single death.

In 1980 drilling started north of the line, and production continues there slowly, concentrating on the promising discoveries already made, not on prospecting for new fields. The government wants to make sure that oil keeps flowing when the old offshore fields of Ekofisk, Frigg and Statfjord become exhausted. It also wants the population north of the 62nd parallel to have the economic benefits of oil–related activities. Much of Norway's economic policy has always revolved around keeping citizens from leaving the sparsely populated parts of the country.

Oil and gas are very important for the country's economy. Through taxes and royalties the state collects about 80% of the revenues from oil and gas production, and in 1999 it accounted for a tenth of total central government revenue, compared with only 1% in 1975 and 5% in 1988. By 1998 petroleum and gas represented 16% of GDP and 40% of export earnings. More than a third of overall investments is in the oil and gas sector. Known petroleum revenues are expected to last until at least 2015. Improving technology steadily opens up previously inaccessible fields.

Since World War II, Norway, under the tutelage of *Labor Party* governments, always centrally planned and steered the country's economy more than did most other Western European countries. The goal always was to distribute income more evenly, and to maintain full employment and stable prices. It is therefore no surprise that the Norwegian state took control of all phases of petroleum activity, and sought to maintain its control through *Statoil*. In the 1980s the *Conservative* government wanted to take away *Statoil's* favored status and to give more opportunities to the other two Norwegian energy companies, Norsk Hydro (51% state owned) and Saga Petroleum (privately owned).

Although foreign companies continue to be active in exploration and drilling, their services are used only as the Norwegians decide they are needed. Such discrimination would have had to stop if Norway had entered the EU. Those foreign firms are preferred which invest money into mainland industries, including the ones which are related to petroleum activity, such as those involved in the production of petrochemicals or of platforms and other offshore equipment. This is particularly important because the weak link in the Norwegian economy is its mainland industry. Norway itself invests heavily abroad, and in 1996 this exceeded foreign investment in Norway for the first time. The bulk of its investments goes to Sweden, France and Ireland. It also sets aside some of its oil earnings in a Petroleum Fund, a national nest–egg that is partially invested in international equities. It was valued at $16 billion by 1999 and is an investment fund the country can use for a rainy day in the future.

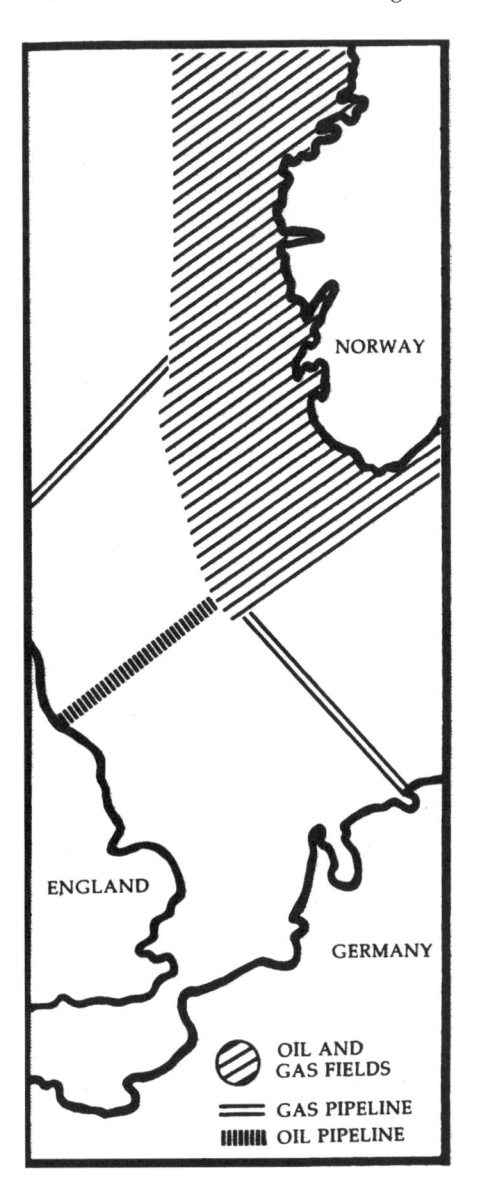

Non–Petroleum Industries

Although Norway is a highly industrialized society, it remains within a non–industrial landscape. This is because Norwegian industries tend to be rather small. Only a few hundred of the more than 14,000 companies have more than 200 employees, although those large companies employ about 40% of the work force in manufacturing. Industries are 91% privately and largely Norwegian owned. They are geographically spread out and are often located in beautiful fjord or coastal districts where they can be close to hydropower sources and ports. In 1997 Norway was ranked as the fifth country in the world in overall economic competitiveness.

Hydroelectric power is very important for industry in general, and especially for industries which produce chemicals, iron, steel and ferro–alloys, aluminum and other metals. The latter are very power–consuming and the approximately 30 companies in these sectors consume about a fourth of all electric power produced. Few other countries could supply such industries with cheap electricity to keep them alive. The largest of these electricity consumers by far is the primary production of aluminum for further processing into finished goods. In this sector Norway is the world's second largest exporter after Canada, although all of Norway's bauxite must be imported. It is the largest producer of aluminum in Western Europe. Much of the other metal industry can be supplied either by domestic ores, which are generally of poor quality and are mined predominantly in the northern half of the country, or by importing the needed ores with money earned from exporting unneeded ores. In the northern mountains new deposits of gold have been discovered in such massive size that they could influence the world price of this precious metal.

Although iron ore resources can be mined for at least another century, and Norway has considerable deposits of titanium (used in paints), sulphur, pyrite, copper, zinc, lead and nickel, the sad fact remains, however, that without state subsidies many of its metal producing industries would fail. In order to maintain high employment, aluminum production is maintained at 90% capacity although the industry loses money on every ton it produces. Other metal industries have been pared down to close to 50% capacity and are still losing money.

Norway

About the only industry which is not in trouble in Norway is the tourist business. Thanks to the beauty of its scenery and to the friendliness of its people, Norway normally attracts as many foreign tourists as its entire population. About 70% come from other Nordic countries. A major benefit of tourism is that it stimulates economic activity in the outlying regions, both in the mountains and along the coast. Tourism and the economy as a whole received a major boost in 1994, when the town of Lillehammer hosted the Winter Olympics.

Shipping

Another major sector which has been hard hit by the world recession of the 1970s is shipbuilding. There are about 80 shipyards in Norway, most of them very small, although the industry is dominated by two large groups, Kvaerner and Aker. As orders for traditional ships declined, many companies converted to constructing offshore rigs and specialized ships. This adjustment has temporarily compensated for the loss of orders for regular ships, but many observers fear that even the market for specialized craft will soon be saturated. The state does subsidize this industry to keep it internationally competitive. But it stopped making new subsidy commitments to shipping companies in the 1980s, and it supported efforts to make the shipbuilding industry more efficient through *rationalization*. These measures had by 1981 already led to a drop in employment in shipbuilding from 25,500 to 22,000.

Like Denmark, Norway has one of the world's largest merchant marine fleets. By the early 1980s it possessed between 5% and 6% of the world's fleet (down from 10% in 1967). By 1991 it was third in the world behind the convenience flags Panama and Liberia. Norwegians also own a fifth of all ships used for off-shore oil drilling. Well over 90% of these ships never dock at Norwegian ports, though. Oil tankers account for more than 60% of the total tonnage, and Norwegian shipping companies operate many oil drilling platforms and many of the cruise ships which circle the Caribbean Sea. Further, the world's largest passenger ship, "France," was purchased by a Norwegian shipowner and rechristened "Norway." Its fleet is very modern and is entirely privately owned. There are very few large shipping companies and most are small or medium-sized. Maritime activities account for 15% of gross exports, making shipping the third largest export industry.

Norway's sophistication in ship equipment caused a serious row with the U.S. in 1987, when it was revealed that Kongsberg Vaapenfabrikk, along with a Japanese company, had sold computerized milling equipment enabling the Soviet Union to manufacture submarine propellers so quiet that they could hardly be detected. Norwegian police uncovered a 10-year pattern of illegal sales of high-tech goods to the Soviets. The Reagan administration resisted congressional efforts to bar the offending companies from selling to the U.S. market, after Brundtland admitted that such illegal sales had been made in violation of government policy and provided assurances to her NATO ally that Norway would adhere to *COCOM* rules.

Forestry and Agriculture

Norway's forests in the central and southern part of the country provide a good part of the raw materials for a wood processing industry, although it does have to import some wood from Sweden. This industry traditionally exports 80% of its products, but heavy competition from Canada and its Nordic neighbors have also forced it to face fundamental reorganization. Much of the wooded area is owned by the farmers, many of whom derive supplemental income from forestry. Regardless of who owns the forests, they can, according to Norwegian law, be used by everybody for recreational purposes.

The country has not been self-sufficient in food for many decades, and Norway's agricultural production covers less than half of the people's food consumption. It is self-sufficient in dairy and meat products, but it must import 90% of its food grains. The problem, of course, is that only about 3% of the land can be used for farming, and the terrain is so rugged that the predominantly small farms make it difficult to combine them in a way which would permit large-scale and more efficient farming, although the state is making an effort to encourage this. Also, the northern climate means that the growing season is very short. The very best agricultural land is around the Oslo fjord, in the large valleys in the south-central region and around Stavenger in the south and the Trøndelag area in central Norway.

The state's coffers have been open to Norwegian farmers for years, to the tune of $1.7 billion annually, in an effort to preserve the present pattern of settlement in the country. The government negotiates an "Agricultural Agreement" every two years with both major farmers' organizations which fixes price levels, subsidies and marketing rules. Many farmers could never hope to survive without such assistance. The state also controls the quantity and price of imported foodstuffs, allowing in only what is in short supply in Norway. This is done to protect Norwegian agriculture, and it is certainly one reason why Norwegians were wary of joining the EU, which would prohibit such practices.

Fishing

Even Norway's most picturesque industry, fishing, could hardly survive without state help. The number of fishermen has declined from about 60,000 in 1960 to 26,700 by 1995, a figure which is less than 1% of the country's total workforce. However, during these two decades, their catch doubled, largely because of more efficient fishing and the declaration of a 200-mile economic zone along the Norwegian coast and around Jan Mayen and of a separate fishery zone around Svalbard. Measured by quantity of catch, Norway is the second-leading fishing nation in Europe, behind Russia. Fishing accounts for 14% of non-petroleum exports and is still important because it supplies raw materials for the country's large fish processing industry.

Fishermen are strongly unionized and have well-developed cooperatives which buy the fish at fixed prices; they do not have to sell their catch by auction. Only 2% of the catches are sold fresh, and close to 80% is reduced to oil and meal, while about 10% is frozen and 8% is salted or dried. About 90% of the entire catch is ultimately exported. Norway suspended its commercial whaling after the 1987 season, but in 1993 it announced that it would kill 296 minke whales. Norway and Russia are the last two countries in the world to hunt whales in violation of the 1993 ban by the International Whaling Commission.

In many coastal communities, especially in the north, these mainly small or medium-sized companies represent the only possible industrial element. Therefore, the state has long given subsidies to them to keep them alive and to keep persons in those communities from migrating south into the larger cities. This form of subsidy may make little sense from a purely economic point of view, but as in so many other instances in Norway, political objectives outweigh economic ones. In the North, the once-feared start-up of offshore oil operations north of the 62nd parallel is now eagerly awaited as the only means of averting the Arctic region's depopulation and subsequent decline.

Economic Problems

For years Norway suffered from chronic inflation. Oslo has become the most expensive city of the world to live in. Inflation disturbed the traditional labor peace, and sparked strikes, which many are experiencing for the first time in their lives. It also drove up public spending. From where did the inflation come?

The extremely prosperous oil and gas

Norway

Fishing boats

activity brought lots of money into the country which ended up more and more in the form of public spending rather than investment in private industry to raise productivity and to develop new technology. The oil operations also attracted much of the country's skilled labor and created a very tight supply in the rest of the country. Fearing a threat to their society and their identity, Norwegians closed their borders to a further influx of foreign workers from outside the Nordic area. Despite appeals by the government, employees in the petroleum sector successfully forced the oil companies to pay ever–increasing wages.

As in all Nordic countries, the guidelines for wage settlements covering the entire country are established in summit meetings between the *LO* and the employers associations. Since these unified wage guidelines apply to *all* sectors of the economy, the unions (to which two–thirds of the labor force belongs) have succeeded in insisting that all wages rise with those in the petroleum industry, regardless of whether a company in the non–oil sector is profitable or not. That is where both government subsidies and inflation come into the picture. The government pays much of the costs of higher wages in the form of subsidies. In the 1980s the government created two–thirds of the new jobs. By 1995 public sector employment had doubled since 1972, while industrial jobs had fallen by 100,000. Rising wage costs increase the price of products which Norwegian companies are trying to sell abroad. To make matters worse, Norway's sale of oil and gas greatly increased the strength of its currency, the *krone* (crown). Such a "hard" currency raises even more the actual prices of Norway's goods to foreign buyers. This caused Norway to lose some of its markets abroad.

No government could risk a dramatic rise in unemployment or a deep cut in the social welfare system. Any substantial dismantling of the social welfare system in a Scandinavian country could be fatal to any politician who would propose it, regardless of whether the system could be paid for or not. Unlike other Nordic countries, Norway can pay for its tightly–woven social security net. It introduced a National Insurance Scheme in 1967, which by 1971 had replaced all private pension or insurance programs. It protects all citizens against sickness, unemployment, invalidism and many other unforeseen calamities. At age 67 a person receives a pension which for the average Norwegian amounts to about two–thirds of the income he earned during his working years. Employers' contributions pay 60% of the costs of the scheme, members' 20% and appropriations from the central and local governments the remaining 20%. As in other Scandinavian countries, welfare assistance is given as a right, not as an alm, and the objective is that no personal calamity or old age should endanger the living standard to which the citizen had become accustomed.

The Norwegian government continues to grapple with economic problems, although things look somewhat brighter in the turn of the century. Its annual economic growth averaged 4% from 1994–9, one of the highest on the European continent. Inflation was 2.1% in 1999. Unemployment stood at 3% in 1999, the lowest in Europe except Luxembourg. It would be slightly higher if persons in training and employment programs were included, but essentially all Norwegians who want to work are employed. Per capita GDP is the third highest in the world and tops the Nordic nations. Its budget surplus in 1996 stood at 3.8% of GDP, and it is one of the few countries in Europe that is not slashing its welfare state. Its competitive position has improved because of productivity improvements following a shake–down of labor in manufacturing. Nevertheless, manufacturing accounted for only 13% of GDP in 1994, compared with 20% a decade earlier. It has made its tax system simpler to administer and understand. Although the real tax level stayed the same for the business sector, it reduced the highest marginal rate from 57.8% to 48.8%, and the middle class pays no more than 35.8%.

Its most important decision was whether to join the EU, to which it formally applied in 1992. In November 1994 voters went to the polls, and 52.2% rejected EU membership. Its strong economy, low unemployment, and overall feeling of security allow Norwegians an alternative to the EU. It is part of the internal market anyway through the EEA. One explanation seemed to sum up the majority's attitude: "We know what we have, but we don't know what we'll get."

Norway is moving steadily closer to Europe whether its people are fully aware of it or not. It is Europe's top oil producer, and a third of its export revenue is derived from North Sea energy sources. Because of Norway's expertise, the U.N. charged it in 1991 to create a special group to monitor Iraq's crude oil sales and to ensure that profits go directly to meet humanitarian needs.

Norwegians are rich because of their oil, but they are confronted with the problem of how to use their wealth. All European countries have oil problems, but Norway has one of a different kind. The more they

Norway

Oslo harbor—naval cadets prepare to board a training vessel Courtesy: Jon Markham Morrow

earn from oil, the more two different economies develop: one a flourishing energy production in the high seas, and the other a traditional mainland industry. Norwegians are still torn between wanting to keep their industry alive by avoiding a predominantly oil–based economy and wanting their standards of living to keep on rising as a result of oil wealth.

The major parties know that oil revenues can bankroll the expanding welfare state and bureaucracy. Government subsidies can keep specific, weak industries alive and thereby fight unemployment. But such use of Norway's riches shelters its industry from change and real competition and robs it of the discipline which would be needed to make its mainland economy healthy again. The government subsidies that flow to industry are hand–outs to pay workers, not investments to improve production techniques. Thus oil and gas help to freeze the status quo, while Norway's competitors gear up for the future. What will happen, though, when the oil and gas run out, or if those two things would lose much of their value due to future technological developments in the energy field? The Midas touch obviously creates problems, as well as opportunities. To provide for a future without oil, the government is putting a large amount of its oil and gas revenues and its budget surpluses into a Petroleum Fund, which is expected to be worth $108 billion by the end of the century. To avoid inflation, this fund is invested entirely abroad.

CULTURE

Rural–Urban Traditional Distinctions

A major characteristic of Norwegian politics and society remains the contrast and tension between the periphery and the center. The center encompasses the leaders of the country's civil service, military, Lutheran Church, industry and shipping in and around Oslo and the major cities. In this political and social center one speaks a Norwegian dialect now called *Bokmål* (earlier *Riksmål*), whereas in the periphery most persons speak another dialect now called *Nynorsk* (which means "New Norwegian" and which was earlier called *Landsmål.)* Both dialects have equal status in the state administration and schools, but the use of one dialect or the other reveals important social distinctions. Until the end of the 19th century the only official dialect was *Riksmål*, which had been influenced by the Danish language during the long period of Danish domination over Norway. Thus, it was the language of the more cosmopolitan and middle–upper class city dwellers.

In the course of the 19th century the dialect of *Landsmål* developed from many diverse rural dialects. *Landsmål* was much closer to the speech used by the common people, who at that time lived mainly in rural areas of the south and west. Among these people, class distinctions were minimal, since most were fishermen or small, independent farmers who owned their own land. They were much more religious than their compatriots in the cities, and their respect for state authority was much weaker. They also spoke a dialect which was looked down upon by the city folk. The people in the periphery were much more supportive of movements calling for popular religious revival, the widened use of *Nynorsk* and the prohibition of alcoholic beverages.

From 1917 until 1927 they were able to have all liquors and strong wines banned entirely, and they still are inclined to support politicians who call for tightened controls on alcoholic consumption. In the sparsely–populated north the contrast with the center was less pronounced, since the society there was more fragmented, with more prosperous trade families having a greater economic influence or control over the small farmers and fishermen. The tensions between the center and the periphery still influence Norwegian politics and parties today and were crucially important in the debate over possible Norwegian entry into the EU in 1972 and in 1994.

Norway is now experiencing another form of tension: toward darker–skinned refugees. Animosity against them is easily exploited by the *Progress Party*. Many frightened parents on the east side of Oslo are taking their children out of their neighborhood schools, where five schools already have immigrant majorities, for fear that the quality of education is dropping. Feelings were running so high that the late King Olaf made a plea for toleration of "our new countrymen."

The Arts

The two principal dialects of Norwegian, *Bokmål* and *Nynorsk,* are spoken by only four million persons, and in contrast to the Swedes, who allow English words to seep freely into their language, the Norwegians try very hard to prevent their language from being anglicized in any way, even though most Norwegians learn English in school. Despite the fact that the Norwegian language is spoken by so few people in the world, Norway is a very active literary nation. It has the world's highest book sales per person, and book publishing is supported by sizable state subsidies. It has had three Nobel Prize winners in literature (Bjørnstjerne Bjørnson, Knut Hamsun and Sigrid Undset).

The earliest Norwegian literature is Eddic poetry from the 9th or 10th centuries, and many fairy tales and folk poems survive from subsequent centuries. After the country's links with Denmark were broken in 1814, Henrik Wergeland won the reputation as the most significant Norwegian lyricist with his visionary romantic poetry. He ignited a literary renaissance in the country. Bjørnson was the first writer whose works became widely known beyond the country's borders; his earlier plays and short stories are infused with nationalist ideas and enthusiasm, but his later works are more characterized by modern realism. Also well–received abroad were the plays of Henrik Ibsen, whose serious, penetrating works explore man's ethical and psychological dimensions. Ibsen, Bjørnson and two other writers in the realist school, Jonas Lie and Alexander Kielland, are generally considered to be the most significant Norwegian authors, although Arne Garborg, Undset and Hamsun should not be overlooked.

Just as the liberation from Denmark sparked a literary outburst, the emancipation from German occupation in 1945 had the same effect. For awhile poetry and exciting narratives were produced, but Norwegian literature quickly moved from the optimistic enthusiasm of national emancipation to pessimism, intellectual indecision, fear and powerlessness. Literature became more experimental. As Norway began its economic flowering and a wealthy consumer society developed, Norwegian literature turned to the alleged absurdity of society and the difficulties which individuals have in establishing their own identity and meaningful contacts with other persons in a cold, consumption–oriented society. Much Norwegian literature became thereby politicized, as authors pointed to a need for radical change.

A particular pride of contemporary Norwegian literature is Herbjørg Wassmo, who in 1987 won the Nordic Literature Prize for her 1986 novel *Hudløs Himmel (Sensitive Sky)*. She is the first Norwegian woman to win it. Her writings depict womens' psyche, chiseled in drastic realism. She commands a sensitive, poetic language.

The society which those authors criticized so mercilessly was, however, a very tolerant one, which not only bore criticism well, but which even chose to pay for such literary attacks against itself. As few Norwegian books could be financial successes on the tiny Norwegian market, the state created a cultural fund which purchased 1,000 copies of each work of Norwegian literature so that every public library could have a copy to circulate. The state also grants three–year scholarships to young authors in order to provide them with the financial wherewithal to work undisturbed.

One author who does not need the state's hand is Jostein Gaader, a high school philosophy teacher. His novel, *Sophie's World,* is a highly readable history

A town nestles by a fjord north of the timber line

Norway

Edvard Grieg

Norwegian film figure is the actress Liv Ullman, who often appears on stage in the U.S. and in many films directed by the Swede, Ingmar Bergman. Because of her fame and activism for the UN Children's Fund, she was named as the UN's first goodwill ambassador to various parts of the world, especially Africa. Recommended in 1997 for an Oscar for best foreign film was Norway's *The Other Side of Sunday,* directed by Otto Nesheim. Set in 1959, it is a delightful portrayal of the maturing of a young girl who grows up in a pious family living in a rural part of Norway where almost everything was forbidden.

Norwegian art and music cross its borders more easily since they appeal to human senses and intellect without the restriction of language. Norway's best-known composer was Edvard Grieg, who composed intimate, soothing romantic pieces. Another widely acclaimed composer, Johann Swendsen, produced symphonic music, which, like that of Grieg, drew inspiration from Norwegian folk music. The country has many active composers today,

"The Scream" by Edvard Munch

of Western thought told in a compelling mystery. After reaching the bestseller lists in Scandinavia and Germany, it was introduced to the American market in 1995.

The state and the municipalities also subsidize all cultural activities with a view to making culture largely decentralized and thereby available to as many persons as possible. It maintains six regional theaters, in addition to the National Theater in Oslo, the country's main stage, and the National Stage in Bergen. Oslo also has the Norwegian Theater, which presents plays only in *Nynorsk,* and the Oslo New Theater. Plays are also televised once a week so that Norwegians can have the chance to experience theater performances in every corner of the country. In 1988 the theaters found themselves in dire financial straits, due to a top-heavy organization, too many employees with too little work, and the fact that government subsidies, which amount to 85% of the total outlays, had not been adjusted in 15 years. Without such subsidies, a single ticket would cost $125, instead of only $15.

State subsidies also keep the Norwegian film industry alive, so that it can produce about 10 feature and 80 short films per year; most are aimed primarily at a Norwegian audience. These subsidies cover 45% of the production costs for black and white and 55% for color films. The state will also guarantee loans for up to 90% of the total production costs. All films shown in Norway must, however, be approved by a state film censor, a requirement which is highly controversial today.

Perhaps the internationally best known

Norway

and there are four symphony orchestras in the major cities. The Norwegian Opera was created under the directorship of the renowned singer Kirsten Flagstad in 1958 in order to provide a suitable setting for both opera and ballet. In 1994 the world heard one of Norway's most popular song artists, Sissel Kyrkjebø, open and close the Winter Olympics in Lillehammer. Many of her CDs and cassettes have been released in the U.S. Also popular in America in the late 1990s is country music star Bjoro Haland and his band. Higher–brow stars are opera singers Kjell Mangus Sandev and his wife Kjersti Sandev.

The giant of Norwegian art is Edvard Munch, who is considered to be one of the fathers of expressionism around the turn of the century. His paintings scream at the viewer and reveal how some human beings can be desperately anxious and torn inside. Most of his works are displayed in the Munch Museum in Oslo, and other works of his are scattered among the 320 art museums and art collections throughout the country. On the day the world's attention was focused on the opening of the Lillehammer Winter Olympics, his (and Norway's) most famous painting, The Scream, worth at least $55 million, was stolen from the National Gallery in Oslo by thieves who brazenly left a postcard reading, "Thanks for the poor security." Norwegians heaved a sigh of relief in May 1994, three months later, when the police recovered it undamaged in a sting operation. In 1996 four Norwegian men were sentenced to six years in prison.

Norwegian artists have been leaders in the production of "monumental art," and as in the other Scandinavian countries, abstract art has become a dominant form. It also has produced recognized sculptors, such as Carl Nesjar, Odd Tandberg, Arnold Haukeland and Nils Aas. The sculptor best known internationally, however, is Gustav Vigeland.

Education

At age seven, Norwegian children enter school, and for at least nine years they must attend an elementary school, which is financed and operated by the municipal governments. About 80% continue their education for an additional three years in schools which are operated and financed by the counties. A recent reform under an earlier *Labor* government combined in 1976 the separate tracks of secondary schools which had prepared young people for the university, for a trade or for some other job, which did not require a university education. The problem with such separate schools was that it was very difficult to change from one secondary school to another type; many critics also believed that such separate schools established and hardened class differences within Norwegian society.

A typical Norwegian family cross-country skiing

Therefore, comprehensive schools, similar to the American high schools, were created, which combined various tracks under one roof and which eased the difficulty of switching from one track to the other. Those who follow the college preparatory course in the new comprehensive schools usually qualify for entrance into one of the four state–funded universities in Oslo, Bergen, Trondheim and Tromsø, into one of several specialized universities (which teach, for example, engineering, agriculture, architecture, business administration, physical education or music), or one of seven regional teachers' colleges. Education is free at all levels, and needy students in the secondary schools can receive extra scholarships. Students at the universities or colleges receive both scholarships and loans which must be repaid within ten to fifteen years. As elsewhere in Europe, the universities are experiencing severe overcrowding.

As in all Scandinavian countries, Norwegian schools have been laboratories for experimentation, especially that kind which seeks to eliminate social differences. Many of these changes have not been well received, and one of the first things which the former *Conservative* government changed was reevaluation of grades in schools, which had been deemphasized or done away with on the grounds that they were discriminatory and were hindrances to learning. The new administration also enhanced the financial basis of private schools and gave them more freedom to run themselves as they chose.

The Media

Considering its small population, the Norwegian press offers both variety and a considerable number of individual publications—in all there are 161 daily newspapers. All are in private hands, although all receive state subsidies in one form or the other. Most generally support the political line of one party or the other without having formal ties to it. It was estimated in 1989 that 40% of the newspapers support leftist parties, and a majority supports the center and right. The only exceptions are newspapers linked with the *Labor* and *Communist* parties. The largest newspapers are the independent to conservative Oslo dailies, *Aftenposten* and *Verdens Gang*, as well as the liberal dailies *Dagbladet* from Oslo and the *Bergens Tidende* from Bergen. Favorite weekly magazines are *Allers*, *Hjemmet* and *Norst Ukeblad*, which are all family publications. The favorite monthlies are *Reader's Digest*, entitled *Det Beste* in Norwegian, and *Donald Duck Co.*, whose hero is very familiar to American and European readers!

Local radio and TV stations compete with the state–owned Norwegian Broadcasting Company. Its activities are free of direct government control, although it is run by a council composed of representatives of the *Storting*, the public service and certain public groups. The director is also appointed by the government. Financing comes from public funds since no advertising is permitted (except on some foreign stations); radio and television must compete with one of the most beautiful natural settings for the people's attention. Norwegians are outdoors people, and they tend to spend their four weeks of

Norway

Sami with reindeer

paid vacation hiking, fishing, swimming, camping and boating in the summer and cross–country skiing or skating in the winter. Prosperity has also enabled one out of six families to buy its own seaside cottage or mountain chalet. This is a striking proportion when one considers that 53% of the families own the houses or apartments in which they live.

The Native Population

One group which lives especially close to nature is the 60,000 or so Sami, about two–third of whom live in Norway's far north, and about a third of whom live in the north of Finland and Sweden. It is believed that about 45,000 Samis live in Norway. Isolated for centuries in the northern periphery of Scandinavia, they preserved their unique Finno–Ugric language, but their exclusive identity with the Sami culture is breaking down as most Sami are being assimilated with the other Scandinavian cultures to one degree or another. The most tightly–knit Sami are the reindeer–raising nomads, who now constitute only a seventh of the total Sami population. However, their grazing areas have been greatly reduced by fences erected along the Norwegian–Swedish border and by the construction of hydroelectric plants at the waterfalls in the north.

The extension of the social welfare system to every corner of Norway has made practices of helping each other largely unnecessary, and therefore a part of the glue within the nomadic community has been destroyed. Of course, many Samis want to become partially or wholly assimilated into the Norwegian culture, but an emotional debate is still taking place in Norway concerning the future of this minority within the larger society. Expressed in a simplified way, some Norwegians argue that the Samis' standard of living should be elevated to the prevailing Norwegian level, while others argue that their cultural independence should be preserved at all costs, even though their culture scorns individual advancement and permits many social inequalities within its own society.

The Norwegian state does finance a Sami school at Karasjok for those children whose parents want them to learn in the Sami language. Other special schools and university courses are also provided. It is certain that the most effective means for the survival of this unique minority is to preserve its language, and subsidized radio and TV programs are aired. Nevertheless, the Sami culture will continue to lose its grip on the lives of most of the group.

The lives of this far–away people was so vividly portrayed in the first Sami film ever made, *Pathfinder*, that it won an Oscar nomination in 1988 for best foreign film. This film was half financed by the Norwegian government and directed by a 32–year–old Sami, Nils Gaup, under appalling conditions. It was shot above the Arctic Circle in temperatures which reached 40 degrees below zero and when there were only two hours of daylight. Cameras had to be stored in a freezer to avoid condensation inside the mechanisms, and sound equipment had to be defrosted with electric hair dryers. The message was worth the extreme effort.

Through councils (called *Siida*), composed of representatives of the various families, the nomads regulate the use of grazing land. The council also traditionally had the function of guiding the community and of arranging for the provision of food and other necessities for the socially weak within the group. In 1989 Samis elected for the first time 39 representatives to their own Sami People's Congress, which convenes in the Finn-

Norway

mark town of Karasjok. It has advisory as well as decision-making powers in matters related to the Samis. At the third opening of this parliament in 1997, King Harald V publicly expressed regret to the Sami people for the repression inflicted on them and their culture: "Today we must apologize for the injustice the Norwegian state once imposed on the Sami people through policies of Norwegianization." A major issue is how to gain control of natural resources of the Sami regions. In Sweden a similar elected *Someting* was created in 1993.

FUTURE

The most difficult and most critical political question facing Norway today is how to find a healthy balance between the North Sea economy and that of the mainland, a balance which would protect traditional industry, environment and society, while providing a stable base for continued elevation in the standard of living and for maintenance of the social security net which the country created for all citizens.

Norway's chief problems will continue to be economic ones. In the long run, though, the country's large oil and gas revenues will help it economically and will certainly enable it to maintain its comprehensive social welfare net. In the future, Russia, which exports many of the same things as Norway—oil, gas, timber—will become a formidable competitor. In general, Norway's oil-related problems will be the kind which most countries would be happy to have. Therefore, to many less fortunate nations, Norway's problems will continue to seem like golden ones.

A national referendum on joining the EU was held November 28, 1994, with the *Labor* and *Conservative* parties supporting entry, while the *Center* and *Socialist Left* parties opposed it. The Norwegian public remains divided on the issue. One skeptic said that "it is no good telling people here that we should join the EU because other European countries want to do the same. We have to find strong Norwegian reasons why we should do so." Also, proponents could not argue that the country would be devastated economically if it stayed out; they made the same argument in 1972, but Norway prospered. Norway is still a young country whose independence and sovereignty will be defended fiercely. This is why voters chose—52.2% to 47.8%—to remain outside the EU. There are still proponents of European integration, but all Norwegians share a reluctance to reopen the acrimonious debate, which cannot be put off forever.

Norway is an enthusiastic NATO member and is the alliance's only country to border on Russia. It sent six combat aircraft and one warship to support the air war against Yugoslavia in 1999, despite the fact that its ambassador's residence in Belgrade was damaged by NATO bombing. It has more than 800 troops deployed in the stabilization force in Bosnia, and it agreed to accept 6,000 Kosovar refugees. It was also awarded the OSCE chairmanship for 1999.

Under a new prime minister since September 1997, Kjell Magne Bondevik, Norway's political system will certainly remain stable even though it will have to muddle through with a minority government. The 1997 elections left Norway with a shaky ruling coalition that will survive or fall on the political skills of Bondevik. He has been left with very little room for maneuver, and pragmatism and careful vote counting are the order of the day.

Towing a concrete oil structure out from Stavanger

The Kingdom of Denmark

Area: 16,629 sq. mi. (43,069 sq. km., slightly more than twice the size of New Jersey, excluding Greenland and the Faroe Islands).
Population: 5.2 million (estimated).
Capital City: Copenhagen (Pop. 1.4 million, including the suburb of Frederiksberg.
Climate: Due to the flow of the Gulf Stream, the temperatures dip to below freezing for about 100 or so days during the winter, and summer days are sunny and bright, with cool nights.
Neighboring Countries: Germany (South); Norway (North); Sweden (East and Southeast).
Official Language: Danish.
Other Principal Tongues: There is a German-speaking minority in the south; English.
Ethnic Background: Germanic, North European.
Principal Religion: Lutheran protestant.
Main Exports: Machinery, ships, meat, pharmaceuticals, electronics, dairy products, textiles, furniture.
Main Imports: Industrial machinery, automobiles, petroleum, textile raw fibers, yarns, metals, chemicals, grain and foodstuffs, wood. Major Trading Partners: Germany, Sweden, UK, France, U.S., Norway.
Currency: Krone.
National Holiday: April 16, Birthday of the Queen.
Chief of State: Her Majesty Queen Margrethe II, b. 1940. (Pronounced Mar-gret). Ascended the throne January 15, 1972. Married (1967) Count Henri de Laborde de Monpezat (France), named *Prince Henrik of Denmark* from that date.
Heir Apparent: His Royal Highness Crown Prince Frederik (b. 1968).
Head of Government: Poul Nyrup Rasmussen, Prime Minister (since January 1993).
National Flag: A red field, crossed in the center by a white stripe, and from top to bottom, by another, the latter being off-center, closer to the pole.

A thousand years ago the Danes were among the roving Vikings who terrorized most of Europe. Even after these marauders settled down, Denmark was a powerful country ready and willing to assert its domination over much of the Nordic area. Today the Danes are a peaceful and inventive people, who spend less than 7% of their budget on defense, and who, characteristically, thought of a way of constructing a super-elliptical peace negotiating table which can seat participants in such a way that all have a sense of prestige. This does not mean that they are not patriotic, though. As in the other Nordic countries, one sees more national flags displayed than in any other Western European country, with perhaps the exception of Switzerland. Also, foreign flags can be displayed in Denmark only with special police permission and only so long as the Danish flag is displayed also. It is true that the Danes feel free to criticize their own state and society. But when any such discussion is over, most still remain firmly convinced that Denmark is by far the best place in the world to live.

Because the country is very poorly endowed with natural resources, Danes for centuries had to make a living primarily from agriculture and fishing, when they were not raiding various other lands dur-

Denmark

ing their medieval history. In this peninsula with its islands, scarcely larger than Vermont and New Hampshire combined, there are still three pigs for every two humans, and Denmark remains the world's largest exporter of pork. It is also the second largest exporter of butter and the third largest of cheese. Since 1945, though, Denmark has become an increasingly dynamic and innovative industrialized country, and its agricultural population has fallen from almost a fourth in 1945 to about 6% today. Danes have learned to make up for their lack of raw materials by know–how and ingenuity, and by the 1970s no more than a third of their exports were derived from agriculture.

Denmark is made up of the Jutland Peninsula which shares a 41–mile–long (68 km.) border with Germany, which always exercised much cultural, economic, political and military influence on Denmark. Since 1815 the only military actions directed against Denmark have originated from Germany, and Denmark's economy has always been considerably oriented toward its neighbor. Today, in spite of World War II, Danes bear little hostility toward Germans, but they do tend to view their southern neighbors as Canadians view the Americans: near, numerous, not intentionally threatening, but a bit too powerful economically and culturally. Germany is Denmark's major creditor and customer today, and for Jutlanders, Hamburg is almost as economically important as is Copenhagen.

The rest of Denmark is composed of 406 islands, and no Dane lives further than 31 miles (52 km.) from the sea. The numerous islands (not including Greenland) give the country a total coastline of 4,380 miles (7,300 km.). This is equivalent to about one–sixth the way around the world at the equator, or the distance from Copenhagen to Bombay, India. With such a long coast, it is not a surprise that Denmark has always been a leading fishing and maritime shipping nation.

Close to a fourth of all Danes live in the capital city. In fact, few countries are so dominated by their capitals as is Denmark. Copenhagen is the governmental, administrative, economic and cultural heart of the country. To the delight of almost all who see it, it has old streets and elegant buildings, a stately royal residence with colorfully dressed guards, and charming canals criss–crossing the city. It is also a vibrant, growing city which almost appears to be bursting at the seams. Copenhagen has a very active free port and a busy airport, which makes it one of the world's major transportations hubs. By opening in 1990 the first international air–link and ferry services to Latvia's capital city of Riga, it is reviving historical ties with other Baltic neighbors. It is hoped that this will stimulate economic growth to help counter–balance the powerful Ruhr–Paris–Milan triangle. As a small and highly prosperous nation with a very open society, this country is inescapably tied in with a heavily interdependent world, and is vulnerable to all major political, military and economic developments in Europe. Its people, therefore, know well that they could never hope to imitate the Prince in Hans Christian Andersen's fairy tale, *The Swineherd,* who "went back into his own country and locked the door behind him."

HISTORY

Early Danish history is discussed under the general section entitled "The Nordic Countries." Following the collapse of Nazi Germany, Denmark quickly reverted to its old pattern of leftist–socialist parliamentary government under its constitutional monarchy. Communists were never a major element and all but disappeared. The welfare state was gradually enlarged, as in other Nordic countries. A new constitution abolished the upper house of parliament in 1953, leaving a unicameral legislature. Government was predominantly by minority coalitions of the left.

GOVERNMENT

The Monarchy

Danish politics is characterized by a great measure of underlying stability despite a multi–party system which makes it both impossible for a single party to win a parliamentary majority and difficult for a combination of parties to form a majority coalition. Such stability is due in large part to the Danes' tradition of tolerance and compromise and to the overall consensus about political aims and democratic means.

Denmark has Europe's longest standing monarchy, established in 985. In 1848 a peaceful revolution put an end to the absolute monarchy, and the constitution which was adopted the following year and which has been revised several times since, is still valid. Today, the monarch

The Danish Royal Family: (left to right) Prince Joaquim, Her Majesty Queen Margrethe II, Prince Henrik, Crown Prince Frederik.
Photo by Klaus Møller

Denmark

Daily changing of the Royal Life Guard in Copenhagen

continues to symbolize the unity of the nation. The last major revision of the constitution in 1953 permitted females to succeed to the throne, and when King Frederick IX died in 1972 his daughter, Margrethe II, became Queen. She is a hardworking, intelligent woman who studied law, social sciences and archeology at universities in Copenhagen, Århus, Cambridge, London and Paris. Despite an annual budget of 22 million krone (about $2–1/2 million), the Queen lives relatively modestly and is far less wealthy than the queens of Britain and Holland.

She did away with much of the court etiquette at Amalienborg Castle in the center of Copenhagen, as well as the clumsy addition to her royal title, Queen of the Vends and Goths, Duchess of Slesvig–Holsten, Stormarn, Ditmarsken, Lauenburg and Oldenburg. Like the Danish government, which in 1946 wisely accepted the permanency of the 1920 border between Denmark and Germany even though the British gave it the chance to reopen the question, Margrethe fully accepts the loss of part of Schleswig to Germany. Unlike her father, she does not hesitate to travel to the lost province.

Her function is chiefly ceremonial. She does not attend cabinet meetings and none of her acts is official without being countersigned by the responsible minister. She is so concerned to be perceived as being politically neutral that she does not even vote in Danish elections. Her only political function is to oversee the formation of a government which can have its program accepted by a majority in parliament. This is, of course, a frequent and important task in a country in which new elections now normally have to be held every other year. But she always must accept the advice of the nation's parliamentary leaders. Since no Danish monarch is permitted to make an important political decision, the crown is kept safely out of the political fray; this insulation from political criticism helps to maintain the popularity of the royal family. Public opinion polls have consistently revealed that about 90% of all Danes are in favor of the monarchy.

The Parliament

Real political authority originates from the popularly elected parliament, called the *Folketing*, which since 1953 has been unicameral. The *Folketing*, which meets in Christiansborg Castle, is composed of not more than 179 members, of which two each must come from Greenland and the Faroe Islands. For electoral purposes, Denmark is divided into three zones—Greater Copenhagen, Jutland and the islands—which are subdivided into 17 districts with a total of 103 constituencies. All Danes 18 years of age or older are eligible to vote. The electoral system is complicated, with proportional representation enabling many parties to win seats in the *Folketing*, despite a requirement that a party must capture at least 2% of the total vote in order to gain *any* seats.

The fact that so many parties are represented in the parliament has prevented any party from gaining a majority of seats during the entire 20th century, and even a majority coalition has become a rarity. Most governments are now minority coalitions which can generally operate for a short while because of a special provision which permits a new government to begin to rule *without* a parliamentary vote of confidence and to continue to rule until a majority can be mustered against it. Nevertheless, few Danish parliaments survive the full four years for which they are elected, and since the 1960s prime ministers have been forced to dissolve the *Folketing* and to call new elections after about two years. The 1988 elections were the 12th in 33 years.

One might expect that under such difficult conditions parliamentary sessions might be tense and uproarious. In fact they are quiet and most civilized. Applause and any form of interruption to show disapproval are strictly forbidden, and members honor extraordinary oratory by quietly handing the person a ten øre coin (a little more than 1 cent). Members now mainly address each other by using the familiar form of the word "you" and often meet together in coffee clubs to make many preliminary decisions.

The growth of government, especially of the welfare portion, has led to the strengthening of the prime minister and his cabinet, whose members are usually, but need not be, members of parliament. Most bills are introduced by the cabinet. It would be a mistake, however, to underestimate the power of the ordinary membership. Because of the absence of steady and reliable majorities, governments must constantly count possible votes in the *Folketing* before making any decision. Further, one–third of the members can demand a referendum on any piece of legislation. This potent weapon is very seldom used, but it is a safeguard against possible disregard by the majority for the concerns of the minority. The constitution also requires a referendum in any case were Denmark agrees to transfer a portion of its sovereignty to an international body. Thus, in 1972, Danes were asked to approve their country's entry into the EC, and about two thirds of them did so.

Since 1955 the *Folketing* has also had the power to appoint an ombudsman, who, with a staff of 12 full–time lawyers and eight clerks, can process the claim of any citizen who thinks he has been treated unjustly by any government official or institution, except the legal courts. The ombudsman may also investigate a matter on his own initiative. He seldom uses his power to initiate legal action, but he frequently makes recommendations to ministries, and they are always acted upon. He can also recommend free legal aid to persons who wish to bring a case against an official, so long as the ombudsman believes that there are good grounds for such proceedings.

A second ombudsman for consumer affairs was created in 1975 with a staff of 22 to process complaints that goods or services were sold through false advertising or unfair marketing methods. In most cases, solutions to these problems have been found through negotiation, rather than through litigation. Whenever businesses are in doubt about the propriety of an advertising or marketing technique, they can request the advice of the ombudsman for consumer affairs in order to find out in advance what might be considered imper-

Denmark

missible. Thus, in Denmark public and business officials alike must be aware that their practices could be investigated by one or the other ombudsman, elected by the *Folketing*.

POLITICAL PARTIES AND GROUPS

Until well into the 1960s parliamentary seats were distributed basically among four parties: the *Social Democratic,* the *Radical–Liberal,* the *Liberal* and the *Conservative.* But the 1960s were in Denmark, as elsewhere in Western Europe and North America, years of ferment. Taxes rose to pay for rapidly expanding social welfare programs. The number of employees in the changing Danish economy threatened the livelihood of some farmers and small merchants. Added to this was a youth revolt which led many persons to ask fundamental questions about the increasingly comfortable technical and materialist society.

These developments gave rise to new parties on the left, while the uneasiness toward rising taxes and budgetary and balance of payments deficits led many Danes to support other unconventional parties. The explosion came in the 1973 elections when five previously unrepresented parties got 36% of the vote, and their percentage has not sunk significantly since. The resulting difficulty in producing a stable government that could confront the pressing economic crisis facing Denmark remains the country's number one political problem.

Danish voters are divided roughly evenly between left and right, but the sheer number of parties that win seats in the *Folketing* makes it difficult to maintain a governing coalition with a stable majority. Ex–Prime Minister Poul Schlüter conceded on New Year's Day 1991: "One certainly can say we don't have Europe's strongest government!" He was right. In January 1993 he resigned after an inquiry found he had lied to parliament. He was replaced by Poul Nyrup Rasmussen, leader of the *Social Democratic Party* and former chief economist of the Confederation of Danish Trade Unions.

The Parties of the Left

Since 1924 the *Social Democratic Party (S)* has been Denmark's most important party and is now headed by Prime Minister Rasmussen. As the party in power in the 1970s, the *Social Democrats* had to pay the price for the chronic economic crisis and for double–digit unemployment and inflation figures. It resigned in 1982. It has always been a relatively unideological reform party with a working class character and close ties to the labor union. In 1961 it eliminated all references to Marx in its party program, and began attracting more and more votes from public servants and employees. One result is that the party became quite heterogeneous, and the intra–party splits between its left and right wings inclined the major trade union federation *(LO)* to become slightly cooler in its support of the party.

In the 1998 elections it won 36% of the votes and climbed from 63 to 65 seats. It faces difficulties as a working–class party in a country in which fewer and fewer people have blue–collar jobs. Also, it is split between leftists who want to move leftward to compete with the *Socialist People's Party*, and those on the right, who wish to move back toward the center. It remains the major governing party in a coalition that has a slender one–vote majority thanks to the smaller *Center Democratic* and *Radical Venstre* parties.

The *Socialist People's Party (SF)* was founded in 1959 by a former head of the Danish Communist Party (DKP) and originally was joined mostly by disaffected communists, who nevertheless advocated a more radical program than that of the *Social Democrats.* (The *DKP* has meanwhile practically disappeared, with only .1% of the votes.) The *SF* is composed mainly of academics and pacifists, and about 60% of its members are employees and civil servants. Its major policies include unilateral disarmament, withdrawal from NATO, an atomic free zone in Scandinavia and increasingly close Nordic economic cooperation rather than Danish orientation toward the allegedly more capitalist EU. It climbed steadily in the 1980s. In 1998 it captured 13 seats with 7.5% of the vote.

Social Democrats have tried to shun this party, but they do depend on its votes on some important issues. By the same token, even limited cooperation with the *Social Democrats* in the past was too much for the *SF's* left wing, which broke away from it in 1967 and formed the *Left Socialist Party.* The latter lost all its seats in 1990, but under the banner *Unity List Red–Green* (EL), it captured 2.7% of the votes and five seats in 1998. Both it and *SF* agreed to support Rasmussen's program in parliament.

One of the four traditional parties and one which is a regular coalition partner of the *Social Democrats* is the *Radical Venstre Party (RV)*, which won seven seats and 3.9% of the votes in 1998. The *RV* was founded in 1905 and is composed of liberals who see themselves as being a little closer to the left than the other non–socialist parties. They advocate the maintenance of an efficient private economy, as well as social reform without socialism. They vote with the conservatives on economic issues, but with the left on foreign and defense policies. When the government collapsed in 1993, *RV*, led by Marianne Jelved, became the king–maker, enabling the *Social Democrats* to rule, on condition that the new government follow Schlüter's fiscal austerity policy. It remained in the government after the 1994 elections.

The Parties of the Center–Right

In recent years the parties of the center and the right have gained ground by promising to reduce taxes and to curb welfare spending. The *Conservative People's Party (KF)*, founded in 1916, is a pragmatic party which defines itself as a party of the political center. It is a staunch advocate of private property and free enterprise, a strong defense and, since the onset of the energy crisis of 1973, of nuclear power. It draws it votes mainly from the middle class and self–employed. In 1998 it declined from 27 seats to 16 and from 15% to only 8.9% of the votes. Its earlier success was due in part to its skillful and popular, Poul Schlüter. In 1982 Schlüter, a lawyer who had never held a ministerial post before, became the first *Conservative* prime minister in Denmark since 1894. Until 1993 he performed as a master at staying in power as the head of shrinking minority governments. *KF* is now in opposition, and its leadership has been assumed by Per Stig Moller.

The *Liberal Venstre Party (V)* was founded in 1870 and was traditionally a farmer's party; now its draws half its votes from cities and towns. It advocates a restriction of the government's activity in the economy, and since the 1970s it has pressed for a reduction of public spending and private consumption in order to cope with the economic crises which have beset Denmark. In 1998 it climbed to 24% of the votes and 43 seats in the *Folketing.*

Prime Minister Poul Nyrup Rasmussen

Denmark

Its leader, Uffe Ellemann–Jensen, resigned after his party's election defeat. This flamboyant former TV newscaster argued that Danes should take advantage of their prosperity to begin reforming the welfare state.

Founded in 1974 by disaffected *Social Democrats* who strongly supported Denmark's entry into the EU and who continue to advocate a strongly European–oriented policy, the *Center Democrats* (CD) define themselves as a middle–of–the–road party. They do cooperate sometimes with the *Social Democrats* in parliament, but they always strongly oppose the influence of the left–wing members of that party. They climbed to 4.3% of the votes and eight seats in 1998. In 1997 it pulled out of the ruling center–left coalition in protest against concessions made to left–wing parties to pass the budget. It finds many votes among the German–speaking minority in northern Schleswig. The *Christian People's Party*, with only 2.4% of the votes and four seats, was established in 1970 as an interdenominational party opposed to such facets of modern Danish society as abortion and pornography.

Without question, the most unusual party and that which has received the most press coverage abroad is the *Progress Party*, which was founded in 1972 around an eccentric, but sharp–witted lawyer and instructor of tax law at the University of Copenhagen, Mogens Glistrup. He was catapulted to prominence in early 1971 when he explained on national television how he legally avoided paying a single øre (penny) of taxes on an income of 3.3 million Danish krone (about $400,000) by taking advantage of tax loopholes. He was able to show to his shocked viewers why, despite the strength of egalitarian ideals in Denmark, wealth is still distributed unevenly. In the 1970s, for instance, one-tenth of all taxpayers owned 62% of the country's wealth; two–tenths owned 81% and three–tenths owned over 92% of the nation's wealth.

The *Progress Party* shot up in 1972, representing a serious revolt against the tax system, high government spending and bureaucracy in general. Glistrup also proposed some bizarre ways to save money, which it must be said, most of the party's voters and members never took very seriously—Denmark should practically disband its diplomatic service, abolish its army and leave NATO. How did he propose that Denmark respond in case of a foreign attack? It should install in advance a telephone answering service with the following recorded message for all aggressors: "Don't get excited. We surrender!" The party is now strongly pro–NATO.

The party's electoral fortunes soared to 16% of the total vote, but by 1998 its percentage had sunk to 2.4% and four seats. This drop was, in part, due to the fact that the party is isolated in parliament, since no party dares to form a coalition with it. The party was weakened by Glistrup's guilty verdict in court two weeks before the 1981 elections; he was sentenced to four years in prison on charges of "gross tax evasion." He had devised for himself and about 20,000 clients an almost perfect system of avoiding paying taxes. In 1990 he was expelled from the party. The *Progressives'* success makes the formation of a conservative alternative to the *Social Democrats* most difficult. Party leader Pia Kjaersgaard explained in 1988: "Higher taxes! People are fed up with being plundered!" Since the government had not lowered tax rates significantly, this anti–tax message continues to draw crowds.

There also is an explosive issue which the *Progress Party* exploited: growing discontent over a flood of refugees, particularly Iranians, into Denmark. Glistrup dared to utter that "they breed like rats." In 1984 parliament introduced a law preventing border police from turning back people who claim political exile. As a result, the flood of refugees soared from several hundred in 1984 to 9,000 in 1985. By 1986 they were pouring in at a rate of 1,000 per week. This resulted in insulting graffiti on Danish walls and unpleasant racial incidents. One sign of discontent was that during the first nine months of 1986, some 15,000 Danes resigned from the Red Cross, the organization responsible for taking care of new arrivals. This dissatisfaction prompted parliament to amend the liberal asylum law. Denmark has only about 180,000 immigrants from outside the EU and Nordic region. Nevertheless, a 1998 poll revealed that almost half of all Danes admitted to being "racist" or "fairly racist," the second–highest ratio in Europe (after Belgium) and the largest in the Nordic world. In 1995 four MPs left the *Progress Party* and formed the *Danish People's Party* (DF), led by Pia Kjaersgaard. With slogans like "Denmark is for the Danes," it did very well in 1998, winning 7.4% of the votes and 13 seats.

The main comic relief in the 1994 elections was provided by the *Party of Consciously Workshy Elements*, "led" by comedian Jacob Haugaard. Campaigning on a platform demanding "a tail wind for cyclists, better Christmas presents, and more nutella [a chocolate–nut breakfast spread] for soldiers," Haugaard captured a seat in his Jutland constituency. He decided that running again in 1998 was simply too much work.

Provincial and Local Government

There are several other levels of government in Denmark—it is divided into 14 provinces, each led by elected provincial councils headed by a mayor (*Amtsborgmester*) elected by the council from among it own members. There are also 270 primary municipalities led by elected municipal councils. Two other major areas under Danish jurisdiction have complete authority in domestic affairs, with only foreign and defense policy emanating from Copenhagen: Greenland and the Faroe Islands. Each is allowed to send two MPs to the *Folketing*.

Outlying Lands: Greenland and the Faroe Islands

Greenland, which at one point is only 14–1/2 miles from Canada, is the world's largest island and is 50 times the size of Denmark and about one–third the size of the U.S. Over 80% of its majestic but dangerous area lies under permanent ice and snow, which continually breaks off into the ocean forming many of the world's icebergs. The narrow coastal strip around much of the island (a strip which itself is eight times the size of Denmark) is tundra, on which trees cannot grow higher than knee level. Only about a fifth of Greenland's 56,000 population is Danish. The rest are natives of Eskimo or mixed backgrounds, who speak an Eskimo dialect, although they learn Danish in schools. Most live in the 120 or so towns or settlements located chiefly along the southwestern coast, the largest being the capital, Nuuk (formerly Godthaab). Nuuk is a modern city of 11,000 inhabitants with first–class Danish hotels and five–story apartment houses, which differ little from European dwellings, except that cod and seal skins often hang on lines from balconies along with jeans and fashionable Danish clothes.

Greenland (which the natives call Kalâdlit Nunât, or "Land of People") was made an integral part of Denmark in 1953, but a new generation of Greenlanders wanted more direct control over their island's destiny. Denmark made it known that it would respect the people's wishes. In 1979, following a referendum in Greenland, the island was granted self–government as a "distinct community within the Kingdom of Denmark." The native population determines its own domestic affairs through a 21–member locally elected assembly called the *Landsting* and an executive called the *Landsstyre*. Denmark continues to determine foreign and defense matters and is represented in Greenland by the Queen's High Commissioner. The autonomy status does not affect the island's inclusion in NATO or the status of the Danish–American air bases at Soendre, Stroemfjord and Narssarssuaq, nor of the installation in Thule. There, a giant radar is located roughly half way along

Denmark

the shortest route between the U.S. and Russia, and Thule therefore plays a crucial role in the American early warning system.

Three years after receiving limited self–rule, Greenlanders voted against remaining in the EU. It thereby became the first element to ever leave the EU. In the first referendum over the membership in 1972, over 70% of the Greenlanders had voted against entry, but they were swamped by the Danish majority. Ten years later, after haggling with Brussels over fishing rights and with Danes over mining rights on the island, and after having achieved political autonomy and more self–confidence, the islanders decided to leave the EU, which had poured from $10 to $20 millions' worth of investments into Greenland every year.

The 1983 electoral victory of the two parties which were committed to withdrawal from the EU—the socialist *Forward Party* and the leftist *Eskimo Movement*—was the prelude for Greenland's final decision in 1985 to leave the EU. Denmark continues to send it costly subsidies, amounting to about $200 million per year, as well as thousands of technicians and advisers, without whom the island could not hope to survive in its present form. With economic and social modernization having only begun in the 1950s, Greenland is very dependent upon Danish expertise to build and operate housing units, hospitals (which have helped double average life expectancy since the 1950s), schools, power plants and communication and transportation facilities. The last is particularly difficult because there are no trains or roads between towns and settlements.

The essential services which Danes perform should not, in the opinion of some islanders, give the Danes control over the island's economy and resources. The people live primarily from fishing and sealing, as well as from jobs in the public sector, and they raise sheep, lamb and reindeer. Under the ice there are also such minerals as zinc, lead and cryolite, which are already mined, as well as iron ore, uranium, nickel, molybdenum and perhaps oil, which may be extracted one day. The compromise to which the Danes and Greenlanders agreed during the negotiations over autonomy was that each side would have a veto right over the exploitation and sale of Greenland's natural resources. This compromise was necessary, but it will undoubtedly bring many disagreements in the future.

In the meantime, Greenlanders and their Danish helpers must cope with many social problems which have emerged as a result of the extremely rapid movement of most natives from an isolated existence at the edge of civilization into modern life. This sudden change risks the collapse of the old way of life before a new one emerges. The results are heavy unemployment among the young, venereal diseases and the familiar scourge of alcoholism. Today, nine out of ten crimes on the island stem from the latter, and any visitor sees its presence in Greenland almost everywhere he looks. The suicide rate is nearly 17 times as great as in 1960 and four times that of of Denmark, which itself has one of the world's highest levels of suicide. Social challenges to Danes and native islanders are very great.

The Faroes, an archipelago of 18 islands in the North Atlantic between Norway, Scotland and Iceland, have a rough and beautiful landscape of mountain peaks, high plateaus, valleys and fjords. These islands are not well suited to farming, but they are ideal for sheep and cattle grazing. Its waters were also full of fish, which provided work for a fourth of the labor force and comprised over 90% of the islanders' exports. Fish were the foundation for the islander's economy until the industry collapsed due to overfishing. This dragged the rest of the islands' economy down with it. By 1994 unemployment had reached 20%, and about 9% of the population had been forced to emigrate. Only a series of emergency aid packages from Copenhagen have staved off bankruptcy. The 43,000 Faroese are descendants of the Norse settlers who came during the Viking era, and they still speak their own language, which is related to Icelandic and certain western Norwegian dialects. Of course, all Faroese also speak Danish.

The islands have been self–governing within the Kingdom of Denmark since 1948. The ancient, locally elected parliament, the *Lögting*, and the executive, the *Landsstýcri*, are responsible for all matters except those involving foreign policy, defense, the police, the courts and the Church. The Faroese have their own flag, postage stamps and paper money. They do use Danish coins. Denmark pays for about a third of all public spending. Such support enabled the islanders to have a higher average income than the Danes themselves until the islands' economy turned sour in the 1990s.

The local inhabitants do not allow the Danes to make the most important economic decisions for them. They decided in 1974 not to be a part of the EU, fearing that the EU's fish policy might threaten that industry. They have also resisted all temptations either to permit the search for oil within their 200–mile economic zone or the establishment of what could be a lucrative tourist industry in the islands. They are in NATO, though, and have a small radar station. While the Faroese do not want to seal themselves off from the outside world, they do wish to avoid anything which could disturb their quiet island life, their cultural independence or their native language.

ECONOMY

Denmark has long ceased being a primarily agricultural country, although its production in that sector is generally efficient and is an important component of its foreign trade. Denmark is now highly industrialized, even though it almost totally lacks raw materials, except salt and newly–discovered North Sea oil and gas, which may eventually be capable of supplying up to a third of the country's energy needs. What the Danes lack in raw materials they must make up for in highly skilled labor and high quality production. They must work with their brains and they must have a sharp eye for niches in the world market which they could fill quickly and with a minimum of materials. This requires imagination and adaptability to customers' tastes, and these requirements are well suited to Danish ingenuity and the small size of Danish firms.

Danes specialize in finished goods and have moved in on highly specialized markets. For example, it is the world's largest supplier of insulin for diabetics and of industrial enzymes. It also has a large share of the world market in marine diesel engines, hearing aids (especially those attached to eye glasses), and radio telephones. It produces Lego toys, which can be found in children's playrooms all over Western Europe and North America; 98% of its sales are abroad. Legoland Park outside Copenhagen attracts more than a million visitors a year and has become Denmark's biggest tourist attraction. Danish furniture is known for quality, design and flair. It also has become the world's largest exporter of a particularly familiar product throughout the world: beer. This is primarily because of the Carlsberg–Tuborg brewery group, which also has sizable operations in the U.S.

As a highly prosperous nation with a small domestic market, Denmark is extremely dependent upon foreign trade. Indeed, it has one of the highest levels of foreign trade per inhabitant in the world. Industrial exports constitute from 35% to 40% of its total production, and few Danish farmers could hope to survive if the country's foreign agriculture markets were lost. More than half its industrial exports go to other EU countries (mainly to the U.K. and Germany). With such dependency upon exporting, it is no surprise that Denmark pursues a liberal (free) trade policy and chooses to remain in the EU, despite lingering opposition to mem-

Denmark

bership. After Sweden and Finland joined in 1995, with the possibility that enlargement will some day extend deep into eastern Europe, a Danish exit from the EU is no longer a feasible option.

Industry is overwhelmingly privately owned. The central or local government authorities operate only the postal service, gas works, electricity generation, ports, certain transportation companies and some other services belonging to the country's economic infrastructure. The state does not engage in industrial production and it is seldom willing to subsidize lame–duck industries! Also, only about one–twelfth of its industry is foreign–owned. Firms are of small or medium size, with an average of 60 employees. Almost half employ less than 20. It is nevertheless true that most industrial exports stem from medium or large–sized firms, but Danes have never tried to build up gigantic industries, such as steel, automobile or aircraft production. Anticipating the single EU market in 1992, mergers took place in basic Danish industries like foodstuffs, sugar and alcohol which amounted to be the most far–reaching restructuring of Danish industry in a century. Finally, industry is geographically dispersed—there is no one concentrated industrial region.

Labor and Employers

Labor and employers are highly organized. The *Confederation of Danish Employers (DA)* represents 159 employer and manufacturer organizations. The *National Organization of Trade Unions (LO)* links 1,699 unions, which organize about 85% of all wage earners, one of the highest percentages in the free world. *DA* and *LO* collectively negotiate wages and working hours every two years, and the government intervenes only if the two sides cannot agree. In that case, the *Folketing* legislates the final proposals presented by an impartial mediator. Strikes are forbidden while a valid agreement is still in force, and there are relatively few strikes.

One highly explosive difference of opinion which exists between employers and the trade unions is the latters' wish to introduce what they call "economic democracy." There are already forms of employee participation in the firms' decision-making, but this does not extend to sharing profits. Supported by the *Social Democratic* and other leftist parties, the *LO* maintains that the unions should be given a portion of the businesses' value which the employees helped to create. There are many different proposals, but all call, in general, for 5% of all wages to be put into special funds under the control of the unions. These funds, provided by the employers, would be used to buy shares in industries, which would then be owned by the unions, not individuals, who would nevertheless derive some kind of financial benefit from this upon retirement.

Employers quickly noted that such a practice would enable the unions to gain quickly a controlling share in most industries, despite the fact that the Danish constitution would forbid this share to exceed 49%. The spectre of the trade unions *controlling* the economy horrifies businessmen and others, but it delights some persons who think that such a measure would make Denmark a more just society. By the end of the 1980s, these funds were already cash–rich and were even being invested in a variety of ways, including agriculture. In 1990 the Schlüter government initiated moves to restrict the unions' power to maintain closed shops and to pass on union dues to political parties, in effect to the *Social Democrats*.

A fish vendor

Agriculture

The percentage of Danes engaged in agriculture and fisheries has fallen to only 5%, although the food industry provides between 12% and 18% of domestic employment. Two–thirds of farms have been merged or converted to other use since the Second World War. About two–thirds of the land is still used for farming, almost entirely by single family, and non–farmers are not allowed to own farmland. However, there are fears similar to those in the U.S. that many family farms may fail. Favorable climate, good soil, and careful, but intensive land use, result in the country's having two to three times as much farmland per inhabitant as do its more densely populated, but less efficient, EU partners—it maintains the highest productivity and export of farm produce per capita in all Europe. Agriculture accounts for 25% of its merchandise exports. This has helped Denmark produce three

Denmark

times as much food as its own citizens need and it sells about 70% of its produce abroad; these sales account for about a third of its foreign currency earnings, making Denmark the world's fifth-largest exporter of food products. EU countries purchase about two-third of its farm exports, which is an important reason why Danes chose to join the EU in 1972. Americans, who have developed a taste for Danish cheese and canned hams, are the second largest purchasers.

About 90% of the farmers' total income is derived from animal products, and only 10% from grain. Its major animal is the pig, almost 80% of which are exported, primarily to the U.K. A few farmers have discovered that mink-raising can be quite profitable, and Denmark is now one of the world's main suppliers of these skins. Farmers have retained powerful clout through the Agricultural Council. The farmers themselves came under severe attack by ecologists, who claim agricultural methods and materials pollute the earth.

Shipping and Fishing

All Danes are surrounded by the sea and have understandably always been a seafaring people. Except for such "flag of convenience" states as Liberia, only Norway and Greece have more shipping tonnage per capita than does Denmark. Most of the fleet *never* docks in Danish ports, but 85% of all ships sailing Baltic waters have Copenhagen as their home port. Shipping provides close to a tenth of the country's total foreign currency earnings, ranking behind industry and agriculture, but ahead of tourism and fishing.

Two of the world's largest shipping companies, A.P. Møller and the East Asiatic Company, are Danish. The crisis in world shipping has undeniably been felt in Denmark. Since 1973 its fleet has declined in numbers, and its share of the world's merchant shipping dropped from 1.76% in the early 1960s to 1.36% at the beginning of the 1980s. Fewer new vessels are on order in Danish shipyards than at any time since 1950, but in the 1990s it remains the world's largest shipbuilder after Japan and Korea. A major reason for the decline in the competitiveness of Danish shipping is, without question, the wage levels, which doubled from 1972 to 1978.

Denmark is among the top ten fishing nations in the world. An unusual feature among fishing nations is that company activity is almost unknown in Denmark. Almost all fishing vessels are owned by the captains; each ship's earnings entirely depend upon the catch, and the crews share in the distribution of profits. It is not surprising that there are no strikes in this sector. Vessels fish mainly in the North and Baltic Seas, but there is an important problem: access to Norwegian, Swedish, or EU countries' waters has been restricted or eliminated. Danes face a general problem in these waters—there are too many fishermen chasing too few fish. The Danes' most important fish for use as food is cod, and for industrial use, the sand eel. Their major buyers are the EU, Sweden, Switzerland and the U.S. About six hundred inland trout farms have sprung up, made possible sometimes by springwater and a cool climate.

The 1970s Oil Crisis

Like most industrialized countries, Denmark underwent a major conversion in the 1950s and 1960s from coal to oil, and by 1972 its dependence on imported oil had swelled to 93% of its energy consumption. Thus, when the first oil crisis shook the world in 1973, Denmark was unprepared. This was especially so since it had seemed to have obtained very little from the portion of the North Sea which had been carved out for it. Danes have so far resisted nuclear energy, but they have switched many power plants from oil to coal, with the goal of fueling at least 80% of them with coal. Power plants are also being geared to provide district heating (whereby heat is pumped into individual dwellings from a central plant) for about 40% of households. About 30% are heated by gas, either in individual furnaces, or from district heating systems. Finally, energy conservation measures help Danes continue to reduce their oil consumption.

Any visitor to the country can see that the average Dane lives a very prosperous life and that there is very little visible poverty in the country. Average per capita income is among the highest in the world. Almost 60% of households own the houses and apartments in which they live. The average Dane spends only a sixth of his income on housing and a fourth on food, drink and tobacco. In 1992 the Washington-based Population Crisis Committee concluded that of 140 countries it studied Denmark has the highest quality of life; Sweden and Finland were not in the top ten.

Social Benefits and Taxation

Most Danes have supported the development of a comprehensive social welfare system, whose underlying philosophy is that a society should be judged by the way it treats its weakest members and that individuals are very seldom personally responsible for the social problems from which they might suffer. Therefore, the public should support any person unable to support himself. As a rule, these assistance funds come directly from tax revenues, *not* from insurance schemes to which the beneficiaries must contribute. Also, one qualifies for benefits merely by being a resident of Denmark, which means that foreigners can receive roughly the same benefits as can citizens. The fact that the state pays the cost of child-bearing, funerals and burials indicates that the country literally has a cradle-to-the-grave welfare system.

Danes work an average of 37.5 hours a week, have four weeks of paid vacation, receive 90% of their previous income for up to three and a half years as well as retraining and relocation expenses in case of unemployment, and can claim a state pension at age 62 (55 for widows). The government's decision in 1998 to raise the retirement from 60 to 62 was understandably unpopular. Medical care is free, unless the patient chooses his own doctor, in which case he pays a portion of the fee. Mothers receive maternity benefits up to 14 weeks. Over four decades of welfare legislation culminated in a comprehensive assistance act of 1976, which guarantees every resident in need economic aid not merely to survive, but also to maintain the standard of living to which the person had become accustomed.

Many foreigners greatly admire such a complete welfare system, but the reverse side of the coin is one of the world's highest tax levels and the highest of any EU country. The income tax, which constitutes about two-thirds of all taxes, is heavily progressive, and even those with middle incomes feel the bite. The marginal personal income tax rate is 68%, and the minimum marginal rate is 51%; a tax reform in 1993 aims to reduce those rates to 63% and 43% respectively within five years. Corporate rates are 34%. Denmark also has the EU's highest taxes on many consumer goods; for instance, cars are taxed at twice their original price. The VAT stands at 25%, the highest in the EU. Over half of the population's earnings is collected by the state.

Many Danes have begun to wonder whether welfare assistance and other forms of government spending have gone too far. Unemployment pay is higher than the minimum wage, so many Danes prefer to collect the unemployment benefits than to go back to work by taking a low-paying job. To stem this trend, Danes voted yes in a 1996 referendum which declares that persons below the age of 25 are no longer permitted to collect full unemployment benefits. Demonstrating how far some people want to extend the welfare state, one prominent *Social Democrat* proposed in 1989 that the six week maternity leave should be supplemented by a special leave to *propagate* (albeit only for those in jobs with a high risk of low fertility). These kinds of questions and abuses

Denmark

have fueled both tax evasion and tax revolts. Taxes on automobiles equal twice their price, and high taxes on electronics, alcohol and tobacco have sent Danes (whose alcohol consumption is the highest in the Nordic world) over the German border in droves to shop for these items.

In 1998 one million Danes of working age, one–fifth of the population, were still in one way or another dependent on welfare for their income. The costly welfare system has not rid Denmark of some seemingly intractable problems. In 1987 about 30,000 persons were considered by researchers to be "down and outs"— homeless who were usually alcoholics or drug addicts and who were entirely dependent on welfare payments for survival. Another 120,000 to 150,000 faced serious economic hardship. Also, the suicide rate is one of the highest in the world.

The desire for a high standard of living despite high tax levels has also contributed to the inclination of more and more women to work; 76% of Danish women between the ages of 16 and 66 have jobs, compared with 37% in 1950. Only one in five children is cared for by a full–time parent. One social by–product of the enormous increase in working wives is that the birth rate is declining. Denmark will increasingly be facing the demographic problem caused by growing numbers of older citizens being supported by a shrinking working population.

Economic Reform

Like many other people, including Americans, Danes lived beyond their means. Public spending grew rapidly; the deficit rose 500% from 1975 to 1984 and it doubled from 1980 to 1982, reaching 13% of the GDP by 1983. The government had had no budget surplus since 1974, and it has had difficulty exercising the kind of financial restraint which would be necessary to check the growth in its foreign borrowing and in inflation. After 1940, prices doubled every seven years.

By 1982, the government's debt had grown to such heights that the total cost of servicing it was equal to the entire income tax revenue. Particularly worrisome was the foreign debt, which rose from 12% of the GDP in 1975 to 38% and which remains a problem, even though it had declined to 30% by 1993. This dizzying growth so damaged the country's credit worthiness that the IMF and Standard and Poor's added Denmark to their "credit watch" list in 1982 and further lowered its rating in 1983. As a Copenhagen banker admitted "we have been living too well on borrowed money. We were on the way to hell, but we were doing it first class."

There was a long–term trend since 1973 toward growing trade and balance of payments deficits. Rising wages negatively affected the competitiveness of Danish exports, and some of its markets were shrinking or lost. Too much of the labor force had shifted from industrial to non–productive public sector jobs. In 1974 there were 550,000 Danes working in the public sector, but only five years later the number stood at 750,000.

Only a partial sacrifice of the high standard of living could put the country's financial books back in order, and that is exactly what the Schlüter and Rasmussen governments did. It made sweeping cuts throughout the economy, including the social welfare programs. It abolished the automatic indexing for wages and welfare benefits which tied them to inflation, and imposed severe statutory limits on wage rises in both the public and private sectors. It also cut public borrowing and vowed to maintain the value of the currency. It consciously slowed down economic growth and placed a higher priority on combatting inflation than on reducing unemployment.

The medicine worked and saved Denmark from the financial abyss. By 1999 it had lowered inflation to 2.3%, reduced the national debt to 66.8% of GDP and its annual budget deficit to only 1% of GDP, improved exports and created a current accounts surplus of 3% of GDP, one of the largest in the OECD in relation to size of economy. Denmark's financial institutions were also strengthened through mergers, and it escaped the serious problems facing banking in the other Nordic countries. Its economic growth averaged only 1% of GDP in the five years before 1993, but by 1997 its annual growth rose to 2.7%. Also, unemployment surged to 12.5% by 1994, but it had declined to 5.9% by 1999.

An ambitious austerity program is not easy for governing coalitions that had no majority in parliament and ruled a nation long–accustomed to annual increases in real wages and welfare spending. But many Danes are encouraged that their country has begun to overcome the addiction to borrowing. Economic optimism has returned. Nevertheless, Denmark will continue for many years to be both wealthy and debt–ridden.

CULTURE

Literature

It is difficult for a small country with its own language to gain the world's attention to certain aspects of its culture. Although the Danish language is understood, albeit with some difficulty, by other Scandinavians, it cannot be understood at all by German and Dutch speakers, although all three languages are of Germanic origin. The geographically restricted reach of Danish has meant that most Danish literature remains unknown in the rest of the world even though it publishes more books per copy than any other nation in the world except Iceland. The major exception is the literary giant, Hans Christian Andersen (1805–1875), whose folk tales filled with fantasies and down–to–earth moral insights have delighted children (and adults!) for generations. Andersen's mind has become a part of many persons' childhood: "The Princess and the Pea," "The Emperor's New Clothes," "The Steadfast Tin Soldier" and "The Little Mermaid" (memorialized by a statue in Copenhagen harbor, which is one of the city's most beloved landmarks) and many other delightful tales. In 1998 the maiden's statue was beheaded for the second time in 33 years. After three days a hooded figure dropped the head off at a television station, and police suspected that the culprits were to be found in the feminist protest milieu.

Andersen has by far the greatest international reputation of any Danish author, but Denmark has many other writers of which it can be proud. In the 18th century Ludvig Holberg wrote many comedies and a novel of fantasy, *Niels Klim's Journey to the World Underground,* which is a delightful plea for religious tolerance. A more intensive Christianity was presented in the lyrics of Johannes Ewald (1743–1781), especially *Ode to the Soul.*

In the 19th century other Danish authors dealt with spiritual matters. Perhaps the most profound and the one with the greatest impact upon philosophical and theological thinking in the western world was Søren Kierkegaard (1813–1855), the father of existentialism. He attempted to get people to reflect on their own existence and to realize that human life is a problem and demands choices and self-creation.

N.F.S. Grundtvig pointed to the spoken, live word as the key to a human and Christian community, and his novel *Adam Homo* is now translated and accessible to the English–reading audience. Another important Danish work, *Seven Gothic Tales,* appeared first in English in 1934 under the pen name of Isak Dinesen, a year before it was rewritten in Danish by its author, Karen Blixen. Her work dealt with man's religious life, and she argues that man is a mere marionette of God and that he should simply live out the destiny to which God assigns him. Blixen is best known throughout the world for her book, *Out of Africa,* later made into a hit film, an engaging portrayal of her two decades living and farming in Kenya. Peter Høeg more recently gave Danish literature a worldwide audience with his

Denmark

The Little Mermaid

best-selling novel, *Miss Smilla's Feeling for Snow*.

Religion has played very little part in post–World War II Danish literature, with the notable exception of Martin Hanson's *The Liar*. Some authors, such as Thorkild Hansen, in his three–volume biography of Knut Hamsun, have dealt with Denmark's experiences under Nazi domination. Others, such as Villy Sørenson, Niels I. Meyer and K. Helveg Peterson, focus on the problems arising from the individual's life in a prosperous, materialist society and offer neo–Marxist solutions to contemporary problems. Dea Trier Mørch, Elsa Gress and Suzanne Brøgger have produced sensitive literature focusing on women's roles in society. They also produced a satirical response by one of Denmark's most popular contemporary authors, Klaus Rifberg, in his 1978 novel *Dobbeltgaenger* ("The Double"). Others, such as Peter Seeberg and Ole Sarvig, have written modern experimental novels and Thorkild Bjørnvig, Marianne Larsen and Henrik Nordbrandt, have written lyrical poetry which commands an attentive audience in Denmark today.

The 1930s brought three outstanding Danish playwrights to public acclaim. Kaj Munk was a clergyman deeply influenced by Kierkegaard. He wrote about strong men who tried to accomplish great things, but who were doomed to failure by man's inherent sinfulness. Munk was executed by the German occupation force for resistance activities. Soya produced realistic drama, and Kjeld Abell in his plays rebelled against the boredom and mediocrity of bourgeois society.

The Arts

It cannot be said that the Danes are passionate theater fans. A 1975 survey revealed that only 16% of the population ever attends a performance. Also, theater in Denmark is not commercially viable. The state provides a variety of subsidies to keep the 15 theaters in Copenhagen and ten in the provinces alive. In general, the state gives financial support to most of the arts, on the principle that it has a duty to provide an economic foundation for Danish culture without interfering with it. Artistic freedom is always to be respected. The Ministry of Cultural Affairs also supports efforts to bring traditional culture to Danes who have little education in order to try to close what some Danes see as a "cultural gap." It finances activity centers and events in working class areas, but the efforts to expand cultural opportunities have not yet proven to be very successful. Such costly programs, as well as financial support for art and artists, are increasingly criticized by many Danes, who feel that tax money could be better spent for other more immediate economic needs.

The only theaters open during the summer months and comprehensible to non–Danish speaking persons is the Pantomime Theater, which has a long tradition of artistic excellence. The Tivoli Gardens, in which this theater is located, is filled with amusements and cafés and is certainly one of the world's most famous and delightful parks.

A Dane, Carl T. Dreyer, was an early film pioneer, with such films as "Jeanne d'Arc." No Danish filmmaker today would dare try to produce a film without state aid. Because of such aid, about 20 films a year are made, most of them focusing on everyday life in a very realistic way. The only Danish director with an international reputation today is Henning Carlsen, but such directors as Henning Kristiansen, Morten Arnfred, Astrid Henning-Jensen, Anders Refn, Edward Fleming, Bille August, Hans Kristensen and Jørgen Leth, create films for an avid Danish audience.

The towering figure in Danish music was Carl Nielsen (1865–1931), who gained a wide international public. Other composers, such as Per Nørgård, Ib Nørholm, Hans Abrahamsen, Erik Norby, Bo Holten and Poul Ruders have also been creative and successful. Thanks to such American

Denmark

artists as Thad Jones, Copenhagen has become one of Europe's major jazz centers. Denmark is also a European ballet center. The Royal Danish Ballet's international fame was established in the 19th century by August Bournonville. It is housed in the Royal Theater in Copenhagen and has its own school, where talented youngsters from age seven to sixteen are trained. It has been particularly successful in producing great male dancers, such as Erik Bruhn, Peter Martins and Peter Schaufuss.

At the forefront of Danish artistic achievement are the sculptor, Bertel Thorvaldsen (1770–1844) and the painter C.W. Eckersberg (1783–1853). Thorvaldsen achieved an international breakthrough in Rome and came to be the most renowned sculptor of his day. Eckersberg also made his breakthrough abroad as a pupil of Jacques Louis David in Paris. From David he learned to observe nature very closely and to reproduce it honestly. His numerous paintings of the Danish coasts, countryside and prominent citizens of Copenhagen provide the modern viewer with a valuable look at 19th century Denmark. He also taught at the Academy of Art, which had been founded in Copenhagen in 1754. There he was able to launch an entire school of Danish painters, which included Christen Købke, who preferred to paint Danish churches and the outskirts of Copenhagen, where town and country met.

In the 1940s, daring Danish painters and sculptors, such as Richard Mortensen, Mogens Andersen and Robert Jacobsen, experimented in modern styles in non-figurative art. Contemporary Danish artists, such as Jørgen Haugen Sørensen, Egon Fischer, Willy Ørskov, Niels Strøbek, Per Kirkeby, Stig Brøgger, Paul Gernes and Tonning Rasmussen, have continued the experimentalist tradition. This has had an important impact on industrial products and furniture, in which Danish design has been very innovative, as well as commercially successful.

Religion

The focus of some of Denmark's greatest literature on religious subjects should not leave one with the impression that Danes are a deeply religious people today. They are not. A recent survey indicated that only 45% of the adults believe that there is a God and the low church attendance on Sundays reveals that Danes are not a people greatly concerned with religious questions and matters. A 1987 survey revealed that more Danes believe in reincarnation than in the Christian doctrine of the resurrection of the body and that there are more full-time teachers of new, non-Christian religions in Denmark than there are priests in the state Church, the Evangelical Lutheran Established Church, which receives financial support from the government.

Nevertheless, the official Church is so enmeshed in Danish society that over 90% of all Danes belong to the Church, although they are free to leave it. In fact, only one person in Denmark is required to belong to the state church: the reigning monarch. More than half the marriages take place in a church, and over 80% of Danish children are christened; over 95% are buried from the Church. The Church is there when desired—sometimes Christmas, Easter, and for family needs. It remains to be seen how many homosexual couples will marry in the Church. A 1988 law grants them the legal status of married couples, including inheritance, tax deductions and alimony, but excluding the right to adopt children. This is the first such law in the world. The social event of 1989 was a group marriage of ten gay couples in Copenhagen's city hall.

Education

All children are required to attend at least nine years of school, from ages seven to sixteen. All public education, which is administered and largely financed by local governments, is free from elementary school through the university. About 5% of the Danish children at the primary or lower secondary level attend private schools. It is very easy to found a private school in Denmark, and the local government authorities ask very few questions about the proposed schools' educational philosophies before granting them the usual 70% state subsidy for non-public schools.

The egalitarian goal of many Danes is revealed by the facts that during the first seven years of schooling, numerical grades and required tests cannot be given. Many Danes fear that lasting social distinctions among citizens could be created if younger children received such grades and tests. However, from the eighth grade on, voluntary examinations can be given to those pupils who want to take them in order to enter institutions of higher education, and pupils also can be issued grades if the parents desire this to be done. Attempts by some left-wing politicians and educators to abolish all grades and examinations have not yet found a political majority.

After the 7th grade, about 30% of the pupils choose to pursue vocational studies, while the rest follow courses which could lead to the grammar school (*gymnasium*) and, after a three-year course, to university or higher technical studies. Grammar school graduates must pass a University Entrance Examination, and others must have passed a separate Higher Preparatory Examination in order to win one of the restricted places at the universities.

The oldest is Copenhagen University, established in 1479 and others are in Arhus, Odense, Roskilde and Alborg. Separate colleges, such as the Dental Colleges of Copenhagen and Arhus, the Royal Danish Conservatory of Music, the Royal Danish College of Pharmacy and the Royal Academy of Fine Arts, teach specialized subjects which are not normally taught at the Danish universities. As a sign of the times, there has been a shift in the subjects which students choose to study. In 1976 half chose liberal arts majors leading to teaching or civil service, while only a fifth chose majors targeting the private sector. By 1991 fewer than a fifth opt for majors relevant to the public sector, while more than 40% prepare for employment in business, computers, and engineering. Men are predominant in these fields, while most of the law and theology students and 80% of the medical students are women. Among the only professions in which women match or exceed their share of the general population are medicine and diplomacy; the foreign service makes sure that half its new recruits are women.

The Media

Radio and television programming is the responsibility of Radio Denmark, a publicly-owned corporation managed independently by 27 persons chosen by the *Folketing*. All broadcasting is financed by license fees, and in 1988 a new second television channel became operational on which commercial advertising is permitted for the first time. This broke the state-run TV monopoly, and almost all observers agree that the presence of a second channel has improved the quality of the government-run station. In 1996 Danes were glued to their televisions watching their Olympic team win more gold medals than anyone expected and the first Dane ever to win the Tour de France bike race, Bjarne Riis.

Many Danes still rely on the 55 daily newspapers, almost a dozen of which are published in Copenhagen, for much of their news. The most respected of the larger newspapers are *Politiken* and *Berlingske Tidender*. The latter is one of Europe's oldest newspapers. It was the first European newspaper to publish the text of the American Declaration of Independence. It is a conservative and middle-class newspaper, which has come very close to bankruptcy in the past, due in part to its employees' resistance to any measures of economic restraint. Many Danes wanted the latter to survive because it is the major non-socialist voice in a predominantly left-oriented mass media landscape. It is now prof-

Denmark

itable. Both of the above newspapers decided in 1986 to launch Sunday editions.

Most Danish newspapers have severed their ties with political parties, with the *Social Democratic Party's Aktuelt* being the only exception. It now publishes a less politicized Sunday edition, *Det Fri Aktuelt*. There are also specialized newspapers, such as *Børsen* for businessmen, and the fast-growing *Information,* for the intellectual left. One non-Copenhagen newspaper has a national outlook and circulation: the slightly conservative *Jyllands-Posten,* published in Århus.

FUTURE

Denmark's major problems will continue to be economic, although there has been much improvement in this regard. Denmark is much more sure of itself now that its economy has become one of Europe's strongest. Danes' tolerance and capacity for compromise will prevent the country's remaining economic difficulties from producing a real political crisis, in which the democratic order would be threatened. The debilitating conflicts over NATO have given way to a broad consensus of support. During the 1991 war in the Persian Gulf, pro-American and pro-NATO attitudes were at a visible high. It supported the NATO air war over Yugoslavia in 1999 and enthusiastically endeavors to establish and tighten links with the Baltic states, especially Lithuania. It helped create a Danish-German-Polish corps that has its headquarters in the Polish city of Szczecin (Stettin) along Germany's border.

It has been openly uneasy about the Maastricht Treaty. Referring to the EU, Foreign Minister Niels Helveg Petersen said: "We are not ardent integrationists." In 1993 Danes nevertheless decided that their future belongs in the EU. In the previous year, a very narrow majority had rejected the Maastricht Agreement in a referendum, expressing concerns heard in other EU countries: unelected bureaucrats in Brussels were concentrating too much power and acting with a heavy hand. Worse, they operated outside of democratic control and were rushing Europeans into greater unity by fiat.

After having negotiated four "opt-outs" from the EU, meaning that Denmark would not take part in the monetary union, common citizenship, cooperation in domestic and justice affairs, or defense, the government again took the question to the people, this time actively campaigning for a yes vote. Also in the yes camp were virtually all of Denmark's political, economic and media establishment. Although 57% of voters said yes, Denmark was left deeply divided. On May 28, 1998, voters decided not to adopt the Euro in the first round. But Denmark agreed to keep the krone in a band within 2.25% of the Euro. Thus it will be ready to join whenever it chooses to do so.

Danes went to the polls in 1994 to decide which economic course their country should take: to try to tackle the unacceptably high unemployment rate while sustaining the welfare state, as the current Rasmussen government insists, or to pursue structural reforms to reduce unemployment, as the opposition *Liberal* opposition proposes. Voters preferred Rasmussen's approach, but they retained him as prime minister only as the head of a minority government. In March 1998 voters again kept Rasmussen's government in office by the narrowest of margins. It won ninety seats in the 179-seat assembly. Despite his one-seat majority, the prime minister said that his economic policy would stay on course.

Tivoli Gardens

The Republic of Finland

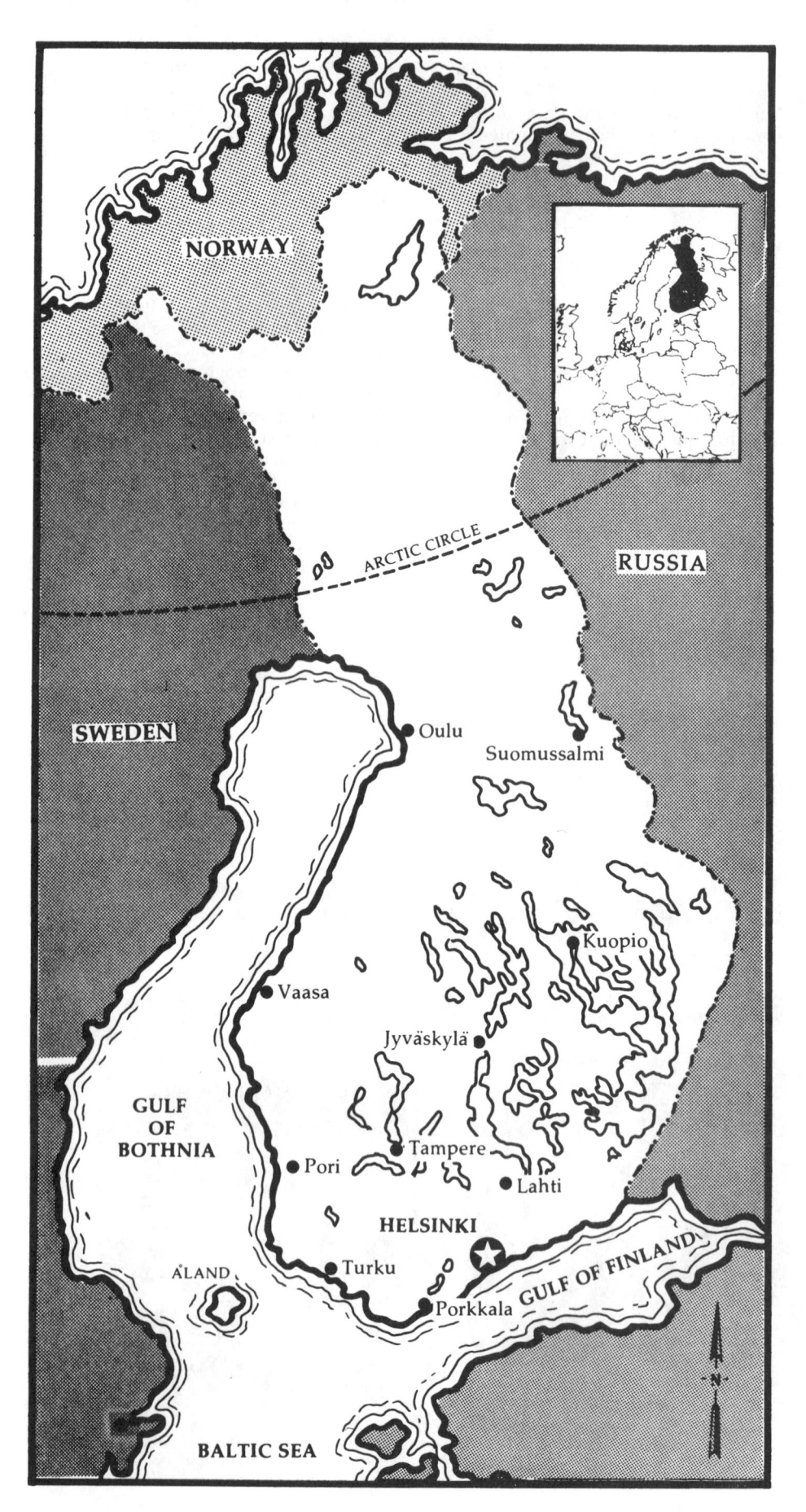

Area: 130,119 sq. mi. (338,144 sq. km., about the size of Washington state).
Population: 5.1 million (estimated).
Capital City: Helsinki (Pop. 500,000, estimated).
Climate: Temperate in the south, but rapidly ascending into Arctic temperatures in the northern areas. Neighboring Countries: Russia (East); Norway (North); Sweden (West).
Official Languages: Finnish, Swedish.
Ethnic Background: Finn 93%, Swede 6%, Gypsy .12%, Saami (Lapp) .11%.
Principal Religion: Evangelical Church of Finland (Lutheran) (89%); Orthodox Church of Finland (1%), other and nonreligious 10%.
Main Exports: High technology (especially electronics) 26%, paper and pulp products 19%, machinery and metal products 19%, iron and steel, timber, ships, clothing and footwear.
Main Imports: Foodstuffs, petroleum, chemicals, autos, textile yarns, fabrics.
Major Trading Partners: Germany, Sweden, Great Britain, Russia, Japan. Half its trade is with the EU.
Currency: Finnmark, to be replaced by the Euro.
National Day: December 6 (1917), Independence Day.
Chief of State: Martti Ahtisaari, President (since 1994).
Head of Government: Paavo Lipponen, Prime Minister (since 1995).
National Flag: White field crossed horizontally, and then vertically by bright blue stripes, the latter being off center, closer to the pole.

In the ancient past, Finland was regarded as a cold land of legendary witchcraft, far off Europe's beaten path. It was very thinly populated by a silent and complicated people, who spoke an extremely baffling language when they chose to speak at all. Now the country is dynamic and forward–looking and is very much in the mainstream of both Western and Eastern Europe.

With a land area about the size of Italy, but with less than one–tenth of the population, the Finns call their rugged and strikingly beautiful country the "land of lakes and marshes." Indeed, one–tenth of the country is under water. But outsiders would probably say "the land of *forests*, lakes and marshes." The ever–present forests provide the country with its most valuable natural resource. They cover 65% of the surface area and are actually growing, not shrinking. Only Russia and Sweden have larger forested areas in Europe. An additional 22% is unforested peatland or marsh. Only 12% of the land area is available for cultivation, pasture and ur-

Finland

ban settlement. Finland has few mountains.

This country is at the head of the Baltic Sea in the northeastern corner of Western Europe and is the northernmost of the world's industrialized countries. Except for Norway's North Cape, which touches Finland, the country extends farther north than any other mainland area of Europe. In fact, one-third is north of the Arctic Circle. It also extends farther east than any other Western European country and shares an 800-mile (1,280 km.) border with Russia. On the south it faces the Gulf of Finland with Estonia beyond, and on the west are the Gulf of Bothnia and Sweden. With 130,000 square miles, Finland is the seventh largest country in Europe, with only Russia, Ukraine, France, Spain, Sweden, and Germany being larger. There are some 20,000 coastal islands, most of which are in the southwestern archipelago, merging into the Åland Islands in the west. Finland extends about 700 miles (1,120 km.) from north to south and 400 miles (640 km. east to west).

Glaciers which were miles thick completely covered Finland during the great ice ages. That is one explanation why the country is relatively flat with thousands of lakes filling the low spots. It also partly explains why much of the land, still recovering after the release 10,000 years ago from the unimaginable weight of the ice, is rising about one foot every 50 years. Where the Baltic is shallow, that uplift movement is giving Finland more land at the expense of the sea. The glaciers are the reason that the most common land type is moraine, a mixture of rocks and soil transported from other locations by the ice.

Finland has three major topographic regions, based on altitude. The uplands north of the Arctic Circle average 600–1,000 feet (183–305 meters) above sea level and include all the high points in Finland, the highest being 4,357 feet (1,328 meters). The coastal plain is less than 300 feet (91 meters) above sea level and extends inland from the Baltic 20 to 60 miles (32 to 96 km.) The lake district fills the remainder of the country south of the Arctic Circle and is intermediate in altitude. The entire country averages about 500 feet (152 meters) in altitude, only half of the average for Europe as a whole.

Although Finland lies between 60° and 70° north latitude, it has a much milder climate than most countries so far north. The Gulf Stream and the prevailing winds are welcome benefactors for the Finns, giving them a climatic advantage over southern Greenland, Canada's Northwest Territories and most of Siberia, which lie in the same latitudes, but which have much more severe weather. A better comparison is Alaska, also between 60° and 70° North, and partly favored by warming ocean currents. The length of the day varies greatly, even in the south, which has six hours of sunlight daily in December and 19 hours in June. In northern Lapland, however, the sun never sets for 73 days in summer and never rises for 51 days in winter.

HISTORY

The Early Periods

When the Indo-European tribes pushed into the Baltic area about 4000 B.C. they found people already there who are believed to be related to the present-day Finns. These early inhabitants probably had moved into the area soon after the continental ice sheet began to melt about 12,000 years ago. As the Indo-Europeans moved up the shores of the Baltic Sea, they pushed some Finns ahead of them. About 2000 B.C. and again at the beginning of the Christian era, waves of immigrants came to Finland from across the water to the south and land from the southeast and gradually pushed the Lapps, who had arrived earlier, into the northern portions of the country. All of these early Finnish tribes moved west from north and central Russia. Finnish is related to Estonian and to the languages of isolated parts of northern Russia. It is also distantly related to modern Hungarian and Turkish.

Scandinavian influence in Finland began during the era of great migrations, about 400 A.D., and continues to the present. Christian missionaries first entered southwest Finland in the 10th century, and the Catholicized Finnish aristocracy developed close links with Poland. The King of Sweden and the Bishop of Uppsala made a crusade into Finland 200 years later, establishing a foothold in the southwest, which was expanded in the following centuries to include all the northern shore of the Gulf of Finland. Swedes colonized the southwestern and southern coastal areas and the Åland islands, areas where Swedish language and culture is still very strong. The Swedes slowly annexed the remainder of Finland and ruled it as a Swedish province, though not as a colony, until 1808.

Following a successful Russian invasion, Finland was declared an autonomous Grand Duchy of Imperial Russia, a status which continued until 1917. During the 19th century Finns were permitted to continue to practice the rudimentary representative government which the Swedes had created. This early period of Russian rule saw very little effort at Russification. It actually gave the Finns a chance to overcome the heavy Swedish cultural and lingual influence and to assert their Finnishness, while retaining those elements of Scandinavian traditions and values, such as the structure of society and the judicial system, which Finns found valuable. Not until the mid-19th century did the educated classes and the country's major newspapers begin to use the Finnish language. But in 1899 a Russification campaign began. The Finns were no longer permitted to practice the Swedish form of government, and Finland was required to provide troops for the Russian army. This provoked Finnish resistance to Russian rule, and in 1905 a general strike paralyzed the country.

In 1906 the Russian government, badly shaken by an unsuccessful revolution, agreed to a Parliament Act for Finland, providing for Finland's system of propor-

A typical countryside panorama

Finland

tional representation voting and a single–chamber assembly. At the same time, Finnish women became the first in Europe to be permitted to vote. When the Tsar renounced these concessions in 1910, Finns again mounted determined resistance. Such opposition to Russian domination made it logical after the outbreak of World War I in 1914 for Finnish nationalists to cooperate with the most powerful country opposed to Russia, namely Germany.

A Nation is Born

When the Russian Revolution occurred in early 1917, the majority in Finland favored remaining within the Russian Empire as an autonomous province. When, however, the Kerensky government was overthrown by the Bolsheviks led by Lenin in late 1917, the majority of the Finnish middle class demanded full independence, and the Finnish parliament declared it on December 6, 1917. But the radical left was determined to unleash a revolution in order to establish a socialist state. Known at the time as "Reds," they seized Helsinki and southern Finland in early 1918, causing the parliament to move north to Vaasa.

Thus, Finland's independence was followed almost immediately by a civil war. Led by the former Finnish general in the Tsarist army, Gustav Mannerheim, Finnish government forces, known as "Whites," won a decisive victory over the Reds at Tampere early in April. Mannerheim's forces were supported by a German division which landed on the southern coast and recaptured Helsinki early in the month. The rebellion was thus put to an end; Finnish society was able to remain western, not Soviet, but the costs of Finland's struggle for independence were enormous. Not only were 20,000 Finns killed, but the nation was split into two hostile halves. Not until the Russians invaded the country two decades later was this wound healed.

In the struggle between monarchists and republicans, the former won a temporary victory. Two weeks before the end of World War I the Finns chose a German to be their king, but the defeat of Germany made such a monarchy utterly unrealistic. Therefore, Finland adopted a democratic and republican constitution in 1919 which is still in effect.

Finland joined the League of Nations in December 1920. As the power of the League began to deteriorate in the 1930s, Finland unsuccessfully attempted to ally itself with Sweden and other Scandinavian countries. Therefore, when the Soviet Union attacked Finland in November 1939, the Finns had no friends who would or could help.

General Mannerheim

The Red Army attacked on the ground in the East and Southeast and by amphibious assaults across the Gulf of Finland. It threw almost one million men into the attack, who were opposed by about 300,000 white–clad Finns, 80% of whom were reservists. The Finns, regardless of their numerical inferiority, put up a fierce and effective defense, often fighting on skis. All the amphibious assaults were repulsed as was the main Russian attack against the Finnish fortifications on the Karelian Isthmus.

Russian drives into Finland from the East proved to be disastrous. They came expecting an easy victory and were pitifully ill–prepared. They were equipped neither with field tents nor with portable woodstoves. Finnish troops, attired in warm white winter clothing, often on skis and familiar with the terrain and cold, cut the Russian columns into small pieces and destroyed them. The Russians were scarcely able to cope with the Finnish "invisible wall"—white–clad soldiers who appeared suddenly, fought fiercely and then disappeared in the landscape of drifting snow. The Battle of Suomussalmi was the most dramatic example, with two Finnish divisions completely destroying two enemy ones, resulting in 27,500 Russians killed or frozen to death and 1,300 captured. The Finns lost only 900 men.

But the Soviet Union's overwhelming manpower eventually proved too much for the brave but outnumbered Finns. After three months the Finns accepted the peace terms offered by the Soviets, which at the time was cooperating with Germany and which was reportedly nervous that the British might come to the aid of Finland via Norway and Sweden. In the end, Finland had sustained 25,000 killed and 43,000 wounded, while Soviet casualties were eight to ten times as high.

One of the principal costs of the Winter War was the loss of most of the Karelia. The entire southeastern corner of Finland, containing 10% of the country's territory and people, went to the Russians in the peace settlement. Much of the Karelian population had to be resettled in the West. A further consequence of the war was that the Germans and many others concluded that the Red Army would be a pushover in any future conflict. This fatal misperception enticed the greedy Hitler to attack the Soviet Union only two years later.

When they did attack in mid–1941, Finland, desiring to regain the territory it had so recently lost, went to war on Germany's side. The Finns tried to keep relatively independent of Germany, however, and did maintain peaceful relations with the U.S. throughout the war. They also refused to participate in the siege of Leningrad and to cut the rail lines linking the vital north Russian port of Murmansk and Moscow. It did take the opportunity to reconquer its lost territories and to seize Eastern Karelia, which had always belonged to Russia, although it was populated by Finns. Sensing the way the wind was blowing after the crushing German defeat at Stalingrad, the Finns began to explore ways to a separate peace in 1943, but they were not permitted to extricate themselves from the war so easily.

Things were, on the whole, very quiet on the Finnish front from late 1941 until the allied landings along the coast of

Finland

France in June 1944. At that time, the Soviet Union decided to launch another attack on Finland through the Karelian Isthmus. It directed some of the most concentrated artillery fire in history toward the Finnish positions, and the Finnish front cracked very quickly. It rapidly became clear that Finland could not withstand this furious Soviet onslaught, so it again sought material German help, and the Soviet attack was brought to a standstill.

However, General Mannerheim, who became president in the late summer of 1944, sued for peace with the Soviet Union. The latter placed very hard conditions on Finland. The most immediate demand was for Finns to expel the 220,000 German soldiers who had been stationed in northern Finland. The Germans nevertheless put up very stiff- necked resistance—during their retreat, the Germans destroyed everything in their path, leaving Finns the postwar task of reconstructing the northern part of their country.

The September 1944 treaty with the Soviets forced it to accept the loss of the same areas as in 1940, and almost 400,000 Finnish refugees were set in motion once again. Further, Finland had to relinquish Petsamo and to allow the Soviet Union to establish a naval base for 50 years on the Porkkala Peninsula, immediately southwest of Helsinki. It had to pay the Soviets heavy reparations (ultimately almost $445 million) which by 1952 it had paid in full. Finally, the Finns were required to reduce their army to its peacetime level within two and one-half months.

The strains of war had helped the Finnish people to draw together and to set aside some of the social and lingual differences which had continued to divide them since independence. Finland was fortunate in that it had been the only belligerent country in continental Europe that was not occupied during the war. But the Finns paid a very high price: about 2.2% of their population had been killed in action, and an equal number had been permanently maimed. They lost 12.5% of their territory and were forced to resettle more than 400,000 refugees, 14% of their population.

Finally, they found themselves in a radically changed strategic situation. Germany had been totally defeated. The Soviet Union, with an 800-mile Finnish border, had emerged as the most powerful country in Europe and virtually the only great power in the Baltic area. Soviet troops had important base rights on Finnish territory within a few miles of Helsinki. Looking south, the Finns saw how the Soviet Union had simply annexed the Baltic states of Estonia, Latvia and Lithuania in the course of the war. They were very well aware that Finland was the only lost part of the pre–1914 Russian Empire which had not been reabsorbed by a revived Soviet Russia. Worst of all, Finland realized that there was not a single country in the world which would risk a war with the Soviets to keep Finland independent. What should a small, western–oriented country do in such a situation in order to maintain its national independence and its right to determine it own domestic political and economic order?

A Balancing Act

The Finns have always been noted for a quality known in Finnish as "sisu," variously translated as perseverance, tenacity or simply "guts." This was a quality necessary for a people which always had to struggle to survive in a harsh natural environment. At the same time, they are a very realistic people whose main political problem since World War II has been one of foreign policy. Like other small countries which share borders with big powers, Finland did and now does have various options. It could disregard the security interests of its powerful neighbor and pay the price for that. Or it could recognize those security interests and see how it could adjust its policies to them without sacrificing its own national sovereignty. More and more Finns realized that the latter option was the only realistic one, and their leaders have long established the country's foreign policy on that foundation.

In order not to irritate the Soviet Union after World War II, Finland was forced to turn down all offers of Marshall Plan assistance from the United States. Moscow had suspiciously viewed such aid as a trick designed to undercut its influence and to establish a U.S. predominance over Europe. Therefore, it forbade all of its newly–developed client states in Eastern Europe from accepting this aid. Finland's subsequent economic recovery and prosperity and the fact that it was the only European country fully to repay its war debts from both world wars are all the more astonishing when one remembers that it received no economic aid from the U.S.

A Finnish peace treaty with the Soviet Union came into force in 1947 which placed maximum limits on Finland's armed forces. This was followed in 1948 by a more important step, the signing of a Treaty of Friendship, Cooperation and Mutual Assistance with its powerful neighbor. The Soviets had already entered into such treaties with the satellite states of Eastern Europe, and so when it was announced in February 1948 that the Soviet Union had also invited Finland to work out a mutual assistance pact, many Finns though that the end of their independence was near.

Yet Finnish leaders acted quickly and skillfully. They politely rejected Stalin's offer to sign a treaty identical to the ones signed with Hungary and Romania, countries which had fought against the Soviets during the war. Instead, Finnish leaders drafted their own treaty, tailored to their own particular needs and circumstances. They drew on earlier proposals which the Russians had made to Finland in 1938 and 1939. Perhaps justifiably suspecting foul play in 1939, the Finns had rejected the Soviet proposals, and the Winter War had resulted.

The Soviet–Finnish Treaty

The Treaty of 1948 obligated Finland to defend itself in the case of an attack "with the help, if necessary, of the Soviet Union or together with the Soviet Union." Such "assistance" would "be supplied as mutually agreed between the Parties." Article 2 adds that both countries "will consult together in case there is found to be a threat of the military aggression referred to in Article 1."

The decisive part of the treaty, as far as the Finns are concerned, is the preamble in which "Finland's desire to remain outside the conflicting interests of the Great Powers" is recognized. This granted Finland a privilege not extended to the Soviet Union's Eastern European satellites: the right to be neutral. It is certainly true that the Russians only chose to use this word in reference to Finland in 1970, and, indeed, until the Soviet Union had withdrawn its troops from the Porkkala Peninsula in 1956, one could hardly speak of genuine neutrality. In large part, this Soviet decision stemmed from its buildup of adequate naval facilities on its own soil. It stemmed also from the changed strategic situation, which moved critical points from the waters south of Finland toward the Baltic area closer to Denmark and the straits leading to the North Sea, as well as toward the northern Norwegian and Bering Seas.

The Finns' basic assumption was that the Soviet Union did *not* want to conquer the entire world, but that its policy was basically defensive and essentially oriented toward stability along its borders. Without question, the Soviets had in Finland a more stable and less threatening neighbor than anywhere along the entire huge Soviet border in Europe or Asia. From the standpoint of the Russians' self-interest, the treaty was also advantageous in that direct Soviet control of Finland, which no country in the world could prevent, would undoubtedly cause the neutral but extremely well-armed Sweden to join NATO and would eliminate

Finland

Finnish soldiers—the "invisible wall"

Norway's policy of restricting NATO activity on its soil. Such an unpleasant event would immensely strengthen an enemy alliance by moving NATO several hundred miles closer to the Soviet Union and by strengthening the NATO presence in the Baltic Sea. Thus, like all good and lasting treaties, the 1948 one rested on a firm foundation of mutual interest.

For this reason, President Koivisto traveled to Moscow in 1983 to renew the treaty for another 20 years. It was not scheduled to expire until 1990, but the early renewal was an expression of the desire for continuity despite leadership changes in both countries. Immediately following the failure of the Soviet coup in August 1991, the Finns decided to renegotiate the treaty. Esko Aho was the first Finnish leader to question it. His government did not want it and the neutrality it imposes to be obstacles to entry into the EU, which occurred in 1995.

In 1990 Finland unilaterally abandoned clauses of the Treaty which limited the size of its military forces and relations with Germany. In 1992 Finland and Russia replaced the 1948 treaty altogether and forged independent Russia's first political treaty with a Western country. Both nations committed themselves to respect the other's borders, to protect the other's citizens on their territories, and to renounce the use of force against each other. The treaty is valid for 10 years and renewable for five-year periods unless annulled by either country.

Neutrality and Foreign Policy

Finland's foreign policy, which did not enjoy a widespread consensus even within the country until a generation had passed after World War II, depended upon almost constant Finnish reassurances to the Russians that it would never again present a threat to their security. J.K. Paasikivi, Finland's president from 1946 to 1956, devoted almost his entire effort to eradicating traditional anti-Russian views within Finland, lest they place Finland's security in danger. This policy, known as the "Paasikivi line" was reinforced and expanded by his successor, Urho Kekkonen. The "Kekkonen line" was based upon the realization that the worse East–West tensions are, the greater the ominous prospect that Finland would be obligated to support the Soviet Union. Therefore, Finland took a very active role in reducing such tensions.

For instance, it hosted the initial Strategic Arms Limitation Talks (SALT) between the U.S. and the Soviet Union which resulted in a milestone agreement in 1972. Further, it actively organized, promoted and hosted the Helsinki Conference on Security and Cooperation in Europe in 1975 which was attended by virtually all the highest political leaders in Europe. The "Helsinki Agreements" were a central element in all superpower and European dialogues.

Some observers in the West distrusted Finland's policy of bending over backward not to irritate the Soviet Union. In the late 1960s, the term "Finlandization" entered the international political vocabulary to refer to a condition in which a country is so frightened by Soviet power that it is no longer able to control its own foreign policy. It implied a loss of sovereignty and a kind of remote control of a country from Moscow. Finland's example was often presented as a warning to other Western European nations, although the Finns never pretended that the relationship they maintained with the Soviet Union should be adopted by other nations. "Finlandization" was viewed as an ideal solution for Eastern European countries, since the Soviet Union decided in 1989 to permit democratic revolutions there. During a highly symbolic visit to Helsinki in 1989, Gorbachev praised Finnish neutrality, stating that "for me, Soviet–Finnish relations are a model for relations between a big country and a little one." The word "Finlandization" now sounds better.

Neutrality was a way of saying no to military cooperation with the Soviet Union. The rationale for this disappeared with the Soviet collapse. It now has other options. Like Sweden and Austria, it accepted observer status in the WEU. It declines to enter NATO although in 1994 it joined the Partnership for Peace, devised by NATO as a transitional form of membership. It believes that for now nonalignment, backed up by a credible national defense and implicit collective security provided by the EU, is best for Nordic regional security. Unlike Sweden it is willing to participate in a common EU defense if such a policy is devised. A poll in 1995 revealed that about half the Finns favor military cooperation with the West, and only a third wish to stay out of military alliances.

Relations with the USSR

Finns bristle with anger when they hear the expression "Finlandization." The term implies indirect criticism of their earlier foreign policy. It was normally used by people who lack deep knowledge of Finland and its history, and who were referring to political situations which had nothing to do with Finland itself.

The Finns practiced careful self-censorship toward unpleasant actions of the So-

Finland

viet Union. Finnish newspapers were expected to be discreet and wholly accurate when criticizing the Soviet Union and such criticism could never be sensationalized. As one Finnish historian wrote, "The Finns deny themselves the luxury of making emotionally satisfying gestures." Another noted, "If we bow West, we present our bad sides to the East. We just can't afford to do that." Where self-censorship was practiced, former President Kekkonen openly appealed to the press to show "responsibility."

In 1986 a case of censorship involved a Finnish film entitled *Born American*, which depicts the imprisonment and harsh treatment of three Americans who cross the Soviet border. The Finnish government's response was to ban it because of its hostile portrayal of the Soviet Union. Such censorship did not determine Finns' personal attitudes toward their powerful neighbor. Opinion surveys in 1987 among high school pupils indicated that the USSR was viewed as an Orwellian society with no freedom and miserable living standards. However, two-thirds believed that the Soviet Union was not a threat to peace.

Finland's response to the Soviet Union's invasion of Afghanistan in 1979 was an example of restraint. This brutal venture was a severe shock to the Finns, especially since Moscow had often referred in official declarations to Finland *and* Afghanistan as "neighboring, non-aligned" countries with which it could entertain good relations. Although Finnish leaders publicly called on the Soviet Union kindly to withdraw its forces from Afghanistan, Finland, unlike most other nations of the world, abstained from condemning the invasion by vote in the United Nations. Further, in the aftermath of the Soviet Union's shooting down of a South Korean passenger jet with hundreds of persons aboard in mid-1983, the Koivisto government appealed to Finnish ground crews not to join an international boycott of flights in and out of the USSR. Finland avoided taking a stand whenever the interests of the great powers, including the United States, were in conflict. Thus, unlike some of the U.S.' allies, Finland almost never criticized American foreign policy in public.

Finland is always extremely sensitive to any development in Northern Europe which might provoke a Russian reaction toward it. Finnish tempers flared in the spring of 1986 when the Soviet Union waited three days to inform the Finns officially about the Chernobyl nuclear disaster. Soviet leaders subsequently reached an agreement that such information would be exchanged immediately.

While western leaders could understand Finnish concerns in these matters, they had greater difficulty understanding Kekkonen's reverent allusions to Lenin, who had lived in Finland, had expressed sympathy and friendship toward the country and had been the first leader to recognize Finland's independence. Kekkonen's pilgrimage to Lenin's birthplace and his willingness to stand with communist dignitaries on top of the Lenin Mausoleum in Moscow on the occasion of the 50th and 60th anniversaries of the Bolshevik Revolution were puzzling. After the failed August 1991 coup in the USSR, Helsinki's Lenin Museum offered to take Lenin's embalmed body if it were forced out of its Red Square Mausoleum. Said the museum's director: "We always gave Lenin a hiding place when times were difficult in Russia."

Western observers asked why the Finns had constantly to repeat their loyalty to their treaty with the Soviet Union. A former Finnish foreign minister explained that such monotonous repetitions are like declarations of love in marriage: "the latter have no news value either, but their omission can give the partner cause for unwarranted suspicion." In the Koivisto era this tedious liturgy of assurances to the Soviet Union was heard less often, but the "Kekkonen line" was still genuinely accepted by Finns. True consensus had replaced repetition. The benefit of Finland's good relations with both superpowers was shown in 1990, when Mikhail Gorbachëv, worried about the Baltic states' drive for independence, asked Koivisto to help. Koivisto informed President George Bush of the former Soviet leader's concerns.

The turbulent events in the former Soviet Union in the 1990s are creating heightened anxiety in Finland, whose leaders fear that the gigantic multi-national neighbor might head inexorably toward dissolution and catastrophe. Such a prospect fills most Finns with horror. It could drive hundreds of thousands of desperate and starved Russians across the 1,200 kilometer border with Finland.

Finnish uneasiness was heightened by the 1993 Russian parliamentary election campaign, in which ultra-nationalist candidate Vladimir Zhirinovsky spoke of reincorporating Finland into a new Russian empire and banishing Helsinki's Finnish residents to Lapland so that Russians could move into their apartments. In January 1994, the Russian ambassador in Helsinki sent a note to the Finnish Foreign Ministry complaining that the existence of two right-wing groups violated the 1947 Treaty of Paris, which bans fascist activity in Finland. Finns regard this treaty as obsolete and were incensed that Russian leaders would try to influence Finland's presidential election in this crude way.

Nevertheless, with Russian nationalism on the rise and with thousands of Russian troops deployed in the region of St. Petersburg, Finns want to avoid upsetting their giant neighbor. This is why President Martti Ahtisaari warned in 1995 against an eastward expansion of NATO, instead recommending opening the EU to Central and Eastern European membership. As the only EU state sharing a land border with Russia, Finland has a special interest in promoting what it calls a "northern dimension" of deeper cooperation with Russia. The idea is to assist Russia to settle down and prosper in the region with sympathetic and helpful Nordic states. When Finland assumed the rotating EU presidency in July 1999 it made improvement of relations with Russia one of its main themes.

Worries about Russia increasingly directed Finns' attention toward Western Europe, especially the EU. Many fear being isolated in a rapidly changing world. As former *Conservative Party* leader, Ilkka Suoninen, asked: "If the world changes from confrontation to more cooperation, then where does neutrality lie?" The government applied in 1992 for entry into the EU. In October 1994, 57% of the voters accepted their country's entry into the EU. This historic event took what had been a Western European bloc right up to the gates of Russia. Finland's Swedish-speaking Åland Islanders, who enjoy a self-governing status, initially voted not to follow Finland into the EU, but they changed their minds in November 1994 and voted to go along with the rest of the Finns. Finland is the Nordic area's biggest enthusiast for the EU and is proud to be the first to adopt the Euro.

Defense

Remembering that the western democracies had left it to fight alone against the Soviet Union, the Finns try to maintain sufficient military preparedness in order to be able to cope with any potential aggressors. Its military doctrine is based on self-reliance and territorial defense. It aims to mobilize at short notice a well-equipped force of a half million soldiers who can retain control of strategically important areas, delay and wear down an attacker until it can concentrate the necessary force to defeat him in areas of Finland's own choosing.

Finland has compulsory military service for all males over 18 years; about 90% of all men serve. Since 1995 women may also volunteer. They are trained for the same duties as men and have the same opportunities and responsibilities. After active duty of 8 to 11 months, a Finn remains in the reserves until age 60. In wartime, it could mobilize 500,000 trained

Finland

and equipped soldiers: 460,000 in the army; 30,000 in the air force; and 12,000 in the navy. Most serve in the southern part of the country, but efforts are now being made to shift more of the country's military capability northward into Lapland, where an eventual violation of Finnish territory would most likely occur. Finland's defense spending is 1.6% of GNP. Spending on 24,000 border troops and civil defense is included in other ministries' budgets.

Because of the country's policy of neutrality, Finnish troops are also welcome participants in UN peace–keeping missions, particularly in the Middle East. That this form of duty is not without risk was demonstrated in 1985 when 21 Finnish soldiers were captured in southern Lebanon and held for eight days before being released by their Christian militia captors. The commander of the UN troops in southern Lebanon was a Finnish major–general. In 1995-7 Finland dispatched a 450–man peacekeeping force to Bosnia to help enforce the Dayton Accords. In 1999 Finland provided forensic scientists to investigate massacres in Kosovo, and President Martti Ahtisaari was a key mediator with Russia and NATO in the search for a peaceful settlement of the conflict.

Although most Finns and all political parties still oppose NATO membership, 43% of respondents said in 1996 that Finland would eventually join. Its ties with NATO are warming, and its minister for Europe, Ole Norrback, publicly stated in 1996 that membership in NATO is "more probable than improbable." His remark sparked a debate, but the very fact that there is talk about NATO membership is a radical departure.

About a third of its military equipment is produced in Finland. It purchased arms from the Soviet Union (MIG jet fighters), Sweden (Draken interceptor aircraft), Britain (Hawker Siddeley jets), France, and 64 American Hornet F–18C interceptors, produced in Finland. In 1992 it bought Russian tanks, artillery, and ammunition from the stockpiles of former East Germany. It sends its officers to the U.S., France, Britain (and earlier, to the Soviet Union) for specialized training. Finland has assumed a special role in assisting the Estonian military. It sends advisers to Estonia, including instructors to the National Defense and Public Service Academy in Tallinn and Baltic Defense College in Tartu. It provides specialized training to some Estonian troops on its own soil. Backed by a well–deserved reputation for fierce and imaginative defense on their own territory, the Finns are able convincingly to show their teeth to any potential attacker.

GOVERNMENT

What the Finns gained from their particular brand of foreign policy was the privilege to have a domestic political and economic order far different from that which the Soviet Union required of its Eastern European neighbors. Finland has the same constitution it adopted in 1919. Unlike three of its Scandinavian neighbors, Norway, Sweden and Denmark, Finland is a republic.

The President

At the time the constitution was written, supporters of a monarchy reached a compromise with supporters of a republic that the President would not be a mere figure–head who cuts ribbons and gives parties for foreign dignitaries. Instead, he would be the leading figure in the political system, and he is required to sever all ties with a particular political party. Until 1988 he was elected for a term of six years through an electoral system very similar to that in the U.S.: voters elected 301 members to an electoral college, who then chose the president from among various candidates. Finns now elect their president directly by universal suffrage. When no candidate receives 50% of the votes on the first round, a runoff election between the top two candidates takes place three weeks later.

The president commands the armed forces and makes foreign policy, although declarations of war and important treaties require parliamentary approval. He has the right to dissolve parliament, to call new elections and to initiate and delay legislation and to appoint the cabinet. He also appoints all bishops for the state–supported Lutheran and Orthodox churches, all university professors and the governors for 11 of Finland's 12 counties (regions). The only exception is the predominantly Swedish–speaking island of Åland, which has been self–governing since 1921. Finland's 464 municipalities are administered by their own popularly elected municipal councils, which exercise the municipalities' power to collect taxes, maintain public order and attend to education, culture, health and social welfare.

The office of the presidency is actually so powerful that may observers have jokingly referred to Finland as the only *real* monarchy in Scandinavia. This seemed particularly appropriate because of the man who occupied the office from 1956 until 1981, Dr. Urho Kekkonen. Thanks to his own efforts, his foreign policy views were accepted by most Finns until the Cold War ended in the early 1990s. Because of Kekkonen's strong personality, the presidency grew even more powerful, a fact which added political stability to a

Dr. Urho Kekkonen

country in which a cabinet sometimes survives less than a year.

In the 1982 presidential elections a record 86% of Finns chose the highly popular Mauno Koivisto. His modesty and unpretentiousness contrasted strongly with Kekkonen's sometimes brash and almost authoritarian style. Further, he was a man who was far less inclined to intervene excessively in domestic politics. His presidency brought a gradual transfer of more responsibilities to the prime minister, the cabinet and parliament. Under his leadership, the Finnish political system began to resemble more closely that of the other Scandinavian countries where the chief focus is on Parliament, not on the head of state.

In 1994 Finns elected a new president, Martti Ahtisaari, a *Social Democrat*. A career diplomat and former U.N. undersec-

President Martti Ahtisaari

Finland

retary general, Ahtisaari had never before run for public office. That fact proved to be his strength because he had not been associated with the economic disasters which had overtaken Finland. He hammered away at the country's unemployment and vowed that he would lead Finland on a different economic course. Actually, the president has very little constitutional power in the economic sphere; his power lies in foreign policy, which is Ahtisaari's area of expertise.

Parliament

There are various reasons for the frequent parliamentary deadlocks. The 200-seat unicameral chamber, the *Edu skunta* (one-fourth of whose members are women) has many powers. They include the power to amend the constitution, to force cabinets to resign, to override presidential vetoes and to approve legislation, which is not subject to judicial review. Its members are elected by a system of proportional representation. This kind of electoral system always permits a large number of parties to win seats in parliament. The greater the number of parties, the greater the difficulty of forming a stable governing coalition which can count on a majority in parliament. Winning a vote on certain kinds of legislation, such as important or urgent economic measures, is particularly difficult, since such measures require majorities of two-thirds or even five-sixths of the members; this is a requirement which is unique to Finland and one which some leading political figures are determined to change.

Politics

At the present time, three big parties occupy most of the seats in the *Eduskunta*. None is a mass, "catch-all" party which attracts voters from all social and occupational groups. Therefore, there is absolutely no prospect of a parliamentary majority being won by any one party, or even by the two left-wing or the two non-socialist parties. This is especially true since the voting strength for all major parties has, on the whole, remained remarkably stable for the past sixty years. In practice, coalitions can be held together only if a minimum of three of the four largest parties participate in them.

Parties of the Left

In the 1999 elections the *Social Democratic Party of Finland* (SDP) dropped to 23% of the votes and 51 of the 200 seats, down from 63. The *SDP* is the chief spokesman for organized labor and for lower-level employees. Although not a heavily ideological party, it is one of the most leftist members in the *Socialist International*. The party officially favors an expansion of the social welfare system and the nationalization of some Finnish industries. The latter objective is particularly difficult, however, because of the requirement for especially large parliamentary majorities to enact economic measures. *Social Democratic* prime ministers, who must always lead coalitions which include non-socialist parties, have shown themselves to be pragmatists who are very willing to pursue a conservative economic policy if Finland's well-being seems to require it.

The party leader, Paavo Lipponen, became prime minister in 1995 at the head of a five-party "rainbow coalition" which included the *National Coalition Party*, *Left Alliance*, *Swedish People's Party*, and the *Greens*. This government remained after the 1999 elections. For the first time, a woman (Tarja Halonen) was foreign minister, and for the second time Finland had a female defense minister, Anneli Taina. Lipponen's second 18-member cabinet includes eight women, the most ever.

The other traditional leftist party was the *Communist Party of Finland (SKP)*, a workers' party. In order to attract a larger following among intellectuals, youth and others who favored a radical change of so-

Prime Minister Paavo Lipponen

ciety, but who did not wish to belong to a rigidly structured communist party, the *SKP* operated within a broader united group called the *People's Democratic League (SKDL)*. The *SKP* broke away from the *SDP* and declared itself a separate party in Moscow in 1918. It was banned from politics in the 1930s, and though legalized in 1944 the party spent the years from 1948, when it was widely suspected of having planned a *coup d'etat*, until 1966 in opposition. It remained organized along the Leninist lines of democratic centralism, requiring absolute obedience to the party line once the party had made a decision. The program dropped the Leninist concept of dictatorship of the proletariat, which granted a communist party, as the allegedly true representative of the people, the right to rule a country without free elections.

In the second half of the 1960s, an intra-party quarrel between an orthodox and a revisionist wing of the party erupted, and the chasm between them was opened wider when the Soviet Union invaded Czechoslovakia in August 1968. The more moderate, majority wing of the party embraces the idea of "Eurocommunism," or that branch of communism in democratic countries which is tailored not to the needs of the Soviet Union, but to the needs of the home countries. Under chairman Alvar Aalto, the leadership launched a new slogan: "Socialism with a Finnish face." This wording is strikingly reminiscent of the former Czech communist leader's call for "socialism with a human face," a call which provoked the Soviet invasion.

Backed by the Soviet Union, the orthodox wing, headed by Taisto Sinisalo, opposed this direction taken by the majority within the party. Therefore, Aalto's revisionist majority expelled the hard-line faction of the party in 1985, leaving Finland with two Communist parties, including the break-away hard-line faction called *Democratic Alternative*. Joining forces under the banner, *Left Alliance*, they 20 seats, down from 22. Although the Communists are often exasperatingly shifty partners, who maneuver to avoid responsibility for unpopular programs, observers generally agree that their sharing of government responsibility has been good both for them and for Finland. It is now in the government.

Parties of the Center and Right

The *National Coalition Party* (KOK, also called "the Conservatives") is a conservative party which stresses the values of nation, private property and enterprise, religious principles and restraint in expanding the social welfare system. It comes the closest of all Finnish parties to being a mass party, and it draws over 60% of its votes from skilled workers and employees. In the 1999 elections, it grew from 39 seats to 46.

Although it supported the "Kekkonen line" in foreign policy, it was distrusted by the Soviet Union as being too nationalist, although it must be remembered that all Finnish parties are nationalist in the sense that their policies are oriented toward *Finnish* interests. The *KOK's* support for some of the government's legislation has been crucial in the past when the governing

Finland

parties were unable to agree. Thus, the *KOK* has long been an essential feature of Finnish politics. So little separates the major parties doctrinally that the *Conservatives* remained in the government in 1995, despite election losses. Since 1994 its leader is Saulio Njinisto.

The fourth major party is the *Center Party (KESK)*. It changed its name in 1965 from the *Agrarian Union* and attempted to expand its base to include more than the farmers. This effort was only partially successful, and although one–fourth of its voters are workers, about 60% are farmers. The party advocates protection of Finnish agricultural interests, private property, individual rights and economic and governmental decentralization. It seeks to balance out the political left and right in Finland. It emerged as the big winner in 1991, garnering a quarter of the votes and 55 seats. It became the senior partner in the ruling coalition in 1991, with its leader, Esko Aho, becoming Finland's youngest–ever prime minister at age 36. Aho's tough economic medicine, which included capping spending on almost everything and raising taxes, put Finland back on the road to recovery. His government also skillfully led the country into the EU, even though his party was deeply divided over the issue. But many voters did not like his austerity measures and deserted the party in 1995. It fell to 44 seats, but in 1999 it rebounded to win 48. It is the main opposition party. In 1996 it won Finland's first elections to the European Parliament.

The Swedish People's Party (SFP) retained its 11 seats and about 5% of the votes in 1999. Over the years it has declined steadily due to the decreasing percentage of Swedish–speaking voters to the present 6.5%. To counter this decline, the *SFP* disassociated itself in 1964 from its purely Swedish language base and proclaimed a socially progressive national policy. Still, the great majority of its voters are found in the Swedish–speaking minority.

The Christian League (SKL) won ten seats (up from seven) in 1999. The *Green* (ecologist) party gained 11 seats (from nine). It had been challenged in 1995 by a new *Ecological Party*, which captured one seat based on .3% of the votes. Another new party entered the 1995 elections—the *Progressive Finnish Party* (also known as "Young Finns"). A free–market liberal party, it won 2.8% of the votes and two seats, but it faded in 1999. The populist *Rural Party*, has dropped from 17 seats in 1983 to only one in 1995. This party, which has practically disappeared, acted as a funnel for protest movements in the countryside and campaigned against alleged government corruption.

From among the ten parties the presi-

Downtown Helsinki

dent must put together a cabinet, called the Council of State. He appoints and dismisses the prime minister and the cabinet ministers, who need not be members of the parliament, but who, as a group, must enjoy a majority in the legislature. Unlike in parliamentary democracies, the cabinet is not the major power center, but is rather a body where contending interests meet and sometimes are resolved. Also, the president chairs the cabinet meetings. The cabinet assumes responsibility for the president's decisions, since they must be countersigned by the appropriate cabinet minister.

Finnish cabinets are very short–lived, and the country had 60 governments before it had celebrated the sixtieth anniversary of its independence. There were 12 governments in the 1970s alone, and Finland now has almost a dozen living ex–prime ministers. Yet, new governments are usually created by merely shuffling around a few cabinet seats. Thus, there is somewhat more cabinet stability than meets the eye. *The Center Party* and the *Social Democratic Party* are crucial participants in almost every government. Until 1995 the *National Coalition* was consistently excluded, and the major non–socialist parties cannot assemble a majority in parliament. Of course, neither can the two leftist parties, so there is no alternative to the delicate broad coalitions which have become the rule in Finland.

ECONOMY

After World War II had ended, the Soviet Union handed the exhausted and defeated Finland a reparations bill which could only make the Finns shudder. They had to give the Russians a large part of their merchant marine and to deliver heavy industrial products—ships, metal and engineering equipment—at prices which the Russians had established arbitrarily. This seemed like a terrible demand to make on a country which had always been primarily agricultural and whose industry was limited almost exclusively to wood products. In the end, the Soviet demands proved to be a great blessing in disguise for the Finns. The sums to be paid were not impossible, and they were paid by 1952. But by having been *forced* to create a heavy industrial base and thereby to diversify its industry in order to pay the reparations, Finland established the very foundation for its present economic prosperity. The Finns have a habit of paying what they owe. It was the only European country to pay off all of its debts from both world wars. It has experienced an extraordinary economic transformation in the second half of the 20th century. Shortly after the war its GDP per capita was a third below that of Sweden, and 70% of its people worked the land; now that latter figure is only 6%, and it is almost even with Sweden in wealth.

Finland

Economic Links with Russia

It established significant trade patterns with the Soviet Union, which was until 1991 Finland's most important single trading partner. Not only did the Soviet Union provide 90% of Finland's oil, half of its electricity, and all of its natural gas, but it was a guaranteed market for Finnish exports, even though this two–way trade declined somewhat in the 1980s, and both Finns and Soviets increased their trade with the West. Russia's share of Finland's total foreign trade had dropped from 26% to 7% by 1995. As the USSR diversified its trade with the West under Mikhail Gorbachev, Finns began to worry about losing business and about their ability to compete. Nevertheless, when the average Finn thought of the Soviet Union, he thought perhaps as much of economic opportunity as of political danger.

The Finnish shipbuilding industry was one of the greatest beneficiaries of the Soviet reparation demands. Finland had to replace its own fleet and it then turned to production of ships for export. Until the 1990s sales to the Soviet Union accounted for more than 8% of Finland's total exports. The Soviet Union was particularly interested in Finnish–made ships suited for Arctic conditions, and more than 80% of the shipyards' orders came from that country. Russia was also an especially good customer in that it pays for these ships as soon as they leave the slipway. Further specialties include high–technology shipping, such as liquid gas carriers, cable layers and Arctic oilfield vessels. Most of the "loveboats" cruising in the Caribbean, half of the world's icebreakers and the drilling rigs used to bore a fourth of the offshore wells in the North Sea, were constructed in Finland.

The Soviet Union was an avid buyer of products from its only immediate neighbor that has an advanced western economy and technology. It bought ships, machinery, paper, chemicals and large quantities of food and drink, tobacco products, clothing and footwear. It also welcomed the large–scale production projects which Finland conducts just over the Soviet border. These include the construction of a wood processing complex at Pääjärvi, the enlargement of a paper and pulp complex at Svetogorsk and the largest of all—the Kostamus project involving construction of an open–cast iron ore mining complex 30 miles (48 km.) inside the Soviet Union. Such projects are far more attractive than similar Finnish projects in the Middle East because Finnish workers can return home on weekends, and the projects stimulate economic activity in the nearby northern and eastern parts of Finland, which badly need economic stimulation.

The Soviet Union gave Finnish firms contracts to build 50 villages deeper in the Soviet Union along the gas pipeline being constructed to transport natural gas from Siberia to Western Europe. In 1987 it also awarded a contract to Finnair (Finland's airline) to renovate and assume partial management of the Berlin Hotel in Moscow. Soviet leaders stated that this deal should be a model for future joint ventures with the West. By 1991 Finnish companies had signed about 260 joint–venture agreements with the USSR, but only a handful had gone into operation.

Finland is one of the highest per capita energy users of the world and has to worry particularly about its supplies. It is one of the richest countries in peat resources, and it does fire some power plants with this material. With no oil, gas or coal of its own, and with hydroelectric resources which do not come close to those of Sweden or Norway, it must import almost 70% of its energy. About half comes from Russia, including not only oil, gas and electricity, but also nuclear fuel services.

In contrast to the Swedes, the Finns have not been split over the question of nuclear power. Two of Finland's four reactors are from the former USSR, and the fuel for its two Swedish–built ones is enriched in Russia. The Russians also promised not only to provide nuclear fuel, but also to dispose of much of the nuclear wastes, thereby largely freeing the Finns from that frightening problem. Nuclear power plants produce a third of Finland's electricity and a seventh of all its energy. Again, Finns saw that the Soviet Union not only gave them headaches, but aspirin as well! Although a parliamentary majority voted against more nuclear power in 1993, the government shelved plans to build a fifth plant.

Since the arrival of *perestroika* in the USSR the former certainties of trade with a reliable Soviet Union have vanished. Finns no longer could be sure who on the Soviet side was making key business decisions, and they complained that they were no longer being paid on time. Because of violence and economic shortages in the USSR, Finnish workers were no longer eager to go there to work, even for short periods of time. The Soviets curbed oil and gas deliveries to Finland. Finns received a particularly rude shock in 1991 when the Soviet government ended the bilateral clearing house system based on semi–barter trade and replaced it with a normal trade arrangement financed through convertible currencies. This had a devastating effect on trade with the Soviet Union. Finnish exports to its neighbor dropped 34% in the first month alone to a level of 7.6% of Finland's total exports, a far cry from the 25% only a decade earlier. Overnight Finland was running a balance of payments deficit with the Soviet Union and was becoming far more dependent upon its markets in Western Europe.

This turn of events plunged Finland into its deepest recession since 1945 and revealed a prominent Achilles heel in the Finnish economy. In 1991 its GDP declined by 5% and its industrial production by 15%, and it faced record unemployment and bankruptcies. By the mid–1990s Finnish efforts to boost trade with Russia were succeeding, rising by a third in 1994. By the end of the century Russia accounted for 7% of Finland's trade. Half its imports were oil and gas, and a growing percentage of its exports were luxury goods for newly rich Russians. Profiting from this burgeoning trade are the ports of Hamina and Kotka, located 36 and 66 kilometers respectively from the Russian border. These are the EU's most easterly ports and are becoming increasingly important hubs for lucrative Russian traffic. St. Petersburg's affluent bourgeoisie are welcome guests, and Russian is replacing English as the first foreign language taught in local schools.

Other Sectors of Economy

Although only 8.6% of its land is arable, Finland was traditionally an agricultural country. But the percentage of Finns who earn a living from the land or from forestry has decreased steadily from almost 70% in 1880 to almost 50% on the eve of World War II, to 36% in 1960 and to 14% by 1978. In 1999 farming employed only 6% of the population and contributed less than 5% of GNP. Because of the small size of most farms, the short growing season and the bitter weather conditions in winter, productivity in agriculture is relatively low, and many farmers can survive only by engaging also in forestry, often in the wooded areas which they themselves own. Yet, Finland remains self–sufficient in all foodstuffs except fruits and vegetables, and, if the harvest is bad, in grain. Dairy and meat products are in surplus and are therefore exported.

The rapid flight from the farms created serious economic and social problems for Finland. From the 1950s to the 1970s many Finns either emigrated to other countries, especially to Sweden, or poured into the urban centers in the southern part of Finland. In the *Economist* of London, one observer described the development this way: "Finland is roughly a jug–shaped country. Imagine the jug filled with the kind of liqueur that has tiny golden specks floating in it. Left alone, nearly all the Finns would, like those specks, drift slowly down to the bottom. Three out of five of them already live in the southernmost fifth of the country."

Finland

The results of this southward drift were urban problems of tight and expensive housing, a proliferation of concrete suburbs, and above all, unemployment.

Finland used to be called a country short on investment capital and long on labor, but many of its citizens who left to find work abroad, especially in Sweden, are returning home. Further, Finland now has larger direct investments in other countries than foreign firms have in Finland. It has poured large sums of money into developing and diversifying the economic base in the northern four-fifths of the country. This is especially difficult given the transportation impediments caused by the great distances, sparse population and cold climate. The only favorable transportation factor is the long water routes branching in many directions.

The main objective is not to make farming more attractive, but to offer tax relief and other subsidies to businesses which locate there and which train or retrain rural inhabitants. It does this primarily through the Regional Development Fund, shortened in Finnish to *Kera*. Though state-owned, *Kera* refuses to rescue lame duck industries. It encourages risk-taking, but it also demands profitability. The Finnish government promotes social, health, cultural and educational services in the North and attempts to shift a portion of administration and decision-making away from the Helsinki area.

It looked to its neighbors, especially Sweden for help; Sweden provided half the foreign capital invested in Finland. However, by the mid-1990s Finland had become more of an equal economic partner with Sweden. Many foreign investments in Sweden are now of Finnish origin. The Nordic Investment Bank has helped to finance joint Finnish-Norwegian and Finnish-Swedish projects in the north of Finland. Nokia, Finland's biggest high-tech company, accounts for nearly a fourth of the global market for mobile telephones and finds a lucrative market in its very own neighborhood. Finland now has more mobile phones than fixed-line telephones. Half the population had a cell phone by 1999, the highest percentage in the world, followed by Norway (46.5%) and Sweden (45.8%).

This country is fortunate to have many valuable raw materials. The most plentiful, and luckily renewable, resource is wood—lots of it! Two-thirds of its forests are privately owned. This, together with its paper products, accounts for 23% of its exports and almost a fifth of its gross production. The wood and paper industry also provides employment for 19% of the work force. Although the financially strong U.S. and Canadian paper mills now meet half of western Europe's wood pulp needs, Finland's new highly efficient paper plants still find their major market in western Europe. In general, Finland's wood and paper industry is thriving, but Finns are having to watch very carefully the less desirable by-product of paper mills: pollution.

Finland is not overly dependent upon its wood industry. About half of the iron ore needed for its domestic market is produced locally, and it has rich deposits of non-ferrous metal as well. It is one of Europe's leading producers of nickel and copper and also mines zinc, chromium, cobalt and produces 10% of the world's vanadium. These generous mineral deposits, along with its forced diversification after 1945, have enabled Finland to build an efficient metal and engineering industry. This sector now produces 19% of exports and a fifth of the gross production. It also employs 34% of the labor force. Diversification has further spread to the chemical and textile sectors, which now produce 9% of exports and provide work for 19% of the labor force.

As might be expected, the economy is very export-oriented. More than a third of total production must be exported, and a quarter of total consumption must be met by imports. Of course, some industrial branches are even more dependent upon exportation than others. For instance, the forest industry exports 80–90% of its production, the textile and clothing factories about 45% and the metal and engineering industries about 40%. This is one important reason why Finland is very sensitive to any changes in the international trade or political climate, and why it has a special Minister for Foreign Trade.

Finland's major market is Western Europe. Half its trade turnover is with EU and EFTA countries; Germany, Sweden and Great Britain are its major Western European trading partners. Within this area, trade has shifted more and more to Sweden and Norway.

Great Britain's and Denmark's entry into the EU made it advantageous for Finland to sign in 1973 an industrial free trade agreement with the EU effective in 1977. Although it did not become a member of the EU's Common Agricultural Program, it enjoyed complete duty-free trade with the EU countries since 1984. Its economic ties with the West were also facilitated by its associate membership in EFTA and its full membership in the WTO, the OECD and the Nordic Council.

The sensitivity on the part of the Soviet Union had earlier dissuaded Finland from seeking EU membership. That changed in the 1990s, and in 1992 the Finns formally applied, and in 1995 it joined. A Finn, Jacob Söderman, became the EU's first ombudsman in 1995. The Finnish government regards full membership as an essential economic and political anchor for the country in the post–Cold War era, especially given the economic problems at home and the instability in neighboring Russia. In 1996 the Finnmark joined the EU's exchange rate mechanism (ERM) as a step toward the European common currency, and in 1999 it became the first Nordic country to adopt the Euro.

During the 1980s Finland's per capita GDP grew 2.8%, compared with an average of 1.6% in the rest of Western Europe.

Finnish paper-making machines sold throughout the world

Finland

Dramatic economic successes despite biting problems of inflation and unemployment stemmed partly from relative labor peace. Unlike in most other Western European countries, Finnish labor unions are gaining members and now represent 80% of the labor force. They are highly politicized and strongly support the *SDP*. Nevertheless, they usually have been willing to enter general income agreements with all governments and industries which are designed to keep the economy efficient and competitive. For instance, they agreed to a wage freeze in 1992 to deal with the recession.

The success also stems partly from a high degree of economic pragmatism. Finns used to view Sweden as their model, but much of their recent economic success was due to their willingness to deviate from that model.

Finns were concerned about unemployment, but it had declined to 10.9% by 1999. It has been hesitant to use public funds to shore up inefficient and unprofitable industries. Further, they have not shirked from cutting public spending or taxes and introducing stringent monetary control and financial restraint to protect their overall economic health. Thus, Finland in the late–1990s has one of Europe's fastest growing economies, increasing an average of 5% per year from 1994–9. It maintains one of the highest levels of prosperity in the industrialized world. It is recovering well from its deepest recession since 1945, during which it suffered the worst decline of any Western European country in recent times. Exports are booming, investment is up, growth is robust, and inflation is down to 1.3% in 1999. The public–sector budget deficit has fallen to 2% of GDP, and its total public debt is down to 58.1% of GDP. The government's attempts to meet the convergence criteria for the EU common currency succeeded spectacularly.

CULTURE

For centuries Finnish culture was heavily dependent upon influences from abroad. Eastern Finland was always exposed to cultural trends from Russia, and Sweden was a conduit for such trends from the rest of Europe. Not until the 19th century did a specifically Finnish identity really awaken, and this was led by the elite's increased use of the Finnish language in literature, journalism, education and politics.

Literature and Arts

A central figure in the break from the tradition of using Swedish was J.V. Snellman, a prominent university professor and statesman and, although of Swedish background himself, the first great author to write in Finnish. In 1835 the first part of Finland's greatest literary work, the *Kalevala,* was published. This monumental national epic by Elias Lönnrot presents traditional Finnish folk poems which tell of myths and legends. It gave a powerful boost to Finnish nationalism and to a yearning for independence. In 1870 another epic, *Seven Brothers,* was published by Aleksis Kivi, who portrayed the Finns of his time with great humor and realism, but with very little romanticism. He established the standard for Finnish prose and drama and soon became universally recognized as Finland's national author.

Both these epic works, the *Kalevala* and *Seven Brothers,* capture the importance which Finns attribute to common people and their identification of man's fate with mysterious, impersonal forces, often associated with forests and nature. This identification gives Finnish literature a sober, almost tragic and often heroic tone. In most Finnish works, though, the reader senses an unmistakable national enthusiasm.

Since 1945 Finnish literature, as well as film, has reflected an intense national self–examination, with much social consciousness and criticism. It has been experimental and "modernist," with much use of loose imagery and collage. Finns have developed a particular passion for the spoken theater; it has more than 40 professional theaters and countless amateur ones as well.

Finland publishes more books per capita than any other nation in the world except Iceland. Because of the complexity of the Finnish language, much of its literature and drama remains untranslated and unknown outside of Finland. Other forms of cultural expression lend themselves better to international audiences. The music of Jean Sibelius (1865–1957) who drew much inspiration from the *Kalevala*, opened the way for a national romantic style and introduced Finnish music to a world audience. The Sibelius Academy in Helsinki is now the country's highest institution for musical studies.

The Finnish opera receives particular support through the annual Savonlinna Festival, which draws large numbers of visitors from outside Finland and which presents important national works with high standards of international artistry. The Metropolitan Opera of New York was so impressed with the quality of the Finnish National Opera that it invited the latter to perform in New York during the 1983 season. This was the first time the "Met" ever invited another opera company to perform in its own home. The Finns also have established a worldwide reputation for imaginative modern design in architecture, industrial arts and city planning.

Ninety percent of Finns belong to one of the two official Finnish churches, the main one being the Evangelic Lutheran Church. However, fewer than 5% attend church services outside the Christmas and Easter holidays. The two churches receive subsidies from taxes paid by registered members, but that income has dwindled so much that the Evangelic Lutheran Church had to dismiss a fourth of the people on its payroll.

Languages and Minorities

A Finno–Ugric language related lingually only to Estonian, Hungarian, and a couple dozen dialects spoken in isolated communities in Russia and the far North, Finnish remains mysterious to the outsider. Finns keep it largely free of foreign words; they prefer inventing words, such as *puhelin* (telephone) or *norsu* (elephant), to borrowing them. They can make up words to be more precise. Finnish has no masculine or feminine, so they do not say

Building ships

Finland

"he" or "she." They have no articles ("a" or "the"). Unlike the Estonians, they have resisted modernizing their spelling, so their words seem bafflingly long.

The percentage of citizens whose primary language is Swedish has declined in the last century from 15% to about 6%, although both remain official languages. There are no longer serious social differences or tensions between the two language groups. In fact, aside from language, very little distinguishes the two groups from each other. Swedish–speaking Finns are still granted a great measure of cultural autonomy. There are 41 Swedish high schools in 31 cities and a Swedish university in Turku. Most Swedish speakers now also speak Finnish, but not vice versa, despite the fact that many Finnish children learn some Swedish in school. Most Finnish school children (91.7%) choose to learn English as their first foreign language, whereas only 7.7% choose to learn Swedish as their first foreign language. Only a tiny percentage of pupils ever enroll in Russian language courses.

There is a third population group in Finland, which has a culture and Finno–Ugric language of its own: Laplanders (who prefer to be called *Sami*, pronounced Sah–meh), a short but strong people toughened by a hard life. Their origins remain obscure, but scholars believe they were Finland's first inhabitants. Finland has only about 3,800 Sami; there are far more in Norway (40,000) and Sweden (17,000). To the disappointment of tourists, they no longer wear their colorful blue, red, yellow and white costumes except on festive occasions; they are mostly settled and make their living chiefly from timbering, farming and tourism. One enterprising tour company tried to create a bonanza by sponsoring honeymoon stays in Lapland during the winter months. The attraction: 24–hour night–time! Surprisingly, the venture failed.

A fourth category of residents is refugees. Finland has hitherto had a tightly restrictive policy. Although it began to open up a bit more in 1987, it still strictly insists on evidence of political, religious or racial persecution. Amnesty International had criticized Finland for returning Soviet seekers of asylum.

Among the 15 former Soviet republics, Finns are culturally closest to their kin 50 miles across the Gulf of Finland in Estonia. They are from the same ethnic stock and can understand each other's language, with a bit of effort. The Estonians have much more practice since they have watched Finnish television for years, thereby making them the former Soviet citizens best informed about the outside world and most familiar with Western problems, pornography and advertising. In fact, their favorite Finn was a jovial TV character who did commercials for sausages and meat, reminding them of how prosperous life could be with a capitalist economic system. There is even a Finnish–speaking minority in Estonia, numbering about 20,000—the Ingrians.

In the Gorbachev era, Finns' interest in Estonia increased to almost a fever pitch. When an Ingrian Lutheran paster came to Finland to seek donations for the church, the response was overwhelming. Also, Finnish farmers sent shiploads of used farming equipment to Estonia to help in the agricultural reform, and Finnish paper was donated for use in greater book publication. Finnish and Estonian firms have established numerous joint ventures. By 1994 half the foreign–owned businesses had Finnish partners, and 13 of 22 commitments made by the government financing corporation, *Finnfund*, were to Estonia. Finns arrive in Tallinn by the ferryload to cash in on low prices in Estonian stores and bars. Some tourists' free–spending and heavy–drinking behavior has given Finns a bad reputation in Estonian eyes. The Finns opened a visa office in Tallinn.

In characteristic fashion, the Finnish government kept its distance from this enthusiasm toward Estonia, not wishing to appear to be undermining Soviet rule there. Finland had recognized *de facto* Soviet annexation of the Baltics in 1940. But in 1991 it joined other nations in recognizing the newly independent Baltic states.

Looking east, Finns also see Slavicized brethren in Karelia, who after the collapse of the USSR are pressing for greater independence from Moscow or, in some cases, outright annexation by Finland; 8,000 Finns from there have already moved to Finland. But not wanting to assume a huge economic burden, Finland wants neither a further influx nor any talk of annexation. Of the 790,000 people who live in Karelia, only about 80,000 are Finno–Ugric–speaking Karelians, of which only 18,000 are Finns and 6,000 Vepps, another nationality related to Finns. Thus, Finns and their relatives represent less than 15% of the population; the rest is Russian. To discourage more emigration to Finland, whose wage level was 100 times as high as that in Russia in 1993, Finnish organizations are founding schools in Karelia and supplying books in Finno–Ugric languages. Also, Finnish companies have two–thirds of the 120 joint–ventures there.

The Media

Finnish–Swedish bilingualism is practiced in the mass media. The Finnish Broadcasting Company (YLE), a state–owned organization, operates or supervises all radio and television broadcasting. It has no radio advertising and two of its television channels have none. It broadcasts Swedish TV programs in western and southern Finland, and there are Swedish–language radio stations. A Sami radio station broadcasts in Lapland, and Radio Finland transmits in various European languages. Domestic production accounts for 57% of all programs, and 54% of foreign programs are from Europe and 29% from the U.S. Foreign programs are transmitted in the original language with subtitles. The Finnish Broadcasting Company gets the large part of its revenues from license fees. There is a privately–owned MTV Ltd (having nothing to do with American MTV), which finances its operations through advertising. There are also private local radio stations (most owned by newspapers and publishers), cable TV companies, and a few local TV stations.

More than 200 Finnish–language and more than 20 Swedish–language newspapers are privately owned. In the decade following independence, Finnish newspapers were mainly tied to political parties, but now more and more are independent of parties. The *Helsingin Sanomat* has become by far the largest in circulation, followed by *Ilta–Sanomat, Aamulehti, Turun Sanomat,* and *Maaseudun Tulevaisuus*.

Education

All Finnish children must attend nine years of school. They have completed the transition to non–tracked comprehensive schools at the secondary level. The goal in establishing such unified schools, similar in some ways to American schools, was to equalize educational opportunities. After completing the comprehensive school, about half the pupils enter a three–year senior secondary school which prepares them for a matriculation examination and access to the universities. Pupils in these advanced schools must pay modest fees, but there are free places for those who have insufficient funds. The country's largest university is the University of Helsinki with approximately 20,000 students. Also located in Helsinki is the Institute of Technology. There are universities at Jyväskylä, Oulu, Tampere and a Swedish–language university in Turku. Because of the flood of students to the universities today, many applicants are turned away, and many students who finish their studies are unable to find employment in jobs for which their studies prepared them.

Finland has adopted an Arena 2000 project that will hook up all Helsinki schools to the internet. In a cold country like Finland, people will be able to meet by Internet when they cannot go physically from one place to the other. By 1997 Helsinki already had twice the number of internet subscribers per 1,000 inhabitants as the U.S. National research and development spending in the computer field is almost 3% of GDP, the highest in the world.

Social Welfare

There is an extensive social welfare system, although it is not yet as sweeping as that in neighboring Sweden. Finland's social welfare is certainly expensive: one fifth of the national budget is devoted to it, and it is one reason why the average Finn spends over a third of his income in taxes. The people receive generous unemployment benefits and pensions. Medical care is not totally free, although Finns do not pay for visits to the doctor or for many medicines, and hospital care is usually not more than $10 per day in public institutions. The economic crisis in the 1990s adversely affects the welfare system. There have been cuts in social benefits and public health care.

Surprisingly, Finns have one of the lowest life expectancies in Western Europe (70 years for men, 78 for women). Some observers attribute this to a predominantly meat and dairy diet which lacks sufficient vegetables. It confronts—as do many nations—a continuing problem of excessive alcoholic consumption. One of the first things independent Finland did was to attempt to prohibit the drinking of alcohol. Prohibition was in effect from 1919 until 1932, but, as in the U.S., its only effect was that of creating a new and prosperous occupation: bootlegging. It has one of the lowest birth rates in Western Europe. This is due only partly to a very liberal abortion law, which has permitted one abortion for every three children born. In 1994 it became the first country in the world to eradicate homegrown cases of measles, German measles and mumps.

One will hardly find a Finn who does not engage in the favorite national sport: cross–country skiing. The loggers' paths through the pine forests are ideal for skiers, When the snow melts, then Finland's long- distance runners attract the world's attention and have done so since the legendary Paavo Nurmi. "The Flying Finn" had built up such a lead in the 1,500 meter run in the 1924 Paris Olympics that he could walk the last 50 meters and still take one of his six Olympic gold medals. In the 1970s Lasse Viren carried the banner by becoming the first person ever to win gold medals in the five and ten thousand meter runs in two successive Olympics. Americans would no doubt blink their eyes in disbelief to see Finns playing Pesäpallo, a very popular modified form of American baseball. Golf is increasingly popular. Most Finns dream of spending part of their year at a country cottage, preferably on one of the many lakes. A fourth of the population owns one and uses it in both summer and winter. There in solitude they enjoy spiritual renewal and such pleasures as sauna bathing.

Perhaps the most widely–known Finnish tradition is the sauna, one of the only Finnish words which has become part of the international vocabulary. Many Finns build them in their basements or in little wooden sheds outside their houses, and there is now one sauna for every five Finns. After sitting in temperatures from 180°F to 210°F (80°C to 100°C), they jump into ice–cold water or take a roll in the snow. They claim that there is nothing better for a person's health or frame of mind!

A sauna bath is also a meeting point for friends or business associates. In fact, the cabinet even conducted a working session once a week in the sauna. If former President Kekkonen had particular difficulty getting the various political leaders to agree on a policy, he merely took them into the sauna, where problems could be ironed out in a more relaxed style! This is no longer possible since the late 1980s because women are now in the cabinet. In Finland, men and women who are not in the same family or are not close friends traditionally do not steam together. In 1992 former Defense Minister Elizabeth Rehn ended the practice of conducting national security debates in the sauna once and for all by declaring: "I believe in making decisions when I am fully clothed, and not when I'm naked. That way I have my notebooks in my hand, and everybody knows what has been decided!" Helsinki's first female mayor, Eva–Riita Siitonen, a modern former TV announcer, no doubt agrees.

FUTURE

Finland's main challenges are how to deal with the effects of change in the former Soviet Union, which hit Finland harder than any other Western European nation. Finns wish to retain good relations with Russia. But they worry about the spread of crime from that chaotic land, which has brought increased black market activity, prostitution, and drugs to the streets of Helsinki. There will certainly be no open door to immigrants from the former Soviet Union although it agreed to visa–free travel with Estonia. Finland must also reexamine the role its neutrality can play in the new Europe.

In 1994 voters decided in a national referendum to accept full membership in the EU. Membership not only helped it recover from its deep recession and steady its economy since the collapse of the USSR. It has lowered food prices by 13% since the trade barriers protecting farmers had to be dropped. This helped bring inflation down. Finns are proud of being the only Nordic country to join the EU's single currency, the Euro, in 1999. In July 1999 it took over the rotating EU presidency and played host to an EU summit in Helsinki in December. Paavo Lipponen barely held on to power after the March 1999 elections. But his five–party "Rainbow Coalition" will continue its course of economic liberalization and rapid integration with Europe.

Finnish-designed products are known worldwide

Iceland

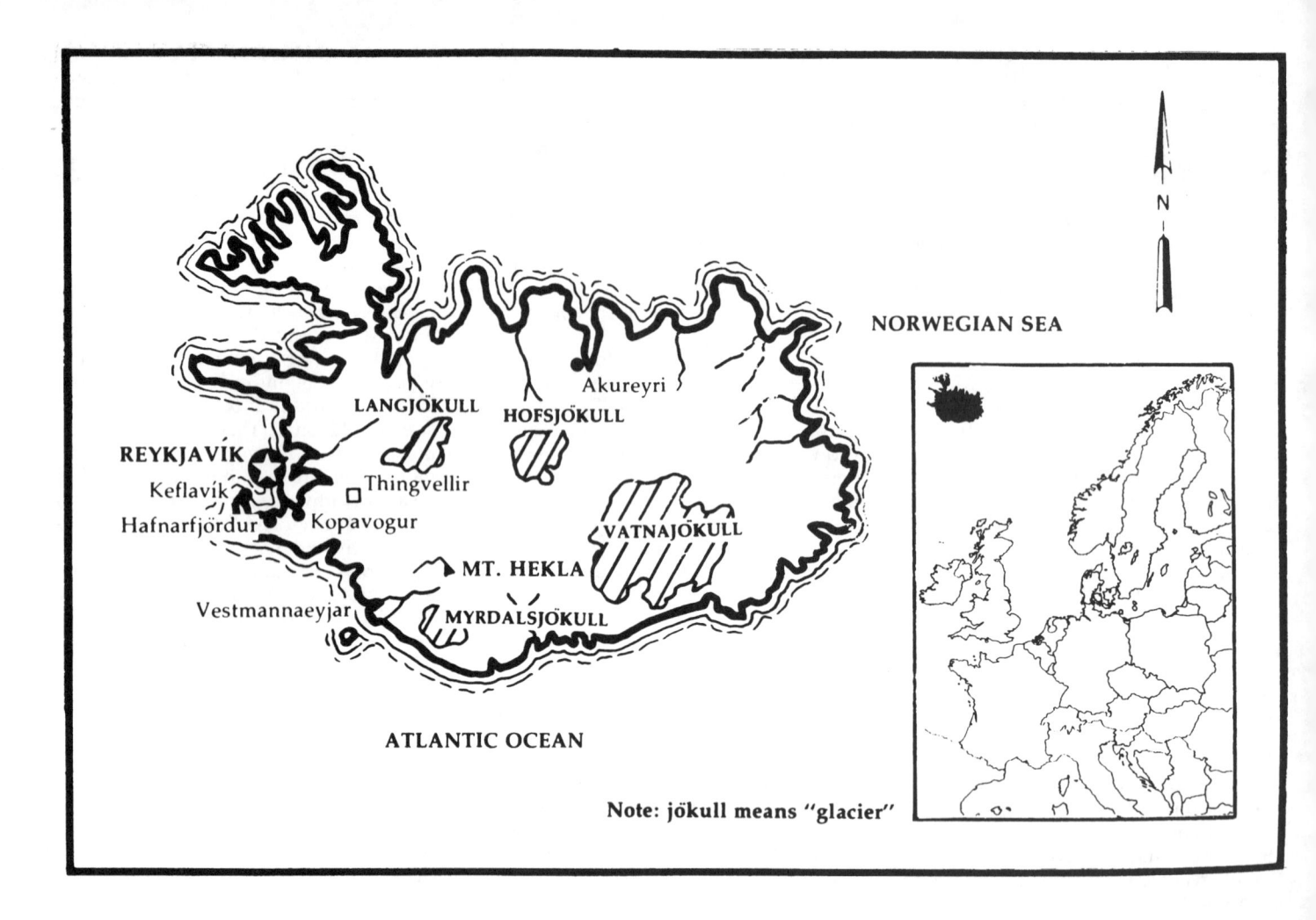

Area: 39,768 sq. mi. (102,952 sq. km., slightly smaller than Ohio and half the size of Great Britain.)

Population: 271,000 (estimated).

Capital City: Reykjavik (Pop. 161,300, estimated; pronounced *Rake*-ya-vic). Over half the country's population lives in Greater Reykjavik.

Climate: Considering its northern position, the climate is cool, yet moderated by the Gulf Stream, with the summers in the mid–50°s (13°C) and the winter about freezing

Neighboring Countries: Iceland lies alone in the North Atlantic, just touching the Arctic Circle, and is about 335 miles northwest of Scotland and approximately 425 miles from the coast of Norway. Greenland lies about 100 miles to the west.

Official Language: Icelandic (based on Old Norse).

Ethnic Background: Nordic, Celtic.

Principal Religion: Lutheran (95%); other Protestant and Roman Catholic (3%); no affiliation (2%).

Main Exports: Fish and fish products (75%), animal products, aluminum.

Main Imports: Machinery, transport equipment, petroleum, food, textiles.

Major Trading Partners: EU, UK, Germany, U.S., Japan, Denmark, France.

Currency: Krona.

National Day: June 17, anniversary of the establishment of the Republic.

Chief of State: Olafur Ragnar Grimsson, President (since July 1996).

Head of Government: David Oddsson, Prime Minister (since 1991), leader of the *Independence Party*.

National Flag: Red Cross, lined in white, upon a blue field.

Hidden beneath the Myrdal Glacier is a treacherous volcanic fissure. When it erupts, the glacier melts instantly, changing from a benign sea of ice to a roaring wall of water racing across the flatland below it. In 1963 an underwater eruption off the southern coast resulted in the birth of a new island (named Surtsey) accompanied by exploding showers of hot lava, clouds of steam and black smoke. These instances only help explain why Iceland is known as the battlefield of fire, ice and steam.

Glaciers cover 12% of the country and its major icecap is the world's third largest. Some 30 of its 100–odd volcanos have erupted since the island's settlement in the late 9th century, and one–third of the world's lava production over the past half–millennium has flowed in Iceland. Icelanders were dramatically reminded of this in October and November 1996 when a new volcano (subsequently named Loki after the Nordic god of fire) erupted under the Vatnajokull glacier; the ice pack is the largest in Europe, measuring 1,800 feet in some places and covering 10% of the island's surface. It melted vast volumes of ice and formed a huge lake under the ice. Smashing through the ice, the volcano spewed black clouds five miles in the air and sent bursts of red lightning over the six–mile long fissure. Then came a torrent of black sulphurous water, ice and mud at times five meters high onto the deserted coastal plain 120 miles east of Reykjavik. Along its 20–kilometer wide path to the sea, it destroyed roads, bridges, tunnels and power and telephone lines.

Prime Minister Oddsson said: "In the space of three or four hours our transport

Iceland

system has been put back 30 years." There are uncounted geysers and hot springs. The colors in Iceland's flag reflect these elements: red for fire, white for ice and dark blue for the sea.

Iceland stands at the northern end of the Atlantic, guarding the boundary between that ocean and the Arctic. The Denmark Strait is to the west, the Greenland Sea to the north and the Norwegian Sea to the east. The island is squarely on the "great circle" air routes between American, Scandinavian and East European cities. The northernmost tip of Iceland touches the Arctic Circle.

It is half the size of Britain and somewhat larger than Ireland. Ohio and Iceland are about equivalent in size. The island is oval-shaped, with many peninsulas extending from the western and northern coasts. The maximum east to west distance is about 300 miles (480 km.) and from north to south it extends about 200 miles (320 km.)

Iceland is the result of thousands of lava flows and volcanic eruptions. Most of the island is plateau, typically 1500 to 2000 feet (457 to 610 meters) in altitude, with volcanic peaks and high tablelands rising above it. Along the north and west coasts, steep cliffs border deep fjords, most of which have good natural harbors and from which broad valleys reach far inland. The largest plain is in the southwest and is Iceland's most fertile grassland.

Although the Polar Current chills the north coast, the Gulf Stream warms the south, bringing a surprisingly mild climate to a land on the doorstep of the Arctic. The average winter temperature is higher than that of New York City, although the almost constant winds greatly lower the chill factor.

When the first settlers arrived, the lower elevations were covered with forests, but they were cut for firewood and prevented from regrowth by sheep grazing and the cooler climate. Moss and grass cover many of these same areas today. Seals, walrus, and arctic fox were the only native wild mammal, but rats, mice, mink, and reindeer have been introduced by humans, deliberately or otherwise. Iceland's coastal waters were teeming with fish.

HISTORY

Iceland had been previously visited by some explorers, especially Irish monks. Norsemen and some Celts settled the island between 870 and 930 A.D. They came mostly from the coastal areas extending from Trondelag to Agder in western Norway, especially the part known as Gulathing, today's Sogn og Fjordana, Hordaland and Rogaland, as well as from the ethnically mixed Viking colonies in Scotland and Ireland. Only the interior, which has always been largely uninhabitable, remained unsettled. The presence of the Celts probably explains the higher percentage of dark-haired people than in other Nordic countries.

Regardless of the original ethnic mix, the population soon became homogeneous. There was little additional immigration. In modern times there has been a steady increase in population because of the low death and high birth rates.

Icelanders continued their explorations beyond their home island in the 10th and 11th centuries. Eric the Red settled Greenland in 986. About 1000 his son, Leif, who was born in Iceland, led the first proven expedition to the American continent, but attempts to settle "Vinland" failed.

At the foot of a great cliff and overlooking a broad lava plain, the *Althingi*, the

Thingvellir—solemn and windswept, ancient site of democratic ideals

Iceland

View of Reykjavik

oldest parliament in the world, began its annual sessions in the year 930, 60 years after the arrival of the first settlers. Recently, a member of parliament suggested that if the British insist on calling their country the "Mother of Parliaments," then Iceland should proclaim itself the "Grandmother of Parliaments"! In 1000 that body decided that Icelanders would thereafter be Christians. Although the *Althingi* now meets in Reykjavik, the original location at Thingvellir is the most celebrated historical site in Iceland. Contacts with Norway remained strong through the first four centuries of Icelandic history. Around 1020 Iceland entered its first agreement with a foreign country: the *Althingi* and King Olav Haraldsson (St. Olav) reached an accord on reciprocal rights. The Icelanders' memory of their earlier independence outlasted centuries of foreign domination, famines, plagues and natural catastrophes. Many of their legends and sagas hark back to the times when they were masters of their own fate.

Iceland was independent until it came under the control of Norway in 1262, then Denmark in 1380. When the Icelandic chieftains (the Godar) accepted the King of Norway as their sovereign under the "Old Covenant" in the years 1262–1264, Iceland became a part of the Norwegian realm. However, it retained its own parliament (*Althingi*), laws, and self–government in most internal matters. The Kingdoms of Denmark and Norway (including Iceland) were united in 1380. But Iceland continued to enjoy considerable self–government throughout the Middle Ages. The 15th century has been referred to as the "English Century" in Icelandic history due to the many contacts between the countries, including much trading and some skirmishing.

With the Reformation, enforced by the Danish Crown in the 16th century, Danish royal power took firm hold, and the introduction of the trade monopoly in 1602 and absolutism in 1662 reduced Iceland, in effect, to the status of a Danish colony. The *Althingi* itself became increasingly powerless and was finally abolished in 1800. The trade monopoly, which meant that Icelanders received low prices for their products and paid high prices for the goods which they had to import on Danish ships, merely stimulated Icelandic resentment toward Copenhagen.

From 1835–1847 Jónas Hallgrímsson and other patriots edited the periodical *Fjölnir.* They advocated a return to the virtues of a golden past, the commonwealth of 930–1262, and the reestablishment of the *Althingi,* which occurred in 1843. In the middle of the 19th century, the Icelanders, led by longstanding *Althingi* president Jon Sigurdsson, continued this campaign finally to sever their ties with Denmark. The Danes were receptive to the idea of loosening their hold on Iceland, but their concessions seldom went far enough for the Icelanders.

Home rule was granted finally in 1904. During World War I Icelanders bolstered their self–confidence by being able to solve their own problems at home without Danish help. In December 1918 an agreement called the "Act of Union" between Iceland and Denmark granted the island full independence. It agreed to continue recognizing Denmark's king as the King of Iceland on the condition that this arrangement be reexamined after 25 years. Until 1944 the state was called "The Kingdom of Iceland."

When the 25 years had elapsed, Denmark was in no position to influence the Icelanders' decision to sever all royal ties between the two countries—it had been overrun by German troops in 1940. The British occupied Iceland that same year. In July 1941 the United States and Iceland concluded an agreement which provided for the stationing of American troops to protect the island. On June 17, 1944, following a referendum, the Republic of Iceland was proclaimed at Thingvellir, the venerated spot where the *Althingi* had been first assembled more than a thousand

Iceland

years earlier. The U.S. was the first country to recognize Icelandic independence.

GOVERNMENT

Iceland is a parliamentary democracy in which the most powerful political figure, the prime minister, must have a majority in the parliament, the *Althingi*. At least every four years, citizens at least 18 years of age elect 63 members of parliament by a system of proportional representation. In 1991 the upper house (*Efri deild*) was abolished, leaving only a unicameral lower house (*Nedri deild*). The prime minister is the head of government.

Political Parties

There is no majority party, and since the 1930s successful government has depended on the formation of a coalition. There are five political parties now represented in the *Althingi*. The *Independence Party (IP—Conservatives)* has been and is the largest. In 1999 it captured 40.7% of the votes and 26 seats. Its leader, the colorful mayor of Reykjavik, David Oddsson, a comic playwright, is prime minister at the head of a coalition government with the *Progressive Party*. Together they command 38 seats in the *Althingi*. IP's program is based on the market economy and on Icelandic membership in NATO, and it is supported by Iceland's major newspaper, *Morgunbladid*.

The *Progressive Party (PP)*, which won 18.4% of the votes and 12 seats in 1999, is a slightly left–of–center party which has traditionally represented agrarian interests. It supports NATO, although it seeks the removal of American troops from Iceland as soon as "conditions" permit. It opposes entry into the EU. It maintains a daily newspaper, *Timinn*. It was the first Icelandic party to use TV advertising. After the 1991 election, *PP* went into the opposition, but it reentered the government in 1995, with its leader, Halldor Asgrimsson, as foreign minister.

The *Social Democrats (SDP)* fell to 11.4% of the votes and seven seats in 1995 and left the government. Its leader, Jon Baldvin Hanibalsson, had as foreign minister called for Iceland to commence negotiations on entering the EU, but no other party supported this. It was damaged by a split and formation in 1995 of a breakaway leftist *Awakening of the Nation* (also called the *People's Movement*), which won 7.2% of the votes and four seats in 1995. The *SDP* has its own newspaper, *Althydubladid*. In 1999 the *Liberals* received 4.2% and two seats.

The most vociferous party of the political left is the *United Left*, which won 26.8% and 17 seats in 1999. Some opponents claim it is dominated by communists. In fact, it must contend with severe internal conflicts between hard–line socialists and more moderate members. It opposed NATO and the stationing of American troops on Icelandic soil. Since 1978 it has not made the realization of these objectives a condition for its entry into a coalition government. A *Left–Green Alliance* captured 9.1% of the votes and six seats in 1999.

Riding partly in the wake of a popular female Icelandic president, the *Women's Alliance* (formerly called the *Feminists*) declined to 4.9% of the votes and three seats in 1995, down from 10.1% in 1982. They do not believe in hierarchy and have no leader, which greatly complicates dealings with them. They also promise to rotate their members of parliament at least every six years so that they will not lose touch with their grass roots. A third of its voters are men.

The voters of the *Women's Alliance* are generally leftist and pacifist in orientation, although their members are split over whether Iceland should withdraw from NATO. They do have issues which Icelandic women consider important, but they do not yet have clear policies. Their general message is that because of womens' experience in child–bearing, they have different values than do men. But despite their crucial contribution to society, they have little influence in a male–dominated country. Although 80% of all women work, their pay is 40% lower than that of the average man. Therefore, in 1985, tens of thousands of women walked off their jobs for 24 hours to protest "male privilege."

The President

The President of the Republic is the head of state and performs primarily ceremonial functions. However, he or she can play an important role in coordinating coalition talks after a parliamentary election. Presidents are elected directly for a four–year term, and there have been only four presidents since the establishment of the Republic in 1944.

Outgoing president, Vigdís Finnbogadóttir, formerly taught literature at the university and was a creative and experimental theater director. Her election seemed highly improbable in a land which has had only one female cabinet member since independence. After she defeated three male rivals, she announced: "I am very proud, not for myself, but for Icelandic women." She was overwhelmingly reelected for a fourth term in 1992, but she declined to run for a fifth time in the July 1996 elections. She was the most high profile president Iceland has ever had.

Local Government; The Judiciary

Iceland is a unitary state. For administrative purposes, it is divided into 23 rural districts. There are also 215 parishes and 14 incorporated towns. The judiciary consists of district and lower magistrates appointed by the Minister of Justice. The Supreme Court, with eight permanent members, is the highest court in the land.

NATO

Although in 1918 the newly independent Iceland intended to follow a policy of "eternal neutrality," the tense world political situation in the late 1940s prompted it to join NATO. Polls indicate that about

President Olafur Ragnar Grimsson

Prime Minister David Oddsson

Iceland

80% of Icelanders are in favor of NATO membership; it has no army, navy or air force of its own, but it is an important member. It occupies a strategic position on the maritime and air routes between the northern seas and the North Atlantic sea lanes so critical to NATO.

As its contribution to the common defense, Iceland permits the stationing of U.S. forces on its territory at the NATO air base of Keflavík, located 30 miles (48 km.) from the capital city. This Iceland Defense Force (IDF) had a total of about 3,000 troops, but in 1993 the U.S. decided to reduce these to 1,400. This hurt the Icelandic economy since the U.S. paid 10.3 billion Icelandic kroner rent, which amounted to 8% of the Iceland's total foreign earnings, and employed many local people.

While the IDF has the responsibility of defending Iceland from foreign attack, Icelanders are responsible for maintaining order at home. There are two groups of personnel who protect the cities. They do it well because there is less crime within the country than in the U.S. These forces are the unarmed 300–member police force and the 12–member "Viking Squad." This squad is the Icelandic equivalent to the American Delta Force. Its troops are heavily armed and well–trained as anti–terrorist commandos.

The IDF has the mission to defend Iceland and to patrol the strategically important waters 140 nautical miles from its coasts. The American aircraft there include AWACS. In 1993 the Americans announced the withdrawal of their F–15 interceptors and Orion P3Cs. Submarine detection devices (SOSUS) under the water are maintained from the base. American forces have two radar stations in southern Iceland, and two new radar stations in the north are manned by Icelandic civilians.

The Icelandic government established several important limitations: there may be no nuclear weapons, even on U.S. ships which enter Icelandic waters. In 1985 the Icelandic parliament declared the coast to be a "nuclear free zone." Reports in 1985 that there may have been American contingency plans to deploy such weapons in time of crisis and that Marines who guard the base have manuals dealing with the handling of atomic weapons created some concern. Secretary of State George Shultz went to Iceland to assure the government that no measure of any kind would ever be taken without its permission. A second limitation is vague: the weaponry at the base must be defensive, not offensive. When the two modern AWACS radar planes were introduced to the base, some critics feared that they could be used as command posts of an offensive war.

Until the late 1990s the stationing of American soldiers in Iceland was a continuous bone of contention among the Icelanders. A vocal minority regarded their presence as a limitation of Icelandic sovereignty and openly advocated a termination of the bilateral agreement of 1951 pro-

A swimming pool in Reykjavik

Iceland

viding for the American defense of Iceland. In 1973 the government of Olafur Jóhannesson even considered closing the American–manned NATO base, but nothing came of the matter. Some Icelanders fear the *cultural* influence of American soldiers and dependents on Icelandic life although this fear diminished as American force levels were scaled down.

In order not to irritate the sensitive and nationalistic Icelanders, the U.S. maintains a low profile, although Americans are given considerable freedom of the country. American TV at the base was once available to Icelanders, but the opposition to it was such that cable TV was installed on the base. American radio can still be heard in Reykjavik, though. U.S. forces and their families must live within the military compound. Unless one of the spouses is an Icelander, soldiers may not leave the base in uniform or remain outside after midnight without special permission. All jobs which are not strictly military must be given to Icelanders. Also, Iceland was perhaps the only country in the world in which the only banned alcoholic beverage was beer. Until this ban was finally lifted in 1989, American GIs had to be careful not to violate that unusual prohibition off base.

Instead of the usual military guards at base gates, there are Icelandic customs officials charged with protecting the country's stringent import restrictions. Americans can leave the base with no more than two packs of cigarettes, and one must be open. Picnickers are not allowed to bring raw meat off base for barbecues and must have filed a list of edible goods they take out of the installation. Said one Icelander, "We don't want Reykjavik to be a Norfolk or a San Diego."

Some Americans show little understanding for the particular sensitivity of Icelanders. A land with only 262,000 inhabitants, with just over a half century of independence, but with a long tradition of relative isolation, is perhaps more inclined to overreact to outside influences which are not entirely wanted. Yet most Icelanders see no alternative to NATO membership and protection by allied forces. They would never dream of creating the kind of well–armed military units which would make foreign troops unnecessary. Therefore, it can be expected that U.S. forces will remain there for some time to come. After all, the American military presence costs the Icelandic taxpayer nothing and accounts for about 8% of the country's export earnings. By the end of the century almost everybody favored the bilateral relationship.

The Icelandic government has decided, however, to change its traditionally passive role within NATO. It has had very little military expertise and has therefore been unable to make competent assessments of the strategic situation as it affects Iceland. It has not sent representatives to the NATO Military Committee or Nuclear Planning Group, and its required contributions to the NATO Infrastructure Fund have always been paid by the U.S. On April 1, 1985, it reorganized and upgraded its Defense Department of the Ministry of Foreign Affairs, which not only handles relations with the IDF, but also with NATO headquarters and defense ministers. This reorganization, which is the greatest change in Iceland's military affairs since 1944, met with no public controversy.

General Secretary Gorbachëv and President Reagan in Reykjavik White House photo by Terry Arthur

Foreign Relations

Since World War II Iceland has established diplomatic relations with more than 76 countries. It was the first country in 1991 officially to recognize the independence of the Baltic states and was among the first to recognize the Yugoslav break–away republics of Slovenia and Croatia. It sent a medical team to Bosnia, development aid to Africa, and food via the Red Cross to Russians around Murmansk. It has joined a number of international organizations. In 1946 it became a member of the UN. It is also a charter member of the Council of Europe, the OECD and many of the institutions associated with the UN, such as the IMF. It joined EFTA in 1970, and has had a free trade agreement with the EU since 1972.

In the 1990s interest in full EU membership came alive in all Nordic countries, which heavily depend on trade with Europe. Iceland is the most wary of the EU, fearing that the sole prop for its economy—fishing—could be endangered. Former Foreign Minister Hannibalson expressed it this way: "We want tariff–free access for all our fish and marine products, but at the same time we need to safeguard our fish resources." It has a 200–mile marine boundary and manages its fish stocks well. Iceland made a move in the direction of harmony with the EU by deregulating its banking industry to permit more competition; in 1990 its first privately–owned bank, Islandbanki, came into existence. Through EEA Iceland's isolation from the EU is prevented because it enjoys free trade in all things but fish and agriculture. There is little interest in full EU membership. In Prime Minister Oddsson's words, "It's just not on the agenda."

Iceland's geographic position has, for the most part, placed it out of the normal travel routes. However, in the recent past, there have been a few occasions when the world turned its eyes toward the island country. In 1972 Bobby Fischer played Boris Spassky in Reykjavik in one of the most celebrated chess matches of the world. A year later then–presidents Nixon of the U.S. and Pompidou of France met with Soviet leader Brezhnev to discuss world issues. Once again, in 1986, the leaders of the world's two most powerful countries came together in the Reykjavik summit. Ronald Reagan and Mikhail Gorbachev pushed diplomats aside and met face–to–face to discuss breath–taking visions of nuclear disarmament. In 1991 Iceland exercized some moral authority by supporting independence moves in the Baltic states within the USSR.

ECONOMY

The most prominent characteristic of the Icelandic economy is its lop–sided dependence upon the fishing industry, itself heavily dependent upon cod. Exports account for over half its GDP, and since 1945 75% of its export earnings are from fish

Iceland

and fish processing, which provide 12% of employment. Cod accounts for 40% of fish exports. Its major fish markets are the EU, which takes about 60% of its fish and fish products, and the United States, which imposes almost no tariff duties on the fish and purchases about 10% of Iceland's total exports in the 1980s. The importance of this single product is so great that Iceland has a separate ministry of fisheries. A decline in fish prices and the government's slashing of fishermen's quota for cod by half in 1994 in order to protect stocks and allow the fish population to recover inevitably hurt the economy in the short term.

In 1986 another segment of Iceland's fish industry was highlighted: saboteurs from an environmentalist group called "Sea Shepherds," operating primarily out the the US and Canada, wrecked Iceland's only plant for processing whale oil and byproducts and sank two of Iceland's four whaling ships. They charge that the country conducts illegal commercial whaling under the guise of scientific research. Whaling is economically unimportant for Iceland, but it remains a controversial issue. Icelandic fishermen contend that the protected whales compete with them for the decreasing fish stocks in their waters. In 1991 Iceland and Norway asked the International Whaling Commission to lift the five–year ban on whaling in the North Atlantic, on the grounds that the stocks had replenished themselves. This request was rejected. In 1992 Iceland left the organization and announced plans to resume commercial whaling.

The country so depends upon fishing that it was understandable for it to want to extend its fishing limit around its own coasts in order to reduce the fishing activities of other countries in these waters. It did so, first to four nautical miles in 1952, then to 12, 50 and finally 200 miles (350 km.) in 1975. Each extension resulted in conflicts called "cod wars" with Britain, whose fishing fleets also worked in Icelandic waters.

In 1976 the third "cod war" flared up with particular intensity; Iceland sent coast guard gun boats against British trawlers, and warning shots were fired, boats were rammed and trawler wires were cut. Britain responded by sending two naval frigates and surveillance flights in and over Iceland's self–declared waters. Iceland even temporarily broke diplomatic relations with London. Finally an agreement was reached in the summer of 1976 when Britain accepted Iceland's conditions on cod fishing.

An important consequence of these conflicts with Britain, which temporarily boycotted Iceland's fish products, was that the Soviet Union stepped in and agreed to

A fishing catch

purchase Icelandic fish and to sell Iceland oil. Iceland now imports most of its oil from other nations, including Britain, but it swaps fish for oil with the Russians.

Much of the rest of Iceland's energy needs are derived from two renewable sources: hydroelectric and thermal. As an island, its electrical power cannot be exported easily. Icelanders have learned to tap the hot lava and waters under their soil. Today, 99% of the home and hot water heating in Greater Reykjavik, where half the country's population lives, comes from these sources. Four–fifths of all Icelandic homes are heated geothermally with hot water being piped around towns and villages from nearby boreholes. A pleasant byproduct of hydro and geothermal energy is that these are "clean" sources. Therefore, Iceland is free of the air pollution and urban grime which are produced by fossil fuels.

Industry now employs more people than agriculture and fishing combined. Most of it, however, processes fish or agricultural products. Machine and building industries are increasing in importance, but the country's almost total lack of wood and metals hampers the operations of such industries.

With about 90% of its energy potential unused, Iceland is well–equipped to house energy intensive industries such as aluminum production. The Icelandic Aluminum Company, a wholly owned subsidiary of the Swiss firm Alusuisse, imports ore from abroad and processes it into finished metal. By 1991, aluminum exports constituted about 15% of Iceland's merchandise exports. But international competition, especially from Russia, have dampened hopes of preserving this industry.

The Achilles heel of the Icelandic economy remains its overdependence upon the fishing industry. The size of the catch varies, and foreign demand and currency values are in constant flux. When catches and markets are good, the country experiences booms which encourage the strong trade unions to demand much higher wages. When the economy turns sour, then Icelanders tend to continue living beyond their means. They do not want to give up their relatively high standard of living, which is generally on a par with other Nordic countries. Almost 90% of all homes are owned by those who occupy them. This is perhaps the world's highest percentage of owner–occupied buildings. While this is not an exclusively Icelandic problem, the maintenance of prosperity is difficult for a largely barren country of active volcanoes, lava fields and glaciers, which must import almost everything it consumes.

The unfortunate consequence was the highest inflation rate in Europe, which by 1985 had reached an annual rate of 100%. In the 1980s the government moved to combat the inflationary cycle. It abolished the indexing of wages (which tied them to the inflation rate), froze wages temporarily and devalued the krona. The result of the government's program was that by 1995 inflation had been lowered to 2%, the lowest in two decades. In 1999 the OECD placed Iceland fifth in the world for what one can buy with his money. The economy was stabilized and restructured: capital markets have been liberalized, the tax system has been completely reformed, the public sector has been downsized, and shares in state banks and telecoms have been sold to the private sector. Membership in the EEA has provided an important impetus to liberalize the economy.

Unemployment stood at 2% in 1999, and Iceland even had to import foreign labor from Poland, the Philippines and Thailand. The Oddsson government's Thatcherist policy of continued slashing of public spending and privatizing state industries transformed him from being the country's most popular mayor to its least popular prime minister. However, the results are positive. Annual economic growth averaged 5% from 1996–9. The welfare system remains generous though more modest than elsewhere in the Nordic world. Some reforms are bound to be unpopular, such as requiring contributions to pensions and the prospect of raising the official retirement age from 67 to 70. Bright spots in the economy are immense renewable energy resources, a well–educated work force and a work ethic which makes the 40–hour week almost unheard of.

Iceland has a rather good transportation system for a country of its size compared to population. It has over 7,500 miles (12,343 km.) of roads. Although efforts are being made to pave more roads, about 6,750 miles (10,893 km.) are still dirt. The country has four major and about 50 minor ports and over a hundred usable air fields. Iceland's best known transportation is a fleet of airplanes which transport passengers over the North Atlantic between Europe and North America. Operating outside of IATA regulations, Icelandair (called Icelandic Airlines until its merger in 1973 with the country's other airline, Loftleidir) flies passengers for bargain prices. Skyrocketing fuel prices and fierce competition from the major com-

Iceland

mercial airlines and other cut–rate companies temporarily threw Icelandair's financial balance into the red. But a good turnaround has been accomplished, and prospects are good that the company will show a profit. A smaller airline, Eagle, also has some international routes.

Agriculture is still important; 11% of the work force is engaged in agriculture, a percentage which will gradually fall. Sheep raising was formerly the nation's most important economic activity, and there are still some 800,000 sheep. In addition, there are over 50,000 cattle. Few grains are grown, although some can thrive in the climate. Geothermally heated greenhouses are a growing business, producing especially tomatoes, cucumbers and flowers.

CULTURE

Icelanders are proud of their Nordic heritage and in many respects are closer to their Viking forebearers than any of the other Nordic countries. Their language (which has given the world such words as "saga" and "geyser") is so close to Old Norse that Icelanders can read the 13th and 14th century sagas in their original form. It was Icelanders who carried out the most dangerous Viking sea voyages of all, those through Greenland and beyond to Newfoundland and Labrador. That heritage, combined with 680 years of rule by distant kings and their own isolation and hardships, has made Icelanders fiercely protective of their independence and their cultural purity. This is a major reason many are uncomfortable with the stationing of foreign forces on their island. An American ambassador to the country, Marshall Brement, who translated and published Icelandic poetry, characterized Icelanders as "inward–looking, perhaps introverted. But above all, they are fiercely devoted to the preservation of their language and culture."

They create their own words for modern things: *simi* (telephone); *ratsjá* (radar); *rafmagn* (electricity). There are no dialects

Kristján Jóhannsson

in Icelandic. Most of the Nordic literature of the Middle Ages, and all of it which is truly world class, came from Iceland. Much of our information about the Viking Age and later centuries in Scandinavia itself comes from those Icelandic writings. The people are fascinated with their own past, and there is scarcely a social conversation which does not touch on their history or geneology. In fact, many families can trace their family tree back almost 30 generations; few peoples in the world are able to give such a complete picture of their heritage.

The vehicle for preserving their national identity and past is their literature, especially their sagas, which tell stories of their gods, heroes and ancestors. President Vigdís, a former language teacher, asserted that "if we lose this identity, which is the language, a great treasure will be lost. We don't have anything from the past except the word." This is why there was such an outpouring of joy in 1966 when the Danish decided to return the body of ancient writings collected by the Icelandic professor, Arni Magnusson (1663–1730). The Danish decision prompted hundreds of Icelanders to assemble before the Danish Embassy in order to praise Denmark and at the same time to sing patriotic songs. When the writings actually arrived in Iceland, the inhabitants streamed into the streets to celebrate.

After the sagas, Icelandic literature declined, not to revive until the 19th century. In the 19th and 20th centuries there appeared a long line of fine poets and novelists. In 1955 an Icelander, Halldor Laxness, won the Nobel Prize for his chronicling the life of modern Iceland. Iceland is the home of world–renowned tenor Kristján Jóhannsson, who has performed in every major opera house including Italy's La Scala, New York's Metropolitan Opera, the Vienna State Opera, the Royal Opera House, and Covent Garden. Icelanders are avid readers. They publish more books per capita than any other country, and five daily newspapers serve only 244,000 people. The largest, a morning edition, has a circulation of more than 40,000, followed by an independent afternoon daily.

Iceland occasionally produces internationally acclaimed films such as "When the Raven Flies" by the Icelandic director Hrafn Gunnlaugsson. This brutally authentic Viking film about violence and revenge captures both the mood of the Norsemen and bleak beauty of the Icelandic landscape.

The country has a state–run radio station. It also has a national television network *(RUV)*, which aims to protect the national culture through higher Icelandic content. It charges a fee of 2,000 krona ($30) per month (including radio). It does not broadcast on Thursdays. The reason given is that this weekly black–out encourages more reading, chess–playing and spending time with the family. Network employees admit that the tradition also is designed to give them a day off

The author and family in Iceland, 1985

Iceland

each week. A live broadcast of President Reagan's arrival in October 1986 was the first time in two decades that Icelanders could watch TV on a Thursday evening. Private radio and television stations are now permitted. A private TV network, the Icelandic Broadcasting Corporation (IBC), maintains two commercial channels that, for a monthly fee of 3,000 krona ($45), compete with the state–backed Channel 1, which some critics call dull. They have at least one advantage: they broadcast on Thursdays! So does BSkyB, a satellite TV service beamed from London. It has no licence to broadcast to Iceland, use of its output is therefore piracy. But by installing a satellite dish, Icelanders can receive its multi–channel offering of entertainment, news, films and sports. With hefty monthly fees of $75 to receive RUV and IBC, it is hardly surprising that many Icelanders choose to tune into Sky for free.

The Danes brought Lutheranism to the island, and the church is the official one. Ninety–five per cent of the people profess to be Lutherans, although few attend church regularly. The state supports it, and any change in its organization must be approved by the *Althing*. There is religious freedom, and other churches are active in the major towns.

Education is compulsory between the ages of seven and 16 and most pupils continue on. All students learn English and Danish. The University of Iceland, with 4,000 students, provides all the higher education on the island, and includes departments or schools of law, medicine, engineering, science, theology, philosophy and economics; 1,500 study abroad. The country's literacy rate is 99%.

Special insurance is mandatory and covers old age, disability, maternity, sickness and unemployment benefits. Some health costs are, however, paid by the individual. There is one physician for every 750 inhabitants. In 1996 Dutch sociologists at Erasmus University conducted a study to determine which European people live the longest and happiest lives. They concluded that Icelanders, who can expect to be happy more than 62 years of their lives, top the list.

Iceland's population is so small and homogeneous, and such complete medical and family records have been maintained since the First World War, that it has decided to become the first country in the world to permit this information to be combined into a single linked computerized database. The aim is to create a genetic inventory that traces the likely chromosomal sites of the genes for a number of inherited diseases. Biotechnology companies will be able to search these linked databases for clues into the nature of diseases. Considerable controversy preceded the decision, but 58% of Icelanders are in favor of the database, according to a 1998 poll.

FUTURE

Iceland's economy remains somewhat fragile because of excessive dependence upon exporting fish products and importing almost everything else. The American–manned base at Keflavík can be expected to remain open at half the former strength. Its presence in Iceland is no longer questioned by many Icelanders. Iceland's wariness toward EU membership will continue despite fears of isolation from its main market; all but one of its Nordic partners (Norway) joined the EU. But it is doing quite well without it. Austerity and economic liberalization will continue thanks to the reelection of David Oddsson's center–right coalition in May 1999.

The spectacular waterfall Godafoss in northern Iceland

The Italian Republic (Italy)

With Detlev Hoffmann

Italy

A rainy morning in Rome

Area: 187,176 sq. mi. (301,225 sq. km., about twice the size of California; about 750 miles—1,200 km.—from north to south and from 95 to 155 miles—152 to 248 km. wide).
Population: 57.8 million (estimated).
Capital City: Rome (*Roma* in Italian; Pop. 2.92 million, estimated).
Climate: From late spring to early winter the days are generally sunny and warm. Midsummer is quite hot in all but the North, where in the winter (the rainy season throughout the country) temperatures can sink to below freezing; the South is consistently warm.
Neighboring Countries: France (West); Switzerland and Austria (North); Slovenia (Northeast), with Croatia, Bosnia–Hercegovina, Montenegro (Yugoslavia), and Albania paralleling its eastern coastline across the Adriatic Sea 50 to 100 miles (80 to 160 km.) away.
Official Language: Italian.
Ethnic Background: Indo–European, North African.
Principal Minorities: Predominantly German–speaking people with Austrian culture in South Tirol (Alto Adige); Albanian–speaking people in Calabria and Sicily; Greek–speaking people in Grecia–Salentin (Puglia) and some places in Calabria; French–speaking minority in Aosta–Valley; Slovene-speaking minority in the Trieste–Gorizia area.
Principal Religion: Roman Catholic.
Main Exports: Machinery and transport equipment, textiles, foodstuffs, chemicals, footwear.
Main Imports: Machinery and transport equipment, foodstuffs, ferrous and non-ferrous metals, wool, cotton, petroleum.
Major Trading Partners: EU (58%), especially Germany and France; OPEC countries, U.S., Japan.
Currency: Lira.
National Day: June 5, (1946), Anniversary of the Republic. Actually the first Monday in June is the day celebrated.
Chief of State: Carlo Azeglio Ciampi, President (since May 1999).
Head of Government: Massimo D'Alema, Prime Minister (since October 1998).
National Flag: From the pole, three equal vertical stripes of red, white and green.

Italy has the second largest population in Western Europe and is easily recognized on every map by its boot shape. This narrow peninsula with the Apennine mountain range as its backbone extends from the Alps almost to the North African coast. It is flanked by the largest islands of the Mediterranean: Sicily (15,500 sq. mi.–25,000 sq. km.) and Sardinia (14,300 sq. mi.–23,000 sq. km.) in the western basin of the Mediterranean. With its own coastline extending almost 5,000 miles (8,000 km.) and its mild climate, Italy has lured people for thousands of years. However, most of its settlers did not come as polite guests with hat–in–hand, but rather as plunderers or conquerors who used force to overrun the land.

In the long course of Italian history, almost all the peoples of Europe have at one time or another either occupied or settled the country. From the ancient Greeks to the Spaniards, from the ancient Germanic tribes and Arab Saracens to the Holy Roman and Austrian em perors, peoples of the world have left their traces in Italy. This almost uninterrupted chain of foreign domination dating back to the classical period has decisively affected the traditions, behavior and mentality of the Italian. At the same time it has provided a basic impulse for Europe. Roman rule, which extended from the Mediterranean area through present day Germany and France as well as all the way to Hadrian's Wall in Britain, and the Renaissance (meaning "rebirth") in the 14th and 15th centuries, decisively shaped western civilization.

Modern Italy is a country full of contradictions and peculiarities. In the very

Italy

same state where most of the citizens are Catholic and where the main seat of the Catholic Church is located, one finds the strongest and most powerful communist party outside of Eastern Europe. Italy's economy is the sixth largest in the industrialized world, and in northern Italy the visitor witnesses a modern industrial and urban life. But in the South one finds the many typical characteristics of a developing nation with illiteracy, high unemployment and unproductive agriculture.

Whoever takes the so–called "sunny freeway," a gigantic masterpiece of modern highway construction, to a village in the region of Abruzzi in central Italy finds himself in two different worlds: on the one hand steel and concrete construction and on the other hand a medieval mountain village which has had electricity for only 40 years! Old women clothed in black sit in front of their houses and look distrustfully at the stranger who perhaps had come from a demonstration for women's rights in Milan or Rome.

Italy, with its strong, influential unions, has more strikes than almost any other country in Europe. Even by Western European standards, Italy is a prosperous nation. At the same time, one is astonished by the social differences between the rich and poor, and by the frequent servility of the worker and employee toward the boss. Half of the defense budget is swallowed up by the almost 360,000–man army, but the borders must still ultimately be protected either by an ally, such as the U.S., or by neutral states to the north or east. Only one–third of the defense budget is allocated to the navy which has the sobering task of defending the 5,000 mile coastline.

Given the strong centrifugal forces of highly diverse regions and countless competing political groups, it is no wonder that Guilio Andreotti wrote in his memoirs that Italy is almost ungovernable.

HISTORY

One of the major contradictions of Italian history is that the heroic epoch that was invoked and emulated by Mussolini, Italy's fascist dictator from 1922 to 1943, is actually not Italian history, but rather the history of a single city, Rome. This city rose to become the ruler of the entire Mediterranean world and much more of Europe. At one time, a person could truly say "all roads lead to Rome." Italians themselves interpret differently the significance of Rome's earlier power and influence. If one were to ask inhabitants of southern Italy, particularly someone from Calabria or Sicily, whether they consider themselves descendants of the Romans, one would immediately receive a vigorously negative response. In contrast to those from the northern and central part of the peninsula, southern Italians view Roman history as the beginning of perpetual foreign or outside control. The present form of this control is the economic predominance of the North over the South.

In a strict sense, Roman history cannot be called Italian national history because the concept of "the nation" was completely unknown in the ancient world. Yet, one cannot understand modern Italy without first viewing some of the principal features of Rome's development. This still vi-

Pordenone (near Venice): Medieval pagentry with modern touches
Photo by Vincent Campi

Italy

brant past has had tremendous impact not only upon Italy itself, but also upon Western Europe as a whole. The most evident examples of Roman heritage are found in the Romance languages, which include modern Italian, Spanish, Portuguese, Romanian and French. Without its Latin components, English would never have developed as it did and certainly would be incomprehensible to people today. The grammatical structure and vocabulary of all modern Germanic languages was strongly influenced by Latin (including the old rule that the verb comes *last* which gives non– Germans so much trouble!). In law, civil administration, literature, art and engineering, ancient Roman civilization established the standards for many centuries.

The Early Period

The history of ancient Rome is long and exceedingly complicated, and is punctuated with magnificent victories and achievements, as well as ignoble failures, corruption and civil war. That history can be divided roughly into three periods: it was ruled by kings from roughly 753 B.C. (according to Roman legend) until 509 B.C., when a revolt led to the establishment of a republic, governed by elected consuls. The Roman Republic lasted until 45 B.C. when Julius Caesar established an empire subsequently ruled by emperors. In 185 A.D. this mighty empire was divided into a Western empire, led from Rome, Milan and Trier in present–day Germany, and an Eastern empire, ruled from Constantinople (now Istanbul) in Turkey. The former empire finally collapsed in 476 A.D., whereas the Eastern one continued to exist for another thousand years.

According to their own legend, the Romans were descendants of a group of Greeks who had accompanied Aeneas, one of the sons of the Trojan King Priam. Aeneas had escaped from the burning city of Troy and had sailed across the Mediterranean Sea before being blown ashore at the mouth of the Tiber River. There he allegedly founded a city called Lavinium. In fact, Italy was settled around 1,200 B.C. by Indo–European tribes which moved into the area from the West, and since the Trojans were Indo–Europeans themselves, there might have been some truth in the Roman belief that they were descended from the Greeks.

The settlers in the Italian peninsula broke up into various warlike tribes: the Etruscans settled around the present city of Viterbo, located about 66 miles (110 kilometers) north of Rome. The Umbrians also settled north of Rome around the present city of Perugia. The Samnites built up their civilization south of Rome, while the Latins were based around the Tiber River. At the bottom of the peninsula and on the island of Sicily, the Greeks and Phoenicians established colonies, which thrived on trade and shipping.

Roman legends tell us that the city of Rome was founded in 753 B.C. by a Latin chief named Romulus, one of the infants allegedly reared by a she–wolf. The new city was situated on a hilly site about 20 miles (32 km.) inland from the former city of Lavinium in order to be out of reach of Phoenician and Greek raiders. Romans believed that Romulus made himself king of Rome and ruled until 716 B.C. He was succeeded by Numa Pomilius, who came from the Sabine tribe and who is said to have introduced Rome's first religious institutions, which were largely copied from those of the Etruscans and Greeks. Many Greek gods were worshipped, although the Romans gave them different names. For instance, Zeus became *Jupiter*, Hera became *Juno*, Hermes became *Mercury* and Athena became *Minerva*.

Under the rule of the Roman kings, the city's influence and control began to expand beyond the original seven hills, named the Palatine, the Capitoline, the Esquiline, the Aventine, the Caelian, the Quirinal and the Viminal. The most powerful foes were the Etruscans, a fierce, but civilized people, who had perfected the use of iron. The Etruscan leader, Tarquin, reportedly defeated the Romans and became King. Although it still became the leading city of the *Latin League,* a loose association of cities bound together for purposes of defense, Rome's subsequent kings were of Etruscan descent and were known as "the Tarquins;" they were elected by a small group of noblemen.

Under the Tarquin kings, Rome's class system became more firmly shaped. On top was the patrician class, consisting of free Romans who had the right to attend the assembly of aristocrats who advised the king. Eventually this assembly became open to all Romans who owned property. The plebeian class was composed of freed slaves who had immigrated to the city. The third class was composed of slaves, who had some rights, but who were not citizens. Only patricians and plebeians were allowed to serve in the army—soldiers were at first required to provide their own uniforms, weapons and supplies, and they were paid by being able to share in the booty gained in victorious campaigns.

The last king was also named Tarquin, but his people called him *Superbus* because of his arrogance. He ruled very badly, involving Rome in expensive wars, arresting and murdering Roman citizens without trial and generally subjecting the city to a reign of terror. Finally in 509 B.C. two patricians staged a successful revolt

An Etruscan soldier

and drove out the last of the kings, although it was not until 496 B.C. that the final attempt by the Etruscans and Sabines to restore the monarchy in Rome was suppressed.

The Republic

Because the kings had made themselves so hated, the Roman Republic was declared, which was ruled by two consuls elected by the People's Assembly each year for a one–year term. The first two consuls were the leaders of the revolt, Brutus and Collatinus, who were the most important founders of the Republic. Later, officials below the level of consuls were elected in pairs, and the normal career path to the post of consul was through a series of lower offices.

The republican constitution was not wholly democratic in the modern sense because it granted considerably more power to the patricians than to the plebeians and because most slaves were entirely excluded from politics. Only the election of the civil servants, consuls and judges by the

Italy

People's Assembly can be regarded as democratic. There can be no doubt that a few influential Roman families wielded a disproportionate amount of power and authority. In general, the nobility and large landowners insured that all political functions were carried out honorably. Yet it was possible for common people with talent to acquire great political prominence and to influence Roman politics. For example, the well–known politician Cicero, who did not come from one of the few influential families in Rome, was the most famous orator of his time. Despite his great influence and fame, he suffered his entire life from an inferiority complex about his humble background.

The Roman constitution succeeded in solving many social crises and enabled Rome to establish and maintain a citizen's army. Realizing that victories were their own, these citizen soldiers were eminently more motivated than the disorderly mercenary armies of oriental dynasties. For the ancient world, the Roman civic virtues such as discipline, obedience and bravery were of great importance—they made their control over other peoples legitimate. Three essential pillars for the Roman state's strength were the exclusively Roman understanding of the commonwealth as *res publica* ("affairs of the people") from which the word "republic" is derived, the right of political participation, which was the highest goal of every distinguished Roman, and the disdain for all purely private matters.

In the Roman Republic important steps toward limited government were made: the very existence of a constitution, so long as it is observed, places limits on rulers' power. The Roman republican constitution, which was unwritten, especially embodied many principles essential for the development of modern democracy and did limit the state's control over citizens in several important ways. It was based on the separation of power between the executive and the legislature. The executive leadership was provided by the two consuls, who were elected by the People's Assembly, composed of all citizens. However, the electoral system gave more votes to those citizens who paid more taxes. Therefore, upper classes always had a majority of votes. The highest executive authority alternated each day from one consul to the other, although the consul not having the highest authority could veto decisions made by the other except in times of war. The yearly election and the mutual control over each other prevented the concentration of power in one person's hands.

The fact that the civilian rulers had command over the military, even in times of crisis, prevented the development of a "state within a state" and the use of war as an end in itself instead of as a political means. The daily alternation of supreme command over the military, however, caused many defeats, the most famous occurring in Cannae in 216 B.C. But these changes helped to prevent a military dictatorship. In time of extreme emergency, the People's Assembly could appoint a dictator to exercise full political powers until the grave dangers to the city had passed. The only exception to such a dictatorship limited in time was Julius Caesar, who at the end of the Roman Republic, was appointed dictator for life.

The Senate wielded limited legislative power and had authority over foreign policy, including the declaration of war and ratification of treaties. In domestic policy it had only advisory power. In contrast to the consuls and other civil servants, Senators, who numbered up to three hundred at any one time, were not elected; rather they consisted of retired high government officials, including all former consuls.

To protect themselves in courts of law, the plebeians forced the establishment of Tribunes for the People, elected by the People's Assembly and to whom any ple-

Built by the first Tarquin king, the *Circus Maximus*, seating 300,000 Romans, saw the first chariot races

Italy

The Roman Senate

beian could turn for help whenever he believed that he was being treated unjustly. These People's Tribunes could even veto decisions made by the Senate and they could eventually veto any law. It was considered to be a very serious crime to attack the Tribunes during their term of office. Plebeians won the right for themselves (and for slaves!) to stand for election to all city offices and thereby ultimately to gain seats in the Senate. Plebeians also won the right to marry patricians, thus making class lines less rigid.

Very significantly, the plebeians were able to have a written legal code adopted in 454 B.C. These laws were published on 12 bronze tablets, known as the Twelve Tablets of Law, and were kept in the heart of the city, known as the Forum. Every Roman schoolchild was expected to know them by heart, and they ultimately became the foundation of Roman law and of the legal systems of many modern European nations. Roman laws embodied all the important rules pertaining to contracts, the protection of private property, marriage and divorce and inheritance. Because private property was at the core of Roman legal thought, offenses were most frequently punished by requiring payment of property. The victims of petty theft and robbery and the families of murder victims were compensated by means of fines and confiscated property. The Romans had no clear-cut criminal law with the exception of a political penal code for corruption, abuse of public office and high treason.

Two important preconditions for the rise of Rome were the still unexplained decline of Etruscan rule over northern and central Italy in the 5th and 4th centuries B.C., as well as the Roman domination of the various tribes in Italy and the Greek cities in the south. Rome had been constantly threatened by various tribes within Italy and by Gauls who poured into the peninsula from the north. Once it was even captured and burned. The city was saved several times by such heroes as Cincinnatus and Camillus.

One Greek city in southern Italy, Tarentum, even sent for the help of Pyrrhus, King of Epirus in northern Greece, who arrived in 280 B.C. with a huge fleet carrying a herd of elephants and 25,000 troops. This army clashed with the Romans outside of Heraclea in 280 B.C.; the Romans fought extremely well, but when Pyrrhus sent his elephants roaring and screaming against the enemy troops, who had never seen such beasts before, the soldiers panicked and retreated. Though he won the battle, Pyrrhus had lost far more soldiers than had the Romans, and his weakened troops therefore were eventually beaten at Benventum. Today, the words "Pyrrhic victory" refer to any success which is achieved at too high a price.

Punic Wars

The victory over Pyrrhus, along with other swift and successful campaigns, established Roman domination over the Italian Peninsula in the first part of the 3rd century and permitted them to cast their sights farther for the first time. It is no surprise that Italy hurled a serious challenge against the major naval power in the western Mediterranean at the time: the Phoenician metropolis of Carthage (located a few miles outside the present city of Tunis in North Africa). Carthage had numerous colonies extending all along the coasts of North Africa and Spain, and it dominated Sardinia and the western part of Sicily.

In the first Carthaginian (Punic) War (264 to 241 B.C.) between the land power Rome and the sea power Carthage, Rome demonstrated its unusual adaptability by skillfully utilizing its allies in order to acquire sea power itself and by gaining the three large islands, Sicily, Sardinia and

Italy

Corsica. From 218 to 202, after the Romans had finally expelled the Gauls from the mainland peninsula, Carthage, which had been provoked by Roman meddling in Spain, sought revenge in a second round of battles known as the Second Punic War.

The Carthaginians, led by a brilliant young general named Hannibal, threatened the very heart of Rome's Italian domain. In 218 B.C. he moved an army of 100,000 foot soldiers, 1,300 cavalry and 40 elephants from Spain over the Pyrenees and Alps right into Italy. But the climate was too cold in the mountains, and he lost all his elephants and many of his troops during this journey. Nevertheless, he was able to assemble an army on its soil in 218 B.C. Although the Romans tried to avoid open battle, except at Cannae, Hannibal's forces succeeded through skillful maneuvering in destroying several Roman armies, but was never able to take Rome; he remained until 203 B.C. when he received word of an end run that the Romans were planning on Carthage itself. He departed hastily to his city's rescue, but to no avail. Roman troops captured the city and destroyed it, salting the soil in the hope that nothing would ever grow again. From this harshness came the expression "a Carthaginian peace." At last, Rome was unchallenged master of the western Mediterranean. (A treaty between Carthage, now outside Tunis, and Rome ending the Punic wars was finally signed . . . in 1987 A.D.!)

Roman Imperialism

Rome could now direct its sights eastward toward Greece. Between 198 and 190 B.C., Rome won victories in Greece, which not only again opened the Roman door wide to Greek cultural influence, but it also gave the Romans a firm foothold in Asia Minor. This was the beginning of Roman imperialism. Hitherto, diplomatic balancing and management of conquered peoples were the primary factors in Roman foreign policy; in the new phase it adopted different methods of power politics. Punitive expeditions against disloyal allies and the destruction of cities like Carthage and Corinth in 115 B.C. revealed the foreign political pattern for the conquest of the eastern Mediterranean area. By 63 B.C. nearly all the countries in the Mediterranean region were paying tribute to Rome.

The burden of constant war and of administering the enormous empire overextended the resources of a small state that started on the banks of the Tiber River at the foot of the Palatine Hill, which had transformed itself into a large and powerful metropolis.

The Romans' encounter with Greece during the conquest of the eastern Mediterranean area influenced Roman life and thought in such a way that the Roman poet Horace could write that the "conquered Greeks conquered their victors." Greek slaves taught the children of the wealthy in the Roman Empire. The Greek language assumed a role during

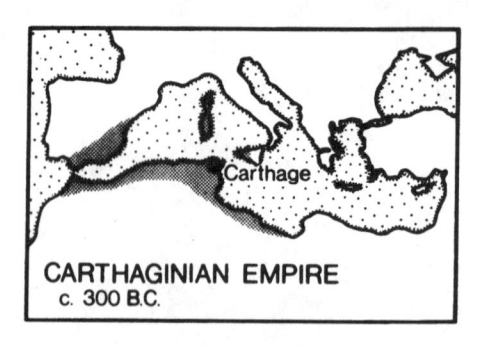

CARTHAGINIAN EMPIRE c. 300 B.C.

the Republic which in some ways corresponded to that of the French language in the 17th and 18th centuries. On the other hand, the Romans clung to their traditional political and cultural norms and deeply mistrusted foreign influences. They were willing to adopt those technical and institutional achievements of other peoples which the Romans considered worthy of copying. For instance, many weapons systems were patterned after those of the conquered peoples. The critical examination and adoption of that which was considered better, combined with the steadfastness of a self–reliant identity, gave Roman policies their dynamism and flexibility.

After many years the Republican constitution became increasingly incapable of solving the many social problems of such a large realm. The defense of the vast empire, with its many administrative requirements, called for an effective central bureaucracy, but the old Republic did not have such an institution and was therefore unable to perform many essential functions. Numerous military campaigns claimed thousands of casualties and therefore left large tracts of land either to fall fallow or into the hands of the large landowners. Further, following the campaigns, many unemployed soldiers drifted into Rome, thereby adding to the city's mounting problems.

In earlier times no one was permitted to enter the city of Rome with weapons. Standing armies with nothing to do and former peasants who had lost their land to large landowners broke down the old customs which had integrated the army with the society and the state. At this point, the earlier observation of the Greek philosopher, Aristotle, applied to Rome: masters of weapons are also masters of the state.

The political order in the Roman Republic began slowly to disintegrate, and widespread dissatisfaction, lawlessness and corruption ran riot throughout the realm. The citizens' rights were gradually whittled away; the parties particularly established themselves in the social circles of the later Republic from 133 to 45 B.C. The *Senate Party* represented the interests of the nobility and the large landowners, while the *Popular Party* was supported by the masses.

The Republic Falls; The Empire Arises

Early in the 1st century B.C. civil war between these two groups broke out which lasted on and off for most of the remainder of the century. The leading figure in this struggle was Gaius Julius Caesar, the best known leader within the *Popular Party*. Born into a patrician's family, but always possessing strong plebeian sentiments, his extraordinary bravery and endurance endeared him with his troops. He was a talented general, politician, orator, poet, historian, mathematician and architect. William Shakespeare called this unique man "the noblest man that ever lived in the tide of times." In 60 B.C. he was elected consul and set about to accomplish his two chief objectives of establishing order in Rome and the empire, and reconciling the conflicting classes. He spent nine years in Gaul (presently France) and Britain, which not only enabled him to win victories for Rome, but to write an eight volume history entitled the *Gallic War*, which remains one of the most important books of ancient history (much to the distress of modern Latin students).

When he wanted to return to Rome in 49 B.C., he was informed by the Senate that he was to disband his army and to return to Rome alone. Sensing that he was about to be arrested, he decided to cross the Rubicon River and to march his army *against* Rome itself. For four years he confronted his enemies, including his former friend and son–in–law, Pompey, in battles in Greece, Egypt, North Africa and Spain, before returning in 45 B.C. as master of the entire Roman world.

Julius was acclaimed dictator in 45 B.C. He proceeded to try to restore order and to introduce such measures as founding colonies inside and outside of Italy to provide new lives for Rome's unemployed, providing grain for the hungry, enabling non–Romans to become members of the Senate and making all residents of Italy Roman citizens. He also made no secret of his conviction that Rome could survive only if it had one ruler with absolute power which included the right to name his successor.

Fearing the restoration of kings, a group

Italy

of senators let by Brutus and Cassius murdered Caesar in 44 B.C. in the theater of Pompeius, which was being used temporarily as the Senate. This act, vividly dramatized by Shakespeare, again thrust Rome into a civil war which touched every part of the realm. Not until Octavian, Caesar's grandnephew, established order in 31 B.C. did the bloody civil war come to an end. He became the first emperor of Rome, under the name of Augustus (meaning "the revered") and his successors bore the title of "Caesar" in honor of Julius. The Roman Republic was dead, and the Roman Empire had commenced. The Caesars served for life and were selected in many different ways. Most of them were not from the city of Rome. Some even came from Spain, (Trajan), Africa (Lucius Septimius Severus) or from what is now Yugoslavia (Diocletian).

Peace and Prosperity

Augustus restored order and revived trade, and his people again experienced the rare combination of peace and prosperity. He launched a building program in the empire and its capital which enabled him to say toward the end of his life in 14 B.C., "I found Rome a city of brick and am leaving it a city of marble." Despite a string of less capable emperors, his life's work lasted almost two centuries.

There are many preconceived ideas about Roman emperors. They are often portrayed as degenerate beasts who practiced tyranny with Caesarian insanity, only to fall victims to palace revolts or poisonous death. This is only an anecdotal and superficial understanding. It is true that they sometimes directed political cruelty against other members of the noble class who might have presented a threat to them, but the Roman Empire and its citizens drew many benefits from the emperors' efforts.

It was precisely the centralized bureaucracy, which the emperors created, which made the Roman Empire the blooming civilization as we know it today. Some were wise and learned men, such as Marcus Aurelius, whose published volume, *Meditations,* is still a highly valued philosophical work. Impressive ruins bear eloquent witness to prosperous Roman cities from Germany to the desert sands of the Sahara. The Empire reached its greatest expansion under Emperor Trajan from 98 to 117 A.D. From Iraq to Scotland, from Cologne to Libya, one spoke Latin and lived according to Roman law and customs.

A dark shadow over the cultural splendor of the Roman classical period was the fact that much of the economic prosperity was achieved by means of slave labor. Modern estimations are that at any one time between 300,000 and 500,000 slaves provided a luxurious life for many citizens of Rome, which by the 2nd century A.D. had grown to a city of over a million inhabitants, including slaves. Our present view of humanity inclines us to judge harshly the treatment of the ancient slaves, who without rights or status could be sold or even killed by their masters. Under Roman law they were considered to be nothing more than "animated tools." However, slaves were actually valuable property, especially an educated Greek.

The degree of suppression endured by a slave depended upon his type of work. Naturally, those slaves who served in public office, including the highest administrative offices, or who as scholars instructed the children of wealthy Romans were much better off than those who worked on the large plantations. The exploitation of the latter led to two slave revolts. In 136 B.C. the slaves in Sicily rose up under their leader, Syrer Eunus, and established a short–lived slave republic in the city of Enna. From 73 to 71 Rome trembled before the legendary slave leader, Spartacus, who led 90,000 rebellious slaves in southern Italy.

Very early the conscience of many persons was stirred by the injustice of slavery. In Plautus' comedies the slaves always played the intelligent and superior roles. Stoic philosophy rejected such servitude entirely. In making a judgment against human bondage in the Roman world, one must remember that slavery existed in modern times as well. In addition, the history of human suppression and exploitation is a very long one. To say that a worker during the period of early capitalism in Manchester or a mercenary Hessian soldier bought by the English to fight against Washington's army during the American Revolution was better off than an ancient slave would be deceptive.

The Decline and Fall of the Empire

The emperors considered their main task to be the security of the Empire's extensive borders. However, as the threat of invasion became greater and greater, the ancient Roman world was unable to withstand after the beginning of the 3rd century A.D. the mounted attacks of Germans, Slavs, Huns, Persians, Turks, Mongolians, Berbers and later, of Arabs.

In 284 A.D. Diocletian, the son of a freed slave from Illyria (now in Yugoslavia) became emperor. He realized that the Roman Empire had grown too large to be governed by one man, so in 285 A.D. he divided it into an Eastern and a Western part. He assumed rule over the eastern portion, with its seat in Nicomedia in Asia Minor, and the subsequent Western em-

Statue of the Emperor Trajan in Rome

perors held court at Milan and Trier. Emperor Constantine, who became sole Emperor of Rome in 324 A.D., continued the reorganization of the Empire initiated by Diocletian. He built a new city on the site of the former Byzantium, a strategically important crossroads between Asia and Europe, and named it after himself: Constantinople. From then on, the Roman Empire was administered from that city and Rome lost much of its significance. There, Roman civilization mingled with that of Greece and of Asia.

Disciples of and converts to Christianity had been circulating amid most parts of the empire since the 1st century A.D., converting many who held the ancient Greek and Roman beliefs in the classical gods to their belief in a single, almighty God. These beliefs and moral teachings were those of a mortal who claimed to be his Son. A gradual Christian penetration of the Roman society and the emergence of Christianity to that of a state religion was not as commonly supposed. They were only persecuted when they directly challenged the traditional classical understanding of a state religion as a form of political loyalty. It would not have been possible for Christian beliefs to spread unless there had otherwise been an attitude of relative religious tolerance. In spite of some use of torture and martyrdom, this faith continued inexorably to grow, even-

Italy

tually becoming the most powerful and dominating concept of the western and mid–eastern world (al though supplanted by Islam to a large degree in the Mideast after the life of the prophet Mohammed).

Constantine decided to accept Christianity and to make it the Empire's official religion. After his death in 337 A.D. there was less and less cooperation and coordination between the eastern and western parts of the Empire. While Constantinople was a safe distance from the marauding tribes of Europe, the western part became the object of sustained attacks by Goths, Visigoths and Vandals. Rome was temporarily captured and sacked in 410 A.D. and in 476 the East Gothic chief, Odoacer, marched his troops into the city and deposed the last western Roman Emperor, Romulus Augustulus. Thereafter, sheep grazed on the overgrown ruins of the Forum, once the scene of the power behind the heart of the Empire.

Rome Destroyed

The destruction of Rome was without precedent. But many aspects of this great Empire have been salvaged for posterity, including its literature, which was protected in the Christian cloisters, and its law. Further testimonies to the splendor of the Roman past are the unique accomplishments in architecture, such as domes, columns and basilicas, and in engineering, such as bridges, aqueducts and highways. Most of the important European roads today follow the same routes established by the Romans. Therefore, Italy's past is significant not only to Italians, but to all persons touched by western civilization.

The "Middle Ages"

During and after the Middle Ages, Italy was so fragmented into feuding and ever–shifting states, Papal holdings, kingdoms and foreign dominions that even well–educated Italians have difficulty comprehending their own history during that time. In the Middle Ages as well as in modern times, Italy was characterized by foreign domination, inner strife and parochialism of the Catholic Church. Over a span of a thousand years Byzantines, Germanic tribes, Arabs, Germans, Normans (Scandinavians), Frenchmen, Spaniards and Austrians marched across the land and levied taxes or subjugated the dependent minor princes in the peninsula to servitude.

Ideals such as freedom, unity and independence first became political realities in 1861 with the "Resurgence," or unification movement. With Italy's past in mind, it should be no surprise that Italians' identification with their state developed very slowly. The political culture was stamped with a combined feeling of powerlessness and distrust toward the state.

After the fall of the Roman Empire, centuries of gloom and of alternating domination, particularly by the Germans and Lombards, afflicted the peninsula until the Frankish King Pippin, father of Charlemagne, introduced in the 8th century A.D. a territorial order in Italy. It was divided into a Lombard–Frankish area in the north and a Byzantine area in the south, ruled ultimately from Constantinople. The results of this fateful division continue to be evident in the economic and cultural contrasts between the North and the South right up to the present day.

Along with the division of Italy, the

The Roman Empire at its height

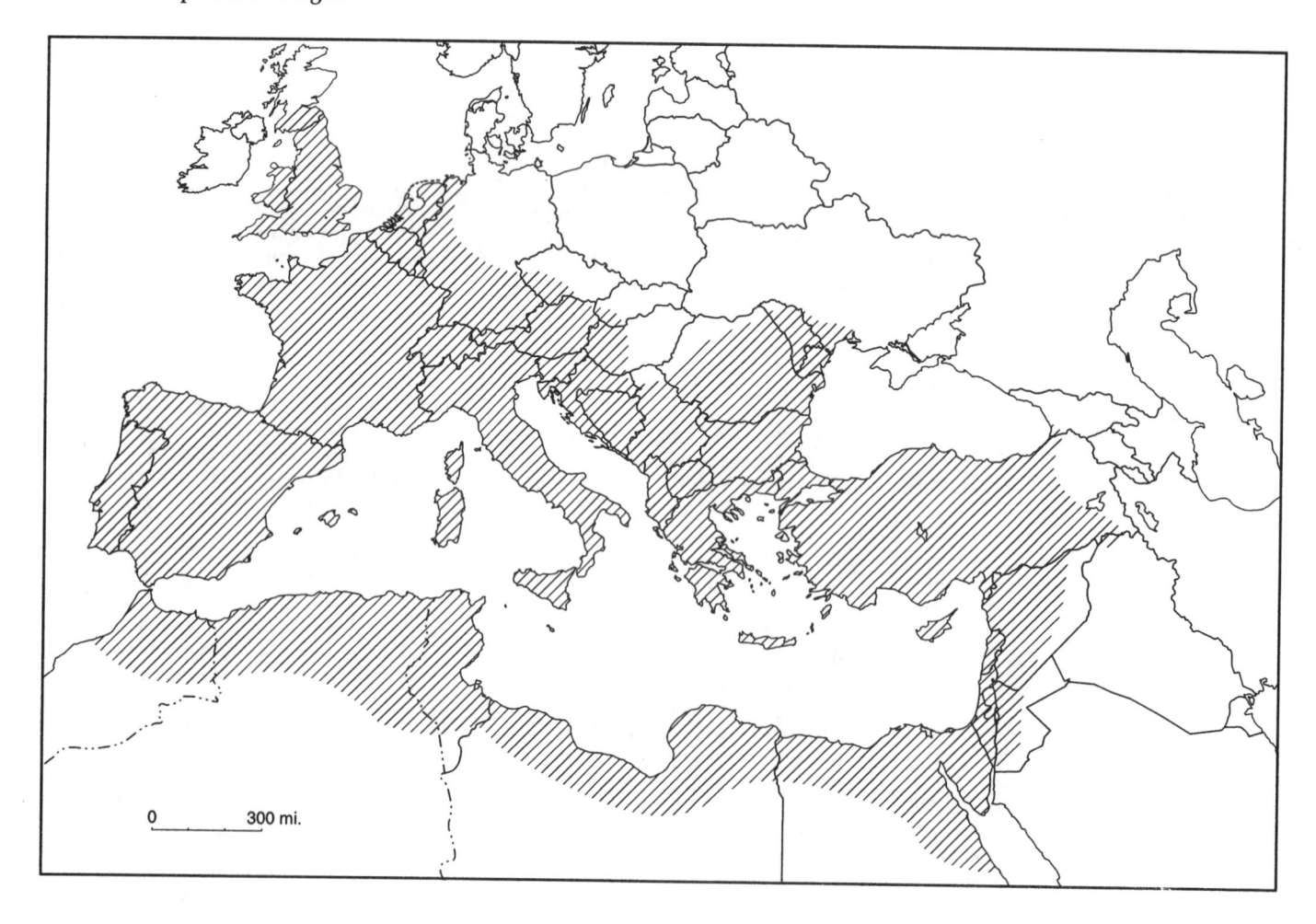

Italy

so-called "Pippin Deed" had another extremely far-reaching consequence for the political development of Italy. The Deed assured the Pope an ecclesiastical state in the middle of Italy, which centuries later was the last political entity in the nation which resisted unification with the national Italian state.

Meanwhile during the later Middle Ages, as the North was involved in and profiting from the constant conflict between the German Emperors and the Popes, the South was undergoing an entirely different development. The Byzantines, who were also occupying Sicily, could no longer fend off the attacks of the Moslem Saracens from North Africa.

The Byzantines, who had become Eastern Orthodox Christians, could not count on the Roman Catholic Church for assistance in upholding their occupation. Around 900 Sicily blossomed into a rich and fertile garden under the new Moslem rule. The Saracens, reputed to be bloodthirsty pirates along the coast of Italy, exercised a clever and tolerant reign in which an enormous cultural flowering unfolded. They introduced lemons, oranges, cotton and pistachio nuts, the last being the island's most important agricultural export today. Only an entirely new actor who entered the world scene could put an end to such a rule.

The Power of the Holy "Roman" Empire

In 1080, through a shrewd marriage policy, southern Italy under the Normans (Vikings) became joined with the Holy Roman (actually German) Empire under Friedrich II of the Staufen dynasty. Known to his contemporaries as "the wonder of the world," Friedrich was an enlightened emperor who was as at home in the world of politics as in the world of scholarship. His reign was the last golden age in Italy before a long period of conservative–clerical foreign domination. Despite their different life-styles, Friedrich succeeded in uniting the original inhabitants of southern Italy, the Byzantine Greeks and the Moslem Saracens, in a life of harmonious co-existence. Under his rule a cultural and economic highpoint was achieved which was unparalleled in Europe at the time.

The new spirit of tolerance as well as the encirclement of the ecclesiastical state by Friedrich's territories did not please the Pope. The long-standing dispute between the German Emperors and the Pope reached a climax with the appeal for a crusade against Friedrich. Many had hoped that divided Italy would develop into a model state under the reign of the House of Staufen. These dreams were shattered, however, when the Frenchman, Charles of Anjou, protégé of the Pope, overthrew Staufen rule in Italy. Southern Italy suffered terribly under the domination of the Anjou family until 1282, when the mounting hate against the uninhibited French arrogance erupted. The absolute monarchy of the French in southern Italy was consumed with uninterrupted wars, and could not withstand the attacks by the Aragonians from Spain, who, through intrigues, were able to undermine every French military unit.

Disunification

As a result of the disputes between the Pope and the German Emperor, the small and fragmented states and cities in northern Italy were able to achieve a certain degree of political independence. Loyalty to one side or the other varied, depending upon the political advantage at the time of a given battle.

The cities knew well how to exploit to their own economic advantage the disputes of the Popes and the German Emperors and the Crusades, which began at the end of the 11th century. The latter were medieval efforts directed at reclaiming Jerusalem from the Arabs. Of all cities, Venice profited most of all from these efforts. The Venetians did not in any way share the religious fervor or self-sacrifice of the German, French and English knights. The knights and the pilgrims enroute to the Crusades and Jerusalem poured into rival Venice and Genoa in droves.

One of the most notable Crusades was the Fourth, which took place from 1198–1204. The aged, composed and politically gifted Doge (leader) Dandolo of Venice was able to redirect the course toward Constantinople and agreed to transport the crusaders to their destination on the condition that they stop along the way and plunder Constantinople for Venice. Thus, instead of becoming conquerors of holy cities held by Moslems, the crusaders attacked and plundered a Christian capital city! The Quadriga, a large statue of four horses from the Hippodrome in Constantinople and now above St. Mark's Cathedral in Venice, bears witness to this strange event. In this way, a troublesome trade rival was seriously weakened. Venice was so powerful that it was not even perturbed by the resulting excommunication of the Venetian leaders by the Pope.

Despite the continuing conflict, no other country in Europe achieved at this time the degree of economic development which took place in Italy. One of the most well-known and powerful families of bankers, the Medici, had gained far-reaching political influence in their home city of Florence, as well as in France, where marriage joined Catherine de Medici with King Henry II. In the economically developed cities of northern and central Italy, the transition had been made from a less productive barter economy to a money economy. The bases of this affluence were the development of industry and trade, especially with the Middle and Far East.

The Re-Awakening—(Renaissance)

In the 14th and 15th centuries northern Italy was the cradle of an intellectual and cultural rebirth known as the *Renaissance*. This reawakening was indirectly stimulated by Venice's refusal to support Constantinople when that city was subjected to a determined Turkish attack. When that last remnant of the Roman Empire finally fell in 1453, many highly cultured Greeks emigrated to Italy from Constantinople and gave the Renaissance movement a significant boost. They helped to reawaken Italian interest in the Greek classical authors. Had it not been for the efforts of the Italian scholars, who laboriously collected and preserved many ancient Greek works, the originals we possess today would have been lost forever.

In the depths of the foaming cauldron of bickering city-states a fundamentally new approach to life was born. Man was no longer the *viator mundi* (pilgrim seeking heavenly salvation) of the Middle Ages, concerned with the universal principle of salvation. He became the *Faber mundi* (the creator and master of the world), who shaped his own destiny. Self-assured individualism and rational thought were reflected in the Renaissance conception of the state. Autonomous states were directed by paid public officials according to the guidelines of "reason of state," and carefully calculated business considerations determined politics and administration. Wars were conducted by mercenary enterprises (known as *condittieri*) who dared to do battle in the same way as one dares to make capital investment, that is, only if a profit is certain. The Florentine, Niccolò Machiavelli, developed the theory of politics which in no way was based upon religious principles.

Correspondingly, scholars who had until that time been considered as *ancillas theologiae* ("slaves of theology") divested themselves of that status and began working independently of theology. Above all, rediscovery of the classical authors advanced this secular conception to that of a rational principle. Spurred on by their Latin predecessors, Dante, Petrarca and Boccaccio, they created new literature in Italian (sometimes intermingled with Latin) but later a total variant of the historic language of Rome.

Italy

Scene typical of the Renaissance—Dante in Florence

The universal man with his comprehensive wealth of knowledge represented the new ideal of the Renaissance man. The universal genius, Leonardo da Vinci, was a painter, artist, engineer, doctor, architect and politician and is a particularly prominent example of vast numbers of creative persons who contributed enormously to his culturally rich times. Inspired by the classical model of rounded arches which tied together the central construction, architects developed a totally new concept of space through emphasis on the vertical, with clear, well-formed proportions. Donatello and Michelangelo surpassed their classical predecessors in expression and monumentality. In painting, the central perspective was developed which strove for ideal anatomical proportion which were at the same time more realistic. Masaccio, Botticelli, Raphael and da Vinci, the best known painters of their time, were the leading lights of an art movement which influenced the entire field of European painting.

Secular-Religious Relations

The Popes themselves were responsible for directing the focus of the Renaissance from the religious realm to the secular princes and scholars. For instance, Pope Julius was Michelangelo's patron. As learned patrons of the arts, the Popes accelerated the inner disintegration of the Church—the reconstruction of St. Peter's Cathedral, sponsored by a member of the Medici family, Pope Leo X, could only be financed by his system of indulgences (paying for forgiveness of sin). This way of raising revenue unleashed the Reformation in the early 16th century. When the Popes became staunch supporters of the counter-Reformation, Italy ceased being the center of the Renaissance, which thereafter found a more congenial setting in France.

In the conflict between the Hapsburgs and the French, which was the central problem for the Western European states until the 18th century, the autonomous Italian city-states lost much of their independence. The plunder and devastation caused by the rival French and Hapsburg armies, as well as pillaging and destruction by pirates from North African Barbary states, came to dominate life in Italy. The South gradually faded under Spanish domination and became unhinged from developments in the rest of Europe. The war of the Spanish Succession (1701–1713), which endangered the European balance of power between the Hapsburgs and France, brought northern Italy under the domination of the Austrians and southern Italy under the control of the Spanish Bourbons. The Popes retained their political hold over much of central Italy. Due to uncontrolled cuttings, the rich forests of Puglia, where Friedrich II had so happily hunted, were reduced to withering grasslands.

It is hardly surprising that the shock waves of the French Revolution of 1789 soon were felt in Italy, where feudal institutions and conditions were still present. French republican forces invaded Savoy and Nice in the fall of 1792 and in March 1796 a concentrated French campaign began in Italy. This resulted not only in temporary French domination of most of northern and central Italy, but also in brilliant victories for a young French general who soon became the leader of France, Napoleon Bonaparte. In early 1798 French forces invaded the Papal states. The Pope fled and a Roman Republic was established. Although the French were temporarily driven out of Italy in the latter part of 1799, Napoleon, who had seized power in late 1799, renewed his Italian conquests and soon secured much of Italy under his control. When Napoleon made himself Emperor of France he also placed an Italian crown on his head, thereby becoming King of Italy, with all of northern and central Italy under his authority. In the spring of 1806 French forces occupied the rest of Italy and on March 30, 1806, Napoleon's brother, Joseph, was pro-

Italy

A FOREIGN DOMINATED, POLITICALLY FRAGMENTED PENINSULA

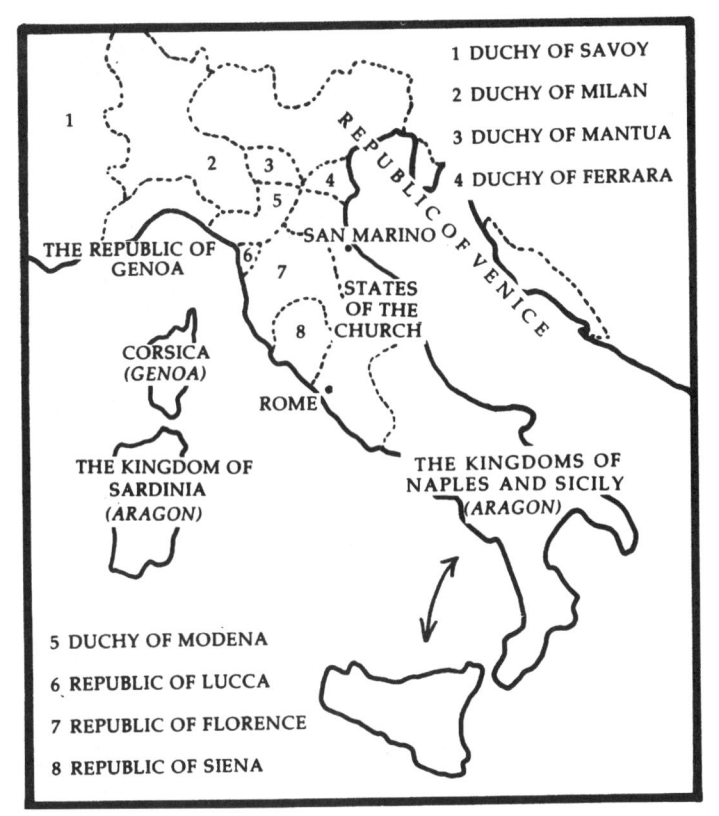

About 1450

About 1722

claimed the King of the Two Sicilies. When Joseph became King of Spain in 1808, a French general, Joachim Murat, was crowned King of Naples.

Exit Napoleon

Although Napoleon's hold on Italy was finally broken in 1815, his legacy remained. He had decreed important reforms in the country. These included the Napoleonic Code, which together with Roman law, remains the foundation of Italian law today. He confiscated much of the Church's property, ended feudal privileges and immunities and improved roads and education. He thereby gave Italians a crucially important impetus for political, social, legal and economic reform.

The restoration of the old regime after the Congress of Vienna reestablished Austrian domination in northern and central Italy. The Pope was granted the Vatican's pre–Napoleonic holdings again and the Bourbon King, Ferdinand I of the Two Sicilies again became ruler of southern Italy. But the spark of the enlightenment, Italian nationalism and the right of Italians to establish a democratic state continued to ferment within a few secret societies of bourgeois intellectuals.

Fragmented Italy

Prince Metternich of Austria stated correctly in 1815 that Italy was not a nation, but rather a "geographic concept." The only state within Italy which played an active role in Europe was Piedmont–Savoy, where the unification movement originated. The remainder of Italy was either under foreign control or ruled by small splinter states. The parochialism which had its roots in Italian history also resisted the liberal ideas of the French Revolution and those of the few "middle and upper–class romantics" who dreamed of Italian national unification. Numerous uprisings, usually started by the secret societies against the established rulers from 1820 to 1831 were all crushed.

The revolutionary movement was not strong enough to overcome Austrian domination without outside help. The major European powers had concluded that the balance of power in Europe was more important than Italian unity. Further, the most important secret resistance movement, the *Carboneria* (literally "Charcoal Burners") had been so loosely organized, so heterogeneous and so unable to define its aims clearly that it was incapable of uniting in crucial moments.

It was these kinds of problems that certain subsequent Italian nationalists tried to avoid. The traveler to Italy notices that in every town, streets and plazas bear the names of Mazzini, Cavour and Garibaldi. They made up the triple constellation of the "Resurgence," the name they gave to Italian political unification in 1861.

Gradual Unification

In 1831 a young Genoan political thinker, Giuseppe Mazzini, founded the "Young Italy" movement. He had remained the intellectual head and prophet of the unification drive for a free, independent and republican Italy although he was unable to lead that movement to success. He died in 1872 bitterly disappointed about the kind of Italian state which had been created.

In 1848 uprisings again occurred throughout Italy, and the Pope was even temporarily driven out of Rome. But with the aid of French troops, the rebellion was quelled. With its failure, nationalists' eyes turned increasingly toward the Kingdom of Piedmont–Sardinia, whose capital was Turin and which was ruled by one of the oldest ruling families in Europe, the house of Savoy. It had been the only regime in Italy which had fought hard for freedom from Austria.

Italy

Under Napoleon, 1804–13

The Unification of Italy, 1849–70

The new Piedmont king, Victor Emmanuel, who was to become the first king of a united Italy, was a man of rough manners and visible virility. He became a popular focus of attention for those who wanted change. But he was also a politically shrewd man, which was revealed by his appointment as Piedmontese Prime Minister of a man whom he personally detested: Count Camillo di Cavour, not a brilliant man, but a pragmatic man who was well aware that Italy could never become independent as a result of spontaneous mass uprisings of idealists. The political hold of Austria had to be broken and he knew that Italians would need the help of a foreign power to do this. Therefore, he turned to the new French Emperor, Napoleon III.

The French leader agreed to support Piedmont in any war against Austria under the condition that in the event of victory, France be rewarded with Nice and Savoy. The deal was sealed by the marriage of Victor Emmanuel's 15-year-old daughter, Clotilde, with Napoleon's lecherous cousin, Jerome. With such a commitment tucked away in his breastpocket, Cavour sought a way to bring about war with Austria. Two blunders by the latter country played directly into Cavour's hands. One was Austria's decision to impose military conscription on its dominions of Lombardy and Venetia, a move which drove many draft-dodgers into Piedmont. The tension which arose as a result of Piedmont's refusal to turn these young men over to the Austrian authorities gave Cavour the excuse he needed to begin military preparations.

The second blunder was committed just when the French Emperor was beginning to have second thoughts about the promises he had made earlier to Piedmont. In the spring of 1859 Austria issued an ultimatum to Piedmont, demanding that it either disarm itself or go to war. Cavour, of course, chose the latter, and with Napoleon's assistance faced the powerful but indecisive Austrian Army and defeated it at Magenta on June 4 and at Solferino on June 24 and conquered all Lombardy and Milan.

After these important victories, Napoleon grew weary of the war and concluded an armistice with the Austrians at Villafranca on July 11. Cavour was understandably furious at the French, but the movement toward Italian unity had gained such momentum that it could no longer be stopped. Revolutionary assemblies in Tuscany, Modena, Parma and Romagna voted in August 1859 to unite with Piedmont; France and Britain spoke out against any foreign (i.e. Austrian) intervention to foil these popular decisions. In March 1860, plebiscites in the four areas confirmed the steps taken by the assemblies. True to his earlier promise, Cavour delivered Savoy and Nice to the French.

Southern Unification

With most of northern and central Italy now unified, the cauldron of unification began to bubble in the South. In the spring of 1860 revolts broke out in Sicily which gave a highly talented military adventurer his chance to reenter the center stage in Italy—Giuseppe Garibaldi. A former member of Mazzini's "Young Italy" movement, he had spent 13 years as a soldier of fortune in Latin America, where he became a master in the leadership of irregular forces and guerrilla warfare. He had raced back to Italy in 1848 when he heard of the revolutionary activity there. He formed military forces first in Lombardy, then in Venice and finally in Rome, where he served under Mazzini to defend the Roman Republic which had just been created. From April to the end of June 1849, Garibaldi's legion, clad in red shirts and Calabrian hats, had defended the "Eternal City" valiantly against French troops which protected the Pope. Prolonged resistance had proved to be impossible, so Garibaldi fled with his troops to the tiny independent republic of San Marino, where he disbanded his army and went into exile.

Revolts in Sicily in 1860 again drew him into southern Italy and in May he

Italy

packed his 1,000 irregulars, mostly students, poets and soldiers of fortune, into rickety steamers and set a course directly to Sicily. When he arrived at Marsala, he declared himself dictator of Sicily and proceeded to defeat piecemeal the confused and divided Neapolitan troops which were supposed to defend the island. By mid–July he poised for his strike against the Bourbon Kingdom of the Two Sicilies with its capital in Naples.

Riding a tide of popular enthusiasm, Garibaldi's army, which had swollen to 10,000 men, crossed the Strait of Messina in mid–1860, and his units produced panic among the Neapolitan troops whenever they appeared. On September 7, a jubilant Garibaldi entered the city of Naples far in advance of his troops. In less than five months he had conquered the Kingdom of the Two Sicilies, a country of 11 million inhabitants.

He immediately set his sights again on Rome, which was still defended by French troops. Not wishing to lose entirely the initiative for unifying Italy, Cavour ordered his own troops to march southward into the Papal States. On September 18 they crushed the Pope's forces at Castelfidardo and then defeated a remaining Neapolitan Army at Capua. These successes prompted the Piedmontese parliament to annex southern Italy. In October plebiscites in Naples, Sicily, the Marches and Umbria revealed overwhelming popular support for union with Piedmont. In February 1861 Victor Emmanuel II was proclaimed King of Italy, and a new Italian parliament representing the entire peninsula except Rome and the province of Venetia assembled. Shortly thereafter Florence became Italy's new capital until 1870.

Differences Among the Union

The historical differences between northern and southern Italy were not overcome through the unification and establishment of a monarchy. Despite the initial enthusiasm in southern Italy for joining the newly unified state, the southern half of the autonomous Italian national state was considered by the northern rulers more as a conquered province of the North. They displayed little respect for traditional practices in the South, regarding the people as backward and rural, and merely included it in a highly centralized governmental administration which was imposed on all of Italy. Therefore, the Italian King's popularity in the South disappeared almost overnight, and southerners again began to look northward with distrust and resentment which has yet to disappear.

The new national leaders next turned to the province of Venetia, which was still in the clutches of the Austrian Empire. When the latter entered a war in 1866 against Prussia, however, Italy immediately sided with the victorious Prussians, who granted their allies the prize which Italians had wanted. Only Rome remained outside the new Italy.

The End of the Church State

The ecclesiastical state, under the Pope, remained a drop of melancholy in the wine of the unification. The Vatican resented the reduction of its secular power in the unification of Italy. As the new Italian state was officially declared in 1861, it was taboo even to speak of Piedmont and that part of Italy ruled by it. But when France became locked in war against Prussia in 1870, French troops could no longer defend Rome against the rest of Italy. Hence, in September royal Italian troops marched into Rome unchallenged, and the national capital was transferred to the city without delay.

The ecclesiastical state came to an end, and the popes withdrew in bitterness behind the Vatican walls with utter contempt for the Italian kingdom. This Papal rejection of the Italian state nipped in the bud all attempts to integrate Catholic elements in politics, and the Catholic prohibition against political participation gained strength especially in the more independent–minded South. It hardened many Italians' distrust toward their state, a problem which remains today. Leading liberals asserted their strong anticlerical position despite the Church's opposition. Only in the first decade of the 20th century did the Church support a *Catholic People's Party* (the *Popolari*), a forerunner of the present *Christian Democratic Party*. Those historians are certainly correct who argue that an earlier integration of moderate Catholic forces would have helped stabilize Italy's political system and would have helped to prevent the later rise of fascism.

Continued Instability

The first years of unification were overshadowed by political instability, social opposition and an ever–growing gap between North and South. The inhabitants of the South continued to be looked down upon as backward, illiterate semi–North Africaners. The people were also disadvantaged by the new liberal leaders' dropping of trade barriers, which clearly favored the industrially powerful North.

The one–crop agrarian society of the South bore the full economic weight of foreign grain imports. Malnutrition, health problems and child labor abuse set in motion an enormous emigration wave from the South. From 1886 to 1890 over 200,000 people left their homeland every year, most of whom sought refuge in the United States. Today, 25 million Americans are of Italian and/or Sicilian descent. The fact that most of their ancestors came from southern Italy helps explain why Americans often have a one–sided view of Italy, namely that of the impoverished South rather than the more opulent North.

Parliamentary proceedings degenerated quickly as deputies became so concerned about clinging to their seats that

Monument in Rome commemorating the unification of Italy

Italy

they avoided taking clearcut stands on the pressing issues of the day. By means of a method which came to be known as *Trasformismo* ("Transformism"), prime ministers and cabinets disregarded party affiliation and made delicate bargains with any interested deputies from the left, right or center in order to patch together a short–lived parliamentary majority. In the process, all political groups became highly fractured, and cabinets changed so constantly that no coherent and consistent governmental policy was possible. Major questions were avoided or postponed, and when domestic pressure for change became too great, governments tended to divert attention from them by taking refuge in such emotional campaigns as anticlericalism or colonialism.

Colonial Ambitions

In order to cope with the problem of a surplus of workers and to divert attention from the domestic political paralysis and tensions, Italy embarked on a colonial policy which was not only unprofitable, but which robbed it of its strength. After a casualty–ridden expedition into the East African coast of Eritrea (now in Ethiopia), Italy temporarily conquered this area in 1889–90. A subsequent campaign in Ethiopia ended in catastrophe soon thereafter, costing the lives of 15,000 poorly–equipped soldiers when the Ethiopians drove them out. Italy took Libya and the southeastern Greek islands (Dodecanese) from Turkey, which was in the process of disintegration.

All of these foreign adventures could not distract from the domestic social tensions and conflicts. Rebellions, violent protests, assassinations and bloody reactions against the forces of order became so commonplace by the turn of the century that many observers believed that the young kingdom could not survive.

The most outstanding politician in the early 20th century was Giovanni Giolitti, who tried to fuse the liberal bourgeoisie and socialists who supported the state from 1903 to 1915. He was able to guide some progressive legislation through a highly undisciplined parliament. Factory laws were passed, insurance companies and railways were nationalized, trade unions were legalized, agricultural cooperatives were subsidized and collective bargaining was encouraged. However, he could not overcome the widespread impression among the people that Italy was not only standing still, but was decaying.

Sick and tired of these internal conflicts, a movement of bourgeois intellectuals under the leadership of the poet Gabriele D'Annunzio, and the political thinkers Gaetano Mosca and Vilfredo Pareto gained respect, and practically declared war on the parliamentary system. D'Annunzio called on young Italians to seek fulfillment in violent action that would put an end to parliamentary maneuvering, general mediocrity and dullness which characterized public life. Mosca and Pareto called for a new political elite which understood how to use power and to put an end to materialist values.

A jingoist *National Party* was created in 1910 under the leadership of Enrico Corradini, who never tired of painting an attractive picture of martial heroism, of total sacrifice of individualism and equality to one's nation, of the need for reestablishing discipline and obedience, of the grandeur and power of ancient Rome and of the personal gratification which comes with living dangerously. Its extremist appeals were heard enthusiastically by many Italians, who needed only the travails of a long and disappointing war to make a dangerous leap toward fascism.

World War I

Although Italy had allied itself with Germany and Austria–Hungary in 1882, it declared its neutrality at the outbreak of World War I in 1914 on the grounds that its allies were waging an aggressive war. For more than ten years it had pursued, under Giolitti's leadership, a policy of peaceful reconciliation in Europe. Italy did, in fact, enter World War I against Austria and Germany in 1915. In Hemingway's *A Farewell to Arms*, one sees that the Italian war against Austria was neither easily won nor advantageous for Italy. It lost 600,000 men in battle, and the Italian economy was wrecked by the war. The public debt swelled, inflation ran out of control and many of the demobilized soldiers left one kind of army for another: that of the unemployed.

To make things worse, the aftermath of the Paris peace settlement following the war never fulfilled Italy's high expectations. Trentino and the city of Trieste did become part of the country, as did the Istrian Peninsula (now a part of Yugoslavia) and the German–speaking part of South Tirol which, even today, remains a bone of contention between Austria and Italy.

Postwar Chaos

Italy had entered the post World War I era as a society badly off balance. Without relief, lawlessness in the countryside and towns, strikes in the cities as well as sharp and often violent domestic differences of opinion, polarized the political scene. The war had brought revolution in Russia, and with that revolution a breaking away in Italy and elsewhere of radically revolutionary communists from the more moderate socialist parties. The establishment of the *Communist Party of Italy (PCI)* scared many anti–Marxist Italians, who became sympathetic to the idea of a strong leader who could protect Italy from the communist revolution. This included many wealthy landowners and industrialists.

The war had also frustrated the dreams of many Italian nationalists, who had believed that Italy should become a major Mediterranean and Balkan power. Millions of returning veterans were bitter about the fact that their country seemed to show no appreciation for the suffering and sacrifice which they had endured. Even appearing on the streets in uniform was bound to evoke abuse. Finally, the traditional Italian parties and elites were almost wholly incapable of coping with the domestic political situation. Therefore, a vacuum and a constituency were created for a charismatic opportunist with extremely flexible principles and an emotionally appealing, but intellectually fraudulent political theory: Benito Mussolini.

Mussolini and the Fascists

Born the son of a blacksmith and a school teacher in 1883, Mussolini had been educated in a seminary, but had been expelled because he reportedly stabbed another student. After teaching school for a few years, he fled to Switzerland in order to avoid military service. He grew tired of exile after a couple of years and returned to Italy to serve in the army, rising like Hitler to the rank of corporal. He then became a journalist, an activity which he did quite effectively and which helped launch a meteoric career in Socialist politics. In 1911 he was jailed briefly for his inflammatory articles against Italy's colonial policy in North Africa, and in 1912 he was named editor–in–chief of the major *Socialist Party* newspaper, *Avanti!* ("Forward") of Milan. His writings and speeches sometimes took excursions into anarchism, and they were always radical. At the *Socialist Party* congress at Reggio in mid–1912, he was among those party members who vehemently rejected a moderate course for the party and insisted that socialism must destroy the "bourgeois experiment" of democracy.

He never veered from his bitter opposition to liberal democracy, but after the outbreak of World War I, he revealed how fluid his political convictions really were. Unlike his former socialist comrades, he strongly supported Italy's involvement in the war. He maintained that it was one of the country's finest hours and that the young heroes had been betrayed by the conniving, greedy politicians at home. He had coined the slogan "war or revolution," which clearly presented the only alternatives as he saw them. The moving and persuasive eloquence with which he

Italy

Mussolini and his "Black Shirts"

used the Italian language, his undeniable charisma and showmanship and his appearance of raw manliness (although he was in reality often a timid man in times of crisis when daring moves needed to be taken) greatly appealed to the lost, the frightened and the bored.

They flocked to the many loosely–knit *Fasci* (groups) which sprang into existence in imitation of the *Fascio di combatt– imento* (fighting group), which Mussolini had founded in Milan in 1919. Mussolini wanted to weld a coalition with the non– communist left, but he found little support for such a union. It took a couple of years for him to gain full control of the *fascist* movement, named after the Latin word *fasces*, which meant a bundle of sticks around an ax, an ancient Roman symbol of state authority. Not until 1921 was the *Fascist Party* formally created. Mussolini quickly saw that the government's inability or unwillingness to step in and bring the rural and industrial violence under control offered a welcome opportunity for the Fascists to present themselves as the protectors of life, property, law and order.

His *Squadristi* (black–shirted bully squads) roamed the streets unimpeded and intimidated voters and opponents. When the Socialists proclaimed a general strike in August 1922, the Italian public became exasperated with this newest in a series of crippling strikes. It did nothing as the Fascists sacked or smashed trade union or Socialist party headquarters and presses all over Italy, including those of *Avanti!*, the paper which Mussolini once edited. They also seized control of the city councils in Cremona, Ferrara, Livorno, Parma and Ravenna. These brazen, but unopposed acts were merely the prelude to a Fascist *coup d'etat* which had been long–planned.

After delicate negotiations with royalist and Church circles to assure their acquiescence, Mussolini mobilized his Black Shirts for a "March on Rome" on October 22, 1922. Mussolini demonstrated that he was not entirely confident such a seizure of power would succeed by remaining close to the Swiss border in order to be able to escape into exile just in case the march failed. The prime minister tried to persuade King Victor Emmanuel III to sign a declaration of martial law in order to deal with the crisis, but the latter refused. Informed that there would be no resistance whatsoever, Mussolini took a night train to Rome, where the King appointed him prime minister. After so much violence and lawlessness, Rome fell to the Fascists without a shot being fired. This outrageous act of political adventurers would have been foiled if the forces of order had only shown the smallest bit of courage.

Step by step, Mussolini (who named himself *Il Duce*—"The Leader") transformed Italy into the first European dictatorship outside of Russia. He combined workers, employers and other groups into organizations called corporations. This corporate structure was intended to convey the mistaken impression that class and other social conflicts had been or were being eliminated. It therefore was used to justify the abolition of trade unions and strikes, which were allegedly no longer necessary to protect workers.

His power was insured through the introduction of censorship, a strict administration, a youth movement led by the state, a sham one–party electoral system, the liquidation of all political opponents and the creation of a feared secret police *(OVRA)*. The slogan *"credere, obbedire, combattere"* ("believe, obey, fight") reflected the new ideal. Although the King remained on the throne and the bicameral parliament was permitted to go through the motions as if it were functioning, all power by 1925 rested with Mussolini and his Fascist Party, whose organization reached from 10,000

Italy

Fasci (local) party groups all the way up to a Fascist Grand Council of about 20 men. All other parties were outlawed.

Fascist "Theory" and Administration

In the Fascist ideology which Mussolini had helped to concoct, freedom had allegedly been created through authoritarianism, and nobility and heroism had been established through discipline and sacrifice. The state was glorified, and liberalism, democracy and socialism were condemned. On top of that allegedly well-ordered state stood the leader, Mussolini, a man with a knack for sensationalism, self-dramatization, effective oratory and heavy-handedness toward those who were weaker than he. The subsequent persecution of all opposition forces was restrained in comparison to the terror in Nazi Germany.

The initial economic successes, which were the result of drastic protective tariffs and grandiose projects sponsored by the state, became corrupted by the dead-end policies to establish an autarchical (internationally independent) economy. The antiquated relationships of the property owners toward the peasants in the agrarian South remained unaffected, and the power of the Mafia, although repressed somewhat, was not broken. Of far-reaching importance, however, were the Lateran Treaties (Feb. 11, 1929) with the Vatican. Mussolini settled the long-standing dispute with the Church over its role in Italian politics by granting it extensive opportunities to influence political and social affairs within Italy (see Vatican City State).

World War II

Italy was ill prepared for the wars which it fought, at first on a small scale against Ethiopia in 1935, and then later against Germany's enemies in World War II. After Mussolini's attempts to conquer Albania and Greece in 1941 had failed, Italy and the *Duce* became more dependent upon Hitler than the Italians had intended. Their initial enthusiasm about the adventure of war soon turned to resignation and disappointment. Although Italy was supposedly a "partner" in the Axis, Hitler and the Germans in some ways considered it as much a problem as an asset insofar as the war effort was concerned. Although Mussolini was arrogant and boastful in public, he was rather timid in reality.

Things got worse when the Americans, British and Canadians began to launch successful attacks against the Italian homeland. In mid-1943 British and Canadian forces landed on the east coast of Sicily and took Syracuse, while General George S. Patton's troops landed in the south of the island and took Marsala and Palermo. They then joined the British forces to expel the Germans who were in control of Sicily. The allies next turned toward the Italian mainland and began bombing Rome on July 19.

The sober reality of war right in the city of Rome brought the downfall of Mussolini. The Fascist Grand Council, formerly a malleable tool in Mussolini's hands, which had not met since 1939, demanded his resignation, which the King ordered the next day. The former *Duce* was arrested as he left the royal palace, but was rescued later by a daring, precision operation by German paratroopers. Totally at the mercy of Germans, Mussolini eked out a temporary existence as head of a puppet fascist state in German-occupied northern Italy until April 28, 1945, when communist partisans murdered him and publicly hanged him and his mistress upside down. A few days later, his protector, Hitler, shot himself and had his body burned in Berlin to escape such ignoble public treatment.

Unfortunately, long, drawn-out negotiations in the summer of 1943 between the Anglo-American allies and the new Italian government under Marshal Pietro Badoglio enabled the Germans to improve their defenses in Italy. Therefore, when an armistice could finally be signed and an amphibious assault could be launched the very same day against the mainland on September 3, 1943, the Germans were well-prepared. The British Eighth Army under General Montgomery landed with little difficulty on the coast of Calabria. By contrast, the American landing at Salerno thereafter was resisted fiercely and almost ended in disaster.

The rugged and hilly Italian terrain, combined with the dogged German resistance under Marshal Kesselring, rendered every mile of northward advance in the Peninsula painful and costly. The Germans had dug in their heels along the so-called Gustav Line, in the center of which was located the almost impregnable 1,700 foot (510 meter) tall Monte Cassino, which guarded the road through the Liri valley toward Rome. In order to try to circumvent these formidable defenses, the Americans made another amphibious landing at Anzio, located only 33 miles (53 km.) south of Rome. But the American troops were pinned to the slopes overlooking the beach under murderous fire for four months until they could finally break free. In April 1944 Monte Cassino finally fell at the cost of thousands of American lives and after the allies had made the much-criticized decision to bomb the Benedictine abbey there, which the Germans were effectively using for observation purposes.

In June 1944 allied troops entered Rome. When seven allied divisions were withdrawn shortly thereafter in order to

Benito Mussolini—*Il Duce*

Italy

take part in an amphibious landing in southern France, the possibility of driving the German armies entirely out of Italy quickly disappeared. Italy therefore remained partially occupied by the Germans until the end of the war. On the plus side, the Italian invasion diverted German troops which otherwise would have been available elsewhere. Tactically, it was a very costly mistake, since Italy presented no threat, and the very terrain made it a defender's battlefield, not an invader's. This is reflected in the tremendous number of allied casualties.

The Italian resistance to the Axis powers was militarily significant in the course of the war. After the war the resistance became a symbol of solidarity and it should have helped the Italians to put aside some of their many regional, political and social differences. Unfortunately, the adhesive effect of the resistance proved to be weaker and more transitory than many had hoped.

After the war, Italy found itself again in the strange position of being both the conqueror and the conquered. Regular troops and partisan units had fought against the Germans ever since the fall of Mussolini in mid–1943. However, the fact that this same Italy had been an ally of Nazi Germany, and had led attacks against Albania, Yugoslavia and Greece, had not been forgotten. In contrast to Germany, Italy was able to preserve its national unity, but this was due chiefly to the crucial assistance of the influential Italians living in the United States.

The peace treaty which took effect September 15, 1947, required Italy to renounce all claims on Ethiopia and Greece and to cede the Dodecanese Islands back to Greece and five small Alpine areas to France. In addition, the Istrian Peninsula (including Fiume and Pola) was awarded to Yugoslavs. The Trieste area west of the new Yugoslav territory was made a free city until 1954, when it and a 90–square–mile (135 sq. km.) zone was transferred to Italy and the remainder to Yugoslavia. In addition, Italy was required to pay reparations to the Soviet Union and Albania.

GOVERNMENT

A majority of Italian voters in a national referendum held in June 1946 chose to abolish the monarchy and to establish a democratic republic. With the unpleasant memories of a dictator and a rigid one–party state fresh in their minds, the framers of the post–war constitution made two important decisions which have made it difficult for the country's political institutions to cope with some of Italy's festering economic and social problems. First, they greatly curtailed the powers of the head of government in order to make the reemergence of a dictator almost impossible. Second, they adopted the proportional representation system of voting which gave parliamentary seats to as many parties as possible.

Italy is a highly centralized, unitary state. As in France, the prefect in each of the 93 provinces is appointed by and accountable to the central government. The 20 regions each elect regional parliaments and wield limited political power, but they still are chiefly administrative units for the central government. Five of these regions have had special statutes for a long time (Sardinia, Sicily, Trentino–Alto Adige, Valle d'Aosta and Friuli–Venezia Giulia). The other 15 were created in 1970. This broadening of regional government may, in time, lead to an actual decentralization of political power in Italy.

Political Crisis

A political earthquake is occurring in Italy which has brought about profound changes in the country's parliamentary system and party politics. Italians have always known that there was corruption in high places, but what they have now learned is taking their breaths away. It began in 1991 with the arrest of a *Socialist Party* official in Milan who was caught taking bribes on a cleaning contract in a home for the elderly. But it developed into an explosion which is demolishing the nation's entire political order.

Investigations (called "Operation Clean Hands") into embezzlement, illicit bribes, and kick–backs to political parties and politicians in return for public–works contracts have produced the greatest public corruption scandal in modern European history. The estimated $11 billion in annual rip–offs is equivalent to the government's annual deficit. The investigations have also uncovered possible evidence that the Mafia and top government leaders might have been cooperating for years. None of the traditional parties escaped unharmed; all were discredited.

Until the collapse of communism in Europe, Italians had grudgingly tolerated misgovernment by leaders mainly preoccupied with party intrigue and devious fund–raising because it seemed like the alternative would have been rule by the *Communist Party of Italy*, which had discomforting links with the Soviet Union. With that danger gone, most Italians see no reason not to confront head on the rot in the political establishment. By mid–1993, more than 2,600 persons in the political and business elite, including top corporate executives, party chairmen, and three former prime ministers, had either been arrested or were under investigation. Entire regional and local governments had been jailed or forced to resign.

Voters' disgust came to a head in an historic referendum on April 18–19, 1993. Voting on eight separate questions, over 90% voted to abolish state financing of political parties, and 83% chose to scrap the system of proportional representation in the Senate. Designed in the post–fascist era to prevent another single party, such as Mussolini's, from gaining power, this system created government by weak coalitions of quarrelsome partners and by an oligarchy of often corrupt party leaders. In a 1999 referendum, 91% voted to abolish the proportional representation system used to distribute 25% of the seats in the lower house, the Chamber of Deputies. But since only 49.6% turned out to vote, just shy of the 50% required, the balloting was not valid. Many of the more than 40 parties that compete for seats were pleased with the result.

Voters abolished the ministries of industry, agriculture and tourism, as well as political appointments of state savings–bank directors; all had been favorite conduits of patronage. The 1993 referendum was a stunning rebuke to politicians and their machinery of power. In the coming years all of the institutions and parties discussed below will be changed or influenced by the rage and determination which were and are being expressed.

Parliament

Italy is a parliamentary democracy with a bicameral legislature. The Chamber of Deputies is composed of 630 members elected until 1994 by proportional representation in 32 electoral districts at least every five years. The Senate is composed of 315 members. Every five years members representing the 20 regions (the exceptions being the valley of Aosta, which sends a senator and the province of Molise, which sends two) are elected. Beginning in 1994, 75% in both houses are elected directly, while a fourth enter under the old system of proportional representation. In contrast to the Chamber of Deputies, the Senate contains some non–elected members. Every ex–president of the republic is a senator for life, and five other senators are appointed for life.

Both houses have *identical* powers. Both function and make decisions independently, and both must pass a bill before it is forwarded to the largely ceremonial president of the Republic for signature. The legislative system is slow and cumbersome, making passage of laws difficult. Because of the electoral system, almost the same constellation of parties is represented in both chambers with the same proportion of parties in the standing committees. The Senate has 11 such committees

Italy

Uniformed police—*carabinieri*   Courtesy: Jon Markham Morrow

and the Chamber of Deputies 14. In both houses party politics determines all aspects of the legislative process.

Since 1988 party discipline is easier to maintain because of the elimination of secret voting, which had permitted dissidents to vote anonymously against their own parties and bring down their own governments; the result was perennially weak government. Secret balloting had been one stumbling block to efficient rule under a constitution which had been designed four decades ago primarily to prevent another Mussolini from coming to power. No Italian legislature has lived its full five–year life since 1968.

Presidency

The president who is elected by the members of both houses of Parliament for a seven–year term, can veto a law, but his veto can be overridden by a simple majority in both houses. The *immovilismo* of the party system and the inability to form governing majorities to handle Italy's ever–increasing problems prompted suggestions that the constitution be changed in order to create a presidential democracy on the French model.

The presidency is gaining in influence even without constitutional change. In 1991 Francesco Cossiga grew tired of his figure–head role and proclaimed his intention "to shake a few pebbles out of my shoes." He startled the nation by becoming more involved in everyday politics. His moves were highly unorthodox and caused a storm of controversy. In 1992 he decided to give "a shock to the political classes" by resigning two months before his term ended. He charged that Italy's traditional politicians had ignored the electorate's reform message in the parliamentary elections that month. Facing a crisis which had paralyzed Italy's major parties, his successor, Oscar Luigi Scalfaro, broke long–standing practices in 1993 by not consulting the ruling parties before selecting the first prime minister not to belong to a political party: Carlo Azeglio Ciampi, a respected civil servant and head of the independent Bank of Italy. Scalfaro charged Ciampi with enacting sweeping political reform, trimming the budget, and then bowing out after early elections. In the past, party leaders dictated the political direction to president. But in 1993 it was President Scalfaro who delivered the marching orders to the party chiefs. In May 1999 Ciampi, whose hobby is German literature, became president.

Normally the most delicate political act in which the president is fully involved is the formation of a cabinet. A prospective candidate for the prime ministerial post is charged by the president to form a government. The prospective candidate suggests the composition of the new government after extensive consultations with the possible coalition partners. Whether the prime minister can win and maintain a majority for his cabinet in *both* chambers is always the decisive question.

Political Parties and Alliances

In May 1996 Italy installed its fifty–fifth government since World War II. The average duration of each has been seven months, although things improved in the

President Carlo Azeglio Ciampi

406

Italy

1980s insofar as longevity was concerned. All governments have been coalitions which are forever shifting, with disagreement on a single point bringing down an administration. To understand why Italian governments are so unstable, one must examine the basic party structure and the consequences of the electoral system.

The multi-party system is highly fragmented, but for the 1996 elections many of the numerous parties grouped themselves into two loose alliances, which the *Washington Post* aptly described as "not coalitions but collages, fragments of political movements thrown together without a cogent denominator other than the aim of power. As such they are prone to instability."

On the political right are the parties that formed the *Freedom Alliance*, which had won the 1994 elections, but declined in 1996 from 366 to 246 seats in the Chamber of Deputies and 155 to 116 in the Senate. They are the totally new *Forza Italia* ("Go, Italy!"), the *National Alliance* (formerly the neo-fascist *Italian Social Movement—MSI*), and the *Christian Democratic Center Party*, a breakaway minority from the former ruling *Christian Democrats*. The *Northern League* dropped out in December 1994.

In the center are the *Italian Popular Party* (PPI, formerly the *Christian Democrats—DC*), the *Italian Republican Party (PRI)*, the *Italian Liberal Party (PLI)*, the *Social Democratic Party of Italy (PSDI)* and *Italian Renewal*. In 1994 most had formed an electoral alliance called *Pact for Italy*, which won only 16% of the votes. On the left are the *Democratic Party of the Left (PDS*, formerly the *Communist Party of Italy—PCI)*, the hard-line *Refounded Communist Party, Socialist Unity,* formerly part of the *Socialist Party of Italy—PSI)*, the *Socialist Party of Proletarian Unity (PSIUP)*, the anti-Mafia party in Sicily, *La Rete* (the Network), and the *Greens*. For the 1994 elections the leftist parties formed the *Progressive* bloc, which won a third of the votes. In 1996 the center and left combined forces to form an "Olive Tree" coalition, a patchwork of ex-Communists, liberals, greens, some former Christian Democrats, and a few independents. Together they made history. By capturing 40% of the votes in April 1996, they became Italy's first leftist government, under the *PPI's* Romano Prodi. They broke a long-standing taboo by including nine former Communists from the *PDS* in the ruling coalition, more than from any other party. The Communists have not always been easy partners. In 1997 Prodi had to resign briefly because they would not support his health care reform. But his government was reinstated five days later, the 57th since 1947, and he announced that "Italy is back on track for Europe."

Until 1993, when the entire political landscape began to change, the political fronts in Italy were polarized and somewhat rigid. The problem was that parties cornering roughly a third of the vote—the *PDS* and the *MSI*—were unacceptable as coalition partners, leaving only two-thirds within which to find a majority. Neither of the two largest parties was capable of winning a majority. No governing coalition could be formed without the participation of the *Christian Democrats* and the *Socialists*. Together with the *Social Democrats*, the *Liberals* and sometimes the *Republicans*, these two parties could paste together a wobbly temporary majority in parliament composed of five parties (called the *Pentapartito*), which were generally more interested in their own survival and in delivering maximum benefits to their own special constituencies than in providing stable government capable of dealing with Italy's pressing problems.

The *DC* and the *Socialists* were never natural partners, for reasons of ideology and strategy. Any coalition between them was by nature unstable because the partners were fierce competitors. The *DC* could not win a majority by itself, and the *Communists* were not accepted by most Italians as ready for a place in the government. Thus, the balance was held by about a dozen small parties. This insured incoherence and produced a string of short-lived governments with narrow attention spans.

Even elections could not always produce a government; they could produce only the raw materials for one. They seldom settled questions; they merely deferred them. Following elections, an acceptable coalition, composed almost invariably of the same parties which were in the last one, was hammered together only after a drawn-out process of bargaining. It could take weeks or months until the many demands of powerful party and factional leaders had been satisfied and balanced. While there was a certain stability inherent in this process, the damage to the political system is clear. Widespread corruption and cynicism toward rulers flourished in a fragmented political scene in which politicians were well entrenched with little possibility of being displaced. Nobody expected major changes. One voter remarked before the 1992 polling, "we all know that when the vote is counted we will be right back where we started." The same could certainly not be said of the 1994 elections.

The Right

Forza Italia

The historic 1994 elections not only produced a parliament in which nearly 80% of the members had never served before and a cabinet in which most members had no previous ministerial experience, they resulted in a governing coalition composed of a party which had not existed six months earlier, a federalist regional group from the North dedicated to weakening the central government, and a former fascist pariah organization which had been carefully excluded from power in Rome for a half century.

None is a conventional political party. Apart from their populist streaks and opposition to the left, they have little in common. The essential prerequisite for this dramatic turnabout was the two-year corruption investigation involving kickbacks from government contracts that ensnared most of Italy's political elite and discredited the *Christian Democrats* and their traditional ruling partners.

Forza Italia's name was derived from a soccer slogan, "Go, Italy!" At the head of this movement is one of Italy's richest men, Silvio Berlusconi, a entrepreneurial superstar whose business empire, Finin-

Silvio Berlusconi

vest, includes three TV networks dominating commercial television, Italy's largest department store chain, the top-selling newsmagazine, and an array of other investments, including the AC Milan soccer club, which has become one of the world's best. His opponents charge that he misused his three TV networks, which control 45% of the Italian audience, to propagandize voters. They also claim that a politician with such vast and varied investments cannot escape from conflicts of interest. A man with telegenic good looks, enormous energy and determination, and an excellent business brain, he called for "a new Italian miracle" which would flow from his program of fostering private enterprise, slashing red tape and debt, intro-

Italy

The Italian Chamber of Deputies (630 members)

MARCH 1994 ELECTIONS

- FREEDOM ALLIANCE: 366
  - *Forza Italia*
  - *National Alliance*
  - *Northern League*
- Pact for Italy: 46
- Others: 5
- PROGRESSIVE ALLIANCE: 213
  - *PDS*
  - *Refounded Communists*
  - *Others*

APRIL 1996 ELECTIONS

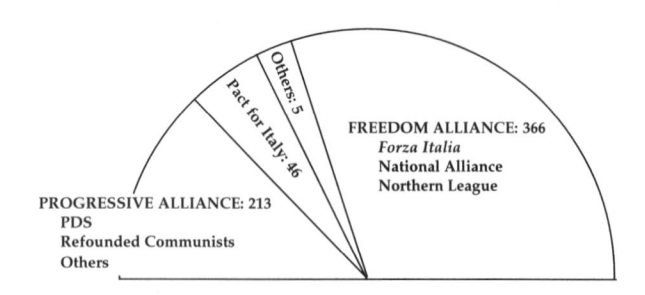

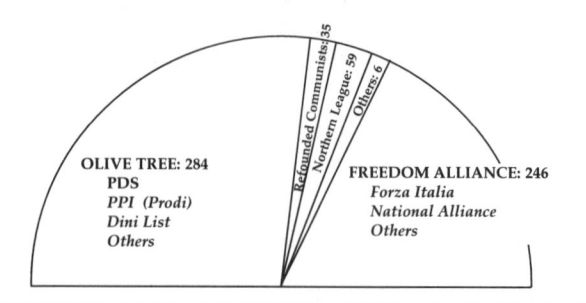

- OLIVE TREE: 284
  - *PDS*
  - *PPI (Prodi)*
  - *Dini List*
  - *Others*
- Refounded Communists: 35
- Northern League: 59
- Others: 6
- FREEDOM ALLIANCE: 246
  - *Forza Italia*
  - *National Alliance*
  - *Others*

> The Chamber of Deputies is confusingly composed of shifting political party alliances, sometimes, as in 1996, blending right and left. A perfect example is the *Olive Tree*. In order to secure the prime ministership, Prodi's *Italian Popular Party* (formerly called *Christian Democrats*) had to draw from both sides of the political spectrum. The current governing coalition now has former communists (*PDS*) as its main pillar. This fragile constellation could change at any time.

ducing a flat–rate tax system, and creating a million new jobs.

Like most of the party's office–holders, Berlusconi had never even run for public office before. He claimed to have been forced into politics "to keep my country from falling into the hands of the communists." Centrist reformers had failed to organize an effective bloc to the powerful momentum the communists had displayed in the 1993 municipal elections. Despite inexperience, *Forza Italia* won about a fourth of the votes and did especially well among young voters. After the elections Berlusconi said: "I know the young generation well. They grew up seeing America through the television shows that I brought to Europe. They have come to believe in the meritocratic philosophy that will help us develop a more liberal and free–market society without losing our cultural roots or traditions."

Its deputies tend to be young, ambitious professionals and business people who helped change the character of the parliament by lowering the average age (40% under age 50 and 25% under 40), raising the percentage of university graduates to 75, and increasing the number of women representatives from 51 to 93 (of whom 47 are from the three conservative ruling parties). *Forza Italia* found itself sandwiched between the autonomy–seeking *Northern League*, with its roots in the rich and industrialized Lombardy region around Milan (Berlusconi's home town), and the *National Alliance*, whose voters are concentrated in the impoverished South and who advocate a strong central government.

This heterogeneous coalition could not give Italy what has eluded it for more than four decades: stable government. In December 1994 it collapsed after only eight months when the *Northern League* walked out. Berlusconi had refused to separate himself from his business empire. In June he had accused the three state–owned RAI TV channels of hostile editorial policy and forced the RAI board to resign. When he was formally placed under investigation for his business dealings, including tax fraud and corruption, he could no longer survive as prime minister.

His quarrelsome government was replaced by one of non–elected technocrats, with Lamberto Dini, a taciturn ex–banker and treasury minister under Berlusconi, with no party affiliation, as prime minister. Dini promised to introduce reforms, especially of the underfunded pension system, and to cut government spending, and then to call new elections. In the 1996 elections, *Forza Italia* slipped only slightly, from 21% to 20.6% of the votes, but the larger *Freedom Alliance* lost 120 of its 366 lower house seats and won only 116 of 315 Senate seats. They find themselves in the opposition and in serious trouble.

Berlusconi was convicted in 1997 for false accounting (though his 16–month sentence was commuted), and he faced five more trials on counts ranging from bribing tax inspectors who were auditing his businesses to illicit soccer transfers. In 1998 he was sentenced to two years and nine months in prison for bribery although his parliamentary immunity and the appeals process keep him out of jail. But he cannot lead the party that was built around him. He had to announce that he would not be a candidate for prime minister after the next elections, and the opposition coalition is on the verge of falling apart.

National Alliance

Until 1994 the neo–fascist *Italian Social Movement–National Right (MSI–DN)* could be found at the outer right fringe of the party spectrum. It understood how to capitalize on the disadvantaged population of southern Italy. Protest against the establishment and disappointment over the center–left governments increased its percentage of votes to 6.8% in 1983, but their support in 1992 fell to 5.4% and 34 seats. One of them was taken by Alessandra Mussolini, granddaughter of the fascist dictator and niece of actress Sophia Loren. In terms of a political program, the *MSI* maintained entirely the tradition of Italian fascism.

But then came a new and intelligent young leader, Gianfranco Fini, who steered the party away from the corporatism and exaggerated nationalism of old fascism and gave it a new program (which he calls "post–fascism") and a more respectable name: *National Alliance*. The *MSI*

The National Alliance's Gianfranco Fini

408

was dissolved in 1995. He studiously avoided contacts with extreme–rightist groups elsewhere in Europe and condemned anti–Semitism, attacks against foreigners, and skinhead violence. Emphasizing clean government, law and order (including reintroduction of the death penalty), stricter immigration controls, family values, and the preservation of Italian unity, he transformed the party into a broad–based mainstream conservative political force, modeled on the French Gaullists, and a major player in Italian politics.

Having been excluded from government for a half century, it could not be blamed for corruption and poor performance, as could Italy's traditional parties. Fini declared during the campaign: "Italy no longer divides itself between fascists and anti–fascists, but between thieves and those with clean hands!"

The reward came in the 1994 elections: it more than doubled its previous electoral score, capturing 13.5% of the votes and five seats in the cabinet. It did especially well among the young, who are the most adversely affected by Italy's frighteningly high unemployment. It captured 23% of the votes from Italians under age 25, versus only 13% for the former Communists, now called *PDS*. Capitalizing on the dramatic decline of the former *Christian Democrats*, who had long dominated the South, the *National Alliance* became the strongest political force in the southern half of Italy, including Rome. But the party lost badly in 1996, capturing only 16% of the vote. It is back in opposition.

Not everyone is persuaded that the party's transformation is genuine. Fini himself reinforced the skeptics shortly after the elections by describing Mussolini as "the greatest statesman of the century." Some party members demand that Italian claims on parts of Istria and Dalmatia in the present Slovenia and Croatia be resurrected, but Fini assured the public that his party would not press this issue. Most Italians, who are accustomed to seeing neo–fascists in every post–war Italian parliament, are not alarmed.

But in other European countries, which must deal with menacing right–wing movements on the rise, there was near–panic. The hostile foreign reaction prompted former President Scalfaro to warn: "Italy does not need to take lessons in democracy from anybody!" Also Berlusconi asserted that "fascists do not exist in my government." Citing polls showing that fewer than 1% of Italians identify themselves as "fascists," he asked, "so how can this be considered dangerous?"

Northern League

In the 1990s all of Italy's established parties anxiously witnessed the rise of leagues seeking regional autonomy in the North. The most successful within this *Lega Nord* (Northern League) is the *Lombard League*, led by Umberto Bossi. The *Northern League* rocketed to 19% of the vote in that region's 1990 elections. In the 1992 national elections it won more than a fifth of the votes in Lombardy and 8.7% nationally, jumping from one to 55 seats in parliament. In 1994 it entered the ruling coalition and claimed five cabinet posts. But Bossi terminated its cooperation with Berlusconi in December 1994, causing a serious split in the party. It captured a respectable 10% of the national vote and 59 lower house seats. In the process it became the largest party north of the River Po, winning up to 40% of the votes in some northern regions.

The *League* stands for federalism and devolution of power to the regions. It capitalizes on local dissatisfaction against what is seen as misrule by Rome, which does not seem to act vigorously enough to stem the wave of immigrants and to reverse Northern Italy's subsidizing of the South. It charges, with considerable justification, that too much of those funds end up in the pockets of Mafia contractors. A clean–government party, the *Northern League* benefitted from the country's massive corruption scandal. Its spokesman, Roberto Maroni, announced that "our purpose of breaking up Italy is not linked to ethnic or religious identities, but to economic issues."

Emboldened by its strong election showing in 1996, the *League* proclaimed northern Italy an "independent and sovereign" republic called "Padania" (for the River Po) and called on the United Nations to recognize its right of self–determination. Unlike the Basque country in Spain and France, Padania has never existed before. Nevertheless, its supporters are playing government. They moved their 15 "ministers" into a Renaissance building in Venice and swore in a self–nominated "parliament" in their "capital city" of Mantua. In 1997 they held unofficial parliamentary elections and charged the assembly with writing a new constitution that would make Padania either independent or loosely confederated with Italy. Advocates wave their own flag, wear green shirts and call themselves "citizens of the North." They call on northerners to refuse to pay their taxes to Rome.

Despite these trappings, opinion polls suggest that most northerners oppose secession although many agree with some of the League's criticisms. Bossi did not help his cause in 1997 by referring to the Pope as a "foreigner" and saying that the Italian flag belongs in the toilet. This remark brought a million Italians into the streets in Milan and Venice to demonstrate for national unity.

The Center

Italian Popular Party

Until 1994 the *Christian Democrats (DC)* had been the dominant party since 1945, and as such was hit the hardest by the political storm that is raging in Italy. It had placed in office all prime ministers until the *Republican*, Giovanni Spadolini, held the office from 1981 to 1982. The *DC* formed coalitions with all parties except the *PDS* and *MSI*. Also, in 1983, 64% of all mayors, 57% of city councilors, 90% of the managers of state–operated businesses, 94% of all savings and loan presidents and

Italy

Secretary of State Madeleine Albright with former Prime Minister Prodi

58% of all bank presidents were members of the *DC*. In addition to the broad spectrum of closely related organizations in all sectors of the society in which the *DC* party exercises influence, the party receives special support from the Catholic Church. Two-thirds of the *DC's* 1,200 sections were founded in 1946 at the insistence and under the influence of local clerics.

Ideologically, the *DC* built upon the two larger middle class parties of the pre-fascist period. The Catholicism of the old *Popular Party* and the economic liberalism of the old *Liberal Party* were the pillars for the *DC's* political conception. In accordance with the Manifesto of Milan of 1943, the *DC* defined itself as a "Catholic People's Party" encompassing all classes. It had no binding party program. Instead, it was the classical example of the "catch-all party."

The *DC's* adaptability and its openness to coalitions toward both the right and the left were reasons why for so long it survived political and economic crises without suffering large electoral losses. However, it refused to agree to a "historical compromise" *(Compromesso storico)* with the Communists. Its heterogeneity helped it to stabilize Italian society and guarantee the proper functioning of the parliamentary system.

Shaken by scandals which left few of its talented leaders untainted, the party not only suffered election losses, but was affected by the liberalization of Catholicism. The first appearance of erosion became evident with the divorce referendum of 1974, in which the *DC* and the Catholic Church sought to abolish the 1972 laws permitting Italians to divorce. At least 3 million women, up to that point the party's most loyal supporters, helped defeat the suggestion to repeal the divorce laws. An even harder nut to crack was the referendum in 1985 to abolish the abortion law which had been passed in 1980, permitting abortion under specific circumstances; the *DC* supported the law, but 70% of the voters opposed it.

The party had failed to take into account the extensive sympathy for the Pope, who had just recovered from an attack on his life, and who was very opposed to the abortion act. Pope John Paul II, who is Polish, generally takes very little interest in Italian politics, a fact which has removed much of the spiritual underpinnings for the *DC*, which the party has in the past known how to exploit. In 1985 the Italian government revised the 55-year-old concordat with the Vatican ending the status of Roman Catholicism as the state religion. The Church accepted the civil court's right to decide on marital annulments, previously the exclusive right of the Church, and it agreed that religious instruction in public schools would be optional.

The *DC* had been further threatened by the continuous economic crises, for which it, as the major governing party, had to bear responsibility. Many workers and employers lost confidence in the party. It experienced a sharp fall in the 1992 elections, winning only 29.7% of the votes and 206 seats in the Chamber of Deputies. This ignited an intra-party crisis. Mario Segni, a former *Christian Democrat* who organized the drive for electoral reform in 1993, broke away and formed a new party, *Democratic Alliance,* aiming to attract a wide spectrum of reform supporters from all parties.

Staring electoral disaster in the face, *DC* party leader, Mino Martinazzoli, led the move in 1994 to rename the party, *Italian*

Italy

Hon. Romano Prodi
President-Designate
European Commission

Popular Party (PPI) in order to try to improve its image and appeal. The "new" name was designed to signal a return to the Catholic values of Luigi Sturzo, the priest who had founded the *Popular Party* in 1919. The 1994 election results indicated that voters were not willing to accept this cosmetic change. Under a new leader, Romano Prodi, an unassuming economics professor and political neophyte, the party itself won only 6.8% of the votes in 1996. But Prodi was the architect of the Olive Tree coalition, which formed the center–left government and brought most parties of the center and left under its umbrella. In October 1998 the Prodi government fell when its ally, the *Communist Refoundation Party*, voted to oppose the budget. Prodi was named president of the European Commission in Brussels the following year.

A minority refused to stay in the *Popular Party*, forming instead the *Christian Democratic Center Party*, which garnered 5.8% of the votes in 1996. To gain some name recognition, it recruited actress Gina Lollobrigida to be a candidate for the 1999 European Parliament elections.

The Republicans

Despite its voter appeal of only 4.4% and 27 seats in 1992, the *Italian Republican Party (PRI)* maintained a noticeable position at the center of the party spectrum through its pragmatically–oriented political goals. The *Republicans'* role consisted in overcoming the lack of innovation in the *DC's* economic policy through constructive criticism aimed at increasing efficiency. Known as the party of "enlightened capitalism," the *PRI* has come to represent especially the interests of the export–oriented companies of northern Italy. For example, Fiat boss Agnelli is a registered member of the *PRI*. The reason for the small percentage of voters is the fact that the party appears too anti–clerical for small farmers, too closely tied to large industry for the workers and too progressive for the conservative element within the middle class.

The Social Democrats

The *PSDI* formed the left wing among the center parties and is a strictly anti–communist leftist party. Despite its low voter strength of about 5% from 1947 to 1976, the *Social Democrats* have participated in over half of the cabinets. Due to the increasing concentration on the large parties, the percentage of *PSDI* votes sank to 2.7% and 16 seats in 1992. Because of its declining fortunes, it has leaned more heavily toward the left. Workers make up 24% of the *PSDI's* electorate, while housewives remain the strongest group among its voters, with 27%.

The Liberal Party

The *Italian Liberal Party (PLI)* was originally the ruling party from the founding of the Italian State in 1861 until World War I. However, the party's strong anti–clerical position and its function as the right

Foreign Minister Lamberto Dini

wing of the centrist governing coalitions cost it much popularity.

Italian Renewal

A new party created in 1996 by former central banker and prime minister, Lamberto Dini, *Italian Renewal* won 4.3% of the votes and barely cleared the threshold for winning seats in parliament. They were enough to clinch victory for Olive Tree, and Dini became foreign minister in the new government.

The Left

The Communists

The *PDS* is the largest party on the left with 1.5 million members. It emerged from the 1996 elections as Italy's largest political party, having captured 21.1% of the votes. It overcame its political and social isolation of the 1950s and 1960s because it was able to reach beyond its traditional base in the industrial working class and to gain new voters from the middle class. A traditionally atheistic party, it can exist in a country closely associated with the Catholic Church because it quietly dropped atheism as a part of its platform. It also ceased being a Marxist–Leninist cadre party and instead became simply a leftist worker's party. It rejected the concept of its first postwar leader, Palmiro Togliatti, who wanted to introduce socialism into Italy through revolution. History had proven that efforts to change Italian society through revolution simply helped to drive an uncertain middle class into the arms of the fascists.

In the 1960s the *PDS* was the first Western European communist party publicly to reject the Leninist doctrine of a revolutionary seizure of power followed by a dictatorship of the proletariat. That is, it turned down the model of the Soviet Union and sought its own path to socialism.

This enabled the *PDS* to accept Italian membership in NATO and the EU, and as Western Europe's largest communist party, to become the leader of so–called "Eurocommunism," a movement which discards Marxist–Leninist orthodoxy as the basis of its ideology. The movement recognizes parliamentary democracy as a prerequisite for socialism, which, it believes, could be achieved through a wide consensus of reform–oriented forces. It also rejects the planned economies found in Eastern Europe, although this rejection does not imply total acceptance of a free market economy. Economically and politically the *PDS* advocates an unclear course which tries to combine overall economic planning by the state with individual economic decisions.

It is no surprise that these policies led to tensions with the Soviet Union. The *PDS* criticized Moscow because of the Soviet occupation of Afghanistan in 1979 and because of the introduction of martial law in Poland in 1981. Such criticism was cautiously welcomed by other Italian parties, although the *DC* recognized that the *PDS's* anti–Moscow course made it difficult for *Christian Democrats* to reap electoral hay by presenting themselves as bulwarks against communism.

In contrast to that of its *voters*, the social structure of the party *members* has not basically changed. The reservoir of the party

Italy

is still industrial workers, who make up approximately three-fourths of its membership. An important lever for accomplishing party goals is the largest union in Italy, the *CGIL,* with 4.316 million members. One thing which has weakened the party is that the number of industrial workers has declined in Italy's modernizing economy. Also, the growth of the service and white collar sectors have reduced the power of trade unions, and that has adversely affected the *PDS.* The new groups in which the party was able to attract voters and members, such as the intellectual and technical elites as well as the civil service workers, remain under-represented in the overall party membership. However, just the opposite can be seen in the party's leadership organs. In the 36-member party directorate, a majority has full university credentials.

To hold on to the votes of young and well-educated people, the *PDS* has loosened the leaders' grip on the rank and file by making public criticism of the party no longer grounds for expulsion and by permitting elections to the party's central committee to be held in public. The formerly closed way of making party decisions has been replaced by free and open votes in all party committees, from the national to the local level. It has formally embraced the market economy and has not opposed the privatization of nationalized industries. It accepts NATO and American nuclear bases in Italy, and it rejects unilateral nuclear disarmament.

In order to escape from its political isolation, the *PDS* abandoned all hope for a coalition with the *DC* and sought links with other leftist parties, including the *Socialists.* This course brought frustration and danger. Just how unreliable the *Socialists* were for the *PDS* was revealed in a string of municipal elections in 1985–86. Since the 1970s, the *Communists* had ruled or co-ruled most large Italian cities. Along with the trade union movement (whose membership is decreasing), city government was a pillar of *Communist* power. There they could prove that they were efficient and largely incorruptible, and therefore capable of participating in national government. However, when the *Socialists* began to ally with the center parties at the local as well as the national level, *Communist* mayors were thrown out of city halls all over Italy: Venice, Milan, Turin, Parma, and, most galling to the *PDS,* Rome. Only the traditional stronghold of Bologna remained secure for the *PDS.*

In an attempt to stem the party's decline, the *PDS,* after open and heated debate, replaced the tired and grey Alessandro Natta in 1988 with a more youthful leader: Achille Occhetto, who represents a more open-minded generation within the party. Occhetto adopted a new language: the words "Marxist" and "Eurocommunism" have vanished, to be replaced by "progressive" and "Euroleft." "Our party isn't a member of a particular political-ideological camp. It's not part of the so-called communist camp. On the contrary, I maintain that there is no longer a real communist movement, and the traditions we represent in Italy are our own." He was replaced in 1994 by another pragmatist, Massimo D'Alema.

In 1991 the *PDS* cast off both its name and hammer and sickle symbol and sought membership in the Socialist International. Occhetto argued that "shattering events" in Eastern Europe had left the party with no choice. One member admit-

Prime Minister Massimo D'Alema, Leader, *PDS*

ted that "in terms of Italian politics, this is our Berlin Wall that has come crashing down." The new insignia is a spreading tree, with the hammer-and-sickle practically hidden in the roots. But the difficulty in transforming this party were shown when Occhetto temporarily lost his job as party secretary; reformers deserted him when he backed the hard-liners' demands that Italy withdraw its air and naval forces from the Gulf War against Iraq.

With the total collapse of Moscow-led communism in Europe, the other parties have lost their rationale for excluding the *PDS* from government. The communists are now in a position to enter a governing coalition with any major party. The *PDS* has become an especially potent political force in central Italy. The *PDS* was the main pillar of the *Olive Tree* coalition with nine ministers in the cabinet.

In October 1998 *PDS* leader Massimo D'Alema became the first ex-Communist to form an Italian government, the country's 56th. A pensive former editor of Italy's largest leftist newspaper, *L'Unità,* and author of many books, the most recent of which is aptly entitled *La Grande Occasione* (*The Big Chance*), D'Alema admires Tony Blair's style of reform and has attacked irresponsible trade unionists. He broke a record by bringing nine parties into his government, sarcastically dubbed "the first center-left government of the center-right open to the radical left." It includes Communists, ex-Communists, various greens, centrists, and a new party, Francesco Cossiga's *Democratic Union for the Republic,* which had been a part of the conservative opposition.

Refounded Communist Party

Hardliners broke from the *PDS* and formed a separate party, *Refounded Communist Party,* led by Fausto Bertinotti. The leader demands that Italy withdraw from NATO and opt out of further European integration. He also calls for a restoration of inflation indexing for wages. The party refused to join the ruling *Olive Tree* coalition, which, in Bertinotti's opinion, is too "heavily weighted on the side of centrists and moderates." But its 35 lower house seats, won through 8.6% of the votes, are crucial for the survival of the government.

The Socialists

Former leader Bettino Craxi, who in 1983 became both the first *Socialist* and youngest prime minister of Italy since 1945, moved the party more toward the political right and replaced the hammer and sickle as the party's symbol with a red rose. The *Socialists* advocate a reformed market economy including returning some state enterprises to private hands, closing highly inefficient state-owned businesses and trimming payrolls in the overmanned nationalized firms. They also staunchly support the western alliance. Since the beginning of the 1960s they have changed structurally from a working-class party to one which is led by intellectuals, and whose electorate is composed of middle class voters.

Craxi was one of the first politicians implicated in the kickback scandal which has shaken Italian politics at the roots. The first revelations were made in his power base, Milan. Craxi aroused indignation in 1993 when he refused to relinquish his parliamentary immunity and answer the corruption charges against him and his party. His successor as party leader, Giorgio Benvenuto, resigned in disgust, charging that political bosses are resisting surrendering their influence and power. His resignation demonstrated how difficult it was for reformers to purge the old political elite, despite the unmistakable message sent by voters in the April 1993 referendum. In parting, Benvenuto said: "Socialism has a future in Italy, but I don't know whether this party can survive." In early 1994 the party split, and the parts sank to irrelevance after the 1994 elections. Facing 20 different graft investigations in 1994, Craxi refused to surrender his passport to magistrates in Milan and fled to Tunisia.

Other Parties and Politicians

Benefitting from the yearning for clean government are the *Greens,* who won 2.5% of the votes in 1996 and entered the governing Olive Tree coalition. The party had once gained some notoriety through one of the most colorful advocates of environmentalist causes, who stimulated both excitement and embarrassment in the Italian parliament—the erotic Hungarian–born porno star, Ilona Staller, known as "Cicciolina" (meaning "little fleshy one"). Her position: "more pornography equals knowledge and nonviolence." To buttress her rhetoric in public appearances, she gave her campaign speeches topless. Her bare breasts in public rallies seemed to underscore how little else there was to think about in some past elections. In 1988 she lost her parliamentary immunity, which had protected her from counts of public indecency. She had gone out in Venice "clad" only in a see–through skirt. In 1989 she was again censured because of her continued public strippings. It is little wonder that the U.S. was reluctant to issue her an official visa to air her views in this country.

Surprisingly, her legislative record became more serious: she introduced bills banning furs and taxing cars to raise funds for planting trees. As she philosophized: "It's better to come up with strong bills than to show off your boobs." She added: "I don't undress in parliament anymore." But she did try her hand at diplomacy in 1990, offering her body to Iraqi dictator Saddam Hussein in exchange for hostages. After he rebuffed that tempting offer, she married and divorced American artist Jeff Koons, whose art, like his wife, blends business with pornography. In 1998 a Rome court ruled that because of her "excessive permissiveness" she was unfit for motherhood. It granted custody of their child to Koons.

Uncivic Culture

When considering Italian government, it must be remembered that the society has often been characterized as an "uncivic culture." According to studies made by Almond and Verba in the late 1950s, two–thirds of the Italians refused to have anything to do with politics or to discuss the subject with anyone. Only 3% were proud of their state institutions, and only 10% approved of political participation.

Silvio Berlusconi and Umberto Bossi

An updated version of this study in 1980 revealed that Italians have become much more inclined to engage in direct political action, especially in the form of demonstrations, strikes, blocking of rail roads or highways or even political violence. Many Italians cling to the view that laws have been made to be evaded, that taxes are hostile acts of the state against the individual, and that one who does not successfully embezzle the government when one has the opportunity is considered a fool. Public institutions were long regarded with an unparalleled carefree air. The citizen's contempt and irritation toward his state was almost nihilistic, as is manifested in the widely used expression *piove, governo ladro* ("It's raining on this corrupt state"). The political revolution in the 1990s has shown that toleration of corruption and indifference toward elected representatives have dramatically changed.

Government Under Constant Challenge

The bad state of government affairs is not simply a result of the continuous public scandals which have brought down many governments and have helped paralyze the bureaucracy. For instance, in 1981 the Cossiga government fell because of an affair centered around an ultra–secret Masonic Lodge named P2 in which many of the country's leading politicians, industrialists and tax officials were closely linked in a scandal. This is rather the result of an historically developed behavioral pattern. For centuries the state meant nothing more to Italians than suppression by foreigners of subordination to the Doge princes, who themselves were dependent upon others. It has been difficult for Italians to believe that the state is working for their interests. One Italian expressed this in 1993: "We expect little of our politicians, and that's what we get."

The permanent crisis of the modern democratic state in Italy is scarcely suitable for developing a stronger sense of public spirit among its citizens. The work of many heterogeneous factions organized into many groups has made the establishment of a political consensus difficult. In Rome alone, over 25,000 politically active organizations have been counted. Some of these groups refuse to observe the democratic rules of the game and have become parts of the powerful terrorist movements which seek to achieve their political goals through violence. Terrorists on the ex-

Italy

Former President Scalfaro addresses the Chamber of Deputies

treme right have tried to upset the political system by means of countless indiscriminate bomb attacks. They have not been brought entirely under control.

The extreme leftists, the Red Brigades, posed a great problem for Italian domestic security through their precisely planned and executed attacks and kidnappings of high–ranking personalities. Their objective is to undermine the state and then to provoke a fascist reaction, which, they hope, would be the prelude to a "proletarian" revolution, although the working class in Italy shows almost no sympathy for such aims. U.S. Brigadier General James L. Dozier, the highest ranking American general stationed in Italy, was kidnapped from his Verona apartment in 1981 and freed by a highly–trained Italian anti–terrorist unit in a daring and brilliant raid in 1982 after he had been held prisoner for over 40 days.

This spectacular kidnapping was intended to be the opening act for a carefully planned spree of further kidnappings, commando–style raids on jails to free arrested terrorists, and as a final bloody crescendo, the massacre of the entire *Christian Democratic* leadership at a *DC* gathering in Rome. Yet this campaign was foiled by the absolute determination of the Italian government to put an end to left–wing terrorism. The government was greatly aided by the crack anti–terrorist units, which had been created in order to achieve the same level of expertise as that of the astonishingly well–informed, well–armed and well–trained terrorists.

In 1982 almost a thousand suspected terrorists were arrested, including many of their known leaders. Bases, conspiratorial apartments and arms dumps were raided. The police and courts also made effective use of a temporary law permitting more lenient sentences for terrorists who tell on their former comrades. The state thus made a significant strike at left–wing terrorism. Very importantly, it did this without abandoning democracy or an observance of civil rights. But the causes of such violence remain: an immobile political system, a corruption–ridden bureaucracy, and the bleak economic outlook for many young Italians. In 1999 there was a frightening reminder of Red Brigade terrorism when one of the government's top advisers, Massimo D'Antona, was gunned down as he walked to work. Prime Minister D'Alema vowed: "We are faced with a terroristic band that the state intends to find and to hit."

The Mafia

Organized crime, particularly the Sicilian Cosa Nostra, whose power extends from Sicily to Rome and the industrialized area further north, and its competitors, *Ndrangheta* from Calabria, responsible for the kidnapping of the young American heir, John Paul Getty, Jr., and Camorra from Naples, is the country's number one plague. The Mafia accumulated enormous wealth from lucrative bogus public works contracts, "protection," and international drug traffic, of which Sicily became the

Italy

European center following the severance of the "French Connection" in the 1970s. The Mafia lost ground in the global drug trade, supplying only an estimated 5% of the American market in 1993. Italian mobsters also face competition from ruthless imitators from Russia, Colombia, and other countries. Italy is not merely a transit point for drugs, which increasingly flow into the veins of Italians themselves, it gives the country the shameful distinction of having the largest number of addicts on the Continent.

With its wealth the Mafia has shifted its emphasis to becoming an entrepreneur, although protection rackets still extort $4.7 billion dollars each year from small businesses alone. A 1996 survey revealed that 23% of businesses paid racketeers an average of 10.7% of their annual sales. The Mafia bought into countless businesses and penetrated a portion of the Italian banking system, which it needs to "launder" its "hot" money. Whereas the Mafia's main profits were once from the drug trade, they are now from government contracts and extortion. In 1996 the Italian trade association, *Confcommercio*, estimated that a fifth of all trade and construction enterprises in Italy are controlled by organized crime and that the authorities discover no more than 8% of illegal businesses.

The competition among Mafia families for larger shares of the drug trade unleashed ruthless gang wars which left the streets and countryside strewn with hundreds of bloody corpses. It also led the Mafia to aim its ugly pistol against the political process itself. In 1979 it began liquidating top Italian political officials in Sicily who stood in its way. The government responded to this deadly challenge by making membership in a Mafia clan a crime, by legalizing the confiscation of suspects' estates if they cannot demonstrate that their income was legally acquired, and by sending the new leader of the secret services to Sicily as that island's regional prefect. In 1987 courageous judges and prosecutors in Palermo, relying heavily on testimony from 14 Mafia members who broke the code of silence, convicted 338 Mafiosi of crimes ranging from murder to drug trafficking in the biggest Mafia trial in Italian history. For the first time, the leading mobster bosses received the stiffest sentences.

In the 1980s and 1990s the Mafiosi maintained a steady wave of killings, not only among themselves, but against the Italian state. In 1988 they murdered an active judge for the first time. The government cooperated with U.S. officials to crack a powerful transatlantic drug ring. Despite the scores of bosses arrested, all agree that only the tip of the iceberg had been shattered. Authorities are able to prosecute criminals more quickly because of a 1989 judicial reform aimed at streamlining the system. As one headline read: "Perry Mason has finally entered Italy's old and decrepit courtrooms."

The criminal families not only expanded their operations into northern Italian cities, but began influencing municipal and regional elections by murdering or intimidating candidates. In 1991 five persons, including a member of a city council, were shot; one victim was even beheaded; his head was used for target practice. This horrified the Italian public and prompted the government to assume the authority to dissolve any city council or local authority infiltrated by the Mafia and to send judges, even against their will, to man under-staffed courts in the three regions most plagued by gangs: Calabria, Sicily, and Campania. The government created in 1991 a special post, dubbed the Italian "FBI," within the Attorney General's office to coordinate the fight against organized crime.

Like some Latin American countries, Italy is fighting to prevent itself from falling under the control of unelected international criminals. At stake is the freedom of Italians to be ruled by leaders they elect, rather than by those who reap undreamed profits from feeding human vices. After the Mafia murdered two top anti-Mafia officials (Giovanni Falcone and Paolo Borsellino) in 1992, the government deployed 7,000 soldiers to Sicily in July to crack down on the mob. This was the most drastic step taken since 1945 against a domestic disorder and the first time troops were used in a large-scale crackdown on the Sicilian mobsters. Also in 1992 law-enforcement officials joined Spanish, British, and American police to arrest Italians working with the Cali (Colombia) cocaine cartel. In November the biggest organized crime sweep in almost ten years put scores of Mafia suspects in jail, including several mayors and three members of parliament.

Armed with strengthened antiracketeering laws permitting wider use of phone taps, property searches, confiscation of property of convicted or suspected Mafia people, state reimbursement to businesses which suffer for defying the racketeers, and guarantees of protection for state witnesses, police maintained this momentum in 1993. A startling development occurred when the Pope broke the Church's long tradition of silence on Mafia matters and lashed out against organized crime. The Mafia's two top leaders, Salvatore ("Toto") Riina and Benedetto Santapaola, as well as the only women known to have headed an Italian crime syndicate (the Camorra around Naples), Rosetto Cutolo, were captured. In 1996 one of the most powerful and ruthless bosses in the history of the Corleone clan, Giovanni Brusca (nicknamed "the Pig"), who had masterminded the murder of Falcone and Borsellino, was captured by 200 black-hooded special police troops.

The key has been a crumbling of the long-standing code of silence. By 1997 more than 1,200 arrested Mafiosi were collaborating with investigators. The growing number of *pentiti* ("penitents") has prompted Mafia organizations to retaliate brutally, departing from the older code of honor not to attack women, children, judges, government officials, and innocent bystanders. It has also been expensive for the taxpayer to take care of more than 6,000 people, including families, who need escorts, protection, money and shelter, special schools and churches. But organized crime really does seem to be on the run.

The resulting confessions of these *pentiti* led not only to the dramatic arrests of Mafia leaders. They opened perhaps the most explosive chapter in Italy's mega-corruption scandal: that top *Christian Democratic* leaders, especially seven-time prime minister, Giulio Andreotti, may have cooperated with and protected the Mafia. No Italian politician had as many revealing nicknames as he: "Machiavelli," "Mephistopheles," and "the Fox." Prosecutors claim that the Mafia had guaranteed his party votes and political control in Sicily in return for government contracts for Mafia-controlled companies and protection from police crackdowns. Andreotti denied the charges but agreed to have his senatorial immunity lifted in order to clear his name in court.

Commencing in 1995, this trial is a humiliating ordeal for Andreotti; two-thirds of respondents in a 1995 poll think he did indeed have a "relationship" with the Mafia. The press calls it "the trial of the century."

Many Italians now believe that organized crime can finally be defeated. No longer able to act with impunity inside Italy, the Mafia and other organized crime groups are increasingly expanding their operations into other European countries. In 1998 one of the new generation's top bosses in Sicily, Vito Vitale, was arrested. Declaring the anti-Mafia crackdown to have been successful, the government announced that 7,000 army troops would be pulled out of Palermo and the rest of Sicily. Many Sicilian politicians find this move too hasty.

The Italian Family

Despite the complicated historical development and the division into numerous interest groups, the Italian family has

Italy

The Galdino Barella family of Paina, near Milan

Photo by John M. Morrow

traditionally been responsible for Italy's national identity and strength. It is the most important institution and focal point of Italian life. Its significance has changed due to the modernization which accompanies industrial life. Italy reached zero population growth in 1987, and by 1998 the average mother produced only 1.2 children, compared with 2.7 in 1964. In most years now, deaths outnumber births, and only immigration somewhat stabilizes the population. Among western European countries, only women in Catholic Spain bear fewer children. But in contrast to most northern European nations, only 6% of Italian babies are born out of wedlock.

An opinion poll in the 1970s revealed that nearly half the women between the ages of 25 and 35 no longer considered motherhood as their most important goal in life. Earlier, Italians would have been shocked by such a result. Because of Italians' desire for higher living standards, the emancipation of women, and the declining influence of the Catholic Church, the birth rate has fallen dramatically, especially in the North of Italy.

The Bureaucracy

Because many political decisions are made within the various interest groups rather than in the official political channels, the Italians have a good understanding for the term "undergovernment" *(sottogoverno)*. Italian bureaucracy, with 1.7 million civil servants, has been reproached for its general inefficiency, inflexibility and corruption. Government employees have alarming absenteeism, and far too many who report for work either do nothing or use their time to do outside work in order to have a second income.

Government officials are, for the most part, recruited from the South, where an administrative position is for many the only opportunity for a job. The emphasis on authority, exaggerated bureaucracy and official government patronage and nepotism which characterizes public offices, can be traced back historically to the behavioral patterns of the pre–capitalistic feudal states of the South. It is a curious phenomenon that in this land of contradictions the North conquered the South during the "Resurgence" partly through its economic predominance; however, the South conquered the North through the Italian bureaucracy.

The South

The main domestic problem remains the structurally underdeveloped South. When describing the Italian social and economic situation, one can speak of an industrialized state which has some characteristics of an underdeveloped country. Four–fifths of the industry is concentrated in the Turin–Milan–Genoa triangle. Although roughly one–third of the population is concentrated in the South, two–fifths of Italy's unemployed live there. In 1998 the jobless rate in the South was 22% vs. 7% in the North. The problem is bound to get worse because the birth rate and illiteracy are considerably higher in the South. The average income per capita in the South is 70% of the Italian average, and it is widening in the 1990s. The per capita productivity in the South is 40% to 60% under that of the North. There are, of course, significant differences between regions within the South. For instance, Calabria and Campania are very depressed, while such areas as Abruzzi and Molise are catching up with the North. Clearly prosperity is not being shared equally throughout Italy.

The traveler coming from the modern, industrialized North to Calabria or the Basilicata in the South has the feeling that he has left a highly developed country and has landed in an underdeveloped one. In order to compensate for this historical disadvantage, a governmental agency called the *Cassa per il Mezzogiorno*

Italy

was established in 1950 to channel resources to the South and thus stimulate improvements. The *Cassa* has accounted for a few worthwhile projects, including a turnpike from Milan to Palermo, which opened up the South to tourism. However, overall results have proved to be disappointing. Profit–seekers in the North benefited excessively from road construction, favorable state credits, as well as cheap, unskilled labor available in and from the South. The Mafia and the Ndrangheta also earned through fraud a massive fortune from the money provided by the *Cassa*.

In order to fill the industrial gap, the government financed a petrochemical and iron works, which achieved high rates of production, but which *Corriere della Sera* called the "cathedral in the desert." This capital–intensive plant employed few persons, contaminated large areas of land and failed to stimulate an economic base around it. The best example of a grandiose government–subsidized project which failed, though, is the mammoth ironworks in Calabria's Gioia Tauro. This made little economic sense because its superfluous steel could hardly be sold in the saturated world market. However, an entire citrus producing area was destroyed in order to build this plant. To transport the steel products, a nearby port was dredged despite the fact that the southern Italian coast was rich with natural bays. Many millions were spent for this project, but much of the money landed in the pockets of the Mafia. Therefore Rome decided to terminate the plant's production.

The culmination point for misery in the South is Naples, the "capital of poverty," as it was described by the Turin newspaper *La Stampa*. The city, with its 1.3 million inhabitants, among which over 100,000 are unemployed, is practically incomprehensible. Speculation on construction projects has been boundless. Also, the absence of a sewage system has transformed the once renowned gulf into a cesspool which is five times more polluted than Italy's other coastal waters. Neapolitan newspapers read many days like a hair–raising chronicle of crime and catastrophe. The number of stolen vehicles is estimated at 40,000 annually. There are not enough orphans' homes to accommodate the deserted children of desperate parents living in a city which is known traditionally to be family–conscious. It is surprising that Naples has not collapsed under the pressure of such massive problems.

Foreign Relations and Defense

Italy joined the UN in 1955, but the two main pillars of its foreign policy are membership in the EU, of which it was a founding member, and NATO. It has 325,000 men under arms, over half (164,000) of whom are doing their basic 10–month military service. These forces are supplemented by more then 8,500 U.S. ground and air force troops, mainly in northern Italy, and more than 4,000 U.S. naval personnel in the 6th fleet based in Naples. Although it occupies a strategically important position on NATO's southern flank, its defense spending accounts for less than 2% of its GDP. This has dire consequences for the Italian navy, which must leave the defense of Italy's extensive coastline to the army and the air force, which are concentrated in the North. The navy is capable of defending only merchant vessels in the Mediterranean.

NATO membership for a country with the largest communist party in Western Europe caused some tensions. However,

The Italian aircraft carrier *Giuseppe Garibaldi* is inspected by former Prime Minister Craxi

Italy

as the *PCI* moved steadily away from Moscow and renamed itself the *PDS*, it increasingly accepted national defense within NATO. The dilemma still gives Italian foreign policy one of its major characteristics: it is normally conducted quietly and with the utmost of discretion in order not to allow foreign policy to become part of the always heated domestic cauldron.

A dramatic exception occurred in 1990 when the prime minister admitted that in 1956 the government, aided by the CIA, had set up a clandestine paramilitary network (code name: *Gladio*, Latin for "sword") to resist a possible Communist occupation. Weapons and explosives were hidden in 139 caches. *Communists* were incensed that they were the targets, and a national scandal ensued when suspicions were aired that renegade *Gladio* agents might have used some of the explosives to make right–wing terrorist attacks in the 1960s and 1970s, a charge which the government vehemently denied. The revelations also stirred debate in other NATO countries, especially Belgium, where right–wing terrorists might have gotten their weapons from similar caches.

Italy has long sought to play a more assertive role in the world, especially in Mediterranean affairs. It became the first European NATO ally to accept, without condition, U.S. medium–range cruise missiles, which began to be deployed at Comiso, Sicily, in 1983. Italian willingness to contribute to strengthening NATO was again shown in 1988 when its government termed the eviction of American F16 fighter aircraft from Spain as "disastrous" and agreed to their being based in Southern Italy. The end of the Cold War made that relocation unnecessary.

Rome's concern for stability in the area is expressed in the 1990s by its support for a Council for Security and Cooperation in the Mediterranean (CSCM), modelled on the OSCE, to include countries on all shores of the Mediterranean. It is worried that its confused domestic politics, its difficulty in meeting the criteria by 1998 for a unified European currency, and the emergence of a dominant Paris–Bonn/Berlin axis might relegate it to second-class status in the EU. To demonstrate that her country cannot be taken for granted, Foreign Minister Susanna Agnelli temporarily refused an American request in the summer of 1995 to deploy F–117 "stealth" fighter–bombers in Italy for use in NATO's Bosnian campaign.

Italy was the first European country to join the multi–national peacekeeping force in the Sinai Peninsula to help preserve the peace between Israel and Egypt, and in 1982 its troops joined the French and Americans in overseeing the withdrawal of the PLO and other foreign belligerents from the war–torn city of Beirut, Lebanon. It is willing to guarantee Malta's neutrality. In 1991 it sent ten Tornado aircraft and five naval vessels to the Persian Gulf to support its allies' war effort against Iraq. In 1993 Italy was one of the first countries to send troops on the UN humanitarian mission to Somalia, part of which had been ruled by Italy until 1960. Links with Somalia remained strong. Most educated Somalis still speak Italian, and many studied in Italy.

When NATO launched an air war against Serbia in 1999 to try to stop ethnic cleansing in Kosovo, Italy stuck with the alliance. Although its own aircraft were not involved, it sent 2,000 troops to Albania to administer humanitarian aid, and it permitted NATO pilots to use 14 bases in Italy, including especially Aviano in the Northeast. American flights from Aviano had become an emotional public issue in 1998–9 when a low–flying Marine Corps EA–6B Prowler aircraft passing through Aviano clipped the cable of a gondola killing 20 skiers. Anti–American and anti–NATO feelings were inflamed when an American military court acquitted the pilot on charges of negligence. However, he was found guilty of obstruction of justice for destroying a video taped record, and the Americans agreed to tighten restrictions and accountability for training flights in Italy. Although some parties, such as the *Northern League* and the *United Communists* opposed the air strikes, Prime Minister D'Alema, a former Communist, declared that "we'll be loyal to the end."

One of Italy's thorniest future foreign policy problems is immigration. By 1999 legal immigrants living there numbered around one million. About 800,000 illegal ones had slipped in, and loopholes in the law make it difficult to deport them. Many Italians fear that some of these illegals are involved in prostitution and drug rings in the major cities. Other European countries fear that Italy could be a gateway into the EU now that Italy has become a member of the EU's Schengen group, which lifts border controls for those persons already inside an EU country. Until recently Italy was a land of emigration, but its long coastline facing North Africa has made it a natural bridge between the burgeoning populations of Africa and the rich nations of Europe. Not wishing to damage its good relations with its Arab neighbors on the other side of the Mediterranean and Adriatic Seas, Italy has not wanted to impose quotas. To encourage its growing number of illegal residents to register with the authorities, it offered its generous welfare benefits to non–EU citizens, but this merely stimulated even greater immigration.

In a country which thought it was above racism, daily headlines now report racial strife. Nowhere was that more visible than in Florence, where the presence of hundreds of North African street vendors sparked protest marches to decry the influx. Gangs of white rowdies set upon the newcomers with baseball bats and iron bars.

To the East, the collapsed communist regimes in Albania and Yugoslavia have enhanced the spectre of an immigration flood. Waves of Albanians, travelling across the Adriatic Sea in overcrowded boats, were washed ashore in 1991, only to be penned into coal docks and a local soccer stadium, which they proceeded to wreck out of anger toward their reception. One Caritas relief worker complained that "the police threw food at them like in a zoo."

Stung by the criticism, the government adopted a new policy to prevent the exodus of impoverished Albanians. Italian naval vessels help Albania patrol its shores. It also established a large emergency aid program within Albania itself. Italian soldiers distribute food and advice on improving the infrastructure, as a forerunner to a longer–term program to help stabilize the Balkan country's ailing economy. In 1997, for the first time since the Second World War, Italy led a multinational force, including 6,000 of its own soldiers, into Albania to restore order. Violence and anarchy had broken out when thousands of people lost their savings in shady financial pyramid schemes. By the end of the year, order had been restored, and thousands of the Albanian refugees began to be deported.

ECONOMY

The motor which keeps the country operating despite all of the crises, scandals, strikes, poverty and natural catastrophes, is the Italians' ability to improvise and adapt to existing conditions. Such extraordinary resilience and resourcefulness have taken shape through centuries of foreign domination and of continuous threats along the coastline from pirates and conquerors. The every–day problems merely stimulate these qualities and enable one to understand why so many informed commentators on the state of Italian affairs are inclined to say with confidence that "the situation is desperate, but not hopeless."

Italy has a private enterprise economy, although the government has a controlling interest in some large commercial and industrial firms. Electricity, transportation, telephone and telegraph are largely owned by the state. Three TV channels are dominated by the state RAI

Italy

A gondolier in the late afternoon, Venice

Photo by Vincent Campi

network, although voters in a 1995 referendum chose to allow private shareholders to buy a stake in them. Three other channels, with 65% of the advertising market, are owned by Silvio Berlusconi's Fininvest, and voters in 1995 decided that he should not be forced to give up control of two of them.

By the 1990s the changes in wage indexation and the remarkable improvement in labor productivity stabilized inflation at 1.5% in 1999, despite a VAT of 19%. Economic growth exceeded that of Germany and France, and the size of its economy had surpassed that of the UK. It is now the world's fifth largest economy, behind the U.S., Japan, FRG and France. Entering the 1990s its economy was growing at an annual rate of about 4%; in 1997 it declined to 0.7%. Italian firms have invested heavily in the latest technology and have some of the most productive factories in Europe. Its companies are also actively investing outside the country. Of the 68 major European takeovers and mergers from 1986 to 1988, Italian companies were involved in 28 of them. Northern Italy shows particular dynamism. Of Italy's 20 regions, the three northern ones—Lombardy, Veneto and Piedmont—produce almost 40% of the GDP. Lombardy alone generates 30% of the country's exports.

Prodded by its strong desire to join the EU's single currency (Euro), Italy has made spectacular economic progress since 1992. By 1999 the budget deficit has declined to 2.7% of GDP, even though its total national debt is equal to 121% of its GDP. Servicing that debt consumes 11% of its GDP and a fifth of government spending. Fortunately, 90% of Italy's debt is funded domestically, thanks largely to Italians' fetish for saving: they save 15% of their earnings, the highest rate in the EU. Much of it is in government securities. Thus, most of the interest payments are recycled into the economy.

Partly because of the shaky ruling coalitions that require expensive concessions to keep all partners satisfied, it has not been easy for any government to make big cuts in government spending and borrowing. The country's financial system both in banking and the stock market must be further modernized. Obstacles to business exist, such as rigid hiring and firing laws, high employers' social security contributions, and widespread price controls. These raise unemployment, which stood at 12% in 1999; half have been out of work for more than a year. Joblessness is higher for the South (22%, and about 50% for youths) than in the North (7%) and for women and youths; a third of adults under 25 have no job.

Nevertheless, Italy remains a visibly prosperous country. A reflection of such prosperity is the fact that almost two–thirds of the adult population were home-owners by the end of the 1980s, and one Italian family in four has a second home. One explanation of such economic well–being which defies the gloomy statistics is the celebrated "submerged economy," a parallel unofficial economy, mainly behind the backs of government statisticians and tax collectors. Tax revenues equal about 41% of GDP (which is below the EU average), and it is conservatively estimated that tax evasion amounts to around 15% of GDP. This kind of economic activity is done at home, in the streets or on the job, while the boss is looking the other way.

If the production of goods and services from such a submerged economy were able to be included in the official economic figures, an estimated 10% to 30% would have to be added to the national wealth. This "black economy" makes the country's double–digit unemployment figure less serious politically than in many other Western European nations. Also, whereas unemployment prevails in large parts of the South and in some cities in the industrial North, there are other regions where the demand for jobs must be filled with guest workers such as Tunisians in Sicily and Yugoslavs in Trieste.

Italy's dependence upon oil and raw material imports is excessive. It has almost no domestic energy sources except

Italy

small amounts of natural gas (chiefly in the Po Valley) and very few other raw materials. Domestic oil production meets only 3.6% of needs. Government plans to expand nuclear power production were dealt a severe blow in a 1987 referendum vote which stopped the building of atomic power stations. Italy still has only three functioning nuclear plants, which produce only 1% of the country's energy needs. As a result, it must continue to import 80% of its energy needs, twice the Western European average. Such extreme dependence on energy imports explains its determination in 1982 to defy President Reagan's embargo on the sale of gas pipeline equipment to the Soviet Union. Russia pays for such equipment by delivering large quantities of natural gas to Italy and other Western European countries. Also, it explains the heavy Italian investment in a trans–Mediterranean gas pipeline, which began in 1982 to bring Algerian gas to the economically depressed southern Italy.

The magnitude of the country's trade deficit results mainly from the import of consumer goods and even agricultural products which Italy itself produces. It is only 80% self–sufficient in food. It does have impressive trade successes, though, in clothing, shoes and mechanical goods; 90% of its total exports are manufactures. Over half its trade is with its EU partners.

Agriculture

Even though the percentage employed in agriculture has dropped over the years from 38% in 1951 to 16.2% in 1975, Italy's agricultural population remains far above the EU average of 9%. The rather unproductive Italian agriculture suffers from the small size of farms and the advanced age of farmers. Also, about a fourth of the farm land is underutilized and about a tenth is not used at all.

A major agricultural obstacle is, of course, the problem of hill farming. More than 40% of Italy is classified as hilly, and such terrain merely intensifies the country's other agricultural problems of fragmentation and low productivity. Only about 23% of the land is classified as plain, most of it in the fertile Po Valley in the North, the Pontine Valley south of Rome and parts of Puglia in the South, although the latter is strapped by severe irrigation problems. The Po Valley is Italy's breadbasket, producing cereals, dairy products and sugar beets. In the South, Mediterranean produce predominates, such as citrus fruits, olive oil, wine and tomatoes. But Italy is faced with a particular dilemma as far as this latter farming is concerned. On the one hand, it is inefficient. Yet, if farming in the South were reorganized, many agricultural workers would lose jobs.

Government–Owned Enterprises

Italy's enormous budget deficits can be partly explained by the huge losses by some of the businesses which are wholly or partially owned by the state, the almost uncontrollable system of social expenditures, and the hostile attitude of the citizens toward taxes. The state's hand in the economy is large. In contrast to many other European countries, where left–wing governments once nationalized many companies, such work was done in Italy by Mussolini. The three large state–owned industrial groups—IRI, ENI and EFIM—account for about 10% of GDP. Some of the firms controlled by these huge holding companies are not profitable. These debt–ridden enterprises are an economic burden in a country in which most private concerns report a profit.

Therefore, the government decided to reduce the state's ownership in the economy. It is in no great hurry to privatize, and it has made no commitment to divest itself totally. But the former "Olive Tree" coalition pledged to get the process started. During the 1990s the proportion of the banking system in state hands declined from 70% to 20%.

Unions

In the view of many analysts, it is an encouraging sign that the Italian trade unions, which organize about 40% of Italy's work force, have lost a considerable portion of their power and influence. In the past the unions had made the Italian worker one of the most protected in Europe, and they had gained a practical veto power over the country's economic and social policies.

The reversal in trade unionists' fortunes has come since the *Communists* have lost votes in successive parliamentary elections, and since a massive strike against the Fiat automotive company collapsed in the fall of 1980. Fiat had to keep its overseas prices competitive with those of other countries. Now only 30% of Fiat's work force is unionized. Italy enjoys better industrial relations as a result: from 1984–8, only 40 million man hours of work were lost each year, compared to an annual av-

The frenzy of last–minute Christmas shopping in a Rome food market

Italy

Coming home from school past the *Piazza San Marco*, Venice

Photo by Vincent Campi

erage of 130 million in the previous decade. Enhanced competitiveness enabled production and export of a somewhat unique item: subway riders on Washington D.C.'s Metro are now riding in cars of Italian manufacture.

The heavy political involvement of the unions has caused them to lose touch with the rank–and–file members, who are more interested in bread–and–butter economic issues. In the midst of a recession, more and more Italians have also come to the conclusion that private enterprise and market–oriented management are necessary if the country's prosperity is to be maintained. Further, the unions were forced to budge on wage indexation, which had kept the motor of inflation well lubricated. The result is a generally favorable economic outlook. At the same time, despite the fact that things Italian miraculously turn out to be less serious than they are usually predicted, the country continues to face some serious economic challenges.

CULTURE

No other country has both profited and been stifled by the wealth of its historical inheritance as has Italy. This inheritance has attracted educated tourists for over 200 years. Annually, 26 million tourists exchange their currencies in Italy in order to see its incomparable art treasures and to enjoy the usually mild climate. In addition, approximately 80 million individual pieces of art await restoration. The most dramatic reappearance in 1999 was Leonardo Da Vinci's *Last Supper*, which had undergone a meticulous 21–year restoration in Milan. Italy possesses 30,000 churches, 20,000 castles, 3,000 archaeological sites which are of value to art historians and shelters in its 712 museums countless important works of art.

Only one who understands the ambivalent attitude of the Italian toward his history and state can excuse the fact that the money used by the state to maintain the irreplaceable wealth of arts corresponds to the amount needed to construct 18 miles of freeway. Since 1909 the immeasurable cultural inheritance has been administered by a small group of 284 highly–placed civil servants. However, Italy alone cannot be expected to bear the burden history has placed upon it; the entire civilized world is also, to some extent, responsible for the vast historical wealth.

UNESCO provided a considerable contribution in order to save Venice, which was threatened by uninhibited industrial exploitation of the hinterlands. Many European and American organizations provided aid to cover damages caused by the catastrophic flood in Florence in 1966. It continues to face flooding, with the low–lying parts of the city inundated about every three years. Florence was again shaken in 1993, when terrorists exploded a car bomb in front of the 16th century Uffizi Gallery, which houses the world's most important collection of classic Italian art, including priceless paintings by Leonardo da Vinci, Michelangelo, Raphael, and Titian, and which is visited by more than a million persons each year. Six people died, three paintings and many Medieval manuscripts in the library were destroyed, and 21 canvases and three statues were damaged.

The unique Byzantine churches of Ravenna are threatened, the cathedral in Milan is unstable and there is danger that the Palatine Hill in Rome will collapse. Unfortunately, the international contribution has never been used in full because of competition and disputes among the different bureaucracies. The burden of history has not only left its imprint on the political culture and on the problem of southern Italy *(Mezzogiorno)* but also literally threatens to slip out of the Italian state's control.

Italy's extraordinary significance for the development of western civilization from antiquity through the Middle Ages and the Renaissance in the areas of science, the arts, architecture and finance is well known. The Italians have also accomplished much in more recent times. The recognition of Italian as the language of music indicates the influence it had on the developing years. During the Baroque period (17th/18th centuries), composers such as Dominico Scarlatti, Antonio Vivaldi and Luigi Boccherini, just to name the most important figures, were prominent; (Bach was a great admirer of Vivaldi's works). The 19th century also produced world renowned composers, such as Gioacchino Rossini, Giuseppe Verdi, Gaetano Donizetti and Giacomo Puccini. Even today, Italian composers such as Luigi Dallapiccola, Bruno Maderna and Luigi Mono are conspicuous. No singer of opera is a star until he performs at the incomparable *La Scala* in Milan.

Without even taking into account the countless artists of the 15th, 16th and 17th centuries, Italian artists include modern painters such as Amadeo Modigliani and

Italy

Giorgio de Chirico and sculptor Marino Marini, who have maintained Italy's reputation in the international art world. In 1906 and 1936 respectively Giosuè Carducci and Grazia Deledda received Nobel prizes for literature. Significant writers such as the novelist Giovanni Verga and the romantic poet, Gabriele D'Annunzio, lead a long list of splendid literary figures. In lyric poetry, Giuseppe Ungaretti, Eugenio Montale and Salvatore Quasimodo (who won a Nobel prize in 1959) have made important contributions. Dramatist Luigi Pirandello and novelists Curzio Malaparte, Cesare Pavese, Tomasi di Lampedusa, Ignazio Silone and Alberto Moravia dominated the Italian literary scene until after World War II. The critical realist, Italo Calvino, enjoys postwar popularity.

International film, opera and theater festivals, as well as modern art exhibits reflect the ever–vibrant cultural life of Italy. In terms of cinema, Rome is to Italy what Hollywood means to the U.S.A. Italian directors have been and still are the leading film figures in Europe. Names such as Vittorio de Sica, Federico Fellini, Luchino Visconti and Pier Paolo Pasolini have decisively affected European films. With his commercial Italian Western (often referred to jokingly as "spaghetti Western") director Sergio Leone captivated masses of movie–goers all over the world. Italian cinema's stellar position was shown in 1999 by Roberto Benigni's *Life is Beautiful*, which won two Oscars, including the best foreign–language film, and the Grand Jury Prize at the Cannes Film Festival. Italians continue to see many American feature films, and in 1999 two–thirds of its foreign TV programs were purchased from the United States.

In the natural sciences, the Italians have also distinguished themselves—Galileo Galilei, Luigi Galvani and Alessandro Volta played a prominent role in the research of electricity. Guglielmo Marconi won a Nobel price in 1909 for his discovery of the wireless telegraph. One cannot overlook another Nobel prize winner, Enrico Fermi, who investigated the peaceful use of the atom.

For the first time since Italy's creation, the press is no longer controlled by political power and parties, but by the normal business groups in the Italian economy. Major dailies include Rome's *La Repubblica*, Milan's *Corriere della Sera* and *Il Giornale*, and Turin's *La Stampa*. *Il Foglio* is a clever four–page daily, and the Communist *L'Unita* is also widely read. Italians buy no more dailies than they did in the 1930s—six million, compared with 22 million in the UK. The major news weeklies include *L'Espresso* and *Panorama*.

Despite its problems, Italy remains a prosperous, democratic country, in which civil rights are protected far better than in most countries of the world. It sometimes looks maddeningly chaotic, but the Italian brand of chaos has a certain refreshing sweetness to it which is precisely why millions of non–Italians are fervent admirers, even lovers of this country and its basically friendly people. Perhaps a touch of chaos is essential to the renowned Italian *dolce vita* ("sweet life").

FUTURE

That Italy will not collapse or capitulate under the weight of its multi–faceted ordeals is due largely to the fact that the Italians have an unshakable ability to adapt to existing circumstances with imagination and practicality. Some tendencies toward integrating the otherwise centrifugal political forces are evident in the widespread rejection and struggle against corruption, terrorism and organized crime.

Pressure for a thorough reform of the political system continues. By 1997, 2,000 prominent figures had been prosecuted for corruption although only two were

A group of television actors and actresses

The Spanish Steps, Rome

Italy

still in jail. Many prominent politicians are being brought to trial and sentenced: Two former prime ministers, Bettino Craxi and Arnaldo Forlani, and *Northern League* leader Umberto Bossi were convicted of illegal party funding; Bossi was sentenced a second time in 1995 for insulting a judge. Silvio Berlusconi was tried on corruption and bribery charges just as he was attempting a political comeback. His legal tangle effectively deprives the political right of its top leader. Corruption is no longer an integral part of political life.

Pressure on the Mafia is also being maintained. The trial of seven-time prime minister Andreotti shed light on the sordid practices of both the Mafia and the country's political elite. Since there are credible allegations that the Mafia and part of the political elite collaborated in the past, the "Clean Hands" campaign can succeed only if it continues on both fronts. But it is unlikely that the Mafia now has protectors at the heart of government. In the traditional heartlands of organized crime in the South, a new bevy of mayors have been elected who are providing more efficient local government and opposing corruption and lawlessness more energetically.

Referring to the country's biggest corruption scandal and shake-up since 1945, Italy's most famous living novelist, Umberto Eco, stated in 1993 that "we are living through our own 14th of July 1789." The difference, he noted, is the heads of the political elite are being chopped off by newspapers and television, not by a guillotine.

Electoral reform was supposed to clarify political choices and allow voters, not parliamentary intriguers, to choose who would govern. Governments were supposed to last longer. But the new election law intended to diminish the number of parties did not have the desired effect. Thus, only shaky governing coalitions result; cobbled alliances remain the Italian way. The political landscape is as fragmented as ever, with two communist and one ex-communist parties, three former socialist parties, four ex-Christian Democratic parties (three on the left and one on the right), one ex-fascist and one currently fascist party in parliament. Despite the 1993 reform which attempted to reduce the number of political parties, Italy's politicians have succeeded in making the new system work more or less like the old one.

The 1996 national elections brought Italy closer to stability as voters gravitated toward two main blocs. Romano Prodi's center-left *Olive Tree* coalition won a near majority of 284 seats and was able to form a minority government. It was the first leftist government in Italian postwar history with former Communists as participants. But its durability was questioned from the start since it was not a harmonious team united behind a clear set of political principles. It also had to depend on the 35 votes of the *Communist Refoundation* party on a case-by-case basis, which opposed *Olive Tree's* policy of cutting public spending and liberalizing the economy. It brought Prodi's government down in October 1998. Taking *Olive Tree's* place was a nine-party government led by Massimo D'Alema, the first former Communist to rule in a western European country since the war.

Lovers in a sunlit piazza in Florence

Photo by Jon M. Morrow

The Republic of San Marino

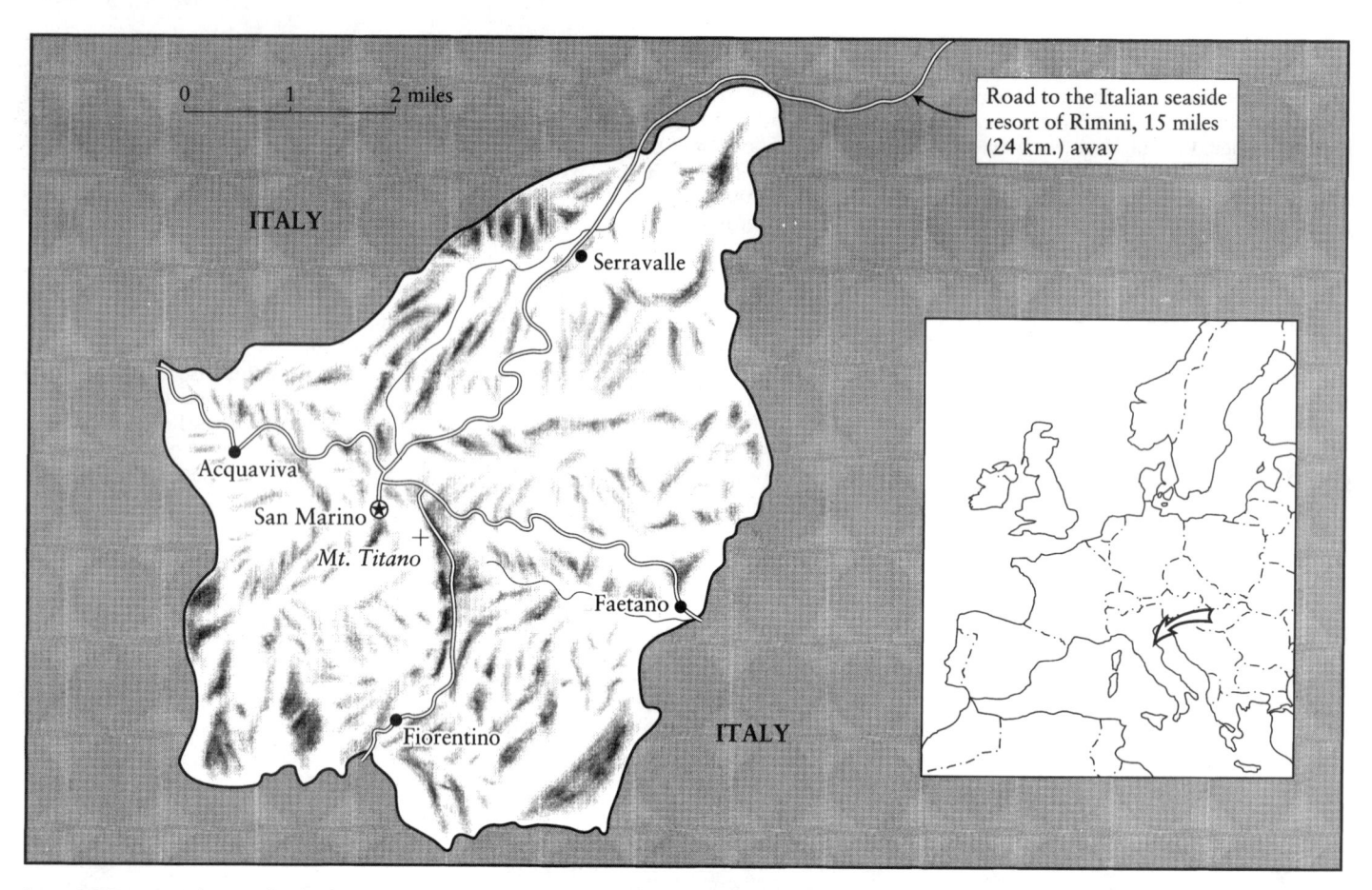

Area: 23.5 sq. mi. (62 sq. km.)
Population: 24,300 (estimated).
Capital City: San Marino (Pop. 4,500, estimated).
Climate: Mild and temperate.
Official Language: Italian.
Ethnic Background: Italian.
Principal Religion: Roman Catholic.
Main Industries: Postage stamps, tourism, cotton textiles, brick, tile, cement.
Main Customer: Italy.
Currency: Italian Lira.
Independence: Fourth Century A.D.
Government: Republic.
Chiefs of State: Two Captains Regent, selected every six months.
Heads of Government: Secretary of State for Foreign and Political Affairs and for Information, Secretary of State for Internal Affairs and Justice.
National Holidays: April 1, October 1.

Known today chiefly to collectors, who prize this tiny country's beautiful postage stamps, San Marino is a historical curiosity situated on the slopes of Monte Titano in the eastern part of central Italy, to which it is linked by a customs union and a treaty of friendship. The last remaining relic of the self–governing Italian city states, San Marino is the smallest republic in the world, and it always has wanted to stay that way. Its residents once refused Napoleon's offer of more territory on the grounds that the country's small size and poverty were the greatest guarantors of its independence. It has an irregular rectangular form with a maximum length of eight miles (13 km.) The country's setting is dominated by the 2,424 feet high (739 meters) Monte Titano, whose three summits are crowned by ancient fortifications. The medieval–looking capital city with its red–roofed stone houses is located directly below one of these fortifications and is surrounded by triple walls. Of its 23,400 residents, roughly 3,000 are non–citizens, mainly Italians. An additional 20,000 of the people (known as Sanmarinese) reside abroad, principally in Italy.

San Marino traces its origin to 301 A.D. when St. Marinus (from whom the country derives its name) and a small group of Christians fled to Monte Titano to escape religious persecution. In memory of their founder, the San Marinese do not date years according to Christ's life, but instead begin counting the years from 301 A.D. For instance, the year 2000 in San Marino is 1699! By the 12th century this tiny territory had become self–ruling. It has always managed to maintain its independence chiefly thanks to its geographic isolation, its mountain fortresses and its skill in playing rival noble families against one another. By the 15th century, it was a republic ruled by a Grand Council composed of 60 men from San Marino's leading families.

During the Italian unification struggles in the 19th century, San Marino offered asylum to revolutionaries, including the hero Giuseppe Garibaldi. This assistance enabled it to gain a guarantee of independence from the Kingdom of Italy in 1862. San Marino remained neutral in World War II until September 1943, and in November of that year it was temporarily occupied by German troops. In June 1944 it was damaged by British bomber pilots who were attempting to dislodge the occupiers.

The Statutes of 1600, enlarged in 1926 and revised in 1939, serve as a constitution. They established a parliament, the Great and General Council, with 60 members elected every five years by universal suffrage since 1960. This Council in turn elects two Captains Regent, largely ceremonial figures who formally exercise executive power for a period of six months. During their semi–annual investitures on April 1 and October 1, the Noble Guard and Great and General Councilors all dress in brightly colored uniforms and parade through the capital's streets. The Captains Regent cannot be elected for a second term until three years have elapsed. In 1981 for the first time in the

The Republic of San Marino

country's history, a woman, Maria Lea Pedini Angelini, was chosen. The Council also elects from among its members ten persons who serve as secretaries of state in the Council of State, the principal organ of executive power. These secretaries of state each head a government administrative department.

The Secretary of State for Foreign Affairs and the Secretary of State for Internal Affairs are in fact the highest and most powerful government executives of San Marino. Finally, the Great and General Council elects a supreme appellate judicial body, the Council of Twelve, which hears appeals from the decisions of San Marino's two full–time judges, who need not be citizens. These judges decide on the basis of San Marino's own civil and criminal legal system, which has understandably been influenced greatly by Italian law.

The country has many political parties, which are heavily influenced by their much larger counterpart parties in Italy. In the 1993 elections, the *Christian Democratic Party (DCS)* won 26 seats; the *Socialist Party (PSS)* 14; the *Left Democrats* 11; The *People's Alliance* 4; the *Democratic Movement* 3; the *Communists* 2. Like their Italian counterparts, these parties are not rigidly bound to doctrine. A unique election feature is that the state pays 75% of the return fare for any Sanmarinese living abroad to come home and vote in general elections. Over 5,400 did just that in 1988, returning from as far as Detroit, where many Sanmarinese live.

This tiny mouse does not hesitate to roar against the United States if it gets an urge to do so. In 1982 its parliament voted to "deplore" American policy in El Salvador and authorized a symbolic $4,500 contribution to the rebel forces in that Central American nation.

Monte Titano dominates San Marino

All parties in San Marino favor a broad social security system which, among other things, provides health care from state funds. Children up to the age of 12 receive a guaranteed summer holiday on the seaside, and up to the age of 14 a free public education. Those wishing to study further are eligible for state scholarships to Italian high schools and universities. Finally, the state of San Marino finds work for all citizens who cannot obtain employment privately. If no work at all can be found, then the state provides unemployment benefits amounting to 60% of the person's normal salary.

This country has no army because Italy provides for its defense. It does have a military corps which performs parade duty during national celebrations. It has a *gendarmerie* which maintains public order. In 1988 San Marino entered the Council of Europe, and in 1992 it joined the United Nations.

There are utterly no natural resources, so earnings must be made from farming (chiefly wheat and grapes), livestock raising, light manufacturing (chiefly cotton textiles, brick and tile, cement and pottery), the sale of postage stamps and tourism. It is the only European microstate which does not attract capital by being a tax haven. Diplomatic relations between the EU and San Marino were opened in 1983. Its goods have free access to the EU.

During the summer months, from 20,000 to 30,000 foreign tourists visit San Marino each day. Unfortunately, the Sanmarinese welcome these tourists with solid rows of souvenir shops on both sides of the principal streets. Without doubt, it has more tourist stands and shops per capita than does any other country in the world. This creates an excessively commercialized air in this naturally beautiful mountain–top republic. But several handsome hotels and restaurants have appeared in recent years, relieving this monotony. There is no radio broadcasting or television of its own, and there are no railroad or airport facilities.

FUTURE

Although legally independent, San Marino has always been very vulnerable to pressure from the Italian government, political parties and trade unions. This situation will certainly continue. Its beautiful setting and the curiosity which this tiny republic stimulates will help assure that tourism will continue to be a lucrative source of income. However, a shortage of energy will continue to exist, and San Marino will have great difficulty finding the necessary funds to finance badly needed expanded water and electric power systems.

The Vatican City State

St. Peter's Square

Area: .15 sq. mi. (.40 sq. km.)
Population: 1,000 (estimated).
Climate: Temperate.
Neighboring Countries: Italy.
Official Languages: Italian, Latin and various modern languages.
Religion: Roman Catholic.
Currency: Vatican Lira, interchangeable with Italian Lira.
National Day: June 30.
Chief of State: His Holiness Pope John Paul II (formerly Karol *Cardinal* Wojtyla), elected Pope October 16, 1978.
Suffrage: Limited to cardinals less than 80 years of age, who elect a Pope for life.
National Flag: Yellow and white stripes parallel to the staff, with the papal insignia on a white field.

Vatican City is the world's second smallest state. One can leisurely stroll around the full length of its borders in less than one hour. Located in the heart of Rome, near the west bank of the Tiber River, and surrounded by medieval walls and the Church of St. Peter, this tiny dot on the Rome city map is often said to wield more influence in the world than the entire nation of Italy. The reason is that this is the headquarters of the Roman Catholic Church, the largest body of Christians in the world. Building began in the 8th century to create a residence for the popes. By the Middle Ages the Vatican had come to control a large part of Italy and was one of the most important and influential powers in European politics. In 1870 the government of the newly founded Italian state annexed the extensive Papal States throughout Italy. The pontiffs rejected all offers of financial compensation, choosing instead to withdraw behind the Vatican's walls in defiance.

In 1929 the Pope chose to sign the Lateran Treaty with the then fascist government of Italy. This treaty established the independence and sovereignty of the State of Vatican City, fixed the relationship between the Italian government and the Catholic Church and set a cash payment for the earlier seizure of papal property. A revision of this treaty in 1984 ended the status of Roman Catholicism as Italy's state religion. Despite the loss of much of its property, the Vatican has very extensive investments throughout the world, especially in Italy.

The Church's wealth is widely assumed to be massive. Financial operations are handled by the Institute for Religious Agencies, better known as the "Vatican Bank," whose depositors are Catholic religious orders, Vatican employees and clergymen. For 2,000 years until 1987 the Vatican kept its financial operations strictly secret. However, an inspection of the books of the bankrupt Milan–based Banco Ambrosiano and the mysterious suicide of that bank's president in 1982 revealed deep Vatican entanglement in questionable financial dealings. The Church hierarchy was so seriously embarrassed by this scandal that the Pope ordered an end to the Holy See's dependence upon investment and speculation for its funds. It would rely instead on "the spontaneous contributions of the faithful and of other men of good will."

The bank scandal made it more difficult to raise money. Money was taken from "Peter's pence," the annual world–wide collection intended to fund works of charity. But appeals to the national churches, whose funds are not controlled by the Vatican, did not produce enough money. In 1998 the Vatican celebrated five years in the black.

In 1987 an Italian court issued an arrest warrant against the head of the "Vatican Bank," American Archbishop Paul Marcinkus, as "accessory to fraudulent bankruptcy." Because the Archbishop, (who the Vatican insisted was innocent)

Vatican City

had moved inside the Vatican walls, he could not be arrested by Italian authorities; Italy has no extradition treaty with the Vatican.

There are no precedents for such a complex legal standoff between the two sovereign states. According to Article 22 of the Lateran Treaty, the Vatican is obligated to surrender to Italian custody anyone who enters its grounds in order to escape from Italian law. However, Article 11 states that "central bodies of the Catholic Church are free from every interference on the part of the Italian state." During the Second World War, even the Mussolini government did not try to get possession of Jews and political refugees who had hidden within the Vatican's walls. Italy's highest court annulled the arrest warrant, and Marcinkus retired from papal service in 1991 and returned to Chicago as a parish priest. Supervision of the bank passed to an international board of five Catholic lay directors.

The Lateran Treaty established extraterritorial status, but technically not papal sovereignty, for 13 areas outside Vatican City. These are chiefly the major Catholic churches in Rome and the Pope's summer residence of Castel Gandolfo. In an agreement of 1951, the Vatican's radio station (Stazione Radio Città del Vaticano) also was placed under Vatican jurisdiction.

Insofar as the purely political functions of the Vatican are concerned, all executive, legislative and judicial authority is vested in the Pope. He appoints a governor and organs to administer the Vatican. The College of Cardinals serves as the chief papal advisers, and the Roman Curia carries on the central administration of the Roman Catholic Church's religious affairs.

Within the Vatican live fewer than 1,000 persons, all of whom have Vatican documents, rather than other passports. They are chiefly permanent Vatican employees, the largest number being priests and nuns. Cardinals are considered to be Vatican residents whenever they are in Rome. When a citizen of the Vatican leaves the city limits of Rome, he automatically becomes a citizen of his original nationality (or of Italy if the original nationality does not permit dual citizenship).

Vatican City has within its borders its own telephone system, a post office (which uses the Vatican's own stamps), a radio station, a pharmacy, a banking system with its own coins, and several stores. In addition to the Church of St. Peter and the Vatican Apostolic Palace (which was expanded in the 15th and 16th centuries to become the largest palace in the world) with all its museums and library, the Vatican contains a score of administrative and ecclesiastical buildings, a "village" of apartments and the beautiful Vatican gardens. There is a small railroad station at the perimeter of the Vatican which is connected by 300 meters of track to the Italian state railway station.

The Vatican's dealing with the outside world are conducted by permanent diplomatic representatives (known as *nuncios*) in capitals throughout the world. By tradition, papal nuncios are granted the first rank at those diplomatic ceremonies which they attend. In 1984 the United States became the 107th nation to establish full diplomatic relations with the Vatican, which also has permanent observer status at the United Nations. It established official ties with the Palestinian Liberation Organization (PLO) in 1994.

Sensitive to allegations that the Vatican had done little to condemn the holocaust or help Jews during the Second World War, the Vatican intervened to support the relocation of a cloister located on the edge of the Auschwitz death camp in Poland. The Holy See's relations with Jews had been strained for 2,000 years. But in 1965 the Vatican repudiated the doctrine of collective Jewish guilt for the death of Jesus. In 1993 it signed an accord with Israel leading to full diplomatic relations the following year, and in 1994 it published a document acknowledging its past mistakes which had contributed to anti–Semitism.

In 1997 the Pope condemned the actions of many Christians before and during the Holocaust, saying that they contributed to the rise of anti–Semitism and then failed to help as Jews were being eradicated. Jewish groups criticized the fact that this strong statement fell short of an apology, which they have been demanding. In 1998 the Church, while defending the actions of Pope Pius XII as having been a quieter form of resistance against the Nazis, officially apologized for failing to take a more active role in stopping Nazi persecution of Jews. It also declared Edith Stein, an Orthodox Jew who had converted to Christianity and died at Auschwitz in 1942, to be a saint.

Until 1975 the foreign diplomatic representatives to the Vatican had to be men. When the West Germans sent a woman counselor to its mission, they were reminded of the Vatican's "tradition which forbids Vatican officials from having business contacts with ladies." Finally the former African dictator of Uganda, Idi Amin, forced the Vatican to accept a female mission chief. The Church's ban on women priests is under increasing attack by Catholics. In 1987 it was revealed that a priest who had served in southern Italy for 25 years had undergone a sex change and become a woman. Church practice holds that an ordained priest remains one whatever his transgressions might be. Therefore, the Church granted her early retirement with the usual pension. The Church often acts slowly: in 1992 it formally rehabilitated Galileo Galilei, whom the Inquisition had condemned in 1633 for daring to prove that the Earth orbited the sun, rather than the other way around.

Italy assumes responsibility for defending the Vatican and for patrolling St. Peter's Square. When the Turkish gunman who shot the Pope in May 1981 was captured, he was taken initially to the Commissariato Borgo, the Vatican police headquarters. He was then bundled very quickly into an armored car and driven to central police headquarters in downtown Rome. There was evidence which was not

His Holiness Pope John Paul II

Fresco in the Sistine Chapel

Vatican City

conclusive that Soviet or Eastern European intelligence agencies, operating through Bulgaria, were involved with this attempted murder.

By the end of the decade, though, Mikhail Gorbachëv's *Glasnost* had led to better relations between the Holy See and Eastern Europe, and the Pope launched a campaign for a "Europe without spiritual frontiers." The reconciliation between communism and Christianity was crowned by Gorbachev's historic audience with the Pope (whom he addressed as "Your Holiness"!) in 1989. Said a Vatican diplomat: "Catholicism and communism are ideologies that cannot be reconciled. . . . But there is space for common endeavor in the social, cultural and humanitarian fields." Gorbachev expressed interest in the Pope's call for a third road between capitalism and socialism, a new social order that would combine social justice with economic efficiency and political pluralism. The USSR wanted to be a full partner in a common European civilization, and the Pope holds one of the keys to that community.

In 1991 he named spiritual leaders for Soviet Catholics, published a social doctrine for societies returning to capitalism, and convened an unprecedented synod of bishops from the two halves of Europe to meet in Rome. In 1996 Pope John Paul II received one of the world's last Communist leaders, Fidel Castro. In return, the Cuban dictator renewed his country's invitation of the Pontiff; Cuba was the only Latin American nation the pope had not yet visited. The Pope arrived in Cuba on January 21, 1998, to large and enthusiastic crowds. The political importance and influence of the Pope were visible in the easing by Castro (who for the first time as president wore civilian clothes in his own country) of religious intolerance before the Pontiff arrived and his public composure while the Pope admonished the Cuban church to fight for "the recognition of human rights and social justice" and to take "courageous and prophetic stands in the face of the corruption of political and economic power."

Order within the small state is provided by a colorfully dressed regular army of Swiss guards. Recruitment is held in the cantons of Freiburg, St. Gallen and Lucerne; the men must be between 20 and 30 years old. They carry old-fashioned halberds, but they always have machine guns hidden close by. Perhaps former Soviet Foreign Minister Andrei Gromyko was wrong in calling them "the world's least frightening army"! Plain-clothes Swiss guards and agents from the papal gendarmes always accompany the Pope everywhere when he confronts audiences and crowds within the Vatican, just as Secret Service men accompany the President of the United States. One difference is that the agents never turn completely away from the Pope in order to scan for potential troublemakers. Paul VI ruled that it was disrespectful for the guards to turn their backs on the Pontiff. In 1998 a disgruntled guard fatally shot his commander and wife and then killed himself. This was the first time in 150 years that this had occurred, and it prompted the Vatican to review its recruiting procedures and administer psychological exams for new guards.

The Vatican possesses priceless cultural treasures, including the Vatican Museums, the frescoes by Michelangelo in the Sistine Chapel, frescoes by Pinturicchio in the Borgia Apartment, Raphael's Stanze and the Church of St. Peter, where such art treasures as Michelangelo's *La Pietà* are displayed. In 1983 more than 200 of these irreplaceable art works toured the United States, where they were viewed by millions of Americans in New York, Chicago and San Francisco. The Vatican Library contains a valuable collection of manuscripts from the pre-Christian era to the present. It also publishes an influential daily newspaper, *L'Osservatore Romano*, and owns a press which publishes books and pamphlets in all languages of the world.

FUTURE

As the health of the formerly active and charismatic Pope John Paul II fails, the influence of the Roman Catholic Church, and therefore of the Vatican, can be expected to continue to decline. All over Europe the Pope's clout is weakening, as was shown by the election of a former Communist as president in his native Poland and by referenda in Ireland permitting divorce and abortion under certain circumstances. Its former political influence in Italy was greatly diminished by the collapse of the *Christian Democracy* party, and it no longer swings much political weight in Spain. In Europe its role has been reduced to trying to influence social issues. But even this is difficult in the face of so many persons who describe themselves as "cultural Catholics" while blithely ignoring the pope's teaching when it does not suit them. The Holy See, which claims over a billion believers or 17.3% of the world's population, now faces a major challenge over the ordination of women. It is not surprising that the Vatican is looking forward to a grandiose diversion to celebrate the dawning of the third Christian millennium in the year 2000. More than 30 million visitors are expected to journey to Rome for the event.

Reprinted with special permission of King Features Syndicate

The Republic of Malta

Chief of State: Guido De Marco, President (since April 1999).
Head of Government: Eddie Fenech Adami, Prime Minister (since September 1998).
National Holiday: Republic Day, December 13.
National Flag: Two large vertical white and red stripes with a gray cross in the upper left–hand corner.

Malta is a small but historically and strategically important group of five islands (two of which are uninhabited) in the central Mediterranean Sea 60 miles (96 km.) south of Sicily and 180 miles (290 km.) north of Libya. For centuries Malta, with its well–sheltered anchorage, has been squarely in the middle of the many struggles to control the Mediterranean Sea and with that, the traffic between Europe, Africa and the Middle East. Because of its strategic importance and small size, Malta has always been dependent upon exterior powers.

Malta's people and culture today clearly reflect the influence of the many conquerors who have dominated the islands. Ethnically, the Maltese people are predominantly of Carthaginian and Phoenician origin. The latter named the islands "Maleth," meaning "hiding place," from which the country's present name is derived. The Maltese culture is a mixture of Italian and Arabic traditions. Maltese is a Semitic language arising from the mixture of Arabic and Sicilian Italian. It is the only Semitic language which is written in Latin script, and to the stranger it sounds very much like Arabic. The official language since 1934, Maltese is the most widely used medium of communication. It is also the language of instruction in the schools, which are patterned on the British educational system, and is used by one television and nine radio networks. Scholars disagree whether the European or the Arabic component predominates in the Maltese character and nature, but they do agree that the Maltese have a distinct culture and identity of their own.

The impressive main corridor of the Presidential Palace in Valletta stirs memories of the courageous Knights of Malta

Area: 122 sq. mi. (316 sq. km., one–tenth the size of Rhode Island).
Population: 370,000 (estimated).
Capital City: Valletta (Pop. 21,000, estimated).
Climate: Mild and sunny Mediterranean.
Neighboring Countries: Italy lies to the north, Libya to the south.
Official Languages: Maltese, English. Italian is also widely spoken.
Other Principal Tongues: Italian is understood.
Ethnic Background: Mixture of Phoenician, Carthaginian, Arab, Sicilian, Norman, Spanish, Italian, British.
Principal Religion: Roman Catholic (98%).
Main Exports: Tourism, ship repair, clothing, food manufacturing and processing, textiles.
Main Customers: Italy (40%), Germany (15%), France (9%), UK (6%); EU (70%).
Currency: Maltese Lira.
Former Colonial Status: British Crown Colony.
Independence Day: September 21, 1964, within the British Commonwealth of Nations; Republic declared on December 13, 1974. Government: Parliamentary democracy.

HISTORY

The Early Period

Archaeologists have uncovered evidence of Neolithic cave dwellers from approximately 3800 B.C. on Malta, and it is probable that the islands were a center of Mediterranean civilization before Crete was. Between the 9th and 6th centuries B.C. the Phoenicians, Greeks and Carthaginians established colonies in Malta and the islands' inhabitants came into contact with Semitic cultures along the southern and eastern rim of the Mediterranean. In

The Republic of Malta

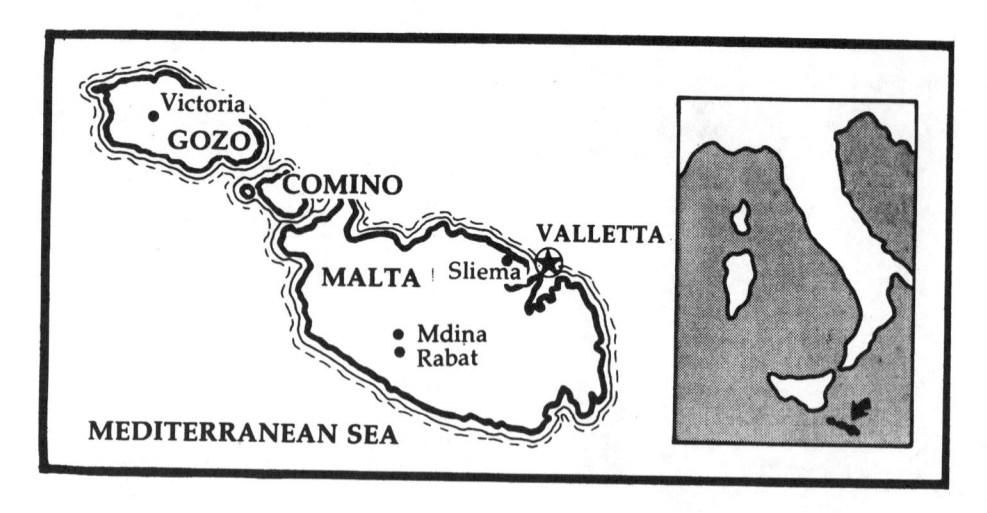

218 B.C. the islands fell under Roman control.

Christian Beginnings

According to Biblical legend, a Roman ship carrying St. Paul crashed on offshore rocks in 60 A.D., and Paul saved himself by swimming shore. The Maltese still use the favorite saying when everything seems to go wrong: "Don't forget that even St. Paul was shipwrecked on Malta!" He wasted no time in converting the population, and the majority of Malta's population has been Christian ever since.

Arabs and Normans

When the Roman Empire approached total collapse in the 4th century A.D., Malta fell under the domination of Constantinople. Until the 16th century the islands were ruled successively by Arabs, who came in 870 A.D. and placed their indelible stamp on the Maltese, by Normans, who displaced the Arabs in 1000 A.D. and who improved Maltese political and legal structures, and later by other European nations.

Control by the Knights

In 1520 Malta came under the control of the Order of the Hospital of St. John of Jerusalem (otherwise known as the "Knights Hospitalers," or the "Maltese Knights"), a Roman Catholic religious order. It had been founded in Jerusalem before the Crusades in order to protect Christian pilgrims. Later, it had established its headquarters on the Greek island of Rhodes before being driven out by the Turks. The Holy Roman Emperor of the time, Charles V, granted Malta to the Knights, which they turned into a fortress against Islam.

Their military mission was to keep the Turks out of the western Mediterranean and to clear the southern Mediterranean of pirates. Their raids on the immense Ottoman Empire so enraged the Turkish Sultan that he sent a huge army of 40,000 men and a navy of 200 ships against the heavily fortified islands. The four-month Turkish siege was one of the bloodiest in history, and of 9,000 Maltese Knights and soldiers, fewer than 1,000 survived unwounded. But their valor, under Grand Master Jean de La Valette, a shrewd military tactician after whom Malta's present capital city was named, forced the Turks to withdraw. Never again did the Turks attempt to penetrate the western Mediterranean.

The victorious and prosperous Knights began to build the capital city of Valleta on a rocky headland. They built innumerable splendid baroque palaces, churches and public buildings, financed primarily by booty from their naval adventures against the Turks. Many of these structures still survive and testify to the great prosperity of that time. The famed Sacra Infermeria Hospital, whose construction began in 1571, was recently converted to a magnificent and modern Mediterranean conference center in an attempt to make Malta a major trade center.

Napoleon and British Rule

Napoleon Bonaparte seized the islands in 1798. Because of sympathetic French Knights, his troops scarcely had to fire a shot. However, realizing that he would be unable to defend the islands against the British Navy, he decided to return them to the Knights soon thereafter. Not wishing this to happen, a sizable number of Maltese rebelled and demanded to be placed under British sovereignty. Always attentive to the strategic needs of its empire and navy, and bracing itself for a bitter struggle against Napoleonic France, Britain gladly accepted in 1800. British sovereignty over Malta was later confirmed by the Treaty of Paris in 1814. The Maltese Knights never returned to the islands as rulers, but each June they return from all over the world in full regalia for the Feast of St. John at St. John's Cathedral.

Throughout the 19th century, Malta was ruled by a British governor, and its economy grew almost entirely dependent upon the proceeds from British military facilities on the islands, a dependence which Malta has never been able to overcome successfully. Immediately following World War I the British granted internal autonomy to the Maltese, but the experiment failed and in 1933 Malta reverted to its status of a Crown Colony. During World War II, this "unsinkable aircraft carrier," as Winston S. Churchill called it, heroically resisted brutal German bombing and refused to surrender even though the islands were frequently cut off from supplies for months at a time. Malta played an extremely significant role in the successful Allied efforts in North Africa, Sicily and southern Europe. In 1947 the islands were again granted self-government, but a British-appointed governor maintained control over foreign affairs, defense and currency.

In 1955 the *Maltese Labor Party* won a parliamentary majority and made a radical proposal for full integration of Malta into the United Kingdom. This proposal, which now appears highly surprising in view of the party's later stand on independence, received the support of three-fourths of the voters in a referendum in 1956. However, negotiations to work out such an integration broke down two years later, and by 1960 the Maltese support for the tie had disappeared. Independence, not integration, became the new goal, and this was achieved in 1964 by the *Nationalist Party*, which had won the parliamentary elections that year.

GOVERNMENT

The constitution of 1964, which had made Malta an independent parliamentary monarchy within the British Commonwealth, was revised in 1974 to create a republican parliamentary democracy. A 65-member unicameral parliament, called the House of Representatives, is selected by universal suffrage of all citizens over the age of 18 on the basis of proportional representation (PR) at least every five years. Since 1987 any party which wins more than 50% of the popular vote is assured a majority of parliamentary seats, despite PR. The majority party appoints the prime minister and cabinet, who exercise executive power, but who remain responsible to the House of Representatives. An indirectly elected, largely ceremonial president serves as the head of state for a five-year term.

The government of the country is highly centralized in the capital city although Sliema is actually the country's largest city. There is little established local gov-

The Republic of Malta

ernment. The major exception to this is the island of Gozo, which has a locally elected Civic Council which rules that small island in conjunction with a commissioner appointed by the central government in Valletta. Malta has an independent judicial system consisting of lower courts and a Constitutional Court, a Superior Court and a Court of Appeal.

POLITICS

Only two political parties have a significant number of seats in the House of Representatives or play an important role in Maltese politics. The opposition *Labour Party* (*LP*) sees itself as a socialist party and depends upon the support of workers and the powerful trade unions. From 1961 until 1971 the *LP* was embroiled in such a bitter struggle with the Catholic Church that the Church declared any vote or other active support for this party to be sufficient grounds for excommunication. The lifting of this ban in 1971 enabled the party to maintain its position.

For many years the character of the *LP* was shaped by the personality of its mercurial former leader, Dom Mintoff, who stepped down as prime minister in 1984. He was succeeded by his hand–picked successor, Carmelo Mifsud–Bonnici. The *LP* favored an independent and neutral Malta playing the role of bridge between Europe and the Arab world and an anti–colonialist foreign policy involving close ties with the "Third World." To strengthen its European credentials, it joined the Council of Europe in 1965.

The *LP* advocates foreign investment and economic help to industrialize the islands. At the same time, it seeks the redistribution of property and income in order to create a more egalitarian society. In many ways, these last two objectives are in conflict with one another. Under Mintoff's premiership the government took over broadcasting, telecommunications, oil and gas and a full or majority interest in all banks. It also established a national airline and shipping line, and his government introduced a minimum wage, a 40–hour work week and mandatory wage increases to keep pace with inflation.

The *LP* clashed with the Catholic Church because of his decision to nationalize hospitals and schools. Mintoff expelled all nuns and doctors who refused to comply with the state takeover of the hospitals. He refused all state assistance to the country's private (mainly Catholic) schools, which educate about a third of all Maltese children. The government's campaign against Catholic schools was stepped up in 1984 when it was announced that private schools could no longer charge tuition. This move was followed by widespread violence, including a raid on Catholic Church headquarters, reportedly led by Mifsud–Bonnici. Hostility between the Church and the *LP* had been intensified when the latter introduced a bill to authorize state seizure of about three–fourths of the Church's property in Malta. Not surprisingly, Vatican spokesmen warned that such action would have "predictable repercussions on religious peace." But in 1985 Mifsud–Bonnici signed an agreement with the Vatican designed to end the controversy over government control of Catholic schools.

Under the leadership since 1992 of Alfred Sant, a pragmatic Harvard PhD in business administration and former diplomat in Brussels, the party shook off its confrontational socialist image. He severed the party's formal links with the trade unions and admits that economic liberalization has benefitted Malta. Not all *LP* militants supported these changes, but they paid off in the 1996 elections. At the end of a spirited campaign opposing Maltese entry into the EU, a 15% value added tax (VAT) required by the EU, and gun controls that were unpopular in this country with a strong hunting tradition, the *LP* won 50.7% of the votes and 35 parliamentary seats, giving it a narrow one–seat majority. But the *Labour* was brought down by disloyalty within its own ranks. The fiery Dom Mintoff opposed his party's plan to lease state land to an American consortium to build a new yacht marina. When he voted against his government, it fell, called an election for September 5, 1999, and lost.

The ruling *Nationalist Party* (*NP*), led by Prime Minister Eddie Fenech Adami, stands much closer to the Catholic Church and to the Maltese middle class. It wishes to safeguard Malta's Catholic Church and European traditions. The *NP* advocates Malta's following the example of other minute European states, such as Andorra, Monaco and Liechtenstein, in lowering taxes so that foreign wealth and business enterprises are attracted to the islands. This reduces the island's dependence on financial handouts from other countries and brings prosperity to Malta. The *NP* advocates closer relations with Western Europe and the U.S.

The *NP* ruled from 1987 to 1996. The transition of power in 1987 went more smoothly than many observers had feared. Fenech Adami vowed that his government would work to bring about national reconciliation in a land bitterly polarized in many ways: labor unions based in the dockyards versus the middle class; clans with generations of hostility; villages divided in their loyalty to competing saints; townships torn by rivalry between clubs which parade on holy days; males by their rooting for Italian or British soccer teams. The transition from violent confrontational politics succeeded. Party allegiance no longer dominates every issue, and the pervasive tension is gone. In 1996 the *NP* captured 47.8% of the votes and 34 seats. In 1998 it regained the reins of power.

A third party, the *Democratic Alternative*, won only 1.46% of the votes in 1996. It is politically active, but it is irrelevant in the House of Representatives. It describes itself as "green–progressive" and focuses on corruption and social and environmental issues. It publishes a monthly newspaper, *XPRESS*.

Foreign and Defense Policy

Malta had difficulty solving its major long–standing economic and foreign policy problem: how to survive economically

Hon. Alfred Sant
Leader, *Labour Party*

Prime Minister Eddie Fenech Adami
Leader, *Nationalist Party*

The Republic of Malta

A pleasant beach on the northern part of Malta

without the rental fees paid by Britain for use of Maltese defense facilities. In 1971 the strong–willed Mintoff abrogated the Mutual Defense and Assistance Agreement of 1964; after months of difficult negotiations a new seven–year agreement was reached tripling the rental fees Britain was required to pay. He again demanded an increase in 1973. Britain finally decided it could live without Malta's base facilities and withdrew from the island in 1979, after 179 years of military presence there. Mintoff hailed this as "the day of light, freedom day, the day of the new Malta."

The economic problems caused by the loss of more than $70 million in revenue were not solved by that freedom. Mintoff's attempts to obtain a quadripartite guarantee of Maltese neutrality and a five–year budgetary subsidy (financial gift with no strings attached) from France, Italy, Algeria and Libya were rejected. Italy's offer of a loan amounting roughly to $5 million at low interest was ridiculed by Mintoff as "crumbs which no government can accept that wants to be taken seriously." Nor was Britain inclined to help Mintoff.

A modest amount of development assistance which the People's Republic of China had given Malta since 1971 to construct a dry dock to handle tankers was much too small to solve Malta's problems. Therefore, Mintoff turned to that oil–rich state to the south, whose leader had shown himself willing to support practically any state or group whose policies are directed against the industrialized west: Libya. Mintoff announced in 1979 that "Europe showed us the cold shoulder, but Libya heartily and spontaneously accepted our suggestions for collaboration." Libya's flamboyant and erratic leader, Col. Moamer al Ghadafi, took a 500–man delegation to the ceremony in Malta marking the British withdrawal, and promised the country unlimited aid.

Ghadafi delivered oil and gasoline to Malta almost without charge, and the Maltese government was able to derive even greater profit from this gift by imposing a stiff local consumption tax on the petroleum. Libya also invested approximately $150 million in the islands, entered a defense pact with Malta and provided helicopters and coastal patrol boats. Ghadafi proudly proclaimed Malta as the "northern outpost of the Arabic world" and even aspired to introduction of pure Arabic as Malta's official language (Arabic is no longer compulsory in secondary schools.). Such pronouncements merely aggravated many Maltese who from the beginning had misgivings toward this strange marriage of convenience. *NP* leaders called it an exchange of "one type of colonialism for another."

The marriage was scarcely a year old when a disagreement erupted. Both governments claimed oil rights in the waters between the two states. An angry Mintoff declared Libya "a danger to peace in the Mediterranean" and expelled as "security risks" 50 Libyan military personnel who had been sent to train Maltese helicopter pilots. By 1984 differences with Libya were settled. Both countries agreed to submit their dispute over oil rights in the sea to the International Court of Justice, which rendered a decision satisfactory to both parties. They signed a military cooperation treaty under which Libya would help to train and supply the Maltese forces and help to protect Malta "in case of threats or acts of aggression." In 1981 Malta had signed an agreement with the Soviet Union, which pledged to respect Malta's neutrality in return for the right to store up to 300,000 tons of oil on the islands. Mintoff claimed that the Soviet Union was not committed to defend the island if Maltese territory were violated.

Under Fenech Adami, Malta steered a more pro–western course. The *NP* has a tradition of strong sympathies with Italy. Under *Labour* rule, Malta had already secured assistance from its nearest northern neighbor. Arguing that Maltese neutrality was in Italy's and NATO's interest and threatening to allow the Soviet navy to use the harbor of Valletta, it persuaded Italy to support Malta. The Italian government rather liked the idea of assuming greater responsibility in the Mediterranean area. In 1980 it promised Malta technical assistance and financial support. Until 1994 Italy covered a third of Malta's budget deficit, enabling that shortfall to remain below 4% of GDP.

The islands, which for five years had maintained a consultative arrangement with NATO, received in 1981 military guarantees from Italy. In exchange, Malta formally declared neutrality and promised not to allow any foreign military bases. In 1987 the Maltese constitution was changed in order to entrench both non–alignment and neutrality and to forbid foreign military bases.

In 1986 the former *LP* prime minister admitted having tipped off Ghadafi minutes before the American bombing raid on Libya, thereby possibly saving the Libyan leader's life. Such "even–handedness" was not shown by the *NP* government. Malta maintained economic ties with Libya and renegotiated its friendship treaty with it. But Fenech Adami emphasized that he had widened the political distance with Ghadafi and that the military clauses, which had obligated Malta to warn Libya of American air strikes, had been removed. Fenech Adami's government severed air links with Libya and honored the UN embargo imposed after Libya's complicity in the bombing of a Pan Am plane over Lockerbie, Scotland, appeared obvious.

Prime Minister Sant informed Brussels that he had put Malta's application for EU membership on hold because joining is not in the tiny country's interest. Its farming sector is too small and vulnerable, and Malta fears open borders. He preferred a less restrictive industrial free–trade agreement with political and security cooperation. "The Maltese people voted for a vision of Malta as an open European country which wants its own space." In one of his first acts, Sant formally withdrew Malta from NATO's Partnership for Peace program "because it contradicts our constitutional neutrality. . . . We do not agree that in our case, with the end of the superpower confrontation, neutrality is no longer relevant." After the 1998 election, the new *NP* government renewed the country's EU application. Although Malta allots about 3.5% ($10 million) of its budget to the

The Republic of Malta

maintenance of its small army and navy, it could never defend itself alone.

ECONOMY

Malta is a highly over-crowded mini-state with four-tenths of a million people on only 122 square miles (316 sq. km). It has no natural resources except limestone, and its terrain is very unsuited to agriculture. It can supply only about 20% of its food needs, and only 6% of its population can find employment in agriculture. Its major agricultural products are potatoes, cauliflower, grapes, wheat, barley, tomatoes, citrus fruit, cut flowers, hogs, poultry and eggs. Desalination plants provide half of Malta's fresh water.

Its major industry, thanks to its deep water harbors, is ship repair. This provides 5% of total employment, although it has fallen on hard times. The government's efforts since independence to diversify the economy have had modest success, and Malta now has some light manufacturing enterprises in the clothing, textile, building and food processing sectors. Foreign investments contributed significantly to this success, but they have meant that more than half of Malta's industrial production is in foreign hands. Maltese industry will be lucky if it can continue employing a fourth of the workforce. Not wanting to compete as a low-wage economy, it faces a particular obstacle in that it must import so many raw materials in order to export finished products at a profit.

An Achilles heel is the fact that more than half of its exports are textile products. In the industrialized nations to which it exports, there are increasingly loud demands to erect barriers against textile imports in order to protect their own clothing industries. Malta must still import most consumer and industrial needs, including fuels and raw materials.

A fourth of its GDP is derived from tourism, its biggest revenue earner. The number of foreign tourists who visit Malta is more than twice as large as the country's population. The government believes that with a million tourists every year (predominantly Britons) the three islands have reached the saturation point. Therefore, it aims to restructure the industry to attract more upmarket tourists. This would bring more income from fewer visitors. They arrive at the country's two usable airfields, one major and two minor harbors.

In order to try to overcome Malta's economic stagnation, the former *NP* government liberalized the economy, which was over-protected and state-dominated. Through "tax holidays," it lured foreign investment from the West. It largely completed its first priority of improving the infrastructure by overhauling the telecommunications network and building a new power station, desalination plants, and a second airport terminal. It attracted some higher-skill and technology industries to replace traditional ones, like textiles, which are threatened by low-cost competition from north Africa and Asia.

In 1997 Malta could look back on a decade of 5% annual economic growth (6% in 1996) and an enviable 3% unemployment rate. Its public-sector finances are solid, with a budget deficit in 1997 of 3.1% of GDP and an overall public debt of 36% of GDP, lower than any EU country except Luxembourg. In 1993 employment in the service sector overtook private direct production for the first time. Malta's per capita income ($9,000 in 1997) exceeds that of Portugal and Greece. With one or more cars per family, there is an air of prosperity in the country. The feeling that Malta is already performing rather well is an important reason why many voters do not view EU entry as an urgent necessity.

Since 1971 Malta has had a special trade relationship with the EU, to which it sent 68% of its exports and from which it bought 78% of its imports in 1990, the year in which it applied for full membership. The *NP* government drafted all its legislation with eventual EU membership in mind. Prime Minister Fenech Adami had announced that "Malta is a European country. To us, this will be a homecoming." Voters saw it differently in 1996, but they changed their minds in September 1998. Malta's EU application was renewed.

FUTURE

With a *Nationalist* government and prime minister and with economic optimism in the air, Malta looks into a future of prosperous alignment with western Europe and in the EU. Prospects for the tiny island nation are good.

Ancient fortifications guard Valletta

The Sovereign Military Order of Malta

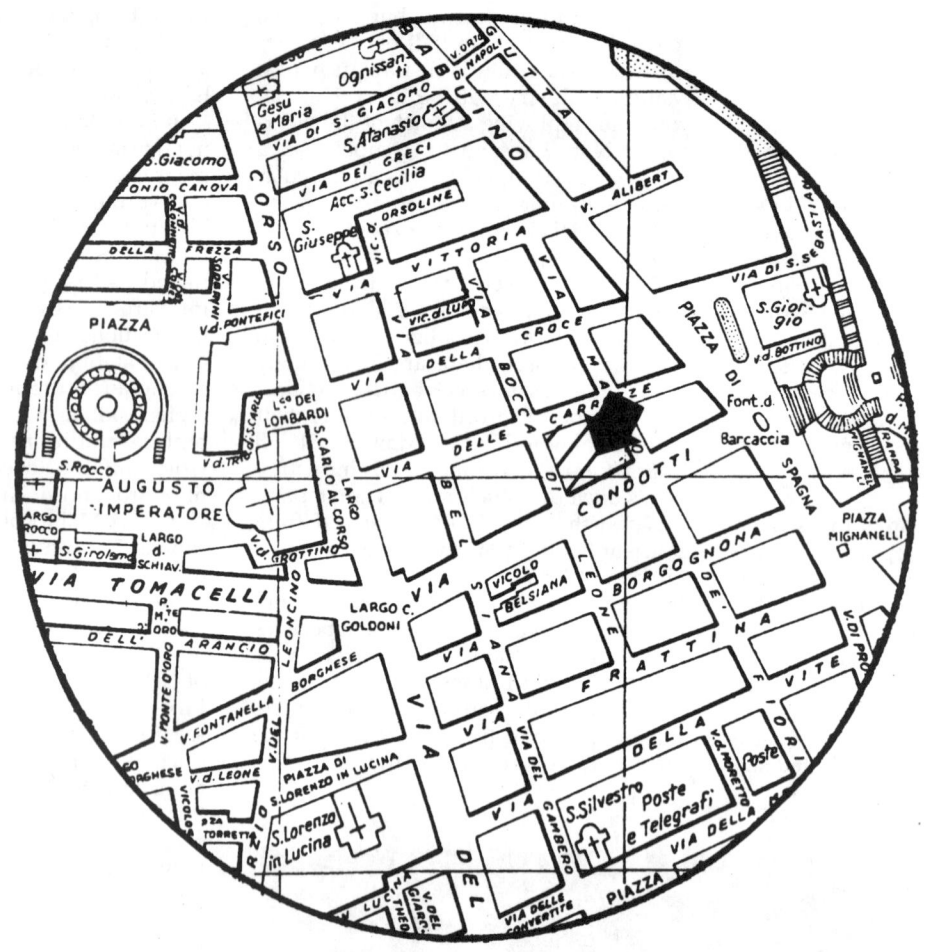

(The Roman Catholic *Sovereign Military Hospitaler Order of St. John of Jerusalem, of Rhodes and of Malta*)

Area: The Malta Palace (*Palazzo di Malta*) and the *Villa Malta*, about three acres.
Population: International membership in the Order is about 9,600, all of whom retain their own nationality.
Neighboring Countries: Located in Rome, Italy.
Religion: Roman Catholicism.
Chief of State (Head of the Order): The Prince and Grand Master (since 1988), His Most Eminent Highness Frà Andrew Bertie (b. 1929).
Flag of State: A plain white cross on a red field, (of the Grand Master)—The white Maltese Cross on a red field.

Only with a magnifying glass can one see the world's smallest country on a Rome city map. Completely surrounded by a wall and with a territorial size equivalent to half a football field, *The Sovereign Military Order of Malta (SMOM)* is the only country in the world which has *no* citizens whatsoever and which is small enough to be assigned a street address: 68 Via Condotti, a very elegant street just a stone's throw from Rome's famous Spanish Steps. By peeping through the keyhole of the main gate of Villa Malta on the Aventine Hill, a palace which is also part of *SMOM*, one can gain the kind of view normally available only to astronauts: one can see three sovereign countries, namely the *SMOM*, Italy and the Vatican.

The Prince and Grand Master was elected in 1988 by the Council Complete of State and was duly confirmed by the Pope. Today this ancient entity maintains diplomatic relations with the Holy See, on which it depends as a religious Order, but not as a sovereign, and with 48 nations (but not with the United States), has delegations to the Council of Europe and UNESCO, and enjoys the same status of extra–territoriality which the Italian government grants to any embassy; that is, it is considered to be *foreign soil*. On January 28, 1961, the Civil Courts of Rome declared the Order an " international sovereign society." Issuing its own passports and conducting its affairs without interference, this tiny state is truly an oddity in the contemporary world.

The hospital–infirmary dedicated to St. John the Baptist was founded in Jerusalem about the middle of the 11th century. It was administered by a monastic community, originally connected with the Benedictines but later independent, which was dedicated to the care for those Christians who fell ill during their pilgrimages to the Holy Land.

In the same century Pope Urban II urged the formation of a great crusade in order to sweep the Moslems from the cradle of Christianity and to expand the reach of the Roman Catholic Church. A growing army, led by French knights and joined by noblemen and simple folk from many nations, in 1096 progressed on horseback and foot across Europe and toward the Holy Land. The crusader knights were young, ranging from 16 to 30 years, and they were brimming with enthusiasm, self–confidence, a strong taste for adventure and (for many) visions of riches. They seized Jerusalem in 1099 and surrounding areas in a series of bloody battles. During the first years the hospital's prior installed some of them into the Order of St. John of Jerusalem as

The Sovereign Military Order of Malta

defenders. To confirm their intense dedication at the time of their induction they held out their swords, which were blessed under flickering torches.

In 1113 the community of the Hospital of St. John was recognized by the Pope as a religious Order of the Church, free from all lay interference. This was the germ of the Order's sovereignty. In the 1130s, because of the need to protect the sick, the pilgrims and the Christian settlements in the Holy Land, the Order acquired the additional military character and became a monastic–chivalric Order, in which monks were knights and knights took the monastic vows. The Order's military edge was first felt in 1118 when its knights did more than protect; they openly attacked the Moslems. Stories of their bravery made them living legends, and new recruits continued to join their ranks every year.

In 1187 the overwhelming forces of Saladin, Sultan of Egypt and Syria, drove the Knights, who suffered terrible losses, from the Latin Kingdom of Jerusalem. All of them were at least wounded, and only a handful survived, including the Grand Master. Those who remained escaped. The Kingdom and the Order continued at Acre (Akka). In even greater numbers than before, knights came from all over Europe to join the struggle against the "infidels." There were eight crusades until 1291, but each grew weaker. The crusaders were never permanently able to wrest Jerusalem from Moslem control. The Kingdom was wiped out in 1291 by the Moslems, and the order moved to Cyprus. But the Knights of St. John remained dedicated to their task of defending Christianity.

They used Cyprus as a base for the next 120 years, continuing to battle the Moslems on or around the Mediterranean Sea. The island was never considered ideal for their purposes because the coastline was too extensive to defend adequately. In 1310 the Knights attacked and captured Rhodes, a beautiful island of meadowlands and forests lying some 25 miles (40 km.) off the southwestern coast of Turkey. Establishing their headquarters there, they continued to expand their navy and constructed a watchtower on the nearly islet of Simi in order to foil any naval attack.

In the following years their control extended over most of the islands off the western coast of Turkey, some little more than outcroppings of jagged rock. Their activity excited admiration throughout Europe because the Knights could effectively challenge Turkish domination in the Mediterranean Sea. In recognition of this role, Pope Nicholas V recognized the Grand Master of the Order as the *Sovereign Prince of Rhodes* in 1446.

The Turks overran Asia Minor and were

The Malta Palace, 68 Via Condotti

H.M.E.H. The Prince and Grand Master

The Sovereign Military Order of Malta

moving into Europe—in 1453 they put an end to the Byzantine Empire and proceeded to launch attacks on Rhodes. Over and over the Turks made massive attacks against the island, but not until 1532 did they succeed in overwhelming the Knights and forced them to leave. During the following eight years the Knights were homeless, but in 1530 the Holy Roman Emperor, Charles V, gave the Order the island of Malta, on which they built the finest hospital in Europe at that time. Included were the nearby islands, as well as the African mainland fortress–city, Tripoli, a city which the Knights soon abandoned.

During the next 268 years they vigilantly patrolled the waters to protect trade routes for Christian merchants. They continued to raid Turkish ships and those of Barbery pirates (see *The Republic of Malta*).

The Prince Grand Master of the Order, who since 1630 has the rank equal to that of a Cardinal, was the undisputed ruler of Malta and was a sovereign who entered into treaties with other nations and enjoyed the usual rights accorded to a chief of state. Of course, the Order's very existence, powers, privileges and immunities remained under the protective umbrella of the Roman Catholic Church, and these were therefore respected throughout Christendom. Splendid architectural monuments, churches, public buildings and fortifications still bear witness to the Order's sovereign rule in Malta.

It took periodic interest in acquiring territory in the New World. In 1653 Louis XIV of France gave the Order four Caribbean islands—St. Kitts, St. Martin, St. Croix and St. Barthélemy—but the Order later decided to sell these small islands to the French West India Company.

In 1794 it approached James Monroe, the U.S. Ambassador to France, with an offer of ports, provisions and protection for American sailors in the Mediterranean in return for lands in America. Monroe responded that the Order was welcome to purchase land, but that such property could not become a part of another sovereign government and would have to remain under the jurisdiction of the United States. Although the Order was not interested in buying under these terms, its personal ties with the United States have remained strong—approximately 1,500 out of 9,600 of the Order's knights are presently living in the U.S., and they include such prominent American Catholics as former Treasury Secretary William E. Simon, the late Clare Boothe Luce, William F. Buckley, Jr., and the late Terrence Cardinal Cooke, Archbishop of New York. However, Americans can never ascend to the highest ranks of the Order because only persons of long–standing nobility are admitted to high leadership positions.

Napoleon's forces, engaged in a campaign against Egypt, occupied the island of Malta in 1798 and drove out the Order. The knights were overwhelmingly French and were reportedly somewhat sympathetic to the French general. But they again found themselves without a home. This was followed by what has been called the Russian *coup d'état* (1798–1803).

Tsar Paul I of Russia was a bitter opponent of the French Revolution and also had hopes of setting up a Russian naval base in the Mediterranean. He had shown himself as a friend of the Order. He now had himself proclaimed Grand Master by a handful of knights who had gone to live in Russia, instead of the Grand Master Frà Ferdinand von Hompesch, who had abandoned Malta to the French. This proclamation of a married non–Catholic as head of a Catholic religious order was wholly illegal and void; it was never recognized by the Holy See, which was a necessary condition for legitimacy. Accordingly, Paul I, who was nevertheless accepted by many knights and a number of governments, can only be regarded as a Grand Master *de facto*, never one *de jure*. This was only a brief interlude. Paul was murdered in 1801 and was succeeded by his 24–year–old son, Alexander I. The new Tsar helped the Order to return to legitimate

Interior courtyard of the Malta Palace

The Sovereign Military Order of Malta

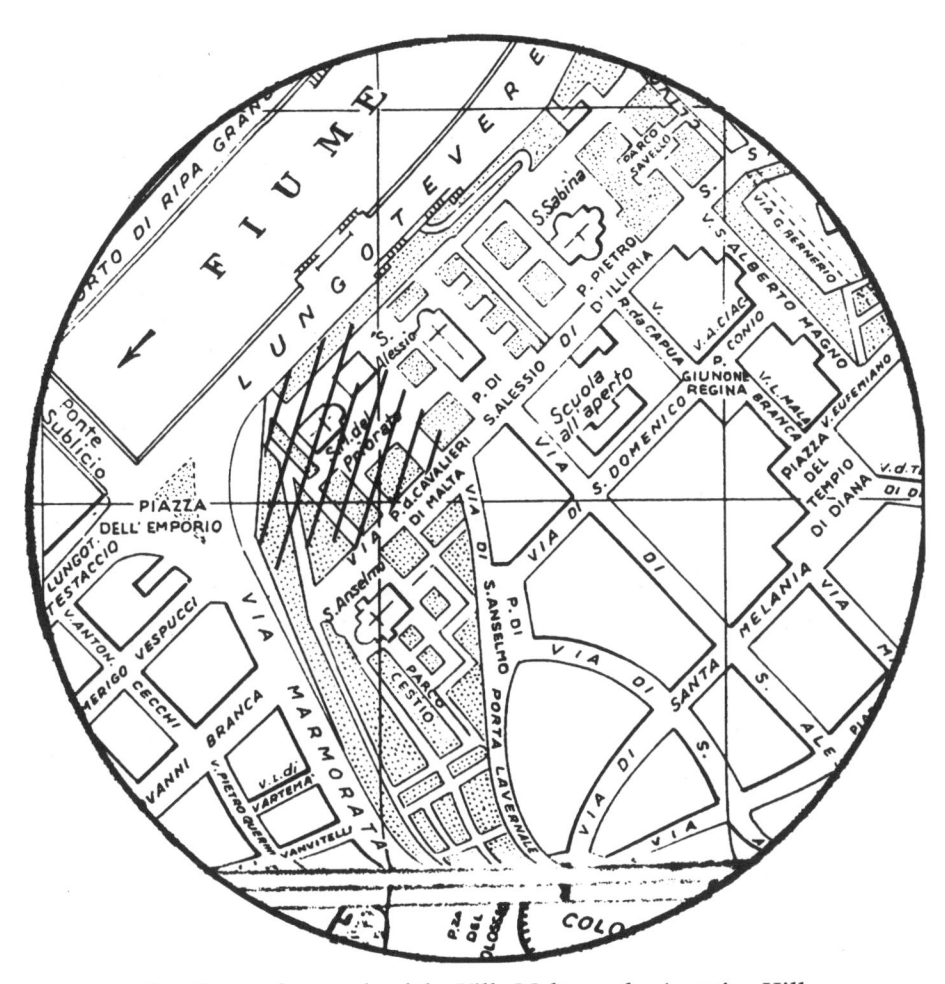

the Order has returned to its original mission of caring for the sick. Yet those persons who dismiss *The Sovereign Military Order of Malta* as being neither sovereign nor military are only half right. It no longer performs a military function, despite the shining swords which the Knights still bear on festive occasions. It does perform an admirable humanitarian function in a world which, in many places, is still largely gripped by disease and misery. And it is a sovereign entity by international recognition, even if it only has three acres in Rome to call its very own.

Location and grounds of the Villa Malta on the Aventine Hill

rule. In 1803 Frà Giovanni Battista Tommasi was elected Grand Master.

In the meantime, the British, who had seized the island of Malta from Napoleon in 1801, specified in the 1802 Treaty of Amiens with France that Malta must be restored to the Order. This never happened, though, and Britain continued to rule the island until it became independent in 1964. Surviving knights scattered throughout Europe attempted after 1802 to persuade European powers once again to give the Order a base. Various islands were considered, but no nation seemed interested in donating even a small one to what they considered to be a fading order of knighthood. The Sovereign Order's headquarters moved to Sicily and then to Ferrara. Finally, in 1834 the 16th century Malta Palace in Rome, which had been the Order's embassy to the Papal State since the early 1600s, became the Order's headquarters and remains so to the present time.

Maintaining health institutions throughout the world, from small dispensaries and leper colonies to ten hospitals,

The Principality of Monaco

Aerial view of Monaco showing the Port of Monaco

Area: .575 sq. mi. (1.5 sq. km.).
Population: 31,700 (estimated).
Capital City: Monaco–Ville.
Climate: Mild Mediterranean.
Neighboring Country: France.
Official Language: French.
Other Principal Tongues: Italian and Monégasque (a mixture of French and Italian) are also spoken.
Ethnic Background: French (50%), Italian (15%), native Monégasques (ca. 4,500), and diverse other European peoples.
Principal Religion: Roman Catholicism is the state religion.
Major Industries: Banking, tourism, postage stamps, gambling, small industries, such as cosmetics, chemicals, food processing, precision instrument manufacture, glassmaking and printing.
Main Customers: France, Italy.
Currency: French Franc.
Year of Independence: 1338.
National Day: November 19.
Chief of State: His Serene Highness Prince Rainier III (b. 1923).
Heir Apparent: Prince Albert (b. 1958).
Head of Government: Minister of State in Charge of Foreign Affairs, Jean Ausseil.
National Flag: Red and white vertical stripes.

The Principality of Monaco is one of the smallest sovereign countries in the world. A densely populated, hilly city overlooking the Mediterranean Sea, Monaco is surrounded on three sides by the French Department of Alpes–Maritimes. The French city if Nice is nine miles (15 km.) to the west of Monaco and the Italian border is five miles (8 km.) to the east. Three picturesque settlements are now unified into one city, and its older section, situated on top of a steep rock, has maintained its medieval flavor. Overlooking crowded Riviera beaches and some of the most luxurious tourist resorts in the world is the 13th century Genoese palace, which was remodeled in the 16th century in Renaissance style. Here resides the Prince of the House of Grimaldi, whose family has ruled Monaco, with periodic interruptions, since 1297. On January 8, 1997, Prince Rainier launched a year–long, $270 million celebration of his family's 700–year reign, the longest of any European dynasty.

Evidence of Stone Age settlements has been found within the present borders of Monaco. Founded much later by the Phoenicians, the city was known to the ancient Greeks and Carthaginians. Under the domination of the Romans (who called the city Herculis Moenaci Portus), Monaco was quite prosperous, and it was from Monaco that Julius Caesar set sail for his campaign against Pompeii. Its wealth was destroyed by the invading barbarians, who brought the once–mighty Roman Empire to its knees. In the 7th century Monaco became a part of the Lombard Kingdom. Later it was absorbed into the Kingdom of Arles and was also subjected to a period of Mohammedan control. In 1191 the Genoese took control of Monaco, but they ceded domination in 1297 to the reining Grimaldi family.

As a minuscule land in a restless world, the independent principality of Monaco always needed the protection of a stronger power in order to survive. It allied itself first with France. In 1524 it accepted Spain's protection instead, but it returned to French safety in 1641. In 1793 the radicalized French National Convention dispossessed the wealthy and aristocratic Grimaldi rulers and annexed the entire Monacan domain to France. After Napoleon's fall from power, the Congress of Vienna awarded Monaco to the Kingdom of Sardinia as a protectorate in 1814. France repossessed the principality in 1848 and after greatly reducing its territory, granted independence to the present tiny remainder in 1861.

France today continues to assume responsibility for Monaco's defense, and a 1918 treaty stipulates that Monaco's policies must conform to French political, military, naval and economic interests. A further treaty of 1919 stipulates that Monaco would be incorporated into France if the reigning prince dies without an heir. Prince Rainier III married the late American actress Grace Kelly in 1956. She epitomized American affluence and Hollywood glamor and attracted the world's attention to the ruling Grimaldi family, but she met an untimely death in an automobile accident on the hilly roads of Monaco in 1982. Their offspring insure survival of the principality for at least an-

The Principality of Monaco

other generation and probably more. Prince Rainier has intimated that he may one day abdicate in favor of his son, Prince Albert, a graduate of Amherst College in Massachusetts. Albert attends government meetings and is already preparing for the transition.

Since 1865, customs, postal services, telecommunications and banking are governed by an economic union with France. Monaco refuses to tax its own citizens, who number only about 20% of the principality's residents. These 4,500 Monégasques also receive housing subsidies and preferential employment. They are guaranteed government service jobs, and all companies must make their first job offers to them. Most Monégasques go to France for higher education, but thanks to the principality's healthy economy, they return.

More than half the residents are French, many of whom chose to reside and to locate their businesses in Monaco in order to avoid French taxation. French protests of this situation in 1962 unleashed a serious dispute. Nevertheless, a compromise was worked out in 1963; all French companies which do more than 25% of their business outside of the principality were brought under French financial control. In 1987 the tiny state acquired another famous resident for the same tax reasons: tennis player Boris Becker. He decided to guard his newly-won fortune against West German tax collectors, despite publicly-aired parliamentary protests.

Monaco has undergone a remarkable economic transformation in recent decades. When Prince Rainier took the throne in 1949, at age 26, his realm was seen, in the words of Somerset Maugham, as "a sunny place for shady people." It was a glitzy but sleazy gambling center. The prince sought to upgrade its image in order to attract wealthy, respectable visitors, depositers, and residents, and to provide long-term employment opportunities for native Monégasques.

His main achievement was to stimulate the local economy by creating thriving banking and tourist industries. Benefiting from tax advantages, banks have doubled in number since the early 1980s to nearly 40. It is estimated that there is one cashier for every 400 residents! Tough laws permitting the seizure of profits from drug operations were introduced in 1993 in an effort to keep the banks' money clean. The principality now attracts 4 million visitors a year, 3 million of whom are day trippers from Italy and France. The annual Grand Prix auto race attracts 150,000 alone. Tourist spending amounts for 25% of GDP. Monaco also has experienced a blooming of commerce and light industry.

In 1967 Prince Rainier won a long struggle with the Greek shipping magnate, Aristotle Onassis, over control of the famed casino of Monte-Carlo. Monaco's native citizens are not permitted to gamble in the casino, and contrary to popular belief, less than 5% of the principality's revenues are derived from its gambling royalties. Still, the social life of Monaco centers around the Place du Casino, with its lovely gardens. The Monte Carlo Philharmonic is one of the world's most recorded orchestras. The principality also boasts first-rate opera and ballet companies, as well as 55 galleries and 50 open-air sculptures.

Monaco's present constitution, which was promulgated December 17, 1962, reduced the prince's powers somewhat and increased parliamentary powers. Executive power is vested in the hereditary prince, who rules through his appointed Minister of State. The latter official must be a French citizen and must be selected from a slate of three candidates put to the principality by the French president. The Minister of State is assisted by three state counselors (one of whom must be French) and palace personnel who are appointed by the prince. Legislative power rests with an 18-member National Council elected by universal suffrage for five-year terms. The prince shares the legislative powers in that he retains the right to initiate legislation. Although four political parties are now active in Monaco, one party, the *National and Democratic Union (UND)*, controls all 18 National Council seats. The French judicial system applies in Monaco, and two Parisian judges form the Court of Appeal.

France controls Monaco's foreign relations, and the principality is included in the EU through its customs union with France. Since 1993 it is a full member of the United Nations, and it serves on several UN specialized agencies. It also maintains four embassies (in Paris, Brussels, Bern and Rome) and 110 consuls of its own, including ones in Washington and New York. In 1994 it signed a cultural convention under Council of Europe auspices. But because it is not considered to be either completely democratic or independent, it has never formally asked nor been invited to join the Council of Europe.

Monaco has no newspapers of its own, but there is a private radio station (Radio-Monte-Carlo) with programming in French, Italian and Arabic. Also, Trans-World Radio has a seat in Monte-Carlo and broadcasts in four languages. One private television station (Tele Monte-Carlo) transmits programs in French and Italian.

FUTURE

As the 20th century closed Prince Rainier could look back on a half century of rule in his mini-state. With an heir to the throne and an active program of home-based economic diversification, this minuscule 700-year-old principality can expect not only to exist, but to prosper in the coming years.

Prince Albert and His Serene Highness Prince Rainier III

The Hellenic Republic (Greece)

Area: 50,961 sq. mi. (131,900 sq. km., somewhat larger than Louisiana).
Population: 10.5 million (estimated).
Capital City: Athens. The population of the *Greater Athens* area, including Athens, Piraeus (its port) and surrounding municipalities is estimated to be 3.1 million.
Climate: Generally mild, with the summer hot and dry, tempered in the vicinity of the coast where sea breezes blow in every afternoon.
Neighboring Countries: Turkey (East, across the Aegean Sea, with many scattered Greek islands lying close to the Turkish coast, bordered on the northeast by *European* Turkey); Albania, Bulgaria, Macedonia (North).
Official Language: Greek.
Other Principal Tongues: There is a small Turkish–speaking minority (about 1.5% of the population) in Thrace.
Ethnic Background: Indo–European.
Principal Religion: Greek Orthodox.
Main Exports: Textiles, chemicals, metal products, cement, fresh fruit, vegetables, olive oil, cotton, tobacco, currants and raisins.
Main Imports: Machinery, automobiles, petroleum, consumer goods, meat and live animals.
Major Customers: Germany, Italy, France.
Currency: Drachma.
National Holiday: March 25 (Independence Day).
Chief of State: Constantinos Stephanopoulos, President (since 1995).
Head of Government: Costas Simitis, Prime Minister (since January 1996).

Greece

National Flag: Four white and five blue alternating stripes, with a white cross on the upper left hand corner.

Greece is a land with many islands which, at times in the past, has been the geographic, military, economic, cultural or philosophical heart of the western world. Its mainland portion is for the most part mountainous and hilly. Its geographical position at the intersection between East and West and between the Balkans and the Mediterranean have made it a springboard to the Orient and a thoroughfare for invasion by Moslem peoples heading west. For ancient Romans, Christian crusaders and European merchants, Greece was the doorway to the East. For Arabs, Turks, Serbians and Bulgarians, it was an important gateway to western culture. Throughout the centuries, Greece's position at the bridgehead of three continents inevitably drew it into most conflicts between the peoples of Europe, the Near East and North Africa.

This central position of Greece remains largely unchanged in the 20th century. For instance, before Germany dared to attack the Soviet Union in 1941, the German dictator, Adolf Hitler, first conquered Greece in order to secure the southern flank of "Europe's soft underbelly." Even today Greece occupies a key strategic position for NATO, bordering as it does, on Albania, Bulgaria and Macedonia and on NATO's easternmost partner, Turkey. With its many islands, it is the heart of the Aegean Sea and the eastern Mediterranean.

As important as is its geographic location, contemporary Greece is much more than a rampart for western defense. It is a society which is feeling the strains of transition from authoritarian political rule to modern democracy and which is experiencing a shift from traditional values and economic ways to those more compatible with Greece's new role as a full partner with the prosperous and advanced states of Western Europe and as a land which is open to the major influences of the modern world. All changes in Greece are always viewed from outside the country with a mixture of hope and anxiety.

HISTORY

Greece is both a very old and a very new country. Not until 1829 were Greeks able to end four centuries of Turkish domination and to create an independent nation–state. However, the Greek state which was proclaimed in that year and the country's contemporary society and culture bear little resemblance to the ancient Greece which so many people have admired throughout the centuries. The large body of Greek classical literature and the many magnificent ruins reflect the grandeur of the ancient past. But the modern Greek's approach to life and his understanding of himself have been shaped far more significantly by the Byzantine past (324 A.D. to 1453), the Orthodox Church and four centuries of Turkish domination than by the Greece of antiquity. At the very most, the modern Greek shares with his ancient forefathers an ardent passion for political discussion, a talent for daring economic activity and a proverbial hospitality.

The Early Periods

Nevertheless, a presentation of Greece without the classical period would be unthinkable, for ancient Greece was the cradle of western culture and civilization. Most western philosophical, political, scholarly and artistic achievements have their roots in Greek antiquity. Ancient Greece has served in many respects as a model worthy of imitation or, at the very least, as an almost inexhaustible, examinable reservoir of human experience and thought. It is rightly referred to as the founder of western thought and culture. That torch still to a degree burns today.

It is often the case in history that the new and the extraordinary emerge at the point

The Parthenon in Athens (temple of Athena, goddess of wisdom) dominates the Acropolis, that flat–topped natural stronghold of early times which was the heart of the city
Photo by Susan L. Thompson

Greece

of contact between various cultures and peoples. From roughly 1600 to 1200 B.C. Greece attracted a flood of Indo–Germanic tribes from the north, who came into contact with older cultures from Crete, Egypt and other areas of the Mideast. These highly intelligent and agile newcomers borrowed the Phoenician letters and numbers and developed a written Greek language; they took the religiously oriented astronomy of the Mideast and developed it into mathematics. They also freed the ancient Egyptians' great, but static, art of sculpture from its immobility and produced an art capable of portraying the idealized likeness of man.

When the first Greek immigrants arrived on the coast of the Aegean Sea, they came upon a highly developed culture, whose mysterious ruins on the island of Crete provide evidence of the Minoan culture, named after the legendary king of the island, Minos. It began to rise around 3000 B.C. and had developed brilliantly by about 2000 B.C. The unearthed palaces, ceramics and frescoes give exciting glimpses into a highly developed and cultivated civilization. The Minoans apparently maintained a very powerful fleet because excavations provide no evidence of fortifications. The origins of this culture, its social structure and its decline remain a mystery to the present day.

The Greeks began to burn and sack the Minoan strongholds around 1400 B.C. and a new culture emerged—the Mycenaean, named after the town of Mycenae in the Peloponnesos—the peninsula forming part of the mainland of Greece. The remains of this culture can be seen around the Peloponnesian coasts and up the eastern seaboard of Greece all the way to Thessaly (Thessaloniki), as well as in the southern islands of the Aegean Sea, the islands of Rhodes and Cyprus, and the west coast of Asia Minor. Through the decoding of many clay reliefs from this period (roughly 1600 to 1150 B.C.) we know that the civilization was organized in small, Greek–speaking governmental structures. Even the names of Greek myths appear as historical realities in these carvings, so this society unquestionably provided material for these myths and system of religion.

It was around 1200 B.C. that the legendary siege and destruction of Troy (a city whose ruins can be seen on the northwestern coast of Turkey) is said to have taken place. This exciting tale, which may even contain a tiny bit of truth, sprang from the alleged kidnapping of Helen, the beautiful wife of the Spartan King, Menelaüs, by Paris, a prince of Troy. King Agamemnon of Mycenae, Menelaüs' brother, led a ten year Greek expedition to Troy to recapture the Queen. Finally the Greeks pretended to give up the fight, leaving behind a large wooden horse as a supposed gift of congratulations to the "victors." During the same night that the gullible Trojans broke a hole in their walls to bring the fatal trophy into the city, Greek soldiers sprang out of the "Trojan horse" and captured the city from within.

A System of Religion

Sometime between 900 and 700 B.C., the Greek poet Homer described the siege in the *Iliad* and the *Odyssey* and the Greek warriors' adventures on their way home. These long poems may not have been written by the same author. Nevertheless, they are the beginning, and, in some experts' view, the best of Greek literature. They quickly became the standard texts which were memorized by Greek pupils and influenced Western literature as have few other works. They also reflected, and may even have influenced, the Greeks' view of the gods which, they thought, took a direct part in their daily lives. Homer poetically presented a host of particular gods, with well–defined characteristics, names and places of residence.

Zeus, ruler of the heavens was of primary importance. **Hera,** his wife and sister, was queen of the heavens. **Poseidon** ruled the sea and unleashed earthquakes, and **Hades** lorded over the underworld. **Athena** was the goddess of wisdom and skills, including those of the household, **Aphrodite** of love and beauty, **Eros**, her son, god of love (thus the word "erotic"), and **Apollo** of youthful manly beauty, of light, healing, young men's arts, such as archery, music, prophecy and poetic inspiration. **Artemis,** sister of Apollo, was goddess of the moon, wild animals and hunting, **Demeter** of grain, **Hephaestus,** god of fire and metalworking, **Hermes,** messenger of the gods and god of the roads, **Ares** of war, and **Dionysus** of wine (and thus, drunkenness).

All Greeks ascribed to the gods at least *some* influence over their lives and cities, but it would be a mistake to think that Greek life was dominated by *fear* of the deities, as was the case in some primitive societies. Greek political, economic and intellectual life was never profoundly shaped by religious dogma, clergy or temples. They sought human achievement and pleasures, and their endeavors were, on the whole, secular rather than religious. In this respect, the Greeks distinguished themselves from most other ancient civilizations. Nevertheless, the authority of the gods continued to be invoked in order to bolster political authority within the cities. Therefore, as the philosopher Socrates experienced in the year 399 B.C., a person could lose his life for defaming the gods in public, especially within the earshot of impressionable young people.

City–States

The onset of a second migratory wave into Greece from 1200 to 900 B.C. led many Greeks to flee across the Aegean Sea to the Near East, on whose coasts they founded cities such as Ephesus and Miletus. Athens was located on the peninsula of Attica, an inverted triangle about 20 miles (30 km.) wide at the base and 35 miles (56 km.) from top to bottom. Attica, which had allegedly been united by the legendary King Theseus, was able to remain an undisturbed enclave during this second migration.

As was often the case, geographic factors left their stamp on Greek history. The mountainous terrain, with small river valleys and almost no large plains except in the North, favored from the beginning the

Detail from a piece of Minoan pottery

Greece

formation of a kind of small political organization known as *Polis* (from this the words "politics" and metropolis" are derived). The *Polis* was a city–state, which in some cases included a number of small towns. Its limited size later made possible the unprecedented development of democracy in some Greek cities, especially Athens, and it helped stimulate the development of political awareness and interest among the citizens of the cities.

The Greeks' passion for politics was one reason why the philosopher Aristotle defined humans as "political beings." However, the intense interest in politics and the small scale of Greek political units were also factors which helped perpetuate the never–ending and exhausting conflicts among the various city–states. These conflicts helped prevent the integration of the Greek settlements into a larger political order, such as a nation state, as we know it today. Citizens in the city–states viewed the world strictly on the basis of their narrow local patriotism and never developed a sense of Greek *national* identity. For the Greeks, including the Athenians, there was hardly a period of more than two years which was free of conflict with other cities. In general, the history of ancient Greece is one of almost constant war.

Had it not been for the temporary predominance during the 8th to the 6th centuries B.C. of the cities' aristocracies (often called "oligarchies") who gradually dislodged the cities' kings from power, and who maintained some close ties among the various city–states, Greece would probably have suffocated very early in the stifling spirit of provincial narrow–mindedness. It is because of this aristocratic class that the poetry of Homer, with its portrayal of the Olympian world of the gods, became standard references for all Greeks. The aristocracy was also responsible for developing the Greek education of man in the arts as well as in athletic competition.

The periodic gathering of Greeks for the Olympic Games, first organized in 776 B.C. at the city of Olympia in the western Peloponnesos, and thereafter held every four years, reflected the spirit of competition which became a precedent for the knightly tournaments in the European Middle Ages. Those with Olympic prowess and the virtues espoused by the noble class greatly overshadowed those persons who merely showed the simpler virtues, such as trading skills and industriousness, and sometimes they even overshadowed sculptors and architects who adorned the cities in which the Greeks lived. There can be no doubt that the Olympic Games brought Greeks together and showed them some common ideals. But these games never succeeded in creating peace

Greek legend tells of Hero, a priestess of Aphrodite, whose lover, Leander, swam to her each night across the strait between Europe and Asia. On one stormy night he drowned, his lifeless body washing to the shore. In grief, she cast herself into the raging waters.

or political unity in the Hellenic world, any more than have the modern Olympic Games eliminated wars or divisions among the peoples of the world today.

The governing cliques of aristocrats did begin to establish the political principles that the privilege of ruling should be passed around periodically and that rulers should not be above an established body of rules of law. Such laws were independent of the will of the temporary ruler and could be invoked if the rulers appeared to be abusing their powers. Thus, a notion of "limited government" by consent of the governed existed in most Greek cites from the 8th century on. This was a principle which was scarcely known in any other civilization of the era.

Politically, the aristocracy's domination over the masses was already being challenged from the 8th century. Rapid population growth, increasing tensions among the social classes and changes in warfare (which made citizen armies militarily superior to ones based primarily on noblemen) became important factors in further Greek developments. Increasing conflicts between the aristocracies and the common

Greece

citizens created the right kind of conditions by about 600 B.C. for dictators to seize power in most of the cities. The threatened or dispossessed noblemen called them *tyrannis,* or "tyrants," a word which had formerly been applied to absolute rulers and one which still retains its negative connotation.

It is true that most tyrants disregarded many previously established laws and conventions. But most came to power by promising to break the power of the aristocracy, and they were usually favored by the common citizens. They frequently launched conspicuous building programs to create public works which would both provide people with jobs and improve the economic base, living conditions, beauty and therefore, the prestige of the city. They also proclaimed laws which would benefit small tradesmen, artisans and farmers, and sometimes they gave subsidies to these groups. To pay for these policies, they often expropriated the property of the noblemen (and of their own opponents!). Such property could thus be dispersed to some persons who had possessed none. They often abused the power they wielded, but because they did tend to have an ear attuned to the wishes of the lower classes of citizens they, too, made a contribution toward the development of democracy in Greece.

Those Greek cities which had only small agricultural hinterlands close by could relieve the pressures created by rapidly growing populations only by founding colonies overseas to which their excess people could emigrate. Between 750 and 550 B.C. such Greek colonies were created along the coasts and on the islands of the entire Mediterranean and Black Sea, including one at Byzantium (later Constantinople, now Istanbul, Turkey). Greek colonies sprung up from the eastern coast of Spain to the mouth of the Dnieper River in what is now the Soviet Union and from what is presently the French Riviera and Sicily (where Syracuse was built) to the toe of Italy, which, along with Sicily, became known as "Greater Greece."

By means of these colonies, the Greek language, culture and influence were extended over much of the known world. Almost all of these colonies quickly broke their umbilical cords which tied them to their mother cities and became politically independent. There was no all-powerful overlord to subordinate the cities through taxes or military means as was the case in the Middle and Near Eastern empires. They continued to share similar viewpoints on ruling, culture and religion, and they almost always maintained sentimental ties. They also traded with the older Greek cities, and such trade was the foundation for an enormous growth of wealth

Frieze of a Greek athlete

in the entire Greek world. This wealth provided some Greeks with leisure, which was essential for their being able to produce beautiful poetry, usually about various forms of love. Leisure was also the starting point for rational, systematic speculation about nature. Thus, the Greeks began to free philosophy from mythology, which had characterized speculation in other ancient cultures.

The philosopher Plato coined the expression that the Greeks sat around the Mediterranean like frogs around a pond. In a short period of time, the Greeks showed themselves to be daring seafarers, traveling as far as Britain. It was the Greeks who gave meaning to the saying that "oceans are bridges," and they established the foundations of a Greek maritime predominance which indirectly continues to exist today.

Athens and Sparta

As could be expected, these cities often became bitter rivals. In the motherland political developments came to be dominated by the rivalry between the land power, Sparta, and the sea power, Athens. By the late 8th century B.C., Sparta had acquired the entire southern part of Peloponnesos. Its expansion had always been of a military rather than of an economic nature, and it did very little colonizing. The political organization of Sparta consisted of the exclusive domination by a warrior caste over the subjugated masses, who practically were kept in a condition of slavery and who were responsible for the economic maintenance of their masters.

According to law, all members of the warrior caste were equal and were not allowed to possess private property. The elite, whose reputation of being unconquerable, lasted until the 5th century B.C., was shaped from early youth by strict breeding and upbringing in a collective (thus the expression "Spartan discipline"). They performed permanent military service until the age 60 and had a very restricted private life. The Spartans' thoughts centered almost exclusively around the triangular fortress, the mess hall and the battlefield. Most standard forms of pleasure and luxury were abolished in order to make military life more attractive. This form of life would enthuse few people today, but a form of it was presented as an ideal state in one of the greatest books ever written, *The Republic* by Plato.

The Spartan political system blended elements of monarchy, aristocracy and democracy. Two kings had limited power

Greece

and had supreme authority only in time of war. A Council of Elders, whose members were elected by an assembly of soldiers, made the really important political decisions. The brand of Spartan perfection, whose purpose was permanent military preparedness, tolerated no change and therefore soon became frozen in conservative rigidity.

Athens, a late bloomer among the Greek city-states, assumed a unique position from its onset because it encompassed the entire Attican Peninsula and became master of the sea. Perhaps most important, it developed a new kind of political order. As we have seen, the domestic political conflicts between the nobility and other classes of citizens had gradually led to the rise of tyrants in most cities. In the course of the 6th century B.C., a few of these cities experienced the emergence of a more democratic political order, in which the principles of equality before the law and the right to vote were extended to that part of the inhabitants who were citizens. Foremost among these was Athens.

Athenian law was codified and made public by 621 B.C. This enabled anyone who could read or who was informed to compare the behavior of the city's rulers with the established laws. In 593 the highly respected public figure, Solon, introduced a complete legal reform which provided the lower classes with financial relief, legal protection and a powerful voice in the city's government. The reform abolished property requirements for participation in the Assembly, which elected the city's leaders and which served as the final court or law for important cases, including those for public officials accused of abusing their power. For such cases, the judges were selected by lot from the entire citizen body.

The reform also transferred from the upper-class to the other classes the right to determine the Assembly's agenda. Thus, the lower classes gained an important influence, perhaps even control, over the election of the city's officials, over legislation and over the Athenian judiciary. These reforms cannot be said to have secured democracy in Athens, but they laid the foundation for the Athenian democratic tradition. It was not until the reform of the statesman Cleisthenes in the years 508–507 B.C. that the power of the aristocracy was completely broken and all the important political decisions began to be made by democratic institutions.

The most important organ in the Athenian political system, and that which wielded legislative authority, was the Assembly, in which all citizens could attend and vote. This form of parliament did have some important drawbacks. One was that citizenship in Athens, as well as other Greek cities, was denied to women, foreign residents and slaves. Slave-ownership was widespread. Small farmers and shopkeepers usually had two or three and the rich could own thousands. In general, slaves were at least as numerous as were citizens. In any case, never did anything close to a majority of adult residents have the right to vote in the Assembly, so Athenian democracy, as advanced as it was for its time, was still ruled by a minority.

A second drawback stemmed from the fact that the Assembly met on a regular basis every nine or ten days. Since such meetings were too frequent even for most of the passionately political Athenians, few citizens attended most sessions, and the wealthier ones, who had more leisure to pursue their political interests, were often able to dominate the proceedings. Not until the 5th century B.C. were citizens paid to attend the sessions so that they could receive financial compensation for being away from their work.

The government's supreme executive functions were performed by the Council, composed of 500 representatives drawn by lot from the ten districts of the city. For the sake of convenience, the Council was divided into ten committees, each of which served a tenth of a year, during which time the chairmanship changed daily. The Council and the committees always remained subordinate to the Assembly, though. The sovereignty of the people was, in principle, exercised through the Assembly, but those who really had the decisive influence were those who could have their point of view accepted by the often fickle and easily changeable majority in the Assembly. This fact put a high premium on the ability to speak eloquently and persuasively in public. Thus, these skills formed the basis of Athenian education. It also gave rise to a whole new profession: sophistry, so named because the sophists claimed to make men wise *(sophos)*. Sophists made good money by teaching people how to win arguments in the Assembly and courts of law.

The volatility and changeability of the majority within the Assembly meant that policy could switch suddenly, and yesterday's powerful and honored leaders could be disgraced and dismissed the very next day. This led to great political instability and to a form of permanently latent revolution in Athenian political life. It is not surprising that many a leader was sent

Simplified map of Sparta and Athens with certain major cities of the area

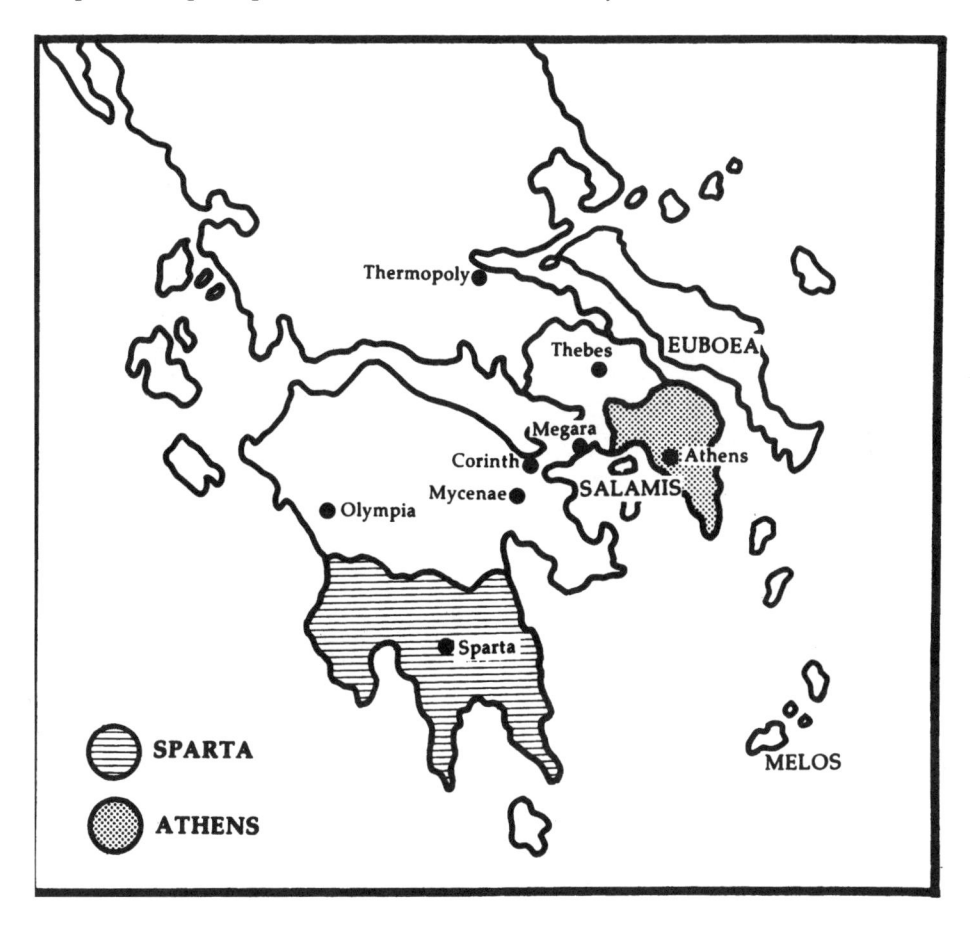

Greece

into exile, not because he had disregarded Athenian law or interests, but because his political opponents had successfully seized the chance to get rid of him. It is clear that such a political order was an ideal setting for golden-tongued demagogues and intriguers. This is one reason why such profound political thinkers as Socrates, Plato and Aristotle condemned democracy as an inferior type of political organization.

Only the most competent politicians, who could persuade the masses at any moment, could conduct a coherent and consistent policy under these circumstances. These leadership qualities were best reflected by Athens' greatest political figure, Pericles, who from 461 to 428 B.C. was able to guide the city to the summit of its power, glory, prosperity and architectural achievements. Of course, there were courts of law in which all citizens' rights were to be protected. But Plato's description in the *Apology* of Socrates' trial in 399 B.C. indicates that court proceedings could be uproarious and outrageous affairs, in which political or personal interests often weighed heavier than the evidence, to say nothing of justice.

With all its shortcomings, though, Athens extended wealth, luxury, leisure and political power more broadly among its citizens than did any other city. Also, democracy was an essential step in the direction of placing ultimate political power in the hands of the ruled, instead of those of arbitrary rulers. In Athens, the citizens exercised final control over all aspects of government. This first great example of democracy in action influenced western political thought from then on and helped to inspire the democratic revolutions of the 18th, 19th and 20th centuries A.D. in America, Western Europe and modern Greece itself.

Athens existed under conditions of almost permanent mobilization and imperialism, maintained by sea power and the exploitation of allies. It was able to survive a grave external threat to itself and to the rest of Greece in the first decades of the 5th century B.C., namely that of the mighty Persian empire to the east. The power of this great empire already extended into India and, by the middle of the 6th century, to the Greek cities along what is today the western coast of Turkey. When these cities, especially Miletus, revolted in 500 B.C., they were brutally crushed by the Persians within a few years.

The easterners, under the Great King Darius, decided to eliminate the sources of support for the Greek cities under their control, and especially to punish Athens for its aid to the rebels. Darius threw his military forces against the Greek mainland in 492 B.C. and conquered Macedonia and Thrace. However, during a violent storm his navy was wrecked off Mount Athos. But he resumed the operation two years later, landing an expeditionary force of 20,000 troops on the Attican coast; these troops were easily defeated by a far smaller force of Athenian citizen soldiers on the Plain of Marathon. A messenger ran as fast as he could for 26 miles (42 km.) in order to bring the news of victory to Athens, where he reportedly died upon arrival. The modern Marathon runs, in which both Olympians and many thousands of avid joggers now participate, commemorate the feats of both the Athenian soldiers and their prodigious messenger. Athens' victory secured for it enormous importance and prestige in all of Greece, and it ushered in the "Golden Age" of Athens, the 5th century B.C., when its power and cultural achievements were at their peak.

After Darius' death his crown prince, Xerxes, laid careful plans for a final blow to Greece. It certainly is wrong to assume that the Greeks displayed solidarity and fraternity with each other in the face of the Persian threat. Such concepts, as well as nationalism, were still unknown in the ancient world, as many Greeks showed in this great struggle. Xerxes was able to persuade the Greek trading power in the western Mediterranean, Carthage (located near the present-day city of Tunis in Tunisia), to tie down the western Greek forces by means of an attack against Sicily. All of northern Greece offered Persia indispensable support. Greek architects and engineers built the pontoon bridge over the Dardanelles and dug a canal in order to spare the Persian fleet from having to sail around the perilous Mount Athos. Most of the sailors in the Persian fleet were Greeks, and Athenians who had been driven out of their city served the Persians as highly paid military advisers. Basically, only a large part of those cities in central Greece and the Peloponnesos, including Corinth, Thebes and a couple of dozen smaller city-states fought under the leadership of Sparta and Athens.

In the summer of 480 B.C. the numerically vastly superior Persian units, with an estimated 100,000 foot-soldiers and 1,000 ships, descended upon central Greece. They confronted the Greeks' first line of defense at Thermopoly, where in a legendary effort, a Greek force of 7,000 courageous soldiers, under the command of Spartan King Leonidas, held back the entire Persian army for a week before withdrawing. The enemy was then able to march almost unopposed into Attica and to occupy and completely destroy Athens, which had been evacuated just in the nick of time.

The Athenians were by no means defeated. In the narrow straits between the Attican coast and the island of Salamis, the Athenian admiral Themistocles lured the Persian fleet into a trap and destroyed it. Also, the land battle at Plateaea in 479 B.C. demonstrated the superiority of well-trained and motivated citizen soldiers over a huge immobile army, which was largely composed of a colorful mixture of diverse peoples who had been involuntarily drafted into service and who had been left on the Greek mainland without logistical support. At the very same time, the news arrived that the Sicilian Greeks had stopped the Carthaginian invasion and that the remainder of the Persian fleet in Asia Minor had been cornered and destroyed at Mount Mycale, located immediately north of Miletus. After these sobering dual victories, the Persian threat was ended, and many of the Greek cities on the Aegean coasts rebelled anew against Persian domination. For the next 280 years the Greek world was spared from any serious external threat until the Roman Empire absorbed all of it in 190 B.C.

The Delian "League" and the "Golden Age"

Athens, which had carried the main burden of the Persian War, took quick advantage of its undisputed mastery at sea in order to construct a widely-spun web of alliances, which extended throughout the entire Aegean area and which Athens dominated. After Sparta had relinquished

An Athenian lady

Greece

An artist's concept of ancient Athens at its height

its leadership in the Greek alliance against Persia, Athens organized in 478–477 B.C. the Delian League, which maintained a common treasury on the island of Delos, where the League's representatives occasionally met. As the largest contributor, Athens was assured political and military predominance within the League. Soon, its allies discovered that they were veritable *subjects* of Athens, especially after 454 B.C., when the treasury was transferred to Athens and when meetings of the council were terminated.

Athens experienced an almost unbelievable economic upswing and it had a democratic order which inspired both loyalty on the part of its own citizens, as well as some admiration and support on the part of the lower classes in the other Greek cities (to the chagrin of their non–democratic leaders!). Conditions were favorable to a cultural flowering which still testifies to Athens' "Golden Age." Out of the rubble of Athens emerged the classical Athens, with its grandiose structures on the Acropolis (literally "high city" which in most Greek cities was first a place of refuge from enemies and, later, the place for temples). Under the leadership of Pericles the living conditions of the poor were improved. After a few unfortunate military adventures, Pericles again launched Athens' deliberate, major policy of colonization, sending settlers to Thrace, Euboea and Naxos in 447 and then on to other Aegean islands, Macedonia, southern Italy and the Black Sea. These settlements provided land for Athens' allies and poorer citizens, as well as markets for its trade.

Art, science and philosophy flourished. Sculpture achieved its eternal classical form under artists such as Phidias and Plyclet. The dramatists, Aeschylus (525–456), Sophocles (496–406) and Euripides (485–408) produced timeless tragedies. It is characteristically Greek that the victory over the Persians did not produce feelings of superiority among the Greeks. In his famous tragedies, Aeschylus portrayed the Persians with sympathy and sorrow. In bitingly critical comedies, Aristophanes took hilarious, but deadly, shots at the politics of the day. He is the only 5th century author of comedies whose complete works survived. On the southern slope of the Acropolis these dramatists presented plays in festivals, at which winners were chosen. A special tax on the rich enabled people from all classes to enjoy the performances.

In the writing of history, Thucydides approached his subjects far more systematically and analytically than had Herodotus in his narrations. Thucydides presented a concept of history as a structure of interlocking effects, which themselves become causes in human affairs. He sought to delve into the motives and interests of conflicting parties in historical events, and his historical method is still important today. In medicine, Hippocrates demanded that the body be studied as a whole. Hippodamus of Miletus redesigned Piraeus (which was and is, in effect, the port of Athens) and introduced gridiron planning for cities, instead of building towns with wildly winding streets.

A Second Round With Sparta

The enormous growth of Athens' power and its imperialist foreign policy again led almost unavoidably to a collision with Sparta, the second greatest power in Greece. When Athens turned on its major trade competitors, Corinth and Megara, which had been joined by Thebes, Corinth appealed to Sparta for help. The tension boiled over in the Peloponnesian War, which lasted almost three decades from 431 to 404 and which ended in Athens' defeat and ruin. This war was conducted with a brutality which had been almost unknown up to that time. Because of the alliance systems which Sparta and Athens had built up, almost every city in Greece was ultimately drawn into the conflict.

Based on what he witnessed in this war, Thucydides, the former Athenian general who had been exiled from Athens during the first part of the war for failing to save Amphipolis from the Spartans, developed his pessimistic view that man's insatiable striving for power was the sole motor of history. In his fascinating classic book, *History of the Peloponnesian War*, he described very impressively the restless and unlimited political passion which was a basic characteristic of the Greeks, along with the yearning for perfection and order in art and philosophy. On the one hand, Greeks were politically volatile and unreliable; on the other, they left timeless works.

As a sobering example, Thucydides described the political mistreatment of a small state by a more powerful one. When the island of Melos refused to join the

Greece

The Lions of Delos, guardians of Apollo's sacred island Courtesy: Dorothy L. Lewis

Athenian naval league, the Athenians stormed the capital city, killed all the men and sold the women and children into slavery. And *that* was done by a *democratic* Athens! Thucydides' observations on foreign relations remain largely valid today. Military power and the willingness to use it are significant factors in international politics. Modern countries, large and small, must still adjust to this reality or suffer the consequences. The challenge to men remains to create a system of international law and widely respected codes of international conduct which would greatly diminish the significance of military force in human affairs.

At the onset of the war, Sparta marched into Attica and drove much of the rural population into the city of Athens, where close quarters and insufficient sanitary conditions created ideal conditions for a deadly plague, which broke out in 430 and which reduced the population by a third. It so frightened the rest of the people that, as Thucydides described so vividly, all respect for morality, social ties and law broke down for a time, since all individuals expected to be dead by the next day. The great leader Pericles died in 429. Fortunately for Athens, the Spartans were unable to launch any decisive attacks, so an armistice was arranged in 423 and a peace treaty in 421.

This first phase of the war accomplished nothing. Athens was interested only in having a temporary breather, and in 415 it sent an expedition under the leadership of the wealthy, brilliant and handsome young general, Alcibiades, to Syracuse (a former colony of Corinth) on the island of Sicily. As happened so often in Athens, Alcibiades no sooner left the city with his large army and navy than his political enemies at home turned on him and demanded that he return home to stand trial. Knowing that he would be returning to sure death, Alcibiades fled instead to the Spartans, whom he persuaded to recommence hostilities against Athens in 414. The next year, the Syracusans proceeded to decimate the Athenian force.

By 412 both Syracuse and Persia had entered the war on Sparta's side, and Athens' allies along the Ionian coast had revolted. These setbacks so discredited the democratic order that an oligarchy was temporarily established, but the people in Athens could not accept this for long. Therefore Alcibiades was called back to Athens as the city's supreme commander, and democracy was restored. However, Athens was so ridden by party squabbles and demogoguery that it could not possibly conduct a successful war against its enemies. After a stinging naval defeat, Alcibiades was again driven into exile, and he was ultimately executed by the Persians. Demagogues in Athens persuaded the volatile majority to execute most of the successful commanders, and after its last fleet was destroyed in 405, the Athenians were exhausted and in 404 they surrendered to the Spartans, and Athenian greatness came to an end. In fact, none of the Greek cities ever fully recovered from the wounds they suffered in this terrible war.

The Athenian empire had existed for a shorter period of time than had any of the famous empires of antiquity; it had risen and fallen in three–quarters of a century. It was also the smallest of the great empires, comprising only a corner of Greece, most of the Aegean islands and colonies along the western coast of Greece, in Asia Minor around the Black Sea and in southern Italy. It probably never had a citizen population of more than about 60,000 and the population of Attica was certainly never more than a half million; in all likelihood it was a lot less.

The Postwar Period; Socrates, Plato and Aristotle

The Peloponnesian War accelerated the breakdown of morality, restraint and harmony among citizens in Athens and elsewhere in Greece. Greek politics was in a state of chaos. The probing, analytical minds of Greek thinkers had revealed that the gods in which Greeks had believed did not really sanction the moral order or back up the laws of the various cities as the people had thought. These insights created problems for the rulers, who now had greater difficulty persuading their people to obey them. If the gods did not determine what was just and what was not, then who did? What was justice? This was the fundamental question which a stonecarver and former private in the Athenian infantry liked to discuss at the Athenian marketplace *(Agora)* with anyone who wanted to talk about it.

His name was Socrates, and he particularly attracted a following of young, rich and ambitious Athenians, who were itching to become rulers themselves. He impressed and entertained them by skillfully cross–examining influential and supposedly wise men in public on subjects dealing with justice and morality. In reality, he was *teaching by questioning*. He was invariably able to reveal that they did not really know much about these subjects. He claimed not to know anything about these difficult concepts, but because of his skepticism and willingness to examine any question at its very roots, the oracle of Delphi (a pronouncement by a religious group with political clout) declared him to be the wisest of all men.

The rulers of Athens did not agree. Aristophanes revealed in his hilarious play, *The Clouds,* that most of the people regarded him as a mere gadfly or hairbrain, who taught young people how to lie, to avoid paying their debts and to turn against their parents with a good conscience. He was perceived to be undermining the already corroded authority of the city, and he was therefore put on trial in 399 B.C. for allegedly defaming the gods and corrupting the youth. He was condemned to death. But this questioning

Greece

stonecarver, who never wrote a word (he was described by others, such as Plato or Xenophon) influenced western civilization as almost no other human being.

After the fall of Athens in 404, the greatest power in Greece was Sparta, which established oligarchies in most cities. Even Athens experienced a "reign of terror," under the "thirty tyrants," led by a former pupil of Socrates and cousin of Plato—Critias—whose bloody deeds did much to assure his teacher's execution. The heavy Spartan hand provoked revolutions everywhere, and Greece experienced a long period of power struggles with Persia, Sparta, Athens and Thebes as the main contenders. By about 370 B.C. Spartan predominance in Greece ended once and for all.

Greece entered the 4th century B.C. in pitiful condition. The constant war had devastated much of the countryside, impoverished or destroyed many of the cities and disrupted the patterns of travel and trade. It was a time of growing piracy and of economic depression. However, it was also a time of continued intellectual achievement. The most influential sculptor of antiquity, Praxiteles, was creating individual statues which could stand alone in their perfection, rather than having to blend into an architectural setting.

The philosopher Plato, a rich Athenian from a very influential family, focused on the legacy of one man who, in his opinion, stood out in the madness of Athens: Socrates. His poetic and literary style, filled with brilliant argumentation, common sense and moral concern, as well as with beautiful myths and metaphors, greatly enhanced his prestige in his own day and his scholarly reputation right up to the present time. He founded a school in the Athenian suburb of Academia (from which the words "academy" and "academic" are derived), which survived until the Christian emperor Justinian closed it in 529 A.D.

Out of this school came his most famous pupil, Aristotle, who classified the various branches of knowledge, created much scientific terminology, advocated close scientific examination and experimentation and established standards of definition and proof. He too created a school, called the Lyceum (after which the French high school "lycée" is named). In 1997 this school was accidentally unearthed on a construction site for a Museum of Modern Art, 600 meters from Athens' central Constitution Square. The large ancient complex that was rediscovered includes a central courtyard and palaestra (wrestling area). Although he had very little impact on his own contemporaries, his writings, which were preserved by Arab scholars and rediscovered in medieval Europe, became the basis of scholarship and university teaching in Europe and the U.S. until the 19th century.

Philip of Macedon and his Son, Alexander

The mainland of Greece had fallen into such political chaos that it was left to the mercy of Philip II of Macedon, a wild kingdom of a half–Greek population in the North (now the independent state calling itself Macedonia). Macedon was culturally attracted to Greece, and Philip brought to his court outstanding Greek artists, writers and scholars, including Aristotle, who tutored the monarch's son, Alexander. Macedon was a different kind of political entity than the city–states of Greece. It was a large kingdom, not a city.

Philip was able to extend his rule into Byzantium in what is now Turkey. He could take advantage of the web of rivalries among the Greek cities to the south so that he brought one city after the other under his influence. The warnings of one of antiquity's most famous speakers, Demosthenes, fell on deaf ears in Athens, and by the time he could organize a coalition of the most important Greek cities against the Macedonian king, it was too late. Philip's victory in 338 B.C. followed up by finishing operations in the Peloponnesos signaled the end of the cities' freedom. The King proclaimed a general peace and organized the Greek cities in a league under his control.

Philip had already begun preparations for war against Persia when he was assassinated in 336. His son, Alexander, later known as "The Great" (356–323), who had just turned 20 when he became king, turned a new page in the book of world history. In a breath–taking campaign, the young commander in only nine years conquered the Persian Empire which had reached its greatest expanse, and he also won parts of south Asia as far as the Indus Valley. By the time he arrived in Susa with his army, which had completed a

Frieze of a water bearer

Greece

Alexander

12,000 mile (20,000 km.) march, Alexander ruled over an empire which stretched from Greece over Asia Minor, the Phoenician coast, Egypt, Mesopotamia, Babylon, Persia and beyond.

It is true that the Persian Empire had been weakened by palace intrigues and rebellions, but nothing fell into his lap without his having to earn it. On the contrary, bitter struggles demanded the entire strategic genius of the young commander, and his army had to engage in constant and exhausting individual combat with wild mountain men, to face inconceivable perils in the extensive deserts and dry highlands, and to master difficult technical challenges, such as the siege of the sea fortress at Tyre in Palestine.

He also had the political sense to assume the right titles in order to win the loyalty of his newly conquered subjects. He became the **Great King** in Persia and the **Divine Pharaoh** and **Son of the God Amon** in Egypt. The Greek cities bent to his demand that he be proclaimed no less than a *Greek God*. Genius, energy, ambition and charismatic leadership so united in the person of Alexander the Great that he could inspire thousands to perform the most incredible feats, and he was honored as a demigod during his own lifetime.

The fascination for this great and unfathomable personality remains alive today, especially since his campaigns of conquest were not like the maraudings of Mongols, who left nothing but devastation and terror in their wake. He placed the stamp of Greek civilization on the entire Near and Middle East, not by simply forcing the Greek culture on conquered peoples, but by attempting to foster an ingenious synthesis of the Greek and Oriental cultures. The most visible expression of this attempt was the mass marriage in Susa (today in western Iran) of 10,000 Greek Macedonians with Persian women in the year 324 B.C.

A by-product of Alexander's success was the release of the Jewish people from Babylonian captivity; they gradually returned to Palestine, but many, referred to in the *Bible* as Samaritans, adopted some Greek customs, much to the consternation of those who had struggled to preserve their faith intact.

When Alexander died on June 13, 323 B.C., at the age of only 33, the gigantic empire which he had created fell into three large parts, which had been divided among his three main generals and which ultimately developed into a relatively consolidated system of states: the kingdoms of Egypt, Macedonia and Seleucid (the latter encompassing the bulk of the former Persian Empire). There were also minor states which developed, such as Pergamum, Rhodes and Syracuse. The thread of Hellenistic culture ran through all of these states. The century following Alexander's death witnessed constant border wars caused by the conflicting interests of the three major kingdoms. Also, a new rising power in the west, Rome, conquered all the Greek cities in Italy by 270 B.C. These conquests not only increased Rome's power, but enhanced the influence of Greek culture on Rome itself. Much of the Roman Empire retained Greek culture and usages, including the grisly custom of execution by crucifixion.

The creative genius of the old Greece had not entirely dried up after the death of Alexander. This was a time when the Greek heritage was preserved in great libraries in Alexandria (a Greek city and the capital of Egypt) and Pergamum (now in Turkey), where scholars carefully collected, classified, evaluated and edited classical texts and theories. Thinkers such as Euclid (in mathematics) Archimedes (in physics) and Theophrastus (in botany) absorbed what had previously been done in their fields. Their works later became the point of departure for the Renaissance in the 15th and 16th centuries A.D. Eratosthenes calculated rather accurately the circumference of the earth in 295 B.C. The astronomer, Aristarchus, even proposed the revolutionary theory that the earth revolves around the sun. His theory was incorrectly refuted by another thinker, Hipparchus, in the 2nd century B.C. Ptolemy's explanation of the astronomical constellation was accepted for many centuries before it was disproved by the discoveries of Kepler and Galileo.

The classical Greek language gradually gave way to dialects and became a learned language of scholarship. The more simplified Greek which emerged facilitated communication among many different peoples. Greek remained the international language of administration, diplomacy, business, teaching and theology. It is no surprise that simplified Greek was the language of the first written New Testament known to exist. Greek knowledge, customs and administrative talents migrated to Rome as Greeks were taken as slaves by the Romans, who used them according to their knowledge and talent, often as civil servants.

The Roman and Byzantine Era

The road from classical to modern Greece passed through the gates of the Roman and Byzantine Empires. Byzantium, along with later Turkish domination, shaped modern Greece far more than did the Greece of Homer, Pericles and Socrates. Rome had conquered the entire Greek world by 190 B.C., and in 394–395 A.D. the Roman Empire was divided into a western and an eastern half. The latter, initially Rome, but later ruled from Byzantium (later Constantinople and now Istanbul), was the offspring of the union of

Greece

classical Greece and Christianity. With Christian faith, Roman administration and Greek thought and language, Byzantium remained the preserver of classical philosophy and culture. This remains the Empire's greatest legacy to the west, providing the foundation for the later Renaissance (see Italy).

In a swift tide of events, the Romans expelled the Jews from Palestine (Israel) in 70 A.D.; they had already widely become dispersed throughout the Mediterranean area prior to that date, but became more so after the *diaspora* (dispersal). Many settled on Greek islands and a substantial number of these, together with Jews in Rome itself, were converted to Christianity in the first centuries A.D. in spite of oppression.

Until the 11th century A.D. the Byzantine Empire, of which Greece was only a small part, was the leading country of its time in terms of military power, area and population, differentiated administrative organization, education level of its people and splendid mosaics and buildings, the most impressive example of which is the Hagia Sofia Church (now a mosque) in Istanbul, Turkey. From Byzantium the Slavic Balkans and Russians were Christianized, not by means of fire and sword, but by means of an alphabet. The monks Cyril and Methodius developed the Cyrillic script, which was molded to display graphically the Slavic languages and which is now used by Russians and other Slavic peoples, such as the Bulgars and Serbs. At its peak, the Empire under Emperor Justinian (527–565) extended to all of Italy, parts of Spain, North Africa and the Middle East, including Syria and Palestine.

This colorful mixture of peoples was ruled by a theocratic (religiously oriented) monarchy. The state and Orthodox Church were united in the person of the Emperor, whose rule was absolute. Tsarist Russia later adopted this term, and the word "Tsar" was derived from the earlier Latin word for "emperor"—"Caesar." For a long time, Byzantium served as a rampart against the onslaught of Islam. However, rivalry with the Roman Catholic West, whose 4th Crusade resulted in the plundering of Constantinople by Catholic knights in the year 1204 brought about a change. For a while, Frankish knights and Italian merchants dominated Greece, and Slavs who were moving southward threatened the Empire. The constant battle against the Moslem pirates and later against the Turks weakened the Empire and reduced it in size to Greece and the capital city. In 1453 the remainder of the Empire fell into the hands of the Turkish Sultan Mohammed II, without the Christian west lifting a finger to help.

Islamic Rule: Church Preservation of Greek Culture

Greece lived under the sign of the Islamic half–moon for almost 400 years until it won its independence in 1829. But it was Byzantine tradition, embodied and preserved by the Orthodox (which literally means "worshipping correctly") Church, which provided the strength of survival and the sense of cultural independence. The Church kept Greek identity alive, operated underground schools, guarded Greek literature and culture, fought any attempt to diminish the use of the Greek language, and, with the approval of the Turkish masters, took full responsibility for such acts as baptism, marriage and burial, which until the early 1980s remained the exclusive privilege of the Church.

The Turks also granted the Orthodox Church tax exemption and the right to conduct court cases in civil matters. Thus, the Church not only was responsible for religious matters, but also for most legal and civil administration over Orthodox Christians. This was because of the Turkish masters' desire largely to avoid contact with "infidels." In contrast to some other Islamic peoples, the Turks placed no importance on the religious conversion of their subjects. Such intense Orthodox political involvement in, and even control over, political, social and religious affairs created in Greece a kind of close union between Church and nation which was almost unique in the world. This union only now is breaking down, as the Greeks are becoming increasingly secular, and as the Church's political and social influence is being strongly challenged. Nevertheless, much of the prestige which the Church still enjoys today stems from the Greeks' awareness that in the past the Orthodox Church kept the Hellenic flame burning

Alexander the Great's empire at its height

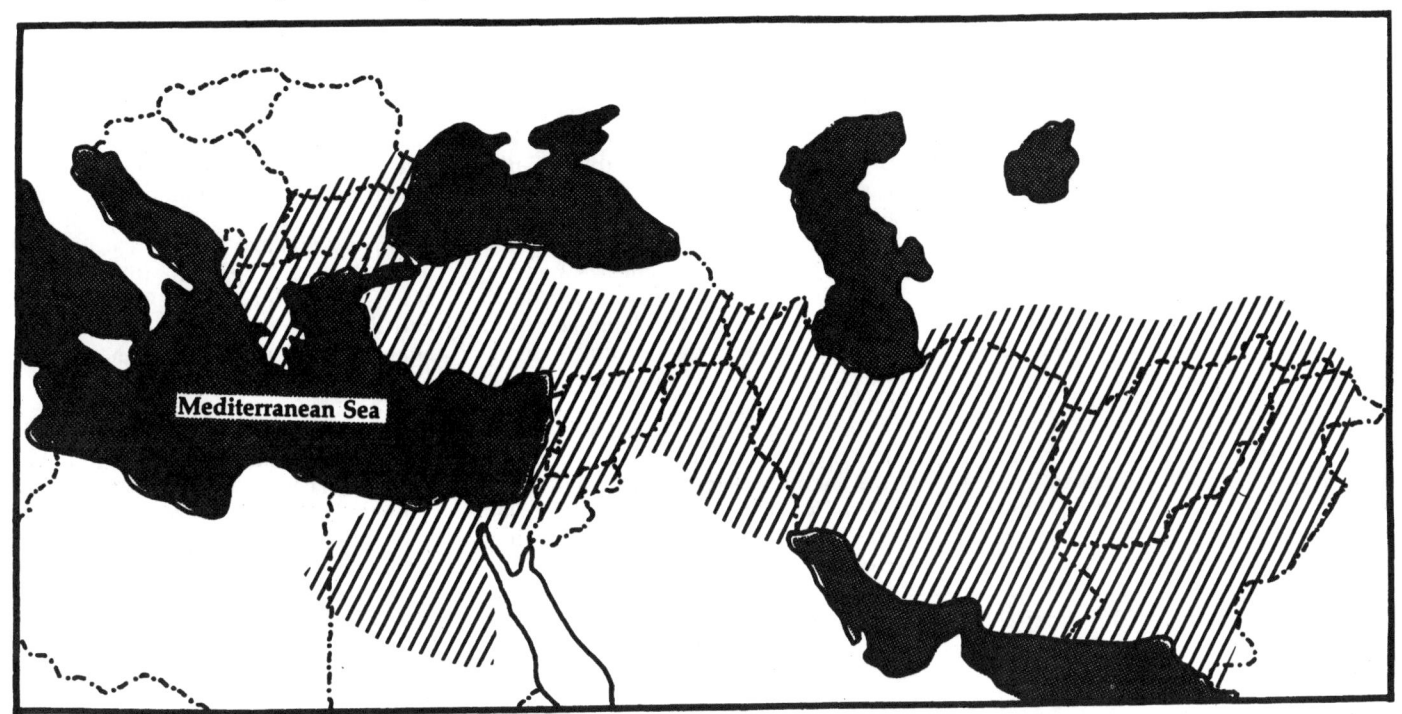

Greece

Greek history kept alive under Turkish occupation

during four centuries of Turkish domination and that, as the chief patron for Greek nationalism, the Church was at the forefront of the struggle for Greek independence in the 1920s.

Without a doubt, the Turks left their traces in Greece, even though the war of independence almost totally removed any visible traces of Turkish rule. Remains of medieval cities or of mosques can hardly be found in the country today. One does notice elements in the Greeks' everyday life, though: the warm hospitality and generosity, the food and the manner in which coffee is prepared and drunk, the men's habit of sitting around cafés in mid-day, while the women are at home working, the music, the distinctly Balkan folklore, the peasant dress and the reels of red tape and almost impenetrable bureaucracy all reflect heavy Mideastern influences.

On the other hand, the unpleasant memory of long Turkish subjugation, the bloody and emotional struggle with the Turks to regain Greek independence in the 1820s and the effort, which continues to this day, to extend Greece's borders to include all Greek-speaking peoples, have combined to create a deep-seated hatred which always plays a prominent role in Greek politics.

Revolt

Exasperated by Turkish maladministration and inspired by the ideals of liberty ignited in Europe by the French Revolution, the Greeks revolted against the Turks in 1821. This struggle immediately stimulated sympathy in all of Western Europe, where the love for Greek antiquity was great and where only a few years earlier the young British poet, Lord Byron, had written of Greece lamentingly in *Childe Harold's Pilgrimage*: "Trembling beneath the scourge of Turkish hand, From birth to death enslaved; in work, in deed, unmann'd." Byron even went to Greece to fight for its independence, and his death as a result of fever at Missolonghi on April 19, 1824, lent the struggle an almost divine consecration in the eyes of many Western Europeans.

As so often in 19th and 20th century Greek history, foreigners' admiration for Greek antiquity helped focus attention on *modern* Greece's problems. The Russian poet Pushkin found this fact disgusting. He wrote acidly: "This enthusiasm of all cultured nations for Greece is unforgivable childishness. The Jesuits have told us all that twaddle about Themistocles and Pericles, and so we imagine that the shabby nation of robbers and traders are their legitimate successors." Pushkin was certainly too hard on the Greeks, but it is true that foreign observers were all too apt to show disgust at Turkish atrocities in this brutal struggle and to overlook such behavior when the Greeks committed them. For instance, there was hardly a reaction to the Greeks' hanging, impaling and roasting alive 12,000 Turkish prisoners who had surrendered at Tripolitsa, but the outcry was deafening when the Turkish governor later systematically executed 30,000 Greek survivors at Chios and sold another 46,000 into slavery. The atrocities which were being committed by both sides did not hinder the French, British and Russians from joining the struggle against the Turks in 1827 and by 1829 Turkey had to sue for peace.

A Wobbly Monarchy

In an ambassadorial conference in London, the major powers and Greece finally defined the boundaries of the new Greek state which was much smaller than present-day Greece. The first border extended only as far north as the line extending from the Gulf of Volos on the east to the Gulf of Arta on the west. This excluded such islands as Crete and Corfu. At the same conference, Prince Otto of Bavaria

Greece

was named king of Greece and was placed on a royal throne which wobbled and shook almost continuously until it was finally abolished once and for all in 1974. The new king made one mistake after another. This foreigner refused to convert from Catholicism to Orthodox Christianity in a land where the Orthodox Church was inextricably linked with the very idea of the Greek nation. Then he tried to impose tightly centralized government upon a people which had just fought for their independence. The first capital of modern Greece was Nauplion, a city with a tradition reaching back to ancient times. For idealistic reasons, Athens, a dusty village of 5,000 inhabitants at the time, was declared capital with the constitution of 1834.

It is not surprising that the Greeks could never settle down under such rule and that the two unfortunate elements in subsequent Greek politics developed like malignant cysts in the very heart of Greek politics. First, an unbridgeable gap between monarchists and republicans was created. Second, the Greek military began meddling in Greek politics. Such activity was partly the consequence of, and partly the cause of, the political instability which afflicted the country for the next century and a half.

This chronic instability and absence of even a minimal consensus ultimately left the Greek political landscape littered with the wreckage of two dynasties. Absence of political stability ultimately resulted in five removals of kings from power (1862, 1917, 1922, 1941 and 1967), seven changes of constitution, three republics, seven military dictatorships, 15 revolutions and *coups* (of which ten succeeded), 155 governments (43 since 1945), 12 wars and a bitter five–year civil war. Thus, in certain ways, modern Greek politics until 1973 was like a pendulum swinging constantly between the extreme democracy of Athens and the iron military sentiments of Sparta.

About the only thing the Greeks could agree on was that their borders had to be extended until all Greeks were citizens of the Greek state (a goal referred to as the "Great Idea"). Thus, where domestic politics divided them, intense nationalism, which can bubble to the surface of any Greek almost instantly, united them. The settlement of 1832 had not created a natural and mutually acceptable frontier between Greece and Turkey, and every Greek government pursued an ingathering policy of some kind to rectify this. This meant constant friction and occasional war with Turkey, which greatly nourished the hatred which Greeks seem almost always to bear toward their neighbor to the east.

It took time, but the Greeks have, with the notable exception of Cyprus and small pockets of Greeks in southern Albania, accomplished their "Great Idea." In 1864 the British turned over to them the Ionian islands, including especially Corfu. In 1881 Greece received a third of Epirus and the bulk of Thessaly, but when it conducted naval actions against the Turks in Crete and the rest of Thessaly a few years later, the Turks declared war on Greece in 1897. They routed the Greek army and even threatened to take Athens—a humiliating defeat for Greece.

The emergence before World War I of one of Greece's greatest 20th century political leaders, Eleutherios Venizelos, brought Greece many benefits. He introduced important reforms to establish a modern state. An admirer of Western European democracy, he created the foundations of a state of law in Greece, expanded the school system, initiated a land reform program, legalized trade unions and created agricultural cooperatives. He was also able to utilize his international prestige and diplomatic skill to win for his country a handsome chunk of the spoils of distribution to the Balkan nations resulting from the Balkan Wars against Turkey in 1912 and 1913. Greece received a part of Macedonia, the island of Crete and the Aegean Islands. These additions enlarged the Greek land area by 75% and its population by 70%.

**World War I and
Another Greek–Turkish Round**

When World War I broke out, King Constantine I tried to remain neutral, but British and French pressure, which included the landing of French troops on Greek soil, caused the King to abdicate. Prime Minister Venizelos was able to have his country declare war on Germany and its allies. Its reward from its new allies was western Thrace, which it received in 1918 and a British promise of a part of Turkey around Smyrna (now Izmir).

On May 15, 1919, British ships transported Greek troops to Smyrna in order to collect its booty, but this adventure ended in a catastrophe. American President Woodrow Wilson opposed any carving up of Turkey in spite of its support of Germany in the war. Further, the greatest political leader in Turkish history, General Kemal Atatürk, who created the modern Turkish state, revived his exhausted and humiliated countrymen, who had been decimated during the war, and organized a heroic defense of Smyrna.

After the British stopped supporting the Greek expeditionary force, the Turks delivered a devastating and fatal blow to the Greeks. In bloody revenge, the Turkish sword swung freely, and practically the entire Greek population was either killed or driven out of the area around the coast of Asia Minor where Greeks had lived for 3,000 years. The French and British declared themselves to be neutral in the face of this massacre and refused to take Greek refugees on board their ships although it had been the British who had made promises to the Greeks which had unleashed this tragic adventure in the first place. In the end, 600,000 Greeks perished, and almost a million and a half were forced out of Turkey. In return, Turkey agreed to the repatriation of about 400,000 Moslems living in Greece.

Continued Political Conflict

The one positive thing which this unfortunate conflict did produce was clearly defined borders between Greeks and Turks (except in Cyprus), with only negligible minorities on the wrong side of the lines. But the disaster sent Greek politics into a tail spin again. Venizelos and the King were forced into exile. The first Greek Republic was established in 1923, followed by military *coups* in 1925, 1926, 1933 and 1935, and a restoration of the monarchy in 1935, but one in which real power was held by General Joannes Metaxas. The latter suppressed most political groups and led a right–wing dictatorship until he was subsequently removed from power by the German conquerors in 1941.

World War II

Greece entered World War II on the side of Britain and France. On October 28, 1940, the Greek government said *ochi* ("no") to a host of unacceptable demands made by the impetuous Italian dictator, Benito Mussolini, who boasted of a "promenade to Athens." Italian troops entered Greece from Albania. Although the British hurriedly sent a limited number of troops to Greece from North Africa, the Greeks themselves were able to drive Mussolini's poor–quality forces back into Albania, where they could have destroyed the entire Italian army if Metaxas had not feared German retaliation.

Since Hitler had already decided that Greece, the "Achilles heel of Europe" should not be allowed to fall into enemy hands it mattered little what the Greek general feared. Hitler sent his storm troopers into Greece; their numerical superiority broke the Greek resistance on April 6, 1941. The last British bastion in Greece was taken within two months, the island of Crete, after the attackers launched the largest airborne operation against the island that the world had ever seen. The Germans then divided Greece into occupation zones, awarding the lion's share to the defeated Italy, which perhaps

Greece

could at least tend to a conquered country.

The suffering and humiliation of occupation created a resistance movement in Greece. Metaxas had destroyed all political parties and thereby had created a political vacuum. Therefore, the Greek communists, who had built up an underground apparatus, were able to form an effective resistance organization, the *Greek Liberation Front (EAM)*, which had a fighting force, the *Greek People's Liberation Army (ELAS)*. Not until 1943 was an anti–communist competitor created, the *Greek Republic Liberation League (EDES)*.

The British supported both partisan groups in order to disrupt the Germans' supply links with their troops in North Africa. When the Italian fascist regime collapsed in 1943, its occupation forces left Greece after selling a large part of their weapons to the Greek partisans. The Germans responded to the resistance activity in Greece by shooting hostages and devastating entire villages. These measures merely drove countless young peasants into the arms of the communists.

Civil War

Even during its struggle against the Germans, *ELAS* began preparing a civil war against its Greek opponents. At first, the Soviet leader, Stalin, honored the agreement he made with British Prime Minister Churchill at the Tehran conference from November 28 to December 1, 1943, to divide the Balkans into spheres of influence with Greece falling into the British sphere. However, from March 1944 on, the Soviets began supporting their Greek comrades. Therefore, when the Germans pulled out of Greece in October, the communists were in a very good position. They controlled about 90% of the country when the exile government arrived at Athens from Egypt accompanied by about 15,000 British troops. Fearing defeat in a democratic election, *ELAS* resisted by force, and it took a full month of bitter house–to–house combat for the British and the Greek government troops to drive the communists out of Athens. Fighting again broke out in December 1944, but the communists suffered such losses they decided to lay down their arms temporarily.

The first elections, which were held on March 31, 1946, under the supervision of 1,200 American, British and French troops, produced a resounding victory for the conservative royalists. Also, in a referendum held on September 1, 1946 to determine the future form of government, 68% of those voting supported the restoration of the monarchy. This referendum and the stern anti–communist measures of the right–wing extremist, Colonel George Grivas, made a reconciliation with the communists impossible. They also made it difficult for non–communist liberals and republicans to give the new regime their enthusiastic support.

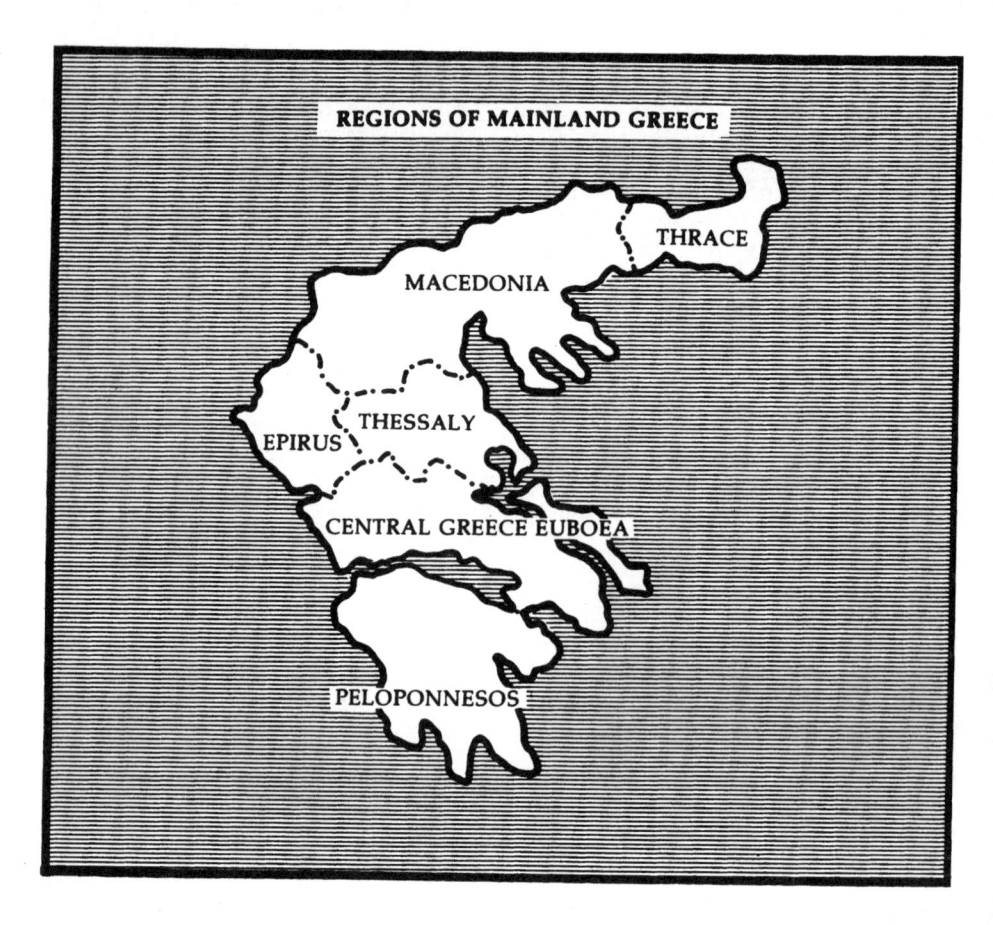

With the aid of the Soviet Union, Yugoslavia and Bulgaria, the Greek communists resumed their armed struggle, which lasted three more years. Key factors in the ultimate non–communist victory were American economic and military assistance to Greece (as a consequence of the "Truman Doctrine," which promised aid against communist threats to Greece and Turkey) and Yugoslavia's break with the Soviet Union in 1948. After the latter event, the Yugoslav leader, Marshal Tito, closed the Yugoslav–Greek border, thereby preventing needed supplies from being shipped to the Greek communist rebels.

In 1949 the communists finally gave up the struggle, which had cost them about 80,000 casualties and the government forces about 50,000. This tragic conflict polarized Greek politics for years, sapped Greece's economic resources and caused considerable destruction in the country. The civil war complicated the problem of reconstruction, despite generous infusions of Marshall Plan assistance from the U.S. Thus, while World War I lasted in reality ten—not four—years in Greece, World War II had also, in effect, lasted a decade in the battered country. The only tangible benefit from the settlement after the second conflict was that Greece was awarded the Dodecanese Islands in 1947.

Restoration and Recovery; the Status of Cyprus

The government turned to the task of restoring and improving the country's economy. It led Greece into NATO in February 1952 and into a Balkan Pact in August 1954, which was supposed to forge a military link among Greece, Turkey and Yugoslavia. This pact has, for all practical purposes, remained a dead letter because of Greece's chronic tensions with Turkey. Such tensions were again rekindled in 1954 as a result of events on the island of Cyprus, which had been a British base since 1878 and a Crown Colony since 1925, and 80% of whose residents are Greek. Cyprus had long aroused the emotions of Greek nationalists and the goal (called *Enosis*) of bringing the island's residents under Greek authority had long existed. *Enosis* was supported on the island by the Orthodox Church and by a large number of educated Greeks.

When some of them launched an indiscriminate terrorist campaign in 1954 in order to try to stimulate international sympathy for their cause, the Turkish minority on the island fought back. Although

Greece

Cyprus was ultimately granted independence, the problems of how the two groups should administer the island and of what kind of relations Cyprus should maintain with Greece and Turkey has been and is a continuing, chronic irritant in the relations between the two NATO allies.

POSTWAR POLITICS

During the postwar period, Greece was a parliamentary democracy; King Paul succeeded his brother, King George II, in 1947. But there also was a strong military involvement in politics. Present party alignments emerged. There was almost continuous political instability after the communists were defeated, and cabinets sometimes lasted only a few months.

From 1954 to 1963 the key figure in Greek politics was Constantine Caramanlis, who later became president and who tried to steer Greece more closely toward Western Europe by establishing economic links with the EC. Almost two decades later, as prime minister and president, he finished his work by overseeing Greece's entry into the EC as a full member in 1981. He and many of his countrymen hoped that entry into the EC would help secure democracy in Greece.

The years from 1963 to 1965 were characterized by the sweeping social reform efforts of Georgios Papandreou and by a situation in which neither the supporters of the monarch nor of parliamentary democracy could prevail. The political temperature in Athens rose extremely quickly in 1965. Young King Constantine II, who had ascended to the throne at the age of 23 when King Paul died in 1964, almost immediately locked horns with Papandreou over a number of constitutional issues, especially that involving control of the army. The King accused the prime minister of trying to infiltrate the military by means of a left–wing organization called *Aspida*, headed by Papandreou's son, Andreas (who became prime minister in 1981 and again in 1993). Papandreou saw the matter differently—he wanted to fire his defense minister because the latter balked at dismissing right–wing plotters within the army. In any case, King Constantine dismissed Papandreou in mid–1965, an act which set off two more confusing years of stop–gap governments, trials, riots, strikes and political polarization, which cleared the way for the military to act.

On the eve of May 1967 parliamentary elections, in which Papandreou's *Center Union Party* was favored to win, perhaps with the electoral help of communist groups, a group of military officers seized power, pointing to the alleged communist danger and claiming to have the support of the King. It turned out that the King had not even been informed about the plan. When they began arresting and exiling parliamentary leaders, including both Papandreou, King Constantine attempted a clumsy *coup* of his own, which failed miserably and which forced *him* to flee the country. Not until 1993 did a stable and democratic Greek republic inform Constantine, who had just announced his hopes of reclaiming the throne some day, that he could leave his London exile and return to Greece as a private citizen any time he wanted.

There are some Greeks (including the present prime minister) who are absolutely convinced that the U.S., through its CIA, had a hand in this military *coup*, even though it is admitted that there is no absolute proof, and even though President Lyndon Johnson publicly denounced the *coup*. One often points to a so–called "Prometheus Plan" worked out by the King and the army, for a military *coup* in the event that the elections produced a government with communist participation. It is alleged that this plan was approved by NATO. Further, Andreas Papandreou frequently reminded his listeners that during the Nixon administration, Vice President Spiro Agnew, himself of Greek descent, traveled to Greece, thereby allegedly giving the dictatorship "full support."

It is, of course, true that the U.S. maintained its military presence in Greece and made arms sales to the new military rulers. Whether the rumors of U.S. complicity or foreknowledge of the *coup* are true or not, these allegations did help to create in Greece a strong anti–American feeling, which remains strong and which the present leader chooses successfully to exploit to the fullest.

Military Dictatorship

The seven–year military dictatorship, first under the leadership of Georgios Papadoupoulos and, after November 1973, under the chief of the secret service, Colonel Demetrios Ioannides, is remembered as a long and brutal period. The "colonels" converted Greece into a military camp in which political opponents were persecuted by all the means of state terror.

October 1944: Prime Minister Georgios Papandreou on the Acropolis as Greek women carry the national flag to be raised over liberated Athens

Greece

The regime put itself on the wrack when in 1974 Ioannides decided to overthrow the government of Cyprus' mercurial Archbishop Makarios and to try to install a government on the island subject to command from Athens. This heavy-handed action merely provoked the Turks to invade Cyprus and ultimately to partition the island. Since the Turks used American weapons in this invasion (referred to as *Attila*), many Greeks place partial responsibility on the Americans' shoulders. This is a deliberate distortion, however, since the Turks were using weapons received as a member of NATO and there was no authorization by the U.S. to use them for an invasion of Cyprus. The use of such weaponry violated American law, and even when the U.S. thereafter cut off all arms sales to Turkey for several years, this event, which was clearly out of American control, created even more resentment in Greece against the U.S. In effect, the Americans were criticized both because they allegedly *supported* the "colonels" and because they allegedly *did not!*

Fortunately the crisis created a situation which the "colonels" could not handle. Greece had been brought to the brink of war with Turkey, so important senior officers withdrew their support from the discredited Ioannides and called for Constantine Caramanlis to return from his Paris exile and to reassume the reins of power as the leader of a government of national unity. Thus, as in Portugal the same year, a foreign policy crisis cleared the way for the establishment of a democratic political order.

After years of intense political instability and harsh military rule, Greeks adjusted very well to democracy after 1974. When Andreas Papandreou called for *allaghi* ("change") in the 1981 parliamentary election, a near majority of his countrymen responded to his call. Greeks knew well that for the first time in decades that change meant a transfer of power from one democratic party to another, not a change of regime involving the destruction of democratic rule.

Despite many political and economic problems, Greece is experiencing unprecedented stability. There is good reason to believe that the traditional Greek cycle of volatile democracy-military dictatorship, often punctuated by *coups*, has come to an end. Now the two largest parties, which received 86% of the votes in 1993, firmly accept the parliamentary system. Also, the soldiers have returned to their barracks once and for all, although all Greek politicians must continue to calculate the military's possible response to any decision. Despite the invariably inflated election rhetoric, the Greek body politic is no longer divided into hostile, enemy camps.

In some Western European countries, monarchs symbolize national unity, but in Greece they almost always tended to divide, not to unite the nation. Therefore, 69% of those who went to the polls voted in a referendum held on December 8, 1974, to abolish the monarchy and to establish a republic.

In 1981 the Greek leadership nervously allowed Constantine II to return briefly to Athens to attend the funeral of his mother, ex-Queen Frederika, at the Tatoi Palace on the outskirts of Athens. They feared that his presence in Greece, after 14 years of absence (first in Rome, now in London, where he is in the sales and public relations business) might destabilize the new regime. They permitted him to land at a military airbase near the palace and remain in Greece a few hours to attend. The leaders' risk paid off because only two thousand chanting admirers appeared to greet the king.

It became clear that what little support the monarchy had enjoyed earlier had largely evaporated. This realization bolstered the confidence and long-term stability of the republic. When the king and his family unexpectedly returned for a two-week holiday in August 1993, scuffles broke out between royalists and leftist protesters, prompting the government publicly to disapprove of the visit. An irritated President Caramanlis noted that "such affairs do not threaten democracy or our system of government but hold the country up to ridicule." In 1994 parliament stripped the king of his citizenship and remaining property in Greece.

PRESENT GOVERNMENT STRUCTURE

On June 7, 1974 a new constitution went into effect which described Greece as a "presidential parliamentary republic." Considering the Greeks' experiences during seven years of military dictatorship, it is not surprising that the new constitution contains extensive guarantees of individual rights and civil liberties. The head of state is a president, who is elected for a five-year term by the parliament, which meets for this purpose as an electoral college. This form of indirect election means that no president can claim to have a direct mandate from the people and thereby challenge the political direction taken by the majority in parliament. The presidential powers are largely ceremonial, and most of his acts must be countersigned by a responsible minister, that is, by the government.

The parliament voted in 1986 to reduce the president's powers even further. He can no longer appoint the prime minister. He can dissolve parliament only if two governments fall in rapid succession. He can no longer call a referendum on what he regards as a major issue, address the people directly when his opinions differ from those of the government, or proclaim a state of siege.

The president's powers and actual influence in Greek politics depend upon the respect which he enjoys in the eyes of the citizens or of the leading politicians. The president until 1985 was Constantine Caramanlis, one of the most highly respected leaders in Greece and widely regarded as one of the major architects and protectors of the democratic regime. His views on important issues could not be overlooked by any prime minister. He was succeeded by Christos Sartzetakis, a respected supreme court justice who became famous for cracking the notorious Lambrakis murder case in 1963 and who was immortalized as the incorruptible judge in the movie "Z", which portrayed Greek politics during the last years of the monarchy. In 1990 Caramanlis was again elected to a five-year term. He was succeeded in 1995 by Constantinos Stephanopoulos, who had sought exile in Paris during the military dictatorship and who had later broken away from Caramanlis' *New Democracy* party. A lawyer known for his modesty and honesty, he has never been implicated in a scandal.

The most powerful political office in Greece is that of the prime minister, who must be able to find a majority for his policies in the 300-seat unicameral parliament. At present, all Greek citizens 18 years or older can vote. The members of Parliament are elected by a modified form of proportional representation which favors the larger parties. This system is designed to increase the chances that one party will have a parliamentary majority even when none wins a majority of the votes cast. For instance, in the 1993 elections, the *Panhellenic Socialist Movement* (PASOK) received 46.9% of the votes, but it won an absolute majority of the seats. In the 14 general elections following 1951, the government has changed the electoral system nine times within six months of the polling in order to maximize its seats. In 1989 the system was brought closer to a strict proportional representation system, which improves the chances of small parties and thereby makes it more difficult to form a majority. Although the *New Democracy* party's Constantine Mitsotakis had approved of this change, he denounced it as unfair after the 1989 election, in which he fell seven seats short of a majority.

Since instability had long been a curse in Greek politics, it is logical that the framers of the present constitution would seek ways to insure stability within a

Greece

democratic framework. Parliament is elected for four years, but the prime minister can arrange for elections to be held earlier in the event he cannot maintain a parliamentary majority.

A deputy's influence depends largely on whether his particular party permits him to disregard the party's recommendations or policy when votes are taken. For instance, under Andreas Papandreou *PASOK* forbade its deputies to vote against the party leadership and would certainly refuse a maverick deputy the chance to seek reelection under the *PASOK* label. A traditional source of influence for the deputy is *rousfeti* ("influence peddling"), by which he uses the bureaucracy to get special favors, including jobs, for his constituents. This is a way for him to win and to maintain votes, but the massive migration from rural areas into the cities has reduced its effectiveness. In the cities people are no longer so inclined to turn to their local political bosses and deputies for help or favors.

The traditional need for some practice like *rousfeti* reflects the difficulty which Greek citizens have had in attracting the attention of an overgrown and often lethargic, indifferent or corrupt bureaucracy in order to find solutions for individual or collective problems. At the same time, *rousfeti* has helped to bloat or paralyze the bureaucracy because jobs are often filled or created for friends or constituents of influential politicians. Appointments and subsequent promotions are too often based more upon friendship and connections that upon merit. Mitsotakis vowed to end *rousfeti*, a move that was resented by many *New Democrats*, who wanted to place their supporters into positions after eight years in opposition.

In Greek political ideology, it is better to have a friend or relative hired or advanced rather than having a merit system. Added to the problem are job security for even the most incompetent workers, exaggerated respect for tradition which leaves little room for new ideas, lack of management skills and excessive fear of being blamed for mistakes (if you don't do *anything*, you can't be blamed for doing *something!*). As many as a dozen signatures were required for even simple transactions. A bureaucrat's typical response is understandably *avrio, avrio* ("tomorrow, tomorrow").

The government tried during the 1980s to do something about these problems within the bureaucracy. Papandreou pledged to end "partisanship and corruption in public administration," and he launched a program of decentralization to transfer some power from bureaucrats in Athens to local councils. His administration began by firing about 300 senior civil servants merely because they had been appointed during earlier administrations. This was too much shock treatment too early, and also many competent officials were sacked in this indiscriminate purge. He appointed hundreds of his own party people, many of whom were conscientious and well-educated, but inexperienced. By distributing so many jobs to *PASOK* supporters, he merely played the old game of *rousfeti* again. Upon assuming office in 1996 Prime Minister Simitis vowed to restrict patronage and to reduce the public-sector payroll by hiring only one qualified civil servant for every three who retire. He faces stiff resistance from the 40% of *PASOK* members who are public-sector employees and who are used to securing jobs for their family and friends.

THE POLITICAL SCENE

One of the most encouraging developments in Greek politics since 1974 is that the military no longer threatens to intervene in politics to the extent that it once did. Although soldiers were apparently still hatching plots in 1975, they concentrate now on purely military duties. Nevertheless, no Greek politician, especially no leftist prime minister, would dare overlook the possibility that the officers might return to their earlier self-appointed political role of "straightening up the mess" of democratic politics.

In order to help pacify the military, Papandreou increased their housing allowances and pay sharply. Also, his stridently nationalistic rhetoric was well received in the mess halls. As irritating and exaggerated as his nationalism may have been to foreigners, it did serve an important domestic political purpose of reconciling, if not totally integrating, ultra-conservative and military circles with the democratic regime.

Greece's two main parties are, in traditional Greek style, personalized in that they are built around, and largely dominated by, respected figures. They are run from the top. Central headquarters selects electoral candidates and controls patronage. In Greece, politics always revolves more around *persons* than *policies*. This characteristic of both major parties, which were created in 1974, produces both weaknesses and strengths. The most obvious disadvantage is that any party which is so dependent on one person could decline or disappear quickly if the leader were no longer there. One bullet could immediately change the party landscape. The advantage is that because of the personalities

Evzone **(a Greek regiment) presidential guard in the traditional white foustanela**
Courtesy: Jon Markham Morrow

457

Greece

President Constantinos Stephanopoulos

and political skill of Papandreou and Caramanlis, both were able to consolidate modern Greek democracy. They created parties of the right and left which are committed to the democratic regime.

PASOK

PASOK grew extremely rapidly since its founding in 1974. It climbed from 14% of the vote in 1974 to 25% in 1977 and to 48% in 1981, to become the first non–conservative government since 1974. In 1985 *PASOK* slipped slightly to 46% of the vote and 161 seats, but it fell badly in 1989 and 1990 to 39% of the votes and 125 seats, thereby losing its majority. In 1993 it bounced back, capturing 46.9% of the votes and a comfortable 171–seat majority in parliament. *PASOK's* rise to power would have been unthinkable without the inspiration and leadership of one man, Andreas Papandreou.

Young Andreas got a Ph.D. in economics from Harvard University and became an American citizen in 1944. After serving in the U.S. Navy, he taught economics at such American universities as Minnesota (where he met and married his first wife, Margarete), Northwestern and Berkeley.

When in 1963 his father asked him and all other Greeks living abroad who could contribute to the nation's development to return to Greece, Andreas agreed. When the "colonels" seized power in 1967, he and his father were imprisoned. Andreas was kept in solitary confinement for eight months before he was released, thanks in large part to the efforts of his American wife and the U.S. Embassy. He again went into exile, first to Sweden and then to Canada, before returning in 1974.

Papandreou was a brilliant speaker with a knack for accurately reading the pulse of his audience. However, his eloquence often lapsed into demagoguery. He is very intolerant of criticism or diverging views. He ran *PASOK* and the Greek government with an iron hand.

PASOK's voter appeal was not limited to one class or group. Young voters were especially attracted to *PASOK*. It established a network of local organizations all over Greece, had a populist strain and it was very nationalistic, directing its venom toward the U.S., Turkey, NATO and the EU. Nationalist appeals always brought in the votes in Greek elections and they combined with the populist appeals to help *PASOK* win votes from a wide spectrum of groups, including farmers, workers, employees and mid–level civil servants.

At first *PASOK* presented itself as a somewhat Marxist movement for national and social liberation, and even shortly before the 1981 election Papandreou announced that "we plan to change the system, not to embellish it." Experience indicates that too much Marxism is bad politics in most democratic countries. The party quickly backed away from it and now merely advocates using certain aspects of Marxist thought "in a creative way."

It saw itself as a left wing party, as European socialist and social democratic parties go. For years it refused to join the Socialist International because Papandreou claimed that it was dominated by the social democratic parties in northern Europe, especially the German SPD, which he had branded as the European representative of "monopoly capitalism." Nevertheless, *PASOK* is extremely flexible (some say "opportunist") and can present itself in almost any democratic way, depending on the political climate and realities of the time.

As a governing party, it faced the typical problems of a radical party which finds itself in power and responsible for confronting concrete problems. The party was aware that the change for which many Greeks voted in 1981 was not socialism, but something less, and the party acted accordingly. This caused tension within the party.

Before the 1989 elections, Papandreou's popularity plummeted because of a serious financial scandal and his public love affair with Dimitra Liana, a divorced airline stewardess half his age. She accompanied him to London to be by his side during his openheart surgery. She began serving as his official consort. Some feared that she influenced his political decisions. Many Greeks were shocked by pictures of her in the nude which were published in Greek newspapers.

There is, of course, a long history of such extramarital relationships in Greek public life. His own father lived with an the actress "Kiveli" for 19 years without being criticized for it, and even Papandreou's *New Democratic* opponent, Mitsotakis, was known to have a mistress in Salonika. Nevertheless, to minimize electoral damage in socially conservative Greece, Papandreou divorced his wife a few days before the election, although for legal technical reasons he was unable to marry Liana before June 18. But he had already sacrificed the respect of many citizens. Many Greeks cringed in 1993 when he named Liana as his chief of staff, a powerful post managing his work schedule as prime minister and controlling access to him.

PASOK regained a majority in the 1993 elections, and the frail Papandreou again became prime minister. He suffered from heart, lung and kidney problems and was able to work only a few hours a day. He

Former Prime Minister Andreas Papandreou

tried to demonstrate that he was firmly in charge by refusing to appoint a deputy prime minister and pushing potential rivals aside. By January 1996, after he had spent 44 days in the hospital on life–support machines, *PASOK* had to act. Polls in the fall had shown that 82.3% of Greek respondents were dissatisfied with the ailing Papandreou, and 87.7% wanted him to retire from politics.

The situation was particularly urgent because it seemed to many that he was determined to make his unpopular wife Dimitra ("Mimi") his successor. They were irritated by the way she interfered in government, screened access to the prime minister, and summoned ministers for meetings. She deepened the divisions within the party and strengthened fears

Greece

that it would be punished severely at the next elections. Her efforts to change her image by having breast–reduction surgery, wearing more dignified clothing, and appearing to be the pious Orthodox wife by visiting churches were foiled by the front–page publication in 1995 of yet another photo of her bathing topless. She did not see a problem: "Should I not enter politics because I once bathed naked?" Her husband's death spelled the end of any serious political ambitions on her part. In 1999 she was charged with fraud and embezzlement of public funds, having evaded taxes on the purchase of land where she and her husband had built a multi–million dollar house.

In January 1996 Papandreou was replaced as prime minister by Costas Simitis, a mild–mannered technocrat and reformer, who had been challenging Papandreou for months. He had studied law in Germany and economics in Britain. Lacking his predecessor's charisma, he is nevertheless one of Greece's most popular politicians. Within days of Papandreou's death in June 1996 Simitis quickly consolidated his power, with the crucial backing of Andreas's son, George Papandreou, by narrowly winning the leadership of the party and of the 200–member central committee, PASOK's main decision–making body. In September 1996 he called an early general election and guided his party to victory, winning 41.5% of the votes and 162 seats in the 300–seat assembly. Most of Andreas Papandreou's staunch supporters lost their seats, leaving Simitis's economic reform faction with about 120 of the 162 seats.

Simitis, whom Papandreou had fired as finance minister in the mid–1980s, has remade PASOK by introducing economic austerity measures, beginning to privatize state industries, and limiting patronage. All are designed to enhance the competitiveness of the Greek economy, reduce inflation and the massive public debt, and prepare the country's entry into the European single currency in 2001. He broke with PASOK's populist tradition of pandering to interest groups, including the powerful farmers, who make up a fifth of Greece's workers. He has changed PASOK so much that it and the opposition New Democracy agree on most major issues, including friendly relations with the United States and continued U.S. military presence in Greece. Rapport with America was enhanced by the appointment in 1999 of the soft–edged George Papandreou as foreign minister. Born in the U.S. by his American mother and speaking perfect American English, he grew up in the U.S., Canada and Sweden and studied at Amherst, Harvard and the London School of Economics.

Communists

One of PASOK's firmest political principles (dictated in part by political pragmatism) was to refuse to establish any direct links with Greek Communists. They are divided into two main parties. The Greek Communist Party (KKE) is a rigid Marxist–Leninist party. It greeted the August 1991 coup against democracy in the USSR as a "welcome return to order." It is the only party in Greece today which had existed before 1974. The KKE has a well–organized and highly disciplined cadre and base. It controls much real estate around Athens, including a shipping company. Its domestic and foreign policy is predictable: state control over the economy and withdrawal from NATO and the EU.

In the 1989 elections, the KKE forged an "Alliance of the Left and Progress" with the Greek Communist Party of the Interior (KKES) and other small groups. KKES is so named because its leaders had remained in Greece after the civil war instead of fleeing to Eastern Europe. It advocates a softer, Euro–communist line, more in tune with the Greek democratic political order. Together they won 13% of the votes and 29 seats, most of which going to the KKE.

Since neither PASOK nor New Democracy won a parliamentary majority, the Communists suddenly found themselves in a situation where they were courted by both large parties and could determine the composition of the Greek government. As the key to power, they attained a measure of influence they had not had since the civil war had ended in 1949 and since they had been legalized in 1974.

The Communists' electoral success brought mixed blessings. On the one hand, disagreements over cooperating with the bourgeois parties fractured the unity and prompted a wave of expulsions

Prime Minister Costas Simitis

and resignations. Their new role in government eroded their popularity, causing them to lose a sixth of their votes and a quarter of their seats in 1989. In 1990 their 10.3% of the votes and 21 seats no longer enabled them to play the role of power brokers. In 1991 Maria Damanaki was chosen as the new chairperson. She had been a daring student leader during the disturbances which helped bring down the military dictatorship in 1974.

The Communists' success gave them political legitimacy and helped all Greeks to bury the hatchet which had been bloodied during the civil war. The term "civil war" officially replaced the previous term for the struggle: "bandits' war." The 40th anniversary of the last battle in the mountains of Epirus was redesignated a celebration of "national reconciliation." Some 16 million files which the security police had kept on politically suspicious persons were burned, and full pension rights and social benefits were extended to anybody who had fought on the losing side. Communist unity did not last until the 1996 elections. The KKE got 5.6% of the votes and 11 seats. The Left Coalition captured 5.1%, which was above the 3% needed to win its 10 seats. Finally, a new party on the left, Democratic Renewal, won 4.4% of the votes and 9 seats.

The New Democracy Party

New Democracy, sprang up quickly around Constantine Caramanlis. He later became a cabinet member before the colonels overthrew the government in 1967. He was jailed briefly and later escaped to exile abroad. Returning to Greece in 1974 he served as minister of economic coordination and foreign affairs until 1981.

It is clearly the more conservative of the two major parties, but it is a party of the center and the reformed right, which is committed to democracy and social reform. It defines itself as a modern, pluralistic party. It is liberal in the European sense in that it favors a limitation of the state's role in the society and economy. It advocates a free–market economy, but one which does not overlook the economic needs of any groups, including those citizens with lower incomes. New Democracy's foreign policy is strongly oriented toward the West, and it was Caramanlis who guided Greece into the EU and back into the NATO command structure.

New Democracy ruled Greece from 1974 to 1981 and again from 1990–93. Although it introduced many needed changes, it became tinged with accusations of corruption and favoritism, whose roots are deeply embedded in Greek politics and society.

PASOK and Papandreou benefitted

Greece

from the unpopularity of *New Democracy's* economic austerity policies by staging a dramatic comeback in the 1993 elections. With 78% of the eligible voters turning out, *New Democracy* fell to 39.3% of the votes and 110 seats. It was seriously hurt by a breakaway group called *Popular Spring,* led by former conservative foreign minister, Antonis Samaras. It won almost 5% of the votes and 10 seats, but it fell to only 2.9% and no seats in 1996. The *New Democracy* party came close to election victory in 1996, capturing 38.1% of the votes and 108 seats. In 1997 it picked a new leader, Costas Caramanlis, nephew of *New Democracy's* founder and the youngest man ever to lead a big Greek party. In 1999 Stefanos Manos, a former finance minister who had been expelled from *New Democracy,* founded the *Liberals,* which campaigns against the failings of old–style Greek politics: patronage, inefficient state services, and the wasteful way EU grants are spent.

Foreign Relations and Defense Policy

Any government in Athens formulating Greece's foreign policy finds a complicated web of problems which confound most people who examine it. The ingredients include U.S. military bases in Greece, Greek membership in NATO *along with* Turkey, the traditional enemy to the east which is competing for Cyprus, air–traffic lanes, territorial waters and offshore oil and mineral rights. None of these problems can be sorted out and dealt with separately, and each problem with Turkey is overladen with heated emotion, the roots of which run more deeply than anyone can imagine.

Greece occupies a very important strategic location in the Mediterranean, which is a major lifeline for Western Europe. Much of Europe's oil moves through the Mediterranean, and this southern flank of NATO is a vital staging area for any possible Western European or American military operation in the Middle East. In order to bolster NATO muscle in this region, the U.S. had an airbase at Heraklion, Crete, where super–sensitive monitoring and communications facilities were located covering the eastern Mediterranean, North Africa, the Middle East and the former Soviet Union. The U.S. government announced in 1993 that this base would be closed, leaving only a naval air facility in Suda Bay, Crete, with an airfield nearby. The U.S. Sixth Fleet is trained and equipped to operate without bases in Greece in case their use would be denied.

Negotiations with Washington on a defense cooperation agreement included U.S. bases in Greece. With scarcely a noise of domestic opposition, the talks ratified Washington's prior unilateral decision to relinquish its two bases on the Greek mainland, reduce its troop presence, and retain only two bases in Crete, whose leases were extended to eight years. This noticeably diminished anti–American rhetoric and terrorism in Greece.

Greece still buys most of its weapons from the U.S., as well as from Germany, France and Britain. The Greek government insists that the ratio of American arms sales to Greece and Turkey should not be lower than 7:10. The Greek and Turkish air and naval forces are roughly equal in numbers. However, with 542,000 troops, the Turkish army outnumbers and outguns the Greek forces. The term of service for conscripts is 19–21 months, depending on the branch. Of 168,300 total troops, 119,200 are conscripts.

Among NATO countries, Greece spends the highest percentage of its GDP for defense: 4.6% in 1996, roughly twice the percentage spent by other EU nations. In 1997 Greece launched a $16 billion weapons modernization program, due for completion in 2007. It includes purchase of an AWACS early warning aircraft, 60 new warplanes and other aircraft, including training and transport planes and helicopters, new tanks, anti–aircraft systems, and new warships, including submarines and nine surface ships. It upgraded its anti–aircraft capability by procuring six long–range American–made Patriot missile systems, 21 short–range Russian–made Tor missiles for the army, and 11 French–built Crotale missiles for the air force and navy. This ambitious acquisition program was justified, in the prime minister's words, to safeguard Greece's "interests from Turkish belligerence."

It is unlikely that Greece will again leave the NATO command structure after having reentered it in 1980. It had left that command structure in protest against the Turkish invasion of Cyprus. However, when Greece sought reentry very quickly, it ran up against a Turkish wall. Any NATO member can veto entry into the alliance or its command structure, and Turkey wanted to use its veto to force Greece to make concessions in the Aegean and in Cyprus. On its part, Greece became so anxious to reenter that it even wanted to make its reentry a precondition for the renewal of the U.S. base agreements, thereby giving the Americans a powerful motive to help Greece. It was primarily American diplomatic efforts that smoothed Greece's path back into NATO.

It is scarcely imaginable that Greece would ever completely withdraw from NATO. It is faced with the unpleasant prospect that it would result in an upgrading of Turkey's military capabilities to fill the gap. In Greek eyes, this could tip the military scales in favor of Greece's traditional enemy. Further, the Greek military might balk at any separation from NATO. The basic problem remains: Greek eyes are cast eastward toward Turkey. Greece contributed to its allies' war effort against Iraq in 1991 by sending one frigate. But Turkey's participation was much more visible. In 1991 the EU decided to include Greece in the WEU, with Turkey becoming an associate member.

In the 1990s both have acquired huge quantities of modern offensive weaponry free of charge, as the U.S. and Germany transferred to them hundreds of helicopters, tanks, and artillery under the

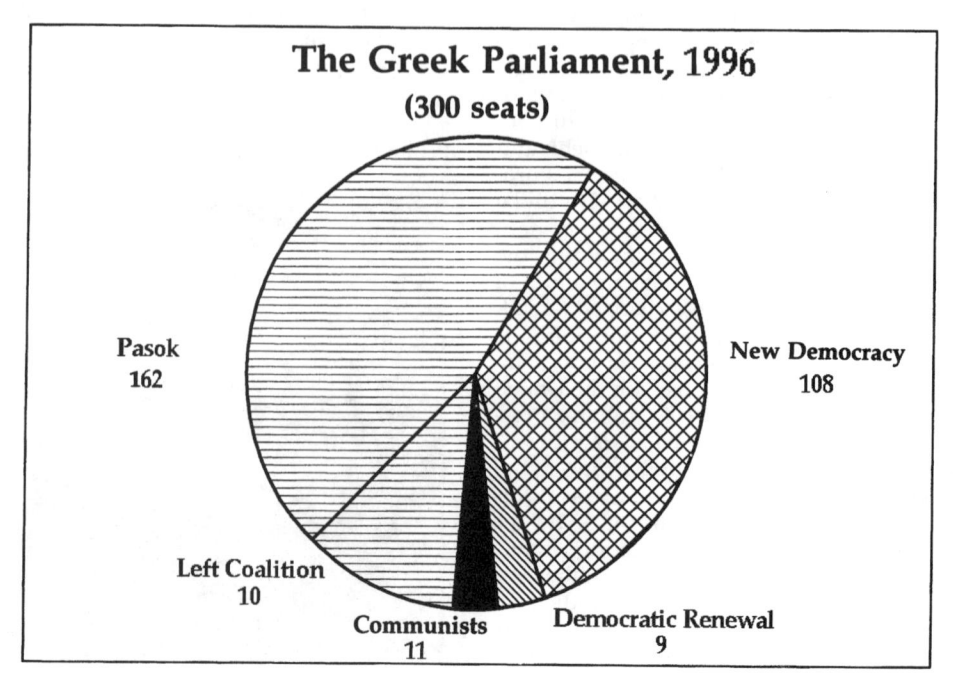

The Greek Parliament, 1996
(300 seats)

- Pasok 162
- New Democracy 108
- Communists 11
- Left Coalition 10
- Democratic Renewal 9

Greece

terms of the 1990 CFE treaty. The purpose of this conventional forces agreement was to diminish the threat of surprise attack in Central Europe. But it was an arms bonanza for Turkey and Greece and, in the opinion of some observers, created less, not more, stability in the Balkans. In 1998 the U.S. stopped all military aid, in the form of credits for purchasing American weaponry, to both Greece and Turkey.

The Balkans

While Turkey remains Greece's top concern, the dramatic changes in the Balkans and the break–up of Yugoslavia are very worrisome to Greeks. They fear that Macedonia to the North could make irredentist claims on their province with the same name. This prompted Athens in 1992 to oppose Macedonia's right to use that ancient Hellenic name when it declared its independence from Yugoslavia. In 1993 a compromise was reached to allow Macedonia to enter the UN under the clumsy temporary name of "Former Yugoslav Republic of Macedonia (FYROM)"; Greece calls the country by the capital's name, Skopje. But no flag was hoisted because of Greece's objection to its 16–point star.

When the U.S. and Greece's EU partners formally recognized Macedonia in 1994, the Greek government imposed a trade blockade on *FYROM*. This deprived the struggling country, in which 500 American soldiers perform peacekeeping duties, of access to the port of Salonika, through which three–fourths of its exports and imports and most of its oil passed. This move was devastating to Macedonia and incomprehensible to Greece's allies, who did not understand why it would want to destabilize a multi–ethnic country which could shield it from the turmoil in the former Yugoslavia. Greece was at odds with all its neighbors.

Through American mediation in 1995, Greece and Macedonia agreed to take steps to end their quarrel. Greece agreed to (1) recognize Macedonia as a sovereign and independent state, (2) lift its trade blockade imposed against Macedonia, which was hurting both countries financially, (3) stop vetoing EU aid to Macedonia, and (4) endorse its membership in the *OSCE*.

In return, Macedonia agreed to redesign its flag and change two articles in its constitution eliminating any hint of a claim on the Greek province of Macedonia. Liaison offices were established in each other's capital, and both countries enjoy mutual "unimpeded movement of people and goods." With the help of U.S. mediator Cyrus Vance the two countries are trying to resolve the dispute about the northern neighbor's name. As a result, trade is now thriving, and in 1997 they even participated in a joint military exercise. In 1999 the Greeks flew supplies to Macedonia to help that country cope with the flood of refugees from Kosovo.

Greeks made a great effort to establish good relations with the new regimes in Bulgaria and Romania. They are already the largest investors in Bulgaria, and overall Greek investment in the Balkans is increasing. Athens utilized its traditionally close ties with Serbia to try to mediate a settlement to the bloody war in Bosnia. This effort led to friction with Turkey, against which Greece and Serbia share a historical antipathy. Greece forbade Turkish planes from flying over its airspace on their way to helping NATO enforce a no–fly zone over Bosnia. It refused in 1994 to endorse NATO ultimatums against Bosnian Serbs or to participate in any military action in Bosnia. In 1995 Turkey used its veto to prevent the establishment of a NATO rapid deployment headquarters in Thessaloniki and a land and air headquarters in Larissa.

Greece welcomed the Bosnian peace agreement in 1995 and the lifting of UN trade sanctions against Serbia–Montenegro, which had hurt the Greek economy. It agreed to send a contingent of 1,000 troops to join NATO's multinational peacekeeping force in Bosnia, and it donated $7 million in reconstruction funds. In 1997 it put pressure on the Serb president to recognize opposition victories in local elections.

Albania presents a special problem. In 1987 Greece had officially ended the state of war with Albania and had sent the first cabinet–level delegation since 1940. In 1991 Mitsotakis became the first Greek prime minister to visit Tirana. By 1994 Greece had become the largest investor in Albania. The partial opening of its borders resulted in thousands of ethnic Greeks from a part of Albania called North Epirus fleeing to Greece. After decrying their plight for decades, Greece could hardly shut them out.

In 1993, after some 300,000 Albanians had poured into Greece, the breaking point was reached. With illegal immigrants being blamed for rising crime and a lowering of wage rates, anti–foreigner sentiment prompted the government to try to detain and expel the estimated half million foreigners who entered Greece illegally in the three previous years. Deportations of Albanians began in 1993, and there was some frighteningly loose talk in Greece about autonomy for the Greek minority in Northern Epirus. Albania retaliated by cutting the number of Greek–language schools. Rarely had Greece's relations with Albania been worse.

A tentative rapprochement was reached in 1995, when Greek police arrested members of the Greek terrorist North Epirus Liberation Front, and the foreign minister visited Tirana. But when Albania later rejected Greece's request for the establishment of three Greek schools in southern Albania, Athens suspended the planned signing of an agreement on employment opportunities for the estimated 150,000 illegal Albanians residing in Greece. In 1997 Greece sent a sizable peacekeeping contingent to Albania as a part of a multinational force to restore public order. To demonstrate impartiality, its troops were not deployed in the south, where the Greek ethnic minority is concentrated. Athens also opened new border crossings and increased its economic assistance to the small destabilized neighbor. By 1999

Greece

there were 400,000 Albanian immigrants in Greece.

Other immigrant waves came from Bulgaria, Poland, Turkish Kurdistan, and Russia. The latter country is home to about a half million Pontians, who are of Greek origin, having once lived along the southern coast of the Black Sea, which the ancient Greeks called "Pontos." Few of them speak modern Greek. By 1991 about 25,000 of them had found their way to Greece. They are a resourceful people who had already become masters of survival in the Soviet Union. Nevertheless, there have been some protests against their being resettled in Thrace, one of Greece's poorest areas and where Muslims predominate.

In 1999 Greece found itself in a difficult situation when NATO launched an air war against Serbia in an effort to stop ethnic cleansing in predominantly Muslim Kosovo. Greek leaders had been friendly to Serb strongman Slobodan Milosevic in the past. Most Greeks are fiercely pro-Serb, as are most of the country's newspapers and TV stations. Both nations are Orthodox Christian, and Greek churchmen are not shy about stirring up emotions against Muslims. But the Simitis government decided that Greece's wider interests—closer ties with Western Europe and joining the Euro—required that it support NATO. As the alliance's sole Balkan country, Athens said it could not join an attack against a neighbor. However, its airbases provided logistical help for AWACS surveillance flights over Yugoslavia, and it permitted supplies to pass through its port of Salonica. Also its good relations with Belgrade enabled Greece to be the only NATO country that could actively support such non-governmental organizations as the Red Cross inside Kosovo.

Greek–Turkish Hostility in Cyprus and the Aegean

Even though it will not leave NATO, many Greeks continue to ask: "What good is NATO to us if it cannot prevent the Turks from invading Cyprus or from threatening Greek interests in the Aegean?" The Greeks and Turks seem to be obsessed with each other, something which is reflected in the fact that both nations spend almost a fifth of their budgets on the military. Tensions have gotten worse since the end of the Cold War. There are many conflicting interests. The biggest is Cyprus, where more than 30,000 Turkish troops still occupy 37% of the island although the Turkish minority comprises only 18% of the population.

Greece suffered a shocking setback in 1983 when Turkish Cypriots declared an independent "Republic of Northern Cyprus," thereby undercutting UN efforts to find a solution to that conflict. Turkey is the only country in the world to recognize the new republic, while all other nations recognize the Greek-dominated Cypriot government. Currently 1,200 UN peacekeepers patrol the line that divides the two communities. The Greeks suspect that the Turks might try to seize other Greek islands lying close to the Turkish coast, such as Rhodes.

Such fears may seem ridiculous to the non-Greek. But Greeks are quick to point out that the Turks maintain a 125,000-man Army of the Aegean equipped with 110 landing craft on their southwestern coast, that Turkish politicians have sometimes in the past refused to recognize that the Aegean islands are Greek, and that the Turks actually demonstrated in Cyprus that they are willing to use military means to back up their aspirations in the area. In 1996 U.S. diplomatic intervention was required to defuse a crisis over Turkish occupation of an uninhabited Greek island. Greeks conveniently forget that the Greek majority in Cyprus, particularly under Archbishop Makarios, sometimes abused the Turkish minority Cypriots.

Greece's position remains unchanged: that Turkish troops and settlers must be withdrawn, and effective guarantees must be given to a Cypriot Republic. In 1997 the EU decided to consider Cyprus' application for membership, but it rejected Turkey's three-decade-old application. Greece refuses to allow a linkage between Greek Cypriot EU entry and a final settlement of the island's division and threatens to veto further EU expansion if such a linkage is made. The EU accepted Greece's position. Turkey strongly objects to any arrangement whereby a Greek Cypriot government might be admitted to the EU, while Turkish Cypriots and Turkey itself are left out. The EU's offer of membership to Greek Cypriots sharpens the divisions. There is no imminent settlement of the thorny issue of Cyprus' division, especially since the 1998 reelection of Glafcos Clerides as Greek Cypriot president. Despite their political differences, Clerides and the leader of Turkish-Cyprus, Rauf Denktash, have been friends since their school days. But this has done little to lessen tensions.

Clerides spurned UN talks on Cyprus and calls for firmer support by Athens. To strengthen his hand, he won Russian agreement to sell 300 sophisticated surface-to-air missiles. The Turks said they would destroy them the moment they arrive. Also, a 1993 defense pact with Greece permits continued construction of a military air base at Paphos that could accommodate Greek F–16s deployed there in time of crisis. One American official noted that "these are acid concerns for Turkey—Greek jets and Russian missiles on Cyprus." To prevent military conflict, an American diplomatic mission in 1997 got Clerides to postpone receipt of Greek F–16s. Clerides also announced that the Russian missiles would not be deployed on Cyprus. Instead they were deployed in 1999 on the Greek island of Crete, placing Turkey well outside of the missiles' 90–mile range.

The Aegean

Greece insists that its airspace extends 10 miles around each island rather than six miles, which Turkey recognized. Also, now that there are proven oil reserves in the Aegean, Greece is determined to maximize its economic rights on the continental shelf. Each country claims that the Aegean is a part of its continental shelf. Actually, both have shown noteworthy restraint in the past, accepting a six-mile offshore limit in the Aegean, compared with the internationally accepted 12 miles.

Rather than improving contacts with Turkey, Greece focused on extracting NATO guarantees against possible Turkish incursions in the area, a guarantee which NATO was understandably unprepared to make against a fellow NATO member. Greece also turned to the Americans to secure a more precise formulation of a vaguely worded guarantee which former Secretary of State Henry Kissinger gave in 1976 that the U.S. would not stand idly by if either Greece or Turkey attempted to resolve their disputes by force. This was a delicate request for the U.S. The Americans hinted that they might be prepared to give Greece a firmer guarantee if it would first try to mend its fences with Turkey.

At NATO's July 1997 summit meeting the American secretary of state got the Greek prime minister and Turkish president to endorse a broad declaration of good neighborly relations in a non-aggression pact. But they rejected Washington's requests to cancel military maneuvers in sensitive areas. Instead they engaged in dogfight challenges over the Aegean, violated a moratorium on military overflights of Cyprus, and steered so closely to each other that two naval vessels nearly collided close to Turkish coast. Nevertheless, in November 1997 Mesut Yilmaz became the first Turkish prime minister to visit Greek territory since 1988. The occasion was the first summit of Balkan leaders since the break-up of Yugoslavia. The meeting was hosted by the Greeks on the island of Crete and ended with a pledge to work together to ease tensions. The Greek and Turkish prime ministers took the opportunity to hold private talks.

Greece granted diplomatic recognition to the Palestine Liberation Organization (PLO) and received its leader, Yassir

Greece

Arafat, in Athens. In 1983 it provided ships to evacuate from Lebanon PLO militiamen loyal to Arafat. In that same conflict it irritated his NATO allies by denying the use of Greek territory to their military aircraft on their way to Lebanon, while allowing Czech planes to refuel on their way to Syria.

In 1988 Greece finally ratified the 1977 European convention providing for the mandatory extradition of terrorists, but it reserved the right not to apply it to "freedom–fighters." In 1988 it freed Abdel Osama Al–Zomar, a Palestinian wanted in Italy. In 1989 it rejected American demands to extradite Muhammad Rashid, a Palestinian in Greek custody wanted in the U.S. in connection with the bombing of a Pan Am airliner over Hawaii in 1982. In 1991 he was put on trial, and in 1992 he was found guilty of premeditated murder. In 1998 American ire was again raised when an Athens court declared that Rashid should be freed for good behavior. The November 17 Movement, Greece's deadliest terrorist group, claimed responsibility for a spate of attacks against U.S. targets in 1998, including an antitank rocket blast at a Citibank branch. The following year left–wing groups protested against the NATO bombing of Yugoslavia by setting off bombs of their own at tourist sites.

Mount Lycabettus, Athens Courtesy: Richard F. Strader

Entry into the EU

Under former prime minister Caramanlis Greece joined the EU in a hurry, primarily in order to strengthen democracy in Greece but also to in order to benefit Greece's economy. Papandreou had often described the EU as a "rich man's club" which discriminated against the weaker economies (although all poor countries in Western Europe entered!). He had promised to pull Greece out of the EU if he were elected.

As on many other issues, he changed his tune after he found himself in the prime minister's chair. The EU, in contrast to NATO, is popular in Greece and that it is quite profitable as well. Greece receives handsome annual subsidies from the EU coffers, more than any other EU member. By 1994 this amounted to $4 billion a year, 5% of its GDP and as much as its shipping and tourist revenues combined. But it also receives stern economic warnings and advice from Brussels. This is bitter but needed medicine; aid does not flow to Greece unconditionally. It cannot be said that Greece made the most of its first decade in the EU. In 1981 its per capita GDP was 58% of the EU average; by 1991 it had fallen to 51%. In 1997 its average per capita GDP, adjusted for purchasing power, was $12,743, the lowest in the EU. Greece ratified the Maastricht Treaty in 1992 and entered the WEU. Now its citizens are asked to make sacrifices in order to get ready for the European single currency. With a government deficit at 5.2% of GDP and a total national debt at 106.9% of GDP in 1997, it did not qualify for the first round, but it hopes to join in 2001.

Social Reform

Some progress was made in the field of social reform, especially in matters involving women's rights. The 1974 constitution

Greece

In traditional costumes of their region, young Macedonian men perform a line dance

includes a provision that all laws that foster inequality between the sexes had to be wiped off the books. Such things are easier written than done in a country with such a powerful state church and in one which the man as head of the household always had the right to decide all family matters literally by decree.

The *PASOK* government was able to break the Church's monopoly on marriage and to permit civil marriages. Before, atheists could not marry in Greece. However, in the late 1980s, only three out of 20 couples in the cities marry outside the church; in the countryside, practically nobody does. Further, there are no more criminal prosecutions for adultery. The government also prepared legislation to permit abortion on demand, although it in fact was already widely available.

Parliament enacted in 1983 a series of important laws to protect women; it permitted divorce on mutually declared grounds of incompatibility and made it possible to name a child without baptism and to register the name with the civil authorities rather than with the Church. It made it legal for a Greek woman to keep her own name after marriage, to have custody of small children, to choose which schools they attend and to travel with them outside the country without her husband's permission. It guaranteed to Greek women equal pay for equal work and forbade employers both to discriminate in hiring and to fire women for being pregnant. The government also proposed family planning centers and social benefits to unmarried mothers.

Perhaps its most explosive move was to abolish dowries which a father had to pay to his daughter's prospective groom. Many wedding plans ended on the rocks because the parents or grooms could not agree on the exact size of the dowry. In Thessaloniki one fiancé broke his engagement with a young woman because her parents refused to meet his demands of a yearly payment, a furnished house, a car and two apartments!

PASOK tried to make good its promise to decentralize power in a highly centralized country. The central government traditionally sent 55 *nomarchs* (governors) into the provinces to exercise nearly total power over local decisions. Local government received all their revenues from Athens and did not even have the right to levy taxes. The Papandreou government doubled the financial grants to local governments and set up committees, composed of city councilmen, farmers, workers and employers, to advise the *nomarchs*, whose control over the city councils was reduced.

ECONOMY

Herodotus wrote almost 2,500 years ago that "Greece always has poverty for a mate." It is the poorest country in Western Europe. OECD classifies it as a "newly industrializing country," which places it in the same general category as countries like Mexico. Of course, it is always tempting to use Western European standards when analyzing the Greek economy. In one sense, this is appropriate because many Greeks do, in fact, want to share the life and values of Western Europeans. But it must be remembered that Greece is geographically isolated from the rest of Western Europe and is Mediterranean and Balkan in character, as well as Western European.

Greece has undeniably changed greatly since the 1940s, when foreign occupation and a destructive civil war stood in the way of economic improvement. In the 1950s it began to experience an economic boom, and in the years 1964 to 1975 it had an annual growth rate of over 10%. By 1999 it had declined to 3.5%, still healthy by EU standards. Personal consumption rose almost as spectacularly, and improvements in living standards were visible. Half of the Greek families living in the cities own their own homes, and the figure is even higher in the countryside.

This is one of those countries in which real earnings and the actual standard of living are higher than official statistics would indicate. The secret lies partly in the flexibility and resilience of the Greeks and in the tightly–knit family, which is marked by hard work, saving for the future and the drive to get ahead. It also lies partly in the extensive "underground" economy similar to that found in Italy. It has almost become the norm for Greeks to hold down second and even third jobs, for which persons are paid in a way which goes unnoticed by the tax collectors and statisticians. It has been estimated that the underground economy may be equivalent to 15% to 20% of Greece's GDP. This thriving underground economy is one reason why more and more foreign refugees and mostly illegal migrant workers are immigrating to Greece, especially from Poland, the Philippines and Africa.

Shipping

Ever since Jason and the Argonauts sailed away to find the Golden Fleece, Greece has been the world's leader in shipping. Today it has the largest merchant fleet in the world owned by one group of nationals. A fifth of the world's merchant fleet is Greek–owned although more ships fly the Liberian and Panamanian flags for reasons of legal convenience. In fact, to get around high European wage costs, two–thirds of Greece's 3,246 ships in 1997 flew Cypriot, Maltese, or Panamanian flags. It also now owns 70% of the EU's total merchant fleet and 51% of its tonnage and was, therefore, given the chairmanship of the EU shipping committee.

Shipping is a vital part of the economy, providing about 114,000 jobs. It is estimat-

Greece

ed that one family out of 11 is directly or indirectly dependent upon shipping for its livelihood. After tourism, it is the country's top foreign exchange earner and has helped to alleviate Greece's chronic balance of payments deficits. Names like Onassis, Niarchos, Goulandris and John Spiros Latsis are inextricably identified with this entire industry.

But the Greek shipping industry has faced serious troubles. The late 80s–early 90s worldwide recession affected it, and several ships still lie idle. Many of the best–known magnates are selling much of their fleets and putting the proceeds into onshore property. In 1977 the dozen largest shipowners had 80% of their equity tied up in ships; by 1987 the percentage had fallen to 25%. Also, the oil glut and the industrialized world's gradual reduction of imported oil hit Greece's large tanker fleet. An increase in protectionism in the world would affect this sector, since only about 1% of its fleet carries cargo to or from Greek ports.

The fleet is relatively older than those of other shipping nations, largely because Greeks prefer to buy used vessels to new ones. The age of its ships, combined with the kind of shipping in which 95% of its vessels engage, created a very bad safety record. While international merchant shipping is becoming increasing specialized, Greece's ships still engage in "tramping," going anywhere on a single–trip basis when a cargo is available instead of traveling regular routes. They are the taxi drivers of the seas, which has been profitable but which makes them more accident–prone as they enter unfamiliar waters.

A final problem is recruiting; Greek law requires that crews be at least 75% Greek, but the rise in living standards on the mainland and islands have made the seaman's life of loneliness, long absences from families and the danger from storms less attractive. Therefore, shipowners are compelled both to pay extremely high wages and benefits, nearly at EU level, and to hire more than 25% of their crews from outside of Greece, especially from Asia. This is illegal, but necessary.

Tourism and Industry

Its ancient ruins, beautiful beaches and almost perpetual sunshine, combined with the people's well–deserved reputation for hospitality and friendliness, have long made Greece a favorite tourist land. It receives over eight million tourists annually, equivalent to more than four–fifths of the Greek population. They leave large amounts of their currencies behind by the time they depart. Tourism is Greece's largest source of foreign currency and its biggest industry, employing a tenth of the population. But there are problems with tourism which unsettle many Greeks. It is seasonal, so many facilities are not used in off–season. Further, it tends to be concentrated in Athens and the islands, which become terribly overcrowded in the high season. Efforts to encourage tourists to visit less–frequented places, particularly the northern part, have not been successful. Turkey, with beautiful beaches, friendly people, low prices, and at least as many ancient Greek ruins as Greece itself, is luring precisely the kinds of middle-class tourists as is Greece.

Finally, Greece lies close to the Arab world and has been subject to terrorist activities. This has not only scared some away, but Papandreou's unwillingness to take energetic measures against terrorism irritated the U.S., whose economic cooperation is important for Greece. In 1988 Arab terrorists took control of a Greek cruise ship, *City of Poros*, and killed nine tourists and wounded 78 in a grisly rampage. The Greek government strongly condemned this savage attack. As the 1991 Gulf War showed, Greece is very sensitive to travel advisories issued by the U.S. government.

Much of the economic growth in the 1960s and 1970s was in medium technology manufacturing industries, such as textiles, cement and metal products, along with ship repair. Manufacturing is concentrated primarily in small, artisan industries. The average number of workers is 45, but about 95% have fewer than ten workers and about 80% fewer than four. Only companies producing basic metals, tobacco, paper, textiles, chemicals and petro–chemicals are in the medium to large–scale category. The hundred largest Greek companies combined do not approach the size of General Motors.

By EU standards Greek production methods are often antiquated and the management style is more appropriate to small artisan family businesses than to modern, aggressive ones. These are all-too–often a "one–man–show" in which the family head runs almost everything and is very hesitant to delegate authority. One result is lower productivity than elsewhere in the EU. For example, manufacturing exports per capita are only about 4% that of the EU average.

Another problem with Greek industry is that it tends to be heavily concentrated in the Athens–Piraeus and Thessaloniki areas. About 30% of the Greek population, 40% of all enterprises and 50% of the total labor force producing half of the country's GDP are located in and around Athens, a sprawling megalopolis of 3.5 million. The capital is growing by 100,000 each year, despite the problems of smog (primarily from a million motor vehicles), high rents, poor sanitation and traffic chaos. There is consensus that the best way of solving the city's traffic and pollution problems is to expand the subway system, and work is proceeding to accomplish this.

Although Greece is not highly developed as a whole, it has pollution problems similar to those of many highly industrialized countries, thanks to the fact that its industry is greatly concentrated. For several years the government has tried to do something about this problem. Athens is formally closed to new industry, and permits for modernization or expansion of existing plants are issued only under the condition that there be no further pollution. Also, large investments have been steered to northern Greece, and this area is now the fastest growing region, in terms of population.

Agriculture

Greek agriculture has always been limited by the facts that the land is 80% mountainous, the soil is rocky and the climate is dry. Only 28% of the land is arable. Greece has the lowest proportion of forest cover of any EU country. That is diminishing rapidly because of fire destruction, which by the beginning of the 1990s had already claimed 1.5 million acres (or 4.8% of Greece's total surface area). Despite the massive exodus to the cities during the past three and a half decades, the farm population is still 36% according to the 1981 census, although those who are actively engaged in agriculture constitute only about 20%. This latter figure is still far above the 9% average in the EU and 3.6% in the U.S.

Living standards of Greek farmers have risen, and such amenities as televisions and autos are commonplace. Their frame of mind has also changed considerably in the last quarter of a century. They are no longer sullen and frightened by the police and the trader. Instead, they are now outspoken and ready to underscore their protests by blocking roads with their tractors, as they demonstrated the end of 1996. They are also far better organized. The former conservative government devoted an increasing share of its budget to modernizing agriculture, but Greek farms are still too small and fragmented to be competitive. That is a major reason why agriculture accounts for less than a sixth of the GDP.

Resources

A further source of foreign exchange has been the remittances sent back to Greece by the 800,000 Greeks living elsewhere in Western Europe (1981 figure). From 1960 until 1975 about 70,000 Greeks per year went to northern Europe in order to accept high paying jobs. However, the

Greece

economic recession forced many of them to return home, and by the 1980s about 25,000 more Greeks were returning annually than were leaving the country.

Greece is not rich in raw materials, but it does mine nickel, bauxite, chrome, zinc, asbestos and lignite (brown coal). It also has deposits of uranium, gold and silver. Heretofore it has had very little domestic oil and rapidly became very dependent upon import sources. By 1981 40% of its export earnings were needed to pay for energy imports. Fortunately, the Greeks' energy consumption is the lowest per capita in Western Europe, mainly because there is little need for heating in the warm climate.

The dry climate prevents a dramatic expansion of hydroelectric power, and the hundreds of scattered islands complicate energy delivery to the far reaches of the country. Greece is nevertheless determined to increase its domestic energy production. With so much sun and coastline, solar and tidal power is a possibility in the distant future. Greeks have been nervous about pressing ahead with plans to construct a nuclear plant which could supply a fifth of the nation's power. The major reason for their hesitation is that the country is very prone to earthquakes, which could dangerously damage a power plant. With its sizable lignite deposits, it plans increasingly to use this brown coal for electricity generation despite the negative environmental consequences. When lignite mining will begin leveling off in the late 1980s, they could begin importing harder and cleaner burning coals to replace the lignite. The goal is to reduce the oil component of electricity from 40% to only 2%.

The greatest hope is that offshore oil extraction can increase. In May 1981 it began extracting its first barrels of low quality Aegean crude oil from Prinos, near the holiday resort island of Thasos in northern Greece. The Prinos production is expected to supply from 8% to 10% of oil needs. Promising oil deposits have also been found off the Ionian islands between Paxoi and Zakinthos, facing Italy. However, the extent to which Greece can use Aegean oil depends upon its ability to settle its differences with Turkey, which also raises conflicting claims in this disputed area. No one should expect these problems to be solved any time soon. Continued dependency on imported oil will be indefinite.

Most of Greece's trade is with the EU, the Middle East and North Africa. While Lebanon was in flames, Athens grew fast as a regional trade center for the Middle East, with many international businesses maintaining regional offices in the Greek capital.

Government Intervention in the Economy

In the 1960s Greece had the fastest growing economy in democratic Europe, but in the 1970s and 1980s Greek governments borrowed heavily to finance an excessive rise in public spending. This left Greece with the largest public sector deficit in Western Europe. It had to devote a third of its budget merely to service its public debt. Before 1990 Papandreou had tried to reduce the government's borrowing, not by reducing spending, but by raising taxes by more than 50%, while increasing spending by 43% He raised the minimum wage by 32%. He reduced the working week by one hour and added a week to all workers' paid vacations. He also sharply raised most social benefits. One might argue that these changes were socially justified, but they fueled inflation, retarded economic growth, kept unemployment high for several years and diminished foreign investment.

Papandreou had to water down his vague promises to "socialize" large sectors of the economy, which many people took to mean nationalization of the major cement, petrochemical, pharmaceutical and ship-building firms. Shipping itself would have had to be exempt, since ship-owners could so easily move their operations to another country. After 1982 he nationalized about 40 ailing industries. A dozen of these were hopelessly non-viable. The high unemployment rate made it difficult to shut them down.

The government made a start in 1986 when it actually closed one and then called in riot police to make sure that the workers did not occupy this textile supply plant. The others remain expensive wards of the state, which already directly or indirectly controls about 60% of the economy, since most industry is owned by the banks and most of the banks have long been owned by the state. Any addition to this would leave the state with almost total control over the economy. Papandreou backed down on any such ambitious schemes and settled for the introduction of a form of workers' participation in the management of large industries rather than mass nationalization.

Mitsotakis pledged to speed up privatization, but it continued to move slowly, complicated by strikes and a European Court ruling that former owners must be compensated. By 1992 only 10 of 208 companies had been sold, but plans were announced to privatize two major oil refineries responsible for 40% of all production. Papandreou promised to end privatization, but within a few months of his reelection in 1993 he abruptly dropped this pledge and announced the partial sell-off of OTE, the state telecoms company.

The trade unions, especially the General Greek Confederation (GSEE), had traditionally been under the thumb of the government, which gave unions their money and usually managed to get their men installed in union leadership. Therefore Greek union leaders were almost always conservative. Papandreou allowed the unions to finance themselves through members' dues, and thereby gave them more independence from the state. Also, strikes became easier by eliminating such

Blessing of the sponge divers

Greece

restrictions as cooling off periods and by making it more difficult for employers to use the "lockout" response to a strike.

The Simitis government has made good progress in stabilizing the economy and keeping the country's course set on the goal of joining the Euro by 2001, a goal supported by 90% of the public, according to 1999 polls. The drachma entered Europe's exchange–rate mechanism (ERM) in 1998 as a prelude to the Euro. The budget deficit was brought down to 2.2% in 1999 and the public–sector debt to 104% of GDP, still high, but lower than that of Italy and Belgium. Inflation had fallen to 3.9%, the lowest figure in more than three decades, and unemployment stood at 10.1% in 1999, close to the EU average. The economy is in need of further restructuring, and Greece still has a long way to go to catch up with the rest of its EU partners.

CULTURE

Before the Byzantine Empire fell under the Turkish onslaught, the Greek culture had largely fallen into a state of religiously–induced rigidity. Under Turkish domination, cultural life oriented itself more around the simple roots of peasant and shepherd life. That is the reason for the fact that modern Greek culture, with its exotic charm, is strongly shaped by and fused with folklore.

Literature and Arts

In modern Greek literature one finds a strong orientation toward folk themes and styles. In the works of its most famous novelist, Nikos Kazantzakis (1883–1957), who was nominated for the Nobel Prize several times, one gains a deep insight into the suffering and the liberation of the Greek people. His novel, *Alexis Zorbas*, which was filmed in the 1960s became an enormous success. Greek music long kept its distance from the Western cultural tradition, and this film, as well as *Never on Sunday*, helped introduce to Western ears the oriental sound of the *bouzouki*, through the artistry of composers Mikis Theodorakis and Manos Hadjidakis. Greece has produced some leading classical musicians, such as singer Maria Callas and composer Dimitri Mitropoulos. Classical music is rapidly gaining in popularity, and Athens has a new concert hall, the Megaro Mousikis, for presentations of all musical styles.

The lyricist, Georgios Seferis (1900–1971) received the Nobel Prize in 1963 for his attempt to synthesize Greek folklore with the western cultural tradition. Odysseus Elytis was also awarded the Nobel Prize for his surrealist poetry.

The hope and the suffering of the Greek left during the turmoil and civil wars of the 1930s and 1940s are chronicled by the astoundingly prolific Yannis Ritsos, one of Greece's most popular poets, especially among those who are young and on the political left. A staunch supporter of the Greek communists, he has published 86 books of his works in 48 languages, and he reportedly has 40 more ready for publication. Like many contemporary Greek artists, he has had much experience with arrests and exile because of his political activities and writings.

This also applied to Mikis Theodorakis, who was an active communist, and to Melina Mercouri, who became the *PASOK* Minister of Culture and Science. The granddaughter of a former mayor of Athens and daughter of a former leftist politician, she played a prostitute in her most famous film, "Never on Sunday," which was shot in the lower–class section of Piraeus, which she represented in the parliament. Forced into exile in Paris and the U.S. when the "colonels" seized power in 1967, she publicly urged tourists to boycott Greece. After 1967 she devoted most of her attention to politics and held high political office until 1994. She created quite a stir in the male–dominated parliament by insisting on wearing trousers to its sessions. In 1990 she was defeated in her bid to become mayor of Athens. When *PASOK* returned to power in 1993, she again became culture minister for a few months until her death of lung cancer in a New York hospital in March 1994. After lying in state at the Athens Cathedral, she effectively shut down the city of Athens by attracting 300,000 admirers to line her funeral procession.

Language

The classical Greek language cannot be understood by modern Greeks, although the modern dialects do retain some features of that earlier, far more complicated, language. Despite the changes over time, the Greeks are the world's only people (except the Chinese) who can look at a 2,500–year–old inscription and recognize it in their own language. A proposal by the education minister in 1987 to restore classical Greek to the higher–education curriculum revived a century–old dispute. Opponents say that teaching two Greek languages would slow down educational reforms, and communists and leftists branded the proposal as reactionary. But classicists responded that even Marx, Engels and Lenin learned ancient Greek! In

Greece

A Greek newspaper reports on the London bombing of the Queen's Horse Guards

1992, after a 16-year hiatus, ancient Greek was reintroduced in junior high schools.

At present there are two modern Greek languages—one is *Katharevousa*, devised in the 19th century to purify the language as much as feasible and return it to a form at least approximating classical Greek. It is used in the Church and was used for a long time in the administration, courts, literature and the universities. The less formal and simpler *Demotiki* ("people's language") is exclusively spoken by 90% of the people. Those who only spoke it felt like quasi-illiterates whenever they entered those circles where *Katharevousa* was spoken. Since the restoration of democracy in 1974, the formal version has lost its privileged position, except in Church life, and it was eliminated from the schools as part of a series of educational reforms which were introduced in 1976.

Educational System

The fact that about 14% of Greek adults (and about 21% of the females) are still illiterate indicates that the school system needs improvement. Given the plenitude of his promises, it is not surprising that Papandreou promised a "revolution" in modern education, which seems to focus on unblocking the bottleneck leading to the Greek universities. Although 90% of all pupils take college preparatory courses, only about 20% of the 100,000-plus university applicants are accepted. This is because the government traditionally limits the number of openings to anticipated numbers of jobs for graduates. In the 1990s the country must face the problem of improving schools ill-equipped and staffed by poorly paid teachers, which has sparked prolonged strikes and disturbing street violence in Athens.

No doubt drawing on his experience in the U.S., Papandreou proposed that a system of junior colleges be established for those applicants not accepted to the universities. Such reforms inevitably run into opposition by educational bureaucrats and the highly-revered professors. Nevertheless, a 1982 Higher Education Law replaced the earlier university system built around a few all-mighty professors with broader American-style departments. It also created about 2,000 new teaching positions and permits undergraduate representatives to participate in university decision making.

In 1987 two new institutions, the University of the Aegean and Ionian University, opened their doors on many Aegean and Ionian islands. These branch campuses strive both to provide practical education and to revive Greek literary and artistic traditions. The professors are required to live at the university sites. This avoids the problems at mainland provincial universities, where professors often appear only briefly during the week before returning to Athens. Greek student life remains highly politicized, and lecture halls and laboratories are still overcrowded in the metropolitian universities.

Cultural Heritage

Many Greeks are aware that the country's rapid economic growth and modernization have sometimes done violence to Greece's cultural inheritance. This is very much the case with Athens. When it was declared to be the capital of the newly-independent Greek nation in 1833, it was "nothing but a pile of filthy ruins," in the words of an Austrian historian, von Prokesch-Osten, who visited the village at that time. When the German archaeologist Ludwig Ross saw the settlement, which had only 5,000 largely poor inhabitants, he was astonished. "One has difficulty believing that one is in Athens!" The new king, Otto I of Bavaria, brought in noted German architects, such as Leo von Klentze, Ernst Ziller and Friedrich von Schinkel, who designed and built glittering neo-classical buildings for the city.

Unfortunately most of these buildings fell victim to the construction boom after World War II, a period when there was little interest in conserving the monuments of the past. "Growth" was the consuming reality, and no major city in Europe grew as fast as Athens. At the turn of the century, it had 120,000 inhabitants. In 1920 it had already 300,000 and by 1950 it had reached a million. At the beginning of the 1960s the number had passed the two million mark, and by now greater Athens has almost four million inhabitants. Every day 350 more citizens stream into the city, a total of 120,000 a year. The basic service problems which are created by this lightning increase are predictable; in the suburbs, water, sewage systems and electricity are often absent. Urban planning has hardly existed and the property speculators dance in delight!

Almost miraculously, there are no slums in Athens and the crime rate is lower than in any other major European city. But one must live amidst countless blocks of unembellished apartment buildings, traffic jams and noxious clouds of smog, called *nefos* by the Greeks; this is a mixture of smoke, dust, sulphur dioxide, carbon monoxide and nitrogen oxides produced by industrial discharges and car exhaust gases. Surrounded by mountains, Athens is as vulnerable to air pollution as is Los Angeles and Denver. When it rains, the sulphur dioxide in the air turns into sulphuric acid which dissolves stone, especially the marble of the city's few remaining monuments.

The previous government tried to make a start at controlling this by limiting the use of high–sulphur oil, but this measure had little effect. It also halted the movement of new industries into the area. The present government is experimenting with banning cars from the center city, but public transportation would have to be greatly improved if this were ever to be made permanent. It also plans to plant more trees in order to beautify the dusty cityscape.

The remaining classical structures in Athens can almost be counted on the fingers of both hands. The previous and present governments have mounted an all–out effort to save the most precious jewel of classical Greece: the Acropolis in Athens. This monument to man's sense of beauty and proportion has led a tortured existence. It has been battered by wars, earthquakes and plunder from such varied groups as barbarian invaders and British diplomats. (Many of the statues and friezes can be seen in the British Museum in London, and the Greek government has formally asked for their return.) During the Turkish occupation, the temples were converted into mosques, and at one point were even used to house the harem of the Turkish commander.

The four major buildings remaining atop the 512–foot (158 meter) hill now face their most serious challenge: tourists and air pollution. Three million tourists visit the Acropolis each year and they not only marvel and walk upon the stones, but in a few cases scratch, pound or etch their names in the stones. The acid rain is an even more formidable enemy, eating away at the marble. Earlier suggestions to cover the entire Acropolis with a plastic dome were rejected as unfeasible. But many original statues are being placed into museums and were replaced by copies. Also, the Parthenon, the huge Doric temple which once housed the gigantic statues of the goddess Passas Athena, was closed to tourists. At one time they could wander and climb unimpeded within this magnificent structure, but now they may view it only from the outside. Work is now being done on all the temples to strengthen them. Also, an Acropolis Museum will house all the sculpture from the temples and will include a space exactly the size of the Parthenon, allowing the original sculptures to be seen in a relation to each other as they once were. In 1991 the government renewed its request for the return of the Elgin Marbles, now in the British Museum; a similar request was declined in 1984.

Another segment of its heritage which it fought hard to bring back to Greece is the Olympic Games, although no one contemplated trying to hold them in the ancient location. The first modern Olympics had been held in Athens in 1896. Greece's hopes to stage the centennial games in 1996 were dashed when Atlanta was picked over Athens. A stunned Melina Mercouri exclaimed: "Coca–Cola has prevailed over the Parthenon!" But jubilant Athenians won their bid to host the 2004 games.

Foreign interest in the treasures of classical Greece remains strong. It is in part maintained by such institutions as the American School of Classical Studies located in Athens. This is an academy for rigorous classical scholarship and archaeological excavation founded a hundred years ago by a group of scholars from Harvard, Yale, Brown, Johns Hopkins and Cornell universities. It now has about 100 students and faculty from the U.S. and Canada and an endowment of $8 million. At the same time, Greeks maintain strong ties abroad, primarily with the U.S. There have been two waves of immigration to the U.S. in the 20th century, and now over three million people of Greek and Greek descent live permanently in the U.S. The third biggest Greek city in the world is Chicago, and Greeks in America have, on the whole, been very successful. They include not only such well–known entertainers as Maria Callas and Telly Savalas (Kojak), but former presidential candidate Michael Dukakis.

These Americans form a potent lobby in the U.S. Congress. Sometimes they can even put pressure on Greece. For instance, in 1963 they erected a statue of President Harry Truman honoring his providing Greece with arms and money to defeat the communists in the Greek civil war. However, some Greeks saw this as a symbol of American tutelage. In 1986 left–wing extremists blew it off its pedestal. The former *Socialist–Communist* majority in the Athens city council voted to get rid of it altogether. At first Papandreou refused to intervene, but Greek–American delegations persuaded him to reconsider.

As elsewhere in the past, the Greek Orthodox Church holds the Greek communities in the U.S. together by organizing schools, cultural events and activities, social welfare and even camping holidays. A Greek wedding is a rite and celebration which is unforgettable.

Orthodox Church

The Greek Orthodox Church remains quite influential in Greece. Except for the Turkish–speaking minority concentrated on Thrace and constituting only about 1.5% of the total Greek population, most citizens are members of the established church, whose position and powers are fixed in the constitution. Greece is the only country in the world in which Orthodox Christianity is the official religion. Although only 4% of Greeks said they attend church regularly, religion remains a part of their daily lives. The Orthodox Church of Greece has as its head His Beatitude Archbishop Seraphim of Athens and all Greece.

The Ecumenical Patriarch of the Orthodox Church (currently Bartholomew) is the spiritual head of world Orthodoxy, but he has no jurisdiction over the Church of Greece. Since the great split with the Roman Catholic Church, he has always resided in Istanbul (formerly Byzantium), Turkey. Life in Islamic Turkey has not been easy for the Patriarch, who must be a Turkish citizen and travel with a Turkish passport. His flock within Turkey has shrunk to only 3,000. During crises between Turkey and Greece, he has had to worry about being expelled from Istanbul, thereby surrendering his primacy over the other Orthodox patriarchs, especially the Russian Orthodox leader, as heir to the Byzantine tradition.

His place as head of world Orthodoxy is tenuous. Relations with the resurgent Russian Orthodox church are not good. By tradition he is considered the first among equals over 135 million adherents of Orthodox Christianity, including 1.5 million in the U.S. He was permitted to restore the shabby buildings of his Patriarchate, in part because of an appeal made to Turkey by former President Carter.

The Church has, in the past, been able to use its influence to delay social reforms. In causing these delays it sacrificed much of its prestige in a society which is in-

**His All Holiness
Ecumenical Patriarch Bartholomew**

Greece

creasingly secular. The government had widespread approval for its plans to cut off state financial aid to the Church and to amend the constitution in order to make all religions equal in the eyes of the law.

It also continued the efforts begun by *New Democracy* aimed at expropriating the landed wealth of the Church, which, after the state, is Greece's largest property and enterprise owner. It owned forest and agricultural land, office and apartment buildings, bank shares, islands and businesses, in addition to churches and monasteries filled with treasures. Much of the Church's land had been abandoned by Turkish land–owners, and the state has often challenged the Church's claim to it. Much of the land is not used at all, in part because it is too hilly or mountainous.

In 1987 parliament approved a bill expropriating the Church's huge, 350,000 acres of land–holdings and distributing them to farm cooperatives. The bill also called for putting laymen in charge of church administration. In an expropriating mood, the government also announced plans to take over most of former King Constantine's property in Greece, estimated to be worth about $40 million. Not surprisingly, the Church announced at first that it would not comply with the new law. An amicable face–saving compromise was found, though. In his first journey to Greece in a quarter of a century, the Patriarch agreed to a church–state committee to administer monastic lands and to leave the rest of the property under the control of the Holy Synod.

The archbishop of the Orthodox Church inside Greece since 1998 is Christodoulos. Although he succeeded the late Seraphim, who was put in power by the rightwing colonels who ruled Greece from 1967 to 1974, he finds himself at loggerheads with the current Greek government. Christodoulos' message is stridently nationalist, and he expounds the tired conspiracy theory that "the world's big powers are working against the interests of Hellenism." He rails especially against the "eastern barbarians" (the Turks) and calls upon Greeks to "liberate Constantinople." Since Orthodoxy is the country's established religion, such populist pronouncements are especially embarrassing to Greece's diplomats.

In general the Church's influence is declining, although it will remain for a long time a political, social and economic force to be reckoned with. In the rural, mountainous areas, attendance at the breathtaking, ritualistic services is very high. A curious custom exists in some of these areas—a shortage of land means a shortage of cemetery land. A person is buried for two or three years; the women of the parish then dig up the bones, clean them

A monastery on the Mount Athos peninsula

and place them in the cellar reliquary of the church together with those of thousands already there. A new burial plot is thus created.

One place where the religious flame also burns brightly is Mount Athos, or the Holy Mountain, as many Greeks call it. It dates back to the 7th century when a group of hermits fled there and founded their "Garden of God," and it is one of the world's oldest Christian communities. Covering 225 square miles in an isolated forested and mountainous peninsula in northern Greece, and overlooking treacherous waters in which many a seaman drowned, Mount Athos contained 180 monasteries sheltering more than 10,000 monks in the 11th century. Now it has shriveled to about 20 monasteries and only 1,400 monks (nevertheless, up from 1,146 in 1972!).

It is beset with numerous problems. One is that its longstanding total ban on women (and even on female animals!) was challenged by female tourists, who sail within sight of the monasteries and sometimes even land illegally. It can no longer maintain the 20 monasteries and 1,700 auxiliary buildings, the 300,000 feet of frescoes, the 20,000 icons, 13,500 Greek manuscripts and a vast collection of relics and treasures which are irresistible objects for thieves.

The Greek state gives it about $300,000 annually, but neither this nor the income it derives from subsistence farming, rent from properties outside Mt. Athos and timber trading enable the monks to make ends meet. The entire area is an autonomous republic within the Greek state, and it rules itself entirely through an annually elected governing body of 20 abbots. All the monks categorically refuse to unite or reconcile their differences with the western churches, which they regard as heretical and corrupt. They all criticize the Greek state's decision to open diplomatic relations with the Vatican, as well as the Orthodox Church's ecumenical steps toward the Catholic Church in Rome.

There is a minority of about 300 zealots within the compound which accuses the other monks of religious impurity. This fanatic minority struggles with them over control of the monasteries. On several occasions, the Greek police have been called in to deal with violent skirmishes between zealots and moderates. Still, all the monks agree that Mount Athos is a gateway to higher spiritual levels and ultimately to heaven. One abbot explained with confidence that "for the rest of the world, we are a lighthouse, battered by the waves, but still lighting the way, as we have done for centuries."

Media

Since 1974 Greece has been a country which enjoys freedom of speech, and Greek newspapers make full use of this liberty. Although the newspaper readership is low by Western European stan-

Greece

dards (about 80 per 1,000), about 85 papers appear daily. Athens alone has 14 morning dailies. Few could survive without the tax–free newsprint and guaranteed loans provided by the state. Greece's large public banks also give aid. Although only two papers are official party organs, *Rizospastis* and *Avgi* of the Moscow–oriented and Eurocommunist parties, respectively, most other papers have a clearly recognizable political line.

Most foreign observers remark that the journalistic standards of the Greek press are rather low, with sensationalism and extreme politicization taking priority over objective reporting. News columns tend to be as politicized as the editorial pages, but this seems to be what most Greek readers expect of their favorite newspapers. Only such Athens morning papers as the independent *Kathimerini* and the pro–socialist *To Vima* even make a stab at objective news reporting. In 1991 the editors of seven newspapers went to jail rather than comply with a new law which, precipitated by the 1989 assassination of Mitsotakis' son–in–law by the November 17 group, prohibited them from publishing statements from terrorists. This measure reminded too many Greeks of the censorship practices during the military dictatorship from 1967 to 1974.

Televisions are found in 96% of Greek households (38% in color). In rural cafes they remain an important source of information, since newspapers often arrive a day late. There are three state–owned television channels: two in Athens (ERT1 and ERT2) and one in Thessaloniki (ERT3). They are financed by the state and by advertising fees. Since 1989 there are also many private channels, which are financed by advertising fees: 10 major ones in Athens and 13 smaller ones in other large cities. Countless local community channels broadcast throughout Greece. The programming consists of American films (70%), Greek films (20–22%), other European programs, and the normal fare of news, sports, documentaries, interviews and entertainment. There is also a mix of state–owned and private radio stations.

After exhaustive consultation among political parties and other interests, a bill for regulating privately–owned press and media was introduced in parliament. The aim is to restrict the excessive concentration of media ownership and the development of communications monopolies. It would prohibit companies that accept contracts with the state to have ownership in a mass media company. Also, no individual would be permitted to own more than a 25% stake in a television station. Finally, it would prohibit simultaneous participation in more than two media categories, such as television and publishing.

FUTURE

Greece is a country which is trying to absorb three decades of rapid economic and social change. A predominantly rural way of life and a traditional system of values have been largely swept away. Greek democracy has become sufficiently robust to absorb a good deal of passionate debate and unrest. Though chronic economic problems are difficult to solve, there is noticeable improvement.

The 1996 elections kept *PASOK* in power. With a new prime minister, Costas Simitis, Greece entered the post–Papandreou era. Simitis is determined to correct the country's financial problems in order to prepare Greece to enter the European single currency by 2001. Some Greeks find his medicine too bitter, but the austere economic policies are working. Greece faces problems along its borders. Tensions with Turkey are serious and can be expected to continue. However, relations with the U.S. are more harmonious than during the Papandreou rule, and those with the Balkan neighbors are also good.

Gazing down from the Acropolis . . . and looking back on the glory of ancient Greece

Iberian Peninsula

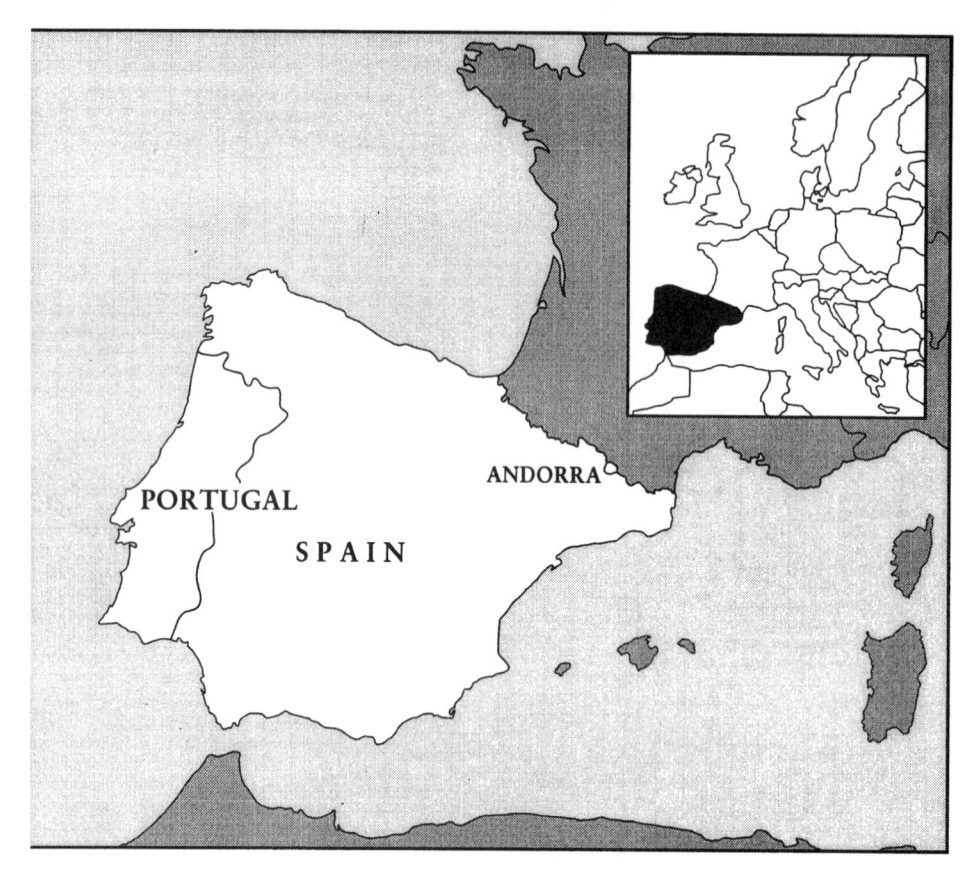

Contemporary Mutual Relations

The Iberian Peninsula is located at the southwest periphery of Europe, separated from the rest of the Continent by the high Pyrenees Mountains. Most of the population is settled around the coastal areas, with certain prominent exceptions, most notably Madrid, where a third of Spain's inland population is concentrated. The land area is distributed very unevenly among the three countries on the Peninsula; Spain occupies about 85% of the space, and Portugal occupies most of the rest. Tiny Andorra has a very small chunk of mountainous land in the Northeast, and Britain still controls a stratgically important toehold on the rock of Gibraltar at the southern tip of Spain.

Spain and Portugal do not have identical characteristics and problems. But they undeniably have very much in common. Perhaps most obviously, if one casts a quick glance at the globe, are their strategically significant locations. They are placed between the continents of Europe and Africa and face the Atlantic and, in the case of Spain, the Mediterranean Sea.

They possess islands in the Atlantic Ocean which are important links between the Western and Eastern Hemispheres: the Canary Islands are Spanish, and the Azores and Madeira are Portuguese. The Spanish also possess the Balearic Islands in the Mediterranean, the largest of which is the tourist mecca of Majorca. Spain also owns a few islands off the Moroccan coast and the cities of Ceuta and Melilla on the northern coast of Morocco. In 1987 the Portuguese agreed to relinquish to China their small enclave of Macao on the southern coast of China. It was their highly valuable strategic positions which enabled Spain and Portugal to escape prolonged international isolation and to regain a status of relative respectability after 1945, despite the fact that until the mid–1970s they had authoritarian political systems which were repugnant to most persons in the democratic countries of the world.

These lands were formerly mighty colonial powers which spread their languages and cultures to colonies in Latin America and Africa, which were many times greater in size and population than the mother countries. Their empires have by now almost completely disappeared. The process of decolonization brought the fascist regime to its knees in Portugal in 1974 and was a consequence of the collapse of fascism in Spain in 1975.

Portuguese and Spaniards speak languages which are derived from Latin and which are very similar to each other. Although their words are spelled and pronounced somewhat differently, they understand the gist of what each other is saying. However, the Spaniard, except in Galicia, generally has more trouble understanding Portuguese than *vice versa*. Both countries are also predominantly Roman Catholic, and the Catholic Church has traditionally wielded considerable power and influence in them.

Both countries have similar political backgrounds, traditions, institutions and problems. They had monarchies which collapsed in the first third of the 20th century because of chronic political turmoil and violence. In neither country did experiments with republican and democratic forms of government go well, and in 1926 in Portugal and 1936 in Spain the military seized power. Such seizure was quick and bloodless in Portugal, but painful and bloody in Spain. The carnage which lasted for three years in Spain was portrayed with great force by Picasso's unforgettable painting, *Guernica*, and by Ernest Hemingway's moving novel, *For Whom the Bell Tolls*.

Both countries lived under fascism for several decades. In the mid–1970s they reemerged from fascism, but experienced different transitions. Portugal dived headlong into revolutionary and democratic government and passed through two tense years of political experimentalism and uncertainty until it could gain its balance in the political center. By contrast, Spain experienced in 1975 a long and carefully planned entry into democracy and a restoration of the monarchy, which has proven to be one of the major bulwarks of democracy.

During the last decade and a half of fascist rule, Spain underwent rapid and extensive industrialization. By contrast, Portugal did not, and it entered its new democratic era as the poorest country in Western Europe. Although Spain remains one of Western Europe's poorest countries, its economic headstart over Portugal has strengthened the inclination of Spaniards to regard the poorer, smaller Portugal in a condescending, patronizing way.

In 1983 the Spanish prime minister traveled to Portugal for a summit conference designed to bury "historical ghosts." He called for "a new era in our relations." His Portuguese counterpart responded by announcing that "the mistrust and reservations which many Portuguese continue to feel toward Spain are no longer justified. Portugal has survived eight centuries of independence and nation identity, and Spain, a great country . . ., has respected and will continue to respect our independence." Clichés remain, though. Some Portuguese still see Spaniards as explosively talkative, opinionated, aggressive, arrogant, sociable and dressed beyond their means, with a barely concealed contempt for Portugal, while the Portuguese are quieter, more reserved and self–deprecating.

In 1986 they again pledged closer cooperation and agreed on frequent and regular meetings between the heads of their

Iberian Peninsula

governments. As a symbol of closer ties, they agreed to have a bridge built over the Guadiana River frontier. In 1989 they adapted their narrow–gauged railway systems to the one used in the rest of Europe so that rail cars will not need to be changed at Iberia's frontier with the rest of Europe. Portugal launched a major effort to streamline and modernize its rail system and highways toward Spain.

The results of their cooperation are clear: Between 1985 and 1989 trade trebled between them, and it doubled again in the 1990s. Only 5.4% of Spain's foreign trade in 1998 was with Portugal, but it is Portugal's second–largest supplier after Germany and its third–biggest market. Spain trades more with it than with all of Latin America. It also invests more heavily in Portugal than anywhere else. By 1998 there were over 3,000 Spanish firms in Portugal, compared with only 400 in 1989. Many multinational corporations deal with Portugal through their headquarters in Madrid. About two–thirds of foreigners visiting Portugal are Spanish. Portugal has over 400 companies operating in Spain. Its trade with Spain as a percentage of its total foreign trade grew from 9.2% in 1986 to 18.5% in 1997. Portugal's income per capita was half that of Spain in 1991, but by 1996 its per capita GDP, adjusted for purchasing power, had increased to $13,100, compared with $14,954 in Spain.

The relationship is asymmetrical, partly because of the different size and partly because of their past: Spain began encouraging competition and entrepreneurship during the Franco years, while Portugal did not. Spain was also largely free of the costly colonial wars, disruptive revolution and political upheaval which set Portugal back.

Portugal and Spain have long traditions of military intervention into politics. Since the 19th century, soldiers in the Peninsula have viewed themselves as the guarantors of their nations' sovereignty and integrity. Although soldiers in both lands symbolically show their loyalty to the state by kissing the respective national flags at ceremonial occasions, their commitment to democracy was not entirely certain, as the attempted coup d'etat in 1981 by elements within the Spanish military revealed. In the constitution of Spain, the military as an institution is granted explicit political powers. In Portugal from the 1974 revolution until 1986 the highest political office, the presidency, was occupied by high–ranking officers. The potential political activity of the military sets these nations off from the rest of Western European nations, where the military is undisputably subordinate to the elected political leadership. Nevertheless, by the 1990s democracy had set deep roots in both countries, and the danger of military intervention had diminished significantly. This adjustment to the Western European norm was strengthened by Spain's entry into NATO in 1982 (Portugal was a founding member), as well as by both lands joining the EU in 1986 and the WEU in 1988.

The Early Period

Many things which Portugal and Spain have in common stem from 2,000 years of shared history. It is likely that the first settlers began arriving on the Iberian Peninsula from 3,000 to 2,000 B.C., and were followed by waves of Celts, Phoenicians, Greeks and Carthaginians from the rest of Europe and Africa. Most of the settlers were firmly unified under Roman rule by 19 B.C., although individual tribes and cultures in the interior and northern parts of the Peninsula continued to exist. Tensions between the center and the periphery have continued to plague Spain and Portugal to the present day, although they are certainly less significant in contemporary Portugal than in Spain. The Romans brought the Latin language to the Peninsula, from which both modern Spanish and Portuguese developed. They also brought Roman law and administrative practices, and in the 4th century they introduced Christianity to the area. From the important Roman cities in the South and East of the Peninsula came many of the Roman Empire's great leaders, such as Hadrian, Lucan, Marcus Aurelius, Seneca and Trajan.

Visigoth and Moslem Rule

The collapse of Rome in the 5th century A.D. was followed by three centuries of rule in Spain by the Visigoths, who had stormed the Peninsula by force. Taking advantage of divisions and quarrels among the Visigoth leaders, Moors from North Africa began crossing the Strait of Gibraltar in 711 A.D. Within a very short time Mohammedans controlled virtually all the Roman cities in the South and East of the Peninsula. Iberian art and commerce bloomed under the new Moslem rule, which was, on the whole, very tolerant toward Jews and Christians.

Christians ensconced in strongholds in northwestern Spain hammered away at the Mohammedan realm in Iberia. It was further weakened by quarrels and intrigues among the Moslem rulers themselves, whose grip on the Peninsula began to loosen. The newly emerging Kingdom of Castile, which combined with Leon and whose military prowess is symbolized by its hero *El Cid,* and the Kingdom of Aragon, which in 1137 combined with Catalonia, slowly but steadily pushed back the Mohammedans. Moslem rule in most of the Peninsula had been broken by the mid 13th century, although a small Moslem kingdom hung on in Granada until 1492.

Moslem Decline; Portugal and Spain Separate

While the reconquest of the Peninsula from the Moslems was taking place, Portugal began to sever its ties with Leon and to establish itself as an independent country. In 1095 Count Henri of the House of Burgundy became the direct ruler over Portugal, and in 1140, after a nine–year rebellion against the King of Leon–Castille,

Spain under Roman rule

Iberian Peninsula

The Iberian Peninsula about 1150

Henri's son, Alfonso Henriques, declared himself to be the King of Portugal. The Burgundians ruled Portugal until 1383, during which time Portugal's borders were expanded from the original Oporto and Coimbra. Lisbon was snatched from the Moslems in 1147. Since the second half of the 13th century, Portugal's boundaries have been the same as today, with the exception of the district of Olivenca, which Spain took in 1801 and continues to hold.

Portuguese Exploration and Conquest

As a country facing the sea, Portuguese sights were always directed outward, and the bulk of the population was attracted to the coast because of this maritime and external commercial orientation. By 1337 their mariners had already landed on the Canary Islands. Overseas exploration was particularly encouraged by Prince Henry the Navigator (1394–1460), a far-sighted and imaginative man who established a maritime school to assemble and extend his country's knowledge of the sea. Portuguese mariners explored the African coast, and in 1488 Bartolemeu Dias rounded the Cape of Good Hope and reached East Africa. In 1497 Vasco da Gama set sail for India. He not only reached it, but he returned to describe the land to a receptive and curious Europe. Pedro Alvares Cabral landed in Brazil in 1500.

Such activity stimulated important advances in cartography and astronomy and also helped redirect the attention of Europe outward toward the larger world. It enabled Portugal to build up a massive empire which included Mozambique, Angola and Guinea–Bissau in Africa, Brazil in South America, East Timor, Macao (which the Chinese gave to Portugal as a reward for its fight against pirates), and Portuguese India (with its capital of Goa) in South and Southeastern Asia, and the Atlantic islands of the Azores and Madeira. Portuguese naval squadrons were stationed permanently in strongholds in or around the Atlantic and Indian Oceans. The Portuguese also began to send settlers to some of these imperial holdings, especially to the Azores, Madeira and Brazil.

These colonial activities brought definite advantages to Portugal, as it did to Spain. It provided it with gold and other precious stones, silks and spices, which were treasured in Europe at that time, and needed foodstuffs, especially wheat. It also provided an occupation for those portions of the feudal nobility which could no longer be supported by domestic agricultural production. Settlement in the colonies offered many Portuguese the hope for a better life. Finally, the desire to convert the peoples of the world to Roman Catholicism furnished the entire enterprise with a spirit of crusade and gave it a religious and spiritual justification.

Spanish Colonial Activities

Portugal's most avid competitor was its only neighbor—Spain. Spanish attention had remained largely focused on Iberia until 1492, which was a very significant date. In that year the Spanish captured Granada, the last Moslem foothold on Spanish soil. The triumphant entry into that city of Ferdinand and Isabella, whose marriage had sealed the unity of Aragon and Castile, signified the end of the seven and one–half century reconquest of the Iberian Peninsula. Thus, Spain took shape as a unified kingdom over an ethnically diverse area three and a half centuries after Portugal. The reconquest sparked a flourish of Spanish literature and artistic achievement which lasted at least two centuries. It also allowed Spaniards to concentrate their energy on overseas expansion and exploration.

As every American school child knows, the year 1492 was significant for another event: Christopher Columbus, a native of Genoa (Italy) working for the Spanish, sailed west in search of India, but instead bumped into the island of Santo Domingo in the Caribbean. His discovery opened the eyes of Europeans to an entirely new part of their world and launched an era of Spanish colonialism which spread Hispanic culture and languages to dozens of modern–day countries.

In order to minimize a potentially dangerous rivalry between Spain and Portugal in the wake of Columbus' discovery, the sovereigns of the two countries agreed in the Treaty of Tordesillas (1494) to divide the world in such a way that Spain would receive the Philippines (named after the Spanish king) and most of the Western Hemisphere (including large chunks of the contemporary U.S., such as California, the Southwest and Florida) with Portugal receiving what is now Brazil, and parts of Africa and Asia. Both countries continued generally to observe this agreement, which had the Pope's approval, but to their consternation, other interested powers, especially Britain, France and the Netherlands, did not.

As Portugal, Spain had several different motives for establishing and maintaining an empire. Dominican and Franciscan friars were always close on the heels of the *conquistadores* in order to convert and ed-

Iberian Peninsula

ucate the native populations. Also, the *conquistadores,* the royal court and the private companies which stood behind them clearly sought wealth, status and power. The Spanish kings insisted that all trade with the colonies be conducted through Seville and be reserved for Castile, although most of the trade was actually organized by Genoese and southern German merchants.

The Spanish kings also claimed one–fifth of all precious metals imported from the New World. Such metals greatly enriched the Spanish treasury, but they also heated inflation within Spain and created serious economic distortions. This wealth was used to add glitter to the royal and noble courts, to finance massive Spanish imports, and also to finance Spanish armies and navies. These military forces were constantly embroiled abroad maintaining an empire which encompassed the present–day BENELUX countries, Italy and, through the Hapsburg throne, all of the Austrian Empire. Throughout the 17th century Spanish money and troops also supported the Catholic struggle against Protestantism. Since almost none of its wealth was invested in productive facilities within the home country itself, Spain remained poor despite its temporary wealth.

Temporary Unity

The 16th century had been Portugal's "Golden Age," but it was dealt a devastating blow in the aftermath of events in Morocco, where King Sabastião and much of the nobility were slain while trying to protect the kingdom's holdings there. Spain claimed the Portuguese throne on the grounds that the mother of King Philip II of Spain was descended from Portuguese nobility. Thus, in 1580 the two countries were united in a dual monarchy, which was supposed to leave the Portuguese with domestic autonomy. In fact, Spaniards were appointed to Portuguese offices.

Despite initial economic advantages which Portugal gained through a dropping of customs barriers between the two lands, it was compelled to enter and to help finance through heavy taxes a costly and protracted war against England. This not only cost Portugal most of its lucrative markets in the Orient, but the bulk of its fleet as well. Both consequences directly benefited England and the Netherlands. Disillusioned about Spanish rule, and taking advantage of a revolt in Catalonia, the Portuguese also revolted. French support helped the rebellion to succeed in 1640, when the House of Bragança was established as the Portuguese ruling family (which it remained until the monarchy fell in 1910). The Spanish did not accept Portuguese independence without a fight, though, and until 1668 struggled unsuccessfully to win back the country.

In order to guarantee that it would never again fall under Spanish domination, Portugal entered an alliance with the sea power, Britain, which always had a sharp strategic eye for coastal countries which could be useful allies. This alliance lasted into the 20th century. The struggle against Spain affirmed and strengthened Portuguese national identity, which still defines itself most clearly in terms of its distinctiveness from the Spanish nation. The loss of many of its colonies and markets in the Orient necessitated a shift of Portugal's colonial attention from the Indian Ocean to Brazil. The revenues from Brazilian sugar, coffee, diamonds, gold and other minerals became extremely important to the Portuguese economy.

Separation

The separation of Portugal from Spain was, for the latter, merely one of a series of foreign political setbacks following the destruction of the Spanish Armada, a mighty fleet sent to subdue England in 1588. Spain squandered its wealth on endless wars on the European Continent, and its European holdings were gradually whittled away. The last blow was the War of the Spanish Succession which erupted after the death in 1700 of Charles II, the last of the Hapsburg rulers in Spain. This conflict ended in the establishment of a Bourbon dynasty in Spain. In practical terms, this meant French domination of Spain's foreign policy. Occasionally Spain seemed to be about able to rear its proud head once again and to assert primacy in its own affairs. However, any chance of Spain's restoring its former imperial grandeur and power was undercut by that social and political convulsion which changed Europe irrevocably—the French Revolution and the accompanying French military conquest of most of Europe.

French troops invaded Spain, and in 1808 Napoleon placed his brother, Joseph, on the Spanish throne. Many Spaniards valiantly resisted this foreign invasion, as Goya's powerful paintings portray. The Grand Army was nevertheless able to conquer most of the Peninsula by 1809. Yet its hold on Spain was only temporary. The English Duke of Wellington supported by Spanish guerrillas advanced from Portugal and delivered crushing defeats at Talavera in 1809 and Vitoria in June 1813.

As an ally of England, Portugal intervened much earlier, in 1793, in the war against revolutionary France. In 1807 the French invaded Portugal, prompting the royal court to flee to Brazil. By 1811, however, the French had been driven out again by British troops and by Portuguese soldiers who had been placed under the command of an English general, Lord Beresford, who in the Portuguese King's absence continued to dominate Portuguese politics long after Napoleon's troops had departed.

Both Spain and Portugal faced the post–Napoleonic era with restored monarchies but with the liberal ideas of the French Revolution in the heads of many of their citizens. These ideas would not permit a quiet return to the authoritarian government of earlier years. Also, these new notions, combined with the long rupture in reliable communication with their American colonies, spelled the end of their empires in the Western Hemisphere. The Spanish and Portuguese had fought heroically for their national independence. Now their American colonies decided to do the same.

Driving the Moors from Spain

The Kingdom of Spain

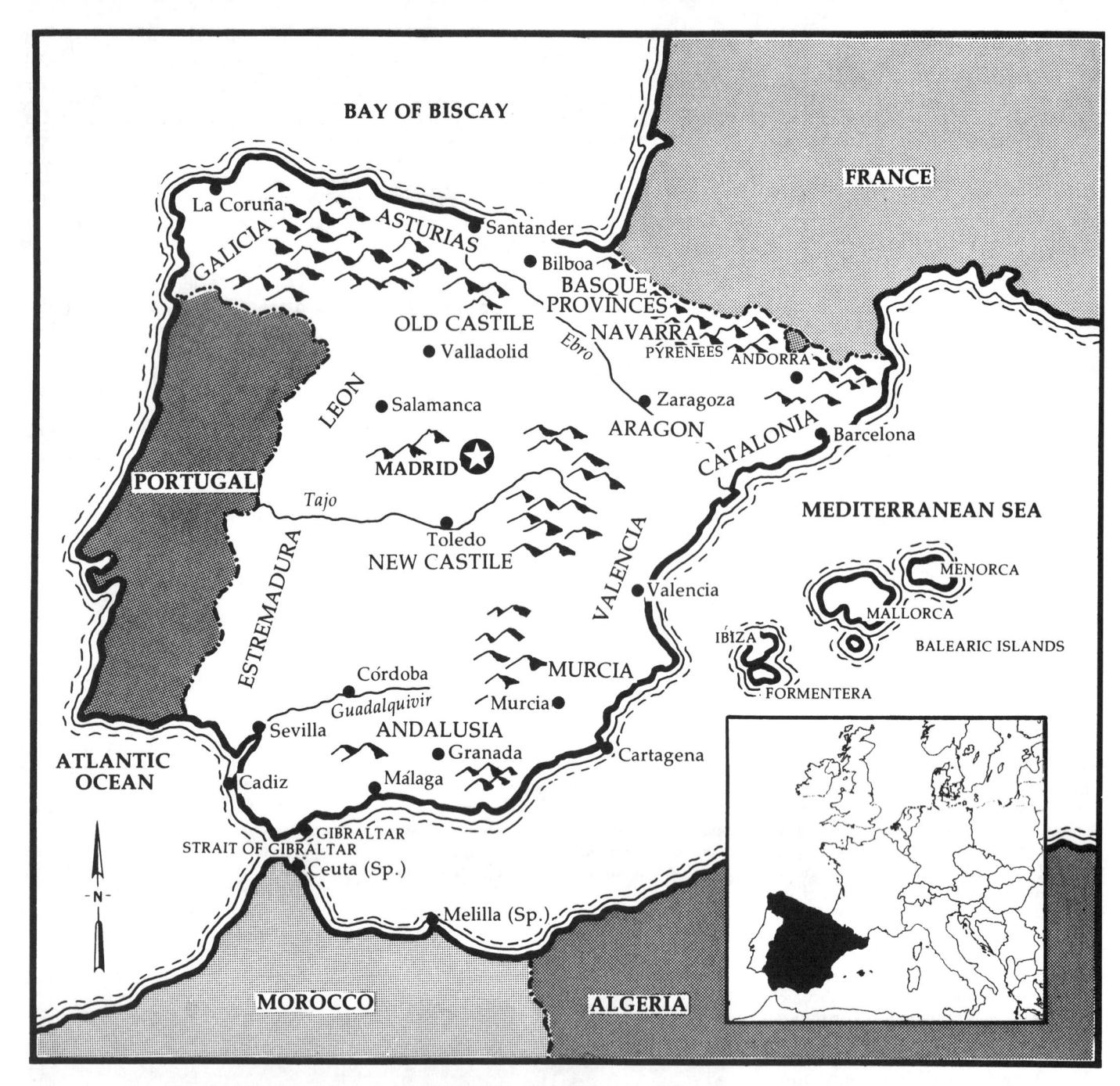

Area: 194,897 sq. mi. (504,750 sq. km.), some 640 miles (1,034 km.) from east to west, 530 miles (848 km.) from north to south.

Population: 40,000,000 (estimated).

Capital City: Madrid (Pop. 4.1 million, estimated).

Climate: Varying from Madrid's 2,000 foot (610 meters) elevation, making the area cold in winter and hot and dry in summer, to the Mediterranean coast which is hot in summer, mild in winter.

Neighboring Countries: France, Andorra (North); Portugal (West); Morocco lies only eight and a half miles across the Strait of Gibraltar.

Languages: Spanish (primarily the Castilian dialect), with Catalan, Basque, Galician, Valencian, regional languages which are once again flourishing and compose an important part of the tongues spoken every day.

Ethnic Background: Indo–European, North African, Arab.

Principal Religion: Roman Catholic.

Chief Commercial Exports: Machinery, iron and steel, fruits and vegetables, footwear, textiles.

Major Customers: France (20%), Germany (15%), Italy (11%), UK (7.5%), Portugal (7.5%), U.S. (6%), EU (71.5%).

Currency: Peseta, to be replaced by the Euro in 2002.

National Holiday: October 12 (1492)—*Dia de la Raza* (Columbus Day).

Chief of State: His Majesty King Juan Carlos I (b. 1938). Married Princess Sophia of Greece, 1962. Proclaimed King of Spain, November 22, 1975.

Heir Apparent: His Royal Highness Crown Prince Felipe, Prince of the Asturias (b. 1968).

Head of Government: José María Aznar, Prime Minister (since April 1996).

National Flag: Three horizontal stripes of red, yellow, and red, with the center yellow stripe twice as wide as the red ones.

Spain

The Spanish royal crest is set off center on the left of the flag.

For as long as most people could remember, Spain was, by European standards, a poor, thinly populated country on the edge of the Continent and separated from the rest of Europe by more than the high peaks of the Pyrenees Mountains. Its people had produced a language and a high culture which had been spread to most countries in the New World, but in politics it appeared excessively passionate, polarized, and generally ungovernable by any other means than authoritarianism. The Spanish Kings had never thoroughly integrated this heterogeneous country, and at times it threatened to split apart, with the Basque and Catalonian provinces in the Northeast leading the way. Unceasing political instability prevailed, punctuated by longer or shorter periods of authoritarian rule. The last such interlude lasted until the end of 1975 and was guided by a diminutive general named Francisco Franco, called *El Caudillo* (the Leader). His fascist regime made Spain an embarrassment to and, for a long time, an outcast in Western Europe.

After Franco's death Spain began to move in a different direction. Indeed, he would scarcely recognize the land he claimed to have "saved" in 1939. Wishing both to create a parliamentary democratic order and to avoid a bloody repeat of the turmoil and civil war of the 1930s, the major contenders for political power have displayed a remarkable willingness to cooperate with each other and to moderate their political demands.

Spain's regions have been offered autonomy statutes which reduce Madrid's hold on the country's politics. Communist and Socialist–led trade unions operate freely and act with moderation and responsibility. Many political parties compete for seats in the national Parliament, but Spanish voters have overwhelmingly supported the moderate democratic parties in the political center, despite a shaky economy whose performance has disappointed many Spaniards' hopes. A king, picked and trained by Franco, has shown unswerving determination to create and to preserve a democratic order and has therefore won the admiration of most of his countrymen. Spain also moved into Western Europe by joining NATO and by entering the EU, which enjoys a broad consensus within the country.

It is true that every November the anniversary of Franco's death still brings some Spaniards out into the streets to wear and wave fascist paraphernalia and to hear inflammatory speeches against the new democratic order. There is also a diminishing minority within the army which has learned little and which vents its dissatisfaction with the new Spain often enough to keep Spain's democrats nervous and willing to go more than an extra mile in order not to provoke the military. But to many people's surprise, democracy in Spain, as well as in Portugal, is working. The Pyrenees are no longer the edge of Western Europe.

CONTEMPORARY HISTORY

The Post–Napoleonic Period

The liberation of Spain from French occupation and the restoration of the Bourbon dynasty by no means brought the country peace and stability. Spain's isolation from its American colonies during the Napoleonic wars had loosened its grip and had given Latin American leaders a taste of local rule which they liked. They therefore revolted. Again, the Spanish treasury was drained by protracted war far from its own territory. After the disastrous Spanish defeat at the battle of Ayacucho in 1825, the vast and mighty Spanish empire had been reduced to the islands of Cuba, Puerto Rico, Guam and the Philippines.

Spanish domestic politics was marred by almost continuous political, social and economic crises. This turmoil began with the King's revocation in 1814 of the admirably liberal Cadiz Constitution, which had been approved in 1812. By 1820 the

The ancient city of Toledo, capital of Spain under Roman rule and home of the illustrious artist El Greco

Spain

dim-witted Ferdinand VII had alienated many important groups, especially the liberals and the military, and in the midst of widespread demonstrations and riots throughout the country, the military revolted. In an unsuccessful attempt to salvage his throne, the King allowed the Cadiz Constitution to be proclaimed again, but it was exactly such democratic constitutions which most of the conservative monarchs of Europe could not tolerate. Therefore, in April 1823 French armies again invaded Spain on behalf of most other European powers. (with the notable exception of England) and restored Ferdinand VII to power.

The next decade and a half were filled with reaction and unrest, followed by another quarter century of rule by generals and a scandal-ridden Queen Isabella II, who was finally deposed in 1868 by military officers. When they tried to appoint a Prussian Hohenzollern to the throne, they provided the spark for a war between France and Prussia in 1870, which resulted in German unification (See *Germany*). A brief and unsuccessful republican experiment ended again in military intervention and the restoration in 1874 of the monarchy under Alfonso XII, the son of Isabella II. A parliament (*Cortés*), for which only property owners could vote, was also created. In order to achieve some measure of stability, the Conservative and Liberal parties agreed to alternate power. However, this system of *turno político* had broken down by the end of the 19th century.

The Spanish-American War and Ensuing Turbulence

Spain was badly shaken in 1898 by its war against the United States. This conflict was sparked by an explosion of dubious origin on a U. S. vessel, the *Maine*, which was anchored in Havana harbor. American soldiers, including those led by Theodore Roosevelt's "Roughriders," entered the battlefield with the cry, "Remember the Maine!" The war left Spain with 200,000 dead in Cuba, a sorely humiliated officer corps, an empty treasury, and a denuded empire. Cuba, Puerto Rico, Guam and the Philippines were taken by the U. S., and Spain retained only a smattering of holdings in West Africa and Morocco.

Wide-spread domestic dissatisfaction increasingly began to manifest itself again, urban workers began to be attracted to Marxism and syndicalism (radically political trade unionism), and anarchism infected the downtrodden workers in Barcelona and the peasants in southern Spain. Also, corruption and inefficiency in Madrid stimulated separatist sentiments in the Basque and Catalonian regions. Political violence became commonplace, and Spanish politics was in a state of utter confusion. Between 1902 and 1923 the country averaged one government every 18 months.

Spain managed to remain neutral in World War I, but in 1921 it experienced such a stinging military reversal at the hands of the Moors at Anual in North Africa that public pressure forced the government to conduct an investigation of that institution which had never contented itself with mere military matters—the army. However, before the investigation could be completed, the military's rage at such "impudence" boiled over. The army seized power in 1923 and formed a government under General Miguel Primo de Rivera. Primo de Rivera's government banned all opposition parties, slapped severe controls on the press and the universities and openly expressed great admiration for the kind of fascist political order which Mussolini was establishing in Italy.

The new Spanish leader did launch an extensive public works program and, with the help of the French, ended the war in Morocco in 1926. But without the support of the masses or of the youth or intelligentsia, Primo de Rivera's authoritarian government could not survive the jolt which the world-wide depression gave to Spain and most other European countries at the end of the 1920s. He therefore resigned in January 1930. Demonstrations in favor of a republic became so intense that King Alfonso XIII was forced to flee the country April 13, 1931. The almost immediate proclamation of the Second Republic (the first being in the early 1870s) unleashed such enthusiasm from its supporters that 200 churches were burned to the ground!

Many Spaniards today look back very carefully to Spain's entry into democracy in 1931 in order to try to insure that earlier mistakes which helped lead to the downfall of the democratic republic would not be repeated. The new constitution of December 1931 legalized all political parties and created a unicameral *Cortés* (Parliament) to which the government was responsible. The constitution declared Spain to be "a workers' republic," and the new government under Manuel Azaña launched a full-scale attack on the old ruling pillars: the Church, the army and the wealthy. The Jesuit order was expelled, and fully state schools were established in order to eliminate religious influence over education. Large estates were confiscated, and the beginnings of a land reform were introduced. Railroads and the Bank of Spain were nationalized, the eight-hour workday introduced, and, perhaps most disastrously, the army officer corps was reduced by almost half.

It soon became clear that many of the new government's reforms were unrealistic. Both the delay in their implementation and the fear that they might actually *be* implemented brought peasants, workers, anarchists, fascists and monarchists out into the streets. Spain was bubbling with conspiracies and intrigues. It experienced one government after the other; in the five years of the Republic, there were 18 different governments! This came to a head shortly after the beginning of 1936 when a Popular Front on the French model, composed of Socialists, Communists, Anarcho-Syndicalists, and Basque and Catalan nationalists, was formed and won an electoral victory. The assassination on July 13, 1936, of the former finance minister under Primo de Rivera, Calvo Sotelo, was the cue for the army to launch a long-planned *coup* against the Republic.

Civil War

On July 18, 1936, a diminutive general, Francisco Franco, flew to Morocco from the Canary Islands and drew his sword against the Republic. Within a few days the revolt spread to garrisons within metropolitan Spain, and within ten days troops were flown in German planes from Morocco to secure strategically important positions. Unlike early military rebellions, which usually succeeded very quickly, this one thrust Spain into a savage three-year civil war which not only destroyed democracy and liberty in Spain, but temporarily moved the country into the center of the world political conflict between the proponents and opponents of fascist dictatorship.

The revolt was successful in certain parts of Spain, but not in such key cities as Madrid. Also, the provinces of Catalonia and Basque strongly supported the Republic because the latter had guaranteed them a large measure of autonomy. Further, Franco did not have the support of the navy, the air force and part of the army.

It is probable that the *coup* would have collapsed within a few months if Franco had not received crucial military assistance from fascist Germany and Italy. The Italians sent more than a thousand planes, four infantry divisions, tanks, artillery and other military equipment. The German contribution was smaller but highly effective. The Germans sent a tank battalion. The major contribution was the Condor Legion, composed of four fighter-bombers, four fighters, one reconnaissance, and two seaplane squadrons. The German aerial bombing of the city of Guernica on April 26, 1937, outraged world opinion and prompted an indignant Pablo Picasso to paint his famous *Guernica*. Sixty years later Germany

Spain

A victim of the civil war amidst the ruins of her home

agreed to donate almost $2 million to the city in symbolic compensation for the destruction.

Franco and Fascism

The Republic called for help, but France and Britain refused to respond to its calls and limited their reactions to verbal protests. It did have on its side some loyal army and naval units, as well as units hastily formed with trade unionists, students, and Catalan and Basque nationalists. In addition, several thousand generally poorly equipped and insufficiently trained international volunteers organized in such units as the Abraham Lincoln and Ernst Thälmann brigades came to fight for the Republic. This conflict inspired to action many idealistic young people throughout Europe and the United States, who saw in Spain the only determined struggle against fascism. The Soviet Union also sent limited aid in the form of advisers, technicians, tanks and aircraft. However, the Soviet Union itself was in the grips of a terrifying purge at home, which spilled over to communist units fighting in Spain. In such a state of paralysis, the Soviets withdrew their aid to the Republic a year before the end of the war.

Ultimately the military balance tipped in favor of Franco's fascists. In the spring of 1939 armed resistance in Catalonia was broken, and soon thereafter Franco's forces entered the severely bombed and starving capital of Madrid. The human costs of this brutal civil war were extremely high: approximately a million Spaniards were either killed or forced to emigrate. The war left most Spaniards with an intense fear of another such armed conflict on their own territory.

Despite Hitler's pressure and threats, Franco did maintain an official policy of neutrality during World War II, although he openly sympathized with Germany and Italy. He even sent a "Blue Division" of volunteers to fight on Germany's side against the Soviet Union from 1941–43. But Franco was always sensitive to the direction political winds blew, and after disastrous German setbacks on the Eastern front in 1943, he decided to maintain his official policy of neutrality more strictly.

Franco created an authoritarian, fascist regime, supported by the army and, initially, by the Catholic Church. This regime remained fundamentally unchanged until his death in November 1975. He always was skillful in playing different groups against each other, but he did not dare create any democratic institutions. The *Cortés* was restructured so that it could not effectively challenge Franco; in reality it was a cheerleader for the rulers. The news media were subjected to close censorship. This was by no means a new phenomenon, since information had been controlled in Spain since the 15th century, except for a brief interlude during the Second Republic. Franco abolished all political parties except his own *Movimiento Nacional* (National Movement).

The right–wing Falangist Movement, which had elaborated fascist ideals for Franco in the early days, gradually declined in influence and ultimately became strictly an agency to administer the bureaucracy. The Catholic Church's support of the regime gradually waned as the years went on, but the Catholic lay organization, *Opus Dei*, did grow in influence, especially within the educational and economic spheres. The *Opus Dei* became more open to progressive ideas and was a force behind Spain's rapid industrialization and robust economic growth which began in the 1960s.

Although Franco was the undisputed dictator from the very beginning, in 1947 he officially made himself chief of state for life, with the right to appoint his own successor. He declared Spain to be a monarchy, but not until 1969 did he name Prince Juan Carlos of Bourbon, whom he had educated and groomed for years to prepare him for his new role, to be the new king upon his death.

Isolation and Economic Progress

Because of Franco's open sympathy with Germany and Italy during World War II, the victorious allies initially isolated Spain in the international community and for years refused to allow it to enter

Spain

the UN. But the Cold War brought many former enemies onto better terms with each other, and Spain was no exception. The emerging hostilities between the Soviet Union and the nations in the Atlantic Alliance greatly enhanced the value of Spain's strategic location. Therefore, in 1953 the U. S. reached an agreement with Franco providing for American financial assistance in return for the right to establish four air and naval bases in Spain. This agreement was of great military significance for the U. S., but it never was regarded kindly by Franco's many opponents. The present Socialist leader, Felipe González, for instance, admitted that his attitude toward the U. S. had always been negative, in large part because the picture of former President Dwight D. Eisenhower smilingly shaking hands with Franco had remained firmly etched in his memory.

All in all, the fascist movement failed to stimulate much mass enthusiasm in Spain. It rested on widespread apathy fed by most Spaniards' intense desire for order after the Civil War. Franco had created a panoply of corporatist organizations, which were designed to mobilize and control the diverse elements of society. But as years passed, dissatisfaction and unrest began to manifest itself since Spain's fundamental problems had by no means been solved. Labor and student unrest, high inflation, growing opposition with the Church, increasing Basque extremism and revolutionary events in neighboring Portugal, beginning in 1974, continually chipped away at the foundations of the fascist state. Yet only one event could wipe away the trappings of fascism and set the process of democracy in motion: the death of Franco, which finally occurred in November 1975.

King Juan Carlos

The most visible sign for a new democratic spirit of reconciliation and national unity quickly became King Juan Carlos de Borbón y Borbón. Even former *Communist Party* chief, Santiago Carrillo, had to admit that "without Juan Carlos, Spaniards would probably be fighting each other again." Few persons had expected that the monarch would become a major linchpin for democracy in Spain.

Franco had chosen Juan Carlos (the grandson of former King Alfonso XIII) over the head of his father, Don Juan, who lived in Portuguese exile and who had always been an outspoken critic of Franco. From his father, Juan Carlos had learned several very important lessons: to install a democracy in Spain, to shun the everyday dealings of political parties, and never to play the army against the people.

Young Juan Carlos was an uninspiring pupil and rather introverted, especially after accidentally shooting his brother with an air gun at age 16. Remembering a suggestion the Italian fascist leader, Benito Mussolini, had once made to him, Franco brought the nine-year old Juan Carlos back to Spain in 1947 and had him educated under his watchful eye. The boy was sent to the army, navy and air force academies in Zaragoza, Martín and San Javier, respectively. He enjoyed his life at these academies, making contacts within the military which later were to be important to him as King. He had plenty of time for his favorite hobbies of athletics, ham radios and fast motorcycles. He also became a jet pilot, and he still flies himself around Spain for official visits.

When Franco decided in 1964 that the young Prince had had enough education, he entered a very trying phase in his life waiting for a task. He married Sophia, the sister of the former Greek King Constantine, who is one of the King's few close friends (and who now is a public relations agent in London). Not until 1969 was he officially proclaimed the crown prince after he had sworn allegiance to Franco's basic principles before the Parliament and after he had had a serious argument with his own father over his decision to accept the Spanish crown from Franco's own hand. He was therefore distrusted by Don Juan and by many Spanish democrats, who thought that the Prince had become *El Caudillo's* stooge.

Many in Franco's coterie also distrusted him because he did not ingratiate himself to them. Their suspicions were fed by the fact that Juan Carlos began establishing contacts with political opponents of the Franco regime, including, through an intermediary, communist leaders in Paris. With Franco on his death bed in late 1975, Juan Carlos gave a revealing glimpse of

General Francisco Franco

his sentiments by flying to Spanish Sahara and telling the troops there that they would have to withdraw because Spanish colonialism had come to an end.

He was installed as King after Franco's death, but he proceeded cautiously. In fact, the Spanish experiment of making a step-by-step transition from a dictatorship to a parliamentary democracy, while continuing to observe the existing laws of the land, was unique in European history. He temporarily retained Franco's last prime minister, Carlos Arias Navarro. Through wise appointments, he gained influence over the Council of the Realm, a small body whose only clear function was to insure that the new regime would remain within the bounds of Francoism. By the summer of 1976 he was able to have Arias eased out of office and to have a man with reformist designs, Adolfo Suárez, appointed in his place. The King gave Suárez unmistakable instructions to proceed as rapidly as possible toward the goal which Juan Carlos shared with most of his countrymen: "to restore sovereignty to the Spanish people."

As King, Juan Carlos set about to demonstrate that the bitter controversies of the past could be ended. When he visited Mexico three years after becoming King, he requested that veteran republicans who had fled from Franco's rule be invited to the Spanish Embassy, where he received them with demonstrative cordiality. Also, in a public speech he called the Civil War a fratricidal tragedy; Franco had always referred to it as a "glorious crusade."

He chooses to live in the relatively small Zarzuela Palace outside of Madrid, rather than the stately palace his ancestors had built in the middle of the capital. He prevents anything like a palace clique to congeal around him. Realizing that most

Spain

Spaniards are not ardent monarchists, he keeps protocol to a minimum and leads a relatively austere private life. But his patience, tact, shrewdness and courage in guiding the nation have won him respect from even those Spaniards who had always considered the very word "monarchist" an insult.

Seeds of Democracy

The National Movement (*Movimiento Nacional*), which Franco had formed out of various political movements, was withering on the vine. The best known component of the National Movement was the fascist–oriented *Falange*, named after the infantry formations which Alexander the Great had called phalanx. The trappings of fascist salutes, paramilitary youth organizations and the calls to revitalize Spain through order, authority and hierarchy remained, but membership in the National Movement had for most Spaniards become a mere formal prerequisite for a government job. In fact, many of Spain's foremost reformers after Franco's death, including Adolfo Suárez, under whose premiership Spain became a modern parliamentary democracy in the second half of the 1970s, had attained political prominence within the *National Movement.*

Spain felt its way slowly and nervously out of the authoritarian political order created and maintained by Franco. Many Spaniards looked back uneasily to the 1930s, and they saw certain parallels between that period and the 1970s. At both times political parties were legalized after dictatorships had ended, and the *Communist Party* supported the young democracy both times. At the beginning of the two democracies the vast majority of Spaniards voted for the moderate parties of the center. Also, world economic crises—the latest in the 1970s—set in at the inception of both Spanish democracies. Basque and Catalonian nationalists demanded autonomy, and a fraction of their numbers resorted to grisly violence to provoke the military and press for their aims. Thus, in both eras, Spanish democratic leaders had to face a declining economy, a wave of strikes and demands for better wages, and extremist violence, while creating a political order which would later be, in the words of King Juan Carlos, "a just order, equal for all," supported by "public activity as much as private activity, under legal safeguards."

Economic Progress

Despite the parallels between the 1930s and the 1970s, one must notice also the many significant differences between Spanish society in the heyday of Franco's rule and in the 1970s. One difference was the evolution of the Church in Spain, tra-

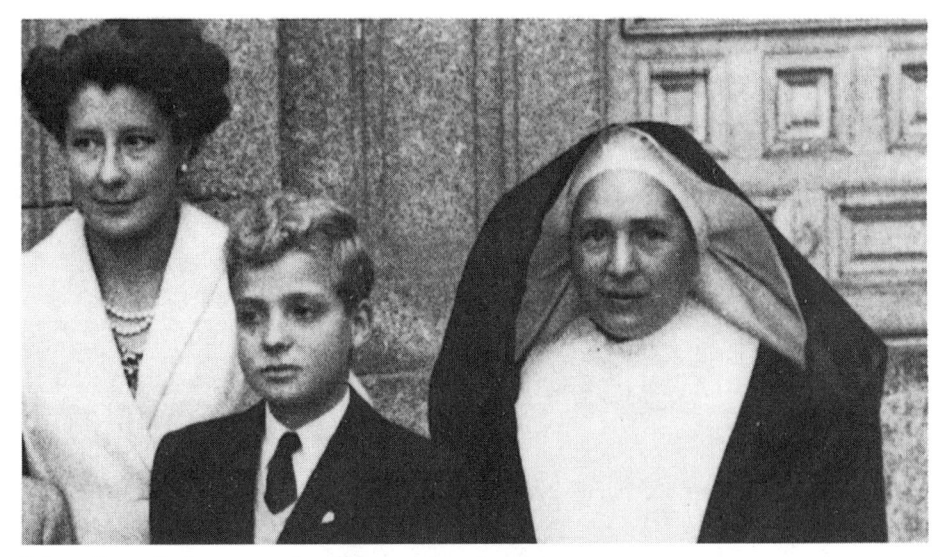

Prince Juan Carlos as a schoolboy

ditionally one of the most conservative in the entire Catholic world. This evolution will be discussed in the culture section of this chapter.

A further development which favored the post–Franco democratic experiment was economic progress. The recession of the 1970s was not nearly as deep as that of the 1930s and did not shake the democratic foundations of the European countries as was the case earlier. Most important, Spain's economic structure has changed drastically since Franco seized power. *El Caudillo* sought to establish complete Spanish self–reliance, which amounted to sealing Spain off economically from the rest of the world. As an international outcast after World War II, Spain was not permitted to receive Marshall Plan assistance. This greatly widened the gap between Spain and most of the rest of Western Europe. But in 1950 the UN lifted the trade boycott against Spain, and capital and modern production and business ideas began to enter the country.

The result was a doubling of industrial production in the course of the 1950s. This upswing did bring a doubling of prices, which stimulated labor unrest, but it also gave Spanish technocrats the courage to draw up a Stabilization Plan in 1959. This significant plan devalued the peseta to a level which would favor Spanish exports, began to eliminate some unnecessary economic controls, buried the old economic isolation policy (known as *autarky*) in theory as well as practice, and headed Spain in a dynamic capitalist direction. This new direction was not only good for the living standards of the people, but also for the later stabilizing of democracy. In the last decade of Franco's rule economic growth in Spain was an enviable 7% per year, one of the highest in Western Europe.

Spain's rapid economic growth not only increased the size of the middle class and gradually began to level out class differences, but it changed the country's outlook and demography. As Spaniards' economic expectations grew, their eyes turned more toward Western Europe, where democracy and prosperity were linked. Their contact with other Europeans was enormously increased by the lightning expansion of the Spanish tourist industry, which soon made Spain the number one tourist country in all of Europe. Although the bulk of Spain's tourists flock to the beaches, seldom venturing into the interior, they brought millions of Spanish into direct contact with Western Europeans and their ideas and spending habits.

Many Spaniards themselves began to pull up stakes and seek a better economic life elsewhere. In the 1960s more than three million Spaniards moved from the poorer countryside into the country's major industrial areas, especially Madrid, Catalonia and the Basque country. Well over two million Spaniards left the rural areas for industrialized countries north of the Pyrenees, especially to France, West Germany and Switzerland, sending much–needed foreign currency remittances back to Spain. Entire villages were deserted.

The new trend greatly reduced the number of Spaniards engaging in agriculture and left many pockets of rural poverty, especially in the South and in the province of Galicia. Such rapid industrial growth also left more polluted air, sea, rivers and tapwater in Spain. It transformed quiet, picturesque fishing villages into loud, overcrowded mass tourist

481

Spain

The Spanish Royal Family: (l. to r.) Princess Elena, Crown Prince Felipe, Queen Sophia, King Juan Carlos I, and Princess Cristina.

places with tasteless and cheaply constructed hotels, an army of souvenir vendors and thieves, and much higher prices. Large parts of the beautiful coastline were scarred with factories, chemical and power plants and blocks of apartments. Also, many of the suburbs around industrial cities shot up almost overnight and were often built without paved streets, or medical, educational and leisure facilities. All too often they became slums and centers for delinquency and crime. Spain paid a high price for its industrialization.

Yet Spain's social base had changed significantly. Workers increasingly began to own their own homes or apartments. They also began to buy cars and take vacations far from home. Although Franco had tried to keep them by and large politically apathetic, more and more Spaniards began under Franco to make public demands on the political system through strikes and demonstrations. Workers began to support the illegal trade union movement which grew out of the 1950s. Workers' Committees (*Comisiones Obreras*) emerged in larger factories to represent workers in negotiations with the management. By the 1970s they had successfully infiltrated the official unions, thereby weakening that prop of the Francoist system. In 1967 workers acquired the right to strike as long as such strikes were peaceful and strictly non–political.

The changes in the Catholic Church, the economy and the social structure had already eaten away at the roots of Francoism long before *El Caudillo* had closed his eyes for the last time. But the main reason why Spain's second attempt at democracy had a better chance to succeed was that Spaniards had a good memory. They remembered that four decades earlier one half of Spain conquered the other after untold suffering and grief and that years of authoritarianism had followed. This time, Spaniards were ready for reconciliation with each other. This willingness to ignore the things they once fought over has been referred to as a *pacto de olvida*, an agreement to forget. For example, after more than a dozen years of *Socialist* rule, many plazas still bear Franco's name.

In 1980 the new democratic regime dared to sponsor the first balanced exhibition of the Civil War. Video tapes, old news films, and tapes of the songs of both sides were played. Documents, flags, weapons, posters and newspapers were shown. Rather than rekindling old passions, the exhibition seemed to strengthen a very powerful sentiment in contemporary Spain—*never again civil war*.

GOVERNMENT

Monarch as Head of State

The King works hard and is informed about the most minute details of his country's policies. However, unlike Franco, he does not attend cabinet meetings, and he usually keeps himself aloof from day–to–day political affairs. He preserves his real political authority for critical issues and times. Some Spaniards were critical of his outspoken support of joining NATO's integrated command structure and the EU's single currency. But communist leader Julio Anguita's demand in 1996 that the king resign unleashed a public furor.

The king operates under strong constitutional constraints. However, he is able to influence the complexion of the government, and he is the supreme commander of the armed forces. Unlike any other monarch in Europe, he deals directly with the political and military leaders in his own country. He is without question Europe's most powerful and influential monarch although he probably is the one with the least personal wealth. He performs all the ceremonial duties of a chief–of–state, but because of his guiding role in Spanish politics, he is a far more important conversation partner for foreign leaders than are most heads of state in Western Europe. A 1990 poll showed that Juan Carlos is more popular than the institution of the monarchy: 82% that he had made a significant contribution to democratic stability, but 42% found the monarchy "out–of–date." Nevertheless, polls in 1996 revealed that the monarchy is Spain's most highly rated institution.

The King influences the selection of the prime minister and the cabinet, and he formally appoints both. The cabinet is technically not responsible to the *Cortés*. However, according to recent practice, a government is expected to have a majority in the Chamber of Deputies.

Spain

Parliament

A national referendum in December 1976 established a bicamaral parliament, and in another referendum in December 1978, 87.8% of all voting Spaniards approved of a new constitution, which contained few traces of Francoism. The upper house of the *Cortés*, the 248 seat Senate, is the less important chamber. In an electoral system which gives each voter four votes, each province elects the four candidates with the highest number. All provinces send four senators regardless of population. This is designed to protect the interests of the smaller provinces and is one indication of the extent to which Spain had become a federal state. The islands and the two Moroccan enclaves send seven senators, and the King is permitted to appoint as many as 41 additional senators.

The 350 members of the lower house, the Chamber of Deputies, are elected by a modified form of proportional representation by which voters choose from a list established by each party. Independent candidates are forbidden to run for election unless they can combine to form a list. Seats are distributed to the various provinces according to population, with the smallest province receiving at least three seats.

The electoral system is designed to favor the large parties at the expense of the smaller ones. The parties are strengthened further by their power to take away a parliamentary seat occupied by any of its members and give it to another. This possibility hardens members' loyalty toward their parties and also makes parliamentary speeches predictable and rather dull. One can only marvel, though, at the way the Spanish, who were not permitted to vote in free elections for more than 40 years, can competently sort their way through more than 60 parties and groups, using two different electoral systems at the same time, and produce a similar result in both houses of the *Cortés*.

Political Parties

In 1977 Spain's major parties signed the Moncloa Pact with each other, named after the small governmental palace in Madrid. By signing this pact, the parties agreed to drop their party dogma for the good of the country. The major parties' moderation was appreciated by the voters. In the first free elections since 1936, the Spanish showed their preference for the parties which are unmistakably in favor of the democratic order. The more radical parties of the left and right found themselves represented in Parliament, but without anything close to a majority.

Political parties entered the post–Franco era with well–founded nervousness. In Spain's past, parties were always plagued by division. Spain was the only country in Europe to experience a civil war in the 20th century, and the political parties had been in the thick of that tragic struggle. From 1939 to 1975 they had been unable to operate freely, and most of them had been driven underground or into exile, where their members were often isolated from each other, and where their leaders had great problems in establishing and maintaining unity. They also had difficulty following political developments within Spain.

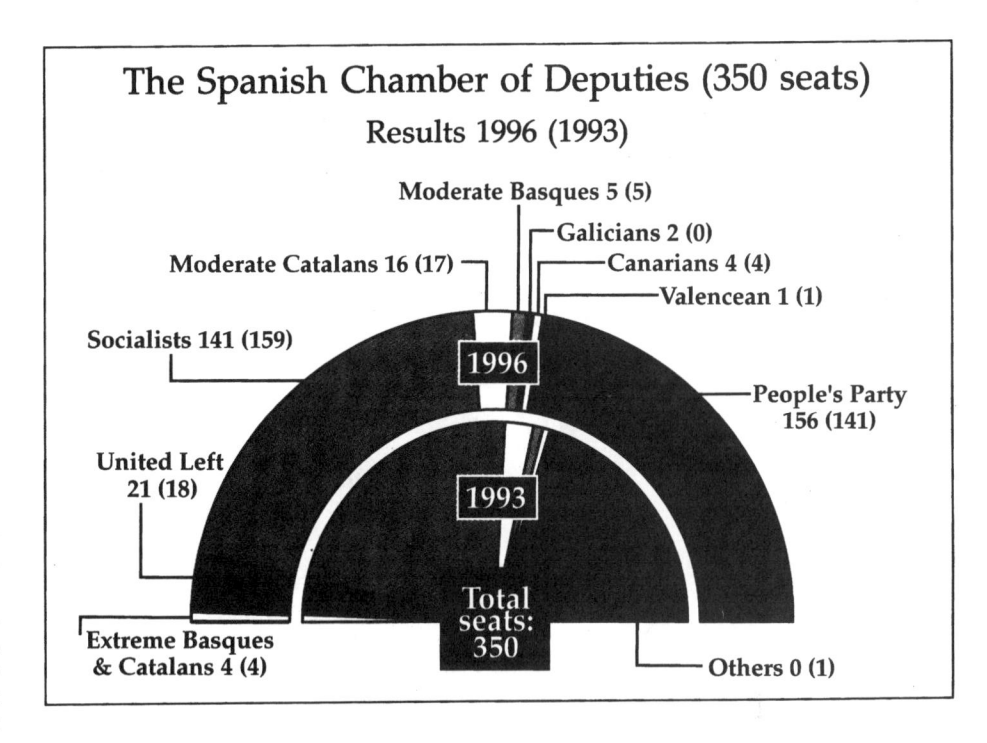

When Franco died, the parties had to organize themselves very quickly. Fortunately Spain had an intelligent and able King who could stabilize the transition while the democratic parties prepared themselves. Portugal had not been so fortunate and had to experience two years of chaos before the moderate democratic parties could gain their footing.

Socialists

Only two of the major parties existed before 1975. The largest party today is the ruling *Spanish Socialist Labor Party (PSOE)* which, together with the *Catalan Socialist Party* and the *Basque Socialist Party*, is generally referred to as *The Socialists*. Founded in 1879, it is the oldest Spanish party. Yet it acquired a young image after a thorough change of leadership in the early 1970s.

Its former leader, Felipe González, is an attractive and charismatic man, who was a labor lawyer and who had engaged in anti–Francoist underground activity. He and the other leaders were able to lead the *PSOE* from a radical leftist Marxist stance during the Franco era to a pragmatic political course which sought to open the party toward the political center. He is a master of compromise, tactics and organization.

A majority within the *PSOE* decided in 1976 to call itself Marxist, over the urgent protest of González. The latter argued that the party should return to the ethical and undogmatic socialism of the party's founders and consider Marxism merely as "an interesting intellectual exercise, but not the holy writ." He, himself, publicly declares that he is not a Marxist. González resigned in protest, and as a result the popularity of the party plummeted. Therefore a special party congress was called in 1979 to vote by 86% to reinstate him as head of a moderate party executive committee. The *PSOE* is still a party with a broad political spectrum, but González brought the left–wing within the party largely under control. The *PSOE* calls for a classless, pluralistic, democratic and decentralized Spain with a market economy. Its slogan is: "Socialism is freedom!"

The party is very strong in Madrid and other industrial centers, and most large cities have Socialist mayors. It is also strong in the agricultural region of Andalusia. It is the only socialist party in southern Europe which has strong support from a significant independent trade union, the *UGT*. It also has a well–developed local base, so it is the only Spanish party with solid roots in the factories, local neighborhoods and national and regional parliaments.

One of the *PSOE's* major advantages

The Spanish Chamber of Deputies (350 seats)
Results 1996 (1993)

- Moderate Basques 5 (5)
- Galicians 2 (0)
- Moderate Catalans 16 (17)
- Canarians 4 (4)
- Valencean 1 (1)
- Socialists 141 (159)
- People's Party 156 (141)
- United Left 21 (18)
- Extreme Basques & Catalans 4 (4)
- Others 0 (1)

Total seats: 350

Spain

had always been its unity in the face of opposing parties' disunity. But that ended as fighting within González's party erupted over the question of what a socialist government should do. One faction, the *renovadores* (renewers), supported González's pragmatic free market policies, aimed at opening up monopolies, curbing the budget deficit, and creating conditions favorable for job creation and business. The *Guerristas,*, named after their leader, Alfonso Guerra, regard themselves as orthodox socialists. The government's economic austerity fueled such strong discontent on the labor front that the unions called several 24–hour general strikes in 1988, 1992, and 1994. The 1988 work stoppage was the first successful general strike in Spain since 1934.

González was sometimes accused of abandoning socialist principles by failing to redistribute wealth. The charge is not entirely fair. During his four terms, education spending rose, as the school–leaving age was raised to 16 and the number of university students doubled. Health services and pension rights were extended to the entire population, and a nation–wide unemployment benefit scheme was created. Overall social spending rose from 27% of GDP in 1977 to 45% in 1997. The magnitude of these expenditures was reflected in the budget deficit, which in 1996 stood at 4.4% of GDP; when he left office in 1996 the overall national debt was a little over 60% of GDP.

His victory in 1993 left him the only socialist ruler in any major Western European country and the only leader in any European country to win a fourth term. In contrast to other Western European socialist parties, his moderate, pragmatic party still personified Spain's post–Franco modernization.

For the first time González had to rule without a parliamentary majority, having fallen from 176 to 159 seats based on 38.7% of the votes. He depended on votes from two regionally–based parties—the *Catalan Convergence and Union* and the *Basque National Party*. The ultimate arbiters and power brokers were the wily Catalan leader, Jordi Pujol, and, to a lesser extent, the Basque nationalist leader, Javier Arzallus. The problem was that these two nationalist leaders subscribe to a different agenda than he did. They do not conceal that their major objective is ever–greater home rule for their regions, and they are willing to use their newly–found leverage in Madrid to press for this. Further complicating the situation was the fact that both of these nationalist parties compete with the *Socialists* for power in Catalonia and the Basque area.

As if these problems were not enough, González's government found itself embroiled in a series of serious financial scandals which severely dented his credibility. His brother–in–law was accused of earning vast sums from influence peddling. He was embarrassed by the flight and recapture of Luis Roldán, the first civilian to head the Civil Guard, accused of amassing a huge personal fortune during his seven years in office. Three ministers and a number of top officials resigned on corruption charges. Then in 1995 it was revealed that Spain's secret service (CESID) illegally tapped the phones of prominent persons, including the king. Not only did this stir memories of Franco's police, but it endangered his shaky alliance with the Catalan nationalists which kept his majority government in power. His deputy, Narcis Serra, and his defense minister, Julian Garcia Vargas, resigned.

The minority González government was also bruised by allegations of illegal party financing schemes and suspicions that he knew about anti–terrorist death squads operating in the 1980s. He maintained that he knew nothing about these squads, and the Supreme Court ruled in 1996 that there was no evidence linking him to their activities and that he therefore could not be called to testify.

Placating his Catalan partners was impossible. Early elections in March 1996 resulted in the defeat of the incumbent by a narrow margin. The *Socialists* captured 37.4% of the votes and 141 seats in the Cortes (down from 159 in 1993). In opposition, González stepped down as leader in 1997 and was replaced by Joaquín Almunia, his close associate.

At the end of González's era, Spaniards reflected on the dramatic transformation their country had undergone during his rule, which lasted longer than any other contemporary Western European leader except German Chancellor Helmut Kohl: Spain is solidly democratic. Francoism has lost its force even though old Francoists have suffered little persecution. The army no longer intervenes in politics. The country is more decentralized, with more power having passed to the regions. The nature of Spanish socialism has changed to the extent that most now refer to themselves as "social democrats," and the middle class is no longer hostile to *Socialists*.

Economically, he championed the free market, was often firm with the trade unions, and privatized some state enterprises. He made Spain look modern, and in 1995 the UN ranked Spain ninth in the world for its "quality of life." In foreign affairs, he led Spain into the EU and NATO, and he permitted the U.S. to retain its military bases in the country.

The Communists

The other party with deep historical roots is the *Spanish Communist Party (PCE)*. Founded in 1920, it was heavily involved in the Spanish Civil War on the republican side. The Communists worked closely with the Soviet Union's participants in the Civil War. This collaboration was too close and gave Spanish Communists a clear look at Marxist–Leninist practices. This fact helps to explain why the exiled party was the first communist party in Europe to reject the Soviet model of communism and the notion of the dictatorship of the proletariat. It condemned the Warsaw Pact invasion of Czechoslovakia in 1968, as well as similar actions against Afghanistan and Poland in 1979 and 1981. In 1977 former party chief Santiago Carrillo published a book, *Eurocommunism and the State*, in which he repeated his contention that the Soviet model had so discredited itself that it was beyond rescue. This moderate, independent course is being continued by the party's present leader, Julio Anguita.

The party's operations within Spain began again long before the death of Franco. It built up party cells in the factories, neighborhoods, youth groups, hospitals and even in the government ministries. It is still the most disciplined and best organized mass party in Spain, despite factional splits. The working class provides 80% of its voters, who are predominantly male. Its strongest areas are in the industrialized zones of Madrid and Catalonia.

Despite its turn from Stalinism and despite its pragmatic approach and support for the democratic regime, it had little electoral success. In the 1979 national parliamentary elections, it received only about 10% of the votes, and in the 1982 elections its vote plummeted to 3.8% and

The PSOE's Joaquín Almunia

Spain

four seats. Combining forces with other elements of the old Marxist left under the banner, *United Left (IU)*, it and its allies won 10.6% of the votes and 21 seats in 1996. Its 21 votes in the *Cortés* have restored its relevance in Spanish politics. While its cells are well entrenched in numerous organizations in the country, it lacks popular support. Its membership had fallen to about 62,000 from its peak of 200,000 in 1978. Although it is firmly supported by the Workers' Commissions, this most powerful trade union federation is losing ground to the *Socialist*–dominated *UGT*.

Many Spanish are still aware of the remorseless and cunning tactics which the Communists used during the Civil War to bring the Socialists and leftist Republicans under their control. Their heavy–handedness caused many Spanish to forget their more moderate actions during the popular front days before the outbreak of hostilities. Although the *PCE* now advocates a "peaceful road to socialism," there are several other ultra–left and violent groups in Spain which call themselves "communist." They therefore help keep alive the inclination of many Spaniards to associate communism with unrest and violence.

Another problem is that although the *PCE* publicly supports democracy, there is still too little democracy *within* the party. Despite periodic purges, there are still wings within the *PCE* which struggle for domination and which are treated harshly by the party leadership. Former leader Carrillo failed in his attempt to win more popular support by breaking away. The party has difficulties with a younger group who call themselves "renovators" and demand the introduction of genuine intra–party democracy and the disavowal of "democratic centralism," which requires absolute obedience after decisions have been made. By 1989 there was even talk of plans to turn the *United Left* into a non–Communist party.

The hardest nut for the splintered *PCE* to crack, though, is the presence of a highly attractive *Socialist Party* for Spanish voters who want a moderate, democratic leftist–oriented party. In fact, the *Communist Party* faces a dilemma: it knows that no party in Spain has a chance without a democratic program and policy. But the more the *PCE* moderates itself and embraces democracy, the more it becomes indistinguishable from the *PSOE*. Thus, there is little reason to vote for the *PCE*.

The Political Right

The existence of two parties on the political left which could together capture about half of the votes presented a serious challenge to the more conservative political forces. The die–hard supporters of the Franco dictatorship had to learn through stinging electoral defeats that Francoism could not survive in Spain without *El Caudillo* himself.

The fact that the two dominant parties in Spain today—the *PSOE* and the *People's Party* (*PP*, until 1989 called the *Popular Alliance* or *AP*)—support the democratic order makes the present political situation far different from the early 1930s. Indeed, the emergence of a basically two–party system strengthens Spanish democracy.

The most conservative of the major parties, the *People's Party*, was refounded, renamed and revamped in 1989. At first it thought it could win votes by hammering against crime and the alleged Marxist danger and by thereby polarizing the society. Young thugs identifying themselves as *AP* adherents roamed the streets with sticks and bicycle chains attacking persons wearing socialist badges. The result was a miserable showing in the 1977 elections.

In post–Franco Spain, the word "right" is still a red flag for many voters, who want to see any conservative policies advocated from the center–right. The party decided to move closer to the political center and to draw a clear line between itself and the anti–regime parties on the right. It rejects violence, supports the monarchy, advocates reforms and a "social market economy," and opposes monopolies. It seeks a broad alliance of voters.

Its former leader was Manuel Fraga Iribarne, one of Spain's most colorful politicians. As almost all earlier leaders of the party, he was a high functionary in the earlier regime. But he became a strong proponent of parliamentary democracy. He was such a skilled and hard–hitting speaker that he even scared some people in his own party. Campaigning energetically on a platform of lower taxes, protection of Spanish business, law and order and strong support for the military, his party became Spain's second largest political force, despite its lingering associations with the Franco era. Fraga left the national scene to become head of Galicia's regional government. This left the party free to construct a more modern alternative to the *Socialist* government.

The party is led by Prime Minister José Maria Aznar, who was able to do what other conservative leaders had failed to accomplish: unite former Francoists, Christian Democrats, and free–market liberals. A master of consensus politics, he insists that "I am a centrist." He narrowly escaped an assassination attempt in 1995. The *People's Party* has the fewest members of any other major party and is well represented only in the upper civil service and the army. Its views are expressed by

Prime Minister José Maria Aznar

the important conservative Madrid daily, ABC, which the party controls.

It is particularly strong in small towns and predominantly rural areas. Its chief problem was that González's pragmatic socialism left little room for a conservative party beyond tax–cutting. But it benefited from the prime minister's difficulties. In the 1993 elections it rose from 106 to 141 seats on the basis of 34.8% of the votes. It was the overwhelming victor of the 1995 municipal elections, capturing majorities in 11 of 17 provincial parliaments and 32 of 52 provincial capitals. Its greatest humiliation of the *Socialists* was its dominance of the under–40 vote.

The *PP* entered the March 1996 elections with a comfortable lead in the polls and was confident it would take power. It captured 38.8% of the votes. But with only 156 seats in the 350–seat lower house, it fell 20 seats short of an absolute majority. Aznar had to negotiate with the regional parties, especially Pujol's Catalans (*CIU*, with 16 seats) and the moderate Basques (*PNV*, with five seats), to scrape together a shaky minority government. The price was another generous increase in regional autonomy. He committed his government to "fully implementing the 1979 statute of autonomy" and to raising the percentage of tax revenues the regions can keep for themselves.

The fact that post–Franco Spain has undergone two peaceful transfers of power, from the center to the left and now from the left to the right, demonstrates that democracy has come of age. In another way Aznar's government represents a *Second Transition* (the title of his 1994 book): it

Spain

brings to power a new generation of leaders in their thirties and forties who were students when Franco died in 1975. The *PP's* leadership has allayed Spanish fears that the old Francoist right would dismantle the welfare state and that fascist intolerance might return to Spain. Aznar, who by temperament prefers politics by accommodation, has a powerful historical motive to operate by consensus. Indeed, most of his policies—privatization of industries, full integration with NATO, and fiscal austerity to qualify for European Monetary Union (EMU)—continue rather than break with the *Socialists'* program.

The Military and Politics

While Spain's parties are doing much to pull Spain's democratic forces together, there are certain elements which place strains on the Spanish constitutional order: the military, regional separatists and a governmental bureaucracy in need of reform.

Although fears of an army coup have subsided, the Spanish military remains the biggest question mark and danger. After Franco's death the civilians carefully removed the 40,000–man National Police from military control and gave the Ministry of the Interior coequal power with the military over the 58,000–man Civil Guard. The latter troops, highly efficient, proud and dressed in dull–green uniforms and black patent–leather tricorn hats, have been used since 1844 as an internal security force by the central government and under Franco as an apparatus of repression. Yet the new regime still cannot be certain that it firmly controls either the police, the Civil Guard or the 230,000–man army. No country can ever make an absolutely clean break with its past, and an essential fact of Spain's past is the military's arrogation to itself of special political responsibility. Every officer takes an oath "to preserve the unity of Spain," and Article 8 of the constitution names the military as ultimate arbiter of Spanish sovereignty and constitutional rights.

Most of Spain's officers are politically conservative and highly disciplined. Most will obey whoever is in power. Since the inception of democracy many officers have openly grumbled about the new kind of politics, which, they say, gives free rein to criminals, terrorists, opponents of a unified Spain, bickering political parties and assertive trade unions. They also resented what they saw as politically motivated military promotions and neglect of the military's needs. By the end of the 1980s only about 9% of the central government's budget was spent on defense.

Soldiers have also criticized the civilian government's failure to cope with domestic terrorism. These groups include the Basque separatists *(ETA)*, a leftist–sounding *GRAPO* (the Spanish initials for "Groups of Antifascist Resistance First of October"), the rightist *Apostolic Alliance* and the *Warriors of Christ the King*. All aim to destroy confidence in the government, polarize society and provoke the armed forces to take over power and establish a dictatorship. Their motives are, of course, different.

The ultra–rightists want a dictatorship for its own sake, and the ultra–leftists want one as a prelude to some kind of Marxist paradise. It cannot be denied that these terrorists know their country's history very well. Domestic violence has time and again destroyed the constitutional order and provoked the establishment of dictatorships to restore order.

The 1981 Attempted Coup

One event especially showed that the essential political issues of parliamentary supremacy and civilian control over the military had not yet been entirely solved. On February 23, 1981, only three weeks after Prime Minister Suárez had announced his resignation thereby plunging Spain into a parliamentary crisis, a colonel in the Civil Guard, Antonio Tejero Molina, led 200 guardsmen into the ornate Chamber of Deputies and held the Parliament and the Cabinet hostage for 18 hours. It was the most outrageous event in the *Cortés* since 1874, when General Manuel Pavia rode his horse up the steps of Parliament and dismissed the horrified deputies.

The intruders roughed up Deputy Prime Minister Manuel Gutierrez Mellado, a liberal general in the army, and unleashed bursts of machine gun fire toward the ceiling, forcing most deputies to take cover under their desks. Since the plotters forgot that the session was being televised, Span-

West of Madrid in the foothills of the bleak Sierra de Guadarrama stands El Escorial, the brooding, magnificent blue-gray slate and stone symbol of the unchangeable spirit of Spain. Combining a royal palace, basilica, monestery and art gallery, it was built by Philip II, heir to the boundless riches of the New World, the most powerful monarch of the 16th century.

Spain

iards outside the *Cortés* were able to witness the shameful spectacle. Tejero, who had received a slap on the wrist only a year earlier for his part in a hairbrained plot to kidnap the Cabinet, was not acting alone. Other officers were also involved. The regional commander in Valencia put his troops on alert and sent his tanks into the streets, and all but two of the nine regional commanders hesitated to do anything while waiting to see if the *coup* (called *el golpe* in Spain) would succeed.

It was at this critical juncture that Juan Carlos, who had fortunately canceled a long-planned trip to the U.S. in order to be in Madrid during the political crisis, acted to save Spanish democracy. He ordered the creation of a "governmental commission" composed of ministerial undersecretaries to assume provisional civilian governmental power while the cabinet was in captivity. He skillfully turned one of the highest-ranking plotters, his military tutor in the 1950s and chief military adviser since 1975, General Alfonso Armada Comyn, away from the venture by declaring that the plotters would "have to put two bullets in me before they take over" and then dispatching Armada to help suppress the uprising.

The King then turned to his many contacts within the army to assure them that he opposed the *coup* and would die to defend Spain's democracy. Ironically, one can thank Franco for having sent the King to the military academies and thereby having provided Juan Carlos with so many friends within the armed forces. He persuaded the officers of the elite Brunete armored division on the outskirts of Madrid to keep their tanks in the camp and out of the streets of Madrid. If the capital city had become filled with tanks, it is likely that the *coup* would have acquired uncontrollable momentum. The King phoned all the captains-general in the nine military districts to coax or pressure them into supporting him.

Finally, at 1:15 A.M. he went on national television, wearing a general's uniform and sitting in front of the royal coat of arms, to announce that "the crown, symbol of the permanence and unity of the nation, cannot tolerate, in any form, actions or attitudes attempting to interrupt the democratic process." This announcement was a tremendous comfort to a people which places great importance on symbols. The next morning Tejero saw that he was alone and gave up.

One *Socialist* deputy announced with relief that "the time of *coups* is over," but centrist politician Antonio Garrigues Walker was more correct in declaring "Thank you Señor Tejero, for pointing out that our democracy is fragile and incomplete." It is true that Spanish democracy had passed an important test. According to opinion polls, only 4% of Spaniards wanted the *coup* to succeed, while 76% were hostile to it. Most soldiers had supported their civilian rulers, but some had revealed that they were divided and hesitant about such support. Clearly, some soldiers still have little faith in parliamentary democracy, and the military still plays an important role in politics and cannot be overlooked. Only hours after the abortive *coup,* the King met with political leaders and warned: "I invite all to reflect and reconsider postures that might lead to greater unity in Spain and more agreement among the Spanish people."

All democratic forces thereafter had to be more cautious and to strive much harder to adopt policies and wage settlements which rest on a consensus, which would

Col. Tejero brandishes a pistol on the podium of the Cortés

include the military. Reforms were slowed down, and a conscientious effort was made to woo the military. For the first time, the army was given an actual role in a stepped-up campaign against Basque terrorism by being deployed along the French border. The *Cortés* passed a law defining states of alarm, siege and emergency, during which times certain civil rights dealing with press freedom, search and detention could be revoked. Finally, Juan Carlos, whose prestige within Spain had soared, had to recognize that his bold actions had alienated him from some elements within the military and that his capacity to prevent another *coup* had probably been reduced.

Treatment of the Plotters

Spain's political leaders were faced with a dilemma as to what to do with the plotters. If they cracked down too hard, they might provoke an unfortunate military response. Spanish history clearly shows that nothing is more dangerous than a humiliated military. However, if the *coup* leaders were not given stiff sentences, then they might be encouraged to try again. After all, most of the key figures in the *coup* had been given the mildest suspended sentences for their part in earlier attempts to overthrow the government.

One year after the *coup* attempt, 32 officers and one civilian were brought to trial before a military tribunal. Tejero had in the meantime become the darling of Spain's ultra-right. In custody, he had enjoyed what he had described as "five-star-hotel treatment" and had received up to 50 admiring visitors each day. Photo books, collections of his jokes (most directed against the new order), and flamenco songs praising him were circulating, and he gave widely published interviews and worked on his memoirs. In his trial in a handsomely furnished hall with soft chairs for the defendants, he supported the slander campaign against the King, which insinuated that Juan Carlos had actually given his advance approval for the *coup*. He also joined other defendants to implicate as many political and military figures as possible in the plot.

Defense attorneys unashamedly cited the many precedents for military intervention in politics. In the closing statements no defendant showed the slightest regret or guilt for his actions, and instead all stressed their love for Spain, their honor as officers and their wish to save the motherland. Tejero probably best expressed the standpoint of a person who learns nothing and understands even less: "I would like to express my utter contempt for those high-ranking officers who have betrayed their motherland." He and the other major conspirator, General Milan del Bosch, were sentenced to thirty years in jail.

The potential strength of the far right was demonstrated by the *Fuerza Nueva* ("New Force"), which had wanted to turn back the wheel of history. Although this and other ultra-right groups never got many votes, they were visible and audible. The leader was Blas Piñar, a highly skilled demagogue who was at his best in rallies complete with outstretched arms giving the fascist salute, fascist paraphernalia everywhere, and the sounds of Franco's hymn, "Cara al Sol" (Face the Sun) blaring in the background. At one time this group could mobilize 300,000 Spaniards in the streets of Madrid every November to honor their dead idol, and their bullies roamed the streets menacingly. The *Fuerza Nueva* idolized the military, especially those soldiers who seized Parliament in 1981, and it promised to help es-

Spain

tablish a "free Spain." Few Spaniards cared much for its notion of freedom. It was scrapped because it had been ignored by those it had hoped to protect: the Church, conservatives and the military.

González bent over backwards to quiet the soldiers' nerves. Shortly after assuming office, he visited the crack Brunete armored division, which had been deeply implicated in the 1981 plot. He picked up on the initiatives of his predecessor to modernize the army by streamlining and professionalizing it and by giving it better equipment. In 1983 the government moved to tighten control over the military by appointing a single chief of defense responsible to the defense minister. It sought to reduce the number of military regions from eight to six and to move the Brunete armored division to Extremadura on the Portuguese border, policies which took a long time to be carried out because officers could refuse to be sent to an uncongenial region.

It reduced the number and rank of Spain's most senior officers. In 1985 the defense minister abolished the guarantee that every officer would be promoted at least to the rank of brigadier general before retirement. But he had to concede the right that all would be made colonels, a policy unheard-of in any other Western army. In 1989 Spain introduced promotions based on merit, and those who cannot perform satisfactorily are retired early. These are important steps toward greater professionalization.

Regionalization and Decentralization

A second element which places a heavy strain on the democratic regime is the attempt to decentralize Spanish government and to grant a satisfactory measure of autonomy to the regions. For reasons related to the Moslem conquest, the prolonged expulsion of them and the vast overextension of imperial power, Spain was never a fully integrated country. Madrid was a somewhat artificial creation, surrounded like a bull's-eye by the harsh, sparsely-populated, mainly Castilian *Meseta*. Around this tableland is the more densely populated and highly diverse periphery.

Tension between the center and the periphery has always been a constant factor in politics. Even today, a fourth of all citizens speak a language other than Castilian Spanish. There are economic disparities. For example, Catalonia, the Basque area and Madrid produce half of Spain's GDP, while almost half the population in Galicia and a third in Estremadura and Castile still work on the land, compared to only 6% in Catalonia and the Basque region. New industries and tourism have helped narrow the gap between these rich and poor regions.

Most Spaniards note regional idiosyncrasies, and many cliches are current: Cordobans are stoic; Galicians are stubborn and moody; Catalans and Valencians are artistic and entrepreneurial; Andalusians are a bit wild and Moorish; and Castilians are austere and noble. Yet all benefit from being a part of the larger Spanish economy and are held together by such strong common interests that no region would vote for secession.

The regions particularly were suppressed under Franco, who in part justified his military *coup* and subsequent rule as the preservation of unity. Franco gained the lasting hatred of the Basques after ordering the devastating bombing of Guernica on April 26, 1937. This situation did not change immediately after Franco's death, and in the Basque country there were some regrettable incidents involving the suppression of cultural events. But in modern Spanish history transitions to greater freedom and democracy were always accompanied by demands for more home rule in the regions, and the post–Franco era was no exception. Fortunately the new leaders had pluralist political sentiments and were therefore willing to make many compromises.

Spain introduced in 1979 the most ambitious plan to decentralize political power since the foundation of the Federal Republic of Germany in 1949. It has already become one of Europe's most decentralized states with 17 autonomous regions, each with its own government and parliament, though with differing degrees of power. Ultimately it is to have a fully federal system, with the central government reserving for itself the exclusive right to conduct foreign, defense, monetary, customs and strategic industrial policy, as well as full responsibility over the national police and criminal law. Health, welfare, local administration, and education were gradually transferred to the regions. Madrid was forced to back down in 1997 when a committee of experts drew up a list of 100 teaching points to be used in history classes all over Spain. Regional minorities, especially in Catalonia and the Basque area, considered the idea that Spain had a unified history to be reactionary and intolerable. The central government negotiates with each of the 17 regions on the powers which should be granted to each.

Relations with the demanding regions is never easy for Madrid. Four regions—Catalonia, the Basque Country, Galicia and Andalucia—have more autonomy than the others. As a price for Catalan support for the Aznar minority govern-

Spanish Provinces

Spain

Plaza de Colón, Madrid

ment in 1996, the central government agreed to raise the proportion of locally raised income taxes the Catalans may keep from 15% to 30% over five years. This percentage differs in each region, so Spain in effect has 17 different tax systems. In 1998 the central government controlled only 58% of public spending, the regions 27% and local governments 15%.

The *coup* attempt in February 1981 prompted the major parties to hammer out a law (called *LOAPA*) in June 1981 which would help insure that the military would not object to the process of devolving roughly half of the central government's administrative and budget responsibilities to the regions. Actual transfer of powers was gradually to take place over years. *LOAPA* established a clearing fund to help reduce economic differences among the regions. It also contained elements which aroused some suspicion, especially in the Basque and Catalan regions. It placed limits on the regional legislative and executive powers, and, some argue, practically eliminated the concept of exclusive regional jurisdiction over certain matters.

Basque Separatism

Basque nationalism remains the Achilles heel of Spanish democracy, and it was the leading argument of the plotters who tried to overturn Spain's democracy in 1981. There are 2.1 million Basques in Spain (just 5% of the country's population) and about 200,000 in France, which declared in 1981 that it would no longer permit its territory to be used as a base for illegal operations in Spain. The relative prosperity of the Basque area had long attracted immigrants from poorer Spanish regions. The result is that half of the residents are not Basque, and only 30% of the people speak Basque.

An ancient people of obscure origins and speaking a language which is unrelated to any language of Europe and which almost no outsiders speak, the Basques have always been sharply aware of their separate identity. This awareness was greatly enhanced by the suppression of things Basque during the Franco era. People were forced to adopt Spanish names, and local administration and police work was placed in the hands of non–Basques who had no comprehension or sympathy with the local language or culture.

Acting more like an army of occupation than a protector of public safety, the Civil Guard antagonized the local population to such an extent that the latter could not help from sympathizing with a group of Basque Catholic nationalists which took shape in 1952 under the name of *Euskadi ta Askatasuna* ("Basque Country and Freedom," or *ETA*). In 1968 *ETA* began resorting to violence to accomplish its aims. This caused it to split into a militant, hyper–nationalist wing, called *ETA–Militar*, staffed by predominantly young, well–educated Basques from middle and working class background and a more moderate wing which now disavows violence. Since 1968 *ETA* was directly responsible for almost 800 deaths by the late–1990s.

ETA–Militar reportedly receives training and material support from Libya, Cuba, Yemen and from Palestinian terrorist organizations. It is closely linked to the only Basque party which opposed regional autonomy in 1980, *Herri Batasuna* ("Popular Unity"), renamed *Euskal Herritarok* (*EH*) in 1998, which climbed to 18% of the Basques' votes in the 1998 regional elections, winning 14 of the 75 seats in parliament. Its parliamentary successes or failures were once irrelevant because it boycotted the national and regional parliaments. That policy changed after *ETA* declared a ceasefire in September 1998, a few weeks before the elections. The large electoral turnout indicated voters' approval of the decision to renounce violence and seek a political path to independence.

Spain

Both organizations demand a revision of the Spanish constitution which would be a prelude for an independent *Euskadi*, based on the right of self–determination. *EH* gave signals that it would like to negotiate with the Spanish government in order to escape from the cycle of violence. But until November 1998 the government refused publicly to enter into such negotiations. The other radical nationalist coalition in *Euskadi*, the more moderate *Euskadiko Ezkerra* ("Basque Left"), fused with the *Basque Communist Party* and publicly disavowed violence.

The major political force in *Euskadi* is the more conservative *Basque Nationalist Party* (PNV), which is rural, conservative and Catholic. It captured 28% of the votes and 21 seats in 1998. A party calling itself *Euska Alkartasuna* (EA) broke away from *PNV*, thereby dividing the moderate Basques. The Basque subsidiary of the *Socialist* party is the *Partido Socialista de Euskadi* (PSE), which regards itself as progressive, modern, and secular; it appeals mainly to non–nationalists. More and more Basques are political moderates. They are no longer so afraid to speak out against *ETA*. The Basque branch of the *People's Party*, which rules in Madrid, rose sharply in 1998 to 16 seats.

The central government has recognized their specific needs by granting Basques the right to raise their own taxes and pay none to the federal treasury, as well as to form an all–Basque police force of 6,000 to replace the Civil Guards and national police. Schools, roads, courts and police are all run by the Basques themselves. There are three types of schooling available: in Spanish, Basque, or a mixture of both languages. A groundswell of opinion sees violence as futile and profoundly damaging to the Basque economy. *ETA* and *EH* supporters came to realize that their extremism was so unpopular that it undermined their cause.

The autonomy measures cut into public support for the separatist alternative. Also, the anti–terrorist campaign by the Spanish police increased French cooperation, and disillusionment among many Basques with the brutality shown by *ETA* reduced the number of terrorist attacks and paved the way to the ceasefire in 1998. Spaniards were greatly relieved that *ETA* terrorists had not disrupted the Barcelona Olympics in 1992. Prior to the games the Spanish and French authorities had launched a determined campaign against *ETA*.

In 1992 ETA's top leaders were arrested, but authorities found the organization to be more complex than had previously been imagined. Its fighters are equipped with advanced technology, weapons, lots of money, and a back–up leadership ready to take over in case the top members were arrested, as was the case. ETA traditionally bases its command and support structures in southwest France. There its armed units are equipped and trained and then sent across the border into Spain to make its bloody strikes.

In 1993 the police delivered a knockout blow by seizing in Bayonne, France, an arms cache of pistols, automatic weapons and plastic explosives so huge that much of it must have been destined for export. One week later, the head of ETA's vast operations, Rafael Caride Simón, was seized while sipping a beer in a Toulouse bar. By that time more than 500 ETA terrorists were behind bars, dispersed in groups of fewer than 15 in jails all over Spain to encourage them to cooperate with police and to prevent them from continuing their operations during incarceration.

As *ETA* became more isolated, it attacked higher–profile targets. In 1995 José Maria Aznar, who became prime minister in 1996, barely escaped death when a car bomb went off near his home. *ETA* also failed in an attempt to assassinate King Juan Carlos in 1995. A year later the mastermind of this abortive plot, Julián Atxurra Egurola, was arrested in France, whose three southwest departments, together with the four northern Spanish regions, the Basque terrorists claim for the independent Basque country they dream of. The house in which Egurola was captured was a true arsenal, containing explosives, timers, grenade launchers, anti-tank rockets, machine guns, pistols and ammunition.

The 1997 killing of a town councillor from the ruling *People's Party* wiped out any remaining support for *Herri Batasuna* outside the Basque area and caused revulsion across Europe and massive protests throughout Spain. In December the entire 23–member leadership of *Herri Batasuna* was sentenced to seven years in prison for helping *ETA* guerrillas. Losing support steadily, the *ETA* declared a ceasefire in 1998.

Madrid kept up its pressure in 1999, arresting *ETA's* top guerrilla in Paris and rounding up one of its main commando units. Some Basques protested that these actions broke a tacit truce. But violence did not reappear. One reason is that the faction within *ETA* that favors a peaceful path to independence had gained the upper hand. The Basque regional parliament asked for UN inspectors to oversee the peace process. The other is that Prime Minister Aznar stuck to his government's policy of seeking a political solution to the problem, while continuing to rule out the Basque nationalists' long–standing demand for a "right to self–determination" to be expressed in a referendum. This would require an alteration of the 1978 constitution that declares Spain to be indissoluble.

Marketplace, Granada Photo by Eugenia Elseth

Catalonian separatist symbol

Spain

The sign was written in both languages—Spanish and Catalan. The Spanish was crossed out, leaving only the Catalan with the added comment: "In Catalonia, in Catalan," meaning that in Catalonia, it has to be written Catalan

Catalonia

Viewed from Madrid, Catalonia appears almost as the model of civic responsibility, when compared with its Basque neighbors. Catalans are Spain's richest and culturally most illustrious minority. The architect Antoni Gaudi, cellist Pablo Casals, and painters Joan Miró and Salvador Dali were all from this region. In the past its literature and language, spoken by about 4 million persons, was suppressed, and under Franco one could be put in jail for singing "El Cant de la Senyera," the Catalan national anthem. But the Catalans are a pragmatic and patient people, who are inclined to wait for more promising times, rather than to revolt. As one Castilian observer noted, "the difference between the Basque and Catalan nationalists is that the Basques want to leave Spain, and the Catalans want to run it." In 1992, the Olympic Games were held in Barcelona, commemorating the 500th anniversary of Columbus's discovery of America. They were a source of great pride for independently–minded Catalans. All events and results were announced first in the Catalan language, and then in Spanish, English and French.

Since 1979 Catalonia has had an autonomy statute similar to that of the Basque country. However, by the time it was able to manage many of its own affairs, an important change had taken place. The region's dynamic industry and commerce had attracted so many immigrants from the poorer Spanish regions that nearly half of the region's population was no longer of Catalan origin. Many of the newcomers refused to learn the Catalan language or to adjust to the cultural traditions in the area. Catalonia had a struggle to define its own identity within the Spanish nation. But by the end of the century the Catalan language had revived remarkably. About 95% of the residents can use it.

In 1993 and 1996 its clout in Madrid was dramatically increased by the fact that both the *Socialist* and *PP* governments became dependent on the *Catalan Convergence and Union's (CIU)* seats to have a majority. The skillful Catalan leader, Jordi Pujol, knows how to use this leverage. With the *Socialists,* he negotiated a measure of fiscal autonomy to keep 15% of the income tax raised in the region. In 1996 he forced the newly elected Aznar to raise that to 30% within five years. He also stepped up his campaign to make Catalan the language used in the schools. He keeps his focus on his central ambition: a loosely federated Spain in which the King of Spain would become the "King of the Spains."

Catalonia is booming economically, and its six million people generate 20% of Spain's GDP. Pujol's favorite statistics are that Catalonia, which his government calls "a country within Spain," has 6% of Spain's territory, 13% of its population, 25% of its exports, and 38% of its industrial exports. Foreign investment poured in, but in the 1990s it was increasingly directed toward other regions, especially Madrid.

Other Regions

The other Spanish regions are also making their way toward one form of autonomy or the other. In Navarra, many residents speak Basque, but waves of immigrants from the Spanish interior have made a great majority of its residents hostile to any form of integration with *Euskadi.* About half the inhabitants of Pais Valencia (the provinces of Valencia, Castellon and Alicante) speak Catalan. However, the majority is in favor of autonomy, while remaining consciously within the Catalan cultural community, which also embraces the Balearic islands, Andorra and Roussillon in France.

Spain's largest region, Andalusia, approved its autonomous statute in the fall of 1981. It is one of Spain's poorest regions, with an illiteracy rate estimated at 30%, but accounting for half of Spain's population growth. Its per capita GDP in 1992 was only 55% of the EU average, compared with 77% for the rest of Spain and 100% for Madrid; a third of its workforce is unemployed. It needs all the financial assistance it can get from the wealthier regions and the EU.

In order to stimulate the region's economy and build up its infrastructure, its capital, Seville, hosted "Expo 92," 500 years since Columbus set foot on Santo Domingo. Visitors saw the pavilions around the 15–century Santa Maria de la Cuevas, where Columbus planned his last voyage to America and where he is buried. His voyages were retraced by reproductions of the *Niña* and *Pinta* and two of the *Santa Maria,* which sailed to San Salvador and New York, where three of the ships will remain as part of the Metropolitan Museum's permanent collection. The second *Santa Maria* proceeded through the Panama Canal and on to Japan, where Columbus had hoped to arrive.

In Galicia, 28.4% of eligible voters went to the polls to approve overwhelmingly its autonomy statute. In the 1996 national elections two candidates of a Galician party won seats in the *Cortés.* Aragon, Asturias and other regions are also moving toward limited self–government. A Valencian party captured one *Cortés* seat in 1996. In the Canary islands the separatist Union of the Canary People, which is discreetly supported by Algeria, won four *Cortés* seats in the 1996 national elections and continues to gain adherents. Although in the minority, this group demands self–determination for the islands and the removal of the Spanish army. To show its free spirit, the islands at first refused in 1989 to lower their tariffs on EU manufactured goods until seven tense weeks of negotiations between the regional government and Madrid brought a peaceful settlement. In 1990 the Canaries decided to adjust its economy to the EU.

Bureaucracy Reform

A third major problem facing Spain is to reform the bureaucracy while maintaining a reasonable level of services. Large numbers of state employees have had some trouble adjusting to the new demo-

Spain

Seaside town of Salobreña on the southern coast
Photo by Eugenia Elseth

cratic environment, where public servants are really expected to *serve* the public. Many functionaries have long regarded their positions as practically their own property, and many old usages have persisted, such as the right of each department to collect fees for the services it performs. Also, financial inspectors expected to receive a percentage of the taxes they collected.

Each department still has a strong sense of self–interest and internal loyalty, which often take priority over serving the public. They are often inefficient and excruciatingly slow, especially when it comes to paying money they owe. They are also greatly overstaffed. This is made worse by such measures as the requirement that 35,000 members of Franco's now disbanded *sindicatos*, or state–controlled unions, be absorbed by the government bureaucracy. Work had to be created for this vast unproductive group, and there is understandably lots of sitting or standing around in many of the departments.

González moved quickly to create the kind of civil service appropriate to a democratic and modern Spanish state. His government began immediately to enforce the conflict–of–interest law passed by the *Cortés* in 1982. Civil servants, cabinet ministers, members of Parliament and top executives of state companies are now allowed to have only one job and one salary. Civil servants, who had become accustomed to a 26 to 28–hour work week, are now required to be at work at 8 A.M. and to work eight and one–half hours, with a half hour lunch break. Also, the first Spanish ombudsman was appointed, with the task of looking into complaints of abuses and neglects inflicted on the people by ministers, administrative authorities or public servants.

Foreign Policy

Franco's death enabled Spain to modify its course in foreign policy. In February 1976 Spain relinquished Spanish Sahara, with its rich phosphate deposits, to Morocco and Mauritania, with the hope that the inhabitants could determine their own future. Algeria greatly resented this solution, and a bloody struggle occurred over control of this colony. Morocco simply annexed the former colony.

The major change in Spain's foreign policy, however, was that it turned its primary attention toward Europe. Spain was the only country in Western Europe which did not belong either to the EU, EFTA or NATO. It had been permitted to join the UN in 1950 and eventually became a member of virtually all world bodies. In 1987 a Spaniard, Frederico Mayor Zaragoza, was named as director of UNESCO.

Spain's entry into Western Europe has signaled certain other foreign policy changes. Franco established a special relationship with Latin America, where there were many authoritarian regimes similar to his own. Now Spaniards openly condemn most Latin American dictatorships. The King left no doubt when he was awarded a prize in Germany for his work toward European unity that although Spain is rooted in Europe, it is also a part of the Hispanic world. Spain's policy during the Falkland Islands conflict underscored this fact.

The *Socialist* government showed its special interest in helping to bring about peace talks in Central America, if Spain had been asked to do so. During a visit to Cuba in 1986, Cuban leader Fidel Castro referred to González as "dear friend Felipe" and pinned Cuba's highest distinction, the order of José Martí, on his lapel. In the mid–1990s Spain became the leading investor and a key Western economic and diplomatic intermediary for Cuba, which, unlike the Philippines, still exerts an emotional pull on Spaniards. Nevertheless, relations cooled after Aznar and the *PP* came to power.

Despite the importance which Spain places on *Hispanidad*, its growing European focus weakens its ties with Latin America. Its historical links with its colonies were severed much earlier than were those of Britain and France, and unlike France, Spain is not the senior member of a currency zone. Its trade with Latin America is also insignificant; the latter provided only 6.2% of Spain's imports and took only 4.3% of its exports in 1987, the major partners being Venezuela and Mexico. Nor could the Spanish ever really dominate; the size of its economy is roughly the same as Brazil's and only about twice the size of Mexico's. In 1992 Spain had hoped to celebrate in grand style the 500th anniversary of Columbus' voyage. But it found at a meeting in Madrid of 19 presidential guests from Latin America and Portugal that the New World now has mixed feelings about that explorer who sailed under the Spanish flag. In 1998–9 Spaniards gave strong support to their most famous investigating judge, Baltasar Garzon, who demanded the extradition of one of Latin America's most notorious military rulers, Augusto Pinochet, who was in London for medical treatment. The charges against him were torture, deaths and disappearances of 94 people.

Franco also established another special relationship with the Arab states. Until 1986 Spain did not recognize Israel, for instance. But after Franco's death the Arab states have shown little gratitude for this long–standing policy. Morocco has refused to help implement self–determination for the almost totally nomadic residents of former Spanish Sahara.

With the backing of over a dozen Arab states, Morocco revived its claims to Ceuta (where 15,000 out of a total population of 70,000 are Muslims, and which is located only 14 kilometers from the Spanish mainland) and Melilla (where 27,000 Moroccans and 45,000 Spaniards, including 15,000 soldiers, live). These are the remnants of a string of fortresses Spain built in North Africa after Andalusia was reconquered. There is tension there between Arab residents (many of whom are illegal) and Spaniards, who show no signs of wanting to be ruled by Morocco. In 1997 Spain fenced off the enclaves to prevent illegal immigrants from using them to gain access to Europe. However, these 2.5 meter high barriers are easy to breach and have not prevented them from becoming centers for illegal immigration to southern Europe. Arabs there do not have rights as Spanish citizens. Muslim leaders negotiated with local Spanish officials to improve their social and political conditions, but resistance to their demands remains strong within the Spanish majority.

Algeria also has intrigued in the Canary Islands to try to lead them away from Spain, and Libya, Yemen and some Palestinian organizations have helped the *ETA* terrorists. Largely because of the proximity and near total dependence on Arab oil, Madrid is still more sensitive to Arab sentiments than are most other Western European countries. It forbade the U.S. from using its two bases in Spain to supply Israel, Saudi Arabia or Egypt. In 1986 it also refused to allow U.S. planes to fly over Spain on their way to make a retaliatory anti–terrorist raid on Libya.

Finally Franco's successors ended the policy of not recognizing the Soviet Union and other Eastern European countries. The King paid a visit to the Soviet Union. However, the opening of diplomatic and commercial links brought in its wake such a high incidence of Soviet espionage in Spain that numerous Soviet officials have had to be expelled. Also, in 1979 former Soviet Foreign Minister Andrei Gromyko offered to help the Spanish end terrorism in their country in return for Spain's refusal to join NATO. He also insinuated that Spanish entry would lead to even greater terrorist activity. This clumsy hint led many Spanish politicians and intelligence officials to conclude that Moscow was actually helping the *ETA*. In 1990 President Gorbachëv visited Spain and advocated closer economic ties.

Defense Policy and NATO

Spain's strategic location brought it into an indirect relationship with NATO through a series of bilateral defense agreements with the U.S. beginning in 1953. According to the provisions of this agreement, the U.S. would provide military assistance to the Spanish armed forces in return for the right to have air bases in Torrejon and Zaragoza, a naval base in Rota, and scattered communications installations throughout the country. About 10,000 U.S. troops are stationed in Spain. The periodic renegotiation of these agreements has never been pleasant or easy.

In 1982 Spain became the first country to enter NATO since Germany did so in 1956. Although a majority within the *Cortés* approved membership, the *PSOE* and *PCE* opposed it, and public opinion polls indicated that more Spaniards were against NATO membership than for it. There is an undercurrent of neutralism in Spain. Nevertheless the earlier government pressed on without a referendum on the issue in order, in the words of the former defense minister, "to bring us back into European and democratic circles and to strengthen the democratic system in Spain."

Thus, not only would Spanish defense be boosted, but its officers would be brought into closer contact with foreign officers who are committed to democracy and civilian rule. Army officers would have to learn foreign languages, travel to other NATO countries and acquire modern military skills. They would have to accept a promotion system based not on mere seniority but on professional competence, as was already the case for young officers in the Spanish air force and navy.

Modernization is also desirable for strictly military reasons. The army is poorly equipped and has very few mobile units which are up to NATO standards. The air force is competent, but it is scarcely large enough to provide for Spain's own air defense needs. Therefore, the government decided to purchase 72 American–made F18A fighter planes. It also acquired an aircraft carrier, called the *Príncipe de Asturias*, equipped with a dozen vertical take–off Sea Harrier jets and leading a task force that will include four new anti–submarine frigates. Still, Spanish studies concluded that Spain has half the necessary capability for defending its own airspace; the U.S. provided the other half from its bases in Zaragoza and Torrejon (now vacated).

The armed forces had been reduced to 230,000 in 1989 and continued to be scaled down until they reached 206,000. About 128,800 young men are selected annually by lottery to do nine months in the military (down from 24 months under Franco and 18 months when the *Socialists* first came to power in 1982). They are led by 78,000 professional soldiers. Soldiers are no longer required to perform non-

Secluded, elegant entrances to several homes in Barcelona

Spain

military duties, such as serving as chauffeur of officers' wives, doing laundry or making house repairs with the commanders taking payment on the black market. Also, morale was lifted by serving better food. When possible, recruits serve near their homes, and they are never posted outside of Spain. The Aznar government announced plans in 1996 to phase out conscription in favor of a smaller, better equipped professional army. It was to be paid for by raising defense spending from 1.5% of GDP in 1997 to over 2%, but this actually declined to only 1% by 1999.

NATO, of course, also derives important advantages from Spain's entry. This large country can serve as a rear base for stockpiling material and for a strategic withdrawal for troops and aircraft in the event that Western Europe is overrun. It is well-situated for resupply from the U.S. Ever since France withdrew from the NATO integrated command in 1967, the alliance has lacked the capacity for "defense in depth." Spain also provides important bases and surveillance posts to protect Mediterranean and Atlantic shipping routes, and it can help deny the exit of enemy ships from the Mediterranean into the Atlantic. It offered in 1988 to take responsibility for a stretch of sea extending from the Balearic Islands, through the Strait of Gibralter, and as far as the Canaries. It also offered Spanish territory for reinforcements and supplies needed on the central front.

The Spanish navy is reputed to be a highly professional fighting force, but some NATO observers have doubts that it could perform all its chosen tasks. In 1990 Spain proposed the establishment of a permanent Conference on Security and Cooperation in the Mediterranean (CSCM) as a way of controlling the effects of growing economic imbalances between the northern Mediterranean states and the impoverished North African states. Like most other European countries, Spain fears uncontrollable illegal immigration.

NATO must accept some restrictions. Spain retains a veto on the stationing of nuclear weapons on Spanish soil. In 1966 a U.S. plane carrying four unarmed hydrogen bombs crashed in the village of Palomares. In 1979 the Spanish required the U.S. to withdraw its nuclear weapons from Rota. This does not necessarily mean that Spain will never create its own nuclear weapons. The country has sufficient technology to manufacture nuclear weapons, but Spain decided in 1987 to sign the nuclear nonproliferation treaty. It had sometimes been reported that Spain might need nuclear weapons in order to protect the enclaves in Morocco—Ceuta and Melilla—which are not included by the NATO nuclear umbrella. The Organization of African Unity has already issued a resolution supporting independence for these enclaves, as well as for the Canary Islands. Partly for that reason, the Spanish have declared the latter to be out of bounds for NATO facilities.

Spain also insists that Spanish officers command all units on Spanish territory. Until January 1, 1999, Spain remained outside NATO's integrated military command structure. It is an active NATO member. It sits on the Atlantic Council and in the defense planning committees; it also has observers in the nuclear planning group. In 1988 it further increased its involvement with Western European defense. It joined the Western European Union, which tries to coordinate a stronger "European pillar." It also concluded an agreement with NATO pledging to defend Spain's territory, airspace and waters, including the Strait of Gibraltar, and allowing its soil to be used for NATO logistics and as a staging platform.

Despite his 1982 electoral rhetoric, González became more pragmatic about his party's opposition to NATO. He brought it to accept the view that Spain's democracy and political stability, as well as its commitment to Europe, would be best served if Spain remained inside of NATO. He considered it the "logical consequence" of Spain's entry into the EU, which took place on January 1, 1986.

Nevertheless, in March 1986, he fulfilled his earlier promise to allow Spaniards to express their opinion in a referendum. This was the first time that a member of either NATO or the Warsaw Pact permitted a popular vote on continued membership. Polls had indicated that a majority was against remaining in NATO. To sweeten the pill, González set terms: Spain would not join the integrated command structure, would not permit the entry or stockpiling of nuclear weapons on its territory, and would negotiate the progressive reduction of the U.S. military presence in Spain.

Sensing that a "yes" vote would be interpreted as a great boost for the *Socialists*, the opposition parties recommended abstention, or, in the case of the communists, rejection. The results stunned many anxious observers: 52.5% voted in favor of continued membership, while fewer than 40% voted for withdrawal. An earlier opponent, *Socialist* Foreign Minister Javier Solana, was named NATO secretary–general in 1995. The opposition parties were left shocked and divided, while González' moderate and pragmatic brand of socialism was reinforced. More important, Spain had finally and dramatically ended centuries of isolation. No longer would the French be able to joke that Africa begins at the Pyrenees!

In 1988 González carried through with his promise to reduce American military forces in the country. No reductions were sought at Rota, which plays a key role in supporting the U.S. 6th Fleet, nor at 11 other key U.S. military installations. But the 5,000 American servicemen and 72 F16 fighters of the 401st Tactical Air Wing at Torrejon, which is located only 12 miles from Madrid and had become a convenient symbol for anti–U.S. protesters, were ordered to leave by 1991. González argued that U.S. use of Torrejon stimulated anti–Americanism and anti–NATO feeling in Spain. This order was the first unilateral reduction of American forces ordered by a European ally since France ordered them out in 1966.

The U.S. and Spain also reached an agreement in 1988 extending for eight years the American lease on four other military bases, including Rota. The major obstacle—Spain's prohibition of nuclear weapons on its territory—was cleared away by the Spanish government's tacit agreement not to inspect American ships in Spanish ports to see whether nuclear weapons are on board. Spain also gave up all the guarantees of specific levels of U.S. aid contained in previous lease agreements.

Spain's government made a crucial decision during the 1991 Gulf war against Iraq to support its allies actively. Before the fighting began it sent three warships to the Persian Gulf to help enforce the UN embargo against Iraq. When the air war commenced, Spain permitted the Americans to launch B–52 bombing raids escorted by Spanish fighter planes from Moron air base near Seville, a base jointly used by both air forces. It ferried bombs to the U.S. planes and even supplied ordnance from its own stocks when the Americans ran low. At first, this was highly unnerving and unpopular in a country whose last war outside its borders was in 1898, when Cuba was lost to the Americans. However, public opinion swung around when reports of Iraqi atrocities in Kuwait began arriving.

It was an enormous political risk for González, but it paid off handsomely. He said: "That is what allies are for," and "for the first time in modern history, Spain has stood where it should be." It marked a defining moment in Spain's effort to end its long isolation and shoulder more international responsibility. It buoyed Spanish confidence and helped sweep away memories of neutrality in the First World War and fascist sympathies in the Second.

In 1992–3 Spain again demonstrated its expanded role in international affairs and the increased professionalism of its military by deploying the Spanish Legion to war–torn Bosnia. This elite unit had been

Spain

View of the port of Gibraltar — Photo by Eugenia Elseth

formed in 1920 as a colonial force for Africa and gained a fearsome reputation in the Civil War on Franco's side. Spanish troops participate in the international force sent to Bosnia in 1995 to implement the peace agreement. The contingent in Bosnia is the largest Spanish force to be deployed outside the country since the Blue Division fought in Russia on the side of Nazi Germany. In 1996 González led an OSCE investigative team to Serbia, which ordered that the country's communist president recognize opposition victories in local elections. In 1999 Spain sent four F–18 fighter aircraft to join NATO's air war against Yugoslavia that aimed to stop ethnic cleansing in Kosovo, and it permitted American military aircraft to stop over at bases across Spain. Public opinion was mixed concerning this action, especially after the Spanish ambassador's residence in Belgrade had been mistakenly damaged in a bombing raid.

Gibraltar

The Spanish government also hopes that NATO membership will prepare the way for Spanish sovereignty over Gibraltar, a piece of rock three and a half square miles (6 sq. km.) in size, where a Muslim army under Tarik ibn Zeyad (thus the Arab name for the rock, *gib al–Tarik*) landed an army from North Africa in 711 to begin the conquest of Spain. England snatched the rock during the War of the Spanish Succession in 1704 and has held it ever since.

The 31,000 Gibraltarians are not of Spanish descent, although they tend to speak more Spanish among themselves than English. Their habits are more English, though. They lunch at noon, not in mid–afternoon, and eat and drink more British fare. They read English newspapers, and their currency is sterling, albeit Gibraltar sterling. They are descendants of various Mediterranean immigrants brought to Gibraltar and include Genoese, Catalans, Jews, Portuguese and Maltese. The Spanish maintain that the population is artificial and the mere remnant of a foreign naval base and is therefore not entitled to self–determination in the decolonization process. The UN has upheld this claim.

Britain, on the other hand, maintains that no change in the status of Gibraltar could be legitimate without the approval of the population, and Gibraltarians remain ardently pro–British and profoundly suspicious of Spain. They have their own miniature Westminster–style democracy, and the attempted *coup* in Madrid in 1981 helped confirm their preference, expressed in a 1967 referendum, when 12,138 voted to remain British subjects; only 44 voted against it.

In 1969 Spain sealed the border between the mainland and the rock. In 1980 Britain agreed to negotiate a settlement. When Prince Charles and his bride decided to visit Gibraltar during their honeymoon cruise, Juan Carlos refused to attend the wedding in London. Also, the Falkland Islands conflict in the spring of 1982 caused further delays. Spain was the only West European land not to support the British in the crisis, and many Spanish see parallels between the Argentines' claim to the islands and the Spanish claim to Gibraltar. Nevertheless, both sides continue to profess the desire to settle their differences. During the Falklands war, Spain did prevent a number of Argentines from launching an attack on Gibraltar from Spanish territory.

Spain made a goodwill gesture in 1982 by opening the border to pedestrians. In 1985 it was opened to vehicular traffic. Britain and Spain reached an agreement in 1988 to share Gibraltar's airport although Spain maintains restrictions on airlines approaching Gibraltar. There are no direct flights, ferry, or ship service between Spain and the Rock. Common NATO, WEU and EU membership no doubt aids in this, as does the fact that Gibraltar no longer has the enormous strategic value it once had. The area is so small that its air strip cannot accommodate large aircraft. Also mines, long–range missiles and nuclear weapons make it far easier to block the strait of Gibraltar than to keep it open. The Rock does contain 30 miles of underground tunnels, a hidden strategic command center and berths for atomic submarines, all of which are important for NATO.

On a visit to London in 1991 González called Gibraltar an "anachronism" and noted that for the British, discussions with Spain about it are like an annual visit to the dentist, while for Spain it is like a permanent stone in its shoe. In 1997 Spain proposed "shared sovereignty" of the Rock. Although the British rejected it, they noted that the Spanish no longer rule out the idea of Gibraltar's independence, only that "independence will never be granted against Spanish wishes." That is not the same as insisting that the Rock must one day be Spanish.

The UK's interest in holding on to the colony has waned, and it would like to be rid of it. In 1991 it withdrew the last of its ground forces stationed there. That was

Hon. Peter Caruana

Spain

an economic blow since spending by British soldiers and their dependents amounted to 18% of Gibraltar's revenues and provided a fourth of the jobs. Some of the losses will be replaced by tourists, whose numbers leaped from 600,000 in 1984, the last full year of the Spanish siege, to more than 3 million annually in the 1990s.

In 1996 Gibraltarians elected a new chief minister, a young pro–business lawyer, Peter Caruana. His *Social Democrats* captured 52% of the votes and eight of 15 seats in the House of Assembly. He tries to improve diplomatic relations with Madrid, while maintaining the Rock's colonial relationship with British. The British welcome this approach, after the more abrasive style of his predecessor, Joe Bossano, whose dream was for the Rock to be independent of both Britain and Spain. Nevertheless, tensions remain. On a visit to EU headquarters in Brussels in 1997, Caruana accused Spain of trying to exclude Gibraltar from EU matters. Spanish leaders are always wary of any moves by Gibraltar to represent itself on the international stage, insisting that it operate through the British foreign office.

ECONOMY

At one time, Spain was a country with a layer of wealthy persons stretched thin over a large population which lived in varying degrees of poverty. Its industry was small, highly protected, unaggressive and suffering from a general mental inertia. Its agriculture was unproductive, by comparison with other Western European nations north of the Pyrenees. The chronically unstable political conditions in the 19th and 20th centuries always hampered economic development and delayed the industrial revolution. In the 1940s Spain's national income had fallen to the level of 1906–07, and not until 1954 was the 1936 level reached.

Much of that has changed by now. The Spanish are now modestly prosperous, and they have the fifth largest economy in the EU. In the cities the shops are filled with luxuries and necessities, which most people have enough money in their pockets to buy. There are plenty of cars on the roads, and 60% of Spanish families own or are buying their own homes (compared with slightly over one–half in Britain and France). It cannot be denied that Spain has come a very long way since the 1950s. Yet the real economic boom for which many Spaniards have hoped after 1975 never came, and important problems remain.

Spain's economy was growing fast (the rate in the late 1980s was 5% annually, 3.4% in 1998). Per capita GDP was still only 76% of the EU average in 1997, down from 78% in 1975. The González government concentrated on containing inflation by restraining wage increases, while spurring growth and structural reform. Unfortunately, the new national wealth has not yet trickled down to all Spaniards.

Economic prosperity is distributed geographically unequally. In Catalonia, the Basque country and Madrid, incomes are 25% higher than the national average, and in most of Andalusia, Estremadura, Galicia and New Castile, incomes are 30% below the national average. In 1999 unemployment stood at a staggering 17.8%, the highest in Western Europe even though it is declining. Although the economy had grown almost threefold in the 30 years prior to 1998 and the population had risen by a quarter, there were few more jobs than there had been in 1964.

As in all Mediterranean countries, Spain has a sizable "submerged economy," which accounts for an estimated one–fifth of GDP. Perhaps as many as one–third of the unemployed has an income from unofficial work. Taking this into account, the real unemployment figure is lower. Joblessness is also unevenly distributed. For instance, in Andalusia and Extremadura, almost one–third of those of working age have no jobs, and almost a fourth of Basques are out of work. For those under age 25, the jobless rate is over 40%. It is a testimony to the resilience of the extended family–based society that the Spanish can bear such joblessness. Only 35% of Spanish women between the ages of 16 and 65 were employed or were seeking a job in 1994, but the fact that 70% of women under age 30 have or are seeking jobs indicates the future trend.

In an attempt to maintain Spanish firms' economic competitiveness, the *Socialist* government introduced the concept of "temporary contracts" in 1984, followed by other labor market reforms in 1994 hoping to make it easier for companies to hire and fire. These measures antagonized labor unions and voters, who had grown accustomed since the Franco era to life–time job guarantees. But enough obstacles remain to make Spain's labor market one of the world's most rigid. Employers must pay 20 days salary for each year of employment to workers "fairly" dismissed, and 45 days to those "unfairly" dismissed. The courts almost always rule that dismissal is "unfair."

Not wishing to hire full–time employees who would receive this kind of protection, employers can, since 1984, hire them on "temporary contracts," which provide no job security. Thus, a two–tier labor market has developed: one for older workers with such protection that they have little incentive to be productive or to restrain their pay demands, and younger ones who stagger from one short–term contract to the other without building real careers. In 1996 fully 97% of all new jobs were in the "temporary" category. To make matters worse, nationwide collective–bargaining agreements are negotiated for each industry, making it hard for individual firms to adjust their employment conditions to their own particular economic circumstances. The result is chronic high unemployment. Fearing the general strikes that plagued the *Socialist* government, Prime Minister Aznar cannot attack this problem head–on, despite his proclamation of 1997 as "employment year."

Inflation fell from 14% in 1981 to 2.4% in 1999, still higher than the EU average. During most of the Franco era, workers and employees were forced to work long hours for low pay. Not until the early 1970s did the lid on the enforced "labor peace" threaten to blow off, so Franco permitted wages to rise in order to buy labor peace. After *El Caudillo's* death, pay continued to rise. Wage settlements above the Western European average, which fed inflation, ceased to make Spain a country with low labor costs and eliminated some of Spain's competitive advantages.

González decided to change this. He viewed inflation as a bigger problem than unemployment and reduced the rise of prices by means of tight fiscal, monetary and wage policies. The austerity policy was not popular, as general strikes in 1988, 1992, 1994 and 1996 revealed. But it worked. Under his successor, the economy is growing, investment is high, and foreign capital pours in. By 1999 the budget deficit had fallen to 1.8% of GDP, the total national debt was 69.8% of GDP, and Madrid still received $1.3 billion in EU subsidies each year.

That inflation is under control is partially due to the largely responsible way in which the major labor unions, the communist–controlled *Confederation of Workers' Commissions (CCOO)* and the *Socialist*–dominated *General Workers' Union (UGT)*, responded to the economic challenges facing the country. Only one worker in seven belongs to a union. Yet Spain has the EU's second worst record for days lost in strikes, after Greece.

As in all Western European countries, the rapid rise in energy prices in the 1970s exacerbated the country's economic problems. Spain is dependent on imported oil for about 60% of its total energy needs. It is only able to produce domestically 2% of the oil it uses. In years of normal rainfall Spain can provide 15% of its power generation through hydroelectricity. It has had modest success in relieving its excessive reliance on imported oil by in-

Spain

creasing its use of this resource, coal and nuclear power. Local opposition to atomic power has caused Spain's nuclear ambitions to be revised downward. Nevertheless, in 1997 nuclear power was generating 30% of Spain's electricity. In 1998 the American energy giant Enron became the first U.S. company to compete in Spain's energy market by building a power station in the South.

Spanish industry under Franco was the most tightly controlled in all of Western Europe. Through his bureaucracy he decreed subsidies, economic privileges, and penalties in a way which created distortions in the economy from which the country still suffers. Yet, while economic competition was tightly controlled, there was precious little control over some things, such as health standards.

Spanish industries are, as a rule, much smaller than in most EU countries. It has few multinational corporations. Of the FT–500 top European companies, only 24 are Spanish. Businesses tend not to be as high–tech as in some competitor countries; Spain spends only 1% of GDP on research and development, half the OECD average. Half of Spain's biggest companies (including all the auto industry—Europe's third biggest—and nine out of ten top exporters) are owned by foreign companies, 12% by banks, and 30% by the gigantic Spanish state holding company, the *National Institute of Industry (INI)*. INI owns or controls more than 60 enterprises and has partial ownership in another 200 or so. It was created by the Franco regime in order to establish industries which could back up Spain's defense and economic self–sufficiency, and it was often forced to rescue lame duck enterprises. INI now encompasses Iberia Airlines, as well as steel, ship–building, chemicals, power production, oil–prospecting, news agencies and banks.

To this list of nationalized industries, the former *Socialist* government added only the crisis–ridden *Rumasa* group. But it sold some profitable state–owned assets. The state automobile manufacturer, Seat, was sold to Volkswagen, but in 1993 VW announced the closure of the outdated Seat plant in Barcelona. In 1989 the state–owned oil company, Repsol, was partially privatized in Spain's biggest stock offering ever. Privatization has proceeded slowly and timidly. The state still accounts for 45% of GDP.

In spite of the many "social" and "national" obligations which compel them to receive subsidies and borrow heavily, most INI firms are economically viable. Also the government is trying to force automation on firms as a price for state subsidies. The state maintains monopolies over petroleum through *Campsa*, telephones through *Telefónica*, and tobacco through *Tabacalera*.

Foreign trade accounts for 38% of Spain's economy, and the emphasis is on Europe; over two–thirds of total Spanish merchandise exports go to the EU, up from half in 1985; 60% of its imports are from the EU, compared with 37% in 1985. Thanks in part to incentives for investment, Spain attracted needed foreign investments. Favorite sectors for their foreign investors are in the auto and chemical industries, financial institutions and the hotel business. But a major problem which continues to cool the enthusiasm of foreign investors and which seriously burdens the economy in certain areas of Spain is the terrorist activity, especially in the Basque country, traditionally one of the most industrialized and economically dynamic regions in Spain. There the *ETA* has forced "revolutionary taxes" on the companies and has kidnapped and even killed some leading industrialists and engineers. These tactics have prompted other businessmen to leave with their families. In short, Spain will not be wholly attractive for business activity and investments until regional terrorism has ended.

About 10% of the Spanish are employed in agriculture, forestry and fishing. This "primary sector" produces 6% of the country's GDP and under 20% of its exports. Its horticulture, poultry farming, wine and fruit growing are

Spain

The seaside resort of Torremolinos on Spain's southeastern coast

Courtesy: Minnie Lee Wilt

highly productive, but its meat and cereal production is low. Despite the large size of its territory and agricultural population, Spain is not entirely self–sufficient in food. However it does produce enough foodstuffs to create fears in France and Italy, which produce many of the same agricultural products as Spain, that the latter's entry into the EU would open the flood–gates to cheaper produce. This situation places Spain in a certain dilemma.

It needs to reorganize its agricultural production. But the results of such improvement would be to increase rural unemployment and thus stimulate the flight into the cities and industrialized countries. Among the rural problems which must be solved in order to improve the country's agricultural output are insufficient water supplies, forest and brush fires, soil erosion, the preponderance of small, uneconomical farms in the North and the West and the existence of large underutilized estates in the South.

A Spaniard eats an estimated three times more fish than the average West European. To supply this immense seafood appetite, the country has built up the largest fishing fleet in the EU and the third largest in the world. This caused concern over Spain's entry into the EU, and members fight bitterly over fishing quotas. Spain accounts for a fifth of the EU's catch. In 1988 a French coast guard vessel fired on Basque fishing boats who were exceeding Spain's quota. Canada captured a Spanish vessel overfishing off its coast in 1994 and found on board doctored records and illegal nets designed to catch undersized fish. Despite being caught red–handed, Spanish public opinion was enflamed by this "act of piracy." One of its diplomats proclaimed: "We may not be big in anything else, but in fish we are a superpower."

Two of Spain's major economic assets have been the sun and the sea, and since the 1960s Spain has been one of Western Europeans' favorite tourist country. In 1996 it overtook France as Europe's leader in terms of tourist earnings. Only the U.S. exceeds its income from tourism. With 41.4 million overnight tourists coming in 1996, it is an important source of income and employment; it is Spain's biggest earner of foreign exchange. However, the tourist industry is vulnerable to recession in the rest of Western Europe and to political instability. For a long time, Spain relied on its beaches and good weather to attract tourists, but as the peseta hardens, prices have risen, and many tourists look elsewhere. This presents challenges to the industry. In order to stimulate both tourism and its economy in general, Spain decided in 1988 to modernize its railroad, which is one of Europe's oldest, slowest and financially troubled, by introducing its first high–speed trains between Madrid and the cities of Barcelona and Seville and by adapting its narrow–gauge railway system to the one used by the rest of Europe.

Spain has had to make some painful adjustments after its entry into the EU. It caught up with many other Western European countries in terms of social welfare benefits. Almost a third of its unemployed receive some form of assistance, and the social security system (known as "SS") is able to provide free or cheap medical care, although its facilities are often overcrowded. The SS provides pensions, welfare and other social assistance. From 80% to 85% of its funds are provided by a payroll tax on employees. This tax increases labor costs, though, by about 35%.

There can be no doubt that Spain's economy has benefitted from EU membership. Trade is booming, and foreign investment poured in. It has also been a net recipient of structural funds from Brussels. It has overtaken Italy as the EU's major receiver of regional development funds. Perhaps most significantly, the historical phenomenon in Spain of disinterest or lack of prestige accorded to business activity has almost disappeared.

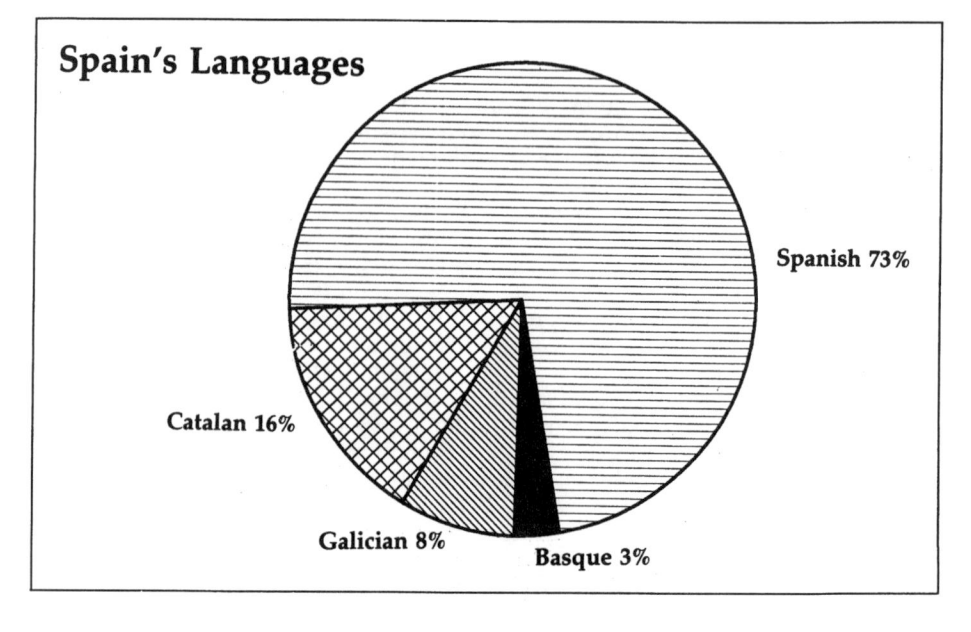

Spain's Languages

- Spanish 73%
- Catalan 16%
- Galician 8%
- Basque 3%

Spain

Goya's epic painting *El 3 de mayo de 1808,* which hangs in the Prado Museum in Madrid, commemorates the French invasion which placed Napoleon's brother, Joseph, on the Spanish Throne.

CULTURE

Languages

Spain's culture and language have taken root far beyond its own borders. In fact, 300 million speak Spanish as a mother tongue, making it the only real challenger to English as a world language. Spanish is the favorite foreign language in American high schools and universities, and as many as 20 million citizens and residents of the U.S. speak Spanish as a mother tongue. The official language in Spain is the Castilian dialect of Spanish, which differs in some respect from the many different dialects of Spanish spoken in South and Central America. The most audible difference is that the "s" or soft "c" sound sounds in Castilian Spanish like the English "th" sound.

There are, of course, many languages spoken within Spain itself, and three are especially important. In Galicia one speaks Gallego, which is more similar to Portuguese than are other Spanish languages. In Catalonia, Valencia and the Balearic Islands, a separate language called Catalan is spoken. It is a Romance language closely related to Provençal and Languedoc, spoken in France. It has a rich written literature and has always been a crucially important cultural tool for preserving Catalan national identity. Catalans requested that the EU recognize their tongue as an official language. Basque, a language with neither Romance or other Indo–European roots, is spoken mainly in the villages of the Basque country and is seldom heard in the two major Basque cities of Bilbao and San Sabastian. It remains, however, a very important vehicle for Basque identity.

Literature and Arts

Spain was always a crossroads between the European and Islamic Oriental cultures. Indeed, some of Europe's greatest writers wrote in Spanish. During the "Golden Age" of the 16th and 17th centuries, Cervantes wrote his classic, *Don Quixote,* a humorous story of chivalry and lofty, idealistic aspirations beyond all human capacity to achieve. Today, the word "Quixotic" is used in English to refer to any naive venture which, because of hopeless odds, is doomed to failure from the very start. In the 20th century Spain has produced several internationally renowned poets, most notably Juan Ramón Jiménez, who won a Nobel Prize in 1956, and Federico García Lorca, who was murdered during the Civil War. Its novelists, such as Ricardo Vasquez Montalban and Soledad Puertolas, have international reputations. In 1989 Camilo José Cela was awarded the Nobel Prize for

Philip II by Sánchez Coello 1531–88

Spain

The horror of April 26, 1937, in Guernica . . .

. . . and Picasso's stark depiction—*Guernica*

Spain

Literature. Author of 60 disturbing and powerful books, Cela lived an exciting, risky and iconoclastic life, disdaining authority in all forms. His regular newspaper columns and television appearances also helped make him a living legend in Spain.

In art Spain has also distinguished itself. El Greco (words which mean "the Greek" and applied to Kyriakos Theotokopoulos, who lived and worked in Toledo) established his own characteristic style in the 16th century. Diego Rodríguez de Silva Velazquez painted revealing and astonishingly uncomplimentary portraits of the Spanish court during the 17th century, and Francisco José de Goya painted powerful portrayals of revolution and resistance in the 18th and 19th centuries.

In the 20th century Salvador Dali, Joan Miró and Pablo Picasso have inalterably influenced modern painting. Because of political disagreements, these artists lived a part of their working lives outside of Spain.

The most ringing protest against Franco, and of course, against war itself, was Picasso's *Guernica,* which he painted for the Spanish pavilion of the Paris World Fair in 1937 in order to invoke the memory of the German bombing of the Basque city of Guernica. He then lent the painting to the Museum of Modern Art in New York and ordered that it not be returned to Spain until democracy had been restored in his homeland. In 1980, after a long legal wrangle with Picasso's heirs, the painting was finally returned to the magnificent Prado Museum in Madrid. In 1992 it was moved to the new modern art museum, Centro de Arte Reina Sofia. Spanish viewers, who often chatter and exclaim in museums, are hushed when face to face with the shrieking victims portrayed in this stark mural.

A major addition to Spanish culture is the Guggenheim Museum in Bilboa, opened in 1997. Costing $171 million to build, this is the anchor project in an effort to preempt Basque violence by emphasizing national pride and culture in a positive way. Basque officials requested that *Guernica,* the work of art most symbolic of the region, be moved or lent to the museum, which is located only 12 miles from the town of Guernica. Citing the painting's deteriorating condition and concerns over its safety in the Basque area, the request was turned down. This decision sparked fierce controversy. Nevertheless, the experiment of stimulating the entire Basque region through this art magnet is a smashing success. In its first 18 months, tourism in the Basque country increased by 28%, most of it attributable to the museum. It has become a symbol of the area's economic and cultural resurgence that could be secured by the permanent end of separatist violence.

Cinema

Over four–fifths of all films shown in Spain are foreign, especially American. Spanish directors have created some very good ones. Luis Buñuel, who for decades lived in exile in France, Hollywood and Mexico, has been especially acclaimed for his playful and charming films. He aims his subtle but deadly arrows toward the Spanish bourgeoisie, from which he himself descended.

The kinds of Spanish films which have won international acclaim are facing almost impossible domestic competition from another kind of movie which has sprung alive after 1975—pornography. Of course, pornography is in the eye of the beholder: one man's treat is another man's horror. But even the most tolerant must be horrified to see a film entitled "Would you like to be my husband's lover?" being shown in a Granada moviehouse named Isabel la Católica (Isabel the Catholic). The main problem is that such films have driven away family audiences from the cinemas, and movie attendance has fallen. By 1978, only 42% of the Spanish regularly went to the cinema, compared to 87% who regularly watched television.

The conservative government announced plans in 1996 to reexamine subsidies to the film industry and to lift screen quotas that had offered some protection for Spanish films against American competitors; 80% of all films shown in Spain were already American. Two–thirds of the foreign TV films purchased at the end of the century are from the U.S. Only slightly more than 10% of Spaniards go to the theater, despite heavy state subsidies of theater tickets. Many people follow bull fighting closely: 40% according to polls, although a small minority is deeply opposed to the sport. It employs about 1% of the entire workforce and nets over one billion dollars every year.

Media

Spain's newsstands have also become inundated with pornographic literature since the repeal of the pornography law. On TV Spaniards can watch programs with such titles as "Let's Talk about Sex," "Erotic Saturday Nights," and "Marriage and Something More." But the lifting of censorship in Spain has also brought a flowering daily and weekly press, even though newspaper readership remains low. Only about 8% of Spaniards buy a newspaper, which is half as many as in France and a fifth as many as in Britain. Three of the best papers in Europe now come from Spain: *Cambio,* a weekly which was modeled on *Time,* the conservative daily, *Vanguardia,* and the liberal daily, *El Pais,* which is unloved by the police, army, and Church, and which has become the most courageous and intelligent watchdog of the new constitution. Even the right–wing dailies, *ABC* and the Catholic–oriented *Ya* have greatly improved their standards and have converted to democracy. However, most papers are partisan in one way or the other. The newest weekly newspaper, *El Independiente,* is seen as close to the *Social and Democratic Center Party.*

There are some black spots in Spanish journalism. The government inherited 30 state–owned newspapers from the Franco era which cannot be abolished suddenly. Also, there are some newspapers which rail against the new order. The most influential is the ultra–right daily, *El Alcazar,* which is named after the famed fortress in Toledo. This fortress became a legend during the Civil War by surviving a two–month Republican siege before being relieved by Franco's troops on September 28, 1936. The newspaper began as a newsletter for Franco's troops and became a mouth–piece for the fascist leadership.

The most regrettable black spot, though, is that the Spanish press still fears to work as freely as in most other Western European countries. For instance, it is still a serious offense to question the honor of the royal family or the legitimacy of the monarchy or the unity of Spain. The press is also forbidden to challenge the honor of the armed forces, including the para–military police. The Spanish military is still the most publicly flattered in all of Western Europe. Despite these continuing limitations on the freedom of the press, it should not be forgotten that for the first time in Spanish history people can generally speak and write about politics and religion without fear of being jailed. Only about 8% of Spaniards buy a daily newspaper. Instead, polls indicate that about two–thirds of adults form their political opinions from television, which 87% watch daily. Although the *Socialist* government has raised the standards of T.V., news reports seldom include opposition criticism of government initiatives. The autonomous governments also run regional channels, but only in Catalonia do they find a large viewer audience. In 1991 private TV was established in Spain.

Catholic Church

The Church had been one of Franco's chief supporters, and he repaid the favor by restoring its role in the schools, and by granting it generous state subsidies. He effectively had the power to appoint bishops, a prerogative which Juan Carlos elim-

Spain

As only the Spanish can dance it—*El Flamenco*

inated. On Spanish coins Franco was called "leader of Spain by God's grace."

In the 1960s, though, the Church's support for *El Caudillo* began to change. Many Spanish priests adopted the ethic of social justice. They began forming social action groups and speaking out in support of disadvantaged workers and peasants. Priests in the Basque country, Spain's most fervently Catholic area, began publicly to support the Basque nationalists.

In the 1960s the Catholic lay organization, *Opus Dei* (Latin for "God's Work"), which began its exisitence in 1928 as a highly conservative effort to become firmly rooted in the society's elite, changed its thinking. It became an important force for rationalizing the economy, improving workers' living standards and taking cautious steps toward political democracy. From a force for reaction, *Opus Dei* became one of Spain's most important forces for innovation. Although it had largely lost its influence on public policy by the end of the 1980s, its membership had grown to about 25,000. This reflects, in part, a renewed flowering in Spain and elsewhere in Europe of lay religious groups. By 1972 most of Spain's bishops were moderate. Franco's displeasure was demonstrated by his government's threat in 1974 to cancel the Concordat (treaty) with the Vatican. In any case, the Church had changed from a major foundation for the Franco regime to a skeptical semi–opponent.

In the 1980s, the Church accepted the *Socialist Party's* law permitting the sale of contraceptives. But it fought hard to prevent the full legalization of abortion and divorce, problems which cannot be so easily hidden in the medicine cabinet. An estimated 300,000 Spanish women each year have abortions either abroad or illegally in back rooms. It is understandable why many Spanish supported the *Socialist* government's reform to depenalize abortion in cases such as rape or where the mother's life is in danger.

The Church hierarchy and the conservative opposition expressed outrage and are helpless against Europe's steepest drop in the birth rate, from 19 births per 1,000 Spaniards in 1975 to 11 by 1989. By 1994 the average woman bears 1.2 children, down from 2.8 in 1975. Spain's overall population is expected to begin declining around 2010. This is influenced by the fact that a third of Spanish women are already in the workforce, and 70% under age 30 have or are seeking employment. Although Spanish families are still cohesive and close, they will continue to become less male–dominated than they once were.

The changed environment in Spain is reflected by opinion polls, which indicated that fewer than 15% of Spaniards considered marriage to be indissoluble. Yet the roots of social conservatism in Spain were also revealed in the fact that it took six years after Franco's death to pass a liberal divorce law, which permits civil divorce by mutual consent one year after the couple has been legally separated. The debate exasperated Church leaders so much that they told Spanish Catholics that the law does not apply to them.

The Church's stand on this issue is not likely to persuade many Spaniards, more than 90% of whom are members of the Church. A Gallup poll in 1987 revealed that Spaniards fell behind the Catholics of Ireland, Portugal and Italy when asked about the importance of God in their lives. Only 42% confessed to being practicing Catholics (with varying degrees of intensity), and 30% regarded themselves as non–practicers. Barely 15% of urban inhabitants attend mass regularly. Since 1988 Spaniards are able to choose between giving a half percent of their income tax to the Church or to the state's culture and welfare budgets. Aid to the Church is no longer simply a part of the budget.

Far more Spaniards go to soccer games regularly than to Church. In fact, the Association for the Defense of Animal Rights, with 5,000 members in 1986, would like even more Spaniards to give up bullfight entertainment for soccer; it has issued stickers saying: *Toros no. Futbol si*. Noting that 24,000 bulls die every year in the spectacle, it maintains that "torture is neither art nor culture." It even launched Spain's first–ever protest march against bullfighting. Although the sport provides employment for 150,000 people and earns more than $100 million per year, most Spaniards do not like it. A survey taken in 1986 found that more than half actively dislike bullfighting, while only a third said they liked it.

Education

The role of the Church in contemporary Spanish society is not a burning political issue. It has turned away from active intervention in politics. But it does raise its voice on certain issues, such as private education, culture and the information media. The Church energetically defends its influence on parochial schools, which are attended by more than a third of all Spanish schoolchildren (twice the figure even of the Franco years) and which are reputed to be academically better than the public schools. The Church is willing to accept some standards and guidelines by the state, such as teacher training and financial accountability. It is also understandably interested in continuing to receive state financial assistance, which reportedly accounts for about 30% of the Church's income. But it wishes to avoid any state control over the content of education in its schools, which it insists must remain religious.

The *Socialists* aroused the ire of the Church by passing legislation guarantee-

Spain

ing the right to free secular education and thereby reducing the Church's influence in the schools. The government also announced that for the first time, books and teaching materials would be distributed free of charge to some 200,000 school children attending rural public and private schools. The school-leaving age was lifted to 16.

When the government tried to raise university tuition slightly in 1987 and to tighten university admissions and academic standards, thousands of students rushed into the streets to protest. Some were concerned that the door might be closing on the accessibility of a university degree, the traditional path to a good job and financial security. Others added that frustration stemming from youth unemployment of more than 40% for ages 16 to 24 and from a crackdown on drugs fueled the flames. One hears criticism that there is too little rigor in the educational system and that some universities have grown too large to be effective. For instance, Madrid's Complutense University has 130,000 enrolled.

Drugs and Immigration

Spain has replaced the Netherlands as the most important conduit into Europe for illegal drugs. European addicts now receive 40% of their cocaine via Spain. In part this is explained by the more open borders to other EU partners, the congenial Spanish-speaking environment for Latin American drug-runners, and the 1983 decriminalization of possession of small quantities of soft or hard drugs for personal use. The González government had made the country's drug laws among the most lax in Europe, and the rapid spread of drug abuse brought a reaction. Spain has Europe's highest incidence of drug abuse and AIDS. It is faced with an epidemic: it has an estimated 100,000 heroin addicts, and cocaine use has spread into the middle-class. It is reckoned that 1.5 million smoke marijuana often. Most of Spain's heavy drug-users are young. The *Socialist* government tried to fight back by increasing maximum prison sentences, fines and indictments for drug traffickers, but critics called these measures too little too late.

Also a shock for Spaniards is racial violence, despite polls which suggest that they are more tolerant of outsiders than are most other Europeans. By the 1990s more than a quarter million legal and 300,000 illegal immigrants were pouring into Spain each year. Former Foreign Minister Javier Solana, now NATO Secretary General, said that "Spain is a country where others have always been taken in with great generosity and solidarity." To try to demonstrate this, the conservative government adopted a law in December 1996 giving the two million legal foreign residents the right both to vote and to run for office in municipal elections starting in 1999.

FUTURE

Spain's future is promising. It has a democratic constitution and a King who has shown that he is willing to die to defend democracy. Spanish voters avoid extremist parties, trade unions show responsibility and moderation, and politicians cooperate with each other. Time has dampened passions over the Civil War, fears of military coups, and emotions over NATO. Separatist terrorism has been dealt devastating blows, and the chances for peace in the violence-torn Basque region have greatly improved since *ETA* declared a ceasefire in September 1998. The liberal, parliamentary order has definitely sunk its roots deeply, and it has already long outlived the earlier Republic, during which 18 governments fell before Franco took full control.

The closeness of the March 1996 elections did not prevent the government of Prime Minister Aznar, the last conservative one in the EU, from delivering on its promises. The economy is buoyant, and the budget deficit has fallen to 1.8% of GDP and the national debt to 69.8% of GDP. Success enabled Spain to enter the European Monetary Union. Aznar pressed on to reform the welfare and tax systems and to reduce the size of the bureaucracy. The sudden resignation of the *Socialists'* candidate for prime minister, José Borrell, left his party in a difficult position to contest the next parliamentary elections, which will be held by May 2000.

Meadows blossom beneath the towering Pyrenees Mountains in the north

The Republic of Portugal

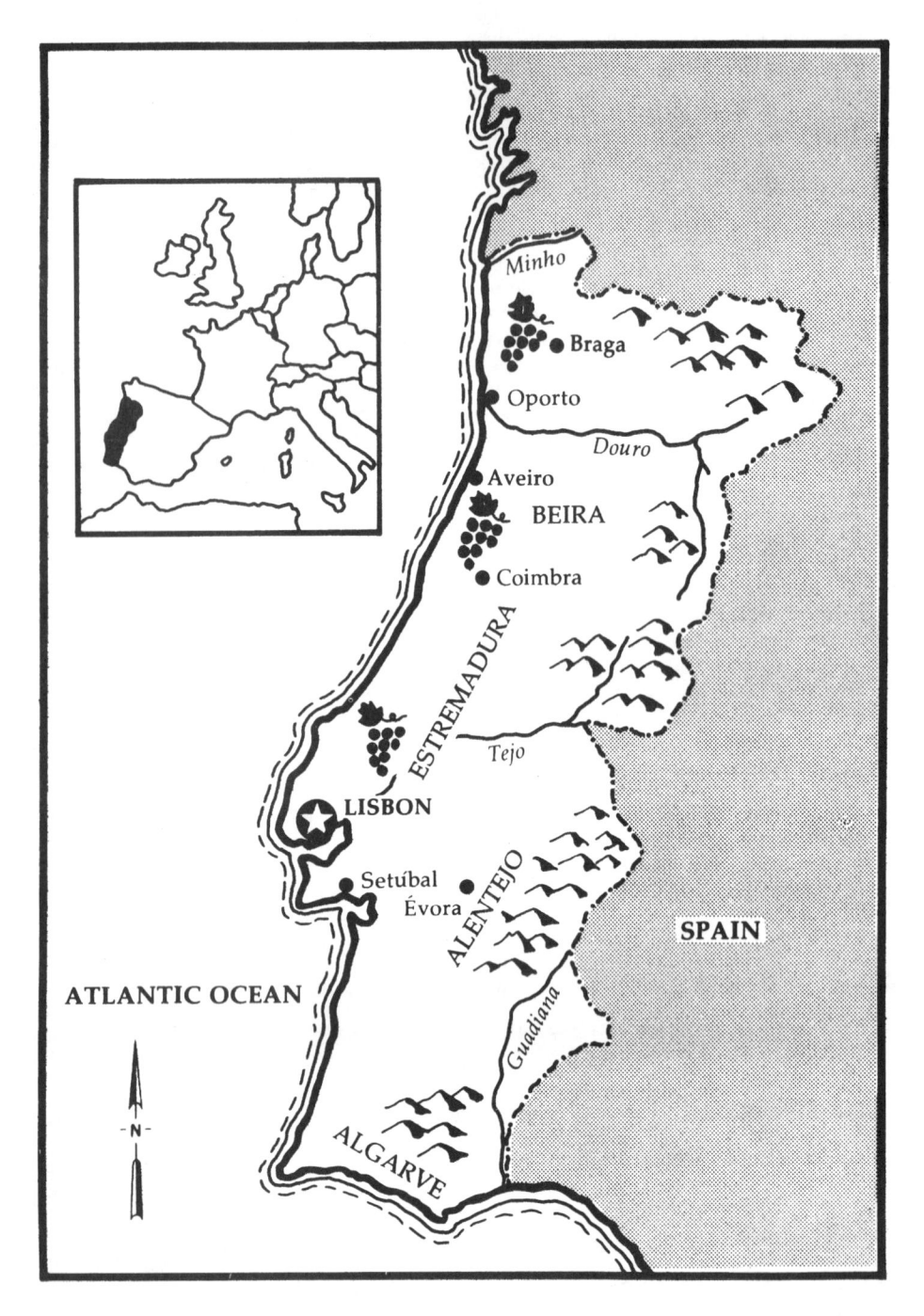

Currency: Escudo, to be replaced in 2002 by the Euro.
National Holiday: June 10 (Luiz de Camões Day, and Day of the Portuguese Communities).
Chief of State: Jorge Sampaio, President (since 1996).
Head of Government: Antonio Guterres, Prime Minister (since 1995).
National Flag: From the hoist, green and red vertical fields, the green being somewhat less than half of the flag. The Portuguese coat–of–arms is imposed where the two fields meet.

Portugal entered the 1970s as a conservative, industrially underdeveloped country at the bottom of Western Europe's economic barrel. It had a fascist political order which suppressed all signs of genuine opposition, and which therefore was an embarrassment to its NATO allies, which sought to defend democracy on both sides of the Atlantic. It was embroiled in a multitude of hopeless colonial wars in an attempt to maintain control over an empire more than 20 times the size of the mother country.

Yet by the 1980s Portugal offered an almost entirely different picture. It had undergone a revolution which, though claiming almost no lives, drastically altered many aspects of the country. It is now a thriving democracy in which persons of all persuasions can speak and act openly. Although it is Western Europe's poorest nation (behind Greece), with the continent's highest infant mortality and illiteracy rates, it was willing to accept the economic challenge of entering the EU. It is a country now almost entirely stripped of its colonial empire, but it is much healthier and stronger as a result. It is a democratically ruled member of NATO with an army radically reduced in size but with military facilities of great strategic importance for the alliance.

The Portuguese are a highly individualistic people, but at the same time they are tolerant, friendly, polite and patient, and form a relatively cohesive society. Without these qualities, the Portuguese would not have survived so well the radical changes which have occurred in the country since 1974. The population is largely homogeneous. But there are about 100,000 blacks from the former African colonies; 10% of Lisbon's population is black, some of whom have been the targets of racist attacks in recent years. There are also about 90,000 gypsies, who have not integrated as well in Portugal as they have in Spain.

Few European countries have such a large portion of its population living abroad as does Portugal. Since the 15th century the Portuguese have emigrated in

Area: 35,553 sq. mi. (92,082 sq. km.), not counting the Azores or Madeira; (about the size and general shape of Indiana—380 miles north to south, and 140 miles at its widest point).
Population: 10 million (estimated).
Capital City: Lisbon (Pop. 2.3 million). *Lisboa* in Portuguese, pronounced Lee's–*boa*.
Climate: Mild and rainy weather in late fall and early winter, but cold and snowy in the mountains. From June to September the days are hot, but the air is rather dry.
Neighboring Countries: Spain (North and East); Morocco lies 140 miles across the ocean to the southeast.
Language: Portuguese
Ethnic Background: Indo–European (predominantly Mediterranean type).
Principal Religion: Roman Catholic.
Chief Commercial Exports: Cork, textiles, clothing and footwear, wood and wood products, wine, canned fish, tomato paste, olive oil, machinery and transport equipment.
Major Customers: EU (75%), principally Germany, France, Spain, UK. Less than 4% of its trade is with the U.S.

Portugal

large numbers, first toward Brazil, and then after Brazilian independence, to such destinations as North America, Venezuela, Angola and Mozambique. However, after 1955 the greatest number of Portuguese emigrants, two–thirds of whom left agricultural areas in Portugal, went to industrialized Western European countries, especially France and Germany, in order to find employment. From 1960 until 1972 a million and a half Portuguese left the country, mainly in the direction of other West European nations. That the number of emigrants to the rest of Western Europe has slowed down considerably is due to the restrictions which those countries have erected since the world recession began in 1974.

The U.S. and Venezuela have become again the favorite destination for Portuguese. The U.S. is now the single country which accepts the greatest annual number of Portuguese emigrants. Indeed, more than a million Portuguese now live there, most of whom are from the Azores. By 1987 the total number of Portuguese living abroad was more than four million—roughly 40% of the country's total population. They send back more than $2 billion in remittances every year, which in 1986 accounted for 13% of Portugal's GDP and more than offset its trade deficit. From 30,000 to 40,000 are returning every year. This intensifies the housing shortage in a country where thousands of impatient residents have already constructed homes without waiting for a building permit.

Portugal is a rectangular–shaped country, a little larger than the state of Maine, but with ten times as many inhabitants. It has a long Atlantic coastline, along which most of the country's inhabitants live, and it has only one neighbor: Spain. The country is separated into northern and southern halves by the Tejo River. The north is cooler and more mountainous, with small family farms and three–fourths of the entire population. The south is hotter and drier, with rolling plains and large farms, called *latifundios*.

Astride the line between the two halves is Lisbon, where the Tejo empties into the Atlantic Ocean. The capital city is located on seven hills and still reflects a physical character shaped by its Moorish past. It is very much the heart of a highly centralized country and has all too often in the past looked down upon the rest of the country and has seemed to be uninterested in the fate and welfare of the regions. With all its suburbs it counts more than a million and a half inhabitants. It and greater Oporto, which is Portugal's only other major city and which has 800,000 residents, have attracted three– fourths of the population which is active in the industrial and service sectors of the economy. Unfortunately Lisbon's historic central shopping district was seriously scarred by a fire in 1988.

Portugal has three main rivers: the Douro in the north, which empties near Oporto, the Tejo in the middle, and the Guadiana, which forms part of the border with Spain and then empties into the Gulf of Cadiz. All originate in Spain, but almost none is navigable between the two countries. Indeed, the transportation links between Spain and Portugal remain very difficult. This is a major reason why both countries have stood for so long with their backs practically toward each other facing somewhat different directions.

CONTEMPORARY HISTORY

In 1882 Portugal became a constitutional monarchy in a setting of bitter power struggles and intrigues among rival claimants to the throne and between conservatives, who supported the Catholic Church and the nobility, and liberals, who wished to reduce the power of those groups. Except for a relatively brief respite between 1853 and 1889, the century preceding the military takeover of power in 1926 was an era of restlessness, discontent and civil disturbances. It was peppered by wars and revolts which so shook the land that conservatives and liberals finally agreed to avoid bloodshed by alternating power in a system called *rotativismo*.

This rotation system could not prevent the steady erosion of support for the monarchy, caused by financial and colo-

The Avenida da Liberdade, Lisbon

Lisbon from the Tejo River

Portugal

nial difficulties and by the rising political ambitions of the middle class, which wanted a greater share in political power. In February 1908 King Carlos I, a man of absolutist inclinations and a lust for personal gratification, and the Crown Prince, were both assassinated, and, after a spell of uncontrollable political turbulence, the monarchy fell in October 1910. As usual, the military was heavily involved in this overthrow.

The monarchy was replaced by a parliamentary republic, whose main accomplishments were to separate Church and state, to end Catholicism's status as the official state religion, and to terminate religious instruction in state schools and state aid to religious schools. But the republic could not find solutions for the country's economic problems or the political factionalism, extremism, terrorism, anarchy, riots, strikes and attempted *coups d'etat*, which continued to be a part of daily political life. The republic was further weakened by Portugal's participation in World War I, which in no way unified the many leading groups behind a common objective.

Not only were many politicians corrupt and incompetent, but the rapid turnover of governments prevented any policy continuity. Portugal had a average of three governments per year until 1926, when the military stepped in again and took political power into its own hands. Because the years of political havoc had not thoroughly polarized Portuguese society, as had been the case in Spain, and because Portugal has, in general, a more homogeneous, less fragmented society than does its neighbor, the military takeover was not followed by a bloody civil war, as in Spain a decade later.

Military–Fascist Rule

In order to attack the financial problems, especially inflation, which the years of chaos had exacerbated, the generals, in 1928, named an economics professor from the University of Coimbra, Dr. Antonio Oliveira Salazar, as finance minister. In 1932 he became leader of the only legal party and prime minister, the post which until 1974 remained the heart of political power in Portugal. He established a fascist state, called the *Estado Novo* ("New State"), which he guided until his incapacitation in 1968. In 1933 a constitution was promulgated which had a few trappings of parliamentary government, such as a unicameral National Assembly and a directly elected president.

The corporatist character of the new constitution was embodied in an advisory organ called the Corporative Chamber. This allegedly united all classes by bringing together representatives of diverse economic and professional groups in order to evaluate all legislation. Also, over the years other organizations were established to encompass workers, employers, craftsmen, landowners, rural laborers, fishermen, women and youth, in order to lock all citizens tightly into a bundle of groups, all directed from the top by Salazar. There was only one legal political party, the *União Nacional* ("National Union"), which never played a central role in Portugal, as did the Nazi or Fascist parties in Germany and Italy.

The Portuguese political system was complicated in theory, but it was rather simple in practice. Salazar, with the advice of trusted cronies from industry, the military and the Church, made all crucial political decisions. Freedom of press and assembly were curtailed, and all written and electronic communications were censored. Critical professors were dismissed, and strikes were outlawed. As every Portuguese knew, the secret police *(PIDE)* was ever–present. It is estimated that one in 400 Portuguese were paid informants.

When the Spanish civil war broke out in 1936, Salazar ordered the creation of a "Portuguese Legion" to fight on Gen. Francisco Franco's side, and about 6,000 Portuguese fought against the Spanish Republic. Portugal also tolerated the transport of munitions from France across its territory until mid–1937, when the British, Portugal's closest ally for three centuries, pressured Salazar into closing its borders to such war material. On March 17, 1939, Franco and Salazar signed a non–aggression and friendship pact, which was amended on July 29, 1940, to obligate both governments to discuss their mutual security interests with one another whenever the "independence or security" of one of the countries is endangered. That pact still remains valid.

Portugal, like Spain, did not become linked militarily and diplomatically with Germany and Italy before and during World War II. Portugal even profited from its neutrality; the country became one of Europe's major centers for spies from all belligerent countries. However, Salazar's sympathies were revealed when he ordered a day of national mourning after Germany's Hitler had committed suicide.

Portugal's valuable strategic position and long–standing relationship with Britain enabled it to become a founding member of NATO, and in 1955 Portugal was admitted to the UN. However, Portugal remained in an economic, social and political condition of stagnation and immobility, ruled and administered by an aging dictator, and a tight clique of generals, admirals and bureaucrats, who, through a swarm of spies, rendered the population submissive, but increasingly dissatisfied and restless.

Salazar greeting Spain's Franco

Portugal

War in Angola: troop carrier swerves to avoid a road trap

In 1968 a law professor, Dr. Marcelo Caetano, assumed leadership over this regime, which was in the process of rapid decay. He had high hopes of reforming and liberalizing the authoritarian system which his predecessor had created, but it had become far too late for such reform. Portugal had just about reached the exploding point, and all that was needed was a spark. That spark came in 1974 from the same institution which had stepped into the Portuguese political sphere many times before and which had established the half–century dictatorship in the first place in 1926—the military.

Colonial Problems

The last straw was the seemingly endless wars in Portugal's African colonies, which the Portuguese preferred to call *Ultramar* (overseas territories). The Portuguese settlers had always mingled more easily with non–white native populations than did the British, French and Belgian colonizers. One still sees the results of this in Brazil, where blacks and whites seem to live together relatively harmoniously (albeit under a predominantly white elite). Also, nothing resembling an *apartheid* ("separateness") policy ever developed in the Portuguese colonies, such as in formerly British and Dutch South Africa.

A certain conviction that Portuguese rule was both good and tolerable for the subject peoples, combined with the economic importance for Portugal and with the fact that there were over a million Portuguese living in the colonies, led Portugal to hang on to its empire long after the other European nations had decided to relinquish theirs. Foreign Minister Franco Nogueira even wrote in 1967 that the Portuguese considered themselves "to be an African nation." The obvious point, however, was that the bulk of the native populations in the colonies did not consider themselves to be *Portuguese!*

In 1961 India simply invaded and annexed the mini–territories of Goa, Damão and Diu. Since 1913 the Portuguese had had to quell occasional native uprisings in Africa. In 1961 these uprisings reerupted, first in Angola around such groups as the *Popular Movement for the Liberation of Angola (MPLA)*, the *Angolan National Liberation Front (FNLA)* and the *National Union for Total Angolan Independence, (UNITA)*, then in 1963 in Mozambique (led by the *Front for the Liberation of Mozambique*) and in Guinea–Bissau. The Portuguese government decided to hold on to the African colonies at all costs, fearing that their loss would spell the doom of the Portuguese state. In fact, it was this decision more than any other which led to the ultimate downfall of the Portuguese fascist regime.

Military Unrest

By 1974 there were 170,000 men in the Portuguese army, 135,000 of whom were stationed in Africa. The lion's share of these troops were four–year conscripts, who increasingly resented their role in quelling native rebellions against a regime which fewer and fewer Portuguese wished to preserve. The need to expand the size of the army to cope with the African wars brought many young men from the lower classes and the universities into the officers' corps. These groups had earlier been largely excluded from the officers' ranks and were more inclined to sympathize with the rebels' aims. These young officers gradually lost faith in the kinds of arguments which had long been used to justify the protracted colonial struggle. Many became inspired by the revolutionary ideas espoused by their African adversaries. They grew to dislike strongly their more traditional military superiors. These radicalized lower–ranking officers formed the illegal *Movement of the Armed Forces (MFA)*, which became the core of opposition to the regime.

Their convictions and confidence were enormously strengthened by the appearance in February 1974 of a book which must be considered one of the most significant in modern Portuguese history: *Portugal and the Future*. It was written by the monacled General António de Spínola, the former commander in Guinea–Bissau, whose legendary bravery in battle had won him the admiration of the lower ranks. Spínola advocated a political solution to the colonial question and the establishment of a sort of Portuguese commonwealth of nations, similar to that of the British. It is not surprising that Dr. Caetano reportedly could not sleep the night after he had read the book!

The "Carnation Revolution"

Plotters in the *MFA* went to work on a plan to overthrow the regime. In the night of April 24/25, 1974, troops numbering about 5,000 occupied Lisbon in a well–planned operation. Since most officers had become indifferent to the survival of the regime, there was no resistance to the surprise *coup*. Some nervous PIDE agents, (which the underground press had called "Gestaportuguese"!) who had fled to their headquarters in panic, had reportedly fired on a crowd of a few persons (reports differ, but the total casualties did not exceed five). Except for these, not a shot was fired to defend a fascist regime which had ruled Portugal for about a half century. Rarely in history has such a fundamental political change occurred with so little loss of life.

The plotters formed a "Junta of National Salvation," which abolished the PIDE and announced that the colonies would be granted the right of self–determination and that political exiles would be permitted to return to Portugal. Political enthusiasm burst into life, and public debates, rallies and street demonstrations seized a nation in which such things had been forbidden for *48 years.*

For two years Portugal was rocked by a succession of provisional governments

Portugal

The military *coup*, April 24/25, 1974

and confusing revolutionary turmoil. While this turmoil was fired by much emotion, it occurred in the traditional Portuguese style of little actual bloodshed. The new leaders were in such a hurry to cut their former colonies totally loose that they made little effort to try at least to introduce a stable transfer of power in the colonies to groups which might have been willing to legitimize their rule through democratic elections. The *MFA's* strong Marxist bias inclined it to hand over power in the colonies to like–minded revolutionaries.

Decolonization and Internal Turmoil

The rapid Portuguese withdrawal from the African territories and Timor in the Far East reduced overnight most of Portugal's land area and its world–wide population by 65%. This created a particularly great refugee problem for the home country. Between 1974 and 1976 at least a half million refugees poured into Portugal, mainly from Angola. In March 1977 the new Marxist leader ordered the expulsion of all persons holding Portuguese passports, so a new wave of expellees began to pour in. The U.S. helped pay for the airlift of the *retornados* and gave Portugal more than $1 billion over five years to help cope with the financial crisis.

The returnees arrived in a chaotic Portugal with few possessions and with currencies which were not accepted in Portugal. Many were convinced that their home government had sold out to revolutionary terrorists and were therefore deeply embittered and inclined toward active, anti–communist and conservative politics. Their bitterness was also stimulated by the facts that there were almost no jobs for them in Portugal and that the government could provide only meager financial assistance. Many only found shelter in shanty towns which cropped up everywhere. In some places, especially in Algarve, the government commandeered luxury hotels for the *retornados,* a logical and humanitarian action which, however, almost bankrupted the country and deprived one of Portugal's most important industries, tourism, of many needed facilities. Ultimately the returnees were dispersed more evenly throughout the country and slowly began to find work. But the initial problems for the shaken country were immense.

There were moderates within the ruling *MFA,* such as General Spínola, whom the *MFA* had appointed immediately as provisional president, who believed that the new leaders had moved too far to the left. As a result of unsuccessful countercoups against the leftist elements within the leadership in September 1974 and again in March 1975, the moderate elements within the government were purged and, in some cases such as Spínola himself, were driven into exile.

Those leaders who remained were highly critical of what they derided as "bourgeois democracy." The avowedly pro–Communist Colonel Vasco Gonçalves advocated the creation of Soviet–style "committees for the defense of the Revolution," and the swaggering admirer of Fidel Castro, General Otelo Saraiva de Carvalho, championed the notion of "people's power" to replace the political parties. These leaders, along with a more pliant presidential replacement for Spínola, General Costa Gomes, allowed the Communists and the far left to assume control of the trade unions, the news media and local governments.

They ordered the soldiers not to intervene when left–wing mobs broke up socialist and conservative political gatherings. They nationalized major industries,

Portugal

insurance companies and banks, and they looked on approvingly as workers seized factories and as peasants took over land in the central and southern provinces. Roughly a fourth of Portugal's forests' and croplands were seized and most of it was converted to forms of collectively owned farms. But these new farms, especially in the province of Alentejo, where farming had traditionally been done on large estates called *latifundios,* were so inefficient that by the end of the 1970s Alentejo produced about a third to half of the grain and livestock it had supplied before the revolution.

The *MFA's* revolutionary economic experiments were devastating for the country, and they aroused intense opposition. It almost seemed that Portugal was going to return to the political havoc which had stricken the country before 1926. But the politically naive and inexperienced captains, who suddenly wore colonels' and generals' brass on their shoulders, lost sight of one important factor: the Portuguese voter.

They had announced that they intended to hold power for three years, but they did not prevent the holding of elections in April 1975 for an assembly which would produce a new constitution. They dismissed the elections casually as a mere opinion poll which could not possibly lessen their grip on political power. However, the results stunned them. In the first free election in a half century, 92% of eligible voters turned out to give a massive vote of non–confidence to the heavy–handed, revolutionary–authoritarian rulers. Over 70% of the voters supported the three moderate democratic parties, and only 17% supported the soldiers' only friends, the Communists and their allies.

When the officers in power made it clear that they had no intention of honoring the results of the election and instead moved to eliminate entirely the freedom of the press, the supporters of the democratic parties poured into the streets to show their disapproval. Beginning in July 1975 anti–Communist riots erupted in the northern part of the country. This massive resistance jolted the majority of military officers out of their state of indifference, and when far–left paratroopers supporting General de Carvalho tried to seize full power for themselves on November 25, 1975, Lt. Col. Ramalho Eanes, who had heretofore been almost unknown, led a crack commando force to foil the uprising. In the aftermath, all Communists and extreme leftists were purged from the *MFA* and from all governing bodies, and the Communists' hopes of taking command over a radical revolution were dashed.

A decade later, de Carvalho was put on trial for his continuing support for leftist revolution. The press dubbed it "trial of the century," and it lasted 19 months. He was convicted in May 1987 of belonging to a terrorist organization, Popular Forces of April 25 (FP–25), which is suspected of being responsible for at least 15 assassinations of businessmen and landowners and for attacks against the U.S. embassy, NATO warships and the residences of German airmen. Forty–seven co–defendents were also convicted.

In the mid–1970s Foreign observers were left dizzy by all the fundamental shifts, from right to left and then back to center, where it was to stay. Most Portuguese had wanted a revolution, but they had wanted a moderate democratic revolution, one which would bring them a stable and just political order, protection of individual rights, and ultimately economic prosperity. The last 50 years had brought them *enough* tyranny and extremist politics. Within a year and a half, the Portuguese revolution had been tamed.

In February 1976 the *MFA* signed a pact with the political parties which greatly restricted the political role of the military. In April 1976 the assembly which had been elected a year earlier to write a new constitution completed its job, and elections in the same month produced another victory for the moderate democratic parties. Eanes, who had been promoted to the rank of general, was elected president in June 1976, an office he occupied for a decade. One month later he swore in Portugal's first truly democratic government since 1926. Within a few months the radically revolutionary military officers disappeared from the political stage. In 1996 Portugal's first contemporary history museum, charting the transition from dictatorship to democracy, was opened in Leiria. It contains official archives of the 1974 armed forces revolt.

GOVERNMENT

The Arrival of Democracy

One of the most astonishing aspects of Portuguese events after April 25, 1974, often called the "carnation revolution" because of its bloodless character, was the speed with which the Marxist flirtation expired and the extent to which the revo-

Former President Eanes

Portugal

Lisbon: panoramic view of the *25th of April Bridge*, showing the Christ the King monument

lution became tamed. Within two years the swaggering officers who had seized power and set Portugal on the fast track toward a radical socialist state had disappeared almost completely, and the rigidly orthodox *Portuguese Communist Party (PCP)* saw much of its electoral support evaporate. Within two years the moderate democratic parties could claim the support of more than 80% of the voters. Also, a president was in office who had snatched the revolution out of the clutches of the extreme left, even though he has moderate leftist sympathies and sees the revolution as something more than the mere establishment of a politically democratic system. He had left no doubt whatsoever that he would support democracy in Portugal with all the vigor that his serious and ram-rod frame could muster.

Of course, the salvation of democracy in Portugal was greatly aided by other important factors. First, the extremists were effectively challenged by a democratically oriented *Portuguese Socialist Party (PS)*, led by Mario Soares, one of the most respected Portuguese political figures. His popularity within Portugal helped him counter the Communist grab for power by presenting a responsible, socialist, democratic alternative to the Stalinist, heavy-handed, Moscow-oriented *PCP*. Also, his immense prestige abroad helped bind Portugal's untried democracy to the West. The *PS* was also aided by the existence of attractive social democratic models in other Western European countries, such as Germany.

A second factor was U.S. financial assistance to Portugal. In addition to helping to finance the return of many refugees from Africa to metropolitan Portugal, the U.S. from 1975 to 1980 granted $1.5 billion in economic assistance to Portugal. This was the largest contribution by any single nation to the $2.3 billion worth of aid given to Portugal by Western countries and institutions during that period. The U.S. also provided Portugal with long-term, low interest credit to purchase grain and animal feeds. This example of enlightened self-interest reflected the earlier insights of the Marshall Plan in the rest of Europe after World War II—the best policy against Marxist appeals is economic success. The U.S. held itself aloof from Portugal's domestic battles and thus enabled the democratic forces to expose the blatant Communist attempts to seize power, backed by money from the Soviet Union.

A final factor, and perhaps the most important, was the fact that the Portuguese were tired of 50 years of dictatorship and wanted desperately an effective economy to scrape the country out of the bottom of the Western European economic barrel and to set it on the path to stability and prosperity.

In spite of the success in grabbing the revolution out of the eager hands of the extremists, there were significant visible traces of revolutionary enthusiasm left in the constitution and the political and economic system, which could only gradually be erased. One was the far-reaching nationalization of much of the economy; Article 10 of the constitution called for "the collectivization of the main means of production." Second, the constitution of 1976 ruled out the idea of a market economy and placed severe limitations on any non-socialist government.

It read like a "Third World" manifesto. For example, Article 1 called for "Portugal's . . . transformation into a society without classes." Article 2 obligated the nation's leaders to "assure the transition to socialism through the creation of conditions for the democratic exercise of power by the working classes." A third remnant was the relegation of the Revolutionary Council, the governing body of the old Armed Forces Movement, as a kind of watchdog of the revolution. Article 273 of the constitution gave the army the duty to "secure the continuation of the revolution." This body was composed of 14 military officers chosen among themselves, the heads of the three branches of the armed services, and the president of the republic, who was chairman of the Council. It had the power to block or even to veto parliamentary legislation, a power which it was not afraid to exercise.

A New Constitution

A fourth remnant is the strong presidency, elected every five years by direct, universal suffrage. A president may be re-elected only once. The president relinquished in 1981 the post of supreme commander, and he can no longer control promotions within the armed forces. He lost his power to appoint and dismiss the government. According to the new 1982 constitution, the government is responsible only to the Parliament, and *not* to the

Portugal

president. The latter can dismiss a government only after consulting the constitutional committee. Although the president's formal powers are limited, his influence is considerable. The reason is that with so many changes in governments (by 1987 there had been 17 in 13 years), the presidency has been the center of political continuity.

The former president, General António Ramalho Eanes, can undeniably take more credit than anyone else for establishing order and discipline among the country's highly politicized military officers and for purging the leftist extremists within the army. In February 1976 he signed a pact with the leaders of the major political parties which demoted the army to a less direct political role. He ruled as a quiet, shy, serious and very hard–working man from a peasant background. Although he is a man who has seldom been seen smiling, he was unquestionably the most popular man in Portuguese politics. This is very important in Portugal, where, as in many young democracies, politics is highly personalized. Names tend to be more important than programs.

The winner of the 1986 presidential election was the *Socialist*, Mario Soares, who jubilantly proclaimed that his election marked "the end of Portugal's transition to a genuine democracy." The event was a watershed in Portuguese politics in that *none* of the candidates was a military man. It signaled the definite return of the soldiers from politics to the barracks. Unlike Eanes, who was always locking horns with the government, Soares went out of his way to get along with the prime minister, despite ideological differences. In fact, he even left his *Socialist Party* and declared himself president of all Portuguese, regardless of their politics. In 1991 he easily won reelection with 70% of the votes, the widest margin since 1974. Soares relinquished the presidency in 1996 to fellow *Socialist,* Jorge Sampaio, a lawyer and former Lisbon mayor who defeated ex–Prime Minister Cavaco Silva 53.8% to 46.2%. This was the first time since 1974 that voters chose a president from the same ranks as the ruling party. Sampaio speaks excellent English, having spent part of his boyhood in Baltimore.

Changes in Government Structure

There are some institutions, policies and trends which have steadily reduced the revolutionary stamp on political life. One is the unicameral parliament, called the Assembly of the Republic, with 230 seats elected for four–year terms by proportional representation. At the head of the majority within the assembly is a relatively strong prime minister. Since 1974 regional governors or parliaments have not been able to block either the prime minister's or the president's powers since Portugal is a highly centralized, unitary state. For administrative purposes Portugal is divided into 18 districts, each with a governor appointed by the Ministry of Internal Administration upon the approval of the prime minister and his cabinet. A plan to devolve more power to the regions failed in November 1998 when an overwhelming 64% of voters in a referendum rejected it; the majority feared that it would destroy national unity, undermine budgetary discipline, and create another wasteful layer of bureaucracy. A few months earlier only a third of voters turned out to express their opinion on the country's strict abortion laws; since a majority did not vote, the results were invalid. This had been Portugal's first–ever referendum, a device whose introduction a year earlier had been hailed as the completion of a finely balanced constitution.

All institutionalized control by the military over the civilian government was eliminated, and military officers were banned from politics. This does not mean that all military influence in Portuguese politics will vanish. Indeed, military intervention in politics has historical roots too deep in Portugal to disappear completely. But it did mean that the Revolutionary Council was replaced by a civilian Council of State and Constitutional Council, appointed jointly by the Parliament, the government and the president. The adoption of the new constitution in 1982 marked the formal end of the "carnation revolution" and the coming of age of Portugal's parliamentary democracy.

A further move to strengthen the Portuguese incentive to remain on the road of democracy was the decision in 1977 to seek entry into the EC and thereby to tighten the links which bind Portugal to the older democracies of Western Europe. Perhaps the most important trend which has reduced the revolutionary stamp on public life in Portugal has been the string of electoral victories for the moderate democratic political parties. This is particularly significant for a country in which all earlier attempts at democratic rule collapsed partly because of a paralyzing multi–party system.

POLITICAL PARTIES

The *Social Democratic Party (PSD)* changed its name from the *People's Democratic Party (PPD),* in order to give itself a sharper programmatic definition. It is a moderate, progressive and organizationally decentralized party without a rigid ideological position. It is an avowedly anti–Marxist party which supports basic democratic freedoms and the market economy. It draws its voters mainly from the middle class in small and medium sized towns, from the independent professions and from mid and upper–level technical cadres. It is traditionally strongest in the Azores and Madeira archipelagos and in northern and central Portugal.

Its former leader, Aníbal Cavaco Silva, became prime minister in a minority government. Buoyed by the popularity he had gained by leading Portugal out of a deep recession, the prime minister led his party to victory in 1987. It received 51% of the votes and 146 seats, giving his party a 22–seat majority. This was the first time since 1974 that a single party won a majority of either votes or seats and the first time that the parties of the left did not win most of the votes. Cavaco Silva's immense appeal and his message of economic modernization through private enterprise had paid off. His government thus had a rare opportunity to carry out its reform plans in a climate of political stability. The Portuguese had wanted a government which could make clear–cut decisions, and they got one.

The 1991 elections demonstrated the steadiness of his free market policies, economic privatization, and encouragement of private initiative and foreign investment. They gave Portugal five years of steady economic growth, averaging 4.6% annually, after entering the EU in 1986. For the first time since the founding of the republic 81 years earlier, a democratically elected party won two consecutive absolute majorities. This was a stunning change for a country whose only previous periods of political stability were under fascist dictatorship. As a result, Portugal has become more assertive and self–confi-

President Jorge Sampaio

Portugal

Prime Minister Antonio Guterres

dent, especially the youth. Cavaco Silva symbolized this new spirit. His 10 years in power brought enormous leaps in living standards and Portugal's belated modernization, including its integration into Europe.

Cavaco Silva did not stand for reelection in October 1995, and he ran unsuccessfully for the presidency in 1996. After a decade in office, a recession since 1992, and some embarrassing scandals, voters had become disillusioned with the *PSD.* Fernando Nogueira replaced him as party leader and led his party to defeat in the October 1995 parliamentary elections. The *PDS* captured 34% of the votes and 88 seats, down from 50.6% and 136 seats.

The biggest loser in 1987 was a party founded by the former president, General Eanes. In its first electoral outing in 1985 the *Democratic Renewal Party (PRD)* had won 18% of the votes. In 1991, this center–left party fell to a disastrous 0.6% of the votes and no seats. It has become politically irrelevant.

The *Popular Party (PP,* formerly called the *Democratic and Social Center—CDS* or *Christian Democrats)* is the newest and most conservative of Portugal's four major parties. It has an anti–Marxist, Euroskeptic, Christian and humanistic orientation and a politically moderate leadership. It is the only major party which rejects socialism as a goal. It finds its members and voters chiefly among industrial management, the service industries, independent farmers and the *retornados* from the former colonies. Women also vote disproportionately for it. The party is strongest in the north, where the influence of the Catholic Church has not sunk as rapidly after 1974 as in Lisbon and the south.

It is decentralized and organizationally weaker than the other major parties. It does have the backing of the major industrialists' association, the *CIP,* but this organization's influence is considerably less than one might think because of the fact that most of Portugal's larger industries had been nationalized. The party was crushed in the 1987 and 1991 elections, winning 4.4% both years and five seats in 1991. Led by Manuel Monteiro in 1995, it tripled its parliamentary seats to 15, based on 9.1% of the votes.

The *Socialist Party (PS),* is led by Prime Minister António Guterres, who replaced current President Jorge Sampaio in 1993. Along with some close associates, Mario Soares founded the *PS* in Münstereifel, Germany, in 1973, with the helping hand of the then ruling *Social Democratic Party of Germany.* When the Portuguese revolution erupted in 1974, Soares rushed back from his Paris exile, and the *PS* was thrust into the forefront of the turbulent events without having time to become well organized for its new role. The *PS* and Soares certainly share much of the credit for channeling the revolution into a democratic direction. But after being the country's most important political party for a few years, its extreme fragmentation and organizational difficulties, along with the wide–spread unsatisfied economic expectations of the Portuguese, caused it to suffer a string of election failures, which shook the party's confidence.

The party is democratically and decentrally organized. Unlike all other Portuguese parties, its voting strength is spread fairly evenly over the entire country and is found primarily in the working and lower middle classes. It is backed by the moderate General Union of Workers, *(UGT),* which, since January 1979, has increasingly challenged *Communist* domination of the organized labor movement. The party program is officially Marxist, but both the economic crisis and existence of a rigid and stubborn *Communist Party* to its left, with which the *PS* refuses to form any coalition, have pushed the party more toward the political center. In the minds of most politically active Portuguese, the desire to overcome Portugal's economic difficulties has replaced earlier aspirations of establishing socialism. This nation–wide change of priorities has understandably forced the *PS* to change its own priorities as well. It now admits that the introduction of socialism in Portugal could only follow a very long transition period.

In 1995 the *PS* won 43.9% of the votes and 112 seats in the 230–seat parliament, up from 29.3% and 70 seats in 1991. This was the party's biggest victory in two decades, and four months later it became the first party since 1974 to capture both the government and the presidency. Although it did not win an absolute majority, Guterres leads a relatively stable government since the two conservative parties would have to team with the *Communists* in order to block its initiatives or bring it down.

Guterres began his career as a radical, and at age 25 he served in Mario Soares's provisional government in 1974. He showed himself to be an ambitious and precocious politician. Now a pragmatic, modern left–wing leader who is a committed Catholic, he vows to maintain Portugal's pro–European stance and its free–market economics, including the policy of privatization. He declared that "change does not mean destroy. Everything we inherit that was positive will be continued." He proclaims that his "priorities of priorities" will be education. Continual strikes in the school system since 1993 point to serious problems.

The final major party is the *Portuguese Communist Party (PCP),* led by Alvaro Cunhal. The *PCP* is not a Eurocommunist party. Indeed, it is the most Stalinist Communist party in all of Western Europe. Perhaps this is not surprising when one considers the fact that during the fascist rule many of its leading functionaries were either in prison or in exile in the Soviet Union. Cunhal himself was in prison eight years and is too bitter and frozen in his thinking to change now. It is Portugal's oldest party and is the only one with roots in the first republic from 1910 to 1926. This is also the country's best organized party. It was a tight, clandestine group during the fascist period, and when the revolution came in 1974 it was immediately prepared to jump into the political fray and attempt to take all the reins of power in its own hands.

Its major base of power since the summer of 1975, when its patrons within the army lost most of their own power, was the landless farmers in the Alentejo region, where the party helped organize collectivized agricultural enterprises *(UCP),* and the trade unions, especially the powerful *General Confederation of Portuguese Workers (CGTP–Intersindical)* which organizes almost three–fourths of all trade union leaders. The *PCP* has also attracted some intellectuals. Geographically the party's electoral fortresses were the agricultural area of Alentejo and the industrial zone around Lisbon. In the north, it faced almost complete rejection, except in the city of Oporto. In 1995 the *PCP* continued its steady decline, falling to 8.6% of the votes (down from 8.8%) and 15 seats (from 17). It was especially punished for its leftist rigidity. The disillusioned, more educated party members are

Hon. Alvaro Cunhal

defecting in droves. Among the party's problems are a general deradicalization of the working class and the rise of a younger wing within the *PCP* which advocates less dogmatic policies.

Foreign and Defense Policies

Portugal's defense policy has long been based on its membership in NATO. In 1988 it joined the WEU. Portugal's major contribution to the alliance has never been in the form of combat troops. During the decade and a half preceding the 1974 revolution, Portugal's army was bogged down in colonial wars, but between September 1974 and November 1975 these millstones were cast off one by one: first Portuguese Guinea (now Guinea–Bissau), then Mozambique, Angola, the Cape Verde Islands, São Tomé and Príncipe. In 1996 Portugal and its six former colonies, including Brazil, fulfilled a long–held ambition by uniting their 200 million people (of whom 162 million are Brazilians) in the Community of Portuguese–Speaking Countries (CPLP). Its task is to protect their common language and promote co-operation. The post of secretary general is rotated alphabetically every two years.

The only actual colony that remained until the end of the century was Maçao, a tiny (six sq. miles) outpost on the southern coast of the People's Republic of China, 40 miles (64 km.) across the Canton River Estuary from Hong Kong. Only about 10,000 of the estimated 427,000 are Portuguese, although 110,000 hold Portuguese passports and can therefore live and work anywhere in the EU if they choose. Few of the Chinese who live there speak Portuguese. In fact, English is used far more than Portuguese. After the 1974 revolution, Lisbon wanted to give up the colony, which is an important trade outlet and source of foreign capital for Beijing. In 1979 officials from both countries met secretly in Paris, where the Portuguese acknowledged Chinese sovereignty over the territory and agreed to administer it until China wanted it back. This agreement was revealed in 1987, when both announced that China would assume full control on December 19, 1999, after 442 years of Portuguese rule.

Even if the Chinese Communists are not directly involved in Maçao's main industry, gambling, they derive considerable profits from Maçao, which has Asia's fastest growing economy. Although nominally under Portuguese administration until the end of this century, Portuguese officials make no pretense of being in charge. They formally appoint Maçao's governor, but only after the Chinese have given their approval behind the scenes. Indeed, all it would have taken for the Chinese to regain control of the colony was a phone call from Beijing. There is little popular agitation for greater democracy, as in Hong Kong. The Chinese promised to respect Maçao's western, capitalist society and economy until at least 2050 and leave it with considerable autonomy in local affairs.

Technically speaking, Portugal still has another colony, namely Portuguese Timor. The annexation of this half of the Timor Island by Indonesia on July 17, 1976, has never been officially recognized by Portugal or the UN. Almost half of East Timor's population died as a result of Indonesia's invasion and a native independence movement still resists Indonesian authority. The situation recaptured the world's attention in 1991, when Indonesian soldiers and police opened fire on peaceful demonstrators, killing dozens in front of Western journalists' cameras. All over Portugal, flags were flown at half–mast, newspapers appeared with black bands, and ceremonies and church vigils were held. Portugal's talks with Indonesia on this issue in 1992 ended with no concrete results.

In 1996 the Nobel Peace Prize was awarded to José Ramos–Horta, a U.S.–educated human rights activist whose leftist Portuguese father had been deported to East Timor, and to Roman Catholic Bishop Carlos Filipe Ximenes Belo, a native of Timor, who had studied in missionary schools in Portugal and Rome. President Jorge Sampaio, whose country had provided refuge for many East Timorese dissidents and had conducted the UN–sponsored negotiations with Indonesia for 12 years, called the award "a wonderful surprise" that reflects the two men's "indefatigable work in the service of human rights and peace in the territory." Portugal was rewarded by being given a two–year non–permanent seat on the UN Security Council in 1997. In the words of Prime Minister Guterres, this recognizes the "prestige and influence of Portugal in the world."

The situation changed dramatically in 1998 when the Indonesian government of longtime ruler Suharto was overthrown, and the new leaders offered the 800,000 Timorese the opportunity to choose autonomy or independence. In May 1999, following more than 15 years of UN–sponsored negotiations in which the Portuguese were more closely involved than any other nation, Portugal signed an agreement with Indonesia calling for a referendum on August 8.

After the 1974 revolution had been tamed, Portugal could afford neither politically nor economically to continue maintaining a large land army. Therefore the size of the armed forces was cut from nearly a half million to about 66,000 politically obedient troops (39,000 army; 14,000 navy; 13,000 air force). Compulsory service has dropped to nine months, and a professional army is being considered. The military's share in the budget fell from 50% in 1970 to less than 10% in the 1990s. What Portugal can contribute to NATO is the use of strategically important facilities on the mainland, where NATO has naval and air facilities, and in the Azores and Madeira island groups, which are autonomous parts of Portugal.

The Azores, nine mountainous and beautiful islands of volcanic origin which are located about 1,000 miles (1,600 km.) west of Lisbon, are a vital stepping stone for NATO airborne forces moving toward the Mediterranean, Middle East, Persian Gulf or Africa. Former President Eanes was certainly correct in calling them "a pillar of support in the defense of Europe." American Air Force General Larry Wright underscored this: "Whoever controls the Azores controls the Atlantic."

Of particular importance is the U.S. air base at Lajes on the island of Terceiram, which the U.S. leases from Portugal. In 1995 the lease was renewed for five years. Lajes is a refueling station, and about 250 U.S. aircraft touch down each month. It is also a base for P–3 Orion maritime surveillance planes which patrol 2.5 million square miles in the North Atlantic.

A serious financial dispute arose in 1988 when the U.S. announced that it would provide less aid. The prime minister noted that "expectations are not being met." Many of his countrymen had the impression that Portugal was being taken for granted, now that democracy had been stabilized. Unlike the situation in Spain concerning Torrejon Air Base, where the issue was political, not financial, there is no public resentment over the American

Portugal

military presence at Lajes. In 1988 the Portuguese government announced that it did not want the F16 fighter bombers which are being evicted from Spain to be redeployed in Portugal. It called for a formal review of the base agreement, and a solution was found in 1989: the U.S. supplied the Portuguese armed forces with 20 F16s, as well as a battery of Hawk ground–to–air missiles, 57 antisubmarine, combat and utility helicopters, air defense radar, and a hydrographic vessel. U.S. financial aid for 1989 was set at $150 million, down from $208 million in 1985. All this assistance enables Portugal to shift its military emphasis in NATO from leasing bases to a more active antisubmarine role in the mid–Atlantic.

In the 1990s the U.S. is pulling some of its military assets out of the Azores after Soviet activity in the Atlantic ended. The U.S., which maintains 1,800 military personnel and 1,900 dependents on the island, also has an underwater terminal on the island of Santa Maria to monitor submarine movements in the Atlantic and a network of underground supply areas throughout the islands whose contents can be airlifted to any transatlantic area within hours. France also operates a missile tracking station on the island of Flores. Because the U.S. is emphasizing a rapid deployment capability for the Middle East, the U.S. is conducting a major buildup of its military facilities here, aimed at providing a "viable support base" eastward and southward.

When, in 1975, the leftist Portuguese government allowed Cuban planes carrying troops to Angola to use Santa Maria for refueling stops, a pro–American Azores separatist movement sprang up, but it withered again when more moderate leaders came to power in Lisbon. This movement indicated the basic strength of the ties between the 200,000 residents of the Azores and the U.S., where more than 600,000 Azoreans now live, mainly on the east and west coasts.

A dispute in 1986 over the elevation of the Azorean flag and anthem to equal status with those of the motherland served as a reminder of local pride. They had been waved and played in official ceremonies since 1980. Nevertheless, because of the symbolic importance, President Soares vetoed the islands' revised autonomy statue, which had been approved by the Portuguese parliament. This was the first use of the presidential veto under the 1976 constitution, and it indicated how a flag and anthem question can revive Lisbon's fears of possible Azorean separatism.

The Madeira archipelago is not only the home of a desirable aperitif wine, which rivals sherry for popularity. It guards the

Wine-growing country around the Douro River Valley

southern approaches to Europe and the Strait of Gibraltar and is the southernmost NATO territory. The island of Porto Santo has excellent airport and deep–water port facilities, which at times has been used for military purposes, such as in 1978 when it was used as a refueling stop for aircraft carrying Belgian troops to Zaire. NATO military planners are very interested in Madeira because the Spanish made it clear that their Canary Islands, which lie only 300 miles (480 km.) south of Madeira, would not be considered NATO territory once Spain entered the Atlantic Alliance.

Portugal is very wary about allowing Madeira to become a military bastion like the Azores. A major reason is that this could create a conflict with the Organization of African Unity, in which voices have long been raised that the Madeira archipelago is colonized African territory and should therefore be liberated. After all, Madeira lies only 350 miles (560 km.) west of Morocco. Lisbon is trying to forge closer links with its former African colonies in order to regain some of their lucrative markets and to send them some of their excess work force.

Both Mozambique and Angola, the two richest of the former colonies, have realized the benefits which the more skilled Portuguese could bring to their countries and have asked the Portuguese to return under a new guise. This reconciliation with its former colonies has been made politically easier since Portugal supported the Black African position toward South Africa. One–seventh of the white South Africans are of Portuguese origin. In 1991 Portugal mediated the "Estoril Accord," ending Angola's 16–year civil war. It also participated, along with American, Russian and Angolan observers, in the political–military commission to supervise the truce and prepare for elections. It also sent peacekeeping forces to Mozambique in the early 1990s. Portugal supported peaceful change in part because it wants to avoid the kind of refugee flood it experienced in the 1970s. Emotional ties with Africa are still strong, but economic links have become much weaker. By the 1990s only about 1% of Portugal's foreign trade was with Angola and Mozambique.

Portugal is also trying to improve its relations with the nations of the Middle East. Portugal was the first ally to heed President Carter's call in 1979 for sanctions against Iran when Iranian mobs had seized the U.S. embassy. It also levied sanctions against the Soviet Union when it invaded Afghanistan, although President Soares' visit to Moscow in 1987 signaled a normalization of relations with Russia.

In 1991 it supported its allies' war to dislodge the Iraqi aggressors from Kuwait. It sent 900 troops to Bosnia to help NATO implement the 1995 Dayton Peace Accord. Its diplomatic support for the U.S. is certainly not due exclusively to the fact that the U.S. still gives Portugal economic and military aid, but to the fact that the two nations now share democratic values and common interests and therefore have a solid foundation for good relations.

ECONOMY

Under fascist rule, Portugal's economy was relatively isolated and sheltered from the rest of Europe. Its industry was primarily in the hands of rather inefficient family businesses, which were protected

Portugal

from stiff Western European competition and which had a comfortable export and import monopoly with their country's African colonies. A third of the Portuguese worked in agriculture. After 1974 much of Portugal's economic situation changed for the better.

The 1974 revolution did, however, create additional economic problems, beyond the temporary scaring away of tourists and their much-needed foreign currencies. Most of the earlier large private industrial and financial groups were broken down, and a wide range of economic activities which were not foreign owned was brought under state control. These included banks, insurance, airlines, railways, electricity, oil, gas, petrochemicals, cement, breweries, tobacco, wood pulp, steel, shipping and ship-building, urban transit, trucking, metallurgy, chemicals, food processing and textiles. Many of these sectors were combined in a huge publicly-owned conglomerate called Quimigal.

In all, 60% of Portugal's industry was nationalized after 1974. These nationalized industries exacerbated Portugal's problems. In 1991 the state still accounted for 40% of GDP. Although many firms escaped the sword of nationalization because of their small size, it is not surprising that an immediate result of this policy was that investment capital was scared away. Productivity dropped and, because wages were doubled after 1974, inflation soared. Such nationalizations merely added to the weight of Portugal's already cumbersome bureaucracy. The state-owned companies also sap up the lion's share of the government's economic subsidies, but these funds are insufficient to convert them into efficient companies able to compete well in international markets.

The Cavaco Silva government vowed in 1985 to end state domination of the economy, which he blamed for keeping Portuguese living standards so far below the Western European average. His reelection in 1987 boosted his program to begin gradually selling off most industries and financial institutions nationalized after 1974. Cavaco Silva noted that "the state should control only companies of particular importance to public service," such as power, water and public-transport utilities. The government's extensive media holdings, including newspapers, are also earmarked for sale, save one television and radio channel. "The era of state paternalism will soon be over." Progress on this privatization program has been slow. One problem is that there are too few large Portuguese groups with enough money to buy what is up for sale. Not wishing to sell most of these assets to foreigners, rigid, but ineffective, limits on how much foreigners can buy were established. Beginning in 1993 foreigners could buy control in state firms on a case-by-case basis.

A welcome reform after the 1974 revolution was the lifting of the ban against strikes and independent trade unions. However, in the heady days after the revolution the well-organized Communists seized control of the major labor union, the CGTP–Intersindical. This union drives an extremely hard bargain and became accustomed to getting what it demands. The CGTP–Intersindical is highly politicized and is able to threaten the government through potentially crippling strikes. In 1988 it sought by means of a 24-hour strike to preserve the stringent dismissal law from 1975 which makes it virtually impossible to fire a worker from his job. For the first time, communist and socialist labor federations united, and factories, airports and banks across the country were shut down, as hundreds of thousands of workers staged the biggest industrial action in Portuguese history. But Cavaco Silva, refused to change a single line of his legislation to make it easier for businesses to fire workers, on the grounds that it is crucial for attracting investment and modernizing the economy.

The decolonization of Portugal's empire forced Portugal to compete with other nations for markets and brought close to a million bitter and penniless *retornados* to the motherland. What was worse, it cut off the country's most important sources of raw materials, especially energy. Even though Portugal has the lowest per capita energy consumption in Western Europe and also the lowest ownership of automobiles per inhabitant (although the number of cars doubled between 1985 and 1990, causing congestion in Lisbon), it can produce only about 20% of the energy it needs. The country must import all of its oil and 83% of its coal. It is usually able to meet 60% of its electricity demand through its own hydro-electricity, but recurrent droughts make this source uncertain. Therefore, it imports substantial amounts of electricity from Spain and France.

Portugal must spend about 10% of its GDP in energy imports, compared with only 1% in 1973, and most analysts expect

Picking grapes in Estremadura

Portugal

Stripping cork

energy demand to rise, as Portugal expands its industry. Perhaps there will be no alternative to using its one untapped energy source, namely the 8,000 tons of proven uranium reserves, mostly located in the northern area of Urgerica, to produce nuclear energy. In the meantime, Portugal will have great difficulty paying for oil, especially since it has a limited range of competitive exports. Therefore, its large trade deficits will probably continue.

Agriculture and Fishing

Portuguese agriculture is traditionally inefficient, and although 12% of all Portuguese are engaged in agriculture, the country must still import half of its food and animal feeds. Farming, fishing and forestry contribute only 9% of Portugal's GDP. Food makes up one-fifth of the nation's total imports. It has the lowest per capita productivity in Western Europe. In fact, its productivity is only a fourth to a third of the EU average and two-thirds that of Spain and Greece. This is due to several factors, including the rocky, hilly soil, the low level of mechanization, the inefficient collective farms in the South, the insufficient size of family farms in the North, and the farmers' general resistance to change. About 30% of Portugal's rural population is estimated to be illiterate, compared with 13% of all Portuguese over age 15. Portuguese farmers' inability to compete successfully within a single European market has left a majority of them living at subsistence levels on incomes a third as big as their Spanish counterparts'.

The revolution of 1974 by no means created Portugal's agricultural problems, but the initial leaders' fervor created particular problems in the south, where the land which was conquered from the Moors in the 13th century was distributed in large tracts to Portuguese nobility. These large land-owners often lived in Lisbon and had their large estates worked by low-paid agricultural laborers. These large estates were ripe for picking in revolutionary times.

The Communists, supported by the ruling leftist military leaders, seized many of the estates and converted them into large collective farms. In other cases, they forced the owners to hire more workers than could be employed profitably. By the 1990s more than half the seized estates had been returned to their original owners, and all owners have received some compensation for their former holdings. Nevertheless, about one-fifth of Portugal's forest and cropland remains collectivized. But these collectively-owned farms have, on the whole, been poorly managed. They therefore now produce only a third to a half of the grain and livestock which they supplied before the revolution. Because of legal tangles, the Cavaco Silva government did not move as fast to de-collectivize farming in the South as it had hoped.

Portugal faces a problem of what to do about its inefficient farming and antiquated fishing fleet which is already unable to withstand competition in its home waters. Also, it has few agricultural products which can compete in the EU. The ones which can are wines, tomato concentrate and cork. The heart of its wine growing is in the Douro River Valley, from which port wine (named for the city of Oporto) comes. Also, the world's largest exporter of a single brand of wine, Mateus Rose, comes from Portugal, the largest importer being the U.S. Actually, the Portuguese seldom drink Mateus Rose, preferring their own dry whites from northern and central Portugal. It is understandable that they prefer not to export these fine wines and, instead, to keep their limited supply for themselves.

Portugal's fishing fleet is the oldest and least productive in all of Western Europe. Many of its vessels have no engines. Portugal leads the world in ship repair; its repair yards are the world's biggest and handle more tonnage than their top four competitors together. In 1969 the Portuguese government granted Spain, which has a fishing fleet that is larger than that of all 15 EU countries combined, unrestricted rights to fish in Portugal's waters. Most leaders in Lisbon now view that decision as a cardinal error and have been trying hard to undo it.

Portugal's chief export is cork, of which it supplies 80% of the world's supply (most of the rest comes from Spain.). This substance is the bark which is stripped off the cork oak trees every 11 years, a process which leaves the trees a bright red color. Cork production suffered a set-back in the mid-1970s, when following the seizure of large estates in Alentejo thousands of cork trees were uprooted to make way for wheat, a crop unsuited for the region. The *Communist*-inspired wheat drive at least temporarily destroyed cork-growing there.

Membership in EU

Portugal's political leaders, supported by a large majority of the population, chose a formidable challenge to prepare their country for a more prosperous future—entry into the EU. Before becoming a full member in 1986, it was a member of EFTA. In 1972 Portugal had entered and agreement with the EU providing free trade of industrial products. Its leaders, as well as those in the EU member countries, hoped that such entry would help solidify the democratic foundations in Portugal, as well as provide a mighty boost for the country's economy. By 1996, 85% of its exports went to Europe (the largest market being Germany), more than double the proportion a decade earlier. It conducts 18.5% of its foreign trade with Spain.

The introduction of greater incentives through a reform of personal taxation, which some observers described as the most punitive in all of Western Europe, stimulated the economy. Portuguese industry enjoys other advantages. Its smallness and fragmented nature lend it some flexibility. The Portuguese could not bear much more poverty. Their poor remain the poorest in Western Europe, and a third of all households still have no running water.

Its basic strength is in the cheapness of labor, the lowest in Western Europe; average wages are only a third of EU average. At $5.60 per hour in 1996, its manufacturing pay was two–thirds lower than in the U.S., three–fourths lower than in Germany, and 60% less than in Spain and Ireland, economies at a similar level of development. The Portuguese labor force, on the whole, works conscientiously and acquires new skills quickly. Of course, there are considerable domestic dangers involved with relying on cheap labor to maintain international competitiveness. It could stimulate even more labor unrest than already exists.

Portugal exports textiles and footwear and faces stiff competition not only in the EU, but also from Third World countries. Portugal is already dependent on the Americans for a large portion of food–stuffs, including 90% of its wheat.

Entry into the EU brought needed social and regional funds to Portugal; 4% of its GDP is derived from financial transfers from Brussels. This country, which was so successful in establishing a democratic political order despite enormous problems and the absence of a democratic tradition, is meeting the economic challenges associated with becoming a full economic partner in Western Europe. By bringing its budget deficit down to 2.9% of GDP and its total national debt to 66% of GDP by 1998, it met the most important qualifications to enter the European Monetary Union (EMU) in 1999, and it adopted the Euro.

Portugal is experiencing rapid economic growth (3.5% in 1998). Inflation, at 2.6% in 1999, is high by Western European standards, but its 4.7% unemployment rate in 1999 is half the EU average. Tourism is booming with about 20 million guests in 1992, primarily British and Spanish; it accounts for 6% to 8% of its GDP. Foreign investment is pouring in, and two–thirds of it comes from the EU. With 75% of its GDP derived from foreign trade, Portugal is one of the most open countries in Europe. It is therefore natural that it became a part of the world's largest economic market, and it is doing quite well. Per capita GDP has risen from 51.4% of the EU average in 1985 to above 64% in 1995.

The existence of a lively "submerged economy" makes it more difficult to get an exact picture of Portugal's economic condition. This kind of activity is done at home, in the streets, or on the job while the boss is looking the other way. It takes place behind the backs of government statisticians and tax collectors. If the production of goods and services from such an invisible economy were able to be included in the official economic figures, an estimated 10% to 25% would have to be added to the GDP, and real unemployment would be below the official figures.

CULTURE

Portugal is a nation whose cultural influence extends far beyond its own borders. Today nearly 200 million people speak Portuguese. Its outward–looking orientation was beautifully reflected in its greatest literary figure, Luiz de Camões (1524–80), who wrote poetry and dramatic comedies. In 1572 he published perhaps the greatest piece of Portuguese literature, *Os Lusíadas* ("The Lusitanians"), a long epic poem celebrating Portuguese history and heroes. His story is linked with that of Vasco da Gama's voyage to India and is infused with much Greek mythology.

Portuguese culture has also been enriched by experiences or influences from abroad. For instance, the novelist, John Dos Passos, and the undisputed king of march music, John Philip Sousa, were both sons of Portuguese emigrants and received their artistic inspiration in the U.S.

In 1998 a Portuguese writer won the Nobel Prize for literature for the first time. Jose Samarago was born into a home with no books, grew up in poverty, never went to the university, and toiled as a metalworker until the fall of dictator Antonio Salazar enabled him, an active *Communist*, to publish his first novel in 1974. The best known of his imaginative novels are *Baltasar and Blimunda* and *The Year of the Death of Ricardo Reis*.

He expressed his hope on receiving the honor that "Portuguese will become more visible and more audible." Earlier in the century Egas Moniz had won the Nobel Prize for medicine.

Influence of Brazil

Perhaps the greatest foreign cultural influence comes from Brazil. For years after 1974 one of the most popular television serials in Portugal was a sort of soap opera from Brazil called "Gabriela." Set in Rio de Janeiro and using an all–Brazilian cast, this *telenovela* (T.V. serial) filled Portugal's air waves with Brazilian slang, songs, accents and dress. Many other such series have subsequently been brought in from Brazil to be aired on Portugal's two state–owned and run channels, RTP 1 and 2, and on its two newer private commercial channels, SIC and TV1.

Chiefly because of its small size and high degree of centralization, there are few different dialects spoken within Portugal, except in Miranda do Douro in the northeast. But of the 150 million persons in the world who speak Portuguese as a native language, only 10 million live in the mother country. At newsstands one finds many Brazilian publications mixed with Portuguese ones: Lisbon alone has five morning and four afternoon papers, the most popular being the tabloid *Correio da Manha*. In 1991 the last state–owned daily newspaper, *Diario de Noticias*, established in 1864, was sold into private hands; it is respected as a serious but rather dull paper, but its look is being modernized. There are also hotselling weeklies, such as *Expresso, O Jornal, Semanario* and *Independente*.

Cork strips ready for transport

Portugal

The National Theater, Lisbon

It is not surprising that the language spoken in this small country is being changed by the Portuguese spoken outside, especially in Brazil. Oral expression is being strongly penetrated by Brazilian words and idiomatic phrases. The economic prowess of Brazil has meant that the Portuguese being learned by foreigners abroad is now primarily Brazilian. Most magazines on Portugal's newsstands are from Brazil.

A passionate debate began in 1986 over whether Portugal should simply recognize this fact and negotiate a linguistic agreement with Brazil and other former colonies. Proponents argue that a common structure of the language must be preserved and that the constant evolution of the language should be incorporated in the mother country. Critics decry the "crime against the patrimony of the Portuguese language" and "a disgusting resignation to Brazil's economic interests." It cannot be expected that, in the long run, any effort to erect a barrier against the flood of foreign cultural influences could succeed in a country like Portugal which is adapting itself so quickly to the changing world which it faces. Millions of Portuguese really want no such barrier anyway. Nevertheless, the government established tough requirements that by 1995 40% of all TV shows must be in Portuguese, three-fourths of which must be produced in Portugal.

Education

Post-revolutionary Portugal inherited considerable educational problems. These included a shortage of schools and teachers, a clear and discriminatory separation of the elite lycée (high school) from the trade schools, a poor geographic distribution of educational facilities throughout the country, and especially the concentration of higher education along the coast. Just before the revolution, the progressive minister of education, Mr. Veiga Simão announced a comprehensive reform, which would have combined all the various educational tracks into one, opened up the path to the universities at Evora, Braga, Aveiro and Lisbon, in addition to the existing universities at Coimbra, Oporto, and Lisbon (where there are two). By the 1990s there were 12 state universities, 14 polytechnic schools, and a growing number of private universities.

Simão was swept out of office along with the entire *ancien regime,* and for a couple years, the educational system became the wet clay in the hands of leftist and Marxist teachers and reformers. Many Marxist textbooks replaced the out-dated books from the Salazar era, schools were taken over by management committees which excluded most parental influence in the schools, and pupils were examined on their "collective work" and even had a voice in the grades they received.

When the *Socialist Party* finally gained a firm grip on the reins of government in the second half of 1975, the textbooks were changed again to reflect the more moderate and pluralistic character of the new leadership. Parents were again given some say in the school system, the former strict grading system was reintroduced, and hundreds of leftists were removed from the schools and the ministry of education. With order restored in the schools, the education system was more or less back where it had been in 1974, but the ground had been laid for important changes.

In 1977 a system of pre-school instruction was introduced, and the pre-university schooling was established at 11 years, with the possibility of a twelfth year later. A special innovation was the introduction of a transition year right before entry into the university, during which time students can review all they had learned in their earlier schooling and begin dealing with common academic material on a university level. Thus, all pupils in Portugal now receive six years of elementary education, which is obligatory, and some secondary schooling. Those who wish to stay in school have five years of secondary school, which about 40% finish.

All children must remain in school until age 15. This is a real strain on the system when one considers that Portugal has one of Europe's youngest populations: al-

Portugal

most a fourth is under age 15. After the one–year transition class, qualified students can enter the university for a "short advanced education" of two to three years, or for the "diverse superior courses" of four or five years. The number of students, at 250,000, is still low with only one in five going on to higher education. But the number is eight times higher than in 1974. In 1998 many of those students participated in a one–day strike to protest the raising of their annual tuition from $7 to $330.

All kinds of scholarly and cultural endeavors are generously supported in Portugal by the Gulbenkian Foundation, established and richly funded by a foreign oil magnate who made Portugal his home. Since the foundation is massively involved in supporting a wide range of cultural activities, is private and has carefully steered clear of government control, it was able to support research with critical political implications, which the politicians in power viewed with some distrust.

Cultural activity also got a boost in late 1986 with a new law (called the "Maecenas Law") that concedes tax breaks to corporations which support cultural initiatives. Up to 60% of any "cultural financing" costs can be written off taxes. Since only about 1% of the national budget is allotted to culture, and public support is very scarce, this new measure is most welcome.

A final view of Lisbon

Religion

Portuguese society has experienced some social transformation in the past decade and a half, but religion has not changed as much as in many other Western European countries. Divorce was permitted after the revolution. The Catholic Church continued to oppose birth control, but Portuguese in child–bearing age are inclined to ignore that opposition. Despite bitter protests by the Catholic Church, Parliament voted in 1984 to permit abortions following rape, or whenever medically advisable. Nevertheless, legal abortion is rare today, and illegal abortions continue.

Religious superstitions and symbols remain strong. One sees "Our Lady of . . ." various things everywhere. A popular cult is the shrine of Our Lady of Fatima, where the virgin reportedly appeared to three shepherd children in 1917. Hundreds of thousands of pilgrims attend candlelight masses at the rural shrine twice a year. Portuguese are conscientious church–goers, by European standards. Although only about a third of all Catholics attend regularly, this compares with fewer than a fifth in Spain and a sixth in France.

FUTURE

Since 1974 Portugal has established a democratic political order which has shown itself capable of surviving. Its extrication from costly colonial wars not only aided its own economy, but it enabled Portugal to concentrate its military attention on common NATO objectives. With the continued need for the U.S. and its allies to be able to project their military presence into the Mediterranean and Middle Eastern regions, Portugal's Azores and Madeira archipelagos in the Atlantic Ocean will continue to have strategic importance. Portugal has benefited from stable, energetic government.

Portugal has undergone a dramatic transformation since joining the EU in 1986. The economy experienced an unprecedented boom and has been modernized and liberalized. Despite poverty which still exists, standards of living have been raised, unemployment is among the lowest in the EU, and most Portuguese have experienced progress. One sees manifestations of economic progress in the construction boom, huge shopping malls, and the emergence of a new technocratic class, although the success is uneven throughout the country. Two showcases of the country's economic development in 1998 were the world exposition in Lisbon, that commemorated the 500th anniversary of Vasco da Gama's first voyage to Brazil and drew millions of visitors, and the opening of the 11–mile Vasco da Gama Bridge spanning the Tejo River.

The economic recession, excessive patronage, and a 1994 scandal involving the bugging of the attorney general's and other leaders' offices put Cavaco Silva on the defensive and opened the way for *Socialist* victories in the 1995 parliamentary elections and 1996 presidential elections.

Prime Minister Guterres succeeded in reducing the budget deficit from 4.2% in 1997 to 2.9% in 1998, below the 3% required for the European currency union, which Portugal joined. The necessary cutbacks hurt. But with the opposition fragmented, his minority government is stable and effective. He faces the October 1999 elections with confidence.

Portugal's democratic constitution has been reformed and strengthened, and Portuguese have rediscovered a sense of national pride. In April 1994 they celebrated the 20th anniversary of the "Carnation Revolution." They can look with satisfaction on the legacies of that revolution: a stable parliamentary democracy, membership in the EU, and sustained economic growth that has raised living standards.

Andorra

The church Sant Cristòfol d'Anyós high in the Andorran Pyrenees dates from the 12th century

Area: 188 sq. mi. (487 sq. km.)
Population: 71,000 estimated. More than 80% are foreigners.
Capital City: Andorra la Vella, population with adjoining Encamp, 22,000.
Climate: Cool, dry summer and snowy, mountain winter climate.
Official Language: Catalan; Spanish and French are also widely spoken.
Ethnic Background: Catalan stock; ca. 15% of residents are native Andorrans, 61% Spanish, 6% French.
Principal Religion: Roman Catholic
Major Industries: Tourism, free port for consumer goods, tobacco products, hydroelectric power, timber.
Major Customers: France, Spain, Germany, Japan.
Currency: The French Franc and the Spanish Peseta.
Year of Independence: 1278.
Government: Since 1993 a self–ruling sovereign state.
Chiefs of State: Figurehead Co–Princes are the President of the French Republic and the Spanish Bishop of Seo de Urgel, who are represented locally by officials called Veguers.
Head of Government: Marc Forné Molné, Prime Minister (since 1994).
National Flag: Three vertical bands of blue, yellow, and red with the national coat of arms in the center.

Perched high in the Pyrenees Mountains is the largest of Europe's six microscopic independent states: Andorra. Mountain peaks rising to 9,000 feet (2,743 meters) overlook six deep valleys on the southern slopes of the Pyrenees. Bordering on France to the north and on Spain to the South, Andorra, with its ruggedly beautiful landscape, is a geographic blend of glacial valleys, lakes, fresh water springs and Alpine meadows. Abundant rainfall and snow give this tiny land a green, rich look half the year and a white mountain look the other half. In the 58 villages and hamlets in the highlands, with their typically granite, wood and slate houses, live many of the native Andorrans, who now comprise only about 15% of the population.

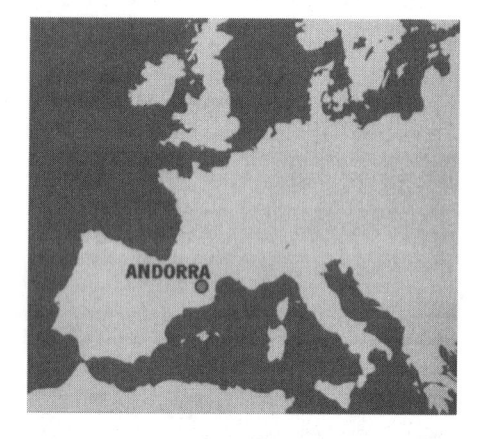

They have a strong affinity with the region of Catalonia in Northern Spain. They speak Catalan, a rich romance language related to Provencal, spoken by approximately six million persons in the region which encompasses French and Spanish Catalonia. In the age of the automobile, Andorra has been ripped from the Middle Ages, and its dizzying economic advancement has attracted thousands of Spaniards and French, who now comprise 61% and 6% of Andorra's residents respectively. These developments have made Andorrans a minority in their own country, but they have also given the land a prosperous, international character.

There is evidence of human settlements in Andorra dating many thousands of years ago, and the first written records date from the third century B.C. It is a local legend that the mountain people in these valleys helped a grateful Charlemagne drive the Moors from the area in 806 A.D. Charlemagne's son, Louis the Pious, granted the six valleys to the Spanish Bishop of Seo de Urgel in 819 A.D. In 1278 the French Count of Foix and the Bishop recognized each other as Co–Princes of Andorra. Over the years, the Count of Foix's claims passed to the King of Navarre, then to the King of France, and finally to the President of the French Republic. Except for a brief period during the French Revolution, when the French occupied Andorra and declared it a republic, it has retained to the present day its co–allegiance to France and the Bishop of Seo de Urgel.

Until 1993 the co–allegiance was formally acknowledged by a token annual tribute (*questia*) of 960 French francs (about $190) to France and 460 Spanish pesetas (about $15) to Spain in alternating years. Because of this tribute and because the country existed as a result of a feudal

Andorra

grant, Andorra was technically not a state, according either to international law or to its own statutes. It was a fief, a feudal carry-over from the Middle Ages with no equivalence in modern Europe.

POLITICAL SYSTEM

In 1990 reformer Josep Maria Beal was elected Sindic, pledging to modernize the country's institutions to enable it to survive in the new Europe. With the support of his successor, Jordi Farras, and other Andorran leaders, such as Oscar Ribas Reig, his pledge was fulfilled. In 1993 the tiny country adopted its first-ever constitution. With three-quarters of the eligible voters participating, 74.2% opted for sovereignty. By choosing self-rule, they acquired the right to have their own judicial system and foreign policy.

Andorrans are now completely free to establish political parties. Traditionally, all Andorran candidates ran as independents. In 1976 Andorra's first political party, the Andorran Democratic Association, was formed. In the February 1997 elections for the 28 seats in the General Council, the *Unio Lliberal* surged to 18 seats. The center-right *Agrupament Nacional Democratic*, fell from eight to six seats. *Nova Democracia* dropped from five to only two seats. A *National Democratic Initiative*, won the two remaining seats.

The right to vote is very restricted. Only the 10,000 or Andorrans whose families have had Andorran citizenship for three generations are permitted to vote. This amounts to only 15% of the population. Women citizens were granted suffrage in 1970. Over time the new constitution is bound to affect every preexisting political institution in the country.

The President of France and the Bishop of Seo de Urgel are figurehead Co-Princes of Andorra and until 1993 had full executive, legislative and judicial power. In practice, they were represented in the country by *Veguers* (their designated representatives) and *Battles* (magistrates). These feudal offices were combined with more modern elected offices.

The country had no constitution before 1993, but a "Plan of Reform," adopted in 1866. It established the groundwork for a General Council of 28 members (at least four of whom are elected from each of the six Parishes in the six valleys—Andorra, Canillo, Encamp, La Massana, Ordino, and Sant Julià). Each member is elected to a four-year term, and half the members

THE CO-PRINCES OF ANDORRA

**His Excellency
The Honorable Jacques Chirac
President of the French Republic**

**His Excellency
The Most Reverend Joan Martí Alanis
Bishop of Seo de Urgel**

Hon. Marc Forné Molné

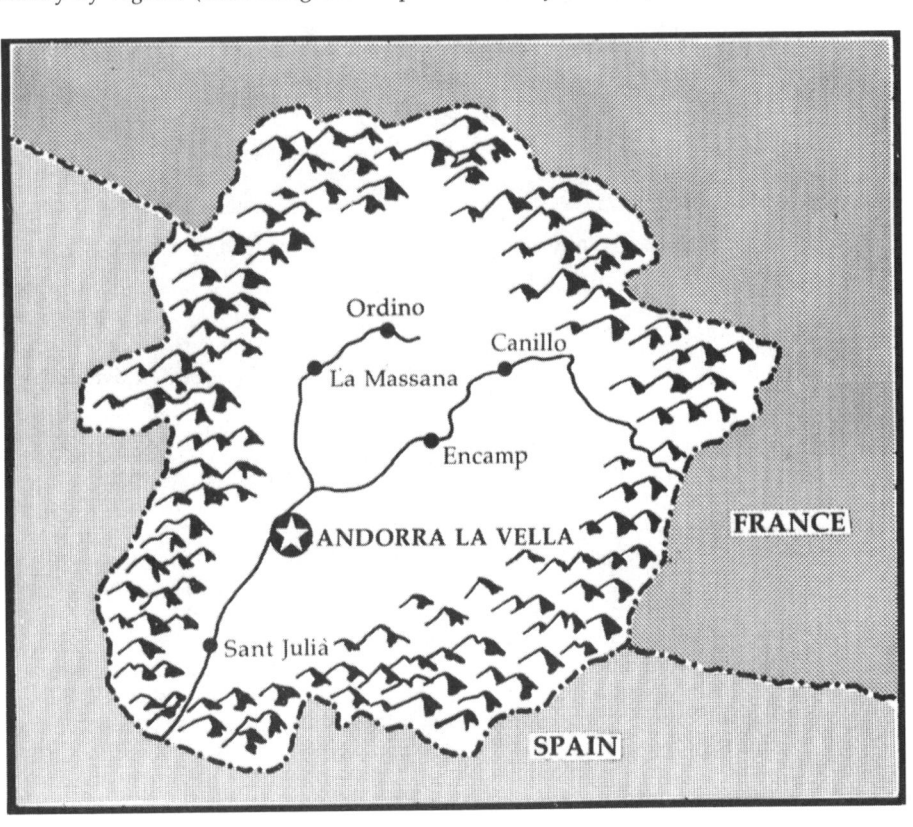

Andorra

Statue in front of the main government building

were elected every two years. Before the new constitution was implemented, the General Council had no formal legislative power, but it was the supreme administrative body. It elected for three–year terms a Sindic (manager) and Sub–Sindic to implement its decisions. There was usually tension within the General Council between the four representatives from the capital city, where two–thirds of the country's population lives, and the remaining 20 representatives from the more rural parishes. When the capital's four representatives request funds for facilities needed by the rapidly growing capital city, the remaining members are inclined to demand similar facilities for their parishes. This often created deadlocks on important issues.

The judicial system is now independent. It is based on French secular and Spanish Ecclesiastical law. That such a hybrid legal system could function in Andorra is demonstrated by the fact that the entire country maintains only six jail cells, most of which usually are empty. The constitution emboldened the judiciary in 1993 to arrest the director of state security and president of the Olympic committee in a new effort to fight corruption. Earlier, the country's main families had been powerful enough to suppress scandals through their dominance of the French and Spanish courts in Andorra.

Andorra has no defense forces, but all able–bodied men between the ages of 16 and 60 are required to arm themselves and be ready to serve without pay or uniforms in the People's Militia, which has not fought in a war for 700 years. This strange, unorganized army regards all its "soldiers" as officers. In practice, France and Spain provide for Andorra's defense, and the Barcelona police and French gendarmerie alternate year by year in assisting the 32–man Andorran police to maintain order within the country.

Andorra is a member of UNESCO, but until 1993 its diplomatic affairs were handled primarily by France, the Bishop of Seo de Urgel having no official international status. Its 1993 constitution permits Andorra to conduct its own foreign policy. It immediately joined the UN as a full member, entered the Council of Europe in 1994, and tightened its ties with the EU. The United States' relations with Andorra have traditionally been conducted through its consulate in Barcelona.

ECONOMY

Since only 4% of the country's land can be cultivated, most of its food must be imported. It owes its livelihood to tourism and to its status as a free port (duty–free marketplace) for manufactured goods from many industrialized nations. This duty–free status makes Andorra one of the most active smuggling centers of Europe, an activity which French and Spanish customs officials have difficulty controlling due to the country's remote and rugged frontier, and due also to the impossibility of checking all the thousands of automobiles which cross its borders daily. Andorra refuses to make smuggling a penal offense. Therefore, dealing in contraband, by either organized criminals or legal merchants, thrives.

This tiny country absorbs 12 million visitors each year—two–thirds of them from Spain. What awaits this throng of visitors are good bargains at gaudy shops, but also long traffic jams, tight parking, exhaust-filled air, shoulder–to–shoulder walking, and almost interminable waiting at the border. For export, it manufactures cigars and cigarettes, matches, anisette liqueur and sandals. It also produces for sale that customary product of microstates: beautiful postage stamps, although no postage whatsoever is required for mail *within* the country.

Both France and Spain want to limit Andorra's duty–free business. Many Andorrans fear that the attractiveness of a shopping trip to their country will decline in the future. Andorra's favorable trade agreements with Spain and France give it legal trade outlets to the entire EU. In

Andorra

1990, for the first time 700 years, Andorra signed an international treaty, approving a trade agreement with the EU. It makes Andorra a member of the EU customs union. It permits industrial goods to flow freely to and from the EU and obligates Andorra to apply the EU's external tariffs on such goods to third countries. Full EU membership must wait. Spain insists that Andorra introduce adequate labor and social security laws for the 20,000 Spaniards who work in Andorra, mainly in tourism, before the tiny country is considered for EU membership. Andorra's 1993 constitution permits the establishment of labor unions, hitherto banned.

It has a hydroelectric plant at Escaldes, which provides electricity for Andorra and which exports a modest amount of power to the northern part of Barcelona province and to southern France. Residents of Andorra pay no personal income taxes.

The 1993 constitution grants freedom of religion although Roman Catholicism remains the established church. Andorra's school system is a cumbersome combination of French secular schools and Spanish parochial schools, financed and staffed by France and Spain, and terminating educational possibilities within Andorra at age 14. Because there is no university, young Andorrans go to France or Spain for higher education. Only half of them return, in part because the exorbitant property prices, which have spiralled to Parisian levels, keep them away.

Andorra has one daily newspaper, *Pople Andorra* and one monthly, *Andorra Magazine*. Radio service is provided by the Spanish–owned *Radio Andorra* and the French–owned *Sud Radio*, and Andorrans can receive one Spanish and two French television stations. There are no railroad or airport facilities, but good roads tie the country to Spain and, except in the winter months, to France.

FUTURE

Andorra has undergone great social, economic, and political changes, from a traditional pastoral and farming fiefdom and economy to a sovereign mini–state thriving on commerce and tourism. This process, which has led to a quadrupling of Andorra's population in 25 years, brings both promise and problems to the future Andorra. Population density has become and will remain very high. Tourism is expected to provide prosperity for years to come, but it is uncertain whether such tourism will destroy Andorra's traditions and mountain tranquility. Western Europe's newest sovereign state, with a new constitution and its first general elections in December 1993, repeated in February 1997, Andorra can face the future with confidence.

Bibliography of Key English—Language Books

GENERAL

Barzini, Luigi. *The Europeans.* New York: Simon Schuster, 1983.

Bell, David S. *Western European Communists and the Collapse of Communism.* Oxford: Berg, 1993.

Black, Cyril E., et al. *Rebirth. A History of Europe Since World War II.* Boulder, CO: Westview, 1992.

Cole, John and Francis. *The Geography of the European Community.* New York: Routledge, 1993.

Craig, Gordon A. *Europe Since 1815.* 3rd ed. New York: Holt, Rinehart Winston, 1971.

Curtis, Michael. *Western European Government and Politics.* New York: Longman, 1997.

Dragnich, Alex N., Rasmussen, Jorgen S, and Moses, Joel C. *Major European Governments.* 9th ed. Chicago: The Dorsey Press, 1994.

Dyker, David. *The European Economy.* New York: Longman, 1992.

———. *The National Economies of Europe.* New York: Longman, 1992.

Duroselle, Jean–Baptiste. *Europe: A History of its Peoples.* New York: Viking, 1990.

Gallagher, Michael, et al. *Representative Government in Western Europe.* New York: McGraw Hill, 1992.

Giustino, David de. *A Reader in European Integration.* A selection of key documents. New York: Longman, 1996.

Hancock, M. Donald, et al. *Politics in Western Europe.* 2d ed. Chatham, NJ: Chatham House, 1998.

Jones, Robert A. *The Politics and Economics of the European Union.* Williston, VT: Edger Elgar, 1996.

Kesselman, Mark, et al. *European Politics in Transition,* 3d ed. Lexington, MA; D.C. Heath, 1997.

Kramer, Jane. *Europeans.* New York: Penguin, 1992.

Lane, Jan–Erik and Ersson, Svante O. *European Politics.* 4th ed. Beverly Hills: Sage, 1998.

Laqueur, Walter. *Europe in Our Time. A History, 1945-1992.* New York: Penguin, 1993.

Mair, Peter, ed. *The Western Europe Party System.* Oxford: Oxford University Press, 1990.

McCormick, John. *The European Union.* Boulder, CO: Westview, 1995.

Miller, Steven L., ed. *European Unification: A Conceptual Guide for Educators.* Bloomington, IN: ERIC Clearing House for Social Studies, 1995.

Pinder, John. *European Community. The Building of a Union.* Oxford: Oxford University Press, 1992.

Perry, Marvin. *An Intellectual History of Modern Europe.* Boston: Houghton Mifflin, 1993.

Pond, Elizabeth. *The Rebirth of Europe.* Washington D.C.: Brookings, 1999.

Roberts, Geoffrey and Hogwood, Patricia. *European Politics Today.* New York: St. Martin's, 1997.

Steiner, Jürg. *European Democracies.* 2d ed. NY: Longman, 1991.

Tsoukalis, Loukas. *The New European Economy.* 3d ed. New York: Oxford University Press, 1996.

Urwin, Derek W. *Western Europe since 1945. A Political History.* 5th ed. New York: Longman, 1997.

———. *The Community of Europe. A History of European Integration since 1945.* New York: Longman, 1991.

Warmenhoven, Henri J. *Western Europe.* Guilford, CT: Dushkin, annually updated.

Young, John W. *Cold War Europe. 1945-1989.* New York: Routledge, 1991.

Germany

Adenauer, Konrad. *Memoirs, 1945–1953.* Chicago, Regnery, 1966.

Ardagh, John. *Germany and the Germans: After Unification* rev. ed. New York, Penguin Books, 1991.

Ash, Timothy Garton. *In Europe's Name. Germany and the Divided Continent.* New York: Random House, 1994.

———, *The File. A Personal History.* (Stasi). New York: Random House, 1997.

Balfour, Michael. *Germany. The Tides of Power.* New York: Routledge, 1992.

Bark, Dennis L. and Gress, David R. *A History of West Germany.* Cambridge, MA: Basil Blackwell, 1989.

Bracher, Karl D. *The German Dictatorship: The Origins, Structure, and Effects of National Socialism.* New York: Praeger, 1970.

Brandt, Willy. *My Life in Politics.* New York: Penguin, 1992.

Buse, Dieter K. and Doerr, Juergen C., eds. *Encyclopedic History of Modern Germany.* 2 vols. Hamden, CT: Garland, 1997.

Cecil, Lamar. *Wilhelm II.* 2 vols. Chapel Hill: University of North Carolina, 1996.

Clay, Lucius. *Decision in Germany.* Garden City, N.Y.: Doubleday, 1950.

Craig, Gordon A. *From Bismarck to Adenauer: Aspects of German Statecraft.* New York: Harper and Row, 1965.

———. *Germany 1866–1945.* New York: Oxford University Press, 1978.

———. *The Germans.* rev. ed. New York: Penguin, 1992.

Conradt, David P. *The German Polity.* 5th ed. New York: Longman, 1993.

———, et al, eds. *Germany's New Politics.* Providence, RI: Berghahn, 1995.

Dalton, Russell J. *Politics in Germany.* 2d ed. New York: Harper Collins, 1993.

Edinger, Lewis and Brigitte Nacos. *From Bonn to Berlin.* New York: Columbia University Press, 1998.

Elias, Norbert. *The Germans.* New York: Columbia University, 1996.

Fisher, Marc. *After the Wall: Germany, the Germans, and the Burdens of History.* New York: Simon Schuster, 1995

Fulbrook, Mary. *A Concise History of Germany.* Cambridge: Cambridge University Press, 1990.

———. *The Divided Nation: A History of Germany, 1918–1990.* Oxford: Oxford University Press, 1992.

———. *Anatomy of a Dictatorship. Inside the GDR, 1949–1989.* New York: Oxford University Press, 1995.

Fest, Joachim. *Hitler.* New York: Random House, 1975.

Fest, Joachim. *Hitler.* New York: Random House, 1975.

Gedmin, Jeffrey. *The Germans. Portrait of a New Nation.* Washington D.C.: AEI Press, 1995.

Giersch, Herbert, et al. *The Fading Miracle. Four Decades of Market Economy.* Cambridge: Cambridge University Press, 1992.

Glaessner, Gert–Joachim and Wallace, Ian, eds. *The German Revolution of 1989: Causes and Consequences.* Oxford: Berg, 1992.

Griffith, William E. *The Ostpolitik of the Federal Republic of Germany.* Cambridge, MA: MIT Press, 1978.

Grosser, Dieter, ed. *German Unification: The Unexpected Challenge.* Oxford: Berg, 1992.

Hamilton, Daniel S. *Beyond Bonn. Crafting U.S. Policy Toward the Berlin Republic.* Washington, DC: Brookings, 1994.

Hamilton, Richard. *Who Voted for Hitler?* Princeton: Princeton University Press, 1982.

Hampton, Mary and Christian Soe, eds. *Between Bonn and Berlin. German Politics Adrift.* Lanham, MD: Rowman & Littlefield, 1998.

Hancock, M. Donald and Welsh, Helga, eds. *German Unification. Process and Outcomes.* Boulder, CO: Westview Press, 1992.

Hancock, M. Donald and Henry Krisch. *Germany.* Boulder, CO: Westview Press, 1999.

Holborn, Hajo. *The History of Modern Germany.* 3rd ed. Princeton: Princeton Univ. Press, 1982.

Jarausch, Konrad and Gransow, Volker, eds. *Uniting Germany. Documents and Debates.* Providence, RI: Berghahn, 1995.

Keithly, David M. *The Collapse of East German Communism. The Year the Wall Came Down, 1989.* Westport, CT: Praeger, 1992.

Koehler, John O. *Stasi. The Untold Story of East Germany's Secret Police.* Boulder, CO: Westview Press, 1998.

Lange, Thomas and Goeffrey Pugh. *The Economics of German Unification.* Williston, VT: Edger Elgar, 1998.

Bibliography

Lankowski, Carl. *Germany and the European Community.* New York: St. Martin's, 1992.

Livingston, Robert Gerald and Sanders, Volkmar. *The Future of German Democracy.* New York: Continuum, 1994.

Mann, Golo. *The History of Germany Since 1789.* New York: Praeger, 1968.

Marsh, David. *The Germans: The Pivotal Nation. A People at the Crossroads.* New York: St. Martin's, 1990.

Merkl, Peter H. *The Origin of the West German Republic.* New York: Oxford University Press, 1965.

Opp, Karl Dieter, et al. *Origins of Spontaneous Revolution. East Germany 1989.* Ann Arbor: University of Michigan Press, 1995.

Padgett, Stephen, ed. *Adenauer to Kohl. The Development of the German Chancellorship.* Georgetown University Press, 1994.

Pommerin, Reiner. *The American Impact on Postwar Germany.* Providence, RI: Berghahn, 1995.

Pond, Elizabeth. *Beyond the Wall. Germany's Road to Unification.* Washington, DC: Brookings, 1993.

Pulzer, Peter. *German Politics, 1945–1995.* New York: Oxford University Press, 1995.

Rippley, LaVern. *Of German Ways.* New York: Barnes and Noble, 1970.

Schoenbaum, David. *Hitler's Social Revolution: Class and Status in Nazi Germany 1933-1939.* Garden City, N.Y.: Anchor Books, 1967.

Schweitzer, C.C., et al, eds. *Politics and Government in Germany, 1944-1994. Basic Documents.* 2d rev. ed. Providence, RI: Berghahn, 1995.

Smith, Gordon, et al, eds. *Developments in German Politics.* Durham, NC: Duke University Press, 1992.

Szabo, Stephen F. *The Diplomacy of German Unification.* New York: St. Martin's, 1992.

Thompson, Wayne C. *In the Eye of the Storm. Kurt Riezler and the Crises of Modern Germany.* Iowa City: University of Iowa Press, 1980.

———. *The Political Odyssey of Herbert Wehner.* Boulder, CO: Westview Press, 1993.

——— and Thompson, Susan L. and Juliet S. *Historical Dictionary of Germany.* (Contains many entries and lengthy chronology and bibliography). Metuchen, NJ: Scarecrow Press, 1994.

Turner, Henry A. *Germany from Partition to Reunification.* New Haven, CT: Yale University Press, 1992.

Turner, Lowell. *Fighting for Partnership. Labor and Politics in Unified Germany.* Ithaca, NY: Cornell University Press, 1998.

Uris, Leon. *Armaggedon.* London: Corgi, 1963.

Wolf, Markus. *Man without a Face. The Autobiography of Communism's Greatest Spymaster.* New York: Times Books Random House, 1997.

Austria

Bader, William B. *Austria Between East and West 1945–1955.* Stanford: Stanford University Press, 1966.

Bischof, Günter, et al, eds. *The Kreisky Era in Austria.* New Brunswick, NJ: Transaction, 1993.

Bluhm, William T. *Building an Austrian Nation. The Political Integration of a Western State.* New Haven: Yale University Press, 1973.

Fitzmaurice, John. *Austrian Politics and Society Today.* New York: St. Martin's, 1991.

Gruber, Helmut. *Red Vienna. Experiment in Working–Class Culture, 1919–1934.* Oxford: Oxford University Press, 1991.

Herzstein, Robert E. *Waldheim. The Missing Years.* New York: Arbor House/W. Morrow, 1988.

Johnson, Lonnie. *Introducing Austria. A Short History.* Riverside, CA: Ariadne, 1992.

Luther, Richard, and Muller, Wolfgang C., eds. *Politics in Austria. Still a Case of Consociationalism?* Portland, OR: Frank Cass, 1992.

Luther, Kurt Richard. *Austria 1945–1995.* Brookfield, VT: Ashgate, 1998.

Mitten, Richard. *The Politics of Antisemitic Prejudice. The Waldheim Phenomenon in Austria.* Boulder, CO: Westview, 1992.

Pelinka, Anton and Plasser, Fritz, eds. *The Austrian Party System.* Boulder, CO: Westview, 1989.

Pelinka, Anton. *Austria: Out of the Shadow of the Past.* Boulder, CO: Westview, 1999.

Schorske, Carl F. *Fin–De Siècle Vienna. Politics and Culture.* New York: Vintage Books, 1981.

Segar, Kenneth and Warren, John, eds. *Austria in the Thirties: Culture and Politics.* Riverside, CA: Ariadne, 1992.

Spaulding, E. Wilder. *The Quiet Invaders: The Story of the Austrian Impact Upon America.* Vienna, 1968.

Sully, Melanie A. *The Haider Phenomenon.* New York: Columbia University Press, 1997.

Switzerland

Bonjour, E., et al. *A Short History of Switzerland.* Oxford: Clarendon, 1972.

Bradfield, B. *The Making of Switzerland: From Ice Age to Common Market.* Zurich: Schweizer Spiegel Verlag, 1964.

Craig, Gordon A. *The Triumph of Liberalism: Zurich in the Golden Age, 1830–1869.* New York: Collier, 1990.

Hilowitz, Janet Eve. *Switzerland in Perspective.* Westport, CT: Greenwood, 1990.

Kieser, Rolf and Spillman, Kurt R., eds. *The New Switzerland. Problems and Policies.* Palo Alto, CA: SPROSS, 1996.

Linder, Wolf. *Swiss Democracy.* New York: St. Martin's, 1994.

Luck, Murray J. *History of Switzerland: The First Hundred Thousand Years From Before the Beginning to the Days of the Present.* Palo Alto, CA: SPROSS, 1985.

McPhee, John. *La Place de la Concorde Suisse.* New York: Farrar/Straus/Giroux, 1983.

Milivojevic, Marko, and Mauerer, Pierre. *Swiss Neutrality and Security. Armed Forces, National Defence and Foreign Policy.* New York: St. Martin's, 1991.

Remak, Joachim. *A Very Civil War. The Swiss Sonderbund War of 1847.* Boulder, CO: Westview, 1993.

Sorell, Walter. *The Swiss.* New York: Bobbs–Merrill, 1972.

Steinberg, J. *Why Switzerland.* 2d ed. Cambridge; Cambridge University Press, 1996.

Steiner, Jürg. *Amicable Agreement Versus Majority Rule: Conflict Resolution in Switzerland.* Chapel Hill: University of North Carolina Press, 1974.

———. *Conscience in Politics.* Levittown, PA: Garland, 1996.

Liechtenstein

Kranz, Walter, ed. *The Principality of Liechtenstein: A Documentary Handbook.* Schaan: Lingg, 1973.

Raton, Pierre. *Liechtenstein: History and Institutions of the Principality.* Vaduz: Liechtenstein Verlag, 1970.

Schlapp, Manfred. *This is Liechtenstein.* Stuttgart: Seewald, n.d.

France

Adams, William James. *Restructuring the French Economy: Government and the Rise of Market Competition Since World War II.* Washington, D.C.: Brookings, 1989.

Ardagh, John. *France Today.* rev. ed. New York: Penguin, 1991.

Bell, David S. *The French Socialist Party.* Oxford: Oxford University Press, 1988.

——— and Criddle, Byron. *The French Communist Party in the Fifth Republic.* Oxford: Oxford University, 1994.

Bernstein, Richard. *Fragile Glory. A Portrait of France and the French.* New York: Alfred A. Knopf, 1990.

Braudel, Fernand. *The Identity of France: History and Environment.* Harper and Collins, 1989.

Bridgford, Jeff. *The Politics of French Trade Unionism.* New York: St. Martin's, 1992.

Brogan, D. W. *France Under the Republic (1870–1939).* New York: Harper and Row, 1940.

Cole, Alistair. *François Mitterrand. A Study in Political Leadership.* New York: Routledge, 1994.

Bibliography

Gross, Maire and Sheila Perry. *Population and Social Policy in France.* Herndon, VA: Cassell, 1997.

De Gaulle, Charles. *The War Memoirs of Charles de Gaulle.* 3 vols. New York: Simon Schuster, 1960.

———. *Memoirs of Hope and Endeavor.* New York: Simon Schuster, 1970.

Doyle, William. *The Oxford History of the French Revolution.* Oxford: Oxford University Press, 1990.

Ehrmann, Henry and Schain, Martin A. *Politics in France.* 5th ed. New York: Harper Collins, 1992.

Friend, Julius W. *The Long Presidency: France in the Mitterrand Years, 1981–1995.* Boulder, CO: Westview, 1999.

Gaffney, John. *The French Left and the Fifth Republic: The Discourses of Communism and Socialism in Contemporary France.* New York: St. Martin's, 1989.

Gildea, Robert. *France Since 1945.* Oxford: Oxford University Press, 1996.

Gordon, Philip H. *A Certain Idea of France. French Security Policy and the Gaullist Legacy.* Princeton: Princeton University Press, 1993.

Hazareesingh, Sudhir. *Political Traditions in Modern France.* Oxford: Oxford University, 1994.

Hirschfeld, Gerhard. *Collaboration in France. Politics and Culture during the Nazi Occupation, 1940–1944.* Oxford: Berg, 1989.

Hoffmann, Stanley and Ross, George, eds. *Continuity and Change in Mitterrand's France.* New York: Oxford University Press, 1987.

Hollifield, James F. and Ross, George, eds. *Searching for the New France.* New York: Routledge, 1992.

Larkin, Maurice. *France Since the Popular Front. Government and People, 1936-1986.* Oxford: Oxford University Press, 1988.

Lewis–Beck, ed. *How France Votes.* Chatham, NJ: Chatham House, 1999.

May, Catherine. *The Black and the Red.* (Biography of Mitterrand). NY: Harcourt Brace Jovanovich, 1987.

McMillan, James F. *Twentieth Century France. Politics and Society in France, 1898–1991.* New York: Routledge, 1992.

Morris, Peter. *French Politics Today.* New York: St. Martin's, 1994.

Northcutt, Wayne. *Mitterrand. A Political Biography.* New York: Holmes and Meier, 1992.

Perry, Sheila. *Voices of France. Social, Political and Cultural Identity.* Herndon, VA: Cassell, 1997.

Safran, William. *The French Polity.* 3d ed. New York: Longman, 1991.

Schoenbrun, David. *Soldiers of the Night: The Story of the French Resistance.* New York: New American Library, 1981.

Stevens, Anne. *The Government and Politics of France.* New York: St. Martin's, 1992.

Tilly, Charles. *The Contentious French: Four Centuries of Popular Struggle.* Cambridge: Harvard University Press, 1986.

Tocqueville, Alexis de. *The Old Regime and the French Revolution.* New York: Doubleday Anchor, 1955.

Wahl, Nicholas, ed. *DeGaulle and the United States, 1930–1970.* Oxford: Berg, 1992.

Wright, Vincent. *The Government and Politics of France.* 4th ed. New York: Routledge, 1994.

Zeldin, Theodore. *The French.* New York: Pantheon Books, 1982.

The Benelux Countries

General

Eych, F. Gunther. *The Benelux Countries: An Historical Survey.* Princeton: Van Nostrand, 1959.

Kossman, E. H. *The Low Countries, 1780–1940.* Oxford: Oxford Univ. Press, 1978.

Stein, George J. *Benelux Security Cooperation.* Boulder, CO: Westview, 1990.

Weil, Gordon L. *The Benelux Nations: The Politics of Small–Country Democracies.* New York: Holt, Rinehart Winston, 1970.

The Netherlands

Anderweg, Rudi B. and Galen A. Irwin. *Dutch Politics and Government.* New York: St. Martin's, 1993.

Bakvis, Herman. *Catholic Power in the Netherlands.* Toronto: McGill–Queen's Univ. Press, 1981.

Cox, Robert H. *The Development of the Dutch Welfare State.* Pittsburgh: University of Pittsburgh Press, 1993.

Daalder, Hans and Irwin, Galen A. *Politics in the Netherlands. How much change?* Portland, OR: Frank Cass, 1989.

Gladdish, Ken. *Governing from the Center. Politics and Policy–Making in the Netherlands.* DeKalb, IL: Northern Illinois University Press, 1992.

Israel, Jonathan I. *Dutch Primacy in World Trade, 1585–1740.* Oxford: Oxford University Press, 1990.

Lijphart, Arend. *The Politics of Accommodation: Pluralism and Democracy in the Netherlands.* Berkeley: University of California Press, 1968.

Wolters, Menno and Coffey, Peter. *The Netherlands and EC Membership Evaluated.* New York: St. Martin's, 1990.

Belgium

Boudart, Marina, et al. *Modern Belgium.* Palo Alto, CA: SPOSS, 1990.

Cowie, Donald. *Belgium: The Land and the People.* Cranbury, NJ: A. S. Barnes, 1977.

Hooghe, Liesbet. *A Leap in the Dark. Nationalist Conflict and Federal Reform in Belgium.* Ithaca, NY: Cornell University Press, 1993.

Fitzmaurice, J. *Politics of Belgium. Crisis and Compromise in a Plural Society.* New York: St. Martin's Press, 1983.

Lijphart, Arend, ed. *Conflict and Coexistence in Belgium.* Berkeley: University of California Press, 1980.

Meerhaeghe, M.A.G. van. *Belgium and EC Membership Evaluated.* New York: St. Martin's, 1992.

Meeus, Adrien de. *History of the Belgians.* New York: Praeger, 1962.

Luxembourg

Barteau, Harry C. *Historical Dictionary of Luxembourg.* Metuchen, NJ: Scarecrow Press, 1996.

Majerus, Pierre. *The Institutions of the Grand Duchy of Luxembourg.* Luxembourg: Ministry of State Press and Information Service, 1976.

Margue, Paul. *A Short History of Luxembourg.* Luxembourg: Ministry of State Press and Information Service, 1976.

Great Britain

Adolino, Jessica R. *Ethnic Minorities, Electoral Politics, and Political Integration in Britain.* Herndon, VA: Cassell, 1998.

Baylis, John. *Anglo–American Relations Since the Second World War.* New York: St. Martin's, 1997.

Blair, Tony. *New Britain.* Boulder, CO: Westview, 1997.

Bartlett, C.J. *The Special Relationship. A Political History of Anglo–American Relations since 1945.* New York: Longman, 1992.

Beer, Samuel H. *Britain Against Itself.* New York: Norton, 1982.

———. *Modern British Politics. Parties and Pressure Groups in the Collectivist Age.* rev. ed. New York: Norton, 1982.

Birch, Anthony H. *The British System of Government.* 8th ed. New York: Routledge, 1990.

Briggs, Asa. *A Social History of England.* London: Weidenfeld Nicolson, 1983.

Budge, Ian, and McKay, David, et al. *The Changing British Political System. Into the 1990s.* New York: Longman, 1988.

Butler, David and Sloman, Anne, eds. *British Political Facts, 1900–1979.* 5th ed. New York: St. Martin's Press, 1980.

Cashmore, E. Ellis. *United Kingdom? Class, Race, and Gender since the War.* Winchester: Unwin Hyman, 1989.

Childs, David. *Britain since 1945.* 3d ed. New York: Routledge, 1992.

Clarke Michael. *British External Policymaking in the 1990s.* Washington, D.C.: Brookings, 1992.

Colley, Linda. *Britons. Forging the Nation, 1707–1837.* New Haven, CT: Yale University Press, 1992.

Bibliography

Croft, Stuart. *British Security Policy. The Thatcher Years and the End of the Cold War.* New York: Routledge, 1992.

Crossman, R. H. S. *Introduction to Bagehot's English Constitution.* London: Fontana, 1963.

Davis, Charlotte. *Welsh Nationalism in the Twentieth Century.* Westport, CT: Praeger, 1989.

Edgell, Stephen and Duke, Vic. *A Measure of Thatcherism. A Sociology of Britain in the 1980s.* New York: Routledge, 1991.

Freedman, Lawrence. *Britain and the Falklands War.* Cambridge, MA: Basil Blackwell, 1988.

Garner, Robert and Richard Kelly. *British Political Parties Today.* 2d ed. Manchester: Manchester University Press, 1998.

Hardie, Frank. *The Political Influence of the British Monarchy, 1868–1952.* London: Batsford, 1970.

Harvie, Christopher. *Scotland and Nationalism. Scottish Society and Politics 1707–1994.* New York: Routledge, 1994.

Havighurst, Alfred F. *Britain in Transition: the Twentieth Century.* Chicago: University of Chicago Press, 1979.

Irwin, John. *Modern Britain. An Introduction.* 3d ed. New York: Routledge, 1994.

James, Simon. *British Cabinet Government.* New York: Routledge, 1992.

Jones, R. Brinley, ed. *The Anatomy of Wales.* Peterson–super–Hy: Gwerin, 1972.

Kavanagh, Dennis A. *British Politics.* Oxford: 3d ed. Oxford University Press, 1996.

———. *Thatcherism and British Politics. The End of Consensus?* 2d ed. Oxford: Oxford University Press, 1990.

King, Anthony, et al. *Britain at the Polls, 1992.* Chatham, NJ: Chatham House, 1992.

———, et al. *New Labour Triumphs: Britain at the Polls.* Chatham, NJ: Chatham House, 1998.

Kirk, Russell. *America's British Culture.* New Brunswick, NJ: Transaction, 1992.

Krieger, Joel. *Reagan, Thatcher, and the Politics of Decline.* New York: Oxford University Press, 1986.

Marwick, Arthur. *Culture in Britain Since 1945.* Cambridge, MA: Basil Blackwell, 1991.

Morgan, Kenneth O. *Labour People.* Oxford: Oxford University Press, 1987.

Norton, Philip. *The British Polity.* 3d ed. New York: Longman, 1994.

Paterson, Alan. *The Law Lords.* London: Macmillan, 1982.

Pearce, Malcolm and Stewart, Geoff. *British Political History 1867–1990.* New York: Routledge, 1992.

Pilkington, Colin. *Representative Democracy in Britain Today.* Manchester: Manchester University Press, 1997.

Rasmussen, Jorgen S. *British Politics.* Belmont, CA: Wadsworth, 1993.

Reitan, Earl A. *Tory Radicalism. Margaret Thatcher, John Major, and the Transformation of Modern Britain.* Lanham, MD: Rowman & Littlefield, 1997.

Riddell, Peter. *The Thatcher Decade. How Britain has Changed During the 1980s.* Cambridge, MA: Basil Blackwell, 1989.

Robbins, Keith. *Nineteenth–Century Britain. England, Scotland and Wales: The Making of a Nation.* Oxford: Oxford University Press, 1988.

Rose, Richard. *Politics in England.* 5th ed. New York: Harper Collins, 1989.

Särlvik, Bo and Crewe, Ivor. *Decade of Dealignment: The Conservative Victory of 1979 and Electoral Trends in the 1970s.* Cambridge: Cambridge University Press, 1983.

Seldon, Anthony, ed. *Conservative Century. The Conservative Party Since 1900.* Oxford: Oxford University, 1994.

Shaw, Eric. *The Labour Party Since 1979. Crisis and Transformation.* New York: Routledge, 1994.

Shell, Donald and Beamish, David, eds. *The House of Lords at Work.* Oxford: Oxford University, 1993.

Sked, Alan and Chris Cook. *Post-War Britain: A Political History.* 2d ed. New York: Penquin, 1990.

Skidelsky, Robert, ed. *Thatcherism.* Cambridge, MA: Basil Blackwell, 1990.

Smith, Martin J. and Spear, Joanna. *The Changing Labour Party.* New York: Routledge, 1992.

Thatcher, Margaret. *The Path to Power* and *Downing Street Years.* 2 vols. New York: HarperCollins, 1993, 1995.

Thompson, Juliet S. and Wayne C. *Margaret Thatcher. Prime Minister Indomitable.* Boulder, CO: Westview, 1994.

Trevelyan, G. M. *History of England.* London: Longmans, 1963.

White, Brian. *Britain, Detente and Chaning East–West Relations.* New York: Routledge, 1992.

Williams, Glyn and Ramsden, John. *Ruling Britannia. A Political History of Britain 1688–1988.* New York: Longman, 1990.

Young, Hugo. *The Iron Lady. A Biography of Margaret Thatcher.* New York: Farrar Straus and Giroux, 1989.

Northern Ireland

Arthur, Paul *Government and Politics of Northern Ireland.* Second Edition. New York: Longman, 1984.

——— and Jeffery, Keith. *Northern Ireland Since 1968.* Cambridge, MA: Basil Blackwell, 1988.

Aughey, A. and Morrow, D. *Northern Ireland Politics.* New York: Longman, 1997.

Barton, Brian and Patrick J. Roche. *The Northern Ireland Question.* Brookfield, VT: Ashgate, 1999.

Bew, Paul, et al. *The Political Future of Northern Ireland.* Vancouver: University of British Columbia Press, 1993.

Boyle, Keven and Tom Hadden. *Northern Ireland: The Choice.* New York: Praeger, 1998.

Bruce, Steve. *God Save Ulster! The Religion and Politics of Paisleyism.* Oxford: Oxford University Press, 1989.

———. *The Edge of the Union. The Ulster Loyalist Political Vision.* Oxford: Oxford University, 1994.

Gaffikin, Frank and Morrissey, Mike. *Northern Ireland. The Thatcher Years.* Atlantic Highlands, NJ: Humanities Press, 1990.

Hull, R. H. *Irish Triangle.* Princeton: Princeton University Press, n.d.

Irvine, Maurice. *Northern Ireland. Faith and Faction.* New York: Routledge, 1991.

McGarry, John, ed. *The Future of Northern Ireland.* Oxford: Oxford University Press, 1991.

Mitchell, Paul and Rick Wilford, eds. *Politics in Northern Ireland.* Boulder, CO: Westview, 1998.

Ruane, Joseph and Todd, Jennifer. *The Dynamics of Conflict in Northern Ireland.* New York: Cambridge University Press, 1996.

Whyte, John and Fitzgerald, Garret. *Interpreting Northern Ireland.* Oxford: Oxford University Press, 1991.

Wichert, Sabine. *Northern Ireland since 1945.* New York: Longman, 1991.

Wilson, Tom. *Ulster. Conflict and Consent.* Cambridge, MA: Basil Blackwell, 1989.

Republic of Ireland

Ardagh, John. *Ireland and the Irish. Portrait of a Changing Society.* New York: Penguin, 1998.

Boyce, D. George. *Nationalism in Ireland.* 2d ed. New York: Routledge, 1991.

Busteed, M.A. *Voting Behavior in the Republic of Ireland.* Oxford: Oxford University Press, 1991.

Carter, R.W. and Parker, A.J. *Ireland. Contemporary Perspectives on a Land and its People.* New York: Routledge, 1990.

Chubb, Basil. *The Government and Politics of Ireland.* 3d ed. New York: Longman, 1992.

Collins, Neil and McCann, Frank. *Irish Politics Today.* 3d. ed. New York: St. Martin's, 1997.

Curtis, Edmund. *A History of Ireland.* London: Methuen, 1961.

Fitzgerald, Garret. *All in a Life.* London: Macmillan, 1991.

Fulton, John. *The Tragedy of Belief. Division, Politics, and Religion in Ireland.* Oxford: Oxford University Press, 1991.

Keatinge, Patrick. *Ireland and EC Membership Evaluated.* New York: St. Martin's, 1992.

Bibliography

Macardle, Dorothy. *The Irish Republic.* Dublin: Irish Press, 1951.

McCaffrey, Lawrence J. *Ireland from Colony to Nation–State.* Englewood Cliffs, NJ: Prentice–Hall, 1977.

Munck, Ronnie. *The Irish Economy.* Boulder, CO: Westview Press, 1993.

Townshend, Charles. *Political Violence in Ireland.* Oxford: Oxford University Press, 1985.

Uris, Leon. *Trinity.* New York: Doubleday, 1975.

Scandinavia

Archer, Claire, and Maxwell, Stephen, eds. *The Nordic Model.* Vermont: Gower, 1980.

Arter, David. *Scandinavian Politics Today.* New York: St. Martin's, 1999.

Connery, Donald S. *The Scandinavians.* New York: Simon Schuster, 1966.

Derry, T. K. *History of Scandinavia: Norway, Sweden, Denmark, Finland and Iceland.* Minneapolis: Univ. of Minnesota Press, 1980.

Einhorn, Eric S. and Logue, John. *Modern Welfare States. Politics and Policies in Social Democratic Scandinavia.* Westport, CT: Greenwood Press, 1990.

Elder, Neil, et al., eds. *The Consensual Democracies: The Government and Politics of the Scandinavian States.* New York: Martin Robertson, 1982.

Erikson, Robert, et al, eds. *The Scandinavian Model. Welfare States and Welfare Research.* New York: M.E. Sharpe, 1987.

Ingelbritsen, Christine. *The Nordic States and European Unity.* Ithaca, NY: Cornell University Press, 1998.

Oberg, Jan, ed. *Nordic Security in the 1990s.* New York: St. Martin's, 1992.

Scott, Franklin D. *Sweden: The Nation's History.* Minneapolis: Univ. of Minnesota Press, 1977.

Sundellas, Bengt, ed. *Foreign Policies of Northern Europe.* Peoria, IL: Bradley University Publishing, 1982.

Turner, Barry, and Nordquist, Gunilla. *The Other European Community: Integration and Cooperation in Nordic Europe.* New York: Martin Robertson, 1982.

Wendt, Franz. *Cooperation in the Nordic Countries: Achievements and Obstacles.* Atlantic Highlands, NJ: Humanities, 1981.

Sweden

Esping–Andersen, Gösta. *Politics Against Markets: The Social Democratic Road to Power.* Princeton: Princeton University Press, 1985.

Hadenius, Stig. *Swedish Politics During the 20th Century.* Stockholm: Swedish Institute, 1985.

Heclo, Hugh, and Madsen, Henrik. *Policy and Politics in Sweden. Principled Pragmatism.* Philadelphia: Temple University Press, 1987.

Koblick, Steven, ed. *Sweden's Development from Poverty to Affluence, 1750–1970.* Minneapolis: Univ. of Minnesota Press, 1975.

Lorenzen, Lilly. *Of Swedish Ways.* New York: Barnes and Noble, 1978.

Metcalf, Michael. *The Riksdag: A History of the Swedish Parliament.* New York: St. Martin's, 1988.

Misgeld, Klaus, et al, eds. *Creating Social Democracy. A Century of the Social Democratic Labor Party in Sweden.* University Park: Penn State Press, 1994.

Miles, Lee. *Sweden and European Integration.* Brookfield, VT: Ashgate, 1997.

Milner, Henry. *Sweden. Social Democracy in Practice.* Oxford: Oxford University Press, 1989.

Oakley, Stewart. *The Story of Sweden.* London: Faber Faber, 1976.

Persson, Inga, ed. *Generating Equality in the Welfare State. The Swedish Experience.* Oxford: Oxford University Press, 1991.

Ruin, Olof. *Tage Erlander. Serving the Welfare State, 1946–1969.* Pittsburgh: University of Pittsburgh Press, 1990.

Samuelsson, Kurt. *From Great Power to Welfare State: 300 Years of Swedish Social Development.* London: George Allen and Unwin, 1968.

Scott, Franklin D. *Sweden: The Nation's History.* Minneapolis: University of Minnesota Press, 1977.

Sundelius, Bengt, ed. *The Committed Neutral: Sweden's Foreign Policy.* Boulder, CO: Westview Press, 1989.

Tilton, Tim. *The Political Theory of Swedish Social Democracy. Through the Welfare State to Socialism.* Oxford: Oxford University Press, 1990.

Norway

Archer, Clive and Ingrid Sogner. *Norway, European Integration, and Atlantic Security.* Thousand Oaks, CA: Sage, 1998.

Derry, T. K. *A History of Modern Norway: 1814–1972.* New York: Oxford University Press, 1973.

Hoidal, Oddvar K. *Quisling. A Study in Treason.* Oxford: Oxford University Press, 1989.

Holst, Johan Jorgen. *Norwegian Foreign Policy in the 1980's.* Oxford: Oxford University Press, 1988.

Jonassen, Christen J. *Value Systems and Personality in a Western Civilization: Norwegians in Europe and America.* Columbus: Ohio State University Press, 1983.

Lind, L., and Mackay, G. A. *Norwegian Oil Policies.* Toronto: McGill–Queen's Univ. Press, 1980.

Lovoll, Odd S. *Norwegian—American Studies.* Northfield, MN: St. Olaf College, 1989.

Popperwell, Ronald G. *Norway.* New York: Praeger, 1973.

Ramsøy, Natalie R., ed. *Norwegian Society.* Oslo/N.Y.: Universitatsvorlaget, 1977.

Selbyg, Arne. *Norway Today.* New York: Oxford University Press, 1986.

Skard, Sigmund. *The United States in Norwegian History.* Westport, CT: Greenwood Press, 1976.

Strom, Kaare and Svasand, Lars, eds. *Challenges to Political Parties: the Case of Norway.* Ann Arbor: University of Michigan, 1997.

Su-Dale, Elizabeth. *Culture Shock! Norway. A Guide to Customs and Etiquette.* Minneapolis: Scandisc, 1995.

Denmark

Anderson, Robert T. *Denmark: Success of a Developing Nation.* Cambridge, MA: Schenkman, 1978.

Arenson, Theo. *The Family of Kings.* London: Castles, 1976.

Einhorn, Eric, and Logue, John. *Welfare States in Hard Times. Problems, Policy, and Politics in Denmark and Sweden.* Kent, OH: Kent Popular Press, 1982.

Fitzmaurice, John. *Politics in Denmark.* New York: St. Martin's Press, 1981.

Holbraad, Carsten. *Danish Neutrality. A Study in the Foreign Policy of a Small State.* Oxford: Oxford University Press, 1991.

Johansen, Hans Christian. *The Danish Economy in the Twentieth Century.* New York: St. Martin's Press, 1987.

Logue, John. *Socialism and Abundance. Radical Socialism in the Danish Welfare State.* Minneapolis: Univ. of Minnesota Press, 1982.

Lyck, Lise, ed. *Denmark and EC Membership Evaluated.* New York: St. Martin's, 1992.

Miller, Kenneth E. *Denmark. A Troubled Welfare State.* Boulder, CO: Westview Press, 1991.

Oakley, Stewart. *A Short History of Denmark.* New York: Praeger, 1972.

Petrow, Richard. *Better Years: The Invasion and Occupation of Denmark and Norway, April 1940–May 1945.* New York: Morrow, 1975.

———. *The Story of Denmark.* New York: Praeger, 1972.

Finland

Arter, David. *Politics and Policy–Making in Finland.* New York: St. Martin's, 1987.

Austin, Daniel F. C. *Finland as a Gateway to Russia.* Brookfield, VT: Ashgate, 1996.

Engman, Max and Kirby, David, eds. *Finland. People, Nation, State.* Bloomington: Indiana University Press, 1989.

Jakobson, Max. *Finland in the New Europe.* Westport, CT: Praeger, 1998.

Jutikkala, Eino, and Kauko, Pirinen. *A History of Finland.* New York: Praeger, 1974.

Bibliography

Koivisto, Mauno. *Landmarks. Finland in the World.* Helsinki: Kirjayhtymä, 1985.

Maude, George. *The Finnish Dilemma.* London: Oxford University Press, 1976.

Nickels, Silvie, ed. *Finland: An Introduction.* London: George Allen Unwin, 1973.

Paasi, Anssi. *Territories, Boundaries and Consciousness: the Changing Geographies of the Finnish-Russian Border.* New York: Wiley, 1997.

Pentila, Risto E.J. *Finland's Search for Security Through Defence, 1944–89.* New York: St. Martin's, 1990.

Rinehart, Robert, ed. *Finland and the United States.* Washington, DC: Institute for the Study of Diplomacy, 1993.

Tiilikainen, Teija H. *Europe and Finland.* Brookfield, VT: Ashgate, 1998.

Wuorinen, John H. *A History of Finland.* New York: Columbia University Press, 1965.

Iceland

Durrenburger, E. Paul and Pálsson, Gísli. *The Anthropology of Iceland.* Iowa City: University of Iowa Press, 1989.

Gislason, Gylfi. *The Problem of Being an Icelander. Past, Present and Future.* Reykjavik: Almenna Bokofelagio, 1973.

Laxness, Halldor. *Independent People. An Epic.* New York: Vintage, 1996.

Tomasson, Richard F. *Iceland. The First New Society.* Minneapolis: University of Minnesota, 1980.

Mediterranean Europe

General

Aliboni, Roberto, ed. *Southern European Security in the 1990s.* New York: St. Martin's, 1992.

Chilcote, Ronald H., et al. *Transitions from Dictatorship to Democracy: Comparative Studies of Spain, Portugal and Greece.* Bristol, PA: Crane Russak, 1990.

Kurth, James, and Petras, James. *Mediterranean Paradoxes. The Politics and Social Structure of Southern Europe.* Oxford: Berg, 1992.

Liebert, Ulrike and Cotta, Maurizio, eds. *Parliament and Democratic Consolidation in Southern Europe. Italy, Spain, Portugal, Greece and Turkey in Comparison.* New York: Columbia University Press, 1990.

Italy

Barkan, Joanne. *Visions of Emancipation: The Italian Workers' Movement Since 1945.* New York: Praeger, 1984.

Barzini, Luigi. *The Italians.* New York: Atheneum, 1977.

Bull, Martin and Martin Rhodes, eds. *Crisis and Transition in Italian Politics.* Portland, OR: Frank Cass, 1997.

Burnett, Stanton H. and Luca Mantovani. *The Italian Guillotine: Operation Clean Hands and the Overthrow of Italy's First Republic.* Washington D.C.: CSIS, 1998

Catanzaro, Raimondo, ed. *The Red Brigades and Left–Wing Terrorism in Italy.* New York: St. Martin's, 1991.

Caesar, Michael, and Hainsworth, Peter, eds. *Writers and Society in Contemporary Italy.* 2d rev. ed. Oxford: Berg, 1993.

Chubb, Judith. *Patronage, Power and Poverty in Southern Italy: A Tale of Two Cities.* Cambridge: Cambridge University Press, 1982.

D'Alimonte, Roberto and David Nelken, eds. *Italian Politics. The Center–Left in Power.* Boulder, CO: Westview, 1997.

DiScala, Spencer M. *Italy. From Revolution to Republic. 1700 to the Present.* Boulder, CO: Westview, 1998.

Duggan, Christopher and Wagstaff, Christopher, eds. *Italy in the Cold War. Politics, Culture and Society 1948–1958.* Oxford: Berg, 1993.

Farneti, Paolo. *The Italian Party System.* London: Frances Pinter, 1985.

Francioni, Francesco, ed. *Italy and EC Membership Evaluated.* New York: St. Martin's, 1992.

Furlong, Paul. *Modern Italy. Representation and Reform.* New York: Routledge, 1994.

Giammanco, Rosanna Mulazzi. *The Catholic–Communist Dialogue in Italy: 1944 to the Present.* Westport, CT: Praeger, 1989.

Gilbert, Mark. *The Italian Revolution. The End of Politics, Italian Style?* Boulder, CO: Westview, 1995.

Ginsborg, Paul. *A History of Contemporary Italy. Society and Politics 1943–1988.* New York: Penguin, 1991.

Hearder, Harry. *Italy: A Short History.* Cambridge: Cambridge University Press, 1990.

Hibbert, Christopher. *Rome: The Biography of a City.* New York: Viking, n.d.

Hine, David. *Governing Italy. The Politics of Bargained Pluralism.* Oxford: Oxford University Press, 1993.

Kertzer, David I. *Comrades and Christians. Religion and Political Struggle in Communist Italy.* Prospect Heights, IL: Waveland, 1992.

Kogan, Norman H. *Political History of Postwar Italy: From the Old to the New Center Left.* New York: Praeger, 1981.

Levy, Carl, ed. *Italian Regionalism. History, Identity and Politics.* New York: Berg, 1996.

Locke, Richard M. *Remaking the Italian Economy.* Ithaca, NY: Cornell University Press, 1997.

Leonardi, Robert and Wertman, Douglas A. *Italian Christian Democracy.* New York: St. Martin's, 1989.

McCarthy, Patrick. *The Crisis of the Italian State.* New York: St. Martin's, 1997.

Moss, David. *The Politics of Left–Wing Violence in Italy, 1969–85.* New York: St. Martin's, 1990.

Mountjoy, Alan B. *The Mezzogiorno.* New York: Oxford University Press, 1973.

Partridge, Hillary. *Italian Politics Today.* New York: St. Martin's, 1998.

Pasquino, Gianfranco and McCarthy, Patrick. *Elections in a Changing Italy.* Boulder, CO: Westview Press, 1993.

Pinter Publishers, *Italian Politics, A Review.* New York: Columbia University Press, annual updated editions.

Pridham, Geoffrey. *Political Parties and Coalitional Behavior in Italy.* New York: Routledge, 1988.

Procacci, Giuliano. *History of the Italian People.* Hammondsworth, UK: Penguin Books, 1973.

Putnam, Robert D. *Making Democracy Work. Civic Traditions in Modern Italy.* Princeton: Princeton University Press, 1993.

Richards, Charles. *The New Italians.* New York: Penguin, 1995.

Sassoon, Donald. *Contemporary Italy. Politics, Economy Society since 1945.* New York: Longman, 1986.

De Scala, Spencer, M. *Renewing Italian Socialism. Nenni to Craxi.* Oxford: Oxford University Press, 1988.

Spotts, Frederic and Theodor Wieser. *Italy. A Difficult Democracy. A Survey of Italian Politics.* New York: Cambridge University Press, 1986.

Trevelyan, J. O. *A Short History of the Italian People.* London: Allen and Unwin, 1956.

Weinberg, Leonard. *The Transformation of Italian Communism.* New Brunswick, NJ: Transaction, 1995.

San Marino

Bent, James T. *A Freak of Freedom or the Repubic of San Marino.* Port Washington, NY: Kennikat, 1970.

Rossi, Giuseppe. *San Marino.* San Marino: Governmental Tourist Body Sport and Spectacle, n.d.

———. *A Short History of the Republic of San Marino.* San Marino: Poligrafico Artioli–Modena, n.d.

San Marino. Milan: Ediz. Garami (Garanzini Milano), 1977.

Malta

Berg, Warren G. *Historical Dictionary of Malta.* Metuchen, NJ: Scarecrow Press, 1995.

Blouet, Brian. *The Story of Malta.* Rev. ed. London: Faber Faber, 1972.

Sire, H. J .A. *The Knights of Malta.* New Haven, CT: Yale University Press, 1996.

Vatican City

Flamini, Roland. *Pope, Premier, President.* New York: Macmillan, 1980.

Kreutz, Andres. *Vatican Policy on the Pales-*

Bibliography

tinian–Israeli Conflict: The Struggle for the Holy Land. Westport, CT: Greenwood, 1990.
La Bello, Nina. *Vatican Empire.* Frieside: SS, 1970.
Nichols, Peter. *The Pope's Divisions.* New York: Holt, Rinehart and Winston, 1981.
Partner, Peter. *The Lands of St. Peter: The Papal State in the Middle Ages and the Early Renaissance.* London: Methuen, 1972.
Walsh, Michael J. *Vatican City State.* Santa Barbara: ABC–Clio, 1983.

Greece

Bahcheci, Tozun. *Greek Turkish Relations Since 1955.* Boulder: Westview Press, 1989.
Clogg, R., *Greece in the 1980's.* London: Macmillan, 1983.
———, ed. *The Struggle for Greek Independence.* London: Macmillan, 1973.
——— and Yannopoulos, G. *Greece Under Military Rule.* New York: Basic Books, 1972.
———. *A Concise History of Greece.* Cambridge: Cambridge University Press, 1994.
Constas, Dimitri, ed. *The Greek–Turkish Conflict in the 1990s. Domestic and External Influences.* New York: St. Martin's, 1991.
Couloumbis, J. A., et al. *Foreign Interference in Greek Politics: An Historical Persective.* New York: Pella, 1976.
———. *U.S. Relations with Greece and Turkey.* New York: Praeger, 1982.
Featherstone, Kevin, ed. *Political Change in Greece: Before and After the Colonels.* Kent: Croom Helm, 1988.
Gianaris, Nicholas V. *Greece and Turkey. Economic and Geopolitical Perspectives.* New York: Praeger, 1988.
Hadjiyannis, Stylianos. *Social Conflict and Change in Modern Greece.* Bristol, PA: Crane Russak, 1991.
Hart, Parker T. *Two NATO Allies at the Threshold of War. Cyprus, a Firsthand Account of Crisis Management, 1965–1968.* Durham, NC: Duke University Press, 1990.
Kazakos, Panos and Ioakimidis, P.C., eds. *Greece and EC Membership Evaluated.* New York: St. Martin's, 1995.
Kourvetaris, Yorgos A. and Dobratz, Betty A. *A Profile of Modern Greece. In Search of Identity.* Oxford: Oxford University Press, 1988.
Macridis, Roy C. *Greek Politics at a Crossroads.* Palo Alto: Hoover, 1984
Mouzelis, Nicos P. *Modern Greece. Facets of Underdevelopment.* New York: Holmes and Meier, 1980.
Nachmani, Amikam. *International Intervention in the Greek Civil War.* Westport, CT: Praeger, 1990.
Pettifer, James. *The Greeks. The Land and People Since the War.* New York: Penguin, 1993.
Salem, Norma, ed. *Cyprus. A Regional Conflict and its Resolution.* New York: St. Martin's, 1992.
Spourdalakis, Michalis. *The Rise of the Greek Socialist Party.* New York: Routledge, 1988.
Stavrakis, Peter J. *Moscow and Greek Communism, 1944–1949.* Ithaca, NY: Cornell University Press, 1992.
Stearns, Monteagle. *Entangled Allies. U.S. Policy Toward Greece, Turkey, and Cyprus.* New York: Council on Foreign Relations Press, 1992.
Theofanides, Stavros, ed. *Greece and EC Membership Evaluated.* New York: St. Martin's, 1993.
Tzannatos, Zafiris. *Socialism in Greece.* Brookfield, VT: Gower, 1986.
Winnifrith, Tom and M. P., eds. *Greece—Old and New.* New York: St. Martin's Press, 1982.
Woodhouse, C. M. *Modern Greece: A Short History.* New York: Faber and Faber, 1977.
———. *Karamanlis:The Restorer of Greek Democracy.* New York: Oxford Univ. Press, 1982.

Iberian Peninsula

General

Baklonoff, Eric N. *The Economic Transformation of Spain and Portugal.* New York: Praeger, 1978.
Kohler, Beate. *Political Forces in Spain, Greece and Portugal.* Woburn, MA: Butterworth, 1982.
Mar–Molinero, Clare and Angel Smith. *Nationalism and the Nation in the Iberian Peninsula. Competing and Conflicting Identities.* New York: Berg, 1996.
Michener, James. *Iberia.* New York: Random House, 1968.
Payne, Stanley G. *A History of Spain and Portugal.* 2 vols. Madison: University of Wisconsin Press, 1973.
Tovias, Alfred. *Foreign Economic Relations of the European Community: The Impact of Spain and Portugal.* Boulder, CO: Lynne Rienner, 1990.
Wiarda, Howard J. *Politics in Iberia. The Political Systems of Spain and Portugal.* New York: HarperCollins, 1993.
———. *Iberia and Latin America. New Democracies, New Policies.* Lanham, MD: Rowman & Littlefield, 1996.

Spain

Alba, Victor. *The Transition in Spain: From Franco to Democracy.* New Brunswick, NJ: Transaction Books, 1978.
———. *The Communist Party in Spain.* New Brunswick, NJ: Transaction Books, 1983.
Ampara, Almarcha and Ortega, Alfonso, eds. *Spain and EC Membership Evaluated.* New York: St. Martin's, 1993.
Arango, R. *The Spanish Political System.* Boulder, CO: Westview, 1982.
Bertrand, Louis, and Petrie, Sir Charles. *The History of Spain. From the Musulmans to Franco.* New York: Collier Books, 1971.
Carr, Raymond, and Fusi, Juan Pablo. *Spain: Dictatorship to Democracy.* 2nd ed. Winchester, MA: Allen and Unwin, 1981.
———. *Spain: 1808–1975.* 2nd ed. New York: Oxford Univ. Press, 1982.
Castro, Americo. *The Spaniards: An Introduction to Their History.* Berkeley: University of California Press, 1985.
Collins, Roger. *The Basques.* London: Blackwell, 1987.
Conversi, Daniele. *Nationalist Mobilization in Catalonia and the Basque Country.* Reno: University of Nevada, 1995.
Eaton, Samuel D. *The Forces of Freedom in Spain, 1974–1979.* Palo Alto: Hoover, 1981.
Fusi, J. *Franco: A Biography.* New York: Harper and Row, n.d.
Gil, Federico G. and Tulchin, Joseph S., eds. *Spain's Entry Into NATO.* Boulder, CO: Lynne Rienner, 1988.
Gillespie, Richard. *The Spanish Socialist Party. A History of Factionalism.* Oxford: Oxford University Press, 1989.
Gilmour, David. *The Transformation of Spain.* Topsfield, MA: Quartet, 1986.
Grugel, Jean and Tim Rees. *Franco's Spain.* New York: St. Martin's, 1997.
Gunther, Richard, ed. *Politics, Society, and Democracy. The Case of Spain.* Boulder, CO: Westview Press, 1993.
———, et al. *Spain After Franco: The Making of a Competitive Party System.* Berkeley: University of California Press, 1988.
Hooper, John. *The New Spaniards..* Rev. ed. New York: Penguin, 1995.
Hunt, Rosemary. *Get to Know Spain.* New York: Heineman, 1979.
Jackson, Gabriel. *The Spanish Repubic and the Civil War, 1931–1939.* Princeton: Princeton University Press, 1965.
Kenwood, Alun, ed. *The Spanish Civil War. A Cultural and Historical Reader.* Oxford: Berg, 1992.
Lancaster, Thomas D. and Prevost, Gary. *Politics and Change in Spain.* New York: Praeger, 1985.
Maravall, Jose. *The Transition to Democracy in Spain.* New York: St. Martin's Press, 1983.
Maxwell, Kenneth, ed. *Spanish Foreign and*

Bibliography

Defense Policy. Boulder, CO: Westview Press, 1991.

———— and Steven Spiegel. *The New Spain. From Isolation to Influence*. New York: Council on Foreign Relations, 1994.

Newton, Michael T. *Institutions of Modern Spain: a Political and Economic Guide*. New York: Cambridge University, 1997.

Parry, J.H. *The Spanish Seaborne Empire*. Berkeley: University of California Press, 1990.

Payne, Stanley G. *Basque Nationalism*. Reno: University of Nevada Press, 1975.

Preston, Paul, ed. *Spain in Crisis: The Evolution and Decline of the Franco Regime*. London: Harvester Press, 1976.

————. *The Triumph of Democracy in Spain*. Methuen, 1986.

————. *The Politics of Revenge. Fascism and the Military in 20th Century Spain*. New York: Harper Collins, 1990.

Salmon, Keith. *The Modern Spanish Economy. Transformation and Integration into Europe*. New York: Columbia University Press, 1991.

Shubert, Adrian. *A Social History of Modern Spain*. New York: Harper Collins, 1990.

Sullivan, J.L. *ETA and Basque Nationalism. The Fight for Euskadi 1890–1986*. Kent: Croom Helm, 1988.

Vilar, Pierre. *Spain. A Brief History*. 2nd ed. New York: Pergamon, 1980.

Woolard, Kathryn A. *Double Talk. Bilingualism and the Politics of Ethnicity in Catalonia*. Palo Alto, CA: Stanford University Press, 1989.

Portugal

Birmingham, David. *A Concise History of Portugal*. Cambridge: Cambridge University Press, 1993.

Bruce, N. *Portugal, The Last Empire*. New York: Wiley, 1975.

Bruneau, Thomas C. *Politics and Nationhood. Post–Revolutionary Portugal*. New York: Praeger, 1984.

————. *Political Parties and Democracy in Portugal*. Boulder, CO: Westview, 1997.

———— and Macleod, Alex. *Politics in Contemporary Portugal: Parties and the Consolidation of Democracy*. Boulder, CO: Lynne Rienner, 1986.

Crollen, L. *Portugal, the U.S. and NATO*. Leuven, Leuven University Press, 1973.

dos Passos, John. *The Portugal Story: Three Centuries of Exploration and Discovery*. New York: Doubleday, 1969.

Figueiredo, Antonio de. *Portugal: 50 Years of Dictatorship*. London: Penguin, 1975.

Graham, Lawrence. *The Portuguese Military and the State*. Boulder, CO: Westview Press, 1993.

———— and Makler, Henry, eds. *Contemporary Portugal:The Revolution and its Antecedents*. Austin: Univ. of Texas Press, 1979.

Hamilton, Kimberly A. *Lusophone Africa, Portugal, and the United States*. Boulder, CO: Westview Press, 1992.

Harsgor, Michael. *Portugal in Revolution*. The Washington Papers, Vol. III, No. 32. Beverly Hills: Sage, 1976.

Harvey, Robert. *Portugal: Birth of Democracy*. New York: St. Martin's Press, 1978.

Janitschek, Hans. *Mario Soares. Portrait of a Hero*. New York: St. Martins, 1986.

Livermore, H. V. *Portugal: A Short History*. Princeton: Scholar's Bookshelf, n.d.

MacDonald, Scott B. *European Destiny, Atlantic Transformations. Portuguese Foreign Policy under the Second Republic, 1974–1992*. New Brunswick, NJ: Transaction, 1993.

Magone, José M. *European Portugal: the Difficult Road to Sustainable Democracy*. New York: St. Martin's, 1997.

Marques, Antonio H. *History of Portugal*. 2 vols. New York: Columbia University Press, 1972.

Maxwell, Kenneth. *The Making of Portuguese Democracy*. New York: Cambridge University Press, 1995.

Nataf, Daniel. *Democratization and Social Settlement. The Politics of Change in Contemporary Portugal*. Albany, NY: SUNY, 1995.

Opello, Walter C., Jr. *Portugal. From Monarchy to Pluralist Democracy*. Boulder, CO: Westview Press, 1991.

Pinto, António Costa, ed. *Introducing Modern Portugal*. Palo Alto, CA: SPOSS, 1998

————. *Salazar's Dictatorship and European Fascism*. New York: Columbia University Press, 1996.

Porch, Douglas. *The Portuguese Armed Forces and the Revolution*. Palo Alto, CA: Hoover Institution, 1991.

Raby, D.L. *Fascism and Resistance in Portugal: Communists, Liberals and Military Dissidents in the Opposition to Salazar, 1941–1974*. New York: St. Martin's, 1988.

Silva Lopes, José de, ed. *Portugal and EC Membership Evaluated*. New York: St. Martin's, 1994.

Wheeler, Douglas L. *Historical Dictionary of Portugal*. Metuchen, NJ: Scarecrow Press, 1993.

Andorra

Carter, Youngman. *On to Andorra*. New York: Norton, 1964.

Deane, Shirley. *The Road to Andorra*. New York: Morrow, 1961.

Morgan, Bryan. *Andorra, the Country in Between*. Nottingham, U.K.: Palmer, 1964.